# Freedom in the World
# 2004

The findings of *Freedom in the World 2004* include events from January 1, 2003 through November 30, 2003.

# Freedom in the World 2004
## The Annual Survey of Political Rights & Civil Liberties

Edited by Aili Piano and Arch Puddington

Freedom House • New York, NY, and Washington, DC
Rowman & Littlefield Publishers, Inc. • Lanham, Boulder,
New York, Toronto, Oxford

ROWMAN & LITTLEFIELD PUBLISHERS, INC.

Published in the United States of America
by Rowman & Littlefield Publishers, Inc.
A wholly owned subsidiary of The Rowman & Littlefield Publishing Group, Inc.
4501 Forbes Boulevard, Suite 200, Lanham, Maryland 20706
www.rowmanlittlefield.com

P.O. Box 317, Oxford OX2 9RU, United Kingdom

British Library Cataloguing in Publication Information Available

**Library of Congress Cataloging-in-Publication Data**

Freedom in the world / —1978–
New York : Freedom House, 1978–
v. : map; 25 cm.—(Freedom House Book)
Annual.
ISSN 0732-6610=Freedom in the World.
1. Civil rights—Periodicals. I. R. Adrian Karatnycky, et al. I. Series.
JC571 .F66 323.4'05—dc 19 82-642048
AACR 2          MARC-S
Library of Congress [84101]

ISBN 0-7425-3644-0 (alk. paper)—ISBN 0-7425-3645-9 (pbk. : alk. paper)
ISSN 0732-6610

Printed in the United States of America

The paper used in this publication meets the minimum requirements of American
National Standard for Information Sciences—Permanence of Paper for Printed Library
Materials, ANSI/NISO Z39.48-1992.

# Contents

# Acknowledgments

*Freedom in the World 2004* could not have been completed without the contributions of numerous Freedom House staff and consultants (please see the section entitled "The Survey Team" at the end of the book for a detailed list of these contributors). Several other Freedom House staff members took time out of their schedules to read and provide invaluable feedback on the country reports, including Mike Staresinic and Sanja Pesek of the Belgrade office; Antonio Stango of the Almaty office; Stuart Kahn of the Bishkek office; Mjusa Sever of the Tashkent office; John Kubiniec and Adam Sauer of the Warsaw office; Patrick Egan and Roland Kovats of the Budapest office; and Margarita Assenova of the Washington, D.C. office. Balazs Jarabik of the Pontis Foundation and Jan Surotchak of the International Republican Institute contributed valuable insights. Amy Phillips of the New York office supplied critical administrative support. Jennifer Windsor, the executive director of Freedom House, provided overall guidance and support for the project.

Generous financial support for the survey was provided by the Lynde and Harry Bradley Foundation, the Smith Richardson Foundation, the Lilly Endowment, and the F. M. Kirby Foundation.

# Gains for Freedom Amid Terror and Uncertainty

Adrian Karatnycky

In 2003, freedom's gains outpaced setbacks by a margin of nearly two to one. Despite deadly, sporadic terrorism around the world and a year of significant political volatility, in all, 25 countries showed significant improvements (with three making gains in their freedom category and 22 improving their numerical scores). The year also saw 13 countries suffer significant erosion of their freedom (with five dropping in category status and eight declining in their numerical scores). Freedom categories—Free, Partly Free, and Not Free—represent a broad assessment of a country's level of freedom, while numerical changes in political rights and civil liberties represent a more nuanced 1 to 7 scale, with 1 representing the highest levels of freedom and 7 representing the most repressive practices.

As 2003 drew to a close, there were 88 Free countries (one less than last year). There were 55 Partly Free countries, the same as last year. And there were 49 Not Free countries, an increase of one from the previous year.

The globe's 88 Free countries account for 46 percent of the world's 192 sovereign states. In 2003, 2.780 billion people (44 percent of the world population) live in Free countries, where rule of law prevails, basic human rights are protected, and there is free political competition. The sole entrant into the ranks of Free countries this year was Argentina, where democratic elections marked the return of rule by a popularly elected president, Néstor Kirchner. The preceding elected president, Fernando de la Rúa, had been forced from office by violent protests in late 2000 and replaced by his main rival in a constitutional process. Argentina's improved status was also a consequence of progress in fighting corruption and military and police impunity.

The world's 55 Partly Free countries account for 29 percent of all states. In Partly Free states, which account for 1.324 billion people (21 percent of the world population), there are some basic political rights and civil liberties, but these are eroded by some or many of the following factors: rampant corruption, weak rule of law, and religious, ethnic, or other communal strife. In many cases, a single party dominates politics behind a façade of limited pluralism. Burundi and Yemen improved their rankings from Not Free to Partly Free. Yemen's progress reflected increased vibrancy in its political life. Burundi made progress as a result of incremental improvements in political rights that resulted from the integration into government of political groups that represent the majority Hutu population. The broadening of Burundi's government helped to improve interethnic relations and increase pluralism in a state emerging from a genocidal civil war. Formerly Free Bolivia and Papua New Guinea are now Partly Free. In Bolivia, the decline is the result of the resignation of the country's

# Freedom in the World—2004

The population of the world as estimated in mid-2003 is 6,296.0 million persons, who reside in 192 sovereign states. The level of political rights and civil liberties as shown comparatively by the Freedom House Survey is:

Free: 2,780.1 million (44.03 percent of the world's population) live in 88 of the states.

Partly Free: 1,324.0 million (20.97 percent of the world's population) live in 55 of the states.

Not Free: 2,209.9 million (35.00 percent of the world's population) live in 48 of the states.

## A Record of the Survey
### (population in millions)

| Year under Review | FREE | PARTLY FREE | NOT FREE | WORLD POPULATION |
|---|---|---|---|---|
| Mid-1992 | 1,352.2 (24.83%) | 2,403.3 (44.11%) | 1,690.4 (31.06%) | 5,446.0 |
| Mid-1993 | 1,046.2 (19.00%) | 2,224.4 (40.41%) | 2,234.6 (40.59%) | 5,505.2 |
| Mid-1994 | 1,119.7 (19.97%) | 2,243.4 (40.01%) | 2,243.9 (40.02%) | 5,607.0 |
| Mid-1995 | 1,114.5 (19.55%) | 2,365.8 (41.49%) | 2,221.2 (38.96%) | 5.701.5 |
| Mid-1996 | 1,250.3 (21.67%) | 2,260.1 (39.16%) | 2,260.6 (39.17%) | 5,771.0 |
| Mid-1997 | 1,266.0 (21.71%) | 2,281.9 (39.12%) | 2,284.6 (39.17%) | 5,832.5 |
| Mid-1998 | 2,354.0 (39.84%) | 1,570.6 (26.59%) | 1,984.1 (33.58%) | 5,908.7 |
| Mid-1999 | 2,324.9 (38.90%) | 1,529.0 (25.58%) | 2,122.4 (35.51%) | 5,976.3 |
| Mid-2000 | 2,465.2 (40.69%) | 1,435.8 (23.70%) | 2,157.5 (35.61%) | 6,058.5 |
| Mid-2001 | 2,500.7 (40.79%) | 1,462.9 (23.86%) | 2,167.1 (35.35%) | 6,130.7 |
| Mid-2002 | 2,717.6 (43.85%) | 1,293.1 (20.87%) | 2,186.3 (35.28%) | 6,197.0 |
| Mid-2003 | 2,780.1 (44.03%) | 1,324.0 (20.97%) | 2,209.9 (35.00%) | 6,314.0 |

\* The large shift in the population figure between 1997 and 1998 is due to India's change in status from Partly Free to Free.

democratically elected president, Gonzalo Sánchez de Lozada, after violent street protests and a bloody police response in October 2003. Papua New Guinea declined from Free to Partly Free as a result of growing corruption and rampant violent crime.

The 49 Not Free countries represent 25 percent of the world's states. There are 2.210 billion people (35 percent of the global population) who live in Not Free countries. In Not Free countries, basic political rights are absent and basic civil liberties are widely and systematically denied. Three formerly Partly Free countries saw their status decline to Not Free. The Central African Republic became Not Free after a March 2003 military coup ousted a civilian president and suspended the National Assembly. Mauritania entered the ranks of Not Free countries amid further erosion in political rights, including signs of pressure on the opposition that further reduce the chances for competitive electoral politics. Azerbaijan entered the ranks of Not Free states after manifestly unfair presidential balloting and a massively fraudulent vote count in October 2003 resulted in Ilham Aliyev succeeding his ailing father as president of the Turkic-speaking, oil-rich former Soviet republic.

While few countries changed their freedom category (three states made gains: Argentina from Partly Free to Free; Burundi and Yemen from Not Free to Partly Free; and five states declined in freedom category: Bolivia and Papua New Guinea from Free to Partly Free; Azerbaijan, Central African Republic, and Mauritania from Partly Free to Not Free), there were significant improvements in political rights and civil liberties in 22 other countries and a decline in freedoms in 8 other states. Although these changes were significant, they fell short of affecting the overall freedom status rating. Together, changes in both freedom status and numerical ratings meant that in all, 25 countries registered gains, while 13 suffered setbacks in political rights and civil liberties—a ratio of nearly 2 to 1.

## FREEDOM IN THE DEVELOPING WORLD

Significantly, this year's *Freedom in the World* survey demonstrates that liberty is not the exclusive province of prosperous and wealthy countries. While as a group low-income countries have significantly lower freedom rankings than middle- and high-income countries, there is nevertheless a surprisingly high number of poor and developing countries that manifest a strong record of respect for political rights and civil liberties. In all, our survey data show there are 38 Free countries with an annual gross national income per capita (GNPpc) of $3,500 dollars or less.[1] Of these, 15 have a per capita income of less than $1,500. As importantly, the survey shows little significant difference in the level of freedom registered by middle income countries ($1,500-$6,000 GNIpc; with a median of $2,960) and high income countries ($6,000-$40,000 GNIpc; with a median of $19,570).

### The Global Trend

|      | Free | Partly Free | Not Free |
|------|------|-------------|----------|
| 1973 | 44   | 42          | 65       |
| 1983 | 52   | 56          | 58       |
| 1993 | 72   | 63          | 55       |
| 2003 | 88   | 55          | 49       |

### Tracking Elecoral Democracy

| Year Under Review | Number of Electoral Democracies |
|-------------------|---------------------------------|
| 1993 | 108 |
| 1998 | 117 |
| 2003 | 117 |

## FREEDOM AND TERRORISM

The *Freedom in the World* findings incorporate the impact on the erosion of freedoms that is caused by the actions of terrorist movements. The findings also take into account the impact of efforts to combat terrorism. Clearly, terrorist actions have negative impact on individual freedoms in a number of countries around the world. Conversely, successful strategies to combat worldwide terrorism must include a vigorous effort to expand freedom in order to change the environment in which terrorism thrives.

On balance, however, the survey finds that since September 2001, 51 countries have made overall gains in their level of freedom and 27 have registered overall setbacks. There has been a net increase of two in the number of Free countries in this period.

Improvements in freedom have generally occurred in settings that have not been the main breeding grounds of global terrorists. Freedom registered most of its gains in the post-9/11 world in East Central Europe, East Asia, and sub-Saharan Africa. In the Middle East and North Africa, a breeding ground for global terrorism, on the other hand, downward trends have outpaced gains post-9/11. In this part of the world over the last three years, there have been overall setbacks to freedom in Egypt, Jordan, Mauritania, Morocco, and the United Arab Emirates, and modest progress in Bahrain, Iraq (post-Saddam), and Yemen. Many of the region's politically closed states—Algeria, Libya, Saudi Arabia, and Syria, for example—remain frozen in patterns of repression. Indeed, the war on terrorism has also enabled some of the world's most repressive states—such as Uzbekistan in Central Asia and the People's Republic of China—to invoke counterterrorism as an explanation for their ongoing harsh and unjustifiable repression and intimidation of dissent.

Despite pressures on civil liberties that efforts to combat terrorism have created in North America and Europe, on balance, the survey has found that these long-standing and durable democracies have to date preserved a broad array of freedoms as a result of a complex interplay between executive power, legislative oversight, judicial influence, civic action, independent media, and vigorous efforts by civil liberties groups. Among stable democracies, the greatest potential impact of anti-terror legislation on freedom was to be found in the United States. Many civil liberties organizations have been highly critical of aspects of the USA PATRIOT Act, which grants federal law enforcement agencies additional powers to investigate those suspected of involvement in terror plots and of measures that, some contend, discriminate against immigrants. The survey, however, has found that while U.S. government policies pose a threat to some aspects of civil liberties, the United States has to date been able to preserve a broad array of rights and liberties. An important factor has been the vigorous ongoing role of the judiciary, the press, and civil society organizations that are working to mitigate the impact of the most problematic actions.

## RELIGION AND FREEDOM

The tragic events of September 11, 2001, brought enhanced scrutiny and debate about the political character of countries with Muslim majorities, which some refer to as the Islamic world. Current counterterrorism efforts have been largely directed against fanatical political movements of extremist Islamists who have misappropriated the language of Islam to further their own political objectives. However, in the last two years, events have prompted a vigorous debate among Muslims and non-Muslims alike on whether the lack of freedom in many Muslim-majority countries is caused by the presence of Islam itself.

It is true the religious extremism of any stripe poses a danger to individual freedoms. However, a particular religious background of people is not deterministic in the existence of freedom within societies. While religion and culture play a role in molding politics within countries, cultures have proven far less immutable than experts and scholars have argued. Cultures can and do change, and progress toward democratization has occurred in societies with diverse religious backgrounds. In the 1970s, for example, the survey found low levels of freedom in majority-Catholic countries. Many scholars at that time argued that Catholic countries were unlikely candidates for further democratic progress. Yet by the 1990s, a wave of democratization had swept and transformed the majority-Catholic world. Similarly, a specific political interpretation of "Confucianism"—in which individual freedoms were urged to be subsumed to the needs of the community—also lost legitimacy as democratization progressed in many East Asian countries.

Countries with significant Muslim populations are diverse and significant numbers of Muslims can be found throughout the world. Indeed, today, about half of the world's 1.5 billion Muslims live under democratically elected governments. The largest populations of Muslims are found in such states as India, Bangladesh, Indonesia, Turkey, and Nigeria, as well as the Muslim minorities that participate in the democratic life of Western Europe and North America. It is only in the Arab world that democracy is completely absent.

In 2003, the survey finds an ongoing freedom gap between countries with a Muslim majority and the rest of the world. There are currently two Free countries with Muslim majorities, Mali and Senegal. There are 17 Partly Free majority-Muslim countries—a drop of one from last year—and 28 Not Free countries, up one from last year. Yemen improved from Not Free to Partly Free, while Azerbaijan and Mauritania declined from Partly Free to Not Free. This contrasts dramatically with the rest of the world, where the number of Free countries stands at 86, the number of Partly Free states is 38, and the number of Not Free states is 21.

All of this, however, should not suggest some kind of inexorable link between Islam and tyranny. Explanations for the continued lack of freedom in many of these countries—which are in diverse regions including Africa, the Middle East, North Africa, and Central Asia—are many and complex. The survey data shows no causal linkage between choice of religion of the majority of the population and level of individual freedom within societies.

## ELECTORAL DEMOCRACIES

In addition to tracking a broad range of political rights and civil liberties, the Freedom House survey monitors the state of electoral democracy around the world. The annual list of electoral democracies reflects a judgment by Freedom House staff using a list of criteria (see accompanying box) to determine whether the last major national elections within a country were considered to meet the established international standards of "free and fair."

In 2003, of the 192 governments, 117 or 61 percent are considered to be electoral democracies. Of that total, 88 countries are considered also to be "Free," i.e., liberal democracies. In addition, 29 countries considered to be electoral democracies are only rated Partly Free. Many of the Partly Free electoral democracies (sometimes referred to as "illiberal democracies" by analysts and scholars) have deficiencies in the other areas of civil liberties and political rights—rule of law, human rights, discriminatory practices—that persist despite gains in the electoral arena.

The number of electoral democracies has declined from last year. Tainted national elections in Georgia and Armenia, a putsch against the freely elected president in Guinea-Bissau, and constraints on the voting rights of nonindigenous citizens of Fiji, who were excluded from participation in the governance of the country, led to their being removed from the electoral democracy list. (Note: While the failure to hold free and fair elections as of November 2003 [the survey cutoff date] meant that Georgia was removed as an electoral democracy, there was significant hope that the country would reclaim its place among electoral democracies during the elections scheduled for January 4, 2004.)

In addition, a number of countries make this list by only a very narrow margin. Two such countries on the edge—as of the survey's November 30, 2003, cutoff date—include Russia and Ukraine, where control of mass media by those in power and pressures against opposition politicians by the state security structures, are threatening their status as electoral democracies.[2]

## REGIONAL PATTERNS

In Western and Central Europe, all 24 of the states are rated Free. Turkey, which is included in the roster of European states, is rated Partly Free—the only NATO member to belong to that category. All 25 European countries, Turkey included, are electoral democracies.

In the Americas and the Caribbean there are 23 Free Countries, 10 Partly Free, and 2 (Haiti and Cuba) Not Free. With the exception of Antigua and Barbuda, Cuba, and Haiti, the remaining 32 Western Hemisphere countries are electoral democracies.

In the Asia-Pacific region there are 17 Free countries (a decrease of one from the previous year), while Partly Free and Not Free states number 11 (an increase of one) and 11, respectively. Twenty-three of the 39 Asia-Pacific states are electoral democracies.

In Eastern Europe and Central Asia there are today 12 Free countries, 8 are Partly Free (a decrease of one), and 7 are Not Free (an increase of one). Dramatic progress in terms of rights has been registered primarily in the East European states, however, where there are 12 Free and 3 Partly Free states. The significant progress that these states have made has been confirmed and reinforced by their rapid integration into the security and economic structures of Europe and the Euro-Atlantic community. By contrast, aside from the three Baltic republics, among the states that once formed the USSR, there is not a single Free country, and Not Free post-Soviet lands outnumber their Partly Free neighbors 7 to 5 in a year that saw Azerbaijan's decline to Not Free status. Seventeen of the regions 27 countries are electoral democracies as of November 30, 2003.

In sub-Saharan Africa, 11 countries are Free, 20 are Partly Free (a decrease of one), and 17 are Not Free (an increase of one). Africa continues to register the greatest variations of any region year-to-year. It has seen significant instability, with steps forward in some countries often followed by rapid reversals. Nineteen of the region's 48 states are electoral democracies.

Among the countries of the Middle East and North Africa, Israel remains the region's sole electoral democracy and Free country. There are 5 Partly Free and 12 Not Free states, an increase of one Partly Free state (Yemen, which was formerly rated Not Free).

### COUNTRY TRENDS: The Year's Gains in Freedom

In addition to Argentina, which went from Partly Free to Free, and Yemen and Burundi, which raised their status from Not Free to Partly Free, 22 countries registered improvements in freedom that were significant but not large enough to warrant a change of category. Brief, alphabetically arranged, summaries follow.

Improvements in democratic Benin's electoral processes, as signified by vigorously contested free and fair legislative elections, led to improvements in political rights.

The island country of Cape Verde, one of Africa's more vibrantly free countries, registered improvements in the rights of women and an increased public awareness of the legal protections that women now enjoy. The year also saw increased private-sector vibrancy and increased business opportunities. These factors led to a cumulative gain in civil liberties.

Chile's ongoing democratic consolidation saw further improvements in political rights as the military's once-overarching political influence waned.

In Congo (Brazzaville), political rights improved as a consequence of the signing of a lasting cease-fire agreement that helped stabilize the country's fragile political environment.

Côte d'Ivoire's civil liberties improved after an internationally negotiated settlement to a civil war. A fragile government of national unity offered hope for an end to a period of extreme violence and strife.

Ghana's civil liberties consolidated and deepened in a year that saw increased openness in civic discourse and general improvements in respect for human rights and the rule of law.

Postwar and post-Saddam Iraq, while ravaged by terrorism and rampant crime, nevertheless saw a relaxation of the former Ba'athist state's controls on independent civic life, more open public and private discussion, and a range of newspapers and broadcast media, which today—despite limited controls by the U.S.-led occupation—are among the most diverse in the Arab world. All these factors on balance contributed to improvements in civil liberties.

Jordan's political rights made modest gains with the restoration of a national legislature with limited powers that was elected in a relatively open election.

The effects of Kenya's free and fair 2002 national elections continued to be felt in 2003, as official transparency and accountability improved while civic and political life showed increased vibrancy. All these factors contributed to incremental improvements in political rights and civil liberties.

Civil liberties in Madagascar improved as normalcy and calm returned to the country's civic, political, and associational life after violence that disrupted and destabilized the country following the bitterly contested elections of December 2001.

Malawi's democratic political rights improved on the nullification of a law that had eroded the rights of legislators and the defeat of a controversial effort to lift term limits for the presidency.

Malaysia's civil liberties improved amid signs of greater resilience in academic freedom and improvements in personal autonomy.

Mali's democracy scored modest improvements in civil liberties as a result of further consolidation of democracy and incremental changes in public discourse.

Nigeria's civil liberties improved as a result of the abatement in intercommunal violence that had beset the country in 2002.

Paraguay showed gains regarding political rights via a free and fair April 2003 election that brought Nicanor Duarte to the presidency and helped to boost official transparency.

Political rights in the genocide-ravaged land of Rwanda improved after multiparty presidential and legislative elections that led to increased political discourse in a setting of circumscribed political choice.

An improved security environment and increased pressures to punish those guilty of civil war atrocities led to modest gains in Sierra Leone's civil liberties.

Sri Lanka's political life may have been shaken by the president's dismissal of three cabinet ministers and a temporary suspension of parliament. However, its civil liberties improved as a result of a significant decline in violence and modest improvements in the rule of law resulting from an ongoing, though tenuous, cease-fire with the Tamil rebels.

Uganda made modest gains in political rights after a Constitutional Court ruling that removed restrictions on political party activity, potentially opening the door to multiparty politics in what has heretofore been a one-party state dominated by long-ruling president Yoweri Museveni.

The survey also recorded upward adjustments in the civil liberties scores of the Pacific Island states of Micronesia, Nauru, and Palau. The Freedom House survey team made these adjustments after refining its evaluation of the scope of freedoms enjoyed by trade unions, media organs, and nongovernmental organizations in these three countries.

## COUNTRY TRENDS: Declines in Freedom in 2003

In addition to category declines in the freedom of Bolivia and Papua New Guinea (from Free to Partly Free) and Azerbaijan, the Central African Republic, and Mauritania (from Partly Free to Not Free), eight countries saw an erosion of political rights, civil liberties, or both.

Djibouti's political rights declined after unfair elections in which the incumbent government had exploited the advantages of office to secure victory.

In the Dominican Republic, corruption scandals and a growing rejection of transparency by the government of President Hipolito Mejia resulted in the erosion of political rights.

Guinea-Bissau registered a decline in political rights as a military coup toppled the unpopular president Kumba Yala. Paradoxically, the military reversed some of the constraints on the country's civil liberties by releasing some opposition members Yala had jailed. Nevertheless, on balance the new dominance of the military in the country's political life represented a net setback for freedom.

In an environment beset by an ongoing Maoist insurgency, Nepal's political rights declined as a result of the continued suspension of an elected parliament and the failure of the King to schedule new national elections.

Political rights in impoverished Sao Tome and Principe declined after a brief coup led to the temporary displacement of that island country's government. The coup was quickly reversed as a result of the active and resolute engagement of Nigeria and its president, Olusegun Obasanjo. Still, the coup attempt traumatized political life in what had previously been an open and successful democracy.

The already-limited political rights enjoyed by the people of Swaziland took another hit from constitutional changes designed to entrench more deeply the institution of rule by royal decree.

The survey also recorded a decline in Vanuatu's political rights rating as a result of a technical reevaluation of the country's political life, rather than from specific changes that occurred in 2003, as well as a decline in the civil liberties rating for the United Arab Emirates due to a reassessment of the state of personal autonomy and equality of opportunity in the country.

## FREEDOM, WEALTH, AND POVERTY

The volatility of politics in poverty-riddled Africa—which experienced two military coups and a failed coup attempt—reinforces by counterexample the impression that prosperity correlates well with stability, democracy, and freedom.

This year's survey examines the relationship between income and levels of freedom in 192 countries. To no one's surprise, the data confirm that the world's most prosperous states are as a group freer than the world's poorest countries. But the correlations also show that countries of middling wealth, including a broad array of developing nations, do nearly as well in terms of freedom as high-income countries.

## Freedom and Economic Development

|  | FREE | PARTLY FREE | NOT FREE |
|---|---|---|---|
| **Low-Income Countries**<br>**GNI per capita less than $1,500** | 15<br>(16 percent) | 39<br>(43 percent) | 37<br>(41 percent) |
| **Middle-Income Countries**<br>**GNI per capita between**<br>**$1,500 and $6,000** | 35<br>(66 percent) | 11<br>(21 percent) | 7<br>(13 percent) |
| **High-Income Countries**<br>**GNI per capita greater than $6,000** | 38<br>(79 percent) | 5<br>(10 percent) | 5<br>(10 percent) |
| GNI per capita = gross national income<br>per capita | | | |

Moreover, our examination shows that a low level of economic development need not always condemn a society to an absence of freedom. Indeed, there is a large cohort of low- and low-middle-income countries that guarantee their inhabitants a broad range of political and civil liberties. Indeed, 38 countries with a per capita annual income of $3,500 or less are rated Free.

As noted above, the biggest cluster of Free countries is found among high-income countries, defined as those with a gross national income per capita (GNIpc) of more than US$6,000 per year. In this group, whose median GNIpc is $19,570 per year, 38 countries are Free, 5 are Partly Free, and 5 are Not Free. The five Not Free countries in this group (Brunei, Oman, Qatar, Saudi Arabia, and the United Arab Emirates) derive the vast proportion of their wealth from natural energy resources and investment income derived from these resources. Two Partly Free countries (Bahrain and Kuwait) have wealth that derives from similar natural resource origins. Thus, among upper-income countries that derive the vast proportion of their wealth from enterprise and knowledge, 38 are Free and only 3 are Partly Free. Societies that are most successful in producing wealth are almost uniformly Free.

Among middle-income countries—i.e., those with an annual GNIpc of $1,500 to $6,000—35 are Free, 11 are Partly Free, and 7 are Not Free. With a median GNIpc of only slightly less than $3,000 per year, this is far from a prosperous set of countries. Yet 66 percent of medium-income countries are Free, a proportion that does not dramatically differ from that of high-income countries (where 79 percent are Free). At the same time, the proportion of Not Free states among middle-income countries stands at 13 percent compared to 10 percent of high-income states—again, only a modest difference. Yet the incidence of freedom among the lower-middle and middle-income states is impressive, and only slightly lower than that boasted by the richest set of countries.

Among the poorest countries, however, where GNIpc is under $1,500 per year, the level of freedom is significantly lower. This lowest-income cohort has only 15 Free countries, 39 Partly Free countries, and 37 Not Free countries. And among the poorest of the poor in this cohort (i.e., the 29 countries with a GNIpc of $300 or less), only three—Ghana, Mali, and Sao Tome—are Free.

Among the 88 Free countries, 38 (or 43 percent) are high-income, 35 (or 40 percent) are middle-income, and 15 (or 17 percent) are low-income. Of the 55 Partly Free countries, 5 (or

9 percent) are wealthy, 11 (or 20 percent) are middling, and 39 (or 71 percent) come from the poorest group. Among the world's 49 Not Free states, 5 (or 10 percent) are high-income, 7 (or 14 percent) are middle-income, and 37 (or 76 percent) are low-income.

Such data indicate that the lowest income levels correlate with significantly lower levels of freedom. But our look at incomes and freedom levels also reveals that low-income countries are fully capable of establishing strong democratic practices and respect for civil liberties rooted in the rule of law. Out of 128 countries with an annual GNIpc of $ 3,500 or less, 38 are rated Free by the survey.

## FREEDOM'S TENURE

This year, we have also taken a closer look at what the survey shows in terms of the tenure of freedom in the world's polities. While 88 countries stand rated as Free at the end of 2003, for the bulk of them, freedom—and in some cases sovereign state-hood—is a recent arrival. Indeed, long-term uninterrupted freedom has been rare for most countries. Of the globe's 192 states, only 24 (or 12.5 percent) have been Free throughout the entire 31 years spanned so far by the Freedom House survey. An additional 20 of today's Free countries have had 15 to 30 years of uninterrupted freedom. This means that 44 of the world's Free states have had high levels of free-dom for fewer than 15 years.

Our time-series data show that over the last 31 years, a total of 112 countries have been rated free and experienced at least some period of democratic governance in an environment of broad respect for human rights. Significantly, of this group of 112 that have at any time in their history been Free, 88 are Free today; while only 2 today are Not Free. This means that 79 percent of all countries that have ever in the last 31 years known high levels of freedom are Free today. As importantly, when a country attains a high degree of freedom (or in other words, merits being ranked as Free in the survey), it rarely slips back into the kind of severe and systematic repres-sion denoted by a Not Free ranking. Indeed, out of the 112 countries that have at-tained high levels of respect for both political rights and civil liberties, only 14 have ever seen their rights status lapse back to Not Free.[3]

Conversely, among the 109 states that have at any time in their history lived under the denial of most basic freedoms as indicated by a Not Free rating, 28 are today Free, 32 are Partly Free, and 49 are Not Free.

The time-series record shows that 80 countries have not experienced broad-based freedom at any time during the 31-year record of the survey.

In all but the few worst cases, even highly repressive Not Free countries have been unable to rob their people completely and lastingly of all civil liberties and political rights. Out of 109 countries that have been rated Not Free in the history of the survey, only 13 (or 12 percent) have sustained in every year the high levels of political control and repression represented by the Not Free rating. These 13 countries are Burma, Chad, China, Congo (Kinshasa), Cuba, Equatorial Guinea, Iraq, Libya, North Korea, Rwanda, Saudi Arabia, Somalia, and Vietnam. This suggests that over time, even the most repressive rulers find themselves hard-pressed to succeed at constantly sup-pressing their citizens' desires for a broad array of political rights and civil liberties.

## CONCLUSIONS

A year of significant momentum for freedom—despite the threats to liberty posed by widespread global terrorism—is encouraging. So, too, is the evidence that suggests political rights and civil liberties can thrive even in conditions of significant economic privation. We also can derive some comfort from evidence in this year's review of long-term data that suggests that countries and populations that have experienced a high degree of freedom find ways of protecting that freedom and preventing its reversal.

At the same time, the survey's findings show that while there is much heartening news this year, important challenges remain. Many states—particularly the Partly Free countries—appear unable to make the transition to stable democratic rule rooted in the rule of law. Other states—a broad array of Not Free countries—have proved resistant to democratic change. Given the fact that Free societies account for 89 percent of the world's wealth, they have the capacity to help solidify and deepen democracy where it is fragile. They also have the capacity and the resources to significantly assist indigenous movements that seek to bring democratic change to closed societies.

*Adrian Karatnycky is senior scholar and counselor at Freedom House.*

## NOTES

1. Economic data are for 2001 and come from World Bank Development Indicators and *www.internetworldstats.com* and are compared with *Freedom in the World* ratings of events through November 30, 2003.

2. Although the current survey reflects findings and trends of events through November 30, 2003, Russia's elections of December 7, 2003, were neither free nor fair, and Russia would no longer remain on Freedom House's list of electoral democracies.

3. These are Argentina, Burkina Faso (formerly Upper Volta), Chile, the Gambia, Ghana, Grenada, Guatemala, Guyana, Lebanon, the Maldives, Nigeria, Seychelles, Suriname, and Thailand.

# Introduction

The *Freedom in the World—2004* survey contains reports on 192 countries and 18 related and disputed territories. Each country report begins with a section containing basic political, economic, and social data arranged in the following categories: **population, gross national income per capita (GNI/capita), life expectancy, religious groups, ethnic groups, capital, political rights** [numerical rating], **civil liberties** [numerical rating], and **status** [Free, Partly Free, or Not Free]. Each territory report begins with a section containing the same data, except for GNI/capita and life expectancy figures. [Note: the polity and economy designations included in previous editions are no longer included in this edition.]

The **population** and **life expectancy** figures are from the *2003 World Population Data Sheet* of the Population Reference Bureau. Population figures for territories are from sources including *The World Almanac and Book of Facts 2004*, the CIA *World Factbook 2003*, the BBC, World Gazetteer, and the Unrepresented Nations and Peoples Organization (UNPO).

The **GNI/capita figures** are from the World Bank's *World Development Indicators 2003* and *www.internetworldstats.com.*

Information about **religious groups** and **ethnic groups** are primarily from the CIA *World Factbook 2003*. For territories, this information was also derived from sources including *The World Almanac and Book of Facts 2004* and the UNPO.

The **political rights** and **civil liberties** categories contain numerical ratings between 1 and 7 for each country or territory, with 1 representing the most free and 7 the least free. The **status** designation of Free, Partly Free, or Not Free, which is determined by the combination of the political rights and civil liberties ratings, indicates the general state of freedom in a country or territory. The ratings of countries or territories that have improved or declined since the previous survey are indicated by asterisks next to the ratings. Positive or negative trends which do not warrant a ratings change since the previous year may be indicated by upward or downward trend arrows, which are located next to the name of the country or territory. A brief explanation of ratings changes or trend arrows is provided for each country or territory as required. For a full description of the methods used to determine the survey's ratings, please see the chapter on the survey's methodology.

Following the section on political, economic, and social data, each country and territory report is divided into two parts: an **overview** and an analysis of **political rights and civil liberties**. The overview provides a brief historical background and a description of major recent events. The political rights and civil liberties section summarizes each country or territory's degree of respect for the rights and liberties which Freedom House uses to evaluate freedom in the world.

# Afghanistan

**Population:** 28,700,000 **Political Rights:** 6
**GNI/capita:** $523 **Civil Liberties:** 6
**Life Expectancy:** 46 **Status:** Not Free
**Religious Groups:** Sunni Muslim (84 percent),
Shia Muslim (15 percent), other (1 percent)
**Ethnic Groups:** Pashtun (44 percent), Tajik (25 percent),
Hazara (10 percent), Uzbek (8 percent), other (13 percent)
**Capital:** Kabul

**Ten-Year Ratings Timeline (Political Rights, Civil Liberties, Status)**

| 1994 | 1995 | 1996 | 1997 | 1998 | 1999 | 2000 | 2001 | 2002 | 2003 |
|------|------|------|------|------|------|------|------|------|------|
| 7,7NF | 7,7NF | 7,7NF | 7,7NF | 7,7NF | 7,7NF | 7,7NF | 7,7NF | 6,6NF | 6,6NF |

**Overview:** With halting progress on several fronts, Afghanistan continued to struggle toward normalcy in 2003. President Hamid
Karzai's Transitional Administration (TA) worked to extend
the writ of the central government and curb the power of regional warlords, while
preparations for national elections and the drafting of a new constitution began during the year. However, the war-ravaged country remained wracked by pervasive
insecurity and some armed conflict. In addition, the slow disbursement of foreign
aid hampered efforts to provide humanitarian assistance as well as to rebuild
Afghanistan's shattered infrastructure and institutions. Although the level of personal autonomy has substantially increased since the fall of the ultraconservative
Taliban regime in 2001, numerous human rights violations, including threats to
women's rights and to freedom of expression, were reported during the year.

Located at the crossroads of the Middle East, Central Asia, and the Indian subcontinent, Afghanistan has for centuries been caught in the middle of great power
and regional rivalries. After besting Russia in a contest for influence in Afghanistan, Britain recognized the country as an independent monarchy in 1921. King Zahir
Shah ruled from 1933 until he was deposed in a 1973 coup. Afghanistan entered a
period of continuous civil conflict in 1978, when a Communist coup set out to transform this highly traditional society. The Soviet Union invaded in 1979, but faced
fierce resistance from U.S.-backed *mujahideen* (guerrilla fighters) until troops finally
withdrew in 1989.

The mujahideen factions overthrew the Communist government in 1992 and then
battled each other for control of Kabul, killing more than 25,000 civilians in the capital by 1995. The Taliban militia, consisting largely of students in conservative Islamic religious schools, entered the fray and seized control of Kabul in 1996. Defeating or buying off mujahideen commanders, the Taliban soon controlled most of the
country except for parts of northern and central Afghanistan, which remained in the
hands of the Tajik-dominated Northern Alliance coalition. Pakistan and Saudi Arabia
were the Taliban's main supporters, while Iran, Russia, India, and Central Asian states
backed the Northern Alliance.

In response to the terrorist attacks of September 11, 2001, the United States
launched a military campaign in October 2001 aimed at toppling the Taliban regime

and eliminating Saudi militant Osama bin Laden's terrorist network, al-Qaeda. Simultaneously, Northern Alliance forces engaged the Taliban from the areas under their control. The Taliban crumbled quickly, losing Kabul to Northern Alliance forces in November and surrendering the southern city of Kandahar, the movement's spiritual headquarters, in December.

As a result of the Bonn Agreement of December 2001, an interim administration headed by Pashtun tribal leader Hamid Karzai, which enjoyed the nominal support of Afghanistan's provincial leaders, took office. The UN-brokered deal that put Karzai in office sought to balance demands for power by victorious Tajik, Uzbek, and Hazara military commanders with the reality that many Pashtuns, who are Afghanistan's largest ethnic group, would not trust a government headed by ethnic minorities. In June 2002, the United Nations administered an emergency loya jirga (gathering of representatives), presided over by the formerly exiled King Zahir Shah, which appointed the TA to rule Afghanistan for a further two years. Karzai won more than 80 percent of the delegates' votes to become president, decisively defeating two other candidates. The Tajik-dominated Northern Alliance filled more than half the cabinet positions, including the key positions of ministers of defense and the interior, while the remainder were given to Pashtuns and representatives of other ethnic groups.

The UN-mandated International Security Assistance Force (ISAF), over which NATO assumed command in August 2003, is responsible for providing security in Kabul, but many areas outside the capital are unstable and conditions deteriorated in parts of the country as the year progressed. Military commanders, tribal leaders, rogue warlords, and petty bandits continue to hold sway. Bolstered by arms, money, and support from the United States and neighboring governments, some warlords maintain private armies and are reluctant to submit to the leadership of the central administration. Recurrent fighting between two northern factions throughout the year left dozens dead or injured. Civilians were affected by an increasing number of bombings, rocket attacks, and other sporadic violence by suspected Taliban sympathizers.

Seeking to curb the power of regional strongmen, President Karzai signed a decree in December 2002 banning political leaders from taking part in military activity; he also undertook several reshuffles of provincial governors and other key officials throughout 2003. Karzai won a crucial battle in May when a number of governors agreed to hand over a greater proportion of customs revenues to the central government. Following an attempt in September to reform the Ministry of Defense by appointing more professionals and non-Tajiks to positions in the ministry, the TA initiated a voluntary program of disarmament, demobilization, and reintegration in October. Preparations for holding a constitutional *loya jirga* (CLJ) and national elections continued during the year, with the formation of a constitutional commission charged with drafting a new constitution and conducting public consultations, and an election commission whose first tasks were to prepare accurate voter lists and register political parties.

**Political Rights and Civil Liberties:** Despite a number of improvements since the fall of the Taliban regime, the political rights and civil liberties of most Afghans remained severely circumscribed in 2003. The emergency loya jirga (ELJ) convened in June 2002 was charged with choosing a head of state and key ministers for the TA, which is mandated to govern while a new constitution is drawn up and elections scheduled for mid-2004 are organized. The majority of the delegates to the ELJ were selected through a two-stage electoral process, but places were also reserved for women and refugees. Although care was taken to ensure a widely representative grouping, some human rights groups charged that the delegate-selection process was characterized by "widespread and systematic" manipulation and intimidation from military commanders. The ELJ itself was marred by complaints of behind-the-scenes deals, some orchestrated by representatives of the U.S. government, which were said to have subverted the voting process. In addition, many delegates complained that warlords and Islamic fundamentalists had threatened them during the proceedings. While the vote on Hamid Karzai's presidency was held by secret ballot, later votes on the arrangement of the government and its key personnel were "highly irregular," according to Human Rights Watch.

Crackdowns on political activity have continued in Kabul and other provinces. Political parties have faced threats after distributing publications critical of certain government officials, and ordinary citizens have been threatened after speaking openly about political issues, according to Human Rights Watch. Nonmilitarized and pro-democracy political parties find it difficult to campaign openly because of the security situation and pressure from military factions. In October, a new law on political parties prohibited the registration of parties backed by armed forces or which oppose Islam or promote racial, religious, or sectarian hatred and violence.

The TA functioned as a central government with both executive and legislative authority, but its writ over areas outside Kabul remained limited. During the year, preparations commenced for the holding of elections in 2004 and the drafting of a new constitution, which was meant to be ratified at a CLJ held in December 2003. Although two women and a broad range of ethnic groups hold positions in the 30-member cabinet, concern has been raised about the government's lack of inclusiveness given the present domination of the Northern Alliance over state structures, particularly the security apparatus.

Afghanistan's media remained fragile in 2003. A press law adopted in 2002 guarantees the right to freedom of expression, subject to certain restrictions. Authorities have granted more than 200 licenses to independent publications, and a number of private radio stations began broadcasting, although some warlords have refused to allow independent media in the areas under their control. In April, cable television services resumed in Kabul and several other cities after being banned by the conservative chief justice of the Supreme Court in January. A number of journalists were threatened or harassed by government ministers and others in positions of power as a result of their reporting. Many practice self-censorship or avoid writing about sensitive issues such as Islam, national unity, or crimes committed by specific warlords. In June, two editors of the Kabul-based newspaper *Aftab* were arrested briefly and charged with blasphemy, and in July, the *fatwa* (religious edict) department of the Supreme Court recommended that they be sentenced to death.

For Muslim Afghans, the end of Taliban rule meant that they were no longer forced to adopt the movement's ultraconservative Islamic practices. Although the new administration attempted to pursue a policy of greater religious tolerance, it remained subject to some pressure from Islamic fundamentalist groups. The minority Shi'a population, particularly those from the Hazara ethnic group, has traditionally faced discrimination from the Sunni majority, and relations between the two groups remain somewhat strained. The small numbers of non-Muslim residents in Afghanistan are now generally able to practice their faith, although Hindus and Sikhs have had difficulty in obtaining cremation grounds and building new institutions of worship.

Academic freedom is not restricted. However, government regulations prohibit married women from attending high school and, during the year, several thousand young women were expelled from school. In some provinces, schools have also been the target of threats and violent attacks by fundamentalist groups.

With the fall of the Taliban, residents of Kabul and most other cities were able to go about their daily lives with fewer restrictions and were less likely to be subjected to harassment from the authorities. Rights to assembly, association, and free speech were formally restored, but were applied erratically in different regions. A November 2002 Human Rights Watch report detailed numerous violations of these rights in the province of Herat. In addition, police and security forces have occasionally used excessive force when confronted with demonstrations or public protests. In late 2002, police forces fired on a peaceful student march at Kabul University, killing 3 students and wounding more than 20. Both international and Afghan nongovernmental organizations (NGOs) are able to operate freely, but their effectiveness is impeded by the poor security situation in much of the country. Despite broad constitutional protections for workers, labor rights are not well defined, and there are currently no enforcement or resolution mechanisms.

Throughout Afghanistan, new rulers faced the question of whether to bring to justice, take revenge on, or simply ignore perpetrators of past abuses. Dealing with past abuses as well as protecting basic rights is particularly difficult in a country where the rule of law is extremely weak. There is no functioning nationwide legal system, and justice in many places is administered on the basis of a mixture of legal codes by judges with minimal training. In addition, the influence of armed power brokers and political factions over the judiciary remains strong. The Karzai administration's plans to rebuild the judiciary have proceeded slowly, as the Judicial Reform Commission tasked with overseeing the process of legal reform has thus far operated with limited effectiveness, and funding from donors has been generally inadequate.

Although the Bonn Agreement recognized the need to create a national army and a professional police force, progress on both fronts has been limited. By June 2003, only 6,500 recruits to the Afghan National Army had been trained, out of a proposed force of 70,000, and attrition levels are already high. However, in October, the TA initiated a voluntary program of disarmament, demobilization, and reintegration that is eventually intended to target 100,000 of the estimated 200,000 armed men in Afghanistan.

In a prevailing climate of impunity, government ministers as well as warlords in some provinces sanctioned widespread abuses by the police, military, and intelligence forces under their command, including arbitrary arrest and detention, torture, extortion, and extrajudicial killings. The Afghan Independent Human Rights Commission, which was formed in August 2002 and focuses on raising awareness of human rights issues in addition to monitoring and investigating abuses, received around 2,000 complaints of serious rights violations during 2003.

Numerous civilians have been killed as a result of bombings, rocket attacks, and other acts of terror by unknown assailants; during localized fighting between ethnic factions, particularly in the north; or during skirmishes between Taliban supporters on one side and government forces and the U.S. military on the other. Both the foreign and Afghan staff of a number of international organizations and nongovernmental aid agencies have been targeted for attack, particularly in the provinces with an active Taliban presence, and several dozen were killed during the year. In October, after months of reluctance on the part of the international community to significantly expand the 5,300-strong International Security Assistance Force (ISAF), the United Nations voted that the ISAF should be allowed to operate beyond Kabul. Although Germany deployed a contingent of troops in the northern city of Kunduz shortly thereafter, other donors remained loath to commit extra troops, and the security situation in much of the country continued to be extremely poor.

Hundreds of thousands of Afghans returned to their homes during 2003, but well over one million refugees remain in both Pakistan and Iran, and in addition, tens of thousands of civilians continue to be displaced within the country. Humanitarian agencies and Afghan authorities were ill-equipped to deal with the scale of the repatriation, while the poor security situation compounded by widespread land-grabbing meant that many refugees were unable to return to their homes and instead congregated in and around major urban centers.

The end of Taliban rule freed women from harsh restrictions and punishments that had kept them veiled, isolated, and, in many cases, impoverished. Women's formal rights to education and employment were restored, and in some areas they were once again able to participate in public life. Karzai named 2 women to his cabinet, and nearly 200 women took part in the ELJ, although some female delegates were threatened by other participants and officials for being outspoken. Women's choices regarding marriage and divorce, particularly their ability to choose a marriage partner, remain circumscribed by custom and discriminatory laws, and the forced marriages of young girls to older men or of widows to their husband's male relations is a problem, according to Amnesty International.

As a result of continued lawlessness and inter-ethnic clashes, women also continued to be subjected to sexual violence. In certain areas, ruling warlords imposed Taliban-style behavioral restrictions on women. A Human Rights Watch report issued in December 2002 detailed the strictures imposed on women by Ismail Khan's administration in Herat, which include mandatory usage of the *burqa*, or head-to-toe covering; a ban on traveling with unrelated men; and gynecological examinations for women suspected of "immodest" behavior. While record numbers of children returned to school, a number of girls' schools were subject to arson and rocket attacks from Islamic fundamentalists during the year.

# Albania

**Population:** 3,100,000
**GNI/capita:** $1,340
**Life Expectancy:** 74
**Religious Groups:** Muslim (70 percent), Albanian Orthodox (20 percent), Roman Catholic (10 percent)
**Ethnic Groups:** Albanian (95 percent), Greek (3 percent), other (2 percent)
**Capital:** Tirana

**Political Rights:** 3
**Civil Liberties:** 3
**Status:** Partly Free

**Ten-Year Ratings Timeline (Political Rights, Civil Liberties, Status)**

| 1994 | 1995 | 1996 | 1997 | 1998 | 1999 | 2000 | 2001 | 2002 | 2003 |
|------|------|------|------|------|------|------|------|------|------|
| 3,4PF | 3,4PF | 4,4PF | 4,4PF | 4,5PF | 4,5PF | 4,5PF | 3,4PF | 3,3PF | 3,3PF |

**Overview:**

The year 2003 proved to be one of treading water for Albania, as a short-lived cooperation agreement between the country's two main political forces, the Socialist Party (SP), led by Fatos Nano, and the Democratic Party (DP), led by former president Dr. Sali Berisha, fell apart early in the year, and local elections held in October again led to charges of fraud and incompetence.

From World War II until 1990, former dictator Enver Hoxha's xenophobic Communist regime turned Albania into the most isolated country in Europe. In 1990, the Communist government collapsed, and in March 1992, multiparty elections brought the DP, led by Berisha, to power. Continuing poverty and corruption, however, weakened Berisha's government, and in 1997, the collapse of several popular pyramid investment schemes resulted in widespread looting and violence.

In the years since the unrest of 1997, during which Albania has been ruled by the SP, the central government in Tirana has been unable to assert meaningful control over much of Berisha's stronghold in northern Albania.

Albania's first parliamentary elections since 1997 were held over four rounds between June and August 2001. Although international monitoring groups admitted that there were "serious flaws" in the election process, the polls were nevertheless deemed valid. Socialists now hold 73 out of 140 seats in parliament, as against 46 by the opposition, the DP-led Union for Victory coalition. After the elections, Berisha's DP announced a boycott of parliament to protest alleged electoral irregularities, and did not return until January 2002.

The 2002 truce between Berisha and Nano proved fragile, and by the beginning of 2003, Albania's short-lived national political unity again broke down, severely threatening its progress toward joining the European Union (EU). More signs of the continued turmoil within Albanian politics came with the resignation of Foreign Minister Ilir Meta, a bitter Nano rival, in July. Disagreements within ruling factions in the government prevented the nomination of a replacement for the rest of the year. Because of such infighting, little serious progress was made in 2003 on the fight against organized crime and on economic reform. Although the EU opened negotiations with Albania for a Stabilization and Association Agreement—generally seen as the first step toward full EU membership—in February, realistic analyses of the country's situation suggest that it has far to go to join the EU.

Municipal elections held on October 12, 2003, revealed some interesting new trends in Albanian politics, with the DP scoring its first victories in southern Albania since the turmoil of 1997. Voter turnout was 52 percent, a 10 percent drop from the local elections in 2000. In the northern town of Skhoder, only 29 percent of the electorate turned out to vote. Overall, the SP gained 34.2 percent of the votes cast for municipal offices, the DP won 32 percent, and the Social Democratic Party (PSD) became Albania's third-strongest party, winning 5.3 percent of the overall vote.

Many observers, however, deemed confusion surrounding the elections (organized under a new electoral code) as a setback. On October 22, the head of the OSCE's Observer Mission to the elections announced that the poor way in which votes were being tabulated in the postelection period "was disappointing" with "a mixture of carelessness, incompetence, and deliberate political obstructionism." The elections were also marred by the practice of "family voting," in which the head of the household votes for all members of the family. In December, Albania's Electoral College ruled that the municipal elections had to be repeated in 130 out of 346 precincts.

**Political Rights and Civil Liberties:** Albanians can choose their public representatives in generally free and fair elections. The last elections to the 140-seat Kuvend Popullor (People's Assembly) were held in 2001. The president of the republic is chosen by parliament. A number of political parties operate throughout the country. Although the most important political organizations are the DP and the SP, the differences between the parties are more a matter of the personalities leading them than of serious programmatic or ideological approaches. Albanian society remains very clan-based, and in very general terms, Berisha's DP commands the allegiance of the Gheg clans in the north, while Nano's SP has the support of the Tosk clans in the south.

The constitution guarantees freedom of expression. Freedom of the press has improved since the fall of communism, but considerable harassment of journalists persists. In October, Albania's Interior Minister Luan Rama (along with his bodyguards) assaulted and seriously beat the editor of Albania's fourth-largest television station. Rama was dismissed as a result of the incident, but it nevertheless exemplified the type of intimidation journalists continue to face.

The Albanian constitution provides for freedom of religion and religious practice, and on the whole Albania has not seen the inter-religious tensions typical of its neighbors. However, there has been a rise in tensions in northern parts of the country between rival Muslim sects, as well as between Roman Catholics and Muslims. In January, a leading Muslim cleric in the city of Skhoder was killed, according to some reports by more extreme adherents of the Wahhabi branch of Islam. Albania's small Greek Orthodox minority has intermittently been subjected to various forms of discrimination. The restitution of church properties confiscated during the Communist period remains unresolved. There were no reports of government attempts to restrict academic freedom.

Although freedom of association and movement are generally respected, significant problems remain. Several trade unions and independent nongovernmental organizations (NGOs) are also active. There were no significant reports of governmental harassment of either foreign or domestic NGOs in 2003.

The Albanian constitution provides for an independent judiciary. Overall, however, the judiciary, along with law enforcement agencies, remains inefficient and prone to corruption, and judges are often inexperienced and untrained. The combination of a weak economy and the growth of powerful organized crime syndicates make judges susceptible to bribery and intimidation. A recent survey by the U.S. Agency for International Development found Albania to be the most corrupt country in the region, and a World Bank study released in 2002 claimed that Albania provided "a startling picture of systemic corruption . . . [that] is deeply institutionalized." There are no reported political prisoners in the country, but at least one individual died after being beaten while in police custody this year.

Widespread lawlessness plagues large parts of Albania. Weak state institutions have increased the power of crime syndicates, and international law enforcement officials claim that Albania has become an increasingly important transshipment point for drug smugglers moving opiates, hashish, and cannabis from southwest Asia to Western Europe and the United States. The weakness of state institutions in northern Albania has also resulted in the resurgence of traditional tribal law in these areas, most importantly the tradition of blood feuds between different families and clans. Up to 2,000 children belonging to rival families engaged in blood feuds are being kept inside their homes for fear of their becoming targets of revenge killings.

The Albanian constitution places no legal impediments on women's role in politics and society, although women are vastly under-represented in most governmental institutions. The 2003 municipal elections especially witnessed a significant reduction in the number of women vying for public office. The Albanian labor code mandates that women are entitled to equal pay for equal work, but data are lacking on whether this is respected in practice. Traditional patriarchal social mores, moreover, pose significant problems for the position of women in Albania. Many segments of Albanian society, particularly in northern Albania, still abide by a medieval moral code according to which women are considered chattel property and may be treated as such. The trafficking of women and girls remains a significant problem; according to some estimates, Albania provides almost 50 percent of the women trafficked in southeastern Europe, and up to 30,000 Albanian women (a figure representing almost 1 percent of the population) work as prostitutes in Western Europe.

# Algeria

**Population:** 31,700,000 **Political Rights:** 6
**GNI/capita:** $1,650 **Civil Liberties:** 5
**Life Expectancy:** 70 **Status:** Not Free
**Religious Groups:** Sunni Muslim (99 percent), Christian
and Jewish (1 percent)
**Ethnic Groups:** Arab-Berber (99 percent), other (1 percent)
**Capital:** Algiers

## Ten-Year Ratings Timeline (Political Rights, Civil Liberties, Status)

| 1994 | 1995 | 1996 | 1997 | 1998 | 1999 | 2000 | 2001 | 2002 | 2003 |
|------|------|------|------|------|------|------|------|------|------|
| 7,7NF | 6,6NF | 6,6NF | 6,6NF | 6,5NF | 6,5NF | 6,5NF | 6,5NF | 6,5NF | 6,5NF |

**Overview:**    Violence in Algeria continued to diminish in 2003, yet the root causes of the 11-year conflict remain. The government's lackluster response to a massive earthquake reinforced staunch popular disaffection with the government that derives from long-standing socioeconomic ills and a lack of public accountability and transparency. Mounting political disarray, stirred by upcoming presidential elections, further clouded the scene. However, the government has made some important steps in the human rights arena.

Algeria gained independence in 1962 following 132 years of French colonial rule that ended with a bloody eight-year revolution. Algeria's current conflict can be traced to the 1986 oil market collapse. As oil prices dropped precipitously, Algeria saw its key source of foreign exchange dwindle. Unemployment, housing shortages, and other social ills fed growing popular resentment. The government embarked on a series of quick-fix economic reforms, but neglected to address the deep political roots of the crisis. With no political outlet, Algeria's young men took to the streets in violent riots during October 1988.

Once peace was restored, President Chadli Bendjedid vowed to open Algeria's political system by amending the constitution and legalizing political parties after more than 30 years of single-party rule. Most significantly, the amended constitution paved the way for the government's controversial 1989 decision to legalize the Islamic Salvation Front (FIS), an umbrella organization of Islamist opposition groups with significant grassroots support. In January 1992, the FIS was poised to win a commanding parliamentary majority when the army stepped in, forced President Bendjedid to resign, and cancelled the vote. The FIS was subsequently banned and its leaders imprisoned. The country was placed under a state of emergency that remains in effect.

Algeria's abortive experiment with democracy quickly deteriorated into violence as Islamist militants took up arms against the regime. The loosely structured coalition undergirding the FIS splintered into rival armed factions. As these groups surged at the expense of political moderates, Algeria's Islamist movement turned increasingly radical. A guerrilla-style insurgency erupted in the countryside, while urban-based extremists resorted to terrorist tactics. The resulting bloodletting has left an estimated 150,000 dead. Hundreds of civilians were killed in a series of massacres perpetrated by Islamic extremists. Meanwhile, government-backed militias are believed to have committed mass killings, and human rights groups have accused the Algerian security forces of being responsible for thousands of "disappearances."

In 1997, the Islamic Salvation Army (AIS), the least radical of the armed groups, announced a unilateral ceasefire. While AIS combatants agreed to lay down their arms, extremist offshoots such as the Armed Islamic Group (GIA) and the Salafist Group for Preaching and Combat (GSPC) continued to conduct terrorist attacks on both civilian and government targets.

The 1999 presidential election was severely flawed. Citing government fraud and manipulation, the entire slate of opposition candidates withdrew from the election at the eleventh hour, leaving Abdelaziz Bouteflika to run unopposed. After Bouteflika took office, the government introduced a "civil harmony" law that granted amnesty or leniency to Islamist rebels who renounced violence. According to government sources, some 5,500 members of the armed groups surrendered between July 1999 and January 2000. The GIA and the GSPC continue to wage attacks, with more than 1,100 civilians killed in 2002 and 2,000 people killed in 2001.

Ongoing violence, while diminishing, continued to plague Algeria in 2003. Some estimates maintain that at least 100 people are killed each month by armed groups, security forces, and state-armed militias. In early 2003, the GSPC kidnapped 32 European Sahara trekkers. All were eventually released, although one died in captivity. Although foreigners had been targeted in the violence during the early 1990s, this incident stands as the first such attack in some years. Algerian security forces also continue to mount operations against suspected militant strongholds.

A massive earthquake in May left 2,200 dead and thousands homeless. As with previous natural disasters, the government's inability to respond effectively drew significant popular criticism. Government officials were visibly absent, while Islamic charitable networks mobilized quickly to provide assistance. Some angry residents threw stones at President Bouteflika when he came out to survey the damage. The government established a commission of inquiry into the faulty construction of the scores of apartment buildings that collapsed in the earthquake. Yet, for the majority of Algerians, the tragedy confirmed their perceptions of a government that remains detached and unaccountable to its people. The earthquake's aftermath will contribute to Algeria's festering social ills that include 30 percent unemployment, persistent housing shortages, and a significant proportion of the population living below the poverty level.

A mounting political crisis is overshadowing preparations for the presidential election, currently slated for April 2004. Specifically, a power struggle has erupted between former prime minister Ali Benflis and President Bouteflika. Differences between the two men initially emerged over the question of reform, with Benflis pushing for deeper reforms while Bouteflika opted for a more cautious approach. Tensions between Bouteflika and the National Liberation Front (FLN), their party, escalated after Bouteflika sacked Benflis as prime minister in May. Bouteflika had attempted to short-circuit nomination procedures by securing the FLN candidacy, but was rebuffed. He, in turn, tried to ban the party congress, which proceeded regardless, nominating Benflis as its presidential candidate.

Political turmoil surrounding the upcoming election emanates from an opaque regime in which a relatively small group of military leaders hold the true reins of power.

Sometimes referred to as the *boite noire* (black box), the military decision-making apparatus is the least understood, yet most critical factor in Algerian politics. The generals broker power among themselves through an informal process of consultation and consensus.

## Political Rights and Civil Liberties:

The right of Algerians to choose their government freely is heavily restricted. Real power in Algeria has always resided with the military. The military leadership's primacy over their civilian counterparts predates Algerian independence, while every leader since Algerian independence has come to power only with the army's blessing. Algeria's civilian president is the nominal head of state, but wields minimal leverage with a small group of generals who retain ultimate authority over political decision making. Parliamentary elections have been largely free of systematic fraud, although the turnout rate in the 2002 elections was the lowest in Algerian history. A Berber electoral boycott coupled with a government ban on the FIS and Wafa parties—two important opposition parties—restricted voter choice, leading to significant apathy.

The press in Algeria is relatively vibrant, although the government often restricts the press either directly through strict defamation laws or indirectly via its control of publishing houses. Journalists have accused the authorities of attempting to silence the media with presidential elections approaching. Several dailies have published searing exposes of government corruption and abuse of power over the last several months, and a number of these papers have met with government harassment. State-run printing houses temporarily stopped printing six dailies on the grounds that the publishing companies were in arrears on outstanding bills. All six papers had published articles implicating high-ranking government officials in various scandals. In one case, the publisher of *Le Matin* was detained at the airport and subjected to legal restrictions following a complaint against him by the Finance Ministry. The paper had recently published an article accusing the interior minister of shady business dealings.

Religious freedom is generally respected. Islam is the state religion, although the government rarely interferes in the practice of non-Muslim faiths. The government monitors closely activities in the mosques, which are closed to the public except during prayer hours.

The government does not restrict academic freedom. During the turmoil of the 1990s, many artists, professors, and intellectuals fled Algeria. However, intellectual life appears to be reawakening. The number of conferences and colloquiums, both international and domestic, is growing, and numerous visas have been granted to international experts in a variety of fields.

Algerian authorities have exploited the state of emergency, in effect since 1992, to curtail sharply freedom of assembly. Citizens and groups are required to obtain government permission prior to holding public meetings. A decree, in effect for the past two years, effectively bans demonstrations in Algiers. In other areas of the country, restrictions on public gatherings are less tight. Emergency laws have also impeded Algerians' rights of association. The government denied registration of certain political parties, nongovernmental organizations, and other associations based on "security considerations."

The 1992 state of emergency laws significantly impinge on due process. While the human rights situation has improved, torture is still prevalent and investigations into human rights abuses are rarely carried out, maintaining a climate of impunity and confusion. The number of political prisoners is estimated to be several thousand, primarily suspected Islamists. Notably, FIS leaders Abassi Madani and Ali Belhadj were released in July at the end of their 12-year sentences.

The initiation of a public debate on human rights issues has been a key positive development. The government has established an ad hoc mechanism to look into the issue of "disappearances," serving as an interface with the thousands of families of the disappeared. The head of a government-established human rights commission has proposed that the Algerian government undertake a number of substantive human rights initiatives. While the degree of independence and freedom to maneuver remain unknown, these developments nevertheless constitute a step in the right direction.

Berbers comprise approximately 20 percent of the population. However, their cultural identity and language are not fully recognized under the law.

Women face discrimination in several areas. The 1984 Family Code, based largely on Islamic law, treats women as minors under the legal guardianship of a husband or male relative, severely restricting their freedoms in several areas.

# Andorra

**Population:** 100,000
**GNI/capita:** $16,990
**Life Expectancy:** na
**Religious Groups:** Roman Catholic (predominant)
**Ethnic Groups:** Spanish (43 percent), Andorran (33 percent), Portuguese (11 percent), French (7 percent), other (6 percent)
**Capital:** Andorra la Vella

**Political Rights:** 1
**Civil Liberties:** 1
**Status:** Free

**Ten-Year Ratings Timeline (Political Rights, Civil Liberties, Status)**

| 1994 | 1995 | 1996 | 1997 | 1998 | 1999 | 2000 | 2001 | 2002 | 2003 |
|------|------|------|------|------|------|------|------|------|------|
| 1,1F | 1,1F | 1,1F | 1,1F | 1,1F | 1,1F | 1,1F | 1,1F | 1,1F | 1,1F |

**Overview:** Efforts by the European Union and the OECD to introduce greater financial transparency in countries across the world threatened Andorra's status as a major tax haven in 2003. Over the year, Andorra was pressured to reform its restrictive nationalization criteria to accommodate its overwhelmingly foreign population.

As a co-principality, Andorra has been ruled jointly for 715 years by the president of France and the Spanish bishop of Urgel, who, as of May 12, was Monsignor Joan Enric Vives Sicilia. The 1993 constitution modified this feudal system, keeping the titular heads of state but transforming the government into a parliamentary democracy. Andorra became a member of the United Nations in 1993 and a member of the Council of Europe in 1994.

In March 2001, the country held elections and returned Marc Forne of the conservative Liberal Party of Andorra (PLA) to head the government. The PLA won an absolute majority with 15 out of the 28 seats in the Consell General, while the Andorran Democratic Center Party (ADCP, formerly the Democratic Party) won 5 seats, the Socialist party (PS) captured 6 seats, and the Unio Laurediana party won 2 seats.

A new European Union (EU) directive passed early in 2003 threatens Andorra's status as a major tax haven. All EU member countries are now required either to exchange information on savings accounts held by noncitizens or to levy a withholding tax on such accounts. As other tax havens have agreed to the EU's directives, it is assumed that Andorra will also fall in line.

The European Commission against Racism and Intolerance (ECRI) criticized Andorra in its 2003 report on the country for having restrictive naturalization criteria. Despite the fact that a majority of those living in Andorra are noncitizens, a person can become a citizen only by marrying an Andorran or by residing in the country for more than 25 years. Although noncitizens receive most of the social and economic benefits of citizens, they lack the right to participate in national politics.

Tourism is the mainstay of the economy and accounts for 90 percent of its gross domestic product. Because of the country's banking secrecy laws and tax haven status, the financial sector is also important. However, the threat of economic sanctions from the EU, which has been trying to introduce greater transparency into the financial sector in Europe, and the OECD, which has blacklisted Andorra for being an "uncooperative tax-haven," minimizes the appeal of this country for investors. In 1991, Andorra established a customs union with the EU that permits free movement of industrial goods. It also adopted the euro, despite the fact that it is not a member of the EU.

The United Nations Security Council named Andorra as one of 58 countries that had failed to meet an October 31 deadline to submit reports on measures to combat terrorist activities.

**Political Rights and Civil Liberties:** Andorrans can change their government democratically and do so enthusiastically. More than 80 percent of eligible voters participated in elections in 2001 to choose the members of the Consell General, which then selects the Executive Council President, who is the head of government. Popular elections to the 28-member parliament are held every four years. Fourteen members are chosen in two-seat constituencies known as "parishes," and fourteen are chosen by a national system of proportional representation. The people have a right to establish and join different political parties, and an opposition vote does exist. However, more than 65 percent of the population consists of noncitizens, who have no right to vote and face a number of hurdles that bar them from becoming citizens. As a result, there is little participation by non-Andorrans in government and politics.

Due to a lack of available information, Transparency International did not review and rank Andorra in its 2003 Corruption Perceptions index.

Freedom of speech and religion are respected across the country. There are two independent daily newspapers (*Diari d'Andorra* and *El Peridico de Andorra*), access to broadcasts from neighboring France and Spain, and unlimited Internet access. Although Catholicism is the predominant religion (90 percent of the whole population) and the constitution recognizes a special relationship with the Roman

Catholic Church, the state has ceased providing the Church with subsidies. According to the ECRI, Andorran authorities have begun to respond to the needs of smaller religious groups, such as Jews, Hindus, and Muslims. However, there is a degree of concern about the lack of a proper mosque for the Muslim community. The country's academic system remains free.

The government generally respect freedom of assembly and association. Although the government recognizes that both "workers and employers have the right to defend their own economic and social interests," there is neither an explicit right to strike nor legislation penalizing antiunion discrimination. Some advances in labor rights, however, were made with the creation of a registry of labor associations in late 2001.

Andorra's judicial system, which is based on Spanish and French civil codes, does not have the power of judicial review of legislative acts. The country has not accepted compulsory International Commission of Jurists jurisdiction.

Immigrant workers, primarily from North Africa, complain that they lack the same rights as citizens. An immigration law in 2002 attempted to remedy the situation by granting legal status to 7,000 immigrants who lacked work permits or resident permits.

Citizens have a right to own property, but noncitizens can own only a 33 percent share of a company unless they have lived in the country for 20 years or more. A law to reduce this to 10 years is pending in parliament.

Women enjoy the same legal, political, social, and professional rights as men, although they are underrepresented in government. Today only four women occupy seats in parliament. Moreover, there are no specific laws addressing violence against women, which remains a problem across the country.

# Angola

**Population:** 13,100,000
**GNI/capita:** $500
**Life Expectancy:** 40
**Religious Groups:** Indigenous beliefs
(47 percent), Roman Catholic (38 percent),
Protestant (15 percent)

**Political Rights:** 6
**Civil Liberties:** 5
**Status:** Not Free

**Ethnic Groups:** Ovimbundu (37 percent), Kimbundu
(25 percent), Bakongo (13 percent), mestico [mixed European and native African]
(2 percent), European (1 percent), other (22 percent)
**Capital:** Luanda

**Ten-Year Ratings Timeline (Political Rights, Civil Liberties, Status)**

| 1994 | 1995 | 1996 | 1997 | 1998 | 1999 | 2000 | 2001 | 2002 | 2003 |
|------|------|------|------|------|------|------|------|------|------|
| 7,7NF | 6,6NF | 6,6NF | 6,6NF | 6,6NF | 6,6NF | 6,6NF | 6,6NF | 6,5NF | 6,5NF |

**Overview:**     Angola continued to sustain peace in 2003, one year after the death of rebel leader Jonas Savimbi ended three decades of civil war. Demobilization of former combatants is going well overall, and a 2002 ceasefire has held between Savimbi's National Union for the

Total Independence of Angola (UNITA) and the ruling Popular Movement for the Liberation of Angola (MPLA). With peace, the government can no longer use the war as an excuse for lack of delivery on collapsed social services. Political debate shows signs of rejuvenation, and civic groups are increasingly urging the government to become more accountable for violations of human rights, slow political reform, and nontransparency in oil transactions. The government in 2003 signaled a desire to hold a dialogue with separatists in the oil enclave of Cabinda, the scene of low-scale guerrilla activity for decades.

Angola was at war continually since independence from Portugal in 1975. During the Cold War, the United States and South Africa backed UNITA, while the former Soviet Union and Cuba supported the Marxist MPLA government. A 1991 peace accord that led to presidential and legislative elections in 1992 disintegrated when Savimbi lost the presidency and fighting resumed. A subsequent peace agreement in 1994 also fell apart. The UN Security Council voted in February 1999 to end the UN peacekeeping mission in Angola following the collapse of the peace process and the shooting down of two UN planes.

The United Nations is playing a leading role in the current humanitarian effort and is shifting its focus from emergency relief to sustainable development. Nonetheless, some two million Angolans depend on humanitarian assistance for survival. UNITA appears committed to ending hostilities for good; about 80,000 former rebel soldiers have been demobilized, with 5,000 of them integrated into the armed forces and the police. However, the MPLA and UNITA disagree about how rapidly political and economic reforms can occur, and both sides will need to demonstrate a commitment to rebuilding the country rather than simply dividing up Angola's diamond and oil riches. The peace process would have a better chance if the economic and political elite included groups other than the two main parties.

The conflict claimed 500,000 to 2 million lives, and sent another estimated 500,000 Angolans to seek refuge in neighboring countries. About half of the 4.1 million internally displaced people and one-fourth of refugees have returned to their places of origin, mostly spontaneously. However, about 1 million of the remaining internally displaced live outside former transit centers and thus lack official assistance from the government or United Nations. These displaced people require shelter, food, clothes, health care, education, and often identification documents. Others, especially those who prefer to live in the capital Luanda, have been coerced into resettling outside the place of their choice. Women are vulnerable to sexual abuse by former combatants and do not generally receive demobilization benefits. Former child soldiers—estimates vary from 7,000 to 11,000—also remain outside the demobilization process. The United Nations expects the return and resettlement process to continue until 2006.

The process has been slowed, too, by untold millions of land mines and by a war-ruined infrastructure, which make large tracts of the country inaccessible to humanitarian aid. At least 70,000 people have lost limbs to mines over the years. It will take years to rebuild roads, bridges, and communications networks.

Angola is Africa's second largest oil producer. Petroleum accounts for up to 90 percent of government revenues, but corruption and war have prevented the average Angolan from benefiting from the wealth. An estimated $1 billion in oil revenue goes missing every year. The country's rich diamond areas have been carved up between MPLA and UNITA elites. Subsistence agriculture supports 85 percent of the population. The government has failed to make significant progress in reforms recommended by the IMF.

Prospects for an eventual negotiated settlement in Cabinda were enhanced by a July meeting between a Angolan authorities and Ranque Franque, a leader of the separatist Front for the Liberation of the Enclave of Cabinda (FLEC).

**Political Rights and Civil Liberties:** Angolans freely elected their own representatives for the only time in the September 1992 UN-supervised presidential and legislative elections. International observers pronounced the vote generally free and fair despite some irregularities. However, Savimbi rejected his defeat to President Jose Eduardo dos Santos in the first round of presidential voting and resumed the guerrilla war.

The two factions of the former rebel group UNITA merged into one political party in 2002. Eighty-seven other opposition groups have formed a coalition but have negligible weight. The National Assembly has little real power, but members engage in heated debates, and legislation proposed by the opposition is sometimes passed. The MPLA dominates the 220-member National Assembly; UNITA holds 70 seats. Presidential elections planned for 1997 have been put off until at least 2005. Dos Santos said in October that a new constitution must be drawn up as a first step. No date has been set for parliamentary or local elections.

Although political debate is lively, UNITA claims that MPLA supporters have harassed or attacked its members and offices in the provinces. The ruling party denies this is an official policy. The MPLA has not fostered the participation of civil society in reconstruction. Corruption and patronage are endemic in the government.

Despite constitutional guarantees of freedom of expression, journalists are often subjected to self-censorship or intimidation by the government. However, severe repression of the media by UNITA and the MPLA eased following the 2002 ceasefire. There are several independent weeklies and radio stations. The only television station is state-owned, although the government announced plans in 2003 to open up the sector to privately owned broadcasters. Defamation of the president or his representatives is a criminal offense, punishable by imprisonment or fines. There is no truth defense to defamation charges. Internet access is limited to a small elite, as most citizens lack computers or even electricity.

Religious freedom is widely respected. The educational system barely functions, although plans are under way to build new schools and train teachers. More than 50 percent of rural children do not attend school. Only 3 out of 10 rural women older than 15 years of age can read and write.

The constitution guarantees freedom of assembly, but in practice authorities do not always grant opposition groups the right to hold demonstrations. Several dozen civic organizations form a small but increasingly vocal group that is demanding greater government accountability in human rights and faster economic and political reform. Churches especially have grown more outspoken with peace. However, civil society organizations require greater coherence to be effective.

The right to strike and form unions is provided by the constitution, but the MPLA dominates the labor movement and only a few independent unions exist. The lack of a viable economy has hindered labor activity.

The government has yet to establish a Constitutional Court, as mandated by the constitution. Local courts rule on civil matters and petty crime in some areas, but an overall lack of training and infrastructure inhibit judicial proceedings, which are also heavily influenced by the government. Only 23 of the 168 municipal courts were operational in mid-2003. Prisoners are commonly detained for long periods in life-threatening conditions while awaiting trial, and overcrowding and unsanitary conditions prevail. Often prisoners have to rely on relatives or outsiders for food.

Severe human rights abuses, including torture, abduction, rape, sexual slavery, and extrajudicial execution, were perpetrated during the war by government and UNITA security forces. Such actions have subsided somewhat across the country, although nongovernmental organizations report human rights violations are continuing in Cabinda. Moreover, the New York-based Human Rights Watch has warned that the government is not doing enough to ensure the safety of displaced Angolans returning home. The rights group said Angolans faced harassment and restriction of movement, and were being forced to relocate where they might risk political persecution and human rights abuses. Police and security forces are rarely held accountable for shakedowns, muggings, rapes, or beatings.

Angolans have the right to own property. However, the government still dominates the economy and the war discouraged the development of a private sector. Prospects look better with peace, and the government in February passed legislation aimed at facilitating private investment.

Women occupy cabinet positions and National Assembly seats. Nevertheless, despite legal protections, de facto discrimination against women remains strong, particularly in rural areas. Spousal abuse is common, and the war contributed to rape and sexual slavery. Women are often the victims of land mines as they forage for food and firewood.

# Antigua and Barbuda

**Population:** 100,000    **Political Rights:** 4
**GNI/capita:** $9,390    **Civil Liberties:** 2
**Life Expectancy:** 71    **Status:** Partly Free
**Religious Groups:** Anglican (predominant)
**Ethnic Groups:** Black, British, Portuguese, Lebanese, Syrian
**Capital:** St. John's

**Ten-Year Ratings Timeline (Political Rights, Civil Liberties, Status)**

| 1994 | 1995 | 1996 | 1997 | 1998 | 1999 | 2000 | 2001 | 2002 | 2003 |
|------|------|------|------|------|------|------|------|------|------|
| 4,3PF | 4,3PF | 4,3PF | 4,3PF | 4,3PF | 4,3PF | 4,2PF | 4,2PF | 4,2PF | 4,2PF |

**Overview:**

In 2003, as a result of pervasive infighting within the ruling Antigua Labour Party (ALP), three members left the party and are now sitting as independents.

Antigua and Barbuda, a member of the Commonwealth, gained independence in

1981. In 1994, the elder Vere Bird stepped down as prime minister in favor of his son Lester. In the run-up to the 1994 election, three opposition parties united to form the United Progressive Party (UPP), which campaigned on a social-democratic platform emphasizing rule of law and good governance. Parliamentary seats held by the ALP fell from 15 in 1989 to 11, while the number for the UPP rose from 1 to 5.

After assuming office, Lester Bird promised a less corrupt, more efficient government. Yet the government continued to be dogged by scandals, and in 1995, the prime minister's brother, Ivor, received only a fine after having been convicted of cocaine smuggling. In the March 1999 elections, the ALP won 12 parliamentary seats, the UPP 4, and the Barbuda People's Movement (BPM) 1.

In June 2003, four dissident legislators of the ALP announced that they no longer had confidence in the leadership of Prime Minister Lester Bird and left the party. At the last minute, one of the dissidents returned to the party, thus preventing an early election. A new election is scheduled for June 2004.

The endemic corruption of state institutions continues unabated, and only 4 of the 14 people named in a Royal Commission of Inquiry, which concluded that there were serious instances of fraud in the medical-benefits program, have been indicted. The Medical Association has alleged official obstruction and emphasizes that improprieties continue. The prime minister's brother, Vere Bird, Jr., continued to serve as minister of agriculture despite an arms-trafficking inquiry that concluded he should be barred from government service.

**Political Rights and Civil Liberties:** The 1981 constitution establishes a parliamentary system: a bicameral legislature is composed of the 17-member House of Representatives (16 seats go to Antigua, 1 to Barbuda) in which members serve five-year terms, and an appointed Senate. Eleven senators are appointed by the prime minister, four by the parliamentary opposition leader, one by the Barbuda Council, and one by the governor-general.

Political parties can organize freely. However, the ruling party's monopoly on patronage makes it difficult for opposition parties to attract membership and financial support. The government has been planning to reform the electoral system by establishing an Independent Electoral Commission to review electoral law and redraw constituency boundaries, create a new voter registry, and introduce voter identification cards; however, the relevant legislation has not yet been introduced. The Electoral Office of Jamaica commission was contracted to prepare a new voter list; deceased and absent voters have not been removed from the list since 1975.

Although the government introduced anticorruption and integrity legislation in parliament in October 2002, no significant action has been taken. If the bills are approved, public officials would be required to make an annual declaration of assets, with failure to comply becoming a punishable offense. The Integrity in Public Life Act 2002 and the Prevention of Corruption Act 2002, which are being submitted as part of Organization of American States and United Nations anticorruption treaties signed by the country, will help establish provisions for regulating and guaranteeing good governance. The administration and enforcement of the acts would fall to an independent commission. The legislation also aims to define corruption.

The ALP government and the Bird family continue to control television, cable, and radio outlets. The government owns one of three radio stations and the television station. One of the prime minister's brothers owns a second station, and another brother owns the cable company. Opposition parties complain of receiving limited coverage from, and having little opportunity to present their views on, the government-controlled electronic media. There is free access to the Internet. The Declaration of Chapultepec on press freedoms was signed in September 2002.

The government respects religious and academic freedom.

Labor unions and civic organizations can organize freely. The Industrial Court mediates labor disputes, but public sector unions tend to be under the sway of the ruling party. Demonstrators are occasionally subject to police harassment.

The country's legal system is based on English common law. The ruling party has manipulated the nominally independent judicial system, which has been powerless to address corruption in the executive branch. The islands' security forces are composed of the police and the small Antigua and Barbuda Defence Forces. The police generally respect human rights; basic police reporting statistics, however, are confidential. The country's prison is in primitive condition and has been criticized for the abuse of inmates, though visits are permitted by independent human rights groups.

A resolution to ratify the International Labour Organization Convention Concerning Equal Remuneration for Men and Women Workers for Work of Equal Value was presented to parliament in late 2002. Social discrimination and violence against women are problems. The governmental Directorate of Women's Affairs has sought to increase awareness of women's legal rights.

# Argentina

**Population:** 36,900,000
**GNI/capita:** $6,940
**Life Expectancy:** 74
**Religious Groups:** Roman Catholic (92 percent), Protestant (2 percent), Jewish (2 percent), other (4 percent)
**Ethnic Groups:** White [mostly Spanish and Italian] (97 percent), other [including mestizo and Amerindian] (3 percent)
**Capital:** Buenos Aires

**Political Rights:** 2*
**Civil Liberties:** 2*
**Status:** Free

**Ratings Change:** Argentina's political rights and civil liberties ratings improved from 3 to 2, and its status from Partly Free to Free, due to the stabilization of the country's electoral democracy and important innovations in fighting corruption and ending military and police impunity.

**Ten-Year Ratings Timeline (Political Rights, Civil Liberties, Status)**

| 1994 | 1995 | 1996 | 1997 | 1998 | 1999 | 2000 | 2001 | 2002 | 2003 |
|------|------|------|------|------|------|------|------|------|------|
| 2,3F | 2,3F | 2,3F | 2,3F | 3,3F | 2,3F | 1,2F | 3,3PF | 3,3PF | 2,2F |

**Overview:**   Peronist governor Nestor Kirchner took office on May 25, 2003, as Argentina's sixth president in 18 months, after former chief executive Carlos Menem, whose tenure in office symbolized the corrupt excesses of the 1990s, abruptly withdrew from participating in a run-off election that Kirchner was widely favored to win. In his inaugural address, Kirchner promised that his government would act as "the great repairer of social inequities," a message greeted with hope by what was once Latin America's most developed country, which, for most of the past decade, endured the worst economic depression in its history.

The Argentine Republic was established after independence from Spain in 1816. Democratic rule was often interrupted by military coups. The end of Juan Peron's authoritarian regime in 1955 led to a series of right-wing military dictatorships that spawned left-wing and nationalist violence. Argentina returned to elected civilian rule in 1983, after seven years of vicious and mostly clandestine repression of leftist guerrillas and other dissidents in what is known as the "dirty war."

As a provincial governor, Carlos Menem, running an orthodox Peronist platform of nationalism and state intervention in the economy, won a six-year presidential term in 1989, amidst hyperinflation and food riots. As president, he implemented, mostly by decree, an economic liberalization program. He also won praise for firmly allying the country with U.S. foreign policy, particularly during the Gulf War with Iraq.

In the October 1997 elections, voter concerns about rampant corruption and unemployment resulted in the first nationwide defeat of Menem's Peronists, whose macroeconomic stabilization stalled as a result of international economic strife and his own government's growing corruption. Buenos Aires mayor and Radical Party leader Fernando De la Rua was chosen as the nominee of the center-left Alliance for presidential elections to be held October 24, 1999. Menem's long-running feud with his former vice president, Eduardo Duhalde, the hapless Peronist Party presidential nominee and governor of Buenos Aires province, sealed the latter's fate. Duhalde was defeated by De la Rua, 48.5 percent to 38 percent.

Weak, indecisive, and facing an opposition-controlled congress, De la Rua sought to cut spending, raise taxes, and push forward an anticorruption agenda and unpopular labor reforms. In October 2000, Vice President Carlos Alvarez resigned after De la Rua stonewalled calls for a serious investigation of the reported buying of congressional votes in order to pass labor legislation, a charge that appeared to receive first-hand corroboration in court testimony in 2003. In December 2000, a judge who himself was under investigation for "illegal enrichment," dropped the charges against the 11 senators named in the scandal.

Unable to halt the economic crisis, De la Rua called on Menem's former economy minister to restore credibility to the government's economic program and to stave off default on Argentina's $128 billion in public sector debt. Record unemployment, reduced and delayed wages to federal and provincial workers, and the closing of public schools created the kind of social mobilization and protest unseen for nearly a generation. In the October 2001 congressional by-elections, the Peronist Party bested the ruling Alliance coalition. However, citizen anger resulted in an unprecedented 21 percent of the votes being spoiled or nullified.

In December 2001, government efforts to stop a run on Argentina's banking system sparked widespread protests. Middle-class housewives—the bulwark of the government coalition's base—turned out in massive street protests. At the same time, riots and looting of supermarkets in poorer districts erupted, some of which appeared to have been organized by rivals within the opposition Peronists and by disaffected serving or former members of the Argentina's intelligence services. As the death toll reached 27, De la Rua resigned. He was replaced by an interim president, who himself was forced to quit less than a week later. On December 31, 2001, Duhalde, the 1999 Peronist standard-bearer, was selected as the new president. A decade-old law prohibiting the use of the military for internal security, a sizable reduction in military strength carried out by the Menem government, and continuing civilian abhorrence of the recent legacy of the dirty war, all helped keep the military from intervening in politics during the weeks-long transition.

The steep devaluation of the peso and a debilitating default on its $141 billion foreign debt left Argentina teetering on the brink of political and economic collapse throughout 2002, as the restrictive fiscal policies urged by the IMF and pursued by the government were not matched by increases in foreign investment. According to official government statistics, between October 2001 and May 2002, about 5.2 million people belonging to the middle class sank below the poverty line. An attempt by congress to impeach a highly politicized Supreme Court loyal to Menem was dropped, after international financial institutions said the move would endanger the country's access to foreign credit, and the legislature itself was the target of persistent accusations of bribery. Unemployment soared to levels unheard of since the founding of the republic, and violent crime spiraled out of control. Several of the country's police forces were roundly criticized both for not being able to stop the crime wave and for contributing to it through deep-seated corruption and frequent use of excessive force. Documents declassified by the U.S. State Department in 2002 and 2003 provided additional proof of former U.S. secretary of state Henry Kissinger's "green light" for the military-led "dirty war."

Nestor Kirchner, a relatively unknown governor from the Patagonian region, succeeded in getting into a runoff in the first round of the April 2003 presidential election, winning 22 percent to Menem's 24.3 percent. Menem's high negative poll ratings convinced him to drop out of the contest.

Kirchner moved to purge the country's authoritarian military and police leadership. The new head of the Federal Police was fired a few months after the election in a corruption scandal—a first in the country's history—and replaced with a well-regarded reformer. Kirchner also took steps to remove justices from the highly politicized Supreme Court, considered the country's most corrupt institution, and signed a decree allowing the extradition of former military officials accused of human rights abuses. The populist Kirchner, a former sympathizer of leftist guerrillas active in the country three decades ago, also moved Argentina into closer alliances with Venezuelan strongman Hugo Chavez and Cuba's Fidel Castro, the world's longest-ruling dictator.

Kirchner's government, buoyed by a projected 7 percent economic growth rate, spent 2003 locked in tough negotiations with the IMF over its demands for sweeping concessions on the renegotiation of Argentina's foreign debt. However, by year's end, the government had yet to tackle needed reforms of an outdated tax system and laws that discouraged domestic and foreign investment. Organized picketers, some of whom appeared to have ties to former members of the intelligence services, showed their muscle by daily blocking key thoroughfares in Buenos Aires and other major metropolitan areas.

**Political Rights and Civil Liberties:** Citizens can change their government democratically. As amended in 1994, the 1853 constitution provides for a president elected for four years with the option of reelection to one term. Presidential candidates must win 45 percent of the vote to avoid a runoff. The legislature consists of the 257-member Chamber of Deputies elected for six years, with half the seats renewable every three years, and the 72-member Senate nominated by elected provincial legislatures for nine-year terms, with one-third of the seats renewable every three years. Two senators are directly elected in the autonomous Buenos Aires federal district.

The 2003 elections were considered to be free and fair, despite claims made by former chief executive Carlos Menem—and considered false by outside observers—that he was withdrawing from the presidential contest out of fear that he would be fraudulently denied the election. The subsequent government of Nestor Kirchner made anticorruption pledges a central theme, and Decree 1172/03 established the public's right to information and other transparency guarantees. However, there are no specific legal protections offered to government or private sector whistleblowers, who must seek redress in inadequate administrative or judicial remedies such as the Public Employees Law or the Work Contract Law.

The press, which was frequently under attack during Menem's presidency, enjoys broad credibility and influence, the latter due in part to the continued discredit of public institutions and the major political parties. In May 2003, the offices of the respected *La Nacion* daily newspaper, critical of the new government's warm relations with Cuba, were the object of a judicially sanctioned raid purportedly meant to probe allegations that some of the paper's shareholders were involved in tax evasion and money laundering.

The constitution guarantees freedom of religion. Nevertheless, the 250,000-strong Jewish community is a frequent target of anti-Semitic vandalism. Neo-Nazi organizations and other anti-Semitic groups, frequently tied to remnants of the old-line security services, remain active. The investigation of the 1994 car bombing of a Jewish community organization, which resulted in 85 deaths, has languished in part because of sloppy police work at the crime scene and the anti-Semitic views of members of the security forces in charge of investigating the crime. New revelations in 2003, suggesting that an investigating judge deliberately sidetracked the investigation by bribing key witnesses with funds from a secret slush fund, increased already strong suspicions that complicity in the attack went high into Menem's inner circle. Academic freedom is a cherished Argentine tradition and in 2003 was largely observed in practice.

The right to organize political parties, civic organizations, and labor unions is generally respected. Labor is dominated by Peronist unions. Union influence, however, has diminished dramatically in the past decade because of corruption scandals, internal divisions, and restrictions on public sector strikes decreed by Menem to pave the way for his privatization program.

Menem's authoritarian ways and manipulation of the judiciary resulted in the undermining of the country's separation of powers and the rule of law. The tenure of scores of incompetent and corrupt judges remains a grave problem. In June, President Nestor Kirchner took an unprecedented step toward establishing an independent judicial system by issuing a decree that limited the president's powers to appoint Supreme Court judges while widening the selection process to include the views of a number of nongovernmental organizations.

Public safety is a primary concern for Argentines, much of it fueled by a marked increase in illegal drug consumption that began during the Menem years. Within a decade, crime in Argentina has doubled, and in Buenos Aires, tripled, including a 50 percent increase in the murder rate in the past five years. In 2003, there were more than 10 murders per 100,000 inhabitants, a number equaled only during the 1970s, when the military dictatorship "disappeared" thousands.

In May 2002, the Argentine penal code was changed; the penalty for being convicted of killing a police officer became a life sentence without the possibility of parole. Police misconduct includes growing numbers of allegedly extrajudicial executions by law enforcement officers. The Buenos Aires provincial police have been involved in drug trafficking, extortion, and vice. Arbitrary arrests and abuse by police are rarely punished in civil courts owing to intimidation of witnesses and judges, particularly in Buenos Aires province. The torture of detainees in police custody in the province is widespread. Prison conditions are generally substandard throughout the country. On a positive note, in 2003, the government's law enforcement minister, Gustavo Beliz, publicly recognized the nexus between political corruption and police misconduct.

Argentina's estimated 700,000 to 1.5 million indigenous people are largely neglected. Approximately 70 percent of the country's rural indigenous communities lack title to their lands.

Women actively participate in politics in Argentina. However, domestic abuse remains a serious problem, and child prostitution is reported to be on the rise. In 2002, the city of Buenos Aires significantly expanded the legal rights of gay and lesbian couples.

# ⬇ Armenia

**Population:** 3,200,000  **Political Rights:** 4
**GNI/capita:** $790  **Civil Liberties:** 4
**Life Expectancy:** 72  **Status:** Partly Free
**Religious Groups:** Armenian Apostolic (94 percent), other Christian (4 percent), Yezidi (2 percent)
**Ethnic Groups:** Armenian (93 percent), Azeri (3 percent), Russian (2 percent), other [including Kurd] (2 percent)
**Capital:** Yerevan
**Trend Arrow:** Armenia received a downward trend arrow for the holding of presidential and parliamentary polls that failed to meet international standards for democratic elections, and for the arrest and detention of large numbers of opposition supporters.

**Ten-Year Ratings Timeline (Political Rights, Civil Liberties, Status)**

| 1994 | 1995 | 1996 | 1997 | 1998 | 1999 | 2000 | 2001 | 2002 | 2003 |
|------|------|------|------|------|------|------|------|------|------|
| 3,4PF | 4,4PF | 5,4PF | 5,4PF | 4,4PF | 4,4PF | 4,4PF | 4,4PF | 4,4PF | 4,4PF |

**Overview:**       The political scene in Armenia was dominated for much of 2003 by developments surrounding the February-March presidential election and the May parliamentary vote, both of which were condemned by international election observers for failing to meet democratic standards. President Robert Kocharian was reelected in a controversial second-round runoff, taking office despite mass street demonstrations against the election results and the detention of hundreds of opposition supporters. Pro-presidential parties gained a majority in parliament and formed a three-party coalition government following legislative elections. The final verdict in the trial of those accused in the October 1999 shootings in parliament had not been reached by November 30, while the brother of a key opposition leader was convicted in a murder case allegedly linked to the parliament killings. Meanwhile, ties with Russia were further strengthened during the year as Moscow extended its control over Armenia's energy sector.

Following a brief period of independence from 1918 to 1920, part of the predominantly Christian Transcaucasus republic of Armenia became a Soviet republic in 1922, while the western portion was ceded to Turkey. Armenia declared its independence from the Soviet Union in September 1991.

The banning of nine political parties prior to the 1995 parliamentary elections ensured the dominance of President Levon Ter Petrosian's ruling Armenian National Movement's (ANM) coalition. In February 1998, Petrosian stepped down following the resignation of key officials in protest over his gradualist approach to solving the conflict over Nagorno-Karabakh, the disputed Armenian enclave in Azerbaijan. Prime Minister Robert Kocharian, the former president of Nagorno-Karabakh, was elected president in March with the support of the previously banned Armenian Revolutionary Federation-Dashnaktsutiun.

Parliamentary elections in May 1999 resulted in an overwhelming victory for the Unity bloc, a new alliance of Defense Minister Vazgen Sarkisian's Republican Party and former Soviet Armenian leader Karen Demirchian's People's Party, which campaigned on a populist platform of greater state involvement in the economy and increased social spending. In June, Sarkisian was named prime minister and Demirchian became speaker of parliament. Kocharian's relationship with Sarkisian and Demirchian was marked by power struggles and policy differences.

The country was plunged into a political crisis on October 27, when five gunmen stormed the parliament building and assassinated Sarkisian, Demirchian, and several other senior government officials. The leader of the gunmen, Nairi Hunanian, maintained that he and the other assailants had acted alone in an attempt to incite a popular revolt against the government. Meanwhile, allegations that Kocharian or members of his inner circle had orchestrated the shootings prompted opposition calls for the president to resign. However, because of an apparent lack of evidence, prosecutors did not press charges against Kocharian, who gradually consolidated his power over the following year. In May 2000, Kocharian named Republican Party leader Andranik Markarian as prime minister, replacing Vazgen Sarkisian's younger brother, Aram, who had served in the position for only five months following the parliament shootings.

The trial of the five gunmen, plus eight others charged with complicity in the parliament shootings, began in February 2001 and finally ended on November 14, 2003. A final verdict had not been reached by the end of November. More than four years after the massacre, many in the country continue to believe that the gunmen were acting on orders from others and accuse the authorities of a high-level cover-up about the identity of the masterminds of the attacks.

Despite earlier pledges by much of the perennially divided opposition to field a joint candidate in the February 19, 2003, presidential election in order to improve its chances of defeating Kocharian, several parties eventually decided to nominate their own candidates. Among the nine challengers in the presidential poll, Kocharian officially received 49.48 percent of the vote, followed by Stepan Demirchian, son of the late Karen Demirchian, with 28.22 percent. Since no candidate received the 50 percent plus 1 vote necessary for a first-round victory, a second-round vote was schedule for March 5 between the top two finishers. According to international election observers, including the Organization for Security and Cooperation in Europe (OSCE), the election fell short of international standards for democratic elections, with the voting, counting, and tabulation processes showing serious irregularities. Other problems noted included media bias in favor of the incumbent and political imbalances in the election commissions.

During the days that followed, thousands rallied in the largest peaceful demonstrations in Yerevan in years to protest alleged election falsification and show support for Stepan Demirchian. According to a highly critical Human Rights Watch report, police used controversial Soviet-era legislation to arrest hundreds of opposition supporters. More than 100 were sentenced in closed-door trials to two weeks in prison on charges of hooliganism and participating in unsanctioned demonstrations.

In the March 5 second-round runoff, Kocharian was reelected with 67.44 percent of the vote, while Demirchian received 32.56 percent. International observers echoed many of the same criticisms as those expressed regarding the first-round vote. The next two months saw further mass protests against the final results of the election and more arrests and detentions reported. The Constitutional Court rejected appeals by opposition leaders to invalidate the election results, although it did propose holding a "referendum of confidence" in Kocharian within the next year to allay widespread doubts about the validity of the election returns. Kocharian promptly replied that he would not comply with the proposal.

The political atmosphere remained tense leading up to the May 25 parliamentary poll. Several hundred candidates were registered to compete for the 56 single-mandate seats, while 17 parties and 4 electoral blocs contested the 75 seats to be distributed under the proportional representation system. The pro-presidential Republican Party, Orinats Yerkir (Country of Law), and Armenian Revolutionary Federation-Dashnaktsutiun secured 40, 19, and 11 seats, respectively. The Artarutiun (Justice) bloc, which was formed in March and is comprised of more than a dozen opposition parties, came in third place with a total of 15 seats. Thus, deputies backing Kocharian, including a number of independent candidates who broadly support the president, secured a majority in parliament. For the first time, the Communist Party failed to pass the 5 percent threshold required to gain seats under the proportional system. The OSCE and Council of Europe noted improvements in the freedom and fairness of the campaign and media coverage when compared with the earlier presidential poll. However, they concluded that the election still fell short of international standards for democratic elections, particularly with regard to the counting and tabulation of votes. Artarutiun refused to recognize the validity of the election returns; a formal appeal of the results was subsequently rejected by the Constitutional Court.

A concurrent referendum on a package of constitutional amendments, representing a wide range of issues and nearly 80 percent of the constitution's articles, was rejected by voters. The amendments reportedly were not widely publicized or well understood by most of the electorate. Although some of the proposed changes were originally intended to curb some of the disproportionate powers of the presidency in relation to other branches of government, opposition parties had argued that the amendments would actually increase them. Other amendments included abolishing a ban on dual citizenship, allowing noncitizens to vote in local elections, and granting foreigners the right to own land in Armenia.

On June 11, the Republican Party, Orinats Yerkir, and the Armenian Revolutionary Federation-Dashnaktsutiun agreed to form a coalition government despite disagreements over some substantive policy issues and the distribution of government posts among the three parties. Andranik Markarian remained prime minister, while Orinats Yerkir chairman Artur Baghdasarian was named speaker of parliament. The following day, Artarutiun and another opposition party elected to parliament, the National Unity Party, boycotted the opening session of parliament to protest the results of the parliamentary election; they finally ended the boycott in early September.

In a politically sensational case, Armen Sarkisian, the brother of former prime ministers Aram and Vazgen, was convicted on November 18 of ordering the December 28, 2002, murder of Tigran Naghdalian, the head of Armenian Public Television and Radio. Sarkisian was sentenced to 15 years in prison, as was the trigger man, John Harutiunian, while another 11 defendants received prison sentences of 7 to 12 years. The prosecution had argued that Sarkisian had ordered the murder in revenge because he believed that Naghdalian was somehow involved in the October 1999 parliament shootings, in which his brother Vazgen had been killed. However, some opposition members maintained that the case was a politically motivated campaign against Armen's brother, Aram, a vocal critic of Kocharian's leadership. They also believed that the murder was part of a government cover-up to prevent Naghdalian from testifying in the ongoing trial over the parliament shootings; Naghdalian had been in the control room of his television station when the shootings, which were recorded on videocassettes, occurred. Critics of the verdict questioned the validity of the evidence in the case against him; in August, Harutiunian retracted pretrial testimony that Armen had ordered the murder, contending that he had signed his original testimony under duress.

Relations with Russia, which counts Armenia as its closest ally in the Caucasus, continued to be strengthened during the year. In exchange for a write-off of its considerable debts to Moscow, Yerevan agreed to transfer key state-owned assets to Moscow, including six hydroelectric power plants. In September, Armenia ratified an agreement to transfer financial control of the Medzamor nuclear power plant to Russia. These deals will provide Moscow, with its already substantial military interests in Armenia, with additional political and economic leverage over Yerevan.

Despite ongoing international pressure to resolve the long-standing Nagorno-Karabakh conflict, little progress was made during the year on reaching a breakthrough. Sporadic exchanges of fire along the ceasefire line continued, but did not escalate into full-scale fighting. At the same time, neither Kocharian nor Azerbaijan's president Heydar Aliev appeared willing to risk the domestic political consequences of making major public concessions over the disputed territory, particularly during a presidential election year in both countries.

**Political Rights and Civil Liberties:** Armenians cannot change their government democratically. The 1995 and 1999 parliamentary and 1996 presidential elections were characterized by serious irregularities. The most recent presidential and parliamentary polls, in February-March and May 2003, respectively, were strongly criticized by international election monitors, who cited widespread fraud particularly in the presidential vote. The 1995 constitution provides for a weak legislature and a strong, directly elected president who appoints the prime minister. Most parties in Armenia are dominated by specific government officials or other powerful figures, suffer from significant internal dissent and division, or are weak and ineffective. President Robert Kocharian formally belongs to no political party, but instead relies on the support of a number of both large and small political groups, including the Republican Party of Prime Minister Adranik Markarian.

Bribery and nepotism are reportedly quite common among government bureaucrats. In November 2003, the government approved a long-awaited anticorruption program that had been drafted with the support of the World Bank.

There are some limits on freedom of the press, and self-censorship among journalists is common, particularly in reporting on Nagorno-Karabakh, national security, or corruption issues. While most newspapers are privately owned, the majority operate with limited resources and consequently are dependent on economic and political interest groups for their survival. There are a number of private television stations, and most radio stations are privately owned. In April 2003, journalist Mger Galechian was assaulted in his office by a group of assailants and was hospitalized with head injuries. Galechian was a correspondent for the opposition newspaper *Chorrod Iskhanutyun*, known for being strongly critical of the government. As of November 30, parliament had not yet adopted the final version of a controversial draft media law. International organizations and media watchdogs criticized provisions, including one requiring media organizations to reveal their sources of funding and another permitting the courts to compel journalists to disclose their sources to protect the public interest. Meanwhile, the criminal code makes libel an offense punishable by up to three years in prison, while insulting a public official could lead to two year's imprisonment.

On April 3, 2002, the independent television station A1+ lost its license after the national television and radio broadcasting commission granted a tender for its broadcasting frequency to an entertainment channel. Journalists and opposition politicians criticized the closure of A1+, which had a reputation for objective reporting, as a politically motivated decision to control media coverage in the run-up to the 2003 presidential and parliamentary elections. Following the decision, thousands of people demonstrated in a number of weekly protests over the station's closure and to demand President Kocharian's resignation. In 2003, additional bids by A1+ for a broadcast frequency were rejected.

Freedom of religion is somewhat respected. The Armenian Apostolic Church, to which 90 percent of Armenians formally belong, enjoys a privileged status and has advocated for restrictions on nontraditional denominations. While 50 religious groups are officially registered, the Jehovah's Witnesses have been denied registration repeatedly because of the group's strong opposition to compulsory military service; 23 members are in prison for practicing conscientious objection. Draft legislation providing for alternative military service was pending in parliament as of

November 2003. The law's adoption is likely to clear the way for the registration of the Jehovah's Witnesses.

In general, the government does not restrict academic freedom. In September 2002, the Ministry of Education ordered the compulsory display of the portraits of Kocharian and the head of the Armenian Apostolic Church in secondary schools. The history of the Apostolic Church is a required school subject.

The government generally respects freedom of assembly and association, although the registration requirements for nongovernmental associations are cumbersome and time-consuming. According to a report by Human Rights Watch, the authorities abused administrative detention regulations to intimidate and punish peaceful demonstrators and political activists following the February 2003 presidential election. More than 100 activists were sentenced to up to 15 days in prison for attending or engaging in acts of hooliganism at rallies that the authorities said were unauthorized, the report stated. The authorities arrested some individuals who were not protest organizers, even though only leaders—and not mere participants— of unauthorized rallies may be penalized under the country's code of administrative offenses. After major international organizations, including the OSCE and Council of Europe, condemned the crackdowns, the authorities began to release some of the arrested at the beginning of March. While the constitution enshrines the right to form and join trade unions, in practice, labor organizations are weak and relatively inactive.

The judiciary, which is subject to political pressure from the executive branch, is characterized by widespread violations of due process. Police frequently make arbitrary arrests without warrants, beat detainees during arrest and interrogation, and use torture to extract confessions. A Human Rights Watch report concluded that police denied access to legal counsel to those opposition supporters who were given short prison terms for participating in unauthorized rallies after the 2003 presidential vote. The accused were sentenced in closed trials and denied the opportunity to present evidence or lodge formal appeals. In April, the Constitutional Court declared that these and other related arrests were unlawful. However, the Council of Justice, a judicial oversight body headed by Kocharian, rejected the Court's recommendation to investigate the mass arrests and the conduct of those judges who had issued the detention sentences.

In September 2003, parliament voted to abolish the death penalty in all cases by ratifying Protocol 6 of the Council of Europe's Convention on the Protection of Human Rights and Fundamental Freedoms. Although the abolition of capital punishment was a major obligation of Armenia's membership in the Council of Europe, the government had delayed ratifying Protocol 6 largely because of widespread support for the use of the death penalty against the suspects in the October 1999 parliament shootings. In November, Kocharian signed amendments to a new criminal code denying parole to those sentenced to life imprisonment for grave crimes, including terrorist acts and assassinations of public figures. The amendments were regarded as a guarantee that those on trial for the parliament shootings would never be released from prison.

Although members of the country's tiny ethnic minority population rarely report cases of overt discrimination, they have complained about difficulties receiving education in their native languages.

Freedom of travel and residence is largely respected. However, registering changes in residency is sometimes complicated by the need to negotiate with an inefficient or corrupt government bureaucracy. While citizens have the right to own private property and establish businesses, an inefficient and often corrupt court system and unfair business competition hinder operations. Key industries remain in the hands of oligarchs and influential clans who received preferential treatment in the early stages of privatization.

Domestic violence and trafficking in women and girls for the purpose of prostitution are believed to be serious problems. In June 2003, the U.S. State Department issued a report that cited Armenia as among those countries making significant efforts to comply with minimum requirements for eliminating trafficking. Traditional societal norms tend to limit women's professional opportunities to more low-skilled jobs.

# Australia

**Population:** 19,900,000   **Political Rights:** 1
**GNI/capita:** $19,900   **Civil Liberties:** 1
**Life Expectancy:** 80   **Status:** Free
**Religious Groups:** Anglican (26 percent), Roman Catholic (26 percent), other Christian (24.3 percent), non-Christian (11 percent), other (12.7 percent)
**Ethnic Groups:** White (92 percent), Asian (7 percent), other [including Aboriginal] (1 percent)
**Capital:** Canberra

**Ten-Year Ratings Timeline (Political Rights, Civil Liberties, Status)**

| 1994 | 1995 | 1996 | 1997 | 1998 | 1999 | 2000 | 2001 | 2002 | 2003 |
|------|------|------|------|------|------|------|------|------|------|
| 1,1F | 1,1F | 1,1F | 1,1F | 1,1F | 1,1F | 1,1F | 1,1F | 1,1F | 1,1F |

**Overview:**
On the domestic front, illegal immigration and the government's responses to it continued to create headlines in Australia's local media in 2003. In international affairs, Australia was an active force in helping to restore peace and order in Bougainville, Papua New Guinea (PNG), and in promoting regional cooperation to counter terrorism. Australia's involvement in fighting terrorism also went beyond the region, with the country committing troops to the U.S.-led Operation Iraqi Freedom.

Claimed by the British in 1770, Australia gained independence in January 1901 as a commonwealth of six states. The government adopted the Northern Territories and the capital territory of Canberra as territorial units in 1911. The Labor Party and the conservative Liberal Party are the dominant parties. Prime Minister John Howard of the Liberal Party and the rural-based National Party coalition has been in power since 1996.

A surge in illegal immigration has prompted the government to tighten immigration laws. There is considerable public support for these new measures despite international criticism and challenges by some human rights advocates. The government tried to limit legal challenges on judgments made by the Refugee Review Tribunal, an independent body that examines decisions of the immigration department. In February 2003, the High Court ruled that applicants would be allowed to challenge judgments if they could prove, within strict time limits, that the tribunal had made mistakes. The government said the appeals system needed reform and that the fourfold increase in court cases overburdened the system and taxpayers when few could be proven. Official figures show that in 2001, only 100 out of more than 2,500 appeals lodged were successful. Nevertheless, a federal court ruled in April that the government has no power to detain asylum seekers prior to deportation when they have been refused permission to enter another country.

As a result of these rulings, the government decided in July to increase the number of refugees taken from offshore immigration detention centers that do not have third-country options. More than 700 refugees processed on Nauru and PNG have been resettled in other countries. The government also agreed to give permanent residency to nearly half of 1,400 East Timorese asylum seekers.

Since a ceasefire was reached in Bougainville in 1998, Australia has sent 3,500 military personnel and 300 monitors to PNG. A new multilateral transition team, led by Australia, took over the peace process from the UN Observers Mission at the end of June. Australia also sent troops, police, and other personnel to the Solomon Islands in July to lead a multinational force to restore law and order after years of ethnic warfare. And in August, Australia pledged $10 million to build a regional police training center in Fiji to support law, justice, and police reforms in South Pacific nations.

An Australian foreign policy white paper warned that weakened states in the South Pacific are vulnerable to terrorist activity, as reflected in growing corruption, lawlessness, and instability. This "arc of instability" north of Australia included PNG, Vanuatu, and Fiji. Australia signed antiterrorism accords with Fiji in February and the Philippines in May, following similar treaties with Indonesia, Malaysia, and Thailand in 2002. The treaties commit these countries to increasing cooperation in law enforcement, intelligence and information sharing, and other initiatives to disrupt terrorists and their financial backers. Canberra's call for public sector reform, improved law and order, policing, judicial reform, and increased accountability for aid money in PNG stirred tensions between the two countries. Australia is the largest donor to PNG, providing aid worth $300 million annually.

Canberra's decision to send 2,000 troops to Iraq sparked sharp debates and antiwar protests in many of the country's larger cities. When order broke down at a protest in Sydney in March, with demonstrators hurling chairs and bottles at the police, the government threatened legal action to prevent further rallies if protest organizers could not commit to peaceful protests.

**Political Rights and Civil Liberties:** Australia is a constitutional democracy with a federal parliamentary form of government. Citizens participate in free and fair multiparty elections to choose representatives to the parliament.

The constitution does not provide for freedom of speech and of the press, but citizens and the media freely criticize the government without reprisal. In a rare instance of government intervention, the government announced in March that it is monitoring and blocking electronic mail messages sent to its troops in Iraq. Messages that are "negative, inappropriate, and not supportive" would be blocked to protect the morale of Australian troops involved in the U.S.-led military action to oust the Iraqi regime. Freedom of religion is respected.

The rights of assembly and association are not codified in law, but the government respects these rights in practice. Workers have the right to organize and bargain collectively, but the Federal Workplace Relations Act of 1996 has imposed numerous restrictions. Critics charge that this law has made it more difficult for unions to get into workplaces and organize workers. This law also abolished closed shops and union demarcations.

The judiciary is independent, but aborigines say they are routinely mistreated and discriminated by police and prison officials. Indeed, the Aboriginal population suffers from general discrimination, a disproportionately high level of unemployment (three times that of the general population), inferior access to medical care and education, and a life expectancy 20 years shorter than that for the nonindigenous population. Aboriginal people are also under-represented at all levels of political leadership and have imprisonment rates 15 times higher than that of the general population.

Aboriginal groups have called for an official apology for the "Stolen Generation" of Aboriginal children who were taken from their parents by the government from 1910 until the early 1970s and raised by foster parents and in orphanages. Government officials have stood firm against such an apology, reasoning that the present generation has no responsibility to apologize for the wrongs of a previous generation.

Australia began to tighten its immigration policy following a marked increase in illegal migrants, mostly from the Middle East, during the 1998-2001 period. In one instance, more than 430 mainly Afghani migrants tried to sail to Australia in 2001. Canberra refused to grant them entry to Australia when a Norwegian commercial freighter that rescued them in the Indian Ocean tried to turn them over to Australia. Canberra transferred them to Australian-funded refugee holding facilities in Nauru and PNG.

Many people, particularly legal immigrants, complained that these boat refugees are "queue jumpers." The government cited this complaint as a reason for the Migration Amendment Bill in 2001. This law removed barred noncitizens from applying for "permanent protection visas" (which allows the person to live and work permanently in Australia as a refugee) if entry was unlawful and occurred in one of several "excised" territories along the country's northern arc: Christmas Island, Ashmore and Cartier Islands, the Cocos Islands, and resource installations designated by the government. All such foreign nationals would be detained and released pending full adjudication of their asylum claim.

Although women enjoy equal rights and freedoms, violence against women is a growing problem, particularly within the Aboriginal population.

# Austria

**Population:** 8,200,000
**GNI/capita:** $23,940
**Life Expectancy:** 79
**Political Rights:** 1
**Civil Liberties:** 1
**Status:** Free
**Religious Groups:** Roman Catholic (78 percent),
Protestant (5 percent), other [including Muslim] (17 percent)
**Ethnic Groups:** German (88 percent), non-nationals
[includes Croats, Slovenes, Hungarians, Czechs, Slovaks,
Roma] (9.3 percent), naturalized [includes those who have lived in Austria at least
three generations] (2 percent)
**Capital:** Vienna

**Ten-Year Ratings Timeline (Political Rights, Civil Liberties, Status)**

| 1994 | 1995 | 1996 | 1997 | 1998 | 1999 | 2000 | 2001 | 2002 | 2003 |
|------|------|------|------|------|------|------|------|------|------|
| 1,1F | 1,1F | 1,1F | 1,1F | 1,1F | 1,1F | 1,1F | 1,1F | 1,1F | 1,1F |

**Overview:**
While the inclusion of the far-right Freedom Party in government since 2000 has caused an international stir, it has also blunted the protest appeal of this formerly radical party. In 2003, Austria returned to focusing on basic socioeconomic issues, such as privatization and pension reform. In a move criticized by the UN High Commissioner for Refugees, Austria tightened asylum laws in 2003.

Modern Austria emerged at the end of World War I, when the Austro-Hungarian Empire was dismembered. It was voluntarily annexed to Nazi Germany in 1938 and suffered the defeat of Hitler's regime. Postwar Austria, by consent of the superpower Allies, remained neutral between the Cold War blocs. Focusing instead on economic growth, Austria has developed one of the wealthiest economies in Europe.

From 1986 until 2000, the two biggest political parties—the center-left Social Democratic Party of Austria (SPO) and the center-right People's Party of Austria (OVP)—governed together in a grand coalition. Members of the two parties shared in the administration of not only cabinet ministries, but also many other government functions. Labor relations were corporatist, with management and unions both represented not only in individual firms' decision making, but also in national policymaking.

The election of October 1999 saw the emergence of the first government since 1970 not to include the Social Democrats. Instead, the People's Party formed a coalition with the Freedom Party, a far-right nationalist party with vestigial Nazi sympathies. The Freedom Party had grown steadily in the polls as voters became disaffected with the power sharing of the two big parties and the near impossibility of major political change. The Freedom Party won its biggest ever share of the vote, 27 percent, in that election, and was thus included in a coalition with the People's Party's Wolfgang Schuessel as chancellor.

The reaction among fellow members of the European Union (EU) was immediate and dramatic. In 2000, the EU officially suspended ties with Austria. Though this had little practical effect, technically it meant that the other 14 EU countries had to deal with Austria on a bilateral basis rather than through the EU. It also saw support for the Freedom Party shoot up, as Austrian voters resented the EU's attempts to interfere with the choice Austrians had expressed at the polls. Later in 2000, however, the EU reinstated Austria.

One effect of the EU sanctions was that Joerg Haider, the Freedom Party's leader, withdrew from that post and contented himself with the governorship of the state of Carinthia. Haider had been both Freedom's biggest vote-winner and the source of its major controversies. For example, he referred to Nazi death camps as "punishment camps" and once told a rally of former SS officers that they were worth "honor and respect," though he also referred to the Nazi regime as a "cruel and brutal dictatorship." With Haider's official withdrawal from national politics, Austrian politics returned to near-normality and Freedom was forced to moderate its far-right stances as it dealt with the day-to-day reality of governing.

However, Haider could not remain absent from the national stage for long, and he continually tried to pull strings with the national Freedom leaders, including Susanne Riess-Passer, the vice chancellor and formal Freedom Party leader. Internal Freedom Party wrangling caused the party to withdraw from the coalition in September 2002. The elections of November 2002 saw the Freedom Party's vote share fall from 27 percent in 1999 to 10 percent. In subsequent cabinet negotiations, the People's Party failed to reach an agreement with the Social Democrats to restore the grand coalition, and similarly failed with the Greens. Thus, the Freedom Party was once again included, but this time as the clearly junior partner, and subsequent local election results in 2003 confirmed its decline in the polls.

The second term under Schuessel has seen the united right government tackle several sensitive questions of political economy, including pensions and privatization. Despite massive—and, for Austria, highly unusual—protest strikes in May, a pension reform was pushed through in June that capped benefits from the costly pay-as-you-go system. The privatization of the Voestalpine steel works also caused some nationalist backlash, with a rumored sale to a Canadian company prompting the finance minister, Karl-Heinz Grasser, to insist that Voestalpine would remain in Austrian hands. Proposed reforms of the federal rail system have also drawn threats of strikes from the labor unions.

In October 2003, the government tightened asylum laws. Austria has the highest number of asylum seekers per capita in Europe, and the asylum issue had been a vote winner for the Freedom Party. Under the new law, criticized by the UN High Commissioner for Refugees, some asylum seekers could be deported while appeals of their cases are held. New arrivals will be asked for full statements within 72 hours. The government insists that it is merely trying to speed up the process and that 85 percent of those who come are actually economic migrants.

**Political Rights and Civil Liberties:** Austrians can change their government democratically. Perhaps ironically, the participation of the Freedom Party in government emphasized this basic right when other European countries tried in 2000 to induce Austrians to forgo their democratic choice.

Though there are competitive political parties and free and fair elections, the traditional practice of grand coalitions in Austria has disillusioned many with the political process. Frustration with the cozy relationship between the People's Party and the Social Democrats helped lead to the rise of the Freedom Party as a protest party. However, Austria is less corrupt than during the 1980s, when campaign donation laws were tightened somewhat.

The media are free, though not highly pluralistic. The end of the monopoly of the state broadcaster ORF has not brought significant competition to the broadcast market, and print media ownership is concentrated in a few hands, particularly the News and the Print-Medien groups. Harassment suits by the Freedom Party against investigative and critical journalists have hampered reporters' work.

Religious freedom is respected in Austria and enshrined in the constitution. However, there are only 12 officially recognized religions, and these have the ability to draw on state funds for religious education. The process of joining that group requires a period of ten years of observation, a practice that the Jehovah's Witnesses have complained violates their freedom of religion. However, the Witnesses are recognized as a "confessional community." Academic freedom is generally respected.

Freedoms of assembly and association are protected in the constitution, and trade unions have traditionally been powerful. They not only are free to organize and strike, but have been considered an essential partner in national policy making. Strikes held in May 2003 against the government's controversial pension reforms did not stop those reforms from going through.

The judiciary is independent, and a constitutional court examines the compatibility of legislation with the constitution. Austria is a member of the Council of Europe, and its citizens have recourse to the European Court of Human Rights in Strasbourg.

Demonstrators protested in July after a man from Mauritania was killed in a disturbance at an exhibition of African culture. Generally speaking, residents are afforded equal protection under the law. However, immigration has fueled some resentment toward minorities and foreigners, and asylum laws are among the tightest in the developed world.

A 1979 law guarantees women freedom from discrimination in various areas, especially the workplace. A 1993 law sought to increase women's employment in government agencies where women were underrepresented.

# Azerbaijan

**Population:** 8,200,000
**GNI/capita:** $710
**Life Expectancy:** 72
**Political Rights:** 6
**Civil Liberties:** 5
**Status:** Not Free
**Religious Groups:** Muslim (93 percent), Russian
Orthodox (3 percent), Armenian Orthodox (2 percent),
other (2 percent)
**Ethnic Groups:** Azeri (90 percent), Dagestani (3 percent),
Russian (3 percent), Armenian (2 percent), other (2 percent)
**Capital:** Baku
**Ratings Change:** Azerbaijan's status declined from Partly Free to Not Free due to
the holding of seriously flawed presidential elections in October and a subsequent
government crackdown on opposition supporters.

**Ten-Year Ratings Timeline (Political Rights, Civil Liberties, Status)**

| 1994 | 1995 | 1996 | 1997 | 1998 | 1999 | 2000 | 2001 | 2002 | 2003 |
|------|------|------|------|------|------|------|------|------|------|
| 6,6NF | 6,6NF | 6,5NF | 6,4PF | 6,4PF | 6,4PF | 6,5PF | 6,5PF | 6,5PF | 6,5NF |

**Overview:**

The October 15, 2003 presidential election marked the end of an era in Azerbaijan, as the ailing President Heydar Aliev, who had long dominated the country's political life, withdrew from the race less than two weeks before the vote. His son, Ilham, who was widely regarded as his father's preferred successor, was voted head of state in an election marred by systematic and widespread fraud. The results of the poll sparked public protests and a violent police crackdown, followed by the detention of hundreds of opposition supporters.

After having been controlled by the Ottoman Empire since the seventeenth century, Azerbaijan entered the Soviet Union in 1922 as part of the Transcaucasian Soviet Federal Republic, becoming a separate Soviet republic in 1936. Following a referendum in 1991, Azerbaijan declared independence from the disintegrating Soviet Union.

In June 1992, Abulfaz Elchibey, leader of the nationalist opposition Azerbaijan Popular Front, was elected president in a generally free and fair vote. A military coup one year later ousted him from power and installed the former first secretary of the Azerbaijan Communist Party, Heydar Aliev, in his place. In the October 1993 presidential elections, Aliev reportedly received almost 99 percent of the vote. Azerbaijan's first post-Soviet parliamentary elections, held in November 1995, saw five leading opposition parties and some 600 independent candidates barred from the vote in which Aliev's Yeni Azerbaijan Party (YAP) won the most seats. In October 1998, Aliev was chosen president with more than 70 percent of the vote in an election characterized by serious irregularities.

In a widely expected outcome, the ruling YAP captured the majority of seats in the November 2000 parliamentary election. The Azerbaijan Popular Front and the Communist Party came in a distant second and third, respectively. International monitors from the Organization for Security and Cooperation in Europe (OSCE) and the Council of Europe cited mass electoral fraud, including the stuffing of ballot boxes and a strong pro-government bias in state-run media. Despite widespread criticism of the elections, the Council of Europe approved Azerbaijan's application for membership just days after the vote, a decision widely criticized by international human rights groups.

An August 2002 national referendum led to the adoption of a series of constitutional amendments, some of which critics charged would further strengthen the ruling party's grip on power. One particularly controversial amendment stipulates that the prime minister becomes president if the head of state resigns or is incapacitated. Critics charged that the aging and ailing Aliev would appoint his son, Ilham, prime minister in order to engineer a transfer of power. Opposition groups and the OSCE charged that the referendum was marred by fraud, including ballot-box stuffing, intimidation of election monitors and officials, and inflated voter-turnout figures of nearly 90 percent.

Throughout 2002, a number of demonstrations were held to demand various political and economic changes, including Aliev's resignation. In June, an unarmed protestor was shot and killed by police in the town of Nardaran, the first time that such a tragedy had occurred since Azerbaijan's independence more than a decade ago. The government blamed the riots on radical Islamic groups, although residents insisted that the authorities used these accusations as a pretext to repress dissent. In April 2003, 15 individuals arrested in Nardaran in 2002 were found guilty of fomenting the unrest and given prison terms or suspended sentences; during the year, the four defendants who had been imprisoned were pardoned and released.

In the months preceding the October 15, 2003 presidential elections, the political atmosphere was marked by uncertainty over Aliev's declining health and its ramifications for his reelection bid. The 80-year old Aliev, who had a history of heart trouble, collapsed during a live television broadcast in April and left Azerbaijan that summer to receive medical treatment in Turkey and the United States. At the same time, government officials continued to deny that his health problems were serious, and he remained the official YAP candidate for the presidential election.

Heydar Aliev's son, Ilham, was officially nominated as a presidential candidate in June by a group of residents from the autonomous exclave of Nakhichevan, the home territory of the Aliev family. He was appointed prime minister in August, but took a leave of absence from his post just days after being appointed so that he could legally run for president (the election code prohibits a serving prime minister from running for president). On October 2, the elder Aliev withdrew his candidacy in favor of his son's.

Final figures released by the Central Election Commission showed Ilham Aliev defeating seven challengers with nearly 77 percent of the vote. His closest rival, opposition Musavat Party leader Isa Gambar, received only 14 percent of the vote, while six other candidates received less than 4 percent each. According to OSCE observers, the election was marred by widespread fraud and failed to meet international standards for democratic elections. Among the irregularities noted were partisan election commissions favoring the governing party and its supporters; the failure of authorities to adequately implement a new electoral code; the use of flawed procedures to deny registration to several potential candidates; serious flaws in the counting and tabulation of votes; limitations on election observation by domestic civic groups; and biased media coverage favoring Ilham Aliev.

Meanwhile, the authorities' obstruction of many opposition rallies and the beating and arrest of hundreds of opposition activists overshadowed much of the campaign and election period. After violent clashes between security forces and demonstrators in Baku on October 15 and 16, in which at least one person was reportedly killed and several hundred were injured, the authorities unleashed a crackdown against the opposition in which more than 600 people were detained. Among those arrested were opposition party leaders and supporters who had not been directly involved in the preceding days' violence, along with many election officials who refused to certify fraudulent election results.

In a region of the world wracked by years of instability, the ramifications of Ilham's victory are being watched closely by both domestic and international observers. A post-election challenge for Ilham, who is described as lacking his father's commanding presence, will be consolidating his power base among the ruling elite. At the same time, Aliev is expected to continue many of his father's economic policies, including supporting the lucrative Baku-Ceyhan oil pipeline, a key energy project for the West.

A lasting settlement for the disputed territory of Nagorno-Karabakh, over which Armenia and Azerbaijan fought in the early 1990s, remained elusive during the year. The region, which is formally part of Azerbaijan, is now predominantly ethnic Armenian and effectively under Armenian control. Several violations of the 1994 ceasefire occurred during the summer of 2003, although they did not erupt into full-scale fighting.

**Political Rights and Civil Liberties:** Citizens of Azerbaijan cannot change their government democratically. The country's constitution provides for a strong presidency, and in practice parliament exercises little independence from the executive branch. The 1993, 1998, and 2003 presidential and 1995 and 2000 parliamentary elections were considered neither free nor fair by international observers. Amendments to the constitution, adopted in a 2002 referendum, included a provision replacing the proportional-representation system, under which one-fifth of the members of parliament were elected, with single-mandate constituency races, under which the remaining four-fifths of parliament were already chosen. Opposition parties argued that the proportional system was the only way for them to participate in elections, since most lack nationwide organizations.

More than 40 political parties are registered. However, most opposition parties are weak and are based on personalities rather than political platforms, and they have been unable to unite in lasting alliances to challenge the government. Hundreds of opposition activists and leaders were detained by police in the weeks surrounding the October 2003 presidential election.

Corruption is endemic throughout Azerbaijani society, with government officials rarely held accountable for engaging in corrupt practices. Transparency International's 2003 Corruption Perceptions Index ranked Azerbaijan 124 out of 133 countries surveyed.

Although the constitution guarantees freedom of speech and the press, journalists who publish articles critical of the president or other prominent state officials are routinely harassed and prosecuted, and self-censorship is common. State-owned newspapers and broadcast media reflect the position of the government. Independent and opposition papers struggle financially in the face of low circulation, limited advertising revenues, and heavy fines or imprisonment of their staff. In March, 400 delegates from some 170 print media outlets gathered to establish a press council to address ongoing pressures faced by the country's media. However, an alliance of six other publications boycotted the meeting over concerns that the selection of members to the council had not been conducted transparently. Libel is a criminal offense. In early 2003, Elmar Huseynov, editor-in-chief of the independent *Monitor* magazine, was convicted of libel in connection with an article he wrote about the prevalence of corruption in Azerbaijan, including comparisons of the government with the Sicilian mafia. Huseynov has been targeted with legal harassment for several years over his criticisms of government policies.

During the run-up and aftermath of the 2003 presidential election, journalists suffered increased intimidation and attacks, including physical assaults while reporting on political opposition rallies. Other restrictions on the nonstate media included editorial interference and lawsuits for criticizing government officials. Rauf Arifoglu, editor of the opposition *Yeni Musavat* newspaper, was arrested for allegedly organizing public demonstrations on October 16 and sentenced to three months in prison; he remained in detention as of November 30.

The government restricts some religious activities of members of "nontraditional" minority religious groups through burdensome registration requirements and interference in the import and distribution of printed religious materials. Islam, Russian Orthodoxy, and Judaism are considered traditional religions, and their members can generally worship freely.

Some faculty members and students reportedly were pressured to support governing-party candidates in the 2003 presidential election and were instructed to attend pro-government events, according to an OSCE report. A number of teachers were allegedly targeted for reduced work hours or dismissal in connection with their membership in opposition political parties, according to the 2003 U.S. State Department human rights report. Security services are believed to monitor some telephone conversations and Internet traffic, particularly of prominent political and business figures, according to the U.S. State Department report.

The government frequently restricts freedom of assembly, particularly for political parties critical of the government. Although a number of political demonstrations took place without incident during the weeks surrounding the 2003 presidential election, local authorities frequently obstructed opposition rallies and beat and arbitrarily arrested many participants of unauthorized protests. Police assaulted dozens of party leaders, journalists, and others at a peaceful campaign event on September 21 in Baku. On the eve of the election, security forces attacked peaceful protestors who had gathered in front of the headquarters of the opposition Musavat Party. The following day, several thousand people gathered at an unsanctioned rally at Azadliq Square in Baku to protest preliminary election figures. After some of the participants began beating security officers and damaging government buildings, police and military troops used excessive force to disperse the demonstrators, killing at least one person and injuring several hundred others. As of November 30, the government had not arrested any law enforcement officials or announced the findings of an investigation in connection with the violent disturbances.

Registration with the Ministry of Justice is required for a nongovernmental organization (NGO) to function as a legal entity, and the registration process has been described as cumbersome and nontransparent. Amendments adopted in 2003 to NGO laws further complicated requirements for registering grants. In 2003, several leading human rights defenders, including Eldar Zeynalov, the chair of the Human Rights Center of Azerbaijan, were subjected to harassment and intimidation believed to be state-sanctioned. Although the law permits the formation of trade unions and the right to strike, the majority of trade unions remain closely affiliated with the government, and most major industries are state-owned. There is no effective collective bargaining system between unions and management representatives.

The judiciary is subservient to the executive branch and is corrupt and inefficient. Arbitrary arrest and detention are common, particularly for members of the political opposition. Detainees are often held for long periods before trial, and their access to lawyers is restricted. Police abuse of suspects during arrest and interrogation reportedly remains commonplace, with torture sometimes used to extract confessions. According to a report by Human Rights Watch, law enforcement officials tortured many of those detained in the post-October 2003 election crackdowns against the political opposition. The group also documented many more cases of police beatings during the 2003 presidential campaign than during the 2000 parliamentary election campaign. Local human rights groups maintain that more than 100 political prisoners are held in detention throughout the country. Prison conditions are reportedly harsh and even life-threatening, with many inmates suffering from overcrowding and inadequate medical care.

Some members of ethnic minority groups, including the small Armenian population, have complained of discrimination in areas including education, employment, and housing. Hundreds of thousands of ethnic Azeris who fled the war in Nagorno-Karabakh have been prevented by the Armenian government from returning to their homes and remain in Azerbaijan, often living in appalling conditions.

Significant parts of the economy are in the hands of a corrupt elite, which severely limits equality of opportunity. Supporters of the political opposition face job discrimination, demotion, or dismissal. In 2003, Human Rights Watch documented more than 100 cases in which opposition supporters or their relatives were fired from their jobs because of their opposition activities.

Traditional societal norms and poor economic conditions restrict women's professional roles; there are 12 women in the country's 125-seat parliament. Domestic violence is a problem, and there are no laws regarding spousal abuse. Azerbaijan is a country of origin and a transit point for the trafficking of women for prostitution.

# Bahamas

**Population:** 300,000
**GNI/capita:** $14,860
**Life Expectancy:** 72
**Religious Groups:** Baptist (32 percent), Anglican
(20 percent), Roman Catholic (19 percent),
other Protestant (18 percent), other (11 percent)
**Ethnic Groups:** Black (85 percent), white (12 percent),
Asian and Hispanic (3 percent)
**Capital:** Nassau

**Political Rights:** 1
**Civil Liberties:** 1
**Status:** Free

**Ten-Year Ratings Timeline (Political Rights, Civil Liberties, Status)**

| 1994 | 1995 | 1996 | 1997 | 1998 | 1999 | 2000 | 2001 | 2002 | 2003 |
|------|------|------|------|------|------|------|------|------|------|
| 1,2F | 1,2F | 1,2F | 1,2F | 1,2F | 1,1F | 1,1F | 1,1F | 1,1F | 1,1F |

**Overview:**

Despite ongoing efforts to curb narcotics trafficking and money laundering, the Bahamas continued to be faced with rising drug-related crime and the illicit use of the country's offshore financial system throughout 2003.

The Bahamas, a 700-island archipelago in the Caribbean, gained independence in 1973 and is part of the Commonwealth. Lynden Pindling served as first prime minister and head of the Progressive Liberal Party (PLP) for 25 years. After years of allegations of corruption and involvement by high officials in narcotics trafficking, Pindling was defeated by the Free National Movement (FNM) in 1992. Prime Minister Hubert Ingraham promised honesty, efficiency, and accountability in government. The FNM won 32 seats in the House of Assembly, to the PLP's 17.

In the 1997 election, Ingraham took credit for revitalizing the economy by attracting foreign investment, and his FNM received 34 seats to the PLP's 6. In April 1997, Pindling resigned as opposition leader and was replaced by Perry Christie.

In the May 2002 parliamentary poll, the PLP won 29 seats, while the FNM received only 8. Prime Minister Ingraham retired from politics, fulfilling a promise he had made prior to the elections. He was replaced by PLP leader Christie who, while not as popular as Ingraham, was able to capitalize on the large majority of his party. Christie and Ingraham are close personal friends and business partners, which may indicate that the new prime minister's economic and political policies are not likely to diverge much from those of his predecessor's.

Rising crime rates in the late 1990s, which undermined the early accomplishments of the Ingraham government, were linked to illegal trafficking in narcotics and gunrunning. Ingraham is credited with having subsequently improved the country's international reputation with policies that reduced money laundering and improved counter-narcotics cooperation with the United States. His administration set up a new antidrug intelligence unit and announced plans to bring the financial sector into full compliance with international standards and practices by strengthening requirements to report suspicious and unusual transactions. The Bahamas has promoted tourism and allowed the banking industry to grow, leading to the country having become one of the Caribbean's most affluent.

However, the Christie administration has not been able to effectively curb narcotics trafficking, and the incidence of violent crime associated with drug gang activity has escalated. In addition, the offshore financial system, despite having undergone reforms, continues to be used for illicit purposes. Several banks have been named in U.S. fraud cases, while at least two individuals have been convicted on fraud and forgery charges.

Following a confrontation with the U.S. ambassador over counter-narcotics policies that were mostly addressed, relations with the United States have improved. Bahamians are sensitive to the perception that their international policy is determined by Washington and have struck to independent foreign relations, including an upgrading of relations with Cuba, with the announcement that a Bahamian consul general will be appointed to Havana in 2004-2005.

**Political Rights and Civil Liberties:** The 1973 constitution provides for democratic changes in government. Political parties can organize freely. There is a 49-member House of Assembly, directly elected for five years, and a 16-member Senate. The prime minister appoints 9 members; the leader of the parliament opposition, 4; and the governor-general, 3. The assembly was subsequently reduced to 40 members, in keeping with a campaign promise by the FNM.

Daily and weekly newspapers, all privately owned, express a variety of views on public issues, as do the government-run radio station and four privately owned radio broadcasters. Opposition politicians claim that the state-run television system, the Broadcasting Corporation of the Bahamas, gives preferential coverage to the ruling party. Full freedom of expression is constrained by strict libel laws. Media laws were amended to allow for private ownership of broadcasting outlets. There is free access to the Internet.

Religious and academic freedom are respected.

Constitutional guarantees of the right to organize civic organizations are generally respected, and human rights organizations have broad access to institutions and individuals. Labor, business, and professional organizations are generally free from governmental interference. Unions have the right to strike, and collective bargaining is prevalent.

The judicial system is headed by the Supreme Court and a court of appeals, with the right of appeal under certain circumstances to the Privy Council in London. Some progress has been reported in reducing both the length of court cases and the backlog of criminal appeals. Nevertheless, some murder suspects have been held up to four years before coming to trial.

Violent crime is a continuing concern and is a focus of the Christie government. Nongovernmental organizations have documented the occasional abuse of prisoners, arbitrary arrest, and lengthy pretrial detention. The Royal Bahamas Police Force has made progress in reducing corruption in the force, including introducing new procedures to limit unethical or illegal conduct. While the police have been recognized for their key role in regional efforts to stem the drug trade, coordination with the Royal Bahamas Defence Force (RBDF) has presented more difficulties that reflect general ambivalence about the RBDF's role in law enforcement.

Although the Ingraham administration made important efforts to relieve overcrowding of prisoners, there are persistent reports of overcrowding, and poor medical facilities are still the norm. Children continue to be housed with adults, and there have been reports of sexual abuse.

The Bahamas is an accessible transit area for illegal aliens seeking entrance to the United States. No laws specifically address trafficking in persons, but there are also no reports of such activity. The Bahamian government forcibly repatriates most asylum seekers, including Haitians and Cubans.

Discrimination against the disabled and persons of Haitian descent persists; 20 to 25 percent of the population is Haitian or of Haitian descent. Between 30,000 and 40,000 Haitians reside illegally in the Bahamas. Strict citizenship requirements and a stringent work permit system leave Haitians with few rights. There is no legislation regulating the processing of asylum seekers. The influx has created social tension because of the strain on government services.

Violence against women is a serious and widespread problem, and child abuse and neglect remain serious.

# Bahrain

**Population:** 700,000
**GNI/capita:** $11,130
**Life Expectancy:** 74
**Religious Groups:** Shi'a Muslim (70 percent), Sunni Muslim (30 percent)
**Ethnic Groups:** Bahraini (63 percent), Asian (19 percent), other Arab (10 percent), Iranian (8 percent)
**Capital:** Manama

**Political Rights:** 5
**Civil Liberties:** 5
**Status:** Partly Free

**Ten-Year Ratings Timeline (Political Rights, Civil Liberties, Status)**

| 1994 | 1995 | 1996 | 1997 | 1998 | 1999 | 2000 | 2001 | 2002 | 2003 |
|------|------|------|------|------|------|------|------|------|------|
| 6,6NF | 6,6NF | 7,6NF | 7,6NF | 7,6NF | 7,6NF | 7,6NF | 6,5NF | 5,5PF | 5,5PF |

**Overview:**
After taking significant steps to reform its political system in 2001 and 2002, Bahrain pursued the reform process more slowly during 2003, effecting few significant developments on political rights and civil liberties.

The al-Khalifa family, which has ruled Bahrain for more than two centuries, comes from Bahrain's minority Sunni Muslim population in this mostly Shi'a Muslim country. Bahrain gained independence in 1971 after more than a hundred years as a British protectorate. The country's first constitution provided for a national assembly with both elected and appointed members, but the king dissolved the assembly in 1975 because the assembly attempted to end al-Khalifa rule; the al-Khalifa family ruled without the national assembly until 2002.

In 1993, the king established a consultative council of appointed notables, although this advisory body had no legislative power and did not lead to any major policy shifts. In 1994, Bahrain experienced protests and clashes that left more than 40 people dead, thousands arrested, and hundreds either imprisoned or exiled. The unrest was sparked by arrests of prominent individuals who had petitioned for the reestablishment of democratic institutions such as the national assembly.

Sheikh Hamad bin Isa al-Khalifa's accession to the throne following his father's death in 1998 marked a turning point in Bahrain. Hamad released political prisoners, permitted the return of exiles, and did away with emergency laws and courts. He also introduced the National Charter, which set a goal of creating a constitutional monarchy with an elected parliament, separation of powers with an independent judicial branch, and rights guaranteeing women's political participation. In February 2001, voters overwhelmingly approved the National Charter, setting into motion political reforms that led to local elections in May 2002 and national parliamentary elections in October 2002. Leading Shi'a groups and leftists boycotted these elections, protesting restrictions on political campaigning and electoral gerrymandering aimed at diminishing the power of the Shi'a majority. Sunni Muslim groups ended up winning most of the seats in the new National Assembly. Despite this boycott, opposition groups fared well at the polls, and the new cabinet included opposition figures such as Majed Alawi, the former leader of the London-based Bahrain Freedom Movement.

Since taking office in 2002, the new government and National Assembly have not pressed forward with any significant steps to reform Bahrain's political system. In the first few months of 2003, the focus was on regional events, with protestors taking to the streets against the war in Iraq. Bahrain served as the headquarters of the U.S. Navy's Fifth Fleet in the Persian Gulf.

**Political Rights and Civil Liberties:** Bahraini citizens do not have the ability to choose the leader with the most power in Bahrain, the king. According to Bahrain's 2002 constitution, the king is the head of all three branches of government. He appoints cabinet ministers and members of the Consultative Council. The National Assembly consists of 40 popularly elected members of the Representative Council and 40 members of the Shura Council appointed by the king. The National Assembly may propose legislation, but the cabinet must draft the laws. Formal political parties are illegal in Bahrain, but the government allows political societies or groupings to operate and organize activities in the country.

Freedom of expression is limited in Bahrain, which received a low 117 ranking in the 2003 press freedom ranking of the media watchdog group Reporters Sans Frontieres. The government owns all broadcast media outlets, but there is a stronger degree of freedom in newspapers, many of which are privately owned. In the fall of 2003, the National Assembly began debating a new press law aimed at expanding press freedoms.

Mansoor al-Jamri, the son of a prominent Shiite dissident living in exile and editor in chief of the independent daily *Al-Wasat*, was brought to court for defying a gag order that sought to prevent press coverage of the March arrest of five men suspected of planning a terrorist attack. Al-Jamri and a journalist for *Al-Wasat*, Hussein Khalaf, were prosecuted for publishing the story of the release of three of the suspects. An estimated one-third of the population has access to the Internet, mostly through the National Telephone Company. Though Internet and e-mail access has generally been unrestricted, there are reports of government monitoring of e-mails.

Islam is the state religion. However, non-Muslim minorities are generally free to practice their religion. According to the law, all religious groups must obtain a permit from the Ministry of Justice and Islamic affairs to operate, although the government has not punished groups that have operated without this permit. Though Shi'a in Bahrain constitute a majority of the citizenry, they are underrepresented in government and face discrimination in the workplace. In 2003, the Bahraini government began debating a proposed unified personal status code that would seek to bridge the Sunni-Shi'a division in legal codes governing family affairs such as marriage, divorce, and inheritance.

The constitution provides for freedom of assembly, and demonstrations and open public discussion are generally permitted. Bahrain has seen strong growth in the number of nongovernmental organizations working in charitable activities, human rights, and women's rights in recent years. Bahrainis have the right to establish independent labor unions without government permission. A royal decree giving workers the right to form labor unions also imposed limits, including a two-week notice to the company before a strike and a prohibition on strikes in vital sectors such as security, civil defense, transportation, hospitals, communications, and basic infrastructure. Labor unions figured prominently on the reform agenda in 2003, with a number of new unions created, including the Bankers' Union. Nearly 200,000 of the 700,000 people living in Bahrain are migrant workers, who are sometimes subjected to mistreatment without legal recourse and protections.

With unemployment among Bahraini citizens estimated at 25 percent, the government began to institute a "Bahrainization" program aimed at replacing foreign workers with Bahraini citizens and extending social protections to the unemployed. Bahrain reportedly plans to cease issuing visas to many migrant workers after 2005, hoping to satisfy the demands of unemployed Bahrainis, many of whom took to the streets in protest against the lack of jobs.

The judiciary is not independent of the executive branch of government. The king appoints all judges, and courts have been subject to government pressure. In September, Bahrain sponsored the Arab Judicial Forum, a conference that brought together government and nongovernmental leaders from the Middle East to discuss judicial independence and reform. The Ministry of the Interior is responsible for public security within the country and oversees the police and internal security services, and members of the royal family hold all security-related offices. The constitution provides rule-of-law protections, and government authorities generally respect these protections. Since the government's abolition of the State Security Act in 2001, the judiciary has refused requests by the police to hold detainees longer than 60 hours

Women are under-represented politically; no woman has been elected to office in municipal or legislative elections. The king appointed six women to the Consultative Council. Women are generally not afforded equal protections under the law. In April, the Women's Petition Committee issued a demand supported by 1,700 people to reform the personal status and family laws, the first petition of this type in Bahrain's history. Leading religious scholars expressed opposition to this proposed reform, and no progress was made on the effort to change the personal status and family laws.

# Bangladesh

**Population:** 146,700,000 **Political Rights:** 4
**GNI/capita:** $360 **Civil Liberties:** 4
**Life Expectancy:** 59 **Status:** Partly Free
**Religious Groups:** Muslim (83 percent), Hindu
(16 percent), other (1 percent)
**Ethnic Groups:** Bengali (98 percent), other, [including
Bihari] (2 percent)
**Capital:** Dhaka

**Ten-Year Ratings Timeline (Political Rights, Civil Liberties, Status)**

| 1994 | 1995 | 1996 | 1997 | 1998 | 1999 | 2000 | 2001 | 2002 | 2003 |
|------|------|------|------|------|------|------|------|------|------|
| 2,4PF | 3,4PF | 2,4PF | 2,4PF | 2,4PF | 3,4PF | 3,4PF | 3,4PF | 4,4PF | 4,4PF |

**Overview:**
Bangladesh continued in 2003 to be plagued by lawlessness, rampant corruption, and violent political polarization, all of which threaten its prospects for consolidating democratic institutions and achieving economic development and reform. The opposition Awami League (AL) remains reliant on parliamentary boycotts and national strikes to impede the effective functioning of the Bangladesh Nationalist Party (BNP)–led coalition government. For its part, the BNP continued to implement a sweeping anticrime drive begun in October 2002 in which army personnel have been periodically deployed to maintain law and order. Official intolerance toward criticism and scrutiny persisted, with journalists, human rights advocates, and leaders and perceived supporters of the political opposition being detained or otherwise harassed throughout the year.

With the partition of British India in 1947, what is now Bangladesh became the eastern part of the newly formed state of Pakistan. Bangladesh won independence from Pakistan in December 1971 after a nine-month war during which Indian troops helped defeat West Pakistani forces stationed in Bangladesh. The 1975 assassination of Prime Minister Sheikh Mujibur Rahman by soldiers precipitated 15 years of military rule and continues to polarize Bangladeshi politics. The country's democratic transition began with the resignation in 1990 of the last military ruler, General H. M. Ershad, after weeks of pro-democracy demonstrations. Elections in 1991 brought the BNP to power under Khaleda Zia.

The political deadlock began in 1994, when Sheikh Hasina Wajed's center-left AL began boycotting parliament to protest alleged corruption in Zia's BNP government. The AL and the BNP differ relatively little on domestic policy. Many disputes reflect the personal animosity between Hasina, the daughter of independence leader Sheikh Mujibur Rahman, and Zia, the widow of a former military ruler allegedly complicit in Mujibur's assassination. The AL boycotted the February 1996 elections, which the BNP won, but then forced Zia's resignation in March and triumphed in elections held in June. Hasina's government signed an accord ending a low-grade insurgency in the Chittagong Hill Tracts. However, political tensions were exacerbated when the government passed a controversial public order law in January 2000, which the BNP said could be used against its members and to break general strikes.

Political gridlock continued in 2001, as the opposition BNP boycotted parliament and organized several nationwide strikes. In October, the AL was voted out of office in elections marred by political violence and intimidation. A new four-party coalition, dominated by the BNP and also including two hard-line Muslim parties, the Jamaat-e-Islami and the Islami Oikyo Jote, was sworn into power with a convincing majority of 214 of the 300 seats in parliament. Zia announced soon after taking office that her top priority would be to free Bangladesh from lawlessness and corruption.

The AL initially refused to accept the election results and since 2001 has intermittently boycotted parliament to protest various government policies. Reneging on a pledge she made during the election campaign, Hasina also organized several nationwide *hartals* (general strikes) during the year.

Faced with mounting domestic and international frustration with the continued deterioration in law and order, in October 2002, the government deployed nearly 40,000 army personnel in "Operation Clean Heart" (OCH) as part of an anticrime drive during which thousands were arrested. A further attempt to crack down on crime and lawlessness was made in June 2003, when authorities announced that they intended to deploy paramilitary forces and that police had been given orders to "shoot on sight." Although the policy was initially popular among Bangladeshis weary of rising crime rates and a general climate of impunity for criminals, police and army excesses, including extortion and torture, led to repeated statements of concern from both domestic and international groups during the year.

**Political Rights and Civil Liberties:** Bangladeshis can change their government through elections. A referendum held in 1991 transformed the powerful presidency into a largely ceremonial head-of-state position in a parliamentary system. Elections to the 300-member unicameral parliament are held in single-member districts under a simple-plurality rule. The June 1996 vote was the first under a constitutional amendment requiring a caretaker government to conduct elections. The October 2001 elections were described as generally free and fair despite concerns over polling irregularities, intimidation, and violence. More than 140 people were killed throughout the campaign period in what was Bangladesh's most violent election to date.

Both major parties have undermined the legislative process through lengthy parliamentary boycotts while in opposition. In recent years, political violence during demonstrations and general strikes has killed hundreds of people in major cities and injured thousands, and police often use excessive force against opposition protesters. Student wings of political parties continue to be embroiled in violent campus conflicts. In addition, several AL politicians were assassinated in August and September.

Aid donors blame corruption, a weak rule of law, limited bureaucratic transparency, and political polarization for undermining government accountability and economic development. In October, Transparency International listed Bangladesh at the bottom of a 133-country list on its 2003 Corruption Perceptions Index and noted that corruption was perceived to be "pervasive." As the Bureau of Anti-Corruption is under the direct control of the prime minister's office, corruption cases filed against senior officials are often politicized and lack credibility, and sitting officials are never prosecuted.

The Bangladeshi press continued to face a number of pressures in 2003. Although the print media are diverse, journalists are regularly harassed and violently attacked by organized-crime groups, political parties and their supporters, government authorities, the police, and Islamic fundamentalists. Most practice some self-censorship. During the year, security forces detained a number of journalists after they reported on topics such as corruption, electoral violence, the rise of Islamic fundamentalism, and human rights abuses. In June, warrants of arrest were filed against two leading news editors for defamation after they published a letter that was critical of a senior government official. Political considerations influence the distribution of government advertising revenue and subsidized newsprint, upon which most publications are dependent. The state owns most broadcast media, whose coverage favors the ruling party.

Islam is the official religion. Hindus, Christians, and other minorities have the right to worship freely but face societal discrimination and remain underrepresented in government employment. Violence against Bangladesh's Hindu minority flared up after the October 2001 elections, when BNP supporters reportedly attacked Hindus because of their perceived support for the rival AL. Atrocities, including murder, rape, destruction of property, and kidnapping, forced hundreds of Hindus from their homes, some across the border into India. There are also occasional reports of violence against members of the Ahmadiya religious minority.

While the government generally respects academic freedom, political polarization at many public universities, which occasionally erupts into protests and clashes between students and security forces, inhibits the ability of some students to receive an education.

The constitution provides for freedom of assembly, but the government frequently limits this right in practice. Demonstrators are occasionally killed or injured during clashes with police. Numerous nongovernmental organizations (NGOs) operate in Bangladesh and fulfill a variety of basic needs in fields such as education, health care, and microcredit. However, those that are perceived to have links to the opposition or that criticize the government, particularly on human rights issues, have been subject to intense official scrutiny and occasional harassment, according to the U.S. State Department's 2002 human rights report.

Union formation is hampered by a 30 percent employee approval requirement and restrictions on organizing by unregistered unions. Employers can legally fire or transfer workers suspected of union activities. The law prohibits many civil servants from joining unions; these workers can form associations but are prohibited from bargaining collectively. The U.S. Agency for International Development has reported that almost half of children aged 10 to 14 are working, mostly as domestic servants, farm workers, or rickshaw pullers.

The Supreme Court displays a "significant degree of independence" and often rules against the executive, according to the U.S. State Department. However, lower-level courts remained subject to executive influence and were rife with corruption. The government continues to delay implementing the separation of the judiciary from the executive as ordered by a 1999 Supreme Court directive. The judicial system is severely backlogged, and pretrial detention is lengthy. Many defendants lack counsel, and poor people have limited recourse through the courts. Prison conditions are extremely poor, and severe overcrowding is increasingly common. Prisoners are routinely subjected to physical abuse and demands for bribes from corrupt law enforcement officials. In a May 2003 report, Amnesty International expressed concern that police frequently detain people without an arrest warrant and that detainees are routinely subjected to torture and other forms of abuse. Local human rights NGO Odhikar registered 43 instances of custodial death during the first half of 2003. The majority of police abuses go unpunished, which results in a climate of impunity.

As part of Operation Clean Heart (OCH), a government-initiated anticrime drive of questionable constitutional legality that took place from October 2002 through January 2003, the army detained nearly 11,000 people, including members of both political parties, over 40 of whom died while in police custody. In February, the president signed legislation that granted the troops involved in OCH immunity from prosecution in civilian courts for the abuses committed during the operation. However, the BBC reported that in March, a military court did find four soldiers guilty of torture and extortion, and in April, a special court convicted eight policemen for similar offenses.

Many of these forms of abuse are facilitated by the existence of legislation such as the Special Powers Act of 1974, which permits arbitrary detention without charge, and Section 54 of the Criminal Procedure Code, which allows individuals to be detained without a warrant. Authorities regularly detain thousands of political opponents and ordinary citizens, and use serial detentions to prevent the release of political activists. In a December 2002 press release, Amnesty International highlighted a pattern of politically motivated detentions, noting that senior opposition politicians, academics, journalists, and human rights activists critical of government policies were particularly at risk of prolonged detention and ill treatment in custody. According to a 2002 UN Development Program report on the Bangladeshi legal system, almost 90 percent of "preventative detention" cases that reach the courts are judged to be unlawful. However, in August 2003, the Supreme Court directed the government to implement a judicial order barring the detention of anyone arrested merely on the suspicion of having committed a crime.

Tribal minorities have little control over land issues affecting them, and minority rights groups say that Bengalis have cheated many tribal people out of their land. A 1997 accord between the government and the Chittagong Hill Tracts (CHT) People's Solidarity Association ended a 24-year insurgency in the CHT that had sought autonomy for indigenous tribes and had resulted in the deaths of 8,500 soldiers, rebels, and civilians. However, Amnesty International's 2002 report noted that while tribal representatives continued to demand implementation of the accord, violent clashes between majority tribal groups and radical groups opposed to the peace process continue to be reported.

Roughly 260,000 Rohingyas fleeing forced labor, discrimination, and other abuses in Burma entered Bangladesh in 1991 and 1992; some 22,000 Rohingya refugees and 100,000 other Rohingyas not formally documented as refugees remain in the country. Bangladeshi authorities speeded up the repatriation process in May under a new agreement reached with the Burmese government. Bangladesh also hosts some 300,000 Urdu-speaking Biharis who were rendered stateless at independence in 1971, many of whom seek repatriation to Pakistan. In May, a landmark high court ruling gave citizenship and voting rights to 10 Bihari refugees.

Rape, dowry-related assaults, acid throwing, and other violence against women occur frequently. A law requiring rape victims to file police reports and obtain medical certificates within 24 hours of the crime in order to press charges prevents most rape cases from reaching the courts. Police also accept bribes not to register rape cases and rarely enforce existing laws protecting women. The Acid Survivors Foundation, a local NGO, recorded 485 acid attacks in 2002, with the majority being carried out against women. While prosecution for acid-related crimes remains inadequate, under the stringent Acid Crime Prevention Act passed in 2002, one attacker was sentenced to death early in 2003. In rural areas, religious leaders occasionally issue *fatwas* (religious edicts) that impose floggings and other punishments on women accused of violating strict moral codes. Women also face discrimination in health care, education, and employment, and are underrepresented in politics and government.

Human rights activists estimate that organized groups traffick nearly 25,000 Bangladeshi women and children each year into Middle Eastern and other South Asian countries for the purposes of prostitution and low-paid labor. Law enforcement officials rarely investigate trafficking, and rights groups allege that the police are often engaged in these and other crimes.

# Barbados

**Population:** 300,000   **Political Rights:** 1
**GNI/capita:** $9,750   **Civil Liberties:** 1
**Life Expectancy:** 73   **Status:** Free
**Religious Groups:** Protestant (67 percent), Roman Catholic (4 percent), none (17 percent), other (12 percent)
**Ethnic Groups:** Black (90 percent), white (4 percent), other (6 percent)
**Capital:** Bridgetown

**Ten-Year Ratings Timeline (Political Rights, Civil Liberties, Status)**

| 1994 | 1995 | 1996 | 1997 | 1998 | 1999 | 2000 | 2001 | 2002 | 2003 |
|------|------|------|------|------|------|------|------|------|------|
| 1,1F | 1,1F | 1,1F | 1,1F | 1,1F | 1,1F | 1,1F | 1,1F | 1,1F | 1,1F |

**Overview:**   The ruling Barbados Labor Party (BLP) retained its legislative majority following May 2003 parliamentary elections. The economy continued to face pressure from the dual onslaught of a fall in tourism following the terrorist attacks of September 2001 in the United States and a reduced demand of its traditional export of sugar due to the downturn of the global economy.

Barbados became independent in 1966 and is a member of the Commonwealth. By 1994, after a recession, the economy appeared to be improving, but unemployment was still at nearly 25 percent. Prime Minister Erskine Sandiford's popularity suffered, and he was increasingly criticized for his authoritarian style of government. He lost a no-confidence vote in parliament when nine BLP legislators were joined by four backbenchers from the opposition Democratic Labor Party (DLP) and one independent legislator who had quit the DLP. David Thompson, the young finance minister, replaced Sandiford.

In the 1994 elections, the BLP won 19 seats; the DLP, 8 seats; and the New Democratic Party (NDP), a splinter of the DLP established in 1989, 1 seat. Prime Minister Owen Seymour Arthur, an economist elected in 1993 to head the BLP, promised to build "a modern, technologically dynamic economy," create jobs, and restore investor confidence. The BLP retained power in 1999 by winning 26 parliamentary seats, leaving Arthur firmly in control of his country.

In the May 23, 2003 elections, the BLP won 23 seats in the House of Assembly, ratifying Prime Minister Arthur's administration. Meanwhile, the DLP has been strengthened under the uncontested leadership of Clyde Mascoll. In June, the Public Accounts Committee's independent oversight of government accounts was strengthened, giving the DLP the ability to better monitor official expenditures.

The Arthur government has made efforts to reduce dependence on tourism—a sector that was badly hurt after the September 2001 terrorist attacks in the United States—and sugar through diversification into the financial and computer services industries. Barbados has not escaped the increase in crime experienced by much of the Caribbean region. Joint patrols of the Royal Barbados Police Force (RBPF) and the all-volunteer Barbados Defense Force have been initiated to patrol the island as violent crimes, many linked to narcotics trafficking, have increased.

**Political Rights and Civil Liberties:** The government is a parliamentary democracy with a bicameral legislature and a party system with universal suffrage. The May 2003 parliamentary elections were free and fair. The 30-member House of Assembly is elected for a five-year term. The 21-member Senate is appointed by the governor-general: 12 on the advice of the prime minister, 2 on the advice of the leader of the opposition, and the remaining 7 at the discretion of the governor-general. The prime minister is the leader of the political party with a majority in the House. Power has alternated between two centrist parties—the Democratic Labor Party (DLP) and the Barbados Labor Party (BLP).

Political parties are free to organize. Apart from the parties holding parliamentary seats, there are other political organizations, including the small, left-wing Workers' Party of Barbados.

Freedom of expression and academic freedom are fully respected. Public opinion expressed through the news media, which are free of censorship and government control, has a powerful influence on policy. Newspapers are privately owned, and there are two major dailies. Four private and two government radio stations operate. The single television station, operated by the government-owned Caribbean Broadcasting Corporation, presents a wide range of political viewpoints. There is free access to the Internet.

The constitution guarantees freedom of religion. The right to organize labor unions, and civic organizations is respected. There are two major labor unions, and various smaller ones are active.

The judicial system is independent, and the Supreme Court includes a high court and a court of appeals. Lower-court officials are appointed on the advice of the Judicial and Legal Service Commission. The prison system is overcrowded and outdated, with more than 800 inmates held in a building built for 350. There are separate facilities for female prisoners and children. The government allows private groups to visit prisons. Although the government has made significant efforts to discharge prison personnel alleged to have beaten inmates, their prosecution has not made significant progress.

In October 2002, Attorney-General Mia Mottley announced that a National Commission on Law and Order would be set up to reduce lawlessness. In dealing with issues that have threatened the island's vital tourism industry, the Commission will address legislative reform, law enforcement, the administration of justice, and penal reform. As part of an effort to reduce the backlog of several thousand legal cases, four judges and two magistrates will also be appointed. Mottley also strongly voiced reservations about the Inter-American Convention on Corruption, claiming that it did not sufficiently regulate private sector corruption. Prime Minister Owen Arthur appointed Mottley, the first woman and youngest person in the post, in 2001.

The high crime rate, fueled by an increase in drug abuse and narcotics trafficking, has given rise to human rights concerns. The number of murders has remained constant. A constitutional change allows convicts to be hanged as soon as possible after their appeals are exhausted. There are occasional reports and complaints of excessive force used by the Royal Barbados Police Force (RBPF) to extract confessions, along with reports that police do not always seek warrants before searching homes. The Caribbean Human Rights Network was disbanded because of a lack of funds.

Barbados has refused to agree to the immunity of U.S. military personnel from proceedings in the International Criminal Court. The U.S. responded by suspending military education programs and military equipment sales. The impasse has dampened efforts to control drug trafficking in the region. Barbados is likely to continue to remain a strong supporter of Trinidad and Tobago, whose former president helped to set up the court.

Women make up roughly half of the workforce. A domestic violence law was passed in 1992 to give police and judges greater power to protect women. Violence and abuse of women and children continue to be major social problems.

# ⬇ Belarus

**Population:** 9,900,000
**GNI/capita:** $1,290
**Life Expectancy:** 69
**Religious Groups:** Eastern Orthodox (80 percent),
other (20 percent)
**Ethnic Groups:** Byelorussian (81.2 percent), Russian
(11.4 percent), other [including Polish and Ukrainian] (7.4 percent)
**Capital:** Minsk

**Political Rights:** 6
**Civil Liberties:** 6
**Status:** Not Free

**Trend Arrow:** Belarus received a downward trend arrow due to increased state attacks on a dwindling number of independent media outlets, intensified state banning of independent civic groups, and increased government pressures on academic freedom.

**Ten-Year Ratings Timeline (Political Rights, Civil Liberties, Status)**

| 1994 | 1995 | 1996 | 1997 | 1998 | 1999 | 2000 | 2001 | 2002 | 2003 |
|------|------|------|------|------|------|------|------|------|------|
| 4,4PF | 5,5PF | 6,6NF | 6,6NF | 6,6NF | 6,6NF | 6,6NF | 6,6NF | 6,6NF | 6,6NF |

**Overview:**

The year 2003 witnessed intensified legal pressures on newspapers, punishments meted out to opposition demonstrators, the disbanding of human rights and civic organizations, and efforts at total state control over independent schools. Harassment of political activists continued with routine arrest, detention, and interrogation of student and civic activists for activities such as the distribution of brochures and leaflets. The closure and suspension of several of the country's dwindling number of independent newspapers forced more independent publications to work outside Belarus's borders.

Belarus declared independence in 1991, ending centuries of foreign control by Lithuania, Poland, Russia, and, ultimately, the Soviet Union. Stanislau Shushkevich, a reform-minded leader, served as head of state from 1991 to 1994. That year, voters made Alyaksandr Lukashenka, a member of parliament with close links to the country's security services, the country's first post-Soviet president. Lukashenka has pursued efforts at reunification with Russia and subordinated the government, legislature, and courts to his political whims while denying citizens basic rights and liberties.

In a 1996 referendum, Belarusian citizens backed constitutional amendments that extended Lukashenka's term through 2001, broadened presidential powers, and created a new bicameral parliament. When the president ignored a court ruling that the referendum was non-binding, Prime Minister Mikhail Chyhir resigned in protest. Since July 1999, when the president's original mandate expired, many Western nations have refused to recognize Lukashenka as the legitimate head of state. Instead, they recognize the pre-1996 Supreme Soviet as the legitimate legislative body.

In October 2000, Belarus held elections to the Chamber of Representatives, parliament's lower house. State media coverage of the campaign was limited and biased, and approximately half of all opposition candidates were denied registration. Nongovernmental organizations reported irregularities such as ballot-box stuffing and tampering with voter registration lists. Seven opposition parties boycotted the elections when the government failed to ensure a fair campaign and to give parliament more substantial duties. Some opposition candidates participated in the election, but only three received a mandate.

Lukashenka won a controversial reelection in September 2001 amid accusations from former security service officials that the president was directing a government-sponsored death squad aimed at silencing his opponents. Formally, Belarusian citizens had three presidential candidates from which to choose. However, the outcome was predetermined, and Western observers judged the election to be neither free nor fair. During the campaign, the government and its supporters harassed would-be candidates and independent media outlets, and state television was used as the exclusive instrument for propaganda on behalf of Lukashenka. On election day, Lukashenka declared himself the victor with 78 percent of the vote over candidates Vladimir Goncharik (12 percent) and Sergei Gaidukevich (2 percent). However, opposition exit polls showed that Lukashenka received 47 percent of the vote and Goncharik 41 percent—an outcome that by law should have forced a second round. At the same time, opposition parties and civil society managed to play an energetic role in the election process. Although the opposition parties backing Goncharik represented a broad political spectrum, they agreed on defeating Lukashenka, a decision that represented an important step in their development. The following year, Lukashenka engaged in political retribution against anyone who had opposed him during the 2001 presidential campaign, including independent journalists and political opposition members.

In 2003, the Lukashenka regime pursued a policy of systematic legal persecution and physical intimidation of its democratic opponents, with courts banning or liquidating nongovernmental organizations, closing down or suspending publication of independent newspapers critical of the Lukashenka government, and harassing independent civic activists and protestors. The year also saw relentless state political pressure on educational institutions and programs, government attacks on academic freedom, and dismissals of educators at a journalism school and an elite secondary school. The government announced the introduction of teaching that will incorporate the "ideas" of President Lukashenka into the national educational curriculum.

The year 2001 marked the five-year anniversary of Belarus's union treaty with Russia. However, Russian enthusiasm for the union has since waned, and there is no serious movement toward implementing the treaty's provisions for the creation of a confederal state.

According to the European Bank for Reconstruction and Development, the country's private sector share of Gross Domestic Product, at 20 percent, is the lowest of all the post-Communist countries. World Bank data also show that more than a quarter of the population lives below the national poverty line.

**Political Rights and Civil Liberties:** Despite a constitutional guarantee of universal, equal, and direct suffrage, citizens of Belarus cannot change their government democratically. The 2001 parliamentary election was marred by serious and widespread irregularities, and most Western governments refused to recognize the results. Western nations declared the 2001 presidential vote, in which Alyaksandr Lukashenka was reelected by a wide majority, to be neither free nor fair. Domestic supporters of opposition candidate Vladimir Goncharik accused the government of massively falsifying the results.

The Lukashenka regime systematically curtails press freedom. State media are subordinated to the president, and harassment and censorship of independent media are routine. Libel is both a civil and a criminal offense. The State Press Committee can issue warnings to publishers for unauthorized activities such as changing a publication's title or distributing copies abroad. It also can arbitrarily shut down publications without a court order.

Harassment and legal attacks against independent newspapers and broadcast journalists continued unabated in 2003. A politically motivated audit of the *Soladarnasts* weekly resulted in significant fines. The newspaper's officials were denied the benefit of independent legal counsel during the proceedings. In 2003, the government brought cases of libel against the Marat independent publishing house and the newspaper *Belorusskaya Delovaya Gazeta*, whose publication was suspended for three months. Periodicals that sought to print materials by the newspaper's staff were prevented from publishing. When the banned newspaper resumed publication in Russia, shipments of its print run were confiscated or blocked by Belarus authorities at the border, and distributors were arrested and detained by authorities. An economic court in the city of Grodno stripped the founder of the newspaper *Novaya Gazeta* of the right to run his business. The local government in Grodno also refused to provide a second independent newspaper with a certificate attesting to its location in the city. Without such attestation, registration of the newspaper was not possible. In June 2003, the country's Ministry of Information promulgated new regulations that required the heads of all FM radio station to provide a complete daily printout of news bulletins and daily playlists to ensure monitoring of content. In 2003, the contents of a draft law on the press were kept secret from the public.

Internet sites within the country are under the control of the government's State Center on Information Security, which is part of the Security Council of Belarus. Independent information, however, is posted by some opposition groups and journalists in Belarus and abroad. The government at times censors and blocks independent sites, particularly during preelection periods. The impact of independent Internet sites is limited. According to the International Telecommunications Union, 8.1 percent of the population has some access to the Internet, while other estimates suggest that only 2 percent of the population enjoys regular Internet access.

Despite constitutional guarantees that "all religions and faiths shall be equal before the law," Belarusian government decrees and registration requirements have increasingly restricted the life and work of religious groups. The government pressures and intimidates members of the independent Autocephalous Orthodox Christian Church, harasses Hindus for public meditation, and represses Baptists for singing hymns in public. Amendments to the Law on Religions, signed into law by President Lukashenka in 2002, provide for government censorship of religious publications and prevent foreign citizens from leading religious groups. The amendments also place strict limitations on religious groups that have been active in Belarus for fewer than 20 years.

Academic freedoms are subject to intense state ideological pressures. In July 2003, the entire staff of the Modern Studies Institute's journalism faculty, some of them active in an independent journalist association, were dismissed after criticism leveled at them by a presidential commission and the Ministry of Education. The leader of the country's most highly regarded secondary school, the National State Humanities Lyceum, was dismissed and a Lukashenka loyalist was appointed in his place, prompting a walkout by students and faculty. In July, the country's education minister announced that in 2004 the educational curriculum would include a new subject—"Belarusian state ideology"—based on the ideas of President Lukashenka. Wiretapping by state security agencies limits the right to privacy

The Lukashenka government limits freedom of assembly and association by groups independent of and critical of his regime. Protests and rallies require authorization from local officials, who can arbitrarily withhold or revoke permission. When public demonstrations do occur, police typically break them up and arrest participants.

In June, the Supreme Court liquidated the Christian Youth Union for "lack of conformity of the organization's program and statute" with national law. In October, the Supreme Court disbanded and declared illegal the activities of the Vyasna human rights organization, in part based on claims that the organization had violated the law during election monitoring activities in 2001. Other nongovernmental organizations were closed in 2003, including the Legal Assistance to the Population group and the Women's Response organization. In August, a local court in Grodno disbanded the independent civic group Ratusha. Other civic groups, including the Lev Sapega Foundation and the Belarusian Helsinki Committee, were issued warnings and subjected to government investigation, steps that are usually a prelude to banning. There were also numerous instances of harassment of the country's independent labor unions, including the confiscation of computer and printing equipment. Leaders of the nationwide protest "To Live Better," in which more than 100,000 citizens took part in March 2003, were sentenced to short-term imprisonment. Among those sentenced were leaders of the civic group Charter 97, a leader of the pro-reform Private Property organization, and a leader of the Strike Committee of Entrepreneurs.

Although the country's constitution calls for judicial independence, courts are subject to heavy government influence. In the last year, numerous independent civic leaders, opposition political activists, independent journalists, and other persons who oppose government policies experienced arbitrary persecution, arrest, and imprisonment. The right to a fair trial is often not respected in cases with political overtones. Human rights groups documented instances of beatings, torture, and inadequate protection during detention in cases involving leaders of the Belarusian Popular Front, members of the student civic group Zubr, and the head of the Belarusian Sociology Association.

An internal passport system that is required for domestic travel and securing permanent housing controls freedom of movement and choice of residence. The country's command economy severely limits economic freedom.

Women are not specifically targeted for discrimination, but there are significant discrepancies in incomes between men and women, and women are poorly represented in leading government positions. Amid extreme poverty, many Belarusian women have become victims of the international sex trafficking trade.

# Belgium

**Population:** 10,400,000
**GNI/capita:** $23,850
**Life Expectancy:** 78
**Religious Groups:** Roman Catholic (75 percent),
other [including Protestants] (25 percent)
**Ethnic Groups:** Fleming (58 percent), Walloon (31 percent),
other (11 percent)
**Capital:** Brussels

**Political Rights:** 1
**Civil Liberties:** 1
**Status:** Free

**Ten-Year Ratings Timeline (Political Rights, Civil Liberties, Status)**

| 1994 | 1995 | 1996 | 1997 | 1998 | 1999 | 2000 | 2001 | 2002 | 2003 |
|------|------|------|------|------|------|------|------|------|------|
| 1,1F | 1,1F | 1,2F | 1,2F | 1,2F | 1,2F | 1,2F | 1,2F | 1,1F | 1,1F |

**Overview:**  Following parliamentary elections in May 2003, the Liberals and Socialists agreed to govern in a coalition, returning the Liberal leader, Guy Verhofstadt, as prime minister for a second term. Both parties held on to a sizable majority of the seats in parliament. Belgium revised a controversial war crimes law that had previously allowed people to file cases against top international political and military figures. A decision by the European Court of Human Rights ruled in favor of four journalists who had accused the state of violating their freedom of expression by searching their offices and homes in 1995 in an effort to identify sources.

Modern Belgium dates from 1830, when the territory broke away from the Netherlands and formed a constitutional monarchy, which today is largely ceremonial. Belgium was one of the founding members of the European Economic Community and still hosts the central administration of the European Union (EU), in Brussels.

Ethnic and linguistic conflicts between the different communities in the country during the 1960s prompted a number of constitutional amendments in 1970, 1971, and 1993 that devolved considerable central government power to the three regions in the federation: French-speaking Wallonia in the South, Flemish-speaking Flanders in the North, and Brussels, the capital, where French and Flemish share the same status. The small German minority in Wallonia, which consists of around 70,000 persons, has also been accorded cultural autonomy. Another 1993 amendment granted the three regional assemblies primary responsibility in a number of important policy areas, including housing, education, and the environment, while keeping issues like foreign policy, defense, justice, and monetary policy in the hands of the central state. In 2002, Belgium became the second country in the world, after the Netherlands, to partially legalize euthanasia.

The Liberals and the Socialists gained strength during parliamentary elections in May 2003, while the Greens dropped from 20 to 4 seats in the lower house and were forced out of the ruling coalition. The Socialists led with 27 percent of the vote compared with 26 percent for the Liberals. Altogether, the new coalition holds 97 of the 150 seats in the lower house. The election was also a success for the far-right Vlaams Blok party, which polled its best results in its 25 years of existence by campaigning on a platform of anti-immigration and cracking down on crime. Vlaams Blok received more than 11 percent of the vote, increasing its seats from 15 to 18. The new government was officially sworn in on July 14 after difficult negotiations over the division of portfolios.

Pressure from U.S. officials influenced Belgium's decision to amend its law on genocide and crimes against humanity. The original law, which had been in effect for 10 years, allowed Belgians and non-Belgians to file charges against foreigners for human rights abuses, even if the alleged crime took place outside Belgium and the plaintiffs were not directly affected. Such liberal standing criteria had led to a number of suits against former U.S. president George H.W. Bush and Israeli prime minister Ariel Sharon over crimes related to the 1991 Gulf War and the 1982 massacres at Palestinian refugee camps in Lebanon, respectively. U.S. Secretary of State Colin Powell threatened to move NATO headquarters, which is located in Brussels, out of Belgium if the government did not revise the law. In the amended law, complainants must show that they are directly affected by the alleged crime. The federal prosecutor involved can also refer cases to the newly created International Criminal Court when the crime involves parties outside the country.

## Political Rights and Civil Liberties:

Belgians can change their government democratically. More than 91 percent of all registered voters turned out at the polls during the last elections. High voter turnout is due in part to compulsory voting laws. The party system is highly fragmented, with few parties gaining more than 15 percent of the vote. In addition, political parties are generally organized along ethno-regional lines, with separate organizations in Flanders and Wallonia, a factor that makes for difficult coalitions. Earlier in the year, the anti-immigrant Vlaams Blok won a case lodged against it by two human rights groups that had claimed the party should have its public funding removed for its use of racist campaign material. The court threw the case out after determining that it was politically motivated.

Transparency International ranked Belgium 17 out of 133 countries surveyed in its 2003 Corruption Perceptions Index, above the United States and France.

Freedom of speech and the press is guaranteed in Belgium. However, Belgium ranked below most West European countries in Reporters Sans Frontiere's index of worldwide press freedom. In July, the European Court of Human Rights ruled that the Belgian state had violated the freedom of expression and the right to confidentiality of several Belgian journalists who were searched by the police in June 1995. A specific Belgian law protecting journalistic sources was tabled in parliament in late 2002. Internet access was not restricted in the country.

Freedom of religion is protected in Belgium, where the state grants subsidies to Christian, Jewish, and Muslim institutions. There are specific antiracism laws in Belgium that prohibit the expression of xenophobia. Such laws, however, are rarely invoked, according to the 2000 report of the European Commission against Racism and Intolerance. Academic freedom in the country was not restricted.

Freedom of association is guaranteed. However, questions were raised in the federal parliament during the year about the large numbers of people arrested in conjunction with peaceful antiwar protests over the conflict in Iraq. According to Amnesty International, during the height of the conflict in March and April, the police put more than 450 demonstrators in "preventive detention" for up to 12 hours.

A gentleman's agreement between workers and employers was reached in 2002 that bolstered the right to strike. Up to this point, employers frequently used the courts to solve strike-related problems, often in their favor. About 63 percent of the Belgian workforce is unionized.

The judiciary is independent in Belgium, and the rule of law generally prevails in civil and criminal matters. However, the UN Committee against Torture examined Belgium on May 6 and 7 and expressed concern about the ill-treatment by police officers of suspects, particularly those who are foreign or non-white Belgian citizens. Amnesty International reported that some people in police custody lacked access to a lawyer during questioning, and/or were denied the right to have relatives or another third party notified of their detention. However, Belgium was congratulated in 2002 for introducing a law against torture and inhuman and degrading treatment.

Equality of opportunity for foreigners is undermined by a relatively high degree of racism in the country, which is frequently propagated by the xenophobic Vlaams Bloc party, whose support has risen in recent years.

Belgium passed a law in 1994 that stipulated that two-thirds of each party's candidates must be of a different sex. Women won more than 35 percent of the seats in the lower house of parliament during elections in 2003, a 10 percent increase since the previous elections in 1999.

# Belize

**Population:** 300,000
**GNI/capita:** $2,960
**Life Expectancy:** 67
**Political Rights:** 1
**Civil Liberties:** 2
**Status:** Free
**Religious Groups:** Roman Catholic (49.6 percent),
Protestant (27 percent), other (23.4 percent)
**Ethnic Groups:** Mestizo (48.7 percent), Creole (24.9 percent),
Maya (10.6 percent), Garifuna (6.1 percent), other (9.7 percent)
**Capital:** Belmopan

**Ten-Year Ratings Timeline (Political Rights, Civil Liberties, Status)**

| 1994 | 1995 | 1996 | 1997 | 1998 | 1999 | 2000 | 2001 | 2002 | 2003 |
|------|------|------|------|------|------|------|------|------|------|
| 1,1F | 1,1F | 1,1F | 1,1F | 1,1F | 1,1F | 1,1F | 1,2F | 1,2F | 1,2F |

**Overview:**　　Belize's ruling People's United Party (PUP) returned to power with an overwhelming victory in the March 2003 parliamentary election. A key challenge for the new government will be tackling the country's violent crime, corruption, and drug trafficking problems.

Belize achieved independence in 1981 and is a member of the Commonwealth. Formerly British Honduras, the name was changed in 1973. The government has changed hands three times, alternating between the center-right United Democratic Party (UDP) and the center-left PUP. In 1993, the UDP and the National Alliance for Belizean Rights (NABR) formed a coalition, winning 16 of the 29 seats in the House of Representatives.

The August 1998 parliamentary elections, in which the PUP won 26 of 29 seats, proved to be a referendum on Prime Minister Manuel Esquivel's largely unfulfilled pledge that his UDP would create jobs. The new prime minister, former attorney general Said Musa, promised adherence to international treaties on indigenous and women's rights. His government later blocked efforts by Indian groups to make claims of their land rights before the Inter-American Commission on Human Rights.

The year 2003 began with a cabinet restructuring that gave Prime Minister Musa direct control over the powerful National Development Ministry, which incorporates economic and governance functions. Parliamentary elections held on March 5 gave Musa's PUP 22 out of 29 seats in the House of Representatives, ratifying Musa's mandate. However, his major challenges continue to be battling the country's violent crime and corruption. The UDP has continued to focus on corruption, and the prime minister cancelled a contract to renovate the Ministry of Foreign Affairs building, which had been awarded to the foreign minister's brother.

In September 2002, the government proposed a constitutional amendment to end appeals to the Judicial Committee of the Privy Council, located in the United Kingdom. The Belize Court of Appeals would be established as the final court of appeals for cases carrying a mandatory death sentence. There has been a moratorium on executions since 1985, but there is concern that a change in the law could lead to a resumption of capital punishment. The legislation had not been passed by the end of November 2003, and appeals to the Privy Council continue to be possible.

In recent years, Belize has experienced increases in the rates of violent crime, drug trafficking, and money laundering. Soldiers of the Belize Defense Force (BDF) routinely participate in joint patrols with the police in an effort to reduce violent crime. Corruption and fraud continue to haunt the Immigration and Nationality Department over nationality applications and passport processing.

Despite encouraging signs, the government of Guatemala in 2003 rejected the border adjudication decision rendered by mediators of the Organization of American States. Belize continued to reject pressure from the United States to sign an Article 98 agreement that would exempt the latter's military from prosecutions by the International Criminal Court. While military aid had been suspended by the United States, other forms of assistance continued.

**Political Rights and Civil Liberties:** Democratic government change takes place with free and fair elections. The 29-seat House of Representatives is elected for a five-year term. Members of the Senate are appointed: 5 by the governor-general on the advice of the prime minister, 2 by the leader of the parliamentary opposition, and 1 by the Belize Advisory Council. There are no restrictions on the right to organize political parties, and there are Mestizo, Creole, Maya, and Garifuna parties in parliament. Transparency International listed Belize for the first time in its 2003 Corruption Perceptions Index, ranking it 46 out of 133 countries surveyed.

There are judicial restrictions on freedom of the press, including prison terms for those who question the validity of financial disclosure statements submitted by public officials. Belize has 10 privately owned newspapers, three of which are subsidized by major political parties. The mostly English-language press is free to publish a variety of political viewpoints, including those critical of the government, and there are Spanish-language media. There are 11 private commercial radio stations and 2 private television stations, along with several cable systems. There is an independent board to oversee operations of the government-owned outlets. There is freedom of religion.

A large number of nongovernmental organizations are active in social, economic, and environmental areas. Labor unions are independent and well organized and have the right to strike, but the percentage of the workforce that is organized has declined. Unionized workers can earn two to three times as much as their neighbors. Disputes are adjudicated by official boards of inquiry, and businesses are penalized for failing to abide by the labor code.

The judiciary is independent and nondiscriminatory, and the rule of law is generally respected. In the past, judges and the director of public prosecutions negotiated the renewal of their employment contracts, which made them vulnerable to political influence. Judges now serve until their mandatory retirement at 65. There are lengthy backlogs of trials, in part because of the high turnover of judges, the result of their low pay. Cases often go on for years while defendants are free on bail. Reports of police misconduct are investigated by the department's internal affairs office or by an ombudsman's office. Extrajudicial killing and use of excessive force are the country's primary rights concerns.

Prisons do not meet minimum standards, though the Hattieville Prison was privatized and is run by a nonprofit foundation that has made some progress in improving the physical conditions of the inmates. Drug trafficking and gang conflict have contributed to an increase in crime. An antinarcotics agreement was signed with the United States in September 2002. Projects aimed at suppressing the cultivation, processing, and trafficking of drugs, curbing violent crime, and eliminating money laundering are funded.

The government actively discourages racial and ethnic discrimination. Although the Maya claim to be the original inhabitants of Belize, the government has only designated 77,00 acres as Mayan preserves out of the 500,000 acres claimed. Most of the indigenous population lives in the south, the poorest part of the country. The Belize Human Rights Commission is independent and effective. Human rights concerns include the conditions of migrant workers and refugees from neighboring countries and charges of labor abuses by Belizean employers. Most of the estimated 40,000 Spanish speakers who have immigrated to the largely English-speaking country since the 1980s do not have legal status. Undocumented Guatemalan, Honduran, and Salvadoran workers, especially in the service and agricultural sectors, continue to be exploited. Chinese and Indian nationals have been found to be working as bonded labor.

The majority of women working in brothels are from Guatemala, Honduras, and El Salvador. In May 2003, the U.S. State Department listed Belize as a candidate for sanctions because of its failure to control human trafficking. Violence against women and children is a serious problem.

# Benin

**Population:** 7,000,000   **Political Rights:** 2*
**GNI/capita:** $380   **Civil Liberties:** 2
**Life Expectancy:** 51   **Status:** Free
**Religious Groups:** Indigenous beliefs (50 percent),
Christian (30 percent), Muslim (20 percent)
**Ethnic Groups:** African [42 ethnic groups, including
Fon, Adja, Bariba, Yoruba] (99 percent), other (1 percent)
**Capital:** Porto-Novo
**Ratings Change:** Benin's political rights rating improved from 3 to 2 due to the holding
of vigorously contested free and fair legislative elections.

**Ten-Year Ratings Timeline (Political Rights, Civil Liberties, Status)**

| 1994 | 1995 | 1996 | 1997 | 1998 | 1999 | 2000 | 2001 | 2002 | 2003 |
|------|------|------|------|------|------|------|------|------|------|
| 2,3F | 2,2F | 2,2F | 2,2F | 2,2F | 2,3F | 2,2F | 3,2F | 3,2F | 2,2F |

**Overview:**  Benin held legislative elections in March 2003 that gave the ruling-party coalition a majority in parliament for the first time since multiparty democracy was introduced more than a decade ago. Parties supporting President Mathieu Kerekou won 53 seats in the unicameral National Assembly, compared with 30 seats for opposition parties. The legislative polls followed local elections that represented the last step in Benin's decentralization process and helped reinstate voter confidence following flawed presidential elections in 2001.

Benin was once the center of the ancient kingdom of Dahomey, the name by which the country was known until 1975, when Kerekou renamed it. Six decades of French colonial rule ended in 1960, and Kerekou took power 12 years later, ending successive coups and countercoups. He imposed a one-party state under the Benin People's Revolutionary Party and pursued Marxist-Leninist policies. However, by 1990, economic hardships and rising internal unrest had forced Kerekou to agree to a national conference that ushered in democracy. The transition culminated in his defeat by Nicephore Soglo in the March 1991 presidential election, and the country's human rights record subsequently improved. Kerekou made a comeback in the 1996 presidential poll.

Presidential elections in 2001 were marred by technical and administrative problems, as well as a boycott by the second- and third-place finishers in the second round of voting. Former president Soglo and Adrien Houngbedji claimed fraud after they won 29 percent and 14 percent, respectively, in the first round of voting, compared with incumbent president Kerekou's 47 percent. The boycott gave Kerekou a solid victory with 84 percent of the vote in the second round of voting, in which he ended up running against an obscure fourth-place candidate. Several members of the Autonomous National Electoral Commission had stepped down in protest before the second round of voting, citing a lack of transparency and poor administration of the election.

Fourteen political parties participated in the March 2003 National Assembly elections. Voter turnout was low, and there were some logistical problems, but the polls were considered free and fair. Opposition party members had accused the ruling party of intimidation ahead of the elections, and the government banned "anti-fraud brigades" that had been organized by the opposition. Pro-Kerekou candidates won 53 assembly seats against 30 by opposition candidates. Corruption and unemployment were subjects that dominated campaigning.

In addition to winning a majority in parliament in the 2003 polls, Pro-Kerekou parties also came out ahead in the local elections, although two opposition leaders won important seats. Former president Soglo was elected mayor of the economic capital, Cotonou, and former presidential candidate Houngbedji was elected mayor of the administrative capital of Porto Novo.

Benin is a poor country whose economy is based largely on subsistence agriculture. The International Monetary Fund in 2002 commended Benin for its economic progress, although poverty indicators have not improved significantly.

**Political Rights and Civil Liberties:** Citizens of Benin can change their government democratically. Benin held its first genuine multiparty elections in 1991 and now has more than 100 political parties. Historically, Benin has been divided between northern and southern ethnic groups, which are the main roots of current political parties; the south has enjoyed more advanced development. Northern ethnic groups enlisted during Kerekou's early years in power still dominate the military, although efforts have been made in recent years to rectify this situation.

Harsh libel laws have been used against journalists, but constitutional guarantees of freedom of expression are largely respected in practice. An independent and pluralistic press publishes articles highly critical of both government and opposition leaders and policies. Benin has dozens of daily newspapers, magazines, and private radio stations. It also has two television stations. Press freedom, however, suffered a slight setback in 2003 with the detention and beating of four journalists from *Le Telegramme*, a daily newspaper. They were detained following the publication of misleading information that was critical of two police authorities, according to Paris-based Reporters Sans Frontieres. Benin's private press observed a "no press day" to protest the detentions and beatings.

The government respects religious and academic freedom.

Freedom of assembly is respected in Benin, and requirements for permits and registration are often ignored. Numerous nongovernmental organizations (NGOs) and human rights groups operate without hindrance. The right to organize and join unions is constitutionally guaranteed and respected in practice. Strikes are legal, and collective bargaining is common.

The judiciary is generally considered to be independent, but it is inefficient and susceptible to corruption at some levels. The executive retains important powers. The Constitutional Court has demonstrated independence, but was accused of bias in favor of the president during the 2001 presidential elections. Lawmakers in 2001 replaced the colonial criminal code. Prison conditions are harsh, marked by poor diet and inadequate medical care.

Human rights are largely respected, although concern has been raised about the operation of anticrime vigilante groups and the failure of the police to curb vigilantism. Smuggling children into neighboring countries for domestic service and meager compensation is reportedly widespread. Many, especially young girls, suffer abuse. Efforts are under way in Benin to fight child abuse and child trafficking through media campaigns and education. Hundreds of children were repatriated from Nigeria in 2003.

Although the constitution provides for equality for women, they enjoy fewer educational and employment opportunities than men, particularly in rural areas. In family matters, in which traditional practices prevail, their legal rights are often ignored. After much debate, a family code that in part strengthened property and inheritance rights for women was approved by the National Assembly in 2002. While female genital mutilation is not illegal, the government has cooperated with efforts by NGOs to raise awareness about the health dangers of the practice.

# Bhutan

**Population:** 900,000
**GNI/capita:** $590
**Life Expectancy:** 66
**Religious Groups:** Lamaistic Buddhist (75 percent), Hindu (25 percent)
**Ethnic Groups:** Drukpa (50 percent), Nepalese (35 percent), indigenous or migrant tribes (15 percent)
**Capital:** Thimphu

**Political Rights:** 6
**Civil Liberties:** 5
**Status:** Not Free

## Ten-Year Ratings Timeline (Political Rights, Civil Liberties, Status)

| 1994 | 1995 | 1996 | 1997 | 1998 | 1999 | 2000 | 2001 | 2002 | 2003 |
|------|------|------|------|------|------|------|------|------|------|
| 7,7NF | 7,7NF | 7,7NF | 7,7NF | 7,6NF | 7,6NF | 7,6NF | 7,6NF | 6,5NF | 6,5NF |

**Overview:**
The ongoing process of political reform undertaken by King Jigme Singye Wangchuk, which is expected to lead to Bhutan's emergence as a constitutional monarchy, continued in 2003. Modest progress was also made on resolving the long-standing issue of repatriating a significant proportion of the Bhutanese refugees currently in Nepal.

Britain began guiding this Himalayan land's affairs in 1865, and in 1907 installed the still-ruling Wangchuk monarchy. However, a 1949 treaty gave India control over Bhutan's foreign affairs. In 1972, the current monarch succeeded his father to the throne.

Reversing a long-standing policy of tolerating cultural diversity in the kingdom, the government in the late 1980s began requiring all Bhutanese to adopt the dress of the ruling Ngalong Drukpa ethnic group. Authorities said that they feared for the survival of Drukpa culture because of the large number of Nepali speakers, also known as Southern Bhutanese, in the south. The situation worsened in 1988, when the government began using a strict 1985 citizenship law to arbitrarily strip thousands of Nepali speakers of their citizenship. The move came after a census showed Southern Bhutanese to be in the majority in five southern districts.

Led by the newly formed Bhutanese People's Party (BPP), Southern Bhutanese held demonstrations in September 1990 against the new measures. Accompanying arson and violence led authorities to crack down on the BPP. As conditions worsened, tens of thousands of Southern Bhutanese fled to Nepal in the early 1990s, many of them forcibly expelled by Bhutanese forces. Credible accounts suggest that soldiers raped and beat many Nepali-speaking villagers and detained thousands as "anti-nationals."

In early 2001, a bilateral team began certifying citizenship documents and interviewing family heads of the estimated 102,000 Bhutanese refugees currently in Nepal. After a number of delays in the process, in October 2003, the Nepalese and Bhutanese governments agreed to repatriate approximately 70 percent of the refugees from the first of the seven camps to undergo the verification procedure.

Bhutan continued to face diplomatic pressure from India regarding the presence in Bhutan of a number of Indian separatist militant groups. After holding talks in 2001 with the Bhutanese government, the United Liberation Front of Assam (ULFA) agreed to reduce its presence within the country, but it appears not to have honored this commitment. In July 2003, the BBC reported that the government intended to give the rebel groups a final chance to vacate Bhutanese territory, after which it would resort to the use of force to displace them.

During 2003, the government made further progress on the issue of political reform. The 39-member constitutional drafting committee submitted a second draft of the constitution to the king in June, and he intends to release it for public discussion as well as solicit comments from outside legal experts. The Speaker of the National Assembly was reelected in August, and a major overhaul of the civil service involving the reshuffling of senior bureaucrats took place in September.

**Political Rights and Civil Liberties:** Bhutanese cannot change their government through elections and enjoy few basic rights. King Wangchuk and a small group of elites make key decisions and wield absolute power, although the king did take several steps in 1998 to increase the influence of the National Assembly. He removed himself as chairman of Bhutan's Council of Ministers; in addition, he gave the National Assembly the power to remove the king from the throne and to elect cabinet members from among candidates nominated by the king. In August, the National Assembly resolved that under the new constitution, all three branches of government should function independently of each other.

The government discourages the formation of political parties, and none exist legally. The 150-member National Assembly has little independent power, although some analysts note that debate within the assembly has become more lively and critical in recent years. Every three years, village headmen choose 105 National Assembly members, while the king appoints 35 seats and religious groups choose 10 seats. For the 105 district-based seats, each village nominates one candidate by consensus, with votes being cast by family heads rather than by individuals. Human rights activists say that in reality, authorities suggest a candidate to the headman in each village and the headman asks families to approve the candidate. Members of all major ethnic groups are represented in the National Assembly.

Bhutanese authorities sharply restrict freedom of expression. The government prohibits criticism of King Wangchuk and Bhutan's political system. Bhutan's only regular publication, the weekly *Kuensel*, generally reports news that puts the kingdom in a favorable light. The only exception is occasional coverage of criticism by

National Assembly members of government policies during assembly meetings. Similarly, state-run broadcast media do not carry opposition positions and statements. Cable television services, which carry uncensored foreign programming, thrive in some areas but are hampered by a high sales tax and the absence of a broadcasting law. Internet access is growing and is unrestricted.

While Bhutanese of all faiths generally can worship freely, government policy favors the Drukpa Kagyupa school of Mahayana Buddhism, which is the official religion. The government subsidizes Drukpa monasteries and shrines and helps fund the construction of temples and shrines, according to the U.S. State Department's 2003 Report on International Religious Freedom. Drukpa monks also wield political influence. Some members of the country's small Christian minority are reportedly subject to harassment by local authorities.

Freedom of assembly and association is very restricted. Citizens may participate in a peaceful protest only if the government approves of its purpose. Nongovernmental groups that work on human rights or other overtly political issues are not legally allowed to operate. In recent years, security forces have arrested Bhutanese for taking part in peaceful pro-democracy demonstrations in eastern Bhutan. They have also arrested and deported Southern Bhutanese refugees living in Nepal who entered and demonstrated inside Bhutan for the right to return home.

The government prohibits independent trade unions and strikes. In any case, some 85 percent of the workforce is engaged in subsistence agriculture. Draft labor legislation under preparation would prohibit forced labor, discrimination, sexual harassment, and child employment in the private sector.

Bhutan's judiciary is not independent of the king, and legal protections are incomplete as a result of the lack of a fully developed criminal procedure code and deficiencies in police training. However, litigants' rights were bolstered by legislation that provided for legal counsel in court cases. In addition, in August, the king approved the establishment of a five-member National Judicial Commission to oversee the appointment of judges and other judicial staff.

Arbitrary arrest, detention, and torture remain areas of concern. According to Amnesty International, approximately 60 political prisoners from southern and eastern Bhutan continue to serve lengthy prison sentences. However, the government's human rights record has improved since the early 1990s, when soldiers and police committed grave human rights abuses against Nepali-speaking Bhutanese.

Conditions for Nepali speakers living in Bhutan have improved somewhat, but several major problems remain. A September 2002 Amnesty International report noted that ethnic Nepalese are still required to obtain official "security clearance certificates" to enter schools, take government jobs, or travel within Bhutan or abroad. At the same time, the government has eased some cultural restrictions that specifically targeted Southern Bhutanese. For example, in recent years, enforcement of a 1989 royal decree forcing all Bhutanese to adopt the national dress and customs of the ruling Drukpas has been sporadic.

The government's expulsion of tens of thousands of Nepali-speaking Bhutanese in the early 1990s, and recent bilateral efforts to repatriate them, have underscored the tentative nature of citizenship in the kingdom. Prior to the expulsions, the government stripped thousands of Southern Bhutanese of their citizenship under a 1985 law that tightened citizenship requirements. The new law required both parents to be Bhutanese citizens in order for citizenship to be conferred on a child. In addition, Bhutanese seeking to verify citizenship had to prove that they or both of their parents resided in Bhutan in 1958.

The UN High Commissioner for Refugees says that the overwhelming majority of Bhutanese refugees who entered camps in Nepal have documentary proof of Bhutanese nationality. Although the Bhutanese government continues to maintain that many of the refugees either left Bhutan voluntarily or were illegal immigrants, a deal to repatriate a first batch of 9,000 refugees was brokered in October under considerable international pressure.

However, since 1998, the government has been resettling Bhutanese from other parts of the country on land in southern Bhutan vacated by those who fled to Nepal. A report published by Habitat International Coalition in 2002 documented specific cases of the appropriation of houses and land and noted that this policy will considerably complicate the refugee repatriation process.

Women participate freely in social and economic life, but continue to be underrepresented in government and politics despite some recent gains. The application of religious or ethnically based customary laws regarding inheritance, marriage, and divorce sometimes results in discrimination against women.

# Bolivia

**Population:** 8,600,000
**GNI/capita:** $950
**Life Expectancy:** 63
**Political Rights:** 2*
**Civil Liberties:** 3
**Status:** Partly Free
**Religious Groups:** Roman Catholic (95 percent), other [including Protestant (Evangelical Methodist)] (5 percent)
**Ethnic Groups:** Quechua (30 percent), mestizo (30 percent) Aymara (25 percent), European (15 percent)
**Capital:** La Paz (administrative), Sucre (judicial)
**Ratings Change:** Bolivia's political rights rating declined from 2 to 3, and its status from Free to Partly Free, due to the removal of an elected president through street protests, continued increases in influence of drug money in politics and political corruption, and security force violence.

**Ten-Year Ratings Timeline (Political Rights, Civil Liberties, Status)**

| 1994 | 1995 | 1996 | 1997 | 1998 | 1999 | 2000 | 2001 | 2002 | 2003 |
|------|------|------|------|------|------|------|------|------|------|
| 2,3F | 2,4PF | 2,3F | 1,3F | 1,3F | 1,3F | 1,3F | 1,3F | 2,3F | 3,3PF |

**Overview:**
In office for little more than a year, President Gonzalo Sanchez de Losada tendered his resignation in October 2003 following a month of protests and road blockages by Bolivia's indigenous groups. The mass demonstrations over a planned energy project and natural gas sales stemmed from the failure of the country's economic and democratic reforms to improve the lives of the country's majority Indian population.

Sanchez de Losada, who fled to Miami, was succeeded in office by Vice President Carlos Mesa.

After achieving independence from Spain in 1825, the Republic of Bolivia endured recurrent instability and military rule. However, the armed forces, responsible for more than 180 coups in 157 years, have stayed in their barracks since 1982.

In the midst of growing social unrest and a continuing economic downturn, in 2002 the Bolivian congress elected Sanchez de Losada, a 72-year-old U.S.-educated millionaire, after he had barely defeated Evo Morales, a radical Indian leader of the country's coca growers and a frequent traveler to Libya, in the popular vote. Sanchez de Losada's selection temporarily eased fears that the country would be converted into a narco-socialist state.

In 1997, as the world's largest exporter of coca, Bolivia produced 270 metric tons of the leaf used to make cocaine. By 2002, U.S.-sponsored antidrug efforts had resulted in that figure dropping to 20 metric tons. However, not only did the country lose an estimated $500 million in revenues from the sales of the leaf, more than 50,000 coca growers and their families were also left without viable alternatives. Morales's showing in the 2002 polls was evidence of how unpopular these policies are among the country's majority Indian population, who use the coca leaf for traditional medicine and who have been shut out from the benefits of U.S.-backed economic reforms.

An anti-coca expeditionary task force paid for by the U.S. Embassy and made up of 1,500 former Bolivian soldiers has been the subject of frequent charges of the use of excessive force and human rights violations ranging from torture to murder. Critics say that the creation of a military force paid for by foreign funds violates both the Bolivian constitution and military regulations. Defenders of the force point out that the coca growers, who demand respect for their own property rights, work closely with narcotics traffickers and claim that the traffickers include snipers and experts in booby traps.

In October 2003, President Sanchez de Losada was forced to resign following a revolt by Bolivian indigenous groups, workers, and students over the planned construction of a $5 billion pipeline, once heralded as Latin America's largest infrastructure development project, and the sale of natural gas supplies through long-time rival Chile to the United States and Mexico. The mass protests against Sanchez de Losada, who privatized state-run businesses and carried out other free-market reforms during his first, corruption-plagued term in office (1993-1997), were fueled by resentment over the failure of nearly two decades of democratic reform and economic restructuring to improve the lot of Bolivia's Indian majority, who speak Spanish as a second language. Per capita income of $930 is the lowest in the Spanish-speaking Americas, and rural poverty and infant mortality compare to sub-Saharan Africa's.

The straw that broke the back of the ruling coalition was dissent in Sanchez de Losada's own cabinet over the brutal repression practiced by the security forces, whose use of large-caliber combat ammunition appeared excessive. The crackdown left some 80 people dead in the days running up to Sanchez de Losada's ouster, and came after a bloody shoot-out in February between soldiers and police that killed 30. As Sanchez de Losada fled to Miami, Vice President Carlos Mesa, a nonpartisan former media personality, assumed office. He immediately appointed a cabinet that has no representative from the country's traditional parties, but includes two indigenous Indian members.

Bolivia remains a hemisphere leader in unequal distribution of wealth, with about 80 percent of its people living in poverty. Official statistics put unemployment at 12 percent. Crime in La Paz and other major cities is increasing steadily, and the national police are considered to be both inefficient and corrupt. Riots protesting tax reforms were joined by striking police in February, pitting the police against their long-time rivals, the military, which was called in to restore order. Despite taking extraordinary measures designed to bring about reconciliation, Mesa appeared in a race against time, all the more so after peasant leader Felipe Quispe announced he was willing to see a civil war take place in order to gain power.

**Political Rights and Civil Liberties:** Citizens can change their government through elections, and Bolivians have the right to organize political parties. The 2002 elections were generally free and fair, although U.S. government officials say they had evidence that Colombian drug lords financed some of Evo Morales's political organization. Evidence abounds that drug money has been used to buy the favor of government officials, including that of police and military personnel.

As a result of recent reforms, presidential terms run five years and congress consists of a 130-member House of Representatives and a 27-member Senate. The principal traditional parties are the conservative National Democratic Action (ADN), the social-democratic Movement of the Revolutionary Left (MIR), and Sanchez de Losada's center-right Revolutionary Nationalist Movement (MNR). In 2002, the Socialist Movement (MAS) and the Pachacutti Indian Movement (MIP) gained significant electoral support as well.

The broad immunity from prosecution enjoyed by legislators is a serious stumbling block in the fight against official corruption. The military justice system generally is susceptible to senior-level influence and corruption and has avoided rulings that would embarrass the military.

Although the constitution guarantees free expression, freedom of speech is subject to some limitations. Journalists covering corruption stories are occasionally subject to verbal intimidation by government officials, arbitrary detention by police, and violent attacks. During 2003, reporters suffered physical assaults both from protestors and from law enforcement officers. The press, radio, and television are mostly private.

Freedom of religion is guaranteed by the constitution. The government does not restrict academic freedom, and the law grants public universities autonomous status.

The right to organize civic groups and labor unions is guaranteed by the constitution. Government-sponsored as well as independent human rights organizations exist, and they frequently report on security force brutality. The congressional Human Rights Commission is active and frequently criticizes the government. However, rights activists and their families are subject to intimidation.

The judiciary, headed by the Supreme Court, remains the weakest branch of government and is corrupt, inefficient, and the object of intimidation by drug traffickers, as are Bolivia's mayoral, customs, and revenue offices. In recent years, the government made serious efforts to improve the administration of justice, including making it more accessible. However, it has not included meaningful efforts to codify and incorporate customary law into national legislation, at least for nonmajor crimes, as a means of reaching out to the indigenous majority. Prison conditions are harsh, with some 5,500 prisoners held in facilities designed to hold half that number, and nearly three-quarters of prisoners are held without formal sentences.

More than 520 indigenous communities have been granted legal recognition under the 1994 Popular Participation Law, which guarantees respect for the integrity of native peoples. The languages of the indigenous population are officially recognized. However, Indian territories are often neither legally defined nor protected, and coca growers and timber thieves exploit Indian lands illegally. Some Indians are kept as virtual slaves by rural employers through the use of debt peonage, with employers charging workers more for room and board than they earn. The observance of customary law by indigenous peoples is common in rural areas. In the remotest areas, the death penalty, forbidden by the constitution, is reportedly sometimes used against those who violate traditional laws or rules. In the 2002 presidential campaign, Indian advocates demanded that the constitution be amended to explicitly grant them greater participation in government and clearer land rights.

Violence against women is pervasive; however, no system exists to record the incidence of cases, and rape is a serious but underreported problem. Women generally do not enjoy a social status equal to that of men. Many women do not know their legal rights.

# ↟Bosnia-Herzegovina

**Population:** 3,900,000    **Political Rights:** 4
**GNI/capita:** $1,240    **Civil Liberties:** 4
**Life Expectancy:** 72    **Status:** Partly Free
**Religious Groups:** Muslim (40 percent), Orthodox (31 percent), Roman Catholic (15 percent), Protestant (4 percent), other (10 percent)
**Ethnic Groups:** Serb (37 percent), Bosniak (48 percent), Croat (14 percent), other (1 percent)
**Capital:** Sarajevo
**Trend Arrow:** Bosnia-Herzegovina received an upward trend arrow due to the passage of several pieces of legislation strengthening central governmental institutions.

**Ten-Year Ratings Timeline (Political Rights, Civil Liberties, Status)**

| 1994 | 1995 | 1996 | 1997 | 1998 | 1999 | 2000 | 2001 | 2002 | 2003 |
|------|------|------|------|------|------|------|------|------|------|
| 6,6NF | 6,6NF | 5,5PF | 5,5PF | 5,5PF | 5,5PF | 5,4PF | 5,4PF | 4,4PF | 4,4PF |

**Overview:** Bosnia-Herzegovina marked some progress in forging stronger central governmental institutions in the year 2003, including the creation of new central government ministries and the introduction of a single value-added tax (VAT). However, other indicators, such as the decrease in the rate of refugee returns, suggest that postwar ethnic divisions within the country remain.

Bosnia-Herzegovina became one of six constituent republics of Yugoslavia in

1945. After Yugoslavia began to unravel and the end of the 1980s, Bosnia-Herzegovina was recognized as an independent state in April 1992. A 43-month-long civil war immediately ensued, which resulted in the deaths of tens of thousands of individuals and the "ethnic cleansing" and forced resettlement of approximately one-half of Bosnia-Herzegovina's population. In November 1995, the Dayton Peace Accords brought an end to civil war by creating a loosely knit state composed of the Bosniac-Croat "Federation of Bosnia-Herzegovina" and the largely Serbian Republika Srpska (RS). The Dayton Accords also gave the international community a decisive role in running post-Dayton Bosnia-Herzegovina, manifested in the significant powers and authorities granted to international civilian agencies such as the Office of the High Representative (OHR). Peace and security in post-Dayton Bosnia-Herzegovina is provided by the NATO-led Stabilization Force (SFOR). Despite these considerable efforts by the international community, however, most aspects of political, social, and economic life in postwar Bosnia-Herzegovina remain divided along ethnic lines.

Bosnia-Herzegovina's latest presidential and parliamentary elections were held in October 2002. Contrary to the hopes of many members of the international community, Bosnian voters across the ethnic divide mainly gave their votes to nationalist parties. The most important nationalist parties—the Bosniac Party of Democratic Action (SDA), the Serbian Democratic Party (SDS), and the Croatian Democratic Union (HDZ)—took control of the joint state presidency, the joint state parliament, and both entities' governments.

Bosnia-Herzegovina made some progress toward creating stronger central governmental institutions in 2003. Early in the year, the international community's High Representative in Bosnia-Herzegovina, Paddy Ashdown, created three new ministries for the central government (justice, security, and transportation). Although Ashdown's move was criticized by observers both inside and outside of Bosnia-Herzegovina for being unconstitutional because it did not have the support of Bosnia-Herzegovina's parliament, publicly elected officials in the country feared being sacked by the international bureaucrat if they protested publicly. In May, it was decided to unify Bosnia-Herzegovina's three ethnically based intelligence services. In November, both entities agreed to the creation of a centralized Indirect Tax Administration (IDA), which should make tax collection more efficient and reduce tax fraud. In December, Bosnia-Herzegovina's parliament passed legislation introducing a single, statewide VAT. Passage of the VAT legislation was an important demand of the European Union (EU). Bosnia-Herzegovina must still pass 47 new laws and create 25 new institutions before the EU will allow the country to begin negotiations leading to a Stability and Association Agreement. Bosnia-Herzegovina also remains heavily dependent on foreign aid for economic survival; according to one recent estimate, 20 to 25 percent of the Bosnian economy depends on foreign aid.

Nevertheless, the gulf between the different ethnic communities in Bosnia-Herzegovina still makes achieving political progress in the country exceedingly difficult. Over the past several years, the OHR has imposed 473 pieces of legislation in Bosnia-Herzegovina that local politicians have been unwilling to do themselves.

On October 22, Bosnia-Herzegovina's wartime president, Alija Izetbegovic, died in Sarajevo. In an important indication of how divided the country remains, while Bosniac-populated areas throughout Bosnia-Herzegovina observed several days of mourning after Izetbegovic's death, in Croat and Serb areas it was business as usual. Just hours before Izetbegovic's funeral in Sarajevo began, the International Criminal Tribunal for the Former Yugoslavia (ICTY) announced that it was closing its investigation into war crimes committed by forces under Izetbegovic's command.

**Political Rights and Civil Liberties:** In general, voters can freely elect their representatives and can form political parties insofar as party programs are compatible with the Dayton Accords. The High Representative, however, has the authority to remove publicly elected officials from office if they are deemed to be obstructing the peace process. In April, the High Representative forced the resignation of the Republika Srpska (RS) president, Mirko Sarovic, because of his alleged involvement in a spying scandal involving the RS secret service monitoring of NATO forces in Bosnia-Herzegovina. The High Representative also has the right to impose laws and regulations on the country when local officials are unable to agree on important matters. Indicative of the limited sovereignty of the country is that the High Representative has no popular mandate; all four of the high representatives in the postwar period have been appointed by the international community, and the peoples of Bosnia-Herzegovina have had no role whatsoever in choosing the most powerful political official in their own country.

A plethora of independent electronic and print media organizations operate in Bosnia-Herzegovina, but the most prominent feature of the country's journalism is its low standard of professional ethics. Bosnian journalism is further hampered by its reliance on foreign donations for survival, and the fact that most media outlets appeal only to narrow ethnic constituencies. During the year, the leading Bosniac daily newspaper, *Dnevni Avaz*, became embroiled in a controversy when a Sarajevo businessman accused the newspaper's editor of being behind a bomb attack on his house. The businessman in question had been the target of a smear campaign by *Dnevni Avaz*. After a four-month investigation, the Sarajevo District Court found the newspaper guilty of printing 52 false and slanderous articles about the businessman over the course of eight months. There were no reports of denial of access to the Internet.

Individuals enjoy freedom of religious belief and practice in areas dominated by members of their own ethnic group, but individuals who are members of a local ethnic minority often face various forms of discrimination or harassment. All three major religious organizations in the country—Islamic, Roman Catholic, and Orthodox—have claims against the government for property confiscated during the Communist period. While the various government's in Bosnia-Herzegovina do not restrict academic freedom, a continuing problem remains ethnic favoritism in appointments to academic positions, and the politicization of such appointments.

The constitution provides for freedom of assembly and association, and the various entity and cantonal governments generally respected these rights. However, the ability of ethnic or religious minorities in a particular area to exercise such rights has sometimes been more difficult than for the local majority population. Although there are no legal restrictions on the right of workers to form and join labor unions, which many workers do, unions are mainly divided along ethnic lines.

The judiciary in Bosnia-Herzegovina is still considered to be unduly influenced by nationalist political parties and executive branches of government. Judges who show some independence are reported to have come under various forms of intimidation. A new criminal code was introduced in March, along with a new Bosnian State Court and State Prosecutor's office. One of the most significant features of the new criminal code allows Bosnian authorities to prosecute individuals who aid or abet persons indicted for war crimes by the International Criminal Tribunal for the Former Yugoslavia (ICTY). It also contains provisions allowing for the dismissal of public officials who fail to arrest, detain, or extradite those so charged and a prison sentence of up to 10 years for such individuals. The most sought-after indicted war criminals from Bosnia-Herzegovina's civil conflict, the former Bosnian Serb political leader Radovan Karadzic and former Bosnian Serb military leader Ratko Mladic, remain at large.

Corruption in the judiciary, police forces, and civil service forms a considerable obstacle to establishing the rule of law in Bosnia-Herzegovina. International officials claim that there is an "imbalance between the components of the rule of law." Local police and corrections personnel have reached a baseline of professional competence and democratic policing, but the judicial system—courts, judges, prosecutors, legal codes, rules of evidence and criminal procedures, and the witness protection program—still require radical reform and restructuring. Many indicted war criminals remain at large.

Refugee returns declined significantly in 2003, partly because of weak economic conditions, and partly because the vast majority of property restitution cases left over from the war have now been resolved. Many people appear to be returning to their prewar homes only to sell their property and move back to areas in which they are members of the local ethnic majority. Nevertheless, there have been some large-scale, permanent returns, particularly in the northern RS in and around the town of Kozarac.

Women are legally entitled to full equality with men. However, they are significantly underrepresented in politics and government and are frequently discriminated against in the workplace in favor of demobilized soldiers. To compensate for the absence of women in public life, political parties have to list three women among the top 10 names on their lists of candidates. A significant problem in postwar Bosnia-Herzegovina has become its emergence as a destination country for trafficked women. UN reports claim that a substantial reason for the market for trafficked women working in brothels in Bosnia-Herzegovina is due to the large international civil and military presence in the country. The new Bosnian criminal code that went into effect in March specifically makes trafficking in human beings a crime and increases penalties available to law enforcement officials for such offenses.

# Botswana

**Population:** 1,600,000
**GNI/capita:** $3,100
**Life Expectancy:** 37
**Religious Groups:** Indigenous beliefs (85 percent), Christian (15 percent)
**Ethnic Groups:** Tswana (79 percent), Kalanga (11 percent), Basarwa (3 percent), other (7 percent)
**Capital:** Gaborone

**Political Rights:** 2
**Civil Liberties:** 2
**Status:** Free

## Ten-Year Ratings Timeline (Political Rights, Civil Liberties, Status)

| 1994 | 1995 | 1996 | 1997 | 1998 | 1999 | 2000 | 2001 | 2002 | 2003 |
|------|------|------|------|------|------|------|------|------|------|
| 2,3F | 2,2F | 2,2F | 2,2F | 2,2F | 2,2F | 2,2F | 2,2F | 2,2F | 2,2F |

**Overview:**

While Africa's longest-lasting multiparty democracy continued to demonstrate solid stability in 2003, AIDS tore at Botswana's social and economic fabric and minority groups complained of persistent marginalization.

Elected governments have ruled the country since it gained independence from Britain in 1966. A referendum on whether the president should be directly elected was withdrawn shortly before a scheduled vote in late 1997. Festus Mogae, a former central bank chief, succeeded Ketumile Masire as president in 1998 and was confirmed as the country's leader in 1999.

The ruling Botswana Democratic Party (BDP), which has held power since independence, won by a wide majority in legislative and local elections in October 1999, soundly defeating a fractured opposition. In that poll, the BDP swept 33 of 40 National Assembly seats. Polling was deemed free and fair, although the BDP had preferential access to state-run media. The next presidential, legislative, and local elections are due in 2004.

Economic progress in Botswana has been built on sound fiscal management and low rates of corruption, and privatization is progressing slowly. Efforts are under way to diversify an economy where diamonds account for 75 percent of all export earnings. However, unemployment is an estimated 40 percent, and AIDS has taken a toll on the economy. More than one-third of Botswana's population is infected with HIV.

Meanwhile, the government of President Festus Mogae was still defending its 2002 policy of coercing the country's indigenous Basarwa off traditional lands in the Central Kalahari Game Reserve.

**Poltical Rights and Civil Liberties:**

Citizens of Botswana can change their government democratically. The National Assembly, elected for five years, chooses the president to serve a concurrent five-year term. The courts confirm the assembly's choice when the winning party receives more than half the seats in parliament. The Independent Election Commission, created in 1996, has helped consolidate Botswana's reputation for fairness in voting.

The House of Chiefs represents the country's eight major tribes and some smaller ones, and mainly serves in an advisory role to parliament and the government. Critics say it favors the Setswana-speaking tribes. In October, the government committed itself to amending discriminatory clauses in the constitution. Under proposed revisions, the eight Setswana-speaking paramount chiefs would retain their automatic membership in the House, while provisions would be made to elect a still-undefined number of representatives at the district level. Critics say this change does not address discrimination, as Setswana speakers could win the district votes.

Groups outside the eight majority tribes tend to be marginalized from the political process, especially the indigenous Basarwa, or San (red people), who live in extreme poverty, having lost their fertile ancestral lands. Under the Chieftainship Act, land in ethnic territory is distributed under the jurisdiction of majority groups. A lack of representation in the House has imposed on minority groups Tswana patriarchal customary law, which often has different rules for inheritance, marriage, and succession.

Botswana has been rated the least corrupt country in Africa by Transparency International and the World Economic Forum. The government in 1994 passed a bill that set up an anti-corruption body with special powers of investigation, arrest, and search and seizure. The conviction rate has been more than 80 percent.

A free and vigorous press thrives in cities and towns, and political debate is open and lively. Several independent newspapers and magazines are published in the capital. The opposition and government critics, however, receive little access to the government-controlled broadcast media. Botswana easily receives broadcasts from neighboring South Africa. The private Gaborone Broadcasting Corporation television system has a limited reach. There are two private radio stations, but state-run radio is the main source of news for much of the rural population, which also lacks Internet access.

Journalists in 2003 protested a draft bill to set up a press council that could impose fines and jail terms against reporters and publishers for violating a government-stipulated code of conduct. The accreditation of all local and foreign journalists would also become mandatory.

Freedom of religion is guaranteed, although all religious organizations must register with the government. Academic freedom is respected.

The government generally respects freedom of assembly and association, which are guaranteed by the constitution. Civic organizations and nongovernmental organizations, including human rights groups, operate openly without government harassment. Concentration of economic power has hindered labor organization. While independent unions are permitted, workers' rights to strike and bargain collectively for wages are restricted.

Botswana's courts are generally considered to be fair and free of direct political interference. Trials are usually public, and those accused of the most serious violent crimes are provided public defenders. Civil cases, however, are sometimes tried in customary courts, where defendants have no legal counsel. Prisons are overcrowded, but the government has been making moves to address the problem by building new facilities.

Botswana has an excellent record in Africa for human rights, although there are occasional reports of police misconduct and poor treatment of the Basarwa. Almost 50,000 San have been resettled from the Central Kalahari Game Reserve to villages or as laborers on farms. The Botswana Center for Human Rights, Ditshwanelo, protested the government's move in 2002 to cut off basic services to the remaining 600 to 700 Basarwa. The government said the cost of keeping them there was prohibitive, and it denied that it had coerced the Basarwa to leave. The government also rejected assertions by critics that it wanted to protect diamond reserves in the region from potential claims by the Basarwa. This year, 242 Basarwa took the government to court to fight for continued habitation in the reserve. The Basarwa tend to be marginalized educationally, and thus do not enjoy the same opportunities as more privileged groups.

Women enjoy the same rights as men under the constitution, but customary laws limit their property rights. Women married under traditional laws are deemed legal minors. Progress in improving women's rights has been slow, but analysts say the election of more women to parliament in 1999 and the appointment of more women to the cabinet were important steps. Domestic violence is reportedly rampant, but security forces rarely intervene in domestic affairs, especially in rural areas.

# Brazil

**Population:** 176,500,000 **Political Rights:** 2
**GNI/capita:** $3,070 **Civil Liberties:** 3
**Life Expectancy:** 69 **Status:** Free
**Religious Groups:** Roman Catholic (80 percent),
other (20 percent)
**Ethnic Groups**: White (55 percent), mixed (38 percent),
black (6 percent), other (1 percent)
**Capital:** Brasilia

**Ten-Year Ratings Timeline (Political Rights, Civil Liberties, Status)**

| 1994 | 1995 | 1996 | 1997 | 1998 | 1999 | 2000 | 2001 | 2002 | 2003 |
|------|------|------|------|------|------|------|------|------|------|
| 2,4PF | 2,4PF | 2,4PF | 3,4PF | 3,4PF | 3,4PF | 3,3PF | 3,3PF | 2,3F | 2,3F |

**Overview:** On January 1, 2003, former leftist anti-dictatorial firebrand and political prisoner Luiz Inacio "Lula" da Silva was inaugurated as president of a Brazil desperately searching for economic security and a respite from crime, including rampant political corruption. The rise of the one-time leader of the metalworkers union broke a historic monopoly on power by members of a small southern elite, military rulers, and local political bosses in a country with one of the worst income distributions in the world and 50 million people living in poverty. After taking office, Da Silva focused throughout the year on tackling issues including the country's economic crisis, corruption, and racial inequality.

After gaining independence from Portugal in 1822, Brazil retained a monarchical system until a republic was established in 1889. Democratic rule has been interrupted by long periods of authoritarian rule, most recently under the military regime that ruled from 1964 to 1985, when elected civilian rule was reestablished.

Civilian rule has been marked by corruption scandals. The scandal with the greatest political impact eventually led to the impeachment, by Congress, of President

Fernando Collor de Mello, who was in office from 1989 to 1992. Collor resigned and was replaced by a weak, ineffectual government led by his vice president, Itamar Franco.

In early 1994, Fernando Henrique Cardoso, a former Marxist who was Franco's finance minister and a market-oriented centrist, forged a three-party, center-right coalition around Cardoso's Brazilian Social Democratic Party (PSDB). Cardoso's "Plan Real" stabilized Brazil's currency and gave wage earners greater purchasing power. In October 1994, Cardoso won the presidency with 54 percent of the vote, against 27 percent for da Silva, the leader of the leftist Workers' Party (PT) and an early front-runner. However, Cardoso's coalition did not have a majority in either house of Congress.

Cardoso embarked on an ambitious plan of free market reforms, including deep cuts in the public sector and mass privatizations of state enterprises. He also ushered in a new era of dialogue with international human rights organizations and good-government groups.

In 1998, Cardoso's first-ballot victory (nearly 52 percent of the votes cast) over da Silva, his nearest rival, was tempered somewhat by a less convincing win at the congressional and gubernatorial levels. His win was also overshadowed by published accounts of corruption among senior government officials. The revelation in 1999 of a vast criminal conspiracy centered in the jungle state of Acre highlighted the lawlessness of Brazil's remote areas and moved Cardoso to take firm measures to combat the growing threat of organized crime. In 2001, however, the PSDB's legacy of reform was badly tarnished by an energy crisis and a growing number of accusations of corruption at senior levels. The energy crisis, in particular, seemed to drive a wedge between the PSDB and its fractious coalition partners, although causes of the crisis went beyond an alleged lack of government foresight and managerial talent.

Faced with rampant street crime, urban sprawl, rural lawlessness, and the devastation of the Amazon basin, Brazilians also increasingly voiced concerns that political corruption severely limited the government's ability to address difficult problems. Long a transshipment country for cocaine produced in the Andean region, Brazil had, by the beginning of the twenty-first century, become the world's second-largest consumer of the illegal drug, after the United States. Violence in several major Brazilian cities, most notably Rio de Janeiro, involving rival drug gangs and the sometimes outgunned police was fueled by the volume of cocaine and its cheaper derivates consumed locally.

During the 2002 presidential campaign, as the economy staggered under the weight of some $260 billion in foreign debt, unemployment soared and the country's currency lost more than 40 percent of its value against the U.S. dollar. Da Silva campaigned by attacking both the government's economic record and the effects of globalization while abandoning his party's previous anti-free-market stands and its willingness to default on Brazil's foreign debt. After far outdistancing his rivals in a first-round ballot on October 6, in the runoff election held three weeks later, Da Silva received 52.5 million votes, besting Jose Serra, a center-left former PSDB health minister and Princeton University alumnus, 61 to 39 percent. The PT, however, won fewer than 20 percent of the seats in both houses of the Congress, while all important governorships in the 5 largest of Brazil's 27 states were won by other parties.

Brazil's economic crisis and its $260 billion debt were among the first items on

Da Silva's agenda. With a mandate for change conditioned on his coalition's lack of a parliamentary majority, Da Silva defied expectations by boosting investor confidence by controlling inflation through fiscal discipline and tight monetary policies, which in turn resulted in a $30 billion credit line from the IMF.

Da Silva formed the Friends of Venezuela to help resolve the political crisis in neighboring Venezuela, instituted anti-corruption measures, and maintained cordial relations with the United States despite his independent foreign policy. He also quickly established himself as one of the world's foremost voice for developing nations, and Brazil led a revolt by 21 lesser-developed countries at a September World Trade Organization meeting in Cancun, Mexico, protesting their lack of access to the developed world's markets. In a country whose class and racial divides give the lie to its idealized self-image as a harmonious "racial democracy," Da Silva focused on racial equality issues. In a precedent-setting series of actions, he named four blacks to his cabinet, appointed the country's first Afro-Brazilian Supreme Court judge, and pressed for the adoption of a Racial Equality Statute to make good on his promise that blacks will make up at least one-third of the federal government within five years. Brazil's progress, however, was marred by rampant police abuses, including torture and murder, and marked increases in the use of narcotics and ther illegal sale by heavily armed gangs. The Wild West atmosphere of lawlessness in many of Brazil's major cities was underscored in March 2003, when gunmen made off with the justice minister's bulletproof car.

**Political Rights and Civil Liberties:** Citizens can change their government through elections. A new constitution, which went into effect in 1985 and was heavily amended in 1988, provides for a president to be elected for four years and a bicameral congress consisting of an 81-member Senate elected for eight years and a 513-member Chamber of Deputies elected for four years. A constitutional amendment was adopted in 1997 permitting presidential reelection, a measure that was touted as enhancing presidential accountability but also allowed the reelection of the incumbent. The 2002 elections, in which the entire Chamber of Deputies and two-thirds of the Senate were renewed, were free, fair, and the cleanest ever, as a result of a new electronic voting system. Despite a constitutionally proclaimed right to access to public information, Brazil does not have specific laws to regulate and guarantee the principle of transparency provided for in the constitution.

The constitution guarantees freedom of expression. The press is privately owned, but foreigners can only acquire a 30 percent share of a media company and are restricted in their ability to influence editorial decisions or management selection. There are dozens of daily newspapers and numerous other publications throughout the country. The print media has played a central role in exposing official corruption. In recent years, TV Globo's near-monopoly over the broadcast media has been challenged by its rival, Sistema Brasileiro de Televisao (STB). Reporters are frequently the target of threats, assaults, and occasionally, even killings, especially those reporters focusing on organized crime, corruption, or impunity issues. Although the government did not impose restrictions on the use of the Internet, federal and state police began to monitor the Internet to detect on-line recruitment by sex traffickers and the activities of hate groups.

The constitution guarantees freedom of religion and the government generally respects this right in practice. Jewish community leaders continue to express concern over anti-Semitic material appearing on Internet Web sites and compiled by neo-Nazi and skinhead groups. The government does not restrict academic freedom.

The right to strike is recognized, as is the right to organize political parties and civic organizations. Industrial labor unions are well organized and politically connected, although they are more autonomous of political party control than is true in most other Latin American countries; many are corrupt. There are special labor courts. Hundreds of strikes have taken place in recent years against attempts to privatize state industries.

The climate of lawlessness is reinforced by a weak judiciary, which is overtaxed, plagued by chronic corruption, and virtually powerless in the face of organized crime; recently, some improvements have been made. Although the judiciary is largely independent of the executive branch, judges have used their autonomy to impede court reform, stop anti-corruption investigations by other government agencies, and often use their highly formalistic legal decisions to overturn government modernization efforts, including those targeted toward privatization of state-owned industries and welfare reform. Public distrust of the judiciary has resulted in poor citizens taking the law into their own hands, with hundreds of reported lynchings and mob executions. On a positive note, the National Coordination for the Protection of Human Rights Defenders, made up of government officials and civil society representatives, was established in 2003.

Brazil has the highest rate of homicide caused by firearms of any country not at war—more than 70 percent. Police say that most violent crime—perhaps as much as 70 to 80 percent—in the country is related, directly or indirectly, to the illegal drug trade, including most of the 37,000 annual murders. An estimated 200,000 Brazilians are employed in the narcotics business, with at least 5,000 heavily armed gang members working for different drug-trafficking groups in Rio de Janeiro alone. Since 1994, the federal government has deployed the army to quell police strikes and bring order to Rio de Janeiro's 400 slums, most of which are ruled by gangs in league, or in competition, with corrupt police and local politicians.

Brazil's police are among the world's most violent and corrupt, and they systematically resort to torture to extract confessions from prisoners. Extrajudicial killings are usually disguised as shootouts with dangerous criminals. "Death squads" operating in at least 15 of Brazil's 26 states, often composed of off-duty state police, terrorize shantytown dwellers and intimidate human rights activists attempting to investigate abuses. In the rare instances when police officers are indicted for such abuses, convictions are never obtained; typically such indictments are dismissed for "lack of evidence." In May, Brazilian human rights secretary Nilmario Miranda admitted that an Amnesty International report accusing the police of torturing and killing thousands the previous year "reflects the truth."

The prison system in Brazil is anarchic, overcrowded, and largely unfit for human habitation, and human rights groups charge that torture and other inhumane treatment common to most of the country's detention centers turns petty thieves into hardened criminals. Some 200,000 people are incarcerated in Brazil, nearly half of them in Sao Paulo.

Large landowners control nearly 60 percent of arable land, while the poorest 30 percent share less than 2 percent of the land. In rural areas, violence linked to organized land invasions continues to be a sporadic problem; courts have increasingly supported the eviction of such land invaders. Thousands of workers are forced by ranchers in rural areas to work against their will and have no recourse to police or the courts.

White Brazilians earn more than 50 percent more than their black colleagues, and on average, whites without high school diplomas earn more than black university graduates. Violence against Brazil's 250,000 Indians mirrors generalized rural lawlessness. A decree issued by former president Fernando Enrique Cardoso opened Indian land to greater pressure from predatory miners and loggers. In some remote areas, Colombian drug traffickers have been using Indians to transport narcotics. In September, the new head of Brazil's Indian agency promised that the government was serious about demarcating wide swaths of ancestral lands as the first step in converting the land into indigenous reserves.

In August 2001, Congress approved a legal code that for the first time in the country's history makes women equal to men under the law. In January 2003, a new civil code took force that formally replaced a 1916 text that contained myriad sexist provisions concerning social behavior in government, business, and at home, giving women equal rights to men in marriage. Violence against women and children is a common problem, and protective laws are rarely enforced. Forced prostitution of children is widespread. Child labor is prevalent, and laws against it are rarely enforced. In June 2001, a decree granted same-sex partners the same rights as married couples with respect to pensions, social security benefits, and taxation. Brazil is a source country for victims of both domestic and international trafficking of human beings, the majority of whom are women and girls. Occasionally, women are employed as domestic servants in conditions tantamount to slavery.

# Brunei

**Population:** 400,000
**GNI/capita:** $13,724
**Life Expectancy:** 76
**Religious Groups:** Muslim (67 percent), Buddhist (13 percent), Christian (10 percent), other [including indigenous beliefs] (10 percent)
**Ethnic Groups:** Malay (67 percent), Chinese (15 percent), other (18 percent)
**Capital:** Bandar Seri Begawan

**Political Rights:** 6
**Civil Liberties:** 5
**Status:** Not Free

**Ten-Year Ratings Timeline (Political Rights, Civil Liberties, Status)**

| 1994 | 1995 | 1996 | 1997 | 1998 | 1999 | 2000 | 2001 | 2002 | 2003 |
|------|------|------|------|------|------|------|------|------|------|
| 7,6NF | 7,5NF | 7,5NF | 7,5NF | 7,5NF | 7,5NF | 7,5NF | 7,5NF | 6,5NF | 6,5NF |

**Overview:**
Sultan Haji Hassanal Bolkiah Mu'izzaddin Waddaulah continued to show few signs of easing his tight grip on power in this Southeast Asian nation. His government, meanwhile,

worked in 2003 to boost the country's oil reserves. Using gunboats and, later, negotiations, it tried to secure prospecting rights in potentially lucrative coastal waters that also are claimed by Malaysia.

Consisting of two tiny enclaves on the northern coast of Borneo, Brunei is an oil-rich, hereditary sultanate that has been under the absolute rule of Sultan Haji Hassanal Bolkiah since 1967.

The 1959 constitution vested full executive powers in the sultan while providing for five advisory councils, including a legislative council. In 1962, Sultan Omar Ali Saifuddin annulled legislative election results after the leftist Brunei People's Party (BPP), which sought to end the sultanate, won all 10 elected seats in the 21-member council. The BPP then mounted an insurgency that was crushed by British troops but whose legacy is still felt today. Sultan Omar invoked constitutionally granted emergency powers, which are still in force, and began ruling by decree. That practice was continued by his son, Sultan Hassanal Bolkiah, who became the 29th ruler in a family dynasty that has spanned six centuries when his father abdicated the throne in 1967. The British granted full independence in 1984.

Now 57 years old and one of the world's richest men, the sultan has done little to reform the ossified political system that he inherited. Today, the legislative council continues to be appointed by the sultan rather than elected, and the only two legal political parties are largely inactive. Both the Brunei People's Awareness Party and the Brunei National Solidarity Party (BNSP) publicly support the sultan. The BNSP is an offshoot of one of two parties banned in 1988.

In a scandal that fueled public resentment of the opulent lifestyles of royal family members, the sultan's brother, Prince Jefri, was accused in the late 1990s of misappropriating some $16 billion of Brunei's foreign reserves as head of the Amedeo Development Corporation. Amedeo was Brunei's largest private employer until its 1998 collapse. A case against Prince Jefri was settled out of court in 2000.

Oil and natural gas exports to Japan and other countries have given Brunei a per capita income rivaling that of many Western societies. Food, fuel, housing, schooling, and medical care are either free or subsidized, and there is virtually no poverty except for small pockets in tiny, remote villages. Energy reserves are dwindling, however, and the government has had limited success in diversifying the economy. Oil and gas production made up more than 50 percent of economic output and nearly 90 percent of export revenues in 2002.

The dispute in 2003 with Malaysia centered on the contested Baram Delta waters off the northern Borneo coast. In the spring, each side used gunboats to ward off drilling ships sent by the other to prospect for oil. After tempers cooled, the two sides began mulling a joint development arrangement for the waters, where Malaysia made a huge oil find in 2002, the Hong Kong-based *Far Eastern Economic Review* reported in July.

**Political Rights and Civil Liberties:** Bruneians cannot change their government through elections. The sultan wields broad powers under a state of emergency that has been in effect since 1962, and no legislative elections have been held since then. Lacking a more open political system, citizens often convey concerns to their leaders through a traditional system under which government-vetted, elected village chiefs meet periodically with top government officials.

Bruneian journalists face considerable restrictions. Legislation introduced in 2001 allows officials to shut down newspapers without showing cause and to fine and jail journalists who write or publish articles deemed "false and malicious." The largest daily, the *Borneo Bulletin*, practices self-censorship, though it does publish letters to the editor criticizing government policies. Another daily, the *News Express*, closed in 2002 after being sued successfully by a private law firm for defamation. Brunei's only television station is state-run, although Bruneians also can receive Malaysian television and satellite channels. In addition to restricting the media, the government has in previous years detained several Bruneians for publishing or distributing antigovernment materials.

The Shafeite sect of Islam is Brunei's official religion and permeates all levels of society in this predominantly Muslim country. In schools, Islamic study is mandatory and the teaching of other religions prohibited. The sultan promotes Islamic values, as well as local Malay culture and the primacy of the hereditary monarchy, through a national ideology called "Malay Muslim Monarchy." Critics say that the ideology, which is taught in schools, is used in part to legitimize an undemocratic system. While promoting Islam, Brunei's secular government has also voiced concern over religious fundamentalism, and one Islamist group, Al-Arqam, is banned. The government also restricts religious freedom for non-Muslims. It prohibits proselytizing, bans the importation of religious teaching materials and scriptures such as the Bible, and ignores requests to build, expand, or repair temples, churches, and shrines, according to the U.S. State Department's human rights report for 2002, released in March 2003.

Brunei's three trade unions are all in the oil sector, and their membership makes up less than 5 percent of that industry's workforce. Strikes are illegal in Brunei, although authorities have tolerated work stoppages by foreign garment workers to protest poor working and living conditions and forced payroll deductions for sponsors or employment agents. A private group called the Consumer's Association of Borneo in 2002 publicized allegations of torture and other abuses by factory managers of Bangladeshi garment workers involved in work stoppages.

Courts in Brunei generally "appeared to act independently," the U.S. State Department report said. The legal system is based on British common law, though Sharia (Islamic law) takes precedence in areas including divorce, inheritance, and some sex crimes. Sharia does not apply to non-Muslims.

While the government has faced few overt threats since the 1960s, authorities occasionally detain suspected antigovernment activists under Brunei's tough Internal Security Act. The act permits detention without trial for renewable two-year periods. Recent detainees include several citizens who distributed allegedly defamatory letters about the royal family and top government officials; at least seven Christians detained in 2000 and 2001, several of whom had converted from Islam; and several leaders of the 1962 rebellion after they began returning to Brunei from self-imposed exile in Malaysia in the mid-1990s. All were freed by the end of 2001.

The 80,000 foreign workers in Brunei generally work under difficult conditions and sometimes face abuse. Foreign household servants, for example, reportedly are often denied rest days and forced to work very long hours. Some employers allegedly hold foreign household workers' passports to prevent them from leaving Brunei, and reports surface occasionally of employers physically abusing or refusing to pay their foreign servants. Officials generally investigate and punish abuse of foreign household workers when complaints are lodged. Other problems include employment agents reportedly luring laborers to Brunei with false promises of well-paying jobs. Separately, many members of Brunei's ethnic Chinese minority are unable to pass the country's strict citizenship test and therefore lack citizenship despite being native-born.

While Brunei remains a highly traditional society, women recently have made gains in education and now make up nearly two-thirds of Brunei University's entering classes. The *tudong*, a traditional head covering, is mandatory for female students in state schools, though in any case most Bruneian women wear it regularly. Many women work for the government, Brunei's largest employer, although female civil servants that lack university degrees are hired only on a month-to-month basis. This results in slightly less annual leave and fewer benefits than what is given to regular state employees. In another concern, Islamic law governing family matters favors men in divorce, inheritance, and child custody.

# Bulgaria

**Population:** 7,500,000
**GNI/capita:** $1,650
**Life Expectancy:** 72
**Political Rights:** 1
**Civil Liberties:** 2
**Status:** Free
**Religious Groups:** Bulgarian Orthodox (83.8 percent), Muslim (12.1 percent), other (4.1 percent)
**Ethnic Groups:** Bulgarian (83.6 percent), Turk (9.5 percent), Roma (4.6 percent), other (2.3 percent)
**Capital:** Sofia

**Ten-Year Ratings Timeline (Political Rights, Civil Liberties, Status)**

| 1994 | 1995 | 1996 | 1997 | 1998 | 1999 | 2000 | 2001 | 2002 | 2003 |
|------|------|------|------|------|------|------|------|------|------|
| 2,2F | 2,2F | 2,3F | 2,3F | 2,3F | 2,3F | 2,3F | 1,3F | 1,2F | 1,2F |

**Overview:**

Bulgaria continued to make steady progress in 2003 toward its goal of gaining European Union (EU) membership, and the country remains on schedule to join the union in 2007. In July, the International Monetary Fund (IMF) issued a positive report about Bulgaria's reform record.

A Communist government was established in Bulgaria after the Soviet Red Army swept through the country toward the end of 1944. From 1954 to 1989, Communist Party leader Todor Zhivkov ruled the country, but his 35-year reign ended when a massive pro-democracy rally in Sofia was inspired by the broader political changes then sweeping across Eastern Europe.

Throughout the post-Communist period, the main political actors in the country have been the Union of Democratic Forces (UDF) and the Bulgarian Socialist Party (BSP). With the exception of a short-lived, UDF-led government elected in 1991, the BSP dominated parliament from 1989 to 1997.

In November 1996, early parliamentary elections sparked by a deepening economic crisis and growing crime and corruption rates brought the UDF into office. In the April 1997 vote for the National Assembly, the UDF and its allied factions won 52 percent of the vote and 137 of the 240 seats. UDF leader Ivan Kostov was named prime minister.

The UDF's tenure in office from 1997 to 2001 made it the first government in Bulgaria's post-Communist history to serve a full four-year term in office. Moreover, according to most observers, the UDF had been the most successful reformist government southeastern Europe had known until then. It was credited with significant success in privatizing and restructuring most of the state economy as well as winning an invitation for EU membership talks.

In 2001, Bulgaria's former king, Simeon II, returned from his European exile and formed the National Movement for Simeon II (NDSV). Promising quicker integration into Europe, Simeon attracted a large segment of the electorate. In the 2001 elections to Bulgaria's unicameral parliament, the NDSV won 120 of the 240 seats; the UDF, 51; the Coalition for Bulgaria (which includes the BSP), 48; and the Turkish Movement for Rights and Freedoms (MRF), 21. The NDSV formed a coalition with the MRF after failing to gain an outright majority. In November 2001, Georgi Parvanov of the BSP was elected president of Bulgaria, winning 53 percent and defeating the incumbent, Petar Stoyanov.

By 2003, however, there were signs that the public's infatuation with Simeon had worn off. In local elections held over two rounds in October and November, Simeon's party won only 7 percent of the votes cast (down from 40 percent it had won in 2001). Of the other major parties, the BSP won 23 percent of the vote, the UDF gained 14 percent, and the MRF gained 9. The remaining 47 percent of the votes went to a variety of minor parties and to independents. Despite the weak showing of the NSDV, however, the relatively poor showing of the other established parties means that Simeon's government is likely to carry out its term until the next regularly scheduled elections in 2005.

Despite the weakness of the government, Bulgaria has made substantial progress towards joining the EU. In July, the IMF issued a report calling Bulgaria's reform record "excellent" and predicting continuing strong economic growth for the next five years. Bulgaria appears on track to join the EU on schedule in 2007, although if its partner in EU accession that year, Romania, lags behind, there is doubt as to whether the EU will accept Bulgaria by itself.

**Political Rights and Civil Liberties:** Bulgarians can change their government democratically. The president is elected for a five-year term, and the unicameral National Assembly, composed of 240 members, is elected every four years. The Organization for Security and Cooperation in Europe (OSCE) deemed the 1999 local and the 2001 parliamentary and presidential elections to be free and fair.

The constitution guarantees freedom of the press, although international observers believe that the government still exerts undue influence over the media, and many journalists complain of feeling harassed about their reporting. The Council of Europe issued a statement during the course of the year criticizing the government's attempts to control public media outlets, as well as criticizing a new media draft law. There were no reports of the government restricting access to the Internet.

Freedom of religion is generally respected in Bulgaria, although the government has in recent years made it difficult for "nontraditional" religious groups to obtain registration permits allowing them to be active. (Those groups considered "traditional" in Bulgaria are the Orthodox, Roman Catholic, Islamic, and Jewish communities.) In December 2002, the government passed the "Confessions Act"—essentially a law on religion—which some observers claim unduly favors the Bulgarian Orthodox Church. The constitution forbids the formation of political parties along religious, ethnic, or racial lines. There were no reports of the government restricting academic freedom.

The constitution provides for freedom of assembly and association, and the government generally respects these rights. However, there have been reports that the government has denied ethnic Macedonians the right to hold public gatherings. The government also prohibits the formation of groups that propagate ethnic, religious, or racial hatred, or that advocate achieving their goals through the use of violence.

The judiciary is legally guaranteed independence and equal status with the executive and legislative branches of government. However, the judicial system continues to suffer from a variety of problems, including corruption, inadequate staffing, low salaries for magistrates, and a perceived unwillingness to prosecute crimes against ethnic minorities. In September, the parliament passed amendments to the constitution designed to limit magistrates' immunity and to increase their accountability. Law enforcement officials' use of excessive physical force and discrimination against the Roma (Gypsy) population remain serious problems.

Women now hold 63 of the 240 seats in parliament, having doubled their membership since the last general elections. Trafficking of women for purposes of prostitution remains a serious problem, as does domestic violence against women. One local nongovernmental organization published a survey showing that one in five Bulgarian women is the victim of some form of spousal abuse. A survey conducted in 2002 showed that 40 percent of women in the country had complained of harassment in the workplace.

# Burkina Faso

**Population:** 13,200,000
**GNI/capita:** $220
**Life Expectancy:** 45
**Religious Groups:** Indigenous beliefs (40 percent),
Muslim (50 percent), Christian (10 percent)
**Ethnic Groups:** Mossi (over 40 percent), other, [including
Gurunsi, Senufo, Lobi, Bobo, Mande and Fulani] (60 percent)
**Capital:** Ouagadougou

**Political Rights:** 4
**Civil Liberties:** 4
**Status:** Partly Free

**Ten-Year Ratings Timeline (Political Rights, Civil Liberties, Status)**

| 1994 | 1995 | 1996 | 1997 | 1998 | 1999 | 2000 | 2001 | 2002 | 2003 |
|------|------|------|------|------|------|------|------|------|------|
| 5,4PF | 5,4PF | 5,4PF | 5,4PF | 5,4PF | 4,4PF | 4,4PF | 4,4PF | 4,4PF | 4,4PF |

**Overview:**

The government of President Blaise Compaore struggled with political instability in 2003, claiming that it had thwarted a coup plot during the year. Meanwhile, the country's economy suffered with the return of migrant workers fleeing violence in neighboring Cote d'Ivoire.

After gaining independence from France in 1960 as Upper Volta, Burkina Faso suffered a succession of army coups. In 1983, Compaore installed himself as president in a violent coup against members of a junta that had seized power four years earlier and had pursued a watered-down Marxist-Leninist ideology. The populist, charismatic President Thomas Sankara and 13 of his closest associates were murdered. More Sankara supporters were executed two years later.

The presidential poll of December 1991, in which Compaore was reelected by default, was marred by widespread violence and an opposition boycott by all five candidates challenging the incumbent. President Compaore was returned to office for a second 7-year term in November 1998 with nearly 88 percent of the vote. The election was marked by heavy use of state patronage, resources, and media by the ruling party.

The 2002 National Assembly elections were overseen by the reconstituted Independent National Electoral Commission and were considered among the most free and fair polls in Burkina Faso to date. The commission includes representatives from the government, civil society, and the opposition. The 2002 polls marked the first time that a simple ballot was used in voting, which was a measure that opposition parties had urged for several years. The ruling Congress for Democracy and Progress party won 57 of the 111 National Assembly seats, compared with 101 during the 1997 polls. Opposition parties in 2002 fared better than they had any time previously.

In October 2003, authorities arrested Norbert Tiendrebeogo, the leader of the opposition Social Forces Front party, along with 15 others in connection with an alleged coup plot. Most of those detained were military personnel. Authorities said the plot was backed by a neighboring country, apparently referring to Cote d'Ivoire. The Burkina Faso Movement for Human and People's Rights said that those detained had been held without charge for more than 20 days; three days are allowed by law.

Burkina Faso's economy was also on shaky ground during the year, suffering the effects of civil war in neighboring Cote d'Ivoire with the return of more than 300,000 Burkinabe migrant workers. Burkinabe, Muslims, and members of northern Ivorian ethnic groups were among those being targeted after Cote d'Ivoire accused Burkina Faso of supporting mutinous Ivorian soldiers in a September 2002 coup attempt that triggered the civil war. Many families in Burkina Faso depend on remittances from relatives working in Cote d'Ivoire. Relations between the two countries were improving toward the end of 2003, and rail links and trade routes were reopened. However, peace is not assured in Cote d'Ivoire, and Burkina Faso could experience further economic and political turbulence.

Burkina Faso is one of the world's poorest countries, although gains have been made in life expectancy, literacy, and school attendance. More than 80 percent of the population relies on subsistence agriculture.

**Political Rights and Civil Liberties:** The 1991 constitution guarantees people the right to elect their government freely through periodic multiparty elections. In practice, this right has not been fully realized.

Burkina Faso has a vibrant free press, and freedom of speech is protected by the constitution and generally respected in practice. There is some self-censorship. At least 50 private radio stations, a private television station, and numerous independent newspapers and magazines function with little governmental interference. The media, which are often highly critical of the government, play an important role in public debate. There is liberal Internet access.

Burkina Faso is a secular state, and religious freedom is respected.

Freedom of assembly is constitutionally protected and generally respected, with required permits usually issued routinely. However, demonstrations sometimes are violently suppressed or banned. Many nongovernmental organizations, including human rights groups, which have reported detailed accounts of abuses by security forces, operate openly and freely. Labor unions and their rights are provided for in the constitution. Unions are a strong force in society and routinely stage strikes about wages, human rights abuses, and the impunity of security forces.

The judiciary is subject to executive interference in political cases, but is more independent in civil and criminal cases. National security laws permit surveillance and arrest without warrants. Police routinely ignore prescribed limits on detention, search, and seizure. Security forces commit abuses with impunity, including torture and occasional extrajudicial killing. Prison conditions are harsh, characterized by overcrowding, poor diets, and minimal medical attention.

Constitutional and legal protections for women's rights are nonexistent or poorly enforced. Customary law sanctions discrimination against women. Female genital mutilation is still widely practiced, even though it is illegal and a government campaign has been mounted against it. Burkina Faso is used as a transit point for the trafficking of women and children for purposes of forced labor and prostitution, but the government has made an effort to stop this criminal activity.

# Burma (Myanmar)

**Population:** 49,500,000
**GNI/capita:** $105
**Life Expectancy:** 57
**Religious Groups:** Buddhist (89 percent),
Christian (4 percent), other (7 percent)
**Ethnic Groups:** Burman (68 percent), Shan (9 percent),
Karen (7 percent), Rakhine (4 percent), Chinese (3 percent),
Mon (2 percent), Indian (2 percent), other (5 percent)
**Capital:** Rangoon

**Political Rights:** 7
**Civil Liberties:** 7
**Status:** Not Free

**Ten-Year Ratings Timeline (Political Rights, Civil Liberties, Status)**

| 1994 | 1995 | 1996 | 1997 | 1998 | 1999 | 2000 | 2001 | 2002 | 2003 |
|------|------|------|------|------|------|------|------|------|------|
| 7,7NF | 7,7NF | 7,7NF | 7,7NF | 7,7NF | 7,7NF | 7,7NF | 7,7NF | 7,7NF | 7,7NF |

**Overview:**

A number of positive developments noted in Burma last year were not sustained in 2003. The increasing latitude granted by the ruling military junta to the opposition National League for Democracy (NLD) was withdrawn in dramatic fashion in May, when supporters of the regime violently attacked an NLD convoy in northern Burma, leaving an unknown number of people dead, injured, or missing. Subsequently, party leader Aung San Suu Kyi and a number of NLD officials were placed under indefinite detention, NLD offices were once again shut down, and universities and schools were closed in a bid to suppress wider unrest. Following these setbacks, the tentative process of national reconciliation begun in 2000 has all but collapsed, and the junta continues to wield a tight grip over all aspects of Burmese life.

After being occupied by the Japanese during World War II, Burma achieved independence from Great Britain in 1948. The military has ruled since 1962, when the army overthrew an elected government buffeted by an economic crisis and a raft of ethnic-based insurgencies. During the next 26 years, General Ne Win's military rule helped impoverish what had been one of Southeast Asia's wealthiest countries.

The present junta, currently led by General Than Shwe, dramatically asserted its power in 1988, when the army opened fire on peaceful, student-led pro-democracy protesters, killing an estimated 3,000 people. In the aftermath, a younger generation of army commanders created the State Law and Order Restoration Council (SLORC) to rule the country. The SLORC refused to cede power after it was defeated in a landslide election by the NLD in 1990. The junta jailed dozens of members of the NLD, which won 392 of the 485 parliamentary seats in Burma's first free elections in three decades.

Than Shwe and several other generals who headed the junta refashioned the SLORC as the State Peace and Development Council (SPDC) in 1997. The generals appeared to be trying to improve the junta's international image, attract foreign investment, and encourage an end to U.S.-led sanctions linked to the regime's grim human rights record. In late 2000, encouraged by the efforts of UN special envoy Razali Ismail, the regime began holding talks with Suu Kyi, which led to an easing of restrictions on the NLD by mid-2002. Suu Kyi was released from house arrest and was allowed to make several political trips outside the capital, and the NLD was permitted to re-open a number of its branch offices. Nevertheless, press reports continued to note that meaningful discussion between Suu Kyi and the junta over the future restoration of democracy was not forthcoming, leading many analysts to remain doubtful about the regime's intentions.

Suu Kyi's growing popularity and her revitalization of the NLD as a political force during the first half of 2003, especially in the sensitive ethnic minority areas, may have rattled hardliners within the regime. On May 30, a deadly ambush on an NLD convoy in northern Burma by SPDC supporters illustrated the lengths to which the SPDC would go to limit a NLD challenge. Suu Kyi and dozens of other NLD officials and supporters were detained, many in undisclosed locations, for several months following the attack. Suu Kyi's detention and the junta's subsequent crackdown led to international outrage. Japan, the country's largest aid donor, has suspended its aid program until Suu Kyi is released. In July, the U.S. government passed the Burma Freedom and Democracy Act, which bans Burmese imports into the United States, authorizes the president to aid Burmese democracy activists, freezes the regime's financial assets in U.S. banks, and imposes a widened visa ban on Burmese officials attempting to enter the U.S.

A major cabinet reshuffle in August left hardliner Than Shwe as head of state, while the more pragmatic intelligence chief Khin Nyunt was promoted to prime minister. Although the regime then announced a new "roadmap to democracy," it did not provide details of a proposed timetable for its implementation. As talks with ethnic communities and the SPDC have evolved, the NLD has been openly excluded from discussions. In September, Suu Kyi was released into house arrest following a major medical operation, in what some analysts saw as a face-saving move to placate the international community. However, the fact that she remains a prisoner and the continuing crackdowns on the NLD cast doubt on the junta's claim that it remains willing to consider meaningful positive reform.

**Political Rights and Civil Liberties:** Burma continues to be ruled by one of the world's most repressive regimes. The junta rules by decree, controls the judiciary, suppresses nearly all basic rights, and commits human rights abuses with impunity. Military officers hold most cabinet positions, and active or retired officers hold most top posts in all ministries. Official corruption is reportedly rampant both at the higher and local levels.

Since rejecting the results of the 1990 elections and preventing the elected parliament from convening, the junta has all but paralyzed the victorious NLD party. Authorities have jailed many NLD leaders, pressured thousands of party members and officials to resign, closed party offices, harassed members' families, and periodically detained hundreds of NLD members at a time to block planned party meetings. After being allowed somewhat greater freedoms during 2002, the NLD was subjected to another crackdown in 2003. Besides the NLD, there are more than 20 ethnic political parties that remain suppressed by the junta. According to a report published in May by the International Crisis Group, ethnic minority groups feel that they are denied a role in national political life and do not have a chance to influence policy decisions that affect their lives.

The junta sharply restricts press freedom, owning or tightly controlling all daily newspapers and radio and television stations. It also subjects most private periodicals to prepublication censorship and restricts the importation of foreign news periodicals. According to the Committee to Protect Journalists, those caught listening to foreign radio broadcasts can be arrested. Local media were forbidden to report on a banking crisis in February, and coverage of the May 30 disturbances was limited to pro-government propaganda. A number of journalists and writers remained in jail throughout the year as a result of expressing dissident views. Publishers faced additional difficulties when the price of newsprint rose by almost 50 percent following the imposition of U.S. sanctions in July, according to the BBC.

Ordinary Burmese generally can worship relatively freely. However, the junta shows preference for Theravada Buddhism, discriminating against non-Buddhists in the upper levels of the public sector and coercively promoting Buddhism in some ethnic minority areas. The regime has also tried to control the Buddhist clergy by placing monastic orders under a state-run committee, monitoring monasteries, and subjecting clergy to special restrictions on speech and association. A number of monks remain imprisoned for their pro-democracy and human rights work. Burma was once again designated a "country of particular concern" by the U.S. Commission on International Religious Freedom, which noted systematic official discrimination against members of minority religious groups. A 2002 Human Rights Watch report alleged that the government had failed to protect Muslims from a significant increase in anti-Muslim violence, and that it had imposed restrictions on Muslim religious activities and travel.

Academic freedom is severely limited; teachers are subject to restrictions on freedom of expression and publication and are held accountable for the political activities of their students. Since the 1988 student pro-democracy demonstrations, the junta has sporadically closed universities, limiting higher educational opportunities for a generation of young Burmese. Most campuses were relocated to relatively isolated areas as a measure to disperse the student population. Following the clashes in May, the junta once again closed the country's high schools and universities, fearing student unrest. Two students were killed when the military violently suppressed a student demonstration held on May 31 to protest the attack on Suu Kyi, according to Amnesty International.

Authorities continued to infringe on citizens' privacy rights by arbitrarily searching homes, intercepting mail, and monitoring telephone conversations. Laws and decrees criminalize the possession and use of unregistered electronic devices, including telephones, fax machines, computers, modems, and software. The Internet, which operates in a limited fashion in the cities, is tightly regulated and censored.

Freedoms of association and assembly are restricted. An ordinance prohibits unauthorized outdoor gatherings of more than five people, and authorities regularly use force to break up peaceful demonstrations and prevent pro-democracy activists from organizing events or meetings. However, nearly all public sector employees, as well as other ordinary citizens, are induced to join the pro-junta mass mobilization organization, the Union Solidarity and Development Association (USDA). Domestic human rights organizations are unable to function independently, and the regime generally dismisses critical scrutiny of its human rights record from international NGOs and journalists, although it did permit Amnesty International to visit for the first time in January. The few nongovernmental groups that are able to work in Burma generally work in health care and other nominally nonpolitical fields.

Independent trade unions, collective bargaining, and strikes are illegal, and several labor activists are serving long prison terms for their political and labor activities. The regime continued to use forced labor despite formally banning the practice in October 2000, just days prior to an unprecedented call by the International Labor Organization (ILO) for its members to "review" their relations with Burma. The ILO and other sources report that soldiers routinely force civilians, including women and children, to work without pay under harsh conditions. Laborers are commandeered to construct roads, clear minefields, porter for the army, or work on military-backed commercial ventures. Forced labor appears to be most widespread in states dominated by ethnic minorities. A plan drafted jointly by the ILO and the junta during early 2003 that outlined measures to address the problem was tabled after the May 30 attack on the NLD.

The judiciary is not independent; justices are appointed or approved by the junta and adjudicate cases according to the junta's decrees. Administrative detention laws allow people to be held without charge, trial, or access to legal counsel for up to five years if the SPDC feels that they have threatened the state's security or sovereignty. Some basic due process rights are reportedly observed in ordinary criminal cases, but not in political cases, according to the U.S. State Department's annual human rights report. Corruption, the misuse of overly broad laws, and the manipulation of the courts for political ends continue to deprive citizens of their legal rights.

A detailed report issued by Amnesty International in July raised a number of concerns regarding the administration of justice in Burma, including laws and practices regarding detention, torture, trial, and conditions of imprisonment. Prisons and labor camps are overcrowded, and inmates lack adequate food and health care. Amnesty International's 2002 annual report noted that torture during interrogation continues to be a problem, and that at least 73 political prisoners have died in custody since 1988. However, conditions in some facilities have reportedly improved somewhat since the junta began allowing the International Committee of the Red Cross access to prisons in 1999.

Although the junta announced in late July that 91 people arrested in the aftermath of the May 30 violence had been released, more than 1,300 political prisoners remain incarcerated, according to Amnesty International. Most are held under broadly drawn laws that criminalize a range of peaceful activities. These include distributing pro-democracy pamphlets and distributing, viewing, or smuggling out of Burma videotapes of Suu Kyi's public addresses. The frequently used Decree 5/96 of 1996 authorizes jail terms of up to 20 years for aiding activities "which adversely affect the national interest." In September, on the eve of another visit by Amnesty International, a handful of prisoners were released, almost all over the age of 80.

The UN Commission on Human Rights in Geneva condemns the regime each year for committing grave human rights abuses. Annual resolutions commonly highlight a systematic pattern of extrajudicial, summary, or arbitrary executions; enforced disappearances; rape, torture, inhuman treatment, and forced labor, including the use of children; forced relocation and the denial of freedom of assembly, association, expression, religion, and movement; the lack of an independent judiciary; and delaying the process of national reconciliation and democratization. Some of the worst human rights abuses take place in Burma's seven ethnic-minority-dominated states. In these border states, the *tatmadaw*, or Burmese armed forces, often kill, beat, rape, and arbitrarily detain civilians with impunity. A report issued in May by Refugees International accused the army of practicing the "widespread and systematic" rape of ethnic minority women in a number of states. Soldiers also routinely destroy property and seize livestock, cash, property, food, and other goods from villagers.

Tens of thousands of ethnic minorities in Shan, Karenni, Karen, and Mon states and Tenasserim Division remain in squalid and ill-equipped relocation centers set up by the army. The army has forcibly moved the villagers to the sites since the mid-1990s as part of its counterinsurgency operations. Press reports suggested that the army continues to uproot villagers forcibly, and that approximately 1.5 million people have been internally displaced by such tactics. In addition, several million Burmese are estimated to have fled to neighboring countries, according to Refugees International. Thailand continues to host at least 135,000 Karen, Mon, and Karenni in refugee camps near the Burmese border, as well as hundreds of thousands more who have not been granted refugee status.

The junta has committed serious abuses against the Muslim Rohingya minority in northern Arakan state. Because the junta denies them citizenship, the Rohingyas face restrictions on their movement and the right to own land and are barred from secondary education and most civil service jobs. More than 250,000 Rohingyas remain in neighboring Bangladesh, where they fled in the 1990s to escape extrajudicial execution, rape, forced labor, and other abuses, according to reports by Human Rights Watch and other sources. The UN High Commission for Refugees closed its offices on the border in July but serious problems remain. A number of ethnic minority groups complain of systematic discrimination at the hands of the regime, including a lack of representation in the government and military, economic marginalization, and the suppression of their cultural and religious rights.

The junta continues to face low-grade insurgencies waged by the Karen National Union (KNU) and at least five smaller ethnic-based rebel armies. A number of other rebel groups, however, have reached ceasefire deals with the junta since 1989, under which they have been granted effective administrative authority of the areas under their control. While army abuses are the most widespread, some rebel groups forcibly conscript civilians, commit extrajudicial killing and rape, and use women and children as porters, according to the U.S. State Department. A 2002 Human Rights Watch report documented the widespread use of child-soldiers by some insurgent groups, as well as by the Burmese army.

Criminal gangs have in recent years trafficked thousands of Burmese women and girls, many from ethnic minority groups, to Thailand and other destinations for prostitution, according to reports by Human Rights Watch and other groups. Although Burmese women have traditionally enjoyed high social and economic status, they are underrepresented in the government and civil service.

# Burundi

**Population:** 6,100,000
**GNI/capita:** $100
**Life Expectancy:** 43
**Religious Groups:** Christian (67 percent), indigenous beliefs (23 percent), Muslim (10 percent), Protestant (5 percent)
**Ethnic Groups:** Hutu [Bantu] (85 percent), Tutsi (14 percent), Twa [Pygmy] (1 percent)
**Capital:** Bujumbura

**Political Rights:** 5*
**Civil Liberties:** 5
**Status:** Partly Free

**Ratings Change:** Burundi's political rights rating improved from 6 to 5, and its status from Not Free to Partly Free, due to the increased political role for a majority Hutu party and the agreement of one of two remaining rebel groups to join the government and participate in the political process.

**Ten-Year Ratings Timeline (Political Rights, Civil Liberties, Status)**

| 1994 | 1995 | 1996 | 1997 | 1998 | 1999 | 2000 | 2001 | 2002 | 2003 |
|------|------|------|------|------|------|------|------|------|------|
| 6,7NF | 6,7NF | 7,7NF | 7,7NF | 7,6NF | 6,6NF | 6,6NF | 6,6NF | 6,5NF | 5,5PF |

**Overview:**

The year 2003 saw significant movement toward resolving the multifaceted crisis that has plagued Burundi since 1993. The country's political space expanded as an ethnic Hutu became president as part of a power-sharing accord. All but one guerilla faction joined the political process.

With few exceptions, the minority Tutsi ethnic group has largely governed this small African country since independence from Belgium in 1962. The military, judiciary, educational system, business sector, and news media have also been dominated by the Tutsi. Violence between the country's two main ethnic groups—the Tutsi and the majority Hutu—has occurred repeatedly since independence. However, the assassination of the newly elected Hutu president, Melchoir Ndadaye, in 1993 resulted in sustained and widespread violence. Since 1993, an estimated 200,000 Burundi citizens, out of a population of 5.5 million, have lost their lives.

Ndadaye's murder fatally weakened the hold on power of the mainly Hutu opposition Front for Democracy in Burundi (FRODEBU). Negotiations on power sharing took place over the succeeding months, as ethnically backed violence continued to wrack the country. Ndadaye's successor was killed, along with Rwandan President Juvenal Habyarimana, in 1994 when their plane was apparently shot down while approaching Kigali airport in Rwanda. This event triggered the Rwandan genocide and intensified killings in Burundi.

Under a 1994 power-sharing arrangement between the main political parties, Hutu politician Sylvestre Ntibantunganya served as Burundi's new president until his ouster in a 1996 military coup led by Pierre Buyoya, who had formerly been president. Buyoya claimed to have carried out the coup to prevent further human rights violations and violence. Peace and political stability within the country continued to be elusive, as armed insurgents sporadically staged attacks and the government security forces pursued an often ruthless campaign of intimidation. The search for peace eventually led to an agreement to allow a measure of political space for parliament, which has a FRODEBU majority, and the beginning of negotiations in Arusha in 1998.

In 2000, the ongoing negotiations in Arusha, mediated by former South African president Nelson Mandela, resulted in agreement in principle by most parties on a future democratic political solution to the conflict. Nineteen organized groups from across the political spectrum agreed to recommendations from committees on the nature of the conflict, reforms in the nation's governing institutions, security issues, and economic restructuring and development.

The form of the political institutions through which power would be shared and the reform of the military proved to be especially sensitive and difficult issues. In October 2001, the National Assembly adopted the transitional constitution and a transition government was installed the next month, with President Buyoya temporarily remaining chief of state and Domitien Ndayizeye as vice president. The failure of key elements of the Hutu-dominated Forces for the Defense of Democracy (FDD) and National Liberation Front (FNL) to participate in the transition resulted in continued negotiations and violence.

The year 2003 saw some successes in resolving the crisis that has wracked the country since 1993. As a result of South African mediated negotiations, by the end of 2002, most of the factions had agreed to stop the violence and participate in transitional arrangements leading to national elections to be held in late 2004. In April 2003, President Buyoya stepped down and was replaced by FRODEBU secretary-general Ndayizeye. In October, the FDD, one of the two remaining rebel groups that had refused to participate in the peace process, reached an agreement with the government. Although hopes were raised that Burundi's civil strife could be nearing an end, the FNL continued to engage in guerilla activities.

## Political Rights and Civil Liberties:

Political rights within Burundi continue to be circumscribed, although parties and civic organizations do function. Burundi does not have an elected president or parliament. As part of the negotiated political agreement, which entered into force in November 2001, President Pierre Buyoya was replaced in April 2003 by Domitien Ndayizeye for the subsequent 18 months until presidential and parliamentary elections are held, in November 2004.

In June 1998, a transitional constitution reinstituted and enlarged the parliament through the appointment of additional members and created two vice presidents. The parliament's powers remain limited in practice, although it provides an outlet for political expression and remains an important player in determining the nation's future. As part of the agreement, the parliament's legitimacy was heightened by the nomination to it of key political figures. Jean Minani, a leading member of the opposition Front for Democracy in Burundi (FRODEBU) who returned from exile, was chosen by the National Assembly to be speaker.

There are more than a dozen active political parties, ranging from those that champion radical Tutsi positions to those that hold extremist Hutu positions. Most are small in terms of membership. FRODEBU and the Tutsi-dominated Unity for National Progress (UPRONA) party remain the leading political parties.

Some different viewpoints are expressed in the media, although media outlets operate under significant self-censorship and the opposition press functions only sporadically. The government-operated radio station allows a measure of diversity. The European Union has funded a radio station. The Hutu extremist radio broadcasts sporadically and has a limited listening range. The press group Reporters Sans Frontiers placed Burundi 92 out of 116 countries in its 2003 press freedom rankings.

Freedom of religion is generally observed. Academic freedom has been constrained somewhat by ongoing civil strife.

There is a modest but important civil society with a key area of focus on the protection of human rights. Constitutional protections for unionization are in place, and the right to strike is protected by the labor code. The Organization of Free Unions of Burundi is the sole labor confederation and has been independent since the rise of the multiparty system in 1992. Most union members are civil servants and have bargained collectively with the government.

The judicial system is seriously burdened by a lack of resources. Not surprisingly, given Burundi's recent history, there are far more existing and potential cases than can easily be handled by the existing judiciary, and many of them are highly sensitive politically. Many crimes go unreported.

Burundians continue to be subject to arbitrary violence, whether from the government or from guerilla groups. Although detailed, specific figures on the number of dead or injured are difficult to obtain, widespread violence continued in parts of the country in 2003. This has been documented by respected independent organizations inside and outside Burundi, including Amnesty International, Human Rights Watch, and the ITEKA Human Rights League. Amnesty International issued several appeals during the year, for example, for investigations into human rights abuses allegedly conducted by both guerilla and government forces. In addition to operations of the government security forces, there has been intense activity in parts of the country by armed opposition groups.

Apart from using artillery and small arms, government forces have also used helicopters to bomb areas of suspected guerilla presence. More than 30,000 civilians are displaced in the area around the capital and in urgent need of assistance. Reprisals by the armed forces have often been brutal and indiscriminate, and have resulted in hundreds of extrajudicial executions, mainly of members of the Hutu ethnic group. For example, the Burundian army admitted killing 173 civilians in the central province of Gitega in September 2002.

According to Human Rights Watch, Burundian army soldiers forced more than 30,000 civilians from their homes in Ruyigi province in eastern Burundi in late April and early May, and authorities refused to allow humanitarian aid groups to provide assistance to the displaced persons, who are suffering from malnutrition and disease. Much of the military's violence has been committed in zones where the local civilian and military authorities ordered the civilian population to leave the area because of counterinsurgency operations. The continued impunity of the armed forces and the weakness of the Burundian judicial system are important contributing factors to the violence.

The prolonged conflict has crippled the economy (25 percent negative gross domestic product over the last five years) and worsened social indicators. According to the Burundi Chamber of Commerce, the country's GDP has fallen to $620 million dollars, half the figure for 1991. Access to basic social and health services has been severely diminished.

Women have limited opportunities for advancement in the economic and political spheres, especially in the rural areas. Only 5 percent of females are enrolled in secondary school.

# Cambodia

**Population:** 12,600,000　**Political Rights:** 6
**GNI/capita:** $270　**Civil Liberties:** 5
**Life Expectancy:** 56　**Status:** Not Free
**Religious Groups:** Theravada Buddhist (95 percent),
other (5 percent)
**Ethnic Groups:** Khmer (90 percent), Vietnamese (5 percent),
Chinese (1 percent), other (4 percent)
**Capital:** Phnom Penh

**Ten-Year Ratings Timeline (Political Rights, Civil Liberties, Status)**

| 1994 | 1995 | 1996 | 1997 | 1998 | 1999 | 2000 | 2001 | 2002 | 2003 |
|------|------|------|------|------|------|------|------|------|------|
| 4,5PF | 6,6NF | 6,6NF | 7,6NF | 6,6NF | 6,6NF | 6,6NF | 6,5NF | 6,5NF | 6,5NF |

**Overview:**　Cambodia's ruling party was forced to form a coalition government with two smaller parties after failing to win the two-thirds majority of seats in the July 2003 parliamentary elections needed by law to form a government on its own. The election campaign was marred by unequal media access and accusations of voter intimidation. Despite gains by his political rivals, autocratic Prime Minister Hun Sen, 51, seems poised to continue his dominance over this impoverished Southeast Asian nation for the foreseeable future.

After winning independence from France in 1953, Cambodia was ruled by King Norodom Sihanouk in the 1950s and 1960s, the U.S.-backed Lon Nol regime in the early 1970s, and the Chinese-supported Khmer Rouge, which seized Phnom Penh in 1975 after several years of fighting. Under the Maoist Khmer Rouge, at least 1.7 million of Cambodia's 7 million people died by disease, overwork, starvation, or execution. In 1979, neighboring Vietnam toppled the Khmer Rouge and installed a Communist regime.

Civil strife continued in the 1980s, as the Hanoi-backed government fought the allied armies of Sihanouk, the Khmer Rouge, and a former premier, Son Sann. Hun Sen, a onetime Khmer Rouge cadre, emerged as the regime's strongman in the early 1980s. An internationally brokered pact in 1991 formally ended the conflict and put Cambodia on the path to multiparty elections, although the Khmer Rouge continued to wage a low-grade insurgency from the jungle.

Cambodia's first free parliamentary elections, in 1993, were won by a royalist party, known as Funcinpec after its French acronym. Its leader, Prince Norodom Ranariddh, a son of Sihanouk's, apparently capitalized on nostalgia among many voters for the stability that Cambodia enjoyed under the monarchy in the 1960s. Following the vote, Hun Sen used his control over the security forces to coerce Funcinpec into sharing power with his Cambodian People's Party (CPP).

Backed by Cambodia's army and police, Hun Sen harassed and intimidated Funcinpec members, opposition groups, and the press in the mid-1990s before ousting Ranariddh in a bloody coup in 1997. Meanwhile, the Khmer Rouge disintegrated in the late 1990s, bringing peace to Cambodia for the first time since the 1960s and ending the last real armed threat to the government. The coup and Khmer Rouge implosion marked a turning point in recent Cambodian history, establishing Hun Sen as the country's undisputed leader.

During the campaign for the July 27, 2003, parliamentary elections, opposition candidates were able to hold dozens of rallies. But observers including the New York-based Human Rights Watch and Washington-based International Republican Institute criticized restrictions on opposition access to radio and television and blamed local officials for intimidating voters and activists in the countryside. Final results gave the ruling CPP 73 seats, Funcinpec 26, and the opposition Sam Rainsy Party (SRP) 24.

The parties failed to reach their coalition agreement until November, a delay that threatened to worsen the donor fatigue felt by many of Cambodia's foreign patrons. When the IMF released a $12 million loan in February, it mixed tepid praise for the government's reform program with a call for further legal, judicial, and administrative reforms and a thinly veiled plea to curb corruption. Cambodia depends on foreign aid for more than half of its annual government budget.

Cambodia's entry into the World Trade Organization in 2003 may boost foreign investment, but lower tariffs under the global trading system will likely bring in cheap agricultural imports that may erode the livelihoods of some impoverished Cambodian farmers. Moreover, Cambodia's garment industry, which accounted for 23 percent of exports in 2002, could collapse when U.S. quotas expire in 2005.

After six years of haggling, Phnom Penh and the United Nations signed a deal in May to create an internationally backed tribunal for former Khmer Rouge leaders. Many observers complained that the tribunal will have a majority of Cambodian judges, who are widely believed to lack independence.

**Political Rights and Civil Liberties:** Cambodia's 2003 parliamentary elections were marred by restrictions on opposition access to radio and television and allegations of intimidation of voters and activists in the countryside. Local officials, most of whom are CPP members, threatened opposition supporters with violence, expulsion from villages, and denial of rice rations and other goods, Human Rights Watch reported in July. The watchdog group said that Funcinpec and the SRP also violated election laws, though less seriously.

The 2003 vote followed local elections the previous year in which some 31 mainly opposition activists were killed under suspicious circumstances prior to or following the vote, according to UN workers. Courts convicted suspects in some of the killings.

Prime Minister Hun Sen faces few democratic checks on his power. The National Assembly is becoming a forum for policy debate, but its members generally do not vigorously scrutinize government actions.

Moreover, although Cambodia's human rights record has improved in some areas, the rule of law is weak and impunity the norm. Police and soldiers are "able to impose their will on the civilian population and commit violations, safe in the knowledge that they will never be called to account for their actions," the human rights group Amnesty International said in a blistering June report.

Radio and television journalists reportedly practice self-censorship, and broadcast news coverage favors the CPP, observers say. Authorities have denied repeated requests from opposition politician Sam Rainsy for a radio station license. Meanwhile, an editor with a pro-Funcinpec radio station in Phnom Penh, Chuor Chetharith, was killed by unknown assailants in October. Cambodia's print journalists are freer than their broadcast counterparts. They routinely criticize government policies and senior officials, including Hun Sen. Authorities, however, recently have used the country's press law to suspend several newspapers for 30-day periods for criticizing the government or monarchy. Moreover, the government in January detained a newspaper editor, and the owner of Cambodia's sole independent radio station, on charges of inciting anti-Thai riots that rocked Phnom Penh by allegedly publishing or broadcasting unchecked rumors.

Religious freedom is generally respected in this predominantly Buddhist society.

Workers, students, political activists, and others held numerous protests throughout the year with little interference, although police or pro-government thugs recently have broken up some demonstrations. Cambodia's 40-odd nongovernmental human rights groups investigate and publicize abuses and carry out training and other activities. However, Amnesty International in January warned of a "continuing pattern of harassment and intimidation towards human rights defenders" in Cambodia.

Cambodia's few independent trade unions are active, but they are small, have limited resources and experience, and generally have little clout in negotiating with management. Factory workers frequently stage strikes in Phnom Penh to protest low wages, forced overtime, and poor and dangerous working conditions. Credible reports suggest that union leaders face dismissal and other harassment at some factories, and hired thugs at times intimidate or physically attack union members and other workers, according to the U.S. State Department's human rights report for 2002, released in March 2003. With some 80 percent of Cambodians relying on subsistence farming, union membership is estimated at less than 1 percent of the workforce.

Cambodia's judiciary is not independent and is marred by inefficiency and corruption. These problems reflect in part the court system's limited resources, severe shortage of lawyers, and poorly trained and underpaid judges. Security forces and local officials at times illegally detain suspects, while suspects who are charged generally spend lengthy periods in detention before their trials, according to local human rights groups and the U.S. State Department report. Police also routinely conduct searches without warrants.

Investigators often torture criminal suspects to extract confessions, and defendants frequently lack lawyers and must bribe judges to gain favorable verdicts. At the same time, delays or corruption allow many suspects to escape prosecution, leading to impunity for some government officials and members of their families who commit crimes. Despite recent reforms, Cambodian jails remain dangerously overcrowded, and inmates often lack sufficient food, water, and health care, human rights groups say.

Amnesty International and other rights groups criticized the investigations and trials in 2001 and 2002 of more than 90 men convicted for their roles in a November

2000 attack on government buildings in Phnom Penh. A California-based antigovernment group, the Cambodian Freedom Fighters, claimed responsibility for the attack, which killed at least eight people.

In a further sign that the rule of law is fragile in Cambodia, police, soldiers, and government officials are widely believed to often tolerate, or even take part in, gunrunning, drug trafficking, prostitution rings, and money laundering. Diplomats, businessmen, and aid workers say that corruption is widespread in government and banking.

The estimated 200,000 to 500,000 ethnic Vietnamese in Cambodia face widespread discrimination. Meanwhile, the government in 2001 and 2002 forcibly returned several hundred ethnic Montagnard refugees to Vietnam.

With the courts largely unable to enforce property rights, and the land registration system a shambles, military and civilian officials have in recent years forcibly evicted several thousand families from their land, according to Cambodian human rights groups such as LICADHO. Observers say that the local committees set up to settle land disputes render inconsistent decisions, operate with limited transparency, and are undermined by conflicts of interest among committee members.

Cambodian women enjoy equal access with men to education, but they play relatively limited roles in government and business management. They also hold an outsized share of the low-paying farming, factory, and service sector jobs. Rape and domestic violence are common, human rights groups say. Trafficking of women and girls within Cambodia for prostitution reportedly continues to be widespread despite some recent prosecutions of traffickers and sporadic crackdowns on Phnom Penh brothel owners. More than 10,000 children live on the streets of the capital, and many teenagers work in small-scale farming or other informal jobs.

# ⬇ Cameroon

**Population:** 15,700,000 **Political Rights:** 6
**GNI/capita:** $580 **Civil Liberties:** 6
**Life Expectancy:** 48 **Status:** Not Free
**Religious Groups:** Indigenous beliefs (40 percent),
Christian (40 percent), Muslim (20 percent)
**Ethnic Groups:** Cameroon Highlander (31 percent),
Equatorial Bantu (19 percent), Kirdi (11 percent),
Fulani (10 percent), Northwestern Bantu (8 percent),
Eastern Nigritic (7 percent), other (14 percent)
**Capital:** Yaounde
**Trend Arrow:** Cameroon received a downward trend arrow due to increased government repression of the media.

**Ten-Year Ratings Timeline (Political Rights, Civil Liberties, Status)**

| 1994 | 1995 | 1996 | 1997 | 1998 | 1999 | 2000 | 2001 | 2002 | 2003 |
|------|------|------|------|------|------|------|------|------|------|
| 6,5NF | 7,5NF | 7,5NF | 7,5NF | 7,5NF | 7,6NF | 7,6NF | 6,6NF | 6,6NF | 6,6NF |

**Overview:** Despite an October 2002 International Court of Justice ruling that awarded the disputed oil-rich Bakassi peninsula to

Cameroon, the country's relations with its neighbor Nigeria, which had also claimed the Bakassi border region, were cordial but tense in 2003. Meanwhile, President Paul Biya's government intensified its efforts to stifle the independent press with a major crackdown on the fledgling private broadcasting sector.

Cameroon was seized during World War I, in 1916, and divided between Britain and France after having been a German colony from 1884. Distinct Anglophone and Francophone areas were reunited as parts of an independent country in 1961. For three decades after independence, Cameroon was ruled under a repressive one-party system.

Prime Minister Biya succeeded President Ahmadou Ahidjou in 1982. In 1996, the constitution extended the presidential term to seven years and allowed President Paul Biya to run for a fourth term. His reelection in 1997, with 93 percent of the vote, was marred by serious procedural flaws and a boycott by the three major opposition parties.

The ruling Cameroon People's Democratic Movement (CPDM) dominated legislative and municipal elections in 2002 that were no more free and fair than previous polls, despite the creation of the National Observatory of Elections. In the June 2002 parliamentary elections, the ruling CPDM increased the number of its seats in the 180-member National Assembly from 116 to 149. The main opposition, the Social Democratic Front, won 22 seats, down from 43 it had held previously. Smaller parties won the remainder. Municipal elections, which had been postponed from January 2001, were also dominated by the CPDM. Opposition leaders were briefly detained by the police on several occasions in 2003.

In 2003, Cameroon moved closer to resolving its dispute with Nigeria over the oil-rich Bakassi Peninsula following meetings between the two countries on the implementation of an October 2002 International Court of Justice ruling awarding the territory to Cameroon. Cameroon and Nigeria have occasionally clashed militarily over the region, and Nigeria maintains a troop presence there. Nigeria initially rejected the court ruling, but in August 2003, a joint commission of the two countries began the process of demarcating their common border. Most Bakassi residents consider themselves Nigerian.

With elections approaching in 2004, the ruling CPDM stepped up repression of political opponents and the privately owned media. Radio and television stations that issued reports critical of the government of President Biya were closed on the grounds that they lacked proper licensing. Journalists were harassed and arrested. Leaders of the Southern Cameroons National Council (SCNC), a secessionist group based in the country's English-speaking provinces, were periodically detained by security forces. The SCNC has reportedly formed a military wing, raising fears of violence and sharper internal divisions in the run-up to national elections next year.

Privatization and economic growth in Cameroon have progressed, but graft and the absence of independent courts inhibit business development. Oil from a joint, World Bank–backed pipeline with Chad hit international markets in October 2003. The oil is expected to boost government revenues by $20 million per year.

**Political Rights and Civil Liberties:** Although Cameroon's constitution provides for a multiparty republic, citizens have not been allowed to choose their government or local leaders by democratic means. Presidential elections have been devalued by rampant intimidation, manipulation, and fraud, and legislative elections have also been fraudulent. Approximately one-fourth of Cameroonians are Anglophone. The administration of President Paul Biya remains largely Francophone, and the country's main opposition is from Anglophone Cameroonians. The linguistic distinction constitutes the country's most potent political division.

The constitution provides for freedom of the press, but criminal libel laws have often been used to silence regime critics. There are at least 20 private newspapers that publish regularly. Eleven years after the National Assembly passed a bill liberalizing the audio and visual media, Biya signed the legislation into force in 2001. A handful of private radio stations were already operating without a license, but they broadcast only religious or music programs locally. There are at least six national Internet service providers, some of which are privately owned. The government has not tried to restrict or monitor these forms of communication.

Repression of the media increased in 2003. In February, the government closed two privately owned television stations, RTA and Canal 2, on the grounds that they were operating illegally. In March, a radio station, Magic FM, was shut down for running programs critical of the government. In May, police shut down a new radio station the day before it was due to go on the air, saying that it lacked government permission to broadcast; local journalists said they believed the licensing requirement was a pretext. In August, the host of a satirical radio program was imprisoned to a six-month sentence following his conviction in absentia a year earlier for criminal defamation. The charges were based on comments the journalist, Remy Ngono, made on the air regarding accusations of embezzlement against a local businessman. Three journalists from Cameroon's only independent daily, *Mutations*, were briefly detained in April for a report discussing the potential turmoil that could ensue in the event of Biya's retirement.

Freedom of religion is generally respected. Although there are no legal restrictions on academic freedom, state security informants reportedly operate on university campuses and many professors fear that participation in opposition political parties could harm their careers.

Numerous nongovernmental organizations generally operate without hindrance. Trade union formation is permitted, but is subject to numerous restrictions. Workers have the right to strike but only after arbitration, the final decisions of which the government can overturn. In April, the government arrested six trade unionists, including the president of the Confederation of Cameroon workers, on sabotage charges.

Cameroon's courts remain highly subject to political influence and corruption. The executive controls the judiciary and appoints provincial and local administrators. Military tribunals may exercise jurisdiction over civilians in cases involving civil unrest or organized armed violence. In the north, powerful traditional chiefs known as lamibee run their own private militias, courts, and prisons, which are used against the regime's political opponents. Torture and ill-treatment of prisoners and detainees are routine. Indefinite pretrial detention under extremely harsh conditions is permitted either after a warrant is issued or in order to "combat banditry." Inmates routinely die in prison.

Various intelligence agencies operate with impunity, and opposition activists are often held without charges or disappear while in custody. Security forces routinely impede domestic travel, repress demonstrations, and disrupt meetings. Steps have been taken in Belgium, under its universal jurisdiction law, by Cameroonian political and civil society groups to institute legal proceedings against Biya for crimes against humanity.

The London-based human rights group Amnesty International called for an investigation into reports that dozens of extrajudicial executions were carried out in 2002 as part of an anticrime campaign. A military court in July 2002 acquitted six of eight gendarmes accused of killing nine young men who had disappeared in January 2001 after having been detained by an anticrime squad called the Operational Command. Two other gendarmes were given suspended sentences.

Cameroon's population consists of nearly 200 ethnic groups. Slavery reportedly persists in parts of the north, and discrimination exists against indigenous Pygmies and other ethnic minorities. The Beti and Bula dominate the civil service and state-run businesses.

Violence against women is reportedly widespread. Women are often denied inheritance and landownership rights, even when these are codified, and many other laws contain unequal gender-based provisions and penalties. Cameroon is a transit center and market for child labor and traffickers.

# Canada

**Population:** 31,600,000 **Political Rights:** 1
**GNI/capita:** $21,930 **Civil Liberties:** 1
**Life Expectancy:** 79 **Status:** Free
**Religious Groups:** Roman Catholic (46 percent),
Protestant (36 percent), other (18 percent)
**Ethnic Groups:** British Isles origin (28 percent),
French (23 percent), other European (15 percent),
Amerindian (2 percent), other (32 percent)
**Capital:** Ottawa

**Ten-Year Ratings Timeline (Political Rights, Civil Liberties, Status)**

| 1994 | 1995 | 1996 | 1997 | 1998 | 1999 | 2000 | 2001 | 2002 | 2003 |
|------|------|------|------|------|------|------|------|------|------|
| 1,1F | 1,1F | 1,1F | 1,1F | 1,1F | 1,1F | 1,1F | 1,1F | 1,1F | 1,1F |

**Overview:**

The year 2003 was marked by a series of important political developments, including the decision of Prime Minister Jean Chretien to retire at the end of the year, the defeat of a once-dominant separatist party in provincial elections in Quebec, the planned merger of the country's two leading opposition conservative parties, and a series of court cases that could lead to the legalization of same-sex marriages throughout the country.

Colonized by French and British settlers in the seventeenth and eighteenth centuries, Canada came under the control of the British Crown under the terms of the Treaty of Paris in 1763. After granting home rule in 1867, Britain retained a theoretical right to overrule the Canadian parliament until 1982, when Canadians established complete control over their own constitution.

The war against terrorism has been a leading item on the government's agenda since the attacks on the United States of September 11, 2001. Shortly after those attacks, Canada joined other members of the Group of 8 industrial countries in devising measures to combat international terrorism, including stopping funds for foreign terror groups. In December 2001, Canada and the United States undertook a comprehensive bilateral agreement on improving cross-border security.

The government has adopted several measures in the name of curbing terrorist organizations. Several have drawn criticism on civil liberties grounds, with two measures in an omnibus antiterrorism bill evoking particular concern. One allows police to make preventive arrests of those suspected of planning a terrorist act. Another requires suspects to testify before a judge, even if they have not been formally accused of a crime. Concern about terrorism was behind passage in 2002 of the Public Safety Act. The law's sections on data sharing drew criticism from civil liberties groups and from the country privacy commissioner, who expressed concern over the possible retention of data on private citizens for long periods of time and for the possibility that information could be used for purposes other than terrorism investigations.

The retirement of Chretien, scheduled for December 2003, brings to an end one of Canada's most successful political careers. Chretien had guided the Liberal Party to a position of dominance during his years as prime minister. The Liberals selected Paul Martin, a somewhat more conservative figure than Chretien, as his successor. Prior to his formal ascension to the prime ministership, Martin asserted that a priority of his government would be to solidify relations with the United States, which had frayed over Canada's refusal to join the U.S.-led coalition in the Iraq war.

A major issue during 2003 was a series of provincial court rulings that extended the sanction of law to same-sex marriages. In response, the government has referred to the Supreme Court the question of whether the country's Charter of Rights validates same-sex marriage. The Chretien government subsequently encouraged provincial governments to adopt laws permitting gay marriage. By year's end, three provinces—Ontario, Quebec, and British Columbia—had done so. The government also submitted legislation that would sanction same-sex marriages throughout the country. The bill's fate is unclear and may depend on the Court's ruling.

In a major gain for Canadian unity, the Liberal Party defeated the separatist Parti Quebecois for control of the provincial government of Quebec. The Liberal triumph is expected to put an end, for the time being, to the debate over Quebec's status, as the Liberals are strongly opposed to secession.

In another major development, plans moved ahead for a reunification of Canada's two principal conservative parties, the Progressive Conservatives and the Canadian Alliance. Neither party fared well in recent elections, which were dominated by the Liberals. In the current Parliament, the Liberals hold 170 seats, the Alliance 63, and the Progressive Conservatives 15. The country's fourth major party, the New Democratic Party (NDP), holds 14 seats. The NDP, which is social-democratic in orientation, elected a new leader, Jack Layton, in January.

During 2003, a law that would decriminalize the use of marijuana was introduced in Parliament.

**Political Rights and Civil Liberties:** Canadians can change their government democratically. The country is governed by a prime minister, a cabinet, and

Parliament. The Parliament consists of an elected 301-member House of Commons and an appointed 104-member Senate. The British monarch remains nominal head of state, represented by a ceremonial governor-general appointed by the prime minister. As a result of government canvassing, Canada has nearly 100 percent effective voter registration. Prisoners have the right to vote in federal elections, as do citizens who have lived abroad for fewer than five years. During 2003, the Supreme Court issued a ruling that compels the federal government to adopt legislation to make it easier for small parties to raise money and appear on the ballot.

The media are generally free, although they exercise self-censorship in areas such as violence on television. Limitations on freedom of expression range from unevenly enforced "hate laws" and restrictions on pornography to rules on reporting. Some civil libertarians have expressed concern over an amendment to the criminal code that gives judges wide latitude in determining what constitutes hate speech in material that appears on-line.

Religious expression is free and diverse. Academic freedom is respected.

Civil liberties have been protected since 1982 by the federal Charter of Rights and Freedoms, but have been limited by the constitutional "notwithstanding" clause, which permits provincial governments to exempt themselves by applying individual provisions within their jurisdictions. Quebec has used the clause to retain its provincial language law, which restricts the use of languages other than French on signs. The provincial governments exercise significant autonomy. Canada's criminal law is based on British common law and is uniform throughout the country. Civil law is also based on the British system, except in Quebec, where it is based on the French civil code.

Freedom of assembly is respected, and many political and quasi-political organizations function freely. Trade unions and business associations enjoy high levels of membership and are free and well organized.

The judiciary is independent. Recently, there have been complaints that the judiciary has become overly activist and has issued decisions that effectively usurp the powers of the legislature. This debate was further inflamed by provincial court rulings permitting same-sex marriages. Other issues on which the judiciary has issued controversial rulings include child pornography laws, native rights, abortion, and the civil rights of prisoners.

Canada maintains relatively liberal immigration policies. However, concern has mounted over the possible entry into Canada of immigrants who were involved in terrorist missions. In 2002, the Immigration and Refugee Protection Act was passed. It seeks to continue Canada's tradition of liberal immigration by providing additional protection for refugees while making it more difficult for potential terrorists, people involved in organized crime, and war criminals to enter the country.

Canada boasts a generous welfare system that supplements the largely open, competitive economy.

Canada has taken important steps to protect the rights of native groups, although some native groups contend that indigenous peoples remain subject to discrimination. During 2003, the federal government reached an agreement whereby it ceded control of a tract of land the size of Switzerland to the Tlicho First Nation. The government encountered opposition from indigenous organizations over a proposed law that would establish standards for internal governance for native groups.

Women's rights are protected in law and in practice. Women have made major gains in the economy and have strong representation in such professions as medicine and law.

# Cape Verde

**Population:** 500,000
**GNI/capita:** $1,290
**Life Expectancy:** 69
**Religious Groups:** Roman Catholic, Protestant
**Ethnic Groups:** Creole [mulatto] (71 percent),
African (28 percent), European (1 percent)
**Capital:** Praia

**Political Rights:** 1
**Civil Liberties:** 1*
**Status:** Free

**Ratings Change:** Cape Verde's civil liberties rating improved from 2 to 1 due to modest improvements in women's rights.

**Ten-Year Ratings Timeline (Political Rights, Civil Liberties, Status)**

| 1994 | 1995 | 1996 | 1997 | 1998 | 1999 | 2000 | 2001 | 2002 | 2003 |
|------|------|------|------|------|------|------|------|------|------|
| 1,2F | 1,2F | 1,2F | 1,2F | 1,2F | 1,2F | 1,2F | 1,2F | 1,2F | 1,1F |

**Overview:**     Cape Verde courts in 2003 sentenced a number of people for election fraud. Meanwhile, the government undertook unpopular measures as part of its move toward a market economy.

After achieving independence from Portugal in 1975, Cape Verde was governed for 16 years under Marxist, one-party rule by the African Party for the Independence of Guinea and Cape Verde, which is now the African Party for the Independence of Cape Verde (PAICV). The Movement for Democracy (MPD) won a landslide 1991 victory in the first democratic elections after Cape Verde became the first former Portuguese colony in Africa to abandon Marxist political and economic systems. In 1995, the MPD was returned to power with 59 percent of the vote. Antonio Mascarenhas Monteiro's mandate ended in 2001 after he had served two terms as president.

Cape Verde had a spectacularly close presidential election in 2001. In the second round of voting, opposition candidate Pedro Verona Rodrigues Pires defeated ruling party contender Carlos Alberto Wahnon de Carvalho Veiga by only 12 votes in an election that overturned a decade of rule by the MPD; both presidential candidates had served as prime ministers. It was a test for Cape Verde's democracy that despite the closeness of the election, trust remained in the country's institutions and the results were accepted.

The PAICV also defeated the MPD in the 2001 legislative polls. The change in voting appeared to be a reflection of the popular attitude that the MPD had grown complacent. The PAICV won 40 seats compared with 30 for the MPD and 2 for the Democratic Alliance for Change. Disagreements within the MPD in 2000 resulted in a split and the formation of a new party, the Democratic Renewal Party, which won no assembly seats.

In 2003, Cape Verde courts sentenced a number of people for election fraud linked with the 2001 presidential polls that brought Pires to power. The election had been declared free and fair, and those found guilty of "election crimes" had apparently acted on a local level. Delegates of both candidates were found guilty of violations such as stuffing ballot boxes and were given light prison sentences. The ruling party was expected to face a tough challenge from the MPD in local elections scheduled for 2004.

Prices for water, electricity, and transportation soared after officials privatized state utilities in 2003. The country's stagnant economy has been bolstered somewhat by increased exports and tourism, but infrastructure improvements are still needed to assist in private sector development. Cape Verde is one of Africa's smallest and poorest lands. Foreign aid and remittances by Cape Verdean expatriates provide a large portion of national income. Faced with a growing hunger problem, Cape Verde in 2002 made its first request for emergency food aid in more than 20 years.

**Political Rights and Civil Liberties:** Since the country's 1991 transition to multiparty democracy, Cape Verdeans have changed their government three times by democratic means. The president and members of the National People's Assembly are elected through universal suffrage in free and fair elections. The 2001 presidential election had been declared free and fair, and those who were later found guilty of "election crimes" had apparently acted on a local level. Delegates of both candidates were found guilty of violations such as stuffing ballot boxes and were given light prison sentences.

Freedom of expression and of the press is guaranteed and generally respected in practice. No authorization is needed to publish newspapers and other publications. Broadcasts are largely state-controlled, but there is a growing independent press. There are six independent radio broadcasters and one state-run radio broadcaster, in addition to one state-run television station and two foreign-owned stations. Criticism of the government by state-run media is limited by self-censorship resulting from citizens' fear of demotion or dismissal. There is liberal access to the Internet.

The constitution requires the separation of church and state, and religious rights are respected in practice. The vast majority of Cape Verdeans belong to the Roman Catholic Church, and followers of the Catholic faith enjoy privileged status. Academic freedom is respected.

Freedom of peaceful assembly and association is guaranteed and respected. Human rights groups, including the National Commission on the Rights of Man and the Ze Moniz Association, operate freely. The constitution also protects the right to unionize, and workers may form and join unions without restriction. Collective bargaining is permitted, but it occurs rarely.

The judiciary is independent, although cases are frequently delayed. Reforms to strengthen an overburdened judiciary were implemented in 1998. Judges must bring charges within 24 hours of arrest. Prison conditions are poor and are characterized by overcrowding.

Ethnic divisions are not a problem.

Discrimination against women persists despite legal prohibitions against gender discrimination, as well as provisions for social and economic equality. Many women do not know their rights or do not possess the means to seek redress, especially in rural areas. At the encouragement of the government and civil society, more women are reporting criminal offenses such as spousal abuse or rape. In 2003, reporting of such crimes to police continued to increase, and violence against women was the subject of extensive public service media coverage in both government- and opposition-controlled media. Although women do not receive equal pay for equal work, they have made modest gains in various professions, especially in the private sector.

# Central African Republic

**Population:** 3,700,000
**GNI/capita:** $260
**Life Expectancy:** 43
**Religious Groups:** Indigenous beliefs (35 percent), Protestant (25 percent), Roman Catholic (25 percent), Muslim (15 percent)
**Ethnic Groups:** Baya (33 percent), Banda (27 percent), Mandjia (13 percent), Sara (10 percent), Mboum (7 percent), other (10 percent)
**Capital:** Bangui

**Political Rights:** 7*
**Civil Liberties:** 5
**Status:** Not Free

**Ratings Change:** Central African Republic's political rights rating declined from 5 to 7, and its status from Partly Free to Not Free, due to a March military coup that ousted a civilian president and suspended the National Assembly.

## Ten-Year Ratings Timeline (Political Rights, Civil Liberties, Status)

| 1994 | 1995 | 1996 | 1997 | 1998 | 1999 | 2000 | 2001 | 2002 | 2003 |
|------|------|------|------|------|------|------|------|------|------|
| 3,4PF | 3,4PF | 3,5PF | 3,5PF | 3,4PF | 3,4PF | 3,4PF | 5,5PF | 5,5PF | 7,5NF |

**Overview:**

The long-time president of the Central African Republic (CAR), Ange-Felix Patasse, was deposed in a March 2003 coup and succeeded by the former head of the CAR's armed forces, General Francois Bozize. After seizing power, Bozize dissolved the National Assembly and inaugurated a politically and religiously diverse 98-member transitional council in May. He enacted a transitional constitution, which does not set a time frame for the transition, although he has promised elections by January 2005.

The CAR, a sparsely populated country, gained independence from France in 1960 after a period of particularly brutal colonial exploitation. Colonel Jean-Bedel Bokassa seized power in 1967 and, as self-declared emperor, imposed an increasingly bizarre personal dictatorship on the CAR, which he renamed Central African Empire. After Bokassa began to murder schoolchildren, French forces finally ousted him in 1979. A French-installed successor was deposed by General Andre Kolingba in 1981.

Kolingba accepted a transition to a multiparty system that led to democratic elections in 1993 and 1999, both of which were won by Patasse. Although international observers judged the 1999 vote to be free, there were reports of irregularities such as ballot shortages in some areas with a strong opposition following, and

Kolingba and other candidates claimed fraud. Until the elections, members of Kolingba's Yakoma ethnic group had occupied a disproportionate number of positions in the government, security forces, and state-owned businesses.

UN peacekeepers withdrew in February 2000 following the elections and were replaced by a peace-building office; the mandate was extended for another year in September 2003. In May 2001, a coup attempt led by Kolingba left at least 250 people dead in the capital, Bangui, and forced 50,000 others to flee their homes.

In the country's fourth coup since independence, Patasse was deposed in March 2003 after six months of fighting between government troops and renegade soldiers loyal to General Bozize. Patasse, who ruled the CAR for 10 years, fled to exile in Togo. Following the coup, Bozize created the National Transitional Council with delegates from the country's 16 provinces, as well as from all political, social, religious, and professional associations. The council has been charged with drafting a new constitution and preparing for a referendum scheduled for mid-2004; the presidential election is planned for the third quarter of 2004, and parliamentary and municipal elections are due at the end of 2004. The council voted to exclude Patasse from the reconciliation conference. However, 350 delegates, including some long-time political rivals, attended month-long talks that concluded in mid-October. Key players, including Bozize and former president Andre Kolingba, issued public apologies for the unrest that has troubled the country and affirmed their commitment to peace and economic development. Meanwhile, Bozize has lifted a death sentence imposed in absentia on Kolingba in 2002 and imposed a general amnesty for the participants in the 2001 failed coup. There are currently some 380 French-backed peacekeepers in the CAR.

Although the CAR was barred from an African Union summit in July because of the coup, neighboring countries have recognized Bozize as the new head of state. In late August, the state prosecutor issued an international arrest warrant for Patasse, accusing him of embezzlement, murder, rape, and other offenses. Patasse has also been accused of war crimes by human rights groups.

Most of the CAR's people are subsistence farmers, while diamonds and forestry are the government's main source of foreign exchange. In July 2003, the CAR joined the Kimberley Process, a global initiative aimed at ending trade in so-called blood diamonds by establishing that exported gems have not come from conflict areas. The CAR government has made the commitment to introduce a certificate-of-origin system for diamonds and to pass a new law regulating the issuing of exploitation licenses, which were usually granted at the whim of the president.

**Political Rights and Civil Liberties:** The 1986 constitution, now suspended by General Francois Bozize, allowed the people to choose their leaders in democratic elections. The 1998 National Assembly elections produced a nearly even split between supporters of Patasse, leader of the Movement for the Liberation of the Central African People, and supporters of his opponents. Presidential and legislative elections held in 1993, in line with the 1986 constitution, gave the CAR's people their first opportunity to choose their leaders in an open and democratic manner. The Independent Electoral Commission was established in 1999, but it was largely controlled by administrators loyal to the president. A decree later subordinated it to the state Organ of Control to oversee the election process.

The UN Security Council has welcomed the government's efforts to stamp out corruption and establish good governance. At least a dozen senior government officials were arrested in 2002 on charges of embezzlement.

Broadcast media are dominated by the state, but there are several independent newspapers. The only licensed private radio stations are music- or religion-oriented, although some carry programming on human rights and peace-building issues. Legislation enacted in 1998 rescinded the government's authority to censor the press, but authorities have occasionally been restrictive and have used draconian criminal libel laws to prosecute journalists. Several journalists fled the country following the May 2001 coup attempt. Some journalists were tortured.

Press freedom showed signs of improving with the release from prison of Mathurin Momet, publication director of the private daily *Le Confident*, in March 2003. He had spent more than three weeks in detention. However, Ferdinand Samba, publication director of the independent daily *Le Democrate*, was detained for four days in July, beyond the legal time limit for detentions in police custody. He was released without charge. Samba had reported that supporters of Patasse had launched an attack on the city of Kaga Bandoro and that 30 people had died in the fighting.

Religious freedom is generally respected, but the government occasionally infringes on this right. University faculty and students generally belong to many political parties and are able to express their views without fear of reprisal. Open public discussion is permitted.

Several human rights and other nongovernmental organizations operate unhindered, although the constitutionally guaranteed freedom of assembly is not always honored by the authorities. The CAR's largest single employer is the government, and government employee trade unions are especially active. Worker rights to form or join unions are legally protected. The law does not provide for collective bargaining specifically, but workers are protected from employer interference.

Corruption, political interference, and lack of training hinder the efficiency and impartiality of judicial institutions. However, some human rights leaders hailed what they called the independent decision of a court in 2001 to acquit a former defense minister who had been implicated in the May 2001 coup attempt. Limitations on searches and detention are often ignored. Conditions for prisoners, including many long-term pretrial detainees, are extremely difficult and sometimes life threatening. Juveniles are not separated from adults. Police brutality is also a serious problem, and security forces act with impunity.

Discrimination against indigenous Pygmies exists.

Societal discrimination in many areas relegates women to second-class citizenship, especially in rural areas, and constitutional guarantees for women's rights are generally not enforced. However, women have made some gains in the political sphere. Female genital mutilation is still practiced, but it was made illegal in 1996 and is reportedly diminishing. Human rights groups said more than 100 women were raped during the October 2002 military uprising.

# Chad

**Population:** 9,300,000
**GNI/capita:** $200
**Life Expectancy:** 49
**Religious Groups:** Muslim (51 percent), Christian (35 percent), animist (7 percent), other (7 percent)
**Ethnic Groups:** Sara (28 percent), Arab (12 percent), other (60 percent)
**Capital:** N'Djamena

**Political Rights:** 6
**Civil Liberties:** 5
**Status:** Not Free

## Ten-Year Ratings Timeline (Political Rights, Civil Liberties, Status)

| 1994 | 1995 | 1996 | 1997 | 1998 | 1999 | 2000 | 2001 | 2002 | 2003 |
|------|------|------|------|------|------|------|------|------|------|
| 6,5NF | 6,5NF | 6,5NF | 6,5NF | 6,4NF | 6,5NF | 6,5NF | 6,5NF | 6,5NF | 6,5NF |

**Overview:**

As the first revenues of a World Bank-sponsored oil drilling project reached state coffers, economic life in Chad in 2003 remained harsh for most citizens. Despite government assurances to the contrary, political stability continued to raise questions as President Idriss Deby announced a sweeping government reshuffle and dismissed a prominent manager of the state's cash reserves.

Chad has been in a state of almost constant war since achieving its independence from France in 1960. President Idriss Deby gained power by overthrowing Hissein Habre in 1990. Turmoil resulting from ethnic and religious differences is exacerbated by clan rivalries and external interference. The country is divided between Nilotic and Bantu Christian farmers who inhabit the country's south, and Arab and Saharan peoples who occupy arid deserts in the north.

Chad was a militarily dominated one-party state until Deby lifted the ban on political parties in 1993. A national conference that included a broad array of civic and political groups then created a transitional parliament, which was controlled by Deby's Patriotic Salvation Movement (MPS). Scores of political parties are registered.

In May 2001, Deby was reelected president with more than 67 percent of the vote. The six opposition candidates, who alleged that the election was marred by fraud and called for the result to be annulled, undertook a civil disobedience campaign and were briefly arrested. The government subsequently banned gatherings of more than 20 people, although political protests continued.

Parliamentary elections in May 2002 increased the dominance of the MPS in the National Assembly. The MPS captured 110 of the 155 seats. Its parliamentary ally, the Rally for Democracy and Progress, won 12 seats, with the opposition Action Federation for the Republic obtaining 9 seats. The elections were boycotted by several opposition parties that claimed the electoral process lacked transparency.

Chad's influence in the region grew with the emergence of a friendly government in the Central African Republic (CAR), where Chadian-backed rebels led by former CAR army commander Francois Bozize succeeded in ousting CAR president Ange-Felix Patasse in March. The announcement in January 2003 of an amnesty for rebels from the National Resistance Alliance (ANR) brought the return of dozens of

Chadian dissidents living in exile in the CAR, raising hopes for an improved security situation in southeastern Chad.

In northern Chad, intermittent fighting continued as part of a long-standing conflict between government forces and Libyan-supported rebels, despite a truce signed at the beginning of 2002. In January 2003, the government reached a more lasting ceasefire and amnesty deal with insurgents operating in the southeast led by the country's former army chief.

President Deby further consolidated his hold on the government and ruling party in 2003 with a cabinet reshuffle that ousted rivals and promoted allies and family members. Deby replaced reformist prime minister Haroun Kabadi with a northern kinsman and former public works minister, Moussa Faki Mahamat. The move broke with a long tradition of executive power sharing between the north and south, and fueled speculation that Deby intends to amend the constitution to allow him to run for a third term in office in 2006.

In July, oil began flowing through a financially lucrative but controversial World Bank–backed pipeline to Cameroon. The first shipments reached world markets in October. Despite legal guarantees that oil revenues would be spent on poverty alleviation and development, serious questions remain about the government's ability to manage these revenues in a transparent and accountable fashion. In May 2003, the president of Chad's central bank and a key member of the oil revenue oversight committee was dismissed from his post without explanation.

Chad's army and political life are largely in the hands of members of the small Zaghawa and Bideyat groups from President Deby's northeastern region. This is a source of ongoing resentment among the more than 200 other ethnic groups in the country. The formal exercise of deeply flawed elections and democratic processes has produced some opening of Chadian society, but real power remains with President Deby.

France, which remains highly influential in Chad, maintains a 1,000-member garrison in the country and, despite a sometimes rocky bilateral relationship, serves as Deby's main political and commercial supporter. Brutality by Chadian soldiers and rebels alike marked insurgencies in the vast countryside, but the large-scale abuses of the past have abated somewhat.

**Political Rights and Civil Liberties:** In theory, Chadians have the right to choose their political leaders, although this right is severely restricted in practice. Chad has never experienced a peaceful, fair, and orderly transfer of political power. Recent legislative and presidential elections have been marred by serious irregularities and indications of outright fraud. The National Assembly, whose members are directly elected for four-year terms, is the country's sole legislative chamber. In a referendum held in March 1996, voters approved a new constitution based on the French model and providing for a unified and presidential state. A law establishing an ostensibly independent election commission was passed in 2000, despite significant opposition. The law gives the predominance of seats to government representatives and those of parties in the ruling coalition.

Newspapers critical of the government circulate freely in the capital, N'Djamena, but have little impact among the largely rural and illiterate population. According to the BBC, radio is the medium of mass communication, but state control over broadcast media allows few dissenting views. Despite high licensing fees for commercial radio stations, a number of private stations are on the air, some operated by nonprofit groups including human rights groups and the Roman Catholic Church. These broadcasters are subject to close official scrutiny.

In February 2003, two journalists from the Chadian weekly, *Notre Temps*, were sentenced to six months in prison for writing an article that accused Hadje Billy Douga, director of social affairs at the Ministry for Social Action and Women and mother-in-law of the president, of torture. The weekly was ordered shut down for three months. They were released in April, but reported particularly harsh prison conditions. The country's sole Internet service provider is a state-owned telecommunications monopoly.

Although religion is a source of division in society, Chad is a secular state and freedom of religion is generally respected. The government does not restrict academic freedom.

Despite harassment and occasional physical intimidation, the Chadian Human Rights League, Chad Nonviolence, and several other human rights groups operate openly and publish findings critical of the government. Workers' right to organize and to strike is generally respected, but the formal economy is small. Union membership is low. Most Chadians are subsistence farmers.

The rule of law and the judicial system remain weak, with courts heavily influenced by the executive. Security forces routinely ignore constitutional protections regarding search, seizure, and detention. Independent human rights groups have credibly charged Chadian security forces and rebel groups with killing and torturing with impunity, and some have pointed to a context of renewed reprisals against journalists and members of civil society in 2003. Overcrowding, disease, and malnutrition make prison conditions life threatening, and many inmates spend years in prison without charges.

In recent years tens of thousands of Chadians have fled their country to escape politically inspired violence. Several of the 20 or more other armed factions have reached peace pacts, but many of these agreements have failed. Chad's long and porous borders are virtually unpoliced. Trade in weapons among nomadic Sahelian peoples is rife, and banditry adds to the pervasive insecurity.

Women's rights are protected by neither traditional law nor the penal code, and few educational opportunities are available. Female genital mutilation is commonplace.

# Chile

**Population:** 15,800,000 **Political Rights:** 1*
**GNI/capita:** $4,590 **Civil Liberties:** 1
**Life Expectancy:** 76 **Status:** Free
**Religious Groups:** Roman Catholic (89 percent),
Protestant (11 percent)
**Ethnic Groups:** White and mestizo (95 percent),
Amerindian (3 percent), other (2 percent)
**Capital:** Santiago
**Ratings Change:** Chile's political rights rating improved from 2 to 1 due to the diminished
vestiges of the country's authoritarian past, including greater civilian control over the
military.

**Ten-Year Ratings Timeline (Political Rights, Civil Liberties, Status)**

| 1994 | 1995 | 1996 | 1997 | 1998 | 1999 | 2000 | 2001 | 2002 | 2003 |
|------|------|------|------|------|------|------|------|------|------|
| 2,2F | 2,2F | 2,2F | 2,2F | 3,2F | 2,2F | 2,2F | 2,2F | 2,1F | 1,1F |

**Overview:**
In 2003, President Ricardo Lagos responded to high-profile corruption scandals by pledging significant reforms to eliminate what he said were their causes. Lagos won high marks for moving Chile's economy away from recession and for the deft handling of the country's thorny civil-military divide.

The Republic of Chile was founded after independence from Spain in 1818. Democratic rule predominated in the twentieth century until the 1973 overthrow of Salvador Allende by the military under Capt. Gen. Augusto Pinochet. An estimated 3,000 people were killed or "disappeared" during his regime. The 1980 constitution provided for a plebiscite in which voters could reject another presidential term for Pinochet. In the 1988 vote, 55 percent of voters said no to eight more years of military rule, and competitive presidential and legislative elections were scheduled for 1989.

In 1989, Christian Democrat Patricio Aylwin, the candidate of the center-left Concertacion for Democracy, was elected president and the Concertacion won a majority in the Chamber of Deputies. However, with eight senators appointed by the outgoing military government, the coalition fell short of a Senate majority. Aylwin's government was unsuccessful in its efforts to reform the constitution and was stymied by a right-wing Senate bloc in its efforts to prevent Pinochet and other military chiefs from remaining at their posts until 1997.

Eduardo Frei, a businessman and the son of a former president, carried his Concertacion candidacy to an easy victory in the December 1993 elections, defeating right-wing candidate Arturo Alessandri. Frei promised to establish full civilian control over the military, but he found he lacked the votes in Congress, as the 48-seat Senate included a senator-for-life position for Pinochet and 9 designated senators mandated by the 1980 constitution. Frei was also forced to retreat on his call for full accountability for rights violations that had occurred under military rule.

The October 1998 detention of Pinochet in London as the result of an extradition order from Spain, where he was wanted for alleged rights crimes against Spanish citizens living in Chile, at first produced a strong political polarization in Chile. His continued imprisonment, however, was viewed as a reaffirmation of the rule of law, even though it was due to foreign intervention.

On December 12, 1999, Ricardo Lagos, a moderate Concertacion socialist, faced right-wing Alliance for Chile candidate Joaquin Lavin, the mayor of a Santiago suburb and a former advisor to Pinochet, winning 47.96 percent to Lavin's 47.52 percent. Lagos won the January 16, 2000, runoff election, taking a 2.6 percent lead over Lavin. Although the Concertacion coalition had 70 seats to the opposition's 50 in the lower house, it held just 20 seats in the Senate to 18 held by the opposition. A bloc of 11 others were either senators-for-life or had been designated under Pinochet's rules. Lagos's strong early performance appeared, by late 2000, to be threatened by soaring unemployment, price increases, and charges of government corruption. In the October 2000 municipal elections, Lavin won 61 percent of the votes in the contest for the Santiago mayoralty.

In December 2000, a judge indicted Pinochet on homicide and kidnapping charges, in a year that saw the judiciary rule that allegations of crimes against humanity, including torture, kidnapping, and genocide, fell within its purview and were not subject to amnesty decrees. In July 2001, an appeals court in Santiago dropped the charges against Pinochet after it found that he suffered from dementia. On July 1, 2003, the Supreme Court ruled that Pinochet was unfit to undergo trial in the infamous "Caravan of Death" case involving the murder of 57 political prisoners following the 1973 coup. A week later, the 87-year-old retired general resigned his honorary lifetime seat in the Senate.

On December 16, 2001, Chileans voted for a completely new lower house and half of the 38 Senate seats were decided by popular vote. Pinochet supporters made big gains in the legislative elections, although they failed to win control of Congress from the governing center-left coalition.

Political corruption scandals dominated the headlines in 2003 in Chile, a country long viewed as a regional leader in clean government and transparency. Incidents of influence peddling, insider trading, and kickbacks resulted in the head of the central bank and two cabinet members—one a presidential confidant—leaving their jobs. Dozens of lower-ranking officials and several congressmen from the ruling coalition were indicted. In response to the corruption scandals, Lagos forged a working alliance with the opposition's strongest party, the Union Democrata Independiente, to push for reforms.

On August 12, Lagos announced a series of measures relating to the criminal prosecution of former members of the military—including transfer of human rights cases currently under review in military tribunals to the jurisdiction of the civilian court system—and to reparations for victims of past rights crimes and their relatives. In September, the IMF issued a glowing report on the government's economic management.

In a civil suit in October 2003, the U.S. District Court for the Southern District of Florida awarded $4 million in damages against a Chilean former army officer for the killing in Chile of an economist after the 1973 coup—the first verdict handed down by a U.S. jury for crimes against humanity.

**Political Rights and Civil Liberties:** Citizens can change their government democratically. The 1999, 2000, and 2001 elections were considered free and fair, although low registration rates among young voters are a cause for concern.

In 2003, in response to public outcry over the political corruption scandals, Congress passed laws to prevent political patronage in high-level civil service jobs, increase government workers' salaries to reduce their susceptibility to bribes, create public funding for political campaigns, and require private campaign contributors names to be listed publicly.

The Chilean media generally operate without constraint, although some Pinochet-era laws remain in effect and some self-censorship continues. Chile has no law guaranteeing access to public information.

The constitution provides for freedom of religion, and the government generally respected this right in practice. The government did not restrict academic freedom.

The right to assemble peacefully is largely respected, although police occasionally use force against demonstrators. The constitution guarantees the right of association, which the government has also generally respected. Workers may form unions without prior authorization as well as join existing unions. Approximately 12 percent of Chile's 5.7 million workers belong to unions.

The constitution provides for an independent judiciary, and the government generally respected this provision in practice. Most sitting judges come from the career judiciary and all judges are appointed for life. The constitution provides for the right to legal counsel, but indigent defendants, who account for the majority of the cases in the Santiago region, have not always received effective legal representation.

Chile has two national police forces—a uniformed force, the Carabineros, one of Latin America's best law enforcement institutions with a history of popular support and respect, and a smaller, plainclothes investigations force. In recent years, the Carabineros have been the subject of complaints about the inadequate number of uniformed police patrolling the streets and allegations of increasing narcotics-related corruption. Police use of excessive force against demonstrators, brutality, and the lack of due process rights for detainees are also alleged. In 2001, courses in human rights became part of the core curriculum in police academies for both rank and file police and officers, and similar courses were introduced at the academy for prison guards and officials. Prisons are overcrowded and antiquated, with facilities nationally running at about 163 percent of capacity.

In 1990, the Truth and Reconciliation Commission was formed to investigate rights violations committed under military rule. Its report implicated the military and secret police leadership in the death or forcible disappearance of 2,279 people between September 1973 and March 1990. Chilean courts have recently convicted several former military officers of heinous crimes, ruling that a 1978 amnesty decree set down by the Pinochet government was inapplicable to cases of enforced disappearance, which, they have held, is an ongoing crime. Hundreds of former military members now face trial. At the same time, the army, the military branch most implicated in rights crimes, has extended limited cooperation to judicial investigations and army commander General Juan Emilio Cheyre has made speeches distancing the institution from the military regime.

Native American groups in the country's southern region are increasingly vocal about their rights to ancestral lands that the government and private industry seek to develop. Chile has some 1.2 million indigenous people, more than 10 percent of the country's total population, two-thirds of them Mapuches. Upon taking office,

Lagos began to make good on a campaign promise that the "Indian question" would receive priority attention. In October 2003, Lagos proposed constitutional recognition for the country's indigenous peoples.

Violence and discrimination against women and violence against children remain problems. Abortion in any form has been banned since 1989. In 2000, Lagos appointed five women to his 16-person cabinet. The Chilean defense minister, Michelle Bachelet Jeria, is the daughter of a Chilean general tortured to death for his opposition to the 1973 coup.

# China

**Population:** 1,288,700,000 **Political Rights:** 7
**GNI/capita:** $890      **Civil Liberties:** 6
**Life Expectancy:** 71     **Status:** Not Free
**Religious Groups:** Daoist (Taoist), Buddhist, Muslim (1-2 percent), Christian (3-4 percent)
**Ethnic Groups:** Han Chinese (92 percent), other, [including Tibetan, Mongol, Korean, Manchu, and Uighur] (8 percent)
**Capital:** Beijing

**Ten-Year Ratings Timeline (Political Rights, Civil Liberties, Status)**

| 1994 | 1995 | 1996 | 1997 | 1998 | 1999 | 2000 | 2001 | 2002 | 2003 |
|------|------|------|------|------|------|------|------|------|------|
| 7,7NF | 7,7NF | 7,7NF | 7,7NF | 7,6NF | 7,6NF | 7,6NF | 7,6NF | 7,6NF | 7,6NF |

**Overview:**
As China completed its biggest leadership shuffle since the 1970s, new party chief Hu Jintao and other top officials pledged to improve conditions for rural Chinese, who formed the vanguard of the Communist revolution but who are now increasingly left behind in the Asian giant's wrenching transition to a market economy. Nevertheless, the new leaders are unlikely to offer bold initiatives to help China's ailing farmers—or its millions of unemployed urban factory workers—choosing instead to continue policies combining gradual reforms with large dollops of public spending. Carefully groomed and selected as they marched up the Communist Party ranks, Hu and his deputies are also unlikely to ease the party's iron grip on power.

The Chinese Communist Party (CCP) took power in 1949 under Mao Zedong after defeating the Koumintang, or Nationalists, in a civil war that began in the 1920s. Aiming to tighten party control, Mao led several brutal mass-mobilization campaigns that resulted in millions of deaths and politicized nearly every aspect of daily life. Following Mao's death in 1976, Deng Xiaoping emerged as China's paramount leader. Over the next two decades, Deng oversaw China's transformation from a hermetic, agrarian, and often tumultuous Communist society into an authoritarian state with a market-led economy, eager to sell its products abroad and expand its role in global affairs even as it trampled on internationally recognized human rights.

Deng and other leaders signaled their intent to maintain power at all costs with the 1989 massacre of hundreds of student protesters in and around Beijing's

Tiananmen Square. Following the crackdown, the party tapped Jiang Zemin, then Shanghai mayor and party boss, to replace the relatively moderate Zhao Ziyang as party secretary-general. Jiang became state president in 1993 and was widely recognized as China's new paramount leader following Deng's death in 1997.

Jiang continued Deng's policies of selling off state firms, encouraging private enterprise, and rolling back China's "iron rice bowl" welfare system. Having cast aside Mao's utopian goals, China's leaders appeared to agree that continued market reforms would be needed in order to boost living standards and stave off broad calls for political reform. They feared, however, that freeing up the economy too fast could increase social hardship in the near term and create a groundswell against the party.

The CCP's sixteenth party congress in November 2002 was carefully stage-managed to project an image of an orderly transfer of power to a younger generation of leaders. Hu became party secretary-general and, along with other new leaders, took control of the powerful, nine-member Politburo Standing Committee. However, Jiang, now 77, apparently solidified his position as leader of China even as Hu and other younger cadres took charge of day-to-day affairs. Jiang remained head of the Central Military Commission—effectively supreme commander of China's 2.5 million–strong armed forces—and stacked the Politburo Standing Committee with several proteges.

At the annual session of China's parliament in March 2003, the final pieces of the leadership shuffle came together. Hu, 61, replaced Jiang as state president, and Wen Jiabao, the party's third-ranking official, took day-to-day charge of the economy by replacing Zhu Rongji as prime minister. Late in the year, the new government appeared set to revise the constitution at the March 2004 legislative session to give greater protection to private property and allow the party to recruit private entrepreneurs.

In addition to planning constitutional reforms, Hu and other leaders took pains to nurture caring images. They promised better schools, more public works for rural Chinese, and efforts to revive the northeast industrial heartland. However, their initial handling of the Severe Acute Respiratory Syndrome (SARS) that broke out in early 2003 was more Communist than compassionate. They initially stonewalled before finally taking steps against the viral outbreak, which killed 349 people before it was contained in June. Chinese authorities, meanwhile, continue to stifle any organized calls for political reform. Since 1998, courts have sentenced more than 30 leaders of a would-be opposition party, the China Democracy Party, to jail terms of up to 13 years.

The privatization of thousands of small- and medium-sized state-owned firms has thrown tens of millions of Chinese out of work in a society that lacks a viable system of pensions, health insurance, and unemployment benefits. These hardships are likely to increase as the government slashes tariffs and takes other steps to open up China's economy to trade and foreign investment to meet its commitments as a World Trade Organization (WTO) member. Analysts suggest that, at least in the short term, China's leaders will try to ease this transition by continuing to stoke the economy through massive, debt-accumulating public spending rather than by taking tough but painful measures to reform large, money-losing state enterprises or cleaning up ailing and corrupt state banks.

Meanwhile, in the countryside, home to 70 percent of the population—or roughly

900 million Chinese—farmers recently have staged thousands of protests against high and often arbitrary local government fees and taxes. China's WTO membership could make matters worse for many peasants if cheaper agricultural imports chip away at their incomes. Already, China has wide income gaps between its rural areas and cities and between its hinterland and booming coastal areas.

Rural China's woes have contributed to a "floating population," officially tallied at 80 to 130 million people, who have left their rural homes in search of work in cities. Urbanization is transforming this historically agricultural society by providing many rural migrants with modest but unprecedented opportunities, though their shaky legal status often makes migrants vulnerable to abuse by police and employers.

Corruption, meanwhile, has flourished in a country that has a rapidly expanding economy but has neither independent courts, regulators, and investigative agencies, nor a free press to probe and punish wrongdoing. Chinese authorities have responded instead with brute force, in recent years executing hundreds, possibly thousands, of people for corruption.

**Political Rights and Civil Liberties:** Chinese citizens do not have the power to change their government democratically. Ordinary Chinese enjoy few basic rights, opposition parties are illegal, Chinese jails hold thousands of political prisoners, torture is widespread in prisons and detention centers, and the judiciary is used as a tool of political control. The CCP Politburo Standing Committee makes nearly all key political decisions and sets governmental policy. Party cadres hold almost all top national and local governmental, police, and military posts.

China's only real experiment with democracy has been at the local level, mainly with elections for village committees that cannot levy taxes and hold few executive powers. While party-backed candidates have lost some elections, "in general the CCP dominates the local electoral process," and roughly 60 percent of those elected to the village committees are party members, according to the U.S. State Department's 2002 human rights report, released in March 2003. Elections in some areas have also been held for township governors, township and county-level people's congresses, local party secretaries, and the leadership of urban neighborhood committees, which help officials maintain order and provide services.

Press freedom is severely limited, and Chinese editors and reporters work under tight constraints. The government bars the media from advocating political reform, criticizing Beijing's domestic and foreign policies, reporting financial data that the government has not released, or covering internal party politics or the inner workings of the government. At the same time, officials often allow journalists to report on corruption and other ills that the party itself seeks to alleviate. All articles in private publications must be vetted by the government before publication.

As of May, the New York-based Committee to Protect Journalists reported that Chinese jails held 38 journalists, 15 of them for publishing or distributing information on-line. Other journalists have been harassed, detained, threatened, or dismissed from their jobs over their reporting. Officials also recently suspended or shut down some liberal magazines, newspapers, and publishing houses.

The government promotes use of the Internet, which it believes to be critical to China's economic development, but regulates access, monitors use, and restricts and regulates content. Amnesty International said in October that it knew of more than 40 Chinese who were detained or jailed for Internet-related offenses. They included students, political dissidents, and Falun Gong practitioners. Some 59 million Chinese use the Internet, a government-funded group reported in 2002, and the number is growing rapidly.

Chinese face severe restrictions on religious practice. The government forces religious groups to submit to the tight control of state-sponsored bodies and cracks down on religious leaders and ordinary worshippers who reject this authority. The five recognized religions are Buddhism, Taoism, Islam, Protestantism, and Catholicism. Buddhism claims the most adherents. For each of the five religions recognized by the government, the respective "patriotic association" appoints clergy and controls clerical education; monitors religious funding, membership, and activities; and controls publication and distribution of religious books and other materials. Beijing bars the Roman Catholic "patriotic association" and its member churches from recognizing the Vatican's authority in matters including the ordination of bishops.

The extent to which congregations must actually submit to these regulations varies by region. In many areas, unregistered Protestant and Catholic congregations—particularly those that are small and unobtrusive—worship freely. Elsewhere, however, zealous local officials sometimes break up underground services. They also at times fine, harass, detain, interrogate, beat, and torture underground church leaders and ordinary worshippers and raid, close, or demolish underground churches, mosques, temples, and seminaries, according to the U.S. State Department report and other sources.

In Xinjiang, officials limit the building of new mosques, keep tabs on mosques and their leaders, and restrict Islamic publishing and education. Officials recently have also shut down some Xinjiang mosques, burned some Uighur books and journals, and restricted the use of the Uighur language.

Many thousands of Falun Gong practitioners remain behind bars in China, with most apparently held without trial in "re-education through labor" camps. Several hundred Falun Gong adherents reportedly have died in detention because of torture, abuse, and neglect since Beijing's crackdown on the group began in 1999. "Anti-cult" laws developed to crush the Falun Gong, which combines qiqong (a traditional martial art) with meditation, have also been used to sentence members of at least 16 other religious groups to long jail terms, the New York-based Human Rights Watch reported in 2002. Authorities at times also crack down on folk religions and unorthodox religious sects. Academic freedom is restricted by ideological controls on what can be taught and discussed at universities.

Workers, farmers, and others have held thousands of public protests in recent years over labor issues and wrongdoing by local officials. Chinese factory workers routinely take to the streets to protest hardships associated with economic restructuring. In spring 2002, tens of thousands of workers demonstrated in Liaoyang and other northeastern rustbelt cities over mass layoffs and low or unpaid wages, pensions, and severance pay. While the government often tolerates these types of protests as an outlet for pent-up grievances, security forces have also forcibly broken up many demonstrations, particularly those with overt political and social messages or where protestors became unruly.

China has hundreds of thousands of nongovernmental organizations (NGOs). All work in areas that, at least on the surface, do not challenge the government's authority, such as the environment and social welfare. Once registered, NGOs must report regularly to specific government departments.

Workers lack vigorous, independent unions, and enforcement of labor laws is poor. All unions must belong to the state-controlled All China Federation of Trade Unions, and several independent labor activists have been jailed for their advocacy efforts. Private factories often arbitrarily dismiss employees, pay workers below minimum wages, and force them to work overtime, sometimes without extra pay. Moreover, factory and coal mining accidents kill thousands of Chinese workers each year. Though workers lack the legal right to strike, officials frequently allow workers to strike or demonstrate over layoffs; dangerous working conditions; or unpaid wages, benefits, or unemployment stipends.

The government controls the judiciary. The CCP directs verdicts and sentences, particularly in politically sensitive cases, according to the U.S. State Department. Despite some recent criminal procedure reforms, trials are often closed and reportedly only one in seven criminal defendants has counsel. Officials often subject suspects to "severe psychological pressure" to confess, and coerced confessions are frequently admitted as evidence. Police frequently conduct searches without warrants and at times monitor telephone conversations and other personal communications to use as evidence against suspected dissidents.

Many political and ordinary criminal detainees lack trials altogether, detained instead by bureaucratic fiat in "re-education through labor" camps. These camps held as many as 310,000 detainees as of early 2001, and the number has likely grown since then, Amnesty International said in October. In a positive development, Chinese officials said in 2003 that they were abolishing another form of administrative detention called "custody and repatriation." This had been used to detain some one million Chinese each year, many of them migrant workers. By law, at least, migrant workers now can no longer be detained and deported from cities for failing to carry proper papers.

In another gain for the rule of law, ordinary Chinese increasingly are able to bring suits against local governments and are occasionally winning damage awards. At the same time, property rights remain rudimentary. Many Chinese are forcibly relocated from their homes each year to make way for commercial development, often for meager compensation.

China executes thousands of people each year, more than all other countries combined, according to Amnesty International. Many are executed immediately after summary trials, raising serious questions about the fairness of their convictions and sentencing. As part of Beijing's national "Strike Hard" campaign against crime that began in 2001, many Chinese have been executed for nonviolent offenses such as corruption, pimping, "hooliganism," or the theft of rice or farm animals.

Moreover, "torture and ill-treatment continue to be widespread and [are] reported in many state institutions as well as in workplaces and homes," Amnesty International said in June. Courts recently have sentenced some officials convicted of torture to heavy jail terms, although most perpetrators go unpunished. Deaths of criminal suspects in custody because of torture continue to be reported.

By most accounts, Chinese prisons, re-education camps, and detention centers hold thousands of political prisoners, although the exact number is unknown. Conditions in Chinese prisons and labor camps for both political prisoners and common criminals generally are "harsh and frequently degrading," according to the U.S. State Department report. The U.S.-based rights activist Harry Wu and others have reported that forced labor is used widely in Chinese jails and labor camps.

Muslims and other minorities in China face discrimination in mainstream society in access to jobs and other areas, and the majority Han Chinese have reaped an outsized share of benefits from government programs and economic growth despite government initiatives to improve minority living standards. China's 55 ethnic minorities make up slightly less than 9 percent of the population, according to official 1995 figures. The government has tried to crush pro-independence movements among the seven million ethnic Uighurs and other, smaller, Turkic-speaking Muslim groups in China's northwestern Xinjiang province. Since the early 1990s, officials have detained "tens of thousands" of Uighurs and other Muslims in Xinjiang, executing several for alleged separatist activities, the human rights group Amnesty International said in 2002. The government has used the U.S.-led campaign against terrorism to link even peaceful Uighur advocacy of independence to terrorism and to justify its repression of Uighur culture and religion. Authorities also have forcibly repatriated thousands of North Koreans in recent years, putting them at risk of execution or other severe punishment.

The economic reforms launched in the late 1970s have freed millions of Chinese from party control of their day-to-day lives. Increasingly, ordinary Chinese are becoming homeowners as housing once owned by government departments or state-owned enterprises is partially or wholly privatized. The national household registration and identification card system is eroding, meaning that Chinese are increasingly free to move around the country to live and work. Many now work for private firms, which account for about 30 percent of China's economic output. For those who still work for the state, the government took steps in 2003 to scale back the powers of the *danwei*—company-based, government-linked work units for state employees. Though the danwei still control certain aspects of daily life for state workers, the changes allow Chinese to marry, divorce, and sell their state-assigned housing without their employers' permission. The economic reforms have also lifted hundreds of millions of Chinese out of absolute poverty, although some 100 to 150 million still live in poverty, according to the World Bank.

Chinese women reportedly face serious discrimination in education and employment and are far likelier than men to be laid off when state firms are slimmed down or privatized. Despite government crackdowns, trafficking in women and children for marriage, to provide sons, and for prostitution remains a serious problem.

Chinese couples cannot freely choose how many children to have. In the name of stabilizing the country's population, a one-child policy is applied fairly strictly in the cities, though less so in the countryside. While urban couples generally are denied permission to have a second child, rural couples usually may have a second child if their first is a girl. Couples who have an unapproved child can be assessed stiff fines, fired from jobs, demoted or barred from promotion, denied access to social services, forced to pay higher tuition costs when the child goes to school, and occasionally have property destroyed. The use of forced abortions or sterilizations by local officials trying to keep within county birth quotas is believed to occur in occasional, isolated cases, though less frequently than in the past.

# Colombia

**Population:** 44,200,000
**GNI/capita:** $1,890
**Life Expectancy:** 71
**Religious Groups:** Roman Catholic (90 percent),
other (10 percent)
**Ethnic Groups:** Mestizo (58 percent), white (20 percent),
mulatto (14 percent), black (4 percent), other [including
Amerindian] (4 percent)
**Capital:** Bogota

**Political Rights:** 4
**Civil Liberties:** 4
**Status:** Partly Free

**Ten-Year Ratings Timeline (Political Rights, Civil Liberties, Status)**

| 1994 | 1995 | 1996 | 1997 | 1998 | 1999 | 2000 | 2001 | 2002 | 2003 |
|------|------|------|------|------|------|------|------|------|------|
| 3,4PF | 4,4PF | 4,4PF | 4,4PF | 3,4PF | 4,4PF | 4,4PF | 4,4PF | 4,4PF | 4,4PF |

**Overview:**
At the end of its first year in office, the government of President Alvaro Uribe Velez continued to be popular as it made limited gains in delivering on promises of peace and prosperity for Latin America's most violent nation. Some improvements were made in 2003 in the fight to dismantle the world's biggest cocaine industry, and civilian casualties in Colombia's four-decades-long civil war were reduced. However, the country continued to be wracked by massacres—the work of both the guerrillas and right-wing paramilitary death squads—drug trafficking, and by the highest rate of kidnapping in the Western Hemisphere. Uribe created a firestorm when he proposed to grant amnesty to the paramilitaries, a controversial move even in Washington, where several death squad leaders have been indicted as terrorists and narcotics traffickers.

Following independence from Spain in 1819, the former "Gran Colombia" broke up into the present-day states of Venezuela, Ecuador, and the Republic of Colombia (established in 1886). The 1904 succession of Panama, engineered by the United States, left Colombia with its present boundaries. Modern Colombia, Latin America's third most populous country, has been marked by the corrupt machine politics of the Liberals and the Conservatives, whose leadership has largely been drawn from the traditional elite; left-wing guerrilla insurgencies; right-wing paramilitary violence; the emergence of vicious drug cartels; and gross human rights violations committed by all sides. In the 1994 legislative elections, the Liberals retained a majority in both houses of Congress. Ernesto Samper, a former economic development minister, won the Liberal presidential nomination. The Conservative candidate was Andres Pastrana, a former mayor of Bogota and the son of a former Colombian president. Both candidates pledged to continue the free market reforms begun by outgoing president Cesar Gaviria.

Samper won in a June 1994 runoff election and, with strong U.S. encouragement, presided over the dismantling of the Cali drug cartel, most of whose leaders were captured in 1995. The arrests, however, netted persuasive evidence that the cartel had given $6 million to the president's campaign, with Samper's approval.

In the June 21, 1998 election, Pastrana won the presidency in an impressive victory over the Liberal Party candidate, Interior Minister Horacio Serpa. In an effort to consolidate the peace process, in November, Pastrana arranged for the leftist Revolutionary Armed Forces of Colombia (FARC) guerrillas to regroup and peacefully occupy a so-called demilitarized zone consisting of five southern districts, from which a dispirited military was withdrawn. The move, which had been strongly resisted by the military, gave the guerrillas de facto control over a territory the size of Switzerland.

The gamble, however, failed, although Pastrana did achieve some success in severing ties between the armed forces and the United Self-Defense Forces of Colombia (AUC), a collection of right-wing paramilitary death squads. Colombia's most notorious death squad leader admitted what has long been an open secret—not only do the paramilitary groups make big money from the drug trade, as do the guerrillas, but they are also financed by local and foreign private enterprise.

In 2001, it became clear that the FARC's "demilitarized zone" was actually a state within a state that the guerrillas used as a sanctuary for coordinating military operations, a rest area for battle-weary insurgents, and a base for criminal activities such as drug trafficking and the warehousing of hostages. On September 10, 2001, U.S. Secretary of State Colin Powell announced that the AUC would finally be labeled an international terrorist organization, a designation that the U.S. government had applied considerably earlier to the FARC and the National Liberation Army (ELN), another left-wing revolutionary organization.

In May 2002, war-weary Colombians gave Uribe, a hard-line former provincial governor who ran independently of the country's two dominant political parties, an unprecedented first-round victory that was a referendum on how best to end Colombia's decades-long civil strife. Uribe, the victim of an assassination attempt by leftist guerrillas just a month before the election, emerged from a six-candidate field with 52 percent of the vote. Serpa, running again as the Liberal candidate, received 32 percent.

Uribe's inauguration in August was marred by guerrilla attacks that left 19 people dead. In response, he decreed a state of emergency, stepped up anti-guerrilla efforts in urban areas, and created "special combat zones" in 27 municipalities in which the U.S.-backed military was allowed to restrict civilian movement and conduct warrantless searches. He also established a "war tax" to finance thousands of additional troops and tightened restrictions on the foreign press. Critics charged that Uribe's support from paramilitary death squads and his own hard-line stance promised to stoke the violence and made a ceasefire less likely.

By late 2002, three months of intensive aerial spraying in the coca-rich province of Putumayo, part of a $1.3 billion U.S. antidrug aid effort, resulted in the almost complete destruction of the cocaine-producing crop. However, in November, Gilberto Rodriguez Orejuela, the former head of the notorious Cali drug cartel that was once responsible for trafficking 80 percent of the cocaine reaching the United States, was released from prison by a court over Uribe's strong objections.

In 2003, Uribe won high marks for his hands-on, take-charge style and his personal courage in traveling to the country's most violent regions. In his first 10 months in office, Uribe allowed the extradition of 64 accused drug traffickers to the United States, more than his predecessor, Andres Pastrana, had allowed during his entire four-year term. Meanwhile, Colombia's highest tribunal dealt Uribe a surprise political setback, stripping him of the emergency powers he had assumed in 2002 to fight leftist rebels. The decision by the Constitutional Court, which annulled the special militarized zones he had created and took away his ability to issue special decrees, signaled the court's willingness to intervene if Uribe, elected in a landslide due to popular clamor for law and order, tried to overstep his powers.

Despite his store of political capital, Uribe, lacking support in congress for his legislative agenda, did little to press ahead with reforms. The country's military, which, although better equipped and trained and increasingly possessing more useful intelligence, retains much of its inefficient and almost feudal structure, continues to rely on mostly peasant conscripts, and even lacks a clear understanding of its missions and of the manpower and equipment needed to carry them out.

Human rights groups charged that an antiterrorism law approved in June 2003 by the Senate, which allows the army to detain suspected terrorists without a warrant for up to 36 hours, would facilitate human rights abuses by government forces. In November 2003, more than 850 members of a right-wing paramilitary group, part of an illegal army responsible for some of the country's bloodiest massacres, laid down their arms and were allowed to return to civilian life. Many had past careers as common criminals, and human rights groups said the move made a mockery of justice. That same month, the commander of the Colombian National Police and his four closest deputies were cashiered in a corruption scandal just days after Uribe replaced three cabinet ministers, including the defense minister, who had taken a hard line on corruption within the military. On a positive note, Uribe publicly denounced what he called the "collusion" between the police and the paramilitaries in various regions of the country.

Also in November, Colombian troops defeated an unprecedented effort by 14 FARC combat units to encircle Bogota and to cut off major roads leading to the capital city of 7 million people. The previous month, Colombians voted down key referendum proposals supported by Uribe that had been intended to freeze government spending in order to provide more funds to wage war against the guerrillas, fight corruption, and streamline a top-heavy political structure.

## Political Rights and Civil Liberties:

Citizens can change their government through elections. In October 2003, municipal elections were held in which 50 governors and 914 mayors were elected. Although they took place in a climate of fear created by the murder of at least 26 candidates, the polls were generally free of violence on election day. Although more than 200,000 police officers were deployed during the elections to watch over the polls, turnout was low. In a major development, a leftist former labor leader won the Bogota mayoralty, considered the country's second most important post. The climate of intimidation that pervades Colombia has caused more than 150 mayors around the country to attempt to govern their municipalities from the safety of provincial capitals.

Public corruption remains one of the most serious problems facing Colombia. It affects virtually all aspects of public life and extends far beyond the narcotics trade. For example, foreign business executives with military procurement contracts complain that the armed forces sometimes do not honor their contracts and that the executives are subjected to intimidation if they protest. Anticorruption activists claim that the annual cost of systemic problems exceeds $2.2 billion and that corruption may be a greater threat to the country's institutional survival than is the internal war.

The constitution guarantees free expression. However, media ownership is concentrated in the hands of wealthy families, large national conglomerates, or groups associated with one or the other of the two dominant political parties. In 2003, the Spanish media conglomerate Prisa acquired majority ownership of the country's largest radio network, thus becoming the first foreign media owner in the country. Journalists are frequently the victims of political and revenge violence, and the Committee to Protect Journalists ranks Colombia as the second most dangerous country in the world for the media, after Algeria. More than 120 journalists were murdered in the past decade, many of whom were killed for reporting on drug trafficking and corruption; most of the cases remain unresolved by the legal authorities. In a positive development, two former soldiers were convicted in 2002 of the assassination of two TV cameramen; each defendant was sentenced to 19 years in prison. In the province of Arauca, threats by paramilitaries and guerrilla forces induced all 16 journalists stationed there to leave. As a result of their mass exodus, the province became a "silent zone" for several months. The government did not limit or block access to the Internet or censor Web sites.

The constitution provides for freedom of religion, and the government generally respected this right in practice. It also did not restrict academic freedom, although threats and harassment caused many professors and students to adopt lower profiles and avoid discussing controversial topics, with some academics opting for voluntary exile. Paramilitary groups and guerrillas maintained a presence on many university campuses in order to generate political support and to undermine their adversaries through both violent and nonviolent means.

Constitutional rights regarding the freedom to organize political parties, civic groups, and labor unions are severely restricted in practice by politically motivated and drug-related violence and by the government's inability to guarantee the security of its citizens. The murder of trade union activists increased significantly in recent years, and Colombia remains the most dangerous country in the world for organized labor, which goes far toward explaining why only about 6 percent of the country's workforce is unionized, one of the lowest percentages in Latin America. More than 2,500 trade union activists and leaders have been killed in little more than a decade. Labor leaders are frequently targeted for attack by paramilitary groups, guerrillas, narcotics traffickers, and other union rivals.

The justice system remains slow and compromised by corruption and extortion. The civilian-led Ministry of Defense is responsible for internal security and oversees both the armed forces and the national police. Civilian management of the armed forces, however, is limited. In 2002, the Colombian national police got a new chief after a corruption scandal involving 71 officers—including the head of antinarcotics operations—were accused of stealing more than $2 million in U.S. aid. Previously, the 85,000-strong force had been considered to be a bulwark against corruption.

Colombia's 165 prisons, which were built for 32,000 people but hold more than 47,000, are frequent sites of murders and riots. A penal code approved by congress in June 2001 is designed to relieve the strain on prisons and allows convicts to be released after serving 60 percent of their sentences, rather than the 80 percent previously required.

Colombia is one of the most violent countries in the world. More than 3,000 people are kidnapped each year in Colombia, and there is a greater risk of being kidnapped there than in any other country. Political violence in Colombia continues to take more lives than in any other country in the Western Hemisphere, and civilians are prime victims. In the past decade, an estimated 40,000 have died and more than 1.5 million have been displaced from their homes. More than 90 percent of violent crimes go unsolved. Human rights violations have soared to unprecedented highs, with atrocities being committed by all sides in the conflict. Human rights workers in Colombia are frequently murdered by a military often lacking in personal and tactical discipline, and by rightist paramilitary forces. In November 2002, Human Rights Watch issued a scathing report in which it accused Attorney General Luis Camilo Osorio of interfering with military and paramilitary human rights abuses. It charged that Osorio had failed to support, and had even fired, prosecutors investigating the cases.

Left-wing guerrillas, some of whom also protect narcotics-production facilities and drug traffickers, also systematically violate human rights, with victims including Sunday churchgoers and airline passengers. The FARC guerrillas also regularly extort payments from hundreds of businessmen throughout the country. Another problem concerns "social cleansing"—the elimination of drug addicts, street children, and other marginal citizens by vigilante groups often linked to police.

There are approximately 80 distinct ethnic groups among Colombia's 800,000-plus indigenous inhabitants, who live on more than 50 million acres of land granted to them by the government, often located in resource-rich, strategic regions fought over by the warring outside armed groups. These Native Americans are frequently the targets of forced recruitment by the guerrillas and selective assassination by the paramilitary forces despite their seeking to remain neutral in the armed conflict. In a three-year period, human rights groups say, more than 1,500 Indians have been forced into service with the guerrillas. In 1999, FARC guerrillas kidnapped and killed three U.S. Native American rights activists. Indian claims to land and resources are under challenge from government ministries and multinational corporations. In 2003, paramilitary groups killed several Indian leaders.

According to the United Nations, some 948,000 children under the age of 14 work in "unacceptable" conditions. An estimated 60 percent of FARC fighters are believed to be under the age of 15, and female child-soldiers are reported to be subjected to sexual abuse. Child-soldiers attempting to leave without permission are executed by firing squad.

Women are active in politics and community organizations. Sexual harassment and domestic violence are still severe problems. The law prohibits rape and other forms of sexual violence, including by a spouse. However, it remains a serious problem, as does the trafficking of women for sexual exploitation.

# Comoros

**Population:** 600,000
**GNI/capita:** $390
**Life Expectancy:** 56
**Religious Groups:** Sunni Muslim (98 percent),
Roman Catholic (2 percent)
**Ethnic Groups:** Antalote, Cafre, Makoa, Oimatsaha,
Sakalava
**Capital:** Moroni

**Political Rights:** 5
**Civil Liberties:** 4
**Status:** Partly Free

## Ten-Year Ratings Timeline (Political Rights, Civil Liberties, Status)

| 1994 | 1995 | 1996 | 1997 | 1998 | 1999 | 2000 | 2001 | 2002 | 2003 |
|------|------|------|------|------|------|------|------|------|------|
| 4,4PF | 4,4PF | 4,4PF | 5,4PF | 5,4PF | 6,4PF | 6,4PF | 6,4PF | 5,4PF | 5,4PF |

**Overview:**

Internal tensions and rivalries between the leaders of the three constituent islands and the federation president in 2003 resulted in continued political instability. In September an agreement was reached that would result in legislative polls in December 2003, although it has yet to be implemented. Key terms of the accord have the central government maintaining control over the country's army, while the police will be administered by local presidents. Another key compromise was the decision to set up a provisional customs council to facilitate the fair distribution of revenue among the three islands.

Two mercenary invasions and at least 18 other coups and attempted coups have shaken the Indian Ocean archipelago of Comoros since independence from France in 1975. In 1990, in the country's first contested elections, Supreme Court justice Said Mohamed Djohara won a six-year term as president. French soldiers reversed a 1995 attempted coup by elements of the Comoros security forces, who were aided by foreign mercenaries. An interim government ruled for five months until President Mohamed Taki Abdoulkarim was elected in 1996 in internationally monitored elections that were considered free and fair. Tadjidine Ben Said Massonde became the interim ruler when Taki died suddenly in November 1998.

Three islands comprise Comoros: Grande Comore, Anjouan, and Moheli. Anjouan voted for self-determination in a 1997 referendum, repulsed an attempted invasion by the government, and then dissolved into violence as rival separatist groups took up arms against each other. Separatists on Moheli also declared independence. Mayotte Island, the fourth island of the Comorian archipelago, had voted to remain a French overseas territory in a 1974 referendum and today enjoys a far higher, French-subsidized standard of living than do the other islands.

Efforts to end the separatist crisis began with the 1999 Antananarivo agreement. Anjouan's refusal to sign the agreement led to violence on Grande Comore and a subsequent coup by Colonel Azali Assoumani. A reconciliation agreement, known as the Fomboni Declaration, was signed in 2000 between the Assoumani government and Anjouan separatists. A national referendum was approved in December 2001 for a new constitution that gave greater autonomy to the three islands of Comoros within the framework of a confederation and provided for a rotating executive presidency among the islands every four years.

In 2002, while elections for the president of each of the three islands that make up the new federation appeared to have been largely free and fair, the poll for the executive leader of the federation was not. President Assoumani won the executive presidency with 75 percent of the vote. He was, however, the only candidate as his two opponents had claimed fraud and dropped out of the race. After the country's electoral commission concluded that the 2002 vote for the executive presidency was not fair, the commission was dissolved and a body of five magistrates ruled that the election would stand.

Internal tensions and rivalries between the leaders of the three constituent islands and the federation president in 2003 resulted in continued political instability. Lengthy negotiations took over minimum conditions for holding postponed legislative elections. In September, an agreement was reached that would result in legislative polls in December 2003, although it has yet to be implemented. Key terms of the accord have the central government maintaining control over the country's army, while the police will be administered by local presidents. Another key compromise was the decision to set up a provisional customs council to facilitate the fair distribution of revenue among the three islands.

Comorians are among the world's poorest people. The country relies heavily on foreign aid and earns a small amount through exports of vanilla, ylang-ylang, and cloves. The political troubles have affected the country's economic relations with the outside world. In March 2003, two of the island presidents signed a resolution calling upon the European Union to "temporarily delay" its payments to the central government for fishing rights. They also asked ComoreTel, the largest telecommunications company on the island, to suspend its revenue payments. This tense political situation created confusion among Comorians who did not know whether to pay their taxes to their island government or to the central government.

**Political Rights and Civil Liberties:** Comorians have the constitutional right to change their government democratically, although this right has been only partially realized. Presidential elections held in 2002 for each of the archipelago's three islands were considered to be largely fair, while the vote for the executive presidency turned into a one-horse race whose outcome was not contested. Comorians exercised their constitutional right to change their government democratically in open elections for the first time in the 1996 parliamentary and presidential elections. Mohamed Taki Abdoulkarim won the presidency in a runoff election with more than 60 percent of the vote. The conservative Islamic main opposition party held several seats in the National Assembly. Parliament has not met since Assoumani's 1999 coup, and parliamentary elections have been postponed until at least December 2003.

The leader of a major opposition party was arrested in September on grounds of destabilization, threatening state security and inciting violence. He was subsequently released from detention, but placed under house arrest and forbidden from undertaking political activities.

Freedom of expression is generally, but not fully, respected. The semiofficial weekly *Al-Watwan* and several private newspapers sharply critical of the government are published in the capital, but they appear only sporadically because of limited resources. All are believed to exercise extensive self-censorship. Two state-run radio stations broadcast, and about 20 regional radio stations and five local private television stations operate without overt government interference. Academic freedom is generally respected.

Islam is the official state religion. Non-Muslims are legally permitted to practice, but there were reports of restrictions, detentions, and harassment. Detainees are sometimes subjected to attempts to convert them to Islam. Christians are not allowed to proselytize.

The government generally respects the rights of freedom of assembly and association. The former is explicitly recognized in the constitution, although the latter is not. Occasionally the police have violently dispersed protesters. Unions have the right to bargain and strike, but collective bargaining is rare in the country's small formal business sector.

The Comorian legal system is based both on Sharia (Islamic law) and on parts of the French legal code and is subject to influence by the executive and other elites. Most minor disputes are settled by village elders or a civilian court of first instance. Harsh prison conditions are marked by severe overcrowding and the lack of adequate sanitation facilities, medical attention, and proper diet.

Women possess constitutional protections. In practice, however, they enjoy little political or economic power and have far fewer opportunities for education or salaried employment than do men. Economic hardship has forced growing numbers of young girls, known as mpambe, into domestic servitude. They receive room and board, but little or no pay.

# ↑ Congo, Democratic Republic of (Kinshasa)

**Population:** 56,600,000  
**GNI/capita:** $80  
**Life Expectancy:** 48  
**Religious Groups:** Roman Catholic (50 percent), Protestant (20 percent), Kimbanguist (10 percent), Muslim (10 percent), other (10 percent)  
**Ethnic Groups:** More than 200 tribes, mostly Bantu  
**Capital:** Kinshasa  

**Political Rights:** 6  
**Civil Liberties:** 6  
**Status:** Not Free  

**Trend Arrow:** Congo (Kinshasa) received an upward trend arrow due to the inauguration of a two-year transitional government and the establishment of a unified national military.

**Ten-Year Ratings Timeline (Political Rights, Civil Liberties, Status)**

| 1994 | 1995 | 1996 | 1997 | 1998 | 1999 | 2000 | 2001 | 2002 | 2003 |
|------|------|------|------|------|------|------|------|------|------|
| 7,6NF | 7,6NF | 7,6NF | 7,6NF | 7,6NF | 7,6NF | 7,6NF | 6,6NF | 6,6NF | 6,6NF |

**Overview:**

The inauguration of a national power-sharing government in June 2003, following the signing of a peace agreement the previous year that ostensibly ended the country's five-year war, led to further stabilization of the Democratic Republic of Congo (DRC). A unified national military, headed by 30 officers from former belligerent forces, was formed to administer the DRC's 10 military zones. The Ituri region remained the scene of the most pervasive fighting and human rights abuses in the DRC, although the numerous militia groups operating there have repeatedly agreed to work with the government to reinforce state authority in the region.

As the Belgium Congo, the vast area of Central Africa that is today the DRC was exploited with a brutality that was notable even by colonial standards. The country became a center for Cold War rivalries on Belgium's withdrawal in 1960 and remained so until well after Colonel Joseph Mobutu came to power with CIA backing in 1964. The pro-Western Mobutu was forgiven by Western governments for severe repression and financial excesses that made him one of the world's richest men and his countrymen among the world's poorest people. Domestic agitation for democratization forced Mobutu to open up the political process in 1990. In 1992, his Popular Revolutionary Movement, the sole legal party after 1965, and the Sacred Union of the Radical Opposition and Allied Civil Society, a coalition of 200 groups, joined scores of others in a national conference to establish the High Council of the Republic to oversee a democratic transition. Mobutu manipulated and delayed the transition.

Despite widespread opposition to his rule, it was the 1994 genocide in neighboring Rwanda that triggered Mobutu's demise; he had allowed Hutu Interahamwe fighters to base themselves in his country, which was then known as Zaire. In 1996, Rwanda and Uganda easily tapped into popular hatred for Mobutu in their seven-month advance on Kinshasa. They installed Laurent Kabila, who at the time was a semi-retired guerrilla fighter, as the head of their rebellion and toppled the Mobutu regime in May 1997. Mobutu fled to Morocco and died of cancer a few months later. A subsequent armed conflict erupted in late 1998 after Kabila fell out with Uganda and Rwanda, whose leaders had helped him seize power. Kabila was assassinated in January 2001. His son, Joseph, revived the 1999 Lusaka peace accord and furthered the consolidation of a ceasefire.

The war at some point has drawn forces from at least eight countries into the fighting: Angola, Chad, Namibia, Sudan, and Zimbabwe on the side of Kabila; and Burundi, Rwanda, and Uganda on the side of the rebels. In 2003, the UN Security Council authorized the expansion of the UN force in the DRC from 8,700 to 10,800. A voluntary disarmament program has met with mixed success.

The conflict in the DRC has directly and indirectly claimed the lives of an estimated 3.3 million people, according to the International Rescue Committee, which makes it the most deadly conflict since World War II. By UN estimates, another 2.7 million were displaced. The UN special rapporteur on human rights in the DRC confirmed that genocide may have occurred in the Uturi region, and reported extrajudicial executions in South Kivu province and throughout the eastern parts of the country in 2003. Amnesty International said that all armed groups continue to recruit and use child soldiers.

A UN panel investigating the plunder of natural resources in the DRC submitted its final report to the Security Council in October 2003. While the conflict was launched by Rwanda, which was concerned about its security, the report confirmed that the war was largely fueled by competition to control the DRC's vast mineral and diamond wealth, and this illicit economic exploitation persists through proxy militias controlled by neighboring countries and government officials. Over its three-year tenure, the UN panel has named more than 150 individuals and companies suspected of complicity in this exploitation. They include many senior political and military officials in several countries party to the war. The Office of the Prosecutor of the International Criminal Court has also announced its intention to investigate the role of Western and Asian business interests in fueling crimes against humanity in the DRC.

Under an accord reached in December 2002 in Pretoria, South Africa, the country is now run by a two-year transitional government headed by President Joseph Kabila. Multiparty elections are mandated by July 2005. Most former rebel groups are now authorized to act as political parties. Kabila's government of national unity consists of 4 vice presidents, 36 ministers, and 24 vice ministers. Extensive executive, legislative, and military powers are vested in the president and vice presidents. Key ministries are shared among the government and the two main former rebel groups—the Congolese Rally for Democracy (RCD) and the Ugandan-backed Movement for the Liberation of Congo (MLC). Human rights groups and the United Nations strongly criticized the military appointments of two officers from the RCD, Laurent Nkunda and Gabriel Amisi, who are accused of leading massacres in Kisangani in May 2002 in which more than 100 civilians were executed.

The peace agreement obliged Rwanda to withdraw its troops, which entered the DRC in 1996 to pursue the Interahamwe, a Rwandan Hutu militia responsible for the massacre of about 800,000 Tutsis and moderate Hutus in 1994. Although the Rwandan government says all of its 20,000 troops have left the country, it is accused by human rights groups of maintaining some forces in the eastern DRC. By the end of 2002, Angola, Namibia, and Zimbabwe had withdrawn from the DRC, while Uganda officially withdrew its forces in May 2003. Diplomatic relations continued to thaw in 2003 with the Great Lakes countries, notably Uganda, which is seeking the DRC government's aid in rooting out Ugandan rebel groups based in the country's northeast.

None of the militias operating in the Ituri region are signatories to the national power-sharing agreement, and they have complained of being excluded from the transition process. Despite assurances of cooperation by these armed groups, the killing, torture, rape, and abduction of civilians to forced labor camps continue to be reported. The International Criminal Court said it had evidence that 5,000 civilians had been killed in Ituri between July 2002 and early 2003; these events possibly constitute genocide, which falls within the court's jurisdiction. In a report issued in July 2003, Human Rights Watch said the fighting in the region has been inaccurately described as a local ethnic rivalry when apparently the combatants were armed and often directed by the governments of the DRC, Rwanda, and Uganda. There are currently some 4,500 UN soldiers deployed in the region, where a UN arms embargo remains in effect.

In October 2003, the Mayi-Mayi militia and the RCD former rebel movement signed a ceasefire agreement. Until then the two groups had maintained hostile relations, and fighting had kept on unabated between their troops, even though both are signatories to the national power-sharing accord.

Most people live marginal lives as subsistence farmers despite the country's vast natural resources. In 2003, the government continued to normalize relations with creditors, implementing an economic reform program and securing an 80 percent external debt reduction from the IMF.

**Political Rights and Civil Liberties:** The people of the Democratic Republic of Congo (DRC) have never been able to choose or change their government through democratic and peaceful means. There are no elected representatives in the entire country. Mobutu Sese Seko's successive, unopposed presidential victories and legislative polls were little more than political theater. Infrastructure and institutions to support a free and fair election are almost entirely absent, although the United Nations is working with the government and the newly created Independent Electoral Commission to provide support for the presidential and legislative polls slated for 2005.

In accordance with a transitional constitution adopted in April, the National Assembly and the Senate convened in the capital, Kinshasa, in 2003. The National Assembly consists of 500 appointed members from the parties to the intra-Congolese dialogue, namely the former Kinshasa government, the unarmed political opposition, civil society, and former rebel movements. The Senate is made up of 120 appointees from the various parties to the national power-sharing accord. Its first task will be to draft legislation in line with the transitional constitution, such as laws on nationality, the functioning and organization of political parties, electoral law, and institutional management, as well as a general amnesty for all former combatants. Civil society representatives head five other constitutionally mandated bodies on human rights, the media, truth and reconciliation, elections, and the fight against corruption.

At least 400 political parties registered after their 1990 legalization, but they were later banned under Laurent Kabila. Restrictions on political parties were eased in May 2001, and there are currently 234 parties legally recognized by the government.

Freedom of expression is limited, although the new constitution contains several articles intended to guarantee free expression, and the government has created a national law reform commission tasked with amending legislation that curtails the media. The UN broadcaster, Radio Okapi, has expanded its coverage of the country to include several local languages. Radio Maendeleo, one of the few independent radio stations in the eastern DRC, came back on the air in July after seven months of silence following its closure by the RCD. Officials said the station had violated the terms of its license by broadcasting political content. However, the station's new permission to operate remains subject to compliance with laws governing "public order and national security." At least 30 independent newspapers are published regularly in Kinshasa, but they are not widely circulated beyond the city. Although the government does not restrict access to the Internet, few people can afford the connection costs.

Despite statutory protection, independent journalists are frequently threatened, arrested, or attacked. The most serious cases include that of Akite Kisembo, an interpreter for Agence France-Presse, who was abducted in July and remains missing. That same month, Donatien Nyembo Kimuni, a reporter for *La Tribune* newspaper, was sentenced to five years in prison for an article critical of the management and working conditions of the Congo Mineral private mining company. In March, Raymond Kabala, a Kinshasa-based journalist, was released from prison after serving more than seven months. Kabala had been convicted of making "harmful accusations" against the former security and public order minister, Mwenze Kongolo, in an article alleging that Kongolo had been poisoned.

Freedom of religion is respected in practice, although religious groups must register with the government to be recognized. Academic freedom is restricted in practice. Fears of government harassment often lead university professors to engage in self-censorship.

Freedom of assembly and association is limited. Numerous nongovernmental organizations, including human rights groups, operate despite intimidation and arrest. Despite the signing of the peace accord, Human Rights Watch recently reported that human rights workers in the DRC were under increasing attack, citing 20 cases of arrest, beating, and intimidation of human rights defenders, civil society activists, and independent journalists during a single three-month period in 2003.

More than 100 new independent unions were registered after the end of one-party rule in 1990. Previously, all unions had to affiliate themselves with a confederation that was part of the ruling party. Some unions are affiliated with political parties, and labor leaders and activists have faced harassment. There is little union activity, owing to the breakdown of the country's formal (business) economy and its replacement by the black market.

Despite guarantees of independence, in practice the judiciary is subject to corruption and manipulation. In October, magistrates in the DRC began an indefinite nationwide strike to protest low pay and lack of autonomy. In January, the Military Order Court sentenced 30 people to death for their role in the assassination of Laurent Kabila; 45 others were acquitted. The government had lifted a moratorium on the death penalty dating to 1997 about one month prior to the verdict. The defendants cannot appeal to a higher judicial authority. In a move hailed by human rights groups, the government abolished the Military Order Court in April. Seventy prisoners unconnected with the assassination were released under a presidential amnesty. Under pressure from human rights groups, the government said it had convened a commission to ensure that the verdicts reached in the assassination trials were fair and impartial.

Ethnic societal discrimination is practiced widely among the country's 200 ethnic groups.

Despite constitutional guarantees, women face de facto discrimination, especially in rural areas. They also enjoy fewer employment and educational opportunities than men and often do not receive equal pay for equal work. Violence against women, including rape and forced sexual slavery, has soared since the onset of armed conflict in 1996. Children continue to face forced conscription by all sides in the conflict, although the government appeared to be scaling back this practice. The Save the Children organization has ranked the DRC among the world's five worst conflict zones in which to be a woman or child.

# Congo, Republic of (Brazzaville)

**Population:** 3,700,000    **Political Rights:** 5*
**GNI/capita:** $640    **Civil Liberties:** 4
**Life Expectancy:** 50    **Status:** Partly Free
**Religious Groups:** Christian (50 percent),
animist (48 percent), Muslim (2 percent)
**Ethnic Groups:** Kongo (48 percent), Sangha (20 percent),
Teke (17 percent), M'Bochi (12 percent), other (3 percent)
**Capital:** Brazzaville
**Ratings Change:** Congo (Brazzaville's) political rights rating improved from 6 to 5 due
to the signing of an apparently durable cease-fire agreement in March that has helped
stabilize the country's fragile political environment.

**Ten-Year Ratings Timeline (Political Rights, Civil Liberties, Status)**

| 1994 | 1995 | 1996 | 1997 | 1998 | 1999 | 2000 | 2001 | 2002 | 2003 |
|------|------|------|------|------|------|------|------|------|------|
| 4,4PF | 4,4PF | 4,4PF | 7,5NF | 7,5NF | 6,5NF | 6,4PF | 5,4PF | 6,4PF | 5,4PF |

**Overview:**

For much of the past decade, the Republic of Congo has been torn by a bewildering civil conflict that in 2003 inched closer to a resolution with the signing in March of a new peace agreement between rebel and government forces. The emerging detente, reinforced by a broad government amnesty for the insurgents and the establishment of a human rights commission, continued to spread at year's end amid conflicting signs of economic revival and a persistent humanitarian crisis in the Pool region.

A decade after Congo's independence from France, a 1970 coup established a Marxist state in the country. In 1979, General Denis Sassou-Nguesso seized power and maintained one-party rule as head of the Congolese Workers' Party. Domestic and international pressure forced his acceptance of a national conference leading to open, multiparty elections in 1992. Pascal Lissouba won a clear victory over former prime minister Bernard Kolelas in a second-round presidential runoff that excluded Sassou-Nguesso, who had run third in the first round.

Disputes over the 1993 legislative polls led to armed conflict. The fighting subsided but flared once again among ethnic-based militias in 1997. Sassou-Nguesso, who has had military support from Angola and political backing from France, built a private army in his native northern Congo and forcibly retook the presidency in October 1997. Peace agreements signed in late 1999 included an amnesty for combatants who voluntarily disarmed. A new constitution was adopted by referendum in January 2002, providing for a multiparty system and establishing wide-ranging powers for the president, who would be directly elected for a seven-year term.

The March 2002 presidential poll was marred by irregularities, and there was no independent electoral commission, but international observers hailed the peaceful nature of the vote. Sassou-Nguesso was virtually assured a victory when his main challenger, former prime minister Andre Milongo, dropped out of the race just before the election, claiming irregularities. Sassou-Nguesso won the election with 89 percent of the vote. Elections for the 137-member National Assembly in May and

June were dominated by Sassou-Nguesso's Congolese Workers' Party and other parties affiliated with it.

Following a year of renewed fighting, in March 2003, the Congolese government reached a new peace agreement with Ninja militias operating in the north. Despite the cessation of hostilities, a grave humanitarian crisis persists in the Pool region, where tens of thousands of people were forced to flee their homes and most infrastructure was completely destroyed. About half of the refugees remain internally displaced. In a bid to consolidate the peace process, the National Assembly subsequently approved an amnesty for all combatants dating from January 15, 2000, until the date Sassou-Nguesso signs the bill into law. UN-backed resettlement and demobilization efforts have begun, but remain slow.

Although Congo is the fourth-largest producer of oil in Sub-Saharan Africa, poverty remains widespread, affecting some 70 percent of the population. Improved oil markets in 2003 boosted growth. The government has proceeded with privatization plans under the direction of the IMF.

**Political Rights and Civil Liberties:** Since the outbreak of civil war in 1997, Congolese have been only partly able to exercise their constitutional right to change their leaders through democratic elections. Competitive multiparty elections were held for the first time in 1992 and 1993. Presidential and legislative elections held in 2002 were not deemed fair, in part because of irregularities and the absence of an independent electoral commission.

The government generally respects press freedom, but continues to monopolize the broadcast media. In 2000, the government abolished censorship and sharply reduced penalties for defamation. About 10 private newspapers appear weekly in Brazzaville, and they often publish articles and editorials that are critical of the government. There are approximately 10 domestic Internet service providers, and no government restrictions on Internet use.

Religious freedom is guaranteed and respected. Academic freedom is restricted, and university professors often exercise self-censorship to conform to the views of the government. However, there were no reports of students or professors being overtly censored.

Freedom of assembly and association is constitutionally guaranteed, and this right is generally respected in practice, although public demonstrations are rare. Nongovernmental organizations (NGOs) generally operate freely. Workers' rights to join trade unions and to strike are legally protected. Collective bargaining is practiced freely. Most workers in the formal business sector are union members, and unions have made efforts to organize informal sectors, such as those of agriculture and retail trade.

The judiciary is subject to corruption and political influence. The court system was generally considered to be politically independent until the civil war. Scarce resources and understaffing have created a backlog of court cases and long periods of pretrial detention. In rural areas, traditional courts retain broad jurisdiction, especially in civil matters. Prison conditions are life-threatening, with reports of beatings, overcrowding, and other ill-treatment. Women and men, as well as juveniles and adults, are incarcerated together. Human rights groups and the International Committee of the Red Cross have been allowed access.

Human rights violations against the civilian population abated with the ceasefire between the government and Ninja militias. A 1999 peace agreement broke down in 2002 when members of the Ninja militia took up arms following reports that security forces were attempting to arrest their leader. Both sides have been accused of atrocities against the civilian population. The August 2003 amnesty covers an estimated 14,000 demobilized Ninja fighters, and potentially government security forces, which have been accused of extrajudicial killings, rape, beatings, physical abuse of detainees and citizens, and arbitrary arrest and detention. Local human rights groups and opposition politicians have criticized the amnesty for excluding opposition activists currently in exile.

Inquiries were opened in 2003 into the disappearance of more than 350 Congolese refugees who returned from exile in the Democratic Republic of Congo (Kinshasa) in 1999. Human rights groups and survivors launched a case in a French court against President Denis Sassou-Nguesso and other high-ranking government officials for alleged crimes of torture, forced disappearance, and crimes against humanity. The Congolese government contends that France does not have jurisdiction over incidents occurring in Congo and has sued France in the Hague-based International Court of Justice to suspend the prosecutions. No decision is expected until the middle of next year. The Congolese government is currently conducting its own parallel hearings into the disappearances before a tribunal in Brazzaville.

In accordance with the country's new constitution, a human rights commission consisting of members from civil society organizations, professional associations, and public institutions was formed in August 2003. While it has been hailed by local rights groups as a positive development, the commission's powers are limited. Members are named by presidential decree and have no authority to summon accused parties. The president also appointed the members of a social and economic council and freedom-of-speech council, completing the range of constitutionally required bodies. In September 2003, the government ratified the Convention Against Torture and Other Cruel, Inhuman, or Degrading Treatment or Punishment, although local human rights groups say police abuse of detainees remains a serious problem.

Ethnic discrimination persists. Pygmy groups suffer discrimination, and many are effectively held in lifetime servitude through customary ties to Bantu "patrons." Members of virtually all ethnic groups practice discrimination in hiring practices.

There is extensive legal and societal discrimination against women despite constitutional protections. Access to education and employment opportunities, especially in the countryside, are limited, and civil codes regarding family and marriage formalize women's inferior status. Violence against women is reportedly widespread. After declining in 2000 and 2001, incidents of rape increased in 2002 with the renewed outbreak of hostilities. NGOs have drawn attention to the issue and provided counseling and assistance to victims.

# Costa Rica

**Population:** 4,200,000
**GNI/capita:** $4,060
**Life Expectancy:** 79
**Political Rights:** 1
**Civil Liberties:** 2
**Status:** Free
**Religious Groups:** Roman Catholic (76.3 percent),
Evangelical (13.7 percent), other (10 percent)
**Ethnic Groups:** White and mestizo (94 percent),
black (3 percent), Amerindian (1 percent), other (2 percent)
**Capital:** San José

**Ten-Year Ratings Timeline (Political Rights, Civil Liberties, Status)**

| 1994 | 1995 | 1996 | 1997 | 1998 | 1999 | 2000 | 2001 | 2002 | 2003 |
|------|------|------|------|------|------|------|------|------|------|
| 1,2F | 1,2F | 1,2F | 1,2F | 1,2F | 1,2F | 1,2F | 1,2F | 1,2F | 1,2F |

**Overview:**

Public support for President Abel Pacheco declined in 2003 over allegations of illegal funding of his 2002 presidential campaign by foreign business interests. While more than half of his cabinet had resigned by mid-year, Pacheco insisted that he would not resign. Meanwhile, an article in the country's constitution banning the reelection of presidents was removed.

Costa Rica achieved independence from Spain in 1821 and became a republic in 1848. The 1949 constitution bans the formation of a national army. In the 1994 elections, Jose Maria Figueres, son of the legendary president Jose "Pepe" Figueres, defeated Miguel Angel Rodriguez of the Social Christian Party (PUSC). The outgoing president, Rafael A. Calderon, Jr., of the PUSC had promoted neoliberal economic policies, and Figueres campaigned against them. Despite his campaign pledges, Figueres's last two years in office saw the passing of free market policies championed by his opponent in the presidential elections. In the 1998 elections, Rodriguez bested Jose Miguel Corrales of the National Liberation Party (PLN).

For many years there has been a consistent flow of Nicaraguans searching for employment in Costa Rica. Simmering tensions with the country's northern neighbor, Nicaragua, were exacerbated in 2001 when the Costa Rican government began to build a seven-foot-high fence along the Penas Blancas border crossing on the Pan-American Highway along the Pacific Coast. Claims that the wall was to control heavy goods traffic in a region that has become a favored route for drug smuggling were dismissed in Nicaragua. There are more than 400,000 Nicaraguans in Costa Rica, many of whom work without papers on farms where they are paid subsistence wages. In 1998, Costa Rica declared a temporary amnesty for these and other illegal Central American immigrants, and more than 200,000 Nicaraguans legalized their status.

After winning the 2002 presidential runoff elections, the government of Pacheco of the PUSC continued to make little progress in passing legislation. Improprieties in the financing of his election further tarnished his image. The 2002 elections were unusual in leading to a four-way draw. After increasing voter dissatisfaction with the two traditional parties—the PUSC and the PLN—two smaller upstarts, the Citizens Action Party (PAC) and the Libertarian Movement (ML), received significant support. Only 69 percent of the population cast votes.

In August 2003, allegations of the illegal financing of President Abel Pacheco's campaign by Panamanian, Nicaraguan, Salvadoran, Taiwanese, and Costa Rican business interests surfaced. Because Pacheco had campaigned on the issues of transparency and a fight against corruption, the existence of secret accounts and illegal financing received extensive media coverage. After claiming that his actions were no worse than those of his predecessors, Pacheco publicly denied in September that he would resign over this scandal. Public opinion support has steadily declined for Pacheco. By mid-year, over half of his cabinet had resigned, often after mass demonstrations were staged against privatization plans.

During 2003, the legislature was embroiled in squabbles over the composition of parliamentary commissions, delaying legislation. In April, the constitutional court voted to eliminate Article 132 of the constitution, which bans presidential reelection.

Despite the relative calm of Costa Rica, the increase in gang-related violent crime led Costa Rican public security forces to coordinate actions with its neighbors in September.

**Political Rights and Civil Liberties:** Democratic government change takes place with free and fair elections. There are guarantees for the right to organize political parties. In response to allegations of drug money financing the elections, new campaign laws have been passed to make party funding more transparent. The president and the 57-member Legislative Assembly are elected for a four-year term and are banned from seeking a second term.

The press, radio, and television are generally free. Ninety percent of the population is literate, and there are six major privately owned dailies. Television and radio stations are both public and commercial, with at least four private television stations and more than 90 private radio stations. Access to the Internet is free. Article 309 of the criminal code, which had allowed up to two years in prison for anyone damaging the reputation or insulting the rank of a government official, was repealed in February 2002. Other similar laws are still on the books, including one allowing people who feel that their reputation was impugned by an item of news to sue and get the author fined. Article 149 of the criminal code places the burden on journalists to prove their innocence, and Article 152 punishes anyone who repeats offensive remarks. A recent poll of journalists found that more than a third were threatened with prosecution. The assassination of a prominent journalist sparked protests around the country.

Freedom of religion is recognized, and there is complete academic freedom.

The constitution provides for the right to organize civic organizations. There are numerous nongovernmental organizations active in all parts of society and the country. Labor can organize freely, but there has been a noticeable reluctance to expand labor rights. Minimum wage and social security laws are often ignored, and the consequent fines are insignificant.

The judicial branch is independent, with members elected by the legislature. The legal system includes a Supreme Court, courts of appeals, and district courts. The Supreme Court can rule on the constitutionality of laws and chooses an independent national election commission. There are long delays in the justice system, partly as a result of budget cuts. Prisons are notoriously overcrowded, but generally meet international standards.

A 1994 Police Code and the 2001 Law for Strengthening the Civilian Police were designed to depoliticize and professionalize the police in order to create a permanent career path within the institution. The law replaced military ranks with civilian titles and required the police academy to develop a course and diploma in police administration. The Ministry of Public Security and the Ministry of the Presidency share responsibility for law enforcement and national security. Several entities, including the Border Guard, Rural Guard, and the Civil Guard, were merged into a single "public force."

Independent rights monitors report increases in allegations of arbitrary arrest and brutality. Human rights complaints are investigated by an ombudsman who has the authority to issue recommendations for rectification, including sanctions against government bodies, for failure to respect rights. Corruption in the public security forces is not considered a serious problem and, when discovered, is usually dealt with in a decisive manner.

Illegal narcotics trafficking and money laundering have increased in Costa Rica. The country is a regional leader in the enactment of progressive antidrug statutes, including the use of wiretaps, controlled deliveries, and undercover agents. Financial institutions must report any transactions involving more than $10,000. In 1999, the Legislative Assembly passed legislation allowing for U.S. antidrug patrols to operate in Costa Rican waters.

Indigenous rights are not a priority.

The government is making significant efforts to combat human trafficking; Costa Rica is a transit and destination country for trafficked persons. Often, women workers are sexually harassed, made to work overtime without pay, and fired when they become pregnant. A law criminalizing sex with minors was passed in 1999 in an attempt to crack down on the country's growing sex tourism industry. Violence against women and children is a problem, although the government has shown concrete support for programs and policies to combat it.

# Cote D'Ivoire

**Population:** 17,000,000
**GNI/capita:** $630
**Life Expectancy:** 43
**Political Rights:** 6
**Civil Liberties:** 5*
**Status:** Not Free
**Religious Groups:** Christian (20-30 percent), Muslim (35-40 percent), indigenous beliefs (25-40 percent)
**Ethnic Groups:** Akan (42.1 percent), Voltaiques, or Gur (17.6 percent), Northern Mandes (16.5 percent), Krous (11 percent), Southern Mandes (10 percent), other (2.8 percent)
**Capital:** Yamoussoukro (official); Abidjan (de facto)
**Ratings Change:** Cote d'Ivoire's civil liberties rating improved from 6 to 5 due to a reduction of hostilities following the signing of a ceasefire.

**Ten-Year Ratings Timeline (Political Rights, Civil Liberties, Status)**

| 1994 | 1995 | 1996 | 1997 | 1998 | 1999 | 2000 | 2001 | 2002 | 2003 |
|------|------|------|------|------|------|------|------|------|------|
| 6,5NF | 6,5NF | 6,5NF | 6,4NF | 6,4NF | 6,4PF | 6,5PF | 5,4PF | 6,6NF | 6,5NF |

**Overview:** The government and rebels signed a ceasefire in January that provided for a broad-based coalition government. The peace process, however, was encountering difficulties toward the end of the year. Press freedom improved and then suffered a setback in 2003 with the murder of a French journalist.

Cote d'Ivoire gained independence from France in 1960, and President Felix Houphouet-Boigny ruled until his death in 1993. Henri Konan Bedie assumed power and won fraudulent elections in 1995 with 95 percent of the vote. Alassane Ouattara, the opposition's most formidable candidate, was barred from the contest. Demonstrations were banned, and the media were intimidated.

General Robert Guei seized power in December 1999 and stood for election in October 2000. When initial results showed Guei was losing to Laurent Gbagbo, he sacked the electoral commission, detained its officers, and declared himself the winner. Tens of thousands of people took to the streets in a popular uprising that toppled him from power. Clashes followed between supporters of Alassane Ouattara's Rally of Republicans (RDR) and Gbagbo's Ivorian Popular Front (FPI). Supported by security forces, Gbagbo refused to call for new polls. The political violence led to a deepening division between the largely Muslim north and mainly Christian south, although the conflict is not strictly rooted in a north-south, Muslim-Christian divide. Gbagbo was eventually declared the winner, with 59 percent, compared with 33 percent for Guei.

The FPI won 96 seats in the December 2000 legislative elections, while 4 went to the Democratic Party of Cote d'Ivoire, and 5 went to the RDR. Twenty-four seats went to smaller parties and independents, and 2 seats in Ouattara's district went unfilled.

Civil war erupted in September 2002 when the government attempted to demobilize and retire some 700 soldiers. In what appeared to be either a coup attempt or a mutiny, General Guei was killed. An insurgent group calling itself the Patriotic Movement of Cote d'Ivoire, which is now part of the rebel New Forces, emerged in the north, calling for Gbagbo to step down and for new elections. The insurgents quickly seized control of more than half of the country. Fighting erupted in the west of the country and two more rebel groups emerged.

President Gbagbo's government and the New Forces signed a ceasefire in January 2003 providing for a broad-based coalition government that would rule until elections in 2005. Violence continued, mainly in the west, but unrest abated considerably. The violent targeting of Muslims as political opponents also diminished. Despite these improvements, Gbagbo appeared to accept the peace accord with reluctance and was preoccupied with his own political survival. In August, authorities detained 18 people on suspicion of planning to assassinate him. Another 13 people were arrested in France that month on suspicion that they were organizing a coup. Meanwhile, the United Nations said there were signs that both sides in the war were re-arming.

By October, the peace process appeared to be unraveling with the withdrawal of New Forces representatives from the government to protest what they said was Gbagbo's reluctance to delegate meaningful authority to their ministers. The New Forces, consisting of one rebel group in the north and two in the west, also put disarmament plans on hold. Authorities detained 11 activists with the opposition RDR in October for several days and questioned them about an alleged plot to assassinate various unnamed politicians and military leaders. A militia group allied with Gbagbo's FPI increasingly raised concern. The government ordered the disbanding of the Grouping of Young Patriots in October after its members attacked French-owned utility companies in Cote d'Ivoire; the group accuses France of siding with rebel forces. The government also banned demonstrations for three months in an effort to avoid possible street violence. Ghana, as chair of the Economic Community of West African States, was leading diplomatic efforts to break the impasse.

Cote d'Ivoire retains strong political, economic, and military backing from France, which has maintained a military garrison near Abidjan for years, mainly to protect French nationals who live in Cote d'Ivoire. Many French, however, fled after the war erupted. Some 4,000 French peacekeepers are in the country, and West African countries have provided 1,300 peacekeepers.

During the Houphouet-Boigny period, Cote d'Ivoire became an African model for economic growth and political stability. A plunge in the 1990s of the world price of cocoa, Cote d'Ivoire's chief export, and later coffee, its fifth-largest export, considerably hurt the economy. Political unrest did further damage.

**Political Rights and Civil Liberties:** The people of Cote d'Ivoire cannot change their government democratically. The 1995 presidential election was neither free nor fair and was boycotted by all the major opposition parties. Voting in the October 2000 presidential election appeared to be carried out fairly, but only 5 of 19 potential candidates were allowed to contest the vote. The Ivorian Popular Front (FPI) of President Laurent Gbagbo won an overwhelming number of seats in the December 2000 legislative election.

Press freedom is guaranteed but not always respected in practice. State-owned newspapers and a state-run broadcasting system are usually unreservedly pro-government. Several private radio stations and a cable television service operate, but only the state broadcasting system reaches a national audience. Dozens of independent newspapers are published, many of which are linked to political parties. There is liberal access to the Internet.

Press freedom improved and then suffered a setback in 2003. The government allowed Radio France Internationale (RFI), the BBC, and Africa No. 1 to resume their FM broadcasts in February after having suspended them five months previously. The government also invited Paris-based Reporters Sans Frontieres to Cote d'Ivoire to provide guidance on how to professionalize the press. Gbagbo announced a draft law that would eliminate prison sentences for press offenses.

However, attacks on the press have not ended. A correspondent for the state-run Agence Ivoirienne de Presse, Kloueu Gonzreu, was found murdered in western Cote d'Ivoire in March, and a correspondent for RFI, Jean Helene, was shot and killed by a policeman in October. Helene was outside police headquarters in Abidjan waiting to interview political detainees who were about to be released. There has been an anti-French campaign in the pro-Gbagbo media, leading to attacks on French journalists. A former RFI correspondent was forced to leave the country. Opposition newspapers temporarily halted publishing in October after pro-Gbagbo militants attacked newspaper delivery trucks.

Religious freedom is guaranteed but is not respected in practice. The government openly favors Christianity, and Muslims have been targeted in the past few years of political unrest and face discrimination. Attacks on mosques and churches diminished in 2003. The government inhibits political expression by requiring authorization for all meetings held on college campuses. The government owns most educational facilities in the country.

Human rights groups generally operate freely in Cote d'Ivoire, and a ministry of human rights has been created. However, in April, the offices of the Ivorian Movement of Human Rights were ransacked, and employees said they had been threatened in their homes. Union formation and membership are legally protected, although only a small percentage of the workforce is organized. Workers have the right to bargain collectively. Child labor and child trafficking are problems, although Cote d'Ivoire has made efforts to stem both practices. Thousands of West African children are believed to be working on Ivorian plantations, while some 100,000 children were estimated to be working in hazardous conditions on the country's cocoa farms.

Cote d'Ivoire does not have an independent judiciary. Judges are political appointees without tenure and are highly susceptible to external interference. In many rural areas, traditional courts still prevail, especially in the handling of minor matters and family law. Security forces generally operate with impunity and prison conditions are harsh. In August, the government released 54 political prisoners.

The New York–based Human Rights Watch (HRW) in November said pro-government militias continue to kill, torture, and harass civilians with impunity. Most of the militia members are from Gbagbo's Bete tribe in south-central Cote d'Ivoire. They have targeted immigrant farmers and members of other ethnic groups. HRW also said there was increasingly lawlessness in the north. It has called on the government to disband militias, set up an international commission of inquiry to investigate human rights abuses committed during the war, and bring perpetrators to justice. The rights organization has documented massacres of civilians, particularly in the west of the country, where Liberian mercenaries and militias have been used by both sides during the war. The international monitoring group Global Witness said in March that Liberia was the driving force behind the training, arming, and deployment of rebel groups based in the west. HRW said both the government and rebels were responsible for summary executions and sexual violence against women and girls that were rooted in ethnic discrimination occurring in a climate of impunity.

Freedom from discrimination is guaranteed but not respected in practice. Human Rights Watch has accused officials of deliberately encouraging a culture of violent xenophobia in Cote d'Ivoire, whose economy has long attracted workers from neighboring countries. More than one-quarter of the country's population is estimated to be African expatriates. Land-use disputes, aggravated by political tension, often trigger violence against African foreigners. At least 500,000 Africans have returned to their respective countries, mainly Mali and Burkina Faso, because of the civil war and another 750,000 people have been displaced.

Women suffer widespread discrimination, despite official encouragement for respect for constitutional rights. Equal pay for equal work is offered in the small formal business sector, but women have few chances to obtain, or advance in, wage employment. In rural areas that rely on subsistence agriculture, education and job opportunities for women are even scarcer. Female genital mutilation is still practiced, although it has been a crime since 1998, and violence against women is reportedly common.

# Croatia

**Population:** 4,300,000
**GNI/capita:** $4,550
**Life Expectancy:** 74
**Religious Groups:** Roman Catholic (87.8 percent),
Orthodox (4.4 percent), Muslim (1.3 percent),
Protestant (0.3 percent), other and unknown (6.2 percent)
**Ethnic Groups:** Croat (89.6 percent), Serb (4.5 percent),
Bosniak (0.5 percent), Hungarian (0.4 percent), Slovene (0.3 percent), Czech (0.2
percent), Roma (0.2 percent), Albanian (0.1 percent), Montenegrin (0.1percent), other
(4.1 percent)
**Capital:** Zagreb

**Political Rights:** 2
**Civil Liberties:** 2
**Status:** Free

## Ten-Year Ratings Timeline (Political Rights, Civil Liberties, Status)

| 1994 | 1995 | 1996 | 1997 | 1998 | 1999 | 2000 | 2001 | 2002 | 2003 |
|------|------|------|------|------|------|------|------|------|------|
| 4,4PF | 4,4PF | 4,4PF | 4,4PF | 4,4PF | 4,4PF | 2,3F | 2,2F | 2,2F | 2,2F |

**Overview:**

Parliamentary elections in November 2003 returned to power a resurgent Croatian Democratic Union (HDZ), the right-of-center party whose nationalist policies had led Croatia through its first decade of independence. Despite the euphoria surrounding its election victory, the HDZ still has to deal with the same serious problems that led to the SDP's downfall—responding to the intense international pressure to cooperate with the International Criminal Tribunal for the Former Yugoslavia (ICTY), and revitalizing an economy increasingly burdened by $20 billion in external debt.

As part of the Socialist Federal Republic of Yugoslavia, Croatia held its first multiparty elections in 1990, electing Franjo Tudjman, a former Communist general turned nationalist politician, as president in May 1990. Tudjman's Croatian Democratic Union (HDZ) ruled Croatia from 1990 to 1999. As rival nationalisms competed with each other in Croatia during 1990 and 1991, Croatia's Serb population in the region known as Krajina declared independence from Croatia, even as Croatia itself was declaring its independence from the former Yugoslavia. The result was a de facto partition of the country between 1991 and 1995. In May and August 1995, a majority of the Serb population of Croatia was forcibly expelled from Krajina during Croatian military offensives to establish control over the contested territory.

On December 11, 1999, Tudjman died, and in the subsequent extraordinary presidential elections in January 2000, Stjepan Mesic of the Croatian People's Party (HNS) was elected president. In legislative elections that also took place in January 2000, a center-left coalition wrested control of parliament from the HDZ. The leader of the SDP (the former League of Communists of Croatia), Ivica Racan, was named prime minister.

In Croatia's latest parliamentary elections, held on November 23, 2003, the HDZ, together with its new leader, Dr. Ivo Sanader, gained 66 seats, making the HDZ the strongest party in the new 152-member parliament. Because of international objections to the formation of a coalition majority government with extreme right-wing nationalist parties, Sanader decided to lead a minority government with the support of the Independent Democratic Serb Party, the Croatian Party of Pensioners (HSU), the Croatian Peasants Party (HSS), and representatives of Croatia's Italian minority. The HDZ's victory ended three years of a relatively weak SDP-led coalition government. The HDZ's return to power was viewed with caution because of the party's past history of engaging in nationalist demagogy, its meddling in neighboring Bosnia-Herzegovina, and its poor record in dealing with Croatia's ethnic minorities. Prime Minister Sanader has claimed that the party is now "reformed" and has evolved into a normal European Christian-democratic party purged of extremists, but many of its more controversial figures from the past remain in influential positions. On a more positive note, it is widely believed that only a party with strong nationalist credentials, such as the HDZ, will have the strength to extradite Croatian citizens indicted by the ICTY, one of the most important preconditions for Croatia's entry into the European Union (EU).

An important test case of how the Sanader government will cooperate with the ICTY will be the fate of General Ante Gotovina, indicted by the ICTY and accused of responsibility for the murders and "ethnic cleansing" of thousands of Serbs during "Operation Storm" in August-September 1995. Gotovina is in hiding, but ICTY pressure on Croatia in 2003 to find and turn him over caused considerable political problems for the previous Croatian government. Britain and the Netherlands refuse to ratify Croatia's Stabilization and Association Agreement with the EU—generally seen as the first step to being formally invited to join the union—until it improves its cooperation with the ICTY. Sanader himself has raised the expectations for his government by promising to return all Serb property back to its owners by the end of 2004—a promise made by the previous government in 2001, but never fulfilled—and to streamline a bloated state bureaucracy. Although Croatia's goal of entering the EU by 2007 seemed increasingly unrealistic in 2003, in February, Croatia submitted its application for candidate member status in the EU.

The new HDZ government will also have to contend with numerous economic problems leftover from the Racan period. Among these are the high external debt estimated to be close to $20 billion, or 70-75 percent of Croatia's annual GDP, and high levels of unemployment of almost 19 percent at year's end. These economic problems are already responsible for the new government's decision to backtrack on a promise to reduce the level of the value-added tax (VAT) it had promised to implement this year.

**Political Rights and Civil Liberties:** Croatian voters can change their government democratically. The parliamentary elections of November 2003 were contested by a record 34 candidates competing for each of the 152 seats in parliament. Although the elections were on the whole free and fair, the Organization for Security and Cooperation in Europe (OSCE) expressed concern over the short time frame available for election administration, the lack of accessibility for out-of-country voters, particularly for refugees in Serbia and Montenegro and Bosnia-Herzegovina, and the lack of transparency in campaign financing. Respect for the separation of powers in the Croatian political system remains problematic, and there have been numerous cases in recent years in which the executive or legislative branch has failed to abide by or implement decisions made by the Constitutional Court.

Croatia's constitution guarantees freedom of expression and the press. On the whole, freedom of the media is respected in Croatia, but more reform of government media regulations is needed. The most important media outlet, HRT (Croatian Radio-Television), is still under substantial political control, despite long-running efforts to transform it into a European-style public-service broadcaster. Most observers regard the 2003 Law on Croatian Radio Television to be a step backward in terms of promoting the institution's independence. Journalistic freedom also remains weak; in a 2003 survey, half of the journalists questioned claimed that they do not feel free in their work. The penal code still allows for prison sentences for journalists found guilty of "defamation" and libel. There are no governmental restrictions with respect to access to the Internet.

Respect for freedom of religion has increased in Croatia in the post-Tudjman period, although ethnic and religious minorities enjoy these rights to a significantly lesser degree than ethnic Croatians. The overwhelming majority of Croatians are Roman Catholic. Consequently, the Roman Catholic Church has a considerable degree of power and influence in the country. An important indicator of how powerful the Church remains in Croatia, is the fact that relatively few candidates in the November elections who held views on social policy opposed by the Church succeeded in winning office. There were no reports of restrictions on academic freedom.

The constitution provides for freedom of association and assembly. A wide variety of both international and domestic nongovernmental organizations (NGOs) operate in Croatia and there were no reported instances of governmental harassment of NGOs during the year. The constitution allows workers to form and join trade unions, and they do so freely. Approximately 64 percent of the workforce is unionized.

Croatia's judicial system suffers from numerous problems, including a large number of judicial vacancies and a shortage of experienced judges, both of which have led to a huge backlog of cases (estimated at 1.4 million in 2003); excessive trial length; and a lack of enforcement of judicial decisions, especially in cases relating to the repossession of property owned by Serbs. The judicial system also faces considerable intimidation in the always difficult field of war crimes prosecutions. Prison conditions generally meet acceptable international standards, and the police are considered to act professionally. However, there are reports that police treat ethnic minorities more harshly than they do ethnic Croatians.

According to international monitoring organizations, Croatia continues to fail to live up to obligations stemming from its accession to the Council of Europe in 1996 to adopt nondiscriminatory laws relating to ethnic minorities. According to a U.S. State Department report released in 2003, "A pattern of often open and severe discrimination continues against ethnic Serbs and, at times, other minorities in a wide number of areas, including the administration of justice, employment, housing, and freedom of movement."

The constitution prohibits discrimination on the basis of gender. Domestic violence against women is believed to be a widespread and under-reported phenomenon. In July, parliament passed a Law on Gender Equality intended to further empower women in the workplace and public life. Women currently make up 27 of the 152 members of parliament, and there are 4 women in the 15 member cabinet. Trafficking in women for the purposes of prostitution continues to be a problem, although Croatia is considered to be primarily a transit country for most trafficked women sent to Western Europe.

# Cuba

**Population:** 11,300,000  **Political Rights:** 7
**GNI/capita:** $1,406  **Civil Liberties:** 7
**Life Expectancy:** 76  **Status:** Not Free
**Religious Groups:** Roman Catholic, Protestant, other
**Ethnic Groups:** Mulatto (51 percent), white (37 percent),
black (11 percent), Chinese (1 percent)
**Capital:** Havana

**Ten-Year Ratings Timeline (Political Rights, Civil Liberties, Status)**

| 1994 | 1995 | 1996 | 1997 | 1998 | 1999 | 2000 | 2001 | 2002 | 2003 |
|------|------|------|------|------|------|------|------|------|------|
| 7,7NF | 7,7NF | 7,7NF | 7,7NF | 7,7NF | 7,7NF | 7,7NF | 7,7NF | 7,7NF | 7,7NF |

**Overview:**  In the midst of growing popular discontent with the Cuban government, the authorities stepped up repression in 2003 against dissidents calling for free speech and other pro-democracy reforms. Dozens of political activists and independent journalists were sentenced to lengthy prison terms in April, while three men were executed following a failed attempt to flee to the United States. Meanwhile, Fidel Castro continued efforts to persuade the United States to end its four-decades-old embargo.

Cuba achieved independence from Spain in 1898 as a result of the Spanish-American War. The Republic of Cuba was established in 1902, but remained under U.S. tutelage due to the Platt Amendment until 1934. In 1959, Castro's July 26th Movement—named after an earlier, failed insurrection—overthrew the dictatorship of Fulgencio Batista, who had ruled for 18 of the previous 25 years.

Following the 1991 collapse of the Soviet Union and the end of some $5 billion in annual Soviet subsidies, Castro has sought Western foreign investment. The legalization of the U.S. dollar since 1993 has heightened social tensions, as the minority with access to dollars from abroad or through the tourist industry has emerged as a new moneyed class, and the majority without access has become increasingly desperate.

Under Castro, cycles of repression have ebbed and flowed depending on the regime's need to keep at bay the social forces set into motion by his severe post-Cold War economic reforms. By mid-June 1998, after the visit of Pope John Paul II five months earlier, the number of dissidents confirmed to be imprisoned had dropped nearly 400 percent. In February 1999, the government introduced tough legislation against sedition, with a maximum prison sentence of 20 years. It stipulated penalties for unauthorized contacts with the United States and the import or supply of "subversive" materials, including texts on democracy, by news agencies and journalists.

U.S.-Cuban relations took some unexpected turns in 2000. The story of the child shipwreck survivor Elian Gonzalez, who was ordered to be returned to his father in Cuba after a seven-month legal battle involving emigre relatives in Florida, received unprecedented media coverage. In response to pressure from U.S. farmers and businessmen who pushed for a relaxation of economic sanctions against the island, the United States eased the 38-year-old embargo on food and medicine to Cuba in October.

In June 2001, Castro, who was then 74, collapsed at a long outdoor rally near Havana. The incident centered attention on what might happen once the world's longest-ruling dictator passes from the scene. In November, Hurricane Michelle, the most powerful tropical storm to hit Cuba in a half-century, left a low death toll but a trail of physical destruction, devastating Cuban crops. In the wake of the storm, the U.S. permitted the first direct food trade with Cuba since the beginning of the embargo in 1962. The renewal of food sales in the wake of Michelle sparked further debate between farmers and others in the United States who want the embargo lifted, and Cuban exile groups and some democracy activists who demand even tougher sanctions.

In 2002, the Varela Project, a referendum initiative seeking broad changes in the four-decades-old socialist system, achieved significant support domestically. Its leader, Oswaldo Paya, was showered with international recognition. In May, project organizers submitted more than 11,000 signatures to the National Assembly demanding that a referendum be held in which Cubans could vote for fundamental reforms such as freedom of expression, the right to own private businesses, and electoral reform. A June visit by former U.S. president Jimmy Carter also added status and visibility to the protest movement. After Carter mentioned the project on Cuban television that month, the regime held its own "referendum" in which 8.2 million people supposedly declared the socialist system to be "untouchable." In October, more than 300 dissident organizations joined together as the Assembly to Promote Civil Society in preparation for a post-Fidel Castro Cuba. Composed of 321 dissident organizations ranging from human rights groups and independent libraries to labor unions and the independent press, the civil society assembly said it would prepare for a post-Castro transition rather than seek reforms from the regime. Meanwhile, Castro faced serious popular discontent, particularly because of the failing sugar industry. In June 2002, the government closed 71 of Cuba's 156 sugar mills.

Although aging Cuban strongman Fidel Castro suffered another fainting spell in Buenos Aires on May 25, 2003 as he exited an inauguration event in Buenos Aires for Argentina's new president, there were few palpable signs during the year that his regime was any closer to collapsing, even though recovery from a 1990s depression faltered and discontent increased. In the midst of the worst rights crackdown in a decade, Cuba was reelected to a seat on the UN Commission on Human Rights. Castro also continued his attempts to whet the appetites of U.S. farm state congressional delegations and enlist their help to break the four-decades-old embargo by diverting $250 million from paying old debts to buy American agricultural products. He appeared to shrug off the decision by the European Union to review its policies toward Cuba because of human rights concerns. In June, the official newspaper *Granma* reported that one of Cuba's most visible black leaders, Esteban Lazo, had been promoted to the post of chief ideologist of the Cuban Communist Party.

In April, speedy one-day sham trials resulted in prison terms ranging from 6 to 28 years for 75 independent journalists, opposition party leaders, and human rights activists rounded up the previous month. After summary trials, the government also sent three men who hijacked a ferry in a failed effort to reach the United States to the firing squad, ending a three-year de facto moratorium on executions. In July, 12 Cubans attempted to sail a 1951 Chevy truck to freedom across the 90-mile Florida Straits. Just six months after the regime's heavy-handed crackdown on dissenters,

Paya delivered more than 14,000 signatures to the National Assembly demanding a referendum for sweeping political changes.

**Political Rights and Civil Liberties:** Cubans cannot change their government through democratic means. Castro dominates the political system, having transformed the country into a one-party state with the Cuban Communist Party (PCC) controlling all governmental entities from the national to the local level. Communist structures were institutionalized by the 1976 constitution installed at the first congress of the PCC. The constitution provides for the National Assembly, which designates the Council of State. It is that body which in turn appoints the Council of Ministers in consultation with its president, who serves as head of state and chief of government. However, Castro is responsible for every appointment and controls every lever of power in Cuba in his various roles as president of the Council of Ministers, chairman of the Council of State, commander in chief of the Revolutionary Armed Forces (FAR), and first secretary of the PCC.

In October 2002, some eight million Cubans voted in tightly controlled municipal elections. On January 19, 2003, an election was held for the Cuban National Assembly, with just 609 candidates—all supported by the regime—vying for 609 seats. All political organizing outside the PCC is illegal. Political dissent, spoken or written, is a punishable offense, and those so punished frequently receive years of imprisonment for seemingly minor infractions.

The press in Cuba is the object of a targeted campaign of intimidation by the government. Independent journalists, particularly those associated with five small news agencies established outside state control, have been subjected to continued repression, including jail terms at hard labor and assaults by state security agents while in prison. Foreign news agencies must hire local reporters only through government offices, which limits employment opportunities for independent journalists. Twenty-eight journalists were among those arrested in April 2003.

In 1991, Roman Catholics and other believers were granted permission to join the Communist Party, and the constitutional reference to official atheism was dropped the following year. However, in October 2002, the U.S. State Department issued a report saying that Cuba was one of six countries that engaged in widespread repression of religion. The report said that security agents frequently spy on worshippers, the government continues to block construction of new churches, the number of new foreign priests is limited, and most new denominations are refused recognition. In a positive development, the regime now tolerates the Baha'i faith.

Cuban state security forces raided 22 independent libraries and sent 10 librarians to jail with terms of up to 26 years.

In Cuba, the executive branch controls the judiciary. The 1976 constitution concentrates power in the hands of one individual—Castro, president of the Council of State. In practice, the council serves as a de facto judiciary and controls both the courts and the judicial process as a whole. In 1999, the Cuban government showed some willingness to enhance anti-narcotics cooperation with the United States.

There are some 320 prisoners of conscience in Cuba, most held in cells with common criminals and many convicted on vague charges such as "disseminating enemy propaganda" or "dangerousness." Members of groups that exist apart from the state are labeled "counterrevolutionary criminals" and are subject to systematic repression, including arrest, beating while in custody, confiscation, and intimidation by uniformed or plainclothes state security agents. Of the 75 dissidents—considered by Amnesty International to be "prisoners of conscience"—who faced charges in April, not a single one was acquitted.

Since 1991, the United Nations has voted annually to assign a special investigator on human rights to Cuba, but the Cuban government has refused to cooperate. Cuba also does not allow the International Red Cross and other humanitarian organizations access to its prisons.

Freedom of movement and the right to choose one's residence, education, and job are severely restricted. Attempting to leave the island without permission is a punishable offense. In the post-Soviet era, the rights of Cubans to own private property and to participate in joint ventures with foreigners have been recognized by law. Non-Cuban businesses have also been allowed. In practice, there are few rights for those who do not belong to the PCC. Party membership is still required for good jobs, serviceable housing, and real access to social services, including medical care and educational opportunities.

About 40 percent of all women work, and they are well represented in most professions. However, violence against women is a problem, as is child prostitution.

# Cyprus (Greek)

**Population:** 900,000
**GNI/capita:** $12,320
**Life Expectancy:** 77
**Religious Groups:** Greek Orthodox (78 percent), Muslim (18 percent), other (4 percent)
**Ethnic Groups:** Greek (85 percent), Turkish (12 percent), other (3 percent)
**Capital:** Nicosia

**Political Rights:** 1
**Civil Liberties:** 1
**Status:** Free

*See also Turkey, Cyprus, in the Related and Disputed Territories section.*

**Ten-Year Ratings Timeline (Political Rights, Civil Liberties, Status)**

| 1994 | 1995 | 1996 | 1997 | 1998 | 1999 | 2000 | 2001 | 2002 | 2003 |
|------|------|------|------|------|------|------|------|------|------|
| 1,1F | 1,1F | 1,1F | 1,1F | 1,1F | 1,1F | 1,1F | 1,1F | 1,1F | 1,1F |

**Overview:** Tension and confidence mounted in early 2003, as it appeared that the two sides of divided Cyprus might reach an agreement on reuniting the island. However, no agreement was reached by the deadline of March 2003 set by the United Nations and Secretary-General Kofi Annan, who has worked hard to bring about a resolution. Though the failure of talks was widely blamed on the intransigence of Rauf Denktash, the long-time Turkish Cypriot leader, an election in Greek Cyprus shortly before the deadline may have contributed as well. In February, Tassos Papadapoulous was elected in place of Glafcos Clerides, the incumbent; Clerides was seen as conceding too much to the Turkish Cypriots in negotiations, and Papadapoulous is expected to take a tougher line in the future. Despite the failure of the peace plan to date,

Greek Cypriots got good news in April 2003, when the treaty enlarging the European Union (EU) by 10 countries was signed. Greek Cyprus will join without the northern part of the island.

Annexed by Britain in 1914, Cyprus gained independence in 1960 after a 10-year guerrilla campaign by partisans demanding union with Greece. In July 1974, Greek Cypriot National Guard members, backed by the military junta in power in Greece, staged an unsuccessful coup aimed at unification. Five days later, Turkey invaded northern Cyprus, seized control of 37 percent of the island, and expelled 200,000 Greeks from the north. Currently, the entire Turkish Cypriot community resides in the north, and property claims arising from the division and population exchange remain key sticking points in the reunification negotiations.

A buffer zone, called the "Green Line," has divided Cyprus since 1974. The capital, Nicosia, is similarly divided. The division of Cyprus has been a major point of contention in the long-standing rivalry between Greece and Turkey in the Aegean. Tensions and intermittent violence between the two populations have plagued the island since independence. UN resolutions stipulate that Cyprus is a single country in which the northern third is illegally occupied. In 1982, Turkish-controlled Cyprus declared its independence, a move recognized only by Turkey.

The UN-sponsored negotiations on reuniting the island broke down in 2003 over a range of issues. On the Greek side, President Clerides was seen as having conceded too much to his Turkish counterpart, Rauf Denktash, especially on the right of Greek Cypriots to return to land lost after the Turkish invasion. (They also note that Turkish Cypriots control 37 percent of the island's land, but are less than 20 percent of its population.) Denktash, on his side, insisted that the plan did not offer Turkish Cypriots strong enough guarantees of equal rights in a united Cyprus.

Shortly before the collapse of the talks, Papadapoulous was elected president in February with 51.5 percent of the vote. He is believed to have won because his predecessor had offered too much to the Turkish Cypriots. His Democratic Party (Diko) has its roots in the so-called rejectionist movement, which once took an uncompromising line on negotiations with the Turkish Cypriots, but which now backs the idea of eventual federation along the general lines of the UN plan. Papadapoulous is backed in parliament by the Progressive Party of the Working People (Akel), a self-described Communist, but essentially Social-Democratic, party.

Though most EU members did not want to accept only part of Cyprus as a member, the EU reluctantly did so after the failure of the talks. Greece had threatened to veto the entire enlargement process, involving nine other countries, if Greek Cyprus was not included. Preparation for EU membership will mean, among other things, implementing liberalizing measures in the economy, which has a large dose of state ownership and intervention, to bring it into line with EU norms.

In April, shortly after the Greek Cypriot government signed the EU accession treaty, the Turkish Cypriot authorities loosened border crossings with the south, in a move greeted with enthusiasm on both sides. This came after some pressure not only from Turkish Cypriots, who strongly back negotiations with their Greek Cypriot neighbors, but from Turkey itself. The new government of Turkey, elected in November 2002, is less willing than past governments to back the Turkish Cypriot hard line on negotiations, because Turkey's own chances of getting into the EU hinge on, among other things, a resolution of the island's division.

**Political Rights and Civil Liberties:** Greek Cypriots can change their government democratically. Suffrage is universal and compulsory, and elections are free and fair. The 1960 constitution established an ethnically representative system designed to protect the interests of both Greek and Turkish Cypriots, and from the Greek Cypriot point of view the constitution still applies to the entire island. There is a clear separation of powers between the executive and legislature. Ministers may not be members of parliament, which has 80 seats, 24 of which are left vacant for Turkish Cypriots.

Freedom of speech is respected, and a vibrant independent press frequently criticizes authorities. Several private television and radio stations in the Greek Cypriot community compete effectively with government-controlled stations.

Freedom of religion is provided for by the constitution and is protected in practice. Around 99 percent of the inhabitants of Greek-controlled Cyprus are Greek Orthodox Christians. An agreement with northern authorities dating from 1975 provides for freedom of worship for both communities in both parts of the island. The government does not restrict academic freedom.

Nongovernmental organizations, including human rights groups, operate without government interference. Workers have the right to strike and to form trade unions without authorization. More than 70 percent of the workforce belongs to independent trade unions.

The independent judiciary operates according to the British tradition, upholding the presumption of innocence and the right to due process. Trial before a judge is standard, although requests for trial by jury are regularly granted. Cyprus is a member of the Council of Europe, and its citizens have recourse to the European Court of Human Rights. In January 2003, a report issued by the Council of Europe (based on a visit to prisons in 2000) expressed concern about ill-treatment of prisoners, including beating, electric shocks, and threats, prompting promises of corrective legislation from the government.

According to the Ministry of the Interior, around 1,200 Turkish Cypriots live in Greek-controlled Cyprus. The 1975 agreement between the two sides governs treatment of minorities. In practice, Turkish Cypriots in the south have reported difficulty obtaining identity cards and other documents, and complained of surveillance by the police.

Women in Cyprus have levels of legal protection equivalent to other European countries. Women hold 6 seats in parliament.

# Czech Republic

**Population:** 10,200,000    **Political Rights:** 1
**GNI/capita:** $5,310    **Civil Liberties:** 2
**Life Expectancy:** 75    **Status:** Free
**Religious Groups:** Roman Catholic (39.2 percent),
Protestant (4.6 percent), other (57.2 percent)
**Ethnic Groups:** Czech (81.2 percent), Moravian (13.2 percent),
Slovak (3.1 percent), other (2.5 other)
**Capital:** Prague

**Ten-Year Ratings Timeline (Political Rights, Civil Liberties, Status)**

| 1994 | 1995 | 1996 | 1997 | 1998 | 1999 | 2000 | 2001 | 2002 | 2003 |
|------|------|------|------|------|------|------|------|------|------|
| 1,2F | 1,2F | 1,2F | 1,2F | 1,2F | 1,2F | 1,2F | 1,2F | 1,2F | 1,2F |

**Overview:**

The year 2003 witnessed Vaclav Havel's passage from the Czech political scene after a decade of service as that country's president. Havel was succeeded in the February presidential poll by his political nemesis, Vaclav Klaus, who, along with Havel, has been one of the Czech Republic's two key political figures since the country's post-Soviet independence. With voters overwhelmingly supporting European Union (EU) membership in a June 2003 national referendum, the country is expected to formally join the EU in May 2004.

In December 1989, an anti-Communist opposition led by dissident Havel and the Civic Forum brought down the Czechoslovak government. The country's first post-Communist elections were held in 1990. In 1992, a new constitution and Charter of Fundamental Rights and Freedoms were adopted, and the country began an ambitious program of political and economic reform under Finance Minister Klaus. A leading figure in the ruling center-right Civic Democratic Party (ODS), Klaus became prime minister the same year. In 1993, the state dissolved into the Czech and Slovak Republics and Havel became president of the new Czech Republic. In 1997, Klaus resigned amid allegations of corruption in the ODS.

Close parliamentary elections in 1998 brought about Czech Social Democratic Party (CSSD) control of the government, although ODS managed to negotiate control of key government positions. This so-called opposition agreement between CSSD and ODS drained meaningful political competition and brought about several years of political gridlock. The last parliamentary election to the Chamber of Deputies (lower house) was held in June 2002, and a by-election to the Senate (upper house) took place in November 2002. The CSSD secured the most votes and the party's chairman, Vlad Spidla, became the new prime minister.

In the February 2003 presidential poll, Klaus was elected on the third round of voting following two inconclusive ballots. Klaus obtained 142 votes, one more than the 141 needed from the 281-member joint parliamentary session. In March, Prime Minister Spidla's cabinet asked the Chamber of Deputies for a vote of confidence, which it received by holding the votes of deputies from the governing coalition. The ruling three-party, CSSD-led coalition government has the support of the thinnest possible legislative majority, 101 of the 200 seats. The governing coalition's tenuous hold on power was underscored when in July 2003 MP Josef Hojdar left the CSSD's parliamentary faction in protest of the government's proposed fiscal measures (though he did not leave the CSSD itself).

Having joined NATO in 1999, the Czech Republic moved closer in 2003 to achieving the second of its key strategic objectives, membership in the EU. With more than three-quarters of the vote cast in favor of membership in a June 2003 national referendum, the Czech Republic is expected to formally join the EU in May 2004. As Czechs are now exchanging the "post-Soviet" label in favor of a "pre-EU" one, political parties are preparing for their first ever European Parliament elections in June 2004, following formal accession into the EU. The Czech Republic will be allotted 24 seats in the European Parliament.

Although significant progress has been made in the Czech Republic toward establishing the mechanisms and institutions of a full market economy, the economic sector requires further reform. A substantial part of state-owned property was privatized during the early to middle 1990s on the basis of a "voucher" program, under which Czech citizens were permitted to buy vouchers entitling them to bid for shares in selected companies. Power stations, oil and gas networks, banks, and the social and pension insurance sectors were among the strategic holdings exempt from the privatization program. Greater strides were made after 1999, when the government initiated an effort to revitalize Czech industry that sought to prepare public enterprises for privatization through internal reform and debt restructuring. Prime Minister Spidla has set forth a package of fiscal reform measures with a goal of overhauling public finances and has threatened to resign if parliament does not approve this reform package.

**Political Rights and Civil Liberties:** Czech citizens can change their government democratically. Since shedding the Soviet yoke more than a decade ago, the Czech Republic has had a sound record of free and fair elections. Voters elect members of the Senate and the Chamber of Deputies, which comprise the National Assembly. The Chamber of Deputies (lower house), has 200 members who are elected for four years, and the Senate (upper house) has 81 members, elected for six years with one third of the senators being replaced every two years. The president, elected by the National Assembly for a five-year term (with a maximum of two subsequent terms), appoints judges, the prime minister, and other cabinet members.

The Czech Republic continues to confront some difficult remnants of the Soviet legacy, including significant corruption that affects many sectors of Czech society. In the 2003 Transparency International Corruption Perceptions Index, the Czech Republic was ranked 54 out of 133 countries.

Freedom of expression is honored in the Czech Republic, although the Charter of Fundamental Rights and Freedoms prohibits threats against individual rights, state and public security, public health, and morality. Libel can be prosecuted as a criminal offense. The country's print and electronic media are largely in private hands. In 2000, the Law on Free Access to Information took effect, and the National Assembly amended broadcasting laws to meet EU standards. In 2001, the assembly passed an important bill designed to limit political influence over Czech Television (CT), the state broadcaster. Passage of the legislation helped end a standoff at CT between journalists and management. Under this law, nongovernmental groups, rather than politicians, make nominations for membership to CT's governing council, the body that controls the selection of CT's director. In July 2003, a Czech court convicted the former secretary general of the Foreign Ministry, Karel Srba, of conspiring to murder an investigative reporter for the Czech daily newspaper *Mlada Fronta Dnes.*

The government generally respects freedom of religion. However, in 2001, President Vaclav Havel vetoed a law on churches that he believed would limit the ability of religious groups to engage in charitable activities. When the Chamber of Deputies overrode the veto in mid-December, Cardinal Miloslav Vlk suggested that the Czech Catholic Church might challenge the law before the constitutional court. Academic freedom is widely respected in the Czech Republic.

Czech citizens may assemble peacefully, form associations, and petition the government. Trade unions and professional associations are free. Judges, prosecutors, and members of the armed forces and police may not strike. In 2003, the government's proposed fiscal reform measures generated considerable opposition from the country's trade unions, including a major one-day strike in September by the teacher's union, in which more than 70,000 teachers reportedly took part.

The Czech Republic's independent judiciary consists of a supreme court, a supreme administrative court, and high, regional, and district courts. There is also a constitutional court. In December 2001, President Havel signed a bill on judicial reform but suggested he might challenge aspects of the law, which he expected to "more widely and consistently separate judicial and executive power."

Property ownership, choice of residence, and fair wages are legally protected. Citizens generally enjoy all of these rights.

The Charter of Fundamental Rights and Freedoms gives minorities the right to help resolve matters pertaining to their group. A 1999 law restored citizenship to many residents, including Roma, who continue to experience discrimination. In 2001, the National Assembly approved legislation for the protection of ethnic minority rights. The law's provisions include the creation of a governmental minority council.

Gender discrimination is legally prohibited. Sexual harassment in the workplace appears to be fairly common. In May, the government amended a resolution setting priorities and procedures for enforcing gender equality in the workplace.

# Denmark

**Population:** 5,400,000    **Political Rights:** 1
**GNI/capita:** $30,600    **Civil Liberties:** 1
**Life Expectancy:** 77    **Status:** Free
**Religious Groups:** Evangelical Lutheran (95 percent),
Muslim (2 percent), other (3 percent)
**Ethnic Groups:** Scandinavian, Inuit, Faroese, German,
Turkish, Iranian, Somali
**Capital:** Copenhagen

**Ten-Year Ratings Timeline (Political Rights, Civil Liberties, Status)**

| 1994 | 1995 | 1996 | 1997 | 1998 | 1999 | 2000 | 2001 | 2002 | 2003 |
|------|------|------|------|------|------|------|------|------|------|
| 1,1F | 1,1F | 1,1F | 1,1F | 1,1F | 1,1F | 1,1F | 1,1F | 1,1F | 1,1F |

**Overview:**

With the drafting of a new EU constitution in 2003, Denmark had to rethink its often troubled relationship with the European Union. Danes had to weigh their skepticism of the EU against the isolation resulting from opting out of its provisions. On the domestic front, the most pressing issue was Denmark's strict immigration laws, which continued to create controversy.

Denmark has been a monarchy since the fourteenth century, but the monarch's power became ceremonial with the first democratic constitution, written in 1849. Denmark was occupied by Germany during World War II, but its sizable resistance movement earned it recognition as part of the Allied powers. In 1949, Denmark abandoned its traditional neutrality and joined NATO, and in 1973, it joined the European Economic Community, forerunner to the European Union. The current Danish constitution, which established a single-chamber parliament, was adopted in 1953.

After World War II, Denmark's politics were dominated by the Social Democrats. However, in the November 2001 elections, immigration became the main issue, and the results brought to power a right-of-center government. The ruling coalition of Prime Minister Anders Fogh Rasmussen's Liberal Party and the Conservative People's Party, which together hold 40 percent of the seats, is supported by the populist Danish People's Party (DPP). The DPP is in favor of withdrawing from the EU and reducing the number of immigrants in Denmark. Although it does not have mainstream Danish support, it does reflect more widespread fears of a threat to the Danish welfare system. Since the election, Denmark has passed a series of stricter immigration and asylum laws.

Denmark has always had a conflicted relationship to the European Union. When the Treaty of Maastricht was written in 1992, extending the EU's competence into justice, foreign, and monetary policy, Denmark's population rejected the treaty in a referendum. Since then, Denmark has opted out of participation in these areas. However, with the EU writing a new constitution in 2003, Denmark began to reconsider its position. Today, the population is slowly moving in favor of participating in EU defense and judicial cooperation, although support for the euro is less clear. The prime minister is committed to holding a referendum on both the new constitution and the "opt-outs" in 2004. Denmark has an active foreign policy that included troop deployments in 2003 to postwar Iraq and to Liberia.

**Political Rights and Civil Liberties:** Danes can change their government democratically. Denmark is a constitutional monarchy, in which Queen Margrethe II has mostly ceremonial duties. The 179 representatives are elected to the unicameral parliament, called the Folketing, at least once every four years in a system of modified proportional representation. Danish governments are most often minority administrations, governing with the aid of one or more supporting parties. Since 1909, no single party has held a majority of seats, helping create a tradition of interparty compromise.

The semiautonomous territories of Greenland and the Faeroes each have two representatives in the Folketing. They also have their own, elected, home rule governments that have power over almost all areas of governance. Greenland formed a new coalition government in September after the previous government had collapsed as a result of a budget scandal.

In the past, there was a concern that power no longer rested with elected representatives but with EU bureaucrats and pressure groups. However, the Power and Democracy Report, launched by the previous prime minister and released in October 2003, found that democracy in Denmark is robust and political institutions have adapted well to the global changes of the 1990s.

Levels of corruption in Denmark are very low. Transparency International rated Denmark second in the world in its 2003 Corruption Perceptions Index, as did the Institute for Public Relations in its 2003 International Index of Bribery for News Coverage.

Denmark's constitution guarantees freedom of expression. Danish media reflect a wide variety of political opinions and are frequently critical of the government. The state finances radio and television broadcasting, but state-owned television companies have independent editorial boards. Independent radio stations are permitted but tightly regulated.

Freedom of worship is guaranteed to all. However, the Evangelical Lutheran Church is subsidized by the government as the official state religion. The faith is taught in public schools, although students may withdraw from religious classes with parental consent. While 95 percent of the population belongs to the Church, membership and church attendance are on the decline, and Danes are widely disgruntled with the Church's basic teachings. In June, Pastor Thorkild Grosboell of Taarbeck was suspended for publicly stating that he does not believe in God, but the suspension was lifted in July. Academic freedom is ensured for all.

The constitution provides for freedom of assembly and association, and workers are free to organize. Rather than being controlled by legislation, the Danish labor market is mainly regulated by agreements between employers' and employees' organizations. If they cannot agree, however, the Folketing will pass laws. Membership in trade unions is around 80 percent.

The judiciary is independent and citizens enjoy full due process rights. The court system consists of 100 local courts, two high courts, and the 15-member Supreme Court, with judges appointed by the queen on government recommendation. Torture is not defined as an offense in Danish law, and Denmark has thus been criticized, although there have not been reports of torture taking place. The Danish-based International Rehabilitation Center for Torture Victims was awarded the prestigious Conrad N. Hilton Humanitarian Award in September.

Discrimination is prohibited under Danish law. Although Denmark has not seen the kind of neo-Nazi movements that have emerged elsewhere in Scandinavia, human rights groups have noted an increase in hate speech in Denmark and in harassment of Muslims. The rise of the anti-immigrant Danish People's Party since its strong electoral showing in 2001 has sparked more public examination of the position in Denmark of citizens and residents of non-Danish descent. After Prime Minister Rasmussen complained in his 2003 New Year's speech of some Muslim imams preaching what he considered to be non-Danish values, the government agreed to form a committee to investigate continuing problems of integration of minorities in Denmark. In addition, members of Rasmussen's Liberal Party have called for a zero-tolerance policy on immigrant crime. More than half of all adults accused of a criminal act in Copenhagen were of foreign origin in 2002, even though immigrants account for just 17.6 percent of the city's population.

The Alien Act, which took effect in 2002, has continued a trend of tightening standards for granting asylum. It also decreased welfare for immigrants to well below the rate for most Danes, which has resulted in many families living below the poverty line. In September, the government agreed to relax restrictions on Danish citizens living in Denmark with their foreign-born spouses after considerable criticism from advocacy groups. Greenlanders are being actively discouraged from moving to Denmark through a new information campaign.

Danish law requires equal pay for equal work, but Danish men earn about 14 percent more than women in blue collar jobs and 20 percent more in professional positions, according to the Confederation of Danish Labor Unions and the Danish Employer Association. Part of the disparity is explained by differences in education level, experience, and work status, but the remainder is "inexplicable," the groups said when publishing their findings; this may be the result of discrimination or Denmark's sexually segregated job market. The number of women in management positions in county and local government rose in 2003.

# Djibouti

**Population:** 700,000
**GNI/capita:** $900
**Life Expectancy:** 43
**Religious Groups:** Muslim (94 percent), Christian (6 percent)
**Ethnic Groups:** Somali (60 percent), Afar (35 percent), other (5 percent)
**Capital:** Djibouti

**Political Rights:** 5*
**Civil Liberties:** 5
**Status:** Partly Free

**Ratings Change:** Djibouti's political rights rating declined from 4 to 5 due to a legislative election in which opposition parties were significantly disadvantaged by electoral rules and the use of government powers of incumbency.

**Ten-Year Ratings Timeline (Political Rights, Civil Liberties, Status)**

| 1994 | 1995 | 1996 | 1997 | 1998 | 1999 | 2000 | 2001 | 2002 | 2003 |
|------|------|------|------|------|------|------|------|------|------|
| 6,6NF | 5,6NF | 5,6NF | 5,6NF | 5,6NF | 4,6PF | 4,5PF | 4,5PF | 4,5PF | 5,5PF |

**Overview:**

Hopes that elections would further promote Djibouti's democratic opening suffered a setback as the January 2003 parliamentary poll resulted in a clean sweep for the ruling Presidential Majority Union (UMP) coalition. The result was due in part to the UMP's incumbency and dominance of the government administrative apparatus and disadvantageous electoral rules. The opposition Union for Democratic Alternance (UAD) subsequently alleged widespread voter fraud, but its case was rejected by the Constitutional Council.

Djibouti was known as the French Territory of the Afar and Issa before gaining independence from France in 1977. Djibouti's people are deeply divided along ethnic and clan lines, with the majority Issa (Somali) and minority Afar peoples holding most political power. In 1991, Afar rebels of the Front for the Restoration of Unity and Democracy (FRUD) launched a three-year guerrilla war against Issa domination. In 1994, the largest FRUD faction agreed to end its insurgency in exchange for inclusion in the government and electoral reforms. However, sporadic attacks continued by a radical wing of the group.

President Hassan Gouled controlled a one-party system until 1992, when a new constitution adopted by referendum authorized four political parties. In 1993, Gouled was declared the winner of a fourth six-year term in Djibouti's first contested presidential elections. Both the opposition and international observers considered the poll fraudulent. In the 1997 legislative elections, which were also considered unfair, the Popular Rally for Progress (RPP), in coalition with the legalized arm of the FRUD at the time, won all 65 National Assembly seats.

Gouled stepped down in 1999 after 22 years in power, opening the way for the country's first change in presidential leadership. The RPP's Ismael Omar Guelleh won the presidential poll that year with 74 percent of the vote, while Moussa Ahmed Idriss of the Unified Djiboutian Opposition (ODU) received 26 percent. Guelleh, who was Gouled's nephew and a former head of state security, had long been considered the de facto head of government and the president's heir apparent. For the first time since elections began in 1992, no group boycotted the vote, which was regarded as generally fair.

In 2001, the government followed up a peace agreement it had signed with the radical wing of the FRUD in 2000 with a more extensive accord. Like the previous agreement, it was aimed at putting an end to the ethnic Afar insurgency that began in 1991.

In the January 2003 parliamentary elections, a pro-government bloc of four parties under the umbrella UMP ran against the opposition UAD bloc of four parties. The ruling UMP captured all 65 seats despite the UAD receiving 37 percent of the votes in a low voter turnout of 48 percent. In addition, although the coalition won 62 percent of the vote, the election law stipulates that the majority victor in each of the country's five electoral constituencies (in this election, the UMP) wins all seats in that district. The Constitutional Council rejected UAD allegations of widespread voter fraud.

The polls came at a time of increasing U.S. interest in Djibouti, which is strategically located on the Red Sea. In 2003, some 2,000 U.S. Army and Special Forces troops were stationed in Djibouti in support of U.S. foreign policy objectives in the Middle East.

Approximately 2,700 French troops are among 8,000 French residents of Djibouti. French advisors and technicians have traditionally effectively run much of the country. Although this is slowly changing, President Guelleh favors retaining strong ties with France.

Djibouti has little industry and few natural resources, although its strategic position has long proved to be an important asset. Services provide most of the national income. Efforts to curb rampant corruption have met with little success.

**Political Rights and Civil Liberties:** The trappings of representative government and formal administration have had little relevance to the real distribution and exercise of power in Djibouti. Although international observers declared the 1999 presidential poll generally fair, the ruling party had the advantage of state resources to conduct its campaign. President Ismael Omar Guelleh announced in September 2002 that Djibouti would have a full multiparty system, as opposed to a four-party system. In the 2003 legislative election, opposition parties were significantly disadvantaged by electoral rules and the use of government powers of incumbency. The country's political opposition has suffered from significant divisions and had previously been unable to achieve any successes in elections that were controlled by the government.

Despite constitutional protection, freedom of speech is not guaranteed. The government owns the principal newspaper, *La Nation*, as well as Radiodiffusion-Television de Djibouti (RTD), which operates the national radio and TV. Journalists have to generally avoid sensitive issues covering human rights, the army, Front for the Restoration of Unity and Democracy (FRUD), relations with Ethiopia, and French financial aid. In July, the leader of an opposition party and a journalist were jailed on charges of libel. As noted by Amnesty International, the case reflected the weakness of the rule of law as it included arbitrary refusal of bail and a prison sentence for what normally would have been a civil case. Djibouti was also identified in 2003 by the press watchdog group Reporters Sans Frontieres as a country in which freedom of speech is significantly limited. Numerous journalists have been expelled or detained for publishing without government approval. There are also internal pressures on the media. Moreover, journalists are largely untrained and poorly paid. There is only limited Internet access.

Islam is the official state religion, but freedom of worship is respected, although the government discourages proselytizing. While freedom is generally respected, education choices are limited and Djibouti has no university.

Freedom of assembly and association are nominally protected under the constitution, but the government has demonstrated little tolerance for political protest. There are complaints of harassment of political opponents and union leaders. Local human rights groups do not operate freely. However, women's groups and other nongovernmental organizations operate without hindrance. Workers may join unions and strike, but the government routinely obstructs the free operation of unions.

The judiciary is not independent. Sharia (Islamic law) prevails in family matters. The former chief of police, General Yacin Yabel Galab, was sentenced to 15 years in prison in 2002 on charges related to an attempted coup in December 2000. Eleven other police, including eight senior officers, received sentences ranging from 3 to 10 years. Galab was chief of police from independence until his dismissal just prior to the coup attempt. Security forces arrest Djiboutians without proper authority, despite constitutional requirements that arrests may not occur without a decree presented by a judicial magistrate. Prison conditions are harsh, with reports of beatings, torture, and the rape of female inmates.

Despite equality under civil law, women suffer serious discrimination under customary practices in inheritance and other property matters, in divorce, and regarding the right to travel. Female genital mutilation is widespread, and legislation forbidding mutilation of young girls is not enforced. Women's groups are making efforts to curb the practice. A record number of seven women were elected to parliament in January 2003.

# Dominica

**Population:** 100,000    **Political Rights:** 1
**GNI/capita:** $3,180    **Civil Liberties:** 1
**Life Expectancy:** 73    **Status:** Free
**Religious Groups:** Roman Catholic (77 percent),
Protestant (15 percent), other (8 percent)
**Ethnic Groups:** Mostly black and mulatto, Carib Amerindian
**Capital:** Roseau

**Ten-Year Ratings Timeline (Political Rights, Civil Liberties, Status)**

| 1994 | 1995 | 1996 | 1997 | 1998 | 1999 | 2000 | 2001 | 2002 | 2003 |
|------|------|------|------|------|------|------|------|------|------|
| 2,1F | 1,1F | 1,1F | 1,1F | 1,1F | 1,1F | 1,1F | 1,1F | 1,1F | 1,1F |

**Overview:**    The government of Prime Minister Pierre Charles, of the Dominica Labour Party (DLP), continued to experience difficulties in 2003. The party lost popular support as a result of the implementation of austerity measures and has only a slender majority in parliament.

Dominica has been internally self-governing since 1967 and an independent republic within the Commonwealth since 1978. The coalition of the DLP and the Dominica Freedom Party (DFP) came to power in the January 30, 2000, elections; 60,000 people registered to participate.

The current governing coalition, which enjoys a slim parliamentary majority, includes the DLP with 11 of 21 seats and the DFP with 1 seat. The opposition United Workers Party (UWP) holds 8 seats and there is 1 independent. The global economic downturn hurt the agriculturally based economy especially hard and contributed to the imposition of an unpopular program of stabilization and adjustment. The austerity measures have led to cabinet resignations and a reshuffling, civil service strikes, and popular protests.

Dominica's economy is primarily agricultural, though there have been efforts to build the infrastructure required to promote tourism and high technology investment. Because of the island's volcanic geology, rugged terrain, and few beaches, most tourist activity is limited to cruise ship visits. Destruction caused by hurricanes, at times devastating, has further strained the banana industry, which has also been affected by changing market forces, especially increasing competition. Unemployment continues to hover around 20 percent. A major escape valve is the continuing emigration of Dominicans to the United States and the francophone Caribbean.

Dominica's offshore business sector includes several thousand international companies, banks, and Internet gambling companies. Offshore banking interests continue to raise concerns about penetration by international organized crime, particularly Russian organizations. Despite the announcement in January 2000 that the practice will end, Dominica continues to raise money by selling passports and "economic citizenship." Foreign investors can purchase passports for $75,000 to $100,000 worth of investment.

**Political Rights and Civil Liberties:** Citizens of Dominica are able to change their government through free and fair elections. Dominica is headed by a prime minister and the House of Assembly, with 21 members elected to five-year terms. Nine senators are appointed—five by the prime minister and four by the opposition leader. The house elects the president for a five-year term. There are no restrictions on political, civic, or labor organizations. There are three major political parties and one minor one.

The press is free, and there is no censorship or government interference. There are four private newspapers and an equal number of political party journals. Though the main radio station is state-owned, there is also an independent radio station. Citizens have unimpeded access to cable television and regional radio broadcasts, as well as to the Internet.

Freedom of religion is recognized. While a majority of the population is Roman Catholic, some Protestant churches have been established. In the past, members of the small Rastafarian community charged that their religious rights were violated by a policy of cutting off the dreadlocks of prisoners, and that Rastafarian women are singled out for drug searches. Academic freedom is respected.

Advocacy groups are free to operate and include the Association of Disabled People, the Dominican National Council of Women, and a women's and children's self-help organization. Workers have the right to organize, strike, and bargain collectively. Though unions are independent of the government and laws prohibit anti-union discrimination by employers, less than 10 percent of the workforce is unionized.

There is an independent judiciary, and the rule of law is enhanced by the court's subordination to the inter-island Eastern Caribbean Supreme Court. However, the judicial system is understaffed, which has led to a large backlog of cases. The only prison on Dominica is overcrowded and has sanitation problems. In addition, minors are housed with adults. Prison visits by independent human rights monitors are permitted.

The Commonwealth of Dominica Police Force (CDPF) became responsible for security after the Dominica Defense Force (DDF) was disbanded in 1981. The DDF had been implicated in an attempted coup staged by supporters of former prime minister Patrick John, who was convicted in 1986 for his role and given a 12-year prison sentence. He was released by executive order in 1990, became active in the trade union movement, and lost as a DLP candidate in the 1995 election.

Occasional instances of excessive use of force by police are among the few human rights complaints heard. In 1997, the commissioner and deputy commissioner of police were forced to retire as a result of recommendations by a commission of inquiry that investigated allegations of mismanagement, corruption, and police brutality. Under new leadership, the police created the Internal Affairs Department late that year to investigate public complaints against the police and to provide officers with counseling. There were continuing allegations of corruption relating to document falsification. Narcotics traffickers use the country as a transshipment point.

There are 3,000 indigenous Carib Indians, many of whom live on a 3,783-acre reservation on the northeast coast created in 1903 and expanded in 1997. The reservation is governed by the 1978 Carib constitution.

There are no laws mandating equal pay for equal work for men and women in private sector jobs. Inheritance laws do not fully recognize women's rights. When a husband dies without a will, the wife cannot inherit their property, though she may continue to inhabit their home.

# Dominican Republic

**Population:** 8,700,000
**GNI/capita:** $2,230
**Life Expectancy:** 69
**Religious Groups:** Roman Catholic (95 percent),
other (5 percent)
**Ethnic Groups:** Mixed (73 percent), white (16 percent),
black (11 percent)
**Capital:** Santo Domingo

**Political Rights:** 3*
**Civil Liberties:** 2
**Status:** Free

**Ratings Change:** The Dominican Republic's political rights rating declined from 2 to 3 due to corruption scandals and a growing rejection of transparency by the government of President Hipolito Mejia

**Ten-Year Ratings Timeline (Political Rights, Civil Liberties, Status)**

| 1994 | 1995 | 1996 | 1997 | 1998 | 1999 | 2000 | 2001 | 2002 | 2003 |
|------|------|------|------|------|------|------|------|------|------|
| 4,3PF | 4,3PF | 3,3PF | 3,3PF | 2,3F | 2,3F | 2,2F | 2,2F | 2,2F | 3,2F |

**Overview:**

In May 2003, the largest bank scandal in the history of the Dominican Republic exploded onto the political landscape, as the powerful Banco Intercontinental collapsed amid accusations of fraud. The scandal was estimated to cost the Dominican Republic the equivalent of 60 to 80 percent of the national budget. The bank's collapse, together with President Hipolito Mejia's failure to boost the Dominican economy and correct its electricity crisis, dimmed his hopes for reelection in May 2004.

After achieving independence from Spain in 1821 and from Haiti in 1844, the Dominican Republic endured recurrent domestic conflict. The assassination of General Rafael Trujillo in 1961 ended 30 years of dictatorship, but a 1963 military coup led to civil war and U.S. intervention. In 1966, under a new constitution, civilian rule was restored with the election of the conservative Joaquin Balaguer.

In the May 16, 2000, presidential elections, Mejia, a former agriculture minister and a Revolutionary Democratic Party (PRD) outsider, struck a chord among those who felt left out of the economic prosperity, particularly the 20 percent who live below the poverty level. Mejia won 49.87 percent of the vote, compared with 24.9 percent for ruling party candidate Danilo Medina and 24.6 percent for Balaguer, who was running for his eighth term in office.

Following the May 2003 collapse of Banco Intercontinental, the government entered into urgent talks with the IMF for help with the crisis, which cost the national treasury at least $2.2 billion. Opposition to the proposed deal with the IMF and to increased prices for fuel and other basic necessities, as well as continued energy blackouts, led to months of protests in which at least 13 people were killed, frequently as the result of alleged use of excessive force by the police. Declining conditions on the island republic resulted in record numbers of Dominicans trying to enter the United States illegally through Puerto Rico. The scandal undercut Mejia's lobbying campaign to get the Dominican Republic included in the Free Trade Pact that the United States is negotiating with six Central American countries, and reduced his reelection hopes in May 2004.

**Political Rights and Civil Liberties:** Citizens of the Dominican Republic can change their government democratically. The constitution provides for a president and a congress elected for four-year terms. The bicameral National Congress consists of the 30-member Senate and, as a result of a recent census, a Chamber of Deputies that in 1998 went from 120 members to 149. At the end of 2001, the Dominican legislature approved constitutional changes allowing presidents to serve consecutive terms, as part of a package of electoral changes that also included reducing from 50 percent to 45 percent the minimum vote required to win presidential elections in the first round. The reforms also established direct election of the president, eliminating an electoral college system in which representative sectors chose the president on the basis of popular votes.

The media are mostly private. On May 15, 2003, in response to the collapse of the Banco Intercontinental, a court ordered the takeover of several media companies, whose main stockholders the government accused of major money-laundering fraud. Two newspapers, *Ultima Hora* and *El Financiero*, were ultimately shut down, and two others, plus four television channels, a cable television company, and more than 70 radio stations were placed under the control of the government. Subsequently, some of the media assets were used to publicize political activity of the ruling party, and radio programs of government opponents were suppressed.

Constitutional guarantees regarding religious and academic freedom are generally respected.

The government generally respects the right to organize political parties and civic groups. Civil society organizations in the Dominican Republic are some of the most well organized and effective in Latin America. Labor unions are well organized. Although legally permitted to strike, they are often subject to government crackdowns. On August 6, 2003, police raided a local trade union and opened fire on those inside, reportedly to prevent them from carrying out a protest later that day. Peasant unions are occasionally targeted by armed groups working for large landowners.

The judiciary, headed by the supreme court, is politicized and riddled with corruption, although significantly less so in recent years. The courts offer little recourse to those without money or influence, although reforms implemented of late show some promise in increasing citizen access to the courts. Extrajudicial killings by police remain a problem, although the government has begun to refer cases of military and police abuse to civilian courts, instead of to nontransparent police or military tribunals. Police salaries are low, and there is a high level of corruption throughout the country's law enforcement institutions. Prisons, in which 9 out of 10 inmates have not been convicted of a crime, suffer from official negligence, gross overcrowding, poor health and sanitary conditions, and routine violence that results in a significant number of deaths. Homosexual and transvestite detainees report frequent incidents of police brutality, including rape, while in detention.

A major transit country for South American drugs to the United States, the Dominican Republic serves local, Puerto Rican, and Colombian drug smugglers as both a command-and-control center and a transshipment point, mostly for cocaine. The government estimates that some 20 percent of the drugs entering the country remain there as "payment in kind." This phenomenon has contributed to increasing drug abuse and street crime.

The migration of Haitians, some legally but the vast majority without legal documents, to the Dominican Republic in search of economic opportunity has long been a source of tension between the two countries. Some of the illegal migration was assisted by the authorities, who profit from it.. Human rights groups report that children born of Haitian parents in the Dominican Republic, generally denied registration as citizens, frequently were among the thousands of people deported each year as illegal Haitians

Violence and discrimination against women is a serious problem, as are trafficking in women and girls, child prostitution, and child abuse. The Dominican Republic is primarily a source country for trafficked women between the ages of 18 and 25, and girls as young as 15, and an estimated 100,000 Dominican women work overseas as prostitutes. Only 25 representatives in the lower house of Congress and 2 senators are women.

# East Timor

**Population:** 800,000
**GNI/capita:** $390
**Life Expectancy:** 49
**Religious Groups:** Roman Catholic (90 percent),
Muslim (4 percent), Protestant (3 percent), other (3 percent)
**Ethnic Groups:** Austronesian (Malayo-Polynesian), Papuan,
small Chinese minority
**Capital:** Dili

**Political Rights:** 3
**Civil Liberties:** 3
**Status:** Partly Free

**Ten-Year Ratings Timeline (Political Rights, Civil Liberties, Status)**

| 1994 | 1995 | 1996 | 1997 | 1998 | 1999 | 2000 | 2001 | 2002 | 2003 |
|------|------|------|------|------|------|------|------|------|------|
| -- | -- | -- | -- | -- | 6,4PF | 6,3PF | 5,3PF | 3,3PF | 3,3PF |

**Overview:**
East Timor continued the arduous process of nation building in 2003 in a scarred land as it prepared for the end of a UN mandate that has helped maintain order and build democratic institutions from scratch. A series of armed attacks on civilians by suspected antigovernment militias early in the year raised questions about the tiny Southeast Asian country's ability to protect its citizens once international troops and police are fully withdrawn by May 2004.

The Portuguese became the first Europeans to land on Timor Island in the sixteenth century. They retreated to the eastern part of Timor in the late eighteenth century following years of fighting for control of the island with the Dutch. After Portugal abruptly abandoned its colony of East Timor in early 1975, two armed Timorese groups—the leftist Fretilin and the right-wing Timorese Democratic Union—fought for control of the territory. Indonesia invaded in December 1975 and formally annexed East Timor in 1976.

As Indonesian forces tightened their grip on the territory, they committed widespread abuses against the local population during counterinsurgency operations against Fretilin's armed wing, the East Timorese National Liberation Army (Falintil). By 1979, civil conflict and famine had killed up to 200,000 Timorese. For the next two decades, poorly equipped Falintil forces continued to wage a low-grade insurgency from the rugged interior.

East Timor's road to independence began with the 1998 downfall of Indonesia's iron-fisted President Suharto, who had rejected even autonomy for the territory. As support for independence mounted in 1999, local militias, armed by the Indonesian army, began attacking pro-independence activists and suspected supporters. Amid the violence, East Timorese voters overwhelmingly approved an August 1999 referendum on independence. In response, militia fighters and Indonesian forces killed more than 1,000 civilians, drove more than 250,000 others into Indonesia's West Timor, and destroyed up to 80 percent of East Timor's roads and buildings before being ousted in late September 1999 by an Australian-led multinational force. An interim UN administration helped rebuild roads, schools, and other infrastructure and set up a legislature and other basic institutions.

The Fretilin party won the most seats in the 2001 constituent assembly vote, which was marred by accusations by smaller parties, not fully substantiated, that Fretilin intimidated voters. In a controversial move, the constituent assembly inserted a clause in the constitution it drafted that automatically transformed the assembly into the nation's parliament upon independence for a full five-year term. That means that legislative elections are not due until 2007. Fretilin's leader, Mari Alkatiri, is prime minister.

President Jose Gusmao, a former resistance commander who had been captured and jailed by Indonesian authorities, took office after easily winning a five-year term in elections in April 2002. East Timor became fully independent in May, its citizens flush with hope but woefully short on economic resources. It is Southeast Asia's poorest country, with 85 to 90 percent of urban adults lacking jobs and small-scale coffee production virtually the only export industry.

Armed attacks in early 2003, in the western Ermera district near the Indonesian border and elsewhere killed at least five villagers. Yet even as security problems continue, the end of the UN mandate in May 2004 will mean a withdrawal of UN security forces that had totaled 3,372 troops and 387 civilian police in mid-2003. The human rights group Amnesty International expressed concern in July that East Timor's fledgling police force lacks the capacity, oversight, and legal and procedural guidelines to protect the public while respecting human rights. It cited in particular the December 2002 shooting by police of some 18 people, two fatally, during riots in the capital, Dili.

Foreign donors in 2002 pledged $440 million to East Timor through 2005. If fully disbursed, these funds should help the government stay afloat financially until it begins earning income under a 2002 deal with Australia that gives East Timor a share of revenues from Timor Sea oil and gas production. The revenues could total $6 billion over 20 years, according to conservative estimates. However, Foreign Minister Jose Ramos Horta, speaking to the Hong Kong-based *Far Eastern Economic Review* in January 2003, warned that the new nation might not yet have the institutions to properly handle large revenue flows.

**Political Rights and Civil Liberties:** East Timorese chose their leaders for the first time in presidential elections in 2002 and balloting for a constituent assembly the previous year. They continue to face the task of building viable democratic institutions in a land plagued by neglect and brutality during two centuries of Portuguese colonial rule and 24 years of Indonesian occupation. Opposition parties have complained that Fretilin has excluded their members from some supposedly nonpartisan government jobs.

The key source of local news and information is the state-run Radio East Timor, though several community and nongovernmental radio stations serve various parts of the half-island country. East Timor's few news publications freely criticize the government. Denied voices or roles under the Indonesian occupation, numerous nongovernmental groups are now providing social services and monitoring and promoting human rights.

East Timor's several trade unions are independent but inexperienced and poorly funded and have made little headway in organizing workers. With an estimated two-thirds to three-fourths of East Timorese dependent on subsistence agriculture, unions are likely to play limited roles for the foreseeable future.

Like other state institutions, East Timor's civil law judiciary is weak and inexperienced, having been built quickly from the ground up by UN administrators and East Timorese leaders. Besides lacking adequate resources, the courts are short on trained lawyers, prosecutors, and translators, who have to work in four languages—Indonesian, the local Tetum dialect, English, and Portuguese. Although its use raises questions about universal access to the judiciary, Portuguese is the primary language of the courts and was used to draft many laws, even though it is spoken by only a minority of East Timorese.

Many criminal suspects are held in pretrial detention without judicial review longer than legally permissible, some for periods longer than the maximum sentence for the crimes for which they were charged, according to the U.S. State Department's human rights report for 2002, released in March 2003. In the aftermath of the January militia attacks, security forces illegally detained 39 people, some for more than a week, according to Amnesty International.

Like other post-conflict societies, East Timor faced the vexing question of whether to deal with past abuses through trials or through some form of reconciliation. It chose trials, and a UN tribunal in Dili, staffed by local and international judges, has convicted and jailed more than 30 East Timorese for their roles in the 1999 violence. Overall, indictments have been handed down against more than 300 suspects, the majority for crimes against humanity. However, more than two-thirds remain in Indonesia, which refuses to extradite them.

Ethnic Malay Muslims and ethnic Chinese face occasional harassment, while many non-Portuguese speakers claim to be at a disadvantage in competing for political and civil service posts. While most returning refugees from Indonesian West Timor have reintegrated fairly easily, there have been isolated cases of local residents stoning, beating, and interrogating returnees suspected of militia links, with some returnees in past years subjected to forced labor.

East Timorese women face problems including domestic violence, the judiciary's relatively poor record of prosecuting suspected rapists, and traditional practices in some regions and villages preventing women from owning or inheriting property.

# ↑ Ecuador

**Population:** 12,600,000   **Political Rights:** 3
**GNI/capita:** $1,080   **Civil Liberties:** 3
**Life Expectancy:** 71   **Status:** Partly Free
**Religious Groups:** Roman Catholic (95 percent), other (5 percent)
**Ethnic Groups:** Mestizo (65 percent), Amerindian (25 percent), white (7 percent), black (3 percent)
**Capital:** Quito
**Trend Arrow:** Ecuador received an upward trend arrow due to a rise in the participation of the country's indigenous peoples in government.

**Ten-Year Ratings Timeline (Political Rights, Civil Liberties, Status)**

| 1994 | 1995 | 1996 | 1997 | 1998 | 1999 | 2000 | 2001 | 2002 | 2003 |
|------|------|------|------|------|------|------|------|------|------|
| 2,3F | 2,3F | 2,4PF | 3,3PF | 2,3F | 2,3F | 3,3PF | 3,3PF | 3,3PF | 3,3PF |

**Overview:**

Lucio Gutierrez, a former coup leader and retired army colonel who had never held political office, was sworn in as president in January 2003 after promising during a hard-fought campaign to eliminate the country's infamous corruption and alleviate its extraordinary rural poverty. Gutierrez was supported in his victory at the head of a leftist coalition in the chronically unstable country by the country's increasingly empowered Indian groups. Despite the unprecedented incorporation of indigenous peoples in Gutierrez's government, by year's end, the conflicting demands placed on Ecuador's still fragmented political system by his heterogeneous coalition and the need for economic reform resulted in the withdrawal of key political support by Indian and peasant communities.

Established in 1830 after achieving independence from Spain in 1822, the Republic of Ecuador has endured many interrupted presidencies and military governments. The last military regime gave way to civilian rule when a new constitution was approved by referendum in 1978.

Vice President Gustavo Noboa took over as president in January 2000 after demonstrators had forced his predecessor to step down. The protests by indigenous groups, reportedly manipulated by putschist senior army commanders, were joined by those of significant numbers of mid-level military officers led by Lucio Gutierrez. Despite the protestors' acclamation of a three-person "junta" that included Gutierrez, congress met in emergency session in Guayaquil to ratify Noboa, who did not belong to any political party, as the new constitutional president.

Gutierrez, a civil engineer who was inspired by another coup plotter, Venezuela's Hugo Chavez, won a surprise first-round victory in the October 20, 2002, presidential election, defeating two former presidents who stood as standard-bearers for Ecuador's traditional political parties. Gutierrez, who had campaigned on a platform of combating corruption and poverty, went on to best the banana magnate Alvaro Noboa, a populist, in the November 24 runoff. Gutierrez was sworn into office on January 15, 2003. His election constituted the first time that Ecuador's chief executive shared the humble background and dark-skinned complexion of the country's majority, and his government included the unprecedented incorporation of indigenous peoples.

After initiating a few reforms, such as an overhaul of the corrupt customs service and some tough fiscal policies, including increases in bus fares and in oil and electricity prices, the Gutierrez government quickly became mired in internal disputes. Dissent over the fiscal reforms as well as over government plans to encourage private investment in the oil industry and controversial labor reforms boiled over into the streets, as one-time Gutierrez supporters expressed their frustration that the cash-strapped government had not done more to fight poverty. Despite government successes in fighting inflation and making vast improvements in Ecuador's balance of payments situation, the decision by the powerful indigenous Pachakutik movement to withdraw support for Gutierrez, at one point calling him a "traitor," appeared to portend serious social tensions in the months and years ahead. In November, a scandal erupted over the alleged ties of Vice President Alfredo Palacio to a businessman detained on drug-trafficking charges who had contributed $30,000 to the Gutierrez-Palacio campaign.

**Political Rights and Civil Liberties:** Citizens can change their government through elections, and the 2002 elections were generally considered to be free and fair. The 1978 constitution provides for a president elected for four years, with a runoff between two front-runners if no candidate wins a majority in the first round. The 77-member unicameral congress (National Chamber of Deputies) is composed of 65 members elected on a provincial basis every two years and 12 elected nationally every four years. In 1998, the national Constituent Assembly decided to retain Ecuador's presidential system. It also mandated that in the year 2002, a presidential candidate would need to win 40 percent of valid votes in first-round balloting and exceed by 10 percent those received by the nearest rival in order to avoid a runoff.

Transparency International has ranked Ecuador as the second most corrupt country in Latin America, after Paraguay. A government report published in 2000 said that corruption costs Ecuador more than $2 billion a year. In July, former president Gustavo Noboa was given asylum in the Dominican Republic, becoming the latest in a long line of politicians, including other former presidents, who opted for exile rather than face corruption charges.

Constitutional guarantees regarding freedom of expression are generally observed. The media, mostly private, are outspoken. The government controls radio frequencies. In 2003, the situation of the press in Ecuador deteriorated, as the media faced attempts to effect a gag law as well as aggressive statements by Gutierrez, members of his government, and members of congress.

The constitution provides for freedom of religion, and the government generally respects this right in practice. The government does not require religious groups to be licensed or registered unless they form NGOs that engage in commercial activity. The government allows missionary activity and religious demonstrations by all religions. The government does not restrict academic freedom.

The right to organize political parties, civic groups, and unions is generally respected. Labor unions are well organized and have the right to strike, although the labor code limits public sector strikes. Ecuador has numerous human rights organizations, and despite occasional acts of intimidation, they report on arbitrary arrests and instances of police brutality and military misconduct.

The judiciary, generally undermined by corruption afflicting the entire political system, is headed by a supreme court that, until 1997, was appointed by the legislature and thus subject to political influence. In reforms approved by referendum in May 1997, power to appoint judges was turned over to the supreme court, with congress given a final chance to choose that 31-member body on the basis of recommendations made by a special selection commission. In a positive development, a new criminal justice procedural code that fundamentally changes Ecuador's legal system entered into force in July 2001. The new code empowers prosecutors to investigate and prosecute crimes, and alters the role of judges to that of neutral arbiter presiding over oral trials. In another positive development, in 2003, an Ecuadoran court initiated a case against ChevronTexaco, alleging that a subsidiary of the California-based multinational oil company polluted the rain forest with billions of gallons of waste from 1971 to 1992.

Torture and ill-treatment of detainees and prisoners remain widespread. However, police courts that are neither impartial nor independent continue to try members of security forces accused of human rights violations.

Ecuador is a transshipment point for cocaine passing from neighboring Colombia to the United States, as well as a money-laundering haven. Widespread corruption in Ecuador's customs service led the government to privatize it in May 1999. The dollarization of the Ecuadoran economy appears to have had the unintended effect of making the country more attractive for money laundering and other financial criminal activity.

A growing number of incursions from both Colombian guerrilla groups and their paramilitary enemies into Ecuadoran territory added to regional concern (including worries in Panama, Venezuela, Brazil, and Peru) about the extent to which the neighboring country's civil war would affect public safety and the survival of democratic institutions. Violent crime has undermined public faith in the police to maintain order.

Despite their growing political influence, indigenous people continue to suffer discrimination at many levels of society and are the frequent victims of abuse by military officers working in league with large landowners during disputes over land. In the Amazon region, indigenous groups have attempted to win a share of oil revenues and a voice in natural resource and development decisions. Although the government tends to consult indigenous communities on natural resource matters, their wishes are not always met.

After the 2002 elections, women held 17 of 100 seats in congress, the largest proportion in the country's history. Gutierrez initially named four female cabinet ministers, including the first female minister of foreign affairs. At year's end, there were two female cabinet ministers, following turnover in the cabinet. Violence against women, particularly in indigenous areas where victims are reluctant to speak out against other members of their community, is common.

# Egypt

**Population:** 72,100,000 **Political Rights:** 6
**GNI/capita:** $1,530 **Civil Liberties:** 6
**Life Expectancy:** 68 **Status:** Not Free
**Religious Groups:** Muslim [mostly Sunni] (94 percent),
other [including Coptic Christian] (6 percent)
**Ethnic Groups:** Eastern Hamitic stock [Egyptian, Bedouin,
Berber] (99 percent), other (1 percent)
**Capital:** Cairo

**Ten-Year Ratings Timeline (Political Rights, Civil Liberties, Status)**

| 1994 | 1995 | 1996 | 1997 | 1998 | 1999 | 2000 | 2001 | 2002 | 2003 |
|------|------|------|------|------|------|------|------|------|------|
| 6,6NF | 6,6NF | 6,6NF | 6,6NF | 6,6NF | 6,6NF | 6,5NF | 6,5NF | 6,6NF | 6,6NF |

**Overview:** In the face of mounting economic problems, the war in Iraq, and American calls for democratization in the Arab world, Egypt witnessed a growing chorus of demands for political change by academics, journalists, and political opposition leaders in 2003. Although the government cracked down on unauthorized demonstrations during the year, it introduced a number of limited reforms and tolerated more open public discussion of the country's political future.

Egypt formally gained independence from Great Britain in 1922 and acquired full sovereignty following the end of World War II. After leading a coup that overthrew the monarchy in 1954, Colonel Gamel Abdel Nasser established a repressive police state, which he ruled until his death in 1970. The constitution adopted in 1971 under his successor, Anwar al-Sadat, established a strong presidential political system with nominal guarantees for most political and civil rights that were not fully respected in practice.

Following the assassination of Sadat in 1981, Hosni Mubarak became president and declared a state of emergency, which he has since renewed every three years (most recently in February 2003). The ruling National Democratic Party (NDP) dominates the tightly controlled political system. In the early 1990s, Islamic fundamentalist groups launched a violent insurgency, prompting the government to jail thousands of suspected dissidents and crack down on political dissent. Although the armed infrastructure of Egyptian Islamist groups had been largely eradicated by 1998, the government continued to restrict political and civil liberties.

High levels of economic growth in the late 1990s temporarily alleviated the underlying socioeconomic problems, particularly poverty and high unemployment among college graduates, that appeared to fuel broader public support for Islamist militancy. However, the country has experienced an economic slowdown over the last three years. Since the September 11, 2001 attacks on the United States, foreign exchange earnings from tourism revenue, oil sales, Suez Canal receipts, and expatriate remittances have declined and foreign direct investment has fallen.

Egypt's economic problems became even more acute in 2003. In late January, the government abandoned its "managed peg" currency regime and adopted a floating exchange rate, causing the pound to depreciate substantially during the course of the year. This devaluation, along with a reduction of subsidies on basic commodities, sparked an estimated 10 to 20 percent increase in the cost of living. In September, the World Bank's country director in Egypt warned that the poverty rate may be increasing for the first time since the mid-1990s.

Economic reforms needed to attract foreign investment have progressed slowly because of fears that austerity measures will undermine political stability. In June, U.S. trade representative Robert Zoellick stated that Egypt had "a long way to go" before it became a serious candidate for a free trade agreement with the United States because of the government's failure to undertake reforms in areas such as intellectual property protection, customs regulations, money laundering, taxation, and privatization. High-profile corruption trials of former government officials and businessmen continued in 2003, but critics allege that the anticorruption campaign has spared leading politicians.

The government's stated position of neutrality in the conflict between Iraq and the U.S.-led coalition exacerbated public anger. In the weeks leading up to the coalition invasion of Iraq in March, small-scale rallies ostensibly organized to protest the war became venues for protesting the government's performance at home. The authorities reacted by deploying riot police to contain illegal demonstrations and arresting dozens of activists suspected of organizing them, while allowing a number of docile, officially sanctioned antiwar rallies. After an estimated 20,000 people gathered in Cairo on the first day of the war to demonstrate against the invasion, thousands of riot police were deployed to prevent a repeat, using water cannons, truncheons, and dogs to disperse demonstrators. Hundreds of people were injured and around 800 were detained, including two members of parliament. Several dozen people arrested during and after the rally were held without charge for weeks.

After the fall of Baghdad, the government initiated a series of limited reforms, such as the abolition of state security courts and hard-labor prison sentences; initiated a wide-ranging dialogue with legal opposition parties; and tolerated more open discussion of previously taboo topics. However, there were few signs that far-reaching political change is on the horizon.

**Political Rights and Civil Liberties:** Egyptians cannot change their government democratically. As a result of government restrictions on the licensing of political parties, state control over television and radio stations, and systemic irregularities in the electoral process, the 454-seat People's Assembly (Majlis al-Sha'b), or lower house of parliament, is perpetually dominated by the ruling National Democratic Party (NDP), as is the partially elected upper house, the Consultative Council (Majlis al-Shura), which functions only in an advisory capacity. There is no competitive process for the election of the president; the public is entitled only to confirm in a national referendum the candidate nominated by the People's Assembly for a six-year term. The assembly has limited influence on government policy, and the executive initiates almost all legislation. The president directly appoints the prime minister, the cabinet, and the governors of Egypt's 26 provinces.

Political opposition in Egypt remains weak and ineffective. A ban on religious parties prevents the Muslim Brotherhood and other mainstream Islamists from organizing politically, although they typically compete in elections as independents or members of secular parties. Political parties cannot be established without the approval of the Political Parties Committee (PPC), an NDP-controlled body affiliated with the Consultative Council. The PPC has approved the formation of only two new political parties in the last 21 years and routinely rejects applications. Most recently, in November, it denied an application by the Social Constitution Party.

Freedom of the press is limited. The government owns and operates all ground-broadcast television stations. Although three private satellite television stations have been established since 2001, their owners have ties to the government and their programming is subject to state influence. In October, Dream TV, owned by business mogul Ahmed Bahgat, canceled a program on well-known political thinker Muhammad Hassanein Heikal after government officials objected to its content. All radio stations are owned by the government, with the exception of two stations owned by a private company, Nile Radio Production, that were allowed to begin broadcasting in the summer of 2003. However, those two stations received licenses only on the condition that they restrict their programming to entertainment. Egypt's three leading daily newspapers are state controlled, and their editors are appointed by the president. The government encourages legal political parties to publish newspapers and exercises indirect control over them through its monopoly on printing and distribution, but heavily restricts licensing of nonpartisan newspapers. Strictly speaking, only foreign publications are subject to direct government censorship, but most privately owned publications, such as the English-language *Cairo Times*, have been forced to register abroad (usually in Cyprus) and are therefore subject to censorship.

Press freedom is further restricted by vaguely worded statutes in the Press Law, the Publications Law, the penal code, and libel laws. Direct criticism of the president, his family, or the military can result in the imprisonment of journalists and the closure of publications. Discussion of tensions between Muslims and Christians in Egypt and expression of views regarded as anti-Islamic are also proscribed. In June, two journalists convicted of slander in 1998 lost their appeal and began serving one-year prison sentences, but they were released three weeks later pending the outcome of a petition by the press syndicate. Later that month, the weekly newspaper of the Takaful party, *Al-Sadaa*, was suspended, apparently because of its harsh anti-American diatribes, although no reason was given. The government does not significantly restrict or monitor Internet use, but publication of material on the Internet has been prosecuted under the same statutes as regular press offenses. Academic freedom is generally respected in Egypt, though professors have been prosecuted for political and human rights advocacy outside of the classroom.

Islam is the state religion, and the government directly controls most mosques, appoints their preachers and other staff, and closely monitors the content of sermons. It is presently implementing a plan to establish control over thousands of small, unauthorized mosques (known as *zawaya*) located in residential buildings. Most Egyptians are Sunni Muslim, but Coptic Christians constitute less than 6 percent of the population, and there are small numbers of Jews, Shiite Muslims, and Baha'is. Although non-Muslims are generally able to worship freely, the government has seized church-owned property and frequently denies permission to build or repair churches. Muslim extremists have carried out several killings of Coptic villagers in recent years and frequently burn or vandalize Coptic homes, businesses, and churches.

Freedom of assembly and association is heavily restricted. Organizers of public demonstrations, rallies, and protests must receive advance approval from the Ministry of the Interior, which is rarely granted. Hundreds of people who attended illegal demonstrations during the year were arrested and detained by State Security Intelligence (SSI) personnel. A new law regulating nongovernmental organizations (NGOs) went into effect in 2003.The Law of Associations prohibits the establishment of associations "threatening national unity [or] violating public morals," prohibits NGOs from receiving foreign grants without the approval of the Ministry of Social Affairs (which generally blocks funding to human rights defenders and advocates of political reform), requires members of NGO governing boards to be approved by the ministry, and allows the ministry to dissolve NGOs without a judicial order. In June, two existing human rights groups were denied registration under the new law— the New Woman Research Center (NWRC) and the Land Center for Human Rights (LCHR). Although an administrative court subsequently overruled the ministry's decision to reject NWRC's application, it is not yet clear whether the ministry will respect this judgment. Some groups have avoided the new NGO restrictions by registering as law firms or civil companies.

In April 2003, the People's Assembly approved sweeping changes to Egypt's socialist-era labor laws. Under the previous laws, workers were prohibited from striking, but enjoyed virtually absolute job protection—an employee who had held his job for over a year could not be legally terminated unless he committed a "grave" breach of his contract obligations. In practice, however, these laws were not enforced outside of the public sector. Private business owners, with the collusion of government regulators, circumvented the rules by not providing their workers with employment contracts or making them sign undated letters of resignation before being hired. According to one study, 82 percent of the jobs added between 1988 and 1998 in the private, nonagricultural sector in Egypt were not protected by a formal employment contract. The new Unified Labor Law allows employers to lay off workers, with compensation, and lifts the ban on strikes. However, the new law requires that strikes be approved by two-thirds of a union's members and limits the right to strike to "nonstrategic" industries. The government-backed Egyptian Trade Union Federation remains the only legal labor federation.

Egypt's regular judiciary is widely considered the most independent and impartial in the Arab world. The Supreme Judicial Council, a supervisory body of senior judges, nominates and assigns most judges. However, political and security cases are usually placed under the jurisdiction of exceptional courts that are controlled by the executive branch and deny defendants many constitutional protections. The State Security Courts, responsible for trying most defendants charged with political offenses, were abolished in June. However, the government also changed the penal code to grant prosecutors in regular cases most of the extraordinary powers that once resided with these courts. For example, prosecutors now have the authority of investigating judges and can detain individuals for up to six months without charge.

Two exceptional court systems remain in place. The Emergency State Security Courts, empowered to try defendants charged with violating decrees promulgated under the Emergency Law, issues verdicts that cannot be appealed and are subject to ratification by the president. Although judges are usually selected from the civilian judiciary, they are appointed directly by the president. Since 1992, civilians charged with terrorism and other security-related offenses have often been referred by the president to military courts. Since military judges are appointed by the executive branch to short, renewable, two-year terms, these tribunals lack independence. Verdicts by military courts are subject to review only by a body of military judges and the president. Moreover, evidence produced by the prosecution in cases before the military courts often consists of little more than the testimony of security officers and informers. Allegations of forced confessions by defendants are routine.

Although Egyptian officials said in mid-2003 that henceforth only terrorism and other security-related offenses will be tried in emergency courts, this pledge has not been upheld. Ashraf Ibrahim, a vocal opposition activist who helped expose police brutality during the March demonstrations, was arrested in April and detained for four months before being charged in the emergency courts with, among other things, "weakening the prestige of the state by disseminating false information."

The Emergency Law restricts many basic rights. Its provisions allow for the arrest and prolonged detention without charge of suspects deemed a threat to national security. In November 2002, the UN Committee against Torture concluded that there is "widespread evidence of torture and ill-treatment" of suspects by the SSI apparatus. According to local and international human rights organizations, at least three people died in 2003 as a result of suspected torture in police or SSI custody. The Emergency Law also empowers the government to wiretap telephones, intercept mail, and search persons and places without warrants. In mid-2003, parliament passed legislation weakening judicial oversight of wiretaps.

Local and international human rights organizations estimate that more than 10,000 people are currently detained without charge on suspicion of security or political offenses, and that several thousand who have been convicted are serving sentences on such charges. In September, the government released several hundred members of the radical Islamist group Gemaa al-Islamiyya, but scores of other suspected Islamist militants were arrested during the year.

Although the constitution provides for equality of the sexes, some aspects of the law and many traditional practices discriminate against women. Unmarried women under the age of 21 are not permitted to obtain passports without permission from their fathers. Muslim female heirs receive half the amount of a male heir's inheritance (Christians are not subject to provisions of Islamic law governing inheritance matters). Domestic violence is common, and there are no laws against marital rape. Job discrimination is evident even in the civil service. The law provides for equal access to education, but the adult literacy rate of women lags behind that of men (34 and 63 percent, respectively). Female genital mutilation is practiced in Egypt, despite government efforts to eradicate it. In January, the government appointed Egypt's first-ever female judge. In September, the ruling NDP initiated legislation that will allow women who marry foreigners to pass Egyptian citizenship on to their children.

# ↓ El Salvador

**Population:** 6,600,000    **Political Rights:** 2
**GNI/capita:** $2,040    **Civil Liberties:** 3
**Life Expectancy:** 70    **Status:** Free
**Religious Groups:** Roman Catholic (83 percent),
other (7 percent)
**Ethnic Groups:** Mestizo (90 percent), white (9 percent),
Amerindian (1 percent)
**Capital:** San Salvador
**Trend Arrow:** El Salvador received a downward trend arrow due to rising crime, especially from gangs, and continuing corruption, impunity, and judicial incompetence.

**Ten-Year Ratings Timeline (Political Rights, Civil Liberties, Status)**

| 1994 | 1995 | 1996 | 1997 | 1998 | 1999 | 2000 | 2001 | 2002 | 2003 |
|------|------|------|------|------|------|------|------|------|------|
| 3,3PF | 3,3PF | 3,3PF | 2,3F | 2,3F | 2,3F | 2,3F | 2,3F | 2,3F | 2,3F |

**Overview:**

In El Salvador's March 2003 parliamentary elections, the Frente Farabundo Marti (FMLN) secured the largest number of seats. Growing violent crime, including by youth street gangs, led to the implementation of a controversial government offensive targeting gang members.

The Republic of El Salvador was established in 1859, and more than a century of civil strife and military rule followed. The civil war that raged from 1979 to 1991, and left more than 80,000 dead and 500,000 displaced, ended with the Chapultepec accords.

In the 1999 presidential election, the Alianza Republicana Nacionalista (ARENA) party's candidate, Francisco Flores Perez, was chosen with 52 percent of the votes, avoiding a second-round runoff. However, the election was marked by a low voter turnout of only 39 percent. Public opinion polls indicate that support for democracy as a preferred form of government has declined over the past decade.

The two earthquakes of 2002, the collapse of coffee prices, and the slowdown of the U.S. economy, where many of the country's exports go, have made governance in El Salvador a challenge a decade after the end of the civil war. High levels of crime, especially on the part of gangs (*maras*), corruption, and government incompetence have led to popular distrust of national political leaders. More than 70 percent of public officials are perceived to be corrupt.

In 2002, two former generals, Jose Guillermo Garcia and Carlos Eugenio Vides Casanova, were on trial in Florida for torture and extrajudicial killings. After a general amnesty was granted to the armed forces in 1993, legal action for human rights abuses committed during the civil war moved to the United States. A case against the generals, accusing them of bearing ultimate responsibility for the killings of three nuns and a lay worker and for covering up the role of senior officers, had been dismissed by a U.S. appeals court. Former U.S. ambassador Robert White, who served in El Salvador at the time of the murders, testified that he long believed that there was a cover-up of the killings by both the Salvadoran and the U.S. governments.

President Flores Perez canceled the 10-year anniversary celebrations of the end of the civil war, set for March 15, 2002, after a boycott was threatened by the FMLN, and he declared the Chapultepec accords finished.

In the March 16, 2003 parliamentary elections the FMLN won 31 seats, the largest number, in the 84-seat Legislative Assembly. ARENA lost 2 seats, down to 27. The Partido de Conciliacion Nacional (PCN) gained 2 seats, up to 16, and moved quickly to establish an alliance with the FMLN to pass legislation. The run-up to the 2004 presidential elections has exposed the polarized relations between the political parties. Schafik Handal, of the FMLN's orthodox faction, has announced his intention to run for the presidency, but he is likely to be challenged by moderates in the party.

The government's support for the Unites States actions in Iraq, including the deployment of Salvadoran troops, received little public support and was perceived to be a result of pressure from Washington.

**Political Rights and Civil Liberties:** Citizens can change their government democratically. The 2003 legislative elections and the 1999 national elections were free and fair. The 1983 constitution, and subsequent reforms, provides for a president elected for a five-year term and the 84-member, unicameral National Assembly elected for three years. Four political parties are represented in the assembly, and five more are recognized.

The media are privately owned. There are five daily newspapers and 16 television stations. One government and five private television stations reach most of the country. Two cable television systems cover much of the capital, and other cable companies operate in major cities. All carry major local stations and a wide range of international programming. There are approximately 20 small cable-television companies across the country, serving limited local areas. There are some 150 licensed radio stations, and broadcasts from neighboring countries are available. A national defense bill approved by the assembly in August 2002 raised concerns that reporters would have to reveal their sources. The law that was passed includes a requirement that public officials provide information related to national defense. Books, magazines, films, and plays are not censored. There is free access to the Internet.

Although the country is overwhelmingly Roman Catholic, evangelical Protestantism has made substantial inroads, leading to friction. Academic freedom is respected.

There is full freedom of assembly and association. A full range of nongovernmental and voluntary organizations are active and represent diverse interests as well as vie for support. There are 133 unions, 16 federations, and 3 confederations representing labor. Public employees are not allowed to have unions; they are represented by professional and employee organizations that engage in collective bargaining.

The judicial system is ineffectual and corrupt, and a climate of impunity is pervasive, especially for those politically, economically, or institutionally well connected. Poor training and a lack of sustained disciplinary action for judges, as well as continued corruption, a lack of professionalism, and a slow system of processing cases, greatly undermine public confidence in the justice system. The Office of the Human Rights Ombudsman, who is elected by the National Assembly for a three-year term, was created by the 1992 peace accords with an amendment to the constitution defining its role. The office has been accused of corruption and is hampered by staffing problems, including a 17-month period when there was no ombudsman.

The peace accords led to a significant reduction in human rights violations. Nevertheless, political expression and civil liberties are still circumscribed by sporadic political violence, repressive police measures, a mounting crime wave, and right-wing death squads, including "social cleansing" vigilante groups. Random killings, kidnappings, and other crimes, particularly in rural areas, have reinforced the country's reputation as one of the most violent in Latin America. The crime wave has also been fed by the deportation of hundreds of Salvadorans with criminal records from the United States; gang violence is pronounced.

In response, the government introduced a controversial state security offensive against the extreme violence of youth street gangs in 2003. The law, which makes membership in a mara (gang) illegal, received strong public support. Over 7,000 young adults have been imprisoned, and the already overburdened legal system has been overwhelmed. Most of the detained have been released by judges who found insufficient cause to support charges of "illicit association." While the measure raises constitutional questions over rights and due process, the supreme court refused to rule on the law. Meanwhile, violent crime, especially armed assaults and kidnapping, has not been reduced.

El Salvador is one of the few Latin American countries to restrict formally military involvement in internal security, but the army occasionally joins the police in patrolling San Salvador and some rural districts in crackdowns on gang violence. The National Civilian Police, which incorporated some former FMLN guerrillas into its ranks, has been unable to curb the country's crime while protecting human rights. Complaints of police brutality and corruption are widespread; scores of police have been imprisoned on human rights charges. Prisons are overcrowded, conditions are shameful, and up to three-quarters of the prisoners are waiting to be charged and tried.

Research conducted in 2003 determined that there were three different indigenous groups in El Salvador: Nahua-Pipiles, Lencas, and Cacaoperas. The research project concluded that indigenous people have lost relationship with the land and that they are generally considered to be peasants. Urban populations do not believe the country to have an indigenous population. Nevertheless, some small nongovernmental organizations represent these peoples' interests.

There are no national laws regarding indigenous rights. According to research done during the year by the Native Land NGO, Jose Matias Delgado University, the Environmental Ministry, and National Geographic, the country has three different classes of indigenous people.

Violence against women and children is widespread and common. Human trafficking for prostitution is a serious problem, and up to 40 percent of victims are children. Child labor is a major problem.

# Equatorial Guinea

**Population:** 500,000   **Political Rights:** 7
**GNI/capita:** $700   **Civil Liberties:** 6
**Life Expectancy:** 54   **Status:** Not Free
**Religious Groups:** Roman Catholic (predominant)
**Ethnic Groups:** Bioko [primarily Bubi, some Fernandinos],
Rio Muni [primarily Fang], other
**Capital:** Malabo

**Ten-Year Ratings Timeline (Political Rights, Civil Liberties, Status)**

| 1994 | 1995 | 1996 | 1997 | 1998 | 1999 | 2000 | 2001 | 2002 | 2003 |
|------|------|------|------|------|------|------|------|------|------|
| 7,7NF | 7,7NF | 7,7NF | 7,7NF | 7,7NF | 7,7NF | 7,7NF | 6,6NF | 7,6NF | 7,6NF |

**Overview:**   Despite the release in 2003 of a number of political detainees, more than two dozen others reportedly remained in custody during the year. Meanwhile, three banned opposition parties announced that they were forming a government in exile in Spain. Revenues from Equatorial Guinea's large oil sector continued to produce few benefits for the lives of most of the country's citizens.

Equatorial Guinea achieved independence in 1968 following 190 years of Spanish rule. It has since been one of the world's most tightly closed and repressive societies. President Teodoro Obiang Nguema Mbasogo seized power in 1979 by deposing and murdering his uncle, Francisco Macias Nguema. Demands from donor countries for democratic reforms prompted Obiang to proclaim a new "era of pluralism" in January 1992. Political parties were legalized and multiparty elections announced, but in practice, Obiang and his clique wield all power.

Following controversial elections in December 2002 in which President Obiang won a third term with nearly 100 percent of the vote, the administration of Equatorial Guinea announced the formation of a "government of national unity" that brought members of eight opposition parties into the cabinet. All eight parties are considered close to the ruling Democratic Party of Equatorial Guinea (PDGE). The country's main opposition, the Convergence for Social Democracy party, declined to participate. Its leaders, who had boycotted the December elections, viewed the offer as a ploy to sideline the opposition's effectiveness. Despite these democratic overtures, real power remains in the hands of the president. Key cabinet positions are held by presidential relatives and loyalists.

The UN Human Rights Commission terminated the mandate of the special investigator for Equatorial Guinea in April 2002, saying it aimed instead to encourage the government to implement a national human rights action plan. No resolutions were tabled against the country in 2003, a course of action that drew complaints from international rights groups.

In August 2003, the government released 18 political detainees charged with trying to overthrow the government, but opposition leaders and human rights activists say more than 30 others remain in custody. The detentions resulted from a mass trial in May and June 2002, in which 68 people were convicted for plotting a coup against the government. The trial was condemned by human rights groups, and some defendants alleged that their statements were exacted under torture during incommunicado detention. Opposition figurehead Placido Miko Abogo of the Convergence for Social Democracy party was one of those given amnesty after he had served 11 months of a 14-year sentence. However, under the terms of the pardon, the government may re-arrest him at any time in the next 10 years.

Asserting the difficulty of operating within the country, in September 2003, three banned opposition parties—the Progress Party (PP), the Popular Action of Equatorial Guinea (APGE), and the Liberal Party (PL)—announced the formation of a government in exile in Spain.

Equatorial Guinea is the continent's third-largest oil producer and boasts one of the highest figures for per capita gross domestic product in Africa. The expanding oil sector has led to more jobs, but the lives of most people have yet to change. U.S. oil companies have invested at least $5 billion in Equatorial Guinea since the mid-1990s. In a move that highlights the government's lack of transparency, President Obiang has declared the disposition of the country's oil revenues a "state secret."

The government continued to work with the World Bank in 2003 after a decade of rocky relations. The U.S. plan to reopen its embassy in the capital, Malabo, following an eight-year hiatus underlines the region's growing importance to American oil security. The Bank of Central African States estimates growth in 2003 at an impressive 14 percent, almost entirely due to soaring oil revenues.

**Political Rights and Civil Liberties:** Equatorial Guinea's citizens are unable to change their government through peaceful, democratic means. Recent presidential and parliamentary elections have not been credible. The four main opposition challengers withdrew from the December 2002 poll, citing irregularities. The candidates said soldiers, police, and electoral officials were present at polling stations and were opening ballot envelopes after votes were cast. President Teodoro Obiang Nguema Mbasogo was declared the winner of his third 7-year term with 99.5 percent of the vote. The 1996 presidential election was neither free nor fair and was marred by official intimidation, a near total boycott by the political opposition, and very low voter turnout.

The 1999 parliamentary elections were also tainted by intimidation and fraud and were neither free nor fair. Many opposition candidates were arrested or confined to their villages prior to the polls. The ruling Democratic Party of Equatorial Guinea (PDGE) won 75 of 80 seats. In September 2003, the government announced that parliament would be expanded from 80 to 100 seats in elections scheduled for early 2004, although this is unlikely to significantly weaken the ruling party's dominance.

President Obiang wields broad decree-making powers and effectively bars public participation in the policy-making process. Most opposition parties are linked with the ruling party, and several remain officially banned. By moving the presidential election up two months and jailing political opponents, Obiang could be hoping to avoid controversy, such as the claims of fraud that followed previous elections.

Press freedom is constitutionally guaranteed, but the government restricts those rights in practice. Nearly all print and broadcast media are state run and tightly controlled. The 1992 press law authorizes government censorship of all publications. Mild criticism of infrastructure and public institutions is allowed, but nothing disparaging about the president or security forces is tolerated. Publications that irk the government are banned from the newsstands without explanation.

Foreign publications have become more widely available in recent years. The shortwave programs of Radio France Internationale and Radio Exterior (the international shortwave service from Spain) can be heard. A few small independent newspapers publish occasionally, but they exercise self-censorship, and all journalists must be registered. Journalists, political leaders, and association heads have complained of increasing difficulties in accessing the Internet. They said illegal wiretapping had increased and that the country's sole Internet service provider allegedly monitors e-mail traffic closely.

About 80 percent of the population is Roman Catholic. Freedom of individual religious practice is generally respected, although President Obiang has warned the clergy against interfering in political affairs. Monopoly political power by the president's Mongomo clan of the majority Fang ethnic group persists. Differences between the Fang and the Bubi are a major source of political tension that often has erupted into violence. Fang vigilante groups have been allowed to abuse Bubi citizens with impunity. The government does not restrict academic freedom.

Freedom of association and assembly is restricted. Authorization must be obtained for any gathering of 10 or more people for purposes the government deems political. There are no effective domestic human rights organizations in the country, and the few international nongovernmental organizations operating in Equatorial Guinea are prohibited from promoting or defending human rights. Dozens of opposition activists remain in prison.

Steps have been taken to reform the labor sector. The country's first labor union, the Small Farmers Syndicate, received legal recognition in 2000 and is independent. The government has ratified all International Labor Organization conventions. There are many legal steps required prior to collective bargaining.

The judiciary is not independent, and laws on search and seizure—as well as detention—are routinely ignored by security forces, which act with impunity. Civil cases rarely go to trial. A military tribunal handles cases tied to national security. Unlawful arrests remain commonplace. Prison conditions are extremely harsh, and abuse combined with poor medical care has led to several deaths.

Constitutional and legal protections of equality for women are largely ignored. Traditional practices discriminate against women, and few have educational opportunities or participate in the formal (business) economy or government. Violence against women is reportedly widespread. There is no children's rights policy.

# Eritrea

**Population:** 4,400,000
**GNI/capita:** $160
**Life Expectancy:** 54
**Religious Groups:** Muslim, Coptic Christian,
Roman Catholic, Protestant
**Ethnic Groups:** Tigrinya (50 percent), Tigre and
Kunama (40 percent), Afar (4 percent), Saho (3 percent),
other (3 percent)
**Capital:** Asmara

**Political Rights:** 7
**Civil Liberties:** 6
**Status:** Not Free

**Ten-Year Ratings Timeline (Political Rights, Civil Liberties, Status)**

| 1994 | 1995 | 1996 | 1997 | 1998 | 1999 | 2000 | 2001 | 2002 | 2003 |
|------|------|------|------|------|------|------|------|------|------|
| 6,5NF | 6,4PF | 6,4PF | 6,4PF | 6,4PF | 7,5NF | 7,5NF | 7,6NF | 7,6NF | 7,6NF |

**Overview:**
The government of President Isaias Afwerki continued its repressive policy of allowing no opposition or independent organizations in the political or civil sphere. A group of political dissidents and journalists imprisoned in 2001 remain in jail despite widespread international calls for their release. In 2003, the government also cracked down on various religious groups.

In 1950, after years of Italian occupation, Eritrea was incorporated into Ethiopia. Eritrea's independence struggle began in 1962 as a nationalist and Marxist guerrilla war against the Ethiopian government of Emperor Haile Selassie. The seizure of power in Ethiopia by a Marxist junta in 1974 removed the ideological basis of the conflict, and by the time Eritrea finally defeated Ethiopia's northern armies in 1991, the Eritrean People's Liberation Front (EPLF) had discarded Marxism. Internationally recognized independence was achieved in May 1993 after a referendum supervised by the United Nations produced a landslide vote for statehood.

War with Ethiopia broke out in 1998. In May 2000, an Ethiopian military offensive succeeded in making significant territorial gains. Eritrea signed a truce with Ethiopia in June 2000 and a peace treaty in December 2000. The agreement provided for a UN-led buffer force to be installed along the Eritrean side of the contested border and further negotiations to determine the final boundary line. The war had dominated the country's political and economic agenda and reflected deeper issues of nationalism and political mobilization by a government that has long used the threat of real or perceived enemies to generate popular support and unity.

In May 2001, a dissident group of 15 senior ruling-party members publicly criticized President Isaias and called for "the rule of law and for justice, through peaceful and legal ways and means." Eleven members of this group were arrested in September 2001, allegedly for treason. Three members who were out of the country at the time escaped arrest and one withdrew his support for the group. The small independent media sector was also shut down, and 18 journalists were imprisoned. An increasingly unpopular policy of obligatory national service—with no conscientious objector clause—for extended and open-ended periods of time has also heightened tension. Critics call it "forced labor."

In addition to the war with Ethiopia, since 1993, Eritrea has engaged in hostilities with Sudan and Yemen and has also had strained relations with Djibouti. Eritrea's proclivity to settle disputes by the force of arms and the continued tight government control over the country's political life have dashed hopes raised by President Isaias's membership in a group of "new African leaders," who promised more open governance and a break with Africa's recent tradition of autocratic rule.

Eritrea's political culture places priority on group interests over those of the individual. This view has been forged in part by years of struggle against outside occupiers and austere attachment to Marxist principles. Eritrea's aggressive foreign policy has contributed significantly to regional instability and to a sense of victimization among Eritreans, which in turn affords a rationale for continued strong central government control.

**Political Rights and Civil Liberties:** Eritreans have never had the opportunity to choose their leaders through open, democratic elections. Created in February 1994 as a successor to the EPLF, the Popular Front for Democracy and Justice (PFDJ) maintains a quasi-complete dominance over the country's political and economic life that is unlikely to change in the short- or medium-term future. No other political movements are permitted. Instead of moving toward creating a framework for a democratic political system, since the end of the war with Ethiopia, the PFDJ has taken significant steps backward. The 2001 crackdown against those calling for greater political pluralism has chilled the already tightly controlled political atmosphere. National elections scheduled for December 2001 have been postponed indefinitely.

In 1994, a 50-member Constitutional Commission was established. In 1997, a new constitution authorizing "conditional" political pluralism with provisions for a multiparty system was adopted. The constitution provides for the election of the president from among the members of the National Assembly by a vote of the majority of its members.

In 2000, the National Assembly determined that the first elections would be held in December 2001 and appointed a committee that issued draft regulations governing political parties. These draft regulations have not been enacted, and independent political parties authorized by the constitution do not exist. Polls were supposed to have been held in 1998, but they were postponed indefinitely following the outbreak of hostilities with Ethiopia.

The new constitution's guarantees of civil and political liberties remain unrealized, as pluralistic media and rights to political organization continue to be absent. Amnesty International estimates the number of arrests of government critics at more than 300. Prison monitors, such as the International Committee of the Red Cross, have been denied access to the detainees.

Government control over all broadcasting and pressures against the independent print media have constrained public debate. The 1996 Press Law allows only qualified freedom of expression, subject to the official interpretation of "the objective reality of Eritrea." There is limited access to the Internet.

In its September 2001 crackdown, the government banned all privately owned newspapers while claiming that a parliamentary committee would examine conditions under which they would be permitted to re-open. According to Amnesty International, the newspapers were accused of contravening the 1996 Press Law, but their alleged offenses were not specified. In the days following the clampdown, the police in Asmara arrested 10 leading journalists. They had protested in writing to the minister of information concerning the arrest of members of the Group of 15 and the closure of the newspapers. Other journalists were arrested in 2002. Some of them began a hunger strike in April 2002 and were then transferred from prison to unknown places of detention. This action and the absence of nongovernmental human rights organizations have had a dissuasive effect on the development of other civil society groups.

According to independent groups such as Human Rights Watch, persecution of certain religious groups is increasing. Evangelical church groups are banned. In early 2003, several hundred members of a dozen Christian minority churches were arrested without any reason given, tortured, and detained without charge for several weeks. A number of churches were closed down in May 2002 and ordered to register and submit details of individual members and any foreign funding, which most denied receiving. Dozens of Muslims have also been detained incommunicado since 1995 on suspicion of links with armed Islamist opposition groups.

Academic freedom is constrained, and high school students are required to spend their twelfth grade year at a high school based at a military camp in Sawa, a city in the far western part of the country near the Ethiopian border.

The government has maintained a hostile attitude toward civil society and has refused international assistance designed to support the development of pluralism in society. The government controls most elements of civil life, either directly or through affiliated organizations. The civil service, the military, the police, and other essential services have some restrictions on their freedom to form unions. In addition, groups of 20 or more persons seeking to form a union require special approval from the Ministry of Labor.

A judiciary was formed by decree in 1993 and has yet to adopt positions that are significantly at variance with government perspectives. A low level of training and resources limits the courts' efficiency. Constitutional guarantees are often ignored in cases relating to state security. Arbitrary arrest and detention are problems. The provision of speedy trials is limited by a lack of trained personnel, inadequate funding, and poor infrastructure. The use of a special court system limits due process.

Official government policy is supportive of free enterprise, and citizens generally have the freedom to choose their employment, establish private businesses, and function relatively free of government harassment. Until recently, at least, government officials have enjoyed a reputation for relative probity.

Women played important roles in the guerrilla movement, and the government has worked in favor of improving the status of women. In an effort to encourage broader participation by women in politics, the PFDJ named three women to the party's executive council and 12 women to the central committee in 1997. Women participated in the Constitutional Commission, filling almost half of the positions on the 50-person committee, and hold senior government positions, including the positions of minister of justice and minister of labor. Equal educational opportunity, equal pay for equal work, and penalties for domestic violence have been codified; yet traditional societal discrimination persists against women in the largely rural and agricultural country.

# Estonia

**Population:** 1,400,000
**GNI/capita:** $3,870
**Life Expectancy:** 71
**Religious Groups:** Evangelical Lutheran, Russian
Orthodox, Estonian Orthodox, other
**Ethnic Groups:** Estonian (65 percent), Russian (28 percent),
other (7 percent)
**Capital:** Tallinn

**Political Rights:** 1
**Civil Liberties:** 2
**Status:** Free

**Ten-Year Ratings Timeline (Political Rights, Civil Liberties, Status)**

| 1994 | 1995 | 1996 | 1997 | 1998 | 1999 | 2000 | 2001 | 2002 | 2003 |
|------|------|------|------|------|------|------|------|------|------|
| 3,2F | 2,2F | 1,2F | 1,2F | 1,2F | 1,2F | 1,2F | 1,2F | 1,2F | 1,2F |

**Overview:**

Estonia voted to join the European Union (EU) in a September 14, 2003 referendum, with more than two-thirds of voters affirming their support for EU accession. Countrywide parliamentary elections in early March produced a centrist government led by Res Publica, a newly formed political party. Despite his party's having received fewer votes than the Center Party, Res Publica chairman Juhan Parts outmaneuvered Center Party leader Edgar Savisaar to form a ruling coalition with the Reform Party and the People's Union. Estonia continued to prepare for its impending membership in NATO.

After gaining its independence from Russia in 1918, Estonia was occupied and annexed by the U.S.S.R. during World War II. Under Soviet rule, approximately one-tenth of Estonia's population was deported, executed, or forced to flee abroad. Subsequent Russian immigration substantially altered the country's ethnic composition, with ethnic Estonians constituting just over 61 percent of the population in 1989. Estonia regained its independence with the disintegration of the Soviet Union in 1991.

The last few months of 2001 witnessed several dramatic political developments, including the September victory of former Soviet Estonian leader Arnold Ruutel to the largely ceremonial post of president. Prime Minister Mart Laar announced in late December that he would resign in January 2002 because of growing infighting among the national ruling coalition members, particularly after the Reform Party's break with the same coalition partners in Tallinn's City Council. On January 8, 2002, Laar fulfilled his pledge to step down and was replaced on January 22 by Reform Party leader and former central bank president Siim Kallas. The new national government mirrored that of Tallinn's city government, with the Reform Party and Center Party agreeing to form the ruling coalition. Also in 2002, both the EU and NATO extended invitations to Estonia for membership in 2004, fulfilling two of Estonia's long-standing foreign policy goals.

In the March 2, 2003 parliamentary elections, both the Center Party and Res Publica garnered 28 seats in the 101-seat Riigikogu, with the Center Party receiving about 4,000 more votes. However, Res Publica chairman Parts was the first to form a viable coalition, and President Ruutel appointed Parts prime minister on April 10. Of the 101 members of parliament, 57 will be serving their first term, including 27 out of 28 Res Publica deputies.

On September 14, Estonia became the seventh Central and Eastern European country to hold and pass a referendum on joining the EU. Despite a formal recommendation by the opposition Center Party to reject EU accession, 66.9 percent of voters voted yes, and voter turnout exceeded 63 percent. The positive result was facilitated by a late starting, but successful, pro-EU campaign waged by the government, including an unequivocal endorsement from Estonia's popular president, Arnold Ruutel.

Estonia continued to prepare to join NATO, signing the accession protocols in March 2003 and drafting a defense plan reflective of the demands of NATO membership. Additionally, Estonia dispatched a mine-clearing unit to Afghanistan and a 32-member peacekeeping unit to serve in Baghdad, Iraq.

**Political Rights and Civil Liberties:** Estonians can change their government democratically. The March 2003 parliamentary elections were free and fair and were conducted in accordance with the comprehensive dictates of the recently implemented Riigikogu Election Act. The 1992 constitution established a 101-member unicameral legislature (Riigikogu) elected for four-year terms, with a prime minister serving as head of government and a president in the largely ceremonial role of head of state. After the first president was chosen by popular vote in 1992, subsequent presidential elections reverted to parliamentary ballot. However, the current governing parties have agreed to endorse direct presidential elections, with a referendum on the necessary constitutional changes to be held in 2004.

Estonia's citizenship law has been criticized for effectively disenfranchising many Russian speakers through an excessively difficult naturalization process. Many ethnic Russians arrived in Estonia during the Soviet era and are now regarded as immigrants who must apply for citizenship. Although noncitizens may not participate in national elections, they can vote (but not serve as candidates) in local elections. In November 2001, parliament approved the abolition of Estonian-language requirements for candidates to parliament and local councils. Also in late 2001, parliament adopted legislation making Estonian the official working language of both parliament and local councils, although the government may grant local councils the right to use another language under special circumstances.

Prime Minister Juhan Parts has made his very popular anticorruption election platform a priority of his administration. However, on September 19, Finance Minister Tonia Palts resigned amidst a Tax Board investigation into alleged tax evasion at Plambos Holdings, an entity owned by Palts. In July, Palts had suspended Aivar Soerd, head of the Tax Board, and ordered an independent inquiry into the workings of the board.

The government respects freedom of speech and the press. There are three national television stations, including two in private hands, which broadcast both Estonian- and Russian-language programs. Dozens of independent newspapers and radio stations offer diverse viewpoints, and Estonia is one of the most Internet-friendly countries in the world.

Religious freedom is respected in law and practice in this predominantly Lutheran country. Estonia has very few restrictions on academic freedom.

The constitution guarantees freedom of assembly, and the government respects this provision in practice. Political parties are allowed to organize freely, although only citizens may become members. Workers have the right to organize freely, to strike, and to bargain collectively, and the main trade unions operate independently of the state.

While the judiciary is independent and generally free from governmental interference, the quality of some court decisions and the heavy workloads of many judges continue to be areas of concern. A courts act adopted in June 2002 is intended to address issues associated with executive monitoring of the judiciary branch, though its effective implementation has yet to be fully recognized. There have been reports that some police officers physically or verbally abuse suspects. Despite ongoing improvements in the country's prison system, overcrowding, a lack of financial resources, and inadequately trained staff remain problems.

Of Estonia's population of 1.4 million, more than 1 million are Estonian citizens, of which some 120,000 have been naturalized since 1992. Approximately 170,000 people are noncitizens, the majority of whom are ethnic Russians. In May 2001, parliament adopted legislation setting out specific requirements of Estonian-language proficiency for private sector employees, such as pilots, rescue workers, and teachers; the law built upon a previous amendment to the language law passed in June 2000 requiring that Estonian be used in areas of the private sector deemed to be in the public interest, such as health or safety.

Although women enjoy the same legal rights as men, they continue to be underrepresented in senior-level business positions and the government. Parliament has yet to pass a gender equality act proposed in 2002.

# Ethiopia

**Population:** 70,700,000
**GNI/capita:** $100
**Life Expectancy:** 42
**Religious Groups:** Muslim (45-50 percent), Ethiopian Orthodox (35-40 percent), animist (12 percent), other
**Ethnic Groups:** Oromo (40 percent), Amhara and Tigrean (32 percent), Sidamo (9 percent), other (19 percent)
**Capital:** Addis Ababa

**Political Rights:** 5
**Civil Liberties:** 5
**Status:** Partly Free

**Ten-Year Ratings Timeline (Political Rights, Civil Liberties, Status)**

| 1994 | 1995 | 1996 | 1997 | 1998 | 1999 | 2000 | 2001 | 2002 | 2003 |
|------|------|------|------|------|------|------|------|------|------|
| 6,5NF | 4,5PF | 4,5PF | 4,5PF | 4,4PF | 5,5PF | 5,5PF | 5,5PF | 5,5PF | 5,5PF |

**Overview:**

The year 2003 witnessed renewed tension with Eritrea in a dispute over borders, which had resulted in open warfare from 1998 until 2000. Press freedoms underwent some further restrictions during the year, including the closure of the Ethiopian Free Press Journalist's Association (EFJA), and the powers of the prime minister's office were strengthened.

One of the few African countries never to have been colonized, Ethiopia saw the end of a long tradition of imperial rule in 1974, when Emperor Haile Selassie was overthrown in a Marxist military coup. Colonel Mengistu Haile Mariam subsequently became the leader of a brutal dictatorship that was overthrown by a coalition of guerrilla groups in 1991. These groups were spearheaded by the Ethiopian People's Revolutionary Democratic Front (EPRDF), itself an alliance of five parties.

The EPRDF government instituted a transition period that resulted in the establishment of formal democratic institutions. However, as expected, the EPRDF gained a landslide victory against a weak and divided opposition in the May 2000 legislative balloting. Although a handful of opposition candidates were elected, parliament subsequently reelected Prime Minister Meles Zenawi to another five-year term. Opposition parties and some observers criticized the government's conduct of the vote. They stated that the polls were subject to government interference, that the opposition was denied some access to the media, and that opposition supporters were subjected to harassment and detention. However, the opposition was able to engage in some criticism of the government in the media during the official election campaign, and a series of unprecedented public debates was broadcast over state-run radio and television during the electoral campaign.

In 2002, Ethiopia was admitted to the joint International Monetary Fund-World Bank Heavily Indebted Poor Countries (HIPC) initiative, which qualifies the country for debt relief.

The Eritrea-Ethiopia Boundary Commission (EEBC), a mediating body established to draw up a new border, announced its decision, which included assigning the border town of Badme to Eritrea in April 2002. The boundary commission's decisions were supposed to be binding on both sides, but Ethiopia formally rejected the EEBC decision, resulting in the indefinite postponement of the physical demarcation of the new border.

The powers of the prime minister and central government were strengthened with regard to intervening in the affairs of the country's states when public security is deemed to be at risk.

There has been continued guerrilla activity by the Oromo Liberation Front and other groups and heavy-handed government intimidation of regime opponents, especially in the southern Oromo-dominated region.

**Political Rights and Civil Liberties:** Ethiopia has yet to experience truly competitive elections. The country is a federation of 11 regions, with a bicameral legislature and an executive prime minister. The Ethiopian People's Revolutionary Democratic Front (EPRDF) has been in power since 1991, although six other major parties and numerous smaller ones participate in the political system. Executive power is vested in a prime minister, who is selected by the Council of People's Representatives. The first official multiparty elections to the council in 1995 were boycotted by the opposition.

The 1995 constitution has a number of unique features, including decentralization based on ethnicity and the right to secession. The government has devolved some power to regional and local governments. However, the reality differs from what is constitutionally mandated, in practice seriously limiting the right of the people to select their government. In 2003, the central government acquired additional powers to intervene in states' affairs in situations where public security was deemed to be at risk.

There are currently more than 60 legally recognized political parties active in Ethiopia, although the political scene continues to be dominated by the EPRDF. Opposition parties claim that their ability to function is seriously impeded by government harassment, although observers note that these parties are often reluctant to take part in the political process. Some parties have supported, either directly or indirectly, armed resistance to the government.

Although a 1992 law guarantees freedom of the press, journalists face an oppressive and restrictive press environment. The law forbids publishing articles that are defamatory, threaten the safety of the state, agitate for war, or incite ethnic conflict. Journalists also can be jailed for publishing secret court records. In 2002, Reporters Sans Frontieres criticized the jailing of three journalists who were imprisoned for "inventing news likely to demoralize the army and make people anxious," libel, and publishing "immoral and indecent material." Harassment and intimidation of the independent print media have led to significant self-censorship. Ethiopia currently has about 80 weekly and 30 monthly newspapers. Broadcast media remain under close scrutiny by the government.

In late 2003, the government closed the Ethiopian Free Press Journalist's Association (EFJA) office on the basis that it had failed to renew its license. This action came, however, after the EFJA had criticized the development of a controversial new draft press law currently under consideration by the government. The International Federation of Journalists has also expressed its strong concerns about the future of the free press, given government actions to limit input from those directly concerned regarding the new press law. Under the proposed law, the government may impose heavy fines and jail sanctions by linking the new press law to the criminal code.

Constitutionally mandated religious freedom is generally respected, although religious tensions have risen in recent years. The Ethiopian Coptic Church is influential, particularly in the north. In the south there is a large Muslim community, made up mainly of Arabs, Somalis, and Oromos.

The government limits academic freedom. In April 2001, students went on strike at the leading institution of higher education, Addis Ababa University, to protest the government's repressive policies and seek an end to police brutality. The strikes and the response by security forces resulted in more than 40 deaths and 200 injuries. Hundreds were arrested, including prominent human rights leaders. According to Human Rights Watch and the Ethiopian Human Rights Council, in early 2002, five students were killed and dozens arrested as Oromiya state police violently dispersed peaceful marches by high school students protesting regional government educational and land policies, and in July continued unrest resulted in additional violence.

Freedom of association is limited. There is a small but growing civil society sector, which has been subject to some restrictions by the government, including arbitrary harassment, suspensions, and bannings. Meetings called by the Addis Ababa Teachers' Association in 2002, for example, were forbidden by the City Administration, which said the association had no legal recognition by the government.

Freedom of trade unions to bargain and strike has not yet been fully tested. The law governing trade unions states that a trade organization may not act in an overtly political manner. Some union leaders have been removed from their elected office or forced to leave the country. All unions have to be registered, although the government still retains the authority to cancel union registration.

The judiciary is officially independent, although there are no significant examples of decisions at variance with government policy. In May 2002, the International Federation of Human Rights charged that "serious human rights violations persist in Ethiopia." These are in part due to the imperial nature of state authority, whereby there is a long history of domination of ethnic groups by others. One flash point has been a decade-long armed struggle for the autonomy of the state of Oromia. The state government, the federal police, and the military have a history of repression and abuse, mainly involving Oromo intellectuals and community leaders who are viewed as sympathetic to the rebel Oromo Liberation Front. Refugees who have fled to neighboring countries in the past decade have told of widespread use of torture and extrajudicial killings in the region.

Women traditionally have few land or property rights and, especially in rural areas, few opportunities for employment beyond agricultural labor. Violence against women and social discrimination are reportedly common despite legal protections.

# ⬇ Fiji

**Population:** 900,000
**GNI/capita:** $2,160
**Life Expectancy:** 67
**Religious Groups:** Christian (52 percent),
Hindu (38 percent), Muslim (8 percent), other (2 percent)
**Ethnic Groups:** Fijian [Melanesian-Polynesian] (51 percent),
Indian (44 percent), other (5 percent)
**Capital:** Suva

**Political Rights:** 4
**Civil Liberties:** 3
**Status:** Partly Free

**Trend Arrow:** Fiji received a downward trend arrow due to the failure of the government to form a new multiparty cabinet, as ordered by the country's supreme court.

**Ten-Year Ratings Timeline (Political Rights, Civil Liberties, Status)**

| 1994 | 1995 | 1996 | 1997 | 1998 | 1999 | 2000 | 2001 | 2002 | 2003 |
|------|------|------|------|------|------|------|------|------|------|
| 4,3PF | 4,3PF | 4,3PF | 4,3PF | 4,3PF | 2,3F | 6,3PF | 4,3PF | 4,3PF | 4,3PF |

**Overview:**

In 2003, Fiji continued to work to recover from a coup in 2000 that threw out the Indo-Fijian Labour Part-led government. Several officials implicated in the attack were tried, including Vice President Ratu Jope Seniloli. The supreme court upheld a proportionality clause of the constitution, although the Fijian-led government refused to give eight cabinet seats to the now opposition Labour Party. Such political tensions and damage from a severe cyclone further hindered the country's economic recovery.

The British colonized Fiji in1874 and began bringing Indians to work in sugar plantations in 1879. Fiji gained independence in 1970, and the indigenous Fijian and ethnic Indian communities were roughly equal in size. The Indo-Fijian Alliance Party ruled until 1987, when Sitiveni Rabuka, a senior army officer backed by indigenous Fijian hard-liners, overthrew the government.

Ethnic rivalry between the indigenous Fijians and the Indo-Fijians, the two dominant groups, has been the main source of political tensions since then. In a May 2000 coup, George Speight, an indigenous Fijian, held Prime Minister Mahendra Chaudhry, an Indo-Fijian, and members of his cabinet hostage in the parliament building. Speight and his followers surrendered after a 56-day standoff with the authorities. In 2002, Speight pleaded guilty to treason and was given the mandatory death sentence, which was later commuted to life imprisonment.

In 2003, the country continued to work to recover from the effects of the coup. Trials for others involved in the coup were held during the year. In May, Vice President Seniloli, the most senior figure to face charges over the uprising, was charged with treason. Speight had appointed Seniloli president of the new government following the attack. A decision to renew the contract of the country's Army Commander, Commodore Frank Bainamarama, became a major political issue tied to the 2000 uprising. The opposition Labour Party, with a predominantly Indo-Fijian membership, called for his contract's renewal when it expires in 2004; Bainamarama supported the prosecution of all soldiers involved in the coup. Media reports that the government was considering his replacement visibly strained public confidence in the government and relations between it and the army.

Laisenia Qarase, prime minister since September 2001, leads the coalition government with the ultra-nationalist Conservative Alliance, an indigenous Fijian party, as a key member of the coalition. Former prime minister Chaudhry's Labour Party charged that Qarase's refusal to appoint Labour Party members to the cabinet violated the proportionality clause of the constitution; a court ruled in February 2002 that Qarase must include ethnic Indian members of the Labour Party in his cabinet. Qarase ignored this ruling when talks between Qarase and Chaudhry made little progress and Chaudhry took the case to the supreme court.

On July 17, 2003, Fiji's supreme court upheld the proportionality clause and ordered Qarase to form a new multiparty cabinet. Election results entitle the Labour Party to 8 seats in the 22-member cabinet. Qarase did not comply with the supreme court ruling and offered Labour up to 14 cabinet posts in a proposal that would expand the cabinet to 36 posts; Labour rejected the proposal. On July 28, President Ratu Josefa Iloilo opened a new parliament session before the supreme court decision to form a new multiparty cabinet could be carried out. The opposition and many civil society groups strongly criticized this government action.

Fiji was hit in January 2003 by the worst cyclone to strike the islands since 1987, resulting in widespread flooding and losses.

Australia announced plans in May to help upgrade Fiji's police, justice, and prison systems over the next five years. Canberra hopes the aid will help revive the economy and that such improvements will also help curb money laundering, drug trafficking, arms smuggling, and terrorist activities in and around the country. Australia then announced in August another transfer of up to $10 million to build a Pacific regional police training center in Fiji.

Also in August, parliament approved a proposal not to send U.S. citizens alleged to have committed an international offense and living in Fiji to the International Criminal Court under the terms of the Rome Statute for the International Criminal Court. Fiji had signed this treaty, but the U.S. did not. Refusal to grant this exemption to U.S. citizens would result in termination of $1 million in annual U.S. military assistance.

**Political Rights and Civil Liberties:** Fiji is a constitutional republic with an elected president, prime minister, and parliament. A new constitution, introduced in 1997, ended the guarantee of parliamentary majority by the indigenous Fijians but continued to give them many political advantages. For example, indigenous Fijians hold more of the reserved seats than do Indo-Fijians in the 71-member lower house. There are 25 seats open to all races and ethnicities, 23 seats reserved for Fijians, 19 for Indo-Fijians, 3 for "general electors" (mainly citizens of Caucasian and East Asian extraction), and 1 for voters on Rotuma Island.

The constitution empowers, in addition to parliament, the Great Council of Chiefs, a traditional indigenous Fijian body, to name the largely ceremonial president, who in turn appoints the 32-member Senate. Successive governments have used this provision to place indigenous Fijians and Rotumans in at least half of public sector jobs at all levels, including most senior positions. In 2003, the Great Council of Chiefs tried to expand its powers into the legislative domain. Fiji TV reported an alleged role of the traditional chiefs in the 1987 and 2000 coup.

The government exercises considerable authority in censoring the media and restricting freedom of speech. Politicians frequently threaten journalists for reporting "negative" stories about the country. The Television Act granted the government powers to influence programming content. The Press Correction Act authorizes officials to arrest anyone who published "malicious" material or to order a publication to print a "correcting statement" to an allegedly false or distorted article. A proposed media bill, intended to regulate the content or conduct of the media, is the latest addition to these controls. Until this bill was proposed, the government had generally refrained from such interference. The government said that inaccurate reporting by some media outlets made this proposed bill necessary for maintaining law and order. The media law is likely to be passed. The government maintains a television monopoly and holds a stake in several newspapers. In October, the government took over the *Daily Post*, of which the government is a majority shareholder, and proposed giving a monopoly license to Fiji TV.

The constitution provides for freedom of religion. Religious affiliation runs largely along ethnic lines with Fijians being Christians and Indo-Fijians being Hindus. The number of attacks on Hindu and Muslim places of worship has increased since the May 2000 coup. In 2003, the government deported three Chinese women who were members of the Falun Gong religious movement. The women arrived from Australia and were arrested and questioned after they were found distributing pamphlets and banners at the opening of the South Pacific Games in the capital, Suva. Police also raided their hotels and seized Falun Gong literature. Fiji has formal diplomatic ties with China, where Falun Gong members are actively suppressed.

Academic freedom is generally respected. Fiji is host to the University of the South Pacific, making it a center for higher education for the South Pacific region.

Civil rights groups have been required to file a petition for proposed meetings since 2000, and approval is granted on a case-by-case basis. The Emergency Powers Act of 1998, a security law that restricts civil liberties during a state of emergency, was criticized by civil rights groups as being too expansive. The law allows parliament to censor the press, ban public meetings, authorize searches without warrants, and seize private property.

The judiciary is independent, and trials are generally free and fair. However, the courts are heavily backlogged for lack of funds, suspects are frequently held for extended periods before their trials, and prison conditions are poor. Lack of funds also contributes to abuse and corruption by law enforcement officers, who are poorly trained and compensated.

Race-based discrimination is common. Affirmative action programs for indigenous Fijians in education and training, land and housing, and employment are not open to other ethnic groups. Political, economic, and social debates are frequently divided along ethnic lines. The main rivalry is between the indigenous Fijians and Indo-Fijians. The former dominate in government and the armed forces, and the latter control much of the Fijian economy, including agriculture and business. Indigenous Fijians make up about 51 percent of the 900,000 population and Indo-Fijians about 42 percent of it. The rest are other Asians, Europeans, and Pacific Islanders.

Discrimination and violence against women is a serious problem. The number of rape, child abuse, and incest cases continues to rise. In May, the government proposed increasing penalties from 10 to 20 years in prison. Women's groups were concerned that most rape sentences were too lenient and that offenders would use traditional reconciliation mechanisms to avoid felony charges.

# Finland

**Population:** 5,200,000
**GNI/capita:** $23,780
**Life Expectancy:** 78
**Religious Groups:** Evangelical Lutheran (89 percent), Russian Orthodox (1 percent), none (9 percent), other (1 percent)
**Ethnic Groups:** Finnish (93 percent), Swedish (6 percent), other, [including Lapp (Saami)] (1 percent)
**Capital:** Helsinki

**Political Rights:** 1
**Civil Liberties:** 1
**Status:** Free

**Ten-Year Ratings Timeline (Political Rights, Civil Liberties, Status)**

| 1994 | 1995 | 1996 | 1997 | 1998 | 1999 | 2000 | 2001 | 2002 | 2003 |
|------|------|------|------|------|------|------|------|------|------|
| 1,1F | 1,1F | 1,1F | 1,1F | 1,1F | 1,1F | 1,1F | 1,1F | 1,1F | 1,1F |

**Overview:**

Following Finland's general elections in March 2003, its first female prime minister, Anneli Jäätteenmäki, served just two months in office before resigning amid scandal. The new prime minister, Matti Vanhanen, was chosen to replace her in June.

Finland was ruled by Sweden until the early eighteenth century and then became a Grand Duchy of Russia until its independence in 1917. The country is traditionally neutral, but its army has had broad popular support ever since it fended off a Russian invasion during World War II. Finland joined the European Union (EU) in 1995 after its friendship treaty with the Soviet Union became void. It has been an enthusiastic member state and is the only Nordic country to have adopted the euro.

In the 2000 presidential election, Tarja Halonen of the Social Democratic Party (SDP) was chosen as the country's first woman president. She defeated four other female candidates—from a total field of seven—from across the political spectrum to serve a six-year term.

The Center Party came to power after winning 55 seats in the general elections held on March 16, 2003. The second-largest party, the SDP, had led the ruling rainbow coalition since 1995. It remains part of the new ruling coalition, which also includes the Center Party and the Swedish People's Party (representing the Swedish-language minority). Anneli Jäätteenmäki replaced the SDP's Paavo Lipponen as prime minister, becoming the first woman to hold the post. However, just two months after she was chosen, Jäätteenmäki stepped down when it was alleged that she had leaked information from classified foreign policy documents and then lied about having done so. Jäätteenmäki had used evidence from the documents in her public attacks against Lipponen's pro-U.S. stance with respect to the war in Iraq. After Jäätteenmäki's resignation in June, Center Party member Matti Vanhanen succeeded her.

At the European Convention in the second half of 2003, Finland was a leader of the smaller EU states. In opposition to a proposal under the draft EU constitution, it pushed for continued permanent representation of all states in the European Commission. Finland also pushed to preserve its neutrality by arguing against a proposed mutual-defense clause, although it does participate in the European security and defense policy.

With its combination of traditional and modern industries, Finland was ranked the most competitive economy in the world by the World Economics Forum in 2003. In addition to timber and metals, the country has a strong telecommunications sector, and the Finnish firm Nokia is the top mobile phone maker worldwide. Still, unemployment is above the average for the EU.

**Political Rights and Civil Liberties:** Finns can change their government democratically. The prime minister in Finland has primary responsibility for running the government. Representatives in the 200-seat unicameral parliament, called the Eduskunta, are elected to four-year terms. The Aland Islands—an autonomous region that is located off the southwestern coast of Finland and whose inhabitants speak Swedish—have their own 29-seat parliament and have one seat in the national legislature. They held elections for their own parliament on October 19. The indigenous Saami of northern Finland also have their own parliament.

Finland has been rated the least corrupt country in the world in Transparency International's Corruption Perceptions Index since 2000. The law against bribery applies both to government officials and business relations between companies.

Finland has a large variety of newspapers and magazines. Newspapers are privately owned, some by political parties and their affiliates; others are controlled by or support a particular party. Finnish law gives every citizen the right to publish and guarantees the right of reply.

Finns enjoy freedom of religion. Both the predominant Lutheran Church and the smaller Orthodox Church are financed through a special tax, from which citizens may exempt themselves. Other religious groups are eligible for tax relief if they register and are recognized by the government. Religious education is part of the curriculum in all public schools, but students may opt out of these classes in favor of more general education in religion and philosophy. The government respects academic freedom more broadly as well.

Freedom of association and assembly are respected in law and in practice. Finnish workers have the right to organize, bargain collectively, and strike. At the start of 2002, more than 70 percent of workers belonged to a trade union.

The constitution provides for an independent judiciary, which consists of the Supreme Court, the supreme administrative court, and the lower courts. The president appoints Supreme Court judges, who in turn appoint the lower court judges.

The rights of ethnic and religious minorities are protected in Finland. Since 1991, the indigenous Saami, who make up less than 1 percent of the population, have been heard in the Finnish parliament on matters concerning them. The constitution guarantees the Saami cultural autonomy and the right to their traditional means of livelihood, which includes fishing and reindeer herding. Their language and culture are also protected through financial support. However, representatives of the community have complained that they could not exercise these rights in practice and that they do not have the right to self-determination in land use.

While Roma (Gypsies) also make up a very small percentage of the population, they are more widely disadvantaged and marginalized. They have particular problems in the areas of housing, education, and employment, despite Finnish government efforts such as an ombudsman for minorities to counter discrimination. More than half of the Roma population in Finland is unemployed, mainly as a result of low levels of training and prevailing prejudice. The Ministry of Justice has engaged in an action plan for combating racism.

Women enjoy a high degree of equality with men in Finland. In 1906, Finland became the first country in Europe to grant women the vote, and the first in the world to allow women to become electoral candidates. In the current parliament, 38 percent of the delegates and 8 of 18 government ministers are women. Tarja Halonen was the first woman to be elected president in Finland. However, women continue to make 10 percent less than men of the same age, education, and profession, and they are generally employed in lower-paid occupations.

# France

**Population:** 59,800,000
**GNI/capita:** $22,730
**Life Expectancy:** 79
**Religious Groups:** Roman Catholic (83-88 percent), Protestant (2 percent), Muslim (5-10 percent), Jewish (1 percent)
**Ethnic Groups:** Celtic and Latin with Teutonic, Slavic, North African, Indochinese, Basque minorities
**Capital:** Paris

**Political Rights:** 1
**Civil Liberties:** 1
**Status:** Free

## Ten-Year Ratings Timeline (Political Rights, Civil Liberties, Status)

| 1994 | 1995 | 1996 | 1997 | 1998 | 1999 | 2000 | 2001 | 2002 | 2003 |
|------|------|------|------|------|------|------|------|------|------|
| 1,2F | 1,2F | 1,2F | 1,2F | 1,2F | 1,2F | 1,2F | 1,2F | 1,1F | 1,1F |

**Overview:**

In 2003, France took a prominent role on the world stage as the most prominent leader of the opposition to the U.S.- and British-led war in Iraq. In a related vein, the country sought to strengthen the capacities of the European Union (EU) in defense and security affairs by proposing, along with Germany, Belgium, and Luxembourg, the creation of a new EU-only military planning cell. At home, President Jacques Chirac's party had a comfortably large majority in parliament and sought modest economic reforms intended to spur sluggish growth. The government's use of fiscal stimulus to aid the economy brought it into conflict with the EU, whose rules limit deficit spending. The year saw numerous anti-Semitic acts (most probably committed by Muslim sympathizers with the Palestinian *intifada*, or uprising, in Israel and the occupied territories), and anti-immigration sentiment continued to be a cause of some concern.

After the French Revolution of 1789, democratic development was uneven. Republics alternated with monarchies (both Bonapartist and Bourbon) until 1871, with the creation of the Third Republic. Invaded and defeated by Germany in World War II, France was split into an occupied northern half and the collaborationist Vichy regime in the south. After the war, democracy was restored and Charles de Gaulle, free France's wartime leader, became president with the creation of the presidential system of the Fifth Republic, which stands today.

President Jacques Chirac was first elected in 1995. In the first round of the May 2002 presidential election, it was expected that he and Lionel Jospin, the prime minister and head of the rival Socialist Party, would receive the most votes and move to the second round. However, Jean-Marie Le Pen, the head of the far-right, xenophobic National Front, stunned France and the world by receiving more votes than Jospin. Chirac defeated Le Pen overwhelmingly in the second round, and in subsequent June parliamentary elections, the newly created Union for a Presidential Majority won a comfortable majority of seats in parliament for Chirac.

In late 2002, France supported UN Security Council 1441, which threatened "serious consequences" against Iraq if it did not comply with weapons inspectors. However, France clearly never supported an early war and fought to prolong inspections. When the United States sought a second resolution explicitly declaring Iraq in breach of its obligations and paving the way to war, France stated that it would veto any such resolution. Along with the opposition of Russia, another permanent veto-holder on the Security Council, France effectively blocked UN authorization for the war in early 2003, in a move that severely strained French relations with the United States but that bolstered Chirac's popularity at home.

After the war, Chirac took the issue further by proposing, along with Germany, Belgium, and Luxembourg, an EU-only military planning cell to be based in Tervuren, in Belgium, giving rise to concerns that the NATO alliance would be weakened. Britain's prime minister, Tony Blair, wanting to keep his country at the center of both NATO and the EU, sought and received assurances that the "Tervuren plan" would complement, not compete with, NATO. Relations between France and the U.S. nonetheless remained tense.

France's domestic policy in 2003 has been focused on reviving the economy. Prime Minister Jean-Pierre Raffarin pushed through a reform that capped benefits and raised the retirement age for some workers. The trade unions expressed their anger, conducting strikes that brought the country to a halt for several days, but they failed to stop the bill's passage. Raffarin also sought to soften, though not abolish, the laws establishing a 35-hour workweek that were passed by the previous Socialist government. Some aspects of economic policy put France in conflict with the EU, of which it is a key member. The government bailout of Alstom, an ailing engineering giant, drew some criticism, as some perceived the move to be against EU rules on state aid. Most notably, France declared that it would, for the second year in a row, run a deficit in excess of 3 percent of gross domestic product in 2003. This figure is the maximum allowed by EU rules for members that have adopted the euro. The EU has considered fining France, which it is allowed to do under the euro-zone's rules, but this remains unlikely, as it would probably provoke a strongly anti-EU backlash in one of the union's driving members.

**Political Rights and Civil Liberties:** French citizens can change their government democratically. The president is elected for a five-year term (reduced from seven years as of the 2002 election). The key house of parliament, the lower National Assembly, is also elected to a five-year term. The prime minister must be able to command a majority in parliament. For most of the Fifth Republic's history, the president and prime minister have been of the same party, making the president the most powerful figure in the country. There have been several periods of "cohabitation," like that which preceded the 2002 elections, in which the president and prime minister are of rival parties. Under these circumstances the prime minister has the dominant role in domestic affairs, while the president retains control over the armed forces and largely guides foreign policy.

Parties organize and compete on a free and fair basis. Political parties with significant support range from the largely unreformed French Communist Party on the left to the anti-immigrant and anti-EU National Front on the right. France remains a relatively unitary state, with some administrative powers devolved to regions and smaller prefectures, but with key decisions being made in Paris. The issue of Corsica continues to fester. In December 2001, the government devolved some legislative autonomy to the island and allowed teaching in the Corsican language in public schools. However, voters on the island, which hosts a sometimes violent separatist movement, rejected a government proposal for devolution of more power to local Corsican institutions in June 2003.

The president has used his office to head off allegations of corruption stemming from his time as mayor of Paris, claiming immunity as head of state to prevent prosecutions so long as he remains president. Transparency International, a corruption watchdog group, ranked France 23 out of 133 countries in its 2003 Corruption Perceptions Index, a slight improvement from the previous year. Members of the French elite, trained in a small number of prestigious schools, often move between politics and business, increasing opportunities for corruption.

The French media operate largely freely and represent a wide range of political opinion. However, they are not entirely free of harassment. Journalists covering events involving the National Front have been attacked by supporters of the party. Seven reporters had their phones tapped between 2000 and 2002 as part of a government investigation into Corsican separatist violence. Two reporters were arrested on December 30, 2002, after filming the deportation of a Malian immigrant. An 1881 law forbids "offending" various personages, including the president and foreign heads of state, but the press remains lively and critical.

Freedom of religion is protected by the constitution, and strong anti-defamation laws prohibit religiously motivated attacks. However, 2003, like 2002, was marred by numerous incidents of anti-Semitic vandalism believed to be connected to the ongoing Palestinian intifada in Israel. Not all branches of the Church of Scientology and the Jehovah's Witnesses are recognized as religious associations for tax purposes. Many public schools continue to deny Muslim girls the right to wear headscarves in schools, and the public debate over this issue continues. Academic freedom is generally respected.

There is freedom of assembly and association. Trades unions are strong in France, though their memberships have declined over the past two decades. Non-governmental organizations operate freely, for example criticizing conditions at prisons and detention centers for asylum-seekers.

France has a well-qualified judiciary, and the rule of law is well established. The legal system is based on Roman code law. French citizens are treated equally under the law. However, the rise of the National Front has tempted the government to tighten immigration and asylum rules, which are perceived to be abused by economic migrants.

Gender equality is protected by law. A law governing the 2002 legislative election threatened to reduce public funding for political parties that ran fewer than 50 percent women candidates for the National Assembly. No party fully complied; the Socialists, who introduced the parity bill, ran 37 percent women. Despite equal legal status and well established social liberty, women earn about three-quarters what men earn. Gay rights are protected and a type of non-marriage civil union, the PACS, is recognized.

# ↓ Gabon

**Population:** 1,300,000
**GNI/capita:** $3,160
**Life Expectancy:** 59
**Religious Groups:** Christian (55-75 percent), animist (25-45) percent
**Ethnic Groups:** Bantu, other Africans, Europeans
**Capital:** Libreville

**Political Rights:** 5
**Civil Liberties:** 4
**Status:** Partly Free

**Trend Arrow:** Gabon received a downward trend arrow due to the lifting of term limits for the president and increased repression of the media.

**Ten-Year Ratings Timeline (Political Rights, Civil Liberties, Status)**

| 1994 | 1995 | 1996 | 1997 | 1998 | 1999 | 2000 | 2001 | 2002 | 2003 |
|------|------|------|------|------|------|------|------|------|------|
| 5,4PF | 5,4PF | 5,4PF | 5,4PF | 5,4PF | 5,4PF | 5,4PF | 5,4PF | 5,4PF | 5,4PF |

**Overview:**

Gabon's politics continued to be dominated by President Omar Bongo's efforts to consolidate power by removing presidential term limits. In 2003, unlike in the tumultuous first half of the 1990s, Bongo's tactless maneuvers barely caused an outcry in or outside Gabon. Meanwhile, however, the country's once bountiful oil reserves have been declining fast, reportedly due to overexploitation and a lack of government initiatives to diversify the embattled economy.

Straddling the equator on Central Africa's west coast, Gabon gained independence from France in 1960. Bongo, whom France raised from soldier to president in 1967, completed the consolidation of power begun by his predecessor, Leon Mba, by officially outlawing the opposition. France, which maintains marines in Gabon, has intervened twice to preserve Bongo's regime. In 1990, protests prompted by economic duress forced Bongo to accept a conference that opposition leaders hoped would promote a peaceful democratic transition. However, Bongo retained power in rigged 1993 presidential elections that sparked violent protests, which were repressed by his presidential guard. The 1996 parliamentary elections were also seriously flawed.

Following 1996 local government polls, which gave the opposition several victories, the government transferred key electoral functions from the electoral commission to the Interior Ministry. Bongo's electoral victory in 1998, with 61 percent of the vote, followed a campaign that made profligate use of state resources and state media. The polling, which was partially boycotted by the opposition, was marked by serious irregularities, while the National Election Commission proved neither autonomous nor competent.

The Gabonese Democratic Party (PDG), which Bongo created in 1968, won parliamentary elections in December 2001. A divided opposition and low voter turnout, as well as government interference in the polls, helped assure the PDG victory. Ruling party candidates won 88 seats compared with 32 for independent and opposition candidates. Some opposition parties boycotted the vote.

Led by the ruling PDG, parliament in 2003 removed a 1997 constitutional amendment that imposed term limits on the head of state, allowing President Bongo to seek reelection indefinitely. The move also replaced the country's runoff system with a single round of voting in all elections. These changes, fiercely opposed by most opposition parties, were interpreted as an attempt to make Bongo, whose current term ends in 2005, president for life. This is the sixth time the constitution has been amended since the introduction of a multiparty system in 1990. Bongo is adept at the use of patronage. In January 2003, he promoted one of his most serious critics, opposition figurehead Paul Mba Abessole, to the post of deputy prime minister, giving Bongo's government the appearance of greater inclusiveness. In July, the PDG held its first national congress in eight years. Bongo was elected as the party's new president, and his son was elected as vice president.

Gabon faced dwindling oil production, heavy external debt, and a stagnant economy throughout the year. The government projects that for the first time in three decades, oil revenue will be lower than non-oil revenue. These pressures have made the country eager to start mending fences with the IMF and other creditors, primarily France. Diplomatic wrangling escalated over a strategic islet in the potentially oil-rich Bay of Corisco that is also claimed by Equatorial Guinea. If joint exploration is ruled out, the case will probably end up in the International Court of Justice.

**Political Rights and Civil Liberties:** Despite a gradual political opening since 1990, Gabon's citizens have never been able to exercise their constitutional right to change their government democratically. With the 2003 lifting of term limits on the presidency and the continued co-optation and marginalization of the political opposition, President Omar Bongo is poised for another landslide victory in the 2005 elections. Although there are numerous political parties, the Gabonese Democratic Party (PDG) has ruled since President Bongo created it in 1968. Bongo has introduced two new laws to fight corruption, which were approved by the National Assembly.

Press freedom is guaranteed, but often restricted in practice. The state is authorized to criminalize civil libel suits. A government daily and at least 10 private weeklies, which are primarily controlled by opposition parties, are published. Almost all Gabonese private newspapers are printed in Cameroon because of the high costs at the only local printing company. At least six private radio and television broadcasters have been licensed and operate, but their viability is tenuous and most of the programming is nonpolitical. At the end of 2002, there were three Internet service providers in the country, two of which are privately owned. The government did not restrict access to or use of the Internet.

In September, Gabon's media watchdog, the National Council on Communications, suspended two private newspapers and renewed the suspension of a third. The council earlier in the year had suspended publication of two magazines and issued warnings to two others. Three of those penalized media outlets had recently issued reports alleging human rights abuses and government corruption. One of the weeklies, *Misamu*, was shut down for three months in 2002 for reporting on the disappearance of $4.4 million from the government treasury.

Religious freedom is constitutionally guaranteed and respected. The government does not restrict academic freedom, including research.

The rights of assembly and association are constitutionally guaranteed, but permits required for public gatherings are sometimes refused. Freedom to form and join political parties is generally respected, but civil servants may face harassment because of associations. Nongovernmental organizations operate openly, but local human rights groups are weak and not entirely independent. Virtually the entire formal private sector workforce is unionized. Collective bargaining is allowed by industry, not by firm. The judiciary suffers from political interference. Rights to legal counsel and a public criminal trial are generally respected. However, judges may deliver summary verdicts, and torture is sometimes used to produce confessions. Prison conditions are marked by beatings and insufficient food, water, and medical care. Arbitrary arrest and long periods of pretrial detention are common. In July, three activists from a small opposition party were arrested and charged with plotting to burn down government buildings.

While no legal restrictions on travel exist, harassment on political and ethnic bases has been reported. Discrimination against African immigrants, including harassment by security forces and arbitrary detention, is a problem. Most of Gabon's several thousand indigenous Pygmies live in the forest and are largely independent of the formal government.

Gabon has come under scrutiny for the exploitation of thousands of child laborers who are sent from other Central or West African countries to work as domestic servants. The government has cooperated with international organizations to fight child trafficking, but says it lacks sufficient funds and resources to tackle the problem. In March, the National Assembly introduced a bill that would criminalize child trafficking in the country.

Three decades of autocratic and corrupt rule have made Bongo among the world's richest men, although some money has trickled down to rural areas and contributed to education. State institutions are influenced or controlled by Bongo and a small elite, with strong backing by the Gabonese army and France. Oil accounts for some 80 percent of the country's exports.

Legal protections for women include equal-access laws for education, business, and investment. In addition to owning property and businesses, women constitute more than 50 percent of the salaried workforce in the health and trade sectors, and women hold high-ranking positions in the military and judiciary. In August, the president announced that government ministries must appoint at least four women as advisers, that is, more than 150 women for the whole government. Women continue to face legal and cultural discrimination, however, particularly in rural areas, and are reportedly subjected to widespread domestic violence.

# The Gambia

**Population:** 1,500,000
**GNI/capita:** $320
**Life Expectancy:** 53
**Religious Groups:** Muslim (90 percent), Christian
(9 percent), indigenous beliefs (1 percent)
**Ethnic Groups:** Mandinka (42 percent), Fula (18 percent),
Wolof (16 percent), Jola (10 percent), Serahuli (9 percent),
other (5 percent)
**Capital:** Banjul

**Political Rights:** 4
**Civil Liberties:** 4
**Status:** Partly Free

**Ten-Year Ratings Timeline (Political Rights, Civil Liberties, Status)**

| 1994 | 1995 | 1996 | 1997 | 1998 | 1999 | 2000 | 2001 | 2002 | 2003 |
|------|------|------|------|------|------|------|------|------|------|
| 7,6NF | 7,6NF | 7,6NF | 7,6NF | 7,5NF | 7,5NF | 7,5NF | 5,5PF | 4,4PF | 4,4PF |

**Overview:**
Anticorruption efforts topped the government's agenda in 2003, and a number of officials faced charges of financial impropriety. The government worked to improve transparency as it sought to win much-needed foreign investment. Meanwhile, an opposition leader who had been detained after calling for mass protests against the government was awaiting trial on sedition charges at the end of the year.

After gaining independence from Britain in 1965, The Gambia functioned as an electoral democracy under President Sir Dawda Jawara and his People's Progressive Party for almost 30 years. A 1981 coup by leftist soldiers was reversed by intervention from Senegal, which borders The Gambia on three sides. The two countries formed the Confederation of Senegambia a year later, but it was dissolved in 1989. Senegal declined to rescue the Jawara government again when Yahya Jammeh struck in 1994. The leaders of the 1994 coup denounced the ousted government's alleged corruption, promising transparency, accountability, and early elections. Instead, they quickly imposed draconian decrees curtailing civil and political rights and the free media. A new constitution, adopted by a closely controlled 1996 referendum, allowed Jammeh to transform his military dictatorship to a nominally civilian administration.

Jammeh secured a victory in the October 2001 presidential poll, defeating opposition leader Ousainou Darboe. Jammeh won 53 percent of the vote compared with 33 percent for Darboe, a human rights lawyer who headed a three-party opposition coalition. Three other candidates won a combined total of 14 percent. In July, Jammeh had repealed the repressive Decree 89, which had prohibited any former ministers from participating in political activity or taking up a government post until 2024. The opposition was given free airtime on state-controlled radio and television. While the Independent Electoral Commission was under some pressure by the ruling party, it generally operated freely. However, there were lingering concerns about Jammeh's commitment to democracy when several opposition supporters, human rights workers, and journalists were detained after the polls. Allegations surfaced after the vote that Jammeh's party had brought in members of his ethnic group living in neighboring Senegal and issued them voter cards.

In the January 2002 National Assembly elections, the ruling Alliance for Patriotic Reorientation and Construction (APRC) won the most seats. Opposition parties made significant gains despite a boycott by some opposition members. The elections showed signs of improvement over the previous highly flawed legislative vote in 1997, although there were some administrative problems with voter registration.

The Gambia is a poor, tiny country with few natural resources that depends on exports of peanuts and other commodities. Jammeh traveled to the United States in 2003 to attend a business forum to help boost The Gambia's profile since it became eligible in December 2002 for benefits under the African Growth and Opportunity Act. The U.S. act offers incentives for African countries to continue efforts to open their economies and build free markets.

President Jammeh launched an anticorruption campaign in 2003 as part of an effort to win foreign investment. The National Assembly supported his "Operation No Compromise" by passing legislation against corruption and money laundering. A number of officials faced charges of financial impropriety, including some officials from Jammeh's inner circle. Among them was the majority leader of the ruling Alliance for Patriotic Reorientation and Construction (APRC) in the National Assembly.

The Jammeh government continued to have little tolerance for outspoken members of the political opposition. Lamine Was Juwara, of the National Democratic Action Movement party, was awaiting trial on sedition charges at the end of 2003 after he called for mass protests against the government in a newspaper article. He accused officials of corruption and economic incompetence in a newspaper interview in September. Juwara has been detained several times since Jammeh has been in power.

**Political Rights and Civil Liberties:** The country's citizens were granted their right to choose or change their government for the first time in several years in the 2001 presidential election, despite sporadic violence preceding the polls. The 2002 legislative elections showed signs of improvement over the previous highly flawed legislative vote in 1997, although there were some administrative problems with voter registration.

Press freedom is guaranteed, but harassment and self-censorship sometimes inhibit free expression of the country's vibrant, independent print media. The National Assembly passed the National Media Commission Bill in 2002, which provided for the creation of a commission that has the power to decide who is and is not a journalist, and to deny the right to confidentiality of sources. The commission can issue arrest warrants for journalists and can jail journalists for contempt for up to six months. Offenses can include the publication or broadcast of "language, caricature, cartoon, or depiction, which is derogatory, contemptuous, or insulting against any person or authority," according to the New York based Committee to Protect Journalists.

Attacks on the press in 2003 were fewer than in previous years. Abdoulie Sey, editor in chief of the private, biweekly *Independent*, was detained incommunicado at the headquarters of the National Intelligence Agency for three days in September. He was interrogated about an opinion piece critical of President Yahya Jammeh that was written by a Gambian journalist based in the United States. Another *Independent* journalist was assaulted by police in August. Internet access is unrestricted.

Private broadcasters and newspapers in The Gambia struggle to pay exorbitant licensing fees. State-run Radio Gambia broadcasts only tightly controlled news that is also relayed by private radio stations. A single, government-run television station operates. Citizen FM broadcasts in a number of indigenous languages and is an important source of independent information for rural Gambians. Authorities shut it down in October 2001, and it remained closed in 2003.

Freedom of religion is guaranteed, and the government respects this right. Academic freedom is guaranteed and respected.

Freedom of assembly is guaranteed, but this right is not always respected. Security forces often crack down violently on demonstrators. Human rights groups and other nongovernmental organizations generally operate freely in The Gambia, although human rights workers, opposition members, and journalists occasionally face harassment.

Gambians, except for civil service employees and members of the security forces, have the right to form unions, strike, and bargain for wages. There are two main labor unions, and about 10 percent of the workforce is unionized.

The constitution provides for an independent judiciary. While lower courts are sometimes subject to executive influence, the judiciary has generally demonstrated its independence on several occasions, at times in significant cases. There are a number of judges from Nigeria, Ghana, and other African countries who tend to operate fairly and vigorously. Local chiefs preside over courts at the village level. The judicial system recognizes customary law, or Sharia (Islamic law), primarily in marriage matters.

Although the Jammeh government has made some steps toward political openness, it still has extensive repressive powers. A 1995 decree allows the National Intelligence Agency to cite "state security" to "search, arrest, or detain any person, or seize, impound, or search any vessel, equipment, plant, or property without a warrant." In such cases, the right to seek a writ of habeas corpus is suspended. Torture in jails and barracks has been reported, although conditions in some of the country's prisons have improved.

Impunity for the country's security forces is a problem. Parliament passed a law in 2001 giving amnesty "for any fact, matter or omission of act, or things done or purported to have been done during any unlawful assembly, public disturbance, riotous situation or period of public emergency." The legislation was backdated to April 2000, when security forces had cracked down on demonstrators, killing 16 people.

Religious and traditional obstacles to the advancement of women are being addressed by both the government and women's organizations. Higher education and wage employment opportunities for women are still far fewer than those for men, especially in rural areas. However, the government has waived school fees for girls, and women occupy senior government posts, including those of vice president and minister of education. Sharia provisions regarding family law and inheritance restrict women's rights. Female genital mutilation is widely practiced, but women's groups are working to eliminate the practice.

# Georgia

**Population:** 4,700,000
**GNI/capita:** $590
**Life Expectancy:** 77
**Religious Groups:** Georgian Orthodox (65 percent), Muslim (11 percent), Russian Orthodox (10 percent), Armenian Apostilic (8 percent), other (6 percent)
**Ethnic Groups:** Georgian (70 percent), Armenian (8 percent), Russian (6 percent), Azeri (6 percent), Ossetian (3 percent), Abkhaz (2 percent), other (5 percent)
**Capital:** Tbilisi

**Political Rights:** 4
**Civil Liberties:** 4
**Status:** Partly Free

**Ten-Year Ratings Timeline (Political Rights, Civil Liberties, Status)**

| 1994 | 1995 | 1996 | 1997 | 1998 | 1999 | 2000 | 2001 | 2002 | 2003 |
|------|------|------|------|------|------|------|------|------|------|
| 5,5PF | 4,5PF | 4,4PF | 3,4PF | 3,4PF | 3,4PF | 4,4PF | 4,4PF | 4,4PF | 4,4PF |

**Overview:**

After a decade as president, Eduard Shevardnadze stepped down in 2003 in the face of a popular uprising against his rule. Widespread reports of serious fraud during the November parliamentary election provoked three weeks of mass, peaceful protests that culminated in the storming of the parliament building during the legislature's opening session. The dramatic confrontation led to the resignation of Shevardnadze the following day, the cancellation of the proportional component of the parliamentary election, and the scheduling of new presidential elections for January 4, 2004. Meanwhile, relations with Russia continued to be marked by tensions, while a final settlement to the protracted conflicts in the separatist regions of Abkhazia and South Ossetia remained elusive.

Absorbed by Russia in the early nineteenth century, Georgia gained its independence in 1918. In 1922, it entered the U.S.S.R. as a component of the Transcaucasian Federated Soviet Republic, becoming a separate union republic in 1936. An attempt by the region of South Ossetia in 1990 to declare independence from Georgia and join Russia's North Ossetia sparked a war between rebels and Georgian forces. Although a ceasefire was signed in June 1992, the territory's final political status remains unresolved.

Following a national referendum in April 1991, Georgia declared its independence from the Soviet Union, which then collapsed in December. Nationalist leader and former dissident Zviad Gamsakhurdia was elected president in May. The next year, he was overthrown by opposition forces and replaced with former Georgian Communist Party head and Soviet foreign minister Eduard Shevardnadze. Parliamentary elections held in 1992 resulted in more than 30 parties and blocs gaining seats, although none secured a clear majority.

In 1993, Georgia experienced the violent secession of the long-simmering Abkhazia region and armed insurrection by Gamsakhurdia loyalists. Although Shevardnadze blamed Russia for arming and encouraging Abkhazian separatists, he legalized the presence of 19,000 Russian troops in Georgia in exchange for Russian support against Gamsakhurdia, who was defeated and reportedly committed suicide. In early 1994, Georgia and Abkhazia signed an agreement in Moscow that called for a ceasefire, the stationing of Commonwealth of Independent States troops under Russian command along the Abkhazian border, and the return of refugees under UN supervision. In parliamentary elections in November and December 1995, the Shevardnadze-founded Citizens' Union of Georgia (CUG) captured the most seats, while Shevardnadze was elected with 77 percent of the vote in a concurrent presidential poll.

The ruling CUG repeated its victory four years later, in the October 1999 parliamentary election. Election observers from the Organization for Security and Cooperation in Europe (OSCE) concluded that despite some irregularities, the vote was generally fair. In the April 2000 presidential poll, Shevardnadze easily won a second five-year term with a reported 81 percent of the vote. While Shevardnadze's win was widely anticipated, the large margin of his victory led to accusations of electoral fraud. Election monitors noted numerous and serious irregularities, including the stuffing of ballot boxes, inflated voter turnout figures, and a strong pro-Shevardnadze bias in the state media.

Following the parliamentary elections, various competing factions developed within the CUG, which had dominated Georgian politics for much of the 1990s. Shevardnadze himself faced growing opposition from prominent members, including then speaker of parliament Zurab Zhvania and then Justice Minister Mikhail Saakashvili, who criticized the president's failure to contain widespread corruption throughout the country. While Shevardnadze resigned as CUG chairman in September 2001, Saakashvili left the CUG to form his own party, the National Movement, and a formal party split was ratified in May 2002. Local elections held in June saw the CUG lose its long-standing dominance to several rival parties, including the New Rights Party, which was formed by many prominent businessmen, the National Movement, and the Labor Party. Subsequently, Saakashvili was named to the influential post of chairman of the Tbilisi City Council.

With Shevardnadze legally required to step down after his second consecutive full term in office, the November 2, 2003 parliamentary election was watched closely as a prelude to the 2005 presidential vote that would determine his successor. According to official Central Election Commission (CEC) results, the For New Georgia pro-presidential coalition—led by Shevardnadze and composed of the CUG, Socialist Party, National Democratic Party (NDP), and Great Silk Road movement—received 21 percent of the vote. The Union of Democratic Revival (UGR), a party led by Aslan Abashidze, the leader of the republic of Ajaria, won almost 19 percent of the vote. Saakashvili's National Movement came in a close third with 18 percent, followed by the Labor Party with 12 percent. The only other two parties to pass the 7 percent threshold to enter parliament were the opposition Burjanadze-Democrats alliance formed by Zhvania and Speaker of Parliament Nino Burjanadze, which captured almost 9 percent of the vote, and the New Rights, which secured 7 percent.

A domestic monitoring organization, the International Society for Fair Elections and Democracy (ISFED), conducted a parallel vote tabulation, concluding that the National Movement had won the election with nearly 27 percent of the vote, with For New Georgia placing second with about 19 percent. Monitors from the OSCE reported that the elections fell short of a number of international standards for democratic elections. Among the violations noted were ballot-box stuffing, inaccurate voter lists, biased media coverage, harassment of some domestic election monitors, and pressure on public employees to support pro-government candidates.

Over the next three weeks, major opposition party leaders, including Saakashvili, Zhvania, and Burjanadze, launched a series of mass public protests against widespread reports of serious electoral fraud. The demonstrations, which received extensive coverage by the popular independent television station Rustavi-2, were a culmination of years of deep discontent over widespread poverty, separatist conflicts, and corruption during Shevardnadze's long tenure in office. A November 9 meeting between Shevardnadze and the opposition failed to resolve the situation. The political crisis climaxed on November 22, when a large group of protestors led by Saakashvili burst into the parliament chamber where Shevardnadze was addressing the legislature's opening session. Saakashvili declared "the velvet revolution has taken place in Georgia," while he and his followers distributed flowers throughout the chamber. A startled Shevardnadze, who was quickly led out of the building by bodyguards, called the revolt a coup d'etat and declared a state of emergency. However, the country's military and police refused to back Shevardnadze against the demonstrators, and no serious incidents of violence were reported.

Russia's foreign minister was dispatched to Georgia to mediate between Shevardnadze and the opposition, while U.S. government officials worked behind the scenes to ensure a peaceful transfer of power. Georgia's stability was regarded as crucial for both Moscow and Washington, which have key—and often competing—strategic and economic interests in the region. After receiving assurances for his personal safety, Shevardnadze announced his resignation the following day, and Burjanadze was named interim president. The Supreme Court cancelled the results of the election under the proportional, party-list system (but not the results the single-mandate races). Snap presidential elections were scheduled for January 4, 2004, with Saakashvili widely considered to be the favorite for president. As of November 30, the date of new parliamentary elections had not yet been approved. Observers view the upcoming polls as an important test of whether the authorities will be willing to hold democratic elections and can restore public confidence in the country's election process.

Georgia's relations with Russia, which had become especially tense during 2002 over charges that Georgia was harboring Chechen rebels in its lawless Pankisi Gorge region bordering Russia, continued to be strained in 2003. In March, parliament ratified a bilateral security pact with the United States, drawing angry reactions from the Russian parliament already concerned by a U.S. antiterrorist training program for the Georgian military initiated the previous year. Tbilisi and Moscow continued to disagree over a timetable for the withdrawal of Russian troops from two military bases in Georgia, with Russia insisting that it needs about a decade to do so. In May, the appeals chamber of Georgia's Supreme Court ruled against extraditing three Chechens to Russia, a decision that further irritated the Kremlin. At the same time, Russia made inroads into Georgia's energy sector when Georgia signed a 25-year deal with the Russian energy company Gazprom in July, and Russia's Unified Energy Systems (UES) purchased a majority of Tbilisi's electricity distribution network, Telasi, in August from the U.S. energy firm AES.

Long-standing demands of greater local autonomy continued unresolved throughout the year. A final agreement to the protracted conflict in Abkhazia remains elusive, as leaders in Tbilisi and Sukhumi, the capital of Abkhazia, continued to disagree on key issues, including the territory's final political status. While the Georgian government has stated its willingness to grant the territory broad autonomy, Abkhazia's leadership continues to insist on full independence. South Ossetia has maintained de facto independence from Tbilisi since 1992. In the southwestern region of Ajaria, Aslan Abashidze exercises almost complete control over the territory, which has retained considerable autonomy since 1991.

**Political Rights and Civil Liberties:** The November 2003 parliamentary elections fell short of international standards for democratic elections. No voting took place in the separatist territory of Abkhazia and parts of South Ossetia, which remained largely outside central government control. Subsequent opposition-led mass public protests resulted in the cancellation of the results of the poll under the proportional, party-list system (but not the results the single-mandate races), the resignation of President Eduard Shevardnadze, and the scheduling of fresh presidential elections for January 4, 2004. As of November 30, the date of new legislative elections had not been decided. Most political parties tend to be more centered around specific individuals than detailed policy platforms.

Although the government initiated a high-profile anticorruption campaign in 2000, corruption remains endemic throughout all levels of Georgian society. The prevalence of corruption undermined the credibility of Shevardnadze's government and is an obstacle to foreign investment. In its 2003 Corruption Perceptions Index, Transparency International ranked Georgia 124 out of 133 countries surveyed.

While the country's independent press often publishes discerning and critical political analyses, economic difficulties limit the circulation of most newspapers, particularly outside the capital. Independent newspapers and television stations face some harassment by the authorities, and journalists in government-controlled media frequently practice self-censorship. In March, several men forced the independent Dzveli Kalaki radio station off the air when they knocked its rooftop antenna to the ground. The station is known for its willingness to report on politically sensitive issues, including corruption. In July, a former police officer was sentenced to 13 years in prison for the 2001 murder of journalist Georgy Sanaya. Many of Sanaya's family members and former colleagues maintain that his killing was politically motivated and that those who masterminded his murder remain unpunished. The independent television station Rustavi-2, which for years faced harassment and politically motivated tax audits for investigative reporting on issues including government corruption, broadcast reports of voter fraud in the November 2003 election and the subsequent protests that led to Shevardnadze's resignation. Libel laws inhibit investigative journalism; the Rustavi-2 investigative program "60 Minutes" lost two separate politically motivated libel cases in 2003. In June, parliament ratified an amendment to the criminal code imposing longer jail sentences for slandering government officials. Although the government does not limit Internet access, widespread poverty limits its availability to much of the population.

Although the government does not restrict academic freedom, the quality of the country's educational system has been compromised by endemic corruption. Students frequently pay bribes to receive high marks or pass entrance examinations.

Freedom of religion is respected for the country's largely Georgian Orthodox population and some minority religious groups traditional to the country, including Muslims and Jews. However, members of nontraditional religious minority groups, including Baptists, Pentecostals, and Jehovah's Witnesses, face harassment and intimidation by law enforcement officials and certain Georgian Orthodox Church extremists. Over the years, police have failed to respond to repeated attacks by followers of defrocked Georgian Orthodox priest Father Basili Mkalavishvili against Jehovah's Witnesses and members of other faiths. The attacks have included burning religious material, breaking up religious gatherings, and beating parishioners. The Georgian Orthodox Church and the government signed an agreement in October 2002 giving the Church a more privileged status than other religions, although it stopped short of naming the Church as the official church of Georgia.

The authorities generally respect freedom of association and assembly. A series of opposition-led demonstrations in November against election fraud proceeded without incident. However, on November 19, a peaceful opposition demonstration was violently attacked by pro-government supporters in the southern Bolnisi district while police did not intervene. Other instances of violence occurred during earlier opposition demonstrations in September in Bolnisi and in October in the republic of Ajaria. Nongovernmental organizations, including human rights groups, are able to register and operate without arbitrary restrictions.

The constitution and Law on Trade Unions allow workers to organize and prohibit anti-union discrimination. The Amalgamated Trade Unions of Georgia (ATUG), the successor to the union that existed during the Soviet period, is the principal trade union confederation. It is not affiliated with and receives no funding from the government. The ATUG has reported cases of workers being warned by management not to organize unions, and some workers have been threatened for engaging in union activities. Collective bargaining practices, though legally permitted, are not widespread.

The judiciary is not fully independent, with courts influenced by pressure from the executive branch. The payment of bribes to judges, whose salaries remain inadequate, is reportedly common. In 2003, Shevardnadze openly pressured the judiciary, including in August when he called on the Constitutional Court to consult with the government before making important decisions. Police reportedly beat prisoners and detainees to extract confessions and fabricate or plant evidence on suspects. Kidnapping for ransom occurs frequently throughout the country, with senior law enforcement officials allegedly involved. In June, three UN hostages were freed after having spent five days in captivity in the Kodori Gorge area located between Abkhazia and Georgia proper. Prison inmates suffer from overcrowding and inadequate sanitation, food, and medical care.

The government generally respects the rights of ethnic minorities in nonconflict areas of the country. Freedom of residence and the freedom to travel to and from the country is generally respected. However, Georgia continues to face serious refugee problems stemming from the long-standing conflicts in Abkhazia and South Ossetia, as well as from the war in the neighboring Russian republic of Chechnya, with repatriation efforts proceeding slowly.

The country's economy continued to suffer from problems including high rates of unemployment, sporadic payment of government pensions, energy shortages, and widespread corruption.

Sexual harassment and discrimination in the workplace are problems that are rarely investigated. Social taboos limit the reporting and punishment of rape and spousal abuse, and the trafficking of women abroad for prostitution remains a problem. In June, parliament approved amendments to the criminal code making human trafficking a criminal offense punishable by 5 to 10 years in prison, or up to 12 years for a repeat conviction.

# Germany

**Population:** 82,600,000
**GNI/capita:** $23,560
**Life Expectancy:** 78
**Religious Groups:** Protestant (34 percent), Roman Catholic (34 percent), Muslim (3.7 percent), other (28.3 percent)
**Ethnic Groups:** German (92 percent), Turkish (2 percent), other (6 percent)
**Capital:** Berlin

**Political Rights:** 1
**Civil Liberties:** 1
**Status:** Free

**Ten-Year Ratings Timeline (Political Rights, Civil Liberties, Status)**

| 1994 | 1995 | 1996 | 1997 | 1998 | 1999 | 2000 | 2001 | 2002 | 2003 |
|------|------|------|------|------|------|------|------|------|------|
| 1,2F | 1,2F | 1,2F | 1,2F | 1,2F | 1,2F | 1,2F | 1,2F | 1,1F | 1,1F |

**Overview:**

Germany, which held a temporary seat on the UN Security Council, was prominent on the world stage in 2003 as it stood with France and Russia in opposing the U.S.- and British-led war in Iraq. The stance, espoused vociferously by Chancellor Gerhard Schroeder, significantly strained relations with the United States. However, it was popular in Germany, where most citizens opposed the war. Having won reelection in September 2002, Schroeder soon saw his poll ratings decline sharply as the economy continued to falter. However, he subsequently began to gather the will for controversial reforms, particularly of the labor market, that might boost economic growth. Germany has also come under censure from the European Union (EU) for admitting it will breach the euro-zone's excessive-deficit ceiling for the second straight year.

The modern German state emerged in 1871 out of the fragmented Germanic states that existed until that point. Defeated in World War I, and again more devastatingly in World War II, Germany was divided into two states—the capitalist and democratic Federal Republic in the west and the Communist German Democratic Republic in the east—during the ensuing Cold War. In 1989, the Berlin Wall keeping East Berliners from fleeing west was opened, and in 1990, East Germany was absorbed into the Federal Republic. Despite more than a decade of massive subsidies, eastern Germany remains considerably poorer than the rest of the country, with higher levels of unemployment. This economic situation is seen to have contributed to higher levels of support for political groups on the far right and far left in the former East.

The current government, a coalition of the Social Democratic Party (SPD) and the Green Party, was first elected in 1998, with the SPD's Schroeder as chancellor.

The government's first term was marked by slow economic growth (just 0.6 percent and 0.2 percent in the 2001 and 2002), and the SPD's poll ratings languished late in 2002. However, Schroeder's vocal opposition to the war in Iraq played well with voters, and the coalition parties bested the opposition alliance of the Christian Democratic Party and Christian Social Union (CDU/CSU) in the September 22, 2002 legislative elections.

Poll ratings sank quickly again after the election, however, and the SPD, the main coalition party, lagged well behind the CDU/CSU in 2003. The primary reason may be dissatisfaction with the economy, especially with the stubbornly high unemployment rate of around 10 percent. Schroeder began to tackle this issue in earnest with labor-market reforms in 2002. His proposals have included making it easier for firms to fire workers, encouraging the creation of part-time and lower-wage "mini-jobs," and cutting benefits to the unemployed if they prove unwilling to move to take a job or to take an available job. The labor unions, which have traditionally been a major supporter of the SPD, reacted angrily and threatened to strike. However, the collapse of a major unrelated strike by the IG Metall metalworkers' union in eastern Germany weakened the unions in general. Moreover, the chancellor has the tacit support of the opposition CDU/CSU for the core of his reforms, which he needs because the CDU/CSU has a majority in the upper house of parliament.

Relations with the EU were strained over budget deficits in 2003. Member states that adopt the euro as their currency must pledge to run budget deficits of no more than 3 percent of gross domestic product or face heavy fines. Though this rule itself is largely a German creation, Germany breached the ceiling in 2002 and projected that it would do so again in 2003. Though it has been repeatedly warned by the European Commission (the EU's executive), there have been no fines levied.

As a result of Germany's opposition to the Iraq war, relations with France tightened, while relations with the United States suffered. Germany held the chairmanship of the UN Security Council during many of the key debates leading up to the war, and the foreign minister, the pacifist Green Party's Joschka Fischer, played a prominent role. After the war, Germany tentatively sought to improve relations with the United States by, for example, offering to train Iraqi police in Germany. It declined to send peacekeepers to Iraq, but in a mollifying move, it bolstered its presence in Afghanistan.

**Political Rights and Civil Liberties:** Germans can change their government democratically. The constitution provides for a lower house (Bundestag) elected by a mixture of proportional representation and single-member districts, to be reelected at least every four years. The chancellor must control a majority in the Bundestag. The upper house, the Bundesrat, represents the states, and it must approve of much key legislation, including economic bills. Its members are delegates from the individual state governments, and each state's delegation must vote as a block. The head of state is a largely ceremonial federal president, chosen by the parliament. Germany is strongly federal; state governments have considerable authority over areas such as education and policing, as well as substantial powers to tax and spend.

Political pluralism in Germany has been constrained by laws restricting the far left and far right. The Communist Party of Germany was banned in the Federal Republic in 1956. However, the former ruling East German Communist Party, now re-named the Party of Democratic Socialism, is a legal and democratic, if far-left, party that has participated in state governments. Several far-right parties, hostile to immi-gration and the EU, receive a small share of the vote. One, the German People's Union, caused consternation by winning 13 percent of the vote in a state election in Saxony-Anhalt in 1998, but it has been kept out of government at both the federal and state levels. Moreover, the alteration of asylum laws has undercut basic support for such parties, which together won less than 3 percent of the vote in 2002 and no seats in parliament. Nazism is illegal, but the government's attempts to ban the neo-Nazi National Democratic Party were hung up in court when it was revealed that many of those testifying against the party were government agents.

Germany's government is accountable through open debates in parliament that are covered widely in the media. The government is free of pervasive corruption and was ranked number 16 out of 133 countries in Transparency International's 2003 Corruption Perceptions Index.

Freedom of expression is protected in the Basic Law (the constitution), and the media are largely free and independent. However, it remains illegal to advocate Na-zism or deny the Holocaust. German authorities have sought to prosecute Internet users outside Germany posting Nazi propaganda aimed at Germany, although this will be technically impossible to prosecute.

The Constitutional Court ruled in March that surveillance of journalists' phone calls could be deemed legal in "serious" cases (on a case-by-case basis) by judges. The lack of a definition of "serious" is a cause for concern to the media watchdog group Reporters Sans Frontieres, which fears that the vagueness of the word invites abuse.

Freedom of belief is protected under law. Religions that fulfill certain require-ments have the status of a "corporation under public law," and the government collects taxes from church members on the churches' behalf, for a fee. However, Germany has taken a strong stance against the Church of Scientology, which it deems an economic organization rather than a religion. Major parties deny membership to Scientologists, and the group has been under surveillance by government intelli-gence agencies. The Jehovah's Witnesses were denied public law corporation sta-tus in 1997 for failing to demonstrate "indispensable loyalty" to the democratic state, but this ruling was overturned on church-state separation grounds by the high court in 2000. However, the case was still under review by the courts, which have expressed concern that the Jehovah's Witnesses' child-rearing practices do not conform to international human rights law. Academic freedom is respected.

Civic groups and NGOs may operate without hindrance, and the right of peace-ful assembly is not infringed, except in the case of outlawed groups such as those advocating Nazism or opposing Germany's democratic order. Trade unions, farm-ers' groups, and business confederations are free to organize, and they have tradi-tionally played a strong role in Germany's consensus-based policy-making system. However, unions have weakened in recent years.

The judiciary is independent, and the rule of law prevails. The Federal Constitu-tional Court vets the compatibility of laws with the Basic Law. In addition to having its own provisions, Germany is a party to the European Convention on Human Rights. Prison conditions are adequate, with two isolated cases of abuse reported in 2003. Anti-immigrant sentiment led to attacks on members of ethnic minorities.

Women's rights are strongly protected, with generous maternity policies and anti-discrimination laws, though the latter do not prevent some wage discrimination. There are six women in the fourteen-member federal cabinet. Limited gay partnership rights are permitted.

# Ghana

**Population:** 20,500,000   **Political Rights:** 2
**GNI/capita:** $290   **Civil Liberties:** 2*
**Life Expectancy:** 57   **Status:** Free
**Religious Groups:** Indigenous beliefs (21 percent), Muslim (16 percent), Christian (63 percent)
**Ethnic Groups:** Akan (44 percent), Moshi-Dagomba (16 percent), Ewe (13 percent), Ga (8 percent), other (19 percent)
**Capital:** Accra
**Ratings Change:** Ghana's civil liberties rating improved from 3 to 2 due to increased openness in civic discourse and general improvements in the respect for human rights and the rule of law.

**Ten-Year Ratings Timeline (Political Rights, Civil Liberties, Status)**

| 1994 | 1995 | 1996 | 1997 | 1998 | 1999 | 2000 | 2001 | 2002 | 2003 |
|------|------|------|------|------|------|------|------|------|------|
| 5,4PF | 4,4PF | 3,4PF | 3,3PF | 3,3PF | 3,3PF | 2,3F | 2,3F | 2,3F | 2,2F |

**Overview:**

Ghana's National Reconciliation Commission began hearing testimony in 2003 from among nearly 3,000 people who have registered complaints covering abuses committed between 1957 and 1993. While political parties were gearing up for presidential and parliamentary elections scheduled for December 2004, the ruling New Patriotic Party (NPP) won crucial by-elections in March that gave it a majority in parliament.

Once a major slaving center and long known as the Gold Coast, Ghana, a former British possession, became black Africa's first colony to achieve independence. After the 1966 overthrow of its charismatic independence leader, Kwame Nkrumah, the country was wracked by a series of military coups for 15 years. Successive military and civilian governments vied with each other in both incompetence and mendacity.

In 1979, Flight Lieutenant Jerry Rawlings led a coup against the ruling military junta and, as promised, returned power to a civilian government after a purge of corrupt senior army officers. However, the new civilian administration did not live up to Rawlings's expectations, and he seized power again in December 1981 and set up the Provisional National Defense Council (PNDC). The radically socialist, populist, and brutally repressive PNDC junta banned political parties and free expression. Facing a crumbling economy, Rawlings, in the late 1980s, transformed Ghana into an early model for the structural adjustment programs urged by international lenders. A new constitution adopted in April 1992 legalized political parties, and Rawlings was declared president after elections that were neither free nor fair. Rawlings's victory in the 1996 presidential poll, which was generally regarded as free and fair, was assured by the former ruling party's extensive use of state media and patronage, as well as by opposition disunity.

In the December 2000 presidential elections, the opposition, led by John Kufuor of the NPP, alleged intimidation and other irregularities as the second round of voting began. However, those claims dissipated as the polling proceeded and Kufuor's looming victory became apparent. He won soundly with 57 percent of the vote in the second round of polling, compared with 43 percent for Vice President John Atta Mills. The elections were hailed as having been conducted both freely and fairly.

During concurrent legislative elections, the opposition also broke the stranglehold of Rawlings's National Democratic Congress (NDC) on parliament. The NPP captured 99 of the 200 seats available, compared with 92 for the NDC, which had previously held 133 seats. Smaller opposition parties and independents won the remainder of seats. The NPP won a majority in parliament in March 2003 through two by-elections, finishing with 101 seats.

Kufuor and his NPP will face their strongest challenge by the NDC in the 2004 presidential and parliamentary elections. The National Commission for Civic Education continued its campaign of public awareness about democracy and voting procedures ahead of the polls.

The National Reconciliation Commission, which is modeled on South Africa's Truth and Reconciliation Commission, called on former president Rawlings to respond to testimony that he witnessed the torture and murder of a political activist when he was president in the 1980s. Commission officials said Rawlings could write a letter to respond instead of appearing before the body. Rawlings has been cool to previous questions linked to abuses committed during his administrations. The complaints are not likely to lead to criminal prosecution, although they could lead to compensation. The aim of the hearings is to help victims move on and help perpetrators come to terms with their acts and obtain forgiveness.

Ghana is considered a model for stability in West Africa. It has contributed troops to peacekeeping efforts in the region and has hosted peace talks on Liberia. Kufuor is the current president of the Economic Community of West African States.

Ghana's economy depends on income from cocoa and gold. The Kufuor government has made efforts to improve transparency and reduce corruption. Unrest in neighboring Cote d'Ivoire has been a boon for Ghana's economy; more ships are turning to Ghana's ports. The government in 2003 ended fuel subsidies.

**Political Rights and Civil Liberties:** The December 1996 presidential and parliamentary elections conducted under the 1992 constitution allowed Ghanaians their first opportunity since independence to choose their representatives in genuine elections. The 2000 presidential and parliamentary polls were hailed in Africa and abroad as a successful test of Ghana's democracy. The presidential poll marked the first time in Ghana's history that one democratically elected president was succeeded by another democratically elected leader.

Freedom of expression is constitutionally guaranteed and generally respected. Fulfilling a campaign promise, the Kufuor government in 2001 repealed Ghana's criminal libel law and otherwise eased pressure on the press. Numerous private radio stations operate and several independent newspapers and magazines are published in Accra. Internet access is unrestricted.

Religious freedom is respected, but there is occasional tension between Christians and Muslims and within the Muslim community itself. Academic freedom is guaranteed and respected. A ban on campus demonstrations has not been enforced or challenged.

The right to peaceful assembly and association is constitutionally guaranteed, and permits are not required for meetings or demonstrations. Numerous nongovernmental organizations operate openly and freely. The government has not interfered with the right of workers to associate in labor unions, but civil servants may not join unions. Arbitration is required before strikes are authorized. The Ghana Federation of Labor is intended to serve as an umbrella organization for several other labor unions.

Ghanaian courts have acted with increased autonomy under the 1992 constitution, but are still occasionally subject to executive influence. Traditional courts often handle minor cases according to local customs that fail to meet constitutional standards. Scarce judicial resources compromise the judicial process, leading to long periods of pretrial detention under harsh conditions. The proceedings of Ghana's National Reconciliation Commission were seen as a test for the flexibility of the country's democracy and how well Ghana can look into its past, acknowledge its failings, and continue to move democratically into the future.

Communal and ethnic violence occasionally flares in Ghana.

Ghana has been coordinating with regional countries and the International Labor Organization to create a comprehensive plan to address the growing problem of child trafficking and child labor. Ghanaian fishermen released from employment hundreds of trafficked children in September 2003. Lawmakers were drafting a bill against the trafficking of persons in 2003.

Ghanaian women suffer societal discrimination that is particularly serious in rural areas, where opportunities for education and wage employment are limited, despite women's equal rights under the law. Women's enrollment in universities, however, is increasing. Domestic violence against women is said to be common, but often remains unreported. Legislation in 1998 doubled the prison sentence for rape. Efforts are underway to abolish the tro-kosi system of indefinite servitude to traditional priests in rural areas and the practice of sending young girls to penal villages in the north after they are accused of practicing witchcraft.

# Greece

**Population:** 11,000,000
**GNI/capita:** $11,430
**Life Expectancy:** 78
**Religious Groups:** Greek Orthodox (98 percent),
Muslim (1.3 percent), other (0.7 percent)
**Ethnic Groups:** Greek (98 percent), other [including
Macedonian and Turkish] (2 percent)
**Capital:** Athens

**Political Rights:** 1
**Civil Liberties:** 2
**Status:** Free

## Ten-Year Ratings Timeline (Political Rights, Civil Liberties, Status)

| 1994 | 1995 | 1996 | 1997 | 1998 | 1999 | 2000 | 2001 | 2002 | 2003 |
|------|------|------|------|------|------|------|------|------|------|
| 1,3F | 1,3F | 1,3F | 1,3F | 1,3F | 1,3F | 1,3F | 1,3F | 1,2F | 1,2F |

**Overview:**

The trial of several people suspected of being members of the November 17 urban guerrilla group dominated the news in Greece during 2003. The country improved its relations with Turkey over, among other things, the situation between Greek and Turkish Cyprus. Greece also amended its law on trafficking in human beings, adding a provision that gives assistance and protection to the victims of trafficking crimes.

Modern Greece began in 1830, when the country gained its independence from the Ottoman Empire. The ensuing century brought continued struggle between royalists and republican forces. During World War II, Greece fell to Germany in 1941 after a failed invasion by Italy the year before. From 1942 to 1944, local Communist and royalist forces put up a strong resistance against the Nazis, which were eventually defeated with the help of British forces in 1944. National solidarity broke down in the early postwar period when royalists won national elections and eventually defeated the Communists in a civil war. In 1967, a group of army officers staged a military coup, suspending elections and arresting hundreds of political activists. A referendum in 1974 rejected the restoration of the monarchy, and a new constitution in 1975 declared Greece a parliamentary republic.

During parliamentary elections in 2000, the Panhellenic Socialist Movement (PASOK) won more than half of the seats, while the more conservative New Democracy party came in a close second. Other parties winning seats include the Communist Party of Greece and Synaspismos, a coalition of smaller left parties. Of those eligible to vote, 89 percent turned out at the polls.

High security and heavy media attention were prevalent during the start of the trial of 19 suspected members of an urban guerrilla group, called November 17, that were caught last year. Four of the suspects were found guilty of committing a number of murders, bombings, and robberies during a 28-year-long terrorist campaign that claimed 23 lives.

Relations between Greece and Turkey improved in 2003 over Cyprus when the Turkish Cypriot leader opened the border on the island with the Greek side, allowing thousands of people to visit. In October, the Turkish foreign minister, Abdulla Gul, visited Athens and declared tensions with Greece a thing of the past. Both Greece and Turkey made progress toward joining the international Mine Ban Treaty.

**Political Rights and Civil Liberties:**   Greeks are free to change their government democratically. All 300 members of the unicameral parliament are elected according to a system of proportional representation. The president is elected by parliament to a five-year term. Greece generally has fair electoral laws and equal campaigning opportunities. However, during the last election, an all-party committee decided to ban all outdoor posters and banners and to reduce the parties' radio and television advertising by 50 percent. Greece has a system of compulsory voting, but it is weakly enforced. Some representatives of the Roma (Gypsy) community complain that certain municipalities failed to register Romanies who did not fulfill basic residency requirements.

Corruption is a serious problem in Greece, which has ranked lowest of all west European countries in Transparency International's Corruption Perceptions Index for two years running. According to a U.S. State Department human rights report released in March 2003, some police officers are on the payroll of organized crime groups and have facilitated human trafficking by these groups.

Although the constitution provides provisions for freedom of speech and the press, there are a number of limits. The constitution forbids speech that incites fear, violence, and disharmony among the population. Publications that offend religious beliefs, are obscene, or advocate the violent overthrow of the political system can be seized by the state. Groups that oppose the system also threaten the press. A gasoline bomb was lobbed at the house of Anna Panayotarea, a journalist who has been covering the trial of the suspected members of the November 17 terrorist group. Sympathizers of the group maintain that the national press follows the government's official line too closely and have attacked several other journalists since the capture of suspected group members in 2002.

Freedom of religion is generally respected, although there are cases of religious discrimination. Because of their religion, non-Orthodox members of the military, police and fire-fighting forces, and civil service face discrimination and career limits. Academic freedom is not restricted.

Although the Greek constitution allows for freedom of association, ethnic and religious minority groups face a number of barriers. The government does not officially recognize the existence of any non-Muslim minority groups, particularly Slavophones. The Greek government, further, does not recognize Macedonian as a language as officials fear the secessionist aspirations of this group. Roma, who may be either Greek Orthodox or Muslim, are not recognized as a minority but rather as a "socially excluded" or "sensitive" group. Moreover, using the term Turkos or Tourkikos ("Turk" and "Turkish," respectively) in the title of an association is illegal and may lead to persecution. The capture and trial of several suspected leaders of the November 17 group has weakened but not eliminated a major source of political terror in the country. Workers are free to organize into trade unions and bargain collectively.

The judiciary is independent, and the constitution provides for public trials. However, the European Committee for the Prevention of Torture (CPT) raised concerns in a 2002 report about the ill-treatment of detainees by law enforcement officials, especially toward immigrants, and the overcrowding of prisons. In 2003, Amnesty International issued a report critical of Greece's treatment of conscientious objectors, who are frequently not given proper civil service options. In June, a conscientious objector, Lazaros Petromelidis, was sentenced to 20 months imprisonment, suspended for three years, for failing to report to alternative civilian service. His civil service would have brought him far away from his wife and child.

Immigrants and ethnic minorities face discrimination and unequal treatment under the law. The European Commission's Committee to Prevent Torture reports that in 2001 the police mistreated immigrants. The Roma community faces systematic discrimination in all spheres of social life and is often the target of abusive police raids based on racial profiling. Although the Greek constitution guarantees equal treatment to any person legally on the territory of the country, there is a lack of effective legislation to ensure this right.

Women lack specific legislation to deal with domestic violence and, in addition, face sex-based discrimination in the workplace, where they get paid about three-quarters less than men for equal work. Women hold only 8.7 percent of the seats in parliament. According to the U.S. State Department, the government of Greece was not fully complying with minimum standards for eliminating human trafficking in 2003 and not making significant efforts to do so. Around 18,000 people—mainly women and children—were trafficked to Greece in 2002. Greece did, however, pass a law in 2002 that outlaws trafficking in human beings and imposes penalties for the sale of human organs, the exploitation of labor, the economic exploitation of sex, and the exploitation of minors for the purpose of armed conflict and pornography. In 2003, parliament went further in combating human trafficking by providing assistance and protection to the victims of these crimes.

# Grenada

**Population:** 100,000   **Political Rights:** 1
**GNI/capita:** $3,500   **Civil Liberties:** 2
**Life Expectancy:** 71   **Status:** Free
**Religious Groups:** Roman Catholic (53 percent),
Anglican (13.8 percent), other [including Protestant]
(33.2 percent)
**Ethnic Groups:** Black (82 percent), mulatto (13 percent),
other [including European and East Indian] (5 percent)
**Capital:** St. George's

### Ten-Year Ratings Timeline (Political Rights, Civil Liberties, Status)

| 1994 | 1995 | 1996 | 1997 | 1998 | 1999 | 2000 | 2001 | 2002 | 2003 |
|------|------|------|------|------|------|------|------|------|------|
| 1,2F | 1,2F | 1,2F | 1,2F | 1,2F | 1,2F | 1,2F | 1,2F | 1,2F | 1,2F |

**Overview:** Parliamentary elections held in November 2003 saw incumbent prime minister Keith Mitchell reelected amidst accusations that he made payments to public sector workers in exchange for their support. Mitchell's New National Party (NNP) gained a bare minimum of seats in the legislature. Meanwhile, the country's Truth and Reconciliation Commission had not yet made a final report to the government by November 2003 regarding the assassination of a former prime minister and his colleagues in the 1980s.

Grenada, a member of the Commonwealth that gained independence from Britain in 1974, includes the islands of Carriacou and Petite Martinique. Maurice Bishop's Marxist New Jewel Movement seized power in 1979. In 1983, Bishop was murdered by New Jewel hard-liners Bernard Coard and Hudson Austin, who took control of the country in the name of the People's Revolutionary Government (PRG). A joint U.S.-Caribbean military intervention removed the PRG. In 1986, Coard and 18 others were sentenced to death; 2 were pardoned and 17 had their sentences commuted to life imprisonment.

Prime Minister Keith Mitchell of the NNP was reelected by a narrow margin in voting held on November 27, 2003. The elections, deemed to be free, were called seven months early. The NNP won 8 seats, down from the 15-seat sweep of the 1999 elections, while the National Democratic Party (NDP), headed by Tillman Thomas, won 7 seats. The Grenada United Labor Party (GULP), the Good Old Democracy Party (GODP), and the Grenada Renaissance Party (GRP) were unsuccessful.

In the run-up to the 2003 elections, the Mitchell government was accused of garnering voter support by paying public workers retroactive payments. Discrepancies in voter lists were also reported by the opposition. The electoral system was revitalized by the 2003 elections, where the NDP obtained 7 out of 15 parliamentary seats. After the crushing defeat suffered by Grenada's opposition parties in the 1999 elections, the parties' role as alternatives in future elections was seen as seriously in doubt.

The Truth and Reconciliation Commission, which was formally inaugurated in September 2001, has a mandate to investigate violence from the period from the mid-1970s to the late 1980s. The commission is expected to review the convictions of the leaders of the former PRG for their roles in the 1983 assassination of former prime minister Bishop and his cabinet colleagues. As of November 2003, it had not yet presented its final report to the government. In October, Prime Minister Mitchell announced that the Grenadian public would decide the fate of the "Grenada 17" accused of the murders.

**Political Rights and Civil Liberties:** Citizens are able to change their government through democratic elections. The 2003 parliamentary elections were considered free, with some allegations of voter list manipulation and government pandering. The bicameral parliament consists of the 15-seat House of Representatives and the 13-seat Senate, to which the prime minister appoints 10 senators and the opposition leader, 3. The British monarchy is represented by a governor-general.

The right to free expression is generally respected. The media, including three weekly newspapers and several other publications, are independent and freely criticize the government. A privately owned corporation, with a minority government share, owns the principal radio and television stations. In addition, there are nine privately owned radio stations, one privately owned television station, and a privately owned cable company. All of the media are independent of the government and regularly report on all political views. There is free access to the Internet.

Citizens of Grenada generally enjoy the free exercise of religious beliefs. There are no official restrictions on academic freedom.

Constitutional guarantees regarding the right to organize political, labor, or civic groups are respected. Workers have the right to organize and to bargain collectively.

Numerous independent labor unions include an estimated 20 to 25 percent of the workforce. All unions belong to the Grenada Trades Union Council (GTUC), which is represented in the Senate. A 1993 law gives the government the right to establish tribunals empowered to make "binding and final" rulings when a labor dispute is considered of vital interest to the state. The GTUC claimed the law was an infringement on the right to strike.

The independent and prestigious judiciary has authority generally respected by the 782-member Royal Grenada Police Force. There are no military or political courts. In 1991, Grenada rejoined the Organization of Eastern Caribbean States court system, with the right of appeal to the Privy Council in London. Detainees and defendants are guaranteed a range of legal rights that the government respects in practice. There is a substantial backlog of six months to one year for cases involving serious offenses, the result of a lack of judges and facilities. Like many Caribbean island nations, Grenada has suffered from a rise in violent, drug-related crime, particularly among increasingly disaffected youth. Prison conditions are poor, though they meet minimum international standards and the government allows human rights monitors to visit. Flogging is still legal, but it is rarely used, and then primarily as a punishment for sex crimes and theft cases.

There are no significant minority issues.

Women are represented in the government, though in greater numbers in the ministries than in parliament. No official discrimination takes place, but women generally earn less than men for equal work. Domestic violence against women is common. Police say that most instances of abuse are not reported and others are settled out of court. Child abuse remains a significant issue.

# ⬇ Guatemala

**Population:** 12,400,000
**GNI/capita:** $1,680
**Life Expectancy:** 66
**Religious Groups:** Roman Catholic, Protestant, indigenous beliefs
**Ethnic Groups:** Mestizo (55 percent), Amerindian (43 percent), other (2 percent)
**Capital:** Guatemala City

**Political Rights:** 4
**Civil Liberties:** 4
**Status:** Partly Free

**Trend Arrow:** Guatemala received a downward trend arrow due to increased violence, mostly criminal but also political, and widespread corruption.

**Ten-Year Ratings Timeline (Political Rights, Civil Liberties, Status)**

| 1994 | 1995 | 1996 | 1997 | 1998 | 1999 | 2000 | 2001 | 2002 | 2003 |
|------|------|------|------|------|------|------|------|------|------|
| 4,5PF | 4,5PF | 3,4PF | 3,4PF | 3,4PF | 3,4PF | 3,4PF | 3,4PF | 4,4PF | 4,4PF |

**Overview:** After great uncertainty and the threat of widespread violence, the November 2003 elections took place relatively peacefully. Neither Alvaro Colom of the Gran Alianza Nacional (GANA) nor Alvaro Colom of the Unidad Nacional de la Esperanza (UNE) received an absolute majority, forcing a runoff election to be held in late December. Parliamentary elections were held the same month saw the Frente Republicano Guatemalteco (FRG) lose its majority in legislative majority. Meanwhile, criminal and political violence are on the rise, prompting the government to institute a controversial program targeting gangs.

The Republic of Guatemala, which was established in 1839, has endured a history of dictatorship, coups, and guerrilla insurgency. Civilian rule followed the 1985 elections, and a 36-year civil war ended with the signing of a peace agreement in 1996. The peace accords led to the successful demobilization of the Guatemalan National Revolutionary Unity (URNG) guerrillas and their political legalization, the retirement of more than 40 senior military officers on corruption and narcotics charges, and the reduction of the army's strength by one-third. A truth commission mandated by the peace accords began receiving complaints of rights violations committed during the conflict. In a May 1999 referendum, voters rejected a package of amendments to the constitution, approved by congress a year earlier, which had been prepared in accordance with the peace plan.

The former guerrillas of the URNG, seriously divided and unable to make electoral gains, offered a blunt assessment of the peace accords in early 2002: "Genocide is no longer state policy." There is a general consensus that with the failure to implement substantive reforms redressing social and economic inequalities, the peace process is dead. This failure includes the government's inability to end the military's political tutelage and impunity, to fully recognize the rights of the Maya Indians, and to reform taxation to pay for health, education, and housing programs for the poor.

In late 2002, the government of President Alfonso Portillo signed an agreement to provide $400 million in compensation to the victims of the nation's 36-year civil war during which more than 200,000 died and over 200 mostly indigenous villages were destroyed. The National Compensation Program is a result of the 1996 UN-brokered peace accords and the ensuing truth commission.

In July 2003, the constitutional court ruled that retired General Efrain Rios Montt could stand for the presidency. He was later chosen as the candidate for the FRG. The court's decision was condemned at home and abroad. On July 24 and 25, violent demonstrations were staged in Guatemala City as the FRG brought armed supporters to bully the court's justices and critics. The UN Verification Mission for Guatemala (MINIGUA) condemned the fighting as a threat to citizen security.

November 9 presidential elections were held with less than the expected violence, though voting was suspended in seven municipalities because of violence. In the run-up to the election, more than 30 political activists were assassinated. The ruling FRG also authorized a first payment of $645, as "compensation" for their service, to each of the 520,000 members of the Civilian Defense Patrols (CAP). These groups had been set up by the armed forces and were made up of volunteers or impressed local men. The payment was seen as an effort to buy electoral support, though all presidential candidates eventually supported the measure.

Oscar Berger, a former mayor of Guatemala City, of the GANA received 34 percent of the vote. Alvaro Colom, who offers a populist message that appeals to Guatemala's "Mayaness," of UNE party obtained 26 percent of the ballot. Rios Montt came in a distant third with 19 percent. Under the constitution, a runoff election will be held between Berger and Colom since no candidate polled more than 50 percent.

In parliamentary elections held the same month, the FRG lost its congressional majority, but will still have 44 seats, with GANA holding 49 and UNE having 34. At the local level, the FRG was the most successful party, having won over 100 municipalities; GANA won 69, and UNE, 33. The significance of this outcome makes governability a serious concern, as the FRG still has significant support at the grassroots level. The FRG's appeal is based partly on a message of law and order that appeals to segments of the population exposed to high levels of lawlessness and violence. While UNE is identified as left-of-center, as a whole, the left did not fare well with the URNG getting 2 seats in congress. By contrast, after the 1999 elections, the URNG coalition was the third political party.

While the civil war is over, assassinations, kidnappings, beatings, break-ins, and death threats are still common. Death squads have reappeared, and hundreds of street children continue to be murdered and mutilated. In response to a dramatic increase in gang-related violence, the government has implemented a controversial jail-based program targeting gangs (maras) called "The Sweep-up Plan" and modeled after Honduras's draconian anti-gang efforts. President Portillo admitted that clandestine groups with military ties exist, but claims to be powerless to combat them. Guatemala's governance problems are on the rise as corruption and lawlessness increase with impunity.

**Political Rights and Civil Liberties:** Citizens can change their government through democratic means. The 1985 constitution, amended in 1994, provides for a four-year presidential term and prohibits reelection. A unicameral congress consisting of 113 members (increased from 80) is elected for four years. Corruption is widespread and efforts to promote transparency have made little progress

The press and most broadcast media outlets are privately owned. Seven dailies are published in the capital, and six are local. There are several radio stations, most of them commercial. Four of the six television stations are commercially operated and are owned by the same financial interest. Reporters Sans Frontieres, a Paris-based organization, has repeatedly noted that journalists and human rights activists were targets of intimidation, including death threats. Access to the Internet is not limited.

The constitution guarantees religious freedom. The government does not interfere with academic freedom; however, academics have been targets of death threats.

The constitution guarantees the right to organize political parties and civic organizations. Nevertheless, human rights groups are the targets of frequent death threats and the victims of acts of violence. In May, the Inter-American Human Rights Commission noted that 11 activists had been murdered since the elections were announced. The commission also indicated that more than 30 human rights abuses had taken place against grassroots leaders in the period between April and July. An appeals court in May annulled the 30-year sentence of Colonel Juan Valencia Osorio, who had been found guilty of organizing the murder of human rights activist Myrna Mack in 1990. General Edgar Godoy Gaitan and Colonel Juan Oliva Carrera, former heads of the presidential military guard (EMP), also convicted for the same crime, were absolved. The decisions were widely seen as evidence of continued impunity and corruption.

Workers are frequently denied the right to organize and are subjected to mass firings and blacklisting, particularly in export-processing zones where the majority of workers are women. Existing unions are targets of intimidation, physical attack, and assassination, particularly in rural areas during land disputes.

The judicial system remains ineffectual for most legal and human rights complaints. In general, it suffers from chronic problems of corruption, intimidation, insufficient personnel, lack of training opportunities, and a lack of transparency and accountability. The indigenous population continues to be shut out from the national justice system. Although indigenous languages are now being used in courtrooms around the country, Guatemalan·authorities mostly dismiss traditional justice systems. Cursory recruitment efforts have resulted in only a handful of indigenous recruits for the National Civilian Police (PNC).

Despite increasing freedoms, Guatemala has yet to end a tradition of military dominance. The demobilization of the presidential bodyguard and military intelligence, the two units held most accountable for human rights abuses, mandated by the peace accords has not taken place. Guatemala remains one of the most violent countries in Latin America. The closing of military barracks throughout the country—the armed forces were the one Guatemalan institution that had a truly national presence—while the PNC was being created and deployed created a vacuum in which criminal activity escalated. One result was an upsurge of vigilantism and lynchings. Neighborhood patrols—some armed with automatic weapons—have sprung up in an attempt to arrest the spiraling crime wave. More than 60,000 private security guards far outnumber the PNC. President Alfonso Portillo has called out army troops to assist the PNC in patrolling urban areas. Drug trafficking is a serious problem, and Guatemala remains a transit point for drugs going to the United States.

Eighty percent of the population lives below poverty levels, and infant mortality among the Maya—some 60 percent of the population—is among the highest on the continent.

Violence against women and children is widespread and common. There is extensive human trafficking, especially of illegal aliens from Asia en route to the United States. Women and children are drawn into prostitution both locally and in neighboring countries. Guatemala has the highest rate of child labor in the Americas, with one-third of school-aged children forced to work on farms or in factories.

# Guinea

**Population:** 9,000,000
**GNI/capita:** $410
**Life Expectancy:** 49
**Political Rights:** 6
**Civil Liberties:** 5
**Status:** Not Free
**Religious Groups:** Muslim (85 percent), Christian (8 percent), indigenous beliefs (7 percent)
**Ethnic Groups:** Peuhl (40 percent), Malinke (30 percent), Soussou (20 percent), other (10 percent)
**Capital:** Conakry

### Ten-Year Ratings Timeline (Political Rights, Civil Liberties, Status)

| 1994 | 1995 | 1996 | 1997 | 1998 | 1999 | 2000 | 2001 | 2002 | 2003 |
|------|------|------|------|------|------|------|------|------|------|
| 6,5NF | 6,5NF | 6,5NF | 6,5NF | 6,5NF | 6,5NF | 6,5NF | 6,5NF | 6,5NF | 6,5NF |

**Overview:**    In advance of presidential elections to be held in December 2003, leading opposition parties were considering boycotting the vote, and it did not appear as though the polls would be held in a free and fair atmosphere. Guinea is surrounded by countries in conflict, and fighting has already spilled over its borders from Liberia and Sierra Leone. There are persistent tensions between impoverished Guineans and the more than 100,000 refugees that Guinea hosts and who receive humanitarian aid.

Under Ahmed Sekou Toure, Guinea declared independence from France in 1958. Alone among France's many African colonies, it rejected the domination of continued close ties with France. Paris retaliated quickly, removing or destroying all "colonial property" and enforcing an unofficial but devastating economic boycott. Sekou Toure's one-party rule became highly repressive, and Guinea was increasingly impoverished under his Soviet-style economic policies. Lansana Conte seized power in a 1984 coup and was nearly toppled by a 1996 army mutiny. Amid general looting in Conakry, he rallied loyal troops and reestablished his rule.

Conte was returned to office in a 1998 presidential election that lacked credible opposition as state patronage and media strongly backed the incumbent. His reelection to another five-year term, with 54 percent of the vote, was unconvincing, although broad manipulation of the electoral process and opposition disunity probably made more blatant forms of vote rigging unnecessary. Although the polls were an improvement over past elections, hundreds of people were arrested after the vote, including the official third-place finisher, Alpha Conde.

The June 2002 National Assembly elections were not considered fair because of an opposition boycott and the government's control of the electoral process. The ruling Progress and Unity Party easily won the two-thirds majority required to enact constitutional changes. The European Union refused to send observers and financial aid for the vote.

Opposition candidates threatened to boycott the December 2003 vote unless an independent electoral commission was formed and access to state media and political rallies were allowed. Government participation in discussions aimed at improving the fairness of Guinea's polls appeared to be insincere because by October no visible effort had been made to level the playing field. President Conte said he would stand for reelection, although he would not be campaigning. Poor health casts doubt on whether Conte would be able to carry out a full seven-year term, and concern is mounting as to whether Guinea could have a peaceful transition of leadership. In addition to the 100,000 refugees from Liberia and Sierra Leone that Guinea hosts, more than 100,000 Guinean migrants returned from Ivory Coast after the outbreak of hostilities there at the end of 2002. Most of the returnees have been hosted by communities along the border, increasing competition for scant resources.

Guinea's economy has suffered from a world drop in the price of bauxite. The country is the world's second-largest producer of the mineral and is also rich in gold, diamonds, and iron ore.

**Political Rights and Civil Liberties:** The Guinean people's constitutional right to freely elect their government is not yet respected in practice. Guinean politics and parties are largely defined along ethnic lines. Guinea held a referendum in 2001 on extending presidential terms from five to seven years, allowing for unlimited terms in office, and eliminating presidential age limits. The provisions in the referendum were approved in a flawed vote that was boycotted by members of the opposition and marked by low turnout. The referendum also granted President Lansana Conte the power to appoint local officials and Supreme Court judges. The cabinet and armed forces leadership include members of all major ethnic groups in Guinea, but there are a disproportionate number of senior military officers from Conte's Soussou ethnic group.

The government has wide powers to bar any communications that insult the president or disturb the peace. All broadcasting outlets, as well as the country's largest and only daily newspaper, are state controlled and offer little coverage of the opposition and scant criticism of government policy. The print media have little impact in rural areas, where incomes are low and illiteracy is high. Several newspapers in Conakry offer sharp criticism of the government despite frequent harassment. A restrictive press law allows the government to censor or shutter publications on broad and ill-defined bases. Defamation and slander are considered criminal offenses. Internet access is unrestricted.

Constitutionally protected religious rights are respected in practice, although the main body representing the country's Muslims, who constitute 85 percent of the population, is government controlled. Academic freedom is generally respected, but the government influences hiring and the content of the curriculum.

Several statutes restrict freedom of association and assembly in apparent contravention of constitutional guarantees. The government may ban any gathering that "threatens national unity." Nevertheless, several human rights groups and many other nongovernmental groups operate openly. The International Committee of the Red Cross has helped teach security forces about respect for human rights. The constitution provides for the right to form and join unions. However, only a very small formal (business) sector exists. Several labor confederations compete in this small market and have the right to bargain collectively. Unions in rural areas sometimes face harassment and government interference.

While nominally independent, the judicial system remains infected by corruption, nepotism, ethnic bias, and political interference, and lacks resources and training. Minor civil cases are often handled by traditional ethnic-based courts. Arbitrary arrests and detention are common, and there are reports of persistent maltreatment and torture of detainees. Prison conditions are harsh and sometimes life-threatening. Security forces commit abuses, including torture and extrajudicial execution, with impunity. Vigilantism is a problem.

Ethnic identification is strong in Guinea. There is widespread societal discrimination by members of all major ethnic groups. The ruling party is more ethnically integrated than opposition parties, which have clear regional and ethnic bases.

Women have far fewer educational and employment opportunities than men, and many societal customs discriminate against women. Constitutionally protected women's rights are often unrealized. Women have access to land, credit, and business, but inheritance laws favor men. Violence against women is said to be prevalent. Spousal abuse is a criminal offense, but security forces rarely intervene in domestic matters. Women's groups are working to eradicate the illegal, but widespread, practice of female genital mutilation.

# Guinea-Bissau

**Population:** 1,300,000
**GNI/capita:** $160
**Life Expectancy:** 45
**Religious Groups:** Indigenous beliefs (50 percent), Muslim (45 percent), Christian (5 percent)
**Ethnic Groups:** Balanta (30 percent), Fula (20 percent), Manjaca (14 percent), Mandinga (13 percent), Papel (7 percent), other (16 percent)
**Capital:** Bissau

**Political Rights:** 6*
**Civil Liberties:** 4*
**Status:** Partly Free

**Ratings Change:** Guinea-Bissau's political rights rating declined from 4 to 6 following a military coup, while its civil liberties rating improved from 5 to 4 because of a general easing of arrests of political opponents and interference in the judiciary.

**Ten-Year Ratings Timeline (Political Rights, Civil Liberties, Status)**

| 1994 | 1995 | 1996 | 1997 | 1998 | 1999 | 2000 | 2001 | 2002 | 2003 |
|------|------|------|------|------|------|------|------|------|------|
| 3,4PF | 3,4PF | 3,4PF | 3,4PF | 3,5PF | 3,5PF | 4,5PF | 4,5PF | 4,5PF | 6,4PF |

**Overview:**

The military overthrew President Kumba Yala in September 2003 and a Transitional National Council, led by a general, was formed. Following consultations with a spectrum of political groups, the council chose a civilian to lead an interim government and prepare for elections.

Guinea-Bissau won independence from Portugal in 1973 after a 12-year guerrilla war. The African Party for the Independence of Guinea-Bissau and Cape Verde (PAIGC) held power for the next 13 years. Luis Cabral became president in 1974 and made Joao Bernardo Vieira his prime minister, but Vieira toppled Cabral in 1980. Constitutional revisions in 1991 ended the PAIGC's repressive one-party rule. Vieira won the country's first free and fair presidential election in 1994, but he eventually came to be seen as the leader of a corrupt ruling class.

An army mutiny broke out in 1998 after Vieira sacked General Ansumane Mane, accusing him of smuggling arms to rebels in the southern Casamance region of neighboring Senegal, which for years had complained that Guinea-Bissau was backing the rebels. Encouraged by France, about 3,000 troops from Senegal and Guinea intervened on behalf of Vieira. They were eventually replaced by fewer than 600 unarmed West African peacekeepers, which made Vieira vulnerable to his overthrow in May 1999 by Mane.

In the November 1999 presidential elections, the populist Yala of the Social Renewal Party (PRS) won a January 2000 second round runoff over Malam Bacai Sanha of the PAIGC. However, fighting broke out in 2000 between military supporters of Yala and those of Mane after Mane declared himself the head of the armed forces; Mane was subsequently killed. In legislative voting, also held in November 1999, the opposition PRS obtained 38 of the 102 seats, followed by the Resistance of Guinea with 29 and the PAIGC with 24. The 11 remaining seats went to five of the ten other parties that fielded candidates. In November 2002, Yala dissolved the National Assembly. He failed to promulgate a constitution approved in 2001, and Guinea-Bissau was governed by decree.

The general public, which had become increasingly frustrated by Yala's erratic rule and the economy's continual slide, applauded a military overthrow of President Yala in September 2003. Civil servants had not been paid for nearly a year, there was no constitution, strikes were rampant, and parliamentary elections had been postponed four times. By the time the military stepped in, a Transitional National Council (TNC), headed by General Verissimo Seabra, who led the coup, was overseeing a pledged return to elected government. Parliamentary elections were to be held in six months and presidential elections in one year. Henrique Rosa, a businessman who had previously led the national electoral commission, was named interim president. Rosa and Prime Minister Artur Sanha were appointed after the 56-member TNC held consultations with the country's spectrum of political leaders. The TNC was serving as the country's parliament; it includes 25 military officers, delegates from 24 political parties, and representatives of 8 civil society groups. After the coup, a blanket amnesty was granted to all those involved. Yala and his cabinet ministers were barred from standing in elections for five years. Yala was detained during the coup and released the next day. Although his overthrow was greeted with public enthusiasm, a smooth transition is not guaranteed, with divisions remaining in the military.

The vast majority of Guinea-Bissau's one million citizens survive on subsistence farming. Cashew nuts are a key export. There are hopes for substantial oil reserves offshore.

**Political Rights and Civil Liberties:** The people of Guinea-Bissau were able to choose their government freely for the first time in 1994, and both direct presidential polls and legislative elections were judged free and fair by international observers. Voting in the 1999 legislative and presidential elections was declared free and fair by international observers despite widespread delays, isolated cases of violence, and other voting irregularities. However, President Kumba Yala was overthrown in a military coup in September 2003.

Freedom of speech and the press is guaranteed, but journalists practice self-censorship and face some harassment. There are several private and community radio stations. Few private newspapers publish, and the lack of vibrant, independent media outlets may be due more to financial constraints than to government interference. In February, the Yala government ordered the independent Radio Bombolom to cease broadcasting for allegedly reporting false information that the authorities said could threaten national stability. In March, Ensa Seidi, the state-run radio station's editor in chief, was assaulted and expelled from his office for reporting about an opposition politician's return to the country and his plan to run for president. Internet access is unrestricted.

Religious freedom is protected and is usually respected in practice. About half of Guinea-Bissau's population is Muslim. Academic freedom is guaranteed and respected.

The right to peaceful assembly and association is guaranteed and usually respected in practice. Nongovernmental organizations and human rights groups operate openly, although their leaders sometimes face harassment. Six opposition activists were detained in February 2003. The right to strike is guaranteed, and strikes over unpaid wages were rampant in 2003. Collective bargaining rights are not guaranteed, but a National Council for Social Consultation has been established, including the government, workers, and employers, to deal with labor issues. Most wages are established in bilateral negotiations.

The judiciary has operated independently of the government, but its freedom was increasingly limited by President Yala. In 2001, he dismissed four members of the Supreme Court, and in 2002, he imposed his choice to head the Supreme Court over the protest of opposition leaders, saying that the court would soon be able to elect its own officers. Judicial performance is often unpredictable owing to political interference, poor training, and scant resources. Traditional law usually prevails in rural areas. Police routinely ignore privacy rights and protections against search and seizure. Severe mistreatment of detainees is reported.

Women face some legal and significant traditional and societal discrimination, despite legal protection. They generally do not receive equal pay for equal work and have fewer opportunities for education and jobs in the small formal sector. Domestic violence against women is common, and female genital mutilation is widespread. The government has formed a national committee to discourage the practice.

# Guyana

**Population:** 800,000
**GNI/capita:** $840
**Life Expectancy:** 63
**Political Rights:** 2
**Civil Liberties:** 2
**Status:** Free
**Religious Groups:** Christian (50 percent), Hindu
(35 percent), Muslim (10 percent), other (5 percent)
**Ethnic Groups:** East Indian (50 percent), black (36 percent),
Amerindian (7 percent), other (7 percent)
**Capital:** Georgetown

**Ten-Year Ratings Timeline (Political Rights, Civil Liberties, Status)**

| 1994 | 1995 | 1996 | 1997 | 1998 | 1999 | 2000 | 2001 | 2002 | 2003 |
|------|------|------|------|------|------|------|------|------|------|
| 2,2F | 2,2F | 2,2F | 2,2F | 2,2F | 2,2F | 2,2F | 2,2F | 2,2F | 2,2F |

**Overview:**

Guyana's political leadership faced growing questions in 2003 about its ability to combat crime and corruption and its commitment to the rule of law. Amidst what some critics called a "crisis of governance," worries grew about the possibility that foreign narcotics traffickers were extending their reach in the country. Meanwhile, the lack of legitimate foreign investment in Guyana spurred an increasing out-migration of its hard-pressed population.

From independence in 1966 until 1992, Guyana was ruled by the autocratic, predominantly Afro-Guyanese, People's National Congress (PNC). Descendants of indentured workers from India—known as Indo-Guyanese—make up about half of the population, while about 36 percent are Afro-Guyanese descended from African slaves.

The first free and fair elections were held in 1992, and 80 percent of the eligible population voted. The PNC lost to the PPP/C, an alliance of the predominantly Indo-Guyanese People's Progressive Party (PPP) and the Civic Party. PPP leader Cheddi Jagan, having moderated his Marxism since the collapse of communism, became president with 52 percent of the vote. Jagan's work was cut short by his death in March 1997, and he was replaced by Samuel Hinds, a member of Civic, the PPP's coalition partner. Hinds called elections for December 15, 1997, in which Jagan's widow, Janet, defeated the PNC's Desmond Hoyte. Ill health forced Janet Jagan to resign in August 1999, and she was replaced by the finance minister, Bharrat Jagdeo, who promised to heal racial and political divides and to welcome foreign investment.

Jagdeo was reelected on March 19, 2001, after 90 percent of eligible voters turned out to cast their ballots in voting that showed the country's continuing deep divisions along racial lines. Jagdeo's first initiative on being declared the winner was to make a televised national appeal to his countrymen to begin a process of national healing. In mid-2001, violence erupted in several small towns in protest against crime, poverty, and poor public services.

A rising crime rate and a parliamentary impasse dominated Guyana's political scene throughout 2002. The PPP/C and the main opposition People's National Congress/Reform (PNC/R) traded bitter words over the issue of payment for opposition members engaged in a boycott of parliament, in effect since March 15. The PNC/R said that unless agreed-upon reforms of the parliamentary system were implemented, it considered participation in National Assembly debates to be meaningless. Independent observers noted that the impasse posed few immediate risks to political stability, given that the PNC/R continued to participate in the Public Accounts Committee, which is the only standing committee in the assembly.

From February to September 2002, nearly a dozen police officers and more than 50 civilians were killed in an outbreak of violent crime that exacerbated uneasy relations between the two main races. In September, the PPP/C-dominated parliament passed four anticrime initiatives. However, PNC/R representatives who boycotted the legislative session claimed that the measures would not solve Guyana's crime problem, but rather were meant "to arm the regime with the draconian powers of dictatorship."

In January 2003, Amnesty International called recently adopted anticrime legislation "draconian" and said that its mandatory death penalty provisions for those committing a "terrorist act" were "in breach of international law." The organization said further said that it was particularly concerned that "the broad and vague definition of 'terrorist act' adopted ... could be interpreted so as to encompass activities which involve the legitimate exercise of rights guaranteed under international law," including the right to strike. The March 1, 2003, shooting by police of an 18-year-old architecture student in disputed circumstances elevated concerns over extrajudicial killings by the security forces.

In September, a new controversy erupted with the publication of a draft World Bank report that claimed there was a "crisis of governance" in Guyana, and that the government in Georgetown, which had yet to demonstrate a "real commitment to political reform," was unable to promote growth and development nor to manage the challenges of endemic crime and corruption. The crisis, the report said, "discouraged investments, severely compromised good governance and fuelled migration." The World Bank report warned that increasing racial tension would result in violent conflict. "Nowhere was the crisis in governance more evident than in the area of security," it said, "to the point where the rule of law, the security and judicial systems, were viewed as having collapsed and confidence in the army, police and judiciary largely evaporated."

In September, President Jagdeo asked U.S. President George Bush for help in combating cocaine trafficking, saying he feared that the Colombian drug trade was gaining a foothold in Guyana.

**Political Rights and Civil Liberties:** Citizens can change their government democratically. The 2001 elections generated a broader consensus about the importance of election reform to the democratic process. Because the constitution lacks explicit guarantees, political rights and civil liberties rest more on government tolerance than on institutional protection. The 1980 constitution provides for a strong president and the 65-seat National Assembly, elected every five years. Twelve seats are occupied by elected local officials. The leader of the party winning the plurality of parliamentary seats becomes president for a five-year term, who in turn appoints the prime minister and cabinet.

Several independent newspapers operate freely, including the daily *Stabroek News*. However, a growing number of journalists charged the government with failure to respect freedom of the electronic media. The government owned and operated the country's sole radio station, which broadcast on three frequencies. There are no private radio stations. Seventeen privately owned television stations freely criticize the government.

Guyanese generally enjoy freedom of religion and the government does not restrict academic freedom.

The freedom to organize political parties, civic organizations, and labor unions are generally respected. Labor unions are well organized. Companies are not obligated to recognize unions in former state enterprises sold off by the government.

The judicial system is independent, although due process is undermined by shortages of staff and funds. Prisons are overcrowded and conditions are poor. Guyana is the only former British colony in the Caribbean to have cut all ties to the Privy Council of London, the court of last resort for other former colonies in the region. The Guyana Defence Force and the Guyana Police Force are under civilian control, the latter invested with the authority to make arrests and maintain law and order throughout the country. Guyana's porous and largely unpatrolled borders have made the country an increasingly attractive transshipment route for South American cocaine, which, together with a small domestic cultivation of marijuana, has caused local consumption of illegal drugs to increase markedly.

The Guyana Human Rights Association, an autonomous and effective group backed by independent civic and religious groups, reported that security forces killed 39 civilians during the year, compared with 28 in 2002. Although authorities have taken some steps to investigate extrajudicial killings, and charges against some officers have been brought, the numbers are further evidence that abuses are still committed with impunity.

Racial clashes have diminished within the last decade. However, long-standing animosity between Afro- and Indo-Guyanese remains a deep concern. A Racial Hostility Bill passed in September 2002 increased the penalties for race-based crimes. In May 2003, the government appointed an ethnic relations commission to help combat discrimination and reduce social tensions.

There are nine groups of indigenous peoples in Guyana numbering approximately 80,000, or 10 percent of the population. Human rights violations against them are widespread and pervasive, particularly concerning the failure of the state to adequately respect indigenous land and resource rights. Indigenous peoples' attempts to seek redress through the courts have been met with unwarranted delays by the judiciary. In 2002, an agreement between the government and Conservation International, establishing southern Guyana as a protected area, was criticized by indigenous groups as "gross disrespect," since the parties did not consult with six Indian communities whose ancestral lands will be encompassed by the accord. On a positive note, recent government collaboration with UN relief agencies had resulted in improvements in health care, education, and food programs in indigenous communities.

Violence against women, including domestic violence, is common in Guyana. There are no legal protections against sexual harassment in the workplace.

# ⬇ Haiti

**Population:** 7,500,000
**GNI/capita:** $480
**Life Expectancy:** 51
**Religious Groups:** Roman Catholic (80 percent),
Protestant (16 percent), other (4 percent)
**Ethnic Groups:** Black (95 percent), other [including
mulatto and white] (5 percent)
**Capital:** Port-au-Prince

**Political Rights:** 6
**Civil Liberties:** 6
**Status:** Not Free

**Trend Arrow:** Haiti received a downward trend arrow due to ongoing political warfare, rampant corruption, and generalized social and political violence.

**Ten-Year Ratings Timeline (Political Rights, Civil Liberties, Status)**

| 1994 | 1995 | 1996 | 1997 | 1998 | 1999 | 2000 | 2001 | 2002 | 2003 |
|------|------|------|------|------|------|------|------|------|------|
| 5,5PF | 5,5PF | 4,5PF | 4,5PF | 5,5PF | 5,5PF | 6,5NF | 6,6NF | 6,6NF | 6,6NF |

**Overview:**

The year 2003 saw no progress in stemming the absolute decline in the political and economic conditions that, for most Haitians, make life extremely difficult. Political violence increased dramatically as parts of the country slipped into chaos, and supporters of President Jean-Bertrand Aristide battled opponents on a regular basis in the streets of Port-au-Prince. Hopes for a brokered solution to the impasse over parliamentary elections scheduled for January 2004 grew dimmer, as the opposition began to insist on the resignation of the president.

Since gaining independence from France in 1804 following a slave revolt, the Republic of Haiti has endured a history of poverty, violence, instability, and dictatorship. A 1986 military coup ended 29 years of rule by the Duvalier family, and the army ruled for most of the next 8 years. Under international pressure, the military permitted the implementation of a French-style constitution in 1987.

Aristide was first elected in 1990. After having called on his supporters to use force in defending his government, he was deposed by a military triumvirate after only eight months in office and sent into exile. While paramilitary thugs terrorized the populace, the regime engaged in blatant narcotics trafficking. The United States and the United Nations imposed a trade and oil embargo. In September 1994, facing an imminent U.S. invasion, the officers stepped down. U.S. troops took control of the country, and Aristide was reinstated. Aristide dismantled the military before the June 1995 parliamentary elections got under way. International observers questioned the legitimacy of the June election, and Aristide's supporters fell out among themselves. The more militant Lavalas Family (FL) party remained firmly behind him, while the National Front for Change and Democracy (FNCD), a leftist coalition that had backed him in 1990, claimed fraud and boycotted the runoff elections. The FL won an overwhelming parliamentary majority.

The FL nominated Rene Preval, Aristide's prime minister in 1991, as its presidential candidate in the fall. In the December 17, 1995 election, marred by irregularities and fraud, Preval won about 89 percent of the vote with a turnout of less than one-third of those eligible; he took office on February 7, 1996. The United Nations had planned to withdraw its troops by the end of the month. The new U.S.-trained Haitian National Police (HNP), however, lacked the competence to fill the void. At Preval's urging, the United Nations extended its stay, but by June cut its presence to 1,300. The final U.S. combat force had withdrawn two months earlier.

In September 1996, Preval purged much of his security force after allegations surfaced that members were involved in the murders of two politicians from the right-wing Mobilization for National Development (MDN) party. Senate elections held in April 1997 were beset by irregularities, and the resulting ongoing election dispute meant that parliament would not approve a new prime minister to replace Rosny Smarth, who resigned in June 1997 following growing criticism of the government's policies. In September, Aristide announced an alliance with other congressional groups to oppose Preval's economic reform plans.

Aristide had been revered as a defender of the powerless and was swept to victory again in November 2000. The elections were boycotted by all major opposition parties and held amidst widespread civil unrest and voter intimidation. Aristide ran on a populist platform of economic reactivation; opponents claimed he was bent on establishing a one-party state. Aristide's nearly 92 percent of the vote in the presidential election was mirrored in contests for nine Senate seats—all won by his FL party—giving his new government all but one seat in the upper house. In parliamentary elections, which opponents claimed were rigged, the FL won 80 percent of the seats in the lower house.

Following a mysterious attack on congress in December 2001 and the subsequent violent retribution, various international efforts, including those of the Organization of American States (OAS), with over 20 visits, have failed to find a negotiated solution to the political impasse that began after the 2000 parliamentary elections. The opposition Democratic Convergence (DC) has refused to cooperate with President Aristide's efforts to stitch together a coalition that will satisfy the reservations of the United States and the OAS and lead to an end to the sanctions imposed on Haiti.

The country has become a dictatorship in all but name, as power has been monopolized by Aristide and his FL party. The FL holds 73 of 83 seats in the Chamber of Deputies and 19 of 27 in the Senate; there are 8 seats vacant in the latter. Two-thirds of the Senate and all members of the Chamber of Deputies are up for election in January 2004. If elections are not held, the president will be forced to dissolve the legislature and govern by decree. The next presidential elections are scheduled for November 2005, and though Aristide may not be reelected, no successor has been named.

Political warfare involving the former military, Aristide supporters, and others continues unabated. Since 2000, the FL itself appears to have fallen victim to open strife between warring factions. In September 2003, Amiot Metayer, a former FL militant who had moved to oppose Aristide, was murdered. As the murder remained unresolved, supporters mounted protests, and on October 1, they attacked government buildings. In the ensuing melee, five people were left dead, with witnesses claiming that the police had shot indiscriminately into the crowds.

Haiti has the lowest life expectancy and highest infant mortality rates in the Western Hemisphere. Haiti's people are among the poorest in the Western Hemisphere and have the lowest levels of human development, including a literacy rate of less than 50 percent.

**Political Rights and Civil Liberties:** Citizens of Haiti cannot change their government democratically. Haiti's 1987 constitution provides for a president elected for five years, an elected parliament composed of the 27-member Senate and the 83-member Chamber of Deputies, and a prime minister appointed by the president. Credible charges of irregularities and fraud have beset every election since 1990. The Lavalas Family (FL) party has manipulated most legislative and general elections, including the presidential election of 2000. In practice, the FL controls the presidential, legislative, and judicial branches, and most local and regional elected leaders are members of the FL.

Haiti received the dubious distinction of being identified as the most corrupt country in the region by Transparency International in its 2003 Corruption Perceptions Index.

Freedom of speech and the press is limited, and violence against journalists is common. International observers find that media outlets tend to practice self-censorship over fear of violent retribution. There is a variety of newspapers, including two French-language newspapers, with a combined circulation of less than 20,000 readers. Many newspapers include a page of news in Creole. While opposition to the government can be found in the written press, access to such views is beyond the reach of most, primarily because of illiteracy and cost. There are 275 private radio stations, including 43 in the capital. Most stations carry news and talk shows, which many citizens regard as their only opportunity to speak out with some freedom. Television is state run and strongly biased toward the government. Satellite television is available, though it has a minimal impact as most Haitians cannot afford access to television. The few stations carrying news or opinion broadcasts express a range of views. There is no censorship of books or films, and access to the Internet is free. There is freedom of religion. The official educational system is hostage to patronage and pressure from the FL.

Freedom of assembly and association, including labor rights, are not respected. Unions are too weak to engage in collective bargaining, and their organizing efforts are undermined by the country's high unemployment rate.

The judicial system is corrupt, inefficient, and dysfunctional. The legal system is burdened by a large backlog, outdated legal codes, and poor facilities; business is conducted in French, rather than Creole, Haiti's majority language. Prison conditions are harsh, and the ponderous legal system guarantees lengthy pretrial detention periods. International reform efforts ended in 2000 following allegations of corruption involving the U.S. Agency for International Development (USAID), U.S. Justice Department contractors, and others.

The 5,200-member Haitian National Police (HNP) force has been politicized by the FL, is inexperienced, and lacks resources. The HNP has been accused of using excessive force and mistreating detainees, and accusations of corruption are frequent. The HNP is increasingly used against protesters attacking the government. Police brutality is on the rise, and there is credible evidence of extrajudicial killings by members of the HNP. Mob violence and armed gangs pose serious threats in urban areas. Former soldiers and others linked to the former military regime, as well as common criminals, are responsible for much of the violence, including political assassinations. Break-ins and armed robberies are commonplace, and many observers tie the growing violence directly to increases in the drug trade and local narcotics consumption. Haitian officials also say that the rise in crime is due to the repatriation of convicted criminals from other countries, particularly the United States. Turf wars between rival drug gangs have resulted in the killing of scores of people, including several policemen. Private security forces that carry out extralegal search and seizure are flourishing.

Trafficking of drugs and people is a serious problem. There is widespread violence against women and children. Up to 300,000 children serve in *restavec* ("live with" in Creole), a form of unpaid domestic labor with a long national history.

# ↓ Honduras

**Population:** 6,900,000     **Political Rights:** 3
**GNI/capita:** $900     **Civil Liberties:** 3
**Life Expectancy:** 71     **Status:** Partly Free
**Religious Groups:** Roman Catholic (97 percent), other
[including Protestant] (3 percent)
**Ethnic Groups:** Mestizo (90 percent), Amerindian (7 percent),
black (2 percent), white (1 percent)
**Capital:** Tegucigalpa
**Trend Arrow:** Honduras received a downward trend arrow due to increased social violence, especially from gangs (maras), and corruption.
**Ten-Year Ratings Timeline (Political Rights, Civil Liberties, Status)**

| 1994 | 1995 | 1996 | 1997 | 1998 | 1999 | 2000 | 2001 | 2002 | 2003 |
|------|------|------|------|------|------|------|------|------|------|
| 3,3PF | 3,3PF | 3,3F | 2,3F | 2,3PF | 3,3PF | 3,3PF | 3,3PF | 3,3PF | 3,3PF |

**Overview:**     The generalized violence product of gang activity and warfare led to the introduction in 2003 of a draconian law that outlawed gang membership and imposed stiff prison sentences. Crime rates have not been significantly reduced, and human rights organizations continue to be concerned over the constitutionality of the measures. Nevertheless, public support for the crackdown continues.

The Republic of Honduras was established in 1839, 18 years after independence from Spain. It has endured decades of military rule and intermittent elected government, with the last military regime giving way to elected civilian rule in 1982. The 1969 armed conflict between Honduras and El Salvador over land, sometimes known as the "Soccer War," ended with a peace treaty in 1980. The International Court of Justice (ICJ) ruled in 1992 that 69 percent of the territory in dispute should go to Honduras; the ICJ ruled in late 2003 against El Salvador's latest appeal.

President Maduro Joest of the center-left National Party of Honduras (PNH) took office on January 27, 2002, after winning the November 2001 elections. He was elected on a "zero tolerance" pledge aimed at ending crime, defeating conservative Liberal Party (PL) candidate Rafael Pineda Ponce by 8 percent of the vote. The elections, which were the sixth held since military rule came to an end, were characterized by international observers as mostly free, fair, and peaceful. On the eve of the election, however, congressional candidate Angel Pacheco, of the PNH, was gunned down outside of his house. Police arrested three employees of the PL, indicating that the crime appeared to be politically motivated.

In November 2002, after being shamed by international publicity over the murder of nearly 1,300 children in four years, the government announced the formation of a special security force, in addition to the 6,000 new police officers already put on the streets. Killers have been identified in less than 40 percent of these cases. Impunity and corruption, much of it official, still characterize the country.

In August 2003, congress unanimously approved a law banning gangs (*maras*) and stiffening the penalties for membership. Membership in a gang is now punishable by up to 12 years in prison. The law also provides for fines of up to $12,000 for gang leaders. The national commissioner of human rights is questioning the constitutionality of the law. The Ministry of Security has reported that there are 35,000 gang members and 65,000 hangers-on in the country, with 129 gangs active in the capital alone. By September, in "Operation Freedom," 300 people had been arrested under the new law. Although gang violence has escalated and includes apparently random attacks against both civilians and the police, the general public continues to support the crackdown on gangs.

Also in August, former president Carlos Roberto Reina, who defied the military and abolished compulsory military service, committed suicide.

Presidential and congressional elections are scheduled for November 2005, and electioneering has begun, with 14 names proposed for the PL, but none by the PNH.

The after effects of Hurricane Mitch, which devastated the country's economy and infrastructure in 1998, continued to be felt in 2003. About two-thirds of households live in poverty, and 40 percent of the population lives on less than one dollar a day.

## Political Rights and Civil Liberties:

Citizens are able to change their government through regularly scheduled elections. The 2001 contest was considered generally free and fair. The constitution provides for a president and a 130-member, unicameral congress elected for four years. Official corruption and the lingering power of the military have dominated the political scene since the return to democracy. Transparency International's 2003 Corruption Perceptions Index identified Honduras as one of the most corrupt countries in the world, with a ranking of 106 out of 133 countries.

Authorities generally respect constitutional guarantees of freedom of speech and of the press. There are, however, important exceptions, including credible reports of repression against journalists. Journalists have admitted to self-censorship when they uncover reports that threaten the political or economic interests of media owners. In 2002, Reporters Sans Frontiers reported that repressive laws restricting the media were still enforced. It cited the case of Sandra Maribel Sanchez, who was arrested and barred from leaving the country after being accused by a former government official, who Sanchez said was corrupt, of spying and also of illegally working as a journalist because she is not registered with the national journalists' institute as the law requires. Sanchez faces 14 years in prison. Newspapers circulate freely, and numerous radio and television stations broadcast freely. There is free access to the Internet.

Freedom of religion is respected. Academic freedom is generally honored.

Constitutional guarantees regarding the right to form political parties and civic organizations are generally respected. Although citizens have the right to freely assemble in groups, repressive measures in the face of peaceful protests and mounting crime have limited political rights and civil liberties. Labor unions are well organized and can strike, although labor actions often result in clashes with security forces. Labor leaders and members of religious groups and indigenous-based peasant unions pressing for land rights remain vulnerable to repression and have been killed.

The judicial system is weak and open to corruption, and due process is generally not available. Death threats and violent attacks continue against judges who take on human rights cases. Prison conditions are deplorable, and prisoners awaiting trial are housed with convicted inmates. A generalized lawlessness has allowed private and vigilante security forces to commit a number of arbitrary and summary executions, including the murder of hundreds of street children. Drug trafficking through Honduras has been on the rise, and drug-related corruption is pervasive.

The police are underfunded, ill-trained, understaffed, and highly corrupt. The military had controlled the police since 1963, but civilian control was reestablished beginning in 1997. In the past, the military has been used for internal security tasks—suppressing labor unrest, quelling street protests, and combating street crime. Extrajudicial killings, arbitrary detention, and torture by the police still take place. Several hundred youth gangs engage in murder, kidnapping, and robbery, as well as drug trafficking. The need to strengthen and professionalize the poorly equipped civilian police is hampered by a lack of public confidence. At the invitation of the government, the UN Special Rapporteur on Extrajudicial, Arbitrary, and Summary Executions visited Honduras in 2001 and noted evidence of 66 minors killed by police and private security forces from January to June of 2001 and the government's negligence in investigating or preventing extrajudicial and summary executions.

The military exerts considerable, if waning, influence over the government. A constitutional amendment established a civilian minister of defense in direct control over the armed forces and replaced the armed forces commander in chief with the chief of the joint staff. Congress also passed the Organic Law of the armed forces to solidify civilian control over the military. The armed forces made public its budget for the first time in 2001. Most criminal cases against the military remained in military court jurisdiction, and charges were usually dismissed. Since 1999, military personnel have no longer been immune from prosecution in civilian courts. Military officers have been found guilty of drug trafficking, including taking sides in cartel turf wars and protecting drug shipments in transit through Honduras.

The government of President Carlos Flores Facusse (1997-2001) had made efforts to give the concerns of indigenous and black peoples in Honduras a more prominent place in the public agenda. The current wave of violent crime has pushed such efforts into the background.

Some 85,000 workers, mostly women, are employed in the low-wage *maquiladora* (assembly plant) export sector. Child labor is a problem in rural areas and in the informal economy.

# Hungary

**Population:** 10,100,000
**GNI/capita:** $4,830
**Life Expectancy:** 72
**Religious Groups:** Roman Catholic (67.5 percent),
Calvinist (20 percent), Lutheran (5 percent),
other (7.5 percent)
**Ethnic Groups:** Hungarian (90 percent), Roma (4 percent),
German (3 percent), other (3 percent)
**Capital:** Budapest

**Political Rights:** 1
**Civil Liberties:** 2
**Status:** Free

**Ten-Year Ratings Timeline (Political Rights, Civil Liberties, Status)**

| 1994 | 1995 | 1996 | 1997 | 1998 | 1999 | 2000 | 2001 | 2002 | 2003 |
|------|------|------|------|------|------|------|------|------|------|
| 1,2F | 1,2F | 1,2F | 1,2F | 1,2F | 1,2F | 1,2F | 1,2F | 1,2F | 1,2F |

**Overview:**
In 2003, Hungary continued its progress toward the European Union (EU) by voting in favor of joining that body in an April referendum. The year also witnessed a polarized domestic political landscape in Hungary, which included a complex financial scandal involving embezzlement of public funds at the country's second largest financial institution.

King Stephen I, who ruled from 1001 to 1038, is credited with founding the Hungarian state. In the centuries that followed, Hungarian lands passed through Turkish, Polish, and Austrian hands. In the mid-nineteenth century, Hungary established a liberal, constitutional monarchy under the Austrian Hapsburgs, but two world wars and a Communist dictatorship in the twentieth century forestalled true independence.

In the late 1980s, the country's economy was in sharp decline. The Hungarian Socialist Worker's Party came under intense pressure to accept reforms. Ultimately, the party congress dissolved itself, and Hungary held its first free, multiparty parliamentary election in 1990. Since that time, government control in Hungary has passed freely and fairly between left- and right-leaning parties. The country has followed an aggressive path of reform and pursued the very popular cause of European integration.

The current political landscape reflects the thin margin of power enjoyed by the governing coalition, which came into power on the basis of a closely contested 2002 parliamentary election that was generally free and fair. After two rounds of voting, Prime Minister Viktor Orban's ruling coalition of the Hungarian Civic Party-Hungarian Democratic Forum (Fidesz-MDF) garnered just over 44 percent of the vote (188 mandates) and was unable to retain control of the National Assembly. The Hungarian Socialist Party (MSZP) won 42.8 percent (178 mandates). The Alliance of Free Democrats (SZDSZ) narrowly exceeded the 5 percent threshold (19 mandates). Voters elected one candidate on a joint MSZP-SZDSZ ticket. Following the election, the MSZP formed a majority government in partnership with the SZDSZ. The new Socialist-Liberal government elected Peter Medgyessy as prime minister.

Corruption remains a genuine problem for Hungary, which was hit mid-year by a sensational scandal concerning K&H Equities, the brokerage arm of the country's second largest financial institution. The investigation got under way as part of the routine audit responsibilities of the Hungarian Financial Supervisory Authority's (PSZAF) and was not initiated at the request of opposition parties. Karoly Szasz, the chairman of the PSZAF, was hospitalized after being assaulted by unknown assailants. The attack occurred the day before the PSZAF disclosed an illegal transaction involving shares of the State Highway Management Company (AAK). The subsequent investigation found that K&H Equities, with the knowledge of AAK management, diverted assets from AAK to private accounts through the brokerage. Further revelations showed that AAK was just one of several state-owned firms from which K&H had been diverting public funds. The PSZAF has extended its investigation to other organizations, including the Hungarian Development Bank (MFB) and the Finance Ministry, and the matter is now the subject of an ongoing criminal investigation. Meanwhile, the government has announced plans to reorganize the PSZAF, provoking sharp criticism from the European Commission.

Hungarians voted overwhelmingly in favor of joining the EU, with 84 percent of the supporting membership in the binding referendum that was held in April 2003. Turnout for the national referendum, 45 percent of those eligible to vote did so, was considered a disappointment when compared with the turnout of other EU candidate countries. Hungary, which joined NATO in 1999, is expected to formally become a member of the EU in May 2004.

Along with other countries that have made NATO and EU membership strategic objectives, and that are eager to have solid relations with both the United States and the EU, Hungary has walked a diplomatic tightrope, especially with respect to the war in Iraq. The contentious debate over the Iraq war has generated intense pressure on the countries of Central Europe, which have discovered that, in the era of global terrorism, finding their role within the transatlantic community has not been as easy as expected.

Elections to the European Parliament are scheduled for 2004 and, in 2006, parliamentary and municipal elections are scheduled for April and October, respectively.

**Political Rights and Civil Liberties:**   Citizens of Hungary can change their government democratically. Voters elect representatives to the 386-seat unicameral National Assembly under a mixed system of proportional and direct representation. The Hungarian parliament elects both the president and the prime minister.

Post-Communist elections in Hungary have been generally free and fair, although some problems persist. During the heated 2002 parliamentary elections, few parties respected campaign spending caps. The OSCE observed that state media coverage frequently favored the ruling Fidesz party and that government-sponsored "voter education" advertisements appeared to mirror Fidesz-sponsored campaign ads. The results of a local-level by-election in October 2003 were annulled by the courts, which cited illegal election-day mobilization, and the Central Election Commission issued a formal finding in fall 2003. In response to complaints related to the 2002 parliamentary elections, the law now prohibits the use of the voter registry for election-day mobilization. Prior to the 2002 election, Fidesz and Lundo Lungo Drom, a national Roma (Gypsy) party, concluded a political cooperation agreement. Despite this development, only four Roma candidates were elected to the National Assembly, the same number as in the previous election. Toward the end of 2002, the European Commission reported that Hungary was not meeting its constitutional obligation to ensure direct parliamentary representation of minorities.

Freedom of speech is respected, and independent media operate freely in Hungary, although within a highly polarized atmosphere. However, political controversy continues to trouble state television and radio. A 1996 media law requires both ruling and opposition parties to share appointments to state media oversight boards. Left-leaning opposition parties had previously accused the Fidesz party of stacking the oversight boards with supporters. After losing power in the parliamentary elections, Fidesz leaders have accused the new Socialist-Liberal government of attempting to inappropriately influence state television and radio. Both the Medgyessy government and the opposition have pledged to amend the current media law, but neither side possesses the two-thirds parliamentary majority necessary to pass the legislation.

The constitution guarantees religious freedom and provides for the separation of church and state. While all religions are generally free to worship in their own manner, the state provides financial support and tax breaks to large or traditional religions such as the Roman Catholic Church. Some critics have charged that these practices effectively discriminate against smaller denominations.

The Hungarian constitution provides for freedom of assembly and the government respects these rights in practice. The government also respects citizens' rights to form associations, strike, and petition public authorities. Trade unions account for less than 30 percent of the workforce.

Hungary has a three-tiered independent judiciary in addition to the Supreme Court and a constitutional court. The constitution guarantees equality before the law, and courts are generally fair, yet limited budget resources leave the system vulnerable to outside influence. While challenges still remain, previous and current governments have taken measures to reform the civil service, introduce stronger penalties for bribery, and implement a long-term anticorruption strategy.

The constitution guarantees national and ethnic minorities the right to form self-governing bodies. All 13 recognized minorities have exercised this right. In 2001, Hungary implemented a legal rights protection network to provide legal aid to the Roma community. The government also created the Roma Coordination Council, appointed special commissioners in the Ministry of Education and Employment and the Ministry of Labor to specifically oversee Roma issues, and named a minister-without-portfolio in the prime minister's office to promote equal opportunity. However, the Roma population continues to face widespread discrimination in many respects. In 2003, the Hungarian government agreed to pay compensation to the relatives of Hungarian Jews who died in the Holocaust. The compensation is to be provided to remaining family members of Hungarian Jews who perished in Nazi death camps or died during forced labor, as well as those persecuted under anti-Semitic laws in Hungary before the Holocaust began.

In 2001, parliament passed the controversial Status Law granting special health and educational benefits to ethnic Hungarians residing outside the country. The governments of Romania and Slovakia expressed deep concern over the discriminatory nature of the law. In 2003, Hungary came to an agreement with Slovakia and Romania on the application of the Status Law, which was modified to meet objections from the EU and neighboring lands.

Women possess the same legal rights as men, although they face hiring and pay discrimination and tend to be underrepresented in senior-level business and governmental positions. Hungary is a primarily a transit point, but is also a source and destination country for trafficked persons.

# Iceland

**Population:** 300,000
**GNI/capita:** $28,910
**Life Expectancy:** 80
**Political Rights:** 1
**Civil Liberties:** 1
**Status:** Free
**Religious Groups:** Evangelical Lutheran (87.1 percent), other Protestant (4.1 percent), Roman Catholic (1.7 percent), other (7.1 percent)
**Ethnic Groups:** Homogeneous mixture of descendants of Norse and Celts (94 percent), population of foreign origin (6 percent)
**Capital:** Reykjavik

**Ten-Year Ratings Timeline (Political Rights, Civil Liberties, Status)**

| 1994 | 1995 | 1996 | 1997 | 1998 | 1999 | 2000 | 2001 | 2002 | 2003 |
|------|------|------|------|------|------|------|------|------|------|
| 1,1F | 1,1F | 1,1F | 1,1F | 1,1F | 1,1F | 1,1F | 1,1F | 1,1F | 1,1F |

**Overview:**   Following parliamentary elections held in May 2003, David Oddsson retained his position as prime minister, but announced that he will step down in 2004. Iceland's Act on Foreigners went into effect on January 1. In the summer, Iceland resumed whale hunting, generating considerable international and domestic criticism.

After being dominated for centuries by Denmark and Norway, Iceland gained independence in 1944. It became a founding member of NATO in 1949, and two years later, it entered into a defense agreement with the United States that has allowed it to keep no military forces of its own. In 1985, Iceland declared itself a nuclear-free zone. Although the United States had proposed a withdrawal from Iceland, it was decided in fall 2003 that the U.S. Air Force base will remain, at least in the short term.

Economic growth in Iceland was at 4.5 percent for five years before dipping slightly in 2002. The UN's Human Development Index ranked Iceland second worldwide in quality of life last year. The country's abundant hydrothermal and geothermal resources make it one of the cleanest environments in the world.

Iceland held general elections on May 10, 2003. Oddsson's right-of-center Independence Party won 34 percent of the votes, giving it only 2 seats more than the left-leaning Social Democratic Alliance. The Independence Party now rules in coalition with the Progressive Party.

In August, Iceland began whale hunting after not having done so since 1989. Although the program was set up for scientific purposes only, it has been severely criticized by environmentalists and Iceland's own tourism industry, which fears that the hunting could damage Iceland's image. Countries such as the United States and the United Kingdom have formally condemned the practice, but about three-quarters of Iceland's population supports it.

While Iceland has strong historical, cultural, and economic ties with Europe, Icelanders are hesitant to join the European Union (EU). The reluctance is primarily because of the EU's Common Fisheries Policy, which Icelanders believe would threaten their own fishing industry, on which Iceland's economy is predominantly dependent. While Prime Minister Oddsson continues to rule out joining the EU, he has expressed a desire to cultivate a knowledge economy in order to wean the country from its dependence on fishing. The largest opposition party, the Social Democrats, favor EU membership for Iceland. In the meantime, the country has access to European markets as a member of the European Economic Area.

**Political Rights and Civil Liberties:** Icelanders can change their government democratically. Iceland's constitution, which was adopted in 1944, vests power in a president, whose functions are mainly ceremonial, a prime minister, a unicameral legislature (the Althingi), and a judiciary. The president is directly elected for a four-year term. The legislature is also elected for four years (subject to dissolution). The prime minister, who performs most executive functions, is appointed by the president but is responsible to the legislature. Elections are free and fair.

Five political movements are represented in the Althingi. The largest is the Independence Party, whose leader, David Oddsson, is Europe's longest-serving prime minister. Although the Independence Party has dominated Icelandic politics since the country's independence, elections are competitive. Since the May 2003 parliamentary election, the second-largest party, the Social Democratic Alliance, has had only two fewer seats than the Independence Party. Of the 63 members of the Althingi, about 30 percent are women.

Corruption is not a problem in Iceland. In October, Transparency International ranked Iceland the second least corrupt country of those included in its 2003 Corruption Perceptions Index.

The constitution provides for freedom of speech and of the press, and Iceland was tied for first place in the latest Reporters Sans Frontieres world press freedom index. A wide range of publications includes both independent and party-affiliated newspapers. An autonomous board of directors oversees the Icelandic National Broadcasting Service, which operates a number of transmitting and relay stations. There are both private and public television stations.

The constitution provides for the right to form religious associations and to practice any religion freely, although nearly 90 percent of Icelanders belong to the Evangelical Lutheran Church. The state financially supports and promotes the Church, both through a church tax and through religious instruction in schools. However, citizens who do not belong to a recognized religious organization may choose to give the tax to the University of Iceland and have their children exempted from religious instruction. The education system is free of excessive political involvement.

Freedom of association and peaceful assembly are respected. About 85 percent of all eligible workers belong to labor unions, and all enjoy the right to strike.

The country's judiciary is independent. The law does not provide for trial by jury, but many trials and appeals use panels consisting of several judges. All judges, at all levels, serve for life. Since amendments made in 1996, the constitution states that all people shall be treated equally before the law, regardless of sex, religion, opinion, ethnic origin, race, property, or other status. However, there is no constitutional provision specifically prohibiting racial discrimination.

The new Act on Foreigners, which went into force on January 1, 2003 specifies the government's powers with regard to foreigners, including refugees and asylum seekers. Given its geographic isolation, Iceland received only 22 asylum applications and just 207 refugees in 2002. Despite the new provisions, nongovernmental organizations have commented that some issues relating to the reception and treatment of asylum seekers remain unclear or unsatisfactorily resolved under the new legislation.

In 2002, Iceland gave its citizens' genetic data to a private, U.S.-backed medical research company, an action that has raised fears over privacy issues. Iceland, the most genetically homogenous nation on earth, went ahead with the plan on the grounds that the data could provide scientists with vital clues into the origin of diseases, thus increasing the chances of discovering cures. While a law was passed requiring doctors to hand over patient information, the law did contain a provision allowing citizens to opt out of providing genetic data; about 7 percent have done so.

Women enjoy equal rights in Iceland. However, there has been some concern about women of immigrant origin, who may not have the opportunity to learn the Icelandic language and customs and may be unaware of their rights and status under the law. The European Commission against Racism and Intolerance has also criticized Iceland over immigrant women who become sex trade workers after being caught by traffickers. However, there has been little research done on the issue.

# India

**Population:** 1,068,600,000
**GNI/capita:** $460
**Life Expectancy:** 63
**Political Rights:** 2
**Civil Liberties:** 3
**Status:** Free
**Religious Groups:** Hindu (81.3 percent), Muslim (12 percent), Christian (2.2 percent), other (4.5 percent)
**Ethnic Groups:** Indo-Aryan (72 percent), Dravidian (25 percent), other (3 percent)
**Capital:** New Delhi

**Ten-Year Ratings Timeline (Political Rights, Civil Liberties, Status)**

| 1994 | 1995 | 1996 | 1997 | 1998 | 1999 | 2000 | 2001 | 2002 | 2003 |
|------|------|------|------|------|------|------|------|------|------|
| 4,4PF | 4,4PF | 2,4PF | 2,4PF | 2,3F | 2,3F | 2,3F | 2,3F | 2,3F | 2,3F |

**Overview:**

With a current focus on good governance rather than Hindu chauvinism, India's ruling coalition government, headed by the Hindu nationalist Bharatiya Janata Party (BJP), seems well placed to emerge victorious in national elections scheduled for 2004. Nevertheless, analysts remain concerned that the rhetoric and actions of the main Hindu nationalist groups threaten India's tradition of vibrant and inclusive democracy as well as the rights of the Muslim and Christian minorities. Justice for the 2002 killings in Gujarat continued to be elusive, with the BJP-dominated state government showing a marked reluctance to provide an adequate level of rehabilitation for the victims or to bring those accused of crimes to trial. However, after a widely publicized acquittal verdict in June, the Supreme Court declared that it had no faith in the Gujarat government's ability to dispense justice and decided to oversee the legal process in a number of prominent cases.

India achieved independence in 1947 with the partition of British India into a predominantly Hindu India, under Prime Minister Jawaharlal Nehru, and a Muslim Pakistan. The centrist, secular Congress Party ruled almost continuously at the federal level for the first five decades of independence. After winning the 1991 elections, the Congress government responded to a balance-of-payments crisis by initiating gradual economic reforms. However, even as the economic crisis receded, the party lost 11 state elections in the mid-1990s, with regional parties making gains in southern India and low-caste parties and the BJP gaining in the northern Hindi-speaking belt. Congress's traditional electoral base of poor, low-caste, and Muslim voters appeared disillusioned with economic liberalization and, in the case of Muslims, the government's failure to prevent communal violence. In December 1992, India experienced some of the worst communal violence since independence after Hindu fundamentalists destroyed a sixteenth-century mosque in the northern town of Ayodhya. Some 2,000 people, mainly Muslims, died in riots and police gunfire.

After the May 1996 parliamentary elections, a series of minority coalitions tried unsuccessfully to form a stable government. In-fighting among centrist and leftist parties enabled the BJP to form a government under Atal Behari Vajpayee in 1998. One of the government's first major acts was to carry out a series of nuclear tests in April 1998. Holding only a minority of seats, the BJP government faced frequent threats and demands from small but pivotal coalition members. The government fell after a regional party defected, but it won reelection in 1999. Final election results gave the BJP-led, 22-party National Democratic Alliance (NDA) 295 seats (182 for the BJP) against 112 seats for Congress.

The government was shaken in 2001 by a scandal over defense contracts, which led to the temporary resignation of Defense Minister George Fernandes and the withdrawal of one partner from the NDA coalition. Perhaps as a reaction to losses during a series of key state elections, the BJP shifted to the ideological right during 2002, with the promotion of hard-liner Lal Krishna Advani to the post of deputy prime minister as well as the selection of Manohar Joshi of the Shiv Sena party as speaker of the lower house of parliament.

In February 2002, at least 58 people were killed when a fire broke out on a train carrying members of a Hindu extremist group. A Muslim mob was initially blamed for the fire, and in the anti-Muslim riots that followed throughout Gujarat, more than 1,000 people were killed and roughly 100,000 were left homeless and dispossessed. The violence was orchestrated by Hindu nationalist groups, who organized transportation and provisions for the mobs and provided printed records of Muslim-owned property. Evidence that the BJP-headed state government was complicit in the carnage led to calls for Chief Minister Narendra Modi's dismissal, but the party leadership continued to support him. In state elections held in December in which Modi campaigned on an overtly nationalistic and anti-Muslim platform, the BJP won a landslide reelection victory.

The rehabilitation of those displaced by the violence, as well as the prosecution of those responsible for the murders, rapes, and destruction of property made little headway during 2003. Witnesses in the few cases that have been brought to trial have faced intimidation and harassment, as have lawyers and activists working on their behalf. In June, 21 people accused of murder in the Best Bakery case were acquitted because witnesses withdrew their testimony after being threatened. However, in October, the Supreme Court ordered the Gujarat government to appoint new public prosecutors to try or retry a number of cases stemming from the violence. The first guilty verdict was announced in late November, when 12 Hindus were convicted of killing 14 Muslims in Ghodasar village and were given life sentences.

Following an attack on the Indian parliament building in December 2001 by a Pakistan-based militant group, relations between India and Pakistan worsened. The two countries came close to war in May 2002, which prompted a flurry of diplomatic activity on the part of the United States. Individuals with connections to Pakistan-based militant groups continued to carry out terrorist attacks, including twin bomb blasts in Bombay that killed more than 50 people in August. Nevertheless, there was some easing of tensions between the two countries by the end of the year, amid hopes that their customary animosity could be put aside and that the political leadership could restart talks on the disputed territory of Kashmir.

**Political Rights and Civil Liberties:** Indian citizens can change their government through elections. The 1950 constitution provides for a lower house, the 545-seat Lok Sabha (House of the People), whose members are directly elected for five-year terms (except for 2 appointed seats for Indians of European descent). Members of the 245-seat upper house, the Rajya Sabha (Council of States), are either elected by the state legislatures or nominated by the president; they serve six-year terms. Executive power is vested in a prime minister and a cabinet, while an indirectly elected president serves as head of state.

India has held regular and reasonably free elections since independence. A large number of regional and national parties participate, and sitting governments are thrown out of office with increasing regularity. Under the supervision of the vigilant Election Commission of India (ECI), recent elections have generally been free and fair, although violence and irregularities have marred balloting in several districts. In the 1999 national elections, guerrilla attacks in Bihar and northeast India and inter-party clashes in several states killed some 130 people. Badly maintained voters' lists and the intimidation of voters are also matters of concern.

Despite the vibrancy of the Indian political system, effective and accountable rule continues to be undermined by political infighting, pervasive criminality in politics, decrepit state institutions, and widespread corruption. Transparency International's 2003 Corruption Perceptions Index ranked India in eighty-third place out of 133 countries. In November, an engineer working on a government-sponsored road project in Bihar was murdered after complaining to the prime minister's office about corruption. The electoral system depends on black money that is obtained through tax evasion and other means. Politicians and civil servants are regularly caught accepting bribes or engaging in other corrupt behavior, but are rarely prosecuted. Moreover, criminality is a pervasive feature of political life, with a number of candidates with criminal records being elected, particularly in the state legislatures. However, after a battle with the government in 2002, the ECI was able to implement a Supreme

Court directive that requires candidates seeking election to declare their financial assets, criminal records, and educational backgrounds.

India's private press continues to be vigorous, although journalists face a number of constraints. In recent years, the government has occasionally used its power under the Official Secrets Act to censor security-related articles. Intimidation of journalists by a variety of actors continues, with one reporter being killed in September and another abducted by militants in November. The press in the southern state of Tamil Nadu came under repeated pressure from authorities during the year. In April, a journalist was charged and jailed under antiterrorism legislation, and in November, the state assembly passed a resolution calling for the arrest and imprisonment of six journalists following the publication of an article in a prominent national paper that criticized the state's chief minister. The broadcast media are predominantly in private hands, but the state-controlled All India Radio enjoys a dominant position and its news coverage favors the government.

The right to practice one's religion freely is generally respected, but violence against religious minorities remains a problem and the government's prosecution of those involved in such attacks continues to be inadequate. Attacks on Christian targets, including the murder and rape of clergy and the destruction of property, have dramatically increased since the BJP came to power in 1998, mainly in the predominantly tribal regions of Orissa, Gujarat, Bihar, and Madhya Pradesh. Members of the sangh parivar, a group of Hindu nationalist organizations including the BJP, and some local media outlets promote anti-minority propaganda. Legislation on the books in several states, including Orissa, Madhya Pradesh, Tamil Nadu, and Gujarat, criminalizes conversions that take place as a result of "force" or "allurement." These laws have been opposed by human rights activists and religious groups, who argue that the vague provisions of these statutes could be misused. The promotion of Hindu nationalist ideology by some government officials has also affected the educational system. According to the U.S. State Department's International Religious Freedom Report for 2003, textbooks intended for use at most government and private schools have been rewritten to favor a Hindu extremist version of history, despite protests from academics, minority leaders, and advocates of secular values.

There are some restrictions on freedom of assembly and association. Section 144 of the criminal procedure code empowers state-level authorities to declare a state of emergency, restrict free assembly, and impose curfews. Officials occasionally use Section 144 to prevent demonstrations, and police sometimes use excessive force against demonstrators. In November, at least 25 demonstrators were injured and several hundred were detained after police forcibly broke up a protest held by Burmese refugees outside the UN High Commissioner for Refugees office in Delhi. Human rights groups say that police and hired thugs have occasionally beaten, arbitrarily detained, or otherwise harassed villagers and members of nongovernmental organizations who protest forced relocations from the sites of development projects.

Human rights organizations generally operate freely. However, Amnesty International's 2003 report noted that the intimidation of human rights defenders by state officials and other actors, including threats, legal harassment, the use of excessive force by police, and occasionally lethal violence, remains a concern. The work of rights activists may also be hindered by a Home Ministry order issued in 2001 that requires organizations to obtain clearance before holding international conferences or workshops if the subject matter is "political, semi-political, communal or religious in nature or is related to human rights."

Workers regularly exercise their rights to bargain collectively and strike. The Essential Services Maintenance Act enables the government to ban strikes in certain key industries and limits the right of public servants to strike. It is estimated that there are roughly 55 million child laborers in India. Many work in the informal sector in hazardous conditions, and several million are bonded laborers.

The judiciary is independent of the executive. Judges have exercised unprecedented activism in response to public interest litigation over official corruption, environmental issues, and other matters. However, in recent years, courts have initiated several contempt-of-court cases against activists and journalists, raising questions about their misuse of the law to intimidate those who expose the behavior of corrupt judges or who question their verdicts. Corruption in the judiciary is reportedly rife, and access to justice by the socially and economically marginalized sections of society remains limited. The court system is severely backlogged and understaffed, which results in the detention of a large number of persons who are awaiting trial. In April, the government-appointed Malimath Committee recommended an overhaul of the Indian criminal justice system. However, rights groups expressed concern that its proposals would weaken the rights of the accused and of women while increasing the power of judges and the police.

Police routinely torture or otherwise ill-treat suspects to extract confessions or bribes. Custodial rape of female detainees continues to be a problem, as does routine abuse of ordinary prisoners, particularly minorities and members of the lower castes. Police brutality appears to be especially prevalent in the north Indian state of Uttar Pradesh, which has high levels of custodial deaths and extrajudicial executions, according to a briefing paper released in August by the New Delhi–based Human Rights Documentation Centre. While the National Human Rights Commission (NHRC) monitors abuses and makes independent assessments, its recommendations are often not implemented and it has few enforcement powers. Reports by the NHRC, Human Rights Watch, and a number of other groups alleged that police in Gujarat had been given orders by the state government not to intervene during the communal violence that engulfed the state in 2002, and that police have been reluctant to register complaints against those accused of murder, rape, and other crimes, or arrest those known to have played a role in the rioting. Since the riots, scores of Muslim men in Gujarat have been illegally detained and interrogated about their involvement in subsequent attacks such as the killing of former minister Haren Pandya in March 2003, according to Amnesty International. More generally, the failure of the Indian criminal justice system to protect the rights of, and provide equal protection under the law to, minorities, *dalits* (untouchables), and other underprivileged groups remains a concern.

Police, army, and paramilitary forces continue to be implicated in disappearances, extrajudicial killing, rape, torture, arbitrary detention, and destruction of homes, particularly in the context of insurgencies in Kashmir, Andhra Pradesh, Assam, and several other northeastern states. The Armed Forces Special Powers Act and the Disturbed Areas Act remain in effect in several states, and these grant security forces broad powers of arrest and detention. Security forces also continued to detain suspects under the broadly drawn National Security Act, which authorizes detention without charge for up to one year. The criminal procedure code requires the central or state governments to approve prosecution of security force members, which is rarely granted. As a result, impunity for security forces implicated in past human rights abuses remains a concern.

In March 2002, the Prevention of Terrorism Act (POTA) was passed by a joint session of parliament, amid protests by journalists, human rights groups, and some members of the government and judiciary. In addition to widening the definition of terrorism and banning a number of terrorist organizations, the bill also increases the state's powers of investigation and allows for up to 90 days of preventative detention without charge. Since its enactment, the act has been used in a number of states against political opponents, members of minority groups, tribals, dalits, and other ordinary citizens, as well as against terrorist suspects. In February, the Gujarat state government charged 131 Muslims under POTA for the Godhra attack, according to Human Rights Watch, while no Hindus were charged under the act for violence against Muslims.

In India's seven northeastern states, more than 40 mainly tribal-based insurgent groups sporadically attack security forces and engage in intertribal violence. The rebel groups have also been implicated in numerous killings, abductions, and rapes of civilians. The militants ostensibly seek either greater autonomy or complete independence for their ethnic or tribal groups. Negotiations between the central government and separatist groups in Nagaland, where some 25,000 people have been killed since 1947, continued during 2003 without resolution, but authorities were able to sign an agreement with a Bodo tribal group in Assam in February. In a number of states, left-wing guerrillas called Naxalites control some rural areas and kill dozens of police, politicians, landlords, and villagers each year. Police also continued to battle the People's War Group, a guerrilla organization that aims to establish a Communist state in the tribal areas of Andhra Pradesh, Orissa, West Bengal, Jharkhand, Bihar, and Chhattisgarh.

The constitution bars discrimination based on caste, and laws set aside quotas in education and government jobs for members of the so-called scheduled tribes, scheduled castes (dalits), and other backward castes (OBCs). However, members of the lower castes, as well as religious and ethnic minorities, continue to routinely face unofficial discrimination and violence. The worst abuse is faced by the 160 million dalits, who are often denied access to land or other public amenities, abused by landlords and police, and forced to work in miserable conditions. Tension between different ethnic groups over land, jobs, or resources occasionally flares into violent confrontation; in November, several dozen people were killed during attacks on Bihari migrants in Assam. Various forms of discrimination against Muslims are sometimes excused in the context of ongoing tensions with Pakistan as well as the global campaign against terrorism.

Each year, several thousand women are burned to death, driven to suicide, or otherwise killed, and countless others are harassed, beaten, or deserted by husbands in the context of dowry and other disputes. Despite the fact that dowry is illegal and that hundreds are convicted each year, the practice continues to spread. Rape and other violence against women remain serious problems, with lower-caste and tribal women being particularly vulnerable to attacks. Muslim women and girls were subjected to horrific sexual violence during the communal violence that engulfed Gujarat in 2002, and there has been no official attempt to provide rehabilitation for those victims still alive or to prosecute their attackers, according to an Amnesty International report issued in March. Muslim personal status laws as well as traditional Hindu practices discriminate against women in terms of inheritance rights. The malign neglect of female children after birth remains a concern. An increasing use of sex-determination tests during pregnancy, after which female fetuses are more likely to be aborted, and the practice of female infanticide by those who cannot afford the tests have contributed to a growing imbalance in the male-female birth ratios in a number of states, particularly in the northwest.

# Indonesia

**Population:** 220,500,000  **Political Rights:** 3
**GNI/capita:** $690  **Civil Liberties:** 4
**Life Expectancy:** 68  **Status:** Partly Free
**Religious Groups:** Muslim (88 percent), Protestant
(5 percent), Roman Catholic (3 percent), other (4 percent)
**Ethnic Groups:** Javanese (45 percent), Sundanese
(14 percent), Madurese (8 percent), Malay (8 percent),
other (25 percent)
**Capital:** Jakarta

**Ten-Year Ratings Timeline (Political Rights, Civil Liberties, Status)**

| 1994 | 1995 | 1996 | 1997 | 1998 | 1999 | 2000 | 2001 | 2002 | 2003 |
|------|------|------|------|------|------|------|------|------|------|
| 7,6NF | 7,6NF | 7,5NF | 7,5NF | 6,4PF | 4,4PF | 3,4PF | 3,4PF | 3,4PF | 3,4PF |

**Overview:**  During 2003, President Megawati Sukarnoputri cracked down on suspected Islamic militants and ordered a renewed army offensive against separatist rebels in Aceh province. Her administration was far less forceful, however, in promoting human rights, tackling widespread official corruption, and reforming Indonesia's graft-prone judiciary and outmoded legal framework.

Indonesia won full independence in 1949 following a four-year, intermittent war against its Dutch colonial rulers. After several parliamentary governments collapsed, the republic's first president, Sukarno, took on authoritarian powers in 1957 under a system that he called "Guided Democracy." Sukarno proved unable to stem the country's political turbulence, while the economy stagnated. In 1965, the army, led by General Suharto, crushed an apparent coup attempt that it blamed on the Communist Party of Indonesia (PKI). In the aftermath, the army reportedly backed the massacre, between 1965 and 1967, of some 500,000 people, mainly PKI members. With the army's support, the conservative Suharto eased aside the populist Sukarno and, in 1968, formally became president.

Suharto's 32-year, autocratic, "New Order" regime jailed scores of dissidents and banned most opposition parties and groups. In the 1990s, Suharto increasingly concentrated power in himself and his family while allowing close friends to run large business monopolies that operated with little oversight.

In part to sustain its power, Suharto's government launched programs that helped lift millions of Indonesians out of poverty. Pundits placed Indonesia in the ranks of the "Asian Tiger" economies as output grew by 7.6 percent a year, on average, from 1987 to 1996. By 1997, however, years of poor investment decisions and profligate borrowing from weakly supervised banks had saddled Indonesian firms with some $80 billion in foreign debt. The economy shrank by 18 percent in less than a year after growing by 13 percent in 1996. To stave off a private sector debt default, the government agreed in October 1997 to a $43 billion loan package set up by the IMF.

Suharto resigned in May 1998 following months of unprecedented antigovernment protests over soaring food prices and three days of devastating urban riots. Vice President B. J. Habibie, a long-time Suharto loyalist, became president.

In June 1999, Indonesia held its first free parliamentary elections since 1955. Megawati's Indonesian Democratic Party-Struggle (PDI-P) won 154 of the 462 contested seats, with Golkar, Habibie's party, taking 120 and smaller parties the remainder. In another break with the Suharto era, Indonesia's national assembly held its first-ever competitive vote for the nation's top offices that October, electing Muslim leader Abdurrahman Wahid president and Megawati vice president. Previously, the body, called the People's Consultative Assembly (MPR), consisting of parliament plus 195 appointed representatives, simply rubber-stamped Suharto's decision to hold another term.

Wahid increased civilian control over Indonesia's powerful armed forces, though he was less successful in jump-starting the economy, or in containing the insurgency in Aceh or deadly ethnic and sectarian violence in the Moluccas, Sulawesi, and Kalimantan. With his administration adrift and dogged by corruption allegations, Wahid was impeached by the MPR in July 2001. Megawati, daughter of the late Sukarno, became president.

Megawati generally is credited with stabilizing Indonesia's volatile post-1997 economy. However, critics charge that she has largely failed to reign in what is widely seen as a corrupt elite whose unchecked self-interest has sapped the economy and stunted political development. Many observers say that corruption has increased since Megawati took office, in part because of both a lack of enforcement and the recent decentralization of government in Indonesia; decentralization has expanded the power of local officials without improving their oversight.

Investors remain wary of sinking capital into Indonesia because of government corruption as well as fickle courts, inadequate laws, and apprehension that the government will ease its fiscal austerity with the completion of its IMF program at year's end. Economists say that Indonesia's recent economic growth rate of around 3.5 percent annually is only about half that needed to keep pace with new entrants in the labor market and to substantially reduce poverty.

By contrast, Megawati has shown greater resolve in pursuing a military solution in Aceh, an oil-rich province of 4.6 million people in northern Sumatra, where the military launched a fresh offensive against separatist rebels in May 2003. The government renewed its counterinsurgency operations against the rebels, known as the Free Aceh Movement (GAM), following the breakdown of a five-month ceasefire over the question of independence versus autonomy for Aceh. The province has been placed under martial law, and the military operates there with near impunity.

Megawati also has taken a tougher line against Jemaah Islamiyah, a network of Islamic militants in Southeast Asia allegedly linked to the terrorist al-Qaeda network. Initially reluctant to tackle homegrown Islamic militancy for fear of offending powerful Muslim constituencies, her government has arrested scores of suspected terrorists since a 2002 bombing on the resort island of Bali killed 202 people.

Courts have convicted several suspects in the Bali bombing, though a court in September acquitted Muslim cleric Abu Bakar Bashir, 65, of being the spiritual head of Jemaah Islamiyah. Though the cleric was jailed for four years on other charges pending appeal, the acquittal was seen as a setback for Indonesia's antiterrorism campaign. Regardless of Bashir's fate, many analysts say that the government must take the sensitive step of investigating the handful of Islamic boarding schools allegedly linked to Jemaah Islamiyah, and further professionalize the gathering and sharing of intelligence, in order to better curb terrorism.

With Indonesia heading towards elections in 2004, Megawati is the front-runner in a wide-open presidential race, while the rejuvenated Golkar Party of former strongman Suharto seems poised for gains in the separate legislative balloting. With few real policy differences among mainstream politicians, the elections are unlikely to shake up Indonesia's mildly conservative politics, unless Islamic parties make unexpectedly big gains in parliament.

**Political Rights and Civil Liberties:** Indonesians can choose their legislators in free and reasonably fair elections and will elect their president directly for the first time in 2004. The country will hold legislative elections in April and presidential elections three months later. While civilian control and oversight of the armed forces recently have improved somewhat, the Indonesian military still wields considerable influence in politics and business. The armed forces are being weaned off their long-standing formal role in politics and are due to give up their 38 appointed parliamentary and MPR seats in 2004. The military continues, however, to have substantial business holdings and an extensive grassroots presence. An estimated 70 percent of the military's funding comes from off-budget business activities. The army also maintains a "territorial network" of soldiers in every district and village and has links with many provincial bosses. Unlike former president Abdurrahman Wahid, moreover, President Megawati Sukarnoputri has not attempted to curb the power of the military. A controversial bill debated during the year would increase the emergency powers of the military, particularly in Aceh and Papua.

Despite these ongoing problems with the military, Indonesia is evolving into a more open society. The private press, while at times shoddy and sensationalist, reports aggressively on corruption, government policy, and other formerly taboo topics. Journalists, however, face some police violence and intimidation and occasional attacks by paid thugs, student activists, and religious extremists. In another troubling trend, several journalists currently are facing criminal defamation charges over their reporting. In war-torn Aceh, the press has been censored heavily.

Indonesians of all faiths can generally worship freely in this predominantly Muslim nation, although officials monitor and have outlawed some extremist Islamic groups. Animists, Confucians, Baha'is, and others whose faith is not among Indonesia's five officially recognized religions have difficulty obtaining national identity cards, which are needed to register births, marriages, and divorces, according to the U.S. State Department's human rights report for 2002, released in March 2003. The five recognized faiths are Islam, Protestantism, Catholicism, Hinduism, and Buddhism.

Professors and other educators generally can lecture and publish freely. In a serious setback for freedom of expression, however, at least 39 Indonesians have been detained or jailed for peacefully criticizing the government since Megawati took office in 2001, the human rights group Amnesty International reported in July. They include independence activists in Aceh, Papua, and Malaku and labor and political activists in Java and Sulawesi. Many were charged under colonial-era defamation laws.

Indonesia has many effective, outspoken human rights groups, including Imparsial, Humanika, and the Indonesian Legal Aid Foundation, that aid victims and vigorously promote rights. They face, however, "monitoring, abuse, and interference by the government," the U.S. State Department report said. Indonesian workers can join independent unions, bargain collectively, and, except for civil servants, stage strikes. Government enforcement of minimum-wage and other labor laws is weak, however, and there are credible reports of employers dismissing or otherwise exacting retribution from union organizers. Moreover, unions allege that factory managers at times use youth gangs or plainclothes security forces—often off-duty soldiers and police—to intimidate workers or break strikes. Roughly 10 to 15 percent of Indonesia's 80 million industrial workers are unionized.

Despite recent reforms, "the judiciary remained subordinate to the Executive and was often influenced by the military, business interests, and politicians outside of the legal system," the U.S. State Department report said. Bribes influence prosecution, conviction, and sentencing in countless civil and criminal cases. Courts also often limit defendants' access to counsel and allow forced confessions to be used as evidence in criminal cases.

The judiciary's weakness has helped perpetuate human rights abuses by the security forces. In Aceh, the army has been implicated in summary killings, disappearances, rapes, illegal detentions, and other abuses against suspected GAM guerrillas or sympathizers, according to Amnesty International and the New York–based Human Rights Watch. For their part, GAM forces have routinely summarily killed both soldiers and civilians, while intimidating and extorting money from ordinary Acehnese, these groups say. Army abuses also continue in Papua, and questions remain about whether the military and Kopassus, the intelligence service, were involved in a 2002 ambush in the province that killed two Americans. The government denies any official involvement in the deaths.

Indonesian forces also enjoy near impunity in encounters with ordinary criminal suspects. Meanwhile, Amnesty International said in an October report that it continued to receive reports of torture by soldiers and police not only of suspects in conflict zones but also of criminal suspects, peaceful political activists, and Indonesians involved in land and other disputes with authorities. In addition, guards routinely mistreat and extort money from inmates in Indonesia's overcrowded prisons.

Efforts to curb military impunity were dealt a setback by the acquittals or relatively short jail terms handed down in the recent trials of 18 suspects, including senior army officials, in the 1999 violence in East Timor that killed more than 1,000 civilians.

In a series of trials that ended in August, a Jakarta court acquitted 12 defendants and handed down jail terms of between three and ten years to 6 found guilty. Amnesty International said that prosecutors failed to present credible cases and gave a sanitized version of the 1999 violence.

Ethnic Chinese continue to face some harassment and violence, though far less than in the late 1990s, when violent attacks killed hundreds and destroyed many Chinese-owned shops and churches. Unlike other Indonesians, ethnic Chinese must show a citizenship card to obtain a passport, credit card, or business license or to enroll a child in school, a requirement that makes them vulnerable to extortion by bureaucrats. Ethnic Chinese make up less than 3 percent of the nation's population, but are resented by some Indonesians for holding the lion's share of private wealth. A few ethnic Chinese have amassed huge fortunes in business, though most are ordinary traders or merchants.

Ethnic Dayaks in Kalimantan and other members of Indonesia's tiny indigenous minority face considerable discrimination. The government at times fails to stop mining and logging companies from encroaching on indigenous land in Kalimantan and other areas—often in collusion with local military and police—and appropriates land claimed by indigenous Indonesians for development projects without fair compensation.

In a positive development, peace is slowly returning to areas of the archipelago that recently have been torn by violence along ethnic or sectarian lines, including the Moluccas, central Sulawesi, and Kalimantan. In Kalimantan and other areas, many disputes between ethnic groups are said to be linked in part to the government's decades-old policy of resettling tens of thousands of Indonesians to remote parts of the archipelago from overcrowded areas such as Java.

Indonesian women face considerable discrimination. They are often steered by factory employers into low-level, low-paying jobs, and female university graduates reportedly receive salaries that are 25 percent lower, on average, than those paid to their male counterparts. Female household servants at times are forced to work without pay, for extremely low wages, or in situations of debt bondage. Female genital mutilation reportedly is still practiced in some areas, although the more extreme forms of the practice apparently are becoming less common. Trafficking of women for prostitution, forced labor, and debt bondage reportedly continues unabated, often with the complicity or involvement of police, soldiers, and officials, despite the recent passage of a child-trafficking bill and of stiffer provisions against trafficking of women.

# Iran

**Population:** 66,600,000
**GNI/capita:** $1,680
**Life Expectancy:** 69
**Religious Groups:** Shi'a Muslim (89 percent),
Sunni Muslim (10 percent), other (1 percent)
**Ethnic Groups:** Persian (51 percent), Azeri (24 percent),
Gilaki and Mazandarani (8 percent), Kurd (7 percent),
Arab (3 percent), other (7 percent)
**Capital:** Tehran

**Political Rights:** 6
**Civil Liberties:** 6
**Status:** Not Free

**Ten-Year Ratings Timeline (Political Rights, Civil Liberties, Status)**

| 1994 | 1995 | 1996 | 1997 | 1998 | 1999 | 2000 | 2001 | 2002 | 2003 |
|------|------|------|------|------|------|------|------|------|------|
| 6,7NF | 6,7NF | 6,7NF | 6,7NF | 6,6NF | 6,6NF | 6,6NF | 6,6NF | 6,6NF | 6,6NF |

**Overview:**

Efforts by reformist politicians who control the presidency and parliament to further expand social and political freedoms remained stymied in 2003 as a result of opposition from appointive bodies controlled by hardline clerics. The authorities significantly increased restrictions on press freedom and began systematic censoring of Internet content during the year. Thousands of participants in antigovernment protests were detained by security forces, and scores of political activists and journalists were indicted for peaceful activities.

In 1979, Iran witnessed a tumultuous revolution that ousted a hereditary monarchy marked by widespread corruption and brought into power the exiled cleric Ayatollah Ruhollah Khomeini. The constitution drafted by his disciples provided for a president and parliament elected through universal adult suffrage, but unelected institutions controlled by hardline clerics were empowered to approve electoral candidates and certify that the decisions of elected officials are in accord with Sharia (Islamic law). Khomeini was named Supreme Leader and invested with control over the security and intelligence services, armed forces, and judiciary. After his death in 1989, the role of Supreme Leader passed to Ayatollah Ali Khamenei, a middle-ranking cleric who lacked the religious credentials and popularity of his predecessor. The constitution was changed to consolidate his power and give him final authority on all matters of foreign and domestic policy.

Beneath its veneer of religious probity, the Islamic Republic gave rise to a new elite that accumulated wealth through opaque and unaccountable means. By the mid-1990s, dismal economic conditions and a demographic trend toward a younger population had created widespread hostility to clerical rule and a coalition of reformers began to emerge within the ruling elite, advocating a gradual process of political reform, economic liberalization, and normalization with the outside world that was designed to legitimize, not radically alter, the current political system. In 1997, former culture minister Mohammed Khatami was allowed by the ruling clerics to run for president; he won nearly 70 percent of the vote. Khatami's administration made considerable strides over the next few years in expanding public freedoms. More than 200 independent newspapers and magazines representing a diverse array of viewpoints were established during his first year in office, and the authorities relaxed the enforcement of strict Islamic restrictions on social interaction. Reformists won 80 percent of the seats in the country's first nationwide municipal elections in 1999 and took the vast majority of seats in parliamentary elections the following year, gaining the power, for the first time, to legislate major changes in the political system.

The 2000 parliamentary elections prompted a backlash by hardline clerics that continues to this day. More than 100 reformist newspapers have been shut down by the conservative-controlled judiciary during the last three years, and hundreds of liberal journalists, students, and political activists have been jailed. Reform legislation approved by parliament has been repeatedly vetoed by hardliners.

Although Khatami was reelected in 2001 with 78 percent of the vote, he has been unwilling to use this popular mandate to advance the reform process or even to preserve the expansion of civil liberties achieved during his first three years in office. He has refused to call a national referendum to approve legislation that would advance the reform process and continually implores citizens to refrain from demonstrating in public. The most powerful weapon at the president's disposal is the threat of resignation; few observers believe that the "rump" clerical regime that would remain after his departure would be able to maintain control of the country. Although Khatami has repeatedly hinted that he will step down if hardline clerics continue to veto reformist legislation, his failure to act on these threats has made them ineffectual.

Khatami's reluctance to challenge ruling theocrats has led many Iranians to abandon hopes that the political system can be changed from within. The results of a government-conducted poll, published by the Iranian daily *Yas-I No* in June 2003, indicated the depths of this disillusionment: 45 percent of the population would support political change brought about by foreign intervention. Record low turnout for municipal elections in February 2003 showed that the ability of reformist politicians to mobilize the public has deteriorated markedly. In major urban centers, hardline candidates captured most city council seats.

Gridlock between government moderates and hardliners has also obstructed much-needed economic reforms. Although Iran possesses the world's third-largest oil reserves and second-largest natural gas reserves, the government has been unable to generate enough economic growth to reduce the country's soaring unemployment rate. Economic reforms have recently been made in some areas, such as trade liberalization, the establishment of private banks, the approval of a foreign direct investment law, and the amendment of tax laws, but there has been no major restructuring of the economy. According to the IMF, Iran has the highest rate of brain drain in the world, with 160,000 people emigrating to greener pastures last year alone. Among those who remain behind, drug use, clinical depression, and suicide rates among youth are at an all-time high.

In June, Iran witnessed the largest wave of antigovernment demonstrations in four years. The unrest began with a rally by a few hundred students at Tehran University, but appeals by dissident Iranian satellite stations in Los Angeles led thousands of ordinary Iranians to join the protests, which spread to other major Iranian cities. Whereas public demonstrations once exclusively targeted Khamenei and other hardline clerics, calls for Khatami's resignation were prevalent. An estimated 4,000 demonstrators were arrested by the authorities, about half of whom were detained for more than a week, and hundreds were wounded by hardline vigilantes. Khatami's tepid response to the mass arrests led prominent student leaders to publicly withdraw their support for the president. Within the broader reform movement, Khatami and other government "moderates" are increasingly accused not just of being ineffective, but of willingly serving as a democratic façade for an oppressive regime.

Meanwhile, Iran faced new foreign policy challenges in 2003. Although Iranian officials welcomed the American-led ouster of Iraqi President Saddam Hussein in April, reformers and hardliners alike remained suspicious of U.S. promises to establish a representative political system in Baghdad. In June, senior American officials publicly called for a change of government in Tehran. In November, the International Atomic Energy Agency (IAEA) issued a report showing that Iran had been conducting clandestine nuclear research for decades. Although Iran agreed to halt illicit research and allow more intrusive inspections, the IAEA report bolstered U.S. claims that the Islamic Republic has an active nuclear weapons program.

**Political Rights and Civil Liberties:** Iranians cannot change their government democratically. The most powerful figure in the Iranian government is the Supreme Leader (Vali-e-Faghih); he is chosen for life by the Assembly of Experts, a clerics-only body whose members are elected to eight-year terms by popular vote from a government-screened list of candidates. The Supreme Leader is commander in chief of the armed forces and appoints the leaders of the judiciary, the heads of state broadcast media, the commander of the Islamic Revolutionary Guard Corps (IRGC), the Expediency Council, and half the members of the Council of Guardians. Although the president and parliament are responsible for designating cabinet ministers, the Supreme Leader exercises de facto control over appointments to the Ministries of Defense, Interior, and Intelligence.

All candidates for election to the presidency and 290-seat unicameral parliament are vetted for strict allegiance to the ruling theocracy and adherence to Islamic principles by the 12-person Council of Guardians, a body of six clergymen appointed by the Supreme Leader and six laymen selected by the head of the judiciary chief (the latter are nominally subject to parliamentary approval). Of the 814 candidates who declared their intention to run in the 2001 presidential election, only 10 were approved.

The Council of Guardians also has the power to reject legislation approved by the parliament (disputes between the two are arbitrated by the Expediency Council, another nonelected conservative-dominated body, currently headed by former president Ali Akbar Rafsanjani). For example, during the year, the Council of Guardians rejected bills that would have eased the ban on satellite dishes, ended its power to screen candidates for elected office, required Iran to adopt UN conventions on eliminating torture and on ending discrimination against women, and allowed jury trials in an open court for journalists.

Freedom of expression is limited. The government directly controls all television and radio broadcasting and succeeded in jamming broadcasts by dissident satellite stations following the June demonstrations (reportedly after receiving assistance from Cuba). The Press Court has extensive procedural and jurisdictional power in prosecuting journalists, editors, and publishers for such vaguely worded offenses as "insulting Islam" and "damaging the foundations of the Islamic Republic." Since 1997, more than 100 publications have been shut down by the judiciary and scores of journalists have been arrested—often held incommunicado for extended periods of time and convicted in closed-door trials. Circulation of pro-reform newspapers has fallen from a peak of more than three million to just over one million.

Scores of journalists were summoned for interrogation during the year, and dozens were detained, with the number of journalists behind bars reaching a high of 22 in July. The authorities greatly increased ad hoc press restrictions and gag orders banning media coverage of specific topics and events. When 135 members of parliament wrote an open letter in May calling on Ayatollah Ali Khamenei to apologize to the public for ignoring their wishes, not a single newspaper dared to publish it (though it circulated widely on the Web).

While journalists had been allowed in the past to report on demonstrations with few problems, on June 12 the Supreme National Security Council (SNSC) issued a decree prohibiting journalists from entering the university campus in Tehran to cover student demonstrations. Vigilantes beat several journalists who defied the order and confiscated their film and equipment. In the weeks after the June riots, eight journalists were arrested for allegedly inciting students to revolt. The SNSC also issued a decree prohibiting journalists from speaking with foreign Farsi-language news services, and a number of those alleged to have done so were prohibited from leaving the country during the year. A ban on publishing articles about Iranian-American relations has remained in effect since May 2002.

The rapid growth of Internet access in Iran—there are now an estimated three million users—and the tendency of newspapers closed by the judiciary to continue publishing online led the government to begin systematically censoring Internet content for the first time in 2003. In May, Internet service providers (ISPs) were instructed by the Ministry of Telecommunications to block access to a list of "immoral sites and political sites that insult the country's political and religious leaders." At least 12 ISPs were shut down during the year for failing to install filters against banned sites. At least three journalists were arrested in connection with material they published on the Internet.

Religious freedom is limited in Iran, which is 89 percent Shi'a Muslim and 10 percent Sunni Muslim. Sunnis enjoy equal rights under the law, but there are some indications of discrimination, such as the absence of a Sunni mosque in the Iranian capital and the paucity of Sunnis in senior government offices. The constitution recognizes Zoroastrians, Jews, and Christians as religious minorities and generally allows them to worship without interference, but they are barred from election to representative bodies (though a set number of parliamentary seats are reserved for them), cannot hold senior government or military positions, and face restrictions in employment, education, and property ownership. In February, Iran released the last 5 of 10 Jews convicted in a closed-door trial of spying for Israel in 2000. In December, the Expediency Council approved legislation equalizing the amount of "blood money" owed to families of Muslim and non-Muslim murder victims. Some 300,000 Baha'is, Iran's largest non-Muslim minority, enjoy virtually no rights under the law and are banned from practicing their faith. Hundreds of Baha'is have been executed since 1979.

Academic freedom in Iran is limited. Scholars are frequently detained for expressing political views and students involved in organizing protests often face suspension or expulsion by university disciplinary committees.

The constitution permits the establishment of political parties, professional syndicates, and other civic organizations, provided they do not violate the principles of "freedom, sovereignty and national unity" or question the Islamic basis of the republic. In 2002, the 44-year-old Iran Freedom Movement was banned on such grounds and 33 of its leading members imprisoned.

The 1979 constitution prohibits public demonstrations that "violate the principles of Islam," a vague provision used to justify the heavy-handed dispersal of assemblies and marches. According to Amnesty International, the authorities arrested up to 4,000 people during the June demonstrations, about half of whom were detained for more than a week, and charged at least 65 people with criminal offenses. Hundreds of students and political activists were arrested in July and August, including three leaders of the Office to Foster Unity (OFU) and four leaders of the Melli Mazhabi (National Religious Alliance).

In recent years, hardline vigilante organizations, most notably the Basij and Ansar-i Hezbollah, have played a major role in dispersing public demonstrations. Shortly after the outbreak of the June protests, Khamenei warned that "the Iranian nation" may "decide to take action against the rioters," a striking indication that such vigilante groups are sanctioned by the conservative establishment. During the year, at least seven reformist members of parliament were beaten or blocked from giving public speeches in cities outside of the capital.

Iranian law does not allow independent labor unions to exist, though workers' councils are represented in the government-sanctioned Workers' House, the country's only legal labor federation. While strikes and work stoppages are not uncommon, the authorities often ban or disperse demonstrations that criticize national economic policies. In 2003, the Ministry of the Interior prohibited the Worker's House from holding a demonstration on International Labor Day (May 1), citing regional tensions.

The judiciary is not independent. The Supreme Leader directly appoints the head of the judiciary, who in turn appoints senior judges. Civil courts provide some procedural safeguards, though judges often serve simultaneously as prosecutors during trials. Political and other sensitive cases are tried before Revolutionary Courts, where detainees are denied access to legal counsel and due process is ignored. The penal code is based on Sharia and provides for flogging, stoning, amputation, and death for a range of social and political offenses.

Iranian security forces subjected thousands of citizens to arbitrary arrest and incommunicado detention in 2003. Suspected dissidents are often held in unofficial, illegal detention centers, and allegations of torture are commonplace. Zahra Kazemi, a Canadian Iranian photo journalist, was arrested in June while taking photographs outside Tehran's high-security Evin prison and was beaten to death in custody.

There are few laws that discriminate against ethnic minorities, who are permitted to establish community centers and certain cultural, social, sports, and charitable associations. However, Kurdish demands for more autonomy and a greater voice in the appointment of a regional governor have not been met and some Kurdish opposition groups are brutally suppressed. At least two members of Komala, a Kurdish political organization affiliated with the Communist Party of Iran, were executed in 2003.

Although women enjoy the same political rights as men and currently hold several seats in parliament and even one of Iran's vice presidencies, they face discrimination in legal and social matters. A woman cannot obtain a passport without the permission of a male relative or her husband, and women do not enjoy equal rights under laws governing divorce, child custody disputes, or inheritance. A woman's testimony in court is given only half the weight of a man's. Women must conform to strict dress codes and are segregated from men in most public places. Several pieces of legislation intended to give women equal rights, such as a bill on divorce law that parliament approved in August 2002, have been rejected by the Council of Guardians. In November 2003, the Expediency Council approved a law giving divorced mothers the right to have custody of boys aged seven and under. The previous law automatically granted divorced fathers custody of male children over the age of two.

# Iraq

**Population:** 24,200,000  **Political Rights:** 7
**GNI/capita:** $1,090  **Civil Liberties:** 5*
**Life Expectancy:** 58  **Status:** Not Free
**Religious Groups:** Muslim (97 percent), Christian or other (3 percent)
**Ethnic Groups:** Arab (75-80 percent), Kurd (15-20 percent), other [including Turkmen and Assyrian] (5 percent)
**Capital:** Baghdad
**Ratings Change:** Iraq's civil liberties rating improved from 7 to 5 due to the expansion of freedoms of expression and association.

**Ten-Year Ratings Timeline (Political Rights, Civil Liberties, Status)**

| 1994 | 1995 | 1996 | 1997 | 1998 | 1999 | 2000 | 2001 | 2002 | 2003 |
|------|------|------|------|------|------|------|------|------|------|
| 7,7NF | 7,7NF | 7,7NF | 7,7NF | 7,7NF | 7,7NF | 7,7NF | 7,7NF | 7,7NF | 7,5NF |

**Overview:**  Following the April 2003 ouster of Saddam Hussein's tyrannical government by a U.S. and British military coalition, the Coalition Provisional Authority (CPA) presided over a sweeping expansion of civil liberties and began implementing an ambitious plan to establish a democratic government by the end of 2005. However, an escalating insurgency, supported by much of the country's once-dominant Sunni Arab minority, perpetuated a climate of instability and hampered reconstruction efforts.

The modern state of Iraq, consisting of three former Ottoman provinces, was established after World War I as a British-administered League of Nations mandate. In 1921, Britain installed a constitutional monarchy in which Sunni Arabs came to dominate most political and administrative posts at the expense of Kurds and Shiite Arabs. Sunni political dominance in Iraq, which formally gained independence in 1932, continued after the monarchy was overthrown in a 1958 military coup. Following a succession of weak leftist regimes, the pan-Arab Baath (Renaissance) party seized power in 1968. In 1979, the Baathist regime's de facto strongman, Saddam Hussein, formally assumed the presidency.

Hussein brutally suppressed all political opposition and sought to establish Iraq as a regional superpower by invading Iran in 1980. During the eight-year war, his regime used chemical weapons against both Iranian troops and rebellious Iraqi Kurds. Iraqi troops invaded Kuwait in 1990 and were ousted the following year by a U.S.-led coalition.

After the Gulf War, the UN Security Council imposed economic sanctions pending the destruction of Iraq's weapons of mass destruction (WMD). While it was originally anticipated that the sanctions would be lifted within a few years, Iraq refused to disclose its WMD capabilities for more than a decade and the sanctions remained in place. In the aftermath of the September 11, 2001 attacks on the United States, U.S. president George W. Bush designated Iraq's WMD a salient threat to American national security and committed his administration to engineering Hussein's ouster. In March 2003, U.S. and British forces invaded Iraq and captured Baghdad within three weeks.

The initial euphoria felt by many Iraqis in the immediate aftermath of the regime's collapse was soon tempered by the security vacuum, widespread looting, and acute electricity and water shortages that followed. Unemployment soared as a result of the CPA's early de-Baathification decrees, which left around 35,000 civil servants out of work, and the disbanding of Iraq's 400,000-man army. After extensive and often contentious negotiations with leading Iraqi political and religious leaders, the CPA appointed a 25-member Iraqi Governing Council (IGC) in July and granted it limited law-making authority. By year's end, however, decision making on major government policies remained in the hands of the CPA.

While care was taken to ensure that the composition of the IGC, as well as provisional local and regional government bodies, reflected Iraq's confessional and ethnic demography, Sunni Arabs viewed the diminution of their political supremacy with trepidation. Loose networks of Baath Party loyalists organized an insurgency in the "Sunni triangle" of central Iraq, which progressively gained strength during the year. Monthly combat fatalities suffered by coalition forces rose from 7 in May to a high of 94 in November, while terrorist attacks on government offices, humanitarian institutions, and civilian areas increased dramatically in the latter half of 2003. Several prominent Iraqis who supported the American occupation were assassinated during the year, including prominent Shiite clerics Abdel Majid Al-Khoei and Muhammad Baqir al-Hakim; IGC member Aquila Hashimi; the deputy mayor of Baghdad, Faris Abdul Razzaq al-Assam; and Mustafa Zaidan al-Khaleefa, a prominent member of a Baghdad neighborhood council. In response to the escalating violence, the CPA accelerated training of Iraqi security forces and relaxed its de-Baathification screening.

Although the CPA initially planned to restore Iraqi sovereignty only after a constitution was drafted and an elected Iraqi government was in place, the increased frequency and lethality of insurgent attacks led the United States to accelerate the transfer of power. Under a plan unveiled in November, the CPA and the IGC will be replaced in June 2004 by an unelected interim government, selected by provincial caucuses; an elected government will assume power by the end of 2005, after a constitution has been ratified. This new arrangement, which remains subject to change, was also intended to offer Sunni Arab leaders, who felt largely excluded from the IGC, a more substantial presence in the transitional assembly.

Several outbreaks of violence between Kurds and Turkmans in and around the northern city of Kirkuk occurred during the latter half of 2003, most notably a spate of clashes on August 24 that left 11 people dead.

**Political Rights and Civil Liberties:** Iraqis cannot yet change their government democratically, as the CPA wields virtually absolute authority, both directly and through its appointment of provisional government bodies. Nevertheless, the CPA consults regularly with political, religious, and tribal leaders in making decisions and has retracted some decrees that met with broad-based opposition.

Freedom of expression in Iraq is respected by the CPA, with some limits. Although domestic television broadcasting is dominated by the Iraqi Media Network (IMN), established in May 2003 by the CPA, independent print publications proliferated after the fall of Saddam Hussein's regime and are allowed to operate without significant interference. Satellite dishes, banned by the former regime, and unrestricted Internet access have become available to those who can afford them. Although critical of the CPA in many respects, a fact-finding mission sent to Iraq in June 2003 by the London-based Arab Press Freedom Watch (APFW) concluded that Iraqis are "free to think, write, print, publish, and distribute without fear and restrictions."

CPA Order 14 (June 2003) prohibits media organizations from publishing or broadcasting material that incites violence or civil disorder, advocates the return to power of the Baath Party, or contains statements that purport to be on behalf of the Baath Party. It also allows for the closure of media organizations that violate these regulations. At least three local media outlets—two newspapers and a radio station—were suspended during the year on such grounds. In November, the Dubai-based satellite TV news channel Al-Arabiya was banned from operating in Iraq after it broadcast an audiotape in which Saddam Hussein urged Iraqis to kill members of the provisional Iraqi government.

Twelve foreign journalists and other international media personnel were killed and two remained missing as a result of combat operations in Iraq in 2003. International human rights groups drew attention to the deaths of two journalists on April 8 by a U.S. tank returning hostile fire at a Baghdad hotel and the August 17 death of a reporter whose camera was mistaken for a rocket-propelled grenade launcher, claiming that internationally recognized rules of engagement were breached. Ahmed Shawkat, the editor of the liberal weekly *Bila Ittijah*, was gunned down by suspected Islamist militants in October. At least a dozen foreign journalists were detained, most of them briefly, by coalition forces and Iraqi police during the year, including several cameramen and photographers from Arab media outlets suspected of having advanced knowledge of insurgent attacks. In November, a Portuguese journalist was kidnapped in southern Iraq and held for ransom.

Islam is the state religion in Iraq and is likely to remain so under the new political system taking shape. Baathist-era restrictions on freedom of worship and controls over religious institutions have been lifted. Newly constructed Shiite mosques proliferated in the latter half of the year. Religious and ethnic groups in Iraq are represented in the IGC (which has 13 Shiites, 5 Sunni Arabs, 1 Christian and 1 Turkman) and civil service in proportion to their demographic strength. Most government restrictions on academic freedom have been abolished by the CPA, but some new limits have been imposed. De-Baathification of Iraq's universities led to the firing of more than sixteen hundred Baathist professors and other university employees in May, though some were later reinstated. While faculties were permitted to elect university administrators for the first time, nominees were vetted by the CPA.

Freedom of association and assembly are generally recognized by the CPA. Although the Baath Party has been banned, political organizations representing a wide range of viewpoints are allowed to organize freely. Public demonstrations, ranging from strikes by public sector workers to pro-Saddam rallies, occurred almost daily during the year without coalition interference. While coalition forces reportedly killed several unarmed demonstrators in 2003, most deaths appear to have resulted from soldiers returning fire at armed militants. Baathist-era laws banning worker strikes are no longer in effect.

The Iraqi judiciary is not independent. In June 2003, the CPA established the Judicial Review Committee to screen judges and prosecutors for past links to the Baath Party, involvement in human rights violations, and corruption, and to appoint replacements. Although Iraq's 1971 Criminal Procedure Code, which stipulates that suspects cannot be held more than 24 hours without an examining magistrate's ruling of sufficient evidence, remains in force and is generally observed in ordinary criminal cases, thousands of people suspected of security offenses were detained without charge by coalition troops and Iraqi police in 2003. At year's end, the CPA had roughly 12,800 such detainees in custody, including around 4,000 members of the Mujahedin-e Khalq Organization, an Iranian dissident group backed by the former Iraqi regime.

Relatives of detainees are rarely granted access to prisons, though most are eventually able to communicate with family members through handwritten messages exchanged through the International Committee of the Red Cross (ICRC). In November, coalition forces began detaining relatives of wanted men, including the wife and daughter of Izzat Ibrahim al-Douri, the former deputy head of the Baath party.

Public security for Iraqi women, who by some estimates constitute nearly 60 percent of the population, deteriorated significantly after the fall of the Baathist regime. In July 2003, Human Rights Watch reported that insecurity in major Iraqi cities and the "low priority" given to cases of sexual violence by police was preventing many female Iraqis from working and attending school. Islamist groups have used their newfound freedom to harassed unveiled women in many parts of the country. Although the CPA has pledged to protect and empower women, only three were appointed to the 25-member ICG and only one was given a ministerial position. In order to secure support from conservative and Islamist groups in Iraq, the CPA has declined to establish quotas for Iraqi women in the transitional assembly to be formed in 2004.

# Ireland

**Population:** 4,000,000
**GNI/capita:** $22,850
**Life Expectancy:** 77
**Religious Groups:** Roman Catholic (91.6 percent),
Church of Ireland (2.5 percent), other (5.9 percent)
**Ethnic Groups:** Celtic, English minority
**Capital:** Dublin

**Political Rights:** 1
**Civil Liberties:** 1
**Status:** Free

**Ten-Year Ratings Timeline (Political Rights, Civil Liberties, Status)**

| 1993 | 1994 | 1995 | 1996 | 1997 | 1998 | 1999 | 2000 | 2001 | 2002 | 2003 |
|------|------|------|------|------|------|------|------|------|------|------|
| 1,2F | 1,1F | 1,1F | 1,1F | 1,1F | 1,1F | 1,1F | 1,1F | 1,1F | 1,1F | 1,1F |

**Overview:**

The coalition government, made up of the Fianna Fail and Progressive Democrat parties, lost popularity and momentum over the course of 2003, as did Prime Minister Bertie Ahern. Economic growth was weak, and old corruption scandals continued to dog some in the ruling Fianna Fail party.

The Irish Free State emerged from the United Kingdom after the Anglo-Irish Treaty of 1921. (Six protestant-majority counties in the province of Ulster remained within the United Kingdom.) A short civil war followed, ending in 1923. In 1937, the Irish Free State adopted a new constitution and a new name—Ireland, or Eire.

Ireland has been independent in its foreign policy, staying out of World War II and out of NATO. It joined the European Community (now the European Union) along with Britain and Denmark in 1973. As a member, thanks in part to large subsidies for poorer regions within the EU, Ireland has enjoyed high rates of economic growth and has gone from being one of the poorest countries in Europe to being richer than Britain (by some measures). It adopted the euro on its launch (as an electronic currency only) in 1999 and introduced euro notes and coins in 2001.

Ireland has resisted any EU moves that would impinge on its neutrality, including the idea of setting up an EU military capability. Partly for this reason, Irish voters rejected the EU's Treaty of Nice in June 2001, temporarily blocking the enlargement of the EU into eastern Europe. In a second referendum, in October 2002, Irish voters approved the treaty.

Growth in the gross domestic product (GDP) averaged an outstanding 8.6 percent from 1998 through 2002. The growth led to inflation and wage increases, which eroded Ireland's competitiveness. That erosion, compounded by a strong euro (which depresses exports), slowed GDP growth sharply, to a forecast of approximately 2.5 percent in 2003. The slower growth hit the government's budget, forcing a step back from the highly generous fiscal policies of previous years.

Partly thanks to the state of the economy, Prime Minister Ahern and his government steadily lost popularity over 2003. Late in the year, just 36 percent of those polled were satisfied with Ahern's performance. The election promise to create a "world-class health service" has not been fulfilled thanks to tighter budgets. In addition, the government mishandled an investigation into child abuse in state-supervised residences run by religious orders. A judge appointed by the government to investigate corruption turned out to be a tax evader, as did a government backbencher. Meanwhile, the 2002 suspension of the Northern Ireland Assembly cast a shadow in the country during the year, as the republic has been a strong supporter of the Good Friday Agreement that set up the assembly.

## Political Rights and Civil Liberties:

The Irish can change their government democratically. The legislature consists of a lower house (the Dail), whose 166 members are elected by proportional representation, and an upper house (the Seanad, or Senate) of 60 members, some appointed, some elected by a body representing various interest groups. The Senate is mainly a consultative body. The president, whose powers are largely ceremonial, is directly elected for a seven-year term.

The political party system is open to the rise and fall of competing groupings. The two largest parties are Fianna Fail and Fine Gael, which do not differ widely in ideological orientation, but mainly represent the opposing sides of the 1920s civil war. The smaller parties are the Labour Party, the Progressive Democrats, Sinn Fein, and the Greens.

Corruption has been an ongoing issue. A former prime minister, Charles Haughey, who headed several governments from 1979 to 1992, was discovered in 1997 to have received up to one million euros from an owner of a food and textile retailer. Many of the scandals have involved members of Fianna Fail. Though there is no direct connection of corruption to Prime Minister Bertie Ahern, he was found to have signed blank checks as party leader. Ireland improved its ranking on the Corruption Perceptions Index published by Transparency International, a watchdog group, from 23 in 2002 to 18 in 2003.

The media are free and independent and Internet access is unrestricted. The print media present a variety of viewpoints. Television and radio broadcasting is dominated by the state broadcaster, RTE, but the growth of cable and satellite television is weakening its influence. The state maintains the right to censor pornographic and violent material, which critics charge is an anachronism and possibly in contravention of the European Convention on Human Rights.

Freedom of religion is provided for in the constitution, and discrimination on the basis of religion is outlawed. Though the country is overwhelmingly Roman Catholic, there is no state religion. Immigrants and noncitizens face little trouble in religious expression. Religious education is provided in most primary and secondary schools, on whose boards sit officials of the Catholic Church. Parents may exempt their children from religious instruction, and the constitution requires equal funding for students wishing instruction in other faiths. Academic freedom is respected.

There is freedom of assembly and organization, and collective bargaining is legal and unrestricted. Civil groups and nongovernmental organizations can operate freely.

The legal system is based on common law, and the judiciary is independent. In a 2003 visit, the Council of Europe found evidence of some ill-treatment, including beatings of detainees by police, mostly at the time of their detention, but that prisons are on the whole well run. There is equal protection for all under the law, but the Irish Travellers, a nomadic group of about 25,000, face social discrimination in housing, hiring, and other areas.

Inequality persists in the pay of men and women, but discrimination in employment on the basis of sex and sexual orientation is forbidden under national and EU law. The past two presidents have been women: Mary McAleese (elected in 1997) and Mary Robinson (elected 1990). Abortion is legal only when the life of the mother is threatened.

# Israel

**Population:** 6,700,000
[Note: includes about
220,000 Israeli settlers
in the West Bank, about 20,000 in the Golan Heights, and
7,500 in the Gaza Strip. Approximately 172,000 Jews and
170,000 Arabs live in East Jerusalem.]
**GNI/capita:** $16,750
**Life Expectancy:** 79

**Political Rights:** 1
**Civil Liberties:** 3
**Status:** Free

**Religious Groups:** Jewish (80.1 percent), Muslim [mostly Sunni] (14.6 percent), Christian (2.1 percent), other (3.2 percent)
**Ethnic Groups:** Jewish (80 percent), non-Jewish [mostly Arab] (20 percent)
**Capital:** Jerusalem
*Note:* The numerical rating and status reflect the state of political rights and civil liberties within Israel itself. Separate reports examine political rights and civil liberties in the Israeli administered territories and in the Palestinian administered areas.

**Ten-Year Ratings Timeline (Political Rights, Civil Liberties, Status)**

| 1994 | 1995 | 1996 | 1997 | 1998 | 1999 | 2000 | 2001 | 2002 | 2003 |
|------|------|------|------|------|------|------|------|------|------|
| 1,3F | 1,3F | 1,3F | 1,3F | 1,3F | 1,3F | 1,3F | 1,3F | 1,3F | 1,3F |

**Overview:**

Israelis suffered greatly from Palestinian terrorism in 2003, even with a nearly two-month ceasefire. Several suicide bombings killed over 200 Israelis, eroding public security. The attacks elicited powerful Israeli reprisals against targets in the West Bank, Gaza Strip, and, for the first time in 30 years, Syria. Notwithstanding the crisis atmosphere, Israelis strived in 2003 to lead normal lives; they enjoyed and exercised substantial political freedom, and most Israelis—with the exception of the country's 20 percent Arab minority—enjoyed full civil rights. The government of Prime Minister Ariel Sharon of the Likud Party, after winning a landslide election early in the year, pushed ahead with construction of a controversial security barrier in the West Bank. The police launched investigations in response to an official inquiry into the shooting deaths of 13 Arab-Israeli citizens by Israeli police officers in 2000. Several Arab citizens and Arab residents of East Jerusalem were charged during the year with aiding and abetting radical Palestinian groups in suicide bomb attacks in Israel. Two joint Israeli-Palestinian nongovernmental peace initiatives garnered limited domestic support on both sides. In November, four former heads of Israel's internal security service warned that the government's strong-arm tactics against the Palestinians were endangering Israelis. Municipal elections in October were marred by hundreds of criminal investigations of local political activists. The government dismantled the Religious Affairs Ministry, further eroding the near-monopolistic control over religious life by the Orthodox establishment. The Israeli economy continued to suffer under the strain of combating terrorism; state subsidies for social programs were slashed, and workers staged several large-scale strikes.

Israel was formed in 1948 from less than one-fifth of the original British Palestine Mandate. Arab nations rejected a UN partition plan that would also have created a Palestinian state. Immediately following Israel's declaration of independence, its neighbors attacked. While Israel maintained its sovereignty, Jordan seized East Jerusalem and the West Bank and Egypt took control of the Gaza Strip. In the 1967 Six-Day War, Israel came to occupy Sinai, the West Bank, Gaza, East Jerusalem, and the Golan Heights. Syria had previously used the Golan to shell towns in northern Israel. Israel annexed East Jerusalem in 1967 and the Golan Heights in 1981.

Prime Minister Yitzhak Rabin's Labor-led coalition government secured a breakthrough agreement with the Palestine Liberation Organization (PLO) in 1993. The Declaration of Principles, negotiated secretly between Israeli and Palestinian delegations in Oslo, Norway, provided for a phased Israeli withdrawal from the Israeli-occupied West Bank and Gaza Strip and for limited Palestinian autonomy in those areas, and for Palestinian recognition of Israel and a renunciation of terrorism. On November 4, 1995, a right-wing Jewish extremist, opposed to the peace process, assassinated Rabin in Tel Aviv.

At Camp David in July 2000 and at Taba, Egypt, in the fall and in early 2001, Prime Minister Ehud Barak and U.S. president Bill Clinton engaged the Palestinian leadership in the most far-reaching negotiations ever. For the first time, Israel discussed compromise solutions on Jerusalem, agreeing to some form of Palestinian sovereignty over East Jerusalem and Islamic holy sites in Jerusalem's Old City. Israel also offered all of the Gaza Strip and more than 95 percent of the West Bank to the Palestinians. However, the Palestinian leadership rejected the Israeli offers. Some analysts suggested that Yasser Arafat, chairman of the Palestinian Authority, was not satisfied that Palestinian territory in the West Bank would be contiguous and that Israel would recognize a "right of return," which would allow Palestinian refugees to live in Israel. Following a controversial visit by Likud Party leader Ariel Sharon to the Temple Mount in Jerusalem in September 2000, the Palestinians launched an armed uprising. Snap Israeli elections in February 2001 took place against the backdrop of continuing Palestinian violence. Sharon, promising Israelis both peace and security from terrorism, trounced Barak at the polls.

As Israelis prepared to go the polls for national elections in January 2003, two Arab members of the Knesset (parliament)—Ahmed Tibi and Azmi Bishara—were banned by Israel's Central Election Committee from running. Both were accused of opposing the existence of Israel as a Jewish state and encouraging Palestinian violence against Jews. The Israeli Supreme Court subsequently overturned the ban, allowing the two to run in the elections.

In late January, voters handed Sharon's Likud Party a landslide victory over the leading opposition Labor Party. Likud gained 37 seats, while Labor picked up only 19. Likud joined forces with the centrist Shinui Party, which gained 15 seats, and with two right-wing parties—the National Religious Party and the National Union

Party—forming a comfortable coalition government with a total of 68 out of 120 Knesset seats. For the first time in Israel's history, an Arab citizen, Salah Tarif, was accorded a full cabinet portfolio.

Sharon's security platform helped divert voter attention from corruption scandals revealed on the eve of elections. Sharon was accused of conspiring with his sons to hide an illegal foreign loan to pay back an illegal foreign donation made to Sharon's campaign coffers. A vote-buying scandal implicating the Likud Party also failed to dissuade voters.

Palestinians carried out several devastating suicide bomb attacks inside Israel in 2003. The attacks, which took place inside buses, cafés, restaurants, bars, markets, shopping malls, and private homes, were random, occurring in large cities, smaller towns, and on kibbutzim. A suicide bombing by Hamas, a radical Palestinian group, aboard a Jerusalem bus in August killed 18 civilians, mostly Orthodox Jews returning from prayers at the Western Wall in Jerusalem's Old City. That attack violated a seven-week cease-fire arranged by radical Palestinian groups and the Palestinian Authority. After Israel retaliated by assassinating Hamas leaders, Hamas and Islamic Jihad called off the cease-fire, which had provided Israelis with an unusual stretch of relative calm and a return to some normalcy. Despite the attacks, Israelis carried on with their daily lives; citizens continued to ride public buses, eat in restaurants, and participate in public gatherings and events. Several suicide bombings were also prevented, including over 20 in November, according to Israeli security services.

In October, after an Islamic Jihad suicide bomber murdered 21 Israelis—including several Arabs—at a restaurant in Haifa, Israeli warplanes bombed a purported Islamic Jihad training camp in Syria. The attack marked the first time Israel had struck within Syria since the 1973 Yom Kippur War. The air strike increased tensions between the two countries; in late October, Syria's foreign minister threatened to attack Israeli civilian communities on the Golan Heights.

Palestinians in the Gaza Strip carried out several rocket and mortar attacks against Israeli town and cities to the north and east of the strip. The rockets were of a longer range than those fired in previous years, suggesting greater sophistication by the attackers and their acquisition of more advanced weaponry.

Israeli Defense Forces (IDF) retaliated for many terrorist attacks throughout the year. The IDF carried out targeted killings of terrorist suspects in the West Bank and Gaza, where it also staged air strikes, demolished private homes, and imposed curfews. The United States and other nations criticized Israel for the killings of innocent Palestinians, during Israeli antiterror operations.

Israeli reprisals for Palestinian attacks led to some divisions within the Israeli military. The air force grounded several active pilots who, concerned about harming innocent Palestinians, refused orders to attack suspects in the West Bank and Gaza.

In November, the IDF's chief of staff, Lieutenant General Moshe Ya'alon publicly criticized Sharon's policies, saying they were strengthening terrorist organizations and undermining moderate Palestinian politicians. General Ya'alon's remarks followed warnings by four former heads of the Shin Bet, Israel's domestic security service, that the government's policies were leading the country to "catastrophe." Tensions were high along Israel's northern border with Lebanon during the year. In August, Hezbollah, a radical Shiite Muslim group backed by Iran and Syria and based in southern Lebanon, shelled northern Israel, killing one person. After Israel's air strike against Syria in October, a Hezbollah sniper fired across the border into Israel, killing an IDF soldier. Hezbollah also shelled Israeli positions.

Hezbollah reportedly took delivery of rockets capable of striking Israeli population and industrial centers. The group has in the past attacked Israeli positions patrolling near the Shebba Farms area. Hezbollah considers the area occupied Lebanese territory, despite UN confirmation in June 2000 that Israel had withdrawn fully from the "security zone" in southern Lebanon it had occupied for 18 years. Israel had held the zone to protect its northern flank from attacks, including repeated Hezbollah rocketing of Israeli towns and farms.

Hezbollah continued to hold at least five Israeli hostages. Widely believed to be among them is Israeli airman Ron Arad, thought to be held in Lebanon or Iran since his plane was shot down over Lebanon in 1986. Hezbollah hinted during the year that it would negotiate for the hostages' release. Israel considered releasing hundreds of Arab prisoners in an exchange deal. There are more than 5,000 Palestinians in Israeli jails.

Peace talks with Syria did not take place during the year. Intensive negotiations broke down in January 2000 over disagreements on final borders around the Golan Heights.

The initiation of approximately 400 criminal investigations of local political activists on allegations of arson, vandalism, fraud, and other election-related malfeasance tainted municipal elections in October.

In the fall, a group of former Israeli and Palestinian politicians revealed a private peace initiative negotiated in secret in Geneva, Switzerland. Based largely on terms discussed by Israeli and Palestinian negotiators at Taba, Egypt, in December 2000-January 2001, the nongovernmental "Geneva accord" envisioned an independent Palestinian state in the West Bank and Gaza Strip, the dismantlement of Jewish settlements in those areas, the division of Jerusalem, and sole Palestinian control of the Temple Mount in Jerusalem's Old City with international monitoring. In return, Palestinians would pledge peace. There was also a vague reference to the Palestinians dropping their demand for a "right of return" of refugees to Israel. While the accord drew some limited support from the Israeli and Palestinian publics, their respective leaders largely ignored it. Another peace plan headed by former Shin Bet chief Ami Ayalon and Palestinian academic and peace activist Sari Nusseibeh also gathered limited support.

The Israeli economy suffered throughout the year from a drop in tourism and the strain of combating the Palestinian uprising. Finance Minister Benyamin Netanyahu instituted strict austerity measures, including budget reductions, layoffs, privatization schemes, and cuts in social security payments. A general strike called by Histadrut, the national labor union, paralyzed the country in April. Banks, school, and airports closed in response to the Treasury's plan to slash $2.3 billion from the state budget. In an effort to boost domestic employment, the government deported 30,000 foreign workers during the year.

A report released in October by the National Insurance Institute, a quasi-government agency, showed that 21 percent of Israelis live below the poverty line. Of 1.3 million said to be in poverty, more than 600,000 are children. Ultra-Orthodox Jews and non-Jews were the most vulnerable segments of the population.

**Political Rights and Civil Liberties:** Israeli citizens can change their government democratically. Although Israel has no formal constitution, a series of basic laws has the force of constitutional principles.

Arab residents of East Jerusalem, while not granted automatic citizenship, were issued Israeli identity cards after the 1967 Six-Day War. However, by law, Israel strips Arabs of their Jerusalem residency if they remain outside the city for more than three months. Arab residents have the same rights as Israeli citizens, except the right to vote in national elections. They do have the right to vote in municipal elections and are eligible to apply for citizenship. Many choose not to seek citizenship out of solidarity with Palestinians in the West Bank and Gaza Strip, and because they believe East Jerusalem should be the capital of an independent Palestinian state. East Jerusalem's Arab population does not receive a share of municipal services proportionate to its numbers. Arabs in East Jerusalem do have the right to vote in Palestinian Authority elections.

Press freedom is respected in Israel. Newspaper and magazine articles on security matters are subject to a military censor, though the scope of permissible reporting is wide. Editors may appeal a censorship decision to a three-member tribunal that includes two civilians. Arabic-language publications are censored more frequently than are Hebrew-language ones. Newspapers are privately owned and freely criticize government policy. In October, a pirate radio station, Arutz Sheva, was forced off the air by the government for operating without a license. The station, supportive of Jewish settlers in the West Bank and Gaza, broadcast from a boat in the Mediterranean Sea. In November, the Israeli Supreme Court upheld an appeal against a decision by the Israel Film Board to ban the screening of a documentary film critical of Israel's armed forces. Publishing the praise of violence is prohibited under the Counter-terrorism Ordinance. Israeli authorities prohibit expressions of support for groups that call for the destruction of Israel. Internet access is widespread.

Freedom of religion is respected. Each religious community has jurisdiction over its own members in matters of marriage, burial, and divorce. In the Jewish community, the Orthodox establishment generally handles these matters. As a result, the law does not allow civil marriages, which prevents a non-Jew from marrying a Jew. In February 2002, the Supreme Court for the first time formally recognized Jewish conversions performed by Reform and Conservative rabbis in Israel. While the ruling allows those converted by non-Orthodox rabbis to be listed as Jews in the official population registry, the Orthodox establishment can still refuse services to Reform and Conservative converts. In March 2003, the government ordered the indefinite suspension of the enforcement of the no-work law during the Jewish Sabbath. While the Orthodox community objected, Israel's large secular establishment celebrated the decision. Christians, Muslims, Bahais, and others enjoy freedom of religion.

In October, the Sharon cabinet disbanded the Religious Affairs Ministry, effectively putting rabbinic courts under control of the Justice Ministry. The decision cleared the way for increased allocations of state resources to non-Orthodox religious institutions, including those attached to the Reform and Conservative movements. The move was seen as a further erosion of the Orthodox monopoly on Israel's religious affairs.

There is widespread academic freedom in Israel, in the midst of which there are trends of growing polarization between right and left academics, including occasional reports of ad hominem attacks on both sides.

Freedom of assembly and association is respected. Demonstrations, including outside government buildings and official residences of the prime minister, are permitted. Israel features a vibrant civic society, which includes many nongovernmental organizations. Workers may join unions of their choice and enjoy the right to strike and to bargain collectively. Three-quarters of the workforce either belong to unions affiliated with Histadrut or are covered under its social programs and collective bargaining agreements. Foreign workers in the country legally enjoy wage protections, medical insurance, and guarantees against employer exploitation. Illegal workers are often at the mercy of employers, and many are exploited.

The judiciary is independent, and procedural safeguards are generally respected. Security trials, however, may be closed to the public on limited grounds. The Emergency Powers (Detention) Law of 1979 provides for indefinite administrative detention without trial. The policy stems from emergency laws in place since the creation of Israel. Most administrative detainees are Palestinian, but there are currently two Lebanese detainees being held on national security grounds. They are believed to have direct knowledge of missing Israeli airman Ron Arad.

In September, an independent commission issued its findings of a public inquiry into the shooting deaths of 13 Arab Israeli citizens by Israeli police in October 2000. The police opened fire on rioters demonstrating in support of the Palestinian uprising. The report focused carefully on discrimination against the Arab minority in Israel, calling it the primary cause of the riots in 2000. The report recommended censuring former Interior Minister Shlomo Ben-Ami and barring him from holding high office again. The report led to the initiation of criminal investigations of several of the police officers who had opened fire, labeling them "prejudiced." While the 800-plus-page report was criticized by some for not going far enough—and by others for excusing Arab violence—it was generally regarded as an important breakthrough in addressing the social and economic disparities between Jewish and Arab Israelis. Prime Minister Ariel Sharon announced that more Arab citizens would be integrated into Israel's business community; he appointed several Arab Israelis to the boards of state-owned companies.

Some Israeli analysts, including supporters of Arab minority rights, raised caution about radicalization of segments of Israel's Arab population and of Arab residents of East Jerusalem. Several Arab Israelis and East Jerusalem residents were arrested in 2003 for transporting Palestinian suicide bombers to their targets. Several other Arab Israelis, including the mayor of the Arab town of Uhm al-Fahm, were arrested in May on suspicion of channeling money to the radical Islamist group Hamas. Eight Jerusalem Arabs with suspected ties to Hamas were also arrested in May for planning a bus hijacking.

In July, the government passed a new law barring citizenship to Palestinians from the West Bank and Gaza who marry Arab Israelis. The law, which expires after one year, would ostensibly lead to the separation of families. The law is not retroactive; it would not affect Palestinians previously granted citizenship. Some human rights groups characterized the new law as racist. Israel said the law was necessary because some Palestinians have opportunistically married Arab citizens of Israel so they can move to the country and more easily carry out terrorist attacks.

Some one million Arab citizens (roughly 20 percent of the population) receive inferior education, housing, and social services relative to the Jewish population. Israeli Arabs are not subject to the military draft, though they may serve voluntarily. Those who do not join the army are not eligible for financial benefits—including scholarships and housing loans—available to Israelis who have served. Most Bedouin housing settlements are not recognized by the government and are not provided with basic infrastructure and essential services.

Freedom of movement is affected sometimes by security alerts and emergency measures that can subject Israelis to long waits at roadblocks and at public places. The Israeli government continued construction of a security barrier in the West Bank designed to prevent Palestinian suicide bombers from infiltrating Israel.

Women have achieved substantial parity at almost all levels of Israeli society. Women are somewhat under-represented in public affairs; 18 women sit in the 120-seat Knesset. In the May 1999 election, an Arab woman, Husaina Jabara, was elected to the Knesset for the first time. Arab women face some societal pressures and traditions that negatively affect their professional, political, and social lives. The trafficking of women has become a problem in recent years.

# Italy

**Population:** 57,200,000
**GNI/capita:** $19,390
**Life Expectancy:** 80
**Religious Groups:** Roman Catholic (predominant)
**Ethnic Groups:** Italian, small minorities of German, French, Slovenian, and Albanian
**Capital:** Rome

**Political Rights:** 1
**Civil Liberties:** 1
**Status:** Free

**Ten-Year Ratings Timeline (Political Rights, Civil Liberties, Status)**

| 1994 | 1995 | 1996 | 1997 | 1998 | 1999 | 2000 | 2001 | 2002 | 2003 |
|------|------|------|------|------|------|------|------|------|------|
| 1,2F | 1,2F | 1,2F | 1,2F | 1,2F | 1,2F | 1,2F | 1,2F | 1,1F | 1,1F |

**Overview:**

Italy's assumption to the presidency of the European Union (EU) in July 2003 was marred by Prime Minister Silvio Berlusconi's comparisons of a German member of the European Parliament to a Nazi. The incident occurred only weeks after Berlusconi had pushed through legislation making himself and four other top members of his government immune from prosecution for a number of cases pending against him in court.

Modern Italy begins with the mid-nineteenth century Risorgimento that brought together the various regions of the peninsula under the control of the northwestern region of Piedmont. Italy's liberal period ended abruptly with the rise to power of Benito Mussolini and the Fascist Party, which ruled the country for 20 years beginning in 1922. During World War II, Italy, under Mussolini, joined Germany and Japan as an Axis power. The Allied invasion in the south, along with the help of the anti-Fascist resistance in the north, led to the eventual liberation of the whole country in 1945. A referendum in 1946 replaced the monarchy with a republican form of government.

In the late 1990s, Italy began a number of institutional reforms to address a list of pressing issues, including revolving-door governments; Italy has had over 50 governments since 1945. In 1993, a new electoral law switched the country from a pure system of proportional representation to a more restrictive plurality system in an attempt to reduce the number of political parties that can obtain seats. Other reforms have included efforts to modernize the judiciary by streamlining the prosecution of cases in the courts and devolving more power to the country's 20 regions. There has also been a move to reduce unnecessary legislation: Italy has more than 90,000 laws compared with France's 7,325.

The "Clean Hands" corruption trials in the early 1990s led to the collapse of the major political parties that had dominated postwar Italian politics—the Christian Democrats, the Communists, and the Socialists. Since that time, many new parties and coalitions have emerged, including the Casa delle Liberta (House of Liberties), which won national elections in May 2001. The Casa coalition includes Berlusconi's Forza Italia, as well as the post-fascist Allianza Nazionale, and the regionalist Lega Nord. About 85 percent of eligible voters went to the polls—a turnout that was lower than the postwar average of over 90 percent. There are currently two leading coalitions in parliament. The main opposition to the Casa delle Liberta is the leftist Ulivo (Olive Tree) coalition, which contains the former Communist Party, now called the Party of the Democratic Left (DS), as well as different Green formations and former leftist Christian Democrats. The constitution forbids the reemergence of the Fascist Party.

Italy took over the presidency of the EU in July 2003 after Greece ended its six-month rotation. The start of Italy's leadership, however, was marred by comments from Prime Minister Berlusconi, who compared Martin Shultz, a German member of the European Parliament, to a Nazi after he accused Berlusconi of transferring his conflict of interest problems in Italy to Europe.

Parliament passed a law in June that grants Prime Minister Silvio Berlusconi and four top members of his government immunity from prosecution while they remain in office. Berlusconi's trial had begun in March but halted with the passing of the bill, which was rushed through parliament to spare the prime minister the embarrassment of being tried while serving his six-month term as the president of the European Union. The new law sparked a government crisis when one of the parties in the ruling coalition, the Union of Christian Democrats (UDC), threatened to leave if prosecutors in Milan were not allowed to continue an investigation into tax fraud and false accounting by Mediaset, Berlusconi's media company. The UDC argued that the law protected Berlusconi from prosecution but not investigation. Cesare Previti, a former lawyer of Berlusconi's, was handed a prison sentence during the year for bribery and corruption.

Several thousand police officers, soldiers, and civilians from Italy were sent by the government to help with the reconstruction of Iraq after the war ended. In November, the country suffered its largest military loss since World War II when a suicide bomb killed 19 Italians, many of them carabinieri, in Nasiriya, Iraq.

**Political Rights and Civil Liberties:** Italians can change their government democratically. The role of the president, who is chosen by parliament and representatives of the regions, is largely ceremonial. The president chooses the prime minister, who is often, but not always, a member of the largest party in the lower house, the Chamber of Deputies. The constitution also provides for 20 subnational administrative districts. Currently, 75 percent of the 630 seats in the Chamber of Deputies are elected in single-member districts while the other 25 percent are elected by proportional representation, with a 4 percent threshold. A new electoral law circumscribes the chances of smaller parties to attain seats on their own, forcing them to align themselves with other parties in large coalitions on the left and right. In 2000, parliament approved a constitutional change that gives the estimated four million Italians abroad the right to vote, effective with the next national elections.

Corruption remains an issue in politics despite the fall of the postwar political parties. Transparency International ranks Italy 35 out of 133 countries in its 2003 Corruption Perceptions Index, one of the lowest rankings of all Western European countries.

Freedom of speech and the press is constitutionally guaranteed. However, in its 2003 report, Reporters Sans Frontieres ranks Italy among the lowest of all Western countries in terms of press freedom. At issue is the prime minister, who continues to combine his role as head of government with that of being the head of Mediaset, the largest privately owned media group in the country. Berlusconi's ownership of three commercial TV channels, as well as his indirect control over the state-run RAI network, enables him to control 90 percent of the country's media; Italy consequently has one of the most concentrated media markets in the world. Efforts to pass a comprehensive conflict-of-interest bill since the first Berlusconi government in 1994 have made little progress. Internet access is restricted by a 2001 law that allows the government to block foreign Internet sites that contravene national laws.

In September, Berlusconi filed a 15-million-euro libel suit against Piero Fassino, the leader of the opposition, for alleging that the prime minister is behind a smear campaign against the left. *Il Giornale*, a newspaper owned by the prime minister's brother, has been investigating allegations that senior members of the Ulivo government in 1997 received kickbacks in a transaction between Telecom Italia and Telekom Srbija. In June 2002, a wide spectrum of members of parliament criticized the judiciary for authorizing wiretaps of journalists, which, in one case, lasted for over four and a half months. The police that year also raided the homes and offices of journalists working for the dailies *La Repubblica, Corriere della Sera,* and *La Stampa* in response to press leaks. The Organization for Security and Cooperation in Europe criticized Berlusconi in the spring of 2002, when RAI dropped two programs that were critical of him.

Freedom of religion is respected and guaranteed by the constitution. There is no state religion although Catholicism is the dominant religion and the Catholic Church is granted some privileges by the state. A revised Concordat in 1984, for example, gave the Church the right to select teachers paid by the state to teach an optional religion class in public schools. However, there have also been conflicts over religion and the privileged status of the Catholic Church. In October, an Italian court ordered that a crucifix be removed from a school after an Egyptian immigrant, whose two sons attend the school, filed a suit claming that the religious symbol contradicted Italy's secular status. A 1927 law says that public schools must display the crucifix. Academic freedom is respected.

Italians are free to organize into social and political associations, and more than 40 percent of the workforce is unionized. Some of the largest antiwar demonstrations against the U.S.-led war in Iraq took place in Italy.

The independence of the judiciary is undermined by long trial delays and the influence of organized crime. In addition, the current government has been vocally critical of the judiciary. In reference to the corruption charges against him, Berlusconi called the country's magistrates a "cancer that must be cured," a comment that drew strong criticism from the International Commission of Jurists. Berlusconi has made similar comments in the past and has maintained his position since his election that the judiciary is politically motivated to cause his government to fall.

The Roma (Gypsy) community faces unequal treatment from judicial authorities, which are more likely to use pretrial detention and harsher sentences on them than with others. The Lega Nord party continues to inject intolerance into national politics by organizing anti-Islamic campaigns, protesting, for example, the building of mosques.

Women benefit from liberal maternity leave provisions and government efforts to ensure parity in the workforce. However, violence against women continues to be a problem, according the U.S. State Department's human rights report for 2002. There are no quotas for women in either house of parliament, although some parties do maintain them. Around 10 percent of the 630 members of the Chambers of Deputies are women. Italy is a transit point and country of destination for trafficked persons. Women are trafficked from Africa and Eastern Europe for sexual exploitation and children from China for sweatshop labor.

# ↓ Jamaica

**Population:** 2,600,000
**GNI/capita:** $2,800
**Life Expectancy:** 75
**Religious Groups:** Protestant (61.3 percent),
Rastafari (34.7 percent), Roman Catholic (4 percent)
**Ethnic Groups:** Black (91 percent), other [including white,
Chinese, and East Indian] (9 percent)
**Capital:** Kingston

**Political Rights:** 2
**Civil Liberties:** 3
**Status:** Free

**Trend Arrow:** Jamaica received a downward trend arrow due to an upsurge in political
violence and lack of police control.

**Ten-Year Ratings Timeline (Political Rights, Civil Liberties, Status)**

| 1994 | 1995 | 1996 | 1997 | 1998 | 1999 | 2000 | 2001 | 2002 | 2003 |
|------|------|------|------|------|------|------|------|------|------|
| 2,3F | 2,3F | 2,3F | 2,3F | 2,2F | 2,2F | 2,2F | 2,3F | 2,3F | 2,3F |

**Overview:**

The failure of the Jamaican government to fully extend the rule of law over its own police department in 2003 dominated the news from the island, with Prime Minister P. J. Patterson reluctant to criticize openly the country's 8,000-member police force for its frequent excessive use of force. Jamaica continued to have one of the world's highest per capita rates of police killings, according to Amnesty International, and local rights groups say police routinely murder suspects in fraudulent "shoot-outs" rather than submit them to the country's inefficient justice system.

Jamaica, a member of the British Commonwealth, achieved independence from Great Britain in 1962. Since independence, power has alternated between the social-democratic People's National Party (PNP) and the conservative Jamaican Labor Party (JLP). In 1992, the PNP elected Patterson to replace Michael Manley as party leader and prime minister. In 1993 legislative elections that were marred by irregularities and violence, the PNP won 52 parliamentary seats and the JLP 8 seats. The parties differed little on continuing the structural adjustment designed to bring economic stability and growth to the country that was begun in the 1980s, although the JLP was hurt by long-standing internal rifts.

The new Patterson government confronted labor unrest and an increase in violent crime carried out largely by former politically organized gangs operating a lucrative drug trade only loosely tied to local party bosses. In 2000, Patterson promised to stanch Jamaica's "rampant criminality" by introducing new efforts to control guns, creating a new police strike force targeting organized crime, and reintroducing the death penalty. The get-tough promises came after criticisms from key leaders of the vital tourism industry joined a crescendo of complaints from Jamaicans of all walks of life demanding an end to a more than two-decades-long upward spiral of mostly drug-related street crime. The fierce crime wave crippled local businesses and created an exodus of middle-class Jamaicans overseas. Gang fighting in West Kingston erupted in May 2001, leaving a toll of 71 dead; 28 others—including at least three police officers and one soldier—were killed in several days of gunfighting as police and soldiers moved into opposition-held communities.

In 2002, Patterson became the only prime minister in Jamaican history to be elected to three consecutive terms. His PNP won 34 of 60 parliamentary seats and retained the prime ministership for an unprecedented fourth term; the JLP took 26 seats. An observer delegation led by former U.S. president Jimmy Carter said that despite a crackdown on voter fraud, such activity remained high in areas controlled by politically linked gangs. Patterson also became the first chief executive to swear allegiance to the Jamaican people and constitution, rather than to the Queen of England. The firsts marked by the election, however, did virtually nothing to change the challenges facing the PNP, including ridding the island of drug kingpins and illegal guns, reviving a flat economy, and rebuilding a slumping tourist industry.

A national crime plan, hammered out with the support of the JLP and the country's business community, helped to bring about large cocaine seizures. The plan included increased training for police, stronger criminal intelligence planning, and greater ties to foreign law enforcement agencies. Patterson vowed to encourage foreign investment and boost tourism by attracting more pleasure boats to the island, constructing 11,000 new hotel rooms in five years, and promoting environment-friendly tourism.

In late May 2003, the government announced that it was disbanding the controversial Crime Management Unit, the paramilitary anti-crime strike force inaugurated three years earlier to combat drug gangs, but also the object of increasing criticism by human rights groups. It also said it was putting 1,000 new police officers on the streets.

In June, the JLP won a landslide victory in bitterly contested local elections that appeared to be a referendum on the PNP's fiscal policies. The JLP secured control of 11 of the 13 municipal councils contested; 23 percent of the candidates were women. Following the vote, 27 people, including two police officers, were killed during security force operations in western Kingston, and 16 others died in gun battles in the eastern part of the city, as gangs loyal to the country's two major political parties battled.

The JLP announced in November it was refusing to support a new antiterrorism bill that it claimed gave the government "draconian powers" to confiscate private property and to suppress antigovernment protests. The PNP also pushed to give the military the power to effect searches and make arrests even in the absence of the police.

**Political Rights and Civil Liberties:** Citizens are able to change their government through elections, although the 56 percent voter turnout in 2002 was the lowest national vote in years. Jamaica is a parliamentary democracy, with the British monarchy represented by a governor-general, who is appointed by the monarch on the recommendation of the prime minister, the country's chief executive. Following legislative elections, the leader of the majority party or the leader of the majority coalition in the House of Representatives is appointed prime minister by the governor-general, with the deputy prime minister recommended by the prime minister. The bicameral parliament consists of the 60-member House of Representatives elected for five years and the 21-member Senate, with 13 senators appointed by the prime minister and 8 by the leader of the parliamentary opposition. In October, the government announced it was considering a proposal to allow Jamaicans residing overseas to vote in the island's national elections.

The constitutional right to free expression is generally respected. The Access to Information Act of 2002 implements the constitutionally guaranteed right to information. However, government whistleblowers who ethically dissent over official acts of waste, fraud, or abuse of power are not well protected by Jamaican law, as required under the Inter-American Convention Against Corruption. Broadcast media are largely public but are open to pluralistic points of view. There are an estimated 1.9 million radios in Jamaica—the highest per capita ratio in the Caribbean—but only 330,000 television sets. Newspapers are independent and free of government control, although newspaper readership is generally low. Journalists are occasionally intimidated during election campaigns. Public opinion polls play a key role in the political process, and election campaigns feature debates on state-run television. The government does not restrict access to the Internet.

The Constitution provides for freedom of religion, and the government generally respects this right in practice. The government does not restrict academic freedom.

The right to organize political parties, civic organizations, and labor unions are generally respected. Labor unions are politically influential and have the right to strike. The Industrial Disputes Tribunal mediates labor conflicts.

The judicial system is headed by the Supreme Court and includes several magistrate's courts and a court of appeals, with final recourse to the Privy Council in London, which is drawn from members of Britain's House of Lords. The justice system is slow and inefficient, particularly in addressing police abuses and the violent conditions in prisons. Despite government efforts to improve penal conditions, a mounting backlog of cases and a shortage of court staff at all levels continue to undermine the judicial system. Before the government announced in October 2003 that it was adding 1,000 new police officers, Jamaica had just 2.9 officers per 100,000 people, compared with regional averages ranging from 3.2 to 6.9.

Jamaica is a main transit point for cocaine being shipped from Colombia through the Caribbean to U.S. markets, and the drug trade is now largely controlled by Colombian organized crime syndicates. Violence is the major cause of death in Jamaica, and the murder rate is one of the highest in the world. Much of the violence is the result of warfare between drug gangs known as "posses." Jamaican-born criminal deportees from the United States and a growing illegal weapons trade are major causes of the violence. Mobs have been responsible for numerous vigilante killings of suspected criminals. Inmates frequently die as a result of prison riots. Jamaican officials complain that the United States was flagrantly applying a double standard by demanding a full effort by Jamaica to help stop the flow of drugs into the United States, while at the same time failing to stem the flow of guns into Jamaica.

Human rights groups report that there are continuing concerns over criminal justice practices in Jamaica, particularly the shooting of suspects by police. Officially, police are allowed to use lethal force if an officer's life is threatened or a dangerous felon is escaping, but in practice, its use is more widespread, and in 2003 officials said they were considering adopting a stricter use-of-force policy. Other disputed practices include the imposition of death sentences following trials of questionable fairness; corporal punishment; alleged ill-treatment by police and prison wardens; appalling detention centers and prisons; and laws punishing consensual sexual acts in private between adult men. The deaths of detainees is also a problem. A mounting crime rate led the government to take controversial steps toward restoring capital punishment and flogging; rights groups protested both measures. Critics charge that flogging is unconstitutional because it can be characterized as "inhuman or degrading punishment," which the constitution prohibits.

In 1998, a woman was for the first time elected speaker of parliament. Persecution against homosexuals is rampant, with same-sex intercourse punishable by 10 years' imprisonment with hard labor. According to Amnesty International, in the past 20 years, 38 gays have been brutally murdered in Jamaica.

# Japan

**Population:** 127,500,000 **Political Rights:** 1
**GNI/capita:** $35,610 **Civil Liberties:** 2
**Life Expectancy:** 81 **Status:** Free
**Religious Groups:** Shinto and Buddhist (84 percent), other [including Christian] (16 percent)
**Ethnic Groups:** Japanese (99 percent), other (1 percent)
**Capital:** Tokyo

**Ten-Year Ratings Timeline (Political Rights, Civil Liberties, Status)**

| 1994 | 1995 | 1996 | 1997 | 1998 | 1999 | 2000 | 2001 | 2002 | 2003 |
|------|------|------|------|------|------|------|------|------|------|
| 2,2F | 1,2F | 1,2F | 1,2F | 1,2F | 1,2F | 1,2F | 1,2F | 1,2F | 1,2F |

**Overview:** Prime Minister Junichiro Koizumi faced renewed criticism of his reform program from within his own Liberal Democratic Party (LDP) after an upstart opposition party made strong gains in Japan's November 2003 elections. Conservative LDP members argued that their ruling party's struggle simply to gain a parliamentary majority showed that the party's core supporters largely reject Koizumi's prescription to end Japan's long economic malaise. Koizumi argued instead that the legislative gains by the reformist opposition party, the Democratic Party of Japan (DPJ), indicated that most voters want precisely the kind of changes that he proposes.

Japan has been a parliamentary democracy since its defeat in World War II. The conservative LDP has dominated postwar Japanese politics, winning all but one election since it was created in 1955. During the Cold War, the LDP presided over Japan's spectacular economic ascent while maintaining close security ties with the United States. In what became known as Japan's Iron Triangle—the close nexus of the LDP, big business, and the bureaucracy—LDP governments spent heavily to benefit big business and their rural stronghold, large corporations in turn filled the ruling party's coffers, and Tokyo bureaucrats imposed a thicket of regulations to protect mom-and-pop businesses, who voted overwhelmingly for the LDP.

The LDP's sole election loss, in 1993, followed a string of corruption scandals in the late 1980s that brought down Prime Minister Noburu Takeshita and other top LDP politicians. After a fractious reformist government collapsed, the LDP returned to power in 1994 as the head of a three-party coalition.

Japan's current economic woes stem from the collapse of its stock and real estate markets in the early 1990s. The crash saddled Japanese banks with tens of billions of dollars worth of problem loans, and successive LDP-led governments in the 1990s largely failed to contain the fallout.

As the banks' problem loans helped drag down the economy by choking off lending and eroding consumer confidence, the government pumped around $1 trillion worth of stimulus spending into the economy during the decade. The extra spending did little to revive Japan's economy, the world's second largest, but helped jack up its huge public debt, now around 150 percent of economic output, the highest proportion among wealthy countries. Many consumers have cut spending because of job insecurity and in order to save more for retirement in the event that Japan's swelling debt and its greying population overwhelm the state pension system.

Koizumi stepped into this economic quicksand in 2001 following the resignation of unpopular Prime Minister Yoshiri Mori. The prime minister wants to slash red tape, cut wasteful rural spending, and force banks to clean up bad loans. The LDP's conservative old guard have blocked many of these changes, which they fear will inflict economic pain on the farmers, small-business owners, and construction companies that are the ruling party's staunchest supporters. For their part, many economists warn that making deep cuts in public spending and forcing banks to clean up bad loans rapidly could, in the short term, accelerate Japan's vicious economic cycle of weak consumer spending, deflation, tight credit, anemic corporate profits, and layoffs. Cleaning up small banks, for example, could require cutting off credit to thousands of small companies that are the economic backbone of provincial cities and rural Japan.

At the heart of Koizumi's agenda are the goals of eroding the political influence of special interests and of putting politicians, rather than Japan's powerful bureaucrats, in charge of policy. These changes resonate with many voters, who recently have elected several governors who ran as independents behind detailed manifestos that emphasized accountability. So far, LDP conservatives have blocked or watered down many of Koizumi's core plans, such as to privatize Japan's highway corporations and $3 trillion postal savings system. The prime minister accuses these bodies of wasteful public works spending aimed at securing LDP votes.

Under a turnout of less than 60 percent, the LDP won 237 seats in the 480-seat house in the November 9, 2003 snap elections for the lower house. After the vote, it gained a simple majority by welcoming three independents into its ranks and merging with the tiny New Conservative Party, which won four seats. The DPJ gained 40 seats to finish with 177. This was the largest tally for any opposition party since 1958, though changes in the size and electoral structure of parliament make comparisons difficult. While most of the DPJ's gains came at the expense of smaller, leftist parties rather than the LDP, its success may herald the emergence of a two-party system in which voters have a credible alternative to the LDP. Many argue that the lack of such an alternative has kept the LDP in power even as Japan has been plagued for more than a decade by recession, deflation, weak banks, struggling firms, and mounting public debt.

The LDP's victory was helped by Koizumi's high personal popularity among Japanese voters, several consecutive quarters of economic growth, and an uptick in employment after the jobless rate equaled a postwar high in May, hitting 5.5 percent. Like Koizumi, the DPJ, led by Naoto Kan, called for deregulation and spending cuts, while also pledging to decentralize power to Japan's provinces and hike taxes to fund social security outlays.

Under Koizumi, Japan has continued to expand its role in international peace-keeping and security. Japanese troops have participated in several UN peacekeeping missions since 1992, Japanese warships provided logistical support to U.S.-led forces during the war in Afghanistan, and in 2003, parliament approved the dispatch of 1,000 troops to Iraq to provide logistical support to U.S.-led troops and humanitarian aid. The ongoing crisis over North Korea's nuclear weapons program has increased debate over the need to boost the capacity of Japan's already formidable military, which is limited to a self-defense role by the country's pacifist constitution.

**Political Rights and Civil Liberties:** Japanese can change their government through elections and enjoy most basic rights. The lower house of parliament has 300 seats that represent single-member districts and 180 that are chosen by proportional representation. The upper house has 152 single-member seats and 100 chosen by proportional balloting. Despite recent reforms aimed at curbing the power of the bureaucracy, senior civil servants, rather than elected politicians, largely shape policy, generally with little transparency.

Japan's press is independent, though not always outspoken. The European Union has formally complained about the exclusive access to news sources that major media outlets often enjoy as members of Japan's 800 or more private press clubs. As club members, these media outlets receive information from government ministries, political parties, and private firms that is often unavailable to reporters from foreign or small publications, who are shut out of some clubs. Journalists who belong to the clubs generally do not report aggressively on the conditions of ailing banks or companies and other sensitive financial issues. In a rare killing of a journalist in Japan, the bound-and-stabbed body of freelance reporter Satoru Someya, noted for his investigative reporting on organized crime in Tokyo, was found in Tokyo Bay in September.

Japanese of all faiths can worship freely. Buddhism and Shintoism have the most followers. In the wake of the 1995 terrorist attacks in the Tokyo subway by the Aum Shinrikyo cult, parliament amended the Religious Corporation Law to give the government greater oversight of the operations and financial affairs of most religious groups. The law applies only to religious groups that register voluntarily as "religious corporations," but most do register in order to receive tax benefits and other advantages.

China, South Korea, and other regional countries frequently lodge protests against passages in Japanese history textbooks that try to justify the country's occupation of other Asian nations before and during World War II and downplay the imperial army's wartime atrocities in occupied lands. These abuses included forcing tens of thousands of women to work as sex slaves. The Education Ministry, moreover, often censors textbook passages that it considers too critical of Japan's wartime record.

Japan has many well-funded and active civic, human rights, social welfare, and environmental groups. Trade unions are independent and vigorously promote workers' interests. In a key labor concern, the International Labor Organization has criticized laws that prevent police, soldiers, and firefighters from joining unions or staging strikes. Civil servants can join unions but cannot strike, and they face restrictions on bargaining collectively. Around 21 percent of Japanese workers belong to trade unions. Private advocacy groups accuse some employers of exploiting or discriminating against foreign workers, who often cannot speak Japanese and are unaware of their rights.

Japan's judiciary is independent, and defendants generally receive fair trials. Human rights groups say, however, that the criminal process is flawed because defendants often have little access to counsel before their trials. This is because the criminal procedure code allows police and prosecutors to restrict a suspect's access to counsel during an investigation and bars attorneys outright from being present during interrogations, even after indictment. Moreover, rights groups, bar associations, and some prisoners allege that police at times use force to extract confessions from suspects or to enforce discipline among detainees. Appellate courts recently have overturned convictions on the grounds that they were based on coerced confessions.

Foreign and domestic human rights groups have long criticized Japanese prisons for subjecting inmates to severe regimentation that at times includes barring them from talking to each other or even making eye contact. Punishments include forcing inmates to sit motionless for hours at a time, preventing them from washing or exercising, and restraining them with leather handcuffs, the human rights group Amnesty International reported in 2002. Amnesty International has also criticized the secrecy surrounding death row and executions in Japan. Death row inmates typically are notified only two hours before their execution, and their family members are not informed until after the execution takes place.

Japan's three million Burakumin, who are descendants of feudal-era outcasts, and its tiny, indigenous Ainu minority continue to face discrimination in mainstream society, according to the U.S. State Department's human rights report for 2002, released in March 2003. The government funds programs to promote Ainu culture and to boost the economic status of Burakumin.

Meanwhile, Japan's 636,000 ethnic Koreans, most of whom are native born, face "deeply entrenched societal discrimination," the U.S. State Department report said. Moreover, Koreans and some 1.77 million other "foreign residents" are not automatically Japanese citizens at birth. Instead, those seeking citizenship must formally apply and submit to extensive background checks. Separately, some foreigners trying to enter Japan allegedly are mistreated while being interrogated by immigration officials. Those who are denied entry sometimes are held under harsh conditions in privately run facilities prior to being deported, and some asylum seekers are denied fair hearings, Amnesty International said in 2002.

Japanese women have full access to education but face employment discrimination in the private sector. They frequently are tracked by their companies into nonmanagerial careers and generally are disadvantaged in hiring and pay, recent statistics and government surveys show. In addition, sexual harassment on the job is widespread. The law bans both sexual discrimination and harassment in the workplace, but authorizes only light sanctions for corporate violators. One in three Japanese women experiences some form of physical abuse in their homes, a 1998 government survey found. In another concern, the government does not respond aggressively to cases of women and girls being trafficked into Japan, the New York-based Human Rights Watch alleged in June, although some traffickers have been prosecuted.

# Jordan

**Population:** 5,500,000 **Political Rights:** 5*
**GNI/capita:** $1,750 **Civil Liberties:** 5
**Life Expectancy:** 69 **Status:** Partly Free
**Religious Groups:** Sunni Muslim (92 percent),
Christian (6 percent), other (2 percent)
**Ethnic Groups:** Arab (98 percent), other [including
Armenian] (2 percent)
**Capital:** Amman
**Ratings Change:** Jordan's political rights rating improved from 6 to 5 due to the restoration
of an elected parliament.

## Ten-Year Ratings Timeline (Political Rights, Civil Liberties, Status)

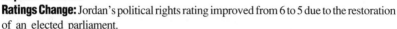

| 1994 | 1995 | 1996 | 1997 | 1998 | 1999 | 2000 | 2001 | 2002 | 2003 |
|------|------|------|------|------|------|------|------|------|------|
| 4,4PF | 4,4PF | 4,4PF | 4,4PF | 4,5PF | 4,4PF | 4,4PF | 5,5PF | 6,5PF | 5,5PF |

**Overview:**
Following King Abdullah's rule by decree for more than two years, reasonably free and transparent, though not fair, parliamentary and municipal elections were held in 2003. In addition, some restrictions on freedom of expression were lifted during the year, and women assumed a higher profile in the government. Nevertheless, it remains to be seen whether King Abdullah's promise of a "new era" of political and civil liberties will come to fruition. With substantial assistance from the United States and other outside donors, Jordan's economy remained strong in spite of the war in neighboring Iraq.

The Hashemite Kingdom of Jordan, known as Transjordan until 1950, was established as a League of Nations mandate under the control of Great Britain in 1921 and granted full independence in 1946. Following the assassination of King Abdullah in 1951, the crown passed briefly to his mentally unstable eldest son, Talal, and then to his grandson, Hussein. King Hussein's turbulent 46-year reign witnessed a massive influx of Palestinian refugees (who now comprise a majority of the population), the loss of all territory west of the Jordan River in 1967, and numerous assassination and coup attempts by Palestinian and Arab nationalists. Although the 1952 constitution provided for a directly elected parliament, political parties were banned in 1956, and parliament was either suspended entirely or emasculated by government intervention in the electoral process for over three decades. While political and civil liberties remained tightly restricted, Hussein proved adept at co-opting, rather than killing, jailing, or exiling, his political opponents. As a result, Jordan avoided the legacy of brutal repression characteristic of other authoritarian regimes in the Arab world.

As a result of the decline of oil revenues in 1980s, which translated into reduced aid and worker remittances from the Arab Gulf countries, Jordan borrowed heavily throughout the decade and was eventually forced to implement economic austerity measures in return for IMF assistance. In April 1989, price increases for fuel and other subsidized commodities provoked widespread rioting. In addition, internal pressure for greater freedom and representation mounted. In response, the government launched a rapid process of political liberalization. Free elections were held later that year, and restrictions on civil liberties were progressively eased. However, the reform process ground to a halt in the mid-1990s and suffered some reversals.

By the time of Hussein's death in February 1999 and the ascension of his son, Abdullah, the kingdom was again faced with severe economic problems. The "peace dividend" expected to follow from Jordan's 1994 peace treaty with Israel, in the form of improved trade with the West Bank and increased investment from Western Europe, had not filtered down to the population at large, which suffered from 27 percent unemployment. Faced with a crippling public debt, Abdullah launched economic reforms needed to attract international investment during the first two years of his rule.

The September 2000 outbreak of the al-Aqsa *intifada* (uprising) in the West Bank and Gaza had an enormous impact on the country, inflaming anti-Israeli sentiments among Jordanians of Palestinian descent, leftists, and Islamists, who dominate much of civil society. As the violence next door continued unabated, the Professional Associations Council (PAC) formed an anti-normalization committee to spearhead mass demonstrations demanding the annulment of Jordan's peace treaty with Israel.

The government reacted by suppressing criticism of Jordanian relations with Israel and banning all demonstrations. In 2001, Abdullah dissolved parliament, postponed general elections scheduled for November, and replaced elected municipal councils with state-appointed local committees. For more than two years, King Abdullah ruled by decree, and issued over 200 "temporary laws," exempt from legislative approval until parliament is reconvened, imposing new restrictions on freedom of expression and assembly, weakening due process protections, and promulgating economic policies that would have almost certainly have been rejected by the outgoing parliament.

As the United States readied for an invasion of Iraq in early 2003, many domestic and foreign observers questioned whether Jordan could cope with the war's fallout. The population's pro-Saddam sympathies, already pronounced during the 1991 Gulf War, had been reinforced in the 1990s by Iraq's shipments of discounted petroleum and preferential access given to Jordanian exports under the UN oil-for-food program. With anti-American sentiment at a peak and more than 400,000 Iraqis living and working in Jordan, the kingdom's decision to allow U.S. troops to operate on Jordanian soil appeared to carry enormous political and security risks. However, an infusion of "oil grants" from the Arab Gulf states and an additional $700 million in economic assistance from the United States (above and beyond its annual $250 million aid package) helped the kingdom avoid an economic crisis, while royal promises to undertake postwar political liberalization persuaded mainstream opposition groups to refrain from mobilizing the public against the government's pro-American alignment. As a result, while the government forcibly dispersed unlicensed demonstrations and detained several antiwar activists for much of the conflict, its suppression of antiwar dissent was far less heavy-handed than that of other pro-U.S. regimes in the Arab world. Within two weeks of the fall of Baghdad in April 2003, Abdullah scrapped a 2001 decree restricting freedom of the press and pledged to hold "free and impartial" parliamentary elections in June.

Although gerrymandering favored representatives of tribes and families traditionally loyal to the Hashemite monarchy, the June parliamentary elections were largely free of fraud. Supervision of elections was transferred from the Interior Ministry to the judiciary, ballots were counted directly at polling stations rather than at a center run by the Interior Ministry, and registered voters were required to produce new identity cards with magnetic strips in order to receive ballots. However, some women may have been deterred from voting by the government's refusal to station female election monitors at polling centers, making it necessary for veiled women to reveal their faces to male monitors before entering polling booths. The Central Elections Committee rejected the applications of two opposition candidates on weak grounds. All major political groups participated in the poll, including the Islamic Action Front (IAF), which captured 16 seats. However, the newly elected parliament has yet to overturn most temporary laws restricting political and civil liberties. In October, King Abdullah unexpectedly replaced Prime Minister Ali Abul Ragheb with Faisal al-Fayez, the minister for the royal court, and unveiled a new cabinet of mostly American- and British-educated technocrats, including three women.

Although municipal elections were held in July, a new law empowering the government to appoint mayors and half of all municipal council seats—a restriction previously imposed only on municipal government in the capital—led the IAF and other opposition groups to boycott the polls in most districts.

**Political Rights and Civil Liberties:** Jordanians cannot change their government democratically. The king holds broad executive powers and may dissolve parliament and dismiss the prime minister or cabinet at his discretion. The 110-seat lower house of parliament, elected through universal adult suffrage, may approve, reject, or amend legislation proposed by the cabinet, but is restricted in its ability to initiate legislation and cannot enact laws without the assent of the 55-seat upper house of parliament, which is appointed by the king. Regional governors are appointed by the central government, as are half of all municipal council seats.

The electoral system in Jordan is heavily skewed toward the monarchy's traditional support base. The single-member-district system, introduced in 1993, favors tribal and family ties over political and ideological affiliations, while rural districts with populations of Transjordanian origin are over-represented relative to urban districts, where most Jordanians of Palestinian descent reside (according to the *Financial Times*, Amman has a member of parliament for every 52,255 voters, while the small town of Karak has an MP for every 6,000 voters). In 2003, only 27 percent of registered voters went to the polls in Amman, a possible indication that many Palestinian Jordanians still feel excluded from the political system.

Freedom of expression is restricted. The state owns all broadcast media and has wide discretionary powers to close print publications. In April, the government repealed Article 150 of the Penal Code, an amendment promulgated by royal decree in 2001 that empowered the State Security Court (SSC) to close publications and imprison individuals for up to three years for publishing information deemed harmful to national unity or the reputation of the state. In January, prior to the repeal of Article 150, the editor in chief, managing editor, and a writer for the weekly *Al-Hilal* were arrested for publishing an article "lacking respect for the family of the Prophet Muhammad" and sentenced by the SSC the following month to prison sentences of two to six months; two of the sentences were commuted to fines, but the author of the article went to jail. The Information Ministry was scrapped in October, and regulation of the media is now the responsibility of an appointed Higher Media Council. Although the law still allows journalists to be jailed by the civilian judiciary, government officials have pledged that journalists will no longer be sent to prison for their writings.

There is no official advance censorship in Jordan, but the authorities are usually tipped off about the contents of potentially offensive articles by informers at printing presses, and editors are then forced to remove the articles. In 2003, the authorities ordered the independent weekly *Al-Wehda* to remove an article about torture in Jordanian prisons from its September 24 issue; when the paper refused, the entire issue was banned. In November, *Al-Wehda* complied with an order to remove a caricature of Fayez and his newly appointed cabinet before its issue hit newsstands. The government has not attempted to censor Internet content. However, government monitoring of telephone conversations and Internet communication is reportedly common.

Islam is the state religion. The government appoints all Islamic clergy, pays their salaries, and monitors sermons at mosques, where political activity is banned under Jordanian law. Sunni Muslims constitute 92 percent of the population, but Christians and Jews are officially recognized as religious minorities and allowed to worship freely. Baha'is and Druze are allowed to practice their faiths, but are not officially recognized. Academic freedom is generally respected in Jordan.

Freedom of assembly is heavily restricted. A temporary law on public gatherings, introduced in August 2001, bans demonstrations lacking written consent from the government. Although the government allowed a number of licensed antiwar demonstrations to take place before and during the U.S.-led invasion of Iraq in March 2003, at least 16 antiwar campaigners were arrested in the weeks leading up to the war, and security forces forcibly dispersed unlicensed demonstrations that erupted after the war began, detaining dozens of protestors. By the end of the war, all had been released and none were charged with criminal offenses. Nongovernmental organizations (NGOs) are routinely licensed in Jordan, and dozens of NGOs address numerous political and social issues. However, professional associations have come under pressure to abstain from political activities. Workers have the right to bargain collectively, but must receive government permission to strike. More than 30 percent of the workforce is organized into 17 unions.

The judiciary is subject to executive influence through the Justice Ministry and the Higher Judiciary Council, whose members are appointed by the king. While most trials in civilian courts are open and procedurally sound, proceedings of the SSC are closed to the public. A temporary law promulgated in 2001 allows the prime minister to refer any case to the SSC and denies the right of appeal to people convicted of misdemeanors, which can carry short prison sentences.

Jordanian citizens enjoy little protection from arbitrary arrest and detention. Under the constitution, suspects may be detained for up to 48 hours without a warrant and up to 10 days without formal charges being filed, but courts routinely grant prosecutors 15-day extensions of this deadline. Even these minimal protections are denied to suspects referred to the SSC, who are often held in lengthy pretrial detention and refused access to legal council until just before trial. Defendants charged with security-related offenses frequently allege that torture is used to extract confessions.

Jordanians of Palestinian descent face discrimination in employment by the government and the military and in admission to universities. Labor laws do not protect foreign workers. Abuse of mostly South Asian domestic servants is widespread.

Women enjoy equal political rights, but face legal discrimination in matters of inheritance and divorce, which fall under the jurisdiction of Sharia (Islamic law) courts, and in the provision of government pensions and social security benefits. Although women constitute only 14 percent of the workforce, the government has made efforts to increase the number of women in the civil service. Women are guaranteed a quota of six seats in parliament. Although the government repealed a law providing for lenient treatment of those convicted of "honor crimes" (the murder or attempted murder of women by relatives for alleged sexual misconduct), the newly elected lower house of parliament rejected the decree in August and rejected an amended version the following month. A royal decree granting women the right to initiate divorce proceedings was also rejected by parliament. In November, King Abdullah appointed seven women to the 55-seat upper house of parliament.

# Kazakhstan

**Population:** 14,800,000 **Political Rights:** 6
**GNI/capita:** $1,350 **Civil Liberties:** 5
**Life Expectancy:** 66 **Status:** Not Free
**Religious Groups:** Muslim (47 percent), Russian
Orthodox (44 percent), Protestant (2 percent),
other (7 percent)
**Ethnic Groups:** Kazakh (53 percent), Russian (30 percent),
Ukrainian (4 percent), German (2 percent), Uzbek (2 percent), other (9 percent)
**Capital:** Astana

**Ten-Year Ratings Timeline (Political Rights, Civil Liberties, Status)**

| 1994 | 1995 | 1996 | 1997 | 1998 | 1999 | 2000 | 2001 | 2002 | 2003 |
|------|------|------|------|------|------|------|------|------|------|
| 6,5NF | 6,5NF | 6,5NF | 6,5NF | 6,5NF | 6,5NF | 6,5NF | 6,5NF | 6,5NF | 6,5NF |

**Overview:** Following an intensified crackdown in 2002 against critics of his government, President Nursultan Nazarbayev continued efforts to silence political opponents and independent journalists throughout 2003. A prominent opposition leader remained in prison, while another was released under an amnesty widely believed to have been granted in exchange for his renouncing future political activities. Meanwhile, new developments in the so-called Kazakhgate corruption scandal, involving alleged illegal payments from Western oil firms to senior Kazakh officials, including Nazarbayev, took place during the year.

This sparsely populated, multiethnic land stretching from the Caspian Sea to the Chinese border was gradually conquered by Russia during the eighteenth and nineteenth centuries. After a brief attempt at independence in 1917 in the wake of the Russian Revolution, Kazakhstan became an autonomous Soviet republic in 1920 and a union republic in 1936.

The former first secretary of the Communist Party, Nazarbayev was elected president on December 1, 1991, just two weeks before Kazakhstan declared independence from the U.S.S.R. The country's first national legislative elections, in March 1994, were invalidated by the Constitutional Court a year later because of numerous irregularities. Nazarbayev subsequently dissolved parliament and called for a referendum on April 29, 1995, in which a reported 95 percent of voters supported the extension of his term until December 2000. An additional referendum in August of that year, which was boycotted by the main opposition parties, approved a new constitution strengthening the powers of the presidency. In December 1995 elections for a new bicameral parliament, Nazarbayev supporters captured most of the seats in the legislature.

In October 1998, parliament approved Nazarbayev's call for presidential elections to be held in January 1999, almost two years before their scheduled date, as well as an amendment to the constitution extending the presidential term of office from five to seven years. The key challenger, former prime minister Akezhan Kazhegeldin, was banned from competing on a legal technicality, while two other candidates were known supporters of the incumbent. Nazarbayev was reelected with a reported 80 percent of the vote.

Otan, a newly formed party loyal to Nazarbayev, won the single largest number of seats in the September 1999 parliamentary vote, which was the first multiparty election in Kazakhstan's history. Despite some improvement since the controversial presidential ballot in January, the parliamentary poll remained deeply flawed. In June 2000, parliament overwhelmingly approved giving Nazarbayev lifetime privileges after the end of his second term in office in 2006, including formal access to key government officials to advise them on policy matters, as well as a permanent place on the Security Council.

Signs of a deepening split within the country's ruling elite became evident following the November 18, 2001 founding of a new political movement, the Democratic Choice of Kazakhstan (DCK). Established by prominent business leaders, some of whom held positions in Nazarbayev's administration, the DCK proclaimed its commitment to democratization, rule of law, and anticorruption efforts. However, some observers questioned the sincerity of its stated goals and maintained that the group's primary purpose was to safeguard its members' substantial political and economic interests while countering those of the president's family and close associates. Apparently sensing that the DCK posed a growing political threat to his regime, Nazarbayev cracked down increasingly on the group throughout 2002. In what critics charged were politically motivated cases, two of the DCK's cofounders—former minister of energy Mukhtar Abliyazov and former governor of Pavlodar Galymzhan Zhakiyanov—were subsequently arrested, convicted of abuse of power and corruption during their tenure in government, and sentenced to prison.

Abliyazov's lawyers announced in April 2003 that they would seek a pardon for their client, and he was freed from prison the following month after receiving amnesty from Nazarbayev. Abliyazov announced that he would cease political activity to concentrate on his business interests, leading to widespread speculation that his release was made conditional on his leaving politics. Zhakiyanov, whose appeal was denied, remained in prison as of November 30.

In September elections to local councils, pro-government parties secured the largest number of seats. Various irregularities, including violations of voting secrecy and campaigning on election day, were reported. Although the councils essentially rubber-stamp decisions made by local appointed leaders, they also play a role in national politics by selecting the majority of members of the upper house of parliament, the Senate.

New developments unfolded during the year in connection with the Kazakhgate corruption scandal, in which Nazarbayev and other top officials allegedly accepted bribes from U.S. oil conglomerates during the 1990s. As part of the U.S. Justice Department's ongoing investigation into the matter, a former U.S. adviser to Nazarbayev, James Giffen, was arraigned in March on two counts of violating the Foreign Corrupt Practices Act. Giffen allegedly funneled millions of dollars in bribes from the Mobil Oil Corporation to Swiss bank accounts held by senior Kazakh officials in order to obtain lucrative energy deals in Kazakhstan. He is free on $10 million bail while the investigation continues. In June, a former senior Mobil executive, J. Bryan Williams, pleaded guilty to tax evasion in connection with money he had received for his role in negotiations over Mobil's purchase of a stake in the Tengiz oil field. Meanwhile, the Kazakh government has denied repeatedly that the president profited from any alleged payments, claiming that funds kept in foreign bank accounts were to be used only in national emergencies.

Although Nazarbayev is immune from prosecution in the U.S. bribery probe, questions have arisen regarding the potential damage to his government from the corruption allegations. In an attempt to silence public debate on the matter, the authorities have harassed and arrested opposition leaders and journalists seeking to publicize the investigation, including independent journalist Sergei Duvanov, who was sentenced to prison in January. There is also speculation that Nazarbayev's daughter, Dariga, is being positioned to succeed him as president, possibly before his current term expires in 2006 if developments in the corruption probe make it expedient for him to step down early. At the same time, the scandal appears to have had minimal impact on foreign interest in developing or investing in Kazakhstan's rich energy sector.

## Political Rights and Civil Liberties:

Citizens of Kazakhstan cannot change their government democratically. The constitution grants the president considerable control over the bicameral legislature, the judiciary, and local governments. President Nursultan Nazarbayev continues to enjoy sweeping executive powers and rules virtually unchallenged. In November 2003, the government submitted a draft of a new election law to parliament. According to representatives from the Organization for Security and Cooperation in Europe (OSCE), the draft did not meet OSCE standards. A parliamentary working group established to propose changes to the draft was deliberating as of November 30. Opposition parties have complained of harassment, surveillance, denial of access to the state-run media, and arbitrary bans on registering candidates.

Corruption is widespread throughout all levels of government, and businesses are forced to pay bribes in order to deal with the government bureaucracy. The U.S.

Justice Department is continuing to investigate the so-called Kazakhgate scandal, in which Western oil companies allegedly paid millions of dollars to top Kazakh officials, including Nazarbayev, in exchange for lucrative contracts. Kazakhstan was rated 100 out of 133 countries in Transparency International's 2003 Corruption Perceptions Index, with 1 representing the least corrupt country.

While the constitution provides for freedom of the press, the government has repeatedly harassed or shut down many independent media outlets. The press is not permitted to criticize the president and his family, and self-censorship is widespread. Libel is a criminal offense, and the country's criminal code prohibits insulting the honor and dignity of the president. All information about the health, financial, and private life of the president and his family is regarded as a state secret. Most newspapers, printing and distribution facilities, and television and radio stations are controlled or otherwise influenced by members of the president's family, including Nazarbayev's daughter Dariga, and trusted government officials. Most local media outlets are not willing to report on the Kazakhgate story about possible illegal payments from Western energy companies to senior Kazakh officials, including Nazarbayev. The content of Web sites has been subject to libel laws, and the government at times has prevented clients of the country's two largest Internet service providers from gaining direct access to several opposition Web sites.

A draft media law proposed by the government was submitted to parliament in August. The draft, which had not been adopted as of November 30, was criticized by international and domestic observers for further restricting media freedom. In a legal case that attracted international attention, journalist Sergei Duvanov was sentenced on January 28 to three and a half years in prison on charges of raping a 14-year-old girl. His supporters insist that the case against Duvanov, who wrote articles accusing Nazarbayev and other political figures of corruption, including the Kazakhgate scandal, was politically motivated. Duvanov was arrested in October 2002, just before he was scheduled to travel to the United States to speak about Kazakhstan's human rights situation. In March 2003, an appeals court upheld Duvanov's conviction, and he remained in prison as of November 30. On April 16, Maksim Yeroshin, editor of the opposition weekly *Rabat*, was hospitalized after being attacked outside of his home. The newspaper's deputy editor maintains that the assault was meant to intimidate the staff of *Rabat*, which has reported on high-level corruption and other controversial issues. In November, Ermurat Bapi, the editor of the opposition newspaper *SolDat*, was found guilty of tax evasion, fraudulent accounting, and illegal business dealings. He received a one-year suspended sentence, was fined, and was barred from practicing journalism for five years. Bapi and his paper, which had ceased publication in August, faced numerous instances of harassment by the authorities, including being fined by the courts in 2003 for libel.

The constitution guarantees freedom of worship, although the government sometimes harasses certain nontraditional groups. Religious organizations must register with the Ministry of Justice to receive legal status, without which they cannot engage in legal transactions, including buying or renting property or hiring employees. Some religious groups have reported lengthy delays in the registration process.

The government reportedly permits most academic freedom, except for criticisms of the president and his family. Corruption in the educational system is widespread, with students frequently paying bribes to professors to earn passing grades. Some government opponents have reported that the authorities monitor their movements and telephone calls, according to the U.S. State Department human rights report for 2002, released in March 2003.

Freedom of assembly is hindered by complicated procedures to obtain necessary permits, including a requirement that organizations must apply to local authorities 10 days in advance of planned demonstrations.

Despite constitutional guarantees, the government imposes restrictions on freedom of association. A 2002 law on political parties raised from 3,000 to 50,000 the number of members that a party must have to register. In addition, there must be at least 700 members in each of the country's regions (oblasts). Opposition parties and the OSCE criticized the law for leading to the likely closure of most of the country's political parties, which had to re-register with the Ministry of Justice before January 17, 2003, under the new regulations. As of November 2003, of the 19 parties previously registered, 8—Ak Zhol, Otan, the Patriots Party, Aul, the Civic Party, the Agrarian Party, Rukhaniyat (Spirituality), and the Communist Party—had successfully re-registered. All, except for the Communist Party, are pro-government. In September, Dariga Nazarbayeva announced her intention to turn her Asar political movement into a political party. Many observers believe that this move is designed to provide an additional base of support for the Nazarbayev family, help Dariga gain a seat in the 2004 parliamentary election, and position her as an eventual presidential successor to her father.

Nongovernmental organizations (NGOs) have reported lengthy delays in the registration process, which is required for them to operate. In 2003, NGOs protested a draft law that defined NGOs as organizations that work for the public good and do not engage in political activity; the government withdrew the draft in October. The government sponsored a Civic Forum on NGOs in mid-October that many members of civic society criticized as an attempt by the authorities to increase state control over the NGO sector.

Workers have the legal right to form and join trade unions and participate in collective bargaining, and a number of unions operate throughout the country. Workers have engaged in strikes, primarily over the nonpayment of wages. However, the government reportedly exercises considerable influence over organized labor. Some union members have been dismissed, transferred to lower-paying jobs, and threatened for their union activities.

The constitution significantly constrains the independence of the judiciary, which is subservient to the executive branch. Judges are subject to bribery and political bias, and corruption is evident throughout the judicial system. Police at times abuse detainees during arrest and interrogation, and arbitrary arrest and detention remain problems. Conditions in pretrial facilities and prisons are harsh. A 2002 Humanization of Criminal Justice Law, which provides for punishments other than imprisonment for more than 100 crimes, has led to a significant reduction in prison overcrowding, according to the U.S. State Department report.

Since Kazakhstan's independence, much of the country's large ethnic Russian population has emigrated, in part because of the enhanced role granted to the Kazakh language. Many of the remaining Russians, most of whom do not speak Kazakh, have complained of discrimination in employment and education. The government reportedly favors ethnic Kazakhs in government employment.

While the rights of entrepreneurship and private property are legally protected, bureaucratic hurdles and the control of large segments of the economy by clan elites and government officials loyal to Nazarbayev limit equality of opportunity and fair competition. In June, parliament adopted a Land Code allowing for private ownership of the country's vast tracts of agricultural land. The law's passage followed heated debates in parliament and the resignation of Prime Minister Imangali Tasmangambetov on June 11; he was replaced two days later by former deputy prime minister Daniyal Akhmetov. Critics charged that the law primarily will benefit those wealthy individuals with close ties to government officials.

Traditional cultural practices and the country's economic problems limit professional opportunities for women, and women's rights experts regard current legislation addressing sexual harassment as inadequate. Domestic violence is a problem, with police often reluctant to intervene in what are regarded as internal family matters. Despite legal prohibitions, the trafficking of women for purposes of prostitution remains a serious problem. Kazakhstan is a place of origin, transit point, and destination country for victims of trafficking.

# Kenya

**Population:** 31,600,000  **Political Rights:** 3*
**GNI/capita:** $350  **Civil Liberties:** 3*
**Life Expectancy:** 46  **Status:** Partly Free
**Religious Groups:** Protestant (45 percent), Roman
Catholic (33 percent), Muslim (10 percent), indigenous
beliefs (10 percent), other (2 percent)
**Ethnic Groups:** Kikuyu (22 percent), Luhya (14 percent),
Luo (13 percent), Kalenjin (12 percent), Kamba (11 percent), Kisii (6 percent), Meru
(6 percent), other African (15 percent), other [including Asian, European, and Arab]
(1 percent)
**Capital:** Nairobi
**Ratings Change:** Kenya's political rights and civil liberties ratings improved from 4 to
3 due to positive post-2002 election developments in 2003, including a constitutional review
process, an anticorruption campaign, and efforts to strengthen judicial independence.

**Ten-Year Ratings Timeline (Political Rights, Civil Liberties, Status)**

| 1994 | 1995 | 1996 | 1997 | 1998 | 1999 | 2000 | 2001 | 2002 | 2003 |
|------|------|------|------|------|------|------|------|------|------|
| 6,6NF | 7,6NF | 7,6NF | 6,6NF | 6,5NF | 6,5NF | 6,5NF | 6,5NF | 4,4PF | 3,3PF |

**Overview:**

The December 2002 presidential and legislative elections, which were the first free and fair elections in Kenya's history, raised hopes in 2003 that the country's long-promised move toward democratic consolidation and respect for the rule of law would finally be under way. During the year, government reform efforts focused on a constitutional review process, an anticorruption campaign to tackle Kenya's endemic corruption, and the strengthening of judicial independence. At the same time, most observers remain cautious regarding the extent to which promised reforms will ultimately be implemented.

Britain effectively colonized Kenya in the late nineteenth century in order to open and control a route to the Nile River headwaters in Uganda. Kenya achieved independence in 1963. The nationalist leader Jomo Kenyatta was president until his death in 1978, when his vice president, Daniel arap Moi, succeeded him. Moi's ascent to the presidency kept the Kenyan African National Union (KANU) in power, but gradually diminished the power of the previously dominant Kikuyu ethnic group in favor of Moi's Kalenjin group.

In 1992, after the country had gone through a lengthy period as a de facto single-party state, domestic unrest and pressure from international aid donors forced Moi to hold multiparty elections. Moi was reelected president in controversial polling. In the December 1997 presidential and parliamentary elections, Moi again secured victory over a divided opposition. His reelection was ensured by massive use of state patronage and the official media to promote his candidacy and by harassment of the divided opposition.

The rule of President Moi was associated with poor governance, limits on political and civil rights, and corruption in the ruling party and government. In 2002, the government-released "Akiwumi Report" on ethnic clashes between 1991 and 1998 stated that public officials, from petty policemen to senior officials, instigated violence. The report cited political factors as the primary cause of ethnic violence that resulted in more than 1,000 deaths during the 1990s, disrupted two general elections, and displaced hundreds of thousands of persons.

Despite these problems, political space continued to open up. As the December 2002 presidential and legislative elections approached, Moi made it clear that Uhuru Kenyatta, the son of former president Jomo Kenyatta, was his preferred successor. However, the opposition succeeded in uniting behind opposition leader Mwai Kibaki, positioning themselves for electoral victory. Kibaki was elected president with 63 percent of the vote, defeating Kenyatta, who received 30 percent. In addition to Kibaki's victory in the presidential poll, his National Rainbow Coalition (NARC)—a coalition of more than a dozen political parties—won the majority of seats in parliament.

The elections heralded a sea change in Kenyan politics. For the first time, power passed from KANU to a coalition offering the promise of meaningful political and economic reform. The new leadership's ambitious reform program includes tackling corruption, addressing economic and social issues, and undertaking institutional reforms designed to promote democracy. Given the early stage of the post-Moi era, the fragility of the NARC coalition, a highly sensitive and complex constitutional reform process, significant constraints on resources, terrorism, and ambiguous attitudes on the part of major donor countries, it is too early to definitively conclude that Kenya is on a sustained trajectory toward full compliance with international norms for transparency and good governance. In 2003, a debate was under way over the extent to which the government should actively seek to right past wrongs and actively pursue alleged wrongdoers, up to and possibly including, former president Moi.

**Political Rights and Civil Liberties:** With the 2002 elections, Kenyans for the first time were able to choose their leaders in genuinely open and competitive elections. Although the elections were widely regarded as legitimate, the country is far from consolidating its nascent and fragile democratic opening, including its electoral processes. Prior to 2002, KANU's election victories were achieved through political repression, media control, and dubious electoral procedures, and power was heavily concentrated in the executive branch of government. Since the resumption of multiparty politics in the early 1990s, many of the core elements necessary for the establishment of a democratic political system have developed. Political parties are active and vocal, and parliament is the setting for much of the nation's political discourse.

An ongoing constitutional review process has included the participation of a wide range of civic and associational groups. It is considering the creation of a senate and an executive prime minister to be elected by parliament; presidential and parliamentary electoral reform; decentralization; and other changes designed to limit the power of the presidency, including giving parliament the power to impeach the president. There is widespread suspicion, however, that the unsolved September 2003 murder of Dr. Odhiambo Mbai, a leader of a committee of the Constitutional Review Commission, which is considering limiting executive branch powers, may have been politically inspired by elements within President Mwai Kibaki's NARC.

Corruption has long been a serious problem in Kenya, which has consistently been ranked in the bottom 10 percent of performing countries on Transparency International's (TI) Corruption Perceptions Index. In its 2003 index, Kenya was ranked 122 out of 133 countries surveyed. However, the press, parliament, and the judiciary are increasingly highlighting examples of government corruption and malfeasance. This process has been accentuated under the government of President Kibaki, who was elected in 2002 due largely to his expressed commitment to uproot corruption. Central to his policy was the launching of a five-year national campaign against corruption, including the establishment of an independent Anti-Corruption Commission, which has begun to exercise its powers to bring charges against suspected corrupt officials. A number of commissions are investigating particular scandals. An investigation of government procurement officers by the Finance Ministry in early 2003 determined that there "is a serious and widespread abuse of office by officers charged with this responsibility." One of Kibaki's early appointments was that of the widely respected head of TI's Kenya chapter, John Githongo, who was placed in charge of the government's Office of Ethics and Governance. A package of reforms has been proposed, and some have been adopted. One of these, an attempt to separate public office from personal interests, is the Public Officer Ethics Bill, under which every public official must annually declare his or her wealth, as well as that of his or her spouse.

The constitution provides for freedom of speech and of the press. The government of former president Daniel arap Moi restricted these rights in practice, with tactics including harassing, beating, and arresting members of the media during the year. Despite this hostile attitude, the print media were fairly free, and in the latter years of Moi's rule, the broadcast media began to show some signs of independence. This trend was accentuated during 2003, and few constraints exist. However, according to the BBC, there are still some reports of journalists being arrested and harassed. The government does not restrict access to the Internet.

In general, the government has respected freedom of religion. However, religious-based tension has risen in recent years, as acts of terrorism associated with Islamic fundamentalism have been committed on Kenyan soil.

One of the core strengths of Kenya's political culture is its energetic and robust civil society. The success of the 2002 elections is a result in large part of the ability of civil society to pry open political space and greater freedoms. Due in large part to their efforts, the public policy process enjoys significant elements of transparency, especially when Kenya is compared to many other countries wrestling with the legacy of decades of authoritarian rule. The role of civil society groups in the ongoing constitutional reform process is a good example, as has been their ability to undertake voter education and election monitoring.

The constitution explicitly permits freedom of assembly, and the Kibaki government, unlike its predecessor, has generally respected this right. All workers other than the police are legally free to join unions of their choice. In December 2001, the labor commissioner registered the Union of Kenya Civil Servants (UKCS), which granted civil servants the right to join unions for the first time since 1980. The government may deregister a union, but the Registrar of Trade Unions must give the union 60 days to challenge the deregistration notice.

Although Kenya's judicial system is largely based on the British model, for much of the independence period, its actions tended to reflect the primacy of the executive branch. In July 2002, a panel of Commonwealth judicial experts from Africa and Canada examined the court system and found it to be among the most incompetent and inefficient in Africa. Judges commonly accept bribes and many are subject to political influence. The courts are also understaffed and underfinanced, and people awaiting trial face long delays that violate their right to due process. The country has officially recognized "Kadhi" Islamic courts that administer Sharia (Islamic law) for such issues as marriage and succession disputes; they are located only in areas with a predominantly Muslim population. Controversial calls from the Muslim community to expand the scope of these courts are being considered in the context of ongoing constitutional discussions.

In recent years, criticism of the judiciary has been aired increasingly freely, and a public policy debate about its shortcomings has ensued. The Kibaki government came into power promising that the rule of law would be upheld and judicial independence strengthened. Kibaki has criticized the extent of corruption in the judiciary and has instructed the minister of justice to establish a process for the immediate identification of corrupt judges. In February 2003, Chief Justice Bernard Chunga resigned after a presidential committee was established to investigate allegations against him of torture, corruption, and interference with the administration of justice. In June, Kibaki appointed eight new High Court judges as part of an initiative to replace judges tainted by corruption. Kibaki suspended 23 senior judges, half of the total number, in October during their investigation into alleged corruption and misconduct.

The Kibaki government has made the protection of human rights a high priority. It has also been considering establishing a commission to investigate the extent of human rights violations undertaken by the former government. However, while there are no current reports of arbitrary arrest, detention without trial, and torture, actions such as mass arrests in August 2003 in the coastal city of Mombasa, where much of the country's Muslim minority live, do raise civil liberties questions. In addition, the government has introduced into parliament a controversial Suppression of Terrorism Bill aimed at combating terrorism. The bill would allow police to arrest and search property without authority from the courts and would permit investigators to detain suspected terrorists for 36 hours without allowing them contact with the outside world.

Kenya's economy has been in long-term decline. Most of Kenya's 29 million people are poor and survive through subsistence agriculture. Nepotism and fraud inhibit economic opportunity and discourage greater foreign investment.

Women in Kenya continue to face serious obstacles in the exercise of their freedoms. A draft gender equity bill created considerable public controversy, with some Muslims protesting that it was too sweeping in scope. Evidence suggests that there is widespread violence against women. According to a study by the Center for Human Rights and Democracy in Eldoret, 60 percent of rape cases in the North Rift region were not reported because women feared unfair treatment by police. Many of the cases have gone unpunished, despite repeated complaints by women's groups that Kenyan laws remain too lenient in sentencing offenders in cases of violence against women.

Traditional attitudes circumscribe the role of women in politics, although there are no legal restrictions and some change is occurring. There were only nine female members of parliament (four elected and five nominated) in the 222-seat National Assembly prior to the 2002 general elections and one female cabinet member. The elections increased the number of women in parliament to eight elected and seven nominated, and three cabinet ministers. The Kibaki government has explicitly targeted improving women's rights as a key policy goal. This issue is also the focus of considerable attention and discussion in the ongoing constitutional review process.

# Kiribati

**Population:** 100,000
**GNI/capita:** $810
**Life Expectancy:** 62
**Religious Groups:** Roman Catholic (52 percent), Protestant (40 percent), other (8 percent)
**Ethnic Groups:** Micronesian, some Polynesian
**Capital:** Tarawa

**Political Rights:** 1
**Civil Liberties:** 1
**Status:** Free

**Ten-Year Ratings Timeline (Political Rights, Civil Liberties, Status)**

| 1994 | 1995 | 1996 | 1997 | 1998 | 1999 | 2000 | 2001 | 2002 | 2003 |
|------|------|------|------|------|------|------|------|------|------|
| 1,1F | 1,1F | 1,1F | 1,1F | 1,1F | 1,1F | 1,1F | 1,1F | 1,1F | 1,1F |

**Overview:**

Controversy over the presence of a Chinese satellite-tracking facility in Tarawa led to a no-confidence vote that brought down the government and to the election of a new president. The controversy also resulted in the termination of ties between China and Kiribati, dismantling of the satellite-tracking facility, and a renewal of ties between Kiribati and Taiwan.

Kiribati has been a constitutional republic since it gained independence from Britain in 1979. The country consists of 33 small islands scattered across nearly 1.5 million square miles of the central Pacific Ocean, as well as Banaba Island in the western Pacific. In 1998, the incumbent president, Teburoro Tito, won a second four-year term, defeating opposition candidates Harry Tong and Amberoti Nikora.

A major issue in the February 2003 presidential election—in which Tito was reelected to a third and final term in office over Taberannang Timeon, a former secretary to the cabinet, by 547 votes—was the presence of a Chinese satellite-tracking facility on the capital atoll of Tarawa. Before the vote, opposition party member Anote Tong (Harry Tong's younger brother) pledged to review the 15-year Chinese lease and "to take the appropriate action at the right time." China's influence became an issue when Harry Tong, a parliament member, asked former president Tito to release details about this lease and Tito refused. Tong also queried Tito about Chinese ambassador Ma Shuxue's acknowledgment that Beijing made a $2,850 donation to a cooperative society linked to Tito. Beijing claims that the facility is part of its civilian space program, but there are allegations that it is used to monitor U.S. missile tests in the Pacific (ultimately, diplomatic ties with Taiwan were resumed on November 1, and China dismantled the tracking station by the end of November).

The controversy led to a no-confidence vote of 40 to 21 against the Tito government in March. Parliament was dissolved and fresh parliamentary and presidential polls were called. In two rounds of parliamentary elections, held on May 9 and 14, the government secured 24 seats against the opposition's 14, with two independent members. However, in July 4 presidential elections, opposition candidate Anote Tong was elected president with 47.4 percent of the vote, defeating rivals Harry Tong of the ruling Maurin Maneaba Party with 43.5 percent and Banuera Berina with 9.1 percent. The race was close, with Anote Tong winning against his brother by only 1,000 votes. Opposition candidates complained that they did not have sufficient access to the government-owned Radio Kiribati station and *Te Uekara* newspaper during the election campaign.

**Political Rights and Civil Liberties:** The 2003 presidential and parliamentary elections were considered free and fair. The president is popularly elected in a two-step process. First, a general election chooses representatives to the 42-member parliament, known as the Maneaba ni Maungatabu. Forty of these representatives are chosen by universal adult suffrage, one is nominated by the Rabi Island Council in Fiji, and the attorney general holds an ex-officio assembly position. ( Rabi Island is a part of Fiji, but many residents there are of Kiribati origin. They were forced to move there from Banabas Islands by the British when phosphate mining left Banabas Island uninhabitable.) Parliament then fields three or four candidates for the presidential round. The president, vested with executive powers by the constitution, is limited to serving three 4-year terms.

Freedom of speech is generally respected. The government owns *Te Uekara*, one of the country's two newspapers. Churches also put out several newsletters and other periodicals. The *Kiribati Newstar*, the only private newspaper in Kiribati, is owned by Ierema Tabai, a former president and member of the opposition party under the government of former president Teburoro Tito. Tabai launched the newspaper after the government blocked his efforts to set up a radio station, Newair FM 101, in 1999. The government closed the station and fined Tabai and other directors of the station for attempting to import broadcasting equipment without a license. In December 2002, the government granted Newair FM 101 a license to broadcast, and the station went into operation in January 2003. Until then, the government had owned the island nation's only radio station, Radio Kiribati. There is one television station and about 1,000 television sets throughout the islands, according to the latest available data from 2000.

Opposition candidates have criticized the Newspaper Registration Act for its vaguely worded restrictions on the printing of offensive materials. The law allows officials to censor articles that could incite or encourage crime or disorder and to shut down any publication against which a complaint has been filed. A single Internet service provider (ISP) supports about 1,000 users. The main constraints to broader Internet access are costs and limited bandwidth.

There were no reports of religious suppression or restrictions on academic freedom.

Freedom of movement and association and the right to organize and bargain collectively are generally respected. There are a number of nongovernmental groups that are involved in development assistance, education, health, and advocacy for women and children. Only about 10 percent of the labor force belongs to unions (90 percent of workers are fishermen and subsistence farmers). The largest is the Kiribati Trade Union Congress with about 2,500 members.

The judicial system is modeled on English common law and provides adequate due process rights. It consists of the High Court, a court of appeal, and magistrates' courts, and appeals may go to the Privy Council in London. The president makes all judicial appointments. The 250-member police force is under civilian control. Traditional customs permit corporal punishment, and island councils on some outer islands occasionally order such punishment for petty theft and other minor offenses.

The government is the main employer in the largely subsistence agricultural economy. The economy also depends considerably on foreign assistance.

Discrimination against women remains strong in a traditional culture of male dominance. Spousal abuse and other forms of violence against women are not uncommon and are often associated with alcohol abuse.

# Kuwait

**Population:** 2,400,000
**GNI/capita:** $18,270
**Life Expectancy:** 78
**Religious Groups:** Muslim (85 percent) [Sunni 70 percent, Shi'a 30 percent], other (15 percent)
**Ethnic Groups:** Kuwaiti (45 percent), other Arab (35 percent), South Asian (9 percent), Iranian (4 percent), other (7 percent)
**Capital:** Kuwait City

**Political Rights:** 4
**Civil Liberties:** 5
**Status:** Partly Free

**Ten-Year Ratings Timeline (Political Rights, Civil Liberties, Status)**

| 1994 | 1995 | 1996 | 1997 | 1998 | 1999 | 2000 | 2001 | 2002 | 2003 |
|------|------|------|------|------|------|------|------|------|------|
| 5,5PF | 5,5PF | 5,5PF | 5,5PF | 5,5PF | 4,5PF | 4,5PF | 4,5PF | 4,5PF | 4,5PF |

**Overview:**

The war in Iraq dominated headlines in Kuwait during the first four months of 2003, as the U.S. military used Kuwaiti territory as the main staging area for its ground war against Iraq in March and April. Despite tensions created by the American military presence, terrorist threats, a handful of missile attacks from Iraqi forces, and a spate of attacks against the American presence, Kuwait was able to maintain law and order during a tense period. On July 5, Kuwait held the tenth elections since independence for its 50-member National Assembly.

The al-Sabah family has played a role in ruling Kuwait for more than 200 years. A year after Kuwait gained its independence in 1961 from Britain, a new constitution gave broad powers to the emir and created the National Assembly. The emir has suspended the National Assembly two times in the last 40 years, from 1976 to 1981 and from 1986 to 1992.

After its restoration in 1992, parliament played an active role in monitoring the emir and the government, forcing government ministers out of office and blocking legislation proposed by the royal family. Parliament, however, has also served as an impediment to progressive political change, rejecting measures that would have granted women the right to vote and accelerated economic reforms.

The 2003 legislative elections did not meet minimal international standards, tainted by the exclusion of women from voting and allegations of widespread government-subsidized vote buying. Pro-government candidates with strong tribal backing did well in the elections, and candidates aligned with Islamists realized some slight gains. Out of 16 liberal candidates, only 3 managed to win seats, a decline of 4 seats from the previous National Assembly. Several analysts contend that the coalition of Islamists and pro-government members with conservative tribal ties may oppose measures to promote women's rights and full political participation, privatize the economy, and update investment laws.

Following the elections, Sabah al-Ahmad al-Sabah, half-brother of Emir Jaber al-Ahmad al-Sabah, became prime minister, taking over for ailing Saad al-Abdallah al-Sabah, who remains the crown prince. Sabah al-Ahmad al-Sabah's appointment as prime minister marks the first time since Kuwait's independence that the prime minister has not been the crown prince. The al-Sabah ruling dynasty is currently led by aging family members; the emir and crown prince are all in their seventies, and unanswered succession questions linger.

The 2002-2003 buildup of American military forces in Kuwait, which served as a staging ground for the land war against Iraq, led to internal tensions and a spate of attacks against American forces. Kuwait designated over half of its territory to serve as staging territory for U.S. forces, and it also donated in-kind assistance such as fuel to the war effort.

In October, the cabinet approved a measure that would allow women to stand for office and vote in municipal council elections. The measure still needs approval from the all-male National Assembly, which has in the past blocked government proposals to open the door to women's full participation in political life.

**Political Rights and Civil Liberties:** Freely elected representatives do not determine the policies of Kuwait's government. The royal family of Kuwait, which is a hereditary emirate, largely sets the government's policy agenda. The country's emir has overriding power in the political system, appointing the prime minister and cabinet. Under the constitution, the emir holds executive power and shares legislative power with the 50-member National Assembly, which is elected by a limited popular vote involving only about 15 percent of the country's 860,000 citizens. The emir has the power to dissolve the National Assembly at will but must call elections within 60 days. The National Assembly is granted powers to overturn decrees from the emir issued during a period when the assembly is not in session, and the assembly has exercised this power in a number of cases. The National Assembly can veto the appointment of the country's prime minister, but then it must choose from three alternates put forward by the emir. Kuwaiti male citizens have only a limited ability to change their government. Women are completely excluded from the political process.

The government bans formal political parties, but it has allowed political groupings such as parliamentary blocs to emerge. The al-Sabah family dominates political life and controls meaningful power. Although the 1962 constitution provides men and women with equal rights, only men aged 21 or over can vote and run for office, according to the current election law.

The government, which owns all broadcast media, places restrictions on freedom of expression. However, it sometimes allows open criticism and debate on politics in the press. Overall, journalists in Kuwait enjoy greater freedom than do some of their regional counterparts, but the government continues to enforce laws that prohibit direct criticism of the emir and senior members of the royal family. In June, the government charged Mohammed Jassem, the editor of *Al-Watan* newspaper and an advocate for political reform, with challenging the authority of and "uttering abusive statements" about the emir. Irritated by satellite television station Al-Jazeera, the government closed the station's offices in Kuwait City.

Kuwaitis have access to the Internet, though Internet service providers have blocked access to certain sites. In May, the Ministry of Communications conducted raids on numerous Internet cafes on the basis that they were not blocking sites deemed immoral by Islamic members of the National Assembly. The Ministry of Communication issued new regulations that require Internet cafe owners to collect the names and civil identification numbers of customers.

Islam is the state religion, and religious minorities are generally permitted to practice their religion freely in private. Academic freedom is generally respected, though some exercise self-censorship. Kuwait has a tradition of allowing relatively open and free private discussions, often conducted in traditional gatherings called *diwayniyas,* and usually only including men.

The government restricts freedom of assembly and protest, and public gatherings require government approval. Kuwait does not have a single legally recognized independent human rights organization, and the civil society sector is small. Workers have the right to join labor unions, but the government restricts freedom of association by mandating that there only be one union per occupational trade.

Kuwait lacks a truly independent judiciary. The emir appoints all judges, and the executive branch of government approves judicial promotions and renewals of judicial appointments. According to Kuwaiti law, authorities may detain suspects for four days without charge. The Ministry of the Interior supervises the main internal security forces, including the national police, the Criminal Investigation Division, and the Kuwait State Security.

An estimated 80,000 stateless residents, known as *bidoon,* are considered illegal residents and do not have full citizenship rights.

Citizens have the right to own property and establish businesses. Oil dominates the economy, accounting for at least 85 percent of public revenues. In the coming year, one thorny issue of contention between the National Assembly and the government is Project Kuwait, a proposal to invite foreign oil majors to develop the emirate's northern oilfields. Lawmakers are seeking provisions that would prevent foreigners from gaining any substantial control over Kuwait's main national resource.

Women face discrimination in several areas of society and remain under-represented in the workforce, although they have made recent gains. According to recent statistics, women account for 34 percent of the workforce and receive two-thirds of the bachelor's degrees in Kuwait. Women have been fighting for full political participation for decades, but have been blocked by conservative male political leaders and Islamist groups.

# Kyrgyzstan

**Population:** 5,000,000
**GNI/capita:** $280
**Life Expectancy:** 69
**Religious Groups:** Muslim (75 percent), Russian
Orthodox (20 percent), other (5 percent)
**Ethnic Groups:** Kyrgyz (52 percent), Russian (18 percent),
Uzbek (13 percent), Ukrainian (3 percent), other (14 percent)
**Capital:** Bishkek

**Political Rights:** 6
**Civil Liberties:** 5
**Status:** Not Free

**Ten-Year Ratings Timeline (Political Rights, Civil Liberties, Status)**

| 1994 | 1995 | 1996 | 1997 | 1998 | 1999 | 2000 | 2001 | 2002 | 2003 |
|------|------|------|------|------|------|------|------|------|------|
| 4,3PF | 4,4PF | 4,4PF | 4,4PF | 5,5PF | 5,5PF | 6,5NF | 6,5NF | 6,5NF | 6,5NF |

**Overview:**

President Askar Akayev's growing authoritarianism was demonstrated by the ratification of a controversial February 2003 constitutional referendum that further consolidated the president's already considerable powers. The referendum, which was portrayed as an effort to enhance the country's stability, came in the wake of deadly clashes between opposition supporters and police the previous year and growing political discontent, including calls for Akayev's resignation. On the international front, Kyrgyzstan continued to juggle its relations with Russia and the United States over strategic matters, while issues related to its border with Uzbekistan remained a source of tension during the year.

Populated by nomadic herders and ruled by tribal leaders for centuries, Kyrgyzstan was conquered by Russia in the mid-1800s and incorporated into the Soviet Union in 1924. The country declared independence from the U.S.S.R. in August 1991. After Akayev, a respected physicist, was elected president in the country's first direct presidential vote two months later, he introduced multiparty elections and pursued economic reforms.

In the 1995 parliamentary elections, no single party won a clear majority, with a mix of governing officials, intellectuals, and clan leaders capturing most of the seats in the legislature. Later that year, Akayev was reelected president in early elections with more than 70 percent of the vote. In a February 1996 referendum, 94 percent of voters endorsed constitutional amendments that substantially increased the powers of the presidency.

Opposition parties, including the Democratic Movement of Kyrgyzstan (PDMK), El Bei-Bechora (The People's Party), and Ar-Namys (Dignity), were barred from competing in the February 2000 parliamentary elections over minor technicalities in rulings that were widely regarded as politically motivated. Ar-Namys chairman Feliks Kulov, who ran as an independent candidate, lost in the runoff by a suspiciously large margin despite having enjoyed a secure lead in the first round. According to official election results, the Communist Party received the largest percentage of votes, followed by the pro-government Union of Democratic Forces. International election observers, including representatives from the Organization for Security and Cooperation in Europe (OSCE), noted serious irregularities such as attempts to bribe voters, violations in vote tabulations, and a state media bias in favor of pro-government parties.

The October 29, 2000 presidential poll was contested by six candidates, including the heavily favored incumbent, who received nearly 75 percent of the vote. Kulov, who was widely regarded as Akayev's main challenger, was denied registration as a candidate for refusing to take a mandatory Kyrgyz language exam, which he charged violated election laws and the constitution. As with the parliamentary elections, international monitors and opposition figures cited widespread irregularities, including the exclusion of candidates for political purposes, the stuffing of ballot boxes, and biased state media coverage.

For the second successive year, Islamic militants conducted armed incursions in August 2000 into the southern region of Kyrgyzstan. The rebels were members of the Islamic Movement of Uzbekistan (IMU), a group seeking the violent overthrow of the secular government of Uzbekistan and its replacement with one based on Islamic law. After several months of battles between the rebels and Uzbek and Kyrgyz troops, the fighting ceased with the onset of winter, with many of the rebels fleeing back to their bases in neighboring Tajikistan.

Following the September 11, 2001, terrorist attacks against the World Trade Center and the Pentagon, Kyrgyzstan offered its support for the U.S.-led war in Afghanistan, including the use of its air bases. For the cash-strapped Kyrgyz economy, U.S. troop deployments promised to be a valuable source of income. Meanwhile, human rights groups expressed concern that the government would use its increased cooperation with the United States to crack down further on sources of domestic dissent, including independent media outlets and opposition political groups.

Years of simmering frustrations in the economically depressed and politically marginalized south culminated in an unprecedented series of public protests in 2002. The demonstrations were sparked by the January arrest of parliament member Azimbek Beknazarov on abuse-of-power charges, although critics maintained that he had been detained because of his public criticism of a controversial 1999 border agreement ceding land to China. On March 17 and 18, a few days after his trial began, thousands of pro-Beknazarov demonstrators marched in the southern district of Aksy. In the first outbreak of deadly political violence since Kyrgyzstan's independence, several protestors were killed and more than a dozen were wounded when police fired into the crowd. In an apparent effort to quell the protests, the authorities released Beknazarov from prison the following day. However, on May 24, he was convicted of abuse of office, given a one-year suspended sentence, and stripped of his seat in parliament.

Thousands of Beknazarov supporters continued to hold rallies, demanding that the charges against him be dismissed and that those responsible for the killings in Aksy be punished. The demonstrators adopted additional demands, including Akayev's resignation and the overturning of a May 8 conviction of Kulov for embezzlement. Kulov was already serving a seven-year prison term, which he had received in January 2001, for abuse of power while national security minister in 1997 and 1998. Most analysts maintained that the cases against him were politically motivated and were intended to exclude him from further activities in politics.

The crisis eased somewhat after an appeals court annulled Beknazarov's sentence on June 28, allowing him to retain his seat in parliament. On December 28, four former regional prosecutors and police officials were sentenced to between two and three years in prison in connection with the Aksy shootings. However, critics charged that senior officials who had authorized the use of force had not been prosecuted and brought to justice.

In the wake of continued criticism of the government's handling of the Aksy crisis and calls for the president's resignation, Akayev called for a constitutional referendum on February 2, 2003 on redistributing power between the executive and legislative branches. Voters were asked to approve or reject an entire package of amendments to the constitution, and they were also asked whether Akayev should serve out the remainder of his term until December 2005. Opposition leaders criticized a decision to have an Akayev-appointed Expert Group make final changes in January to the amendments—which had been drafted by a Constitutional Council consisting of both pro-government and opposition supporters—before their submission for the referendum. The final text, which further strengthened the authority of the president at the expense of parliament, differed substantially from that presented by the Constitutional Council. Among the amendments included in the referendum were the abolition of party-list voting in parliamentary elections in favor of the first-past-the-post system, which could further weaken political parties; a reorganization of parliament from a bicameral to a unicameral body; and the granting of immunity to former presidents and their families.

According to official results, more than 76 percent voted in favor of the proposed amendments and 79 percent supported allowing Akayev to remain in office until the end of his term. Voter turnout was reported to be around 86 percent. Local and international observers noted various irregularities during the referendum, including polling officials' stuffing of ballot boxes and pressuring of voters to support the amendments, the hampering of independent observers monitoring the voting, and inflating of voter turnout figures. The OSCE declined to send observers, citing a lack of time to prepare an effective monitoring mission since the government had announced the referendum date only three weeks before it was held.

Kyrgyzstan continued to balance its strategic and economic relations with Russia and the United States throughout the year. In October, Russia formally established a military base in the town of Kant near Bishkek under the auspices of the Commonwealth of Independent States Collective Security Treaty Organization. Although Kyrgyz and Russian officials insisted that the Russian and U.S. bases in Kyrgyzstan would serve complementary, rather than competing, strategic roles, the Kant air base is widely seen as an attempt by Moscow to counter the growing U.S. influence in Central Asia after September 11, 2001. Meanwhile, the economic benefits of a continued U.S. presence in the country are likely to lead Kyrgyzstan to maintain good relations with both Washington and Tashkent.

Kyrgyzstan's border with Uzbekistan continued to be a source of tension between the two countries throughout the year. Following the 1999 and 2000 IMU incursions into Kyrgyzstan, Uzbekistan placed land mines along the Kyrgyz-Uzbek border to prevent renewed IMU invasions. Tashkent has refused repeated demands by Bishkek to remove the mines, which have killed a number of Kyrgyz civilians. Meanwhile, Uzbek border guards have indiscriminately shot ethnic Kyrgyz suspected of being terrorists.

**Political Rights and Civil Liberties:**  Citizens of Kyrgyzstan cannot change their government democratically. International election observers described the 2000 parliamentary and presidential elections as neither free nor fair. The constitution codifies strong presidential rule and a weak parliament, and the post of prime minister is largely ceremonial. The current bicameral legislature is composed of a 45-member upper chamber, which meets only occasionally to approve the budget and confirm presidential appointees, and a 60-seat lower chamber. Constitutional amendments adopted in a February 2003 referendum will create a unicameral legislature with 75 deputies after the 2005 parliamentary poll; all seats will be distributed through a first-past-the-post system, rather than by party-list voting. Although the constitution limits the president to only two terms in office, President Askar Akayev was allowed to run in 2000 after the Constitutional Court ruled that his first term had begun in 1995, after the country's first post-Soviet constitution was adopted, rather than in 1991, when he was first elected. Despite public pledges by Akayev that he will step down at the end of his current term in 2005, speculation continues as to whether he intends to amend the constitution to run again or if he is working behind the scenes to control the succession process.

The government harassed some members of opposition political groups, including Ar-Namys party deputy chairman Emil Aliyev, who was arrested in July on embezzlement charges that are suspected of being politically motivated. In August, Kyrgyzstan's Supreme Court upheld the 2002 guilty verdict against Ar-Namys party leader Feliks Kulov that had resulted from a politically motivated prosecution. Most political parties are weak, poorly organized, and centered around a specific leading figure.

Corruption is widespread throughout Kyrgyz society. Critics charge that the latest government anticorruption campaign, initiated in April 2003, is unlikely to focus on top-level officials who are government loyalists and will instead target mostly political opponents of the regime. Kyrgyzstan was ranked 118 out of 133 countries in Transparency International's 2003 Corruption Perceptions Index.

Both state and private media are vulnerable to government pressure, which causes many journalists to practice self-censorship. The new constitutional amendments adopted in February contain vague restrictions on journalists' rights to gather and distribute information. Many of the country's media outlets are reportedly increasingly owned or controlled by individuals with close ties to the government. All media are required to register with the Ministry of Justice and wait for formal approval before commencing operations; the registration process is often lengthy and includes background checks on owners and sources of financing. The state printing house, Uchkun, which is the country's primary newspaper publisher, has at times refused to print some independent and opposition newspapers. An internationally funded printing press established by Freedom House and operated by the nongovernmental Media Support Center Foundation was opened in November to allow independent papers to be published without fear of censorship or reprisals. There are no credible reports of government interference in or censorship of the Internet.

The authorities increasingly used libel laws in 2003 to harass media outlets reporting on sensitive issues or critical of the government. The newspaper *Moya Stolitsa Novosti*, which investigated high-level corruption, was forced to close in June because of nearly $100,000 in fines stemming from numerous politically motivated libel lawsuits; the paper was subsequently relaunched as *MSN*. Another newspaper, *Kyrgyz Ordo*, closed in January because of high court fines related to defamation suits against it. Acts of violence against journalists continued in 2003. In September, *Kyrgyz Ruhu* newspaper journalist Ernis Nazalov was found dead in a canal in the southern town of Osh. The fact that Nazalov was investigating government corruption at the time increased suspicion that his death was politically motivated. *Moya Stolitsa Novosti* journalist Alexandra Chernykh—the daughter of the paper's political editor Rina Prizhivoit—was assaulted by unidentified assailants in January, while the car of the paper's editor in chief, Alexander Kim, was set on fire in a separate incident.

Freedom of religion is generally respected. To obtain legal status, all religious organizations must register with the Ministry of Justice, a process that is often cumbersome. However, unregistered groups have not reported restrictions or problems in functioning. The government has increased efforts to monitor and restrict Islamic groups that it regards as extremist and a threat to national security, particularly Hizb-ut-Tahrir, an international movement calling for the creation of an Islamic caliphate throughout the Muslim world. The country's schools, particularly in rural areas, suffer from a severe lack of resources and shortage of qualified teachers. Corruption is widespread throughout the educational system, with bribes often required to obtain admission to schools or universities.

Freedom of assembly is respected inconsistently. A series of demonstrations throughout 2002 included a March protest in which several people were killed by police. Amendments to the constitution adopted in 2003 require that authorities be notified of public gatherings and give officials the right to prohibit gatherings under certain conditions. In some cases, officials, particularly at the local level, have refused to issue permits for demonstrations to critics of the government. While numerous protests and rallies took place across the country in 2003, most without interference from the authorities, security forces forcibly disrupted some demonstrations. In May, a group of mothers of Aksy victims were arrested, and some were beaten by police when they tried to hold a demonstration in Bishkek. The labor law provides for the formation of trade unions and protects members from anti-union discrimination, and unions generally are able to conduct their activities without obstruction.

Although freedom of association is generally respected and many nongovernmental organizations (NGOs) operate with little or no state interference, some have faced harassment by the authorities. Human Rights Watch (HRW) documented numerous complaints of intimidation of NGOs by law enforcement in the period surrounding the February constitutional referendum, including pressuring NGO members to remove their signatures from petitions objecting to the draft constitution. A constitutional prohibition on NGOs pursuing political goals that was adopted during the referendum has raised concern that it could be used to ban legitimate civil society activities, including election monitoring. The Coalition for Democracy and Civil Society had its application for re-registration rejected several times by the Ministry of Justice before finally being approved in October 2003; the ministry had cited the constitutional ban in its earlier refusal to register the group. In February, authorities used the pretext of a medical exam to hospitalize the head of the coalition, Edil Baisalov, against his will for several days before he was scheduled to speak at a conference on human rights defenders. In September, the Kyrgyz Committee for Human Rights (KCHR) was re-registered under an alternative leadership allegedly not elected by the group's membership. HRW expressed concern that the main objective was to silence criticism of the government by supplanting the legitimate leadership of the KCHR.

Despite various legislative reforms in the court system, the judiciary is not independent and remains dominated by the executive branch. Corruption among judges is reportedly widespread. Police at times use violence against suspects during arrest and interrogation and to extract confessions. Defendants' rights, including the presumption of innocence until proven guilty, were not always respected. The country's prisons suffer from high mortality rates, severe overcrowding, poor medical care, and inadequate nutrition.

Ethnic minority groups, including Uzbeks, Russians, and Uighurs, have complained of discrimination in employment and housing. Members of the country's sizable ethnic Uzbek minority have been demanding more political and cultural rights, including greater representation in government and more Uzbek language schools.

The government of Kyrgyzstan, which abolished the Soviet-era exit-visa system in 1999, generally respects the right of free travel to and from the country. However, certain policies complicate internal migration, including a requirement for citizens to obtain official permits to work and settle in particular areas of the country.

Personal connections, corruption, organized crime, and widespread poverty limit business competition and equality of opportunity. In October, a new regulation requiring merchants at bazaars to use expensive cash registers to report sales and improve tax collection led to protests by thousands of merchants in Bishkek.

Cultural traditions and apathy by law enforcement officials discourage victims of domestic violence from seeking legal help. The trafficking of women and girls into forced prostitution abroad is a serious problem, and some victims report that the authorities are involved in trafficking. In August, the government adopted a criminal code amendment punishing trafficking with up to 20 years in prison. Declining economic conditions in the country have had a negative impact on women's professional and educational opportunities.

# Laos

**Population:** 5,600,000    **Political Rights:** 7
**GNI/capita:** $300    **Civil Liberties:** 6
**Life Expectancy:** 54    **Status:** Not Free
**Religious Groups:** Buddhist (60 percent), other
[including animist] (40 percent)
**Ethnic Groups:** Lao Loum [lowland] (68 percent),
Lao Theung [upland] (22 percent), Lao Soung [highland]
including the Hmong (Meo) and the Yao (Mien) (9 percent),
ethnic Vietnamese/Chinese (1 percent)
**Capital:** Vientiane

**Ten-Year Ratings Timeline (Political Rights, Civil Liberties, Status)**

| 1994 | 1995 | 1996 | 1997 | 1998 | 1999 | 2000 | 2001 | 2002 | 2003 |
|------|------|------|------|------|------|------|------|------|------|
| 7,6NF | 7,6NF | 7,6NF | 7,6NF | 7,6NF | 7,6NF | 7,6NF | 7,6NF | 7,6NF | 7,6NF |

**Overview:**
With its command economy, Brezhnev-era politics, and sporadic political violence, Laos is likely to remain among the world's poorest and least developed countries for years to come. The Communist ruling party in 2003 continued to jail dissidents and showed few signs of speeding the pace of limited economic reforms introduced nearly two decades ago. Meanwhile, a string of attacks on buses in remote areas of this Southeast Asian nation killed at least two dozen people, while stepped-up attacks by Laotian forces against antigovernment rebels in the rugged north reportedly led to scores of civilian deaths.

Landlocked, mountainous Laos won independence in 1953 after being a French protectorate for six decades and occupied by the Japanese during World War II. Backed by Vietnam's Viet Minh rebels, Communist Pathet Lao (Land of Lao) guerrillas quickly tried to topple the royalist government in Vientiane. Following several years of political turmoil, Communist, royalist, and so-called neutralist forces in 1960 began waging a three-way civil war.

Amid continued internal fighting, Laos was drawn into the Vietnam War in 1964, when the United States began bombing North Vietnamese forces operating inside Laos. The Pathet Lao seized power in 1975 shortly after the Communist victory in neighboring Vietnam. The guerrillas set up a one-party Communist state under Prime Minister Kaysone Phomvihane's Lao People's Revolutionary Party (LPRP). By the mid-1980s, the Laotian economy was in shambles, reeling from the LPRP's central planning and tight political control and the legacy of civil war. In response, the LPRP in 1986 began freeing prices, encouraging foreign investment, and privatizing farms and some state-owned firms. Partially unshackled, the economy grew by 7 percent a year, on average, from 1988 to 1996.

At the same time, the LPRP continued to reject calls for political reforms, jailing two officials in 1990 who called for multiparty elections. Meanwhile, Kaysone's death in 1992 ushered in a new strongman to lead the country. Veteran revolutionary Khamtay Siphandone, now 79, took the reigns of the all-powerful LPRP and later became state president.

Besides rejecting political change, Khamtay and other leaders also have been unwilling to pursue deeper economic reforms, including privatizing the large, creaking state firms that dominate the economy. They apparently fear that reducing the party's control over the economy could undermine its tight grip on power by giving ordinary Laotians more control over their daily lives.

Diplomats in Vientiane blamed the bus attacks in 2003 on ethnic Hmong rebels, although no group claimed responsibility and little hard evidence linked the insurgents to the attacks. The Hmong rebels are the remnants of an army that was backed by the U.S. CIA during the Vietnam War to fight Communist forces. The rebels are divided and poorly equipped, and experts caution that claims of heavy fighting in 2003 by a U.S.-based Hmong exile group were very likely exaggerated.

Late in the year, a group of several hundred rebels and their families remained surrounded by Laotian forces in Khouang Province, northeast of Vientiane, a situation first reported by *Time Asia* in May. The human rights group Amnesty International said in October that the holed-up rebels were unable to obtain food and that it had received reports of scores of civilian deaths from conflict-related injuries and starvation.

Laos is Southeast Asia's least developed country and depends on foreign aid and loans. Around four-fifths of Laotians are subsistence farmers, most of whom live on less than $2 per day. Trade, tourism, and sales of hydroelectric power to neighboring Thailand are key sources of foreign revenue. The economy has yet to recover from the regional financial crisis that began in 1997, when the country's mainly Thai foreign investors pulled out in droves; most have not returned.

## Political Rights and Civil Liberties:

Laotians cannot change their government through elections and are denied most basic rights. The 1991 constitution makes the ruling LPRP the sole legal political party and gives it a leading role at all levels of government. The LPRP vets all candidates for election to the rubber-stamp National Assembly; elections are held once every five years. At the last election, in 2002, all but one of the 166 candidates for the assembly's 109 seats were LPRP cadres.

Laotian media are state controlled and parrot the party line. The law authorizes jail terms for journalists who step out of line and criminalizes most criticism of the state or LPRP. Two European journalists and their American interpreter, arrested in June while covering the insurgency, were released in July after being sentenced to 15-year prison terms for the killing of a village guard. Two Hmong assistants arrested with them remain jailed under long sentences. The government controls all domestic Internet servers, and authorities at times block access to Web sites that they consider pornographic or that are critical of the government.

Religious freedom is tightly restricted. Dozens of Christians recently have been detained on religious grounds, some for months, and several have been jailed for proselytizing or other peaceful religious activities. A campaign launched in some provinces in 1999 to shut churches and force Christians to renounce their faith appears largely over, though there continue to be sporadic reports of harassment of worshippers in those provinces. Moreover, local officials in some parts of Laos prevent Christians from celebrating major religious holidays, and some minority religious groups reportedly are unable to register new congregations or obtain permission to build new places of worship, according to the U.S. State Department's human rights report for 2002, released in March 2003. In this predominantly Buddhist society, the LPRP controls training for the Buddhist clergy and oversees temples and other religious sites. Recently, however, officials have permitted some Buddhist temples to receive foreign support, expand the training of monks, and emphasize traditional teachings rather than state doctrine.

Academic freedom is highly restricted. University professors generally cannot teach or write about democratization, human rights, and other politically sensitive topics.

Laos has some nongovernmental welfare and professional groups, but they are prohibited from having political agendas and are subjected to strict state control. Laotian trade unions have little influence, partly because they are state controlled but also because few Laotians are wage-earning workers. All unions must belong to the official Federation of Lao Trade Unions, and workers lack the right to bargain collectively. Strikes are not expressly prohibited, but workers rarely stage walkouts. Most wage earners work for the government, although privatization is moving more workers into the private sector.

Laos's party-controlled courts do not provide fair trials or allow citizens to redress government rights abuses and other grievances. "The judiciary was subject to executive, legislative, and LPRP influence, was corrupt, and did not ensure citizens due process," according to the U.S. State Department report. The report noted, however, that officials appear to be easing somewhat their control of the courts. Security forces often illegally detain suspects, and some Laotians have spent more than a decade in jail without trial, according to a 2002 Amnesty International report. Prisoners are routinely tortured and receive inadequate food and health care. In addition, some must bribe jail officials to obtain their freedom once a court has ordered their release. Authorities continue to brook little dissent from ordinary Laotians. Laotian jails hold hundreds of short- and long-term political detainees, according to the U.S. State Department report. They also hold at least nine political prisoners who have been formally charged and tried.

Both Laotian forces and Hmong rebels reportedly have committed some killings and other human rights abuses related to the Hmong insurgency. The Hmong—one of the largest of several upcountry hill tribes in Laos—and other ethnic minorities face some discrimination in mainstream society and have little say in government decisions on how land is used and natural resources are allocated.

Ordinary Laotians enjoy somewhat greater freedom in their daily lives than they did in the years following the Communist takeover. Many now work for themselves or private employers rather than for tightly monitored state firms. Moreover, the government has scaled back its surveillance of the population, although intelligence agencies still keep tabs on some Laotians, and officials at times conduct searches without warrants.

Many Laotian women hold key civil service and private sector jobs, though relatively few are in the top ranks of government. An estimated 15,000 to 20,000 Laotian women and girls, mainly highland ethnic minorities, are trafficked each year for prostitution, mostly to Thailand.

# Latvia

**Population:** 2,300,000
**GNI/capita:** $3,230
**Life Expectancy:** 71
**Religious Groups:** Lutheran, Roman Catholic, Russian Orthodox
**Ethnic Groups:** Latvian (57 percent), Russian (30 percent), Byelorussian (4 percent), Ukrainian (3 percent), Polish (3 percent), other (3 percent)
**Capital:** Riga

**Political Rights:** 1
**Civil Liberties:** 2
**Status:** Free

**Ten-Year Ratings Timeline (Political Rights, Civil Liberties, Status)**

| 1994 | 1995 | 1996 | 1997 | 1998 | 1999 | 2000 | 2001 | 2002 | 2003 |
|------|------|------|------|------|------|------|------|------|------|
| 3,2F | 2,2F | 2,2F | 1,2F | 1,2F | 1,2F | 1,2F | 1,2F | 1,2F | 1,2F |

**Overview:**

Latvia became the last of several candidate countries to vote in favor of accession to the European Union (EU) in a September 20 referendum. Despite severe bouts of disunity and dissension, Prime Minister Einars Repse's ruling coalition became more stable during the year. On June 20, President Vaira Vike-Freiberga, running unopposed, was reelected to her post by the Latvian parliament.

After having been ruled for centuries by Germany, Poland, Sweden, and Russia, Latvia gained its independence in 1918, only to be annexed by the U.S.S.R. during World War II. More than 50 years of Soviet occupation saw a massive influx of Russians and the deportation, execution, and emigration of tens of thousands of ethnic Latvians. In 1991, Latvia regained its independence in the wake of the disintegration of the Soviet Union.

In the October 1998 parliamentary elections, the newly created People's Party received the most votes. However, the parliament approved a minority coalition government, excluding the People's Party and its leader, Andris Skele. The coalition was led by Vilis Kristopans and his center-right Latvia's Way, and included the right-wing nationalist For Fatherland and Freedom/LNNK (FF/LNNK) and the center-left New Party. In June 1999, Latvian-Canadian academic Vaira Vike-Freiberga was elected the country's first female president.

After only nine months in office, Prime Minister Kristopans, whose brief term had been plagued by various policy defeats and political crises, stepped down, precipitating the collapse of his government. Latvia's Way, the People's Party, and FF/LNNK agreed to form a new 62-seat majority coalition led by Kristopans's political rival, Andris Skele.

Following months of growing strains within the ruling coalition over privatization issues and personality conflicts, the government collapsed, and Prime Minister Skele resigned in April 2000. On May 5, Riga mayor Andris Berzins of Latvia's Way was chosen prime minister to lead the new government, which included the previous coalition's three parties.

In parliamentary elections held on October 5, 2002, the newly formed center-right New Era Party, led by Einars Repse, gained the most votes. Repse was named the new prime minister to lead a majority coalition government composed of the New Era Party, Union of Greens and Farmers (UGF), Latvia First Party (LFP), and FF/LNNK. Latvia's Way, the longest-serving party in parliament, failed to win enough votes to enter the legislature. Voter turnout was estimated at more than 70 percent.

On June 20, 2003, President Vaira Vike-Freiberga, running unopposed, was re-elected to a second 4-year term by the Latvian parliament in a convincing 88-6 vote.

Almost 73 percent of Latvian voters participated in a September referendum on EU accession, with 67 percent voting to join the body in April 2005. Prime Minister Repse hailed the vote as one of the three most important events in the country's history, along with the brief spate of independence between the two world wars and the collapse of the U.S.S.R. in 1991.

Shortly after referendum polling stations closed, however, deep fissures were exposed in Repse's coalition. Subsequently, the UGF and FF/LNNK joined the LFP in issuing a statement declaring that they had lost faith in Repse and that the government was failing. Nevertheless, by mid-November, the parties seemed to have reconciled their differences, signing a memorandum of understanding that outlined the coalition's "principles of cooperation."

The impending privatization of the majority share of the Ventsplis Nafta oil terminal has resulted in rising tensions with Russia. Transneft, the Russian state-owned oil transport company, has avoided using the Ventsplis Nafta terminal as part of a conspicuous takeover strategy to both discourage Western buyers and drive down the value of the terminal. As a result, oil traffic at the terminal has been reduced by more than 23 percent.

In August, Latvian customs officials intercepted 28 tons of Russian-made military equipment reportedly bound for Iran; the government has opened an investigation into the smuggling of "goods of strategic importance." Also in August, 105 peacekeeping soldiers were deployed to Iraq to serve in a Polish-led multinational stabilization force.

**Political Rights and Civil Liberties:** Latvians can change their government democratically. The constitution provides for a unicameral, 100-seat parliament (Saeima), whose members are elected for four-year terms by proportional representation, and who in turn select the country's president. According to international observers, the most recent national legislative elections in 2002 were free and fair. Latvia's citizenship laws have been criticized for disenfranchising those who immigrated to Latvia during the Soviet period and who must now apply for citizenship. While EU accession is likely to produce less rigorous citizenship requirements, those residents who remain noncitizens will become stateless people within the EU.

The government has adopted various anticorruption measures, including the establishment of a Corruption Prevention Bureau and laws to prevent conflict of interest among state officials. In 2003, almost 20 high-ranking officials in ministries, tax offices, and the police force either have resigned or have been dismissed due to charges of corruption, and Repse has called for an investigation into the Latvian Privatization Agency. However, a January 7 cabinet decision to triple ministers' salaries has been regarded with suspicion by the parliamentary opposition and the public.

The government respects freedom of speech and the press. Private television and radio stations broadcast programs in both Latvian and Russian, and newspapers publish a wide range of political viewpoints. However, many media outlets routinely report rumors and accusations as fact without benefit of hard evidence.

Freedom of worship is generally respected. However, an education law stipulating that secondary-school classes be conducted in Latvian will go into effect in 2004. The law has been met by substantial resistance by the ethnic Russian community. Most notably, on May 23, more than 10,000 people protested the policy before the Eurovision concert in Riga. Currently, some 120,000 students attend Russian-language schools throughout Latvia.

Freedom of assembly and association is protected by law, and gatherings occur without governmental interference. Workers have the right to establish trade unions, strike, and engage in collective bargaining.

While the government generally respects constitutional provisions for an independent judiciary, reform of the courts has been slow and judges continue to be inadequately trained and prone to corruption. Severe backlogs in the court system have led to lengthy delays in reviewing cases and to pretrial detention for large numbers of persons. The U.S. State Department reports that detainees awaiting trial spend an average of two years in prison. Incarceration facilities remain severely overcrowded, and cases of excessive force by security officials have been reported.

Nearly one-fifth of Latvia's residents are noncitizens, who are barred from participating in state and local elections and from holding some civil service jobs. They are also barred from some private sector jobs such as lawyers, notaries, and commercial pilots. Moscow continues to accuse Riga of discriminating against the country's 700,000 Russian-language speakers, mostly ethnic Russians.

Women possess the same legal rights as men, although they frequently face hiring and pay discrimination.

# Lebanon

**Population:** 4,200,000
**GNI/capita:** $4,010
**Life Expectancy:** 73
**Religious Groups:** Muslim [Mostly Shi'a] (70 percent), Christian (30 percent)
**Ethnic Groups:** Arab (95 percent), Armenian (4 percent), other (1 percent)
**Capital:** Beirut

**Political Rights:** 6
**Civil Liberties:** 5
**Status:** Not Free

**Ten-Year Ratings Timeline (Political Rights, Civil Liberties, Status)**

| 1994 | 1995 | 1996 | 1997 | 1998 | 1999 | 2000 | 2001 | 2002 | 2003 |
|------|------|------|------|------|------|------|------|------|------|
| 6,5NF | 6,5NF | 6,5NF | 6,5NF | 6,5NF | 6,5NF | 6,5NF | 6,5NF | 6,5NF | 6,5NF |

**Overview:**
During 2003, Syria carried out two major troop redeployments, reducing its occupation force in Lebanon to fewer than 20,000 soldiers. However, its firm control of Lebanon's

government continued to be the greatest impediment to freedom in Lebanon. The state's reaction to several major corruption scandals and security incidents during the year highlighted its continuing inability to investigate alleged wrongdoing by allies of Syria.

For more than a thousand years, the rough terrain of Mount Lebanon attracted Christian and heterodox-Muslim minorities fleeing persecution in the predominantly Sunni Muslim Arab world. After centuries of European protection and relative autonomy under Turkish rule, Mount Lebanon and its surrounding areas were established as a French mandate in 1920. After winning its independence in 1943, the new state of Lebanon maintained a precarious democratic system based on the division of parliamentary seats, high political offices, and senior administrative positions among the country's 17 officially recognized sectarian communities. As emigration transformed Lebanon's slight Christian majority into a minority, Muslim leaders demanded amendments to the fixed 6-to-5 ratio of Christian-to-Muslim parliamentary seats and to exclusive Maronite Christian control of the presidency. In 1975, war erupted between a coalition of Lebanese Muslim and leftist militias aligned with Palestinian guerrilla groups on one side and an array of Christian militias bent on preserving Christian political privileges on the other.

After the first few years of fighting, a loose consensus emerged among Lebanese politicians regarding a new power-sharing arrangement. However, following the entry of Syrian and Israeli troops into Lebanon in 1976 and 1978, the various militias and their foreign backers had little interest in disarming. The civil war lost much of its sectarian character over the next decade, with the bloodiest outbreaks of fighting taking place mainly within the Shiite, Christian, and Palestinian communities. Outside forces played a more direct role in the fighting. The Syrians battled Israeli forces in 1982, attacked a Palestinian-Islamist coalition in the mid-1980s, and fought the Lebanese army in 1989 and 1990, while the Israelis combated Palestinian and Shiite groups.

In 1989, the surviving members of Lebanon's 1972 parliament convened in Taif, Saudi Arabia, and agreed to a plan put forward by the Arab League that weakened the presidency, established equality in Christian and Muslim parliamentary representation, and mandated close security cooperation with occupying Syrian troops. After the ouster of General Michel Aoun from east Beirut by Syrian forces in October 1990, a new Syrian-backed government extended its writ throughout most of the country.

Over the next 12 years, Syria consolidated its control over Lebanese state institutions, particularly the presidency, the judiciary, and the security forces. However, in return for tacit Western acceptance of its control of Lebanon, Damascus permitted a degree of political and civil liberties in Lebanon that exceeded those in most other Arab countries. While those who directly criticized the occupation risked arbitrary arrest and imprisonment, criticism of the government was largely tolerated. The motley assortment of militia chiefs, traditional elites, and nouveaux riches who held civilian political positions in postwar Lebanon were persuaded to accept continued Syrian hegemony, primarily through a system of institutionalized corruption fueled by massive deficit spending on reconstruction during the 1990s. By the end of that decade, Lebanon's government debt exceeded its own gross national product and the economy was in deep recession.

As a result of this dismal economic downturn, vocal opposition to the Syrian presence began spreading across the political and sectarian spectrum. Mass demonstrations against the occupation grew in size and frequency throughout 2000 and 2001, while traditional Christian political and religious leaders, who had previously been silent about the issue, began denouncing it openly. Syria downsized its military presence in 2001, but demands for a complete pullout persisted.

After the September 11, 2001, attacks on the United States, Western pressure to preserve civil liberties subsided, in exchange for Syrian and Lebanese cooperation in the war against al-Qaeda. A number of unprecedented measures were taken to stifle freedom in 2002. Security forces closed an independent television station that had given voice to political dissidents, the government invalidated an opposition victory in a parliamentary by-election, and several opposition figures were placed under investigation for alleged ties to Israel and other foreign powers.

In April 2003, Damascus appointed a new cabinet widely seen as more solidly pro-Syrian. A deadlock between allies of Prime Minister Rafiq Hariri and President Emile Lahoud paralyzed government decision making on important economic matters. The year witnessed a number of unresolved corruption scandals, most notably in connection with a debt crisis at Electricite du Liban, a state-owned company that provides power to most of the country, and the collapse in July of Bank al-Madina.

Numerous politically related security incidents occurred during the year, all of which remained conspicuously unsolved. In June, Prime Minister Hariri's television station was damaged by rockets. In July, political opposition figures traveling to a luncheon in the hometown of Interior Minister Elias Murr came under machine-gun fire and were forced to turn back. Later that month, the wife of Johnny Abdo, a former intelligence chief and presidential aspirant, was assaulted.

**Political Rights and Civil Liberties:** The Lebanese people have only a limited capacity to choose their own government. The Lebanese president is formally selected every six years by the 128-member parliament. In practice, however, this choice is made after Syrian authorization, known as "the password" in the Lebanese media. Syria and its allies also influence parliamentary and municipal elections more indirectly. The distribution of parliamentary seats is skewed in favor of regions where Syrian forces have been stationed the longest, such as the Beqaa Valley, and electoral districts are blatantly gerrymandered to ensure the election of pro-Syrian politicians. There has also been widespread interference during the elections themselves, with Lebanese security forces often present inside the polls. Prior to the June 2002 by-election in Metn, Interior Minister Elias Murr declared that using voting booth curtains to ensure secrecy was "optional," a remarkably blatant move to facilitate vote buying. A September 2003 by-election in the Baabda-Aley district was relatively free and fair, but local monitors reported some irregularities.

Political corruption in Lebanon is widely considered to be the most egregious in the Arab world. Transparency International listed Lebanon as the most corrupt of 11 Middle Eastern and North African countries surveyed in its 2003 Corruption Perceptions Index.

Lebanon has a long tradition of press freedom. Five independent television stations and more than 30 independent radio stations operate in Lebanon, though they are owned by prominent political and commercial elites. Dozens of independent print publications reflect a diverse range of views. Internet access is not restricted. However, in September 1991, the government signed a treaty with its larger neighbor explicitly pledging to "ban all political and media activity that might harm" Syria. This treaty, and a variety of subsequent laws drafted to comply with it, allows judges to censor foreign publications and to indict journalists for critical reporting on Syria, the Lebanese military, the security forces, the judiciary, and the presidency. In practice, such laws are mainly used to pressure the media into exercising self-censorship and rarely result in the imprisonment of journalists or the closure of media outlets. However, journalists who persistently violate taboos can be indicted and imprisoned on more serious charges. Permanent closure of licensed media outlets was rare until the closure of Murr Televisions (MTV) in 2002, which generated palpable anxiety among media owners of all political persuasions. MTV's appeal of the decision was rejected in April 2003.

Lebanese University professor Adonis Akra, the author of a newly published book about his experience in detention during an August 2001 crackdown against anti-Syrian activists, was indicted in February 2003 on charges of tarnishing the reputation of the judiciary and harming relations with Syria, and Dar al-Talia, the publishing house that printed the book, was shut down. On July 17, Amer Mashmoushi, the managing editor of the daily *Al-Liwa*, was indicted on charges of defaming the president after criticizing his handling of the Bank al-Madina scandal.

Freedom of religion is guaranteed in the Lebanese constitution and protected in practice, though sectarianism is formally enshrined in the political system. Nearly 350,000 Palestinian refugees living in Lebanon are denied citizenship rights and face restrictions on working, building homes, and purchasing property. Academic freedom is long-standing and firmly entrenched. The country's universities are the region's most open and vibrant.

Freedom of association and assembly is restricted. Although political parties are legal, a 1994 ban on the Christian Lebanese Forces (LF) party remains in place. Nongovernmental organizations, including human rights groups, are permitted to operate freely. Public demonstrations are not permitted without prior approval from the Interior Ministry, which does not rule according to uniform standards, and security forces routinely beat and arrest those who demonstrate against the Syrian occupation. Clashes between police and student activists occurred periodically throughout the year. Police forcibly dispersed a May 3 demonstration against the occupation using water cannons and batons, injuring 7 protestors and detaining 15 people.

All workers except those in government may establish unions, and all have the right to strike and to bargain collectively. Several major strikes occurred in 2003.

The judiciary is strongly influenced by Syrian political pressure, which affects the appointments of key prosecutors and investigating magistrates. The judicial system consists of civilian courts, a military court, and a judicial council. International standards of criminal procedure are not observed in the military court, which consists largely of military officers with no legal training, and cases are often tried in a matter of minutes. In recent years, the nominally independent Beirut Bar Association (BBA) has become less willing to confront the judiciary, allegedly because of widespread corruption. Muhamad Mugraby, a prominent human rights attorney who launched a campaign for "judicial integrity," was disbarred by the BBA in January

2003. After continuing to practice law, he was arrested in August on charges of "impersonating a lawyer" and detained for three weeks.

Arbitrary arrests and detentions by Lebanese (and, occasionally, Syrian) security forces are commonplace, and both have used torture in the past to extract confessions. It is widely known that the Syrian-controlled security agencies monitor the telephones of both cabinet ministers and political dissidents. Dozens of Islamist militants were arrested in 2003 on national security grounds. In May 2003, Hanna Chalita, a Christian political activist, was arrested by Syrian forces at the Lebanese-Syrian border and detained for more than a week. In July, one of the scores of Lebanese political prisoners still held by Syria, Joseph Huways, died in custody after reportedly being denied medical treatment.

Foreign domestic workers are exploited routinely and physically abused by employers. Women enjoy most of the same rights as men, but suffer social and some legal discrimination. Since family and personal status matters are adjudicated by the religious authorities of each sectarian community, Muslim women are subject to discriminatory laws governing marriage, divorce, inheritance, and child custody. Women are underrepresented in politics, holding only three parliamentary seats and no cabinet positions, and do not receive equal social security provisions and other benefits. Men convicted of so-called honor crimes against women usually receive lenient sentences.

# Lesotho

**Population:** 1,800,000
**GNI/capita:** $530
**Life Expectancy:** 37
**Political Rights:** 2
**Civil Liberties:** 3
**Status:** Free
**Religious Groups:** Christian (80 percent), indigenous beliefs (20 percent)
**Ethnic Groups:** Sotho (99.7 percent), other, [including European and Asian] (0.3 percent)
**Capital:** Maseru

**Ten-Year Ratings Timeline (Political Rights, Civil Liberties, Status)**

| 1994 | 1995 | 1996 | 1997 | 1998 | 1999 | 2000 | 2001 | 2002 | 2003 |
|------|------|------|------|------|------|------|------|------|------|
| 4,4PF | 4,4PF | 4,4PF | 4,4PF | 4,4PF | 4,4PF | 4,4PF | 4,4PF | 2,3F | 2,3F |

**Overview:**     The Lesotho government moved forward with its historic prosecution of corrupt officials and Western companies in connection with a bribery scandal surrounding the World Bank–backed Lesotho Highlands Water Project. Despite signs of economic growth, Lesotho slid deeper into a severe drought that could leave more than a quarter of the country's 2.2 million people dependent on food aid in 2004.

Lesotho's status as a British protectorate saved it from incorporation into South Africa. King Moshoeshoe II reigned from independence in 1966 until the installation of his son as King Letsie III in a 1990 military coup. Democratic elections in 1993 did not lead to stability. After violent military infighting, assassinations, and a suspension of constitutional rule in 1994, King Letsie III abdicated to allow his father's reinstatement. He resumed the throne following the accidental death of his father in January 1996.

Troops from South Africa and Botswana were sent to this mountain kingdom at the request of Prime Minster Pakalitha Mosisili, under the mandate of the 14-country Southern Africa Development Community (SADC), in 1998 to quell army-backed violence and a potential overthrow of the government. The violence was touched off by the results of National Assembly elections. Although international observers described the voting as free and fair, the appearance of irregularities and the absence of opposition voices in government prompted demonstrators to reject the results that gave the ruling Lesotho Congress for Democracy (LCD) 79 of 80 National Assembly seats. At least 100 people were reportedly killed before order was restored. An agreement, drafted by the Commonwealth in 1998, allowed the elected, but highly unpopular, government to retain power, but stipulated that new elections be supervised by an independent election commission.

The 2002 legislative election was marked by a turnout of 68 percent. The ruling LCD captured 55 percent of votes cast, winning 77 of 78 constituency seats. The Lesotho People's Congress (LPC) won 1 seat. There are 80 constituency seats, but elections in two constituencies failed. The Basotho National Party won 21 of the 40 seats chosen by proportional representation, while the National Independent Party won 5 and the LPC won 4. Smaller parties won the remainder.

In August 2003, the country's High Court confirmed the conviction of Canadian construction conglomerate Acres International for paying bribes to Masupha Sole, the former head of the multi-billion-dollar dam and watershed project. Other multinational companies either have been convicted or remain under investigation. Sole is currently serving a 15-year prison sentence for his role in the scandal.

Entirely surrounded by South Africa, Lesotho is highly dependent on its powerful neighbor. Its economy is sustained by remittances from its many citizens who work in South African mines. Retrenchments at the mines, however, have contributed to high unemployment in Lesotho. Increased growth in the textile industry has party offset these losses, although some 40 percent of the population remains in absolute poverty.

**Political Rights and Civil Liberties:** The people of Lesotho are guaranteed the right to change their leaders through free and fair elections. The new "mixed member" voting system expanded the number of National Assembly seats by 40, to 120. The additional seats were chosen by proportional representation, while the others continued to be chosen by the first-past-the-post system of awarding seats to whoever gets the most votes. The Senate, the upper house of the bicameral legislature, includes royal appointees and Lesotho's 22 principal traditional chiefs, who still wield considerable authority in rural areas. Any elected government's exercise of its constitutional authority remains limited by the autonomy of the military, the royal family, and traditional clan structures.

The government generally respects freedom of speech and the press, but journalists have suffered occasional harassment or attack. The several independent newspapers routinely criticize the government. There are four private radio stations, and extensive South African radio and television broadcasts reach Lesotho.

Freedom of religion in this predominantly Christian country is generally respected. The government does not restrict academic freedom.

Freedom of assembly is generally respected, and several nongovernmental organizations operate openly. While labor rights are constitutionally guaranteed, the labor and trade union movement is weak and fragmented. Approximately 10 percent of the country's labor force is unionized. Of the remainder, most are engaged in subsistence agriculture or employment in South African mines. However, the textile industry has become increasingly important to the economy as a result of the United States' Africa Growth and Opportunity Act; the industry now provides 43 percent of all foreign exchange. Collective bargaining rights and the right to strike are recognized by law, but there are signs of an escalating crackdown on trade unions. In November, the police shot and killed two textile workers during a demonstration to demand wage increases, and arrested the secretary-general of Factory Workers' Union.

Courts are nominally independent, but higher courts are especially subject to outside influence. The large case backlog often leads to lengthy delays in trials. Mistreatment of civilians by security forces reportedly continues. Prison conditions are poor, but not life-threatening.

The constitution bars gender-based discrimination, but customary practice and law still restrict women's rights in several areas, including property rights and inheritance. Lesotho's constitution perpetuates the minority status of Basotho women married under customary law. A woman is considered a legal minor while her husband is alive. Domestic violence is reportedly widespread but is becoming increasingly socially unacceptable. Women's rights organizations have highlighted the importance of women's participation in the democratic process as part of a broader effort to educate women about their rights under customary and common law.

# ⬆ Liberia

**Population:** 3,300,000     **Political Rights:** 6
**GNI/capita:** $140            **Civil Liberties:** 6
**Life Expectancy:** 49        **Status:** Not Free
**Religious Groups:** Indigenous beliefs (40 percent),
Christian (40 percent), Muslim (20 percent)
**Ethnic Groups:** Indigenous tribes (95 percent), other
[including Americo-Liberians] (5 percent)
**Capital:** Monrovia
**Trend Arrow:** Liberia received an upward trend arrow due to a ceasefire and the departure of President Charles Taylor that led to an easing of violence and repression.

**Ten-Year Ratings Timeline (Political Rights, Civil Liberties, Status)**

| 1994 | 1995 | 1996 | 1997 | 1998 | 1999 | 2000 | 2001 | 2002 | 2003 |
|------|------|------|------|------|------|------|------|------|------|
| 7,6NF | 7,6NF | 7,6NF | 4,5PF | 4,5PF | 4,5PF | 5,6PF | 6,5PF | 6,6NF | 6,6NF |

**Overview:**     As rebel troops struck Monrovia in July 2003, President Charles Taylor abandoned the presidency and sought asylum in Nigeria. West African leaders negotiated an end to the fighting and Nigerian-led peacekeepers arrived in Liberia ahead of the installation of a transitional government. Before seeking asylum, Taylor was indicted by the UN-backed Special Court for Sierra Leone for war crimes.

Liberia was settled in 1821 by freed slaves from the United States and became an independent republic in 1847. Americo-Liberians, descendants of the freed slaves, dominated the country until 1980, when army Sergeant Samuel Doe led a bloody coup and murdered President William Tolbert. Doe's regime concentrated power among members of his Krahn ethnic group and suppressed others. Forces led by Taylor, a former government minister, and backed by Gio and Mano ethnic groups that had been subjected to severe repression, launched a guerrilla war from neighboring Cote d'Ivoire against the Doe regime on Christmas Eve 1989. In 1990, Nigeria, under the aegis of the Economic Community of West African States (ECOWAS), led an armed intervention force, preventing Taylor from seizing the capital but failing to protect Doe from being captured and tortured to death by a splinter rebel group. A peace accord in 1996 led to elections in 1997 that Taylor won.

The peace accord, however, was not entirely effective. Long-standing grievances were not resolved, and Taylor made little effort to seek genuine reconciliation. Many of his rivals were forced to flee the country. Some used neighboring Guinea as a staging ground from which to launch their rebellion against Taylor. New York–based Human Rights Watch reported in November 2003 that Guinea had imported arms that were used by the rebel Liberians United for Reconciliation and Democracy (LURD).

In 2003, as Liberians placed their dead in front of the U.S. Embassy in the capital, Monrovia, international pressure mounted for Washington to intervene militarily to stop the rebel assault on the city that began in March. A handful of U.S. marines eventually arrived to support West African peacekeepers with logistics, but the most significant step the United States made was calling for President Taylor to step down. Spurred on by his indictment for war crimes in neighboring Sierra Leone, he resigned, handing over power to Vice President Moses Blah and accepting Nigeria's offer of asylum.

Taylor's departure from Liberia in August 2003 almost immediately stopped the war. ECOWAS helped negotiate an end to the fighting between Taylor's forces, LURD, and the rebel Movement for Democracy in Liberia (MODEL). The West African peacekeepers were to be part of an eventual 15,000-strong UN-led force that is to oversee disarmament and demobilization. Human rights abuses abated following the ceasefire, but violations continued, especially in the countryside, where peacekeepers continued to have problems gaining access.

Delegates to the peace talks in 2003 chose businessman Gyude Bryant as Liberia's interim president after Taylor fled to Nigeria. The delegates allocated posts in the transitional parliament to the former ruling National Patriotic Party (NPP), LURD, MODEL, other political parties, and civil society groups. Under the terms of the peace deal, the NPP and the two rebel groups can each name five ministers to the 21-member cabinet.

The task of rebuilding Liberia is enormous. The country lacks electricity, running water, a functioning educational system, and proper medical facilities. A generation has been scarred by war. An estimated 38,000 combatants are to be disarmed, including some 15,000 child soldiers. More than 300,000 Liberians have fled the country, and about 500,000 are internally displaced.

Fourteen years of intermittent civil war in Liberia have brought fighting to three neighboring countries and claimed 200,000 lives in Liberia alone. The best chance for lasting peace is to find a regional solution. Peacekeeping troops have been deployed to neighboring Sierra Leone and Cote d'Ivoire as well. Fighters have routinely crossed the borders of those two countries, as well as into Guinea. Taylor reportedly was still pulling strings in Liberia from Nigeria, and a UN panel monitoring sanctions against Liberia said that Taylor had tried to take government revenues while in exile. The panel said it would maintain a diamonds and timber exporting embargo on Liberia, as well as an arms purchasing embargo.

## Political Rights and Civil Liberties:

Charles Taylor and his party assumed power after the 1997 elections, which were generally free and fair. The votes for the presidency and the National Assembly, on the basis of proportional representation, were held under provisions of the 1986 constitution. The polls constituted Liberia's most genuine electoral exercise in decades but were conducted in an atmosphere of intimidation. Taylor's victory reflected more of a vote for peace than for a particular ideology, as many people believed that the only way to stop the war was to make him president. After Taylor fled to Nigeria in August 2003, a transitional government was installed to lead the country to elections in 2005.

Liberia's independent media have survived at the cost of extensive self-censorship. Employees have suffered from constant surveillance, harassment, threats, detentions, and beatings. Taylor owned KISS-FM, the only countrywide FM radio station. State television and one private station broadcast only irregularly.

Independent radio stations broadcast religious programming, but the Roman Catholic radio station, Veritas, has had programming on human rights issues. Its offices suffered a mortar attack during the fighting in Monrovia in July, and it was off the air for a month. Talking Drum Studios, which is run by Search for Common Ground and broadcasts programs promoting peace, was looted. Taylor closed down six rural radio stations in March. Internet access was not specifically restricted under the Taylor government, but many Liberians believed e-mail was monitored.

Liberian journalists were targeted by government forces and rebel soldiers during the fighting in and around Monrovia in 2003. Two foreign journalists were injured. The Ghana-based Media Foundation of West Africa in February urged the Taylor government to stop "the unending spate of physical assault, cruel torture, and sheer impunity" perpetrated against journalists and human rights activists. The foundation said journalist Throble Suah of the independent *Inquirer* newspaper had been beaten into a coma by forces of the government's Anti-Terrorist Unit.

Religious freedom is respected in practice, but Muslims have been targeted because many Mandingos follow Islam. Academic freedom was restricted under the Taylor government. Students feared expressing political views opposed to the government. Exiled student leaders returned to the country after the transitional government was installed.

Numerous civil society groups, including human rights organizations, operate in the country, but their employees are subject to repeated harassment by security forces. Human rights workers have been allowed access to prisons, where condi-

tions are harsh and torture is used to extract confessions. The right to strike, organize, and bargain collectively is permitted by law, but there is little union activity
because of the lack of economic activity. Two umbrella unions cover some 60,000
workers, but most of them are unemployed. There is forced labor in rural areas, and
child labor is widespread.

The judiciary is subject to executive influence, corruption, and intimidation by
security forces, which operate with impunity. International human rights groups have
urged Nigeria to hand Taylor over to the UN-backed Special Court for Sierra Leone,
which has indicted him for war crimes linked to his alleged involvement in the arms-
for-diamonds trade that helped sustain Sierra Leone's civil war.

Civilians were often the casualties during the civil war, suffering at the hands of
both rebel groups and government troops. Abuses included torture of captives while
in incommunicado detention, rape of women and girls, forced labor, forced military
recruitment of men and boys, and extrajudicial killings.

Societal ethnic discrimination is rife, and the Taylor government discriminated
against indigenous ethnic groups that opposed Taylor during the civil war, especially the Mandingo and Krahn ethnic groups.

Treatment of women varies by ethnic group, religion, and social status. Many
women continue to suffer from physical abuse and traditional societal discrimination, despite constitutionally guaranteed equality. Rape, including gang rape, was
rampant during the civil war. Women and girls were often abducted as laborers and
sex slaves, while others joined rebel groups or militias to protect themselves.

# Libya

**Population:** 5,500,000    **Political Rights:** 7
**GNI/capita:** $5,944    **Civil Liberties:** 7
**Life Expectancy:** 76    **Status:** Not Free
**Religious Groups:** Sunni Muslim (97 percent),
other (3 percent)
**Ethnic Groups:** Arab-Berber (97 percent), other [including
Greek, Italian, Egyptian, Pakistani, Turkish, Indian] (3 percent)
**Capital:** Tripoli

**Ten-Year Ratings Timeline (Political Rights, Civil Liberties, Status)**

| 1994 | 1995 | 1996 | 1997 | 1998 | 1999 | 2000 | 2001 | 2002 | 2003 |
|------|------|------|------|------|------|------|------|------|------|
| 7,7NF | 7,7NF | 7,7NF | 7,7NF | 7,7NF | 7,7NF | 7,7NF | 7,7NF | 7,7NF | 7,7NF |

**Overview:**
Libya made significant progress in its bid to break out from
international isolation with the lifting of UN sanctions in
September 2003. Despite limited cooperation from Libya on
the war against terrorism, the U.S. government opted to maintain its unilateral sanctions against Libya, citing concerns with Libya's possible development of weapons
of mass destruction, its lingering ties to terrorism, and its abysmal human rights record.
In June, Libyan leader Mu'ammar al-Qadhafi appointed a new prime minister and
announced broad economic reforms.

Libyan independence dates to 1951, when King Idris assumed power following a UN resolution establishing Libya as an independent and sovereign state. French and British forces had occupied Libya during World War II. Prior to the Allied occupation, Libya had been an Italian colony since an invasion in 1912. In the previous centuries, Libya was under Ottoman rule.

In 1969, Colonel Qadhafi seized power at the age of 25 in a military coup that deposed the staunchly pro-West King Idris. Qadhafi railed against Western control of Libya's oil fields and the presence of foreign military bases in Libya. He ushered in a highly personalized style of rule that combines elements of pan-Arabism with Islamic ideals. Qadhafi purported to find a "third way" that rejects both Western-style democracy and communism.

In the years following Qadhafi's rise to power, Libya gained international pariah status with its sponsorship of various acts of terrorism, as well as its support of insurgencies throughout sub-Saharan Africa. During the 1980s, Libyan meddling in the war in neighboring Chad proved to be a costly military failure. Libyan involvement in the 1988 bombing of Pan Am flight 103 over Lockerbie, Scotland, led the United Nations to impose sanctions on Libya in 1992. The sanctions included embargoes on air traffic and the import of arms and oil production equipment. The United States has maintained its own sanctions against Libya since 1981, citing Libyan sponsorship of terrorism.

Beginning in 1999, Qadhafi embarked on a strategy aimed at ending Libya's international isolation. He surrendered two Libyan nationals suspected in the Pan Am 103 bombing and agreed to compensate families of victims of the 1989 bombing of a French airliner over Niger. The Libyan government also accepted responsibility for the 1984 death of British police officer Yvonne Fletcher, killed by shots fired from the Libyan embassy in London. Qadhafi also expelled members of the Palestinian terrorist organization headed by Abu Nidal.

In response to Libya's surrendering of two terrorism suspects, the United Nations opted to suspend sanctions against Libya in 1999, although the permanent lifting of sanctions was withheld pending Libya's unequivocal renunciation of terrorism. The United States eased some of its restrictions by allowing for the limited sale of food and medicines to Libya, but maintained its travel ban as well as other restrictions. Britain opted to resume diplomatic ties with Libya, reopening its embassy in Tripoli in March 2001. The European Union followed suit by lifting sanctions, but maintains an arms embargo.

The two terrorism suspects went on trial in March 2000 at the International Court of Justice in the Netherlands, but under Scottish law. One of the suspects was found guilty of murder in January 2001 and sentenced to life imprisonment, while the other suspect was acquitted of all charges and freed. Following the trial, the United States and Britain repeated demands that Libya formally accept responsibility for the bombing, compensate the victims' families, and renounce terrorism.

In August 2003, the Libyan government struck a deal with the families of the Pan Am 103 bombing victims, offering to pay $2.7 billion in compensation. The victims' families will be awarded roughly $10 million each. In response, the United Nations voted to lift sanctions on Libya in September, removing a significant hurdle to Libya's reintegration into the global community. The Libyan government remains deadlocked with the French families of the victims of the 1989 UTA airliner bombing over Niger. Libya has already paid a total of $33 million to the victims' families and proposed to pay an additional $1 million per family, but the UTA families have said the compensation package is still too low.

The U.S. government continues to maintain unilateral sanctions against Libya. Washington remains concerned about Libya's potential links to terrorism as well as its long-range missiles and chemical weapons programs. These sanctions include a prohibition of U.S. investment in Libya, a ban on U.S. oil companies doing business in Libya, and a travel ban that forbids the use of American passports for travel to Libya. Libya has also remained on the U.S. government's list of state sponsors of terrorism. In addition, the United States maintains a freeze on Libyan assets. U.S. officials are discussing the possibility of extending the travel ban for only 90 days as opposed to the typical year-long extension. This reduced period is intended to signal to the Libyan government that Washington might be willing to upgrade relations if Libya is more forthcoming on the issues of terrorism and weapons of mass destruction.

Despite its oil wealth, the Libyan economy remains hobbled by inefficient state controls and corruption. Libya's rapid population growth has also led to rising unemployment, currently estimated at 30 percent. In addition, years of sanctions have taken a toll on the lucrative oil sector, with production down to 1.3 million barrels per day from 3.7 million barrels per day in the 1970s. Acknowledging the need for change, Qadhafi has authorized wide-ranging economic reforms. In June, the Libyan leader announced a plan to privatize the economy and promote direct foreign investment. In a bid to attract foreign investment, the exchange rate was liberalized and trade licenses were abolished to allow integration with the global market. Libya has also applied to join the World Trade Organization.

**Political Rights and Civil Liberties:** Libyans cannot change their government democratically. Colonel Muammar al-Qadhafi rules by decree with little accountability or transparency. Libya's governing principles stem from Qadhafi's *Green Book*, a treatise that combines Islamic ideals with elements of socialism and pan-Arabism. Qadhafi rejects Western-style democracy and political parties, claiming instead that his country is a *jamahiriyah*, or state of the masses. As such, Qadhafi calls for direct popular rule. The reality, however, is that power is tightly held by Qadhafi and a relatively small inner circle of advisers.

Libyans do not have the right to organize into different political parties. While people do play a role in popular congresses, they do not affect the balance of power that remains squarely in Qadhafi's control. Extra-governmental bodies, including the revolutionary committees and people's committees, aid Qadhafi and serve as tools of repression. There is no significant legal opposition in Libya, and people's political choices are subject to the domination of Qadhafi and his esoteric political system.

Free media do not exist in Libya. The government severely limits freedom of speech and of the press, particularly any criticism of Qadhafi. The state owns and controls all print and broadcast media outlets and thereby maintains a monopoly on the flow of information. Satellite television is widely available, although foreign programming is censored at times. Internet access is limited, as there is only one service provider (owned by Qadhafi's son). However, reportedly, the number of Internet users is growing.

Freedom of religion is restricted, and the government controls most mosques and Islamic institutions in Libya, which is 97 percent Sunni Muslim. Islamic organizations whose teachings and beliefs differ from the official, government-approved version of Islam are banned. Academic freedom is severely restricted.

Freedom of assembly, demonstration, and open public discussion are severely restricted. Qadhafi maintains an extensive internal security apparatus. The Libyan leader is ruthless with suspected opponents and is able to mobilize his multilayered security apparatus quickly. These multiple and overlapping security services rely on an extensive network of informers that are present throughout Libyan society.

The judiciary is not independent. Security forces have the power to pass sentences without a trial, and the government has used summary judicial proceedings to suppress domestic dissent. Political trials are held in secret with no due process considerations. Arbitrary arrest and torture are commonplace. In October, Amnesty International called on the Libyan authorities to release or grant new trials to 151 students and professionals who have been detained since 1998. They were charged with belonging to an unauthorized group, the Libyan Islamic Group, and have been denied access to a fair trial since that time.

The largely Berber and Tuareg minorities face discrimination. While women's status has improved in some areas like education and employment, discrimination continues in other areas where local traditions predominate. Female genital mutilation is still practiced in remote rural areas. Violence against women also continues to be a problem.

# Liechtenstein

**Population:** 40,000   **Political Rights:** 1
**GNI/capita:** $25,000   **Civil Liberties:** 1
**Life Expectancy:** na   **Status:** Free
**Religious Groups:** Roman Catholic (76.2 percent),
Protestant (7 percent), unknown (10.6 percent),
other (6.2 percent)
**Ethnic Groups:** Alemannic (86 percent), other
[including Italian and Turkish] (14 percent)
**Capital:** Vaduz

**Ten-Year Ratings Timeline (Political Rights, Civil Liberties, Status)**

| 1994 | 1995 | 1996 | 1997 | 1998 | 1999 | 2000 | 2001 | 2002 | 2003 |
|------|------|------|------|------|------|------|------|------|------|
| 1,1F | 1,1F | 1,1F | 1,1F | 1,1F | 1,1F | 1,1F | 1,1F | 1,1F | 1,1F |

**Overview:** Liechtenstein underwent a major constitutional reform in March 2003 that strengthened the monarch's powers considerably, giving the Council of Europe reason to consider placing the quality of its democracy under monitoring. However, the council decided against monitoring, and there is no evidence yet that the prince plans to use the full extent of his constitutional powers to undermine Liechtenstein's democracy.

Liechtenstein was established in its present form in 1719 after being purchased by Austria's Liechtenstein family. Native residents of the state are primarily descendants of the Germanic Alemanni tribe, and the local language is a German dialect. From 1938 to 1997, the principality was governed by a coalition of the Progressive Citizens' Party (FBP) and the Fatherland Union (VU). The FBP was the senior coalition partner for most of this period. Otmar Hasler of the FBP became leader of his party and prime minister after the FBP won a majority of seats in parliament in February 2001 elections.

Liechtenstein's traditional banking secrecy laws have been relaxed in the face of international scrutiny. In 2000, the Organization for Economic Cooperation and Development's Financial Action Task Force labeled the principality "noncooperative" on money laundering thanks to its secrecy laws. Under pressure, Liechtenstein passed a law ending anonymity for account holders. It was removed from the noncooperative list in June 2001, but after the terrorist attacks in the United States on September 11, 2001, concerns reemerged that Islamic terrorists could be laundering money there. The IMF reported in September 2003 that Liechtenstein had made progress updating its banking regulations, but worried that there might not be enough staff to enforce regulations fully.

An amendment legislating a major constitutional reform was passed by a referendum in March 2003, with just over 64 percent of voters approving. It concentrated a good deal more power in the hands of the monarch, currently Prince Hans-Adam II. The prince had threatened to leave Liechtenstein for Austria if the measure was not passed.

The new law gives the prince the power to dismiss the government, veto legislation, and appoint judges. However, it removed the prince's right to rule by emergency decree. The Council of Europe, which monitors democracy among its member countries, expressed concern and considered placing the democratic standards of Liechtenstein's political system under formal monitoring. It decided against doing so (probably thanks in part to extensive lobbying from the principality). Though the measure makes Hans-Adam possibly the most powerful monarch in Europe, there is no sign yet that the prince plans to abuse his powers. He has announced that he will hand over his governmental power to his son and heir, Prince Alois, in August 2004 while remaining head of state.

**Political Rights and Civil Liberties:** The people of Liechtenstein can change their government democratically, but the unelected monarch won greater powers in 2003, making him perhaps the most powerful in Europe. He has the power to dismiss the government, veto legislation and appoint judges. These powers were granted to him democratically by a solid majority of Liechtenstein's citizens in the March 2003 referendum. The legislature consists of 25 deputies chosen in fair elections carried out under proportional representation.

Parties are able to organize freely, and two have dominated Liechtenstein's politics over the last half-century. There are a few independents in the legislature. Switzerland and Austria, the two countries that surround Liechtenstein, have a good measure of influence on the tiny principality, and Liechtenstein is a member of the European Economic Area, a free-trade area of countries that are not members of the European Union. Its currency is the Swiss franc. Freely elected representatives determine the policies of the government, but the monarch can now theoretically veto policies and threaten the government with dismissal.

The constitution guarantees freedom of expression and of the media. There is one private television station competing with the state broadcaster, and the only radio station is in private hands. The two daily newspapers are aligned roughly with the two major political parties. Austria's and Switzerland's broadcasts are available and popular in the country. Internet access is unfettered.

The constitution establishes Roman Catholicism as the state religion but protects freedom of belief. Catholic or Protestant religious education is mandatory, but exceptions are routinely granted. All religious groups are tax exempt. The government respects academic freedom.

The right of association is protected, and the principality has one small trade union.

Judges are appointed by the prince. Due process is respected, and conditions in prisons are acceptable. After the controversy over the monarch's new powers, the Council of Europe's secretary-general sought to reassure those concerned about democracy that "Liechtenstein's status as a law-based state is unarguable." The IMF rated the financial-services regulators, important to a country so reliant on banking, as capable but too few to police all banks and account holders fully.

The abortion law is restrictive, allowing the procedure only when the life or health (including mental health) of the woman is threatened.

# Lithuania

**Population:** 3,500,000
**GNI/capita:** $3,350
**Life Expectancy:** 73
**Religious Groups:** Roman Catholic, Lutheran, Russian Orthodox, other
**Ethnic Groups:** Lithuanian (80 percent), Russian (9 percent), Polish (7 percent), Byelorussian (2 percent), other (2 percent)
**Capital:** Vilnius

**Political Rights:** 1
**Civil Liberties:** 2
**Status:** Free

**Ten-Year Ratings Timeline (Political Rights, Civil Liberties, Status)**

| 1994 | 1995 | 1996 | 1997 | 1998 | 1999 | 2000 | 2001 | 2002 | 2003 |
|------|------|------|------|------|------|------|------|------|------|
| 1,3F | 1,2F | 1,2F | 1,2F | 1,2F | 1,2F | 1,2F | 1,2F | 1,2F | 1,2F |

**Overview:**

In a highly publicized referendum in May 2003, 90 percent of voters voiced their approval of Lithuania's proposed European Union accession. A second-round runoff presidential election on January 5 saw former Prime Minister Rolandas Paskas defeat the heavily favored incumbent, Valdas Adamkus. Barely ten months after assuming office, Paskas was facing an increasing threat of impeachment following allegations that his campaign's main financial backer and some of his aides were deeply involved with organized crime.

Lithuania merged with Poland in the sixteenth century and was subsequently absorbed by Russia in the eighteenth century. After gaining its independence at the end of World War I, Lithuania was annexed by the Soviet Union in 1940 under a secret protocol of the 1939 Hitler-Stalin pact. The country regained its independence with the collapse of the U.S.S.R. in 1991.

Following the 1996 parliamentary elections, the Homeland Union/Lithuanian Conservatives (HU/LC) and Christian Democrats formed a center-right coalition government with Gediminas Vagnorius of the HU/LC as prime minister. In January 1998, the Lithuanian-American independent candidate, Valdas Adamkus, was narrowly elected president.

Growing tensions between Adamkus and Vagnorius eventually led to the resignation of Vagnorius, who was succeeded by Vilnius mayor and HU/LC member Rolandas Paksas in May. However, Paksas stepped down just five months later in protest over the controversial sale of part of the state-owned Mazeikiu Nafta oil complex to the U.S. energy firm, Williams International. HU/LC member and parliamentary First Deputy Chairman Andrius Kubilius succeeded Paksas as prime minister in November.

Apparently because of the public's dissatisfaction over the government's economic austerity policies, the ruling HU/LC experienced a resounding defeat in the October 2000 parliamentary election. The Social Democratic Coalition secured the most votes. However, the informal New Policy electoral bloc, composed of an ideologically diverse cohort of right- and left-wing parties, bypassed the Social Democratic Coalition to form a bare-majority centrist government. Paksas was chosen again to be prime minister.

After only eight months in power, this unstable ruling coalition collapsed following disagreements over the budget and privatization plans for the country's energy sector. Paksas was replaced in July by Algirdas Brazauskas, the chairman of the Lithuanian Social Democratic Party (LSDP). The more ideologically compatible LSDP and New Alliance (Social Liberals) subsequently formed a new ruling coalition government.

In presidential elections held on December 22, 2002, President Adamkus received 35 percent of the vote, not enough for a first-round victory, which requires a candidate to receive more than 50 percent. Adamkus faced Paksas, the second-place winner with 20 percent of the vote, in a January 5, 2003, runoff election. Surprisingly, Paskas defeated Adamkus, who had successfully secured Lithuania invitations to both the EU and NATO. Waging a media-savvy campaign that focused on poverty, corruption and bad government, Paksas received 54.9 percent of the vote to Adamkus's 45.1 percent.

Despite early fears that Lithuanian voters would fail to meet the 50 percent turnout threshold needed to validate the May 10 to 11 EU accession referendum, 63.3 percent of voters cast their ballots, with 90 percent voting to accept Lithuania's invitation to join the EU in April 2005. On September 16, the Lithuanian parliament overwhelmingly ratified the EU Accession Treaty, which was signed into law by President Paksas three days later.

Impeachment seems increasingly likely for the newly elected Paksas. His administration has been rocked by the leaking of a security services report in late October alleging that the main financial backer in Paksas's presidential campaign, Russian Jurijus Borisovas, sold illegal arms to Sudan and that Borisovas, along with some of Paksas's close advisers, were linked with organized crime. Subsequently,

Paskas was charged with illegally granting Borisovas Lithuanian citizenship. In late November, thousands of Lithuanians demonstrated in Vilnius, demanding Paskas's resignation. The parliamentary committee investigating Paskas will announce its findings on December 1, 2003.

A plan negotiated by Lithuanian, Russian, and EU officials for a transit system that allows residents of the Russian exclave of Kaliningrad to visit the rest of the Russian Federation was implemented on July 1, effectively finalizing Lithuania's borders with Russia.

Lithuania supported the U.S.-led war in Iraq and has sent 100 troops to serve in the occupation force in that country.

**Political Rights and Civil Liberties:** Lithuanians can change their government democratically. The 1992 constitution established a 141-member parliament (Seimas), in which 71 seats are selected in single-mandate constituencies and 70 seats are chosen by proportional representation, all for four-year terms. The president is directly elected for a five-year term. The 2000 national legislative election and the 2002-2003 presidential vote were conducted freely and fairly. All permanent residents are allowed to run for office and vote in local government elections, while only citizens can participate in national elections.

Lithuania suffered a series of corruption scandals in 2003, most notably the impending impeachment of President Rolandas Paskas over charges that his campaign's major financial backer, Jurijus Borisovas, sold illegal arms to Sudan and that Borisovas and some of Paskas's closest aides have strong ties to organized crime. Paskas is also being investigated for granting Borisovas Lithuanian citizenship on questionable grounds. In addition, diplomats at Lithuanian consulates in Belarus and Russia have been dismissed because of bribery charges, and several judges were removed from office after a smuggling ring involving senior civil servants and police officers was exposed. In August, the head of the National Payments Agency, Evaldas Cljauskas, was forced to resign amid charges of embezzlement. The ongoing scandal involving the 1999 privatization of part of the Mazeikiu Nafta oil complex continued to take its toll, with charges of embezzlement levied against 20 individuals, including 2 former ministers and a deputy minister.

The government generally respects freedom of speech and of the press. There is a wide variety of privately owned newspapers, and several independent, as well as state-run, television and radio stations broadcast throughout the country. On September 30, a Vilnius court overruled the shutdown of a pro-Chechen rebel Web site, Kavkaz-Center, hosted on a Lithuanian server. In January, a Lithuanian state security agent was videotaped attempting to solicit "comprising information" about two Lithuanian dailies, *Respublika* and *Vakaro zinios*, prompting a government investigation.

Freedom of religion is guaranteed by law and largely enjoyed in practice in this predominantly Roman Catholic country. Academic freedom is respected.

Freedom of assembly and association is generally respected. Workers have the right to form and join trade unions, to strike, and to engage in collective bargaining. However, ongoing problems include inadequate or employer-biased legislation, management discrimination against union members, and the court system's lack of expertise in labor-related issues.

The judiciary is largely independent of the executive branch, and the recently revised Law of Courts has fortified its autonomy. However, there is a severe lack of qualified judges, who consequently suffer from excessive workloads. There have been credible reports of police abuse of suspects and detainees, and prison overcrowding and pretrial detention remain serious problems.

The rights of the country's ethnic minorities are protected in practice. In 1992, Lithuania extended citizenship to all those born within its borders, and more than 90 percent of nonethnic Lithuanians, mostly Russians and Poles, became citizens. In October 2003, the Seimas ratified Protocol 13 of the Convention for the Protection of Human Rights and Fundamental Freedoms, abolishing capital punishment in all cases.

Women are under-represented in upper-level management positions and earn lower average wages than men.

# Luxembourg

**Population:** 500,000  **Political Rights:** 1
**GNI/capita:** $39,840  **Civil Liberties:** 1
**Life Expectancy:** 78  **Status:** Free
**Religious Groups:** Roman Catholic (87 percent),
Protestant (13 percent), other [including Jewish and Muslim]
**Ethnic Groups:** Celtic, Portuguese, Italian, Slavs, other
**Capital:** Luxembourg

**Ten-Year Ratings Timeline (Political Rights, Civil Liberties, Status)**

| 1994 | 1995 | 1996 | 1997 | 1998 | 1999 | 2000 | 2001 | 2002 | 2003 |
|------|------|------|------|------|------|------|------|------|------|
| 1,1F | 1,1F | 1,1F | 1,1F | 1,1F | 1,1F | 1,1F | 1,1F | 1,1F | 1,1F |

**Overview:**

In 2003, Luxembourg's coalition government remained broadly popular, though the poll numbers of the junior party, the Democratic Party (PD), saw a decline. In foreign policy, Luxembourg aligned itself with France, Belgium, and Germany in supporting the creation of a European-only military planning cell, widely seen as a reaction to the American-led war in Iraq.

The Grand Duchy of Luxembourg was established in 1815, after the Napoleonic wars. Following a brief merger with Belgium, it reemerged with its current borders in 1839. The country has always faced the possibility of domination by its neighbors—it was occupied by Germany in both world wars—and it abandoned neutrality in favor of joining NATO in 1949. After joining in an economic union with Belgium and the Netherlands in 1948, Luxembourg became one of the six founding members of the European Community (now the European Union) in 1957. Because it has a small, open economy, Luxembourg's relationship with the EU is highly important in its politics; it adopted the euro as its currency in 1999. A former prime minister, Jacques Santer, served as president of the EU's commission from 1995 to 1999.

Over the course of 2003, the PD's opinion ratings fell in polls, while the opposition Socialist Worker Party's (POSL) rose. The Christian Social Party (PCS) has been in coalition with both parties and there was speculation that in the elections due by June 2004, a new coalition of the PCS and POSL would emerge. However, the POSL's new leader, Jean Asselborn, may be too left-wing for many undecided voters. The government itself remained relatively popular in 2003, despite several years of lackluster economic growth: just 1.2 percent gross domestic product growth in 2001, 1.1 percent in 2002, and a forecast of similar results in 2003.

After the end of the war in Iraq, in April 2003, France, Germany, Belgium, and Luxembourg announced their intention to create a military planning cell based in the Belgian town of Tervuren. This was interpreted by many as a French-led move to undermine the U.S.-dominated NATO, and it caused deep divisions in Europe. Luxembourgers generally opposed the war.

Luxembourg is a strong proponent of greater European integration and has supported the adoption of a new EU draft constitution without watered down amendments. The draft would strengthen European cooperation in many areas and create a new presidency of the European Council (representing the member states rather than the EU itself). Luxembourg's prime minister, Jean-Claude Juncker, has been spoken of as a likely candidate for this presidency.

**Political Rights and Civil Liberties:** Luxembourgers can change their government democratically. The head of state is the unelected Grand Duke Henri, but his powers are largely ceremonial. The unicameral legislature consists of 60 deputies elected by proportional representation. Voting is compulsory for all who are registered. (Residents from EU countries may vote after six years' residence but are not obliged to do so; non-EU residents may not vote. Foreigners comprise a third of Luxembourg's population.)

The political party system is open to the rise of new parties, as seen by the growth of the Action Committee for Democracy and Pension Reform, originally a one-issue party focusing on higher pensions, which first had deputies elected in 1989 and is now a significant fourth party. There are three traditionally strong parties in Luxembourg's politics: the Christian Social Party (PCS), traditionally aligned with the Catholic Church; the Democratic Party (PD), which favors free-market economic policies and a smaller welfare state; and the Socialist Worker Party (POSL), a formerly radical but now center-left party representing the working class. The current government, elected in 1999, is a coalition of the PCS, which has taken part in almost all governments in Liechtenstein's modern history, and the PD.

The government is largely free from corruption; Transparency International, a corruption watchdog, ranked Luxembourg the eleventh cleanest of the 133 countries it surveyed in 2003.

Freedom of expression is guaranteed by the constitution, and Luxembourg has a vibrant media market. A single media conglomerate, RTL, dominates the broadcast radio and TV market, and its broadcasts are popular in Luxembourg's neighboring countries. Newspapers represent a broad range of opinion. Internet access is unrestricted.

Roman Catholicism is the dominant religion, but there is no state religion and the state pays the salaries of ministers from a variety of religions. Students may choose to study either the Roman Catholic religion or ethics; most choose the former. Protestant education is available on demand.

Civic groups and NGOs may operate freely. Freedom of assembly is protected, and Luxembourgers may organize in trade unions. The right to strike is constitution-ally guaranteed.

The judiciary is independent, but its judges are appointed by the grand duke. Prisoners are humanely treated in police stations and prisons.

In part because of its conservative social mores, women comprise just under 40 percent of the labor force, and there remains a significant gap between men's and women's wages. Though abortion law does not technically provide for abortion on demand, a woman who has had an abortion while under "distress" is considered not to have violated the law, and "distress" is interpreted liberally.

# ↑ Macedonia

**Population:** 2,100,000
**GNI/capita:** $1,690
**Life Expectancy:** 73
**Political Rights:** 3
**Civil Liberties:** 3
**Status:** Partly Free
**Religious Groups:** Macedonian Orthodox (67 percent),
Muslim (30 percent), other (3 percent)
**Ethnic Groups:** Macedonian (64 percent),
Albanian (25 percent), Turkish (4 percent), Roma (2 percent),
Serb (2 percent), other (3 percent)
**Capital:** Skopje
**Trend Arrow:** Macedonia received an upward trend arrow due to the achievement of some progress in implementing the 2001 Ohrid Accords, including the legalization of Tetovo University, and the disbanding of an extremist paramilitary group.

**Ten-Year Ratings Timeline (Political Rights, Civil Liberties, Status)**

| 1994 | 1995 | 1996 | 1997 | 1998 | 1999 | 2000 | 2001 | 2002 | 2003 |
|------|------|------|------|------|------|------|------|------|------|
| 4,3PF | 4,3PF | 4,3PF | 4,3PF | 3,3PF | 3,3PF | 4,3PF | 4,4PF | 3,3PF | 3,3PF |

**Overview:**

The nature of Macedonian statehood continued to be precarious throughout 2003. During the course of the year, three of the five signatories to the 2001 Ohrid Accords—which had barely averted a civil war in the country—repudiated the agreement, and two of those parties calling for an outright partition of the country into Macedonian and Albanian sections. Tensions in Macedonia also increased significantly in late summer as a government hunt for an Albanian criminal threatened to again spark intercommunal violence. Nevertheless, there were some significant positive developments: in January, a paramilitary group was disbanded, while in June, the government agreed to legalize the long-disputed Albanian language university in Tetovo.

Macedonia, a republic in the former Yugoslav Communist federation, was recognized as an independent state in 1992. Parliamentary elections in 1998 resulted in the first transfer of power from the left-of-center governmental coalition that had ruled Macedonia since independence to a grouping of right-of-center parties led by former prime minister Ljupco Georgievski's Internal Macedonian Revolutionary Organization-Democratic Party of Macedonian National Unity (VMRO-DPMNE).

Relations between the country's two primary ethnic groups—Macedonian Slavs and ethnic Albanians—deteriorated precipitously after the 1999 Kosovo war. By 2000, Albanian guerrillas who had participated in the Kosovo conflict were operating in Macedonia, often using NATO-occupied Kosovo as their base. Among the guerrillas' political demands were changes to the Macedonian constitution, greater use of the Albanian language in official institutions, and an increase in the number of ethnic Albanians in the civil services. In August 2001, an agreement reached in the town of Ohrid produced a temporary lull in the conflict, which was estimated to have cost the fragile Macedonian economy more than $800 million.

In mid-September 2002, the latest set of parliamentary elections were held. The elections returned to power the left-of-center Social Democratic Party of Macedonia (SDSM), led by Branko Crvenkovski, which succeeded in ousting Georgievski's right-of-center coalition. As in previous governments, ethnic Albanian parties were included in the governing coalition. After the 2002 elections, the Democratic Union for Integration (BDI) became Crvenkovski's coalition partner. The elections, however, were not interpreted as a significant change in the ideological mood of the population, but rather as a vote against the corruption of the incumbents; indeed, government corruption has become a recurring theme in post-1991 Macedonian politics.

Implementation of the 2001 Ohrid Accords has proceeded in fits and starts. On the negative side, three of the five signatories to the 2001 agreement repudiated it in 2003, and two of those three have called for an outright partition of the country. Nevertheless, some progress has been made. In January, the government disbanded a paramilitary group, the "Lions," after a two-day standoff with police north of Skopje. The Lions were a purely ethnic-Macedonian paramilitary group composed largely of criminals and ethnic extremists.

In late August and early September, a return to fighting was barely averted when ethnic Albanian extremists kidnapped two individuals. The extremists belonged to the so-called Albanian National Army (AkSH), which has been active in attempting to create a "Greater Albania" throughout the region; in April, UN officials had declared the AkSH a terrorist organization. Although an escalation of violence was prevented when the two hostages were released the same day, the military mobilization that followed and a series of bomb attacks in the capital indicated how unstable the situation remains.

Since gaining independence, Macedonia has suffered from disputes with most of its neighbors over a number of issues: the name "Macedonia," with Greece; the status of the Macedonian language, with Bulgaria; and Macedonia's northern border, with Serbia and Montenegro. Most of these external disputes have been successfully resolved. The international community has tried in a number of ways to support Macedonia's fragile existence, most notably in April 2002, when the European Union (EU) signed a Stabilization and Association Agreement (considered the first step toward full EU membership) with Skopje.

**Political Rights and Civil Liberties:** Citizens of Macedonia can choose their political representatives in free and fair elections. The September 2002 parliamentary elections were deemed by international organizations to be "largely in accordance with . . . international standards for democratic elections." Voter turnout was approximately 70 percent of the electorate.

Although the constitution provides for freedom of the press, Macedonian media are often aligned with particular political interests that render them less than independent. Many senior positions in state-owned media, from which the majority of the population gets its information, are filled by political appointees rather than by professional journalists. The media in Macedonia are frequently criticized for their lack of professionalism and unwillingness to uphold recognized journalistic standards. In November, three journalists were convicted of slander of government officials, with sentences ranging from financial penalties to three months' imprisonment. Journalists' groups claimed that the verdicts were a direct attempt to intimidate independent media outlets. There were no reports of restrictions of access to the Internet during the year.

The constitution guarantees freedom of religious belief and practice. A number of religious sites were destroyed or damaged in the fighting in 2001, although vandalism against religious sites has decreased significantly since then. Another blow to Macedonia's fragile unity occurred in June 2002, when at least one bishop of the unrecognized Macedonian Orthodox Church decided to break ranks with the Macedonian church hierarchy and accept the canonical authority of the Orthodox Patriarch of Serbia.

There were no reports of restrictions on academic freedom. In June, the Branko Crvenkovski government agreed to recognize the long-disputed Tetovo University, with a primarily ethnic Albanian student body, as the third state university in Macedonia. However, in an indication of the continuing volatility of the issue, parliament had yet to pass the accompanying legislation by the end of November. Ethnic Albanians have claimed that the university is needed to give them more access to higher education in Macedonia. Ethnic Macedonians maintain that the exclusively Albanian-language university will increase ethnic segregation in the country and become a hotbed for Albanian separatism.

The constitution provides for freedom of assembly and association, and there were no reports that the government infringed on these rights in 2003. There are 64 registered political parties in Macedonia. The constitution also recognizes workers' rights to organize and for collective bargaining, although given the poor state of the Macedonian economy, workers generally have little leverage. Nevertheless, strikes and work stoppages are frequent occurrences. Over 50 percent of the legal workforce is unionized.

The judicial system has been criticized for not having a representative ethnic balance among its judges and prosecutors and for having a large backlog of cases. Judicial independence has been questioned, as judges are nominated by parliament in less than transparent procedures. International experts believe a thorough overhaul of the Macedonian criminal justice system is necessary to increase the pace of prosecutions and judicial efficiency. A number of international watchdog groups have charged Macedonian police forces with serious cases of ill-treatment and torture of prisoners.

Macedonia's most important political and societal problem remains satisfying the demands of the ethnic Albanian minority for a more privileged status within the country. In accordance with the Ohrid Accords, references in the constitution to Macedonia as the "land of the Macedonian people" have been eliminated, and the Albanian language has been made an "official" language in municipalities where

Albanians comprise at least 20 percent of the population. The constitutional reforms envisioned by the Ohrid Accords include granting more self-government to local municipalities, increasing the number of ethnic Albanians in the police force, devolving some of the powers of the central government from Skopje to local municipalities, and granting amnesty to ethnic Albanian insurgents.

Enacting these reforms will be extremely difficult. Currently, 85 percent of the positions in the government bureaucracy are held by ethnic Macedonians, and only 11 percent by ethnic Albanians. In total, the civil service has 128,000 people on its payroll, while the IMF claims that Macedonia's civil service is bloated and should be cut to approximately 20,000 to 30,000 people. Consequently, any serious attempt to implement the IMF's recommendations would result in a huge number of dismissals for the Macedonian majority.

Ethnic Macedonians are afraid that these changes will possibly be the prelude either to the secession of ethnic Albanian-populated areas or to their annexation by a "Greater Kosovo." These fears are exacerbated by current demographic trends within the country; according to the recent census, Macedonia's ethnic Albanian population increased by 68,000 over the past decade, while the ethnic Macedonian population increased by only 2,000.

Women in Macedonia enjoy the same legal rights as men, although lingering patriarchal social attitudes limit women's participation in nontraditional social roles in the economy and in government. Twenty-two of the 120 members of parliament are women (21 ethnic Macedonians and one ethnic Albanian). Violence against women is considered a particular problem within the ethnic Albanian and Roma (Gypsy) communities. Domestic violence and trafficking of women from former Soviet republics remain serious problems. In Muslim areas, many women are effectively disenfranchised because proxy voting by male relatives is common.

# Madagascar

**Population:** 17,000,000   **Political Rights:** 3
**GNI/capita:** $260   **Civil Liberties:** 3*
**Life Expectancy:** 55   **Status:** Partly Free
**Religious Groups:** Indigenous beliefs (52 percent),
Christian (41 percent), Muslim (7 percent)
**Ethnic Groups:** Malayo-Indonesian tribes, Arab, African,
Indian, French
**Capital:** Antananarivo
**Ratings Change:** Madagascar's civil liberties rating improved from 4 to 3 due to the country's progress in recovering from widespread civil strife.

**Ten-Year Ratings Timeline (Political Rights, Civil Liberties, Status)**

| 1994 | 1995 | 1996 | 1997 | 1998 | 1999 | 2000 | 2001 | 2002 | 2003 |
|------|------|------|------|------|------|------|------|------|------|
| 2,4PF | 2,4PF | 2,4PF | 2,4PF | 2,4PF | 2,4PF | 2,4PF | 2,4PF | 3,4PF | 3,3PF |

**Overview:**   Madagascar continued to recover in 2003 from the disastrous aftermath of the controversial 2001 presidential election, from which opposition candidate Marc Ravalomanana emerged victorious amidst considerable civil strife. Local elections that were held in 2003 further strengthened Ravalomanana's position.

Madagascar, the world's fourth-largest island, lies 220 miles off Africa's southeastern coast. After 70 years of French colonial rule and episodes of severe repression, Madagascar gained independence in 1960. A leftist military junta seized power from President Philbert Tsiranana in 1972. A member of the junta, Admiral Ratsiraka, emerged as leader in 1975 and maintained power until his increasingly authoritarian regime bowed to social unrest and nonviolent mass demonstrations in 1991.

Under a new 1992 constitution, opposition leader Albert Zafy won the presidency with more than 65 percent of the vote. President Zafy failed to win reelection after being impeached by the Supreme Court in 1996. Ratsiraka won a narrow victory in a December 1996 presidential runoff election that was deemed generally legitimate by international and domestic observers.

Until the recent presidential crisis, Madagascar had made some progress in consolidating its democratic institutions, although a weak party system complicated efforts at governance. Legislative elections in May 1998 were viewed as more problematic than preceding polls since Madagascar's transition to multiparty politics in 1992. The Council of Christian Churches and several political groups, for example, noted that the elections were marred by fraud and other abuses. The then ruling Vanguard of the Malagasy Revolution (AREMA) party won 63 of 150 parliamentary seats and emerged as the leading force in a coalition government.

A decentralization plan was narrowly approved in a 1998 referendum that was boycotted by the country's increasingly fractious opposition. November 1999 municipal polls resulted in overall success for independents who did not have close identification with a particular party. Elections were held in December 2000 for provincial councils, as the next step in the government's decentralization policy. In 2001, the first-ever Senate elections, part of a policy to extend democratic governance, finally took place after a long delay.

A presidential election was held in December 2001. Insisting that he had been denied an outright victory by polling irregularities, and refusing to take part in a postponed second round, Ravalomanana declared himself president in February 2002. After considerable violence between supporters of the two rival candidates, the High Constitutional Court announced in April that Ravalomanana had indeed won election on the first round, and he was sworn into office in May. Ratsiraka refused to acknowledge this result. Fighting continued until July 2002, when Ratsiraka left the country and the last of his forces surrendered. The extended crisis had a seriously negative effect on the Malagasy economy.

Parliamentary elections took place in December 2002. Ravolamanana's I Love Madagascar party (TIM) won a large majority, gaining 131 out of 160 seats. Observers from the European Union said the conduct of the poll was "generally positive" despite a few reported "lapses," while the International Francophone Organization said it was "credible and transparent." One provincial governor, a nephew of former president Ratsiraka, charged that the vote was marred by serious irregularities and nepotism. Municipal elections in 2003 furthered strengthened Ravalomanana's hand.

**Political Rights and Civil Liberties:** Citizens of Madagascar have the right to change their government democratically, although the most recent presidential election demonstrates that this right is not yet fully enshrined in the country's political culture. The head of state is a president, directly elected by universal adult suffrage. The president's term of office is five years. The legislature is bicameral. The lower chamber, the National Assembly (Antenimieram Pirenena), has 150 members, directly elected for a five-year term. The upper chamber, the Senate, has 90 members—two-thirds of them elected by an electoral college and the remainder nominated by the president—serving six-year terms. A 1998 constitutional referendum gave the president the power to appoint or dismiss the prime minister, who may come from a party that has a minority of seats in the assembly; formerly the National Assembly had this power. Approximately 150 parties are registered amid a welter of shifting political alliances. A variety of parties are active, but they suffer from internal divisions and a lack of clear ideology and resources.

Madagascar was ranked 88 out of 133 countries in Transparency International's 2003 Corruption Perceptions Index. In August, former president Didier Ratsiraka was condemned in absentia to 10 years' hard labor for embezzling public funds.

According to the BBC, since the departure of former President Ratsiraka in July 2002, the media in Madagascar have become less polarized, even though the division of the country into two political camps following the disputed December 2001 presidential elections is still felt in some quarters. Madagascar's 16 million people have six daily newspapers and a number of weeklies and monthlies, as well as numerous TV and radio stations. Because of the low literacy rate, the print media are mostly aimed at the French-educated urban elite. Some formerly pro-Ratsiraka radio stations, which operated like "hate radios" during the crisis, have switched to more mainstream forms of broadcasting. Internet use, although not widespread, is becoming more popular.

The government does not interfere with religious rights. More than half of the population adhere to traditional Malagasy religions and coexist with Christians and Muslims. In 1997, the Rally for Madagascar's Muslim Democrats was registered as the country's first Islamic political party. There are no limitations on academic freedom.

The right to free association is respected, and hundreds of nongovernmental organizations, including lawyers' and human rights groups, are active. As has been evidenced by recent events, political and civic organizations do exercise their right to affect the public policy process. Without massive civic protests against President Ratsiraka's attempts to cling to power, it is unlikely that Marc Ravalomanana would have prevailed in the most recent presidential election. (Similarly, civic action had led to the fall of Ratsiraka's dictatorship in 1992.)

Workers' rights to join unions and to strike are exercised frequently. Some of the country's labor organizations are affiliated with political groups. More than four-fifths of the labor force is employed in agriculture, fishing, and forestry at subsistence wages. Madagascar ranked 145 out of 173 countries in the UN Development Program's 2002 Human Development Index.

In general, the judiciary is demonstrating increasing autonomy. A lack of training, resources, and personnel hampers the courts' effectiveness and case backlogs are prodigious. Most of the 20,000 people held in the country's prisons are pretrial detainees who suffer extremely harsh conditions. In many rural areas, customary law courts that follow neither due process nor standardized judicial procedure often issue summary and severe punishments.

With the stated intent of reestablishing a rule of law, President Ravalomanana has sought to arrest and prosecute individuals who were involved in acts of "terrorism" and killings during the recent crisis. Most of these people were pro-Ratsiraka and *cotiers* (coastal people). Ravalomanana's opponents say the government is cracking down on them for political motives and that the legal system is biased against them. A report by Amnesty International has identified some instances of detention without trial and arbitrary arrest. Pro-government supporters say, however, that those who sought to undermine the country's democracy and promote ethnic and regional discord should not be immune from legal sanctions.

Race and ethnicity are important factors in Madagascar's politics. Its mostly very poor population is divided between highland Merina people of Malay origin and coastal peoples mostly of mixed (Malayo-Polynesian, Arab, and African) descent or of black African origin.

Approximately 45 percent of the workforce is female. Malagasy women hold significantly more government and managerial positions than women in continental African countries. At the same time, they still face societal discrimination and enjoy fewer opportunities than men for higher education and official employment.

# Malawi

**Population:** 11,700,000
**GNI/capita:** $160
**Life Expectancy:** 38
**Religious Groups:** Protestant (55 percent), Roman Catholic (20 percent), Muslim (20 percent), indigenous beliefs (3 percent), other (2 percent)
**Ethnic Groups:** Chewa, Nyanja, Lomwe, Ngonde, Tumbuku, Yao, Sena, Tonga, Ngoni, Asian, European
**Capital:** Lilongwe

**Political Rights:** 3*
**Civil Liberties:** 4
**Status:** Partly Free

**Ratings Change:** Malawi's political rights rating improved from 4 to 3 due to the defeat of a controversial bid to lift term limits for the presidency and the nullification of a law that limited the rights of lawmakers.

**Ten-Year Ratings Timeline (Political Rights, Civil Liberties, Status)**

| 1994 | 1995 | 1996 | 1997 | 1998 | 1999 | 2000 | 2001 | 2002 | 2003 |
|------|------|------|------|------|------|------|------|------|------|
| 2,3F | 2,3F | 2,3F | 2,3F | 2,3F | 3,3PF | 3,3PF | 4,3PF | 4,4PF | 3,4PF |

**Overview:**

President Bakili Muluzi's move in 2003 to amend Malawi's constitution to allow him to run for a third term failed. Moreover, the ruling party's popularity was significantly eroded by the famine of 2002 and subsequent charges of government corruption.

After the country gained independence from Britain in 1963, President (later President-for-Life) Hastings Kamuzu Banda ruled Malawi for nearly three decades.

Banda exercised dictatorial and often eccentric rule through the Malawi Congress Party (MCP) and its paramilitary youth wing, the Malawi Young Pioneers. Facing a domestic economic crisis and strong international pressure, he accepted a referendum approving multiparty rule in 1993. Muluzi won the presidency in an election in 1994 beset by irregularities, but seen as largely free and fair. The army's violent December 1993 dispersal of the Young Pioneers had helped clear the way for the polls.

In the June 1999 presidential poll, Muluzi won 51 percent, compared with 44 percent for leading opposition candidate Gwanda Chakuamba, of the MCP and the Alliance for Democracy (MCP-AFORD). Three presidential contenders sued the electoral commission, contending that Bakili Muluzi failed to win votes from more than half of the eligible electorate. The Supreme Court upheld the results of the election. In polls for the National Assembly in 1999, the ruling United Democratic Front (UDF) managed to retain a narrow majority. Violence erupted in opposition strongholds of northern Malawi after the 1999 election results indicated wins for the UDF. Supporters of MCP-AFORD attacked mosques, shops, and homes of suspected UDF supporters.

An unpopular campaign to amend the constitution to allow President Muluzi to run for a third term was effectively ended in April 2003, when the ruling UDF chose his successor for the 2004 elections, Bingu wa Mutharika, a relative political outsider. Muluzi disbanded his cabinet shortly thereafter, expanding the number of posts to 46 and bringing in several opposition members who had backed his third-term bid.

Despite its firm grip on the broadcast media, the ruling party's popularity has waned significantly because of its mishandling of the severe hunger crisis that afflicted Malawi and the subsequent suspension of all donor funding. The country has largely recovered from that disaster, but widespread poverty and government corruption are likely to be key themes in the election.

In a move that bolstered the political opposition, the High Court struck down a two-year-old constitutional amendment that allowed the expulsion of legislators who were elected on the platform of one party, but subsequently defected to another political organization. The ban on "floor-crossing" had been used primarily to punish dissenters within the UDF. The decision paved the way for several prominent expelled legislators to challenge the ruling party in next year's polls.

Agriculture in Malawi employs 80 percent of the labor force, and the economy is dependent on tobacco. Wealth is concentrated in the hands of a small elite. Foreign donors accused the government of corruption and mismanagement in 2002, in part because of the $38 million sale of the country's strategic grain reserves. President Muluzi sacked the former agriculture minister in connection with the scandal and appointed a commission to investigate the grain sale. At least three million Malawians faced serious food shortages as the result of floods, drought, and the sale of grain reserves. In October 2003, the IMF approved its first loan disbursements to the country since aid was frozen in 2001, opening the way for other major international donors to resume support.

**Political Rights and Civil Liberties:** The citizens of Malawi are guaranteed the right to choose their leaders. Suffrage is universal except for serving members of the military. The 1994 presidential elections were considered Malawi's first generally free and fair multiparty elections. The country's electoral commission has shown bias in favor of the ruling party in the past, and there have been problems with voter registration. Parliament is currently debating a bill to shorten the registration period from 14 to 7 days, and limit to two the number of representatives of political parties at voter registration sites, among other amendments to the electoral law. The changes, strongly protested by the opposition, would also give the president powers to determine null-and-void votes.

The Malawi Human Rights Commission warned in November 2003 that political violence was on the rise as party and regional divisions deepened ahead of the elections in May 2004. Members of the Young Democrats, linked to the ruling United Democratic Front (UDF), were blamed for numerous acts of intimidation and violence against opponents of President Muluzi's third-term bid in 2002. No arrests were made in those cases.

Freedom of speech and of the press is guaranteed and is generally respected in practice. Despite occasional restrictions and harassment, a broad spectrum of opinion is presented in Malawi's two dozen newspapers. Nevertheless, there were a number of attacks on the press in 2002, allegedly committed by members of the Young Democrats, who are linked to the ruling UDF. A government ban on broadcasts of news by community radio stations came under growing criticism in 2003. The Paris-based press freedom group Reporters Sans Frontieres denounced the ban, saying that the state-owned Television Malawi and the Malawi Broadcasting Corporation are mouthpieces of the ruling UDF and that community radio stations are the sole independent source of information for much of the population. The ban affects the Roman Catholic Church's Radio Maria, as well as Radio Islam, Transworld Radio, Radio Calvary Church, and MIJ FM, a station founded by the Malawi Institute of Journalism that was threatened with loss of its broadcasting license in 2002 for airing news. There are no restrictions on access to the Internet, although it is not widely used.

Religious freedom is usually respected, but Muslims were targeted in post-election violence in 1999 in protest against the ruling party. President Muluzi is a Muslim. The government does not restrict academic freedom.

The government generally respects freedom of association and assembly. Many human rights organizations and other nongovernmental organizations operate openly and without interference. The right to organize and to strike is legally protected, with notice and mediation requirements for workers in essential services. Unions are active but face harassment and occasional violence during strikes. Collective bargaining is widely practiced.

The judiciary has demonstrated broad independence in its decisions, but due process is not always respected by an overburdened court system that lacks resources and training. Local and international human rights groups criticized the secret deportation in June of five alleged al-Qaeda sympathizers to Zimbabwe at the request of the United States, in defiance of a High Court ruling. The government has declared the deportations of the five foreign nationals, who were later cleared and released in Sudan, a matter of national security. Police brutality is still said to be common, either while detainees are in custody or when they are just released. Arbitrary arrest and detention are common. Appalling prison conditions lead to many deaths, including suffocation from overcrowding.

There are no laws limiting the participation of ethnic minorities in the political process. A citizen of European origin, one of Asian origin, and several citizens of mixed ethnicity are members of the National Assembly. The constitution prohibits discrimination based on language or culture.

Despite constitutional guarantees of equal protection, customary practices maintain de facto discrimination against women in education, employment, and business. Traditional rural structures deny women inheritance and property rights, and violence against women is reportedly routine. The Malawi Human Rights Commission issued a report in 2003 charging that a sex-slave trade flourishes in remote areas of the north, with young girls sold by their parents to pay off debts. However, there has been increased attention to domestic violence and a greater effort to improve the rights of widows. Women employees recently won the right to maternity leave.

# Malaysia

**Population:** 25,100,000  **Political Rights:** 5
**GNI/capita:** $3,330  **Civil Liberties:** 4*
**Life Expectancy:** 73  **Status:** Partly Free
**Religious Groups:** Muslim, Buddhist, Daoist, Hindu, other
**Ethnic Groups:** Malay and other indigenous (58 percent), Chinese (27 percent), Indian (8 percent), other (7 percent)
**Capital:** Kuala Lumpur
**Ratings Change:** Malaysia's civil liberties rating improved from 5 to 4 due to the lifting of a ban on political rallies ahead of the 2004 parliamentary elections and a modest trend toward judicial independence.

**Ten-Year Ratings Timeline (Political Rights, Civil Liberties, Status)**

| 1994 | 1995 | 1996 | 1997 | 1998 | 1999 | 2000 | 2001 | 2002 | 2003 |
|------|------|------|------|------|------|------|------|------|------|
| 4,5PF | 4,5PF | 4,5PF | 4,5PF | 5,5PF | 5,5PF | 5,5PF | 5,5PF | 5,5PF | 5,4PF |

**Overview:**  Malaysia's new prime minister, Abdullah Badawi, faced the challenge in 2003 of shoring up support for the ruling coalition in elections that are expected in the first half of 2004. As deputy prime minister, the largely untested Badawi was elevated to the top post in October after Mahathir Mohamad decided to step down as the nation's leader after more than two decades in office.

Malaysia gained independence from Britain in 1957 and in 1963 merged with the British colonies of Sarawak, Sabah, and Singapore (Singapore left in 1965). The ruling National Front coalition has won at least a two-thirds majority in all 10 general elections since 1957. The Front consists of 14 mainly ethnic-based parties, led by the conservative, Malay-based United Malays' National Organization (UMNO).

UMNO's Mahathir, 77, became prime minister in 1981. During his tenure, Mahathir helped transform Malaysia from a sleepy backwater, dependent on tin, rubber, and palm oil exports, into a hub for multinationals and local firms exporting high-tech goods. However, he also stunted democratic institutions, weakened the rule of law by bullying the press and political opponents, and fostered allegations of cronysim with his state-led industrial development. In addition, he was a polarizing figure at home and abroad, criticizing Malaysia's conservative Muslim leaders for failing to promote a more modern brand of Islam while rankling outsiders with anti-West and anti-Semitic views.

Malaysia's economy grew by more than 8 percent per year, on average, for nearly a decade until 1997, when the regional financial crisis caused growth to slow sharply. By then, poor banking regulation—and, many Malaysians argued, outright cronyism—had left companies saddled with huge debts. As the economy slid into recession in 1998, Mahathir and Deputy Prime Minister Anwar Ibrahim locked horns over how best to revive the economy.

Many felt that beneath this policy dispute was a bitter power struggle between the country's top political leaders. Matters came to a head in September 1998 when Mahathir sacked Anwar, who later was convicted and jailed for 15 years in a trial that international and domestic observers called politically motivated.

Mahathir's jailing of Anwar, on sodomy and corruption charges, divided the majority ethnic Malays and helped the opposition Islamic Pas party make inroads into the Malay heartland in the November 1999 elections. While the National Front kept its two-thirds majority in parliament with 148 out of 193 seats, UMNO itself lost 20 seats and Pas rose to 27 from 7, overtaking the Chinese-based Democratic Action Party (DAP) as Malaysia's largest opposition party. Many Pas supporters are poor, rural Malays who feel left out of the nation's recent economic boom. The National Justice Party (Keadilan), a new secular party formed by Anwar's wife, Wan Azizah Ismail, won 5 seats.

Since the 1999 election, both UMNO and Pas, led by opposition leader Abdul Hadi Awang, have wooed ethnic Malay voters with appeals to Malay unity and their competing visions of the proper role of Islam in a modern nation. Long a champion of Muslim Malay interests but within a secular, religiously tolerant society, Mahathir used the September 11 terror attacks on the United States to link Pas to Islamic extremism. For its part, Pas stridently condemned the U.S.-led military campaign in Afghanistan. Pas's stance proved too divisive for the DAP, which in 2001 pulled out of a loose electoral alliance with Pas and Keadilan. This move could prove critical in the 2004 elections, because ethnic Chinese and other non-Malays provide crucial swing votes in Malaysia's newly drawn electoral districts, which give non-Malays greater influence in some areas.

While fighting for support in the Malay heartland, Mahathir increasingly used Malaysia's draconian Internal Security Act (ISA) against opponents. In 2001, ten secular opposition activists (most of them senior Keadilan members) were arrested for allegedly planning armed antigovernment protests, and 12 Pas members or supporters were arrested for allegedly planning an Islamic-based revolt. All of the Keadilan activists were freed by June 2003. Anwar apparently is the only political prisoner among the secular dissidents. The government made further arrests under the ISA in 2002, mainly of suspected Islamic militants. In a related development, police in 2003 seized bomb-making materials believed to be linked to Islamic terrorists.

In October 2003, Deputy Prime Minister Abdullah Badawi took over the post of prime minister from Mahatir, who made good on a pledge to leave office. Under Badawi, the National Front is expected to win the 2004 elections, but as always, the size of the opposition vote will be scrutinized as an indication of the government's popularity. On the economic front, Malaysia faces the challenge of finding new economic niches now that low-cost manufacturers in China are increasingly attracting the foreign investment that helped fuel Malaysia's roaring, electronics-led economic growth in the 1980s and 1990s. Badawi is expected to follow Mahathir's recent policies of emphasizing the role of small firms, rather than corporate heavyweights and megaprojects, in driving economic growth and of scaling back some of the economic privileges long accorded ethnic Malays.

## Political Rights and Civil Liberties:

Malaysians choose their leaders in elections that are free but not entirely fair, in part because of restrictions on basic rights that tilt the playing field toward the ruling party. Despite these obstacles, the opposition Pas in 1999 retained control of Kelantan state and captured oil-rich Terengganu for the first time.

Malaysia has a parliamentary government within a federal system. Executive power is vested in a prime minister and cabinet. The House of Representatives, which has 193 members, is directly elected for a five-year term, while the 70-seat Senate serves a six-year term. Mahathir Mohamad's 22-year-tenure was marked by a steady concentration of power in the prime minister's hands.

The ruling National Front coalition gives itself significant advantages in elections through its selective allocation of state funds to supporters, use of security laws to restrict the rights to free expression and peaceful assembly, and partisan use of broadcast media. In a move seen widely as an effort to weaken Pas, Kuala Lumpur began disbursing offshore oil revenues directly to local projects rather than to the Terengganu state government nine months after Pas won control of the state in 1999. In addition, the National Front–controlled states of Malacca and Penang withdrew some state business in 2000 from banks, contractors, and professionals suspected of supporting opposition parties. Moreover, redistricting ahead of the 2004 elections by the supposedly neutral election commission created more districts in certain areas where UMNO, the lynchpin of the coalition, polls well among Malays.

Malaysia's constitution provides for freedom of expression, but gives the government the power to limit this right by legislation for security reasons. In practice, the government restricts freedom of expression both through legislation and by intimidating much of the media into practicing self-censorship. State-run Radio Television Malaysia and the two private television stations offer flattering coverage of the government and rarely air opposition views. Moreover, political news coverage and editorials in Malaysia's main private newspapers strongly support the government line. Most major papers are owned by businessmen, companies, and political figures close to the ruling National Front. Many journalists practice self-censorship.

The government uses the Printing Presses and Publications Act (PPPA) to require all publishers and printing firms to obtain an annual operating permit, which can be withdrawn without judicial review. In practice, this provision has been used to restrict some independent and opposition publications. Authorities in 2000 refused to renew the permits of several opposition political weeklies and forced the Pas newspaper, *Harakah*, to print only twice-monthly rather than twice-weekly. Officials have also denied a license to an opposition DAP paper in East Malaysia to print in the rest of the country. Following an unprecedented eight-year trial, social activist Irene Fernandez was sentenced to 12 months in jail in 2003 under the PPPA for a report by her organization alleging poor treatment of migrant workers in Malaysian detention camps. She remained free on bail pending an appeal.

In addition to the PPPA, the Sedition Act, the Broadcasting Act, the Official Secrets Act, and criminal defamation laws also impose restrictions on freedom of expression. The government uses these laws not only to suppress outspoken publications but also to curb dissent and restrict discussion of several allegedly sensitive issues including ethnicity and religion. While Malaysians often publicly criticize the government, opposition politicians recently have been detained or fined for acts including distributing political leaflets and discussing Malaysia's 1969 race riots during an election speech. In a positive development, fewer defamation suits have been filed in recent years. The government generally has not restricted Internet access or content.

Islam is Malaysia's official religion, but Sikhs, Hindus, Christians, Buddhists, and other religious minorities worship freely in this secular country. The government, however, monitors the activities of the Shia minority and periodically detains members of "deviant" Shia sects under the ISA. Partly to prevent the opposition Pas from spreading its political message through mosques, some state governments monitor sermons and have banned certain Muslim clergymen from delivering sermons at state-affiliated mosques.

The government restricts academic freedom by sanctioning faculty and students who take part in antigovernment activities. Authorities recently revoked the scholarship of a university lecturer who was pursuing his doctorate and dismissed several students, apparently based on their political activities.

Freedoms of assembly and association are severely limited. Opposition groups have faced an additional hurdle to reaching supporters ever since the government banned all political rallies in 2001, although late in 2003 authorities again were permitting opposition rallies. Even before the ban, police forcibly broke up many of the dozens of antigovernment demonstrations held in the wake of Deputy Prime Minister Anwar Ibrahim's jailing. Many of the hundreds of protesters arrested were acquitted, though some were sentenced to jail terms of between one and three months. Many were accused of violating Malaysia's 1967 Police Act, which requires permits for all public gatherings except those of workers on picket lines.

Malaysia has thousands of active nongovernmental organizations (NGOs), but authorities over the years have refused to register some groups. The 1966 Societies Act requires any NGO with more than six members, including political parties, to register with the government. University students are legally barred from being active without their schools' permission in any NGO, political party, or trade union. The Universities and University Colleges Act also bans political rallies and meetings on campuses.

Most Malaysian workers, with the exception of police officers, defense officials, and small numbers of "confidential" and "managerial and executive" workers, can join trade unions. However, the law, by permitting a union to represent only workers in single, or similar, trades, industries, or occupations, prevents the formation of broad-based unions spanning multiple industries. In the export-oriented electronics industry, moreover, the government discourages national unions in favor of factory-level unions. Labor laws restrict strikes by allowing the government to refer labor disputes to the Industrial Court and prohibiting strikes while disputes are before that court. In practice, workers rarely strike. Unions, however, bargain collectively in many industries, although public sector workers lack the right to bargain collectively. Only 8 percent of Malaysian workers are unionized. Employers sometimes abuse, and fail to honor contracts with, their household servants.

Malaysia's secular legal system is based on English common law. In addition to the secular courts, Sharia (Islamic law) courts in each of Malaysia's 13 states have jurisdiction over Muslims in some civil and relatively minor criminal matters. The judiciary apparently has become more impartial under Chief Justice Mohamed Dzaiddin Abdullah, appointed in 2000. Still, "In recent years, a number of high-profile cases cast doubts on judicial impartiality and independence, and raised questions of arbitrary verdicts, selective prosecution, and preferential treatment of some litigants and lawyers," according to the U.S. State Department's human rights report for 2002, released in March 2003.

In two recent controversial cases, Ezam Mohamad Noor, youth leader of the Keadilan party, was convicted in 2002 under the Official Secrets Act of leaking state secrets (he was freed early from jail in 2003), and courts rejected appeals by former deputy prime minister Anwar of his 15-year prison term. At the same time, courts recently have ruled against the government in sensitive cases. Judges ordered the release of two opposition leaders detained under the ISA and voided the election of a ruling coalition candidate to the Sabah state assembly because of irregularities in the voting rolls.

The government's use of the ISA and other security laws not only chills political debate but also raises broader civil liberties concerns over detention without trial. Enacted in 1960 under British rule to mop up the remnants of a Communist insurgency, the ISA has been used in recent years to jail mainstream politicians, alleged Islamic militants, trade unionists, suspected Communist activists, ordinary criminal suspects, members of "deviant" Muslim sects, and others. The human rights group Amnesty International said in November that 94 alleged Islamic militants currently were being detained without charge or trial under the ISA in the Kamunting Detention Center in northern Malaysia. Amnesty's figures included 13 students who subsequently were released. The lack of trials makes it difficult to assess the government's claims against suspected militants. ISA detainees have reported being physically assaulted, deprived of sleep, food, and water, and told that their families would be harmed, Amnesty said.

Overall, the government detains hundreds of suspects each year under the ISA and two other laws that also permit long-term detention without formal charges— the 1969 Emergency Ordinance and 1985 Dangerous Drugs Act (DDA). Both the ISA and the Emergency Ordinance allow authorities to detain suspects for up to two years, renewable for ISA detainees. The DDA allows the government to detain suspected drug traffickers for successive two-year periods subject to initial court approval, with periodic review by an advisory panel.

In another concern, police in recent years have killed dozens of criminal suspects while apprehending them. Press reports suggest that at least some of the killings may have been appropriate under the circumstances. Authorities have prosecuted officers in some death cases. Police also at times torture, beat, or otherwise abuse detainees and prisoners, according to Amnesty International.

Pas has moved to implement its strict, conservative Islam in the two northeastern states that it controls. The legislature in Terengganu approved a bill in October
authorizing stoning, flogging, and amputation for offenses by Muslims including
theft, adultery, and consumption of alcohol. Kuala Lumpur says that the law violates Malaysia's secular constitution and, since law enforcement is largely in the
hands of the federal government, refuses to enforce the measures. The Pas government in Kelantan has introduced a similar bill in that state's legislature. The two Pas
administrations also have imposed some dress, dietary, and cultural restrictions on
Muslims. Dozens of Muslim women in Kelantan have been fined for not adhering to
the state's new, conservative dress code in state offices. In November, Pas also unveiled a blueprint to make Malaysia an Islamic state should the party come to power
nationally.

The government recently has tightened its policies on illegal workers in response
to leaner economic times. The immigration law was amended in 2002 to provide for
caning, heavy fines, or imprisonment of illegal workers and those who recruit and
employ them. Moreover, many illegal workers reportedly were abused during mass
deportations from Malaysia in August 2002. Despite some improvements, NGOs and
former detainees allege that government camps for illegal immigrants continue to
provide detainees with inadequate food and medical care and that some detainees
suffer abuse at the hands of guards. Moreover, illegal foreign workers have no legal
protection under Malaysia's labor laws and no legal recourse if abused by employers.

Many ethnic Chinese and Indians, as well as many Malays, criticized the
government's 2001 decision to extend by 10 years a long-standing policy that aims
to boost the economic status of the *bumiputras*—or "sons of the soil," referring to
ethnic Malays and indigenous Malaysians—through favored treatment in many
areas. These include property ownership, higher education, civil service jobs, and
business affairs, although under Mahathir the system was scaled back somewhat.
Critics say that any affirmative action should be based on need rather than race.
They note that Malaysians of South Asian origin, mainly Tamils, lack both the relative wealth of the Chinese community and the preferred status of the ethnic Malays,
and that many individual ethnic Chinese are poor. The government says that the
quotas have improved racial harmony by helping to lift many Malays out of poverty.
The quotas were introduced in 1970 in response to anti-Chinese riots in 1969 that
killed nearly 200 people.

Indigenous people in peninsular Malaysia and the Borneo states generally have
little input into government and business policies affecting them. State and private
logging and plantation companies continue to encroach on land traditionally held
by the Orang Asli and other indigenous groups, particularly in the Borneo states.
State governments in peninsular Malaysia are moving slowly in carrying out federal
orders to transfer individual land titles to many of the roughly 100,000 indigenous
people there, the U.S. State Department report said.

Despite government initiatives and continued gains, women still are under-represented in politics, the professions, and the civil service. The government sponsors many programs to promote women's equality in education and employment. It
also has adopted a law against domestic violence and created programs to help victims of spousal abuse and rape. Some convicted rapists receive heavy punishments,
including caning, but women's groups say that many others receive sentences that

are too light and that, overall, relatively few rape cases are prosecuted. In another concern, some women and girls are trafficked into Malaysia for sexual exploitation, and some Malaysian women are trafficked abroad, though few traffickers are prosecuted, according to the U.S. State Department report.

Islamic courts do not give equal weight to the testimony of women, and activists allege that women sometimes are subject to discriminatory interpretations of Islamic law in divorce and inheritance matters. The interpretation of Islamic inheritance law varies by state but tends to favor male offspring and relatives.

# Maldives

**Population:** 300,000  **Political Rights:** 6
**GNI/capita:** $2,090  **Civil Liberties:** 5
**Life Expectancy:** 67  **Status:** Not Free
**Religious Groups:** Sunni Muslim
**Ethnic Groups:** South Indian, Sinhalese, Arab
**Capital:** Male

**Ten-Year Ratings Timeline (Political Rights, Civil Liberties, Status)**

| 1994 | 1995 | 1996 | 1997 | 1998 | 1999 | 2000 | 2001 | 2002 | 2003 |
|------|------|------|------|------|------|------|------|------|------|
| 6,6NF | 6,6NF | 6,6NF | 6,6NF | 6,5NF | 6,5NF | 6,5NF | 6,5NF | 6,5NF | 6,5NF |

**Overview:**

The Maldives's reputation as a tranquil island paradise was shaken in 2003, when unprecedented antigovernment civil unrest erupted in September following a violent altercation at a prison. Analysts believe that President Maumoon Abdul Gayoom is facing increased pressure both from a pro-reform opposition party and from young Maldivians, who desire greater political freedom. Nevertheless, Gayoom was chosen for a sixth term in an October presidential referendum in which 77 percent of the electorate participated.

Consisting of a 500-mile-long string of 26 atolls in the Indian Ocean, the Maldives achieved independence in 1965 after 78 years as a British protectorate. A 1968 referendum set up a republican government, ending 815 years of rule by the ad-Din sultanate. The Maldives' first president, Amir Ibrahim Nasir, introduced a number of changes to the political system, abolishing the post of prime minister in 1975.

President Gayoom has held power since 1978, when he won his first term under the country's tightly controlled presidential referendum process. The most serious threat to Gayoom's survival came in 1988, when Indian commandos crushed a coup attempt by a disgruntled businessman reportedly backed by Sri Lankan mercenaries. In the aftermath, the autocratic Gayoom strengthened the National Security Service (NSS) and named several relatives to top governmental posts.

In September 2003, after an inmate was killed during a fight in the Maafushi prison, unrest broke out at the prison and riots engulfed the capital. Security forces reportedly opened fire on other prisoners, killing three more and wounding over a dozen. Meanwhile, protestors in the capital, Male, attacked government buildings, including the parliament, the election office, the high court, and two police stations, setting several on fire. In response, Gayoom ordered the arrest of a number of NSS personnel and promised to conduct an inquiry into the circumstances of the initial killing.

The most recent presidential referendum, held in October to confirm Gayoom as president, was approved by just over 90 percent of participating voters. After being sworn in for a record sixth presidential term in November, he promised to reform national institutions and to establish a human rights commission. However, a day later he sacked his attorney general and a cabinet minister, both of whom had supported reformers in their efforts to register an opposition political party.

**Political Rights and Civil Liberties:** Maldivians cannot change their head of government through elections. Under the 1968 constitution, the Majlis (parliament) chooses a single presidential nominee from among a list of candidates. The nominee is then approved or rejected by a national referendum held every five years. A 1998 constitutional amendment allowed citizens to declare their candidacies, but not campaign for the presidential nomination. The constitution grants the president broad executive powers and allows him to appoint 8 of the Majlis' 50 members (the remainder are directly elected) as well as the speaker and deputy speaker. Nevertheless, in recent years, the Majlis has rejected some governmental legislation and has held lively policy debates.

In addition to making arrests prior to the 1999 parliamentary elections, authorities also banned public campaign events, permitting only small meetings on private premises. Political parties are officially discouraged, and candidates for the Majlis run as individuals. Amnesty International reported that 42 people, including academics, intellectuals, businessmen, and three members of parliament, petitioned the Minister for Home Affairs in 2001 for permission to set up the Maldivian Democratic Party. The president decided against the petition, and several of the signatories have been subjected to harassment and periodic arrest.

The law allows authorities to shut newspapers and sanction journalists for articles containing unfounded criticism of the government. Moreover, regulations make editors responsible for the content of material they publish. Four writers for *Sandhaanu*, an Internet magazine, were arrested in early 2002, and after being held in detention and charged with defamation, three were sentenced to life imprisonment. In this environment, some journalists practice self-censorship, although less so than in the past. Today, newspapers are critical of government policies, and the state-run television station's news and public affairs programs discuss timely issues and criticize government performance. All broadcast media are government owned and operated.

Freedom of religion is restricted by the government's requirement that all citizens be Sunni Muslims, a legal ban against the practice of other religions, and a constitutional provision making Islam the state religion. In 2002, four individuals were arrested for distributing Islamist and antigovernment literature, and three were sentenced to life imprisonment, according to the U.S. State Department Report on International Religious Freedom. Non-Muslim foreigners are allowed to practice their religion privately. There were no reported restrictions on academic freedom.

The government limits freedom of assembly and association, and it has in recent years imprisoned several dissidents under broadly drawn laws. The penal code bans speech or actions that could "arouse people against the government." A 1968 law prohibits speech considered inimical to Islam, libelous, or a threat to national security. The Maldives has no known nongovernmental human rights groups.

Workers lack the legal rights to form trade unions, stage strikes, or bargain collectively. In practice, no unions exist, although some workers have established informal associations that address labor issues. The Maldives has about 27,000 foreign workers out of a total workforce of 70,000 to 75,000. Most workers are in the informal (unorganized) sector, although some work in the country's high-end tourism industry, which provides 70 percent of foreign exchange revenues.

Because President Maumoon Abdul Gayoom can review High Court decisions and appoint and dismiss judges, "the judiciary is subject to executive influence," according to the U.S. State Department's 2002 human rights report. Civil law is generally used in civil and criminal cases, although it is subordinate to Sharia (Islamic law). The latter is used in matters not covered by civil law as well as in certain cases such as those involving divorce or adultery. Under Sharia, the testimony of two women is equal to that of one man, and men are favored in divorce and inheritance matters. Punishments such as flogging and banishment to a remote island, which are provided for under the country's interpretation of Sharia, are occasionally carried out.

In a positive move, the government amended the 1990 Prevention of Terrorism Act (PTA) in 1998 to place some limits on police detention of suspects under investigation. Judges, however, can still authorize suspects to be detained without trial, on a monthly basis, if authorities have not started legal proceedings within 22 days of the arrest. The NSS functions as the police, army, and intelligence services, and human rights groups allege that it acts with virtual impunity. Incidents of torture or other forms of ill-treatment of detainees held at police stations or prison facilities continue to be reported, according to Amnesty International.

The government has in recent years detained or kept several political prisoners under house arrest, and some have been sentenced to long prison terms after being convicted in trials in which they have been denied legal representation. After the September 2003 civil protests, authorities arbitrarily arrested more than 100 people, and Amnesty International alleged that over a dozen remained in detention at the end of the year. Most are held after expressing views critical of the government.

More women are entering the civil service, increasingly receiving equal pay to that of men for equal work. Women enjoy a 98 percent literacy rate, compared with 96 percent for men. However, traditional norms that oppose letting women lead independent lives outside their homes continue to limit educational and career opportunities for many women. The government has in recent years sponsored programs to help make women aware of their rights. Children's rights are incorporated into law, and government policy provides for equal access to educational and health programs for both male and female children.

# Mali

**Population:** 11,600,000    **Political Rights:** 2
**GNI/capita:** $230    **Civil Liberties:** 2*
**Life Expectancy:** 45    **Status:** Free
**Religious Groups:** Muslim (90 percent), indigenous
beliefs (9 percent), Christian (1 percent)
**Ethnic Groups:** Mande (50 percent), Peul (17 percent),
Voltaic (12 percent), Tuareg and Moor (10 percent),
Songhai (6 percent), other (5 percent)
**Capital:** Bamako
**Ratings Change:** Mali's civil liberties rating improved from 3 to 2 due to modest improvements in human rights, including legislative reform and efforts to eliminate child trafficking.

**Ten-Year Ratings Timeline (Political Rights, Civil Liberties, Status)**

| 1994 | 1995 | 1996 | 1997 | 1998 | 1999 | 2000 | 2001 | 2002 | 2003 |
|------|------|------|------|------|------|------|------|------|------|
| 2,4PF | 2,3F | 2,2F | 3,3F | 3,3F | 3,3F | 2,3F | 2,3F | 2,3F | 2,2F |

**Overview:**    Mali continued its process of decentralization in 2003 and was commended by the UN Human Rights Committee for its progress on improving human rights. Tens of thousands of Malian migrant workers returned to the country after fleeing unrest in neighboring Cote d'Ivoire.

After achieving independence from France in 1960, Mali was ruled by military or one-party dictators for more than 30 years. After soldiers killed more than 100 demonstrators demanding a multiparty system in 1991, President Moussa Traore was overthrown by his own military. Traore and his wife, Mariam, were sentenced to death in January 1999 for embezzlement. Traore had also received the death sentence in 1993 for ordering troops to fire on demonstrators two years earlier. Sentences for both Traore and his wife have been commuted to life imprisonment.

After the 1991 coup, a national conference organized open elections that most observers judged to be free and fair, with Alpha Oumar Konare of the Alliance for Democracy in Mali (ADEMA) party winning the presidency in 1992. In 1997, a little more than a quarter of registered voters participated as Konare was overwhelmingly reelected against a weak candidate who alone broke an opposition boycott of the presidential contest.

Konare's ADEMA party suffered a split in 2001, adding more competition to the May 2002 presidential election, in which 24 candidates participated. Amadou Toumani Toure, a former general who led Mali during the transition period to multiparty politics in the early 1990s, ran as an independent. After the first round of voting, the Constitutional Court canceled more than 500,000 ballots cast, citing voting by non-registered voters and missing election reports as some of the irregularities. Several presidential candidates had petitioned the court to annul the results entirely, alleging fraud and vote rigging. Toure and Soumaila Cisse, of ADEMA, went to a second round of voting, with Toure securing 64 percent of the vote compared with 36 percent for Cisse. International observers said the polls were well managed and conducted in a spirit of transparency, although they also noted several logistical and administrative irregularities.

The coalition Hope Party dominated voting for National Assembly elections in July 2002, gaining 66 seats, while a coalition led by ADEMA won 51 seats. Smaller parties captured the remainder of seats.

Toure, like his predecessor, has a strong international profile for having been active in regional peace and humanitarian efforts as a UN envoy. In 2003, Konare took office as chairman of the African Union, which was formerly the Organization of African Unity.

The UN Human Rights Committee praised Mali in April 2003 for its progress in improving human rights in the country, citing legislative reform and efforts to eradicate child trafficking. However, the committee called on the government to improve the status of women.

Although a ceasefire was in effect in neighboring Cote d'Ivoire, migrant workers from Mali were still targets of violence by Ivorians who resent their presence. Although the return of the migrants did not hurt Mali's economy as much as expected, a drop in the world price of cotton, which is one of the country's key exports, did increase economic hardship. However, neither development appeared to destabilize the new administration of President Toure.

Despite steady economic growth, Mali remains desperately poor. About 65 percent of its land is desert or semidesert, and about 80 percent of the labor force is engaged in farming or fishing. Hundreds of thousands of Malians are economic migrants across Africa and Europe. An Algerian militant Islamist group took more than 30 European tourists hostage in a remote region of Mali in 2003 and held some for more than five months before the government was able to secure their release. Officials worried that the incident could further hurt the economy by damaging the country's tourism industry.

**Political Rights and Civil Liberties:** Citizens of Mali can choose their government democratically. Since the end of military rule, Mali's domestic political debate has been open and extensive. Despite some irregularities noted by international observers, the 2002 presidential elections were regarded as having been well managed and conducted in a spirit of transparency. There are at least 75 political parties in the country.

The government has established a special commission to help eradicate corruption. Mali was ranked 78 out of 133 countries surveyed in Transparency International's 2003 Corruption Perceptions Index.

Although libel is still considered a criminal offense and press laws include punitive presumption-of-guilt standards, Mali's media are among Africa's most open. At least 40 independent newspapers operate freely, and more than 50 independent radio stations, including community stations broadcasting in regional languages, broadcast throughout the country. The government controls one television station and many radio stations, but all present diverse views, including those critical of the government. The government does not impede access to the Internet.

Mali is predominantly Muslim. However, it is a secular state and minority and religious rights are protected by law. Religious associations must register with the government, but the law is not enforced. Sectarian violence occasionally flares between Muslim groups. A clash over the building of a mosque left several people dead in August. Academic freedom is guaranteed and respected.

Many civic groups and nongovernmental organizations, including human rights groups, operate without interference. Workers are guaranteed the right to join unions, and nearly all salaried employees are unionized. The right to strike is guaranteed, with some restrictions.

Although the judiciary is not independent of the executive, it has shown considerable autonomy in rendering anti-administration decisions, which the government has in turn respected. The UN Human Rights Committee praised Mali in April for its progress in improving human rights, citing the country's extensive legislative reform and a moratorium on capital punishment. Local chiefs, in consultation with elders, decide the majority of disputes in rural areas. Detainees are not always charged within the 48-hour period set by law, and there are often lengthy delays in bringing people to trial. Mali's human rights record is generally good, although there are reports of police brutality. The government permits visits by human rights monitors to prisons, which are characterized by overcrowding and inadequate medical care and food.

No ethnic group predominates in the government or the security forces, and political parties are not based on ethnicity. There have been long-standing tensions between the marginalized Moor and Tuareg pastoralist groups and the more populous nonpastoralist groups; these tension have been a main cause of political instability and violence, including the Tuareg rebellions of the early 1990s. A 1995 agreement ended the brutal, multisided conflicts between Tuareg guerrillas, black ethnic militias, and government troops.

Although the constitution prohibits forced labor, thousands of Malian children have been sold into servitude on coffee and cocoa plantations in neighboring Cote d'Ivoire by organized traffickers. Mali now requires children under 18 to carry travel documents; a law that made child trafficking punishable by up to 20 years in prison was enacted in 2001.

The UN Human Rights Committee concluded in April that further work needs to be done to improve women's rights, specifically regarding marriage, divorce, inheritance, land ownership, and domestic violence. Most formal legal advances in protection of women's rights have not been implemented, especially in rural areas. Societal discrimination against women persists, and social and cultural factors continue to limit their economic and educational opportunities. Legislation gives women property rights, but traditional practices and ignorance prevent many from taking advantage of the laws. Violence against women, including spousal abuse, is tolerated and common. Female genital mutilation remains legal, although the government has conducted educational campaigns against the practice. Numerous groups promote the rights of women and children.

# Malta

**Population:** 400,000
**GNI/capita:** $9,200
**Life Expectancy:** 77
**Political Rights:** 1
**Civil Liberties:** 1
**Status:** Free
**Religious Groups:** Roman Catholic (98 percent), other [including Muslim, Jew, and Protestant] (2 percent)
**Ethnic Groups:** Maltese [mixed Arab, Norman, Spanish, Italian, and English]
**Capital:** Valletta

**Ten-Year Ratings Timeline (Political Rights, Civil Liberties, Status)**

| 1994 | 1995 | 1996 | 1997 | 1998 | 1999 | 2000 | 2001 | 2002 | 2003 |
|------|------|------|------|------|------|------|------|------|------|
| 1,1F | 1,1F | 1,1F | 1,1F | 1,1F | 1,1F | 1,1F | 1,1F | 1,1F | 1,1F |

**Overview:**

A national referendum in March 2003 narrowly approved the country's accession to the European Union. The referendum was followed by national elections the next month and a victory for the center-right, which had run on a pro-Europe platform, beating out the more anti-Europe center-left.

Malta is a small island nation with ties to both the European and Arab worlds. After it gained independence from the British in 1964, Malta became a republic in 1974. From 1964 to 1971, the country was ruled by the Nationalist Party (PN), which pursued a pro-Western alliance. In 1971, the European alliance broke down when the (Labour Party) MLP took power and moved the country toward nonalignment and a special friendship with leftist governments in Libya and Algeria. The PN returned to power in 1987, and in 1990 the country submitted its application for full membership in the EU (then the EC).

After a brief interlude with the return to power of the MLP from 1996 to 1998, Malta continued in a pro-European direction that culminated in a national referendum on March 8, 2003 on EU accession. Malta was the first among the 10 current candidate countries to hold a referendum on the issue of EU membership, which was approved by a vote of 53.65 percent.

The referendum was hotly contested between the two leading parties, which also ran for national office only a month later, on April 12. The PN, which ran a pro-EU campaign, won the elections with 52 percent of the vote and 35 seats. The MLP, which campaigned on an anti-EU platform, received 48 percent of the vote and 30 seats. The smaller Alternattiva Demokratika (AD) lost support compared with the elections in 1998. By the end of the summer, the MLP had changed its position on the EU, dropping its efforts to scuttle the country's membership.

**Political Rights and Civil Liberties:**

The Maltese are free to change their government democratically. Malta has a unicameral legislature with 65 seats that are decided by a national system of proportional representation with an additional single-transferable-vote (STV) arrangement. STV is different from the traditional "list" proportional representation system because it allows the voter not only to choose a party but also to rank-order the candidates running for office. Parliament is elected for a five-year term, and members of parliament, in turn, elect the president to serve five years.

There was no apparent increase in the level of corruption, which remained low, within the government over the year. However, in 2002, a chief justice had to resign after a bribery scandal over a prison sentence appeal.

The constitution guarantees freedom of speech and of the press. There are currently 4 daily newspapers, 10 weeklies, 19 radio stations, and 6 television stations. There is free Internet access.

Although the country is overwhelmingly Roman Catholic, other religious groups are tolerated and respected. There are small communities of Muslims, Jews, and Protestants, the latter being mostly British retirees. The constitution establishes Catholicism as the state religion, and the state grants subsidies only to Catholic schools. The government recently approved a site for a 500-grave Muslim cemetery.

Academic freedom is respected, and there is generally free and open discussion in the country. However, a recent amendment to the criminal code makes incitement to racial hatred a crime that can carry a prison term between 6 and 8 months.

The constitution provides for freedom of assembly and association, and the law recognizes the right to form and join trade unions. Limits on the right to strike were eased in 2002. However, the ILO continues to criticize Malta for the compulsory arbitration clause in its Employment and Industrial Relations Act, which allows the government to force a settlement on striking workers. Such clauses are usually limited to situations involving essential services, or acute national crises, or when the two sides request arbitration.

The judiciary is independent, and the rule of law prevails in civil and criminal matters. However, the Commission on Administrative Justice issued a report in the early part of the year that details a significant backlog in court cases and magisterial inquiries. Amnesty International also released a report in 2002 critical of the forcible deportations of more than 220 Eritreans from Malta in September and October of that year. Primarily a transit country for asylum seekers, Malta has done little to integrate immigrants who generally go on to the United States, Canada, or Australia.

The government respects personal autonomy and freedom. However, divorce is illegal and violence against women continues to be a problem on the island. Additionally, of the 65 seats in parliament, women occupy only 6. A total of 16 women competed for national office during the elections this year. The criminal code has been amended to include a provision to prohibit trafficking in persons. Prostitution is illegal on the island and violators face stiff penalties.

# Marshall Islands

**Population:** 100,000
**GNI/capita:** $1,970
**Life Expectancy:** 68
**Religious Groups:** Christian (mostly Protestant)
**Ethnic Groups:** Micronesian
**Capital:** Majuro

**Political Rights:** 1
**Civil Liberties:** 1
**Status:** Free

### Ten-Year Ratings Timeline (Political Rights, Civil Liberties, Status)

| 1994 | 1995 | 1996 | 1997 | 1998 | 1999 | 2000 | 2001 | 2002 | 2003 |
|------|------|------|------|------|------|------|------|------|------|
| 1,1F | 1,1F | 1,1F | 1,1F | 1,1F | 1,1F | 1,1F | 1,1F | 1,1F | 1,1F |

**Overview:**
The major event in the Marshall Islands in 2003 was the renewal of the Compact of Free Association agreement with the United States to replace the one that expired on September 30. The compact provides nearly half of the Marshall Islands' national budget in exchange for allowing the United States to set up military bases in its territory. In November parliamentary and presidential elections, President Kessai Note's United Democratic Party won a majority of seats in the legislature and Note secured a second term in office.

Following decades of Spanish and German colonial rule, the United States wrested the Marshall Islands from the occupying Japanese during World War II. Beginning in 1997, the Marshall Islands was under U.S. trusteeship administration for nearly four decades. In 1986, the country gained full independence, but ties with the United States remained close. A bilateral Compact of Free Association provides the Marshall Islands with U.S. defense protection and assistance in exchange for access for hosting United States missile bases; the Federal States of Micronesia and Palau have similar agreements with the United States.

Renewal negotiations regarding the compact began four years ago. A key issue was rent for the missile testing range on Kwajalein Atoll, which has been the primary U.S. testing ground for long-range missiles and anti-missile defense since 1964; activities at the testing range have increased since 2000.

In November 2003, the U.S. Senate approved the new $3.1 billion compact, which extends use of the Kwajalein missile-testing range through 2066 for $2.3 billion and establishes an $800 million trust fund that will replace direct U.S. aid in 20 years. Rent payments to landowners for the Kwajalein site were increased to $15 million, plus $5.1 million in annual development funding. By contrast, the old compact guaranteed annual payments of $11.3 million in rent and $1.9 million in aid. Marshall Islanders will continue to have visa-free entry to the United States to live, work, and study, but will lose $800,000 in annual college scholarships.

However, Marshallese landowners want $19.1 million in rent per year. Their rejection of land-use agreements with their own government could block ratification of the new compact. Survivors of U.S. nuclear tests at the Bikini and Enewetak atolls in the 1950s also objected to the absence of any reference to America's continuing obligation to provide them with health care and compensation in the new compact. In exchange for increased funds, the Marshallese government promises to crack down on illegal passport sales. The government expanded the number of inspectors to 10 persons, and a new regulation empowers the police to apprehend and deport visitors who overstay their visa. Persons from China are a particularly serious problem. Illegal passport sales have been a problem since the mid-1990s, when about 2,000 people, mostly from China, Taiwan, and Hong Kong, were found to have purchased fake documents.

President Kessai Note's United Democratic Party won a majority of seats in parliamentary elections in November. In presidential elections held the same month, Note was reelected by members of parliament to a second term.

In August, an outbreak of measles that was linked to persons traveling from Guam affected some 400 people. The government banned inter-island travel and imposed mass immunization to stop the spread of the disease.

**Political Rights and Civil Liberties:** Citizens of the Marshall Islands can change their government democratically. The president is the head of state and chief executive and is chosen by the House of Representatives, or Nitijela, from among its members. The 33-seat House is directly elected for four-year terms. The upper house, the Council of Chiefs, or Iroji, consists of 12 traditional leaders who provide advice on customary law. Political parties are legal, but there are none. The United Democratic Party of President Kessai Note is more of a loose caucus than a formal party. Note was elected to the post in January 2000 and is the first commoner to hold the office.

Freedom of speech is respected. A privately owned newspaper publishes articles in English and Marshallese. Two radio stations, one government owned and one church owned, carry news broadcasts from overseas. The government station carries public service announcements and live broadcasts of legislative sessions. A cable television station offers foreign news and entertainment programs and occasional videotaped local events. The government does not restrict Internet access. Religious and academic freedoms are respected in practice.

The government broadly interprets constitutional guarantees of freedom of assembly and association to cover trade unions. There is no formal right to strike or engage in collective bargaining, but in practice there are no restraints on such activity.

The constitution provides for an independent judiciary, but past governments have attempted to influence the judiciary. Three former chief justices either resigned or were fired by the Kabua administration in the late 1990s. Chief Justice Charles Henry, a U.S. citizen, was tried in August on 29 charges of alleged cheating, misuse of government funds, and criminal libel. In October, the government moved to remove Henry, who had refused to return for his hearing. Nearly all judges, prosecutors, and public defenders are foreigners because few Marshallese have law degrees. To improve the judiciary, President Note raised judges' salaries to attract and retain more qualified foreign judges. The government has cracked down on tax evasion and money laundering after being placed on an international watch list.

Social and economic discrimination against women is widespread even in this matrilineal society, where traditional rank and inheritance of property are through female bloodlines. Growing urbanization and movement from traditional lands have eroded some traditional authority exercised by women. Spousal abuse is not uncommon and is often alcohol related.

# Mauritania

**Population:** 2,900,000
**GNI/capita:** $360
**Life Expectancy:** 54
**Religious Groups:** Muslim (100 percent)
**Ethnic Groups:** Mixed Maur and black (40 percent),
Maur (30 percent), black (30 percent)
**Capital:** Nouakchott

**Political Rights:** 6*
**Civil Liberties:** 5
**Status:** Not Free

**Ratings Change:** Mauritania's political rights rating declined from 5 to 6, and its status from Partly Free to Not Free, due to presidential elections that were held in an atmosphere of intimidation and were not conducted fairly.

**Ten-Year Ratings Timeline (Political Rights, Civil Liberties, Status)**

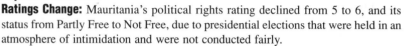

| 1994 | 1995 | 1996 | 1997 | 1998 | 1999 | 2000 | 2001 | 2002 | 2003 |
|------|------|------|------|------|------|------|------|------|------|
| 7,7NF | 6,6NF | 6,6NF | 6,6NF | 6,5NF | 6,5NF | 6,5NF | 5,5PF | 5,5PF | 6,5NF |

**Overview:**  President Maaouya Ould Sid Ahmed Taya won presidential election in November 2003 that lacked transparency and was held in an atmosphere of intimidation. Authorities detained Taya's main challenger and several of his supporters the day after the election. A coup attempt was put down during the year.

After nearly six decades of French colonial rule, Mauritania's borders as an independent state were formalized in 1960. A 1978 military coup ended a civilian one-party state led by Moktaar Ould Daddah. Another coup in 1984 installed Colonel Taya as Mauritania's leader. The absence of an independent election commission, state control of broadcasts, harassment of independent print media, and the incumbent's use of state resources to promote his candidacy devalued Taya's presidential victories in 1992—the country's first, and deeply flawed, multiparty poll—and again in 1997. Taya's Social Democratic Republican Party (PRDS) ruled the country as a de facto one-party state after the main opposition parties boycotted National Assembly elections in 1992 and 1996.

In 2001 municipal and National Assembly elections, Mauritanians were, for the first time, permitted to exercise their constitutional right to choose their representatives in relatively open, competitive elections. More than a dozen parties participated in the elections to choose 81 members of the National Assembly. However, the ruling PRDS was the only party to present candidates in every constituency, and the electoral law was modified to ban independent candidates, whose seats went mainly to the PRDS. The PRDS won 64 assembly seats, while opposition parties won 17. The banning of two political parties in 2002 devalued opposition gains in the National Assembly elections. In the municipal polls, the opposition secured 15 percent of available posts.

In June 2003, the Taya government weathered a coup attempt that triggered two days of fighting in the capital. More than 30 soldiers faced trial late in the year in connection with the coup attempt, and more than 50 Muslim clerics and opposition activists were also arrested.

The November 2003 presidential election saw the issuance of new voter cards that were difficult to falsify, the publication of a list of registered voters, and the use of transparent ballot boxes. However, although each of the six candidates was allocated equal time on state-run broadcast media, Taya received more than his share. Civil society groups were barred from forming an independent body to monitor the poll, and many foreign observers declined to participate after Taya's main challenger, Mohamed Khouna Ould Haidalla, was briefly detained on the eve of the election. Police raided the home of Haidalla, whom Taya had overthrown nearly two decades ago, reportedly on suspicion that he and his supporters were plotting to overthrow Taya if Haidalla lost the election. Opposition members said some voters were allowed to cast ballots without proper identification and that opposition representatives were barred from polling stations. They also reported double voting, voting by proxy, and vote buying.

Taya was reelected to another six-year term with 67 percent of the vote compared with 19 percent for Haidallah. The day after the election, authorities detained Haidallah, and he and more than a dozen of his supporters were to go on trial for allegedly threatening state security. Although opposition candidates disputed the results of the election, they did not choose to take their complaints to court.

Mauritania has been cultivating closer ties with the United States and is undergoing free-market reform. The country is one of three Arab League states, along with Egypt and Jordan, that has diplomatic relations with Israel, despite domestic criticism. Diplomatic ties were established in 1999.

Mauritania is one of the world's poorest countries, although recently oil has been discovered offshore. Much of the country's wealth is concentrated in the hands of a small elite that controls an economy based on iron ore exports and fishing.

**Political Rights and Civil Liberties:** Mauritanians cannot choose their government democratically. The National Assembly exercises little independence from the executive. The country's narrowly based, authoritarian regime has gradually become liberalized, but most power remains in the hands of the president and a very small elite. The November 2003 presidential poll lacked transparency and was held in an atmosphere of intimidation.

Prepublication censorship, arrests of journalists, and seizures and bans of newspapers devalue constitutional guarantees of free expression. The state owns the only two daily newspapers and monopolizes nearly all broadcast media. Independent publications openly criticize the government, but all publications must be submitted to the Interior Ministry prior to distribution. The constitution forbids dissemination of reports deemed to "attack the principles of Islam or the credibility of the state, harm the general interest, or disturb public order and security." The government does not impede Internet access.

Mauritania is an Islamic state in which, by statute, all citizens are Muslims who may not possess other religious texts or enter non-Muslim households. The right to worship in another faith, however, is generally tolerated. Non-Muslims are permitted to worship privately, and some churches operate openly. President Maaouya Ould Sid Ahmed Taya has targeted Muslim extremism. Academic freedom is guaranteed and is not restricted, although security forces have cracked down violently on student demonstrations in the past.

Freedom of association is restricted, and infrequent demonstrations are often violently suppressed. The law requires all recognized political parties and nongovernmental organizations (NGOs) to apply to the local prefect for permission to hold large meetings or assemblies. While numerous NGOs, including human rights and antislavery groups, operate, a handful of black African activist groups and Islamist parties are banned. The banned El Hor (Free Man) Movement promotes black rights, while widespread discrimination against blacks continues.

The constitution provides for the right of citizens to unionize and bargain for wages. All workers except members of the military and police are free to join unions. Approximately one-fourth of Mauritania's workers serve in the small formal (business) sector. The right to strike is limited by arbitration.

Mauritania's judicial system is heavily influenced by the government. Many decisions are shaped by Sharia (Islamic law), especially in family and civil matters. A judicial reform program is under way. Prison conditions in Mauritania are harsh, but the construction of a new prison has reduced crowding and improved treatment.

Mauritania's people include the dominant Beydane (white Maurs) of Arab extraction and Haratine (black Maurs) of African descent. Other, non-Muslim, black Africans inhabiting the country's southern frontiers along the Senegal River valley constitute approximately one-third of the population. For centuries, black Africans were subjugated and taken as slaves by both white and black Maurs. In 2003, the government passed a law that makes slavery a crime and provides for punishment of violators. Although the government does not officially sanction slavery, a few thousand blacks still live in conditions of servitude. A government campaign against the mainly black southern part of the country in the late 1980s culminated with a massive deportation of blacks to Senegal, and relations between the two countries remain strained.

Societal discrimination against women is widespread, but is improving. In 2003, for the first time, a female candidate participated in the presidential election and the first Haratine female was appointed to the cabinet. Under Sharia, a woman's testimony is given only half the weight of a man's. Legal protections regarding property and equality of pay are usually respected only in urban areas among the educated elite. At least one-quarter of women undergo female genital mutilation; the government has intensive media and education campaigns against this practice.

# Mauritius

**Population:** 1,200,000
**GNI/capita:** $3,380
**Life Expectancy:** 72
**Political Rights:** 1
**Civil Liberties:** 2
**Status:** Free
**Religious Groups:** Hindu (52 percent), Roman Catholic (26 percent), Protestant (2.3 percent), Muslim (16.6 percent), other (3.1 percent)
**Ethnic Groups:** Indo-Mauritian (68 percent), Creole (27 percent), Sino-Mauritian (3 percent), Franco-Mauritian (2 percent)
**Capital:** Port Louis

**Ten-Year Ratings Timeline (Political Rights, Civil Liberties, Status)**

| 1994 | 1995 | 1996 | 1997 | 1998 | 1999 | 2000 | 2001 | 2002 | 2003 |
|------|------|------|------|------|------|------|------|------|------|
| 1,2F | 1,2F | 1,2F | 1,2F | 1,2F | 1,2F | 1,2F | 1,2F | 1,2F | 1,2F |

**Overview:**   In September 2003, Paul Berenger became the first person from outside Mauritius' Indian-origin majority to hold the post of prime minister. The mostly symbolic powers of the president were modestly strengthened during the year.

Mauritius, which has no indigenous peoples, was seized and settled as a way station for European trade to the East Indies and India. Its ethnically mixed population is primarily descended from immigrants from the Indian subcontinent who were brought to the island as laborers during its 360 years of Dutch, French, and British colonial administration. Since gaining independence from Britain in 1968, Mauritius has maintained one of the developing world's most successful democracies. In 1992, the island became a republic within the Commonwealth, with a largely ceremonial president as head of state.

In a surprise move in August 2000, President Cassam Uteem dissolved the National Assembly and called early elections, in large part because of a series of corruption scandals that had led to the resignation of several cabinet ministers. Some 80 percent of eligible voters went to the polls. The previous prime minister, Dr. Navin Rangoolam, had served since 1995. In the 2000 elections, the victorious opposition alliance was led by the Socialist Militant Party (MSM). Its leader, Sir Aneerood Jugnauth, had served as prime minister between 1982 and 1995, when he was voted out of office. The MSM is allied with the Mauritian Militant Movement (MMM), whose leader, Berenger, was subsequently appointed minister of finance and deputy prime minister.

In a planned power shift, Berenger assumed the prime minister's position in September 2003, becoming the first person from outside the island's Indian-origin majority to hold the post. As part of the same pact, former prime minister Jugnauth moved up to the largely symbolic presidency.

President Jugnauth and Prime Minister Berenger have long played key roles in Mauritian politics and reflect the diversity of the country's social and political makeup. While Jugnauth has come from the established elite, Berenger had a reputation as a Marxist-oriented firebrand during his early days in politics. His approach and policies have become tempered with the passage of time.

Mauritius has achieved a stable democratic and constitutional order, and its focus on political competition rather than violent conflict demonstrates a level of political development enjoyed by few other African states. The political process is used to maintain ethnic balance and economic growth rather than dominance by any single group. In addition, political parties are not divided along the lines of the country's diverse ethnicities and religions.

The country's political stability has been underpinned by steady economic growth and improvements in the island's infrastructure and standard of living. Per capita income is one of the highest in Africa, and adult literacy is 84 percent. In 2003, the World Economic Forum rated Mauritius as sub-Saharan Africa's third-best country in which to do business. Mauritius' integrated, multinational population has provided a capable and reliable workforce that, along with preferential European and U.S. market access for sugar and garment exports, is attracting foreign investment.

At the same time, after expanding at a robust pace of 4 percent in 2001-2002, gross domestic product growth was expected to slow in 2002-2003 to about 3.5 percent, according to IMF figures. In 2003, the unemployment rate was nearly 10 percent. The export processing zone and tourism sectors continue to be adversely affected by the weak global environment. In addition, significant environmental degradation has occurred as the economy has developed.

**Political Rights and Civil Liberties:** Citizens have the right to change their government democratically. The head of state is a president, elected by the National Assembly for a five-year term. Executive power resides in the prime minister. The National Assembly is unicameral; it has 62 members that are directly elected by universal adult suffrage and a maximum of 8 (currently 4) members appointed from unsuccessful parliamentary candidates who gained the largest number of votes. The members serve for a five-year term. The next elections are due in 2005. Decentralized structures govern the country's island dependencies. The largest of these is Rodrigues Island, which has its own government and local councils and two seats in the National Assembly.

Constitutional amendments that modestly strengthened presidential powers were passed in 2003. These deal with the duties of the president, the appointment of the president and members of the electoral commission, the dissolution of the National Assembly, and the exercise of the prerogative of mercy.

In recent years, there have been a number of corruption cases, and recent efforts to market Mauritius as an international financial center have been impeded by a number of domestic banking market scandals. Mauritius was ranked 43 out of 133 countries in Transparency International's 2003 Corruption Perceptions Index.

According to the BBC, the constitution guarantees freedom of expression and of the press. The state-owned Mauritius Broadcasting Corporation (MBC) operates radio and TV services and generally reflects government thinking. A small number of private radio stations have been authorized, but the state-run media enjoy a monopoly in broadcasting local news. Several private daily and weekly publications, however, are often highly critical of both government and opposition politicians and their policies. Four daily newspapers and eight weeklies offer balanced coverage in several languages. They are often critical of both the government and the opposition parties. Internet access is available.

The government respects freedom of religion.

Freedom of assembly and association are respected, although police occasionally refuse to issue permits for demonstrations. Numerous nongovernmental organizations operate. Nine labor federations include 300 unions.

The generally independent judiciary is headed by the Supreme Court. The legal system is an amalgam of French and British traditions. Civil rights are generally well respected, although cases of police brutality have been reported. There are no known political prisoners or reports of political or extrajudicial killings.

Various cultures and traditions flourish in peace, though Mauritian Creoles, descendents of African slaves who make up a third of the population, live in poverty and complain of discrimination. In addition, tensions between the Hindu majority and Muslim minority persist, despite the general respect for constitutional prohibitions against discrimination. These tensions constitute one of the country's few potential political flashpoints.

Women constitute approximately 20 percent of the paid labor force and generally occupy a subordinate role in society. The law does not require equal pay for equal work or prohibit sexual harassment in the workplace. Women are underrepresented at the national university and are also significantly under-represented in the nation's political life. According to a recent Southern African Development Community report, the percentages of women in the National Assembly and in the cabinet (5.9 and 4 percent, respectively) were the lowest of the 14 member countries.

# Mexico

**Population:** 104,900,000  **Political Rights:** 2
**GNI/capita:** $5,530  **Civil Liberties:** 2
**Life Expectancy:** 75  **Status:** Free
**Religious Groups:** Roman Catholic (89 percent),
Protestant (6 percent), other (5 percent)
**Ethnic Groups:** Mestizo (60 percent), Amerindian
(30 percent), white (9 percent), other (1 percent)
**Capital:** Mexico City

**Ten-Year Ratings Timeline (Political Rights, Civil Liberties, Status)**

| 1994 | 1995 | 1996 | 1997 | 1998 | 1999 | 2000 | 2001 | 2002 | 2003 |
|------|------|------|------|------|------|------|------|------|------|
| 4,4PF | 4,4PF | 4,3PF | 3,4PF | 3,4PF | 3,4PF | 2,3F | 2,3F | 2,2F | 2,2F |

**Overview:**     As President Vicente Fox Quesada reached the halfway mark of his six-year presidency in 2003, his greatest achievement remained having bested the long-ruling Institutional Revolutionary Party (PRI) in the 2000 presidential contest. Mexicans complained that they saw little progress in addressing the problems of poverty, corruption, and unemployment the charismatic rancher-politician had promised to fix. A July 2003 midterm election resulted in a stunning loss of congressional seats for the Fox's National Action Party (PAN), which already lacked a working majority in the legislative body, and striking gains for the opposition PRI, itself in the midst of internecine warfare, as well as for the leftist Democratic Revolutionary Party (PRD).

Mexico achieved independence from Spain in 1810 and established itself as a republic in 1822. Seven years after the Revolution of 1910, a new constitution was promulgated under which the United Mexican States became a federal republic consisting of 31 states and a federal district (Mexico City). From its founding in 1929 until 2000, the PRI dominated the country by means of its corporatist, authoritarian structure maintained through co-optation, patronage, corruption, and repression. The formal business of government took place mostly in secret and with little legal foundation.

In 1999, the PRI nominated, in first-ever open-party competition, former interior minister Francisco Labastida, hailed by some as the politician's return to the helm of a party ruled during the three previous administrations by technocrats. In September, the PAN nominated Vicente Fox, governor of Guanajuato. Cuauhtemoc Cardenas took leave of the Mexico City mayoralty and announced he would again lead the PRD's national ticket. Despite election-eve polls suggesting Fox would lose, on July 2, 2000, he won Mexico's presidency with 42.5 percent of the vote. Labastida won 36 percent, and Cardenas, just 16.6 percent. By nearly becoming the largest party in the lower house of congress, the PAN won enough state governorships to put the long-ruling PRI in danger of becoming a regional party.

Following his election, Fox selected an eclectic cabinet whose new faces signaled an end to the revolving door of bureaucrats in top positions, and included leftist intellectuals, businessmen, and, as attorney general, a serving general—the latter choice bitterly opposed by human rights groups. The business-oriented Fox also announced plans to overhaul the notoriously corrupt and inefficient law enforcement agencies, breaking the political ties between the police and the presidency. In his inaugural address, Fox pledged to make Mexico an international leader in human rights, saying he would "protect them as never before, to respect them as never before."

In 2003, Fox was able to maintain his personal popularity even as the PAN suffered the consequences of the government's inability to deliver on millions of promised jobs, a migration accord with the United States, and serious economic reforms, including labor-market restructuring and privatization of the country's electrical sector. At the same time, inflation was reduced to just 4 percent; interest rates dropped 11 percent, to 6 percent, in three years; and a surge in investor confidence suggested that the country was on the verge of an economic takeoff.

In the run-up to the July 2003 midterm legislative elections, Fox's supporters pointed to a string of achievements, such as serious anticorruption initiatives, the opening of secret government files and investigation of past political crimes, and the capture and imprisonment of a number of once-elusive drug kingpins. However, as Mexico's drug cartels were decapitated, a new breed of crime leaders came to the fore whom experts say are less violent, but also more efficient.

The July elections not only reaffirmed the dominate roles of opposition parties in both houses of congress, but also resulted in the PAN's losing the governorship in the prosperous industrial state of Nuevo Leon, long a party stronghold. The PAN's congressional vote dropped from 38 percent in 2000, to 30.5 percent, while the PRI won 38 percent and the PRD received 18 percent. The PRD not only increased its own congressional representation, but also consolidated its hold on Mexico City, the Western Hemisphere's largest urban area, winning the presidency of 14 of the city's 16 boroughs. The elections, in which 11 parties spent more than $500 million, were the most expensive in recent memory, but yielded a record low voter turnout. Fox was also criticized for spending millions of dollars on a media blitz touting his achievements in the immediate run-up to the elections.

Despite post-election promises by Fox to work harder to collaborate with the opposition on a reform agenda, the PAN's bickering with Fox over indigenous rights and fiscal reform, combined with jockeying within the unreformed PRI for the party's 2006 presidential nomination, made that possibility seem remote. The inability to achieve a meaningful reform of immigration policy with the United States, and the continued marginalization of Mexico's indigenous peoples added to concerns about whether Fox could achieve his goals. With its new international prominence as a nonpermanent member of the UN Security Council, the Fox government was unable to escape the limelight for its refusal to support military intervention by the United States and its allies in Iraq. The economic slowdown in the United States and increased competition from Asia continued to hurt Mexico's economic recovery.

**Political Rights and Civil Liberties:** Mexicans can choose their government democratically. In 2001, 2002, and 2003, opposition parties made gains in state and municipal contests in elections that were generally considered to be free and fair. The president is elected to a six-year term and cannot be reelected. A bicameral congress consists of the 128-member Senate elected for six years, with at least one minority senator from each state, and the 500-member Chamber of Deputies elected for three years, 300 directly and 200 through proportional representation. Each state has an elected governor and legislature. In 2003, serious consideration was being given to a proposal to allow as many as one million Mexicans living in the United States to cast absentee votes in Mexican elections.

According a recent study by the Mexico chapter of Transparency International, some $2.3 billion (approximately 1 percent) of the country's economic production goes to officials in bribes, with the poorest families paying nearly 14 percent of their income in bribes. Corruption at the state-owned petroleum giant Pemex alone is estimated to cost the company more than $1 billion a year. The U.S. Drug Enforcement Administration estimates that between $25 billion and $30 billion of illegal drug money is laundered each year in Mexico and says that the country's financial, political, military, and judicial institutions facilitate those crimes. In November, the Mexican Senate approved a legislative package designed to prevent and detect terrorist financing by clamping stricter reporting requirements on financial institutions and setting down strict penalties for violations of those rules.

The media, while mostly private, largely depend on the government for advertising revenue. In 2000, President Vicente Fox pledged to end the PRI practice of buying favorable stories and vowed to respect media independence. Despite the improvements, however, violent attacks against journalists continue, although with a lower frequency than in past years. Reporters investigating police issues, narcotics trafficking, and public corruption remain at particular risk. Radio and television stations still operate under a law that allows the government to grant broadcast licenses at its discretion, rather than on the basis of professional criteria. In 2002,

Mexico enacted its first freedom of information law, which expressly prohibits the government from withholding for any reason information about crimes against humanity or gross human rights violations. The law went into effect in June 2003. The government did not restrict Internet access, which was widely available across the nation, although much less so among the poor and the elderly, due to economic constraints or lack of computer literacy.

The constitution was amended in 1992 to restore the legal status of the Roman Catholic Church and other religious institutions. Priests and nuns were allowed to vote for the first time in nearly 80 years. Fox himself is the most conservative, fervently devout Mexican president in recent memory and was fined after the 2000 election for breaking election laws prohibiting the use of religious symbols. In 2003, a Roman Catholic cardinal who oversaw Vatican spending in Mexico was investigated in the wake of allegations he was using drug money to build churches. The government does not restrict academic freedom.

Constitutional guarantees regarding political and civic organizations are generally respected in the urbanized northern and central parts of the country. Political and civic expression, however, is restricted throughout rural Mexico, in poor urban areas, and in poor southern states. Civil society participation has grown larger in recent years; human rights, pro-democracy, women's, and environmental groups are active. In June, Fox signed legislation that banned all forms of discrimination, including that based on ethnic origin, gender, age, or religion.

The *maquiladoras* (export-processing zones) have fostered substantial abuses of workers' rights. Most maquiladora workers are young, uneducated women who accept lower pay more readily, with annual labor turnover averaging between 200 and 300 percent. Workers have no medical insurance, holidays, or profit sharing, and female employees are frequently the targets of sexual harassment and abuse. In 2003, Amnesty International released a report that criticized investigations by Mexican police to resolve the murders of at least 263 women and the disappearances of 4,587 more in Ciudad Juarez along the U.S. border. The report said that police in the state of Chihuahua used false evidence, torture, and inadequate forensic tests to investigate the killings of the women, who mostly worked in maquiladoras.

The justice system is based on the cumbersome nineteenth-century Napoleonic code, in which judges decide cases by reading documentary evidence. There is virtually no body of law governing juvenile justice. In most rural areas, respect for laws by official agencies is still tenuous at best, particularly in towns and villages that receive large influxes of dollars from relatives involved in narcotics trafficking in the United States. Lower courts and law enforcement in general are undermined by widespread bribery, despite efforts by the Fox administration toward reform. Torture, arbitrary arrest, and abuse of prisoners persist in many areas, although an investigation released in April by the Boston-based Physicians for Human Rights, conducted with the support of the Mexican government, said that torture was probably not as pervasive as it had been five years earlier. In a recent positive development, the Supreme Court of Mexico ruled in November that the "disappearances" of leftist activists in the 1960s and 1970s were kidnappings not subject to the statute of limitations. The decision paved the way for the arrest of former senior officials implicated in the rights crimes.

The role of the military in internal security—ostensibly to combat domestic terrorism, drug trafficking, and street crime—has contributed to grave human rights problems, particularly in rural areas. Because Mexico has no foreign enemies, the military, which operates largely beyond public scrutiny, serves mainly as an auxiliary police force. In places such as the states of Chiapas and Guerrero, army counterinsurgency units, moving through local civilian populations like an occupying force, continue to cause numerous rights violations. The military justice system allows for soldiers accused of rights violations to be tried in secret, and the outcomes of their trials are only occasionally made public. After the 2003 elections, informed observers said that it was much less likely that Fox would continue to make an issue of corruption and human rights violations committed under the PRI, given the need to cultivate the former ruling party's congressional delegation and Fox's reluctance to anger its powerful military allies.

Mexico's soaring crime rate and lack of effective law enforcement, characterized by an entrenched culture of bribery and disrespect for the law, are serious barriers to economic development. In Mexico City, approximately 80 percent of crimes go unreported because the notoriously underpaid police are viewed as either inept or in league with the wrongdoers; only about 6 percent of reported crimes are solved. Ten percent of all extortive kidnappings in Mexico are believed to be carried out by former or serving police officers. While Colombia is still the hemispheric leader in kidnappings, those are primarily political in nature; experts say that Mexico may hold the world's record for abductions for money. In early 2001, Fox announced a crusade to clean up Mexico's law enforcement system, urging Mexicans to report common crimes and announcing a citizen program to make the police more accountable by making their files more accessible to the public. In 2002, the center-left mayor of Mexico City announced he was hiring former New York mayor Rudolph Giuliani as a security consultant, a move questioned by rights activists familiar with the New York City Police Department's record during the 1990s.

Dozens of labor and peasant leaders have been killed in recent years in ongoing land disputes, particularly in the southern states, where Indians constitute close to half the population. Most Native Americans are relegated to extreme poverty in rural villages lacking roads, running water, schools, and telephones. Indian groups said that a 2001 constitutional reform designed to strengthen their rights fell far short of addressing their concerns.

Domestic violence and sexual abuse remain serious problems, although the Fox government has pledged to fight a problem that some experts say affects 50 to 70 percent of women. Mexico is a source country for trafficked persons to the United States, Canada, and Japan, and a transit country for persons from various places, especially Central America and China. Internal trafficking is also a problem. In 2003, women held only one cabinet ministry, no governorships, and 23 percent of the seats in the lower house of congress.

# Micronesia

**Population:** 100,000
**GNI/capita:** $1,980
**Life Expectancy:** 66
**Religious Groups:** Roman Catholic (50 percent),
Protestant (47 percent), other (3 percent)
**Ethnic Groups:** Micronesian, Polynesian
**Capital:** Palikir

**Political Rights:** 1
**Civil Liberties:** 1*
**Status:** Free

**Ratings Change:** Micronesia's civil liberties rating improved
from 2 to 1 due to a reevaluation of the scope of freedom of the media and association.

**Ten-Year Ratings Timeline (Political Rights, Civil Liberties, Status)**

| 1994 | 1995 | 1996 | 1997 | 1998 | 1999 | 2000 | 2001 | 2002 | 2003 |
|------|------|------|------|------|------|------|------|------|------|
| 1,1F | 1,1F | 1,1F | 1,2F | 1,2F | 1,2F | 1,2F | 1,2F | 1,2F | 1,1F |

**Overview:**

The major issue for the government of the Federated States of Micronesia (FSM) in 2003 was the conclusion of a new Compact of Free Association with the United States. The compact provides U.S. funding to the FSM in exchange for allowing the United States to set up military bases in its territory. A new president, Joseph Urusemal, was elected in May.

FSM was administered by the United States from 1947 to 1979 as one of the U.N. Trusteeship territories. A constitution was adopted in 1979, and full independence was reached in 1984. FSM is composed of four states—Chuuk (or formerly Truk), Kosrae, Pohnpei, and Yap—that cover a total of 607 islands.

In 2003, a new lease agreement was concluded with the United States. The Compact of Free Association provides FSM with financial assistance representing a third of its national income and defense by the United States in exchange for allowing the United States the right to establish military bases in its territory. In May, a new $1.8 billion compact that provides $92 million a year to FSM for 20 years and allows continued access to U.S. services and programs, as well as visa-free access to the United States for FSM citizens, was signed. Many FSM citizens are worried about the lower level of funding, inflation rate adjustments, and the termination of disaster assistance from the U.S. Federal Emergency Management Agency (FEMA). The new compact also provides for a trust fund invested and overseen by a joint board of United States and FSM trustees in response to past mismanagement of funds.

Another major national issue was a call by the people of Faichuk in the state of Chuuk in February to withdraw from the federation. They want a greater share of compact funds, even a separate bilateral agreement with the United States, to garner more funds for their own development needs. This complaint resonated with the other states and spurred debates on federal-state relations. In November, the government announced that it would increase the share of compact funds to the four states.

A general election was held in March 2003, and President Leo Falcam was defeated. On May 11, the thirteenth congress was launched to elect a new president and vice president. Joseph Urusemal was elected the sixth president of the FSM, and Redley Killion was chosen as the vice president. Urusemal is a former governor of Yap, one of the constituent states of the federation, while Killion was vice president in Falcam's administration.

**Political Rights and Civil Liberties:** Citizens of Micronesia can change their government democratically. A unicameral, 14-member legislature is composed of 1 representative each from the four constituent states for four-year terms and 10 representatives from single-member districts for two-year terms. All representatives are popularly elected. Chuuk, the largest of the four states, holds nearly half of the country's population and a proportionate number of congressional seats, which has been a source of resentment among the three smaller states. The president and vice president are chosen from among the four state representatives in the legislature to serve four-year terms. By informal agreement, these offices are rotated among the representatives of the four states. Each state in the Federated States of Micronesia (FSM) has its own constitution, elected legislature, and governor. State governments have considerable power, particularly with the implementation of budgetary policies. As with many other Pacific Island states, traditional leaders and institutions exercise considerable influence in society, particularly at the village level. There are no formal political parties, although there are no restrictions against their formation.

The media are free, and media outlets consist of government newsletters, several small private papers, and television stations in three of the four states. Each state government runs its own radio station, and a religious group runs another station. Satellite television is increasingly available. There is no restriction on Internet access, but small user communities in FSM (about 1,700 users) and other Pacific Island states do not generate sufficient revenue for Internet service providers to bring down costs and expand bandwidth.

Religious freedom is respected in this mainly Christian country. There were no reports of restrictions on academic freedom.

Citizens are free to organize civic groups. There are a few student and women's groups. There are no laws against formation of trade unions, but no unions exist. No specific laws regulate work hours, recognize the right to strike and bargain collectively, or set workplace health and safety standards. Unemployment is high at 22 percent. The economy is dependent on subsistence agriculture, fishing, tourism, and U.S. assistance.

The judiciary is independent. However, cultural resistance to using the courts, particularly for sexual crimes, means many offenders are not brought to justice. Lack of funds hampers efforts to improve the functioning of the courts and prison conditions.

Women continue to suffer from social and economic discrimination in the male-dominated culture. Domestic violence is a serious problem, and cases are often not reported to the authorities because of pressure from within the family, fear of further assault, or an expectation of inaction by the authorities. Even when they were reported, offenders rarely go to trial or those found guilty usually receive light sentences. In October, the government ratified the Convention on the Elimination of all Forms of Discrimination Against Women, but it refused to implement certain parts, including an article requiring employers to give women full pay and social benefits when they take maternity leave.

# Moldova

**Population:** 4,300,000    **Political Rights:** 3
**GNI/capita:** $400    **Civil Liberties:** 4
**Life Expectancy:** 68    **Status:** Partly Free
**Religious Groups:** Eastern Orthodox (98 percent),
Jewish (1.5 percent), other [including Baptist] (0.5 percent)
**Ethnic Groups:** Moldovan/Romanian (64 percent),
Ukrainian (13.8 percent), Russian (13 percent), Bulgarian
(2 percent), Jewish (1.5 percent), other [including Gagauz] (5.7 percent)
**Capital:** Chisinau

**Ten-Year Ratings Timeline (Political Rights, Civil Liberties, Status)**

| 1994 | 1995 | 1996 | 1997 | 1998 | 1999 | 2000 | 2001 | 2002 | 2003 |
|------|------|------|------|------|------|------|------|------|------|
| 4,4PF | 4,4PF | 3,4PF | 3,4PF | 2,4PF | 2,4PF | 2,4PF | 2,4PF | 3,4PF | 3,4PF |

**Overview:**

Two rounds of local elections held in May and June 2003 were deemed by outside observers to be generally in line with international standards. However, concerns were raised about favoritism shown toward the ruling authorities in government-owned media. Some bright signs regarding the economic situation emerged as the economy continued to show strong growth for the third consecutive year.

The Moldavian Soviet Socialist Republic declared independence from the Soviet Union in 1991. Mircea Snegur, chairman of the Communist Supreme Soviet, became the first president of the democratic Republic of Moldova. Snegur's centrist Agrarian Democratic Party (ADP) subsequently won a majority of parliamentary seats in the country's first free and fair popular election in 1994. Two years later, Petru Lucinschi, also a former Communist, defeated Snegur in the 1996 presidential elections. While the Party of Moldovan Communists (PCM) won a plurality of votes in the 1998 elections for Moldova's unicameral parliament, three centrist parties united to form a majority coalition. During this time, Moldova undertook much-needed economic reforms, drafted a new constitution, and joined NATO's Partnership for Peace program.

In the 2001 parliamentary elections, the PCM won a landslide victory on the promise of a return to Soviet-era living standards, and in April, PCM leader Vladimir Voronin was elected president. Moldova thus became the first former Soviet republic to elect a Communist Party member as president.

Under Voronin, the government reinstated Soviet-style territorial administration, restored the November 7 holiday commemorating the October Revolution, introduced measures to make Russian an official second language, and proposed regulations requiring mandatory Russian-language instruction in schools. These Russification initiatives met fierce resistance from the opposition Christian-Democrat People's Party (CDPP) and sparked a continual series of public protests in early 2002. In short order, opposition leaders began to issue calls for the government's abdication, and by February, the government had reversed its previous decision on mandatory Russian-language instruction. The Constitutional Court later voided a draft law that would have made Russian an official state language.

The CDPP protest campaign to force the government to resign slowly lost momentum during the course of 2002, partly because the CDPP draws its strength from a limited portion of Moldovan society, one that generally identifies with Moldova's Romanian heritage. While focusing largely on the issue of cultural identity, the CDPP was slow to develop a fully viable solution to the country's other pressing concerns, such as Moldova's desperate economic situation.

In retribution for the CDPP's efforts to remove it from power, the Communist-controlled government briefly suspended the CDPP in 2002 and moved to lift the parliamentary immunity of the CDPP chairman and two party deputies in the first step toward criminal prosecution. The Council of Europe responded by intervening to negotiate a cessation of the open political hostilities. The CDPP agreed to drop its call for the government's resignation, and the government retracted the threat of prosecution. As part of this agreement, the government also agreed to make good on a variety of council demands relating to political and civil rights in the country. While this compromise agreement demonstrates the extent to which Voronin's government is open to influence from Euro-Atlantic institutions, it also underscores the delicate nature of Moldova's developing democracy and the need for further council monitoring.

Local elections were held nationwide in two rounds in May and June (except in the Gagauz autonomous region; the Gagauz are a Christian Turkic minority). Although the Organization for Security and Cooperation in Europe (OSCE) generally deemed the elections to have been "conducted mostly in line with international standards," some observers expressed concerns about media coverage of the elections. The elections themselves showed that the PCM remained overall the strongest political party in the country, gaining 41 percent of all the mayoral positions contested, while the Social Liberal Alliance "Our Moldova" came in second, winning 21.19 percent.

Separatist elements have declared a "Dniester Republic" in Transnistria, situated between the Dniester River and Ukraine, in which Russian troops continue to maintain a presence. Transnistria is home to approximately 750,000 of Moldova's 4.35 million people. During 2003, Russian and American diplomats in the OSCE tried to resolve the Transnistria issue by putting forth a federalization plan in which Chisniau would share power with the Transnistrian capital, Tiraspol, but by year's end little progress had been made. Voronin's PCM favored the federalization plan, while the CDPP opposed it.

Moldova is one of Europe's most impoverished countries. Official unemployment hovers around 30 percent. By the government's own estimates, some 80 percent of the population subsists on less than the officially designated minimum, and the shadow economy accounts for between 30 and 70 percent of all economic activity. In this grim economic environment, thousands of Moldovans have elected to sell one of their kidneys to black market dealers in Turkey. Harsh economic conditions have likewise led a substantial number of women into prostitution. Despite these problems, Moldova was accepted into the World Trade Organization in 2001, and there has been strong economic growth over the past three years—6.1 percent growth in 2001, 7.2 percent in 2002, and 5.3 percent in 2003. A symbolic token of confidence in Moldova's progress came in May when Moldova was allowed to assume the chairmanship of the Council of Europe's Committee of Ministers.

**Political Rights and Civil Liberties:** Citizens of Moldova can change their government democratically. Although international observers believe that Moldova's Electoral Code provides a sound framework for the conduct of free and fair elections, some needed reforms include improving the accuracy of voter lists and increasing transparency of the tabulation of election results. In 2000, Moldova ended direct presidential elections. Voters elect members to the 101-seat parliament by proportional representation to four-year terms. Parliament then elects the prime minister and president. The self-declared government in Transnistria, however, severely limits the ability of voters in that region to participate in Moldova's national elections. More than 30 political parties are registered and compete in elections. Nevertheless, government security forces are believed to monitor political figures and to conduct unauthorized wiretaps.

The constitution guarantees freedom of expression and of the press. Electronic media, especially television, remain the most important source of information for most citizens. An OSCE report on the 2001 parliamentary elections found that while state broadcasters adhered to the rules of the Electoral Code regarding impartiality in reporting, private broadcasters often aligned themselves with specific political parties or candidates. Although the constitution prohibits censorship, nearly 500 journalists and media workers at the state-owned TeleRadio Moldova held demonstrations in March 2002 to protest alleged censorship and demand greater media independence. Under an agreement with the Council of Europe, the government subsequently passed legislation transferring state control of TeleRadio Moldova to an independent corporation. In March, the new Law on Combating Extremism went into effect. Critics believe it may strengthen the government's ability to limit freedom of expression, although by late in the year no actions had been taken under the law. Concerns remain about the extent of government control over TeleRadio Moldova, however. There were also accusations that state media engaged in biased reporting during the May-June local elections, granting government candidates significantly more coverage than opposition figures. The government did not restrict access to the Internet in 2003.

Moldova's constitution guarantees religious freedom. Although this right is generally respected, there have been some legal impediments to the functioning of various religious groups and sects. Although there is no state religion, the Moldovan Orthodox Church receives some favored treatment from the government. All religious groups are required to register with the government, and unregistered groups are not allowed to buy property or obtain construction permits. A number of groups, including the Church of True Orthodox–Moldova, the Church of Jesus Christ of Latter Day Saints (Mormons), and a local Muslim organization have faced difficulties in recent years in dealing with the government bureaucracy. Nondenominational "moral and spiritual" instruction is mandatory in primary schools and is optional for secondary and university students. Restitution of church properties confiscated during the Communist era remains a problem. In a constitutional first for Moldova, the country's Supreme Court of Justice in April overruled its own earlier ruling, from 1997, which had denied registration to the Bessarabian Metropolitan Church, to some extent bowing to pressure from the Council of Europe and the European Court of Human Rights. No government restrictions of academic freedom were reported in 2003.

Citizens may participate freely in nongovernmental organizations and political parties. Private organizations must register with the state, and demonstrations require permits from local authorities. Worker are allowed to strike, petition the government, and form and join trade unions. The law allows collective bargaining but prohibits strikes by government employees and essential workers.

Moldova's constitution provides for an independent judiciary. It also guarantees equality before the law and the presumption of innocence. There is evidence that some prosecutors, judges, and law enforcement officials accept bribes and are subject to official pressure from governmental figures. Prison conditions are exceptionally poor, and malnutrition and disease are high in penal institutions.

Although ethnic minorities constitute some 30 percent of the population, international observers believe that legislation makes it difficult for them to organize politically. Nevertheless, ethnic minority representation in parliament after the 2001 elections rose from 16 percent to 30 percent. The Roma (Gypsy) community is the victim of particular discrimination in Moldovan society.

There are no official restrictions on women's rights in Moldova, although they are considerably under-represented in public life. Women currently hold 13 of 101 seats in parliament. Domestic violence against women is believed by human rights groups to be widespread. Trafficking in women and girls is an exceptionally important problem. Although the law prohibits trafficking in human beings, the country's poverty makes young women, especially from poor rural areas, vulnerable to promises made by traffickers for jobs in Western Europe. Moldova remains a major source for women and girls trafficked to other countries for purposes of forced prostitution.

# Monaco

**Population:** 30,000
**GNI/capita:** $27,000
**Life Expectancy:** na
**Religious Groups:** Roman Catholic (90 percent), other (10 percent)
**Ethnic Groups:** French (47 percent), Italian (16 percent), Monegasque (16 percent), other (21 percent)
**Capital:** Monaco

**Political Rights:** 2
**Civil Liberties:** 1
**Status:** Free

**Ten-Year Ratings Timeline (Political Rights, Civil Liberties, Status)**

| 1994 | 1995 | 1996 | 1997 | 1998 | 1999 | 2000 | 2001 | 2002 | 2003 |
|------|------|------|------|------|------|------|------|------|------|
| 2,1F | 2,1F | 2,1F | 2,1F | 2,1F | 2,1F | 2,1F | 2,1F | 2,1F | 2,1F |

**Overview:**

National elections in early 2003 led to one of the most significant shifts in postwar Monegasque politics.

The Principality of Monaco is an independent and sovereign state, although it remains closely associated with neighboring France. The royal Grimaldi family has ruled the principality for the past 700 years, except for a brief period of French colonial rule from 1789 to 1814. Under a treaty ratified in 1919, France pledged to protect the territorial integrity, sovereignty, and independence of the principality in return for a guarantee that Monegasque policy would conform to French interests.

Prince Rainier III has led the country since 1949 and is largely responsible for Monaco's impressive economic growth. Since his ascension, the country has ended its dependence on gambling and increased other sources of revenue, principally tourism, financial services, and banking. In August 2002, Monaco added a huge new floating pier to its harbor, which is known as a major port for expensive yachts and fancy cruisers. The pier, the largest in the world, cost almost $250 million and doubles the capacity of the country's port. In February 2002, Monaco adopted the euro despite the fact that it is not a member of the European Union (EU). A new EU directive intended to crack down on tax evasion and fraud that was passed in 2003 threatens Monaco's status as a major tax haven.

Elections in February 2003 led to a major upset for the National and Democratic Union (UND), which lost after dominating national politics in Monaco for the past several decades. The opposition Union of Monaco (UPM) received 58.5 percent of the vote and 21 of the 24 seats in the Conseil National, while the UND received 41.5 percent of the vote. The UPM's victory represented widespread support for Monaco's bid for membership in the 45-member Council of Europe, an issue the party had promoted strongly.

**Political Rights and Civil Liberties:**  Citizens of Monaco can elect their parliamentary representatives democratically. However, the prince has the sole authority to initiate laws and change the government. The 24 members of the Conseil National are elected every five years; 16 are elected by a majority electoral system, and 8 by proportional representation. The head of state is not elected but inherits the position. Prince Rainier III has ruled the country for the past 54 years, and his son, Prince Albert Alexandre Louis Pierre, is his likely successor. The head of government—the Minister of State—is traditionally appointed by the monarch from a list of three candidates who are French nationals presented by the French government. The current Minister of State, Patrick Leclercq, has held the post since 2000. In addition to the Minister of State, the prince also appoints three other ministers (counselors) who collectively make up the government. All legislation and the budget, however, require the assent of parliament.

Because of a lack of available financial information, the level of corruption is difficult to measure in Monaco. As of today, Monaco remains on the OECD's list of uncooperative tax havens. Although it is not a member of the EU, Monaco will have to exchange information or impose a withholding tax to minimize money laundering and prevent capital flows from the EU. As other tax havens have agreed to the EU's directives, it is assumed that Monaco will also fall in line.

The media in Monaco are free and independent. Monaco was one of only 12 of the 55 OSCE member states that had no press freedom violations recorded in 1999–2000. The constitution provides for freedom of speech and the press, although the penal code prohibits denunciations of the ruling family.

The constitution provides for freedom of religion, although Roman Catholicism is the state religion and Catholic ritual plays a role in state festivities. There are free religious institutions and no laws against proselytizing by formally registered religious organizations, although it is strongly discouraged. The government does not restrict academic freedom.

The government does not impose restrictions on the formation of civic and human rights groups. Workers have the legal right to organize and bargain collectively, although they rarely do so. Only 10 percent of the workforce is unionized. All workers except those in the government have the right to strike.

The legal right to a fair public trial and an independent judiciary is generally respected. The constitution requires that the prince delegate his judicial powers to the judiciary.

The constitution also differentiates between the rights of nationals and those of residents. Of the estimated 32,000 residents in the principality, only about 7,000 are actual Monegasques, who alone may participate in the election of the Conseil National. Monegasques also benefit from free education, unemployment assistance, and the right to hold elective office.

A woman can lodge criminal charges against a husband for domestic violence, and women generally receive equal pay for equal work. Although naturalized male citizens in Monaco can transfer citizenship, naturalized women cannot. There were no reports of trafficking in persons into, from, or within Monaco over the year.

# Mongolia

**Population:** 2,500,000
**GNI/capita:** $400
**Life Expectancy:** 65
**Political Rights:** 2
**Civil Liberties:** 2
**Status:** Free
**Religious Groups:** Tibetan Buddhist Lamaism (96 percent), other [including Muslim] (4 percent)
**Ethnic Groups:** Mongol (85 percent), Kazakh (7 percent), other (8 percent)
**Capital:** Ulaanbaatar

**Ten-Year Ratings Timeline (Political Rights, Civil Liberties, Status)**

| 1994 | 1995 | 1996 | 1997 | 1998 | 1999 | 2000 | 2001 | 2002 | 2003 |
|------|------|------|------|------|------|------|------|------|------|
| 2,3F | 2,3F | 2,3F | 2,3F | 2,3F | 2,3F | 2,3F | 2,3F | 2,2F | 2,2F |

**Overview:**

Mongolians in 2003 grappled with acute poverty, high unemployment, and rising violent crime as their landlocked, sparsely populated nation, nestled between China and Russia, continued its rocky transition to a market economy. Prime Minister Nambariin Enkhbayar's former Communist ruling party faces elections in 2004 that will offer Mongolians a choice between his government's incremental approach to economic reform and the opposition's shock therapy agenda.

Once the center of Ghengis Khan's sprawling empire, Mongolia was dominated for much of the past three centuries by its neighbors. China controlled Mongolia for two centuries until 1921. A Soviet-backed, Marxist revolt that year led to the creation in 1924 of a single-party Communist state, the world's second ever, under the Mongolian People's Revolutionary Party (MPRP).

Mongolia's transition from Soviet satellite to democratic republic began in 1990, when the MPRP responded to anti-government protests by legalizing opposition parties and holding the country's first multiparty elections. Facing an unprepared and underfunded opposition, the MPRP easily won parliamentary elections that year and again in 1992.

The key political issue in post-Communist Mongolia has been the pace and extent of economic reform. Market reforms have helped create a fledgling private sector, but also have contributed to soaring unemployment and other social miseries. MPRP governments in the early 1990s privatized small businesses and ended collectivized herding, but had difficulty retooling the economy to survive the loss of Soviet subsidies. Many large firms went bankrupt, and thousands of Mongolians were thrown out of work.

With hardship mounting, the MPRP was swept out of parliamentary power, after 72 years, in the 1996 elections. The coalition of reformist parties that took office, however, also had difficulty stabilizing the economy. Prescribing shock therapy to speed Mongolia's transition to a market system, the Democratic Union Coalition (DUC) cut spending, pensions, and tariffs and freed prices.

This tough economic medicine, however, coincided with steep drops in world prices for two of Mongolia's biggest foreign exchange earners, copper and cashmere. The resulting fall in export revenues gave Prime Minister Mendsaihan Enksaikhan's government little room to boost social spending at a time when its radical policies were helping to send inflation and unemployment soaring.

The MPRP regained power with victories in the 1997 election for the largely ceremonial presidency and the more important 2000 parliamentary vote. The ex-Communists' victories suggested that many Mongolians hoped that the MPRP would rebuild the country's shattered social safety net.

In the 1997 presidential contest, the MPRP's Natsagiin Bagabandi, a former parliamentary chairman, defeated incumbent Punsalmaagiyn Orchirbat of the DUC. The MPRP's parliamentary election victory three years later saw the party gain an overwhelming majority in the legislature, taking 72 of 76 seats. New prime minister Enkhbayar, the MPRP chairman, pledged to stake out a "third way" between his party's still-powerful Marxist wing and the DUC's rapid-liberalization policies.

The 44-year-old Enkhbayar's cash-strapped government has found it tough to deliver on its campaign pledges to create more jobs and boost social services. Observers believe that Mongolia's real jobless rate is around 17 percent rather than the official 4.6 percent. Nature has added to the hardship. Between 1999 and 2002, rural Mongolia was devastated by three straight winters with a brutal ice-and-snow phenomenon, known locally as zud, that killed off around one-third of the nation's livestock. This wiped out the livelihoods of many nomadic herding families and sent thousands of them to Ulaanbaatar. Many former herders who once roamed the steppe now live in shantytowns that ring the capital. Mongolia is likely to depend on donor aid for years to come, although recent foreign investment in gold and copper deposits could eventually help stabilize the government's finances.

**Political Rights and Civil Liberties:** Mongolians can change their government through elections, and they enjoy most basic rights. The 1992 constitution created a hybrid presidential-parliamentary system. Most executive powers are vested in a prime minister, who is chosen by the party or coalition with the most seats in parliament. The president, however, must approve parliament's choice of prime minister and can veto legislation, subject to a two-thirds parliamentary override. Both the president and 76-seat parliament, known as the Great Hural, are directly elected for four-year terms. President Natsagiin Bagabandi easily won reelection in 2001.

Mongolia's press is largely free but faces some government pressure. Newspapers and magazines carry a wide range of party and independent views that often criticize the government. The government, however, has at times filed libel suits and launched tax audits against publications in the wake of critical articles. Libel charges are hard to defend against because Mongolian law places the burden on the defendant to prove the truth of the statement at issue. A court in 2002 sentenced the editor in chief of *Word* newspaper to one year in jail for libel, drawing widespread criticism from journalists. In a still-controversial move, the government shut down two papers in 2000 for failing to comply with tax laws, as well as for their coverage of violence and allegedly pornographic content. In this environment, many journalists practice some self-censorship.

While newspapers are popular in cities, the main source of news in the vast countryside is the state-owned Radio Mongolia. Both Radio Mongolia and state television generally are free of political control. The government, however, has been slow to comply with a 1999 law requiring state broadcast media to be transformed into public corporations. Besides the state broadcast services, Mongolians have access to local private television, English-language broadcasts of the BBC and VOA on private FM stations and, in Ulaanbaatar, foreign television on cable and commercial satellite systems. Political reporting by both print and broadcast journalists is hampered by limited access to official information and a lack of transparency in government.

Mongolians of all faiths worship freely in this mainly Buddhist nation. Some religious groups seeking to fulfill mandatory registration requirements, however, have faced demands for bribes by local officials, according to the U.S. State Department's human rights report for 2002, released in March 2003. Mongolian professors and other teachers generally can write and lecture freely.

The country has many active environmental, human rights, and social welfare groups, though most depend on foreign donors. Mongolian trade unions are independent and active, though the government's slimming down or sale of many state factories has contributed to a sharp drop in union membership, to less than half the workforce. Many laid-off state employees now work in small, non-unionized firms or are self-employed. Collective bargaining is legal, but with Mongolia's poor economy employers enjoy considerable leverage and often set wages unilaterally. The government prohibits strikes in sectors that it considers essential, including utilities, transportation, and law enforcement. Laws on child labor and workplace health and safety are poorly enforced. Private land ownership is not permitted, although the law allows land to be leased for up to 100 years.

Mongolia's judiciary is independent, but corruption among judges persists, according to the U.S. State Department report. In a holdover from the country's Communist past, defendants are not presumed innocent.

Post-Communist reforms have created a more disciplined police force, though anecdotal evidence suggests that officers in rural Mongolia occasionally beat suspects and prisoners. Despite recent reforms, conditions in jails and pretrial detention centers continue to be life threatening because of insufficient food, heat, and health care. Tuberculosis has killed dozens of inmates in recent years, though the percentage of prisoners who die each year from tuberculosis continues to drop. Inmates often come to prison already suffering from illnesses because of the long periods that many spend in pre-trial police detention, where conditions are even worse.

Women make up the majority of university graduates, doctors, and lawyers and have helped set up and manage many of Mongolia's new trading and manufacturing firms. They also are at the forefront of Mongolian civil society, running several influential nongovernmental groups that educate voters, lobby government officials, and promote women's rights and child welfare. Women, however, hold relatively few senior judicial and governmental posts. Anecdotal evidence suggests that many Mongolian women continue to be victimized by domestic violence, which often is linked to alcohol abuse.

# Morocco

**Population:** 30,400,000  **Political Rights:** 5
**GNI/capita:** $1,190  **Civil Liberties:** 5
**Life Expectancy:** 70  **Status:** Partly Free
**Religious Groups:** Muslim (98.7 percent),
Christian (1.1 percent), Jewish (0.2 percent)
**Ethnic Groups:** Arab-Berber (99 percent),
other (1 percent)
**Capital:** Rabat

**Ten-Year Ratings Timeline (Political Rights, Civil Liberties, Status)**

| 1994 | 1995 | 1996 | 1997 | 1998 | 1999 | 2000 | 2001 | 2002 | 2003 |
|------|------|------|------|------|------|------|------|------|------|
| 5,5PF | 5,5PF | 5,5PF | 5,5PF | 5,4PF | 5,4PF | 5,4PF | 5,5PF | 5,5PF | 5,5PF |

**Overview:**     Shaken by five simultaneous suicide bombings on May 16, 2003 that left 45 dead and nearly 100 injured, Morocco has engaged in a security crackdown that has prompted criticism from press freedom and human rights organizations. A new antiterrorism law that erodes human rights protections and increased reports of torture have raised significant concerns. Meanwhile, the Islamists are on the defensive, downplaying their political ambitions during the September 12 municipal elections. King Muhammad VI proposed significant reform of the Mudawana, Morocco's personal status code, which would grant broad new rights to women if passed by parliament.

Moroccan independence dates to 1956, when power passed to King Muhammad V following 44 years of French colonial rule. King Hassan II ascended the throne five years later on the death of his father. In 1975, Morocco laid claim to the Western Sahara following the withdrawal of Spanish forces from the territory. The status of the territory remains in dispute. Hassan II oversaw much of Morocco's modern development; however, despite Hassan's gestures at establishing a constitutional monarchy, power remained concentrated entirely in the hands of the king. The country's stability was shaken during the early 1970s, when two assassination attempts on the king were thwarted. King Hassan embarked on a slow path toward political reform in the 1990s. In 1996, the king established a directly elected lower house of parliament via a constitutional amendment. Hassan also moved to improve the human rights situation and modestly expand political freedoms.

At age 35, King Muhammad VI came to power in July 1999 after the death of his father. While Morocco had made tentative steps toward political and economic liberalization, Muhammad inherited a country with severe social and economic problems. More than 20 percent of the population was unemployed, nearly half remained illiterate, and a third lived below the poverty line. Mounting public debt impinged on the government's ability to provide social services. Islamist charitable networks quickly filled the gap, providing services and gaining support at the grassroots level.

King Muhammad has continued to pursue political opening, although at a measured pace. Soon after he ascended the throne, the young king distinguished himself through a series of bold maneuvers. One of his first acts was to dismiss Driss Basri, long considered one of the most powerful men in Morocco and, in many ways, the embodiment of corruption and repression that marked the monarchy. Thousands of prisoners were released, and the king allowed exile opposition figures to return to Morocco.

In 2002, Morocco held parliamentary elections that were widely considered to be the most representative in the country's history. While the vote did not alter the fundamental distribution of power in Morocco, the resulting diversity in parliament—with 10 percent women and a significant Islamist presence—constituted an important step toward greater political openness.

Five suicide bombings in May 2003 shattered Morocco's sense of stability. Arrests of Islamic extremists, including three Saudi members of al-Qaeda, had taken place during 2002, but the terrorist attack signaled a new and disturbing escalation in terrorist activity. Victims were primarily Moroccans, and the targets included visible symbols of Morocco's Jewish community. While Moroccan officials initially blamed foreign extremists, the 14 attackers were Moroccan and believed to be part of a local extremist group identified as As-Sirat al-Mustaqim, the Righteous Path. The group is based in the slums of Casablanca and could be responsible for a series of assassinations of "unbelievers" from the neighborhood. However, the attackers may have received external funding and training. The extremists' links to al-Qaeda remain unclear; in an audiotape purportedly made by Osama bin Laden in 2002, Morocco was listed among countries "ready for liberation."

The Moroccan government's response to the attacks has been both swift and harsh. Approximately 1,100 terrorism suspects were arrested in the ensuing crackdown. The courts have sentenced more than 50 people to life in prison and 16 people to death. Meanwhile, the Moroccan Human Rights Association has said that the trials appear to be seriously flawed. Few witnesses are called, and acquittals are rare.

Municipal elections were held on September 12; the government postponed the elections from June in the wake of the May suicide bombings. The Islamist Justice and Development Party (PJD) made a conscious decision to lower its profile and run fewer candidates in the local election. Although the PJD denounced the terrorist bombings, the party has found itself under fire in a political atmosphere that is less tolerant of Islamists. As a result, the PJD ran for only 18 percent of the council seats contested, including the Islamist stronghold of Casablanca and the key cities of Fez and Rabat. The Islamist party put up only 3 percent of all candidates. Under pressure from the government, the Islamist party opted to step down rather than risk a greater government crackdown. Yet, the two principal secular parties—the Socialist

Union of Popular Forces (USFP) and the Istiqlal—failed to capitalize on the Islamists' absence, despite running candidates in nearly every jurisdiction. Neither party was able to capture the town halls of Casablanca, Marrakesh, or Tangiers.

**Political Rights and Civil Liberties:** Moroccans' right to change their government democratically is limited. The monarch retains ultimate authority. He may appoint or approve the government and can, at his discretion, dismiss any member of the cabinet, dissolve parliament, call for new elections, and rule by decree. Legislative powers are shared by the king and a bicameral legislature that includes a directly elected lower house. Unlike previous votes, the 2002 parliamentary elections and the 2003 municipal elections were regarded as the most representative in the country's history.

Opposition parties remain weak. The government crackdown on Islamic extremists clearly has deterred moderate Islamist elements from political participation, as witnessed by their decision to roll back dramatically their presence in the local elections. Secular opposition parties have yet to make significant inroads at the grassroots level, nor have they found common cause with the Islamists who have pushed for greater reforms.

Press freedoms remain somewhat restricted. Broadcast media are mostly government controlled and largely reflect official views, although foreign broadcasting is available via satellite. The Committee to Protect Journalists noted a disturbing trend toward censorship with the Moroccan print media. Since May, eight Moroccan journalists have been detained in connection with their work and five remain in jail. The journalists were convicted on charges of "insulting the king" and undermining the monarchy. Prison sentences range from 18 months to three years. Meanwhile, publication of two Casablanca-based satirical weeklies has been suspended. The deterioration in press freedoms appears to be a result of the government crackdown following the May bombings. An antiterrorism law passed soon after the attacks has been used repeatedly to detain reporters.

Islam is the official religion of Morocco, and almost 99 percent of the population is Sunni Muslim. Morocco's Jewish community, while quite small (approximately 5,000), has been able to worship freely. However, in 2003 a disturbing trend of attacks on the Jewish community became apparent. Aside from the May bombings, where four out of the five sites were Jewish or had Jewish connections, a Jewish merchant was assassinated in Casablanca on September 11.

Freedom of association is limited. Nongovernment organizations must receive government permission to operate legally. The Interior Ministry requires permits for public gatherings and has forcibly dispersed demonstrations in the past. However, peaceful protests are generally tolerated.

The judiciary lacks independence and is subject to corruption and bribery. Days after the May bombings, parliament adopted a tough anti-terrorism law that allows terror suspects to be held up to 12 days without being charged; the law also broadens the definition of terrorism and expands the number of crimes punishable by death. Amnesty International says the practice of torture has widened in Morocco as part of the antiterrorism campaign. Some terror suspects interviewed by Amnesty told of being held for weeks in secret detention and subject to various forms of torture. Human rights groups have also criticized the trials of terror suspects that often last only two or three days. Many suspects are convicted on the basis of their statements to police without any material proof of their guilt. Among those convicted are 14-year-old twins who were sentenced to five years in prison for plotting to blow up the liquor aisle of a supermarket.

While Moroccan women are guaranteed equal rights under the constitution, the reality in both the political and social spheres has been one of marked inequality. However, in October 2003, King Muhammad VI proposed far-reaching reforms of Morocco's personal status code. The changes include raising the marriage age from 15 to 18 for women and allowing women the right to initiate divorce. The reforms would also make polygamy quite difficult and, in general, cede greater rights to women in the areas of marriage and divorce. The reforms still need to be approved by parliament. Similar changes were proposed for the Mudawana in 2000, but met with stiff opposition from the Islamists. King Muhammad appears to be taking advantage of the Islamists' defensive posture to push through these significant reforms. Many women pursue careers in the professions or in government, but they face restrictions in advancement. Domestic violence is common, and the law is lenient toward men who kill their wives for alleged adultery.

# Mozambique

**Population:** 17,500,000
**GNI/capita:** $210
**Life Expectancy:** 34
**Religious Groups:** Indigenous beliefs (50 percent), Christian (30 percent), Muslim (20 percent)
**Ethnic Groups:** Indigenous tribal groups, [Shangaan, Chokwe, Manyika, Sena, Makua] (99.7 percent), other (0.3 percent)
**Capital:** Maputo

**Political Rights:** 3
**Civil Liberties:** 4
**Status:** Partly Free

**Ten-Year Ratings Timeline (Political Rights, Civil Liberties, Status)**

| 1994 | 1995 | 1996 | 1997 | 1998 | 1999 | 2000 | 2001 | 2002 | 2003 |
|------|------|------|------|------|------|------|------|------|------|
| 3,5PF | 3,4PF | 3,4PF | 3,4PF | 3,4PF | 3,4PF | 3,4PF | 3,4PF | 3,4PF | 3,4PF |

**Overview:**

Mozambique's nascent democracy continued to mature in 2003, a decade after civil war ended. However, deep political divisions remain, as the ruling Mozambique Liberation Front (FRELIMO) maintains dominance of government institutions. Meanwhile, several men were convicted in January in the 1990 murder of a prominent journalist.

Portuguese traders and settlers arrived in Mozambique in the late fifteenth century, and full-scale colonization began in the seventeenth century. FRELIMO was established in 1962 and launched a guerrilla campaign to oust the Portuguese. In 1975, Mozambique gained independence. FRELIMO was installed as the sole legal party, and its leader, Samora Machel, as president. Independence was followed by 16 years of civil war waged by the Mozambique National Resistance (RENAMO), which was supported first by Rhodesia (Zimbabwe) and later by South Africa.

In 1986, Machel died in an airplane crash and Joachim Chissano became president. In 1989, FRELIMO formally abandoned Marxism-Leninism for democratic socialism and a market economy. In 1992, a ceasefire was signed, followed by a full peace agreement. RENAMO agreed to operate as an opposition political party. The first multiparty elections were held in 1994, which attracted a 90 percent turnout. The elections were judged a resounding success by the international community, despite a brief preelection boycott called by RENAMO, which accused FRELIMO of fraud. RENAMO leader Alphonse Dhlakama captured 33.7 percent of the presidential vote, versus 53.3 percent for Chissano. FRELIMO won a narrow, but workable, majority in parliament in concurrent legislative polls.

Chissano and FRELIMO were reelected in general elections in 1999, despite a strong showing by the opposition. The polls were marred by logistical and administrative difficulties, and RENAMO complained of fraud. However, many Mozambicans and the international community viewed the elections as expressing the people's will. RENAMO's claims of election fraud created a highly polarized political environment. In protest of alleged fraud, RENAMO deputies repeatedly walked out of parliament or interrupted proceedings in 2000 and 2001. At one point, RENAMO threatened to form its own government in six northern and central provinces.

In 2000 and 2001, major floods killed more than 650 people and disrupted the economy. Tens of thousands of the 500,000 who fled their homes have been resettled.

Widespread corruption has damaged the standing of Chissano's government. In January 2003, six men were found guilty of murdering the prominent journalist Carlos Cardoso, who died in 1990 while investigating bank scandals. While the convictions were a triumph of judiciary independence, no charges have been lodged against the president's son, Nyimpine Chissano, who was alleged by three of the accused to have ordered the assassination.

Municipal elections in November were deemed generally fair by the U.S.-based Carter Center, although there were some logistical problems such as lack of transport for voter education agents. RENAMO took part, after boycotting the last round in 1998.

President Joachim Chissano's announcement that he would not run in 2004 appears to reflect an acceptance of democratic practice. Armando Guebeza, a former interior minister and hard-line Marxist, is FRELIMO's nominee for president.

Mozambique boasts one of Africa's best-performing economies, thanks partly to extensive foreign aid. However, the country remains among the world's poorest, with one of the highest infant mortality rates.

**Political Rights and Civil Liberties:** Mozambicans can select their president and parliament through competitive electoral processes, although this freedom is constrained by vestigial economic ravages of war and unfamiliarity with democratic practices. Democratic consolidation is tenuous, but dialogue is present in the young democratic institutions. Parliament is an important player in the political process, although the executive branch overshadows its power. The influence of smaller opposition parties is negligible, which leaves RENAMO the only viable electoral challenge to the status quo.

Parliament agreed in 2002 to change electoral law provisions regarding settling disputes, deploying observers, and naming members to the electoral commission. Procedural changes undertaken in 2001 within parliament, including a strengthening of the committee system, have resulted in that body's increased effectiveness, although partisan tensions sometimes impede work.

Corruption is pervasive. In 2002, Mozambique's attorney general, in a report to parliament, admitted that corruption plagued the legal system. He cited incompetence, corruption, and abuse of power at all levels of the administration of justice, including police, attorneys, judges, lawyers, and prison personnel. He also blamed prosecuting attorneys for failing to press charges against suspects when enough evidence existed.

The constitution provides for media freedom, but the state controls nearly all broadcast media and owns or influences the largest newspapers. The independent media have enjoyed moderate growth, but publications in Maputo have little influence in the largely illiterate rural population. The most important media company to arise is the cooperative Mediacoop, which owns Mediafax (which is faxed to hundreds of subscribers but read very widely), the periodical *Mozambique Interview*, and the weekly *Savana*. Criminal libel laws deter open expression. The more than a dozen licensed private radio and television stations exercise some self-censorship. The opposition receives inadequate coverage in state-run media, especially radio and television.

There is no reported interference with religious practice.

Freedom of assembly is broadly guaranteed, but limited by notification and timing restrictions. Nongovernmental organizations, including the Mozambican Human Rights League, operate openly, as do international human rights and humanitarian groups. FRELIMO's grip is loosening on the labor movement. The Organization of Mozambican Workers, the major trade confederation, is now nominally independent. The Organization of Free and Independent Unions, a more independent group, was formed in 1994. All workers in nonessential services have the right to strike. The right to bargain collectively is legally protected.

The judicial system is hobbled by a dire shortage of judges, magistrates, and defense lawyers. Bribery of judges by lawyers is alleged to be common. Detainees often wait months, sometimes years, before appearing in court without any formal defense. They are tried only in Portuguese, which many Mozambicans speak poorly. Moves were under way in 2003 to set up the Constitutional Council, which will decide whether laws and governmental decisions are constitutional. The supreme court has been exercising the council's powers, which were set forth in the 1990 constitution but never implemented.

Abuses by security forces still occur. An antigovernment demonstration in 2000 resulted in the deaths of more than 40 RENAMO supporters, and approximately 80 prisoners, mostly RENAMO backers, were suffocated under mysterious circumstances. Prisons are severely overcrowded with appalling health conditions.

The government and organized crime influence the business elite. However, Western donors praise Mozambique's privatization drive, which continued in April with the awarding of the management of the main port, Maputo.

Women suffer from legal and societal discrimination, and domestic violence is common. Only formally married women have full rights; for example, widows can lose their possessions. However, draft legislation introduced to parliament in April recognizes all monogamous unions.

# Namibia

**Population:** 1,900,000
**GNI/capita:** $1,960
**Life Expectancy:** 49
**Religious Groups:** Christian (80-90 percent),
indigenous beliefs (10-20 percent)
**Ethnic Groups:** Black (87.5 percent), white (6 percent),
mixed (6.5 percent)
**Capital:** Windhoek

**Political Rights:** 2
**Civil Liberties:** 3
**Status:** Free

**Ten-Year Ratings Timeline (Political Rights, Civil Liberties, Status)**

| 1994 | 1995 | 1996 | 1997 | 1998 | 1999 | 2000 | 2001 | 2002 | 2003 |
|------|------|------|------|------|------|------|------|------|------|
| 2,3F | 2,3F | 2,3F | 2,3F | 2,3F | 2,3F | 2,3F | 2,3F | 2,3F | 2,3F |

**Overview:**

Frustration grew over the slow pace of Namibia's land reform program in 2003, with black farm workers threatening to occupy 15 designated white-owned farms in November.

Namibia was seized by German imperial forces in the late 1800s. Thousands of people were massacred by German troops in efforts to crush all resistance to colonial settlement and administration. The territory became a South African protectorate after German forces were expelled during World War I and was ruled under the apartheid system for 42 years after 1948. After 13 years of violent guerrilla war, Namibia achieved independence in 1990. During a UN-supervised democratic transition, Sam Nujoma was chosen president that year by a freely and fairly elected National Assembly.

The Southwest Africa People's Organization (SWAPO) scored a sweeping victory, and Nujoma was reelected in 1994. Nujoma, the leader of the country's struggle against apartheid, adopted an increasingly authoritarian governing style. He was easily returned to power with 77 percent of the vote for a third 5-year term in the 1999 presidential election. The party had succeeded in passing a bitterly contested constitutional amendment to allow Nujoma to seek a third term. He has repeatedly said he does not intend to seek a fourth term in elections scheduled for 2004.

A concurrent legislative poll saw SWAPO retain its two-thirds majority in the 72-member National Assembly, increasing its number of seats from 53 to 55. The Congress of Democrats and the Turnhalle Alliance each got 7 seats. The United Democratic Front won 2, and the Monitor Action group got 1 seat. The ruling party's main base is among the country's largest ethnic group, the Ovambo, whose prominence within SWAPO has evoked allegations of ethnic discrimination.

In April 2002, the Angolan government and the National Union for the Total Independence of Angola (UNITA) signed a ceasefire agreement. Fighting in Namibia's Caprivi region had flared in October 1998 and in August 1999, and UNITA was accused of supporting Caprivi insurgents. Under a 1999 mutual defense pact, the governments of Angola and Namibia agreed that each could pursue suspected rebels on the other's territory. Caprivi, a finger of land poking eastward out of northern Namibia along its borders with Angola and Botswana, differs geographically, politically, and in its ethnic makeup from the rest of Namibia. It was used by South Africa in that country's operations against SWAPO guerrillas.

In 2003, whites, who make up about 6 percent of the population, owned just under half of Namibia's arable land. The country's land policy of "willing buyer–willing seller" has resulted in the state's acquisition of 123 farms thus far, only about 2 percent of the area estimated to be owned by white farmers and far short of the program's target. Soaring land costs have also hindered government efforts to resettle black farmers. Although Nujoma said last year that he supported the controversial land seizures being carried out by the government of President Robert Mugabe in neighboring Zimbabwe, the Namibian government warned in November 2003 that it would not tolerate any farm invasions. The farm workers' union is currently in talks with the government and commercial farmers.

Capital-intensive extractive industries, such as diamond and uranium mining, have drawn significant foreign investment and are the centerpiece of Namibia's economic growth. Most Namibians, however, continue to live as subsistence farmers, and many lack basic services. Insecurity in the northern Kavango region has taken its toll on the country's important tourism industry.

**Political Rights and Civil Liberties:** Namibians can change their government democratically. The 1999 elections were judged to be largely free and fair and allowed Namibians to exercise their constitutional right to choose their representatives for the third time. There were some instances of government harassment of the opposition, as well as unequal access to media coverage and campaign financing.

Namibia's constitution guarantees the right to free speech and a free press, and the country's press in considered one of the freest on the continent. Private radio stations and critical independent newspapers usually operate without official interference, but reporters for state-run media have been subjected to indirect and direct pressure to avoid reporting on controversial topics. There are at least eight private radio stations and one private television station. The state-run Namibia Broadcasting Corporation has regularly presented views critical of the government. There are no government restrictions on the Internet, and several publications have popular Web sites.

Freedom of religion is guaranteed and respected in practice. The government does not restrict academic freedom.

Freedom of assembly is guaranteed, except in situations of national emergency. Local and international human rights groups operate freely without government interference. Constitutionally guaranteed union rights are respected. Collective bargaining is not practiced widely outside the mining and construction industries. Informal collective bargaining is increasingly common. Essential public sector workers do not have the right to strike. Domestic and farm laborers remain the country's most heavily exploited workers, in part because many are illiterate and do not know their rights.

The constitution provides for an independent judiciary, and the government respects this. However, in rural areas, local chiefs use traditional courts that often ignore constitutional procedures. In November 2003, after a four-year delay, the trials began of 120 defendants accused of high treason and other crimes in relation to the separatist rebellion in Caprivi. Human rights groups have called for independent investigations into the deaths of 13 Caprivi suspects in police custody since 1999.

Authorities have dismissed allegations of torture. Conditions in prisons and military detention facilities generally meet international standards.

Respect for human rights in Namibia is good, and the country's National Society for Human Rights (NSHR) said that the overall civil and political situation in the formerly volatile Caprivi, Kavango, and Ohangwena regions improved considerably. Nevertheless, Caprivians accuse the government of neglect in the province, which is among the country's poorest. Despite some improvements, the NSHR warned that the overall human rights situation in the country deteriorated in 2003. It cited the continued demonization of opposition political parties and the assassination of Bernard Nakale Shevanyenga, the head of a local organization campaigning for the Namibian-Angolan border to be shifted from north of the Kwanyama tribe's communal areas to a line inside Angola.

The Herero and Damara peoples are among the minority ethnic groups demanding larger government allocations for development in their home areas. Herero leaders have filed a $2 billion lawsuit in the United States to demand reparations for abuses they suffered at the hands of German colonists. The Herero were nearly wiped out during colonialism. The government has made efforts to end discrimination of indigenous San (Bushmen), although the NSHR says that the San remain marginalized and subject to rights abuses.

Despite constitutional guarantees, women continue to face serious discrimination in customary law and other traditional societal practices. Violence against women is reportedly widespread, although greater attention is being focused on the problem. Women are increasingly involved in the political process, but remain underrepresented in government and politics.

# Nauru

**Population:** 10,000
**GNI/capita:** $3,540
**Life Expectancy:** 61
**Religious Groups:** Christian (two-thirds Protestant, one-third Roman Catholic)
**Ethnic Groups:** Nauruan (58 percent), other Pacific Islander (26 percent), Chinese (8 percent), European (8 percent)
**Capital:** Yaren

**Political Rights:** 1
**Civil Liberties:** 1*
**Status:** Free

**Ratings Change:** Nauru's civil liberties rating improved from 2 to 1 due to a reevaluation of the scope of freedom of the media, association, and rule of law.

**Ten-Year Ratings Timeline (Political Rights, Civil Liberties, Status)**

| 1994 | 1995 | 1996 | 1997 | 1998 | 1999 | 2000 | 2001 | 2002 | 2003 |
|------|------|------|------|------|------|------|------|------|------|
| 1,3F | 1,3F | 1,3F | 1,3F | 1,3F | 1,3F | 1,3F | 1,3F | 1,2F | 1,1F |

**Overview:**
Severe party and factional competition resulted in several changes in national leadership in 2003. The tussle involved a no-confidence vote in parliament, a supreme

court ruling, and the sudden death of a competitor. Such intense political rivalry has been a major hindrance to sustaining policies and good governance for economic development.

Nauru, a tiny Pacific island nation located 1,600 miles northeast of New Zealand, was a German protectorate from 1888 until the close of World War I, when Australia began administering it under a League of Nations mandate. The Japanese occupied Nauru during World War II. Australian administrators returned to Nauru after the war under a UN mandate, and Nauru gained independence from Australia in 1968.

On January 8, 2003, President Rene Harris was ousted by a parliamentary vote of no confidence following opposition allegations of economic mismanagement and corruption. Harris and six of his ministers boycotted the vote. On January 17, Nauru's chief justice ruled that the 8 to 3 no-confidence vote was invalid without an absolute majority in the 18-member parliament and ordered that Harris be reinstated.

Parliament voted Bernard Dowiyogo to replace Harris, but the Supreme Court barred Dowiyogo from claiming the presidency, and the speaker of parliament resigned in protest. Both acts blocked Dowiyogo from passing a new budget. Parliament then refused to nominate a new speaker, without whom a new parliament session cannot convene to pass legislation.

This impasse ended with Dowiyogo's death in March in Washington, D.C., following heart surgery. Derog Gioura was appointed acting president to lead the caretaker administration until new elections in May. Ludwig Scotty was elected to replace Gioura, but in less than four months, Scotty was ousted by a vote of no confidence. Parliament subsequently chose Harris to lead the government.

Apart from troubles in the political arena, the economy continued its downward spiral. Nauru has become highly dependent on foreign aid. Phosphate, which was plentiful and mined by Australia for use as fertilizer, is almost entirely exhausted, leaving behind broken lands and other environmental problems. More than 80 percent of this eight-square-mile island republic is uninhabitable. Although phosphate mining had made Nauru one of the richest in the world in per capita income, government financial mismanagement squandered much of this wealth. A trust fund built on phosphate royalties will likely be depleted in a few years. The country is also saddled with a large foreign debt relative to its size.

Recent administrations had been seeking new ways to generate income. As an offshore tax and banking center, Nauru has been implicated in international money laundering and is still working to reform its banking sector. The country was also under international pressure, particularly from the United States, to crack down on passport sales when two alleged al-Qaeda operatives were arrested in Malaysia carrying Nauruan passports.

The country also switched diplomatic recognition back and forth between China and Taiwan to secure the most financial aid from the two competitors. Nauru switched recognition from Taiwan to Beijing in July 2002. In 2003, Nauru closed its embassy in Beijing to resume ties with Taiwan. Taiwan agreed to pay Nauru's outstanding loan of $2.7 million on a 737-jet aircraft owed to the Export-Import Bank of the United States.

Since 2001, Nauru has served as a refugee processing and detention center for Australia in exchange for financial aid. Nauru provides temporary housing for hundreds of mainly Middle Easterners seeking asylum in Australia. Additional U.S. financial assistance was also agreed to in exchange for the establishment of an intelligence listening post in the islands.

**Political Rights and Civil Liberties:** Citizens of Nauru can change their government democratically. Suffrage is universal and compulsory for all citizens 20 years and older. The 18-member unicameral legislature is elected by popular vote for three-year terms. Members of parliament choose from among themselves the president and vice president.

There have been no reports of government monitoring or censorship of any media. The government owns and operates the only radio station. Nauru TV is government owned, and there is a private sports network. The government is the sole provider of Internet services. Nauru's telecommunications system is fragile; telephone service was unavailable for nearly two months when a frequency amplifier was damaged in January.

The constitution provides for freedom of religion, and the government generally respects this in practice. There were no reports of any government suppression of academic freedom.

The government respects the right of assembly and association in practice. There are a few advocacy groups for women, development-focused groups, and religious organizations, but there are no trade unions or labor protection laws in this largely agriculture-based subsistence economy. In September, workers at the Nauru Phosphate Corporation, the country's largest employer, went on permanent strike to demand six months of back pay.

The judiciary is independent, and defendants generally receive fair trials and representation. Appeals can be lodged with the High Court of Australia. Nauru has no armed forces. Defense is the responsibility of Australia under an informal agreement. A police force of fewer than 100 persons is under civilian control.

Strict immigration rules govern foreign workers. Those who leave Nauru without their employer's permission cannot reenter, and immigrant workers must leave Nauru within 60 days of termination of employment.

The law provides equal freedoms and protection for men and women, but societal pressures limit opportunities for women to fully exercise these rights. Prostitution is illegal and not widespread. Sexual harassment is a crime, but spousal rape per se is not a crime. Domestic violence is frequently associated with alcohol abuse. Although the government and judiciary generally respond seriously to cases filed, most incidents are reconciled informally within the family or communally by traditional leaders. Consequently, reliable figures are not available.

# Nepal

**Population:** 25,200,000
**GNI/capita:** $230
**Life Expectancy:** 59
**Religious Groups:** Hindu (86.2 percent), Buddhist
(7.8 percent), Muslim (3.8 percent) and other (2.2 percent)
**Ethnic Groups:** Brahman, Chetri, Newar, Gurung, Sherpa,
Magar, Tamang, Bhotia, Rai, Limbu
**Capital:** Kathmandu

**Political Rights:** 5*
**Civil Liberties:** 4
**Status:** Partly Free

**Ratings Change:** Nepal's political rights rating declined from 4 to 5 due to the continued suspension of an elected parliament and the failure to hold new national elections.

**Ten-Year Ratings Timeline (Political Rights, Civil Liberties, Status)**

| 1994 | 1995 | 1996 | 1997 | 1998 | 1999 | 2000 | 2001 | 2002 | 2003 |
|------|------|------|------|------|------|------|------|------|------|
| 3,4PF | 3,4PF | 3,4PF | 3,4PF | 3,4PF | 3,4PF | 3,4PF | 3,4PF | 4,4PF | 5,4PF |

**Overview:**

Political instability and the ongoing Maoist insurgency continued to destabilize Nepal in 2003. A ceasefire between the government and the Maoists was declared in January, but after the two sides held three rounds of inconclusive peace talks, the ceasefire collapsed in August. In the wake of the resumption of hostilities, the incidence of extrajudicial murders, abductions, and other human rights violations by both sides once again rose dramatically. Meanwhile, King Gyanendra appears unwilling to install an all-party interim government or to restore more fully the democratic process by holding elections, and the relationship between the palace and the main political parties remains unproductive.

King Prithvi Narayan Shah unified this Himalayan land in 1769. Following two centuries of palace rule, the left-leaning Nepali Congress (NC) party won Nepal's first elections in 1959. King Mahendra abruptly dissolved parliament and banned political parties in 1960, and in 1962 began ruling through a repressive *panchayat* (village council) system. Many parties went underground until early 1990, when the NC and a coalition of Communist parties organized pro-democracy rallies that led King Birendra to re-legalize political parties. An interim government introduced a constitution that vested executive power in the prime minister and cabinet and turned Nepal into a constitutional monarchy.

In Nepal's first multiparty elections in 32 years, Giraja Prasad Koirala, a veteran dissident, led the NC to victory and formed a government in 1991. Riven by intraparty conflicts, the NC was forced in 1994 to call early elections, which it lost to the Communist Party of Nepal (United Marxist-Leninist), or CPN-UML. The Communists, however, failed to win a majority in parliament. Hopes for a more stable government rose after the NC won a majority in elections held in 1999. The campaign centered on the problems of rampant official corruption, stagnant economic growth, and the Maoist insurgency. Led by Baburam Bhattarai and Pushpa Kamal Dahal, the Communist Party of Nepal–Maoist (CPN-M, or Maoists) has said that it wants an end to the constitutional monarchy and the feudal structure that persists in many parts of the country.

In June 2001, Gyanendra ascended the throne after a palace massacre in which the crown prince apparently shot to death the king and nine other members of the royal family before killing himself. After Sher Bahadur Deuba became prime minister in July, the rebels agreed to a ceasefire. However, when the rebels broke the ceasefire in November, King Gyanendra declared a state of emergency. The government's subsequent decision to use the army to fight the Maoists marked a sharp escalation in the conflict; an estimated 5,000 people were killed in 2002, and Nepal's infrastructure and economy have been devastated.

Political instability heightened in May 2002 when the prime minister dissolved parliament and called for fresh elections to be held in November. When caretaker Prime Minister Deuba, citing the worsening security situation, asked the king in October to postpone the elections, King Gyanendra dismissed Deuba and assumed executive powers himself. While postponing elections indefinitely, he also installed an interim administration headed by Lokendra Bahadur Chand, a former prime minister and leader of a small royalist party. Mainstream political parties termed his decision undemocratic, but were divided on a suitable solution to the political stalemate.

Another ceasefire between the rebels and government forces took effect in January 2003, but the lack of an independent verification process meant that accusations of persistent violations on both sides could not be acted on, according to a report published by the International Crisis Group. Meanwhile, the king appointed a new prime minister in June, choosing Surya Bahadur Thapa, a member of a right-wing royalist party, instead of a consensus candidate that had been agreed on by the main political parties. When a third round of peace talks collapsed over disagreements about the possible formation of a constituent assembly, hostilities quickly resumed in August, and a three-day strike called by the Maoists in September further crippled the economy. Prospects for a resolution to the crisis remain dim, with the political parties continuing to protest the indefinite suspension of the democratic process and the Maoists appearing unwilling to engage in sustained and serious negotiations with a monarchy that is currently operating with limited constitutional legality.

**Political Rights and Civil Liberties:** Citizens of Nepal cannot change their government democratically. The 1990 constitution provides for a 205-seat lower house of parliament that is directly elected for a five-year term and a 60-seat upper house whose members are either elected by national or local government bodies or appointed by the king. During 2003, these constitutional provisions remained suspended; polls that would have elected a new parliament in November 2002 have been indefinitely postponed, and King Gyanendra rules through an interim prime minister and cabinet that he appointed in October 2002. The king's influence is bolstered his authority to wield emergency powers and suspend many basic freedoms in the event of war, external aggression, armed revolt, or extreme economic depression. He also serves as commander in chief of the army.

A wide range of political parties have been allowed to operate since 1990, although the constitution bans political parties that are formed along religious, caste, ethnic, tribal, or regional lines. Recent elections have been free, though not entirely fair. In the 1999 elections, interparty clashes led to several election-related deaths, and Maoist violence caused balloting to be postponed in dozens of districts.

As a result of the escalation in the insurgency, government institutions have all but fallen apart in much of rural Nepal. Elected governments have made few reforms to Nepal's bloated, inefficient civil service, and ministries operate with little openness or accountability. Corruption is perceived to be endemic in politics and government administration. Legislation passed in 2002 disqualified those convicted on corruption charges from contesting political elections for five years and placed the burden of proof in corruption cases on the accused. In May, an anticorruption panel began questioning more than 40 politicians and officials about details of their property holdings. However, compliance with anticorruption regulations remains weak and the prosecution of high-level officials is rare, which contributes to a climate of impunity.

Conditions for journalists deteriorated sharply as the insurgency escalated in late 2001 and have remained poor. Although emergency regulations were lifted in August 2002, journalists are still regularly arrested and detained, and a number have reportedly been subjected to harassment and torture. Media professionals are also under considerable pressure from the Maoists. Suspected rebels murdered a journalist with the state-owned news agency in September, and other reporters have been abducted and threatened as well as being expelled from rebel-held areas. Both the constitution and the Press and Publications Act broadly suppress speech and writing that could undermine the monarchy, national security, public order, or interethnic or intercaste relations. While many private publications continue to criticize government policies, self-censorship as a result of official intimidation is a growing concern. The government owns both the influential Radio Nepal, whose political coverage favors the ruling party, and Nepal's main television station.

Although the constitution describes Nepal as a Hindu kingdom, there is a considerable Buddhist minority. The constitution provides for freedom of religion, but proselytizing is prohibited and members of religious minorities occasionally complain of official harassment. Although the government does not restrict academic freedom, more than 100 teachers have been killed both by security forces and by Maoists, and Maoists regularly target private schools in the rural areas.

Freedom of assembly and association is sometimes restricted. In September, after the Maoists called off the ceasefire, the government ordered a temporary ban on public demonstrations in the Kathmandu Valley and detained hundreds of people who defied the ban. Police sometimes use excessive force against peaceful protestors. The head of the Nepal Progressive Students Union was shot and killed by police during an antigovernment demonstration in April. The government generally allows nongovernmental organizations (NGOs) to function freely. However, both police and Maoist guerrillas occasionally threaten human rights activists to deter them from investigating rights violations. The insurgency has forced a number of NGOs working in rural Nepal to substantially curb their activities.

Trade unions are independent, but they have notched few real gains for workers. By law, workers in certain essential services cannot stage strikes, and 60 percent of a union's membership must vote in favor of a strike for it to be legal. While export-oriented carpet factories have reduced their use of child workers, smaller carpet factories and several other industries continue to depend on child labor. Although bonded labor was outlawed in 2000, it persists in rural areas.

The Supreme Court is viewed as largely independent of the executive. However, lower-level courts are subject to political pressure and endemic corruption, and effective access to justice for many Nepalese remains limited. Because of heavy case backlogs and a slow appeals process, suspects often spend longer in pretrial detention than they would if convicted of the crimes for which they stand accused. Prison conditions are poor, with overcrowding common and detainees sometimes handcuffed or otherwise fettered.

In ordinary criminal cases, police at times commit extrajudicial killings and cause the disappearance of suspects in custody. They also occasionally torture and beat suspects to punish them or to extract confessions. The government generally has refused to conduct thorough investigations and take serious disciplinary measures against officers accused of brutality. Nevertheless, in September, four soldiers were handed down prison sentences after being charged with attempted extortion and kidnapping. Set up in 2000, the official Human Rights Commission has a mandate to investigate alleged human rights violations, such as the extrajudicial killing of 19 people in the Ramechhap district by the army in August. However, the commission lacks enforcement powers and the resources to pursue cases in court.

Both the government and the Maoists have been accused of increased human rights violations in the context of the insurgency, which has affected the majority of Nepal's 75 districts and has claimed more than 8,000 lives since 1996. The poorly equipped police force has been implicated in extrajudicial killings, disappearances, arbitrary arrests and detentions, rapes, and the torture of suspected Maoists and alleged supporters. In a report issued in October, Amnesty International noted that it had recorded more than 250 disappearances countrywide.

Domestic human rights groups accuse the government of using tough security laws such as the Public Security Act (PSA) and the Terrorist and Disruptive Activities Act (TADA), promulgated in April 2002, to deter civilians from supporting the Maoists. Both laws allow officials to detain suspects for up to six months without filing charges. The government has detained dozens of civilians under TADA, including journalists, teachers, lawyers, and political activists. In addition, as of August 2002, authorities had arrested more than 9,900 suspected Maoists or alleged followers, of whom 1,722 remained in custody, according to Amnesty International.

The Maoists have killed, tortured, or kidnapped civilians, including suspected informers, landowners, local officials, teachers, and members of mainstream political parties. The rebels have also set up "people's courts" in some parts of Nepal that hand down summary justice. Adding to civilian hardship, the guerrillas fund themselves in part through extortion and looting, and they ordered a number of national strikes throughout the year that paralyzed major urban centers. The Maoists also use forcibly recruited children as soldiers, human shields, and couriers, according to a December 2002 Amnesty International report.

Members of the Hindu upper castes dominate parliament and the bureaucracy, and low-caste Hindus, ethnic minorities, and Christians face discrimination in the civil service, courts, and government offices. Despite an August 2001 provision that banned caste-based discrimination, *dalits* (untouchables) continue to be subjected to particularly severe exploitation and exclusion. Nepalese officials at times extort money from, or otherwise harass, Tibetan asylum seekers who cross the border into Nepal, and occasionally hand Tibetans back to Chinese authorities, according to the U.S. State Department's human rights report. Some 2,000 to 3,000 Tibetans es-

cape into exile via Nepal each year, with most ending up in India. Nepal also provides asylum to more than 100,000 Bhutanese refugees. International organizations
estimate that approximately 100,000 Nepalese are currently internally displaced as a
result of the Maoist insurgency.

Women rarely receive the same educational and employment opportunities as
men, and there are relatively few women in government and civil service. Although
a 2002 law legalized abortion and broadened women's property rights, many other
laws relating to property, divorce, and several other areas discriminate against women.
Domestic violence and rape continue to be serious problems. The government has
taken few steps to curb violence against women or to assist victims, and authorities
generally do not prosecute domestic violence cases. Organized gangs traffick some
5,000 to 12,000 Nepalese girls to work in Indian brothels each year, according to
estimates by local NGOs. Because the majority of prostitutes who return to Nepal
are HIV-positive, nearly all returnees are shunned and are unable to obtain help to
rebuild their lives.

# Netherlands

**Population:** 16,200,000    **Political Rights:** 1
**GNI/capita:** $24,330    **Civil Liberties:** 1
**Life Expectancy:** 78    **Status:** Free
**Religious Groups:** Roman Catholic (31 percent),
Protestant (21 percent), Muslim (4.4 percent), unaffiliated
(43.6 percent)
**Ethnic Groups:** Dutch (83 percent), other [including Turks,
Moroccans, Antilleans, Surinamese and Indonesians] (17 percent)
**Capital:** Amsterdam

**Ten-Year Ratings Timeline (Political Rights, Civil Liberties, Status)**

| 1994 | 1995 | 1996 | 1997 | 1998 | 1999 | 2000 | 2001 | 2002 | 2003 |
|------|------|------|------|------|------|------|------|------|------|
| 1,1F | 1,1F | 1,1F | 1,1F | 1,1F | 1,1F | 1,1F | 1,1F | 1,1F | 1,1F |

**Overview:**    The Christian Democrats (CDA) narrowly won in national
elections in January 2003 and, after four months of talks,
formed a coalition government with the People's Party for
Freedom and Democracy (VVD) and the Democrats-66 (D66). In April, Human Rights
Watch (HRW) issued a report critical of Dutch asylum policy, which HRW argued
violates human rights standards issued by international bodies.

After the Dutch won their independence from Spain in the sixteenth century,
the House of Orange assumed sovereignty over the United Provinces of the Netherlands. A constitutional monarchy emerged in the 1800s with a representative government. The Netherlands remained neutral in both world wars, but was invaded by
Nazi Germany in 1940. The occupation ended in 1945, after five years of harsh rule
during which Dutch workers were forced to work in German factories and Dutch
Jews were deported to concentration camps. The Netherlands ended its neutrality

when it joined NATO in 1949; it then became, in 1952, one of the founding members of the European Coal and Steel Community, the precursor of the European Union (EU).

Following the shooting death in May 2002 of far-right politician Pim Fortuyn, his newly formed party, the Pim Fortuyn List (LPF), went on to win second place on an anti-immigrant platform in national elections that same month. The fortunes of the LPF were short-lived, however, when infighting within the party led to a collapse of the new government in October and new elections were called for 2003.

During the January 2003 elections, 80 percent of those registered voted and nine parties won seats in parliament. The CDA received more than 28 percent of the vote and 44 seats, just above the Labor Party (PvdA), which received around 27 percent and 42 seats, and the VVD, which received 18 percent and 28 seats. The LPF dropped to fifth place with only around 6 percent of the vote and 8 seats. Following four months of talks and a failed attempt to form a broad center-left coalition with the PvdA, the CDA brought the VVD and D66 into a center-right coalition with a slim majority of only 6 seats.

In April, an animal rights activist, Volkert van der Graaf, was sentenced to 18 years in prison for the 2002 murder of Pim Fortuyn.

A report by HRW in April targets the Netherlands's Aliens Act, which went into force in 2001 and is intended to discourage economic migrants while accelerating the process for people seeking political asylum. HRW argues that the new policy violates fundamental asylum and refugee rights.

**Political Rights and Civil Liberties:** The Dutch can change their government democratically. The 150-member lower house, or Second Chamber, is elected every four years by proportional representation and passes bills on to the 75-member upper house, or First Chamber, for approval. Foreigners resident in the country for five years or more are legally eligible to vote in local elections. Uniquely among the EU member countries, mayors are not elected in the Netherlands but appointed from a list of candidates submitted by the municipal councils. The queen appoints the Council of Ministers (cabinet) and the governor of each province on the recommendation of the majority in parliament.

The Netherlands has little or no problem with corruption. Transparency International's Corruption Perceptions Index has ranked the Netherlands seventh two years in a row, from 2002 to 2003, with scores in the "highly clean" area.

The country's media are free and independent. Restrictions against insulting the monarch and royal family exist but are rarely enforced. Despite a concentration of newspaper ownership, a wide variety of opinion is expressed in the print media. Internet access is not restricted.

The Dutch constitution provides for freedom of religion. Religious organizations that provide educational facilities can receive subsidies from the government. Members of the country's small Muslim population have encountered an increase in racist incidents in the last two years, including vandalism, arson, defacing of mosques or other Islamic institutions, harassment, and verbal abuse. The LPF won significant support in 2002 running on a platform that characterized Islam as a backward and intolerant culture that oppressed women and homosexuals. In late 2002, Hilbrand Nawijn, an LPF member of parliament who was the immigration minister, caused an international stir when he suggested that only Dutch should be spoken in the country's 450 mosques. Academic freedom is not restricted.

People have the right to assemble, demonstrate, and generally express their opinions. Workers have the right to organize, bargain collectively, and strike.

The judiciary is independent, and the rule of law prevails in civil and criminal matters. The police are under civilian control and prison conditions meet international standards. The population is generally treated equally under the law, although HRW has criticized certain aspects of the accelerated asylum determination procedure (AAC), which is part of the new Aliens Act. The new procedure, which is used to screen out 60 percent of asylum claims and seeks to discourage economic migrants while accelerating the process for people seeking political asylum, gives applicants little time to prepare their cases to prove their need for protection or challenge a negative decision or appeal, or to receive meaningful advice from a lawyer. A report by Human Rights Watch also pointed out shortcomings in the treatment of migrant and asylum-seeking children and poor reception conditions for immigrants.

The Dutch are known for their liberal values and laws; among these are tolerant attitudes toward so-called soft drugs like marijuana and the legalization of euthanasia in 2001. The Netherlands, along with Belgium, is the only state that allows homosexual marriage. In 2001, four homosexual couples were married in Amsterdam as a result of a law that also allows gay couples to adopt children.

The Netherlands is a significant destination as well as a transit point for trafficking in persons, particularly women for sexual exploitation. The Dutch government, however, has made significant efforts to investigate and prosecute traffickers through the National Rapporteur on Trafficking in Human Beings. The 2000 Prostitution Law makes illegal employment of prostitutes a crime. Women currently hold 37 percent of the seats in parliament.

# New Zealand

**Population:** 4,000,000
**GNI/capita:** $13,250
**Life Expectancy:** 78
**Political Rights:** 1
**Civil Liberties:** 1
**Status:** Free
**Religious Groups:** Anglican (24 percent), Presbyterian (18 percent), Roman Catholic (15 percent), other or none (43 percent)
**Ethnic Groups:** New Zealand European (74.5 percent), Maori (10 percent), other European (4.5 percent), Pacific Islander (4 percent), other [inlcuding Asian] (7 percent)
**Capital:** Wellington

**Ten-Year Ratings Timeline (Political Rights, Civil Liberties, Status)**

| 1993 | 1994 | 1995 | 1996 | 1997 | 1998 | 1999 | 2000 | 2001 | 2002 | 2003 |
|------|------|------|------|------|------|------|------|------|------|------|
| 1,1F | 1,1F | 1,1F | 1,1F | 1,1F | 1,1F | 1,1F | 1,1F | 1,1F | 1,1F | 1,1F |

**Overview:**  Native Maori claims for land and compensation made almost daily headlines throughout 2003. Although public support remains high for an 1840 treaty between the Maoris and the British that leased Maori land in perpetuity to the white "settlers," public opinion has become more divisive toward Maori claims and the government has taken a harder stand against them. On the international scene, New Zealand joined the Australian-led multinational mission to restore peace and order in the Solomon Islands and was part of a UN mission to support the peace process in that country that concluded at the end of June.

New Zealand became self-governing prior to World War II and gained full independence from Britain in 1947, establishing itself as a parliamentary democracy. The Labor Party has been in office since 1999, when it won an election dominated by questions about the mildly conservative National Party's privatization plans and management of state agencies. Like its victory in 1999, Labor's reelection in 2002 left the party with 52 seats in the 120-seat parliament. Following the election, Labor formed a minority government with the populist Progressive Coalition Party, which had won two seats, and received a pledge of support from the centrist United Future Party (UFP), which had won eight. Meanwhile, the National Party was forced to ponder its future strategy after winning only 27 seats, its worst-ever finish.

The Maori population has increased its claims on land, resources, and compensation from the government. The Waitangi Tribunal, which hears Maori claims for land and compensation, supported a multimillion claim in a report it issued in May. The government said the report's findings were "useful information," but not legally binding. Recent claims for rights to gas and oil fields in the Marlborough Sounds on the South Island, in particular, have created ill will with the non-Maori population. In June, the Court of Appeal ruled that Maori tribes could pursue their claim of the Marlborough Sounds, which currently are used for commercial operations, including marine farms and tourism. In response, the government proposed a new law to prevent Maori tribes from claiming exclusive ownership of the nation's coastline and seabed. Under the proposed law, Maori tribes would be able to use the coastline for fishing but would not be able to deny access to anyone.

The opposition National Party called for the abolition of seven Maori seats in parliament, which have been part of the nation's electoral system for 136 years. In the current legislature, 18 members identify themselves as Maori or part-Maori. Maoris comprise 11 percent of the voting population and 15 percent, or 530,000, of the country's four million people.

As one of the most progressive welfare states in the world, parliament legalized prostitution in June. It was, however, a close vote, with 60 voting for and 59 against the proposed measures. A new law will establish a legal framework for the sex industry, including strict health, safety, and employment guidelines for licensed brothels.

On the international front, the country committed itself to joining an Australian-led, multinational, transition-monitoring group to continue to restore peace and order to the Solomon Islands. New Zealand was also a member of a multinational UN Observer Mission to secure the Solomon Islands and to collect weapons surrendered by former combatants as part of the peace process. This UN group completed its mission in 2003 and left the Solomon Islands at the end of June. To help the country's recovery, New Zealand pledged $8 million in assistance, making New Zealand the single largest donor to the Pacific Island state. Apart from this commitment to the Solomon Islands, New Zealand made a significant shift in its overseas development assistance policy, announcing in May plans to increase funds for business training and small business.

In January, New Zealand granted asylum to some 150 Afghan refugees who were held in Australian refugee detention centers in Nauru and on Manus Island in Papua New Guinea. These refugees were part of a 1,500-person group picked up by a Norwegian freighter in August 2001; in 2002, New Zealand accepted 202 people from Nauru and Manus.

**Political Rights and Civil Liberties:** Citizens of New Zealand can change their government democratically. The government is led by the prime minister and a 20-member cabinet. Queen Elizabeth II is the chief of state and is represented by the governor-general. The country has a mixed-member electoral system that combines voting in geographic districts with proportional representation balloting. The two main political parties are the center-left Labor Party and the mildly conservative National Party. Prime Minister Helen Clark of the Labor Party was elected in 1999. Within the 120-member parliament, seven seats are reserved for the native Maori population.

The media are free and competitive. There is no government control on Internet access, and competitive rates are offered by a number of Internet service providers.

Religious and academic freedom are respected by the government in practice.

The government respects freedom of association. Various nongovernmental and civil society groups are active throughout the country, working to promote community health, minority rights, education, children's welfare, and other issues. Many receive considerable financial support from the government, in addition to private donations.

The New Zealand Council of Trade Unions is the main labor federation. Less than 20 percent of the country's wage earners are members of trade unions. New Zealand is a progressive welfare state, but slow economic growth in the last decade forced the government to end universal free health care. New laws were also introduced to prohibit sympathy strikes, secondary strikes, and walkouts over social or political issues in an environment where unions aggressively advocate workers' rights and collective bargaining is widely practiced. Collective bargaining was further promoted by the passage of the Employment Relations Act in 2000.

The judiciary is independent, and defendants can appeal to the Privy Council in Britain. Police treatment of Maoris, who comprise 15 percent of the general population but more than half of the prison population, had been an issue.

A special tribunal hears Maori tribal claims to land and other resources stemming from the white settlement of New Zealand. The 1840 Treaty of Waitangi between the Maoris and the British leased Maori land in perpetuity to the white "settlers." Maoris now seek higher "rents" for their land and compensation from the government. These claims have become a source of tension with the non-Maori population. Successive governments have introduced programs to boost the social and economic status of Maoris and Pacific Islanders, but most appear to have been only marginally successful.

Violence against women remains a major issue, with reports by the U.S. State Department and civil society groups in New Zealand noting an increase in the number of assaults against women in recent years. The problem had been particularly serious among the Maori population; although Maori women and children make up less than 10 percent of the population, half of them had reported abuse. The number of abuse cases is also disproportionately high among Pacific Islanders, who make up only about 5 percent of the population. There are many governmental and non-governmental programs to prevent family violence and provide victim support, and special programs also target the Maori community. However, these efforts have not significantly improved the situation. The Domestic Violence Act of 1995 broadened the definition of violence to include psychological abuse, threats, intimidation, harassment, and allowing children to witness psychological abuse. It also expanded police powers to address these cases and provided legal services and aid. In 2001, the government introduced "Te Rito," a national strategy to combat domestic violence.

# ⬇ Nicaragua

**Population:** 5,500,000    **Political Rights:** 3
**GNI/capita:** $473    **Civil Liberties:** 3
**Life Expectancy:** 69    **Status:** Partly Free
**Religious Groups:** Roman Catholic (85 percent), other [including Protestant] (15 percent)
**Ethnic Groups:** Mestizo (69 percent), white (17 percent), black (9 percent), Amerindian (5 percent)
**Capital:** Managua
**Trend Arrow:** Nicaragua received a downward trend arrow due to failing government reforms to combat widespread corruption and extend basic legal protection beyond major urban areas.

**Ten-Year Ratings Timeline (Political Rights, Civil Liberties, Status)**

| 1994 | 1995 | 1996 | 1997 | 1998 | 1999 | 2000 | 2001 | 2002 | 2003 |
|------|------|------|------|------|------|------|------|------|------|
| 4,5PF | 4,4PF | 3,4PF | 3,4PF | 2,3PF | 3,3PF | 3,3PF | 3,3PF | 3,3PF | 3,3PF |

**Overview:**    President Enrique Bolanos sparred with the Supreme Court and the judicial system in 2003 in an ongoing effort to reduce widespread corruption throughout the country. The protracted legal battle to bring former president Arnoldo Aleman to justice on corruption charges destabilized Nicaraguan politics during the year. Meanwhile, Nicaragua's economy continued to suffer from the lingering effects of the civil war of the 1980s, a recent hurricane, and a severe drought.

The Republic of Nicaragua was established in 1838, seventeen years after independence from Spain. Its history has been marked by internal strife and dictatorship. The authoritarian rule of the Somoza regime was overthrown in 1979 by the Sandinistas. Subsequently, the Sandinista National Liberation Front (FSLN) attempted to establish a Marxist government, which led to a civil war. The United States intervened indirectly, using Argentine military veterans of that country's "dirty war" on behalf on the right-wing irregular army known as the Contras. The FSLN finally agreed in 1987 to a new constitution that provides for a president and the 96-member National Assembly elected every six years.

In 1990, the newspaper publisher Violeta Chamorro easily defeated the incumbent, President Daniel Ortega, a Sandinista leader. Her 14-party National Opposition Union (UNO) won a legislative majority in the National Assembly. In February 1995, after passage of a law ensuring the military's autonomy, Humberto Ortega—Daniel's brother—turned over command of the military to General Joaquin Cuadra. The army was reduced from 90,000 to 15,000 troops, and former Contras were integrated into its ranks; however, the leadership remained essentially the same. The armed forces continued to own a profitable network of businesses and property amassed under the Sandinistas.

Chamorro was forbidden by law to seek a second term. The 1996 elections were held under the auspices of the five-member Supreme Electoral Council, an independent branch of government. During the campaign, Daniel Ortega portrayed himself as a moderate committed to national unity and reconciliation. Arnoldo Aleman ran on a platform that promised economic reforms, the dismantling of the Sandinista-era bureaucracy, the cleaning up of the army, and the return of property confiscated by the Sandinistas to its original owners. He defeated Ortega 51 to 38 percent, avoiding a runoff. President Aleman's first priority was to reform the army and the police. Aleman named a civilian minister of defense, and a new military code was adopted. The size of the National Police was reduced from 16,000 to 6,800.

In 1999, a governability pact was agreed to by Aleman's right-wing Liberal Constitutionalist Party (PLC) government and the opposition, led by Daniel Ortega. The reforms guaranteed Aleman a seat in both the Nicaraguan and the Central American parliaments, thus assuring him immunity from prosecution. Throughout his presidency, Aleman was dogged by charges that he enriched himself in office, although he never faced formal legal proceedings. In the November 4, 2001 elections, ruling Liberal Party candidate Enrique Bolanos, a conservative businessman respected for his personal integrity, defeated Daniel Ortega, 54 to 45 percent, in a bitterly fought contest in which the two major parties stacked the deck against smaller-party participation.

On January 10, 2002, Bolanos was sworn in as Nicaragua's third post-Sandinista-era president, with a mandate to tackle widespread and systemic corruption, fraud, and incompetence throughout government. One of the major challenges has become the confrontation with former president Arnoldo Aleman, who, along with family members and cronies, is accused of having stolen $100 million. Aleman, as president of the National Assembly, had immunity from criminal prosecution, and this status was seen by many as an example of the widespread impunity of officials that makes a mockery of justice. The protracted effort to indict, prosecute, and convict Aleman for fraud and embezzlement exposed the weakness of the legal system in resisting political pressure, although the system ultimately worked as it was supposed to. Different appeals, including a regional one, were exhausted, and Aleman was convicted of money laundering; additional charges are pending.

The government of Bolanos also faces major economic challenges. Nicaragua is the poorest country in Central America and the second-poorest in the Western Hemisphere. Income distribution in Nicaragua is among the most unequal in the world. Up to 50 percent of the population is unemployed or underemployed. Although the civil war of the 1980s is over, the legacies of that conflict have proven difficult to overcome. This is especially true in terms of the ravaged infrastructure, which was also hit hard by Hurricane Mitch in 1998. A severe drought has further affected the ability of a third of the population to consume even the basic nutritional requirement of 2,200 calories a day. In August 2003, the World Food Programme concluded "that out of a population of 5.4 million, more than 1.6 million are malnourished, with 680,201 enduring 'very high food insecurity', and 947,463 facing 'high' insecurity." The same report noted that, in a country without a famine, 16 people died of hunger in the northern region of Matagalpa in 2002.

The offer to send troops in support of U.S. actions in Iraq was somewhat of a surprise, and was seen as a result of pressure from Washington, D.C. Nevertheless, the road to rapprochement had been cultivated for some time. Popular support for the troop deployment was limited.

**Political Rights and Civil Liberties:** Nicaraguans can change their government democratically. Political and civic activities continue to be conditioned on occasional political violence, corruption, and drug-related crime. Nicaragua was ranked 88 out of 133 countries in Transparency International's 2003 Corruption Perceptions Index.

The print media are varied and partisan, representing hard line and moderate Sandinista, as well as pro- and anti-government, positions. Before leaving office, the Sandinistas privatized the national radio system, mostly to Sandinista loyalists. There are five television stations, three of which carry news programming with partisan political content. Media outlets covering government corruption have been intimidated and/or closed by the government. There is free access to the Internet.

Freedom of religion is respected, and academic freedom is generally honored.

Nongovernmental organizations are active and operate freely. As a whole, civic society has blossomed in the post-Sandinista era. Labor rights are complicated by the Sandinistas' use of unions as violent instruments to influence government economic policy. By means of the public sector unions, the Sandinistas have managed to gain ownership of more than three dozen privatized state enterprises. The legal rights of non-Sandinista unions are not fully guaranteed. The Ministry of Labor has declared strikes illegal. Citizens have no effective recourse when labor laws are violated either by the government or by violent Sandinista actions. Child labor is also a problem.

The judiciary is independent but continues to be susceptible to political influence and corruption. Large case backlogs, long delays in trials, and lengthy pretrial detention have caused the Supreme Court and National Assembly to initiate comprehensive structural reforms of the judicial system.

The Ministry of Government oversees the National Police, the agency that is formally charged with internal security; in practice, the police share this responsibility with the army in rural areas. The conduct of security forces, reflecting enhanced civilian control, continues to improve, although abuses of human rights still occur. Forced confessions to the police remain a problem, as do cases in which security forces arbitrarily arrest and detain citizens. Prison and police holding-cell conditions are poor.

Violent crime is increasing in Managua and other major Nicaraguan cities, although the country remains relatively tranquil compared with some of its Central American neighbors. With long coastlines on both the Atlantic and Pacific, a high volume of land cargo, and myriad jungle airstrips, Nicaragua is an important trans-shipment point for drugs making their way to the north from South America. The Pan-American Highway in Nicaragua's southwest region is a primary venue for narcotics traffickers, although smuggling by air is increasing and small aircraft are occasionally commandeered by traffickers for flights to other countries. The growing level of exposure of Nicaraguan society to the drug trade is evidenced by the significant increase in the local use of cocaine.

Like most Latin American countries, Nicaragua nominally recognizes the rights of its indigenous communities in its constitution and laws, but in practice those rights have not been respected. Approximately 5 percent of the population is indigenous and lives mostly in the Northern Autonomous Atlantic Region (RAAN) and Southern Autonomous Atlantic Region (RAAS). These regions are 50 percent of the national territory, but account for only 10 percent of the population. The largest community is that of the Miskito, with 180,000 people, and the smallest is the Rama, with 1,000; there are 10,000 Sumo and 3,000 Garifuna. The 2001 ruling of the Inter-American Commission for Human Rights over logging rights in favor of these communities has not been fully implemented, although the legislation has been passed. In July 2003, the National Assembly finally approved the codification of the 1987 Autonomy Law that created these areas.

Violence against women, including rape and domestic abuse, remains a serious problem.

# Niger

**Population:** 12,100,000
**GNI/capita:** $180
**Life Expectancy:** 45
**Religious Groups:** Muslim (80 percent), other, [including indigenous beliefs and Christian] (20 percent)
**Ethnic Groups:** Hausa (56 percent), Djerma (22 percent), Fula (9 percent), Tuareg (8 percent), Beri Beri (4 percent), other (1 percent)
**Capital:** Niamey

**Political Rights:** 4
**Civil Liberties:** 4
**Status:** Partly Free

**Ten-Year Ratings Timeline (Political Rights, Civil Liberties, Status)**

| 1994 | 1995 | 1996 | 1997 | 1998 | 1999 | 2000 | 2001 | 2002 | 2003 |
|------|------|------|------|------|------|------|------|------|------|
| 3,5PF | 3,5PF | 7,5NF | 7,5NF | 7,5NF | 5,5PF | 4,4PF | 4,4PF | 4,4PF | 4,4PF |

**Overview:**     The government of Niger continued to infringe on freedom of the press in 2003 with the detention of several journalists. The sentencing of one journalist to six months in prison for defamation led to protests by members of the political opposition and civil society that were not repressed by the authorities.

After gaining independence from France in 1960, Niger was governed for 30 years by one-party and military regimes dominated by leaders of Hausa or Djerma ethnicity. After 13 years of direct military rule, Niger was transformed into a nominally civilian, one-party state in 1987 under General Ali Seibou. International pressure and pro-democracy demonstrations led by the umbrella organization Niger Union of Trade Union Workers forced Niger's rulers to accede to the Africa-wide trend toward democratization in 1990. An all-party national conference drafted a new constitution that was adopted in a national referendum in 1992.

Mahamane Ousmane, of the Alliance of Forces for Change, won a five-year term as the country's first democratically elected president in 1993 in elections deemed to be free and fair. General Ibrahim Bare Mainassara overthrew Ousmane in January 1996 and won fraudulent elections six months later. Parliamentary elections in November were held in an atmosphere of intense intimidation and were boycotted by most opposition parties.

In April 1999, Mainassara was assassinated by members of the presidential guard. The head of the guard led a transitional government that held a constitutional referendum in July and national elections in November. In the presidential election, Mamadou Tandja won in a second round of polling with 60 percent of the vote, defeating former president Ousmane. Tandja's party, the National Movement for the Development of Society, and its partner, the Democratic and Social Convention, achieved a two-thirds majority in the National Assembly by winning 55 of the 83 seats. The other coalition—the Nigerian Party for Democracy and Socialism, and the Rally for Democracy and Progress—won the remaining 28 seats. Both elections were deemed to be free and fair by international observers.

Although press freedom continued to suffer in 2003, the authorities did not respond with a crackdown against demonstrators who protested the sentencing of a journalist to prison. Opposition members of parliament tabled a no-confidence motion against Prime Minister Hama Amadou for poor management and threats to press freedom; the motion was defeated. Fifteen independent radio stations were also closed, but the move appeared to stem from a disagreement over protocol rather than a desire to limit press freedom. However, President Tandja warned the media against airing programs that could "disturb the social peace and public order."

Niger is struggling to implement unpopular structural reforms. The economy is based mainly on subsistence farming, small trading, herding, and informal markets. Uranium is the most important export, but world demand has declined. Niger drew international attention in 2003 because of U.S. claims that Iraq had approached the country to acquire uranium for its nuclear program. The claims were later proven to have been unfounded.

**Political Rights and Civil Liberties:** The people of Niger can change their government democratically. Both the presidential and legislative polls in November 1999 were considered to be free and fair. In 2003, members of the opposition criticized President Mamadou Tandja for what they said was an attempt to drive through a revision of the country's electoral law without the consultation of opposition parties. A new law would no longer oblige government ministers to resign before seeking electoral office. It would also abolish a requirement that the head of the Independent National Electoral Commission be a judge or magistrate.

Constitutional protections for free expression are guaranteed, but these rights are not always guaranteed in practice. Criminal penalties are exacted for violations such as slander. A government newspaper and several private publications circulate. There are dozens of private radio stations, some of which broadcast in local languages. Parliament opened a radio station in 2001 as the Voice of the National Assembly. In 2003, authorities closed 15 independent radio stations, but the move appeared to stem from a dispute over how licenses were issued, rather than from a desire to limit press freedom. The government does not restrict Internet access, although service frequently has technical difficulties.

The government restricted press freedom in 2003 with the detention of several journalists. Maman Abou, director of the weekly *Le Republicain*, was tried in absentia and his lawyers were not told of his trial, according to Paris-based Reporters Sans Frontieres. He was arrested in November and found guilty of defamation for an article alleging that the government awarded contracts to several businesses close to the prime minister without going through the competitive bidding process. He was sentenced to six months in jail. Three journalists from Anfani FM were briefly detained in November for broadcasting information about a conflict between farmers and cattle herders. The publication director of the weekly *L'Enqueteur* received a one-year suspended sentence and was banished from the capital for an article that authorities said incited ethnic hatred.

Freedom of religion is respected, although, at times, Muslims have not been tolerant of the rights of minority religions to practice their faith. Islam is practiced by 80 percent of the population. The government in 2000 banned six fundamentalist-oriented organizations following rioting by fundamentalist groups. Academic freedom is guaranteed but is not always respected. Officials closed the Abdou Moumouni University for two weeks in October following student protests over scholarship arrears and other problems.

Constitutional guarantees of freedom of assembly and association are generally respected. The University of Niamey was closed for two weeks in October because of student demonstrations and strikes over funding problems. Human rights and other nongovernmental organizations operate openly and freely in Niger and publish reports that are often highly critical of the government. Niger's workers have the right to form unions and bargain for wages, although more than 95 percent of the workforce is employed in the nonunionized subsistence agricultural and small-trading sectors.

The constitution provides for an independent judiciary, and courts have shown signs of independence. However, the judiciary is overburdened, limited by scant training and resources, and occasionally subject to executive interference and other outside influence. Efforts at reform are underway. Respect for human rights has improved under the government of President Tandja. However, prolonged pretrial detention remains a problem. Prisons are characterized by overcrowding and poor health and sanitary conditions. The International Committee of the Red Cross and other humanitarian groups have unrestricted access to prisons and detention centers.

Discrimination against ethnic minorities persists, despite constitutional protections. The Hausa and Djerma ethnic groups dominate government and business. Tandja is the country's first president who is from neither group. Nomadic peoples, such as the Tuaregs and many Peul, continue to have less access to government services.

Women suffer extensive societal discrimination, especially in rural areas. Family law gives women inferior status in property, inheritance rights, and divorce. In the east, some women among the Hausa and Peul ethnic groups are cloistered and may leave their homes only if escorted by a male and usually only after dark. Domestic violence against women is reportedly widespread. Sexual harassment and performing female genital mutilation (FGM) were made illegal in 2001. The law against FGM was rescinded and was under review in 2003. Several women's rights organizations operate in the country.

# Nigeria

**Population:** 133,900,000
**GNI/capita:** $290
**Life Expectancy:** 52
**Religious Groups:** Muslim (50 percent), Christian (40 percent), indigenous beliefs (10 percent)
**Ethnic Groups:** Hausa and Fulani (29 percent), Yoruba (21 percent), Ibo (18 percent), other (32 percent)
**Capital:** Abuja

**Political Rights:** 4
**Civil Liberties:** 4*
**Status:** Partly Free

**Ratings Change:** Nigeria's civil liberties rating improved from 5 to 4 due to an abatement of violence between Muslim and Christian communities that had beset the country in 2002.

**Ten-Year Ratings Timeline (Political Rights, Civil Liberties, Status)**

| 1994 | 1995 | 1996 | 1997 | 1998 | 1999 | 2000 | 2001 | 2002 | 2003 |
|------|------|------|------|------|------|------|------|------|------|
| 7,6NF | 7,7NF | 7,6NF | 7,6NF | 6,4NF | 4,3PF | 4,4PF | 4,5PF | 4,5PF | 4,4PF |

**Overview:**

Nigeria made its first peaceful transition from one democratically elected government to another in 2003 when President Olusegun Obasanjo of the People's Democratic Party (PDP) was elected to a second term. Anticipated widespread unrest during the elections did not materialize, although there was violence leading up to the polls that were marred by irregularities. Meanwhile, clashes between Muslim and Christian communities diminished in 2003 compared with the previous year.

The military ruled Nigeria for all but 10 years since independence from Britain in 1960, until 1999. Generals and their backers argued that they were the only ones who could keep a lid on simmering tensions between Muslims and Christians—the north is largely Muslim, while the south is mainly Christian—and among the country's 250 ethnic groups.

Nigeria initially appeared to be emerging from several years of military rule under General Ibrahim Babangida in 1993, when presidential elections were held. Moshood Abiola, a Muslim Yoruba from the south, was widely considered the winner, but the military annulled the results. It continued to rule behind a puppet civilian administration until General Sani Abacha, a principal architect of previous coups, took power in November 1993. A predominantly military Provisional Ruling Council (PRC) was appointed, and all democratic structures were dissolved and political parties banned. Abiola was arrested in June 1994 after declaring himself Nigeria's rightful president. He died in detention, after suffering from a lack of proper medical care, just five weeks after Abacha himself died suddenly in June 1998.

The departure of the two most significant figures on Nigeria's political landscape opened possibilities for democratic change. General Abdulsalami Abubakar, the army chief of staff, emerged as the PRC's consensus choice to be the country's next leader, and he promised to oversee a transition to real civilian rule in 1999. However, Obasanjo—a former general who had led a military regime in Nigeria from 1976 to 1979 and had spent three years in prison under Abacha—won the presidential poll in February. In legislative elections held that year, Obasanjo's PDP won the most seats in both the Senate and House of Representatives.

In the April 2003 presidential poll, Obasanjo faced 19 opposition candidates. However, in the end, the race was between the southern Christian Obasanjo and former general Muhammadu Buhari, a northern Muslim and member of the All Nigeria People's Party (ANPP). Obasanjo won the presidency with 62 percent of the vote compared with 32 percent for Buhari. Buhari filed a petition on behalf of about 20 opposition parties to nullify the election results. The petition accused the Independent National Electoral Commission of not complying with the country's electoral law by failing to get polling agents of contesting parties to certify electoral materials as genuine.

Local and international observers witnessed serious irregularities during the election. The Transition Monitoring Group, a coalition of Nigerian civic organizations, deployed some 10,000 monitors who reported ballot-box stuffing, multiple voting, falsification of results, and voter intimidation. They maintained that fraud and intimidation were particularly prevalent in the southeast of the country. According to Human Rights Watch, the authorities took no action to investigate and prosecute perpetrators of political violence in the run-up to the April elections in which hundreds of people reportedly had been killed.

Obasanjo's PDP won 52 Senate seats and 170 House seats in the April legislative poll. The ANPP captured 25 seats in the Senate and 81 in the House, while the Alliance for Democracy won 5 Senate seats and 30 House seats. Smaller parties secured the remainder of seats.

The majority of Nigerians are engaged in small-scale agriculture, while most wealth is controlled by a small elite. Nigeria's agriculture and manufacturing sectors have deteriorated considerably in the pursuit of oil, which accounts for more than 98 percent of the country's export revenues and almost all foreign investment. Corruption has bled the country of billions of dollars in oil revenue. However, in 2003, the government made significant steps toward improving accountability, including joining the British-led Extractive Industries Transparency Initiative.

**Political Rights and Civil Liberties:** Nigerians can change their government democratically. Although the 1999 presidential and legislative elections were free, they were not fair in many areas. International observers noted irregularities during the 2003 presidential vote that reelected Olusegun Obasanjo, including ballot-box stuffing and alteration of results. Obasanjo's PDP also dominated the year's legislative elections. Members of the bicameral National Assembly are elected for four-year terms to 109 seats in the Senate and 360 in the House of Representatives.

Freedom of speech and expression is guaranteed, and the Obasanjo government generally respects these rights in practice. Several private radio and television stations broadcast throughout the country, and numerous print publications operate largely unhindered. However, criminal defamation laws are still used against journalists. Sharia (Islamic law) in 12 northern states imposes severe penalties for alleged press offenses. The Paris-based Reporters Sans Frontieres (RSF) expressed concern in August about a growing climate of lawlessness that journalists have to work in, especially beyond Lagos. RSF also noted that local authorities regularly target journalists who criticize them, and that the media in northern Nigeria were most at risk. The government does not impede Internet access.

The New York-based Committee to Protect Journalists in April urged lawmakers to pass the Freedom of Information Bill, which is modeled on the U.S. Freedom of Information Act. The bill has been stalled in the lower house of parliament for more than three years, although it has been endorsed by all Nigerian journalism and civil society groups. It would allow journalists and citizens to access information held by government agencies and would require state agencies to publish a list of records in their possession in the government newsletter, the *Federal Gazette*. The bill would also weaken the powers of the Nigeria Press Council, which can accredit and register journalists and suspend them from practicing.

Religious freedom is guaranteed by the constitution, but many sectors of society, including government officials, often discriminate against those of a religion different from their own. Religious violence had become increasingly common, often corresponding to regional and ethnic differences and competition for resources. However, violent clashes between Muslims and Christians diminished in 2003 compared with the previous year. Academic freedom is guaranteed, but security forces harassed and arrested students during protests in 2003.

Freedom of assembly and association are generally respected in practice. However, there were instances in 2003 when security forces cracked down on demonstrations that they believed would turn violent. Up to 10 people were killed when police fired on demonstrators protesting a hike in fuel prices in July, according to petroleum union leaders. Human Rights Watch said that 30 people were arrested in the same month after protesting the visit of U.S. president George Bush. In the southern state of Imo, reports said, police in March arrested up to 300 people who were traveling in a convoy of the Movement for the Actualization of the Sovereign State of Biafra.

Despite several statutory restrictions on the rights of trade unions, workers, except members of the armed forces and those considered essential employees, may join trade unions, and the right to bargain collectively is guaranteed. About 10 percent of the workforce is unionized. The week-long strike in July to protest a hike in fuel prices ended when petroleum unions accepted a compromise price deal offered by the government in which prices would be raised by 30 percent instead of 54 percent. The government, in proceeding with economic structural adjustment, has been attempting to remove subsidies, such as those for fuel. An earlier oil strike, in April, had left nearly 100 foreigners and 170 Nigerians trapped on oil rigs for almost two weeks.

The judiciary is subject to political influence and is hampered by corruption and inefficiency. Many trials in Islamic courts in several northern states have been characterized by absence of due process. Defendants do not always have legal representation and are often ill-informed about procedures and their rights. Lengthy pretrial detention remains a problem. Caning and amputation have been carried out for violations such as adultery and theft. The country's prisons are overcrowded, unhealthy, and life threatening. Nevertheless, the government has allowed international organizations to visit detention facilities, and some improvements have been made.

Members of the security forces committed serious violations in 2003, including extrajudicial killings, arbitrary detention, torture, and beatings. Human Rights Watch sent an open letter to President Obasanjo in July, calling on him to end impunity for human rights abuses and saying that he had failed to do so during his first term in office. The letter said that there had been no action to investigate and prosecute perpetrators of extrajudicial killings and political violence in the run-up to the April elections; hundreds of people had reportedly been killed. The rights group also noted that Obasanjo had failed to publish the findings of the Nigerian Human Rights Violations Investigations Commission more than one year after the final report had been submitted. The commission had investigated and heard testimony about abuses dating back to the country's civil war in the 1960s.

The constitution prohibits ethnic discrimination and requires government offices to reflect the country's ethnic diversity. The Hausa-Fulani from northern Nigeria dominated the military and the government from independence until the southern Christian Olusegun Obasanjo was first elected in 1999. Obasanjo's government is both ethnically and religiously diverse, but societal discrimination is practiced widely, and clashes frequently erupt among the country's 250 ethnic groups. A number of armed youth groups have emerged to defend their ethnic and economic interests. Nigerian human rights groups said in 2002 that intercommunal violence had claimed up to 10,000 lives across the country since 1999. The government in 2003 said that more than 750,000 people had been displaced by communal violence during the previous two years.

Ethnic minorities in the oil-rich Niger Delta region feel particularly discriminated against, primarily with regard to receiving a share of the country's oil wealth. Clashes among ethnic groups and communities competing for resources escalated in 2003. At least 200 people were killed in and around the southern Delta city of Warri in conflicts between rival Ijaw and Itsekiri ethnic groups. Some of the violence was triggered by the drawing of electoral boundaries in the run-up to elections. According to Human Rights Watch, entire communities in the Delta were indiscriminately targeted by security forces in response to local demands for resource control and protests against environmental damage. The group said that the government failed to understand the underlying causes of communal violence and that in the past similar military operations had led to hundreds of extrajudicial killings for which no one had been tried. In addition, oil spills and acts of sabotage frequently disrupt petroleum production, and the taking of foreign oil workers as hostages continued during the year.

Nigerian women face societal discrimination, although educational opportunities have eroded a number of barriers over the years. Women play a vital role in the country's informal economy. Women of some ethnic groups are denied equal rights to inherit property, and marital rape is not considered a crime. About 60 percent of

Nigerian women are subjected to female genital mutilation. Women's rights have suffered serious setbacks in the northern states governed by Sharia. A Muslim woman, Amina Lawal, was sentenced in 2002 to death by stoning after she had a child out of wedlock. Her case gained international attention and an Islamic appeals court in September 2003 acquitted her.

Child labor, marriages, and the trafficking of women for prostitution remain common, and no law specifically prohibits the trafficking of persons. However, efforts were under way during the year to combat the practice. More than 200 children were repatriated to Benin during the year. Children are trafficked throughout West Africa to work on plantations or as domestic servants.

# North Korea

**Population:** 22,700,000  **Political Rights:** 7
**GNI/capita:** $440  **Civil Liberties:** 7
**Life Expectancy:** 63  **Status:** Not Free
**Religious Groups:** Buddhist, Confucian, other
**Ethnic Groups:** Korean
**Capital:** Pyongyang

**Ten-Year Ratings Timeline (Political Rights, Civil Liberties, Status)**

| 1994 | 1995 | 1996 | 1997 | 1998 | 1999 | 2000 | 2001 | 2002 | 2003 |
|------|------|------|------|------|------|------|------|------|------|
| 7,7NF | 7,7NF | 7,7NF | 7,7NF | 7,7NF | 7,7NF | 7,7NF | 7,7NF | 7,7NF | 7,7NF |

**Overview:**  Already isolated because of its nuclear saber rattling, North Korea's Stalinist regime further escalated what appeared to be a high-stakes game of blackmail. Having previously confessed to possessing a uranium enrichment program and having taken steps to fire up a mothballed reactor, Pyongyang in 2003 told U.S. officials that it possessed nuclear weapons and continued its bellicose rhetoric against Japan, South Korea, and the United States. It offered to scrap its nuclear weapons program in exchange for increased aid, diplomatic recognition, and a nonaggression pact with Washington.

The Democratic People's Republic of Korea was established in the northern part of the Korean Peninsula in 1948 following three years of post-War Soviet occupation. At independence, North Korea's uncontested ruler was Kim Il-sung, a former Soviet army officer who claimed to be a guerrilla hero in the struggle against Japan, which had annexed Korea as a colony in 1910. North Korea invaded South Korea in 1950 in an attempt to reunify the peninsula under Communist rule. Drawing in China and the United States, the ensuing three-year conflict killed as many as two million people and ended with a ceasefire rather than a peace treaty. Since then, the two Koreas have been on a continuous war footing.

Kim Il-sung solidified his power base during the Cold War, purging rivals, throwing thousands of political prisoners into labor camps, and fostering a Stalinist personality cult that promoted him as North Korea's "Dear Leader." The end of the Cold

War, however, brought North Korea's command economy to the brink of collapse, as Pyongyang lost crucial Soviet and East Bloc subsidies and preferential trade deals. By some estimates, between 1993 and 2000 economic output shrunk by half.

With the regime's survival in doubt, Kim's death in 1994 ushered in even more uncertainty. Under his son, the reclusive Kim Jong-il, the regime has maintained its rigid political control but has taken modest steps to free up North Korea's centrally planned economy. During the initial years of Kim Jong-il's rule, the situation grew even bleaker as natural disasters, economic mismanagement, and restrictions on the flow of information combined to kill, according to the U.S. State Department, an estimated 1 to 2 million North Koreans between 1995 and 1997.

While the famine threat has receded thanks in part to foreign food aid, a 2002 UN study found that more than half the population suffered malnutrition. Moreover, North Korea's state-run health system has all but collapsed, hospitals lack adequate medicine and equipment, and clean water is in short supply because of electricity and chlorine shortages.

Against this backdrop, economic reforms launched in July 2002 have made life tougher for ordinary North Koreans by igniting inflation and increasing unemployment. The regime eased price controls and promised to raise salaries to offset the higher prices. It also gave factories more autonomy. Many of the promised salary hikes, however, have not materialized, and the Hong Kong–based *Far Eastern Economic Review* reported in March that many factories, suddenly forced to pay their own way, have shut down.

In addition to liberalizing prices, the regime recently has also allowed farmers to set up small markets in cities, something it has quietly tolerated for decades in the countryside. These markets now sell consumer goods as well as food. Prospects appear dim, though, for more far-reaching market reforms. The regime is reluctant to take any measures that would grant North Koreans significantly greater control over their daily lives for fear of undermining its tight grip on power.

The latest crisis over North Korea's nuclear weapons program began in October 2002, after Washington said that Pyongyang had admitted to having a program to produce enriched uranium, a component of nuclear bombs. This program apparently violated a 1994 deal under which North Korea had pledged to abandon its separate plutonium nuclear program. In return, Japan, South Korea, and the United States agreed to provide North Korea with two light-water nuclear reactors, which cannot be used to produce weapons-grade plutonium.

Escalating tensions further, North Korea in December 2002 threw out international inspectors monitoring its Yongbyon reactor, which was shuttered under the 1994 agreement because it could be used to produce plutonium. In 2003, Pyongyang not only made a series of boasts about its alleged nuclear capabilities and threatened to test a nuclear weapon, but also pulled out of the Nuclear Non-Proliferation Treaty.

Washington has rebuffed Pyongyang's efforts to win concessions in return for dismantling its nuclear weapons program, insisting instead that Pyongyang disarm before any negotiated settlement, including a multilateral nonaggression commitment, is considered. For its part, China, North Korea's main patron, recently has appeared eager to reign in Kim Jong-il. Beijing fears that his brinkmanship could provoke Japan and South Korea into building nuclear weapons or even touch off a war that could send refugees streaming into China. Many analysts say, however, that the greatest threat from North Korea is its potential to sell plutonium to rogue states or terrorists for hard cash.

As 2003 ended, ordinary North Koreans faced another winter of hardship. They are among the most impoverished and tightly controlled people on earth, condemned to dehumanizing lives of extreme scarcity, subject to relentless indoctrination, and threatened with execution or incarceration in a labor camp for offenses as trivial as listening to foreign radio.

## Political Rights and Civil Liberties:

North Korea is one of the most tightly controlled countries in the world. The regime denies North Koreans even the most basic rights; holds tens of thousands of political prisoners under brutal conditions; and controls nearly every facet of social, political, and economic life.

Kim Jong-il, the North Korean leader, and a handful of elites from the Korean Worker's Party (KWP) rule by decree, although little is known about the regime's inner workings. Kim formally is general secretary of the KWP, supreme commander of North Korea's 1.1 million–strong army, and chairman of the National Defense Commission. The latter post officially is the "highest office of state" since the 1998 abolition of the presidency.

North Korea's parliament, known as the Supreme People's Assembly, meets only a few days each year and simply rubber-stamps the ruling elite's decisions. In an effort to provide a veneer of democracy, the government occasionally holds staged elections for parliament as well as for provincial, county, and city bodies.

In classic totalitarian fashion, officials subject the masses to intensive political indoctrination through the school system, the state-controlled media, and work and neighborhood associations. Radios and televisions are designed to receive only government stations.

Religious freedom is severely repressed. The government requires all prayer and religious study to be supervised by the state and severely punishes North Koreans for worshipping independently in underground churches. Officials have killed, beaten, arrested, or detained in prison camps many members of underground churches, according to foreign religious and human rights groups. Some reports suggest, however, that house churches often are tolerated if they do not openly proselytize or have contact with foreign missionaries.

The right to privacy is virtually nonexistent in North Korea. The state closely monitors North Koreans through informers as well as security checks on homes. Pyongyang also assigns to each North Korean a security rating that partly determines access to higher education, employment, and health services, as well as place of residence. By some foreign estimates, nearly half the population is considered either "wavering" or "hostile," with the rest rated "core."

North Koreans face death or long prison terms for any peaceful dissent. Some reportedly have been executed merely for criticizing the regime. Authorities have also executed some repatriated defectors, military officers accused of spying or other antigovernment offenses, and North Koreans who were forcibly returned by Chinese border guards after crossing into China.

The regime controls all trade unions and uses them to monitor workers; mobilize them to meet production targets; and provide them with health care, schooling, and welfare services. Strikes, collective bargaining, and other basic organized-labor activities are illegal. The law also bans independent civic, human rights, and social welfare groups.

North Korea's government-controlled courts serve mainly to help the regime control the population. The regime also runs a network of jails and "re-education through labor" camps that are notorious for their brutal and degrading treatment of inmates. Torture and ill-treatment reportedly are widespread in these prisons and labor camps, as well as in detention centers where refugees who have been forcibly returned from China are held for interrogation. In camps for political prisoners, inmates are kept on starvation diets, and up to three generations of a family are often imprisoned for life for the political crimes of a single member, according to an October report by the U.S. Committee for Human Rights in North Korea, a bipartisan, Washington-based advocacy group. In detention centers for repatriated North Koreans, pregnant women are forced to have abortions or, in cases of advanced pregnancy, their babies are killed at birth, the report said.

North Korean camps held some 200,000 political detainees in 2002, according to a U.S. State Department human rights report released in March 2003. In addition to maintaining camps for political prisoners, the regime reportedly has some 30 forced-labor camps for common criminals serving shorter terms, the report added. The number of ordinary prisoners is not known. Separately, the regime maintains special camps that detain orphaned and homeless children under inhuman conditions, according to refugees who have escaped from the camps into China.

Authorities have forcibly relocated "many tens of thousands" of North Koreans to the countryside from Pyongyang, including disabled persons and those considered politically unreliable, according to the U.S. State Department human rights report. The regime is also once again rigorously enforcing a permit system for travel outside one's home province after having relaxed it in the mid-1990s, the *Far Eastern Economic Review* reported in October, citing North Korean refugees in northeastern China.

Despite recent market reforms, North Korea's economy remains centrally planned. The government assigns all jobs, prohibits private property, and directs and controls nearly all economic activity. Besides being grossly mismanaged, the economy is hobbled by creaking infrastructure, shortages of energy and raw materials, and an inability to borrow on world markets or from multilateral banks because of sanctions and a past foreign debt default.

Little is known about how problems such as domestic violence or workplace discrimination may affect North Korean women. There were widespread reports of trafficking of women and girls among the tens of thousands of North Koreans who have recently crossed into China.

# Norway

**Population:** 4,600,000
**GNI/capita:** $35,630
**Life Expectancy:** 79
**Religious Groups:** Evangelical Lutheran (86 percent), other Christian [including Protestant and Roman Catholic] (3 percent), none and unknown (11 percent)
**Ethnic Groups:** Norwegian, Sami (20,000)
**Capital:** Oslo

**Political Rights:** 1
**Civil Liberties:** 1
**Status:** Free

**Ten-Year Ratings Timeline (Political Rights, Civil Liberties, Status)**

| 1994 | 1995 | 1996 | 1997 | 1998 | 1999 | 2000 | 2001 | 2002 | 2003 |
|------|------|------|------|------|------|------|------|------|------|
| 1,1F | 1,1F | 1,1F | 1,1F | 1,1F | 1,1F | 1,1F | 1,1F | 1,1F | 1,1F |

**Overview:**

Police campaigned against a neo-Nazi organization in October 2003, fearing that the group might turn to violence. Norway's new marriage law, which requires that both partners agree that they have equal right to a divorce, was criticized by the Roman Catholic Church.

Following Denmark's rule from 1450 to 1814, Norway enjoyed a brief spell of independence during which the Eisvold Convention, Norway's current constitution, was adopted. Subsequently, Norway became part of a Swedish-headed monarchy. Norway gained independence in 1905 and has since functioned as a constitutional monarchy with a multiparty parliamentary structure.

The current, center-right government took power in October 2001 after the Labor Party suffered its worst election result in 90 years. The ruling coalition is made up of the Conservative Party, the Christian Democratic Party, and the Liberal Party, which together hold 122 seats. Kjell Magne Bondevik of the Christian Democratic Party is in his second term as prime minister. However, the largest party in parliament remains the Labor Party, with 43 seats. Under the constitutional monarchy, King Harald ascended to the throne in 1991.

Norwegian citizens narrowly rejected European Union (EU) membership in referendums in both 1972 and 1994, despite government support for joining. Norwegians feared the threat that membership would pose to the country's energy, agriculture, and fishing industries, in addition to wanting to preserve their sovereignty. As part of the European Economic Area, Norway has nearly full access to European markets. Nevertheless, while 75 percent of Norwegian exports go to EU countries and Norway has adopted almost all EU directives, it has little power to influence EU decisions as long as it remains outside. In order to maintain the current ruling coalition, which includes both pro- and anti-EU parties, the government has agreed not to reopen the question of EU membership during the term of the current parliament, which is scheduled to end in September 2005. The public remains divided over this issue.

A founding member of NATO, Norway has developed an increasingly active foreign policy over the past decade. In particular, the government has sent envoys and negotiators to help resolve some of the world's most contentious disputes, most notably for the Israeli-Palestinian conflict and that in Sri Lanka. Norway runs 10 percent of the world's charities and gives one of the highest levels of overseas development aid as a percentage of its GDP, a policy that has the support of 80 percent of the Norwegian public.

Norway was ranked as the best country to live in worldwide in the past two UN Human Development Indexes. Its high standard of living is due in large part to the discovery of energy deposits in the 1960s, which has made Norway the world's third-largest oil exporter. The government has put 80 percent of oil revenues in a petroleum fund that is invested overseas, thus helping to ensure that the benefits are enjoyed for many years.

**Political Rights and Civil Liberties:** Norwegians can change their government democratically. The 165-member parliament, or Storting, is directly elected for a four-year term by a system of proportional representation. It then selects one-quarter of its members to serve as the upper chamber, or Lagting, while the remaining members make up the lower chamber, or Odelsting. Neither body is subject to dissolution. A vote of no confidence in the Storting results in the resignation of the cabinet, and the leader of the party that holds the most seats is then asked to form a new government.

The indigenous Sami population lives in the north of the country. The Sami have their own consultative constituent assembly, or Sameting, which has worked to protect the group's language and cultural rights and to influence the national government's decisions about Sami land and its resources.

Norway remains one of the least corrupt countries in the world, rated 8 of 133 countries surveyed in Transparency International's 2003 Corruption Perceptions Index. However, a 2003 Gallup survey found that nearly half of all Norwegians believe that bribery in the business world will be an increasing problem in the coming years; Norway was the most pessimistic of 47 nationalities in the survey. In 2003, the chief executive of partially state-owned Statoil resigned as a result of a police probe into alleged bribery of consultants linked to contracts in Iran.

Freedom of the press is constitutionally guaranteed, and many newspapers are subsidized by the state in order to promote political pluralism. The majority of newspapers are privately owned and openly partisan. However, subsidies have been cut in recent years, and there are fears that some special interest publications will be forced to close. A government ban on political commercials, designed to ensure equal opportunity to the media for all candidates regardless of varying resources, violates the European human rights convention, which Norway has signed. In August, TV2 tested the ban by airing a Progress Party commercial. The station was fined Nkr 70,000 (US$9,500) by the Mass Media Authority the next month. In October, the national film board lifted a 90-year ban on films censored for sex or violence. Almost 300 previously banned films may now be released. Norway continues to ban hardcore pornography in movie theaters, on television, and on video and DVD.

The king is the constitutional head of the Evangelical Lutheran Church of Norway, the state church, to which about 86 percent of the population belongs. Other denominations must register with the state to receive support, which is determined by size of membership. By law, a course on religion and ethics, which focuses on Christianity, is mandatory for students, with no exemptions provided. A case submitted to the European Court of Human Rights in 2002 challenges the law on the grounds that it violates parents' rights to control the religious education of their children. Academic freedom is ensured for all.

The constitution guarantees freedom of peaceful assembly and association, as well as the right to strike. Unions play an important role in consulting with the government on social and economic issues, and about 60 percent of the workforce belong to unions. Uncharacteristically, police allegedly used excessive force when restraining protestors during March 2003 protests in Oslo against the Iraq war.

The judiciary is independent in Norway. The court system is headed by the Supreme Court and operates at the local and national levels. The king appoints judges under advisement from the Ministry of Justice.

The Norwegian security police began a nationwide campaign in October against the neo-Nazi organization Vigrid. Police personally visited members of the group in hopes of reducing membership and preventing them from turning to violence.

The government helps protect the heritage of the Sami population through Sami language instruction, broadcast programs, and subsidized newspapers in their regions. A deputy minister in the national government deals specifically with Sami issues. However, Sami dialects are at risk, according to UNESCO. The proposed Finnmark Bill would settle the question of land-use rights by placing all resources under national control; the bill has been criticized by the UN Committee on the Elimination of Racial Discrimination for limiting Sami land rights.

The populist, free market, anti-immigrant Progress Party is the furthest to the right in the Storting, and currently the third-largest party in representation. The party's popularity is due in part to that of its charismatic leader, Carl Hagen. Although the majority of Norwegians have a positive attitude toward immigrants, citizens are increasingly in favor of a stricter immigration policy, according to Statistics Norway. At the start of 2003, 4.3 percent of the population were foreign citizens; about 40,000 immigrants arrived in 2002. Polls suggest that discrimination in housing and employment against ethnic minorities is widespread.

A new marriage law, which includes a clause under which both couples must vow that they are getting married voluntarily and have an equal right to a divorce, has been criticized by the Roman Catholic Church. The Gender Equality Act provides equal rights for men and women, and a Gender Equality Ombudsman enforces the law. Traditionally, 40 percent of the cabinet is female; 8 of the current 19 ministers are women, and women make up 36 percent of the Storting. A new law requires that firms have at least 40 percent women on their boards; the figure currently stands at about 7 percent.

# Oman

**Population:** 2,600,000
**GNI/capita:** $7,720
**Life Expectancy:** 73
**Religious Groups:** Ibadi Muslim (75 percent,) other [including Sunni Muslim, Shi'a Muslim, Hindu] (25 percent)
**Ethnic Groups:** Arab, Baluchi, South Asian, African
**Capital:** Muscat

**Political Rights:** 6
**Civil Liberties:** 5
**Status:** Not Free

**Ten-Year Ratings Timeline (Political Rights, Civil Liberties, Status)**

| 1994 | 1995 | 1996 | 1997 | 1998 | 1999 | 2000 | 2001 | 2002 | 2003 |
|------|------|------|------|------|------|------|------|------|------|
| 6,6NF | 6,6NF | 6,6NF | 6,6NF | 6,6NF | 6,6NF | 6,5NF | 6,5NF | 6,5NF | 6,5NF |

**Overview:**

Oman took a small step forward in opening up its political system in October 2003 by holding the first full election in its history, for its Consultative Council. Nevertheless, the Consultative Council, which is the lower chamber of the bicameral Council of Oman, has advisory rather than legislative powers.

Oman has been an independent nation since Sultan bin Seif's expulsion of the Portuguese in 1650, ending more than a century of Portuguese involvement in certain regions of Oman. After the expulsion of the Portuguese, the sultan conquered neighboring territories, building a small empire that included parts of the eastern coast of Africa and the southern Arabian Peninsula.

During the 1950s and 1960s, Oman experienced a period of internal unrest centered mostly on the interior regions of the country. In 1964, a group of separatists supported by Communist governments, such as the People's Democratic Republic of Yemen, or former South Yemen, started a revolt in Oman's Dhofar province. This insurgency was not completely quelled until the mid-1970s, with Oman's government receiving direct military support from its traditional ally the United Kingdom, as well as from Iran and Jordan.

The current ruler, Sultan Qaboos, came to power more than 30 years ago, after overthrowing his father, Sultan Said bin Taimur, who had ruled for nearly four decades. Sultan Qaboos launched a program to modernize Oman's infrastructure, educational system, governmental structure, and economy.

In 1991, Sultan Qaboos established the Consultative Council, or Majlis Ash-shura, an appointed body aimed at providing the sultan with a wider range of opinions on ruling the country. The 1996 basic law, promulgated by a royal decree from Sultan Qaboos, transformed the Consultative Council into an elected body, but the right to vote in these elections was not granted to all citizens; only a limited number of citizens selected by tribal leaders were allowed to participate in the first elections. The basic law granted certain civil liberties, banned discrimination on the basis of sex, religion, ethnicity, and social class, and clarified the process for royal succession.

This limited political reform in the 1990s was overshadowed by a stronger effort to reform Oman's oil-dependent economy. In 1995, Sultan Qaboos spearheaded an effort to liberalize Oman's economy, reduce its dependence on oil exports, and attract international investments. In preparation for its eventual accession to the World

Trade Organization (WTO) as a full member in 2000, Oman lifted restrictions on foreign investment and ownership of enterprises in the country. In 2000, Oman launched its sixth five-year plan for the economy, which places emphasis on the "Omanization" of the labor force and job creation in the private sector, and more specific focus on Oman's interior regions, which continue to lag behind the coastal regions. Today, the petroleum sector contributes about 40 percent of Oman's gross domestic product, down from 70 percent in the 1980s.

In October 2003, Oman held the first full election in its history, for its 83-member Consultative Council. Though the powers of the Consultative Council remain limited, the election marked the first time that Oman gave the right to vote to all adult citizens, both men and women. Nearly three-quarters of registered voters participated in the election, which marks another modest step in introducing political reforms.

## Political Rights and Civil Liberties:

Citizens of Oman do not have the right to elect their country's leaders democratically. Citizens can express their views only in a very limited way, by electing members to the Consultative Council, which has no legislative powers and may only recommend changes to new laws. The Consultative Council is half of a bicameral body known as the Council of Oman; the other half, a 57-member State Council, is appointed by the sultan. The sultan has absolute power and issues laws by decree. Mechanisms for citizens to petition the government through local government officials exist, and certain citizens are afforded limited opportunities to petition the sultan in direct meetings. Political parties are banned by law, and no meaningful organized political opposition exists.

Freedom of expression and democratic debate is limited in Oman, with laws prohibiting criticism of the sultan. The government owns and controls all broadcast media outlets, which have the broadest reach to the Omani population. During 2003, the government allowed state television to broadcast sessions in which members of the Consultative Council questioned government ministers. As with other countries in the Arab world, the number of households with access to satellite television has increased, leading to an expansion in the diversity of sources of information. However, this information is mostly focused on regional issues. Oman's government permits private print publications, although many of these publications accept government subsidies and practice self-censorship. Omanis have access to the Internet through the national telecommunications company, and the government censors politically sensitive and pornographic content.

Islam is the state religion, and Sharia (Islamic law) is the source of all legislation, according to the basic law. Non-Muslims have the right to worship, although non-Muslim religious organizations must register with the government. The Ministry of Awqaf (Religious Charitable Bequests) and Religious Affairs distributes standardized texts for mosque sermons and expects imams to stay within the outlines of these texts. The government restricts academic freedom by preventing the publication of politically sensitive topics.

The basic law allows the formation of nongovernmental organizations, but civic and associational life remains quite limited in Oman. All public gatherings require government permission. In March 2003, police used moderate force to disperse public demonstrations against the war in Iraq. Oman has no labor or trade unions. In April 2003, the government issued a decree that removed a previous prohibition on strikes. Complaints related to labor and working conditions are managed by the Ministry of Social Affairs and Labor and mediated by the Labor Welfare Board.

Although the basic law states that the judiciary is independent, it remains subordinate to the sultan and the Ministry of Justice. Sharia courts are responsible for family law matters such as divorce and inheritance. In less populated areas, tribal laws and customs are frequently used to adjudicate disputes. According to the law, arbitrary arrest and detention are prohibited. In practice, the police are not required to obtain an arrest warrant in advance. Many of the civil liberties guarantees expressed in the basic law have not been implemented.

Oman currently has a population of approximately 2.6 million people, less than 2 million of whom are Omani citizens. Most noncitizens are immigrant workers. Foreign workers at times have been placed in situations amounting to forced labor, according to the U.S. State Department's human rights report for 2002, released in March 2003.

Although the basic law prohibits discrimination on the basis of sex, women suffer from legal and social discrimination. Women must have the permission of a male relative to travel abroad. Women remain under-represented in political life in Oman, with only two women having won seats on the 83-member Consultative Council in the 2003 national elections.

# Pakistan

**Population:** 149,100,000
**GNI/capita:** $420
**Life Expectancy:** 60
**Religious Groups:** Muslim (97 percent) [Sunni (77 percent), Shia (20 percent)], Christian, Hindu, and other [including Christian and Hindu] (3 percent)
**Ethnic Groups:** Punjabi, Sindhi, Pashtun, Baloch, Muhajir
**Capital:** Islamabad

**Political Rights:** 6
**Civil Liberties:** 5
**Status:** Not Free

**Ten-Year Ratings Timeline (Political Rights, Civil Liberties, Status)**

| 1994 | 1995 | 1996 | 1997 | 1998 | 1999 | 2000 | 2001 | 2002 | 2003 |
|------|------|------|------|------|------|------|------|------|------|
| 3,5PF | 3,5PF | 4,5PF | 4,5PF | 4,5PF | 7,5NF | 6,5NF | 6,5NF | 6,5NF | 6,5NF |

**Overview:**

Having consolidated his hold on power through a dubious referendum that extended his term as president, as well as a series of constitutional amendments that cemented the future role of the military in governance, General Pervez Musharraf held flawed elections in October 2002, and a new parliament and prime minister were in place by the end of the year. Nevertheless, despite the return to nominal civilian rule, the military continued to wield control over Pakistan's government. The new parliament did not effectively function for much of 2003 because of a protracted standoff between the general and the political opposition over the legality of his amendments, and the judiciary remained subservient to the executive. Facing continued pressure from Islamist groups as well as the secular political opposition, the regime appeared to grow less tolerant of criticism from journalists and human rights activists as the year progressed. The increased influence of Islamist parties in government, coupled with their stated aim of "Islamizing" society, remains a concern and will prevent meaningful progress on human rights issues, particularly legalized discrimination against women and religious minorities.

Pakistan came into existence as a Muslim homeland with the partition of British India in 1947. Following a nine-month civil war, East Pakistan achieved independence in 1971 as the new state of Bangladesh. Deposing civilian governments at will, the army has directly or indirectly ruled Pakistan for 29 of its 56 years of independence. As part of his efforts to consolidate power, the military dictator General Zia ul-Haq amended the constitution in 1985 to allow the president to dismiss elected governments. After Zia's death in 1988, successive presidents cited corruption and abuse of power in sacking elected governments headed by Benazir Bhutto of the Pakistan People's Party (PPP) in 1990 and 1996, and Nawaz Sharif of the Pakistan Muslim League (PML) in 1993.

After the PML and its allies decisively won the 1997 elections, Sharif largely ignored Pakistan's pressing economic and social problems while undermining every institution capable of challenging him. This included repealing the president's constitutional power to dismiss governments, forcing the resignations of the chief justice of the Supreme Court and of an army chief, and cracking down on the press. After Indian troops bested Pakistani forces that had made incursions into Indian-held Kashmir, Sharif was blamed by the army for agreeing to a hasty withdrawal. When he attempted to reshuffle the army's leadership, he was deposed in October 1999 in a bloodless coup. Army chief Musharraf then appointed himself "chief executive," declared a state of emergency, and issued a Provisional Constitution Order suspending parliament, the provincial assemblies, and the constitution. In December 2000, 18 of Pakistan's political parties, including archrivals PML and PPP, joined to form the Alliance for the Restoration of Democracy (ARD), an umbrella group calling for an end to military rule. However, Musharraf was able to successfully neutralize Sharif and Bhutto, his primary political opponents, through a combination of court convictions and exile.

While successfully managing to curtail the activities of the political opposition, Musharraf has been less willing to rein in Islamic fundamentalist groups. Although several groups have been banned since September 2001, when Musharraf pledged to support the United States in its war on terrorism, and hundreds of activists have been periodically arrested, the groups continue to function under new names and their leaders have not been prosecuted. Heightened tensions with neighboring India over the disputed territory of Kashmir during 2002 led to growing international pressure on Musharraf to crack down on the militant groups responsible for incursions into Kashmir and suicide attacks within India. However, the increased political presence in the new parliament of religious parties with ties to radical *madrasas* (religious schools) and militant groups suggests that the influence of the Islamists will continue to be strong. In June 2003, the provincial assembly in the North-West Frontier Province passed a bill that declared Sharia (Islamic law) the supreme law of the province and empowered the government to Islamize the economy, the legal system, and education.

Musharraf's primary aim since gaining power has been to ensure a dominant role for the military after Pakistan made the nominal transition back to democratic rule. Constitutional amendments proposed in mid-2002 gave him in his role as president effective control over parliament and restricted the ability of opposition parties to contest the elections. The regime also openly promoted pro-government political parties, such as the newly formed Pakistan Muslim League Quaid-i-Azam (PML-Q). In elections held in October 2002, no single party won a majority of seats; the PML-Q won 126 seats, while the PPP won 81 and the PML, 19. A coalition of five religious parties, the Muttahida Majlis-i-Amal (MMA), performed unexpectedly strongly, winning 63 seats in the national parliament and a majority of seats in two provinces. After over a month of wrangling among the three largest parties, the PML-Q was able to muster enough support from independents and deserters from the other main parties to form a government, and Musharraf's nominee, Mir Zafrullah Jamali, became prime minister in November. The PML-Q consolidated its position by winning a majority of seats in elections to the Senate held in February 2003.

Parliament remained deadlocked throughout most of 2003, with the main opposition parties insisting that Musharraf rescind his amendments and relinquish his position as army chief if he wished to continue as president. Both the MMA and the ARD opposed Musharraf's power grab and vociferously criticized his policies. However, while Musharraf remained unwilling to confront the religious parties, the secular opposition faced continued pressure from intelligence agencies. In October, Javed Hashmi, the leader of the ARD alliance, was arrested and charged with treason after he publicly criticized the army.

**Political Rights and Civil Liberties:** Despite the election of a civilian National Assembly in October 2002, the Pakistani military, headed by General Pervez Musharraf, continues to wield effective control over the structures of government. The 1973 constitution provided for a lower National Assembly, which is directly elected for a five-year term, and a Senate, whose members are appointed by the four provincial assemblies for six-year terms. The constitution also vested executive power in a prime minister, who must be Muslim, and authorized an electoral college to choose a largely ceremonial president. Shortly after the coup, Musharraf suspended the provincial and national assemblies. In 2001, he declared himself president, and in April 2002 extended his term as president by five years with a rigged referendum. In preparation for national elections (the Supreme Court had mandated that they be held by October 2002), Musharraf further strengthened the powers of the presidency and formalized the military's role in governance. The Legal Framework Order (LFO) gives him the right to unilaterally dismiss the national and provincial parliaments, as well as establishes a National Security Council dominated by military figures that would supervise the work of the civilian cabinet.

The LFO also restricts the right of individuals to stand for elected office, by introducing provisions that disqualify criminal convicts, defaulters on loans and utility bills, and candidates without a bachelor's degree or its equivalent. Other rules restrict political parties in their choice of leadership. Some of these measures were explicitly aimed at preventing former prime ministers Benazir Bhutto and Nawaz Sharif from contesting the 2002 elections. Although the government lifted the long-standing ban on political rallies shortly before the elections, significant restrictions remained in place, and the ability of opposition parties to mount effective campaigns was circumscribed. In its statement on the elections, the independent Human Rights Commission of Pakistan (HRCP) noted that governmental machinery had been used to intimidate opposition candidates. The European Union Election Observation Mission expressed concern about the degree of impartiality of the Election Commission, the ability of political parties and candidates to campaign effectively, the partisan misuse of state resources by public authorities, equality of access to the state media, the accuracy of voter lists, and last-minute alterations in the electoral system. Their report concluded that there had been "serious flaws" in the electoral process.

Pakistan's government operates with limited transparency and accountability. Over the past four years, military officers have assumed an increasing role in governance through "army monitoring teams" that oversee the functioning of many civilian administrative departments. The army now has a stake in continuing to influence both commercial and political decision-making processes, as well as maintaining its traditional dominance over foreign policy and security issues. During 2003, because of the continuing standoff between Musharraf and opposition parties who refused to accept the provisions of the LFO, the parliament effectively did not function and the government continued to rule by decree.

On the positive side, women and minorities now have enhanced representation in the parliament. After repeated complaints by religious minorities, the government abolished the system of separate electorates in January 2002, enabling them to vote alongside Muslims and thus participate more fully in the political system. In addition, 10 seats in the reconstituted National Assembly were reserved for minorities and 60 were reserved for women.

Corruption is pervasive at almost all levels of politics and government; Transparency International's 2003 Corruption Perceptions Index ranked Pakistan in a tie for 92nd place out of a total of 133 countries. Although Musharraf has publicly stated that eliminating official corruption is a priority, the National Anti-Corruption Strategy approved in October 2002 focuses on politicians, civil servants, and businessmen, while virtually ignoring the military and security personnel.

The constitution and other laws authorize the government to curb freedom of speech on subjects including the constitution, the armed forces, the judiciary, and religion. Blasphemy laws have also been used to suppress the media; in July, a sub-editor at the *Frontier Post* was convicted of blasphemy and sentenced to life in prison. Islamic fundamentalists and thugs hired by feudal landlords continue to harass journalists and attack newspaper offices, and unidentified assailants murdered one Sindhi journalist in October. On several occasions, police or security forces also subjected journalists to physical attacks or arbitrary arrest. While journalists practice some self-censorship, Pakistan continues to have some of the most outspoken newspapers in South Asia. However, military authorities used increasingly aggressive tactics in 2003 to silence critical journalists, according to Human Rights Watch, which documented several cases of independent journalists being pressured to resign from prominent publications or being arrested on charges of sedition and tortured while in custody. The Web site of an online newspaper established by editor Shaheen Sehbai, who remains in exile, was blocked by Pakistani telecommunications authorities in May. Although restrictions on the ownership of broadcast media were eased in late 2002, most electronic media are state owned and follow the government line.

Pakistan is an Islamic republic, and there are numerous restrictions on religious freedom. Section 295-C of the penal code mandates the death sentence for defiling the name of the prophet Muhammad. Human rights groups say that instances of Muslims bribing low-ranking police officials to file false blasphemy charges against Ahmadis, Christians, Hindus, and occasionally other Muslims have been increasing sharply in recent years. Ahmadis consider themselves to be Muslims, but the constitution classifies them as a non-Muslim minority and the penal code prohibits Ahmadi religious practice. According to the U.S. State Department, as of October 2003, there were 67 blasphemy cases pending in the courts. To date, appeals courts have overturned all blasphemy convictions, but suspects are generally forced to spend lengthy periods in prison, where they are subject to ill-treatment, and they continue to be targeted by religious extremists after they are released. Religious minorities also face unofficial economic and societal discrimination and are occasionally subjected to violence and harassment. The U.S. Commission on International Religious Freedom designated Pakistan as a country of particular concern for the first time in 2002, citing the failure of the government to protect minorities from sectarian violence as well as discriminatory legislation, which created a climate of "religious intolerance."

The government generally does not restrict academic freedom. However, student groups, some of whom have ties to radical Islamist organizations, violently attack or otherwise intimidate students, teachers, and administrators at some universities, which contributes to a climate of intolerance.

After initially permitting some demonstrations, the military government banned all public political meetings, strikes, and rallies in March 2000. Following the ban, authorities have forcibly dispersed some protests and arrested activists to prevent other demonstrations. Some Islamist leaders have been held under house arrest or in preventative detention under the Maintenance of Public Order ordinance, which allows for three months' detention without trial. Laws governing sedition, public order, and terrorism have been used to raid party offices and detain political activists and leaders in Punjab and Sindh. The military regime generally tolerates the work of nongovernmental organizations (NGOs). However, government officials detained a regional coordinator for the independent HRCP in March. In recent years, Islamic fundamentalists have issued death threats against prominent human rights defenders and against female NGO activists who work in rural areas.

Despite legislation outlawing bonded labor and canceling enslaving debts, illegal bonded labor continues to be widespread. Trade unions are independent. The law restricts the right to strike, and workers in certain essential industries face restrictions on bargaining collectively and generally cannot hold strikes. The enforcement of child labor laws continues to be inadequate.

The judiciary consists of civil and criminal courts and a special Sharia (Islamic law) court for certain offenses. Lower courts remain plagued by corruption; intimidation by local officials, powerful individuals, and Islamic extremists; and heavy backlogs that lead to lengthy pretrial detentions. The military regime undermined the Supreme Court's reputation for independence in January 2000, when it ordered all high-ranking judges to swear to uphold the Provisional Constitutional Order issued by Musharraf. When the chief justice and a number of other judges refused, they were replaced. Since then, the courts have rejected subsequent challenges to the legality of military rule. During 2003, the courts' refusal to overturn the LFO led to a showdown between the judiciary and members of the legal profession, who boycotted court proceedings and released a white paper to the media that criticized the judiciary's lack of independence.

Other parts of the judicial system, such as the antiterrorism courts, operate with limited due process rights. A November 1999 ordinance vested broad powers of arrest, investigation, and prosecution in a new National Accountability Bureau and established special courts to try corruption cases. Musharraf has used both to prosecute rival politicians and officials from previous civilian governments. The Sharia court enforces the 1979 Hudood Ordinances, which criminalize nonmarital rape, extramarital sex, and several alcohol, gambling, and property offenses, and provide for Koranic punishments, including death by stoning for adultery, as well as jail terms and fines. According to Human Rights Watch, an estimated 210,000 cases are currently being processed under the ordinances. In part because of strict evidentiary standards, authorities have never carried out the Koranic punishments. The Federally Administered Tribal Areas (FATA) are under a separate legal system, the Frontier Crimes Regulation, which authorizes tribal leaders to administer justice according to Sharia and tribal custom. Feudal landlords and tribal elders throughout Pakistan continue to adjudicate some disputes and impose punishment in unsanctioned parallel courts called *jirgas*. A 2002 report issued by Amnesty International raised concerns that the jirgas abuse a range of human rights and are particularly discriminatory toward women.

Anecdotal evidence suggested that police continue to routinely engage in crime; use excessive force in ordinary situations; arbitrarily arrest and detain citizens; extort money from prisoners and their families; accept money to register cases on false charges; rape female detainees and prisoners; commit extrajudicial killings; and torture detainees, often to extract confessions. Political opponents, former government officials, and other critics of the regime are particularly at risk of arbitrary arrest or abduction, torture, and denial of basic due process rights at the hands of military authorities, according to Human Rights Watch. Prison conditions continue to be extremely poor. A report issued in November by Amnesty International noted that the Juvenile Justice System Ordinance of 2000 remains largely unimplemented and several thousand children continue to be jailed alongside adults.

Violence among rival factions of the Karachi-based Muttahida Quami Movement (MQM), which represents Urdu-speaking migrants from India, and between the police and the MQM, killed several thousand people in the 1990s, but has abated in recent years, although harassment of their activists continues. Press reports indicate that there may be as many as 200,000 armed militants currently active in Pakistan. Sunni and Shia fundamentalist groups continue to engage in tit-for-tat killings, mainly in Punjab and Karachi. An attack on a Shia mosque in Baluchistan in July 2003 left 54 worshippers dead and dozens wounded, and Shia professionals in Karachi, including a large number of doctors, continue to be targeted. Perhaps in retaliation, Azam Tariq, a member of parliament and leader of Sipah-e-Sahaba Pakistan, a Sunni extremist group, was murdered by unknown assailants in October. The South Asia Terrorism Portal has estimated that just over 100 people were killed in sectarian violence in 2003, a slight decrease from the previous year.

A combination of traditional norms and weak law enforcement continue to contribute to rape, domestic violence, acid attacks, and other forms of abuse against women. Although less frequently than in the past, women are still charged under the Hudood Ordinances with adultery or other sexual misconduct arising from rape cases or alleged extramarital affairs, and 20,000 are currently estimated to be in prison as a result of being wrongfully charged. The threat of being charged with adultery may prevent some women from reporting rape. The government-appointed National Commission on the Status of Women recommended in August that the ordinances be repealed, but because of the influence of Islamist parties in parliament, the suggestion is unlikely to be acted on. According to the HRCP, at least 450 women were killed by family members in so-called honor killings in 2003. Usually committed by a male relative of the victim, honor killings punish women who supposedly bring dishonor to the family. Authorities generally do not aggressively prosecute and convict the perpetrators of violence against women. Pakistani women face unofficial discrimination in educational and employment opportunities.

# Palau

**Population:** 20,000
**GNI/capita:** $7,140
**Life Expectancy:** 69
**Religious Groups:** Roman Catholic (49 percent), other [including Protestant and indigenous beliefs]
**Ethnic Groups:** Paluan (70 percent), Asian (28 percent), white (2 percent)
**Capital:** Koror

**Political Rights:** 1
**Civil Liberties:** 1*
**Status:** Free

**Ratings Change:** Palau's civil liberties rating improved from 2 to 1 due to a technical reevaluation of the degree of the country's freedom of association.

**Ten-Year Ratings Timeline (Political Rights, Civil Liberties, Status)**

| 1994 | 1995 | 1996 | 1997 | 1998 | 1999 | 2000 | 2001 | 2002 | 2003 |
|------|------|------|------|------|------|------|------|------|------|
| 1,2F | 1,2F | 1,2F | 1,2F | 1,2F | 1,2F | 1,2F | 1,2F | 1,2F | 1,1F |

**Overview:**
Palau sought to gain U.S. recognition in 2003 for dual citizenship for Palauans, a large number of whom live and work in the United States.

Palau, consisting of 8 main islands and more than 250 smaller islands that lie about 500 miles southeast of the Philippines, was under U.S. trusteeship administration from the end of World War II until it approved its own constitution and became self-governing in 1981. Full independence was achieved in 1994 under an accord with the United States. This accord, known as the Compact of Free Association, provides Palau with $442 million in aid from Washington over fifteen years with the U.S. shouldering responsibility for Palau's defense. Under this accord, the United States has the right to set up military bases in the island state. The current president, Tommy E. Remengesau, Jr., took office after winning the November 2000 elections.

The country has been plagued by reports of human and drug trafficking, prostitution, and money laundering by criminal groups in recent years. International organizations cited Palau for failing to fully implement anti-money-laundering measures. However, the government cited inadequate resources, rather than a lack of political will, as the reason for failing to meet the target.

In 2003, the government sought to obtain U.S. recognition of dual citizenship for its citizens so that they can maintain voting and land rights in Palau, which is restricted to Palauans, while working and living in the United States. About 25 percent of all Palauans are in the United States, while only about 14,000 reside in Palau. Under the Compact of Free Association, Palauans can live and work in the United States without a visa.

In addition to the question of dual citizenship, two other major issues for the upcoming 2004 general election include whether to change the current bicameral legislature into a unicameral one and whether to elect the president and vice president as a team rather than separately, as is currently the practice. In October, President Remengesau announced that he will push for constitutional amendments to adopt these proposed changes through a public referendum after having waited for two years for parliament to address them.

Former governor Albert Ngirmekur of the state of Ngardmau was sentenced to six months in prison in February on a range of corruption and official misconduct charges.

**Political Rights and Civil Liberties:** Citizens can freely change their government, and elections are held regularly. A bicameral legislature, the Olbiil Era Kelulau, consists of the 9-member Senate and the 16-member House of Delegates. Legislators are elected to four-year terms by populate vote. The president and vice president are also elected to four-year terms by popular vote; the two are elected separately rather than as a team. Both can serve for only two consecutive terms. President Tommy E. Remengesau, Jr., was elected in the November 2000 general elections, and Senator Sandra S. Pierantozzi became the first woman vice president. The country is organized into 16 states, each headed by a governor.

Freedom of speech and the press is respected. The Internet, though not significantly widespread in use, is easily accessible with no government intervention.

Citizens of Palau enjoy freedom of religion, and there were no reports of restrictions on academic freedom.

Freedom of association is respected, and civic organizations and nongovernmental organizations (NGOs) can operate freely. Several NGOs focus on youth, health, and women's issues. Palau has no trade unions, although there are no laws or government policy against their formation.

The judiciary is independent. Palau has no armed forces. Order is maintained by a 140-person police force, and defense is provided by the United States under the Compact of Free Association agreement. The compact, which will end in 2009, also provides Palau with financial and other assistance in exchange for the right to maintain military bases in the island state until 2034.

The economy is heavily dependent on transfer payments from the United States under the compact agreement, as well as money sent back to the island by its citizens working overseas. Subsistence agriculture and fishing are widely practiced. The government and tourist industry are the main employers.

According to a May 2000 census, foreign workers account for nearly 30 percent of the population and 73 percent of the paid workforce. Reports of discrimination and abuse against certain foreign workers have surfaced in recent years, and the government has instituted strict measures to keep out foreign workers who are not on active employment in the island state. In April, the police arrested 200 Chinese garment workers following a 20-hour confrontation. They were left stranded without return airfare when their employer, a Taiwanese business, closed down. In July, the government announced that it would tighten supervision to prevent marriages of convenience between foreigners and Palauans. Foreigners are said to have used bogus marriages to extend their stay in the island state and to enter the United States. There have been reports of human trafficking from China, the Philippines, and Taiwan, with some seeking employment in Palau and others using it as a conduit to enter the United States.

Women are active in both traditional and modern sectors of the economy, including politics. As a matrilineal society, there is a tradition of high regard for women. A handful of reports of domestic violence against women, most of which are linked to alcohol and drug abuse, are registered by the police each year. Although the problem is not severe compared to other Pacific Island states, civil society groups believe there is underreporting.

# Panama

**Population:** 3,000,000
**GNI/capita:** $3,260
**Life Expectancy:** 74
**Religious Groups:** Roman Catholic (85 percent), Protestant (15 percent)
**Ethnic Groups:** Mestizo (70 percent), West Indian (14 percent), European (10 percent), Amerindian (6 percent)
**Capital:** Panama City

**Political Rights:** 1
**Civil Liberties:** 2
**Status:** Free

**Ten-Year Ratings Timeline (Political Rights, Civil Liberties, Status)**

| 1994 | 1995 | 1996 | 1997 | 1998 | 1999 | 2000 | 2001 | 2002 | 2003 |
|------|------|------|------|------|------|------|------|------|------|
| 2,3F | 2,3F | 2,3F | 2,3F | 2,3F | 1,2F | 1,2F | 1,2F | 1,2F | 1,2F |

**Overview:**

Though Panama's presidential elections are scheduled for May 2004, early electioneering dominated the national scene during 2003. President Mireya Moscoso's government has been unable to improve economic growth or seriously reduce dishonesty. The effects of the civil war in neighboring Colombian continued to spill over throughout the year.

Panama was part of Colombia until 1903, when a U.S.-supported revolt resulted in the proclamation of an independent Republic of Panama. A period of weak civilian rule ended with a 1968 military coup that brought General Omar Torrijos to power. After the signing of the 1977 canal treaties with the United States, Torrijos promised democratization. The 1972 constitution had been revised to provide for the direct election of a president and a legislative assembly for five years. After Torrijos's death in 1981, General Manuel Noriega emerged as Panamanian Defense Force (PDF) chief; he subsequently rigged the 1984 election that brought to power the Revolutionary Democratic Party (PRD), then the political arm of the PDF. The Democratic Alliance of Civic Opposition (ADOC) won the 1989 election, but Noriega annulled the vote and declared himself head of state. He was removed during a U.S. military invasion, and ADOC's Guillermo Endara became president.

In May 1999, Mireya Moscoso, the widow of three-time president Arnulfo Arias and herself an unsuccessful presidential candidate in 1994, won 44.8 percent of the vote, more than 7 percent above the amount garnered by her rival, Martin Torrijos, son of Omar Torrijos, as the head of a PRD-led coalition. In the years following the U.S. handover in 1999, the Panama Canal continued to operate smoothly, although the departure of the remaining U.S. troops and the closure of U.S. military bases meant the loss to Panama of some $250 million in revenues.

President Moscoso's government continues to be hampered by its inability to effectively reduce corruption and incompetence in the public sector. There is generalized discontent with the government's efforts to fight corruption and with its running of the state and handling of the economy. High unemployment and underemployment are among the principal concerns among Panamanians.

Early electioneering has begun in anticipation of the general elections in May 2004, and has built upon the popular disappointment with the government's overall performance. The leading candidate is Martin Torrijos, but former president Guillermo Endara is also in the running. Several polls conducted by the Latinobarometro and CID-Gallup gave failing job ratings to the government, leaving no branch unscathed. A celebration of the country's 100 years of independence was marred by partisanship as well as widely broadcast comments over the country's corruption.

Effective governability is in question as armed violence has increased significantly in Panama in the past several years. Weekend police checkpoints are now commonplace both in Panama City and in crime-ridden Colon, although the country remains relatively safe when compared with many of its regional neighbors.

Repeated incursions into Panamanian territory by Colombian guerrillas, self-defense armed irregulars, and drug traffickers continue to spark concerns in the region about the spillover effects of Colombia's civil war. Since being invaded by the United States in 1989, Panama has had no military. It relies on the police to provide both internal security and defense of its borders. Dozens of confrontations between armed Colombian groups and the Panamanian police, who suffered several injuries as a result of the fighting, raised questions about whether the latter are up to the challenge provided by the seasoned Colombians. In October 2003, the Coordinadora Nacional de Pueblos Indigenas de Panama warned that indigenous people in the border with Colombia were victimized by armed groups active in the Darien region.

**Political Rights and Civil Liberties:** Panama's citizens can change their government democratically. The 1999 national elections were considered free and fair by international observers. The constitution guarantees freedom of political organizations. In early 1999, Panama's largest political parties agreed to ban anonymous campaign contributions in an effort to stem the infiltration of drug money into the political process. Nevertheless, the widespread corruption of the governmental apparatus indicates the difficulty in enforcing any such bans. In November, accusations resurfaced that President Mireya Moscoso's campaign had received suspect contributions.

Panama's media include an assortment of radio and television stations, daily newspapers, and weekly publications. There are 5 national dailies, 4 private television stations, 2 educational television broadcasters, and 100 or so radio stations. Restrictive media laws dating back to the regime of General Manuel Noriega remain on the books. The law permits the government to prosecute individual reporters and media owners for criminal libel and calumny. Officials can remand anyone who defames the government to jail without trial. A censorship board can fine radio stations for use of abusive language. There is free access to the Internet.

Freedom of religion is respected, and academic freedom is generally honored.

The judicial system, headed by the Supreme Court, was revamped in 1990. However, it remains overworked and its administration is inefficient, politicized, and prone to corruption. An unwieldy criminal code and a surge in cases, many against former soldiers and officials of the military period, complicate the judicial process.

The Panamanian Defense Force (PDF) was dismantled after 1989, and the military was formally abolished in 1994. However, the civilian-run Panamanian Public Forces (the national police) that replaced the PDF, although accountable to civilian authorities through a publicly disclosed budget, are poorly disciplined and corrupt. There are four components: the Panamanian National Police, the National Maritime Service, the National Air Service, and the Institutional Protection Service. Criminal investigations are the responsibility of a semiautonomous Judicial Technical Police. Like the country's prison guards, officers frequently use "excessive force." The penal system is marked by violent disturbances in decrepit facilities packed with up to eight times their intended capacity. About two-thirds of prisoners face delays of about 18 months in having their cases heard.

Nongovernmental organizations are free to organize. Labor unions are well organized, but only 10 percent of the labor force is unionized. However, labor rights were diluted in 1995 when President Ernesto Perez Balladares pushed labor code revisions through congress. Furthermore, the government has issued decrees that do not allow union organization in export processing zones.

Discrimination against darker-skinned Panamanians, especially those from Colon, is widespread. The country's Asian, Middle Eastern, and Indian population is similarly singled out. Indigenous populations continue to be marginalized and often do not speak Spanish. Their living conditions are significantly lower than those of the general population and they face significant discrimination in employment. Since 1993, indigenous groups have protested the encroachment of illegal settlers on Indian lands and delays by the government in formally demarcating the boundaries of those lands. Indian communities do enjoy, however, a large degree of autonomy and self-government.

Violence against women and children is widespread and common. Panama is both a destination and a transit point for human trafficking.

# Papua New Guinea

**Population:** 5,500,000
**GNI/capita:** $580
**Life Expectancy:** 57
**Religious Groups:** Roman Catholic (22 percent),
Protestant (44 percent), indigenous beliefs (34 percent)
**Ethnic Groups:** Melanesian, Papuan, Negrito, Micronesian,
Polynesian
**Capital:** Port Moresby

**Political Rights:** 3*
**Civil Liberties:** 3
**Status:** Partly Free

**Ratings Change:** Papua New Guinea's political rights rating declined from 2 to 3, and its status from Free to Partly Free, due to growing corruption and rampant violent crime.

**Ten-Year Ratings Timeline (Political Rights, Civil Liberties, Status)**

| 1994 | 1995 | 1996 | 1997 | 1998 | 1999 | 2000 | 2001 | 2002 | 2003 |
|------|------|------|------|------|------|------|------|------|------|
| 2,4PF | 2,4PF | 2,4PF | 2,4PF | 2,3F | 2,3F | 2,3F | 2,3F | 2,3F | 3,3PF |

**Overview:**

The country continued during 2003 to work with international partners to restore peace and stability after a decade of fighting in Bougainville. UN peace monitors completed their mandate by the end of June and were replaced by a multinational force led by Australia to continue to reform the country's police and defense force.

Papua New Guinea (PNG), which consists of the eastern part of New Guinea and some 600 smaller islands, gained independence from Australia in 1975. The country is heavily dependent on natural resource exports, particularly mining. In 1988, miners and landowners on Bougainville Island began guerrilla attacks against the Australian-owned Panguna copper mine, which provided 40 percent of the country's total export revenues. A ceasefire collapsed in 1996, and fighting resumed. A new peace treaty between the government and the Bougainville Revolutionary Army was signed in August 2001. By this time, the civil war had claimed more than 10,000 lives and crippled the economy.

UN peace monitors were sent in to collect weapons from former combatants in Bougainville to help pave way for the election of an autonomous government there in 2004. However, peace remains fragile. Bougainville independence hard-liners announced just one day after the UN peace monitors left the country on July 1, 2003 that they will not participate in the peace process. A small band of fighters still controlled zones around the former Panguna copper mine.

An Australia-led multinational force has downsized the PNG army to 2,000 soldiers, and 200 Australian federal police were brought in to provide training to police throughout the country as part of the reform of the PNG defense force. In August, the government launched formal plans to start framing a constitution to prepare for elections in Bougainville.

In connection to the Bougainville conflict, sedition charges resurfaced against the former defense chief Brigadier Jerry Singirok in May. Singirok led a military revolt against the government's plans to use mercenaries in the Bougainville conflict. Singirok can seek amnesty under special laws that were adopted to end the Bougainville conflict.

A number of leadership changes took place throughout the year. In March, Puka Temu, a senior minister, was ousted from parliament by a court ruling for attempted bribes to voters. In August, four ministers (tourism, the environment, lands, and internal security) were dismissed to placate coalition partners in the government. In September, Sir Albert Kipalan was elected the new Governor-General, a symbolic constitutional post with no executive powers.

Crime is a growing problem in the country's urban areas. Ten people were killed in the Tete Settlement in the capital, Port Moresby, and a woman was raped by as many as 70 men. In early July, a new wave of violence led to calls from a growing number of officials for implementation of the death penalty and reintroduction of the vagrancy act; PNG has not used the death penalty since 1975.

In external affairs, the government decided in May to abandon plans to repatriate hundreds of border crossers from the Indonesian province of Papua. The police were suspected of allowing entry to more than 10,000 illegal migrants.

**Political Rights and Civil Liberties:** Citizens of Papua New Guinea can change their government democratically. Voters elect a unicameral parliament with 109 members from all 19 provinces and the National Capital District. The last general election was held in June 2002, resulting in a coalition government headed by Prime Minister Michael Somare.

There are two weekly papers, one in English and one in Melanesian Pidgin (the national lingua franca). The media provide independent coverage and report on controversial issues such as alleged abuses by police, cases of alleged corruption by government officials, and political opposition views. However, there are concerns that press freedom is threatened. The government has cautioned against publication and broadcast of any "negative" comments about the country. The threat applies to journalists as well as academics who write papers on the economy and against the government.

The government generally respects freedom of religion.

The constitution provides for freedom of association, and the government generally respects this right in practice. However, the government continues to restrict freedom of assembly in the form of marches and demonstrations, which require 14 days' notice and police approval. In 2001, police fired on students during a demonstration in Port Moresby, killing 4 persons and injuring about 20.

The judiciary is independent and the legal system is based on English common law. The Supreme Court is the final court of appeal and has original jurisdiction on constitutional matters. The National Court hears most cases and appeals from the lower district courts established at the provincial level. There are also village courts headed by laypersons, who judge minor offenses under both customary and statutory law. The government increased the number of full-time judges in 2002 and took steps to expand training of the judiciary.

Law enforcement officials have committed arbitrary or unlawful killings, used excessive force when arresting and interrogating suspects, and engaged in excessively punitive and violent raids. Police report that most killings occur during gunfights with criminal suspects resisting arrest. The prison system is seriously underfunded and prison conditions in several areas continue to be poor.

Violence between tribes, which is exacerbated by lack of police enforcement, is a serious problem rooted in a cultural tradition of revenge for perceived wrongs. The number of deaths in the last few years has risen due to the availability of modern weapons.

Discrimination and violence against women are serious problems. Domestic violence is a crime, but is commonly considered a private matter. Few victims press charges and prosecutions are rare. Polygamy and the custom of paying a bride price reinforce the view that women are property. Sexual harassment is not illegal and is a widespread problem. The Office of Women's Affairs in the Office of Church and Family Services of the Ministry of Provincial Affairs has had little effect on the government's policy toward women.

# Paraguay

**Population:** 6,200,000
**GNI/capita:** $1,350
**Life Expectancy:** 71
**Religious Groups:** Roman Catholic (90 percent), other [including Mennonite and Protestant] (5 percent)
**Ethnic Groups:** Mestizo (95 percent), other [including Amerindian and white] (5 percent)
**Capital:** Asuncion

**Political Rights:** 3*
**Civil Liberties:** 3
**Status:** Partly Free

**Ratings Change:** Paraguay's political rights rating improved from 4 to 3 due to improvements in electoral politics and promises of governmental transparency made by the incoming government of President Nicanor Duarte Frutos following elections in April.

**Ten-Year Ratings Timeline (Political Rights, Civil Liberties, Status)**

| 1994 | 1995 | 1996 | 1997 | 1998 | 1999 | 2000 | 2001 | 2002 | 2003 |
|------|------|------|------|------|------|------|------|------|------|
| 4,3PF | 4,3PF | 4,3PF | 4,3PF | 4,3PF | 4,3PF | 4,3PF | 4,3PF | 4,3PF | 3,3PF |

**Overview:**                    Paraguayans chose change and reform in national elections held on April 27, 2003, but within the confines of the long-ruling Colorado Party, as insurgent Colorado leader Nicanor Duarte Frutos won his bid for the presidency. Duarte quickly began to inaugurate the good-government agenda that he had promised during the campaign. Skeptics, however, questioned whether the new anticorruption regime would be selectively applied to Duarte's rivals inside and outside the Colorado Party, or whether the elections would truly usher in a new period in Paraguayan politics.

Paraguay, which achieved independence from Spain in 1811, has been wracked by a series of crises since civilian rule was restored in 1989 and the 35-year reign of right-wing Colorado dictator Alfredo Stroessner was ended. The fragility of the country's democratic institutions has resulted in nearly 15 years of popular uprisings, military mutinies, antigovernment demonstrations, bitter political rivalries, and unbroken rule by the Colorados. Disillusionment with the entire political system was evidenced by the low turnout in the 2001 municipal elections, where participation by young people, who constitute nearly three-fourths of the population, was almost nonexistent.

President Luis Gonzalez Macchi assumed the presidency in 1999 after his predecessor fled the country amid charges that he had orchestrated the murder of his vice president. International concern about individuals and organizations with ties to Middle Eastern extremist groups operating in Ciudad del Este and along the tri-border area, where Paraguay, Brazil, and Argentina meet, followed the September 11, 2001, terrorist attacks on the World Trade Center and the Pentagon in the United States.

In December 2002, Gonzalez Macchi offered to leave office three months early, just a week after lawmakers voted to start impeachment hearings against him. Accused of buying an armor-plated BMW stolen from Brazil, mishandling millions of dollars in state revenues, and embezzling $16 million from two banks in the process of liquidation, Gonzalez Macchi barely survived an impeachment trial in early 2003. Even his supporters did not defend the president, who allegedly doubled his personal wealth during his four years in power, by saying that it was inadvisable to oust him so late in his term. Gonzalez Macchi and much of the Colorado Party were discredited, too, by their unsuccessful efforts to reverse the downward economic spiral in one of Latin America's poorest countries.

Favoring populist, anti-globalization rhetoric during the April 2003 presidential campaign, former education minister and journalist Duarte Frutos emerged victorious after having promised to purge the public sector and the judiciary of corruption and inefficiency, create jobs, and return fiscal stability to the country. Although the Colorado Party lost ground in congress in the concurrent legislative elections, it retained a majority of the 17 state governorships.

Faced with concern from the international financial community about the health of Paraguay's highly dollarized banking system and a tax system in which two-thirds of what should be collected is never paid or is siphoned off owing to corruption, on taking office on August 15, Duarte Frutos moved to take control of the tax, ports, and customs authorities to combat tax evasion and smuggling. However, in October, Duarte's law enforcement minister, the commandant of the national police, and the head of customs were forced to resign following revelations about a smuggling and corruption scandal.

A growing number of sometimes violent land seizures by armies of homeless people in and around the capital city, Asuncion, contributed to a growing debate about the distribution of wealth in the country. One out of every three Paraguayans lives below the poverty line, and emigration to Argentina, the traditional escape of the poor, has become unattractive in the aftermath of that country's own economic crisis. Paraguay's economy remains heavily based on agriculture and various forms of contraband, and the country has one of the most unequal distributions of land in the world.

**Political Rights and Civil Liberties:** Citizens of Paraguay can change their government democratically. The 2003 national elections were considered to be free and fair. The 1992 constitution provides for a president, a vice president, and a bicameral congress consisting of a 45-member Senate and an 80-member Chamber of Deputies elected for five years. The president is elected by a simple majority, and reelection is prohibited. The constitution bans the active military from engaging in politics.

Transparency International (TI) consistently ranks Paraguay as the most corrupt country in Latin America. In TI's 2003 Corruption Perceptions Index, Paraguay was ranked 129 of 133 countries surveyed worldwide.

The constitution provides for freedom of expression and the press, and the government generally respects these rights in practice. There is only one state-owned media outlet, Radio Nacional, which has a limited audience. A number of private television and radio stations exist, as do a number of independent newspapers. However, journalists investigating corruption or covering strikes and protests are often the victims of intimidation or violent attack by security forces. Free expression is also threatened by vague, potentially restrictive laws that mandate "responsible" behavior by journalists and media owners. The government does not restrict use of the Internet, nor does it censor Internet content.

The government generally respects freedom of religion. All religious groups are required to register with the Ministry of Education and Culture, but no controls are imposed on these groups, and many informal churches exist. The government generally does not restrict academic freedom.

Although the constitution guarantees freedom of association and assembly, these right has been undermined by the previous government's tolerance of threats and the use of force, including imprisonment, by its supporters against the opposition. There are numerous trade unions and two major union federations, although they are weak and riddled with corruption. The constitution gives public sector workers the right to organize, bargain collectively, and strike, and nearly all these workers belong to the ruling Colorado Party. A new labor code designed to protect workers' rights was adopted in October 1993.

The judiciary, under the influence of the ruling party and the military, is susceptible to the corruption pervading all public and governmental institutions. Corruption cases languish for years in the courts, and most end without resolution. According to the comptroller-general, corruption has cost the Paraguayan treasury $5 billion since the country returned to democracy in 1989. In April 2003, the prosecutor who had almost single-handedly brought then-president Luis Gonzalez Macchi to justice himself faced removal from office by a judicial panel just hours after the prosecutor claimed that the head of the panel owned a stolen Mercedes-Benz.

There have been continuing reports of illegal detention by police and torture during incarceration, including of minors, particularly in rural areas. Reportedly corrupt police officials remain in key posts and are in a position to give protection to, or compromise law enforcement actions against, narcotics traffickers. Colombian drug traffickers continue to expand operations in Paraguay, and accusations of high official involvement in drug trafficking date back to the 1980s. Overcrowding, unsanitary living conditions, and mistreatment are serious problems in the country's prisons. More than 95 percent of those held are pending trial, many for months or years after arrest. The constitution permits detention without trial until the accused completes the minimum sentence for the alleged crime.

The lack of security in border areas, particularly in the tri-border region, has allowed large organized-crime groups to engage in piracy and in the smuggling of weapons, narcotics, and contraband. In the aftermath of the September 11, 2001 attacks, attention focused on the serious lack of governmental control over Paraguay's lengthy and undeveloped land borders, extensive river network, and numerous airstrips (both registered and unregistered). The Islamic extremist organization Hezbollah and other militant organizations are active in the so-called Iguazu triangle region, which extends from the cities of Ciudad del Este in Paraguay, Foz do Iguacu in Brazil, and Puerto Iguazu in Argentina. A joint intelligence center run by Argentina, Brazil, and Paraguay monitors the region, and all three countries use their air forces for surveillance and interdiction efforts.

The constitution provides indigenous people with the right to participate in the economic, social, political, and cultural life of the country. However, in practice, the indigenous population is unassimilated and neglected. Low wages, long work hours, infrequent payment or nonpayment of wages, job insecurity, lack of access to social security benefits, and racial discrimination are common.

Peasant and Indian organizations that demand and illegally occupy land often meet with police crackdowns, death threats, detentions, and forced evictions by vigilante groups in the employ of landowners. According to the Ministry for Social Action, 66 percent of the country's land is held by 10 percent of the population, while nearly one-third of Paraguayans have no land of their own. The top 10 percent own 40 percent of the wealth.

Sexual and domestic abuse of women, which is both widespread and vastly under-reported, continues to be a serious problem in Paraguay. Spousal abuse is common.

# Peru

**Population:** 27,100,000
**GNI/capita:** $1.980
**Life Expectancy:** 69
**Religious Groups:** Roman Catholic (90 percent), other (10 percent)
**Ethnic Groups:** Amerindian (45 percent), mestizo (37 percent), white (15 percent), other (3 percent)
**Capital:** Lima

**Political Rights:** 2
**Civil Liberties:** 3
**Status:** Free

**Ten-Year Ratings Timeline (Political Rights, Civil Liberties, Status)**

| 1994 | 1995 | 1996 | 1997 | 1998 | 1999 | 2000 | 2001 | 2002 | 2003 |
|------|------|------|------|------|------|------|------|------|------|
| 5,4PF | 5,4PF | 4,3PF | 5,4PF | 5,4PF | 5,4PF | 3,3PF | 1,3F | 2,3F | 2,3F |

**Overview:**
The government of President Alejandro Toledo appeared to take a nosedive in popularity by late 2003, as Peruvians took to the streets in increasing numbers to express their frustration with his questionable ethics and failure to make good on campaign promises of more jobs. The popular disenchantment grew despite the country's posting an annual inflation rate of just 1.5 percent—the lowest in decades—and holding its position as Latin America's economic growth leader for the second year in a row. In August, Peru's Truth and Reconciliation Commission presented its report on the scope and origins of the political violence that had wracked the country from 1980 to 2000. While it said that the Maoist Shining Path guerrilla group was the "principal perpetrator of the human rights violations," which included 69,000 people killed—

double the previously accepted figure—the commission also accused the military and security forces of serious and repeated atrocities.

Since independence in 1821, Peru has seen alternating periods of civilian and military rule, with elected civilians holding office since a 12-year dictatorship ended in 1980. However, that same year, the Maoist Shining Path guerrilla group launched its two-decades-long insurgency. Alberto Fujimori, a university rector and engineer, defeated the novelist Mario Vargas Llosa in the 1990 election.

In 1992, Fujimori, backed by the military, suspended the constitution and dissolved congress. The move was popular because of people's disdain for the corrupt, elitist political establishment and fear of the rampaging Shining Path. In November, Fujimori held a state-controlled election for an 80-member constituent assembly to replace the congress. The assembly created a constitution that established a unicameral congress more closely under presidential control. The constitution was approved in a state-controlled referendum following the capture of the Shining Path leader, Abimael Guzman.

Congress passed a law in August 1996 allowing Fujimori to run for a third term, despite a constitutional provision limiting the president to two terms. The law evaded this restriction by defining Fujimori's current term as his first under the 1993 constitution.

In the April 9, 2000, presidential election, Fujimori defeated Toledo, a U.S.-educated economist who had been raised in an Indian shantytown, by 49.9 percent to 40.2 percent. Fujimori, however, came in 20,000 votes short of an outright win, and a runoff election was slated for May 28. Toledo refused to participate in the second round, emphasizing that in addition to being victimized by election-day voting irregularities, he had been repeatedly assaulted by Fujimori supporters in the earlier campaign, had suffered constant death threats and phone taps, was virtually blacked out from media coverage, and was the target of smear campaigns in the press.

In early September, a videotape was released showing Vladimiro Montesinos, the de facto head of the national intelligence service, bribing an opposition congressman at the same time that the spy chief was also being linked to the illegal shipment of arms to Colombian guerrillas. The ensuing scandal raised suspicions that Fujimori had secured a parliamentary majority—after having failed to win one outright in the April 9 general elections—by bribing opposition congressmen to change sides. In late November, Fujimori was removed from office; opposition forces assumed control of congress; and a highly respected opposition leader, Valentin Paniagua, was chosen as interim president.

Following Fujimori's overthrow, the new opposition-controlled congress began a process of renewing the constitutional tribunal, which had been gutted because some of its members had opposed the third-term law, and reforming the constitution. At the end of 2000, Fujimori announced he was availing himself of his dual citizenship to remain in Japan. In July 2001, Paniagua announced the appointment of a Truth and Reconciliation Commission to investigate two decades of rebel and state-sponsored violence.

Running on the slogan "Toledo Trabajo" (Toledo Means Jobs), Toledo bested former president Alan Garcia in runoff elections held on June 3, 2001. During the campaign, Toledo was accused of having used cocaine in a 1998 orgy with five prostitutes and of repeatedly lying about his past; Toledo claimed he was forced to take the drug after having been kidnapped. In August, Toledo sacked Peru's top military chiefs and promised to thoroughly restructure the armed forces.

The 2002 reform of Peru's highly centralized political structure gave new regional governments almost a quarter of the national budget and a range of powers that had long been the province of the central government. However, Toledo's standing suffered from a host of personal incidents, ranging from his having allegedly procured a sweetheart job for his wife at Peru's second-largest bank, to his denial, later reversed, of having fathered a child out of wedlock in the 1980s—a situation that led opponents to accuse him of manipulating the judiciary to his advantage. In June, antigovernment riots protesting the sell-off of state-owned companies left two people dead and nearly $100 million in damages. The Shining Path also made a small comeback, killing 10 people in a car bomb attack outside the U.S. Embassy in March and making a limited effort to disrupt the November 2002 regional elections.

Toledo's government suffered a serious setback at the polls in those elections, as voters selected the main opposition party and a group of independents for 25 new regional governments, whose establishment was meant to end Lima's top-down monopoly on political control. The vote against Toledo's 16-month-old government was a boost for former president Garcia, positioning him as the early favorite for the 2006 presidential election. Toledo's Peru Possible Party, which won only 1 of the 25 contests, was hampered by voter disillusionment over perceived disarray and cronyism in the government, as well as by cynicism about government efforts to spur the economy by selling off state enterprises.

The failure of Peru's macroeconomic gains to translate into economic relief, particularly for the half of the population still mired in poverty, led to a wave of protests in May 2003, including roadblocks that paralyzed the country's highways. As a result, Toledo was forced to declare a 30-day state of emergency and to send the military to restore order in half of the country's 24 departments.

Fallout from Toledo's reputation for high living increased considerably in November, when Peru's first vice president, businessman Raul Diez Canseco, was accused of providing his young girlfriend with official favors and jobs, and was forced to make a public apology and to resign his post as foreign commerce minister.

The Truth and Reconciliation Commission presented its nine-volume report in August on the country's political violence that occurred in the 1980s and 1990s. The report, which accused both the Shining Party and the military of atrocities, shocked many observers by more than doubling the estimated number of deaths during the protracted insurgency. These findings reflected the fact that nearly three-fourths of the victims of both the guerrillas and the military were Indian peasants living in rural areas, and that these rural poor have long suffered neglect at the hand of the central government. Serious questions remained about some of the commission's other findings—including its failure to credit certain once-controversial anti-insurgency strategies with actually reducing rights violations—which was reflected to some extent by concern over the commission's mostly one-sided composition.

**Political Rights and Civil Liberties:** Peruvians can change their government through free and fair elections, and the November 2002 elections were held largely without incident. In preparation for the 2001 vote, congress reformed the constitution, replacing a single nationwide district for congressional elections with a system of multiple districts based on the departments (provinces) into which the country is divided for administrative purposes. The move provided fair representation for the almost 50 percent of the population who live outside the four largest cities and guaranteed them some attention from the state and from political parties, which traditionally have ignored them.

In September, President Alejandro Toledo fired the head of the national intelligence service, a retired admiral, after it was discovered the spy agency had tapped the president's phone line and leaked the tape to a scandal-driven television program. The government has cut the service's budget and personnel, but has yet to conduct the deep-rooted reforms necessary in an agency still suffering from the serious professional deformations promoted by Vladimiro Montesinos, its de facto head under President Alberto Fujimori. In August, Switzerland repatriated to Peru $77.5 million from bank accounts controlled by Montesinos, who is suspected of having obtained the cash from bribes linked to arms and aircraft sales.

The press is largely privately owned and is now considered to be free, but Peru's judicial branch appears unable to provide the guarantees necessary for full press freedom, in part because of high levels of corruption. Radio and television are both privately and publicly owned. The government did not limit access to the Internet.

The constitution provides for freedom of religion, and the government generally respects this right in practice. However, the Catholic Church receives preferential treatment from the state. By law, the military can hire only Catholic clergy as chaplains, and Catholicism is the only recognized religion of military personnel. Academic freedom is not restricted by the government.

The constitution provides for the right of peaceful assembly, and the authorities generally respect this rights in practice. The human rights community has reported that the Toledo administration continues to work toward strengthening relations between the government and civil society. The government permits numerous nongovernmental organizations dedicated to monitoring and advancing human rights to operate freely. In contrast to previous years, these groups reported no harassment or other attempts by the authorities to hinder their operations in 2003.

During his period in office, Fujimori conducted a purge of the judiciary that removed 70 percent of the judges. He replaced them with new appointees having "provisional" status, meaning they lacked job tenure and thus were potentially unduly responsive to the government in cases where it had an interest. Since Alejandro Toledo assumed office in July 2001, the Ministry of Justice has worked to put into place a broad anticorruption effort. However, popular perceptions of the justice system—that it is an inefficient, overloaded bureaucracy riddled by political influence and greed—are hard to change. Scant resources have resulted in most of Peru's more than 3,000 judges being overworked and underpaid.

Peru's financial woes are the most notable factor contributing to spiraling national crime. The National Statistics Institute estimates that rapid increases in poverty have now placed fully half of the population in need. Public safety, particularly in Lima, is threatened by vicious warfare by opposing gangs and violent crime; police estimate that there are more than 1,000 criminal gangs in the capital alone. Conditions remain deplorable in prisons for common criminals. Torture and ill-treatment on the part of the military and security forces remain a concern.

Racism against Peru's large Indian population has been prevalent among the middle and upper classes, although the Fujimori government made some effort to combat it. The election of Toledo, who boasted of his indigenous heritage, is considered a watershed. However, the provisions of the 1993 constitution, and subsequent legislation regarding the treatment of native lands, are less explicit about the lands' inalienability and protection from being sold off than were earlier constitutional and statutory laws.

Spousal abuse is perhaps the greatest problem facing women in Peru today, although recently the government has taken some steps to address the issue. Forced labor, including child labor, exists in the gold-mining region of the Amazon.

# Philippines

**Population:** 81,600,000  **Political Rights:** 2
**GNI/capita:** $1,030  **Civil Liberties:** 3
**Life Expectancy:** 70  **Status:** Free
**Religious Groups:** Roman Catholic (83 percent),
Protestant (9 percent), Muslim (5 percent),
other [including Buddhist] (3 percent)
**Ethnic Groups:** Christian Malay (91.5 percent), Muslim Malay
(4 percent), Chinese (1.5 percent), other (3 percent)
**Capital:** Manila

**Ten-Year Ratings Timeline (Political Rights, Civil Liberties, Status)**

| 1994 | 1995 | 1996 | 1997 | 1998 | 1999 | 2000 | 2001 | 2002 | 2003 |
|------|------|------|------|------|------|------|------|------|------|
| 3,4PF | 2,4PF | 2,3F | 2,3F | 2,3F | 2,3F | 2,3F | 2,3F | 2,3F | 2,3F |

**Overview:**  President Gloria Macapagal-Arroyo was the favorite to win the May 2004 presidential elections after she announced in October 2003 that she would stand for reelection, reversing an earlier decision not to run. Arroyo is credited with boosting tax revenues and stabilizing the budget deficit but has been less successful in tackling the Philippines' rampant crime and chronic corruption, whose burdens fall heaviest on poorer Filipinos. Her administration also has struggled to reign in armed Islamic groups making their bases in the southern jungles.

The Philippines won independence in 1946 after being ruled for 43 years by the United States and occupied by the Japanese during World War II. Once one of Southeast Asia's wealthiest nations, the Philippines has been plagued since the 1960s by insurgencies, economic mismanagement, and widespread corruption.

The country's economic and political development was further set back by Ferdinand Marcos's 14-year dictatorship. Marcos was finally chased out of office in 1986 by massive "People Power" street protests and the defections of key military leaders and units. He was succeeded by Corazon Aquino, who had been cheated out of victory in an election rigged by the strongman's cronies.

Though she came to symbolize the Philippines's emergence from authoritarian rule, Aquino managed few deep political or economic reforms while facing seven coup attempts. Her more forceful successor, former army chief Fidel Ramos, ended chronic power shortages, privatized many state firms, and trimmed bureaucratic red tape.

With the popular Ramos constitutionally barred from running for reelection, Vice President Joseph Estrada won the 1998 presidential election behind pledges to help poor Filipinos. Almost from the outset, the Estrada administration was dogged by allegations that it was corrupt and that it gave favorable treatment to the business interests of well-connected tycoons. The House of Representatives impeached him on these and other grounds in November 2000, but Estrada's supporters blocked prosecutors from introducing key evidence during his trial in the Senate. The resulting massive street protests and public withdrawal of support by military leaders forced Estrada to resign in January 2001.

As vice president, Arroyo became president under the constitutional line of succession. In the first major test of her administration's popularity, Arroyo's coalition won 8 of 13 contested Senate seats and a majority in the House in the May 2001 legislative elections. Nevertheless, Arroyo has been dogged by questions about the legitimacy of her unelected administration, while her establishment image—she is the daughter of a former president of the Philippines—makes her an easy political target for populist backers of former president Estrada.

Far from the political bickering in Manila, the southern Philippines continues to be wracked by Islamic militancy. Arroyo acknowledged publicly in October 2003 that Jemaah Islamiah, the Islamic terrorist group blamed for the 2002 Bali bombing, trains militants on southern Mindanao Island. Meanwhile, the administration has been unable to secure a durable ceasefire with the country's main Islamic rebel group, the separatist Moro Islamic Liberation Front (MILF) on Mindanao. Separately, Arroyo temporarily brought in U.S. soldiers in 2002 to train and equip Filipino forces chasing guerrillas belonging to the Abu Sayyaf, a Muslim kidnapping and extortion outfit in the far southern Sulu Archipelago.

Meanwhile, Arroyo's government has made little progress in reviving stalled talks with Communist rebels, known as the New People's Army (NPA), who have been waging a low-grade rural insurgency since 1969. The NPA's extortion of local businesses and attacks on military and civilian targets in the countryside have helped cripple rural development.

In an incident that added to Arroyo's challenges, some 300 soldiers led a 21-hour mutiny in July, protesting what they described as rampant corruption in the armed forces. Officials alleged that the mutiny was a remnant of an aborted coup plot and accused several leading opposition figures, some with links to Estrada, of backing the mutineers.

Arroyo's main challengers in the May 2004 presidential elections are likely to be movie actor Fernando Poe, Jr., and opposition Senator Panfilo Lacson. The senator has been accused of ordering summary executions when he was national police chief, a charge Lacson denies.

**Political Rights and Civil Liberties:** Filipinos can change their government through elections. However, many foreign and domestic observers said that the street protests and military pressure that forced President Joseph Estrada to resign in 2001 amounted to a "soft coup." Elections continue to be violent, though less so than in the past. Some 100 Filipinos were killed in violence linked to the 2001 national elections, and the military said that 86 people were killed in violence related to local elections in 2002.

The Philippines has a presidential system of government, with the directly elected president limited to a single six-year term. Because she is serving out the remainder of Estrada's term, however, President Gloria Macapagal-Arroyo is eligible to run in the 2004 presidential election. Congress consists of a Senate with 24 directly elected members and a House of Representatives with 201 directly elected members and up to 50 others appointed by the president. Despite recent economic reforms, a few dozen powerful families continue to play an overarching role in politics and hold an outsized share of land and corporate wealth.

Corruption, cronyism, and influence peddling are widely believed to be rife in business and government. The Berlin-based Transparency International ranked the Philippines in an eight-way tie for 92nd place out of 133 countries in its 2003 Corruption Perceptions Index.

The private press is vibrant and outspoken, although newspaper reports often consist more of innuendo and sensationalism than investigative reporting. Seventeen Filipino journalists have been killed since 1998, including six in 2003 as of mid-November, according to the Center for Media Freedom and Responsibility in Manila. Like their print counterparts, most television and radio stations are privately owned and outspoken but lack strict journalistic ethics. The government does not restrict Internet use.

Filipinos of all faiths can worship freely in this mainly Christian society. However, Muslims who live on Mindanao, known as Moros, say that they face economic and social discrimination in mainstream society at the hands of the country's Roman Catholic majority. Muslim-majority provinces lag behind Christian-majority ones on Mindanao on most development indicators, a 1998 Asian Development Bank survey found. University professors and other teachers, meanwhile, can lecture and publish freely.

Citizens can hold protests, rallies, and other demonstrations without government interference. The Philippines has many active environmental, human rights, social welfare, and other nongovernmental groups. Trade unions are independent, though Filipino workers face strict labor laws. The International Labor Organization (ILO) in 2003 renewed its criticism of labor law provisions requiring a union to represent at least 20 percent of workers in a bargaining unit before it can be registered, and imposing stiff sanctions against workers who participate in illegal strikes. Officials have not recently penalized striking workers. The global labor body also said that the labor law provides inadequate protections for female and foreign workers in certain areas. Aside from these tough laws, private employers often violate minimum-wage standards and dismiss, or threaten to dismiss, union members, according to union leaders. Around 5 percent of Filipino workers are unionized.

Despite many gains since the Ferdinand Marcos era, the rule of law continues to be weak. The judiciary is generally independent but at times dysfunctional. "Judges and prosecutors remained poorly paid, overburdened, susceptible to corruption and the influence of the powerful, and often failed to provide due process and equal justice," according to the U.S. State Department's human rights report for 2002, released in March 2003. The result is "impunity for some wealthy and influential offenders," the report added. Because of backlogs, suspects often spend long periods in jail awaiting trial.

Prison conditions are harsh, with inmates kept in overcrowded jails where they receive inadequate food, have limited access to sanitary facilities, and are often at the whim of corrupt officials. Police and prison guards at times rape and sexually abuse female detainees or inmates with impunity, the human rights group Amnesty International said in 2001.

The Philippines's poorly disciplined national police force is regularly described by the official Commission on Human Rights as the country's worst rights abuser. Most notably, police continue to be accused of illegal killings of criminal suspects, although officials frequently allege that any killings of suspects occur during shootouts. Moreover, police and other security forces continue to torture suspects, Amnesty International said in a January report. To combat torture and other abuses, the government has expanded human rights training for the police and military and dismissed, and in some cases prosecuted, dozens of police officers accused of rights violations.

The long-running conflict between the government and the MILF, the separatist Islamic rebel group, has caused severe hardship for many of the 15 million Filipinos on southern Mindanao and nearby islands. Amnesty International in April accused Filipino forces of summary killings, disappearances, torture, and illegal arrests during counterinsurgency operations on Mindanao. MILF guerrillas are widely accused of killings and other abuses and have attacked many Christian villages. Separately, the smaller Abu Sayyaf group has kidnapped and tortured many civilians and beheaded some of its captives. Islamic militants are suspected in a string of bombings on Mindanao in recent years, including two bombings in Davao City in March and April that killed at least 38 people.

In the countryside, the 10,000-strong NPA and smaller Communist groups continue to summarily execute soldiers, police, political figures, and ordinary civilians, according to the U.S. State Department report. The army and pro-government militias operating in Mindoro Oriental and other provinces are responsible for summary killings, disappearances, torture, and illegal arrests while fighting Communist rebels, Amnesty International said in April.

Further signs abound of a society plagued by a weak rule of law. Businesses and powerful landowning families in rural areas often maintain private security teams that operate with near impunity. Meanwhile, vigilante "death squads" reportedly have killed dozens of suspected criminals since 1995 in several Mindanao cities. In late 2003, President Arroyo was facing calls to use the death penalty against convicted kidnappers following a wave of more than 100 kidnappings during the year.

Members of the Philippines's indigenous minority have limited access to some basic government services and at times are pushed off their ancestral lands by mining and other commercial projects, the U.S. State Department report said. The government is slowly implementing legislation passed in 1997 aimed at increasing the amount of ancestral land held by indigenous communities.

Filipino women have made many social and economic gains in recent years, and more women than men now enter high schools and universities. In the job market, though, women face some discrimination in the private sector and have a higher unemployment rate than men, according to the U.S. State Department report. Both the government and civil society groups have programs to protect women from violence and abuse. Still, rape, domestic violence, sexual harassment on the job, and trafficking of Filipino women and girls abroad and at home, for forced labor and pros-

titution, continued to be major problems. An estimated 500,000 women work as prostitutes in the Philippines, according to a 1998 ILO study.

The Philippines also has up to 200,000 street children and at least 3.7 million
working children, according to studies by the government and international agencies. The NPA, MILF, and Abu Sayyaf have been accused of using child soldiers.

# Poland

**Population:** 38,600,000
**GNI/capita:** $4,230
**Life Expectancy:** 74
**Religious Groups:** Roman Catholic (95 percent), other
[including Eastern Orthodox and Protestant] (5 percent)
**Ethnic Groups:** Polish (98 percent), German (1 percent),
other [including Ukrainian and Byelorussian] (1 percent)
**Capital:** Warsaw

**Political Rights:** 1
**Civil Liberties:** 2
**Status:** Free

**Ten-Year Ratings Timeline (Political Rights, Civil Liberties, Status)**

| 1994 | 1995 | 1996 | 1997 | 1998 | 1999 | 2000 | 2001 | 2002 | 2003 |
|------|------|------|------|------|------|------|------|------|------|
| 2,2F | 1,2F | 1,2F | 1,2F | 1,2F | 1,2F | 1,2F | 1,2F | 1,2F | 1,2F |

**Overview:**
Poland, which joined NATO in 1999, moved closer in 2003
to achieving the second of its key strategic objectives,
membership in the European Union (EU). In a referendum
held in June, the country voted overwhelmingly in favor of joining the EU, with 77
percent in support of membership.

From the fourteenth to the eighteenth centuries, Poland and Lithuania maintained a powerful state that Prussia, Austria, and Russia destroyed in three successive partitions. Poland enjoyed a window of independence from 1918 to 1939, but
was forced into the Communist sphere at the end of World War II. Polish citizens
endured decades of Soviet rule until 1989, the year Lech Walesa and the Solidarity
trade union movement forced the government to accept democratic reforms.

Fundamental democratic and free-market oriented reforms were introduced dur-
ing the 1989-1991 period. Later changes were stimulated by a need to adjust the
Polish legal system to EU requirements. Political parties with a background in the
Solidarity Movement stayed in power from 1989 to 1993 (several coalitions) and from
1997 to 2001 (Solidarity Election Action or AWS). In 1995, former Communist
Alexander Kwasniewski replaced the previous president, Solidarity leader Lech
Walesa. Kwasniewski began his reelection campaign in 2000 with a strong lead in
the polls. He defeated 11 opponents in the first round of voting with 53.9 percent of
the vote.

In September 2001, voters handed the government of Prime Minister Jerzy Buzek
a decisive defeat in parliamentary elections. Democratic Left Alliance (SLD) leader
Leszek Miller became the new prime minister. In the election to the Sejm (lower house
of parliament), a coalition of the center-left SLD and the Labor Union (UP) took 41.04
percent of the vote and 216 seats, but failed to win an outright majority. The two

parties formed a government with the leftist Polish Peasants' Party (PSL), which had won 42 seats. Civic Platform (PO), a new centrist party, finished second in the election with 12.68 percent of the vote and 65 seats. The following parties divided the remaining seats: the Leftist-popular agrarian Self Defense Party (Samoobrona), 53 seats; the center-right Law and Justice (PiS), 44; the right-wing League of Polish Families (LPR), 38; and the German minority, 2. The AWS and the Freedom Union (UW) failed to secure a single seat. In the Senate election, the SLD-UP won 75 seats; the bloc Senate 2001, 15; the PSL, 4; the LPR, 2; and Samoobrona, 2. Voter turnout was 46 percent.

In a June 2003 referendum, Polish voters overwhelmingly approved joining the EU, with 77 percent voting in support of membership. Turnout for the national referendum was 59 percent of eligible citizens, surpassing the 50 percent needed to make the vote binding. In November, the European Commission in its annual progress report on future members and candidates identified nine areas of "serious concern" with respect to Poland's preparation for joining the EU. The commission urged that Poland accelerate the harmonization of its laws and regulations with those of the EU in areas ranging from anticorruption efforts to food safety.

Over the past several years, Poland has sought to carve out a twenty-first century leadership role for itself in Europe. Such aspirations have manifested themselves both in the political and security spheres. Polish leadership has been in evidence, for example, in its efforts to shape the EU's future constitution and in maintaining engagement with the poorly performing lands on Poland's—and the future EU's—eastern frontier.

Poland's advocacy on behalf of Europe's developing an interventionist approach to the Iraq crisis and its prominent role in the stabilization of that country following the ouster of Saddam Hussein's regime are among the boldest, and most contentious, Polish initiatives. In charge of one of the four postwar stabilization zones in Iraq, Polish officers command 9,000 troops from some 20 countries. In total, the Polish armed forces placed 2,300 troops on the ground in Iraq. Poland's role in Iraq has generated consternation in a number of capitals in Western Europe that had opposed any military action in Iraq from the outset. Along with other countries that have made NATO and EU membership strategic objectives and that are eager to have solid relations both with the United States and the EU, Poland has confronted the pressures of dealing with the competing and often divergent interests within the transatlantic community.

**Political Rights and Civil Liberties:** Polish citizens can change their government democratically. Voters elect the president and members of parliament. The president's appointment of the prime minister is subject to confirmation by the Sejm (the lower house of parliament). Elections to the European Parliament are scheduled for June 2004. The next parliamentary and presidential elections are scheduled for September and October 2005, respectively.

Over the course of 2003, the SLD-led government continued to confront allegations of party figures' links to organized crime and corruption. The "Rywin affair," which involves allegations that film producer Lew Rywin sought a bribe from a major newspaper publisher in return for using his political connections to influence the shape of the draft media law, remains a festering issue on the country's political scene.

The 1997 constitution guarantees freedom of expression and forbids censorship. However, the country's libel law treats slander as a criminal offense. Journalists, in particular, oppose the growing number of related lawsuits. In 2002, several actions by the Leszek Miller government raised concerns about its respect for media independence. Infringements on media freedoms include gag orders and arbitrary judicial decisions concerning investigations of individuals affiliated with parties in power.

The state respects freedom of religion and does not require religious groups to register. Registered religious groups enjoy a reduced tax burden. In 2003, the Roman Catholic Church for the first time met with serious accusations of sexual impropriety by clerics. The Church responded with investigations and dismissals, including that of a bishop.

Polish citizens can petition the government, assemble freely, organize professional and other associations, and engage in collective bargaining. Public demonstrations require permits from local authorities. Since the 1980s, when shipyard workers in Gdansk launched a national strike and formed the Solidarity labor union, Poland has had a robust labor movement. Although Solidarity's political strength has waned in recent years, labor groups remain active and influential.

Poland has an independent judiciary, but courts are notorious for delays in administering cases. In 1989, the country began a reform process that has sought to increase the efficiency, and professionalism of the judiciary. In its 2002 accession report, the European Commission acknowledged "steady progress" and "improved efficiency" in this process, but noted that Poland should continue efforts to increase public access to justice, address public perceptions of corruption within the judiciary, and improve the treatment of detainees by the police. State prosecutors have dragged their feet on investigations into graft and corruption, contributing to concerns that they are subject to considerable political pressure.

The constitution outlines a range of personal rights and freedoms, including the right to privacy, the inviolability of the home, freedom of movement, and choice of residence.

Ethnic minorities generally enjoy generous protections and rights provided under Polish law, including funding for bilingual education and publications and privileged representation in parliament. In 2003, there were efforts to close several Lithuanian-language schools because of shortages of funding. However, the decision was reversed, and the schools remain open.

Domestic violence against women is a problem in Poland. Women have made inroads in the professional sphere and are employed in a wide variety of professions and occupations. A number of women hold high positions in government and in the private sector.

# Portugal

**Population:** 10,400,000   **Political Rights:** 1
**GNI/capita:** $10,900   **Civil Liberties:** 1
**Life Expectancy:** 77   **Status:** Free
**Religious Groups:** Roman Catholic (94 percent), other
[including Protestant] (6 percent)
**Ethnic Groups:** Portuguese, African minority
**Capital:** Lisbon

**Ten-Year Ratings Timeline (Political Rights, Civil Liberties, Status)**

| 1994 | 1995 | 1996 | 1997 | 1998 | 1999 | 2000 | 2001 | 2002 | 2003 |
|------|------|------|------|------|------|------|------|------|------|
| 1,1F | 1,1F | 1,1F | 1,1F | 1,1F | 1,1F | 1,1F | 1,1F | 1,1F | 1,1F |

**Overview:**   The government was strongly criticized for its handling of massive forest fires that swept across the country during the summer of 2003. Allegations of organized child abuse in state-run orphanages created a national crisis as a number of well-known politicians and television stars were indicted. Following his Spanish counterpart, Prime Minister Jose Manuel Durao Barroso supported the U.S.-led war in Iraq.

Portugal was proclaimed a republic in 1910, after King Manuel II abdicated during a bloodless revolution. Antonio de Oliveira Salazar became prime minister in 1932 and ruled the country as a fascist dictatorship until 1968, when his lieutenant, Marcello Caetano, replaced him. During the "Marcello Spring," repression and censorship were relaxed somewhat and a liberal wing developed inside the one-party National Assembly. In 1974, a bloodless coup by the Armed Forces Movement, which opposed the ongoing colonial wars in Mozambique and Angola, overthrew Caetano. A transition to democracy began with the election of a constitutional assembly that adopted a democratic constitution in 1976. A civilian government was formally established in 1982 after a revision of the constitution brought the military under civilian rule, curbed the president's powers, and abolished the unelected Revolutionary Council. Portugal became a member of the European Economic Community (later the European Union) in 1986, and in early 2002, the euro replaced the escudo. In 1999, Portugal handed over its last overseas territory, Macau, to the Chinese, ending a long history of colonial rule.

During the last parliamentary elections in March 2002, more than five parties won seats. The center-right Social Democratic Party (PSD) took a narrow lead with 40 percent of the vote, followed by the Socialist Party (PS) with 38 percent, the small Popular Party with around 9 percent, and the Communists with 7 percent. The PSD formed a governing alliance with the right-of-center Popular Party, effectively ending six year of PS government. Only about 63 percent of those registered voted.

In the summer of 2003, the government was blamed for acting ineffectively to stem the largest forest fires in modern Portuguese history. The fires destroyed about 10 percent of the country's forests, killing 18 people and causing over one billion dollars in damage. In reaction to the criticism, the prime minister called for a radical restructuring of the forest management procedures. The country also received money from the European Union solidarity fund to help pay for reconstruction after the fires.

A pedophilia scandal in the long-established Casa Pia orphanages rocked the country in early 2003. The scandal hurt, in particular, the opposition PS, whose deputy leader was in prison on charges of pedophilia for four months before being released. The allegations go back 30 years and are considered the greatest upheaval in Portuguese society since the revolution of 1974.

Prime Minister Barroso gave unequivocal support for the U.S.-led invasion in Iraq, even hosting the Azores summit that effectively marked the declaration of hostilities. In the fall, Portugal sent a contingent of the National Republican Guard to Iraq. The 128 police officers, though, were rerouted from their original destination, Nasiriya, after a suicide bomb at an Italian paramilitary base there killed over two dozen people.

**Political Rights and Civil Liberties:** The Portuguese can change their government democratically. Turnout at the polls, however, has dropped in recent years. The 230 members of the unicameral legislature, the Assembly of the Republic, are elected every four years by popular vote using a system of proportional representation. The president is popularly elected for a five-year term, renewable once. The president receives advice from the Council of State, which includes six senior civilian officers, former presidents elected under the 1976 constitution, five members chosen by the assembly, and five members selected by the president. While the president holds no executive powers, he can delay legislation with a veto and dissolve the assembly to call early elections. The constitution was amended in 1997 to allow immigrants to vote in presidential elections. The Portuguese have the right to organize in different political parties and other political groupings of their choice, except for fascist organizations. The autonomous regions of Azores and Madeira are relatively independent, with their own political and administrative regimes, and their own legislative and executive powers.

There is relatively little corruption. Transparency International ranked Portugal 25 out of 133 countries in its 2003 Corruption Perceptions Index.

Freedom of the press is guaranteed by the constitution, and laws against insulting the government or the armed forces are rarely enforced. Commercial television has been making gains in recent years, providing serious competition for the public broadcasting channels that lack funds. Internet access was not restricted.

Although the country is overwhelmingly Roman Catholic, the constitution guarantees freedom of religion and forbids religious discrimination. The Religious Freedom Act that was adopted in 2001 provides religions that have been established in the country for at least 30 years (or recognized internationally for at least 60 years) with a number of benefits formerly reserved for the Catholic Church, such as tax exemptions, legal recognition of marriage and other rites, and respect for traditional holidays. Academic freedom is respected.

There is freedom of assembly, and citizens can participate in demonstrations and open public discussion. Workers have the right to organize, bargain collectively, and strike for any reason, including political ones. A public sector strike in November 2002 and a general strike a month later crippled the country. Both strikes were to protest a proposed labor law that would make it easier to hire and fire workers.

The constitution provides for an independent court system. However, in late 1999, the government began to take some exceptional measures to deal with a backlog of nearly one million cases pending in the judicial system. A number of prominent politicians signed a manifesto in July demanding an investigation into the judicial system during the controversy over the current pedophilia scandal. The manifesto drew attention to the leaking of information during the prosecution process of the scandal and also questioned the length of time that suspects can be held for interrogation.

The constitution guarantees equal treatment under the law and nondiscrimination. However, Amnesty International issued a report in 2003 that expresses concern about a number of human rights abuses in the country, including unlawful police shootings, deaths in police custody, and poor prison conditions that amount to cruel, inhuman, and degrading treatment. Other issues include allegations of racist abuse by police and the slow pace of the administration of justice. However, according to the European Commission against Racism and Intolerance, Portugal has taken a number of steps to combat racism, including passing laws against discrimination and launching initiatives that seek to promote the integration of immigrants and Roma (Gypsies) into Portuguese society.

Portugal is a destination and transit point for trafficked persons, particularly women from Eastern Europe and former Portuguese colonies in South America and Africa. In 2000, a law was introduced that makes domestic violence a public crime and obliges the police to follow through on reports of battering. There are also penalties for sexual harassment in the workplace. Despite these gains, women make only 77 percent of men's earnings. During the election in 2002, about 19 percent of the 230 seats in the legislature were held by women.

# ↑ Qatar

**Population:** 600,000 **Political Rights:** 6
**GNI/capita:** $20,701 **Civil Liberties:** 6
**Life Expectancy:** 72 **Status:** Not Free
**Religious Groups:** Muslim (95 percent), other (5 percent)
**Ethnic Groups:** Arab (40 percent), Pakistani (18 percent),
Indian (18 percent), Iranian (10 percent), other (14 percent)
**Capital:** Doha
**Trend Arrow:** Qatar received an upward trend arrow due to progress on political reforms, including the approval of a new constitution and the first election of a woman to public office.

## Ten-Year Ratings Timeline (Political Rights, Civil Liberties, Status)

| 1994 | 1995 | 1996 | 1997 | 1998 | 1999 | 2000 | 2001 | 2002 | 2003 |
|------|------|------|------|------|------|------|------|------|------|
| 7,6NF | 7,6NF | 7,6NF | 7,6NF | 7,6NF | 6,6NF | 6,6NF | 6,6NF | 6,6NF | 6,6NF |

**Overview:** Despite concerns about regional stability resulting from the war in Iraq, Qatar took limited steps forward to introduce political reform by organizing municipal elections on April 7, 2003 and holding a national referendum on a new draft constitution on April 29. The municipal elections resulted in the first election of a woman to public office, and nearly 97 percent of the voters in the referendum approved the new constitution.

For the first half of the nineteenth century, the al-Khalifa family of Bahrain dominated the territory now known as Qatar. The Ottoman Empire occupied Qatar from 1872 until World War I, when the United Kingdom recognized Sheikh Abdullah bin Jassim al-Thani as the ruler of Qatar and Sheikh Abdullah signed a series of treaties of friendship and commerce with the United Kingdom. Following World War II, Qatar rapidly developed its oil production industry, and the oil wealth contributed to economic and social development in the country.

Qatar became formally independent in 1971. From 1971 to 1995, Emir Khalifa bin Hamad al-Thani ruled as an absolute monarch, with few government institutions checking his authority. In 1995, the emir was deposed by his son Hamad, who began a program to introduce gradual political, social, and economic reforms. Hamad dissolved the Information Ministry shortly after taking power, an action designed to demonstrate his commitment to expand press freedom.

In 1996, Hamad permitted the creation of Al-Jazeera, which has become one of the most popular Arabic language satellite television channels. Al-Jazeera, however, generally does not cover Qatari politics and focuses instead on regional issues such as the situation in Iraq and the Arab-Israeli conflict. In the past few years, Sheikh Hamad accelerated a program to build Qatar's educational institutions, attracting foreign universities to establish branches in Qatar; Cornell Medical School opened a branch in Doha in 2002. In 1999, Qatar held elections for a 29-member municipal council and became the first state of the Gulf Cooperation Council (GCC) to introduce universal suffrage.

In 2002, a 38-member committee appointed by Hamad presented a draft constitution, which was refined and presented to the public in a referendum in April 2003. This new constitution, which was approved by almost 97 percent of voters, slightly broadens the scope of political participation without eliminating the monopoly on power enjoyed by the al-Thani family. This limited progress on political reform took place despite regional tensions over the war in Iraq; Qatar was the location of the forward headquarters for the United States Central Command.

**Political Rights and Civil Liberties:** Qataris do not have the power to change the top leadership in their government democratically. They possess only limited power to elect representatives who serve in local government positions, which have circumscribed powers and report to the minister of municipal affairs and agriculture, who is appointed by the emir. The head of state is the emir, and the al-Thani family controls a monopoly on political power in Qatar. The emir appoints a prime minister and the cabinet. The constitution states that the emir appoints an heir after consulting with the royal family and other notables. The new constitution, ratified by public referendum in 2003, provides for elections to 30 of the 45 seats in a new advisory council, and the government announced tentative plans to hold these elections in 2004. The government does not permit the existence of political parties.

The new constitution guarantees freedom of expression, and the state has generally refrained from direct censorship. However, content in the print and broadcast media is influenced by leading families. The five leading daily newspapers are privately owned, but their owners and board members include royal family members and other notables. Although the satellite television channel Al-Jazeera is privately owned, the Qatari government has reportedly paid operating costs for the channel since its inception. Qataris have access to the Internet through a telecommunications monopoly, which has recently been privatized, but the government censors content and blocks access to certain sites deemed pornographic or politically sensitive.

Islam is Qatar's official religion, and the new constitution explicitly provides for freedom of worship. The Ministry of Islamic Affairs regulates clerical affairs and the construction of mosques. Converting to another religion from Islam is considered apostasy and is a capital offense, but there have been no reports of executions for apostasy since 1971. Qatar's government has also begun outreach efforts to build better relations between Islam and other religions by sponsoring a dialogue on Muslim-Christian understanding and establishing diplomatic relations with the Vatican. The new constitution provides for freedom of opinion and research, but scholars often practice self-censorship on politically sensitive topics.

The constitution provides for freedom of assembly and the right to form organizations, but these rights are limited in practice. Public protests and demonstrations are rare, with the government placing strict limits on the public's ability to organize demonstrations. All nongovernmental organizations require state permission to operate, and the government closely monitors the activities of these groups. There are no independent human rights organizations, but a National Committee for Human Rights, consisting of members of civil society and government ministries, has done some work on investigating allegations of human rights abuses.

The law prohibits labor unions, but allows joint consultative committees of employers and workers to deal with disputes. Foreign national workers, who make up most of the workforce in Qatar, face severe disadvantages in labor contract cases. Several strikes took place in 2003, including one in May by 350 employees at an engineering firm over five months of unpaid wages and a sit-in by several hundred workers in a construction company to protest a salary payment dispute.

Although the constitution guarantees that the judiciary is independent, this is not true in practice. The majority of Qatar's judges are foreign nationals who are appointed and removed by the emir. Qatar's judicial system consists of two sets of courts: Sharia (Islamic law) courts, which have jurisdiction over a narrow range of issues, such as family law; and civil courts, which have jurisdiction over commercial and civil suits. These two sets of courts have been united under the Supreme Judiciary Council. The constitution protects individuals from arbitrary arrest and detention and bans torture, and defendants are entitled to legal representation. There are no reports of widespread violations of human rights in Qatar. Prisons meet international standards, and the police generally follow proper procedures set in accordance with the law.

Women have the right to participate in elections and run for elective office. In the April 2003 municipal elections, Sheikha Yousef Hassan al-Jufairi became the first woman elected to public office. However, legally and socially, women face discrimination. For example, women must have permission from a male guardian to obtain a driver's license or travel abroad.

# Romania

**Population:** 21,600,000    **Political Rights:** 2
**GNI/capita:** $1,720    **Civil Liberties:** 2
**Life Expectancy:** 71    **Status:** Free
**Religious Groups:** Eastern Orthodox [including all
subdenominations] (87 percent), Protestant
(6.8 percent), Catholic (5.6 percent), other (1 percent)
**Ethnic Groups:** Romanian (90 percent), Hungarian (7 percent),
Roma (2 percent), other (1 percent)
**Capital:** Bucharest

**Ten-Year Ratings Timeline (Political Rights, Civil Liberties, Status)**

| 1994 | 1995 | 1996 | 1997 | 1998 | 1999 | 2000 | 2001 | 2002 | 2003 |
|------|------|------|------|------|------|------|------|------|------|
| 4,3PF | 4,3PF | 2,3F | 2,2F | 2,2F | 2,2F | 2,2F | 2,2F | 2,2F | 2,2F |

**Overview:**

Romania made some progress in implementing macroeconomic structural reforms during the course of 2003, as well as adopting better ethnic minority legislation. However, widespread corruption throughout the political system and reported intimidation of the media prevented faster progress on reforms.

Throughout the latter half of the Cold War, Romania was ruled by Nicolae Ceaucescu, one of Eastern Europe's most repressive dictators. In late 1989, popular dissatisfaction with Ceaucescu's rule led to his overthrow and execution by disgruntled Communists. A provisional government was formed under Ion Iliescu, a high-ranking Communist and the leader of the National Salvation Front (NSF). The 1992 parliamentary elections saw the NSF split into neo-Communist and reformist factions. In November 1996, Emil Constantinescu of the Democratic Convention of Romania (CDR) defeated Iliescu in presidential elections. The CDR was prone to considerable instability and lack of unity, however, as was evident in the dismissals of Prime Minister Victor Ciorbea in 1998 and Prime Minister Radu Vasile in 1999.

In the November 2000 parliamentary elections, the former Communist Party, rechristened the Party of Social Democracy (PDSR), won 65 of the 140 seats in the Senate (the upper house of parliament) and 155 of the 327 seats in the Chamber of Deputies (the lower house). A surprising development in these elections, however, was the extent of support for the nationalist Greater Romania Party (PRM) led by Vadim Tudor, which gained 37 seats (or 21 percent of the vote) in the upper house and 84 seats (20 percent) in the lower house; Tudor himself came in second in the 2000 presidential elections. The remaining seats in parliament were won by the National Liberal Party (PNL), with 13 in the upper and 30 in the lower house; the Democratic Party (PD), 13 and 31, respectively; and the Democratic Alliance of Hungarians in Romania (UDMR), 12 and 27, respectively. Since 2000, Adrian Nastase of the PDSR has served as prime minister.

Romania's 2000 presidential elections, held over two rounds in November and December, provided further evidence of the strength of Tudor's right-wing party. In the first round of the elections, Tudor gained 28.5 percent of the vote, coming in second to the PDSR's Iliescu, who gained 36.5 percent in the first round. In the runoff elections in December, most left-wing and center parties shifted their support to Iliescu, allowing him to win the second round with approximately 67 percent of the vote.

Romania received mixed reviews on its progress on implementing political and economic reforms in 2003. While an IMF report on the government's economic program praised progress in structural reforms and the adoption of sound macroeconomic policies—as well as predicting economic growth in the 5 percent range for the next five years—a European Union (EU) report issued in November claimed that Romania could not yet be considered a "functioning market economy" and noted extremely high levels of corruption, even by regional standards; in 2003, Transparency International found Romania to have the worst degree of corruption of any of the 28 EU member or candidate countries. A World Bank study issued in 2003, meanwhile, ranked Romania last among EU candidate countries in terms of the responsiveness and efficiency of its administration, the quality of government regulations, the rule of law, and political stability. Doubt is beginning to grow that Romania will be able to meet all the requirements for its scheduled 2007 accession to the EU. A possible political hurdle to Romania's EU accession that year could be the ultimate electoral strength of Tudor's PRM in the 2004 presidential elections.

Despite these problems, Romania is making some progress in implementing reforms required by the EU. Constitutional changes required by the EU were adopted by referendum in October; turnout for the referendum was 55.7 percent, of which (in an important indicator of the population's support for EU membership) 89.7 percent of those voting endorsed the constitutional changes.

**Political Rights and Civil Liberties:** Romanians can change their government democratically. Elections since 1991 have been considered generally free and fair by international observers. According to international monitoring groups, the legal framework for elections and laws related to the formation of political parties and the conduct of presidential and parliamentary elections, as well as governmental ordinances, provide an adequate basis for democratic elections. In the second round of presidential elections in 2000, voter turnout was 57.5 percent.

Corruption remains a serious problem in Romania. In October, three government ministers were forced to resign after revelations emerged that they had engaged in or failed to stop corruption in their respective ministries. Property rights are secure, although the ability of citizens to start businesses continues to be encumbered by red tape, corruption, and organized crime.

The 1991 constitution enshrines freedom of expression and the press, and the media are characterized by considerable pluralism and a general absence of direct state interference. There are, however, limits to free expression resulting from provisions prohibiting "defamation of the country and the nation." Libel against government officials can still be punished with imprisonment. Some 80 percent of the population gets most of its news and information from the four largest television stations in the country, and media watchdog groups claim that their coverage is generally biased in favor of the government. One domestic nongovernmental organization (NGO) reported 10 major incidents of government harassment of journalists during the year. There were no reports of government attempts to restrict access to the Internet during 2003.

Religious freedom is generally respected, although "nontraditional" religious organizations, including Jehovah's Witnesses, sometimes encounter difficulties in registering with the state secretary of religions. Lack of registration denies adherents the right to exercise freely their religious beliefs and prevents them from building places of worship and cemeteries. The government formally recognizes 17 religions in the country, each of which is eligible for some level of state support for such activities as the building of houses of worship and salaries for the clergy. In May, Jehovah's Witnesses were granted such recognition, the first addition to the list since 1989. In June 2002, parliament passed a law restituting church property held by the state since the Communist period. No government restrictions on academic freedom were reported during the year.

The constitution provides for freedom of assembly, and the government respects this right in practice. In general, the government does not place restrictions on the work of NGO's, which usually find government officials to be cooperative. Workers have the right to form unions and to strike.

Executive institutions exercise undue control over the judicial system. The Public Prosecutor is considered by many international observers to have excessive powers, and much of the judiciary is still packed with Ceaucescu-era holdovers. In 2002, the European Commission called for "comprehensive reform" of the Romanian judiciary. As part of the reform process, constitutional changes adopted in October 2003 formally make the judiciary independent of the government. Prisons are considered to be overcrowded and conditions "harsh," although some improvement in prison conditions was noted during the year.

The 1991 constitution provides for additional seats to be allotted to national minorities if they are unable to pass the 5 percent threshold needed to enter parliament. In the 2000 elections, 18 seats were awarded to national minorities on this basis. The adoption of the Local Public Administration Act in January 2001 grants minorities the right to use their native tongue in communicating with authorities in areas where they represent at least 20 percent of the population. The act also requires signs to be written in minority languages and local government decisions to be announced in those languages. Constitutional changes adopted by referendum in October 2003 allow ethnic minorities the right to use their native languages in court.

There are no restrictions on travel within the country, and there are no legal barriers for citizens who want to change their place of residence.

The constitution guarantees women equal rights with men, but gender discrimination remains widespread. Women are considerably under-represented in government: only 10.4 percent of deputies and 5.7 percent of senators currently in parliament are women. Trafficking in women and girls for purposes of forced prostitution has become a major problem. Romania is considered a country of origin, a transit country, and a minor destination country for trafficked women and girls. Parliament passed a law in November 2001 outlawing trafficking in human beings, and the country is involved in an extensive public education effort to warn people about the dangers of trafficking.

# ↓ Russia

**Population:** 145,500,000   **Political Rights:** 5
**GNI/capita:** $1,750   **Civil Liberties:** 5
**Life Expectancy:** 65   **Status:** Partly Free
**Religious Groups:** Russian Orthodox, Muslim, other
**Ethnic Groups:** Russian (82 percent), Tatar (4 percent),
Ukrainian (3 percent), other (11 percent)
**Capital:** Moscow
**Trend Arrow:** Russia received a downward trend arrow due to increased state pressures
on the media, opposition political parties, and independent business leaders.

### Ten-Year Ratings Timeline (Political Rights, Civil Liberties, Status)

| 1994 | 1995 | 1996 | 1997 | 1998 | 1999 | 2000 | 2001 | 2002 | 2003 |
|------|------|------|------|------|------|------|------|------|------|
| 3,4PF | 3,4PF | 3,4PF | 3,4PF | 4,4PF | 4,5PF | 5,5PF | 5,5PF | 5,5PF | 5,5PF |

**Overview:**   For Russia, 2003 was marked by further movement toward authoritarianism by President Vladimir Putin and the government, signaling the consolidation of power and influence by a ruling elite dominated by former military and security service officers, who now occupy 25 percent of key government and legislative positions. In mid-year, the country's last remaining independent television network was taken over by the government and replaced by an all-sports channel. Restrictive new legislation was passed that for three months threatened free media comment on politics and policies, until it was reversed by the country's constitutional court. In October, with end-of-year parliamentary elections and March 2004 presidential elections nearing, Russian authorities launched a far-reaching prosecution of an economic magnate who supported liberal opposition parties, precipitating a steep decline in Russia's stock exchanges. At the same time, the headquarters of a political consulting firm working for a major opposition party was raided by police.

With the collapse of the Soviet Union in December 1991, the Russian Federation reemerged as a separate, independent state under the leadership of Boris Yeltsin, who had been elected president in June of that year. In 1993, Yeltsin put down an attempted coup by hard-liners in parliament, and a new constitution creating a bicameral national legislature, the Federal Assembly, was approved. The December 1995 parliamentary elections, in which 43 parties competed, saw the victory of Communists and nationalist forces. In the 1996 presidential elections, Yeltsin, supported by the country's most influential media and business elites, easily defeated Communist Gennady Zyuganov. The August 1998 collapse of the ruble and Russia's financial markets ushered in a new government that returned to greater state spending and economic control. One year later, Federal Security Service head Vladimir Putin was named prime minister. Yeltsin, whose term was to expire in 2000 and who could not run for a third term, declared Putin his preferred successor in the next presidential elections.

Conflict with separatist Chechnya, which included a brutal two-year war, from 1994 to 1996, was reignited in 1999. After a Chechen rebel attack on neighboring Dagestan in August and deadly apartment house bombings in several cities blamed by the Kremlin on Chechen militants, Russia responded with an attack on the breakaway region. The second Chechen war dramatically increased Putin's popularity and, after December 1999 elections to the lower house of parliament (Duma), pro-government forces were able to shape a majority coalition.

A frail President Yeltsin resigned on December 31, 1999, turning over power to Putin, who, in March 2000, secured a 53 percent first-round victory over Zyuganov, who received 29 percent. After taking office in March 2000, Putin consolidated his power. He pushed through legislation removing Russia's 89 governors from positions in the upper house of parliament (the Federation Council) and allowing the president to suspend them from office if they violated federal law. Putin created seven new "super regions" headed by Kremlin appointees and introduced personnel changes that have considerably altered the composition of the ruling Russian elite through the influx of representatives of the security and military services; they now represent more than 25 percent of the country's ministers, deputy ministers, legislators, governors, and "super governors." He also challenged the political clout of some economic magnates—including media owners Vladimir Gusinsky and Boris Berezovsky—through a series of criminal investigations and legal proceedings claimed to be part of an anticorruption campaign, but which critics suggested were selective political persecutions.

In October 2002, Chechen militants took approximately 750 people hostage in a raid on a Moscow theater. Russian special forces stormed the building, killing all the Chechen fighters (approximately 50). The raid employed a powerful sedative gas that resulted in the deaths of more than 120 hostages.

Throughout most of 2003—and with the December 2003 parliamentary elections and a March 2004 presidential race looming—Russia saw a significant deterioration of fundamental rights and the emergence of an increasingly assertive foreign policy, reflecting the consolidation of power by former security and military officers.

In June, there was further consolidation of state control over broadcast media with the closure of TVS, the country's last independent television station. The station was taken over by the government for what it said was financial insolvency, although authorities rejected a new investor ready to assume the network's debt. Reporting on politics had been threatened by onerous new constraints after Putin signed legislation passed in July that made media susceptible to closure for criticizing positions of candidates for office. In October, Russia's constitutional court struck down key provisions of the law that banned journalists from making positive or negative observations about candidates or parties. Still, the law's operation had a chilling effect on media coverage of politics for several months. Russia's Federation Council Chairman Sergei Mironov had noted that "as a result of this law, the mass media has been forced to be silent about the election campaign."

In September, Russian authorities took control of VTsIOM, the All Union Institute on Public Opinion, the country's most respected polling firm. VTsIOM staff suggested that Russian authorities acted after the research firm had published a series of polls showing dwindling support for the ongoing war in Chechnya and majority support for a negotiated solution. The VTsIOM management and staff subsequently established a new privately held concern.

Emblematic of worsening domestic trends was the October 25 arrest of Mikhail Khodorkovsky, chairman of the Yukos energy concern and Russia's richest and most influential economic magnate. Speculation concerning Khodorkovsky's arrest and pending prosecution of other Yukos officials centered on politics rather than alleged corruption. Khodorkovsky had actively supported pro-market opposition liberal parties. Indeed, many of the charges against him stemmed from the early period of Russia's economic transition from communism, when a maze of contradictory laws meant that many people engaged in business were not fully compliant with Russian law.

Russia pursued efforts at greater integration among neighboring former Soviet republics with the creation in September of a Unified Economic Space that would eventually link Russia, Ukraine, Kazakhstan, and Belarus. However, plans for the new economic area were set back by the Russia-Ukraine border dispute that erupted in the fall and signaled significant hardening in the policies of the Russian state. In late September, Russia unilaterally and unexpectedly began construction of a dam that eventually encroached on Ukraine's territory. The action raised tensions and was accompanied by assertions from high-ranking Russian government officials that the island of Tuzla—heretofore recognized by Russia as part of Ukraine—was disputed territory. The head of the Russian parliament's foreign affairs committee claimed that both Tuzla and Ukraine's port city of Sevastopol were Russian.

Political assassinations remained a feature of Russian life. In April, unknown assailants shot dead Sergei Yushenkov, a respected member of the Duma and head of the Liberal Russia Party.

Strife in Chechnya continued with Russian counterinsurgency operations, and guerrilla warfare, assassinations, and acts of terrorism by Chechen rebels. Russia moved forward with a new constitution for the disputed territory. An October 5, 2003 election boycotted by Chechen rebels and their supporters saw the victory of Akhmad Kadyrov, the Kremlin's hand-picked candidate, who captured 81 percent of the vote from a claimed turnout of 88 percent. International observers questioned the accuracy and legitimacy of the flawed ballot.

**Political Rights and Civil Liberties:** There are growing questions whether Russians can change their government democratically, particularly in light of the state's far-reaching control of broadcast media and growing harassment of opposition parties and their financial backers. The 1999 Duma election was regarded as generally free and fair despite some irregularities, including biased media coverage. In the run-up to the December 2003 legislative election, opposition political parties widely criticized distorted and unbalanced coverage of their campaigns. The 2000 presidential vote was marred by irregularities. A comprehensive six-month investigation by the *Moscow Times* concluded that incumbent president Vladimir Putin would have faced a second-round runoff if not for widespread fraud; but it also concluded that Putin would most likely have won in the second round. Among the reasons cited for his victory were biased coverage by large media outlets controlled by the state and by Kremlin supporters. The 1993 constitution established a strong presidency with the power to appoint, pending parliamentary confirmation, and dismiss the prime minister. The bicameral legislature consists of a lower chamber (the Duma) and an upper chamber (the Federation Council).

Corruption throughout the government and business world is pervasive. Russia ranked 86 out of 133 countries in Transparency International's 2003 Corruption

Perceptions Index. Tough legislation to combat money laundering entered into force in 2002, leading the Financial Action Task Force of the Organization for Economic Cooperation and Development to remove Russia from its list of noncooperating countries. However, at the end of 2003, the arrest of Yukos Chairman Mikhail Khodorkovsky and several of his associates, coming on the heels of the persecution and prosecution of media owners Vladimir Gusinksy and Boris Berezovsky, confirmed perceptions by many independent Russian analysts that Putin's anticorruption efforts have been applied selectively and have often targeted critics and emerging political adversaries.

Although the constitution provides for freedom of speech, the government continues to put pressure on media outlets critical of the Kremlin. In June, Russia's last independent national television network—TVS—was seized by the government, allegedly to settle the company's debts. The action followed similar takeovers that had resulted in government control of two other independent television networks—NTV, in April 2001, and TV-6, in January 2002. The government routinely intimidates media for unsanctioned reporting on issues related to terrorism. In 2002, authorities temporarily closed a television station for allegedly promoting terrorism, threatened to shut down the independent Ekho Moskvy radio station for airing a phone interview with a hostage taker, and allowed NTV television to broadcast only edited statements made by the Chechen rebel leader inside a theater where hostages were being held.

In July, the government introduced a restrictive new law banning "illegal campaigning" by journalists. The legislation prohibited the publishing or broadcasting of information on candidates that could create a "positive or negative image of the candidate." Its far-reaching character meant that it could be used to suppress unfettered media discussion of policies and platforms of government officials and candidates during an election period. On October 30, the Constitutional Court ruled the legislation unconstitutional, but for over three months the law had sent a chill over open media coverage on politicians and politics.

Throughout Russia's regions, journalists continue to be subjected to physical attack and sometimes murder. On October 9, Alexei Sidorov, editor of the Togliatti newspaper *Tolyatinskoye Obozreniye*, which was known for publishing reports on organized crime and local government corruption, was knifed to death outside his apartment building. His predecessor as editor, Valery Ivanov, had been murdered outside his home in April 2002. In the breakaway republic of Chechnya, the military continued to impose severe restrictions on journalists' access to the war zone, issuing accreditation primarily to those of proven loyalty to the government.

On January 23, amid generally distressing trends in media rights, a civilian court in Ussuriysk ordered the early release of Grigory Pasko, a journalist who had been found guilty on charges of espionage and had served 33 months of a four-year sentence. Press freedom organizations regarded the conviction as a politically motivated effort intended to punish Pasko for reporting on the environmental dangers posed by the Russian navy's nuclear-waste-dumping practices.

With print broadcast media increasingly under government control, the Internet, where there is wider access to independent information, is used regularly by 4.2 percent of the population. This cohort of regular users is growing by 20-40 percent per year, according to a Russian Federation government report.

Freedom of religion is respected unevenly in this predominantly Orthodox Christian country. A 1997 law on religion requires churches to prove that they have existed for at least 15 years before being permitted to register. As registration is necessary for a religious group to conduct many of its activities, new, independent congregations consequently are restricted in their functions. Regional authorities harass nontraditional groups, with the Jehovah's Witnesses and Mormons among the frequent targets. Foreign religious workers are denied visas to return to Russia. In recent years, several Roman Catholic priests have been deported, barred from entry, or refused visa renewals. Following a July suicide attack by Chechen women terrorists that claimed 15 victims attending a Moscow rock-and-roll concert, rights groups reported widespread harassment and unwarranted police identity checks in major urban centers of women wearing Islamic headscarves.

Academic freedom is generally respected, although the academic system is marred by some corruption at the higher levels and by very low levels of pay for educators. A wave of prosecutions against scientists exposing alleged environmental crimes has created a chill in some research institutes, resulting in new worries about academic freedom.

The government generally respects freedom of assembly and association. However, a July 2001 law significantly limits the number of political parties in Russia by requiring that parties have at least 10,000 members to be registered, with at least 100 members in each of the country's 89 regions. In 2002, parliament adopted legislation that gives the authorities the right to suspend parties or nongovernmental organizations whose members are accused of extremism. Critics argue that the law offers an excessively broad definition of extremism, giving the government great latitude to suppress legitimate opposition political activities. The nongovernmental sector is composed of thousands of diverse groups, with many of them dependent on funding from foreign sources. There is increasing evidence that Russia's new rich are beginning to support the nongovernmental sector through charitable giving.

While trade union rights are legally protected, they are limited in practice. Although strikes and other forms of worker protest occur, some unions have criticized a labor code that entered into force in 2002 for placing further limits on the right to strike. Hundreds of thousands of public sector workers held a nationwide, one-day, work stoppage and protest on March 26 in 70 of the country's 89 regions. Anti-union discrimination and reprisals for strikes are not uncommon, however, and employers often ignore collective bargaining rights. In a rapidly changing economy in transition from the former system of total state domination, unions have proved unable to establish a significant presence in much of the private sector.

The judiciary is subject to corruption and suffers from inadequate funding and a lack of qualified personnel. Following the judicial reforms of 2002, the government has made progress in greater due process and timely trials. Since January 2003, Russia's reformed criminal procedure code has provided for jury trials throughout the country, but the legislature has voted to postpone introducing jury trials in certain parts of the country by up to four years because of financial and technical difficulties. The new code also gives the right to issue arrest and search warrants to the courts, not prosecutors, and abolishes in absentia trials.

On October 23, Russian authorities raided the offices of a consultant advising the election campaign of the Yabloko political party, one of several liberal groupings supported by oil magnate and Kremlin critic Mikhail Khodorkovsky. The October 25 arrest of Khodorkovsky signaled the increasing politicization of the legal system. The arrest had been preceded by the jailing on July 2 of Khodorkovsky's associate, Platon Lebedev, head of the Menatep Financial Group. Khodorkovsky's arrest was followed by the Russian government's freezing of 44 percent of Yukos's assets he and his associates controlled. The government action precipitated a steep, one week decline of 15 percent in the Russian RTS market and raised fears about further state encroachments on the private sector.

After the arrest, the president's chief of staff resigned and there were other signs of a fierce policy struggle in which hard-liners from the security services and military had prevailed. "The law enforcement bodies have seized power," declared Russia's *Novaya Gazeta* newspaper. The arrests and investigations in 2003 of Mikhail Khodorkovsky, the Yukos energy company, and the Menatep Group reinforced perceptions that the rule of law is subordinated to political considerations and the judiciary is not independent of the president and his inner circle.

Critics maintain that Russia has failed to address ongoing problems such as the widespread use of torture and ill-treatment by law enforcement officials to extract confessions, and that the courts will be unable or unwilling to handle their expanded duties.

While prisons suffer from overcrowding, inadequate medical attention, and poor sanitary conditions, authorities took steps during in 2003 to reduce the prison population, including introducing alternative sentences to incarceration. The new criminal procedure code limits pretrial detention to six months and has reduced overcrowding in pretrial detention centers (known as SIZOs). In 2001, Putin disbanded the presidential pardons commission, which was viewed as a safeguard against the harsh penal system and had resulted in the release of about 60,000 inmates since its inception in 1991, and ordered the creation of commissions in each of the country's 89 regions.

Ethnic minorities, particularly those who appear to be from the Caucasus or Central Asia, are subject to governmental and societal discrimination and harassment. Racially motivated attacks by skinheads and other extremist groups occur occasionally.

The government places some restrictions on freedom of movement and residence. All adults are legally required to carry internal passports while traveling, documents that are also necessary to obtain many government services. Some regional authorities impose residential registration rules that limit the right of citizens to choose their place of residence freely. Police reportedly demand bribes for processing registration applications and during spot checks for registration documents, and these often unfairly target the Caucasian and "dark-skinned" population.

In recent years, property rights have continued to be legally strengthened. A land code that established the legal framework for buying and selling nonagricultural land was adopted in late 2001. In June 2002, parliament passed a law allowing the sale of agricultural land to Russian citizens; such sales had been severely restricted since the 1917 Bolshevik Revolution. Analysts, however, regarded the end-of-year prosecution of the principal owners of the Yukos group, and the unprecedented step by Russian authorities to freeze their assets in the company, as an ominous assault on the free market system.

Widespread corruption remains a serious obstacle to the creation of an effective market economy and an impediment to genuine equality of opportunity. According to a 2002 report by the Moscow-based Indem think tank, Russians spend an estimated $37 billion annually on bribes and kickbacks, ranging from small payments to traffic police to large kickbacks by companies to obtain lucrative state contracts. Members of the old Soviet elite have used insider information to obtain control of key industrial and business enterprises.

Domestic violence remains a serious problem, while police are often reluctant to intervene in what they regard as internal family matters. Economic hardships contribute to widespread trafficking of women abroad for prostitution. There is credible evidence that women face considerable discrimination in the workplace, including lower pay than their male counterparts for performing similar work.

# Rwanda

**Population:** 8,300,000  **Political Rights:** 6*
**GNI/capita:** $220  **Civil Liberties:** 5
**Life Expectancy:** 40  **Status:** Not Free
**Religious Groups:** Roman Catholic (56.5 percent),
Protestant (26 percent), other (17.5 percent)
**Ethnic Groups:** Hutu (84 percent), Tutsi (15 percent),
Twa [Pygmy] (1 percent)
**Capital:** Kigali
**Ratings Change:** Rwanda's political rights rating improved from 7 to 6 due to the passage of a new constitution permitting political pluralism, and presidential and legislative elections that reflected a modest amount of political choice

**Ten-Year Ratings Timeline (Political Rights, Civil Liberties, Status)**

| 1994 | 1995 | 1996 | 1997 | 1998 | 1999 | 2000 | 2001 | 2002 | 2003 |
|------|------|------|------|------|------|------|------|------|------|
| 7,7NF | 7,6NF | 7,6NF | 7,6NF | 7,6NF | 7,6NF | 7,6NF | 7,6NF | 7,5NF | 6,5NF |

**Overview:**  A new constitution that officially permits political parties to exist, under certain conditions, was unveiled in 2003. Presidential and legislative elections that were held in August and September, respectively, provided Rwandans with some political choice. However, the primacy of the ruling Rwandan Patriotic Front (RPF) was not challenged, and a major Hutu-supported political party was declared illegal.

Rwanda's ethnic divide is deeply rooted. National boundaries demarcated by Belgian colonists led to often violent competition for power within the fixed borders of a modern state. Traditional and Belgian-abetted Tutsi dominance ended with a Hutu rebellion in 1959 and independence in 1962. Hundreds of thousands of Tutsis were killed or fled the country in recurring violence during the next decades. In 1990, the Tutsi-dominated RPF launched a guerrilla war to force the Hutu regime, led by General Juvenal Habyarimana, to accept power sharing and the return of Tutsi refugees. The Hutus' chauvinist solution to claims for land and power by Rwanda's Tutsi minority, which constituted approximately 15 percent of the pre-genocide population, was to pursue the complete elimination of the Tutsi people.

The 1994 genocide was launched after the suspicious deaths of President Habyarimana and Burundian president Cyprien Ntaryamira in a plane crash in Kigali in April. The ensuing massacres were well plotted, with piles of imported machetes distributed and death lists broadcast by radio. A small UN force in Rwanda fled as the killings spread and Tutsi rebels advanced. French troops intervened in late 1994, not to halt the genocide, but in a futile effort to preserve a territorial enclave for the crumbling genocidal regime that was so closely linked to the French government.

International relief efforts that eased the suffering among more than two million Hutu refugees along Rwanda's frontiers also allowed retraining and rearming of large numbers of former government troops. The United Nations, which had earlier ignored specific warnings of an impending genocide in 1994, failed to prevent such activities, and the Rwandan army took direct action, overrunning refugee camps in the Democratic Republic of Congo.

Nearly three million refugees subsequently returned to Rwanda between 1996 and 1998. Security has improved considerably since 1997, although isolated killings and "disappearances" continue.

The government, led by the RPF, closely directs the country's political life. In 1999, it extended the transition period leading to the holding of multiparty national elections for an additional four years, arguing that the move was necessary because of the poor security situation in the country. In 2000, President Pasteur Bizimungu resigned and was replaced by Vice President Paul Kagame, who had already been the de facto leader of the country. A new prime minister, Bernard Makuza, was appointed. The president of the National Assembly fled into exile in the United States and was replaced. The security situation remains generally peaceful, with refugee reintegration continuing to take place.

Nonpartisan municipal elections, a controversial step in the country's political transition, were held in 2001. Candidates were elected to councils, which in turn chose 106 district town mayors who previously had been appointed by the central government. Political parties were forbidden to campaign, and candidates could present themselves only as individuals.

Rwanda's extended post-genocide political transition period officially ended in 2003, but the extent to which this is a move toward institutionalizing pluralist democracy remains unclear. President Kagame overwhelmingly defeated opposition candidate Faustin Twamirungu in presidential elections in August. The RPF's preeminent position in Rwandan political life, combined with a short campaign period, the material advantages of incumbency and the continuing effects of the genocide, which inhibit free expression of political will, ensured Kagame's victory and that of the RPF and its allies in the September parliamentary polls. The largely Hutu Democratic Republican Movement (MDR) was declared illegal by the authorities for allegedly sowing "divisionism," a code word for the fanning of ethnic hatred. In a sign of the extent of the RPF's influence, even the MDR parliamentary delegation voted to ban the party.

Rwanda remained generally peaceful internally, and in November, a group of Hutu guerrillas in the Congo peacefully negotiated a return to Rwanda. Continued instability in the region, however, including tensions with neighboring Uganda, pose considerable challenges to the country's peaceful development and complicate efforts to improve the exercise of human rights and fundamental freedoms.

**Political Rights and Civil Liberties:** The 2003 presidential and parliamentary elections gave Rwandans a limited amount of political choice. A new constitution passed in a 2003 referendum includes provisions for a semi-presidential regime giving strong powers to the president, who has sole authority to appoint the prime minister. The president can dissolve parliament, but only once during a five-year term. Only two succeeding presidential terms are allowed. The constitution officially permits political parties to exist, under certain conditions. Political parties closely identified with the 1994 massacres are banned, as are parties based on ethnicity or religion. The cabinet must consist of representatives from several different parties, and the largest party is not allowed to occupy more than half of the cabinet seats. The constitution also provides that the president, prime minister, and president of the lower house cannot all belong to the same party.

The constitution restricts political campaigning at the grassroots level. It raises the possibility that parties officially distinct from, but in reality subservient to, the RPF could emerge. The constitution's emphasis on "national unity" as a priority and a provision outlawing the incitement of ethnic hatred could be interpreted to limit the legitimate exercise of political pluralism. The constitution also includes a "forum" of parties that is ostensibly designed to foster communication between parties, but could also serve to control party actions.

Hutus have some representation in the government, including Prime Minister Bernard Makuza, who was from the MDR party prior to its banning. In recent years, a number of leading government critics have fled the country. Former president Pasteur Bizimungu remains under arrest for announcing that he intended to set up an independent political party.

The media reflect the RPF's predominant role and are constrained by fear of reprisals. During the genocide, 50 journalists were murdered, while others broadcast incitements to slaughter. The 2003 Rwanda report by Reporters Sans Frontieres, a press watchdog group, concludes that press freedom is not assured. Journalists interviewed admitted that they censor their own writing and that the authorities have made it clear that certain topics cannot be discussed. As a result, newspaper coverage is heavily pro-governmental. The broadcast media are government controlled, although a media bill passed in June 2002 paved the way for the licensing of private radio and TV stations. There are a growing number of newspapers in the country.

Religious freedom is generally respected in Rwanda. Numerous clerics had been among both the victims and the perpetrators of the 1994 genocide.

Local nongovernmental organizations, such as the Rwandan League for the Protection of Human Rights, operate openly, even though they are at times viewed with suspicion by the government. International human rights groups and relief organizations are also active. Constitutional provisions for labor rights include the right to form trade unions, engage in collective bargaining, and strike. There are 27 registered unions under two umbrella groups. The larger group is the Central Union of Rwandan Workers, which was closely controlled by the previous regime, but that now has relatively greater independence.

Constitutional and legal safeguards regarding arrest procedures and detention are unevenly applied. The near destruction of the legal system and the death or exile of most of the judiciary have dramatically impeded the government's ability to administer post-genocide justice. About 120,000 suspects are incarcerated in jails built for 10,000. To help address this problem, the traditional justice system of *gacaca* was re-instituted in 2002. In this system, local notables preside over community trials dealing with the less serious genocide offenses. Some observers have expressed concern about the potential for partiality or for the application of uneven or arbitrary standards. Amnesty International has criticized the process, which moved ahead slowly in 2003, stating that gacaca courts "fall short of international standards of fairness, particularly in terms of competence, independence and impartiality."

The International Criminal Tribunal for Rwanda (ICTR) in Arusha, Tanzania, continues its work. The tribunal, similar to that in The Hague dealing with those accused of genocide and crimes against humanity in the former Yugoslavia, is composed of international jurists. Relations between Rwanda and the court in Arusha have deteriorated in recent years, with Rwanda accusing the ICTR of incompetence and the court accusing Rwanda of refusing to cooperate in war crimes investigations involving its army.

There is ongoing de facto discrimination against women in a variety of areas despite legal protection for equal rights. Economic and social dislocation have forced women to take on many new roles, especially in the countryside.

# St. Kitts and Nevis

**Population:** 50,000
**GNI/capita:** $6,370
**Life Expectancy:** 71
**Religious Groups:** Anglican, other Protestant, Roman Catholic
**Ethnic Groups:** Predominantly black, British, Portuguese, Lebanese
**Capital:** Basseterre

**Political Rights:** 1
**Civil Liberties:** 2
**Status:** Free

**Ten-Year Ratings Timeline (Political Rights, Civil Liberties, Status)**

| 1994 | 1995 | 1996 | 1997 | 1998 | 1999 | 2000 | 2001 | 2002 | 2003 |
|------|------|------|------|------|------|------|------|------|------|
| 2,2F | 1,2F | 1,2F | 1,2F | 1,2F | 1,2F | 1,2F | 1,2F | 1,2F | 1,2F |

**Overview:**
The process for Nevis to secede from St. Kitts gained momentum during 2003, as the country celebrated two decades of independence from the United Kingdom.

European colonization of Nevis began in the seventeenth century with the arrival of English and French colonists. The English settled mostly on Nevis, while the French chose St. Kitts. Intermittent warfare led to changes in sovereignty, but the Treaty of Paris in 1783 awarded both islands to Britain. In 1967, together with Anguilla, they became a self-governing state in association with Great Britain; Anguilla seceded late that year and remains a British dependency. The Federation of St. Kitts and Nevis attained full independence on September 19, 1983.

Going into the March 6, 2000 elections, Prime Minister Denzil Douglas was able to tout his government's efforts at promoting resort construction in St. Kitts, combating crime, and raising public employees' salaries. Critics of the St. Kitts Labour Party (SKLP) claimed that the country had accumulated $192 million in debt and that the government had failed to reinvigorate the islands' sugar economy. The SKLP won a stronger parliamentary majority in elections, taking all 8 seats on St. Kitts, out of the 11-member National Assembly. Opposition leader Kennedy Simmonds's People's Action Movement (PAM), which had hoped to oust the SKLP by winning 3 seats in St. Kitts and forming a coalition with the winners of seats in Nevis, instead lost its only seat on the island to the SKLP, which had previously held 7 seats.

In 2002, the Financial Action Task Force removed the twin island federation from the list of jurisdictions that were uncooperative in the fight against money laundering and other financial crimes.

Beginning in mid-2003, momentum gathered for Nevis to secede from St. Kitts, a process that cast a shadow over the twentieth anniversary of independence from Great Britain, which was celebrated on September 19. Nevis is accorded the constitutional right to secede if two-thirds of the elected legislators approve and two-thirds of voters endorse succession through a referendum. Though a 1998 referendum on independence failed the required two-thirds majority, Nevisians continue to feel neglected. No Nevisian is a member of the governing cabinet, and the island holds only 3 of 11 seats in the legislature.

A major new resort hotel opened in November, a possible sign of economic recovery, although tourist visits have not recovered to the pre-September 11, 2001 levels. Sugar is still the mainstay of the economy, and depressed global prices continued to hurt the local economy during the year.

**Political Rights and Civil Liberties:** Citizens are able to change their government democratically. The 2000 elections were free and fair. Nevertheless, drug trafficking and money laundering have corrupted the political system. The St. Kitts and Nevis national government consists of the prime minister, the cabinet, and the unicameral National Assembly. Elected assembly members—eight from St. Kitts and three from Nevis—serve five-year terms. Senators, not to exceed two-thirds of the elected members, are appointed—one by the leader of the parliamentary opposition for every two by the prime minister. Nevis also has a local assembly, composed of five elected and three appointed members, and pays for all of its own services except for those involving police and foreign relations. St. Kitts has no similar body. The country is a member of the Commonwealth with a governor-general appointed by the Queen of England.

Constitutional guarantees of free expression are generally respected. Television on St. Kitts is government owned, although managed by a Trinidadian company, and there are some government restrictions on opposition access to it. Prime Minister Denzil Douglas has kept pledges to privatize radio, with the selling of the government radio station. There are eight radio stations on the islands and two daily newspapers. In addition, each major political party publishes a weekly or fortnightly newspaper. Opposition publications freely criticize the government, and international media are available. There is free access to the Internet.

The free exercise of religion is constitutionally protected, and academic freedom is generally honored.

The right to organize political parties, civic organizations, and labor unions is generally respected, as is the right of assembly. The main labor union, the St. Kitts Trades and Labour Union, is associated with the ruling SKLP. The right to strike, while not specified by law, is recognized and generally respected in practice.

The judiciary is generally independent. However, in March 1996, when an earlier drug and murder scandal came to trial, the public prosecutor's office failed to send a representative to present the case. The charges were dropped, which raised suspicions of a government conspiracy. The highest court is the West Indies Supreme Court in St. Lucia, which includes a court of appeals and a High Court. Under certain circumstances there is a right of appeal to the Privy Council in London.

The traditionally strong rule of law has been tested by the increase in drug-related crime and corruption. In 1995, it appeared that the police had become divided along political lines between the two main political parties. In June 1997, despite concerns of its cost to a country of some 50,000 people, parliament passed a bill designed to create a 50-member Special Services Unit, which receives light infantry training, to wage war on heavily armed drug traffickers. The intimidation of witnesses and jurors is a problem. The national prison is overcrowded, and conditions are abysmal. In July 1998, the government hanged a convicted murderer, ending a 13-year hiatus in executions and defying pressure from Britain and human rights groups to end the death penalty.

The deportation of a number of felons from the United States under the U.S. Illegal Immigration Reform and Immigrant Responsibility Act of 1996 has contributed to local law enforcement agencies in the region feeling overwhelmed. In 1998, the drug lord Charles "Little Nut" Miller threatened to kill U.S. students at St. Kitts's Ross University if he were extradited to the United States. A magistrate had twice blocked Miller's extradition, but it was approved by the High Court after police stopped and searched his car, finding two firearms, ammunition, and a small amount of marijuana.

Reports suggest that the country's economic citizenship program, which allows for the purchase of passports through real estate investments with a minimum of $250,000 and a registration fee of $35,000, has facilitated the illegal immigration of persons from China and other countries into the United States and Canada.

Violence against women is a problem. The Domestic Violence Act of 2000 criminalizes domestic violence and provides penalties for abusers. The Department of Gender Affairs, a part of the Ministry for Social Development, Community, and Gender Affairs has offered counseling for victims of abuse and conducted training on domestic and gender violence. There are no laws for sexual harassment.

# St. Lucia

**Population:** 200,000
**GNI/capita:** $3,840
**Life Expectancy:** 72
**Religious Groups:** Roman Catholic (90 percent),
Protestant (7 percent), Anglican (3 percent)
**Ethnic Groups:** Black African (90 percent), mulatto (6
percent), East Indian (3 percent), white (1 percent)
**Capital:** Castries

**Political Rights:** 1
**Civil Liberties:** 2
**Status:** Free

**Ten-Year Ratings Timeline (Political Rights, Civil Liberties, Status)**

| 1994 | 1995 | 1996 | 1997 | 1998 | 1999 | 2000 | 2001 | 2002 | 2003 |
|------|------|------|------|------|------|------|------|------|------|
| 1,2F | 1,2F | 1,2F | 1,2F | 1,2F | 1,2F | 1,2F | 1,2F | 1,2F | 1,2F |

**Overview:**     As St. Lucia faced an escalating crime wave, the establishment of a commission to examine the country's constitution with regard to law and order issues was announced in November 2003. Parliament also approved the Caribbean Court of Justice agreement.

St. Lucia, a member of the British Commonwealth, achieved independence in 1979. In May 1997, Kenny Anthony led the St. Lucia Labour Party (SLP) to victory in legislative elections. On taking office, Anthony began to address concerns of an electorate weary of economic distress and reports of official corruption. In 1999, his government faced a series of issues concerning the hotel and airline industries, both vital for the tourism industry. In 2000, Anthony and the SLP gave their approval for regulated casino gambling, brushing aside objections from religious groups and the UWP, to seemingly focus even more of their energies on revitalizing the country's tourism trade.

In June 2001, Anthony announced a two-month crackdown on crime, including increased police patrols and heavy penalties for gun crimes. He maintained that these measures were necessary to combat a wave of murders and armed robberies that he blamed, in part, on a U.S. policy of deporting hardened criminals to the island.

The SLP swept to victory in the December 3, 2001 general elections, winning 14 of 17 seats in parliament, just short of the 16-1 majority it had achieved in 1997. However, in an election called six months ahead of schedule, constituencies dominated by banana farmers registered their discontent with Anthony's party, reflecting a measure of popular discontent with his efforts to keep the island's ailing banana industry afloat. Anthony was the only party leader to survive the election. Although her United Workers Party (UWP) won the other 3 seats, Morella Joseph—the first woman to lead a party into a general election—lost her seat, and National Alliance leader George Odlum and former UWP prime minister Vaughan Lewis failed in their efforts to be elected.

In November 2003, the government and opposition announced the establishment of a Constitution Review Commission to examine St. Lucia's constitution as it relates to issues of law and order. The level of violence has increased noticeably, with police blaming much of the violence on drug-related gangs. The United States has named St. Lucia as a principal transit point in the eastern Caribbean for South

American cocaine. Local authorities are also troubled over the increasing number of travelers coming through the island with fraudulent passports.

**Political Rights and Civil Liberties:** Citizens are able to change their government through democratic elections. The 2001 elections were considered free and fair, although fewer than 50 percent of those eligible actually voted; 60 percent of registered voters had turned out in 1997. The British monarchy is represented by a governor-general. Under the 1979 constitution, a bicameral parliament consists of the 17-member House of Assembly, elected for five years, and an 11-member Senate. Six members of the Senate are appointed by the prime minister, three by the leader of the parliamentary opposition and two in consultation with civic and religious organizations. The island is divided into eight regions, each with its own elected council and administrative services.

The media carry a wide spectrum of views and are largely independent of the government. There are five privately owned newspapers, two privately held radio stations, and one partially government-funded radio station, as well as two privately owned television stations. There is free access to the Internet.

Constitutional guarantees of the free exercise of religion are respected. Academic freedom is generally honored.

Constitutional guarantees regarding the right to organize political parties, civic groups, and labor unions are generally respected. Civic groups are well organized and politically active, as are labor unions, which represent the majority of wage earners. Nevertheless, legislation passed in 1995 restricts the right to strike.

The judicial system is independent and includes a High Court under the West Indies Supreme Court (based in St. Lucia), with ultimate appeal under certain circumstances to the Privy Council in London. In July, a treaty replacing the Privy Council with a Caribbean Court of Justice (CCJ), to be based in Trinidad and Tobago, was approved by St. Lucia. On November 19, parliament passed the Caribbean Court of Justice 2003 agreement, with St Lucia pledging to contribute $2.5 million toward the establishment of the regional court. The CCJ is to have an appellate function and will also interpret the Caribbean Community (Caricom) Treaty.

Traditionally, citizens have enjoyed a high degree of personal security, although there are episodic reports of police misuse of force. In recent years, an escalating crime wave—including drug-related offenses, violent clashes during banana farmers' strikes, and increased violence in schools—has created concern among citizens. The island's nineteenth-century prison, built to house a maximum of 80 inmates, houses close to 500. In late 2002, the government finished construction of a new, $17 million prison facility on the eastern part of the island.

Though there are no official barriers to their participation, women are underrepresented in politics and the professions. A growing awareness of the seriousness of violence against women has led the government and advocacy groups to take steps to offer better protection for victims of domestic violence.

# St. Vincent and the Grenadines

**Population:** 100,000
**GNI/capita:** $2,820
**Life Expectancy:** 72
**Political Rights:** 2
**Civil Liberties:** 1
**Status:** Free
**Religious Groups:** Anglican (47 percent), Methodist (28 percent), Roman Catholic (13 percent), other [including Hindu, Seventh-Day Adventist, other Protestant] (12 percent)
**Ethnic Groups:** Black (66 percent), other [including mulatto, East Indian, and white] (34 percent)
**Capital:** Kingstown

**Ten-Year Ratings Timeline (Political Rights, Civil Liberties, Status)**

| 1994 | 1995 | 1996 | 1997 | 1998 | 1999 | 2000 | 2001 | 2002 | 2003 |
|------|------|------|------|------|------|------|------|------|------|
| 2,1F | 2,1F | 2,1F | 2,1F | 2,1F | 2,1F | 2,1F | 2,1F | 2,1F | 2,1F |

**Overview:**

In 2003, an intergovernmental body removed St. Vincent and the Grenadines from a list of countries seen as not cooperating to combat money laundering.

St. Vincent and the Grenadines achieved independence in 1979, with jurisdiction over the northern Grenadine islets of Bequia, Canouan, Mayreau, Mustique, Prune Island, Petit St. Vincent, and Union Island. The country is a member of the Commonwealth, with the British monarchy represented by a governor-general.

In the March 2001 elections, the social-democratic United Labour Party (ULP) captured 12 of the 15 contested parliamentary seats and Ralph Gonsalves became prime minister. The incumbent conservative New Democrat Party (NDP) won only 3 seats. The election, which had been preceded by serious political unrest and popular mobilization, was monitored by international election observers for the first time in the country's history.

Gonsalves, a one time radical opposition figure, in 2001 led a successful initiative to save the financially ailing Organization of Eastern Caribbean States by relieving it of some administrative requirements now carried out by its individual members. After a controversial trip to Libya, also in 2001, Gonsalves was criticized for not revealing publicly that the Arab nation had promised to buy all the bananas that the Caribbean could produce.

In June 2003, the Paris-based Financial Action Task Force (FATF) removed St. Vincent and the Grenadines from its list of jurisdictions deemed noncooperative in the fight against money laundering. This was seen as a major victory by the government of Prime Minister Gonsalves. In the same month, the U.S. Coast Guard detained eight ships when it discovered that several officers had licenses that were improperly issued by St. Vincent and the Grenadines. The periodic destruction caused by tropical weather has further burdened the island's troubled economy and made efforts of diversification more difficult. Crime continues to discourage tourism, which had begun a slow recovery from the September 11, 2001, attacks in the United States.

**Political Rights and Civil Liberties:**

Citizens can change their government through elections. The constitution provides for the 15-member unicameral

House of Assembly elected for five years. In addition, six senators are appointed—four by the government and two by the opposition.

The March 2001 election was considered free and fair by international observers. However, penetration by the hemispheric drug trade is increasingly causing concern. There have been allegations of drug-related corruption within the government and the police force, and of money laundering through St. Vincent banks. In 1995, the U.S. government described St. Vincent as becoming a drug-trafficking center and alleged that high-level government officials were involved in narcotics-related corruption. Since then, St. Vincent has taken steps to cooperate with U.S. antidrug trade efforts, such as signing an extradition treaty in 1996 with the U.S.

The press is independent, with two privately owned independent weeklies and several smaller, partisan papers. Some journalists believe that government advertising is used as a political tool. The only television station is privately owned and free from government interference. Satellite dishes and cable are available to those who can afford them. The radio station is government owned, and call-in programs are prohibited. Equal access to radio is mandated during electoral campaigns, but the ruling party takes advantage of state control over programming. There is free access to the Internet.

The right to freedom of religion is constitutionally protected and reflected in practice. Academic freedom is generally honored.

Civic groups and nongovernmental organizations are free from government interference. Labor unions are active and permitted to strike.

The judicial system is independent. The highest court is the West Indies Supreme Court (based in St. Lucia), which includes a court of appeals and a High Court. A right of ultimate appeal reports, under certain circumstances, to the Privy Council in London. Murder convictions carry a mandatory death sentence.

Human rights are generally respected. However, in 1999, a local human rights organization accused police of using excessive force and illegal search and seizure, and of improperly informing detainees of their rights in order to extract confessions. The regional human rights organization, Caribbean Rights, estimates that 90 percent of convictions in St. Vincent are based on confessions. The independent St. Vincent Human Rights Association has criticized long judicial delays and the large backlog of cases caused by personnel shortages in the local judiciary. It has also charged that the executive branch of government at times exerts inordinate influence over the courts. Prison conditions remain poor—one prison designed for 75 inmates houses more than 300—and prisons are the targets of allegations of mistreatment. Juvenile offenders are also housed in inadequate conditions.

In December 1999, a marijuana eradication effort in St. Vincent's northern mountains stirred up controversy after U.S.-trained troops from the Regional Security System (RSS) were accused of brutality and indiscriminate crop destruction in what the Barbados-based RSS claimed was a highly successful exercise. One person, who police said was fleeing from a search scene armed with a shotgun, was killed.

Violence against women, particularly domestic violence, is a major problem. Some protection is offered by the Domestic Violence Summary Proceedings Act that provides for protective orders. The punishment for rape is generally 10 years in prison, while sentences of 20 years for sexual assaults against minors are handed down.

# Samoa

**Population:** 200,000
**GNI/capita:** $1,420
**Life Expectancy:** 69
**Religious Groups:** Christian (99.7 percent),
other (0.3 percent)
**Ethnic Groups:** Polynesian (93 percent), Euronesian
[mixed] (7 percent)
**Capital:** Apia

**Political Rights:** 2
**Civil Liberties:** 2
**Status:** Free

**Ten-Year Ratings Timeline (Political Rights, Civil Liberties, Status)**

| 1994 | 1995 | 1996 | 1997 | 1998 | 1999 | 2000 | 2001 | 2002 | 2003 |
|------|------|------|------|------|------|------|------|------|------|
| 2,2F | 2,2F | 2,2F | 2,2F | 2,3F | 2,2F | 2,2F | 2,2F | 2,2F | 2,2F |

**Overview:**   In 2003, the Samoan government took steps to curb the power of traditional chiefs as the public became more concerned about abuse of power issues and whether some of the chiefs' decisions violate constitutional rights and freedoms. On the international front, the government's decision to reject a bilateral treaty with the United States cost it $150,000 in military assistance.

The islands then known as Western Samoa were controlled by Germany between 1899 and World War I. New Zealand occupied and subsequently administered the islands under a League of Nations mandate and then as a trust territory until Western Samoa became independent in 1962. In 1998, the country changed its name to Samoa. Samoa is not to be confused with American Samoa, which consists of the eastern group of these Polynesian islands located between New Zealand and Hawaii.

The centrist Human Rights Protection Party (HRPP) has dominated the country's political process, winning six consecutive elections since 1982. Tofilau Eti Alesana, who became prime minister in 1982, resigned in 1998 for health reasons. He was replaced by Deputy Prime Minister Tuilaepa Aiono Sailele Malielegoai, who led the HRPP to another victory in March 2001 by winning 30 of the 49 parliamentary seats.

In August 2003, the number of government departments and ministries was reduced from 27 to 14, mainly through mergers and appointments of new executive heads, in order to streamline the government. The government also announced increased police efforts to battle growing youth crime, particularly drug use and violence.

The government established a new Law Reform Commission to address conflicts between traditional customs and Christianity. Traditional village chiefs exercise considerable power, particularly in villages where the government's reach is limited, and people defer in many matters to traditional leaders. However, the powers of these traditional leaders have come under question in recent years. In April, the Supreme Court ruled that the village chief's decision to banish nine people from the village of Falealup in 2002 for joining new churches was unconstitutional and violated freedom of religion.

Samoa decided to forgo $150,000 in annual military aid from the United States when it refused to sign a bilateral treaty with Washington by a July deadline. The treaty would have granted exemptions from the Rome Statute of the International Criminal Court to U.S. citizens who are alleged to have committed an international offense and currently live in Samoa. Samoa can ill afford to lose this money, as its economy is heavily dependent on foreign aid and remittances from more than 100,000 Samoan citizens living and working outside of the country.

**Political Rights and Civil Liberties:** Samoans can change their government democratically. Executive authority is vested in the head of state. The 90-year-old Malietoa Tanumafili II holds this position for life; his successor will be elected for five-year terms by the Legislative Assembly. The head of state appoints the prime minister, who is the head of government and chooses the 12-member cabinet. All laws passed by the 49-member unicameral legislature also need approval from the head of state to take effect. Tofilau Eti Alesana, who became prime minister in 1982, introduced universal suffrage; previously, only the *matai* (family chiefs) could vote. In 2003, there were five political parties, two of which were represented in the legislature. Although candidates are free to propose themselves for electoral office, approval of the matai is essential.

The government generally respects freedom of speech and the press. Two English-language and many Samoan newspapers are printed regularly. Journalists are legally required to reveal their sources in the event of a defamation suit against them, although no court case has invoked this law. The government operates the sole television station. There are four major private radio stations, and a satellite cable system is available in parts of the capital. Internet use is growing rapidly.

The government respects freedom of religion in practice, and relations among religions are generally amicable. There were no reports of restrictions on academic freedom.

Freedom of assembly and association are respected in practice. Human rights groups operate freely, and about 20 percent of wage earners belong to trade unions. More than 60 percent of adults work in subsistence agriculture.

The judiciary is independent and upholds the right to a fair trial. The Supreme Court is the highest court with full jurisdiction on civil, criminal, and constitutional matters. The head of state, on the recommendation of the prime minister, appoints the chief justice. The country has no armed forces; the small police force is under civilian control, but has little impact beyond the capital. Most internal disputes are settled by the *fono* (Council of Chiefs) in each village. Punishments imposed by the fono usually involve fines, while banishment from the village is reserved for more serious offenses. Fono vary considerably in their decision-making style and in the number of matai involved in decisions. The 1990 Village Fono Act gives legal recognition to fono decisions.

Abuses by some fono officials have caused the public to question the legitimacy of their actions and the limits of their authority. Such actions include home searches or seizure of property without a warrant. In 2000, the Supreme Court ruled that the Village Fono Act could not be used to infringe on villagers' freedoms of religion, speech, assembly, and association. This ruling followed a fono decision in the village of Saluilua that banished a Bible study group after calling it illegal.

Freedom of movement within the country, as well as the freedom to pursue foreign travel, emigration, and repatriation are guaranteed in the constitution and respected in practice.

Discrimination and violence against women are widespread, and violence against children is growing. Domestic abuses typically go unreported; the police and village fono consider these private affairs and rarely intervene. Spousal rape is not illegal.

# San Marino

**Population:** 30,000
**GNI/capita:** $34,330
**Life Expectancy:** 81
**Religious Groups:** Roman Catholic
**Ethnic Groups:** Sanmarinese, Italian
**Capital:** San Marino

**Political Rights:** 1
**Civil Liberties:** 1
**Status:** Free

### Ten-Year Ratings Timeline (Political Rights, Civil Liberties, Status)

| 1994 | 1995 | 1996 | 1997 | 1998 | 1999 | 2000 | 2001 | 2002 | 2003 |
|------|------|------|------|------|------|------|------|------|------|
| 1,1F | 1,1F | 1,1F | 1,1F | 1,1F | 1,1F | 1,1F | 1,1F | 1,1F | 1,1F |

**Overview:**
After having been in place for only six months, San Marino's governing coalition entered into a crisis during the summer of 2003 that would last into the fall due to infighting among the two coalition member parties.

Founded in A.D. 301, San Marino is the world's oldest and second smallest republic, after Vatican City. Although the Sammarinesi are ethnically and culturally Italian, they have succeeded in maintaining their independence against great odds since the fourth century. The papacy recognized San Marino's independence in 1631, as did the Congress of Vienna after the Napoleonic Wars in 1815. In 1862, San Marino signed a customs union and treaty with Italy, beginning a long period of friendship with the country that surrounds it. Despite its dependence on Italy, from which it currently receives budget subsidies, San Marino maintains its own political institutions. It became a member of the Council of Europe in 1988 and the United Nations in 1992.

Early elections were called in June 2001, leading to the return of a coalition of the Christian Democrats (PDCS) and the Socialist Party (PSS). The PDCS won 25 seats, the PSS 15, the Democratic Party (PPDS) 12, the Popular Party (APDS) 5, the Communist Party (RC) 2, and the National Alliance (AN) 1. In October, Giovanni Lonfernini (PCDS) and Valeria Ciavatta (Popular Alliance of Democrats) were installed as captains-regent—joint heads of state—positions that are elected every six months by parliament.

The latest government crisis came about in 2003 after infighting broke out between the ruling PDCS and Socialists.

On the international front, the foreign minister traveled to Russia in October to mark 10 years since the opening of diplomatic relations between the two countries.

In April, San Marino ratified Protocol No. 12 to the European Convention of the Protection of Human Rights and Fundamental Freedoms, which prohibits discrimination on any grounds by any public authority.

**Political Rights and Civil Liberties:** The Sammarinesi can change their government democratically. The 60 members of the Great and General Council (a unicameral parliament) are elected every five years by proportional representation. The executive power of the country rests with a 10-member Congress of State (cabinet), which is headed by the two captains-regent elected every April 1 and October 1. Although there is no official prime minister, the secretary of state for foreign affairs has assumed some of the position's prerogatives.

Freely elected representatives determine the policies of the government in San Marino, where there are few problems with corruption. Although San Marino is an offshore jurisdiction, the country has made commitments to cooperate with the Organization for Economic Cooperation and Development (OECD) to address harmful tax practices. San Marino has never been blacklisted by the OECD or sanctioned by the EU for its tax practices as an international banking center. Although companies and individuals do pay taxes in the country, the tax rates—about 12 percent for individuals and 24 percent for corporations—are much lower than in the rest of Europe and Canada.

Freedom of speech and of the press are guaranteed in San Marino. There are daily newspapers, a state-run broadcast system for radio and television called RTV, and a private FM station, Radio Titiano. The Sammarinesi have access to all Italian print media and certain Italian broadcast stations. San Marino was one of only 12 of the 55 Organization for Security and Cooperation in Europe (OSCE) member states that had no press freedom violations recorded in 1999–2000.

The law prohibits religious discrimination. Roman Catholicism is the dominant, but not the state, religion. People can request a donation of 0.3 percent of their income through their taxes to be allocated to the Catholic Church, the Waldesian Church, or the Jehovah's Witnesses. Academic freedom is respected.

People are free to assemble, demonstrate, and conduct open public discussions. Workers are free to organize into trade unions and bargain collectively with employers. They are also free to strike, if they do not work in military occupations. Approximately half of the country's workforce is unionized.

The judiciary in San Marino is independent. Lower court judges are required to be noncitizens—generally Italians—to assure impartiality. The final court of review is San Marino's Council of Twelve, a group of judges chosen for six-year terms from among the members of the Grand and General Council. The country's prison system generally met international standards and civilian authorities maintained effective control over the police and security forces.

The population is generally treated equally under the law, although the European Commission against Racism (ECRI) has raised some concerns about the status of foreigners in the country. Most of the foreign-born population are Italians; only about 2 percent—mostly women from Central and Eastern Europe who work as private nurses for the elderly and ill—come from outside the EU. San Marino has no formal asylum policy, and a foreigner has to live in the country for 30 years to be eligible for citizenship. The European Convention on Nationality recommends that the period of residence before a foreigner can apply for citizenship should not exceed 10 years. In 2001, San Marino ratified the international Convention on the Elimination of All Forms of Racial Discrimination (ICERD).

Women are given legal protections from violence and spousal abuse, and gender equality exists in the workplace and elsewhere. There are, however, slight differences in the way men and women can transmit citizenship to their children.

# Sao Tome and Principe

**Population:** 200,000
**GNI/capita:** $290
**Life Expectancy:** 65
**Political Rights:** 2*
**Civil Liberties:** 2
**Status:** Free
**Religious Groups:** Christian [Roman Catholic,
Evangelical Protestant, Seventh-Day Adventist]
(80 percent), other (20 percent)
**Ethnic Groups:** Mestico [Portuguese-African], African minority
[primarily descendants of slaves and indentured servants from Angola and Mozambique],
European [primarily Portuguese]
**Capital:** São Tomé
**Ratings Change:** Sao Tome and Principe's political rights rating declined from 1 to 2 due
to a brief military coup in July.

**Ten-Year Ratings Timeline (Political Rights, Civil Liberties, Status)**

| 1994 | 1995 | 1996 | 1997 | 1998 | 1999 | 2000 | 2001 | 2002 | 2003 |
|------|------|------|------|------|------|------|------|------|------|
| 1,2F | 1,2F | 1,2F | 1,2F | 1,2F | 1,2F | 1,2F | 1,2F | 1,2F | 2,2F |

**Overview:**
Sao Tome and Principe sat on the verge of a dramatic economic transformation even as political instability dogged the country in 2003. A brief military coup in July ousted the country's president, who returned to power one week later. The country, which remains one of the poorest in Africa, was poised to obtain large revenues for leasing to foreign companies the rights to explore its offshore oil reserves.

Sao Tome and Principe consists of two islands approximately 125 and 275 miles off the coast of Gabon in the Gulf of Guinea. Seized by Portugal in 1522 and 1523, they became a Portuguese Overseas Province in 1951. Portugal granted local autonomy in 1973 and independence in 1975. Upon independence, the Movement for the Liberation of Sao Tome and Principe (MLSTP), which was formed in 1960, took power and functioned as the only legal party until a 1990 referendum established multiparty democracy. In 1991, Miguel dos Anjos Trovoada, an independent candidate backed by the opposition Democratic Convergence Party, became the first democratically elected president.

In presidential elections in 2001, Fradique de Menezes, of the Independent Democratic Alliance (ADI), replaced Trovoada, who had ruled the country for 10 years. In the first round of voting, de Menezes won with 56 percent, compared with 38 percent for Manuel Pinto da Costa of the MLSTP. The MLSTP captured 24 seats in parliamentary elections in March 2002. The Democratic Movement of Forces for

Change won 23 seats, and the remaining 8 seats went to the Ue Kadadji coalition. De Menezes called on parliament to introduce laws against vote buying, which he said had been rampant in the March parliamentary poll. Nevertheless, international observers declared the polls to be free and fair.

In January 2003, de Menezes attempted to dissolve parliament and call early elections. However, he backed down when legislators threatened to ignore the decree. The parliament had previously approved a constitutional reform package reducing presidential powers, which de Menezes vetoed.

President de Menezes was briefly ousted by a military coup in July, although he returned to power after one week with the backing of Portugal and numerous African countries. The coup was staged by officers disgruntled over persistent poverty in the country and allegations of state corruption. Tensions escalated in part because Sao Tome is poised to receive an economic windfall of some $200 million next year by leasing the exploration rights to its offshore oil reserves to U.S. and Nigerian companies. After two years of wrangling, the government agreed to divide some of the proceeds with Nigeria, with which it shares territorial waters in the Gulf of Guinea. Following the July coup, de Menezes shuffled his cabinet and overrode a resignation bid by his prime minister, Maria das Neves.

Sao Tome and Principe has been in the process of strengthening its relationship with the United States, which plans to build a sheltering port on the archipelago for the U.S. Navy to patrol waters surrounding the country and protect its oil resources there.

Sao Tome and Principe has mostly relied on external assistance to develop its economy. Unemployment is about 45 percent, and it is one of the poorest countries in Africa. The upcoming oil bonanza has drawn comparisons with Equatorial Guinea, where an influx of petroleum dollars failed to bring benefits to the vast majority of the population. However, Sao Tome has a stronger democratic tradition, and its government has pledged transparency in managing the country's oil revenues.

**Political Rights and Civil Liberties:** The people of Sao Tome and Principe have the right to change their government democratically. Presidential and legislative elections in 1991 gave the country's citizens their first chance to elect their leader in an open, free, and fair contest.

Constitutionally protected freedom of expression is respected in practice. One state-run and six independent newspapers and newsletters are published. While the state controls a local press agency and the only radio and television stations, no law forbids independent broadcasting. Opposition parties receive free airtime, and newsletters and pamphlets criticizing the government circulate freely.

Freedom of religion is respected within this predominantly Roman Catholic country. The government does not restrict academic freedom.

Freedom of assembly is respected. Citizens have the constitutional right to gather and demonstrate with an advance notice of two days to the government. The rights to organize, strike, and bargain collectively are guaranteed and respected. Few unions exist, but independent cooperatives have taken advantage of the government land-distribution program to attract workers. Because of its role as the main employer in the wage sector, the government remains the key interlocutor for labor on all matters, including wages. Working conditions on many of the state-owned cocoa plantations are harsh.

An independent judiciary, including a Supreme Court with members designated by, and responsible to, the National Assembly, was established by the 1990 referendum on multiparty rule. The Supreme Court has ruled against both the government and the president, but is occasionally subject to manipulation. The court system is overburdened, understaffed, inadequately funded, and plagued by long delays in hearing cases. Prison conditions are harsh.

The constitution provides for equal rights for men and women, but women encounter significant societal discrimination. Most have fewer opportunities than men for education or formal (business) sector employment. However, several women have been appointed to cabinet positions, including that of prime minister. Domestic violence against women is reportedly common. Although legal recourse is available, many victims are reluctant to bring legal action against their spouses or are ignorant of their rights.

# Saudi Arabia

**Population:** 24,100,000   **Political Rights:** 7
**GNI/capita:** $8,460   **Civil Liberties:** 7
**Life Expectancy:** 72   **Status:** Not Free
**Religious Groups:** Muslim (100 percent)
**Ethnic Groups:** Arab (90 percent), Afro-Asian (10 percent)
**Capital:** Riyadh

### Ten-Year Ratings Timeline (Political Rights, Civil Liberties, Status)

| 1994 | 1995 | 1996 | 1997 | 1998 | 1999 | 2000 | 2001 | 2002 | 2003 |
|------|------|------|------|------|------|------|------|------|------|
| 7,7NF | 7,7NF | 7,7NF | 7,7NF | 7,7NF | 7,7NF | 7,7NF | 7,7NF | 7,7NF | 7,7NF |

**Overview:** Saudi Arabia continued to place severe restrictions on its citizens' political rights and civil liberties in 2003, even as hints of possible political reforms emerged in an eventful year. Throughout the year, the country faced threats to its internal stability from terrorist groups and calls for political reform from dissidents and regime opponents. The government of Saudi Arabia responded by offering several signs of possible limited political reforms: the approval of the formation of the first Saudi human rights organization, the first official sanction of a human rights conference in the kingdom, the establishment of a center for dialogue on reform, and announcements of local elections to be held next year.

In the 71 years since its unification in 1932 by King Abdul Aziz Al-Saud, Saudi Arabia has been controlled by the Al-Saud family, with King Fahd, the current king, the fifth in the Al-Saud ruling dynasty. The Saudi monarchy rules in accordance with the conservative school of Sunni Islam. In the early 1990s, Fahd embarked on a limited program of political reform, introducing an appointed consultative council, or Majlis Ash-shura. This step did not lead to any substantial shift in political power. In 1995, King Fahd suffered a stroke, and since 1997, Crown Prince Abdullah has taken control of most power and decision making.

With the largest oil reserves in the world, Saudi Arabia is the world's leading oil producer and exporter. Saudi Arabia's oil wealth and importance to the global economy are key features impacting the country's external relations and shaping Saudi Arabia's internal politics by giving the Al-Saud dynasty unmatched wealth to maintain its control.

Saudi Arabia has been under intense scrutiny since the September 11, 2001 attacks against the United States—15 of the 19 hijackers were Saudi citizens, and the leader of al-Qaeda, Osama bin Ladin, is from a wealthy Saudi family. In 2003, the Saudi monarchy took some first steps to stop the flow of financial support to terrorist groups, agreeing for the first time to set up a joint task force with the United States to target suspected terrorist financiers. The government passed the country's first anti–money laundering law, making financing of terrorist organizations a punishable offense. Saudi Arabia banned all charities from sending money abroad without official approval, audited hundreds of domestic organizations, and closed dozens of charities for suspected involvement in terrorist financing. Saudi Crown Prince Abdullah traveled to Russia in the first high-level Saudi visit to Moscow in 75 years to discuss measures to cut off Saudi financing of separatists in Chechnya.

The threat of terrorist attacks has also posed a challenge to the stability of the Saudi regime. A triple suicide bombing that killed 35 people in Riyadh on May 12, 2003 was a wake-up call for the Saudi monarchy, leading to a crackdown that included the interrogation of thousands of Saudi citizens. In early November, another suicide attack left 18 more Saudis dead. The government fired numerous clerics for inciting hatred and preaching an intolerant version of Islam. The Saudi Interior Ministry, fearing that children might have been recruited by militants, made a public appeal to families to report any missing children.

The Saudi government's dominance of the economy, endemic corruption, and financial mismanagement has led to mounting economic woes, with the world's largest oil producer seeing a decline in real GDP per person over the last decade. Unemployment is estimated at 30 percent, and this year, the Saudi government recognized the growing problem of poverty by announcing a strategy to create jobs and build housing for the underprivileged.

Amid these growing economic difficulties and increased access to outside sources of information through satellite television and the Internet, pressure for political change has mounted. Foreign Minister Prince Saud Al-Faisal announced this year a royal decree approving the establishment of Saudi Arabia's first nongovernmental human rights organization. During the summer, Saudi Arabia established the King Abdul Aziz Center for National Dialogue, which is aimed at starting internal discussions on political reform. In September, more than 300 prominent professionals, including 51 women, sent a petition to Crown Prince Abdullah demanding an elected legislature to replace the appointed consultative council, an independent judiciary, and the creation of civil society organizations to promote greater tolerance.

In October, Saudi Arabia organized the country's first human rights conference, a three-day event that examined human rights in an Islamic context. The conference, however, focused on double standards in Western countries rather than the massive human rights abuse problems within the kingdom. During this conference, protestors demanding political reform took to the streets, inspired by the Movement for Islamic Reform in Arabia, a London-based group of Saudi dissidents who set up the first opposition broadcasting network in Saudi Arabia.

In the face of these demands to make its government more open and accessible, Saudi Arabia announced plans to hold local elections in 2004. In November, the Saudi regime said it would start televising 30-minute excerpts of weekly sessions of the Shura Council. Time will tell if these limited reform measures are the start of something broader and more consequential.

**Political Rights and Civil Liberties:** Saudi Arabia is an absolute monarchy, and its citizens have no power to change the government democratically. The country's 1992 Basic Law declares that the Quran is the country's constitution. Saudi Arabia has a 120-member consultative Shura Council appointed by the monarch, but this council has limited powers and does not impact decision making or power structures in a meaningful way.

The country has never held elections for public office at any level. On October 13, 2003, the Saudi government announced it would hold its first elections to select half of the members of municipal councils in parts of the country in 2004. However, the government released few details about these planned elections, and several questions remained, such as whether or not women would be allowed to participate.

Saudi Arabia does not have political parties, and the only semblance of organized political opposition exists outside of the country. Many Saudi opposition activists are based in London. The Al-Saud dynasty dominates and controls political life in the kingdom.

The Council of Ministers, an executive body appointed by the king, passes legislation that becomes law once ratified by royal decree. The Saudi monarchy has a tradition of consulting with select members of Saudi society, but this process is not equally open to all citizens. Corruption is one consequence of the closed nature of Saudi Arabia's government and society, with foreign companies reporting that they often pay bribes to middle men and government officials to secure business deals.

Government authorities frequently ban or fire journalists and editors who publish articles deemed offensive to the country's powerful religious establishment or the ruling authorities. This year, Hussein Shabakshi, a journalist who advocated for elections, human rights, and women's equality in one of his weekly columns in the Saudi daily *Okaz*, was banned by the Saudi Ministry of Interior. Jamal Khasshogi, editor of the reformist newspaper *Al-Watan*, was fired for writing articles critical of the religious establishment.

Religious freedom does not exist in Saudi Arabia, the birthplace of Islam and the location of the two holiest cities of Islam, Mecca and Medina. Islam is Saudi Arabia's official religion, and all citizens are required by law to be Muslims. The government prohibits the public practice of any religions other than Islam. Although the government recognizes the right of non-Muslims to worship in private, it does not always respect this right in practice. Academic freedom is restricted in Saudi Arabia, and informers monitor classrooms for compliance with limits on curriculums, such as a ban on teaching Western philosophy and religions other than Islam.

Saudi citizens do not have any associational or organizational rights, and there is no freedom to form political organizations or to hold protests. In October, Saudi security officials detained hundreds of protestors calling for political reform. Trade unions, collective bargaining, and strikes are prohibited.

The judiciary lacks independence from the monarchy. The king appoints all judges on the recommendation of the Supreme Judicial Council, and the monarchy serves as the highest court of appeal. The rule of law is regularly flouted by the Saudi regime, with frequent trials falling short of international standards. Secret trials are common, and political opponents of the Saudi regime are often detained without charge and held for indefinite periods of time. Allegations of torture by police and prison officials are frequent, though access to prisoners by independent human rights and legal organizations is strictly limited.

Although racial discrimination is illegal according to Saudi law, substantial prejudice against ethnic, religious, and national minorities exists. Foreign workers from Asia and Africa are subject to formal and informal discrimination and have difficulty obtaining justice.

Citizens have the right to own property and establish private businesses, but much private enterprise activity is connected with members of the ruling family and the government. Although Saudi Arabia first joined the General Agreement on Tariffs and Trade in 1993, its slow process of privatization and economic reform has prevented it from becoming a member of the World Trade Organization (WTO). In the past year, Saudi Arabia has taken steps to diversify its economic structures and establish government regulatory organizations to strengthen its market economy. The Saudi government passed a new foreign investment law that would ease restrictions on investment and announced plans to cut tax rates and custom duties. As a result, WTO head Supachai Panitchpakdi announced in 2003 that Saudi Arabia would likely be invited to join the WTO in early 2004.

Women are not treated as equal members of Saudi Arabian society. Women legally may not drive cars, and their use of public facilities is restricted when men are present. By law and custom, women cannot travel within or outside of the country without a male relative. Saudi laws discriminate against women in a range of matters including family law, and a woman's testimony is treated as inferior to a man's in court. The Committee to Prevent Vice and Promote Virtue, a semiautonomous religious police force commonly known as the *mutawa'een*, enforce a strict policy of segregation between men and women and oftentimes use physical punishment to ensure that women meet conservative standards of dress in public.

# Senegal

**Population:** 10,600,000    **Political Rights:** 2
**GNI/capita:** $490            **Civil Liberties:** 3
**Life Expectancy:** 53        **Status:** Free
**Religious Groups:** Muslim (94 percent), other [including
Roman Catholic and indigenous beliefs] (6 percent)
**Ethnic Groups:** Wolof (43.3 percent), Pular (23.8 percent),
Serer (14.7 percent), Jola (3.7 percent), Mandinka (3 percent),
Soninke (1.1 percent), European and Lebanese (1 percent),
other (9.4 percent)
**Capital:** Dakar

**Ten-Year Ratings Timeline (Political Rights, Civil Liberties, Status)**

| 1994 | 1995 | 1996 | 1997 | 1998 | 1999 | 2000 | 2001 | 2002 | 2003 |
|------|------|------|------|------|------|------|------|------|------|
| 4,5PF | 4,5PF | 4,4PF | 4,4PF | 4,4PF | 4,4PF | 3,4PF | 3,4PF | 2,3F | 2,3F |

**Overview:**    Two incidents in Senegal in 2003 outraged advocates for a free press and political freedom in the country. In October, the government of President Abdoulaye Wade expelled a correspondent for Radio France Internationale (RFI) after RFI aired an interview that the reporter conducted with a hard-line member of the separatist Movement of the Democratic Forces of Casamance (MFDC). A violent attack on an opposition leader during the same month led human rights activists, labor leaders, and political opposition leaders to protest in November against what they said were recent acts of political violence that had gone unpunished.

Since independence from France in 1960, Senegal has escaped military or harshly authoritarian rule. President Leopold Senghor exercised de facto one-party rule under the Socialist Party for more than a decade after independence. Most political restrictions were lifted after 1981. Abdou Diouf, of the Socialist Party, succeeded Senghor in 1981 and won large victories in unfair elections in 1988 and 1993.

Wade's victory in the presidential poll in 2000—his fifth attempt to win the presidency—overturned four decades of rule by the Socialist Party. Wade captured 59.5 percent of the runoff vote, against 41.5 percent for Abdou Diouf. The election was judged to have been free and fair by international observers.

The people of Senegal adopted a new constitution by an overwhelming majority in January 2001, reducing presidential terms from seven to five years, setting the number of terms at two, and giving women the right to own land for the first time. President Wade dissolved the National Assembly, which had been dominated by the former ruling Socialist Party, and elections were held in April. A coalition led by Wade won 89 of the 120 seats available, followed by the Socialist Party with 10; smaller parties captured the remainder of seats.

The government indicated its sensitivity over problems in the southern Casamance region when the Interior Ministry in 2003 accused an RFI reporter of trying to sabotage the peace process that is aimed at ending a two-decades-old conflict there between secessionist forces and government troops. The journalist, who reported about divisions within the MFDC, was expelled. One impediment to achieving lasting peace has been divisions within the MFDC between moderate and hard-line members.

A growing number of Westerners working in the region are moving to Senegal's capital, Dakar, from Abidjan, in Cote d'Ivoire, where violent acts of xenophobia are on the increase. Senegal is considered one of the most stable countries in West Africa.

Senegal's population is mostly engaged in subsistence agriculture. The country's economy has enjoyed modest growth since the mid-1990s.

**Political Rights and Civil Liberties:** Citizens of Senegal can change their government democratically. Changes to the 1992 Electoral Code lowered the voting age to 18, introduced secret balloting, and created a nominally fairer electoral framework. The National Observatory of Elections, which was created in 1997, performed credibly in overseeing the 1998 legislative polls and the presidential elections in 2000.

Freedom of expression is generally respected, and members of the independent media are often highly critical of the government and political parties. There are about 20 independent radio stations, some of which broadcast in rural areas. The government does not carry out formal censorship, but some self-censorship is practiced because of laws against "discrediting the state" and disseminating "false news" that President Abdoulaye Wade had promised to repeal. International press freedom organizations maintain that media rights have become more restricted under Wade. It is not unusual for journalists to be detained for questioning by authorities and pressured to reveal confidential sources. There are no official impediments to Internet access.

A Dakar-based correspondent for RFI, Sophie Malibeaux, was expelled in October after the station aired an interview she conducted with Alexandre Djiba, a member of the MFDC, who has taken a harder line in negotiations with the government to end the Casamance conflict. The government accused Malibeaux of trying to sabotage the peace process. In August, Abdou Latif Coulibaly, the author of a recent book that was critical of Wade, said he had been receiving anonymous death threats. Coulibaly, director of the independent Sud FM radio station, blamed the threats on members of the ruling party.

Religious freedom in Senegal, which is 94 percent Muslim, is respected. Rivalries between Islamic groups have sometimes erupted into violence. Academic freedom is guaranteed and respected.

Freedom of association and assembly are guaranteed, but authorities have sometimes limited these right in practice. Human rights groups working on local and regional issues are among many nongovernmental organizations that operate freely. Thousands of people marched through Dakar in November to protest what they said were recent acts of political violence that had gone unpunished. The demonstration was triggered by a violent attack in October on an outspoken member of the political opposition, Talla Sylla, who was beaten with a hammer; Sylla is seeking redress in court. The protesters also demanded an explanation for arson attacks on the National Confederation of Workers and the independent Wal Fadjri radio station. An assailant linked to the attack reportedly was a member of the presidential guard and had been questioned by authorities; he later died in a car accident.

Although union rights to organize, bargain collectively, and strike are legally protected, there are some restrictions on freedom of association and the right to strike. Most workers are employed in the informal business and agricultural sectors. Nearly all of the country's small industrialized workforce is unionized, and workers are a potent political force.

Poor pay and lack of tenure protections create conditions for external influence on a judiciary that is, by statute, independent. In high-profile cases, there is often considerable interference from political and economic elites. Uncharged detainees are incarcerated without legal counsel far beyond the lengthy periods already permitted by law.

There are credible reports that authorities beat suspects during questioning and pretrial detention, despite constitutional protection against such treatment. Prison conditions are poor. Reports of disappearances and extrajudicial killings in connection with the conflict in Casamance occur less frequently. Peace accords between the government and MFDC were signed in 2001. Although the conflict has not come to a definitive end, armed resistance has all but ceased.

Constitutional rights afforded women are often not honored, especially in the countryside, and women have fewer opportunities than men for education and formal sector employment. In 2001, Senegal's first female prime minister was appointed. Despite governmental campaigns, domestic violence against women is reportedly common. Many elements of Sharia (Islamic law) and local customary law, particularly those regarding inheritance and marital relations, discriminate against women. Although Senegal banned female genital mutilation in 1999, it is still practiced among some ethnic groups.

# ⬇ Serbia and Montenegro

**Population:** 10,700,000   **Political Rights:** 3
**GNI/capita:** $930   **Civil Liberties:** 2
**Life Expectancy:** 73   **Status:** Free
**Religious Groups:** Orthodox (65 percent),
Muslim (19 percent), Roman Catholic (4 percent),
other (12 percent)
**Ethnic Groups:** Serb (63 percent), Albanian (17 percent),
Montenegrin (5 percent), Hungarian (3 percent), other (12 percent)
**Capital:** Belgrade
**Trend Arrow:** Serbia and Montenegro received a downward trend arrow due to the
assassination of Prime Minister Zoran Djindjic and the government's subsequent
response to the killing, as well as increased reports of corruption within the ruling
governments of both Serbia and Montenegro.

*Name Change*: On February 5, 2003, the Yugoslav parliament adopted a constitutional charter establishing the state of Serbia and Montenegro. Unless specifically
noted, references to Serbia and Montenegro in this chapter do not pertain to Kosovo.

**Ten-Year Ratings Timeline (Political Rights, Civil Liberties, Status)**

| 1994 | 1995 | 1996 | 1997 | 1998 | 1999 | 2000 | 2001 | 2002 | 2003 |
|------|------|------|------|------|------|------|------|------|------|
| 6,6NF | 6,6NF | 6,6NF | 6,6NF | 6,6NF | 5,5PF | 4,4PF | 3,3PF | 3,2F | 3,2F |

**Overview:**   The dangers facing reformers in post-Communist southeastern Europe became evident in 2003 when Serbian prime
minister Zoran Djindjic was assassinated in Belgrade on
March 12. His assassins came from a mixed group of organized crime figures and
members of Milosevic-era security structures. In the wake of Djindjic's assassination, the government declared a state of emergency, and police conducted a massive operation to apprehend those responsible that drew criticism from human rights
groups. In November, presidential elections in Serbia were declared invalid after less
than 50 percent of the electorate participated, as required by law. Meanwhile, in
Montenegro, the political situation remained tense as allegations emerged that
government officials at the highest levels were involved in smuggling and sex
trafficking.

In April 1992, the former Yugoslav republics of Serbia and Montenegro jointly
proclaimed the formation of the Federal Republic of Yugoslavia (FRY) after Marshal
Josip Broz Tito's Socialist Federal Republic of Yugoslavia (SFRY) disintegrated in
1991. Throughout the 1990s, Slobodan Milosevic's Socialist Party of Serbia (SPS)
ruled the country by virtue of its control over the country's security forces, financial and monetary institutions, and state-owned media. The first serious damage to
Milosevic's power came in 1996, when the Serbian opposition won numerous municipal elections and the SPS lost control of the main urban areas in the country. In
1997, an anti-Milosevic coalition of political forces came to power in Montenegro. In
1999, NATO occupied one of the FRY's two autonomous provinces, Kosovo, after

conducting a 78-day bombing campaign. The final end for the Milosevic regime came on October 5, 2000, when a botched attempt to steal the September presidential elections resulted in hundreds of thousands of people converging on Belgrade to overthrow the Milosevic regime. On October 6, Milosevic publicly conceded to the DOS's Vojislav Kostunica, who had defeated Milosevic in the September poll.

The Democratic Opposition of Serbia (DOS), a coalition of 18 political parties and one independent trade union, took power following parliamentary elections in December 2000. Despite the DOS's victory in Serbia, however, improving relations between the constituent republics of the FRY has been difficult throughout the post-Milosevic period. In March 2002, the European Union (EU) brokered what has become known as the Belgrade Agreement. It created a new state, now simply called "Serbia and Montenegro," that would preserve some vestiges of a common state but also provide each republic with its own currency, central bank, and separate customs and taxation systems. Since that time, the EU has begun voicing support for a stronger union of the two republics. Nevertheless, the new union was proving problematic, as it gave Montenegro—which is only one-tenth the size of Serbia in population and contributes a negligible part of the overall Serbia and Montenegro economy—parity representation in most organs of government, and also because of differences over cooperation with the International Criminal Tribunal for the former Yugoslavia (ICTY). Ratification of the Belgrade Agreement took place only in January 2003.

Despite the ratification of the Belgrade Agreement, the future of Serbia and Montenegro remains unclear. There is some debate within Serbia itself over whether it would be preferable for Serbia to go it alone in its efforts to gain EU accession, rather than maintaining ties with Montenegro. Moreover, in light of the still unresolved issue of the Serbian territory of Kosovo and the uneasy truce in Serbia's Presevo Valley (which contains a sizable Albanian population), Serbia and Montenegro continues to face a very uncertain future. On the more positive side, Serbia and Montenegro is expected to be invited to join NATO's Partnership for Peace in 2004.

Within Serbia itself, the dominant parties and political leaders of the DOS for most of the post-Milosevic period were the Democratic Party of Serbia (DSS), led by Kostunica, and the Democratic Party (DS), led by the late Serbian premier Zoran Djindjic. On March 12, Djindjic was assassinated by a group of organized crime figures and members of Milosevic-era security structures. With Djindjic's killing, Serbia lost one of its most capable politicians, and over the summer, revelations emerged of the involvement of some members of the DS in a variety of corruption scandals. Further eroding the DS's public support was the revelation that it had orchestrated a controversial quorum in the parliament to elect a new National Bank governor.

Presidential elections held in November failed because the most attractive candidates, Kostunica and former federal vice premier Miroljub Labus, refused to participate. Only 37 percent of the electorate turned out, far short of the required 50 percent required for a valid election, which precipitated new parliamentary elections in December. It was unclear to what extent the parliamentary elections would resolve the country's governmental crisis.

In Montenegro, Milo Djukanovic, the president since 1998, decided to step down from his post in 2002 and assume the republic's prime ministerial position. Two attempts to elect a new president that year failed after the elections did not attract the required 50 percent voter turnout. In February 2003, a new presidential law came into force that dropped the 50 percent rule. Subsequently, in May, Filip Vujanovic, the Djukanovic party candidate, was elected. Vujanovic won 64 percent of the votes, with 48.3 percent of eligible voters participating. Opposition parties refused to field candidates, although the Organization for Security and Cooperation in Europe (OSCE) deemed the elections to be generally in line with international standards.

Frequent charges of corruption against high-ranking members of Djukanovic's regime continued to harm the government's reputation. In June, an Italian judge in Naples investigating organized crime and smuggling issued formal arrest requests for several Montenegrin officials, including Djukanovic himself, though most observers believed Djukanovic would enjoy immunity because of his high-level government position. Djukanovic's reputation suffered a further blow when the former interior minister in his government accused him of being personally involved in the trafficking of sex slaves.

Montenegro remains split between the majority of the Orthodox Christian population that declares itself to be Montenegrin and/or Serb and wants to maintain ties with Belgrade, and a minority of the Orthodox Christian population, supported by ethnic Albanians in Montenegro and some Muslims in the mainly Muslim Sandzak region, who prefer independence. (Many Muslims, however, prefer maintaining the union because separation would mean the division of Sandzak region between two independent states.) The pro-independence cause suffered a setback in 2003 when a new census showed that 30 percent of the Montenegrin population declared itself to be Serb, an increase of some 21 percent over the past decade and a further indication of how strong ethnic and emotional ties between Serbia and Montenegro remain.

**Political Rights and Civil Liberties:** Citizens of Serbia and Montenegro can change their government democratically. Throughout the 1990s, the Milosevic regime manipulated and falsified election results. Opposition parties were routinely denied access to the main electronic media in the country, and the tabulation of votes was extremely suspect. However, the DOS victory in October 2000 significantly changed the way in which elections are conducted. Citizens in both Serbia and Montenegro can now choose their leaders in generally free and fair elections. In Montenegro's February 2003 presidential vote, monitoring organizations reported that Milo Djukanovic's Democratic Party of Socialists (DPS) threatened workers in state-owned enterprises to vote for the DPS candidate.

Freedom of the press has improved vastly since the Milosevic period, when the regime enjoyed the support of state-owned media and some prominent members of the independent media were assassinated by "unknown" assailants. However, during the state of emergency imposed after the assassination of Prime Minister Zoran Djindjic on March 12, 2004, many journalists and media watchdog groups criticized the government for going too far in censoring critical coverage of the government's crackdown on organized crime groups.

Libel is still listed as a criminal offense in Serbia, and several government officials filed libel charges against journalists and political opponents during 2003. In July 2002, the Montenegrin parliament passed several changes to its Media Law that drew criticism from domestic and international watchdog groups. The new regulations require editors to consult political parties about the content and even the headlines of articles, and restrict the number of articles that can be published about parties during the campaign. There were no reports of the government restricting access to the Internet, although there were reports that the police monitored e-mail traffic during the massive operation undertaken to apprehend those responsible for Djindjic's assassination.

According to the constitution, all citizens enjoy freedom of religious belief. However, with ethnic and religious identities closely intertwined in the region, increases in interethnic tensions often take on the appearance of religious intolerance. Restitution of church property nationalized by the Communists remains a point of dispute between church and state. There were no reports that the government attempted to restrict academic freedom during the year.

Citizens enjoy freedom of association and assembly. Numerous political parties exist and compete for power in elections. Foreign and domestic nongovernmental organizations (NGOs) enjoy the freedom to pursue their activities. New laws are currently being drafted to codify relations between trade unions and the government.

Significant legal and judicial reform is under way. However, the judicial system is still plagued by a large backlog of cases, underpaid judges and state prosecutors, and an excess of judges left over from the Milosevic era. There are reports that the system takes an excessively long time in filing formal charges against suspects. Moreover, the authority and independence of the judicial system continue to suffer as a result of the failure of legislative institutions to heed judicial rulings. In 2002, for instance, the Constitutional Court of Serbia ruled that the government's revocation of the mandates of some 40 members of parliament belonging to the DSS was unconstitutional. However, the Djindjic government consistently refused to comply with the court's order to reinstate the DSS deputies. An EU report issued in March 2003 noted that little progress had been made in reforming the police and the judiciary in the post-Milosevic period. Prison conditions generally meet international standards.

After Djindjic's assassination in March, the government declared a state of emergency and the police conducted a massive operation code-named "Operation Sabre" to apprehend those responsible. Some 10,000 people were taken into custody in the ensuing months. Human rights groups warned that the government campaign was excessive and that many aspects of the crackdown, such as media restrictions and a suspension of the rights of the accused to legal representation, were violating civil liberties. There were also serious reports that many individuals taken into custody were victims of torture and other forms of police abuse.

Cultural and ethnic minorities have their own political parties, access to media in their mother tongue, and other types of associations. Nevertheless, the number of individuals from ethnic minorities participating in government does not represent their percentages in the entire population. An important constitutional and political challenge facing Serbia and Montenegro is to satisfy increasing demands from regions with large ethnic minorities, such as Kosovo, Sandzak, and Vojvodina. Similarly, there are frequent complaints of unfair treatment and police harassment of the Roma (Gypsy) community.

Although women are legally entitled to equal pay for equal work, traditional patriarchal attitudes prevalent throughout the Balkans often limit women's roles in the economy. In 2003, women held several highly visible governmental positions, including acting president of Serbia and governor of the National Bank of Serbia. However, in general, women are underrepresented in higher levels of government. Domestic violence remains a serious problem. According to one estimate, 50 percent of the women in Serbia and Montenegro have been the victims of domestic violence.

Some towns in southern Serbia have become an important part of the network trafficking women from the former Soviet Union to Western Europe for purposes of forced prostitution. In one especially noteworthy case in 2003, a Moldovan woman accused senior Montenegrin officials of involvement in human trafficking and the promotion of sex slavery. The case collapsed in May, allegedly because of a "lack of evidence." The Council of Europe and the OSCE both criticized the way the Montenegrin judiciary handled the case, and the investigating judge in the case claimed she had been harassed by the Djukanovic government's security services.

# Seychelles

**Population:** 100,000
**GNI/capita:** $6,530
**Life Expectancy:** 70
**Religious Groups:** Roman Catholic (86.6 percent), Anglican (6.8 percent), other (6.6 percent)
**Ethnic Groups:** Seychellois [mixture of Asian, African and European]
**Capital:** Victoria

**Political Rights:** 3
**Civil Liberties:** 3
**Status:** Partly Free

**Ten-Year Ratings Timeline (Political Rights, Civil Liberties, Status)**

| 1994 | 1995 | 1996 | 1997 | 1998 | 1999 | 2000 | 2001 | 2002 | 2003 |
|------|------|------|------|------|------|------|------|------|------|
| 3,4PF | 3,3PF | 3,3PF | 3,3PF | 3,3PF | 3,3PF | 3,3PF | 3,3PF | 3,3PF | 3,3PF |

**Overview:**     The long-time president of Seychelles, France Albert Rene, indicated in 2003 that he would begin transferring some of his presidential functions to his heir apparent, Vice President James Michel.

Seychelles, an archipelago of some 115 islands in the western Indian Ocean, was a French colony until 1810. It was then colonized by Britain until its independence in 1976. The country functioned as a multiparty democracy for only one year before Rene, then prime minister, seized power, in June 1977, by ousting President James Mancham. Mancham and other opposition leaders operated parties and human rights groups in exile after Rene made his ruling Seychelles People's Progressive Front (SPPF) the sole legal party.

Rene won one-party "show" elections in 1979, 1984, and 1989. By 1992, however, the SPPF had passed a constitutional amendment to legalize opposition parties, and many exiled leaders returned to participate in a constitutional commission and multiparty elections. Rene won a legitimate electoral mandate in the country's first multiparty poll in 1993.

The March 1998 presidential and legislative elections were accepted as generally legitimate by opposition parties, which had waged a vigorous campaign. The Seychelles National Party (SNP), led by the Reverend Wavel Ramkalawan, emerged as the strongest opposition group; the party espouses economic liberalization, which Rene has resisted. However, SPPF control over state resources and most media gave ruling-party candidates significant advantages in the polls, and both Rene and the SPPF were returned to power.

The political dominance of President Rene and the SPPF was shaken in the August 2001 presidential election. The opposition increased its vote total from 20 to 45 percent, and Rene's narrow victory engendered widespread opposition complaints of fraud. An official observer delegation from the Commonwealth concluded that the elections were peaceful, but not entirely free and fair.

The SNP subsequently filed a complaint with the Seychelles Constitutional Court, claiming that the incumbent extended his campaign beyond the official period, overtly intimidated voters, and put the names of deceased or under-aged persons on the lists of registered voters. The case was rejected by the Constitutional Court.

In October 2002, Rene dissolved parliament and called for early legislative elections in December. The SPPF won the poll, but the SNP made significant inroads, winning 43 percent of the vote.

In 2003, Rene indicated that he would begin to transfer some of his presidential duties to his vice president and chosen successor, James Michel. President Rene also currently heads the country's Defense, Interior, and Legal Affairs ministries. The next presidential election is due in 2006.

## Political Rights and Civil Liberties:

Citizens of the Seychelles can change their government democratically, though with some limitations. The current constitution was drafted in 1993 by an elected constitutional commission. Seychelles had become a one-party state under the regime established following the 1977 military coup, but legislation to allow opposition parties was passed in December 1991.

The president and the National Assembly are elected by universal adult suffrage for five-year terms. As amended in 1996, the constitution provides for a 34-member National Assembly, with 25 members directly elected and 9 allocated on a proportional basis to parties with at least 10 percent of the vote. Other amendments have strengthened the powers of the president, whose term of office is five years with a maximum of three consecutive terms. Local governments composed of district councils were reconstituted in 1991 after their abolition two decades earlier.

The leadership of the opposition SNP claims that its sympathizers are harassed by police and are victims of public sector job-related security investigations, which are generally carried out by agents of the ruling SPPF at the district level.

Freedom of speech has improved since one-party rule was abolished in 1993. There is one daily government newspaper, *The Nation*, and at least two other newspapers support or are published by the SPPF. Independent newspapers are sharply critical of the government, but government dominance and the threat of libel suits restrict media freedom, and some self-censorship persists. The opposition weekly

*Regar* has been sued repeatedly for libel under broad constitutional restrictions on free expression. The Seychelles Broadcasting Corporation's board of directors includes only SPPF partisans and a single official from former President James Mancham's Democratic Party. High licensing fees have discouraged the development of privately owned broadcast media.

The government respects freedom of religion in this predominantly Roman Catholic country.

Private nongovernmental organizations, including human rights–related groups, operate in the country. The right to strike is formally protected by the 1993 Industrial Relations Act, but is limited by several regulations. The SPPF-associated National Workers' Union no longer monopolizes union activity, and two independent unions are now active.

The judiciary includes the Supreme Court, the Constitutional Court, a court of appeals, an industrial court, and magistrates' courts. Judges generally decide cases fairly, but they still face interference in cases involving major economic or political actors. There are no Seychellois judges, and the impartiality of the non-Seychellois magistrates can be compromised by the fact that their tenure is subject to contract renewal. Security forces have been accused of using excessive force, including torture and arbitrary detention, especially in attempting to curb crime.

The government does not restrict domestic travel, but may deny passports for reasons of "national interest." Nearly all of Seychelles' political and economic life is dominated by people of European and Asian origin. Islanders of Creole extraction face de facto discrimination, and discrimination against foreign workers has been reported. President France Albert Rene and his party continue to control government jobs, contracts, and resources.

Women are less likely than men to be literate, and they enjoy fewer educational opportunities. While almost all adult females are classified as "economically active," most are engaged in subsistence agriculture. Domestic violence against women, reportedly widespread, is rarely prosecuted and only lightly punished.

# Sierra Leone

**Population:** 5,700,000
**GNI/capita:** $140
**Life Expectancy:** 43
**Religious Groups:** Muslim (60 percent), indigenous
beliefs (30 percent), Christian (10 percent)
**Ethnic Groups:** Temne (30 percent), Mende (30 percent),
other tribes (30 percent), Creole (10 percent)
**Capital:** Freetown

**Political Rights:** 4
**Civil Liberties:** 3*
**Status:** Partly Free

**Ratings Change:** Sierra Leone's civil liberties rating improved from 4 to 3 due to improved security in the country and increased pressures to punish those guilty of war crimes.

**Ten-Year Ratings Timeline (Political Rights, Civil Liberties, Status)**

| 1994 | 1995 | 1996 | 1997 | 1998 | 1999 | 2000 | 2001 | 2002 | 2003 |
|------|------|------|------|------|------|------|------|------|------|
| 7,6NF | 7,6NF | 4,5PF | 7,6NF | 3,5PF | 3,5PF | 4,5PF | 4,5PF | 4,4PF | 4,3PF |

**Overview:** Sierra Leone began pursuing war crimes suspects in 2003 through the UN-backed Special Court for Sierra Leone to address abuses committed during the country's decade-long civil war. In November, the UN High Commissioner for Human Rights said that the human rights situation in Sierra Leone had improved markedly in 2003, but noted that the country still faced the challenge of punishing offenders and dealing with ongoing abuses. During the year, UN peacekeepers continue a phased withdrawal from the country.

Founded by Britain in 1787 as a haven for liberated slaves, Sierra Leone became independent in 1961. The Revolutionary United Front (RUF) launched a guerrilla campaign from neighboring Liberia in 1991 to end 23 years of increasingly corrupt one-party rule by President Joseph Momoh. Power fell into the lap of Captain Valentine Strasser in 1992, when he and other junior officers attempted to confront Momoh about poor pay and working conditions at the front. Momoh fled the country. The Strasser regime hired South African soldiers from the security company Executive Outcomes to help win back key diamond-rich areas. In January 1996, Brigadier Julius Maada-Bio quietly deposed Strasser. Elections proceeded despite military and rebel intimidation, and voters elected Ahmad Tejan Kabbah, a former UN diplomat, as president.

The following year, Major Johnny Paul Koroma toppled the Kabbah government, established the Armed Forces Revolutionary Council, and invited the RUF to join the junta. Nigerian-led West African troops, backed by logistical and intelligence support from the British company Sandline, restored Kabbah to power in February 1998, but the country continued to be racked by war. A peace agreement in July 1999 led to the beginning of disarmament, but the process stopped in May 2000 with a return to hostilities and the taking of about 500 peacekeepers as hostages. British troops flew in to help, and disarmament resumed in May 2001.

In the May 2002 presidential poll, in which eight candidates competed, Kabbah was reelected with 70 percent of the vote, compared with 22 percent for Ernest

Koroma of the All People's Congress (APC). The RUF candidate, Alimamy Pallo Bangura, lagged with barely 2 percent of the vote. Kabbah's Sierra Leone People's Party (SLPP) dominated parliamentary elections the same month, winning 83 of 112 available seats, followed by the APC with 27; Koroma's party won 2 seats.

A phased withdrawal of the 17,300-strong UN Mission in Sierra Leone, the world's largest peacekeeping mission, began in October. Only 2,000 peacekeepers are expected to remain in Sierra Leone by December 2004. More than 45,000 fighters have been disarmed, but their reintegration into civilian life has been slow. Although Sierra Leone's decade-long war has ended, Kabbah still faces daunting problems, many of which contributed to causing the war. Entrenched corruption, a culture of impunity, rampant poverty, and unequal distribution of the country's diamond wealth must be adequately addressed if the country is to enjoy lasting peace.

During 2003, victims, perpetrators, and witnesses told their stories to the Truth and Reconciliation Commission. The special court indicted more than a dozen people, including Charles Taylor, who stepped down as president of Liberia in August and accepted Nigeria's offer of asylum. Taylor was accused of backing the former rebel RUF with weapons in exchange for diamonds.

The departure of Taylor and the growing prospect for peace in Liberia bodes well for lasting peace in Sierra Leone. However, insecurity along the borders of Liberia, Sierra Leone, Guinea, and Cote d'Ivoire is perilous for the entire region. The UN Commission for Human Rights said that there had been some progress in providing reintegration opportunities for former combatants, but that long-term reintegration could only be achieved through revival of the economy.

Sierra Leone has vast diamond resources, but smuggling and war have turned it into one of the world's poorest countries. A ban on rough-diamond imports from Sierra Leone does not include diamonds that carry proven certificates of origin from the government. Although the country's annual diamond production is valued at $200 million to $400 million per year, recorded shipments were worth a little more than $40 million in 2002 because of smuggling.

**Political Rights and Civil Liberties:** Citizens of Sierra Leone can change their government democratically. Presidential and legislative elections in February and March 1996 were imperfect, but were considered legitimate. Politicians, former combatants, and civil society representatives joined together in a conference in 2001 and approved a new electoral system for polls scheduled for the following year. Despite some logistical problems, the May 2002 presidential and parliamentary elections were considered the country's fairest since independence. President Ahmad Tejan Kabbah and his SLPP enjoyed the advantage of incumbency and state resources for both elections. Dozens of political parties have been formed, but many revolve around a specific personality and have little following.

Freedom of speech and of the press is guaranteed, but the government at times restricts these rights. Criminal libel laws are used occasionally to jail journalists. Several government and private radio and television stations broadcast, and newspapers openly criticize the government and armed factions. Dozens of newspapers are printed in Freetown, but most are of poor quality and often carry sensational or undocumented stories. The parastatal Sierratel communications company exercised a monopoly over land-line access to the Internet, although access was not officially impeded.

Freedom of religion is guaranteed and respected in practice. Academic freedom is guaranteed.

The rights of freedom of assembly and association are guaranteed, and these rights are generally respected. Several nongovernmental organizations and civic groups, including human rights groups, operate openly and freely. Workers have the right to join independent trade unions of their choice. About 60 percent of workers in urban areas, including government employees, are unionized. There is a legal framework for collective bargaining.

The judiciary is active, but corruption and a lack of resources are impediments. Despite these obstacles, the judiciary has demonstrated independence, and a number of trials have been free and fair. Local courts resumed sitting in all districts of the country in 2003. There are often lengthy pretrial detentions in harsh conditions. Eight judges—from Sierra Leone, Canada, Austria, The Gambia, the United Kingdom, and Nigeria—were appointed to sit on the UN-backed Special Court for Sierra Leone. Among those indicted for war crimes in 2003 included former RUF leader Foday Sankoh, who died while in detention. RUF commander Sam Bockarie, who was also indicted, was killed in Liberia.

Sierra Leone's Truth and Reconciliation Commission, modeled on South Africa's truth commission, was expected to hear testimony from some 700 perpetrators of human rights abuses, victims, and witnesses. The aim of the commission, which has collected about 6,000 written statements, is to create an impartial historical record of violations and abuses, address impunity and the needs of victims, and promote healing and reconciliation.

Sierra Leone once had one of Africa's worst human rights records. Abduction, maiming, rape, forced conscription, and extrajudicial killing were commonplace. Although security has improved considerably, lack of equipment for security forces and poor infrastructure could hinder longer-term efforts to keep a lid on unrest in Sierra Leone, especially if demobilized combatants lack opportunities for employment. A number of national and international nongovernmental organizations and human rights groups operate openly in Freetown.

Despite constitutionally guaranteed equal rights, women face extensive legal and de facto discrimination, as well as limited access to education and formal (business) sector jobs. Married women have fewer property rights than men, especially in rural areas where customary law prevails. Abuse of women, including rape, sexual assault, and sexual slavery, were rampant during the war. Female genital mutilation is widespread.

# Singapore

**Population:** 4,200,000  **Political Rights:** 5
**GNI/capita:** $21,500  **Civil Liberties:** 4
**Life Expectancy:** 79  **Status:** Partly Free
**Religious Groups:** Buddhist, Muslim, Christian, other
**Ethnic Groups:** Chinese (77 percent), Malay (14 percent),
Indian (8 percent), other (1 percent)
**Capital:** Singapore

**Ten-Year Ratings Timeline (Political Rights, Civil Liberties, Status)**

| 1994 | 1995 | 1996 | 1997 | 1998 | 1999 | 2000 | 2001 | 2002 | 2003 |
|------|------|------|------|------|------|------|------|------|------|
| 5,5PF | 5,5PF | 4,5PF | 5,5PF | 5,5PF | 5,5PF | 5,5PF | 5,5PF | 5,4PF | 5,4PF |

**Overview:**  Battered by the effects of war in Iraq, slowdowns in key export markets, and Asia's severe acute respiratory syndrome (SARS) virus, Singapore's trade-dependent economy shrank sharply in the spring of 2003 and grew only slowly for the rest of the year, throwing tens of thousands of people out of work. Meanwhile, Prime Minister Goh Chok Tong formally named Deputy Prime Minister Lee Hsien Loong as his successor. Lee is expected to make few major changes to the city-state's authoritarian politics or market-driven economic policies after he takes over sometime before the next election, which is due by 2006.

Located along major shipping routes in Southeast Asia, Singapore became a British colony in 1867. Occupied by the Japanese during World War II, the city-state became self-governing in 1959, entered the Malaysian Federation in 1963, and became fully independent in 1965 under Prime Minister Lee Kuan Yew. Under Lee, the ruling People's Action Party (PAP) transformed a squalid port city into a regional financial center and an exporter of high-tech goods. At the same time, Lee restricted individual freedoms and stunted political development.

The PAP won every seat in every election from 1968 to 1981, when the Workers' Party's J. B. Jeyaretnam won a seat in a by-election. In 1990, Lee handed power to Goh, who has largely continued Lee's conservative policies and has kept the PAP dominant in parliament. Although the PAP easily won the 1997 elections, the campaign featured a rare airing in Singapore of diverse views on policy issues. Goh responded by warning that neighborhoods voting against the PAP would be the lowest priority for upgrades of public housing estates, where some 85 percent of Singaporeans live.

During the campaign for the 2001 parliamentary elections, opposition candidates criticized the government for not doing more to help Singaporeans hurt by the country's first recession since independence. The PAP campaigned on the theme that no other party had the skills and experience to revive the economy. Repeating a tactic from the 1997 election campaign, the PAP also linked priority for public housing upgrades to support for the ruling party. On election day, the PAP received 75 percent of the vote and won 82 of parliament's 84 seats. Opposition parties contested only 29 seats, with the leftist Workers' Party and centrist Singapore People's Party winning 1 seat each. Veteran opposition politician Jeyaretnam was barred from contesting the elections after the court of appeal declared him bankrupt for being one day late in paying an installment on a damages award to PAP politicians who had successfully sued him for defamation. As a bankrupt individual, Jeyaretnam was barred from practicing law, thrown out of parliament, and prevented from running for office.

The triple blow in 2003 of SARS, the Iraq war, and the global economic slowdown highlighted yet again tiny Singapore's vulnerability to external forces. The SARS virus, which originated in China, killed at least 33 people in Singapore, kept consumers at home in the city-state, and caused many travelers to steer clear of the region. Singapore's economy shrank by 4.3 percent year-on-year in the second quarter before growing slightly in the second half of 2003. Unemployment rose to a 17-year high of 5.9 percent in the third quarter, up from 4.5 percent the previous quarter. Part of this unemployment is structural, with some workers losing jobs as Singapore makes the transition to a more high-end economy in the face of competition from China and other low-wage countries.

The 62-year-old Goh's long-expected announcement that Lee Hsien Loong would succeed him as the PAP's leader, and thereby become Singapore's next prime minister, came with a pledge not to stand down until there are signs of an economic recovery. While Lee, the eldest son of Singapore's founding prime minister, Lee Kuan Yew, is not expected to make any major policy changes, he is likely to bring a more no-nonsense leadership style to the top office. By contrast, Goh, who made the announcement during his National Day speech on August 17, has tried to put a gentler face on the PAP's authoritarian rule.

During the year, authorities remained vigilant to terrorist threats after having arrested some three dozen suspected Islamic militants since 2001.

**Political Rights and Civil Liberties:** Citizens of Singapore cannot change their government democratically. Singapore's 1959 constitution created a parliamentary system where the prime minister and other lawmakers are directly elected for five-year terms. Two amendments authorize the government to appoint additional members of parliament in order to ensure that the opposition has at least three seats. Separately, a 1993 amendment provides for direct elections for the largely ceremonial presidency and gave the president some budget-oversight powers and authority over civil service appointments and internal security matters. The government has used a strict vetting process to prevent any real competition for the office. The current president, S. R. Nathan, a PAP veteran and former ambassador, won the 1999 election by default after the Presidential Election Commission barred three other candidates on the grounds that they lacked either the requisite competence or integrity.

The PAP runs an efficient, competent, and largely corruption-free government and appears to enjoy genuine popular support. It chalks up its electoral success to its record of having helped to build Singapore into a modern, wealthy society and, it says, the opposition's lack of credible candidates and ideas. Opposition parties, however, say that the playing field is uneven because of the government's influence over the press and its use of an array of laws to limit dissent.

Another factor arguably working against the opposition is its difficulty in fielding viable slates for parliament's multimember districts. Each Group Representation

Constituency (GRC) has three to six seats, and each GRC candidate slate must include at least one ethnic minority candidate. The party with a plurality in the district wins all the seats. The current parliament has 15 GRCs and only 9 single-member districts.

Moreover, the government requires candidates for all seats to pay a deposit of S$13,000 (US$7,123) that is forfeited if the candidate does not win a certain percentage of the vote. Parties and candidates also face restrictions on the types of materials that they can distribute during election campaigns and cannot advertise using political films or videos. Opposition politicians are also constrained by the PAP's record of winning civil defamation suits against political foes.

Singapore's press is somewhat freer than in past years, although most major media outlets are linked to the government and journalists face subtle pressure from the ruling party. Journalists often avoid reporting on sensitive topics, including alleged government corruption or nepotism or on the supposed compliance of the judiciary. Although editorials and news coverage generally reflect government policies, newspapers increasingly are carrying letters, columns, and editorials critical of government policies.

The government has not wielded Singapore's harsh Internal Security Act (ISA)—which allows the government to restrict publications that incite violence, might arouse tensions among racial or religious groups, or might threaten national interests, national security, or public order—against the press in recent years. Nevertheless, the ISA's broad provisions leave editors and reporters unclear about what may safely be published. Moreover, occasional statements by senior officials that certain topics are considered to be "out-of-bounds" are widely seen as implicit threats to invoke the ISA.

The Newspaper and Printing Presses Act allows authorities to restrict the circulation of any foreign periodical whose news coverage allegedly interferes in domestic politics. Foreign newspapers and magazines are available, although authorities at times have restricted the circulation of foreign publications that carried articles that the government found offensive.

The government screens and sometimes censors films, television, videos, music, books, and magazines, mainly for excessive amounts of sex, violence, and drug references. The PAP, however, in recent years has loosened some restrictions on the arts.

Companies with ties to the government run Internet service providers. Regulations from 1996 forbid Singaporeans from airing over the Internet information that is against the "public interest" or "national harmony," or that "offends against good taste or decency." In practice, however, authorities mainly block access to some pornographic Web sites. They have tolerated Web sites that host forums for political chat, which have become rare outlets in Singapore for lively political discussion.

Singaporeans of most faiths can worship freely. The Jehovah's Witnesses, however, is banned under the Societies Act because its roughly 2,000 members refuse to perform compulsory military service. Jehovah's Witnesses adherents can still practice their faith, but meetings are illegal. Moreover, several students who are Jehovah's Witnesses members recently have been suspended indefinitely from school for refusing to sing the national anthem or to salute the flag. Separately, several Muslim schoolgirls were suspended from school in 2002 after they defied a government ban preventing girls from wearing traditional Muslim headscarves in class.

The PAP prohibits public discussion of sensitive racial and religious issues and closely regulates political speech. Singaporeans must get police permits to hold public talks or to make political speeches or else face fines under the Public Entertainment and Meetings Act. Chee Soon Juan of the opposition Social Democratic Party has served a number of jail terms in recent years for making speeches without the necessary license or on sensitive issues and refusing to pay the resulting fines. Chee was fined S$3,000 ($1,700) for a speech in 2002. Under the constitution, Singaporeans who are fined more than S$2,000 ($1,100) cannot contest a parliamentary election for five years. The only place where Singaporeans can make public speeches without a license is Speakers' Corner, which is located in a downtown park. Speakers, however, must register with the police in advance. In addition, any public assembly of more than five people must receive police approval.

The government restricts freedom of association by wielding the strict provisions of the 1966 Societies Act, including one provision that permits only groups registered as political parties or associations to engage in organized political activities. For example, authorities in 2001 reclassified two groups that had been critical of the government—the Think Centre and the Open Singapore Centre—as political associations, which barred them from receiving foreign funding, among other restrictions. The Societies Act covers most organizations of more than ten people, and the government historically has denied mandatory registration to groups it considered a threat to public order.

Most unions are affiliated with the National Trade Unions Congress (NTUC), which freely acknowledges that its interests are closely aligned with those of the PAP. NTUC policy prohibits union members who support opposition parties from holding office in affiliated unions, and in 2002, a union official was stripped of his position after being elected secretary general of the opposition Singapore Democratic Alliance. The law prevents uniformed employees from joining unions. Around 15 percent of Singapore's workers are unionized. Workers have not staged a strike since 1986, in part because labor shortages have helped employees secure regular wage increases and have given them a high degree of job mobility.

The judiciary's independence has been called into question by the government's overwhelming success in court proceedings, particularly defamation suits against political opponents. It is not clear, however, whether the government pressures judges or simply appoints judges who share its conservative philosophy. Many judges have ties to the PAP and its leaders. In any case, the judiciary is efficient, and in criminal cases, defendants enjoy a presumption of innocence and the right to confront witnesses and other due process rights.

The government has the power to detain suspects without trial under both the ISA and the Criminal Law Act (CLA). While the ISA historically has been applied mainly against suspected Communist security threats, the government recently has used the law to detain suspected Islamic terrorists. The ISA allows authorities to detain suspects without charge or trial for an unlimited number of two-year periods. A 1989 constitutional amendment prohibits judicial review of the substantive grounds of detentions under the ISA and of the constitutionality of the law itself. In 2001, authorities arrested 15 suspected terrorists under the ISA. In 2002, during another sweep, 21 alleged members of Jemaah Islamiyah, the regional Islamic terrorist group, were detained. It is not clear how many remain in jail.

The government uses the CLA to detain mainly organized-crime or drug-trafficking suspects. Under the law, authorities may place a suspect in preventive detention for an initial one-year period, which the president can extend for additional one-year periods, subject to habeas corpus appeal to the courts. Meanwhile, the Misuse of Drugs Act allows authorities to commit without trial suspected drug users to rehabilitation centers for up to three years. In any given year, several thousand Singaporeans are in mandatory treatment and rehabilitation.

Police reportedly at times mistreat detainees, although the government in recent years has jailed several officers convicted of such abuses. The Penal Code mandates caning, in addition to imprisonment, for around 30 offenses involving the use of violence or threat of violence, and for nonviolent offenses including vandalism, drug trafficking, and certain immigration violations. Caning is discretionary for certain other crimes involving the use of force.

The government actively promotes racial harmony and equity in a society where race riots between Malays and the majority Chinese killed scores of people in the late 1960s. Ethnic Malays, however, have not on average achieved the schooling and income levels of ethnic Chinese or Tamils and reportedly face unofficial discrimination in private sector employment. Several government programs aim to boost educational achievement among Malay students.

Singaporean women enjoy the same legal rights as men in most areas, and many are well educated and hold professional jobs. Relatively few women, however, hold top positions in government and the private sector.

# Slovakia

**Population:** 5,400,000    **Political Rights:** 1
**GNI/capita:** $3,760    **Civil Liberties:** 2
**Life Expectancy:** 74    **Status:** Free
**Religious Groups:** Roman Catholic (60.3 percent),
Protestant (8.4 percent), other (11.6 percent)
**Ethnic Groups:** Slovak (86 percent), Hungarian
(11 percent), Roma [Gypsy] (2 percent), others [including
Czech] (31.3 percent)
**Capital:** Bratislava

**Ten-Year Ratings Timeline (Political Rights, Civil Liberties, Status)**

| 1994 | 1995 | 1996 | 1997 | 1998 | 1999 | 2000 | 2001 | 2002 | 2003 |
|------|------|------|------|------|------|------|------|------|------|
| 2,3F | 2,3F | 2,4PF | 2,4PF | 2,2F | 1,2F | 1,2F | 1,2F | 1,2F | 1,2F |

**Overview:**

In 2003, Slovakia continued its progress in 2003 toward joining the European Union (EU) and NATO. The country voted in favor of joining the EU in a May referendum and will formally become a member of that body in May 2004. In April, Slovakia's parliament ratified the country's accession to NATO, which it is expected to join in mid-2004.

Anti-Communist opposition forces brought about the collapse of the Czechoslovak government in 1989, and the country held its first free elections the following year. After elections in June 1992, negotiations began on increased Slovak autonomy within the Czech and Slovak Federative Republic. These discussions eventually led to a peaceful dissolution of the federation and the establishment of an independent Slovak Republic on January 1, 1993.

From 1993 to 1998, Vladimir Meciar—who served twice as prime minister during this period—and the Movement for a Democratic Slovakia (HZDS) dominated politics in newly independent Slovakia. Meciar battled with then president Michal Kovac over executive and governmental powers, opposed direct presidential elections, flouted the rule of law, and intimidated independent media. His policies resulted in Slovakia's failure to meet the criteria necessary to open EU accession talks and to join NATO.

In the 1998 parliamentary elections, voters supported a major shift in Slovakia's political orientation by rejecting Meciar's rule and electing a broad right-left coalition. The new parliament selected Mikulas Dzurinda as prime minister and pursued policies to enhance judicial independence, combat corruption, undertake economic reforms, and actively seek membership in the EU and NATO.

In September 2002, twenty-five parties competed in free and fair parliamentary elections, although only seven parties exceeded the 5 percent representation threshold. Meciar's HZDS obtained 19.5 percent of the vote (36 mandates), but his party did not receive sufficient support to form a new government. Prime Minister Dzurinda's Slovak Democratic and Christian Union (SDKU) finished second and succeeded in forming a center-right government in partnership with the Party of the Hungarian Coalition (SMK), the Christian Democratic Movement (KDH), and the Alliance of the New Citizen (ANO). Seventy percent of eligible voters participated in the election.

Slovak nongovernmental organizations (NGOs) were particularly active during the campaign, organizing get-out-the-vote initiatives, publishing voter education materials, and monitoring media coverage. By law, public television channels provided equal airtime to candidates during the official campaign period. While parties were free to advertise in newspapers, laws prohibited campaign advertising on private television. Although state and private television generally respected laws regarding objective political reporting, the government broadcast council cited the private TV Markiza for overly supportive coverage of the ANO party, led by Markiza's majority owner at that time, Pavol Rusko. Rusko, who in 2003 became minister of economy, subsequently divested himself of his ownership interest in Markiza but continued to influence the station's editorial policies.

In April 2003, parliament ratified Slovakia's accession to NATO, which is expected to take place in 2004. In a binding national referendum that was held the following month, Slovaks voted overwhelmingly in favor of joining the EU, with 92 percent supporting membership. Turnout for the referendum was a disappointing 52 percent of eligible voters, just slightly above the 50 percent needed to make the vote valid.

In November 2003, the European Commission in its annual progress report on future members and candidates stated, "Slovakia has reached a high level of alignment with the acquis communautaire [body of EU regulations] in most policy areas." The commission, however, urged that Slovakia take stronger measures to root out corruption, especially in the areas of conflict of interest, financing of political parties, and lobbying.

Along with other countries that have made NATO and EU membership strategic objectives and which are eager to have solid relations both with the United States and the EU, Slovakia has sought to find an appropriate political and diplomatic balance in its relations with the United States and the EU. The contentious debate over the Iraq war has generated intense pressure on the countries of Central Europe, which have discovered that finding their role within the transatlantic community has not gone as smoothly as anticipated in the era of global terrorism.

**Political Rights and Civil Liberties:** Slovak citizens can change their government democratically. Voters elect the president and members of the 150-seat National Council. A 2001 law grants voting privileges to foreigners, allowing permanent residents to vote in elections for municipal and regional governments.

Slovakia's media are largely free but remain vulnerable to criminal libel laws and political interference. In 2003, revelations that the Slovak Secret Service wiretapped the editorial offices of *SME*, one of the country's leading daily national newspapers, raised fears of more widespread illegal surveillance. The government does not limit access to the Internet.

The government respects religious freedom. Registered churches and religious organizations are eligible for tax exemptions and government subsidies. The Roman Catholic Church is the largest denomination in the country and consequently receives the largest share of government subsidies. Although Slovakia has not banned or impeded any groups from practicing their faith, the U.S. State Department notes the persistence of anti-Semitism among some parts of the population. The government respects academic freedom.

The government respects the right to assemble peacefully, petition state bodies, and associate in clubs, political parties, and trade unions. Judges, prosecutors, firefighters, and members of the armed forces may not strike.

The constitution provides for an independent judiciary and a Constitutional Court. The European Commission has noted the perception of a high level of corruption in the Slovak courts and expressed concern over the judiciary's perceived lack of impartiality. Corruption and illegal wiretapping incidents involving senior government officials have raised questions about the judicial system's capacity to function at EU levels.

There are more than 10 recognized ethnic minorities in Slovakia. While minorities and ethnic groups have a constitutional right to contribute to the resolution of issues that concern them, Roma (Gypsies) continue to experience widespread discrimination and inequality in education, housing, employment, public services, and the criminal justice system. In 2003, there were reports of coerced or forced sterilization of Roma women. Roma also face the persistent threat of racially motivated violence. Even though the law criminalizes such acts, reports indicate that law enforcement officials do not always investigate crimes against Roma. In response to these problems, the government began a new program to improve Roma education and housing in 2002. The government has also established an informal advisory board to widen dialogue with the Roma community. As of November 30, Slovakia was poised to reach an agreement with Hungary on the application of Hungary's Status Law, which grants special health and educational benefits to ethnic Hungarians residing outside of Hungary.

Slovak citizens enjoy a range of personal rights and liberties, including the right to move and travel freely.

Slovakia has a market economy in which the private sector accounts for approximately 80 percent of gross domestic product and 75 percent of employment. Official unemployment remains high at approximately 14 percent, but the government contends that as many as 5 percent of those who collect unemployment benefits may simultaneously be working on the black market.

Although women enjoy the same legal rights as men, they continue to be underrepresented in senior-level business positions and the government.

# Slovenia

**Population:** 2,000,000
**GNI/capita:** $9,760
**Life Expectancy:** 76
**Political Rights:** 1
**Civil Liberties:** 1
**Status:** Free
**Religious Groups:** Roman Catholic [including Uniate (2 percent)] (70.8 percent), Lutheran (1 percent), Muslim (1 percent), other (27.2 percent)
**Ethnic Groups:** Slovene (88 percent), Croat (3 percent), Serb (2 percent), Bosniak (1 percent), other (6 percent)
**Capital:** Ljubljana

**Ten-Year Ratings Timeline (Political Rights, Civil Liberties, Status)**

| 1994 | 1995 | 1996 | 1997 | 1998 | 1999 | 2000 | 2001 | 2002 | 2003 |
|------|------|------|------|------|------|------|------|------|------|
| 1,2F | 1,2F | 1,2F | 1,2F | 1,2F | 1,2F | 1,2F | 1,2F | 1,1F | 1,1F |

**Overview:**
Slovenia continued to make steady progress in 2003 toward joining Euro-Atlantic institutions, as referendums held in March on entering the European Union (EU) and NATO passed with large majorities.

The territory now constituting Slovenia was part of the Hapsburg Empire from 1335 to 1918. At the end of World War I, Slovenia became a part of the new Kingdom of Serbs, Croats, and Slovenes (renamed the Kingdom of Yugoslavia in 1929), and after World War II, it became a constituent republic of the Socialist Federal Republic of Yugoslavia. In 1990, Slovenia held its first postwar, multiparty, democratic elections, in which the Democratic United Opposition (DEMOS) secured victory. Voters also elected former Communist leader Milan Kucan president. Kucan was reelected in Slovenia's first post-independence polls in 1992, and again in 1996.

Slovenian society has enjoyed remarkable consensus in the post-independence period in comparison with the other former Yugoslav republics. Citizens agree that foreign policy should focus on Slovenia's entering European and trans-Atlantic organizations, and domestic policy on maintaining a social-democratic model. For most of the this period, Slovenia has been ruled by center-left governments whose most important component has been Janez Drnovsek's Liberal Democratic Party (LDS).

Slovenia's latest presidential elections were held over two rounds in 2002. In the first round, held in November, Drnovsek gained 44.3 percent of the vote. He comfortably outdistanced his nearest rival, Slovenian state prosecutor, but political newcomer, Barbara Brezigar of the Social Democratic Party (SDS), who gained 30.7 percent. In the second-round runoff in December, Brezigar secured surprisingly strong support, winning 43 percent of the vote, although that was not enough to defeat Drnovsek's 56 percent. Seventy-one percent of the electorate turned out to vote in the first round of the elections and 65 percent for the second round.

In March, Slovenes voted in referendums on both EU and NATO accession, and the electorate approved the measures by large margins, with 89.61 percent in favor of joining the EU and 66.95 in favor of joining NATO. Slovenia is scheduled to join the two organizations in 2004.

Nevertheless, as Slovenia's media began to discuss the pros and cons of membership over the subsequent months, it became clearer to the public that EU membership would not be a panacea for many of the economic problems facing the country. In addition, many citizens have voiced strong concerns over the fate of Slovenian identity in the EU, given that Slovenes will constitute only 2.7 percent of the new, enlarged union and will have only 7 of the 732 seats in the European parliament. Issues of cultural and national survival in Slovenia receive considerable prominence, especially given widespread concern over the nation's low fertility rate.

The votes on EU and NATO accession were only part of a series of referendums held in Slovenia during the course of the year. By September, the public had participated in five referendums to voice their views on, among other issues, whether to privatize railways and telecommunications systems and whether to allow stores to be open on Sundays. By the fifth such referendum, however, electoral turnout was less than 30 percent.

Also in September, Slovenia officially ended compulsory military service, in accordance with plans to professionalize the military. The new plan calls for the military call to be downsized to a 14,000-strong force.

One outstanding human rights issue in Slovenia that continued to cause problems in 2003 was the fate of the "erased": non-Slovene citizens of the former Yugoslavia who remained in Slovenia after independence, but who were administratively removed from all official records after they failed to apply for citizenship during a brief period in 1992. The "erased" were subsequently denied driver's licenses, access to state health care, and pensions. Under pressure from the EU, the Slovenian government began drafting legislation to restore these rights, but no changes to legislation had been adopted as of November 30.

Slovenia's major foreign policy problem in 2003 was with its southern neighbor, Croatia, over the latter's moves to declare an exclusive economic zone in the Adriatic, which would effectively cut off Slovenia's access to international waters. Evidence of the extent to which passions became inflamed in the two former Yugoslav republics over the issue was seen in a poll released in a Croatian newsweekly over the summer, which showed that the largest number of respondents to the question "Who is Croatia's worst neighbor?" answered "Slovenia."

**Political Rights and Civil Liberties:**  Citizens of Slovenia can change their government democratically. Voters directly elect the president and members of the 90-seat National Assembly (parliament), which chooses the prime minister. The 40-seat National Council, a largely advisory body, represents professional groups and local interests. The political opposition to the government plays a constructive, cooperative role in public policy making. Elections held in 1992, 1996, 2000, and 2002 have been considered free and fair. The government respects the constitutional rights of freedom of speech and of the press, although insulting public officials is prohibited by law. Most print media outlets are privately owned and support themselves with advertising revenues. Some electronic media outlets, such as Slovenia Radio-Television (RTV), remain state-owned. RTV has three radio stations and two television networks. A major complaint against the various media is that they do not represent a wide range of political or ethnic interests. There are also reports of some degree of self-censorship resulting from indirect political or economic pressures on media outlets. There were no reports of government attempts to restrict access to the Internet during the year.

The constitution guarantees freedom of conscience and religion. The most outstanding issue over the past several years regarding religious freedom has been the consistent refusal of authorities to allow the small Muslim community to build a mosque in Ljubljana. Restitution of religious properties confiscated during the Communist period is nearing its end. According to published reports, 86 percent of claims filed by religious organizations for de-nationalization of their property were resolved by the end of September 2003. There were no reports of government restrictions on academic freedom during the year.

The government respects the right of individuals to assemble peacefully, to form associations, to participate in public affairs, and to submit petitions. Military and police personnel may not join political parties. Workers enjoy the right to establish and join trade unions, to strike, and to bargain collectively.

According to the EU, the Slovenian judiciary enjoys "a high degree of independence." The judiciary consists of the Supreme Court, an administrative court, regional and district courts, and an appeals court, and there is also a Constitutional Court. The constitution guarantees individuals due process, equality before the law, and a presumption of innocence until proven guilty. The main problem facing the judicial system is the fact that it is overburdened, with some criminal cases taking two to five years. Prison conditions are in line with international standards, although some overcrowding has been reported.

Slovenia's treatment of ethnic minorities is generally considered to be good. Incitement to racial hatred is prohibited under the Criminal Code. The constitution entitles Italian and Hungarian ethnic communities to one deputy each in the National Assembly. However, there have been persistent reports of police harassment of Roma (Gypsies) and of residents from other former Yugoslav republics, the so-called new minorities. International watchdog groups report some governmental and societal discrimination against Serbs, Croats, Bosnians, Kosovo Albanians, and Roma now living in Slovenia.

According to the constitution, Slovenian citizens enjoy all recognized personal rights and freedoms, including the freedom to travel, to choose one's place of residence, and the right to own private property.

Women enjoy the same constitutional rights and freedoms as men under the law. Currently, there are 12 women serving in the 90-seat parliament and 3 women in the 40-seat National Council. Domestic violence remains a concern. In recent years, Slovenia has become both a transit country and a country of destination for women and girls trafficked from other parts of Eastern Europe for purposes of prostitution.

# Solomon Islands

**Population:** 500,000    **Political Rights:** 3
**GNI/capita:** $570    **Civil Liberties:** 3
**Life Expectancy:** 71    **Status:** Partly Free
**Religious Groups:** Anglican (45 percent), Roman
Catholic (18 percent), other [including indigenous
beliefs] (37 percent)
**Ethnic Groups:** Melanesian (93 percent), Polynesian
(4 percent), Micronesian (1.5 percent), other (1.5 percent)
**Capital:** Honiara

**Ten-Year Ratings Timeline (Political Rights, Civil Liberties, Status)**

| 1994 | 1995 | 1996 | 1997 | 1998 | 1999 | 2000 | 2001 | 2002 | 2003 |
|------|------|------|------|------|------|------|------|------|------|
| 1,2F | 1,2F | 1,2F | 1,2F | 1,2F | 1,2F | 4,4PF | 4,4PF | 3,3PF | 3,3PF |

**Overview:**      Restoring peace and order to the Solomon Islands were top
priorities in 2003 for this country recently torn apart by fierce
ethnic conflict. The government called for military help from
Australia and New Zealand in June 2003 and approved an Australian-led intervention force on July 29. In another move toward ensuring peace and stability, one of
the major militant groups involved in the conflict handed over a large number of its
weapons to the Australian forces.

The Solomon Islands, which is composed of more than 27 islands and 70 language groups, gained independence in 1978 after having been a protectorate of the
United Kingdom. However, clan identity remains much stronger than national identity and a deep source of ethnic rivalry. Tensions between the two largest groups,
the Guadalcanalese, natives of the main island of Guadalcanal, and the Malaitans,
who come from the nearby province of Malaita, over jobs and land rights erupted
into open warfare in 1998. The Isatabu Freedom Movement (IFM) claimed representation of native Guadalcanalese interests and forced the eviction of some 30,000
Malaitans from Guadalcanal. Scores were injured or killed in the fighting that followed between the IFM and the Malaita Eagle Force (MEF), formed from groups of
armed Malaitans.

Prime Minister Bartholomew Ulufa'ala, a Malaitan, was taken hostage in June
2000 by the MEF, which seized control of the capital, Honiara. Ulufa'ala was forced
to resign and was replaced by Mannasseh Sogavare. Fighting officially ended with
the Townsville Peace Agreement of October 2000, which was brokered by Australia
and New Zealand. The agreement provides for the "restructure of the police force, a
weapons amnesty, and reconciliation." Both countries sent unarmed peacekeepers
to supervise the handover of arms, many of which had been brought in from
Bougainville in Papua New Guinea when fighting ended there in 1998. However, the
Malaitan militants' refusal to accept the treaty hindered the peace process. Harold
Keke, leader of the militants, was alleged to have killed 50 people and burned entire
villages in the Weather Coast region of Guadalcanal after the accord was signed.
Armed gangs also continued to operate in many parts of the country, including the
capital city, causing the prime minister to stay out of Honiara for security reasons

and cabinet meetings to be held in secret locations. Parliamentary elections in December 2001 brought a new government to power under Prime Minister Sir Allan Kemakeza.

Australia and New Zealand provide the bulk of resources, including 2,000 personnel (200 police, 200 military personnel, and 1,500 support staff) to assist the Solomon Islands in its recovery. The Australian-led "Operation Help a Friend" was approved by the Solomon Islands government on July 29, 2003 and endorsed by the United Nations in August. This operation continues where a UN mission left off when its commitment ended in June. The first personnel arrived on Guadalcanal island on July 23, and the operation will continue until local police regain control and government structures and legal systems are operating effectively. Australia stated that the mission is also necessary to prevent the islands from becoming a haven for drug trafficking and money laundering. Australia also committed to doubling its bilateral financial aid to the islands from the current $37 million.

Another step toward consolidating peace and order was realized in August when MEF chief Jimmy Rasta ordered his men to surrender their weapons to the Australian led intervention force. By the end of September, nearly 4,000 weapons were collected. Also in August, Harold Keke, leader of a band of Malaitan militants, surrendered. The government charged Keke and his top lieutenants in September with the murder of seven Anglican brothers.

As stability was slowly being reestablished, Prime Minister Kemakeza attempted to reform the government, including removing eight department heads in September for failure to perform their duties. However, the challenges remain considerable. For example, the province of Rennell-Bellona, south of Guadalcanal, declared in August its desire to secede and proposed a federal system. A government study also reported greater support for a federal system.

On another front, the country signed a bilateral agreement with the United States that provides U.S. citizens with immunity from prosecution by the International Court of Justice created by the Treaty of Rome, which the United States opposes and is not a party to. The refusal to conclude this agreement would have risked a loss to the Solomon Islands' of all U.S. military assistance.

The country's economy, which has contracted by 25 percent since 2001, is in shambles. Debt arrears reached $35 million, or the entire basic revenue collected for 2003.

**Political Rights and Civil Liberties:** Citizens of the Solomon Islands can change their government democratically. The government is a modified parliamentary system with a 50-member, single-chamber Legislative Assembly. Suffrage is universal for persons 18 years and over. A parliamentary majority elects the prime minister, the chief executive, who appoints his own cabinet.

Freedom of expression and of the press are generally respected in practice. Media reports on corruption and abuses by politicians frequently make headlines. Those alleged of wrongdoing sometimes use legal and extralegal means to intimidate journalists. However, the government has not systematically suppressed press freedom, leaving matters to the courts for adjudication.

Freedom of religion is generally respected in practice. Academic freedom is also respected despite serious disruptions in instruction and research as a result of the recent violence and lack of government funding.

Numerous domestic nongovernmental organizations operate freely, with most engaging in developmental or religious activity. In 2001, the Civil Society Network, an umbrella group, was formed to provide oversight to government activity; the group regularly criticizes corruption and abuses by government officials. Workers are free to organize, and strikes are permitted. Wage earners represent 10 to 15 percent of the workforce in the country's formal economy.

The judicial system has barely functioned since the coup attempt in 2000. A lack of resources limits defendants' right to counsel, while those in prison face lengthy pretrial detentions due to delays in court hearings. Threats against judges and prosecutors weaken the independence and rigor of the judiciary. Moreover, the government's decision to grant amnesty for crimes committed in connection with the June 2000 coup and events leading up to it as part of the Townsville accord has encouraged an atmosphere of impunity.

The constitution provides for an ombudsman, with the power to subpoena and investigate complaints of official abuse, mistreatment, or unfair treatment. The ombudsman's office has potentially far-reaching powers but is limited by a lack of resources.

Law enforcement relies on a civilian-controlled police force of about 1,000 persons, which has become factionalized and has not functioned effectively since the 2000 coup, when many Malaitan officers joined the MEF. The hiring of about 1,200 untrained former militants as "special constables" to stop fighting has also caused problems. For example, members of this group and the paramilitary Police Field Force have been implicated in many criminal activities. When the police chief attempted to demobilize 800 of the special police in 2003, some 300 protested to demand outstanding salaries and claims before termination. The country has no army.

Despite legal guarantees of equal rights, discrimination limits the economic and political roles of women. No laws prohibit domestic violence, although rape and common assault are illegal. Reports of violence against adult and teenage women have increased since the coup in June 2000.

# Somalia

**Population:** 8,000,000
**GNI/capita:** $120
**Life Expectancy:** 46
**Religious Groups:** Sunni Muslim, Christian minority
**Ethnic Groups:** Somali (85 percent), other [including Bantu and Arab] (15 percent)
**Capital:** Mogadishu

**Political Rights:** 6
**Civil Liberties:** 7
**Status:** Not Free

**Ten-Year Ratings Timeline (Political Rights, Civil Liberties, Status)**

| 1994 | 1995 | 1996 | 1997 | 1998 | 1999 | 2000 | 2001 | 2002 | 2003 |
|------|------|------|------|------|------|------|------|------|------|
| 7,7NF | 7,7NF | 7,7NF | 7,7NF | 7,7NF | 7,7NF | 6,7NF | 6,7NF | 6,7NF | 6,7NF |

**Overview:**    A year of talks hosted by Kenya failed to make much headway in securing a lasting peace in Somalia and establishing an elected national government in 2003. Delegates to Somalia's Transitional National Government (TNG) missed deadlines to select members of parliament and schedule presidential elections. The three-year mandate of the TNG expired in August 2003, but it remained in place to prevent a power vacuum in the country. The president of the TNG, Abdiqassim Salad Hassan, and other key faction leaders have boycotted the Kenya talks since September 2003 following disagreements over the adoption of an interim constitution. The self-declared republic of Somaliland in the north has not participated in the TNG. Intermittent fighting among clan leaders and factions for control of Mogadishu and other areas claimed at least 200 lives in the last year. Concerns that Somalia harbors members of al Qaeda and other terrorist organizations further complicate the picture.

Somalia, a Horn of Africa nation, gained independence in July 1960 with the union of British Somaliland and territories to the south that had been an Italian colony. Other ethnic Somali-inhabited lands are now part of Djibouti, Ethiopia, and Kenya. General Siad Barre seized power in 1969 and increasingly employed divisive clan politics to maintain power. While flood, drought, and famine racked the nation, the struggle to topple Barre has caused civil war, starvation, banditry, and brutality since the late 1980s. When Barre was deposed in January 1991, power was claimed and contested by heavily armed guerrilla movements and militias divided by traditional ethnic and clan loyalties.

Extensive television coverage of famine and civil strife that took approximately 300,000 lives in 1991 and 1992 prompted a U.S.-led international intervention. The armed humanitarian mission in late 1992 quelled clan combat long enough to stop the famine, but ended in urban guerrilla warfare against Somali militias. The last international forces withdrew in March 1995 after the combined casualty count reached into the thousands. Approximately 100 peacekeepers, including 18 U.S. soldiers, were killed. The $4 billion UN intervention effort had little lasting impact.

The Conference for National Peace and Reconciliation in Somalia adopted a charter in 2000 for a three-year transition and selected a 245-member transitional assembly, which functions as an interim parliament. Minority groups are represented, and 30 of the members are women. A government security force in Mogadishu has been cobbled together from members of the former administration's military, the police, and militias.

The TNG and more than 20 rival groups signed a ceasefire in October 2002 in Kenya as a first step toward establishing a federal system of government. However, over the next year, the talks deadlocked when some faction leaders dropped out to form their own parallel talks in the Somali capital of Mogadishu. The TNG was intended to comprise all the country's various clans, but is opposed by a number of warlords, some allegedly supported by Ethiopia; Somalia and Ethiopia have been at odds over a long-running border dispute. A final meeting of Somali leaders, billed as a last-ditch "retreat," is planned in Kenya for the second week of December.

In November, the UN Security Council extended its mandate in the country until 2005. Despite an arms embargo, the Security Council noted a "persistent flow of weapons and ammunitions" to Somalia in 2003. In October, a Somali delegate to the TNG was murdered, along with two Kenyan associates, in what appeared to be a business deal gone sour. The police arrested a former Kenyan member of parliament in connection with the murders.

Somalia is a poor country where most people survive as pastoralists or subsistence farmers. The country's main exports are livestock and charcoal. Three years of drought have led to a humanitarian disaster in the Sool and Sanaag districts in Somaliland, as well as parts of Bari district in Puntland, where some 60,000 people faced food shortages in 2003. The TNG has unsuccessfully called on the international community to unfreeze the assets of Somalia's Al-Barakaat telecommunications and money-transfer company to help the country's battered economy. Al-Barakaat was Somalia's largest employer, and hundreds of thousands of Somalis depended on it to receive money transfers from abroad. U.S. authorities froze the assets of Al-Barakaat in 2001 on suspicion that its owners were aiding and abetting terrorism, a charge the owners deny.

**Political Rights and Civil Liberties:** Somalis cannot change their government democratically. However, the 2000 elections marked the first time since 1969 that Somalis have had an opportunity to choose their government on a somewhat national basis. Some 3,000 representatives of civic and religious organizations, women's groups, and clans came together as the Inter-Governmental Authority for Development, following Djibouti-hosted peace talks, to elect a parliament in August 2000. The 245 members of the Transitional National Assembly (TNG) elected the president. More than 20 candidates contested the first round of voting for the presidency. The Inter-Governmental Authority chose the lawyers who drafted the country's new charter. Under the transitional constitution adopted by the TNG in 2003, the country's main clans will each receive a quota of the 351 parliamentary seats, although the process has bogged down in disputes over the nomination process.

Somaliland has exercised de facto independence from Somalia since May 1991. A clan conference led to a peace accord among its clan factions in 1997, establishing a presidency and bicameral parliament with proportional clan representation. Somaliland is far more cohesive than the rest of the country, although reports of some human rights abuses persist. Somaliland has sought international recognition as the Republic of Somaliland since 1991. A referendum on independence and a new constitution were approved in May 2001, opening the way for a multiparty system. Dahir Riyale Kahin of the ruling Unity of Democrats party emerged as the winner of historic presidential elections in 2003. Kahin had been vice president under Mohamed Egal, who died of kidney failure in 2002. Somaliland's constitutional court dismissed a challenge to the poll results filed by Kahin's rival, Solidarity Party candidate Ahmed Muhammad Silanyo, after ordering a recount. International observers from 14 countries declared the voting to be free and fair. Municipal elections in December 2002 also drew 440,000 people to the polls.

Puntland established a regional government in 1998, with a presidency and a single-chamber quasi-legislature known as the Council of Elders. Political parties are banned. The traditional elders chose Abdullahi Yusuf as the region's first president for a three-year term. After Jama Ali Jama was elected to replace him in 2001, Abdullahi Yusuf refused to relinquish power, claiming he was fighting terrorism. Yusuf seized power in 2002, reportedly with the help of Ethiopian forces.

Somalia's charter provides for press freedom. Independent radio and television stations have proliferated. Most of the independent newspapers or newsletters that circulate in Mogadishu are linked to one faction or another. Although journalists face harassment, most receive the protection of the clan behind their publication. The transitional government launched its first radio station, Radio Mogadishu, in 2001. There are three private radio stations and two run by factions.

Somalia is an Islamic state, and religious freedom is not guaranteed. The Sunni majority often views non-Sunni Muslims with suspicion. Members of the small Christian community face societal harassment if they proclaim their religion.

Several indigenous and foreign nongovernmental organizations operate in Somalia with varying degrees of latitude. The charter provides workers with the right to form unions and assemble freely, but civil war and factional fighting led to the dissolution of the single labor confederation, the government-controlled General Federation of Somali Trade Unions. Wages are established largely by ad hoc bartering and the influence of clan affiliation.

Somalia's charter provides for an independent judiciary, although a formal judicial system has ceased to exist. Sharia (Islamic law) operating in Mogadishu has been effective in bringing a semblance of law and order to the city. Efforts at judicial reform are proceeding slowly. The Sharia courts in Mogadishu are gradually coming under the control of the transitional government. Most of the courts are aligned with various subclans. Prison conditions are harsh in some areas, but improvements are under way.

Human rights abuses, including extrajudicial killing, torture, beating, and arbitrary detention by Somalia's various armed factions remain a problem. Many violations are linked to banditry. Several international aid organizations, women's groups, and local human rights groups operate in the country. In October, two elderly British teachers with the humanitarian group SOS Children's Villages were shot dead in their home. That same month, an Italian aid worker was also killed. The Somali authorities have made arrests in both cases.

Although more than 80 percent of Somalis share a common ethnic heritage, religion, and nomadic-influenced culture, discrimination is widespread. Clans exclude one another from participation in social and political life. Minority clans are harassed, intimidated, and abused by armed gunmen.

Women's groups were instrumental in galvanizing support for Somalia's peace process. As a result of their participation, women occupy at least 30 seats in parliament. The country's new charter prohibits sexual discrimination, but women experience intense discrimination under customary practices and variants of Sharia. Infibulation, the most severe form of female genital mutilation, is routine. UN agencies and nongovernmental organizations are working to raise awareness about the health dangers of this practice. Various armed factions have recruited children into their militias.

# South Africa

**Population:** 44,000,000   **Political Rights:** 1
**GNI/capita:** $2,820   **Civil Liberties:** 2
**Life Expectancy:** 53   **Status:** Free
**Religious Groups:** Christian (68 percent), Muslim
(2 percent), Hindu (1.5 percent), other [including
indigenous beliefs and animists] (28.5 percent)
**Ethnic Groups:** Black (75 percent), white (14 percent),
mixed (9 percent), Indian (2 percent)
**Capital:** Pretoria

**Ten-Year Ratings Timeline (Political Rights, Civil Liberties, Status)**

| 1994 | 1995 | 1996 | 1997 | 1998 | 1999 | 2000 | 2001 | 2002 | 2003 |
|------|------|------|------|------|------|------|------|------|------|
| 2,3F | 1,2F | 1,2F | 1,2F | 1,2F | 1,2F | 1,2F | 1,2F | 1,2F | 1,2F |

**Overview:**   In 2003, South Africa continued to provide a remarkable
example of a democratic transition in an extremely diverse
country. However, President Thabo Mbeki undermined his
country's stature as a regional leader by refusing to condemn publicly increasing
repression in neighboring Zimbabwe. Meanwhile, more than one in nine South Africans is HIV-positive, the highest infection rate in the world, which poses enormous political and economic problems for the country.

South Africa's apartheid government, which came to power in 1948, reserved
political power for the white minority while seeking to balkanize the black, Indian,
and mixed-race, or colored, communities. International economic sanctions and civil
unrest eventually forced the South African government to negotiate with its adversaries. Momentum for change accelerated with the accession to power of Frederick
de Klerk and global moves toward democratization in the late 1980s. In 1990, de Klerk
freed African National Congress (ANC) leader Nelson Mandela from 27 years of
imprisonment and initiated a negotiation process that resulted in legitimate multiparty elections in 1994. These elections brought Mandela and the ANC to power at
the national level. The ANC's electoral primacy was confirmed in national elections
in 1999.

In recent years, tension has increased between the ruling ANC on the one hand
and trade unions, independent media outlets, traditional leaders, and the white minority on the other. Key areas of disagreement between the ANC and labor have
included the government's conservative economic policies and its approach to the
AIDS epidemic.

The ANC leadership has focused blame for the country's problems on the former
white-supremacist regime. This argument has begun to lose potency with time and
with the growing economic empowerment of a minority of black South Africans.
Protests have taken place over the pace of essential-service delivery to disadvantaged people. Serious challenges exist regarding economic development, and the
government has not kept promises to improve vastly education, health care, and
housing. The durability of the new democratic structures is uncertain since South
Africa remains deeply divided by ethnicity and class.

South Africa has one of the fastest-growing AIDS rates in the world, and the health crisis poses serious political, economic, and social problems. About 11 percent of the population is afflicted. Up to 360,000 South Africans die yearly from AIDS, which has orphaned more than 650,000 children in the country. After having spent considerable political capital trying to keep the drugs from the public health system, mystifyingly arguing that the virus did not necessarily cause AIDS, Mbeki yielded to international and domestic pressure to endorse anti-HIV drugs  Besides overwhelming the health care system, the pandemic threatens the economy by depleting future generations of workers. Mbeki's slowness in getting the epidemic under control and the country's astronomical crime rates have scared off much foreign investment.

South Africa is looked to as a regional leader, but Mbeki lacks the moral authority of his predecessor, Mandela. Mbeki's pursuit of "quiet diplomacy" with the ANC's historic ally, Zimbabwe President Robert Mugabe, has been ineffectual in resolving authoritarianism and economic collapse in that country. Such passivity is shortsighted as the crisis has a direct impact on South Africa.

**Political Rights and Civil Liberties:** South Africa's young democracy has been maturing since the new constitution took effect in February 1997 and South Africans can change their government democratically. Two successful national elections have taken place since 1994. Elections for the 400-seat National Assembly and 90-seat National Council of Provinces are by proportional representation based on party lists. The National Assembly elects the president to serve concurrently with the five-year parliamentary term. The next presidential and parliamentary elections are due in 2004, and local ones are scheduled for 2005.

In general, the electoral process, including extensive voter education, balanced state media coverage, and reliable balloting and vote counting, has worked properly. An exception occurs in KwaZulu/Natal, where political violence and credible allegations of vote rigging have devalued the process. Violence there is decreasing, however, as the result of a peace process between the ANC and the Inkatha Freedom Party.

South Africa's constitution is one of the most liberal in the world and includes a sweeping bill of rights. In 2000, the parliament approved legislation outlawing discrimination on the basis of race, ethnicity, or sex. Parliament has passed more than 500 laws relating to the constitution, revamping the apartheid-era legal system. This legislation is now being implemented: for example, some lower courts have been designated "equality courts," with a particular mandate to review instances of unfair discrimination. In 2000, the cabinet endorsed a code of ethics for politicians, covering items such as conflict of interest and disclosure of financial assets and large gifts. Corruption is not widespread, but concerns about increasing incidents led to the introduction into parliament of the 2002 Prevention of Corruption bill.

The press and other independent institutions play important roles in articulating a wide variety of interests. Freedom of expression is generally respected, although the government is sensitive to criticism. The state-owned South African Broadcasting Corporation (SABC) suffers from self-censorship. However, a variety of newspapers and magazines publish opinions sharply critical of the government and the ANC. Scores of small community radio stations operate, as well as one commercial television station, e-TV. Internet access is growing rapidly but remains elusive for disadvantaged people, particularly in rural areas where computers and electricity are scarce.

The final version of the Broadcasting Amendment Bill passed by parliament in 2002 reflects the maturity of the democratic processes. Original draft legislation contained a clause requiring that the SABC report to the minister of communications regarding editorial content. The legislation was revised after considerable debate; the constitutionally mandated Independent Communications Authority of South Africa will ensure that the SABC fulfills its mission of broadcasting in the public interest.

Religious and academic freedom thrive.

The government generally respects the rights of freedom of assembly and association, and a lively protest scene prevails. In recent years, the ANC has seen increased tension with its traditional political allies, the Congress of South African Trade Unions and the South African Communist Party. Labor rights codified under the 1995 Labor Relations Act (LRA) are respected, and more than 250 trade unions exist. The right to strike can be exercised after reconciliation efforts. The LRA allows employers to hire replacement workers. The ANC government has introduced several labor laws designed to protect the rights of workers, although it has taken other actions that weaken trade union positions in bargaining for job security, wages, and other benefits. Half a million jobs have been lost since 1994.

The country's independent judiciary continues to function well. The 11-member constitutional court, created to enforce the rules of the new democracy, has demonstrated considerable independence. In its Treatment Action Campaign ruling in 2002, the court challenged Mbeki by requiring the government to provide treatment to women with HIV or AIDS. Lower courts generally respect legal provisions regarding arrest and detention, although courts remain understaffed. The Bill of Rights prohibits detention without trial, but lengthy pretrial detentions are common as a result of an overwhelmed judiciary. The death penalty was abolished in 1995.

Efforts to end torture and other abuses by the national police force have been implemented, although such incidents still occur. Deaths in police custody continue to be a problem. The constitutionally mandated Human Rights Commission was appointed by parliament to "promote the observance of, respect for, and the protection of fundamental rights." Prisons often do not meet international standards and are characterized by overcrowding, poor health conditions, and abuses of inmates by staff or other prisoners.

The now-concluded Truth and Reconciliation Commission sought to heal divisions created by the apartheid regime through a series of open hearings. From 1996 to 1998, the commission received more than 20,000 submissions from victims and nearly 8,000 applications for amnesty from perpetrators. In 1998, the commission released a report on human rights abuses during the apartheid years that largely focused on atrocities committed by the white-minority government, but which also criticized the ANC. The controversial issue of reparations for victims of apartheid is actively debated within and between the civil society and government.

The breakdown of law and order is a serious problem. An estimated four million illegal firearms circulate in South Africa, and in recent years, the country has ranked first in the world in the per capita number of rapes and armed robberies. Only 1 in 10 violent crimes results in conviction. Self-styled Muslim vigilantes, some with links to criminals, have been charged with violent actions in the Cape Town area.

In response to the September 11, 2001, attacks in the United States, the South African government drafted an antiterrorism bill, whose latest draft was presented to parliament in 2003. Some clauses alarmed South Africans who remembered the days when the ANC was persecuted as a terrorist organization. Further amendments are possible as parliament reviews the proposed legislation.

South African society is characterized by ample personal freedom, and a small black middle class is emerging. However, the white minority retains most economic power. Some three-quarters of South Africans are black, yet they enjoy less than a third of the country's total income. Unemployment stands at about 40 percent among blacks and 4 percent for whites. The quality of schooling differs for the two groups. The government sought to lessen these disparities by improving, although slowly, housing and health care in disadvantaged areas. It has launched initiatives such as the Mining Charter, negotiated in 2002, which requires 25 percent of that industry to be black-owned in five years.

Equal rights for women are guaranteed by the constitution and promoted by the constitutionally mandated Commission on Gender Equality. Laws such as the Maintenance Act and the Domestic Violence Act are designed to protect women in financially inequitable and abusive relationships. These laws, however, do not provide the infrastructure for implementation. Discriminatory practices in customary law remain prevalent, as does sexual violence against women and minors. Forty percent of rape survivors are girls under 18. The Criminal Law (Sexual Offences) Amendment Bill, introduced to parliament in 2003, seeks to widen protection for sexual victims, but human rights groups say it does not go far enough.

# South Korea

**Population:** 47,900,000  **Political Rights:** 2
**GNI/capita:** $9,460  **Civil Liberties:** 2
**Life Expectancy:** 76  **Status:** Free
**Religious Groups:** Christian (49 percent), Buddhist (47 percent), Confucian (3 percent), other (1 percent)
**Ethnic Groups:** Korean
**Capital:** Seoul

**Ten-Year Ratings Timeline (Political Rights, Civil Liberties, Status)**

| 1994 | 1995 | 1996 | 1997 | 1998 | 1999 | 2000 | 2001 | 2002 | 2003 |
|------|------|------|------|------|------|------|------|------|------|
| 2,2F | 2,2F | 2,2F | 2,2F | 2,2F | 2,2F | 2,2F | 2,2F | 2,2F | 2,2F |

**Overview:** A major fundraising scandal that implicated both major parties in 2003 added urgency to longstanding calls from many quarters for an overhaul of South Korea's campaign finance laws. Late in the year, prosecutors were investigating allegations that former top aides to President Roh Moo-hyun, as well as legislators from across the political spectrum, accepted millions of dollars in illegal corporate donations before and after the 2002 presidential election. The opposition-led parliament put off consideration of several bills as it remained at loggerheads with Roh over how to investigate the scandal, which came as Roh was struggling to find his leadership footing after taking office in February. Elected on pledges to improve corporate governance, bring greater transparency to state institutions, and engage, rather than contain, bellicose North Korea, Roh was forced to shuffle his priorities in the face of a slowing economy and new threats from Pyongyang.

The Republic of Korea was established in 1948, three years after the Allied victory in World War II ended Japan's 35-year colonization of Korea and led to the division of the Korean Peninsula between U.S. and Soviet forces. During the Cold War, South Korea's mainly military rulers crushed left-wing dissent and kept the nation on a virtual war footing in response to the continuing threat from the North following the Korean War in the early 1950s. They also led an industrialization drive that transformed a poor, agrarian land into the world's eleventh-largest economy.

South Korea's democratic transition began in 1987, when military strongman Chun Doo-hwan gave in to widespread student protests and allowed his successor to be chosen in a direct presidential election. In voting that December, Chun's protégé, Roh Tae-woo, defeated the country's best-known dissidents, Kim Young-sam and Kim Dae-jung.

After joining the ruling party in 1990, Kim Young-sam defeated Kim Dae-jung in the 1992 presidential election to become South Korea's first civilian president since 1961. As president, Kim cracked down on corruption, sacked hard-line military officers, curbed the domestic security services, and successfully prosecuted former presidents Chun and Roh for corruption and treason.

Amid these gains, South Korea in 1997 went through its worst financial crisis in decades. Slowing exports, a tumbling currency, and years of often reckless, state-directed borrowing brought South Korean companies close to default on $150 billion in debt. Seoul agreed to a $57 billion IMF-led bailout in return for pledging to restructure companies and end lifetime job guarantees. Angry over the government's failure to better supervise the country's banks and business conglomerates, South Koreans in December 1997 elected as president former dissident Kim Dae-jung, who became the country's first opposition candidate to win a presidential election.

Under Kim Dae-jung, South Korea's economy rebounded to become one of the most robust in Asia. This return to prosperity, however, eased pressure on the country's large, family-owned business conglomerates, known as chaebol, and other firms to adopt better business practices. At the same time, Daewoo Motors and other firms seeking foreign suitors or pressed by foreign creditors laid off thousands of workers.

Anger over these layoffs, as well as a series of corruption scandals and criticism that Kim Dae-jung's policy of engagement with North Korea had reaped few benefits, helped the opposition Grand National Party (GNP) take the most seats in the 2000 parliamentary elections. It won 133 out of parliament's 273 seats, with Kim's Millennium Democratic Party (MDP) taking 115.

With Kim Dae-jung constitutionally barred from seeking a second term, Roh, 56, won the December 2002 presidential elections on the MDP ticket. Roh narrowly beat the GNP's Lee Hoi-chang after a campaign in which Roh mixed populist promises with anti-American rhetoric.

Roh took office in February 2003 facing an economic slowdown, an opposition-led parliament, and public moves by Pyongyang to revive its nuclear weapons program. His administration initially made some headway on its reformist agenda, shaking up the state prosecutor's office and launching investigations into the accounting practices of some chaebol.

Many questioned, however, this decision to investigate Korea's industrial powerhouses at a time when economic growth was slowing to around 3 percent, down from 6.3 percent in 2002. Korean firms are also facing competition from lower cost manufacturers in China, and many have responded by sacking workers and moving factories offshore.

Moreover, Roh's calls for engaging North Korea came under opposition attack as Pyongyang took steps to unlock a mothballed nuclear reactor, just months after admitting to having a uranium-enrichment program. While many support Roh's North Korea policy, critics called for a tougher approach and questioned whether Seoul should risk undermining its critical security alliance with Washington, which favors isolating Pyongyang.

As the fundraising scandal put further pressure on the president, Roh vetoed a GNP bill in November calling for an independent counsel to investigate allegations of corruption in his administration. The president said that any independent investigation should wait until prosecutors currently investigating three of his former aides finished their work. Many observers called for new fundraising laws that would ease restrictive caps on contributions but greatly increase the transparency of any donations.

**Political Rights and Civil Liberties:** South Koreans can change their government through elections and enjoy most basic rights. The 1988 constitution vests executive powers in a directly elected president who is limited to a single five-year term. The National Assembly is directly elected for a four-year term.

Anecdotal evidence suggests that bribery, influence peddling, and extortion by officials continue to be pervasive in politics, business, and daily life. The Berlin-based Transparency International in 2003 ranked South Korea in a three-way tie for 50th place out of 133 countries it surveyed for corruption, where higher-ranked countries are considered freer of corruption.

South Korea's press generally is competitive. Newspapers are privately owned and report fairly aggressively on governmental policies and alleged official and corporate wrongdoing. Aggressive reporting, however, has landed several journalists in jail in recent years under criminal libel laws, some for reports that were critical but factually accurate. In a move that raised concerns of selective prosecution, authorities in 2001 fined 23 media companies a record $390 million for tax evasion and filed related criminal charges against five media executives, including the owners of South Korea's two largest papers, *Chosun Ilbo* and *Dong-a Ilbo*. Both papers were particularly critical of then President Kim Dae-jung, whose administration denied any political motives behind the move.

South Korean jails also hold at least 1,000 conscientious objectors, mostly Jehovah's Witnesses, Amnesty International said in March. They typically receive sentences of between 18 months and three years. Apart from this concern, religious freedom is respected. Protestantism claims the most adherents – around 40 percent of the population.

Human rights, social welfare, and other nongovernmental groups are active and operate freely. South Korea's independent labor unions strongly advocate workers' interests, often by organizing high-profile strikes and demonstrations that sometimes lead to arrests. Workers and police clash frequently in some years, particularly during strikes that the government considers illegal. The law bars strikes in government agencies, state-run enterprises, and defense firms. In addition, workers must observe notification and cooling-off provisions before striking and can be forced to submit to arbitration. Under these provisions, the Roh administration in June declared illegal a railway strike called to protest a privatization plan, sending in riot police who detained hundreds of workers in the ensuing clashes. Companies and state-owned enterprises won damages from unions in 2003 for losses that resulted from illegal strikes. Courts in some cases awarded damages out of the salaries of union leaders.

Beginning in 2006, multiple unions will be permitted at the company level, a change expected to give workers greater choice of representatives. The law, however, still bars defense industry and white-collar government workers from forming unions and bargaining collectively, although government workers can form more limited workplace councils. Around 12 percent of South Korean workers are unionized. Among non-union workers, some of the more than 300,000 foreign laborers in South Korea at times are beaten or detained by employers or have their wages withheld or passports seized, according to the U.S. State Department's human rights report for 2002, released in March 2003. The government sponsors programs to protect foreign workers.

South Korea's judiciary generally is considered to be independent. Police abuse of suspects in custody continues to decline, local human rights groups say. Still, criminal suspects and prisoners at times face abuse by law enforcement officials.

In a key human rights concern, the government continues to use the vaguely worded and broadly drafted National Security Law (NSL) to jail not only South Koreans accused of espionage but also some peaceful dissidents. South Koreans have been arrested for peaceful activities including discussing Korean reunification; traveling to North Korea without official permission; praising the North, its leaders, or its state creed of "self-reliance"; or publishing, possessing, or distributing pro-Pyongyang literature.

During his presidency, Kim Dae-jung released dozens of long-term political prisoners held under the NSL. At the same time, he used the NSL to arrest more than 990 people, many for peaceful, allegedly pro-Pyongyang activities, the human rights group Amnesty International said in 2002. Many recent NSL detainees have received suspended sentences or short prison terms, although others have been handed long jail sentences. Amnesty reported in March 2003 that South Korean jails still held 26 NSL detainees, many for nonviolent activities. The incoming Roh administration released nine NSL detainees in April. The government says that it needs to use the NSL against suspected dissidents because of the continued military threat from North Korea.

Because South Korean citizenship is based on parentage rather than place of birth, many of the 20,000 ethnic Chinese born and resident in South Korea face difficulties in obtaining citizenship. Lack of citizenship bars them from the civil service and makes it harder to be hired by some major corporations.

South Korean women enjoy equal access to education, but they face job discrimination in the private sector and are disadvantaged by some government agencies' preferential hiring of military veterans, most of whom are men. Rape, domestic violence, and sexual harassment of women continue to be serious problems despite recent legislation and other initiatives to protect women. Women's groups say that rape and sexual harassment generally are not prosecuted, in part because women are reluctant to bring cases, and convicted offenders often receive light sentences.

# Spain

**Population:** 41,300,000
**GNI/capita:** $14,300
**Life Expectancy:** 79
**Religious Groups:** Roman Catholic (94 percent), other (6 percent)
**Ethnic Groups:** Mediterranean and Nordic
**Capital:** Madrid

**Political Rights:** 1
**Civil Liberties:** 1
**Status:** Free

## Ten-Year Ratings Timeline (Political Rights, Civil Liberties, Status)

| 1994 | 1995 | 1996 | 1997 | 1998 | 1999 | 2000 | 2001 | 2002 | 2003 |
|------|------|------|------|------|------|------|------|------|------|
| 1,2F | 1,2F | 1,2F | 1,2F | 1,2F | 1,2F | 1,2F | 1,2F | 1,1F | 1,1F |

**Overview:**

In March 2003, the Supreme Court agreed to the government's request to impose a permanent ban on the Basque separatist Batasuna party, which is widely regarded as the political expression of the armed Basque separatist group, Euskadi Ta Askatasuna (ETA, or Basque Fatherland and Freedom). On the international front, Prime Minister Jose Maria Aznar supported the U.S.-led invasion in Iraq in the face of popular opposition in Spain and the rest of Europe to the war. In September, Judge Baltasar Garzon, who had become famous for his attempts to extradite Augusto Pinochet to Spain, handed down an indictment of Osama bin Laden and 34 other members of al-Qaeda, the Islamic terrorist network.

The unification of present-day Spain dates from 1512. After a period of colonial influence and wealth, the country declined as a European power and was occupied by France in the early nineteenth century. By the end of the century, after a number of wars and revolts, Spain lost its American colonies. The Spanish Civil War, from 1936 to 1939, led to the deaths of more than 350,000 Spaniards and the victory of Franco's Nationalists, who executed, jailed, and exiled the opposition Republicans. During Franco's long rule, many countries cut off diplomatic ties, and his regime was ostracized by the United Nations from 1946 to 1955. ETA was formed in 1959 with the aim of creating an independent Basque homeland. After a transitional period on Franco's death in 1975, Spain emerged as a parliamentary democracy, joining the European Economic Community, the precursor to the European Union (EU), in 1986.

In national elections held in March 2000, Prime Minister Aznar's Popular Party (PP) enjoyed a resounding victory, capturing 183 out of 350 seats in the Congress of Deputies and 127 in the 208-seat Senate. The opposition Socialist Party (PSOE) posted its worst showing in 21 years, winning just 125 seats in the Congress of Deputies and 61 in the Senate. Surpassing all expectations at the polls, Aznar secured the firm victory with support from traditional Socialist voters. The creation of two million jobs during his first term, and other popular economic policies such as a privatization program, apparently helped propel him to victory.

The Spanish government began negotiations with ETA in 1998, which announced its first indefinite cease-fire since its campaign of violence that had begun in the early 1960s. The talks, however, broke down only a year later, and violence returned in 2000 with a car bombing in Madrid. In 2002, Judge Baltasar Garzon suspended Batasuna for three years on the grounds that the party had links with ETA. In March 2003, the judge banned the Basque party permanently in response to a government request; this is the first party to be banned in Spain since Franco's death. ETA was blamed for the killing of a PSOE activist in Andoain shortly before municipal elections in February. In October, the Basque regional government approved a plan that calls for more independence from Spain.

Prime Minister Aznar gave U.S. president George W. Bush unwavering support for the war in Iraq, despite significant opposition from Spaniards and protests attended by millions of people. Numerous demonstrators were reportedly injured during peace rallies on March 21 and 22, when the Spanish police allegedly fired rubber bullets into the air, charged into a crowd, and beat some demonstrators with truncheons. The actions of the police were strongly criticized by opposition parties as excessive and disproportionate and have sparked 30 formal complaints with the courts.

Despite such widespread criticism, Aznar's PP held its ground in municipal elections in May, dropping only slightly under its main competitor, the PSOE. During the summer, the regional parliament investigated accusations that real estate interests and the PP itself had bribed two PSOE deputies of the Madrid regional legislature.

**Political Rights and Civil Liberties:** The Spanish can change their government democratically. In 2000, around 69 percent of those registered voted in one of the lowest turnouts since the first democratic elections in 1977. The country is divided into 17 autonomous regions with limited powers, including control over such areas as health care, tourism, local police agencies, and instruction in regional languages. The bicameral federal legislature includes the territorially elected Senate and the Congress of Deputies, elected on the basis of proportional representation and universal suffrage.

People generally have the right to organize in different political parties and other competitive political groups of their choice. However, in March, the Supreme Court upheld a law that permanently bans the Basque separatist Batasuna party for its alleged ties with the armed group ETA.

Spain's ranking in Transparency International's Corruption Perceptions Index dropped from twentieth in 2002 to twenty-third in 2003. An investigation into two PSOE members of the Madrid regional legislature, who had defected to the PP on a key vote and allegedly took bribes from real estate developers that were seeking to block PSOE efforts to limit land speculation, ended with no official conclusion. The scandal led to a collapse of the Madrid regional government and new elections in October that returned the PP to power.

Spain has a free and lively press with more than 100 newspapers that cover a wide range of perspectives and are active in investigating high-level corruption. However, in February a National Court judge ordered the precautionary closure of *Euskaldunon Egunkaria*, the only newspaper written entirely in the Basque language, for allegedly disseminating "terrorist" ideology. The paper has denied any role in tipping off the terrorist group to police actions. Some people arrested in connection with the Basque paper were held incommunicado under antiterrorist legislation; a draft law in January reformed the Code of Criminal Procedure, allowing a judge or court to extend incommunicado detention beyond the current five-day maximum. Journalists have also been the target of the ETA, which has allegedly sent letter bombs and assassinated some media professionals over the past few years. The government does not restrict Internet access.

Freedom of religion is guaranteed in Spain through constitutional and legal protections. Roman Catholicism, however, is the dominant religion and enjoys privileges that other religions do not, such as financing through the tax system. Religious conflicts have erupted between the local population and immigrants, as in the region of Catalan, where more than 5,000 people protested the building of a mosque in 2002.

The government does not restrict academic freedom. However, ETA and other Basque nationalists, through a campaign of street violence and vandalism in the region, continue to intimidate unsympathetic academics, journalists, and politicians.

People are free to assemble, demonstrate, and speak publicly. With the exception of members of the military, workers are free to organize and join unions of their choice. Workers also have the right to strike, although there are limitations imposed on foreigners. The Basic Act on Rights and Freedoms of Foreigners in Spain, which went into force in 2001, limits the rights of foreign workers to organize and strike. The law, which forces foreigners to "obtain authorization for their stay or residence in Spain" before they can organize, strike, or freely assemble, is intended to distinguish between "legal" and "irregular" foreigners.

The constitution provides for an independent judiciary. However, there are concerns about the functioning of the judicial system, including the impact of media pressure on sensitive issues like immigration and Basque terrorism, to the emergence of "celebrity judges" like Baltasar Garzon, who focus too much on high-profile extradition demands for international criminal suspects, like Pinochet, bin Laden, and a number of former military leaders that were involved in Argentina's "dirty war" from 1976 to 1983. In September, Judge Baltasar Garzon ordered Tayseer Alouni, a Syrian-born reporter for Al-Jazeera who worked as a war correspondent in Kabul, Afghanistan, arrested at his home in Alfacar, Spain, and placed him under police custody in Madrid for supposed links to the Spanish cell of al-Qaeda, the Islamic terrorist network.

The Spanish government has endorsed a judicial reform plan that would enhance the transparency of judicial offices, adopt a charter on the rights of citizens, and increase the number and preparation of judges and magistrates. The judiciary has also been affected by Basque terrorism, as judicial officials and law enforcement officers have been the target of ETA and ETA-related extremist groups. In October 2001, around 79 judges and 9 prosecutors were reportedly on a "hit list" drawn up by ETA.

A new immigration law that passed the lower house and is expected to pass the Senate seeks to stem the flow of illegal immigrants by imposing penalties on employers who hire them. The reform also obliges airline companies to turn in the names of people traveling to Spain who never use their return tickets. Rights groups argue that the law does little to integrate immigrants, encouraging more intolerance and xenophobia.

Women enjoy a number of legal protections against rape, domestic abuse, and sexual harassment in the workplace. Despite the existence of these provisions, women still earn about 28 percent less than men do, and women are under-represented in senior management positions in the labor force. In the current parliament, women hold 28.3 percent of the seats in the lower house. There is no national quota system to boost female representation in parliament. Spain is also a destination and transit point for trafficked persons, particularly women for sexual exploitation.

# Sri Lanka

**Population:** 19,300,000  **Political Rights:** 3
**GNI/capita:** $880  **Civil Liberties:** 3*
**Life Expectancy:** 72  **Status:** Partly Free
**Religious Groups:** Buddhist (70 percent),
Hindu (15 percent), Christian (8 percent),
Muslim (7 percent)
**Ethnic Groups:** Sinhalese (74 percent), Tamil (18 percent),
Moor (7 percent), other (1 percent)
**Capital:** Colombo
**Ratings Change:** Sri Lanka's civil liberties rating improved from 4 to 3 due to a significant decline in violence and modest improvements in the rule of law resulting from an ongoing, though tenuous, cease-fire with the Tamil rebels.

**Ten-Year Ratings Timeline (Political Rights, Civil Liberties, Status)**

| 1994 | 1995 | 1996 | 1997 | 1998 | 1999 | 2000 | 2001 | 2002 | 2003 |
|------|------|------|------|------|------|------|------|------|------|
| 4,5PF | 4,5PF | 3,5PF | 3,4PF | 3,4PF | 3,4PF | 3,4PF | 3,4PF | 3,4PF | 3,3PF |

**Overview:**
Progress on the peace talks between the Sri Lankan government and the Tamil Tiger separatist rebels ground to a halt as 2003 progressed, largely because of worsening tensions between Prime Minister Ranil Wickremasinghe's coalition government and President Chandrika Kumaratunga, whose People's Alliance (PA) coalition serves as the opposition in parliament. The two long-time political rivals differ mainly on their approach to the peace process, with Kumaratunga repeatedly criticizing the government's willingness to make concessions to the Tigers as negotiations have progressed. Although the February 2002 cease-fire continued to hold, the Tigers pulled out of participating in formal talks in April and did not attend a donors' conference held in June. The absence of armed conflict led to a further reduction in human rights violations by security forces in the north and east of the country. However, the Tigers continued to commit abuses, including the forcible conscription of child soldiers, politically motivated killings, and restrictions on freedom of expression and of association, throughout the year.

Since independence from Britain in 1948, political power in this island nation has alternated between the conservative United National Party (UNP) and the leftist Sri Lanka Freedom Party (SLFP). While the country has made impressive gains in literacy, basic health care, and other social needs, its economic development has been stunted and its social fabric tested by a long-standing civil war that has killed an estimated 65,000 people. The conflict initially pitted several Tamil guerrilla groups against the government, which is dominated by the Sinhalese majority. The war, although triggered by anti-Tamil riots in 1983 that claimed hundreds of lives, came in the context of long-standing Tamil claims of discrimination in education and employment opportunities. By 1986, the Liberation Tigers of Tamil Eelam (LTTE, or Tamil Tigers), which called for an independent Tamil homeland in the Northern and Eastern Provinces, had eliminated most rival Tamil guerrilla groups and was in control of much of the northern Jaffna Peninsula. At the same time, the government was also fighting an insurgency in the south by the leftist People's Liberation Front (JVP). The JVP insurgency, and the brutal methods used by the army to quell it in 1989, killed 60,000 people.

In 1994, Kumaratunga ended nearly two decades of UNP rule by leading an SLFP-dominated coalition to victory in parliamentary elections and then winning the presidential election. Early in her term, she tried to negotiate a peace agreement with the LTTE, but following a renewal of hostilities by the LTTE, she reverted to focusing on a military solution to the conflict. Kumaratunga won early presidential elections in 1999, but in parliamentary elections held in December 2001, the UNP and its allies won 114 out of a possible 225 seats. Wickremasinghe, the UNP leader, became prime minister, although Kumaratunga remains in office as president.

In response to an LTTE cease-fire offer in December 2001, the new government declared a truce with the rebels, lifted an economic embargo on rebel-held territory, and restarted Norwegian-brokered peace talks. A permanent cease-fire accord with provisions for international monitoring was signed in February 2002. Shortly before the first round of talks took place in September, the government lifted its ban on the LTTE, and by December 2002, the government and Tigers had agreed to share political power in a federal system. Although the LTTE suspended their participation in peace talks in April 2003, they stated that they remained committed to a political solution. In June, bilateral and multilateral donors at a conference held in Tokyo pledged a total of $4.5 billion over a four-year period to support Sri Lanka's reconstruction, although much of the aid is conditionally tied to further progress in reaching a settlement with the Tigers.

However, such progress remained constrained in 2003 by growing tensions between the president and the UNP-led government. On November 4, Kumaratunga declared a state of emergency, sacked three cabinet ministers—of defense, the interior, and information—assumed their portfolios, and temporarily suspended parliament. In order to justify these steps, she expressed concern that proposals made public by the LTTE on October 31 concerning the establishment of a Tiger-dominated interim authority in the northeast were a threat to national security. However, analysts noted that an equally compelling impetus for her actions was the declaration by UNP members that they intended to put forward in parliament an impeachment motion against the chief justice, whom the president views as a key ally.

The state of emergency was pulled back, and parliament resumed functioning on November 19, but Sri Lanka remained at a political impasse. Meanwhile, the 20-month old cease-fire with the LTTE continued to hold, despite an increasing incidence of violations since March 2003, the majority of which have allegedly been committed by the LTTE. The government refused to enter into further negotiations with the Tigers, claiming that it was pointless to do so while the president controlled the defense ministry. Although all three actors insist that they are committed to a peaceful resolution of the conflict, observers believe that meaningful peace talks will not resume until the political standoff between the PA and UNP is resolved.

**Political Rights and Civil Liberties:** Sri Lankans can change their government through elections based on universal adult suffrage. The 1978 constitution vested strong executive powers in a president who is directly elected for a six-year term and can dissolve parliament. The 225-member unicameral parliament is directly elected for a five-year term through a mix of single-seat, simple-plurality districts and proportional representation. Elections are open to multiple parties, and fair electoral laws and equal campaigning opportunities ensure a competitive political process. While elections are generally free, they are marred by some irregularities, violence, and intimidation. The independent Center for Monitoring Election Violence recorded 2,734 incidents of election-related violence during the December 2001 parliamentary election campaign, including 47 murders and more than 1,500 assaults, threats, and other abuses. The LTTE refuses to allow elections in the areas under its control and continues to intimidate rival nonmilitarized Tamil political parties.

In recent years, the fact that the executive and legislative branches of government have been controlled by competing parties headed by long-standing political rivals has led to tension and, at times, an inability to effectively resolve issues and construct coherent state policies. The cohabitation between the two rival leaders—President Chandrika Kumaratunga of the SLFP and Prime Minister Ranil Wickremasinghe of the UNP—became increasingly tense throughout 2003. In particular, differences of opinion over the correct way to approach the peace process have led to an inability to formulate a united strategy toward the LTTE and its specific demands during the ongoing negotiations. In addition, the fact that the president can dismiss the government at any time limits the latter's ability to be a strong and effective negotiator who can follow through on its commitments.

Official corruption is a growing concern. In response to increasing pressure from the media and from members of the government, Wickremasinghe appointed a committee in May to look into charges of corruption against ministers and senior ruling coalition politicians, suspended four politicians at the local government level, and attempted to introduce a code of ethics for members of his party. However, the legal and administrative framework currently in force is inadequate in terms of either promoting integrity or punishing the corrupt behavior of public officials. No current or former politician has thus far been sentenced for bribery or corruption, although more than a dozen cases were under investigation or prosecution during the year.

Freedom of expression is provided for in the constitution, and independent media outlets can generally express their views openly. However, the LTTE does not permit freedom of expression in the areas under its control and continues to intimidate and threaten a number of Tamil journalists and other critics. The government controls the largest newspaper chain, two major television stations, and a radio station; political coverage in the state-owned media favors the ruling party. During the state of emergency declared in November, Kumaratunga briefly deployed troops outside government-run media outlets and sacked the chairman of the government-owned Lake House media group. Reporters, particularly those who cover human rights issues or official misconduct, continued to face harassment and threats from the police, security forces, government officials, political activists, and the LTTE. In July 2003, Fisheries Minister Mahinda Wijeskera threatened to kill Lasantha Wickrematunga, the editor of *The Sunday Leader*, after the newspaper published a series of articles accusing the minister of corruption. Business interests wield some control over content in the form of selective advertising and bribery.

Religious freedom is respected, and members of all faiths are generally allowed to worship freely, although the constitution gives special status to Buddhism and there is some discrimination and occasional violence against religious minorities. The LTTE discriminates against Muslims in the areas under its control and has attacked Buddhist sites in the past. According to the U.S. State Department's 2003 Report on International Religious Freedom, evangelical Christian missionaries are occasionally harassed by Buddhist clergy and others opposed to their work.

The government generally respects academic freedom. However, the LTTE has a record of repressing the voices of those intellectuals who criticize its actions, sometimes through murder or other forms of violent intimidation. Groups such as the University Teachers for Human Rights-Jaffna (UTHR-J) have faced particularly severe harassment at the hands of the LTTE.

Freedom of assembly is generally respected, although both main political parties occasionally disrupt each other's rallies and political events. Except in conflict-affected areas, human rights and social welfare nongovernmental organizations generally operate freely. However, the LTTE does not allow for freedom of association in the regions under its control and reportedly uses coercion to force civilians to attend pro-LTTE rallies.

Trade unions are independent and engage in collective bargaining. Except for civil servants, most workers can hold strikes. However, under the 1989 Essential Services Act, the president can declare a strike in any industry illegal. Kumaratunga has used the act to end several strikes. Employers on tea plantations routinely violate the rights of the mainly Tamil workforce.

Successive governments have respected the constitutional provision for an independent judiciary, and judges can generally make decisions in an atmosphere free of overt intimidation from the legislative or executive branches. However, there is growing concern about the perceived politicization of the judiciary, in particular regarding the conduct of the present chief justice. According to the Colombo-based Free Media Movement, he has narrowed the scope of human rights litigation, dismissed a number of judges without holding an inquiry or disciplinary hearing, and consistently defended the president and her party in legal actions relating to political disputes. At the lower levels of the judiciary, corruption is fairly common among both judges and court staff, and those willing to pay bribes have more efficient access to the legal system.

Despite an overall reduction in the number of human rights abuses committed by police and security forces since the February 2002 cease-fire, the rule of law remains weak, and torture and prolonged detention without trial continue to be issues of concern. Such practices are facilitated by legislation such as the Prevention of Terrorism Act (PTA), under which security personnel can arrest and detain suspects indefinitely without court approval. Although no new arrests under the PTA were reported during the year, many of those detained previously under the PTA remain in detention.

There has been little progress in reducing acts of torture by the security forces and police, particularly of detainees during routine interrogations. In August, the Hong Kong–based Asian Human Rights Commission demanded action against policemen in the central province of Kandy, who allegedly tortured two teenage boys in July and then framed false charges against them. Cases of custodial death and custodial rape continue to be reported. A lack of aggressive prosecution of the majority of past abuses contributes to a climate of impunity for those who have overstepped the bounds of the law.

The LTTE has effective control on the ground in large sections of the north and east of the country and operates a parallel administration that includes schools, hospitals, courts, and police and other law enforcement personnel. The Tigers raise money through extortion, kidnapping, theft, and the seizure of Muslim property, and have used threats and attacks to close schools, courts, and government agencies in their self-styled Tamil homeland. Despite their involvement in the peace process, the rebels continued to be responsible for summary executions of civilians, "disappearances," arbitrary abductions and detentions, torture, and the forcible conscription of children to be used as soldiers during the year. Press reports as well as a report issued by the UTHR-J in March indicated that the Tigers continued to recruit teenage children in 2003 despite promises to end the practice. The LTTE has also targeted Tamil political parties that challenge its claim to represent the Tamil people, particularly the Eelam People's Democratic Party (EPDP) and the Eelam People's Revolutionary Liberation Front-Varathar (EPRLF-V), with several dozen party members and supporters having been killed since February 2002, according to a briefing paper released by Human Rights Watch in August.

Tamils maintain that they face systematic discrimination in several matters controlled by the state, including government employment, university education, and access to justice. Thousands of Tamils whose ancestors were brought from India to work as indentured laborers in the nineteenth century did not qualify for Sri Lankan citizenship and faced discrimination and exploitation by the native Sinhalese. However, in October, the parliament approved legislation granting citizenship to about 170,000 previously stateless "Indian" Tamils. Tensions between the three major ethnic groups (Sinhalese, Tamil, and Muslim), which lead to occasional violence, remain a concern. In April, rioting between the Tamil and Muslim populations of the northeast left a number of people dead or injured and hundreds displaced. Overall, nearly a third of the estimated one million internally displaced refugees have returned to their homes since February 2002, but many more remain unwilling or unable to return to the northeast and continue to live in camps throughout the country, according to Refugees International.

Women are under-represented in politics and the civil service. Female employees in the private sector face some sexual harassment as well as discrimination in salary and promotion opportunities. Rape and domestic violence against women remain serious problems, and authorities weakly enforce existing laws. Although women have equal rights under national, civil, and criminal law, matters related to the family, including marriage, divorce, child custody, and inheritance, are adjudicated under the customary law of each ethnic or religious group, and the application of these laws sometimes results in discrimination against women.

# Sudan

**Population:** 38,100,000
**GNI/capita:** $340
**Life Expectancy:** 57
**Religious Groups:** Sunni Muslim (70 percent),
Indigenous beliefs (25 percent), Christian (5 percent)
**Ethnic Groups:** Black (52 percent), Arab (39 percent),
Beja (6 percent), other (3 percent)
**Capital:** Khartoum

**Political Rights:** 7
**Civil Liberties:** 7
**Status:** Not Free

**Ten-Year Ratings Timeline (Political Rights, Civil Liberties, Status)**

| 1994 | 1995 | 1996 | 1997 | 1998 | 1999 | 2000 | 2001 | 2002 | 2003 |
|------|------|------|------|------|------|------|------|------|------|
| 7,7NF | 7,7NF | 7,7NF | 7,7NF | 7,7NF | 7,7NF | 7,7NF | 7,7NF | 7,7NF | 7,7NF |

**Overview:**

Long-elusive peace in Sudan finally seemed at hand at the end of 2003. While some fighting did take place throughout the year, including alleged massacres, the government and the main rebel group in the country's south agreed to sign a comprehensive peace agreement that would end nearly twenty years of continuous war that has claimed more than two million lives. Some internally displaced refugees returned to the south, and more humanitarian aid was delivered to war-affected areas. The United States hinted that sanctions against Sudan would be lifted if there was meaningful progress in the peace process and cooperation in the war against global terrorism. International enthusiasm over progress in the peace process, however, overshadowed the emergence of a new and separate battlefront in the country's west, which had claimed thousands of lives and generated a massive refugee crisis by the autumn. Hassan al-Turabi, a leading Sudanese Muslim cleric and former leader of the ruling governing party, was released from prison.

Africa's largest country has been embroiled in civil wars for 37 of its 47 years as an independent state. It achieved independence in 1956 after nearly 80 years of British rule. The Anyanya movement, representing mainly Christian and animist black Africans in southern Sudan, battled Arab Muslim government forces from 1956 to 1972. In 1969, General Jafar Numeiri toppled an elected government and created a military dictatorship. The south gained extensive autonomy under a 1972 accord, and for the next decade, an uneasy peace prevailed. Then, in 1983, General Jafar Numeiri restricted southern autonomy and imposed Sharia (Islamic law). Opposition led again to civil war, and Numeiri was overthrown in 1985. Civilian rule was restored in 1986 with an election that resulted in a government led by Sadiq al-Mahdi of the moderate Islamic Ummah Party, but war continued. Lieutenant General Omar al-Bashir ousted al-Mahdi in a 1989 coup, and al-Mahdi spent seven years in prison or under house arrest before fleeing to Eritrea. Until 1999, al-Bashir ruled through a military-civilian regime backed by senior Muslim clerics including Hassan al-Turabi, who wielded considerable power as the ruling National Congress (NC) party leader and speaker of the 360-member National Assembly.

Tensions between al-Bashir and al-Turabi climaxed in December 1999; on the eve of a parliamentary vote on a plan by al-Turabi to curb presidential powers, al-

Bashir dissolved parliament and declared a state of emergency. He introduced a law allowing the formation of political parties, fired al-Turabi as NC head, replaced the cabinet with his own supporters, and held deeply flawed presidential and parliamentary elections in December 2000, which the NC won overwhelmingly. Al-Turabi formed his own party, the Popular National Congress (PNC), in June 2000, but was prohibited from participating in politics. In January 2001, the Ummah Party refused to join al-Bashir's new government despite the president's invitation, declaring that it refused to support totalitarianism.

Al-Turabi and some 20 of his supporters were arrested in February 2001 after he called for a national uprising against the government and signed a memorandum of understanding in Geneva with the southern-based, rebel Sudanese People's Liberation Army (SPLA). In May 2001, al-Turabi and four aides were charged with conspiracy to overthrow the government, and al-Turabi was placed under house arrest. In September 2002, he was moved to a high-security prison.

Al-Bashir began to lift Sudan out of international isolation by sidelining al-Turabi, who was seen as the force behind Sudan's efforts to export Islamic extremism. Although Vice President Ali Osman Mohammed Taha—who replaced al-Turabi as Islamic ideologue—maintains a firm commitment to Sudan as an Islamic state and to the government's self-proclaimed jihad against non-Muslims, al-Bashir has managed to repair relations with several states, including Iran, Eritrea, Saudi Arabia, and even the United States. Following the September 11, 2001 terrorist attacks against the United States, al-Bashir issued a statement rejecting violence and offered his country's cooperation in combating terrorism. Sudan had previously provided safe haven for Osama bin Laden and his al-Qaeda network.

Sudan's civil war has pitted government forces and government-backed, northern Arab Muslims against southern-based black African animists and Christians. The government also has sponsored the Popular Defense Force, a volunteer, militant Islamic militia that fights against southern rebels. Some pro-democracy northerners, however, have allied themselves with the SPLA-led southern rebels to form the National Democratic Alliance (NDA), while northern rebels of the Sudan Allied Forces have staged attacks in northeastern Sudan. Some southern groups have signed peace pacts with the government, but there is fighting among rival southern militias. A convoluted mix of historical, religious, ethnic, and cultural tensions has made peace elusive, while competition for economic resources has fueled the conflict. Past cease-fire attempts have failed, with Khartoum insisting on an unconditional cease-fire and the SPLA demanding the establishment of a secular constitution first. In 1999, Khartoum inaugurated an oil pipeline, helping to finance its war effort and ultimately bring greater urgency to the peace initiatives.

Throughout the war, the government has regularly bombed civilian as well as rebel targets. International humanitarian relief efforts have been hampered by cease-fire violations and have sometimes been deliberately targeted by parties to the conflict. The government has denied humanitarian relief workers access to rebel-held areas or areas containing large concentrations of internal refugees.

A peace plan proposed in December 2001 by former U.S. senator John Danforth called for "one country, two systems" in Sudan, with an Islamic government in the north and a secular system in the south.

The international community stepped up its mediation efforts in the civil war in

2002, in part to prevent Sudan from becoming a breeding ground for terrorism, as Afghanistan had prior to September 11, 2001. Peace talks under the auspices of the Intergovernmental Authority on Development (IGAD), which continued in 2003, focused on southern self-determination, borders, and the application of Sharia in the south.

In January 2002, U.S.-mediated peace talks between the government and rebels took place in Switzerland, leading to a breakthrough agreement affecting the Nuba mountain region, a 30,000-square-mile area in the heart of Sudan. The black Africans native to the Nuba region numbered more than one million in 1985, but have been reduced to some 300,000 today. The government has bombed the region frequently and enforced blockades preventing food, fuel, clothing, and medicine from entering.

While in 2002 the government agreed to extend the Nuba agreement and participated in further talks in Machakos, Kenya, rebels reported government-sponsored attacks in several towns and villages. The government also bombed southern villages with MiG fighters and helicopter gunships.

In the fall of 2002, the United States passed the landmark Sudan Peace Act, which recognized Sudan as guilty of genocide. The act authorized direct aid to the south to prepare the population for peace and democratic governance. It also specified sanctions against Khartoum if Sudan is deemed to be hampering humanitarian efforts or judged not to be negotiating in good faith. At the same time, the Canadian oil company Talisman quit drilling operations in Sudan after enduring years of pressure from human rights organizations. It also sold its 25 percent stake in Sudan's Greater Nile Petroleum Operating Company. Human Rights Watch has documented how the Sudanese government has used roads, bridges, and airfields built by international oil companies to wage war in the south, especially in the oil-rich Western Upper Nile region. The report charges some of the companies with complicity in human rights abuses, claming that executives ignored government attacks against civilian targets.

In 2003, substantive peace talks finally resulted in a relaxation of hostilities and the highest degree of optimism yet that a final resolution of the conflict was within reach. However, reports of fighting and massacres surfaced during the year. Canadian and U.S. nongovernmental groups reported a massacre by army regulars in a village in the upper Nile region, citing the discovery of the remains of approximately 2,000-3,000 villagers, including children.

Despite the massacre reports, U.S. President George W. Bush announced in April that the Sudanese government and the SPLA were negotiating in good faith. The Sudan Peace Act requires the president to determine the state of talks every six months. The U.S. State Department, however, reported to the U.S. Congress about possible war crimes in Sudan, including possible genocide in the Upper Western Nile region.

In October, the government and the SPLA agreed to sign a power-sharing agreement at the end of 2003. The deal would effectively end the war and begin a six-year transition period leading to a referendum on southern secession, during which time the government would withdraw 80 percent of its troops from the south. Outstanding issues included whether to extend Sharia law to the capital, Khartoum, home to many non-Muslim southerners, and how to share profits accrued from southern oil fields.

In November, amidst ongoing negotiations and an overall improved security climate, refugees began returning to the south, raising the specter of an enormous logistical challenge and a potential health crisis. There are approximately 500,000 Sudanese refugees in neighboring countries and 3-4 million internally displaced people.

The United States still maintains sanctions against Sudan based on the country's human rights abuses and its apparent support for terrorism. Sudan tried to demonstrate its cooperation in the war against terrorism during the year. In May, security forces conducted a raid on an alleged terrorist training camp in Kardofan, killing four Saudi nationals. Seventeen other Saudis were arrested for taking part in weapons-training exercises in a remote part of western Sudan. Thought to be possible al-Qaeda operatives, they were deported to Saudi Arabia. However, Sudan's commitment to combating terrorism was called into question in June, when Greek authorities operating in the Mediterranean Sea seized a vessel carrying 680 metric tons of explosives destined for a Sudanese port. The listed recipient, a Khartoum-based chemical company, turned out not to exist. Sudan claimed the explosives were for peaceful purposes.

In June, Sudanese Foreign Minister Osman Ismail met with U.S. Secretary of State Colin Powell in Washington to discuss the removal of Sudan from the U.S. list of state sponsors of terrorism. On the day of the meeting, Sudanese forces reportedly attacked ten villages in Eastern Upper Nile, killing at least 60 villagers and abducting several children.

In February, a separate warfront opened in western Darfur province; armed conflict over competing land claims erupted between mostly black agriculturalists and government-backed nomadic Arab militias, known as Janjaweed. The Sudan Liberation Movement (SLM) rebel group was formed in defense of farmers and landowners, who demand greater regional economic rights and self-determination. Despite a cease-fire between the SLM and the government in November, attacks by Janjaweed against farming villages continued. The government said it no longer backed the Janjaweed, but it also restricted humanitarian access to the conflict areas. The United Nations reported that the fighting displaced 500,000 people, with many fleeing west to neighboring Chad. According to the United States, several thousand people were killed in the fighting.

In October, Hassan al-Turabi was released from prison. Analysts suggested that with the government now negotiating closely with the SPLA, there was little need to continue holding al-Turabi, who, as a political rival to President Omar al-Bashir, had previously signed a peace deal with the rebel group.

**Political Rights and Civil Liberties:** Sudanese cannot change their government democratically. The December 2000 presidential and parliamentary elections cannot credibly be said to have reflected the will of the people. The major opposition parties, which are believed to have the support of most Sudanese, boycotted in protest of what they said were attempts by a totalitarian regime to impart the appearance of fairness. The EU declined an invitation to monitor the polls to avoid bestowing legitimacy on the outcome. Omar al-Bashir, running against former president Jafar Numeiri and three relative unknowns, won 86 percent of the vote. NC candidates stood uncontested for nearly two-thirds of parliamentary seats. Voting did not take place in some 17 rebel-held constituencies, and government claims of 66 percent voter turnout in some states were denounced as fictitious. The president can appoint and dismiss state governors at his discretion. There is little press freedom in Sudan. Journalists practice self-censorship to avoid harassment, arrest, and closure of their publications. There are several daily newspapers and a wide variety of Arabic- and English-language publications. While all of these are subject to censorship, some do criticize the government. Radio and television stations are owned by the government and are required to reflect government policy in broadcasts. Penalties apply to journalists who allegedly harm the nation or economy or violate national security. A 1999 law imposes penalties for "professional errors."

In March, state security police detained without explanation a journalist with the *Khartoum Monitor*, an English-language daily. This marked the beginning of year-long harassment of the paper by the government. In July, the Sudanese Court of Crimes Against the State revoked the paper's publishing license because of a 2001 article on slavery in the country's south. Shortly afterward, the paper's editor, Nhial Bol, was involved in a car accident, which many believed to be a deliberate attempt by the state to kill him. In October, Bol fled to Kenya and reported receiving death threats. The government also seized copies of the Arab-language *As Sahafa* and closed the daily *Alwan* for "inciting sedition."

Islam is the state religion, and the constitution claims Sharia as the source of its legislation. At least 75 percent of Sudanese are Muslim, though most southern Sudanese adhere to traditional indigenous beliefs or Christianity. The overwhelming majority of those displaced or killed by war and famine in Sudan have been non-Muslims, and many have starved because of a policy under which food is withheld pending conversion to Islam. Officials have described their campaign against non-Muslims as a holy war. Under the 1994 Societies Registration Act, religious groups must register in order to gather legally. Registration is reportedly difficult to obtain. The government denies permission to build churches and destroys Christian schools, centers, and churches. Roman Catholic priests face random detention and interrogation by police.

Emergency law severely restricts freedom of assembly and association. Students are forbidden to participate in political activities according to the Acts of Student Codes, introduced in 2002 after several university students in Khartoum were suspended for engaging in human rights activities, including organizing symposiums on women's rights and attending a conference on democracy. Other students have been expelled for organizing political activities, and security forces have forcefully broken up demonstrations. In November 2002, the government closed the University of Khartoum indefinitely after students protested attacks on dormitories by pro-government student militias. Several students were injured and arrested. The clashes erupted following student celebrations of the thirty-eighth anniversary of protests against Sudan's first military government and against the banning of the University Students Union four years ago, when opposition groups were poised to win campus elections. The student's union remained banned in 2003. While many international nongovernmental organizations operate in Sudan, the government restricts their movement and ability to carry out their work, which often includes providing essential humanitarian assistance.

There are no independent trade unions. The Sudan Workers Trade Unions Federation is the main labor organization, with about 800,000 members. Local union elections are rigged to ensure the election of government-approved candidates. A lack of labor legislation limits the freedom of workers to organize or bargain collectively. Equality of opportunity and business and property rights are generally restricted to Sudan's Arab, Muslim community.

The judiciary is not independent. The chief justice of the Supreme Court, who presides over the entire judiciary, is government-appointed. Regular courts provide some due process safeguards, but special security and military courts, which are used to punish political opponents of the government, provide none. "Special courts" often deal with criminal matters, despite their use of military judges. Criminal law is based on Sharia and provides for flogging, amputation, crucifixion, and execution. Ten southern, predominantly non-Muslim states are officially exempted from Sharia, although criminal law allows for its application in the future if the state assemblies choose to implement it. Arbitrary arrest, detention, and torture are widespread, and security forces act with impunity. Prison conditions do not meet international standards. In June, the Sudanese Organization Against Torture reported the arbitrary arrest and torture of several people, including students suspected of engaging in political activities or harboring SPLA sympathies. Early in the year, three men in northern Darfur accused of bank robbery were hanged after quick trials in which the accused were denied legal representation. Their appeals and attendant entreaties from the European Union went unheeded.

Serious human rights abuses by nearly every faction involved in the civil war have been reported. Secret police have operated "ghost houses"—detention and torture centers—in several cities. Government armed forces have reportedly routinely raided villages, burning homes, killing residents, and abducting women and children to be used as slaves in the north. Relief agencies have discovered thousands of people held captive in the north and have purchased their freedom so that they could return to the south. International aid workers have been abducted and killed. In 2002, the International Eminent Persons Group—a fact-finding mission composed of humanitarian relief workers, human rights lawyers, academics, and former European and American diplomats—confirmed the existence of slavery in Sudan. After conducting extensive research in the country, the group reported a range of human rights abuses, including what under international law is considered slavery. The report also addressed abductions and forced servitude under the SPLA's authority.

Although there has been no organized effort to compile casualty statistics in southern Sudan since 1994, the total number of people killed by war, famine, and disease is believed to exceed two million. Up to four million people are internally displaced due to government efforts to clear black Africans from oil fields or potential oil drilling sites. In recent years, the government has blocked aid shipments and relief workers to areas affected by war and prevented relief workers from reaching civilians.

Women face discrimination in family matters such as marriage, divorce, and inheritance, which are governed by Sharia. Women are represented in parliament and hold 35 of the assembly's 360 seats. Public order police frequently harass women and monitor their dress for adherence to government standards of modesty. Female genital mutilation occurs despite legal prohibition, and rape is reportedly routine in war zones. According to Amnesty International, women have less access to legal representation than men. President al-Bashir announced in January 2001 that Sudan would not ratify the International Convention on Eradication of All Forms of Discrimination Against Women because it "contradicted Sudanese values and traditions." Children are used as soldiers by government and opposition forces in the civil war.

# Suriname

**Population:** 400,000
**GNI/capita:** $1,890
**Life Expectancy:** 70
**Political Rights:** 1
**Civil Liberties:** 2
**Status:** Free
**Religious Groups:** Hindu (27.4 percent),
Muslim (19.6 percent), Roman Catholic (22.8 percent),
Protestant (25.2 percent), indigenous beliefs (5 percent)
**Ethnic Groups:** East Indian (37 percent), Creole (31 percent),
Javanese (15 percent), other (17 percent)
**Capital:** Paramaribo

**Ten-Year Ratings Timeline (Political Rights, Civil Liberties, Status)**

| 1994 | 1995 | 1996 | 1997 | 1998 | 1999 | 2000 | 2001 | 2002 | 2003 |
|------|------|------|------|------|------|------|------|------|------|
| 3,3PF | 3,3PF | 3,3PF | 3,3PF | 3,3PF | 3,3PF | 1,2F | 1,2F | 1,2F | 1,2F |

**Overview:**

The spillover effects of narcotics trafficking and the drug trade's ties to top political leaders—including former dictator and current member of parliament Desi Bouterse—continued to make the news in Suriname in 2003. Bouterse was one of more than 30 people accused of participating in the 1982 slaying of 15 critics of his military regime. However, as of November 30, no trial date has been set in that case.

The Republic of Suriname achieved independence from the Netherlands in 1975, which had acquired it as a result of the Treaty of Breda with the British in 1667. Five years after independence, a military coup, which brought Desi Bouterse to power as the head of a regime that brutally suppressed civic and political opposition, initiated a decade of military intervention in politics. In 1987, Bouterse permitted elections that were won handily by the New Front for Democracy and Development, a four-party coalition of mainly East Indian, Creole, and Javanese parties. The National Democratic Party (NDP), organized by the military, won just 3 seats.

In 1990, the army ousted President Ramsewak Shankar and Bouterse again took power. International pressure led to new elections in 1991. The center-right New Front won a majority, although the NDP increased its share to 12. The National Assembly selected the New Front's candidate, Ronald Venetiaan, as president. Bouterse quit the army in 1992 in order to lead the NDP. In the May 25, 2000 legislative elections, the New Front won the majority of 51 National Assembly seats—three times as many as its closest rival.

The May 2001 death of a labor leader who was to be the star witness in a trial against Bouterse and others accused of 15 political killings on December 8, 1982 initially appeared to rob the prosecution of key testimony needed to convict the former narcotics-running strongman. However, the government vowed that testimony given by the witness during a preliminary hearing would be submitted in the trial by the judge who questioned him, a move defense lawyers said they would oppose, claiming they would be denied the right to cross-examine the witness. The death of the lone survivor of the December 1982 massacre came amid a renewed push by the Dutch to bring Bouterse to account for the murders and for his role in the 1982 coup. He had already been tried and convicted by a Dutch court in absentia on charges of having introduced more than two tons of cocaine into the Netherlands between 1989 and 1997. Suriname did not extradite Bouterse to the Netherlands because of a bilateral agreement not to extradite their own citizens to each other's country.

In June 2002, the Surinamese police deported to the United States Carlos Bolas, a member of the Colombian Revolutionary Armed Forces (FARC) guerrillas, to face charges of drug trafficking and murder. U.S. authorities say that Bolas, in addition to providing cocaine to Colombian traffickers in exchange for arms, money, and equipment, also was involved in the murder of three American activists in 2000. In October, authorities from neighboring Guyana complained that Suriname is a major supply route for illegal arms used in a crime wave gripping the Guyanese capital of Georgetown.

In October 2003, Dino Bouterse—the son of Desi Bouterse—was acquitted by a military court of stealing more than 80 guns, including twenty-one AK-47 assault rifles, from the government's secret service compound. The court ruled that there was insufficient evidence to convict him. The father, now a member of parliament, said that the charges were part of a political conspiracy by his political opponents.

The trial of a former finance minister in the Wijdenbosch government on fraud and corruption charges began in April. The accused maintained his innocence and said that the government was looking for a scapegoat to blame for the country's economic woes. In October, a judge gave more than 50 convicted cocaine traffickers light sentences in an effort by the government to reduce overcrowding in the country's jails. The UN Drug Control Agency estimates that 20 tons of cocaine is smuggled annually through Suriname to Europe alone.

**Political Rights and Civil Liberties:** Citizens of Suriname can change their government democratically. The constitution provides for a directly elected, 51-seat National Assembly, which serves a five-year term and selects the state president. Political parties largely reflect the cleavages in Suriname's ethnically complex society. A record of 23 parties competed in the 2000 elections.

The Heritage Foundation/*Wall Street Journal* 2003 Index of Economic Freedom rated Suriname a 4 on a 1/5 scale, with 5 indicating that corruption is rampant, regulations are applied randomly, and the general level of regulation is very high.

The government generally respects freedom of expression. Radio is both public and private. A number of small commercial radio stations compete with the government-owned radio and television broadcasting system, which generally offer pluralistic viewpoints. The government does not restrict access to the Internet.

The government generally respects freedom of religion and does not restrict academic freedom.

Although civic institutions remain weak, human rights organizations function freely. Workers can join independent trade unions, and the labor movement is active in politics. Collective bargaining is legal and conducted fairly widely. Civil servants have no legal right to strike.

The judiciary is weak and susceptible to political influence and suffers from ineffectiveness and a large backlog of cases. Both the courts and prisons have become seriously overburdened by the volume of people detained for narcotics trafficking. The civilian police abuse detainees, particularly during arrests; guards mistreat prisoners; and prisons are dangerously overcrowded, with as many as 16 inmates sharing a two-person cell.

Discrimination against indigenous and tribal peoples is widespread. Tribal peoples, called Maroons, are the descendants of escaped African slaves who formed autonomous communities in the rain forest in the seventeenth and eighteenth centuries. Their rights to their lands and resources, to cultural integrity, and to the autonomous administration of their affairs are not recognized in Surinamese law.

Constitutional guarantees of gender equality are not enforced, and the Asian Marriage Act allows parents to arrange marriages for their children without their consent. Several organizations specifically address violence against women and related issues. Despite their central role in agriculture and food production, 60 percent of rural women, particularly those in tribal communities, live below the poverty level.

# Swaziland

**Population:** 1,200,000
**GNI/capita:** $1,300
**Life Expectancy:** 45
**Religious Groups:** Zionist [a blend of Christianity and indigenous ancestral worship] (40 percent), Roman Catholic (20 percent), Muslim (10 percent), other (30 percent)
**Political Rights:** 7*
**Civil Liberties:** 5
**Status:** Not Free

**Ethnic Groups:** African (97 percent), European (3 percent)
**Capital:** Mbabane
**Ratings Change:** Swaziland's political rights rating declined from 6 to 7 due to the adoption of a constitution designed to entrench more deeply the institution of rule by royal decree.

**Ten-Year Ratings Timeline (Political Rights, Civil Liberties, Status)**

| 1994 | 1995 | 1996 | 1997 | 1998 | 1999 | 2000 | 2001 | 2002 | 2003 |
|------|------|------|------|------|------|------|------|------|------|
| 6,5NF | 6,5NF | 6,5NF | 6,5NF | 6,4NF | 6,5NF | 6,5NF | 6,5NF | 6,5NF | 7,5NF |

**Overview:**
Swaziland's long-awaited new constitution was unveiled in May 2003 and was swiftly denounced by pro-democracy activists, trade union members, and civil society represen-

tatives. International observers concluded that parliamentary elections held in October were neither free nor fair.

Swaziland's King Mswati III is the latest monarch of the Dlamini dynasty, under which the Swazi kingdom expanded and contracted in conflicts with neighboring groups. Britain declared the kingdom a protectorate to prevent Boer expansion in the 1880s and assumed administrative power in 1903. Swaziland regained its independence in 1968, and an elected parliament was added to the traditional kingship and chieftaincies. In 1973, Mswati's predecessor, Sobhuza II (who died in 1983) repealed the 1968 constitution, ended the multiparty system in favor of the *tinkhundla* (local council) system, and declared himself absolute monarch.

Voting in October 1998 legislative elections was marked by very low turnout and was neither open nor fair. It was based on the Swazi tinkhundla system of closely controlled nominations and voting that seeks to legitimatize the rule of King Mswati III and his Dlamini clan. Security forces arrested and briefly detained labor and other pro-democracy leaders before the elections and after a series of bomb blasts. The 55 elected members of the National Assembly were approved by the government and were joined by 10 royal appointees.

The country's new constitution, a product of five years of work by the country's Constitutional Review Commission, was unveiled in May 2003. The document maintains a ban on political opposition to royal rule and reaffirms the palace's absolute control over the cabinet, parliament, and the courts. Although it provides for limited freedom of speech, of assembly and of association, and limited equality for women, King Mswati III may waive these rights at his discretion. The Swaziland Democratic Alliance, an umbrella group of banned political parties and human rights, civil, and labor groups, said in September that it planned to draft an alternative constitution that envisions a multiparty system.

A Commonwealth monitoring team reported that the October parliamentary 2003 elections were not credible, citing a lack of free expression in the country, police repression of pro-democracy activists, and the ban on political parties. The Swaziland Democratic Alliance had called on voters to boycott the elections. The number of women legislators increased to an impressive 30 percent, or a total of 16 of 55 seats.

Most Swazis remain engaged in subsistence agriculture. Many families depend on income from men working in South African mines. The country has been hit hard by the AIDS pandemic. According to a UNAIDS report released in November 2003, an estimated 39 percent of the adult population is infected with HIV.

**Political Rights and Civil Liberties:** Swazis are barred from exercising their right to elect their representatives or to change their government freely. King Mswati III is an absolute monarch, and royal decrees carry the full force of law. Of the 65 members of the National Assembly, 55 are elected and 10 are appointed by the king. The king also appoints 20 members of the Senate, with the remaining 10 selected by the National Assembly.

Freedom of expression is severely restricted, especially regarding political issues or matters concerning the royal family. Legislation bans publication of any criticism of the monarchy and self-censorship is widespread. However, broadcast and print media from South Africa are received in the country. There is one independent radio station, which broadcasts religious programming. In April, the new information minister, Abednego Ntshangase, announced that the state media would not be permitted to cover anything that has a "negative bearing" on the government. The ban affects the country's only television station and news-carrying radio channels. The government does not restrict access to the Internet.

Freedom of religion is respected, although there are no formal constitutional provisions protecting the practice. Academic freedom is limited by self-censorship. The government restricts freedom of assembly and association. The trade union movement remains a target of repression, and the American Federation of Labor-Congress of Industrial Organizations (AFL-CIO) petitioned the U.S. Trade Representative in September 2003 to remove Swaziland's trade privileges. At the same time, the Swaziland Federation of Trade Unions, the country's largest labor organization, has been a leader in demands for democratization. Workers in all elements of the economy, including the public sector, can join unions, and 80 percent of the private workforce is unionized. Wage agreements are often reached by collective bargaining.

The dual-system judiciary, which is based on Western and traditional law, is generally independent in most civil cases, although the royal family and the government can influence the courts. Swaziland's judicial system suffered a setback in December 2002, when six South African judges on the country's court of appeals resigned after the prime minister said that the government would ignore court judgments that curbed the king's power.

There are regular reports of police brutality, including torture and beatings. Security forces generally operate with impunity. In November, the Swaziland Red Cross met with prisoners, who complained of beatings with metal chains, of overcrowding, and of neglect of inmates suffering from HIV and AIDS.

The Legal Code provides some protection against sexual harassment, but Swazi women encounter discrimination in both formal and customary law. Employment regulations requiring equal pay for equal work are obeyed unevenly. Married women are considered minors, requiring spousal permission to enter into almost any form of economic activity, and they are allowed only limited inheritance rights. Violence against women is common despite traditional strictures against it.

# Sweden

**Population:** 9,000,000
**GNI/capita:** $25,400
**Life Expectancy:** 80
**Religious Groups:** Lutheran (87 percent), other [including Roman Catholic, Orthodox, Baptist, Muslim, Jewish and Buddhist] (13 percent)
**Ethnic Groups:** Swedish (majority), Finnish, Sami
**Capital:** Stockholm

**Political Rights:** 1
**Civil Liberties:** 1
**Status:** Free

**Ten-Year Ratings Timeline (Political Rights, Civil Liberties, Status)**

| 1994 | 1995 | 1996 | 1997 | 1998 | 1999 | 2000 | 2001 | 2002 | 2003 |
|------|------|------|------|------|------|------|------|------|------|
| 1,1F | 1,1F | 1,1F | 1,1F | 1,1F | 1,1F | 1,1F | 1,1F | 1,1F | 1,1F |

**Overview:**

The political landscape in 2003 was marked by Sweden's rejection of the euro, the European common currency, in a September 14 referendum and by the murder of Foreign Minister Anna Lindh just days earlier. The referendum ensured Swedish sovereignty at the potential expense of influence in the European Union (EU), while Lindh's murder led Swedes to revisit the tradeoff between the safety and approachability of their public figures.

After a series of monarchical alliances with Finland, Denmark, and Norway in the eleventh through nineteenth centuries, Sweden emerged as a modern democracy. Its tradition of neutrality, beginning with World War I, was altered somewhat by its admission to the EU in 1995, and further eroded by a more pragmatic approach to security first presented in 2002. However, Sweden has retained its commitment to stay outside of military alliances, including NATO.

The Social Democrats, led by Prime Minister Goran Persson, have dominated politics since the 1920s. With their partners, the Left (formerly Communist) Party and the Greens, the Social Democrats won 191 out of 349 seats in the 2002 parliamentary elections, promising not to cut back the generous welfare system. An impressive 79 percent of eligible Swedes voted in the poll.

The population overwhelmingly rejected the adoption of the euro in a referendum on September 14, 2003. The country's mainstream political parties generally supported the euro, as did the business community. However, despite strong support from Prime Minister Persson, his Social Democratic Party was split internally on the issue, and Persson criticized members of his party who openly opposed the euro. The general public feared that adopting the euro would lead to a deterioration in Sweden's generous welfare state benefits, for which Swedes are willing to pay high taxes, and that it might hurt Sweden's strong economy, which outperforms most economies in the euro area. The no vote may also have been a reflection of skepticism about the EU as a whole. The rejection of the euro is not expected to have a strong impact on Sweden's economy, although some predict that it will mean a loss of political influence for Sweden in the EU.

On September 10, just days before the referendum, Foreign Minister Lindh was mortally wounded in a knife attack in a Stockholm department store. Although Lindh was one of the most vocal supporters of the euro, it is not thought that the murder was politically motivated. However, the killing did spark considerable debate about security in Sweden, where violence is very rare and politicians regularly travel without bodyguards in order to maintain direct contact with citizens.

**Political Rights and Civil Liberties:** Swedes can change their government democratically. The unicameral parliament, the Riksdag, has 349 members, 310 of whom are elected every four years in a proportional system. The remaining 39 seats are awarded on a national basis to further secure a proportional representation. A party must receive at least 4 percent of the votes in the entire country or 12 percent in a single electoral district to qualify for any seats. The prime minister is appointed by the Speaker of the House and confirmed by the Riksdag. King Carl XVI Gustaf, crowned in 1973, is head of state, but royal power is limited to official and ceremonial functions.

The Liberal Party and the Moderates are the largest opposition parties. Unlike in other parts of Europe, no populist anti-immigrant party has won national representation. The principal religious, ethnic, and immigrant groups are represented in parliament. Since 1993, the Sami community elects its own parliament, which has significant powers over education and culture and serves as an advisory body to the government.

Corruption is very low. Transparency International ranked Sweden the sixth least corrupt country in the world in its 2003 Corruption Perceptions Index. In 2003, some 80 employees of the state-owned alcohol retail monopoly were brought to court on bribery charges, the largest such scandal in Swedish history.

Sweden's media are independent. Most newspapers and periodicals are privately owned, and the government subsidizes daily newspapers regardless of their political affiliation. The Swedish Broadcasting Corporation and the Swedish Television Company broadcast weekly radio and television programs in several immigrant languages. The ethnic press is entitled to the same subsidies as the Swedish-language press. Reporters Sans Frontieres has reported that journalists who investigate extreme right-wing groups are regularly threatened and even physically attacked by neo-Nazi militants.

Religious freedom is constitutionally guaranteed. Although the country is 87 percent Lutheran, all churches, as well as synagogues and mosques, receive some state financial support. Academic freedom is ensured for all.

Freedom of assembly and association are guaranteed, as are the rights to strike and participate in unions. Trade union federations are strong and well organized and represent approximately 85 percent of the workforce.

Sweden's judiciary, which includes the Supreme Court, district courts, and a court of appeals, is independent. A Swedish court overturned a 25-year ban on alcohol advertisements in February, which has led to a dramatic increase in alcohol sales. The ban was judged to be in violation of EU regulations on free circulation of goods and services.

The Swedish intelligence service reports that neo-Nazi activity is increasing in Sweden, which is one of the world's largest producers of racist and xenophobic Web sites. However, popular support for neo-Nazi groups is in fact quite small. The movement's main political party, Sweden Democrats, won only 1.4 percent of the vote in the 2002 general election, which was not enough to win seats in the Riksdag.

While some advocacy organizations have urged a tougher stance against neo-Nazi groups, others fear infringement of the groups' right to freedom of expression. In March, five people were arrested for unruly protestation against a neo-Nazi demonstration.

Amnesty International criticized Sweden in March for its decision to freeze Iraqi asylum requests during the U.S.-led war. Sweden is generally very welcoming of refugees, but its immigration policy has become stricter in recent years.

Sweden is a leader in gender equality. At 45 percent, the percentage of females in the Riksdag is the highest in the world, and half of government ministers are women. Although 79 percent of women work outside the home, women still make only 70 percent of men's wages in the public sector and 76 percent in the private sector. Prime Minister Goran Persson has announced that the government will tighten already strict laws on gender equality if the gap remains in three years. Women are under-represented on company boards as well, and the government has threatened to introduce quotas if this does not change.

Sweden gave formal recognition to adoption by gay couples for the first time in October, which was made possible by a change in law that came into effect in February.

# Switzerland

**Population:** 7,300,000
**GNI/capita:** $38,330
**Life Expectancy:** 80
**Religious Groups:** Roman Catholic (46 percent), Protestant (40 percent), other (14 percent)
**Ethnic Groups:** German (65 percent), French (18 percent), Italian (10 percent), Romansch (1 percent), other (6 percent)
**Capital:** Bern

**Political Rights:** 1
**Civil Liberties:** 1
**Status:** Free

**Ten-Year Ratings Timeline (Political Rights, Civil Liberties, Status)**

| 1994 | 1995 | 1996 | 1997 | 1998 | 1999 | 2000 | 2001 | 2002 | 2003 |
|------|------|------|------|------|------|------|------|------|------|
| 1,1F | 1,1F | 1,1F | 1,1F | 1,1F | 1,1F | 1,1F | 1,1F | 1,1F | 1,1F |

**Overview:**

The October 19, 2003 parliamentary election shook up Switzerland's long-quiet political system by which seats in the cabinet are proportioned in a fixed formula among the major parties. The Swiss People's Party (SVP), a right-wing party with a xenophobic bent, won the biggest share of the vote and may demand a second ministerial seat in the council, where it has long had just one.

Switzerland, which has been a loose confederation of cantons since 1291, emerged in its current borders after the Napoleonic wars in 1815, where its tradition of neutrality was also sealed. The country's four official ethnic communities are based on language: German, French, Italian, and Romansh (the smallest community). Switzerland has stayed out of international wars and only joined the United Nations after a referendum in 2002.

Membership in international institutions has long been a controversial issue in Switzerland. The country is surrounded by members of the European Union (EU), but the Swiss, who fiercely value not only their military neutrality but their political independence, have resisted EU membership. The country has even resisted membership in the European Economic Area, a halfway-house to EU membership that has a trade agreement with the EU.

Hostility not only to EU membership, but also to immigration, has been a hallmark of the right-wing SVP. The other main political parties are the center-left Social Democratic Party (SP), the right-wing Radical Democratic Party (FDP), and the center-right Christian Democratic Party (CVP). Traditionally, these last three parties had held two seats each in the seven-member Bundesrat (Federal Council), with the SVP holding just one. However, the SVP's vote share increased gradually over the 1990s—corresponding with a rightward move by the party—as it poached voters initially from small far-right parties, and then increasingly from the Radicals.

During the October 2003 legislative election, the SVP made blatantly xenophobic appeals, including a newspaper advertisement blaming "black Africans" for crime. The SVP insisted that it had nothing against legal immigrants, who make up a fifth of Switzerland's population, and that it was merely opposed to illegal immigration and abuse of the asylum policy. The SVP won the biggest share of the vote, while the Social Democrats finished just behind the SVP. The Christian Democrats received just under 15 percent of the vote, barely half the total of the SVP.

The SVP's success in the election gave its leader, Christoph Blocher, backing for calling for a second Bundesrat seat for his party. Blocher demanded that he and another minister be appointed to the council, with a seat being taken from the CVP. If his demands are not met, he has threatened to take his party into opposition, which would be unprecedented in modern Swiss politics. A stint in opposition, he hinted, might only increase his party's popularity, as voters could feel that their democratic choice of the SVP was thwarted and flock to it in sympathy. Taking Blocher into the government, on the other hand, might somewhat neutralize his appeal, as he would be under pressure to tone down his fiery rhetoric and operate in the traditionally collegial atmosphere of Swiss federal politics.

The SVP's success also strained relations with the EU. Switzerland and the EU had hoped to conclude an agreement by the end of 2003 that included cooperation on tax evasion, justice, and home affairs. However, the success of the most Euroskeptic of Switzerland's major parties clouded the possibility of an early conclusion to the agreement.

**Political Rights and Civil Liberties:** The Swiss can change their government democratically. The constitution of 1848, significantly revised in 1874 and 2000, provides for two directly elected legislative chambers, the Council of States (in which each canton has two members and each half-canton one) and the National Council. The Federal Council is a seven-person executive; the presidency is ceremonial and rotates annually among the Federal Council's members. Collegiality and consensus are hallmarks of Swiss political culture.

The Swiss institutional system is characterized by decentralization and direct democracy. The cantons and half-cantons have control over much of economic and social policy, with the federal government's powers largely limited to foreign affairs and some economic policy. The rights of cultural, religious, and linguistic minorities are strongly protected. Referendums are also a common feature; any measure that modifies the constitution must be put to a referendum. Any new or revised law must be put to a referendum if 50,000 signatures in favor of doing so can be gathered, and voters may even initiate legislation themselves with 100,000 signatures.

The government is free from pervasive corruption. Transparency International rated Switzerland eighth (tied with Norway and Australia) on its 2003 Corruption Perceptions Index. However, the country has traditionally drawn fire for its banking secrecy laws, which financial watchdogs claim enable money laundering and other crimes.

Switzerland has a free media environment. The Swiss Broadcasting Corporation dominates the broadcast market. The penal code prohibits racist or anti-Semitic speech. Consolidation of newspapers in large media conglomerates has forced the closure of some small and local newspapers. Internet access is unrestricted.

Freedom of religion is guaranteed by the constitution. Most cantons support one or several churches. The country is split roughly evenly between Roman Catholicism and Protestantism, although there are now over 300,000 Muslims, the largest non-Christian minority. Religion is taught in public schools, depending on the predominant creed in the canton. Students are free to choose their creed of instruction or opt out of religious instruction. In 2001, a cantonal court ruled that the Church of Scientology could not be a "real church" because it does not advocate belief in God. Academic freedom is respected.

There is freedom of assembly and association, and the right to collective bargaining is respected. Approximately a third of the workforce is unionized.

The judiciary is independent, and the rule of law prevails in civil and criminal matters. Most judicial decisions are made at the cantonal level, except for the federal supreme court, which reviews cantonal court decisions when they pertain to federal law. Refusal to perform military service is a criminal offense for males. Prison conditions are generally good.

Women were only granted universal suffrage at the federal level in 1971, and the half-canton Appenzell-Innerrhoden denied women the vote until 1990. Abortion laws were liberalized to decriminalize abortion in the first 12 weeks of pregnancy following a referendum in 2002, which 72 percent of voters supported. The law gives women 10 weeks of maternity leave but no salary guarantee.

# Syria

**Population:** 17,500,000
**GNI/capita:** $1,040
**Life Expectancy:** 70
**Religious Groups:** Sunni Muslim (74 percent), other
Muslim [including Alawite and Druze] (16 percent),
Christian [various sects] (10 percent)
**Ethnic Groups:** Arab (90 percent), other, [including Kurd
and Armenian] (10 percent)
**Capital:** Damascus

**Political Rights:** 7
**Civil Liberties:** 7
**Status:** Not Free

## Ten-Year Ratings Timeline (Political Rights, Civil Liberties, Status)

| 1994 | 1995 | 1996 | 1997 | 1998 | 1999 | 2000 | 2001 | 2002 | 2003 |
|------|------|------|------|------|------|------|------|------|------|
| 7,7NF | 7,7NF | 7,7NF | 7,7NF | 7,7NF | 7,7NF | 7,7NF | 7,7NF | 7,7NF | 7,7NF |

**Overview:**
In the face of growing international pressure to end his government's sponsorship of militant terrorist groups and the fall of a sister Baathist government in neighboring Iraq, Syrian President Bashar Assad came under mounting domestic pressure in 2003 to reform the repressive and corrupt political system built by his father. Although some nominal political and economic reforms were introduced, government suppression of political and civil liberties continued, with dozens of people arrested during the year for peacefully expressing their opinions.

Located at the heart of the Fertile Crescent, the Syrian capital of Damascus is the oldest continuously inhabited city in the world and once controlled a vast empire extending from Europe to India. The modern state of Syria is a comparatively recent entity, established by the French after World War I and formally granted independence in 1946. The pan-Arab Baath Party, which seized control of Syria 40 years ago, has long sought to extend its writ beyond Syrian borders. For all its pan-Arab pretensions, however, the Syrian government has been dominated by Alawites, adherents of an offshoot sect of Islam who constitute just 12 percent of the population, since a 1970 coup brought Gen. Hafez Assad to power. For the next 30 years, the Assad regime managed to maintain control of the majority Sunni Muslim population only by brutally suppressing all dissent. In 1982, government forces stormed the northern town of Hama to crush a rebellion by the Muslim Brotherhood and killed as many as 20,000 insurgents and civilians in a matter of days.

In 2000, Assad's son and successor, Bashar, inherited control of a country with one of the most stagnant economies and highest rates of population growth in the region, with unemployment estimated at more than 20 percent. In his inaugural speech, the young Syrian leader pledged to eliminate government corruption, revitalize the economy, and establish a "democracy specific to Syria, which takes its roots from its history and respects its society."

The first six months of Assad's tenure brought dramatic changes. Loose networks of public figures from all sectors of civil society were allowed to discuss the country's social, economic, and political problems in informal gatherings. Assad released more than 600 political prisoners, closed the notorious Mazzeh prison, allowed scores of exiled dissidents to return home, reinstated dissidents who had been fired from state-run media outlets and universities, and instructed the state-run media to give a voice to reformers. The "Damascus Spring" reached its zenith in January 2001 with the establishment of the country's first privately owned newspaper.

In February 2001, however, the regime abruptly reimposed restrictions on public freedoms and launched an escalating campaign of threats, intimidation, and harassment against the reform movement. By the end of the year, ten leading reformists had been arrested. In 2002, the "Damascus Ten" were sentenced to prison terms, while the security agencies arrested over a dozen additional journalists, human rights activists, and political dissidents. The regime's renewed assault on political and civil liberties initially elicited little criticism from Western governments, in part because of Assad's cooperation in the war against al-Qaeda. Economic reform also fell by the wayside as dozens of reform laws remained unimplemented or were put into effect half-heartedly; hopes for a much-needed influx of foreign investment faded.

The March 2003 U.S.-led invasion of Iraq, a country hitherto ruled by a rival branch of the Baath Party, posed serious problems for the Assad regime. The downfall of Saddam Hussein brought an end to Iraqi shipments of cut-rate petroleum supplies, which had helped the government weather dismal economic conditions without implementing major reforms. Scenes of Iraqis celebrating the downfall of a regime so similar to the one in Damascus inspired Syria's pro-democracy movement to reassert itself. In late May, nearly 300 intellectuals signed a petition demanding the release of all political prisoners, the cancellation of the state of emergency, and other political reforms.

After the fall of Baghdad, the Syrian government introduced a number of largely cosmetic social and political reforms. The requirement that Syrian school children wear military-style khaki uniforms was lifted, and the ministry of education was given the authority to make decisions without prior approval from the Baath Party's education bureau. In June, the government decreed that Baath Party membership would no longer affect advancement in the civil service. On the economic front, Assad eased laws on foreign currency transactions, approved the establishment of the country's first private banks and universities, and announced plans to set up a stock market. In September, Assad appointed a new prime minister and cabinet ostensibly committed to economic reform.

Syrian relations with the United States rapidly deteriorated during the invasion of Iraq, when U.S. officials publicly accused Damascus of shipping weapons to the Iraqi military and sending "volunteers" across the border to fight coalition forces. The Bush administration also intensified its calls for Syria to stop sponsoring terrorist groups opposed to the Israeli-Palestinian peace process and abandon its weapons of mass destruction (WMD) programs. In October, the Bush administration publicly endorsed an Israeli air strike on an alleged terrorist training camp outside of Damascus and announced its support for congressional sanctions on Syria.

**Political Rights and Civil Liberties:** The Assad regime wields absolute authority in Syria and Syrians cannot change their government through democratic means. Under the 1973 constitution, the president is nominated by the ruling Baath Party and approved by a popular referendum. In practice, these referendums are orchestrated by the regime, as are elections to the 250-

member People's Assembly, which holds little independent legislative power. The only legal political parties are the Baath Party and six small parties that comprise the ruling National Progressive Front (NPF).

Parliamentary elections in March 2003 were boycotted by five major opposition groups. All 167 of the NPF's candidates were elected, with "independent" candidates taking the remaining 83 seats. At least two people were arrested by the authorities for distributing pamphlets calling for a boycott.

Freedom of expression is heavily restricted. Vaguely worded articles of the Penal Code and Emergency Law give the government considerable discretion in punishing those who express dissent. The Penal Code prohibits the publication of information that opposes "the goals of the revolution," incites sectarianism, or "prevents authorities from executing their responsibilities." The broadcast media are entirely state owned, apart from a handful of non-news radio stations licensed in 2003. While there are some privately owned newspapers and magazines, a new press law enacted in September 2001 permits the government to arbitrarily deny or revoke publishing licenses for reasons "related to the public interest," and compels privately owned print media outlets to submit all material to government censors on the day of publication. Syrians are permitted to access the Internet only through state-run servers, which block access to a wide range of Web sites. Satellite dishes are illegal, but generally tolerated. In July 2003, the government revoked the publishing license of the country's leading independent newspaper, *Al-Doumari*. In May, the authorities released the Damascus bureau chief of the London-based Arabic daily *Al-Hayat*, Ibrahim Humaydi, who had been arrested in December 2002 on charges of "publishing false information."

Although the constitution requires that the president be a Muslim, there is no state religion in Syria and freedom of worship is generally respected. The Alawite minority dominates the officer corps of the military and security forces. Since the eruption of an Islamist rebellion in the late 1970s, the government has tightly monitored mosques and controlled the appointment of Muslim clergy. Academic freedom is heavily restricted. University professors have been routinely dismissed from state universities in recent years due to their involvement in the pro-democracy movement, and some have been imprisoned.

Freedom of assembly is largely nonexistent. While citizens can ostensibly hold demonstrations with prior permission from the Interior Ministry, in practice only the government, the Baath Party, or groups linked to them are allowed to organize demonstrations. In May 2003, according to the London-based Syrian Human Rights Committee, 11 people in Daraya, a suburb of Damascus, were arrested after they demonstrated against local corruption. All 11 were subsequently sentenced by the Supreme State Security Court (SSSC) to prison sentences ranging from three to four years. At least eight Kurdish activists who participated in a peaceful protest outside the Damascus headquarters of UNICEF in June were arrested and remained in prison at year's end.

Freedom of association is restricted. All nongovernmental organizations must register with the government, which generally denies registration to reformist groups. Three unregistered human rights groups have been allowed to operate in Syria, though individual members of the groups have been jailed for human rights related activities. In July 2003, Assad issued a presidential pardon for four members of the Syrian Human Rights Association arrested in 2002.

All unions must belong to the General Federation of Trade Unions (GFTU). Although ostensibly independent, the GFTU is headed by a member of the ruling Baath Party and is used by the government to control all aspects of union activity in Syria. While strikes in non-agricultural sectors are legal, they rarely occur.

While regular criminal and civil courts operate with some independence and generally safeguard defendants' rights, most politically sensitive cases are tried by two exceptional courts established under emergency law: the SSSC and the Economic Security Court (ESC). Both courts deny or limit the right to appeal, limit access to legal counsel, try most cases behind closed doors, and admit as evidence confessions obtained through torture. Abdel Rahman Shagouri was arrested in February 2003 for distributing an e-mail newsletter from a banned Web site and remained in detention throughout the year awaiting trial before the SSSC. Fourteen people were arrested in August for attending a lecture about the state of emergency in Syria and charged by the SSSC with inciting "factional conflict." A July 2003 decree reportedly stipulated that economic crimes previously tried by the ESC will henceforth be tried by criminal courts, but it is not clear whether the ESC has been abolished.

The state of emergency in force since 1963 gives the security agencies virtually unlimited authority to arrest suspects and hold them incommunicado for prolonged periods without charge. Many of the several hundred remaining political prisoners in Syria have never been tried for any offense. The security agencies, which operate independently of the judiciary, routinely extract confessions by torturing suspects and detaining members of their families. Government surveillance of dissidents is widespread. At least seven opposition figures who returned from exile in Iraq in 2003 were arrested and detained on their arrival in Syria, as were at least four exiles returning from other countries. Most were released within a few weeks, but a few reportedly remained in detention at year's end. One Syrian opposition figure who remained in Iraq, Riad al-Shouqfeh, narrowly escaped assassination on July 23. There were many reports of torture by the security forces during the year. In November, Maher Arar, a Syrian-born Canadian citizen released after ten months of detention by the authorities, publicly described the torture he experienced in captivity. According to Amnesty International, Kurdish activist Khalil Mustafa died two days after his arrest on August 8 as a result of torture.

The Kurdish minority in Syria faces cultural and linguistic restrictions, and suspected Kurdish activists are routinely dismissed from schools and jobs. Some 200,000 Syrian Kurds are deprived of citizenship and unable to obtain passports, identity cards, or birth certificates, which in turn prevents them from owning land, obtaining government employment, or voting. The September 2001 press law requires that owners and editors in chief of publications be Arabs. At least thirteen suspected Kurdish activists were arrested and jailed in 2003. Two Kurdish organizers of a December 2002 demonstration against government discrimination were put on trial before the SSSC in late 2003 on charges of advocating Kurdish secession, but no ruling had been issued by year's end.

Although most Syrians do not face travel restrictions, relatives of exiled dissidents are routinely prevented from traveling abroad and many Kurds lack the requisite documents to leave the country. Equality of opportunity has been compromised by rampant corruption and conscious government efforts to weaken the predominantly Sunni urban bourgeoisie.

The government has promoted gender equality by appointing women to senior positions in all branches of government and providing equal access to education, but many discriminatory laws remain in force. A husband may request that the Interior Ministry block his wife from traveling abroad, and women are generally barred from leaving the country with their children unless they can prove that the father has granted permission. Syrian law stipulates that an accused rapist can be acquitted if he marries his victim, and it provides for reduced sentences in cases of "honor crimes" committed by men against female relatives for alleged sexual misconduct. Personal status law for Muslim women is governed by Sharia ( Islamic law) and is discriminatory in marriage, divorce, and inheritance matters. Violence against women is widespread, particularly in rural areas.

# Taiwan

**Population:** 22,600,000   **Political Rights:** 2
**GNI/capita:** $13,392   **Civil Liberties:** 2
**Life Expectancy:** 76   **Status:** Free
**Religious Groups:** Mixture of Buddhist, Confucian, and Taoist (93 percent), Christian (4.5 percent) other (2.5 percent)
**Ethnic Groups:** Taiwanese [including Hakka] (84 percent), mainland Chinese (14 percent), aboriginal (2 percent)
**Capital:** Taipei

**Ten-Year Ratings Timeline (Political Rights, Civil Liberties, Status)**

| 1994 | 1995 | 1996 | 1997 | 1998 | 1999 | 2000 | 2001 | 2002 | 2003 |
|------|------|------|------|------|------|------|------|------|------|
| 3,3F | 3,3F | 2,2F | 2,2F | 2,2F | 2,2F | 1,2F | 1,2F | 2,2F | 2,2F |

**Overview:**   As campaigning heated up for Taiwan's March 2004 presidential election, the focus was on two related issues that have dominated the island's politics in recent years: economic links with China and the question of Taiwanese independence. Trailing in the polls, President Chen Shui-bian tightened the race late in 2003 with calls for a new constitution that, he hinted, would promote Taiwan's formal independence from China. Opposition leader Lien Chan, however, maintained the lead, in most polls, that he had seized after teaming up with a former rival to contest the election. A Lien victory could help break the stalemate with Beijing that has prevented Taiwan and China from establishing direct air and shipping links.

Located some 100 miles off the southeast coast of China, Taiwan became the home of the Koumintang (KMT), or Nationalist, government-in-exile in 1949, when Communist forces overthrew the Nationalists following two decades of civil war on the mainland. While Taiwan is independent in all but name, Beijing considers it to be a renegade province of China and has long threatened to invade if the island formally declares independence.

Taiwan's democratic transition began in 1987, when the KMT government lifted a state of martial law imposed 38 years earlier. The KMT's Lee Teng-hui in 1988 became the first native Taiwanese president. His election broke a stranglehold on politics by mainland refugees, who, along with their descendants, make up 14 percent of Taiwan's population.

In his 12 years in office, Lee oversaw far-reaching political reforms including the holding of Taiwan's first multiparty legislative elections in 1991 and the first direct presidential elections in 1996. Lee also played down the KMT's historic commitment to eventual reunification with China, promoting instead a Taiwanese national identity that undermined Beijing's claim that there is only "one China."

With Lee barred by term limits from seeking reelection, Chen's victory in the 2000 presidential race, in which he ran as the standard-bearer of the pro-independence Democratic Progressive Party (DPP), broke the KMT's grip on politics and signaled that Taiwan would continue promoting an independent identity. Chen, a former Taipei mayor, downplayed but did not renounce his DPP's core position that Taiwan should eventually be independent. With an 82 percent turnout, Chen took 39 percent of the vote to defeat James Soong, a KMT defector who ran as an independent and took 37 percent, and Vice President Lien Chan, who captured 23 percent. Despite Chen's victory, the combined support for his two conservative opponents, totaling around 60 percent of the vote, suggested that many Taiwanese are wary of the DPP's pro-independence platform and its potential to cause trouble with China.

Still, the DPP swept the conservative KMT out of parliamentary power for the first time in the December 2001 legislative elections. While the question of independence loomed large in the campaign, many voters appeared to be swayed at least partly by the DPP's pledges of cleaner government. The DPP won 87 of parliament's 225 seats, up from 70 in 1998, while the KMT took 68, down from 123. The new People First Party, headed by KMT defector Soong, won 46 seats. The Taiwan Solidarity Union, backed by former president Lee, won 13 seats, and two minor parties and independents took the remainder.

Chen's hopes for reelection dimmed in April 2003 after Lien and Soong, his rivals in 2000, teamed up to contest the 2004 vote on a ticket headed by Lien. A KMT alliance in parliament with People First also made it harder for the DPP to pass legislation. A widely anticipated banking reform bill was defeated in July.

Chen gained ground in opinion polls, however, with his surprise proposal in September that Taiwan adopt a new constitution through an islandwide referendum by 2006. Chen said that a new constitution would improve governance by streamlining Taiwan's complicated presidential-parliamentary system. Chen also hinted that he was seeking to delete provisions in the 1946 constitution that formally link Taiwan to the mainland. Along with an economic rebound that coincided with the containment of Asia's severe acute respiratory syndrome (SARS) virus, the buzz surrounding the proposal helped Chen close the gap with Lien to single digits by November from around 20 percentage points in August, according to some polls.

The KMT proposed its own constitutional reforms in November that included changing the presidential election rules to require an outright majority for victory. In late November, the opposition-controlled parliament passed a bill permitting islandwide referendums but, in a setback to Chen, gave the legislature, not the president, the power to decide what questions are put to voters. Undaunted, Chen proposed using a special provision in the law, allowing the president to hold a "defensive" referendum when the island faces an imminent external threat, to hold a referendum during the 2004 presidential election. Chen said that China's longstanding threats against Taiwan justified using the defensive referendum procedure. China sharply rebuked Taiwan, particularly after the administration announced that the referendum would ask whether Taiwan should boost its missile defenses in response to China's build-up of missiles aimed at the island, and whether Taiwan should seek peace talks with the mainland.

Despite Chen's late-year bounce in the polls, the KMT has benefited from frustration among many Taiwanese over the lack of any breakthrough in relations with China. Taiwanese businessmen have poured some $100 billion into China in the past decade or so but say that the lack of direct air and shipping links pushes up their costs. Beijing, however, refuses to negotiate on opening direct links between Taiwan and the mainland unless Taipei concedes that such links are a domestic matter rather than a state-to-state affair. The DPP generally favors closer economic ties but argues that accepting Beijing's one-China precondition would be tantamount to Taiwan's formally renouncing independence.

Beyond their differences over cross-strait relations, the KMT and DPP share similar economic policies. Moreover, a general consensus exists that Taiwan needs to respond to the exodus of Taiwanese factories to the mainland in recent years by boosting its high-end services, research, and manufacturing industries.

**Political Rights and Civil Liberties:** Taiwanese can change their government through elections and enjoy most basic rights. The 1946 constitution, adopted while the Kuomintang (KMT) was in power on the mainland, created a hybrid presidential-parliamentary system. The president, who is directly elected for a four-year term, wields executive power, appoints the prime minister, and can dissolve the legislature. The prime minister is responsible to the legislature, which is directly elected for a three-year term.

The Chen Shiu-bian administration has worked to crack down on vote buying and on the links between politicians and organized crime that were widely believed to have flourished under KMT rule. The Justice Department, for example, has indicted more than 100 Taiwanese for vote buying related to recent legislative and local elections; dozens of legislators, magistrates, and local officials have been indicted for corruption.

Two alleged scandals in 2002, however, stoked concerns over official corruption. The chief shareholder in a development company admitted that she had made large loans to several Democratic Progressive Party (DPP) and KMT politicians. Meanwhile, police in Kaohsiung, Taiwan's second-largest city, detained Chu An-hsiung for allegedly paying several other city councillors to vote for him as speaker of the municipal body. The Berlin-based Transparency International ranked Taiwan in a tie for thirtieth place out of 133 countries rated in its 2003 Corruption Perceptions Index, with top-ranked Finland being the least corrupt country.

Taiwanese newspapers report aggressively on corruption and other sensitive issues and carry outspoken editorials and opinion pieces. In a setback for press freedom, the High Court in July sentenced journalist Hung Cheh-cheng to 18 months in jail for sedition over an article that it said contained classified information about Taiwanese military exercises. The Court granted Hung a three-year suspended sentence. Moreover, criminal defamation laws used by past governments to jail journalists are still on the books. In a positive development, the High Court in 2000 upheld a lower court ruling that raised the legal barrier for news outlets to be convicted of libel.

Broadcast television stations reportedly are subject to some editorial influence by their owners. The DPP, KMT, government, and armed forces each are the largest shareholder in, or otherwise are associated with, one of Taiwan's five island-wide broadcast television stations. The fifth is run by a nonprofit public foundation. Any political influence over regular television is offset, however, by the fact that more than 80 percent of Taiwanese households can access roughly 100 private cable television stations. The government defends a controversial requirement that radio station owners have roughly $1.45 million in capital on the grounds that the amount is based on the actual costs of running a station. Moreover, the amount is reduced for stations serving designated ethnic groups or for certain other socially beneficial purposes.

Taiwanese of all faiths can worship freely. Adherents of Buddhism and Taoism make up around 40 percent of the population. Taiwanese professors and other educators can write and lecture freely. Laws barring Taiwanese from advocating communism or independence from China remain on the books, though they are no longer enforced.

Taiwanese human rights, social welfare, and environmental nongovernmental groups are active and operate without harassment. Trade unions are independent, and roughly 30 percent of workers are unionized. However, teachers, civil servants, and defense industry workers are barred from joining unions or bargaining collectively. Moreover, the law restricts the right to strike by, for example, allowing authorities to order mediation of labor disputes and ban work stoppages while mediation is in progress. Some union leaders have been dismissed without reasonable cause or laid off first during lean times. In another concern, some employers take advantage of illegal foreign workers by confiscating their passports, deducting money from their wages without their consent, and having them work extended hours without overtime pay, according to the U.S. State Department's human rights report for 2002, released in March 2003.

Taiwan's judiciary is largely independent, and trials generally are fair. However, corruption and political influence over the courts remain "serious problems," the U.S. State Department report said, despite recent judicial reforms. Moreover, police reportedly at times use force to extract confessions from suspects and, while confessions obtained through torture are inadmissible, courts sometimes accept confessions even when they contradict other evidence or plain logic, the report added. In a case that the human rights group Amnesty International called a "miscarriage of justice," three men in October began their tenth trial on the same 1991 murder charges. The charges are based almost entirely on confessions that allegedly were extracted by torture.

Taiwan's 400,000 aborigines face discrimination in mainstream society and, in general, have little input into major decisions affecting their land, culture, and traditions. Ethnic Chinese developers often use "connections and corruption" to gain title to aboriginal land, according to the U.S. State Department report. Aborigines say that they also are prevented from owning certain ancestral land under government control. In another concern, anecdotal evidence suggests that child prostitution is a serious problem among aboriginal children despite initiatives by the government and private groups, such as the Garden of Hope Foundation, to protect children.

Taiwanese women have made impressive gains in recent years in business, but reportedly continue to face job discrimination in the private sector. The government in 2001 passed a law banning gender discrimination in the workplace in response to charges by women's advocates that women are promoted less frequently and receive lower pay than their male counterparts and sometimes are forced to quit jobs because of age, marriage, or pregnancy.

Rape and domestic violence are serious problems in Taiwan, the U.S. State Department report said, despite government programs to protect women. Although the law allows authorities to investigate complaints of domestic violence and to prosecute rape suspects without the victims formally pressing charges, cultural norms inhibit many women from reporting these crimes.

# Tajikistan

**Population:** 6,600,000
**GNI/capita:** $180
**Life Expectancy:** 68
**Religious Groups:** Sunni Muslim (85 percent),
Shi'a Muslim (5 percent), other (10 percent)
**Ethnic Groups:** Tajik (65 percent), Uzbek (25 percent),
Russian (4 percent), other (6 percent)
**Capital:** Dushanbe

**Political Rights:** 6
**Civil Liberties:** 5
**Status:** Not Free

**Ten-Year Ratings Timeline (Political Rights, Civil Liberties, Status)**

| 1994 | 1995 | 1996 | 1997 | 1998 | 1999 | 2000 | 2001 | 2002 | 2003 |
|------|------|------|------|------|------|------|------|------|------|
| 7,7NF | 7,7NF | 7,7NF | 6,6NF | 6,6NF | 6,6NF | 6,6NF | 6,6NF | 6,5NF | 6,5NF |

**Overview:**

President Imomali Rakhmonov moved to further strengthen his position after winning a controversial constitutional referendum in June that grants him the right to run for two more seven-year terms in office. The vote, which some observers characterized as a first step in legitimizing a possible "president-for-life" scenario, was criticized by members of the international community and opposition political groups. Meanwhile, Tajikistan continued to expand its cooperation with the United States while balancing relations with Russia, which retains considerable influence over this former Soviet republic.

Conquered by Russia in the late 1800s, Tajikistan was made an autonomous region within Uzbekistan in 1924 and a separate socialist republic of the U.S.S.R. in 1929. Tajikistan declared independence from the Soviet Union in September 1991, and two months later, former Communist Party leader Rakhman Nabiyev was elected president.

Long-simmering clan-based tensions, combined with various anti-Communist and Islamist movements, soon plunged the country into a five-year civil war for central government control. In September 1992, Communist hard-liners forced the resignation of President Nabiyev, who was replaced later that year by leading Communist Party member Rakhmonov. The following month, Rakhmonov launched attacks against anti-government forces that caused tens of thousands to flee into neighboring Afghanistan.

As the fighting continued, Rakhmonov was elected president in November 1994 after most opposition candidates either boycotted or were prevented from competing in the poll. The March 1995 parliamentary elections, in which the majority of seats were won by pro-government candidates, were boycotted by the United Tajik Opposition (UTO), a coalition of various secular and Islamic opposition groups that emerged during the war as the main opposition force fighting against Rakhmonov's government.

Following a December 1996 cease-fire, Rakhmonov and UTO leader Said Abdullo Nuri signed a formal peace agreement in Moscow on June 27, 1997, officially ending the civil war, which had claimed tens of thousands of lives and left several hundred thousand as refugees. The accord called for the merging of opposition forces into the regular army, granted an amnesty for UTO members, provided for the UTO to be allotted 30 percent of senior government posts, and established a 26-member National Reconciliation Commission, with seats evenly divided between the government and the UTO. The commission was charged with implementing the peace agreements, including preparing amendments for a referendum on constitutional changes that would lead to fair parliamentary elections.

During the next two years, the government and the UTO took steps toward implementing the peace accord. In a September 1999 referendum, voters approved a series of constitutional amendments permitting the formation of religion-based political parties. This move paved the way for the legal operation of the Islamic opposition, including the Islamic Renaissance Party (IRP), which constituted the backbone of the UTO. The referendum also included an amendment extending the president's single term in office from five to seven years. In November, Rakhmonov was reelected with a reported 97 percent of the vote in a poll criticized by international election observers for widespread irregularities.

As the final stage in the implementation of the 1997 peace accord, Tajikistan held elections in February 2000 for the 63-seat lower house of parliament. Rakhmonov's People's Democratic Party (PDP) received nearly 65 percent of the vote, followed by the Communist Party with 20 percent, and the IRP with 7 percent. Although the participation of six parties and a number of independent candidates in the poll provided some political pluralism, international election observers, including a joint mission by the Organization for Security and Cooperation in Europe (OSCE) and the United Nations, cited serious problems, including the exclusion of certain opposition parties, biased state media coverage, and a lack of transparency in the tabulation of votes. In the March elections to the 33-seat upper house of parliament, in which regional assemblies elected 25 members and Rakhmonov appointed the remaining 8, the PDP obtained the overwhelming majority of seats.

After the elections, the National Reconciliation Commission was formally disbanded, and a UN observer mission withdrew in May 2000 after nearly six years in Tajikistan. However, important provisions of the peace accord remained unimplemented, with demobilization of opposition factions incomplete and the government failing to meet the 30 percent quota of senior government posts to be awarded to the UTO.

Following the September 11, 2001, attacks on the World Trade Center and the Pentagon, Tajikistan agreed to open its airspace for humanitarian flights during the U.S.-led war in Afghanistan. However, it denied having plans to allow U.S. troops or warplanes to use its territory for military strikes against Afghanistan's then-ruling Taliban. Tajikistan's cautious reaction stemmed from fears of possible retaliatory measures by Taliban forces, as well as from other radical Islamist groups. Meanwhile, the government's growing strategic and economic ties with the United States strained relations with Russia, which already had a strong military presence in the country and generally opposed a long-term U.S. role in the region.

President Rakhmonov's already substantial powers were further consolidated in a June 22, 2003 constitutional referendum. Voters were asked to approve or reject a package of 56 constitutional amendments, the most controversial of which would permit the president to serve two additional seven-year terms beyond the next presidential election in 2006; the constitution previously limited the president to a single seven-year term. Rakhmonov, who argued that this change would better reflect post-civil war circumstances and bring the country continued stability, could theoretically remain in office until 2020. Other amendments included abolishing the legal right to free higher education and free universal health care, which de facto already require payments.

Official results showed that 93 percent of those voting in the referendum supported the amendments, while turnout was reported to be more than 96 percent. The OSCE, which did not send observers because the Tajik government invited the group too late for it to prepare a monitoring mission, nevertheless questioned the accuracy of the results. Critics also charged that most voters were not fully aware of the proposed changes, which were not printed on the ballot papers and had not been given much media coverage. The opposition Democratic Party urged its supporters to boycott the vote, while the opposition Social Democratic Party and the IRP adopted less openly confrontational positions.

On the international front, negotiations with Moscow were ongoing during the year over upgrading a Russian military division in Tajikistan to a military base, a move seen as an effort by Moscow to reassert its influence in the region. Meanwhile, the living and working conditions of the many Tajik migrant workers in Russia, who often face official harassment and discrimination, caused tensions between the two countries. Tajikistan continued to benefit from substantial technical and financial assistance from the United States, which began constructing a permanent embassy in Dushanbe. Relations with Uzbekistan, its more powerful Central Asian neighbor, remained uneasy, with Tajik civilians continuing to be killed accidentally by land mines laid by Uzbekistan along the Uzbek-Tajik border. Uzbekistan refused to remove the mines, which were designed to prevent renewed invasions by Islamic radical groups that had entered into Uzbekistan via Tajikistan several years earlier.

**Political Rights and Civil Liberties:** Citizens of Tajikistan cannot change their government democratically. The 1994 constitution provides for a strong, directly elected executive who enjoys broad authority to appoint and dismiss officials. Amendments to the constitution adopted in a 1999 referendum further increased the powers of the president by extending his term in office from five to seven years and creating a full-time, bicameral parliament whose members would be appointed directly by the president or elected by indirect vote through local parliaments led by presidential appointees. Constitutional amendments adopted in a 2003 referendum allow the president to run for two additional seven-year terms in office. Neither the presidential polls in 1994 and 1999 nor the parliamentary elections of 1995 and 2000 were free and fair.

Patronage networks and regional affiliations are central to political life, with officials from the Kulyob region—the home of President Imomali Rakhmonov—dominant in government. The pro-Rakhmonov PDP is the dominant political party. Secular opposition parties, including the Democratic Party and Social Democratic Party, are weak and enjoy minimal popular support. A 1998 ban on religion-based parties was lifted the following year, leading to the registration of the IRP, currently the only legal religiously-based party in Central Asia. While the IRP has limited political influence within government structures, it also faces opposition criticism of having been co-opted by the authorities.

With parliamentary elections due in 2005, the government increased its pressure during the year on leading officials of the IRP and other perceived potential challengers to the president's authority. Rakhmonov has recently tried to discredit the IRP by hinting at links to terrorist or extremist Islamist groups. In June, the party's deputy chair, Shamsiddin Shamsiddinov, was arrested on charges of murder, setting up an armed group, and other crimes; he was reportedly physically abused while in detention. Another senior IRP official, Qosim Rakhimov, was arrested in July on statutory rape charges. The trials of both men were ongoing as of November 30. The authorities have also targeted exiled opponents, including Yakub Salimov, a former ally of Rakhmonov, who was arrested in Moscow in July on charges including participating in a coup attempt; as of November 30, Russia was denying extradition requests by the Tajik government.

Corruption is reportedly pervasive throughout society, with payments often required to obtain lucrative government positions. Tajikistan was ranked 124 out of 133 countries in Transparency International's 2003 Corruption Perceptions Index.

Despite constitutional guarantees of freedom of speech and the press, independent journalists continue to face harassment and intimidation, politically motivated tax audits, and denial of access to state printing facilities. The penal code criminalizes publicly defaming or insulting a person's honor or reputation. Consequently, journalists often avoid reporting on sensitive political issues, including corruption, and directly criticizing the president and other senior officials. Most newspapers in this impoverished country are weeklies and suffer from low advertising revenues and poor circulation. Television and radio are dominated by state-run channels. The process of obtaining broadcast licenses is cumbersome and expensive, and licenses are sometimes withheld for political reasons.

In late 2003, the state-run printing house refused to print the independent weekly *Ruzi Nav* after the paper published articles critical of government officials. The editor of the independent *Nerui Sukhan* was questioned during the year by the prosecutor's office after publishing an interview with an opposition leader, and the paper was visited by tax inspectors after printing a series of articles criticizing government policies. In September, the country's broadcasting commission rejected a television broadcasting application by the media holding company Asia-Plus, which in 2002 had established the first private radio station to broadcast in the capital. Dozens of journalists were murdered during the country's five-year civil war in the 1990s, and most of the cases have not been solved. In July, two suspects were convicted of the murders of the head of the BBC's Persian language service bureau, Muhiddin Olimpur, and Russia's ORT TV journalist, Viktor Nikulin, in 1995 and 1996, respectively. The high cost of Internet service puts it out of reach of most citizens, who live in poverty. In mid-2003, authorities blocked access to an Internet news site run by exiled opposition journalist Dodojon Atovulloev.

The government generally respects religious freedom in this predominantly Muslim country, although it monitors the activities of religious institutions to prevent them from becoming overtly political. Religious communities must register with the State Committee on Religious Affairs, a process that some local authorities have used to prevent the activities of certain groups, including Jehovah's Witnesses. Authorities closed down a number of unregistered mosques in 2002, a process that continued in 2003. Members of Hizb-ut-Tahrir, which calls for the establishment of an Islamic caliphate throughout the Muslim world, have been given lengthy prison sentences on charges of subversion for distributing copies of the group's literature; several alleged members of the group claim they were tortured while in police custody.

According to the 2002 U.S. State Department's human rights report, released in March 2003, the government does not restrict academic freedom. However, the country's educational system suffers from inadequate funding and resources, declining enrollments of pupils due to poverty, and corruption in the grading system.

Although a number of nongovernmental organizations (NGOs) operate in the country without restrictions, the state strictly controls freedom of assembly and association for organizations of a political nature. Registered groups must obtain permits to hold public demonstrations, and organizers of protests have at times faced government reprisals. Citizens have the legal right to form and join trade unions and to strike, but the country's poor economic climate deters workers from engaging in strikes.

The judiciary is influenced directly by the executive branch, on which most judges depend for their positions, as well as by some criminal groups. Many judges are poorly trained and inexperienced, and bribery is reportedly widespread. Police routinely conduct arbitrary arrests and beat detainees to extract confessions. Detainees are frequently refused access to legal counsel and face lengthy pretrial detention periods. Prison conditions have been described as life threatening because of overcrowding and unsanitary conditions. Since the collapse of the Taliban regime in neighboring Afghanistan, narcotics trafficking across the porous, mountainous border with Tajikistan is reportedly on the rise. Organized crime groups involved in the drug trade allegedly have connections with members of the country's security and police forces.

Most of the population live in poverty and survive on subsistence agriculture, remittances from relatives working abroad, mainly in Russia, and foreign humanitarian aid. Widespread corruption, patronage networks, regional affiliations, limited privatization of land and industry, and the growing narcotics trade restrict equality of opportunity and limit economic growth.

Although women are employed throughout the government and the business world, they continue to face traditional societal discrimination. Domestic violence is reportedly common, and there are credible reports of trafficking of women abroad for prostitution. In August, parliament adopted criminal code amendments that punish trafficking with 5 to 15 years in prison. The participation of women in criminal activities, including the drug trade, has increased as a result of the country's widespread poverty.

# Tanzania

**Population:** 35,400,000    **Political Rights:** 4
**GNI/capita:** $270    **Civil Liberties:** 3
**Life Expectancy:** 45    **Status:** Partly Free
**Religious Groups:** Christian (30 percent), Muslim
(35 percent), indigenous beliefs (35 percent); Zanzibar:
Muslim (more than 99 percent)
**Ethnic Groups:** African (99 percent), other [including Asian,
European, and Arab] (1 percent)
**Capital:** Dar-es-Salaam

**Ten-Year Ratings Timeline (Political Rights, Civil Liberties, Status)**

| 1994 | 1995 | 1996 | 1997 | 1998 | 1999 | 2000 | 2001 | 2002 | 2003 |
|------|------|------|------|------|------|------|------|------|------|
| 6,6NF | 5,5PF | 5,5PF | 5,5PF | 5,4PF | 4,4PF | 4,4PF | 4,4PF | 4,3PF | 4,3PF |

**Overview:** Significant progress occurred in 2003 in Tanzania's long-festering political crisis regarding the semiautonomous islands of Zanzibar and Pemba, with elections that resulted in a victory by the opposition Civic United Front (CUF). Controversial legislation approved by parliament in 2002 that circumscribes the ability of nongovernmental organizations to function was not implemented, although it is expected to be implemented after administrative regulations are enacted.

After Tanzania gained independence from Britain in 1961, the ruling Chama Cha Mapinduzi (CCM) party under President Julius Nyerere dominated the country's political life. The Zanzibar and Pemba Islands were merged with Tanganyika to become the Union of Tanzania after Arab sultans who had long ruled the islands were deposed in a violent revolution in 1964. For much of his presidency, President Nyerere espoused a collectivist economic philosophy known in Swahili as *ujaama*. Although it may have been useful in promoting a sense of community and nationality, this policy resulted in significant economic dislocation and decline, the effects of which continue to be felt. During Nyerere's tenure, Tanzania also played an important role as a "Front Line State" in the international response to white-controlled regimes in southern Africa. Nyerere retained strong influence after he officially retired in 1985 until his death in 1999. His successor, Ali Hassan Mwinyi, held the presidency from 1985 to 1995.

The CCM's landslide legislative victory in the 1995 parliamentary elections was seriously tainted by poor organization, fraud, and administrative irregularities. In addition, extensive use of state broadcasting and other government resources during the campaign favored the ruling party. The CCM won 80 percent of the 232 directly elected seats in the National Assembly. The voting in Zanzibar was plainly fraudulent, with the island's High Court summarily rejecting opposition demands for fresh polls.

Tanzania held legislative and presidential elections in October 2000, the second since the reintroduction of multiparty politics. Incumbent president Benjamin Mkapa won reelection with about 70 percent of the vote, and the CCM won an overwhelming victory in the parliamentary election. Although the conduct of these elections represented a modest improvement over that of the 1995 vote, they were marred by fraudulent polls biased in favor of the ruling party in the federated semiautonomous isles of Zanzibar and Pemba; the status of these islands in relation to the mainland has long provoked tension. The opposition CUF and independent observers convincingly demonstrated that the ruling CCM engaged in fraud to retain power. Subsequent rioting in Zanzibar in early 2001 resulted in the deaths of more than 40 people. In October 2001, the CCM and the CUF announced a reconciliation agreement designed to resolve the political crisis and allow for more transparent government.

The Tanzanian parliament passed restrictive antiterrorism legislation in 2002 that gives the police and immigration officials sweeping powers to arrest suspected illegal immigrants or anyone thought to have links with terrorists. Concerns over President Benjamin Mkapa's health grew as he undertook prolonged medical treatment in Switzerland.

By-elections held in May 2003 were generally regarded as free and fair, with an absence of violence. The CUF won 11 out of 17 seats in the Zanzibar House of Representatives and all 15 seats that were being contested for the national parliament, while the CCM won 6 seats. The seats had fallen vacant after CUF members elected in 2000 were expelled for boycotting parliamentary sessions to protest the 2000 general elections, which the CUF claimed were rigged in favor of the CCM.

Tanzania's economy is growing modestly, but there are a number of serious issues that have complicated prospects for the country's long-term stability. These include relations between the mainland and the Zanzibar archipelago; the presence in Tanzania of 500,000 refugees from Burundi, the Democratic Republic of Congo, and Rwanda; and the need for relief from the country's foreign debt, which in 2001 totaled more than $6 billion.

**Political Rights and Civil Liberties:** The ability of Tanzanians to freely choose their political leaders is not yet firmly entrenched in practice. Although opposition parties were legalized in 1992, the ruling CCM continues to dominate the country's political life. Progress toward democratic consolidation and strong economic growth remain inhibited by high levels of corruption and weak opposition parties. Executive power rests with the president, who is elected by direct popular vote for a five-year term. The president can serve a maximum of two terms. The constitution provides for legislative power to be held by a unicameral National Assembly with members serving a term of five years, and for universal adult suffrage. The legislative body, the Bunge, has 274 members, with 232 elected for a five-year term in single-seat constituencies.

Although the 2000 national elections avoided the massive logistical and administrative chaos of the preceding elections, the CCM continues to enjoy considerable advantages of incumbency that inhibit the realistic prospect of alternation of power. The 2003 elections in Zanzibar raised hopes that 2005 parliamentary and presidential elections (at which President Benjamin Mkapa is not expected to stand) may represent a positive step forward.

Thirteen opposition parties have formal status. Some of them are active, but they tend to be divided and ineffective. The opposition CUF has sought to establish significant support on the Tanzanian mainland. Another major opposition party, the National Convention for Constitution and Reform (NCCR-Mageuzi), whose leader, Augustine Mrema, was runner-up to Mkapa in the 1995 presidential election, has split. Parties with parliamentary representation receive government subsidies, but they criticize the low level of funding and the formula by which it is allocated. In 2003, most opposition parties came together in an electoral alliance, but the CUF did not join.

Corruption remains a serious problem, although the government has made some attempts to address it, including developing a national anticorruption action plan. The Prevention of Corruption Bureau recorded an increasing number of reported incidents on corruption from 432 cases in 1998 to 1,461 cases at the end of 2000. However, it is not clear whether this represents an increase in corruption or increased reporting and improved detection of corruption. Tanzania ranked 92 out of 133 countries on Transparency International's 2003 Corruption Perceptions Index.

Print and electronic media are active, but media impact is largely limited to major urban areas. In terms of numbers, the Tanzanian news media are experiencing their greatest growth. The country has more than 50 regular newspapers, including 17 dailies. It also has 26 radio stations, 15 television stations, and 20 cable operators. The number of journalists has also increased from only 230 in 1991 to more than 4,000 currently, but journalists in general have serious concerns about press laws that could limit freedom of expression. The government has been using its powers selectively to deny nationality to reporters. Jenerali Ulimwengu, a prominent journalist, became the first victim in 2001, followed by Ali Nabwa, editor of the weekly newspaper *Dira*, who saw his citizenship revoked in March.

Freedom of religion is respected, although the 1998 bombing of the U.S. Embassy served notice that Tanzania was not immune from religiously oriented international tensions.

Many nongovernmental organizations (NGOs) are active, and some have been able to influence the public policy process. However, an NGO act passed by parliament in 2002 contains many serious flaws, including compulsory registration backed by criminal sanctions, lack of appeal to the courts, aligning of NGO activities with government plans, prohibition of national networks and coalitions of NGOs, and inconsistencies with other related existing legislation. The International Federation for Human Rights and the World Organization against Torture have warned that several provisions of the proposed act contravene the Tanzanian constitution, the UN Declaration on Human Rights Defenders, and the International Covenant on Civil and Political Rights. As of November 2003, the act had not been implemented, though it is expected to be in the future.

Constitutional protections for the right to freedom of assembly are generally, but not always, respected. Laws allow rallies only by officially registered political parties, which may not be formed on religious, ethnic, or regional bases and cannot oppose the union of Zanzibar and the mainland.

Workers do not have the right to organize and join trade unions freely. Essential workers are barred from striking; other workers' rights to strike is restricted by complex notification and mediation requirements. Collective bargaining effectively exists only in the small private sector. Approximately 85 percent of Tanzania's people survive through subsistence agriculture.

Tanzania's judiciary has displayed signs of autonomy after decades of subservience to the one-party CCM regime, but it remains subject to considerable political influence. Arrest and pretrial detention laws are often ignored. New legislation designed to strengthen the government's ability to deal with terrorist threats has raised civil liberties concerns; police will not need warrants to detain people suspected of committing certain terrorism-related crimes. Prison conditions are harsh, and police abuses are said to be common. According to government estimates, there are approximately 45,000 inmates in the country's prisons, although the prisons' collective capacity is only 21,000. Such overcrowding has caused widespread concern. Questions have been raised regarding the safety and health of prisoners, including minors and women, who have been subjected to sexual harassment and human rights abuses.

The broad distribution of Tanzania's population among many ethnic groups has largely diffused potential ethnic rivalries that have wracked neighboring countries.

Women's rights guaranteed by the constitution and other laws are not uniformly protected. Especially in rural areas and in Zanzibar, traditional or Islamic customs discriminatory toward women prevail in family law, and women have fewer educational and economic opportunities. Domestic violence against women is reportedly common and is rarely prosecuted. Human rights groups have sought laws to bar forced marriages, which are most common among Tanzania's coastal peoples.

# Thailand

**Population:** 63,100,000    **Political Rights:** 2
**GNI/capita:** $1,940    **Civil Liberties:** 3
**Life Expectancy:** 71    **Status:** Free
**Religious Groups:** Buddhist (95 percent),
Muslim (3.8 percent), other (1.2 percent)
**Ethnic Groups:** Thai (75 percent), Chinese (14 percent),
other (11 percent)
**Capital:** Bangkok

**Ten-Year Ratings Timeline (Political Rights, Civil Liberties, Status)**

| 1994 | 1995 | 1996 | 1997 | 1998 | 1999 | 2000 | 2001 | 2002 | 2003 |
|------|------|------|------|------|------|------|------|------|------|
| 3,5PF | 3,4PF | 3,3PF | 3,3PF | 2,3F | 2,3F | 2,3F | 2,3F | 2,3F | 2,3F |

**Overview:**

Backed by high approval ratings and a comfortable parliamentary majority, Prime Minister Thaksin Shinawatra continued in 2003 to carry out populist spending programs, which have helped spark a demand-driven economic recovery. Critics, however, continued to allege that Thaksin has concentrated power in his hands and muted media criticism of his policies. These have included a three-month police crackdown on drug trafficking in 2003 during which some 2,200 suspects were killed.

Known as Siam until 1939, Thailand is the only Southeast Asian nation never colonized by a European country. Beginning with a 1932 coup that transformed the kingdom into a constitutional monarchy, the army ruled periodically for the next six decades. The military last seized power in 1991, when it overthrew a hugely corrupt elected government. After soldiers shot dead more than 50 pro-democracy protesters in Bangkok in March 1992, Thailand returned to civilian rule when the country's revered monarch, King Bhumibol Alduyadej, convinced the military to appoint a civilian prime minister.

Thailand's export-led economy notched up strong growth in the decade prior to 1997, before being dragged down by the regional financial crisis. After spending billions of dollars fruitlessly defending the *baht* against speculators, the government floated the currency in July 1997 and agreed to a $17.2 billion bailout led by the IMF. Amid noisy street protests by middle-class Thais in Bangkok against corruption and economic mismanagement, parliament approved a reformist constitution and elected the Democrat Party's Chuan Leekpai, a former prime minister with a clean reputation, to head a coalition government. The new constitution created independent election and anticorruption bodies and introduced direct election of the Senate. While Chuan's tight monetary policy helped to stabilize the baht, the opposition blamed high interest rates for pushing the economy into recession in 1998.

Criticizing the government for supposedly favoring the urban middle class over ordinary Thais, Thaksin, a former deputy prime minister who built his fortune in telecommunications, unseated Chuan in the January 2001 elections. During the campaign, Thaksin pledged to help poorer Thais hurt by the financial crisis by introducing cheap health care, a debt moratorium for farmers, and investment funds for each village. Thaksin's Thai Loves Thai (TRT) party won 248 out of parliament's 500 seats and then formed a coalition government with three other parties, two of which it has since absorbed. The TRT won the elections despite a December 2000 ruling by Thailand's new National Counter-Corruption Commission that Thaksin had deliberately falsified wealth-disclosure statements in 1997 as a cabinet minister; he was cleared by the Constitutional Court in August 2001.

Thaksin's government has won praise from many Thais for largely sticking to its electoral promises by introducing programs to help the poor and small businesses. Low interest rates and populist spending programs have fueled a consumption-driven economic growth spurt. Moreover, while Thaksin arguably has concentrated power in his hands, he does not always get his way. His government has backed away from introducing a tough press law and from a measure that would have benefited his family's mobile phone business. Thaksin's coalition seems set to win reelection in polls that are due by January 2005 but will probably be held in 2004.

Still, many of Thaksin's moves, taken together, seem to run against the reformist spirit of the 1998 constitution. Some government policies directly help companies that are held by Thaksin's family or the families of cabinet members; Thaksin denies any conflicts of interest. While the constitution requires the prime minister and cabinet members to divest shares in companies they owned when they entered government, many of their families retain considerable business interests. Moreover, Thaksin has filed a series of libel suits against opposition lawmakers, a senior Democrat Party member told the Hong Kong-based *Far Eastern Economic Review* in November. Anecdotal evidence suggests that state-owned firms have placed fewer advertisements in publications perceived to be critical of the government.

Despite the high number of killings involved in a three-month police crackdown against narcotics traffickers in 2003, polls showed a majority of Thais appeared to support Thaksin's campaign to eradicate illicit drugs from the country. Thailand has recently been deluged with methamphetamines and other narcotics from neighboring Burma. The government claimed that most of the more than 2,000 dead were traffickers killed by other traffickers to keep them from becoming police informants. The regional human rights group Forum Asia, however, cited evidence that it said implicated police in at least some summary killings of alleged traffickers.

After denying that Islamic terrorist groups were operating in Thailand, the government took a more forceful approach to Islamic militancy in 2003. Authorities in the spring arrested at least four alleged members of Jemaah Islamiah, the regional Muslim terrorist group suspected in the 2002 Bali bombing.

Like other Southeast Asian countries, Thailand faces the challenge of diversifying its economy now that China increasingly is attracting the foreign investment that powered the region's export-led economic boom in the 1980s and much of the 1990s. Thaksin's government has pushed state banks to lend to certain industries, championed small and medium-sized businesses and rural export sectors, and promoted several industrial megaprojects. Critics allege that many programs carry high risk and could undermine the government's finances.

**Political Rights and Civil Liberties:** Thais can change their government democratically, although violence and corruption have undermined the integrity of elections. Thailand's constitution created a parliamentary system with a two-house legislature. The House of Representatives has 400 seats chosen by first-past-the-post balloting and 100 chosen by proportional representation, all directly elected for four-year terms. The Senate has 200 members who are directly elected for six-year terms.

As in previous elections, candidates spent huge sums to buy votes in the January 2001 balloting—at least 20 billion baht ($465 million), according to Bangkok's Nakhon Ratchsima Rajabhat Institute, which monitors poll fraud. The Election Commission ordered fresh polls in some districts but took little or no action on many of the more than 1,000 allegations of electoral fraud, leading some critics to suggest that Prime Minister Thaksin Shinawatra's party might have pressured commission members to overlook violations.

Anecdotal evidence suggests that official corruption is widespread, involving both bureaucrats demanding bribes in exchange for routine services and law enforcement officials being paid off to ignore trafficking and other illicit activities. The Berlin-based Transparency International's 2003 Corruption Perceptions Index ranked Thailand in a six-way tie for seventieth place out of 133 countries rated. In a positive development, the Anti-Money Laundering Office has indicted many small-time money launderers and ordered police to seize assets and property of many drug traffickers.

Although several legal and constitutional provisions formally restrict freedom of expression on specific topics such as the monarchy and on broad public order, national security, and other grounds, freedom of expression generally is respected in practice. Thai print media are among the most robust in Asia. Newspapers freely criticize government policies and report allegations of official corruption and human rights abuses. Several journalists, however, have been jailed in recent years on libel charges filed by politicians. Journalists, moreover, practice some self-censorship when reporting on the monarchy and national security issues. Broadcast media tend to be less outspoken than their print counterparts. ITV, a major television network, has become more muted since a company owned by Thaksin family members, Shin Corp., increased its ownership stake in ITV to 50 percent in 2000. In addition, the government or armed forces either directly or indirectly own or oversee most other radio and television stations. The 1941 Printing Act gives authorities the power to shut down media outlets, although this power rarely is used. The government does not restrict Internet use.

Thais of all faiths can worship freely in this predominantly Buddhist society. However, Muslims, who make up around 5 to 10 percent of Thailand's population and are in the majority in four of the five southernmost provinces bordering Malaysia, face some private sector job discrimination. Academic freedom is respected, and university professors and other educators can write and lecture without interference.

In a sharp setback for grassroots advocacy, several environmental and land rights activists and community leaders have been killed in recent years in cases that remain unsolved, according to a November report by the human rights group Amnesty International. Thai trade unions are independent, though fewer than 2 percent of Thai workers are unionized. Unions can bargain collectively on behalf of workers, though in practice private employers enjoy considerable economic leverage and generally set wages unilaterally. The law does not protect workers seeking to establish unregistered unions, and private employers often discriminate against, and at times fire, union organizers. Private employers, moreover, often breach the country's poorly enforced labor laws with violations that include using child and sweatshop labor and paying workers less than the minimum wage. Strikes are legal for private sector employees but not for state enterprise workers.

Though the judiciary is generally regarded as independent, it sometimes is subject to corruption, according to the U.S. State Department's human rights report for 2002, released in March 2003. Suspects frequently spend long periods in detention before trial because of heavy case backlogs, and trials often take years to complete. Still, defendants generally receive adequate due process rights at trial.

While the government denied that police had wrongfully killed suspects during the 2003 antidrug trafficking campaign, the high death toll appeared to continue a trend in which Thailand's poorly trained police often are implicated in wrongful killings of criminal suspects. While police occasionally may be justified in using lethal force against Thailand's increasingly well-armed drug traffickers and other criminal suspects, at least some of the killings are unwarranted, according to the press and nongovernmental groups.

Police and, at times, soldiers also continue to be implicated in torture and other abuse of suspects and prison inmates, according to the November Amnesty International report. The poor, foreign workers, and ethnic minorities are particularly vulnerable, the report said. Officers recently have also been accused of raping and extorting sex from female detainees. Thai prisons and immigration detention centers are severely overcrowded, and prison inmates generally lack proper medical care. Many of Thailand's estimated one million members of hill tribes, who live mainly in the north, have never been fully integrated into society. Reportedly, roughly half of hill tribe members lack citizenship, rendering them ineligible to vote, own land, or be covered under labor laws and making it harder for them to access education and health care. The government in 2000 made it easier for hill tribe members to gain citizenship, but corruption and inefficiency reportedly have slowed citizenship processing. Police and soldiers at times carry out warrantless searches of hill tribe villages for narcotics, a practice permitted in some instances by law, but that often is carried out in a way that some academic groups say violates the villagers' civil rights.

Maintaining its long-standing policy of harboring refugees from neighboring Southeast Asian nations, the government provides, in its border areas, temporary asylum to more than 130,000 Burmese refugees. Authorities, however, at times arrest as illegal aliens Burmese living outside designated camps, generally taking them to the border and releasing them. Separately, foreign workers often face extortion and physical abuse at the hands of smugglers, employers, or local police, the November Amnesty International report said. Some Burmese workers who protested against labor violations recently have been arrested and deported to Burma, the report added.

Women make up more than half of university graduates in Thailand and increasingly are entering the professions, but they continue to face discrimination by private employers in hiring and wages. Anecdotal evidence suggests that domestic violence is a serious problem in Thailand. Police, however, do not vigorously enforce relevant laws, and strict evidentiary rules make prosecuting offenders difficult, according to the U.S. State Department report. The government has taken some positive measures such as deploying teams of female police officers in some station houses to encourage women to report sex crimes.

Some 200,000 or more Thai women and children work as prostitutes, according to government and private estimates, many of them after being trafficked to cities from their villages. Many prostitutes work under debt bondage, forced to repay loans by traffickers to their parents. Authorities prosecute relatively few traffickers, and many police, soldiers, local officials, and immigration officers reportedly either are involved in trafficking or take bribes to ignore it.

# Togo

**Population:** 5,400,000
**GNI/capita:** $270
**Life Expectancy:** 54
**Religious Groups:** Indigenous beliefs (51 percent),
Christian (29 percent), Muslim (20 percent)
**Ethnic Groups:** Native African (99 percent), other
[including European and Syrian-Lebanese] (1 percent)
**Capital:** Lomé

**Political Rights:** 6
**Civil Liberties:** 5
**Status:** Not Free

**Ten-Year Ratings Timeline (Political Rights, Civil Liberties, Status)**

| 1994 | 1995 | 1996 | 1997 | 1998 | 1999 | 2000 | 2001 | 2002 | 2003 |
|------|------|------|------|------|------|------|------|------|------|
| 6,5NF | 6,5NF | 6,5NF | 6,5NF | 6,5NF | 5,5PF | 5,5PF | 5,5PF | 6,5NF | 6,5NF |

**Overview:**

Africa's longest-serving leader, Gnassingbe Eyadema, won another five-year term as president in elections held in June 2003 that made a mockery of the democratic process. His main rival was barred from competing, and the electoral code was amended to favor Eyadema's candidacy.

Togoland, a German colony for more three decades until France seized it at the outset of World War I, gained independence in 1960. The country's founding president, Sylvanus Olympio, was murdered in 1963 as Eyadema, then a demobilized sergeant who had served in France's colonial wars, led an army coup to topple the country's democratically elected government. After assuming direct power in 1967, Eyadema suspended the constitution and extended his repressive rule through mock elections and a puppet political party.

In 1991, the organizing of free political parties was legalized, and multiparty elections were promised. The transition faltered, however, as soldiers and secret police harassed, attacked, or killed opposition supporters. Eyadema won fraudulent elections in 1993 and 1998.

Leading opposition parties boycotted the October 2002 legislative vote to protest preparations for the polls, which they said would prevent the holding of a free and fair election. The ruling Rally of the Togolese People party won 72 of 81 parliamentary seats.

Eyadema supporters in the National Assembly began setting the stage in 2002 for his victory in the June 2003 presidential election by changing the constitution to allow him to run for a third term. Lawmakers also altered the composition of the Independent National Electoral Commission, transferred responsibility for organizing the elections from the commission to the Ministry of the Interior, designated the ministry to select polling officers, and stipulated that presidential candidates were to reside in Togo for at least one year prior to elections. To help assure Eyadema's win, the Constitutional Court barred the president's main rival and opposition leader, Gilchrist Olympio, from participating in the polls. The electoral commission denied the candidacy of Olympio, who had been living in exile, on the grounds that he lacked a certificate of residency and could not prove that he had paid his taxes. Olympio appealed, but the commission's decision was upheld by the Constitutional Court.

Eyadema won the election with 57 percent of the vote, compared with 34 percent for Emmanuel Bob-Akitani of Olympio's Union of Forces for Change Party. Four other candidates shared the remainder of the vote. The European Union declined to send observers, saying it was unlikely that the vote would be fair. Monitors from the African Union and the Economic Community of West African States, however, claimed that the elections were free and fair. Opposition members maintained that they were intimidated or barred from polling stations, that ballot boxes were stuffed, that fictitious polling centers were created, and that some legitimate voting stations did not receive ballots.

Eighty percent of Togolese are engaged in subsistence agriculture. Corruption, military spending, and large, inefficient state-owned companies impede economic growth.

**Political Rights and Civil Liberties:** The Togolese people cannot change their government democratically. Presidential elections in 1993 and 1998 were blatantly fraudulent. The National Assembly, which is dominated by President Gnassingbe Eyadema's Rally of the Togolese People, amended the electoral code prior to the 2003 presidential election to favor his candidacy. The measures reduced the power of the electoral commission and compromised its impartiality. The October 2002 legislative elections were neither free nor fair.

At least 15 private newspapers publish in Lome, but independent journalists are subject to harassment and the perpetual threat of various criminal charges. There are more than a dozen independent newspapers that publish sporadically and some 30 private radio stations, most of which operate as pirate stations. Most of the independent broadcast media outlets, however, offer little vibrant local news coverage or commentary. The Press and Communication Code of 1998 declares in its first article that the media are free, but restricts press freedom in most of the 108 other articles.

The National Assembly in 2002 passed an amendment to the media bill that imposes heavy sentences for "defaming or insulting" the president, state institutions, courts, the armed forces, and public administration bodies. The amendment increases the penalty for "insulting the head of state" from the previous penalty of one to six months imprisonment to a jail term of one to five years. Authorities have seized newspaper print runs, harassed and jailed journalists, and shuttered media outlets. The U.S.-based Committee to Protect Journalists said Togo "has one of the most repressive climates for journalists in Africa."

Several journalists were detained in 2003 and faced charges such as disseminating false information and threatening public order. Sylvestre Djalin Nicoue, managing director of the weekly *Le Courier du Citoyen*, was detained for four months without trial before he was released in May. Officials also closed the independent Tropik FM radio station in February. The government does not restrict Internet access.

Constitutionally protected religious freedom is generally respected. Academic freedom is not respected, and government informers and security forces maintained a presence on campuses in 2003.

Freedom of assembly is allowed, but is often restricted among the government's political opponents. Demonstrations are often banned or violently halted. Opposition protests that followed the 2003 presidential polls were suppressed by security forces. Human rights groups are closely monitored and sometimes harassed. Togo's constitution includes the right to form and join unions, except for "essential" workers. Only 20 percent of the labor force is unionized. Unions have the right to bargain collectively, but this right is restricted.

The judiciary is heavily influenced by the president. Traditional courts handle many minor matters. Courts are understaffed and inadequately funded, pretrial detentions are lengthy, and prisons are severely overcrowded. Killings, arbitrary arrests, and torture continue. Security forces commit abuses with impunity, and illegal detention is common.

Ethnic discrimination is rife among the country's 40 ethnic groups. Political and military power is narrowly held by members of a few ethnic groups from northern Togo, especially Eyadema's Kabye ethnic group. Southerners dominate the country's commerce, and violence occasionally flares between the two groups.

Despite constitutional guarantees of equality, women's opportunities for education and employment are limited. A husband may legally bar his wife from working, or he may legally choose to receive her earnings. Customary law bars women's rights in divorce and denies inheritance rights to widows. Violence against women is common. Female genital mutilation is practiced widely by the country's northern ethnic groups, and a 1998 law prohibiting the practice is not enforced. Several organizations promote the rights of women.

Child trafficking for the purpose of slavery is a problem in Togo as it is in much of West Africa. New York-based Human Rights Watch said in a March 2003 report that hundreds of children each year were trafficked from, received in, or trafficked through Togo on false promises of education, professional training, and paid employment. The report said the children were transported at times under life-threatening conditions and were subjected to physical and mental abuse.

# ⬇ Tonga

**Population:** 100,000
**GNI/capita:** $1,410
**Life Expectancy:** 68
**Religious Groups:** Christian (Free Wesleyan Church claims over 30,000 adherents)
**Ethnic Groups:** Polynesian, European
**Capital:** Nuku'alofa

**Political Rights:** 5
**Civil Liberties:** 3
**Status:** Partly Free

**Trend Arrow:** Tonga received a downward trend arrow due to the adoption of new restrictive media laws and efforts to increase the king's already considerable powers.

**Ten-Year Ratings Timeline (Political Rights, Civil Liberties, Status)**

| 1994 | 1995 | 1996 | 1997 | 1998 | 1999 | 2000 | 2001 | 2002 | 2003 |
|------|------|------|------|------|------|------|------|------|------|
| 5,3PF | 5,3PF | 5,3PF | 5,3PF | 5,3PF | 5,3PF | 5,3PF | 5,3PF | 5,3PF | 5,3PF |

**Overview:**

Tonga's government intensified efforts in 2003 to further restrict media freedoms, leading to the largest political demonstration in the country's history. The authorities also pressed for constitutional amendments that would increase the power of the country's king, who has ruled Tonga for nearly six decades.

Tonga, situated in the southwest Pacific, consists of 169 islands, only 36 of which are inhabited. The archipelago was unified as a kingdom under King George Tupou in 1845 and became a British protectorate in 1990. Tonga achieved independence in 1970 and is a member the Commonwealth. Tonga, which is a monarchy, has been under the rule of King Taufa'ahau Tupou IV since 1945. The king appointed his son, Prince Lavaka ata 'Ulukalala, as prime minister in 2000.

Although few citizens want to end the monarchy, more people have called for democratic change, usually emphasizing the importance of greater government accountability. Elections in March 2002 showed strong support for pro-democracy candidates on the main island of Tongatapu. Pro-democracy candidates won seven of the nine directly elected seats reserved for commoners, up from five in a 1999 legislative poll. Shortly before the 2002 elections, Kotoa (Together), a royalist political group, emerged as a serious movement with support from Princess Pilolevu, the king's eldest daughter. Under such pressure, the government launched an economic and public sector reform program in June 2002.

In February 2003, the government banned the import of the New Zealand-based *Tongan Times* (Taimi O Tonga), declaring that the paper undermined the Tongan government. One article alleged that the king has $350 million in overseas bank accounts. The Supreme Court overturned the ban in June, calling it "an ill disguised attempt once again to restrict freedom of the press." The government defied the court injunction and confiscated all copies of the newspaper, while a second government order made it illegal to import, sell, or distribute the newspaper.

Subsequently, the government proposed a Media Operator's Bill to ban foreign ownership of media in Tonga; the *Tongan Times* is owned by Kalafi Moala, a Tongan who holds U.S. citizenship. After Moala won a court case against the ban, the authorities enacted a revised Media Operator's Bill in August that limits foreign ownership to 20 percent. A more restrictive Newspaper Act that followed soon afterward allows the government to shut down any newspaper regardless of its origin. These measures were opposed by some members of the ruling elite, including Prince Uluvalu Tu'ipelehake, a nephew of the king and chair of the Legislative Assembly. Popular opposition to the new media restrictions brought nearly 9,000 people, nearly a tenth of the entire population, to the streets in October for the largest demonstration ever in the island state.

During the year, the government also pushed for proposed constitutional amendments that would increase the king's powers. While the Supreme Court ruled against the government's claim that the king enjoys a royal prerogative above the law and the constitution, parliament—which is dominated by the king and nobles—proposed an amendment to the constitution to exclude laws passed by the Legislative Assembly and ordinances passed by the king from judicial review.

On another front, the U.S. government cited Tonga as a potential launch site for terrorist attacks. The U.S. government alleged involvement between al-Qaeda and Tongan shipping services, specifically in providing flags of convenience; the kingdom refuted these charges.

**Political Rights and Civil Liberties:** Citizens of Tonga cannot change their government democratically. Politics in this former British colony are dominated by King Taufa'ahau Tupou IV—who has reigned since 1945—thirty-three hereditary nobles, and a few prominent commoners. The latter exert influence largely through control of substantial landholdings and their large numbers in parliament. The king appoints his cabinet without election and for life terms, and the cabinet takes up 12 of the 30 seats in the unicameral Legislative Assembly. Nine nobles elected by their peers and nine representatives elected by general election occupy the remaining seats. Cabinet members and nobles usually vote as a bloc. The king appoints the prime minister and presides over the privy council, which makes major policy decisions. Prince Ulukalala Lavaka Ata, who was appointed prime minister in 2000, also heads five government ministries, including defense and foreign affairs.

Despite constitutional guarantees for freedom of speech and the press, the government has a history of suppressing criticism of the monarchy and government. A government effort to ban the New Zealand-based *Tongan Times* in 2003 was followed by a confiscation of all copies of the newspaper. The government also adopted media legislation during the year that would further limit freedom of the press. In September, the Tongan Supreme Court dismissed a Crown suit against the *Tongan Times* for defamation against the minister of police.

Freedom of religion is generally respected in this predominantly Christian society. The Free Wesleyan Church has the most adherents. The state-run Radio Tonga requires that any on-air references to religion relate to mainstream Christian practices. There are no reports of government restrictions against academic freedom.

Freedom of assembly and association are generally respected for groups that avoid politics or criticizing government policies. Many civil society organizations are active in promoting education, public health, culture, and women's issues. The 1963 Trade Union Act gives workers the right to form unions and strike, but regulations on union formation were never promulgated. The economy's substantial trade deficit is largely offset by remittances from citizens working overseas, foreign assistance, and tourism.

The judiciary is generally fair, efficient, and independent of the king and the executive branch. The king's privy council presides over cases relating to disputes over titles of nobility and estate boundaries.

Citizens enjoy freedom of travel, movement, and emigration. Immigration laws have tightened after the illegal sale of Tongan passports, particularly to citizens from China and Taiwan, became sore points in Tongan relations with its major assistance donors. Relations between native Tongans and Chinese immigrants have also worsened in recent years, as evidenced by attacks against Chinese-owned shops.

Women are frequent victims of discrimination and abuse. There are few legal protections for women, and the police and courts generally consider domestic abuse cases better handled by families or village elders.

# Trinidad and Tobago

**Population:** 1,300,000
**GNI/capita:** $5,960
**Life Expectancy:** 71
**Religious Groups:** Roman Catholic (29.4 percent),
Hindu (23.8 percent), Anglican (10.9 percent), Muslim
(5.8 percent), Presbyterian (3.4 percent), other (26.7 percent)
**Ethnic Groups:** Black (40 percent), East Indian (40 percent),
mixed (18 percent), other (2 percent)
**Capital:** Port-of-Spain

**Political Rights:** 3
**Civil Liberties:** 3
**Status:** Partly Free

**Ten-Year Ratings Timeline (Political Rights, Civil Liberties, Status)**

| 1994 | 1995 | 1996 | 1997 | 1998 | 1999 | 2000 | 2001 | 2002 | 2003 |
|------|------|------|------|------|------|------|------|------|------|
| 1,2F | 1,2F | 1,2F | 1,2F | 1,2F | 1,2F | 2,2F | 3,3PF | 3,3PF | 3,3PF |

**Overview:**

Local elections held in July 2003 saw the People's National Movement (PNM) capture a majority of electoral districts. In August, a parliamentary integrity commission was established, an indication of the continuing effort to fight corruption. Meanwhile, an increasing crime rate was a critical problem throughout the year.

Trinidad and Tobago, a member of the Commonwealth, achieved independence from Britain in 1962. In July 1991, Jamaat-al-Muslimeen, a small radical Muslim group, staged a coup attempt in the capital, Port-of-Spain. The prime minister and eight cabinet members were held hostage for four days, and 23 people died in bombings at the police headquarters, the state television station, and the parliamentary building. Yasin Abu Bakr, the leader of the Muslimeen, was arrested in August on charges of conspiracy to murder, but was released on bail.

A stalemate in parliament, with 18 members of each party in a nine-month deadlock, led to street demonstrations and a legal challenge. Prime Minister Patrick Manning of the PNM eventually called for legislative elections in October 2002. The polling was generally peaceful and saw the participation of six parties representing more than 100 candidates contesting the 36 open seats. The PNM won 20 seats, while the United National Congress (UNC) had a heavy showing, reinforcing the domination of these two parties. Manning was sworn in for the third time since 1991, as the seventh prime minister of independent Trinidad and Tobago. His cabinet showed few changes and included his wife, Hazel, who again serves as minister of education; nepotism does not seem to be an issue for the electorate. In previous elections there were concerns over the impartiality of the Elections and Boundaries Commission, but no major improprieties surfaced during the recent national or local polls.

In local elections held in July 2003, the PNM won a majority of seats and took control of two districts that had been strongholds of the UNC, which won just 5 of 14 councils. Also during the year, the UNC became increasingly confrontational, forcing the government of Prime Minister Patrick Manning into compromises when legislation required a two-thirds majority in parliament.

**Political Rights and Civil Liberties:** Citizens of Trinidad and Tobago can change their government democratically. The 1976 constitution established the two-island nation as a republic, with a president, elected by a majority of both houses of parliament, replacing the former governor-general. Executive authority remains vested in the prime minister. The bicameral parliament consists of the 36-member House of Representatives, elected for five years, and the 31-member Senate, with 25 senators appointed by the prime minister and 6 by the opposition. Political parties are free to organize, but in practice, the dominance of the PNM and UNC has led to a two-party system.

In July 2001, Prime Minister Baseo Panday of the UNC lashed out at a Transparency International (TI) report that rated Trinidad, for the first time, as a country with high levels of official corruption. Panday, who was engaged in a long-running feud with prominent members' of the local press, denied that there was corruption in his administration. In its 2003 Corruption Perceptions Index, Trinidad was ranked 43 out of 133 countries. An Integrity Commission, established under the 2000 Integrity in Public Life Act, has the power to investigate the financial and ethical performance of public functionaries. Prime Minister Baseo Panday was the first person to be investigated by the Commission.

Press outlets are privately owned and vigorous and offer pluralistic views. There are four daily newspapers and several weeklies. The broadcast media are both private and public. Prime Minister Panday refused to sign the Inter-American Press Association's Chapultepec Declaration on press freedom until it addressed instances of media dissemination of "lies, half-truths and innuendoes." In April 1999, Information Minister Rupert Griffith reminded the media of the government's power to grant and revoke broadcast licenses and warned that local media operations were being examined "under a microscope." In 2000, a High Court judge ordered Panday to pay newspaper publisher Ken Gordon, an Afro-Trinidadian, $120,000 for defamation, after Panday had called him a "pseudo-racist." There is free access to the Internet.

Freedom of religion is guaranteed under the constitution, and the government honors this provision. Foreign missionaries are free to operate, but the government limits representatives of a denomination to 35. Academic freedom is generally respected.

Freedom of association and assembly are respected. Labor unions are well organized, powerful, and politically active, although union membership has declined. Strikes are legal and occur frequently.

The judicial branch is independent, although subject to some political pressure and corruption. As a result of rising crime rates, the court system is severely backlogged, in some cases for up to five years, with an estimated 20,000 criminal cases awaiting trial. However, the government permits human rights monitors to visit prisons, which are severely overcrowded.

Street crime is on the rise, with the consumption and trafficking of illegal drugs considered to be largely responsible for the increase in violent crime. The increasing frequency with which illicit drugs are used on the islands has been accompanied by significant growth of the drug trade. Drug corruption extends to the business community, and a significant amount of money is believed to be laundered through front companies. Recently, legislation was approved that provides severe penalties for money laundering and requires that major financial transactions be strictly monitored. The government works closely with U.S. law enforcement agencies to track drug shipments in and out of the country.

In May 1999, the government withdrew as a state party from the American Convention on Human Rights, which prohibits countries from extending the death penalty beyond those crimes for which it was in effect at the time that the treaty was ratified. There are more than 100 prisoners on death row. In June 2000, the country withdrew entirely from the International Covenant on Civil and Political Rights. In an indication of the seriousness of the country's crime wave, in January, the Trinidad and Tobago Chamber of Industry and Commerce asked the government to enforce laws strictly, including the execution of convicted murderers.

Corruption in the police force, which is often drug related, is endemic, and law enforcement inefficiency results in the dismissal of some criminal cases. In December 2000, Prime Minister Panday admitted that despite government efforts to finance reforms, something was "fundamentally wrong" with the police force. The police have won praise, however, for establishing a branch of Crime Stoppers, an international organization that promotes community involvement in preventing and informing on crime through a hotline.

Tensions persist between the black and East Indian communities, each roughly 40 percent of the population, as the latter edges toward numerical, and thus political, advantage. The most recent elections are emblematic of the racial tensions that continue to dominate electoral contests.

Violence against women is extensive and remains a low priority for police and prosecutors. However, in a 1999 landmark ruling, the court of appeals overturned a death sentence and reduced the charge from murder to manslaughter in the case of a woman defendant that the court said had suffered from battered-wife syndrome.

# Tunisia

**Population:** 9,900,000
**GNI/capita:** $2,070
**Life Expectancy:** 73
**Religious Groups:** Muslim (98 percent), Christian (1 percent), Jewish (1 percent)
**Ethnic Groups:** Arab (98 percent), other (2 percent)
**Capital:** Tunis

**Political Rights:** 6
**Civil Liberties:** 5
**Status:** Not Free

**Ten-Year Ratings Timeline (Political Rights, Civil Liberties, Status)**

| 1994 | 1995 | 1996 | 1997 | 1998 | 1999 | 2000 | 2001 | 2002 | 2003 |
|------|------|------|------|------|------|------|------|------|------|
| 6,5NF | 6,5NF | 6,5NF | 6,5NF | 6,5NF | 6,5NF | 6,5NF | 6,5NF | 6,5NF | 6,5NF |

**Overview:**
The Tunisian government continued its repressive practices against suspected opposition figures during 2003. In its first report on Tunisia in more than a decade, Amnesty International accused the Tunisian government of systematic human rights abuses, including the arbitrary arrest and torture of suspected government opponents. Presi-

dent Zine el-Abidine Ben Ali announced his intention to seek an unprecedented fourth term in office.

Nationalist pressures for Tunisian independence began in the 1930s under the leadership of Habib Bourguiba, leader of the Neo-Doustour party. Bourguiba became the country's first president when Tunisia gained independence in 1956 after more than 70 years as a French protectorate. Bourguiba's vision for Tunisia led to significant initiatives in the areas of social and economic development, including the promotion of one of the most liberal personal status codes in the Arab world that ceded significant rights to women and remains unmatched in the Arab world today. He also furthered education and spending on economic development projects. However, political rights and civil liberties were severely restricted under Bourguiba's rule.

In 1987, President Ben Ali, formerly the minister of the interior, led a bloodless coup, deposing the aging Bourguiba and promising to open the political system. After an initial period of minor political reform, Ben Ali cracked down harshly on the Islamist opposition. Over time, the government's repressive practices extended beyond the Islamist opposition, with hundreds of dissidents having been jailed over the last 15 years for peacefully exercising their civil liberties.

The government's tolerance for dissent continued to diminish in 2003, which saw the continuation of widespread and systematic government abuse of human rights. Amnesty International issued a 40-page report that chronicled Tunisia's "cycle of injustice" and that pointed out a disturbing discrepancy between laws and practice. According to the report, government opponents—or anyone critical of the government—are subjected to arbitrary arrest, incommunicado detention (without access to a lawyer or family), torture, and imprisonment. While certain changes in Tunisian law provide more human rights guarantees, other legal changes, including a vague definition of "terrorism," undermine basic human rights. In other cases, rights have improved in law, but are widely violated in practice.

In July, Ben Ali—who won the last election in 1999 with 99.4 percent of the vote—announced plans to seek an unprecedented fourth 5-year term in office in 2004. A constitutional referendum last year removed the three-term limit on the presidency, paving the way for Ben Ali's decision. The referendum also raised to 75 the maximum age to become president, which means that Ben Ali will be eligible to stand again for office in 2009. Under this scenario, Ben Ali could be president until 2014.

**Political Rights and Civil Liberties:** Tunisians cannot change their government democratically. The 1959 constitution accords the president significant powers, including the right to select the prime minister and cabinet, to rule by decree when the legislature is not in session, and to appoint the governors of Tunisia's 23 provinces. The legislature, by contrast, serves as a rubber stamp for the president's policies and does not provide a check on executive power. Presidential elections lack any pretense of competition. Although parliamentary elections are contrived to allow for the appearance of a multiparty legislature, the ruling Constitutional Democratic Rally (RCD) holds 148 of the 182 seats. Opposition parties play a symbolic role at best. The authorities have used "security concerns" as a pretext for repression of political dissent and critical discourse across the political spectrum.

Tunisia's press freedoms are among the most restricted in the Arab world. The government controls domestic broadcasting, as well as the circulation of both domestic and foreign publications. In addition, the government uses newsprint subsidies and control over public advertising revenues as a means for indirect censorship. Since President Zine el-Abidine Ben Ali's ascent to power, Tunisian journalists who are critical of the regime have been harassed, threatened, imprisoned, physically attacked, and censored. Two Tunisian journalists, Zouhair Yahyaoui and Hamadi Jebali, are currently in prison. Internet access is tightly controlled, and the government will at times intervene to block access to opposition Web sites.

While Islam is the state religion, the government allows for the free practice of all religions as long as it does not disturb the public order. The government controls and subsidizes mosques and pays the salaries of prayer leaders. The 1988 law on mosques stipulates that only those appointed by the government may lead activities in the mosques, which are required to remain closed except during prayer times. Academic freedom is severely restricted.

Freedom of association and assembly are sharply curtailed. After one opposition party, the Democratic Forum for Labor and Freedom, was legalized last year— eight years after its formation—the number of authorized political parties in the country increased to seven. However, several parties continue to be denied authorization. In addition, a number of politically oriented nongovernmental organizations remain unauthorized. For example, the founders of two organizations—the Tunisian Center for the Independence of the Judiciary and the International Association for the Support of Political Prisoners—have repeatedly faced obstructions in trying to become legally established. The government refuses to legalize most independent human rights organizations; their property has been subjected to vandalism and their offices to suspicious break-ins.

Human rights defenders, particularly lawyers, have been subjected to increased government harassment, including physical beatings. In August, a disabled former political prisoner was beaten on a Tunis street by four men in plainclothes; he had previously been assaulted twice in a similar fashion by state security officers. Another former political prisoner received a nine-month sentence on politically motivated charges. Both men had been helpful to international human rights organizations conducting research on Tunisia. Dissidents are frequently subjected to heavy police surveillance, travel bans, dismissals from work, interruptions in phone service, and harassment of family members. In October, Radhia Nasraoui, a leading human rights activist, initiated a hunger strike to protest systematic government harassment, beatings, and police surveillance.

There is no independent judiciary in Tunisia, with the government having used the courts to convict and imprison critics. Amnesty International has documented a pattern of executive interference in the administration of justice. At all stages of criminal proceedings, guarantees for a free trial under Tunisian and international law are disregarded. Defendants' files at times are confiscated or tampered with at trials, and political prisoners are subjected to harsh prison conditions, including solitary confinement. Arbitrary arrests and incommunicado detention occur with frequency, and torture is often used to coerce confessions. Numerous political trials failed to comply with international standards for a fair trial.

Women enjoy substantial rights, and the government has worked to advance women's rights in the areas of property ownership and support to divorced women.

However, inheritance law still discriminates against women. Unlike in many countries in the Arab world, citizenship rights to a child are conveyed through either the mother or the father.

# Turkey

**Population:** 71,200,000     **Political Rights:** 3
**GNI/capita:** $2,530         **Civil Liberties:** 4
**Life Expectancy:** 69        **Status:** Partly Free
**Religious Groups:** Muslim [mostly Sunni] (99.8 percent), other (0.2 percent)
**Ethnic Groups:** Turkish (80 percent), Kurdish (20 percent)
**Capital:** Ankara

**Ten-Year Ratings Timeline (Political Rights, Civil Liberties, Status)**

| 1994 | 1995 | 1996 | 1997 | 1998 | 1999 | 2000 | 2001 | 2002 | 2003 |
|------|------|------|------|------|------|------|------|------|------|
| 5,5PF | 5,5PF | 4,5PF | 4,5PF | 4,5PF | 4,5PF | 4,5PF | 4,5PF | 3,4PF | 3,4PF |

**Overview:**     In 2003, the ruling Justice and Development (AK) party sought to reform some of Turkey's harsher laws, in hopes of eventually being invited to negotiate with the European Union (EU) for membership. These reforms included the easing of laws restricting the use of the Kurdish language, the curbing of the power of the military in political affairs, and an offer of an amnesty to Kurdish militant separatists who were not involved in violence. While the government has made a great deal of progress on the legal aspects of these reforms, actual practices have changed far more slowly.

Turkey emerged as a republic out of the breakup of the Ottoman Empire at the end of World War I. Its founder and the author of its guiding principles was Kemal Mustafa Ataturk ("Father of the Turks"), who declared Muslim Turkey a secular state. Ataturk sought to modernize the country by pursuing Western learning, abolishing the Arabic script in favor of the Roman alphabet for writing Turkish, and abolishing the Muslim caliphate.

Turkey stayed out of most of World War II, but joined the Allies in February 1945. After the war, the republic joined NATO in 1952 to guarantee its protection from the Soviet Union. Modern Turkish political history has been unstable, with the army pushing out civilian governments four times. The army sees itself as a bulwark against both Islamism and Kurdish separatism.

The role of political Islamism has been one of the main defining questions of Turkish politics in the 1990s and in the first decade of the twenty-first century. In 1995, an Islamist party, Welfare, won the general election but failed to reach a majority, and none of the other parties would join it in a coalition. Two other parties formed a coalition instead, but a breakup of that coalition in 1997 forced the Democratic Party to form a coalition with Welfare. The army, however, soon forced the Welfare prime minister out of power.

The governments that followed failed to stabilize a shaky economy, and in November 2002, a party with Islamist roots, the AK, won a large majority of seats in the general election. The AK sought to distance itself from political Islamism, but its leader, Recep Tayyip Erdogan, a former mayor of Istanbul, had been banned from politics for reading a poem seeming to incite religious intolerance. Instead of Erdogan, Abdullah Gul was selected prime minister. Gul sought to offer Turkey's support to the United States for the war in Iraq. However, his plan to open a northern front in the war failed in the Turkish parliament, which refused to allow the U.S.-led coalition to use Turkey as a staging point. Turkey watched the conflict in Iraq with some trepidation, worried that the end of Saddam Hussein's regime in Iraq would mean the creation of a Kurdish state within Iraq that would provide inspiration to Turkey's own restive Kurds.

The military conflict with the separatist guerrillas of the Kurdistan Workers' Party (PKK) remained on a low boil in 2003, as it has since the PKK announced an end to its insurrection in 2000. This followed the capture of Abdullah Ocalan, the PKK's leader, in Africa. He is being held by Turkey, sometimes in solitary confinement, a fact criticized by the human rights group Amnesty International. However, Mr. Ocalan's death sentence was commuted to life in prison in October 2002.

Shortly before the war, the law banning Erdogan was repealed and he entered parliament in a March 2003 byelection, soon formally taking the post of prime minister. Throughout the summer, he used his party's large parliamentary majority to push through several bills that were key to Turkey's application to join the EU. One law rescinds the ban on some broadcasting in Kurdish and allows the teaching of Kurdish in some private schools. Another law curbs the formal power of the military, expressed through its control of the National Security Council, which is reduced to having an advisory role. A third offers amnesty to Kurdish rebels, but only to those who were not involved in violence. Disappointingly few Kurds accepted the offer, however. Yet another law formally bans torture, but again, practices have lagged behind principle.

EU accession has been a major incentive in Turkey's efforts to reform. In 2001, the European Union praised Turkey's progress in that year toward enacting laws that would bring Turkey closer to the European norms it is expected to follow if it is to be admitted to the EU. However, in 2002, Valery Giscard d'Estaing, a former French president who headed the convention writing a constitution for the EU, stated publicly that Turkish membership in the EU would "destroy" the Union. Talk of inserting a nod to Europe's Christian heritage into the preamble of the constitution, which did not take place, was alienating to mostly Muslim Turkey. The EU again lauded Turkey's efforts in a report in November 2003, but noted that on-the-ground implementation of reforms had been "uneven," and Turkey has yet to be given the chance officially to begin negotiations for membership.

In November, terrorists bombed two synagogues, and then a week later, two British targets (a bank and the British consulate). The government identified two men from the Kurdish region as responsible for the synagogue attacks. Two separate militant Islamist groups claimed responsibility for the anti-British attacks, citing Turkey's membership in the "crusader" NATO alliance and its friendly relations with Israel as its cause. Turkey had not previously been a major target of Islamist terrorism.

**Political Rights and Civil Liberties:** Turkish citizens can change their government democratically, although democratic choice has been undercut by the army in the past. The military retains considerable influence over the government, particularly in security and in some aspects of diplomatic affairs, notably over Cyprus. The 1982 constitution provides for a parliament, the Grand National Assembly, which is elected to five-year terms. The prime minister is the head of government, but the assembly chooses a mostly symbolic president as head of state currently Ahmet Necdet Sezer, a former constitutional court judge. The National Security Council, dominated by the military, had its policy-setting role downgraded to a purely advisory one by a law passed in 2003. A constitutional amendment in 2001 increased the number of civilians on the council.

There are numerous restraints on freedom of expression, although some legal restrictions were relaxed by the AK government in 2003. For example, advocating school instruction in Kurdish no longer necessarily invites a conviction for conspiring to break up the Turkish state. However, laws against "insulting" the state remain on the books, and it is still illegal to defame Mustafa Kemal Ataturk, the father of modern Turkey. Journalists are frequent targets of prosecution; criticizing the military or Kurdish policy is particularly dangerous. One journalist, Hasan Ozgun, who served in prison from 1996 to 2003 for belonging to the PKK, was threatened with re-imprisonment later that year for writing that the military committed abuses, including murder, in southeastern Turkey. Prosecutors asked for a 12-year sentence. Reporters Sans Frontieres ranked Turkey one-hundred-and-fifteenth in the world in its 2003 ranking of press freedom. The government does not restrict access to the Internet, but it does reserve the right to require Internet service providers to provide advance copies of content to be posted.

The overwhelming majority of Turks—around 99 percent—are Sunni Muslims. Secularism remains the state's official creed, and despite the presence of the AK party in government, pressure against Islamists and openly pious Muslims remains strong. It is illegal for women to wear the *hijab* (headscarf) in government or at universities. Though the government is sympathetic to lightening restrictions on the headscarf, it is not willing to offend the military or secular conservatives by pushing this as an issue. A 1998 law placed all mosques under government administration. Three non-Muslim groups—Greek and Armenian Orthodox Christians and Jews—are officially recognized, while other groups lack legal status and their activities are subject to legal challenges. The government does not restrict academic freedom, although self-censorship on sensitive topics like the role of Islam and the Kurdish problem are common.

Authorities may restrict freedom of association on the grounds of public order. Pro-Kurdish political parties and nongovernmental organizations face harassment. The high vote threshold of 10 percent required for a political party to enter parliament shuts out many parties with a reasonable support base, including the Democratic People's Party, DEHAP (formerly HADEP), the main Kurdish party.

With the exception of public servants and workers engaged in the protection of life or property—including those in the mining and petroleum industries, sanitation, defense, law enforcement, and education—workers may form unions, bargain collectively, and strike.

The government influences judges by its control of appointments and promotions. The head of the High Council of Judges and Prosecutors is appointed by the president, and its decisions are not subject to review. Those held for state security offenses can be detained for days without access to a lawyer or families, and conditions are worse in the Kurdish areas of the southeast. The death penalty is now legally only applied to those who commit terrorism or during times of war. While many remain under death sentences, an unofficial moratorium on carrying out these sentences has been in effect since 1984. Ending the death penalty is crucial to Turkey's EU application.

The prison system remains brutal. Despite an official ban, torture—including blindfolding, beating, death threats, deprivation of food and sleep, and in some cases, electric shocks—remains commonplace. Women are frequently sexually assaulted in custody. Although the problem is widely known and even acknowledged by some high officials, few perpetrators are ever convicted, and much remains to be done to bring prison conditions in line with the new laws and with European norms.

Turkey claims that all Turkish citizens are treated equally, but its unwillingness to recognize Kurdish differences results in de facto unequal treatment under the law. Broadcasting in Kurdish was made legal, but the government still officially denies the existence of a Kurdish language and forbids teaching in Kurdish in public schools.

Although women have the same legal status as men, much of Turkey is socially conservative, and women have far lower status in practice. Probably scores of women are killed each year in "honor killings," often by stoning, for transgressions such as having a lover before marriage or for going to the cinema with a man before marriage. An article in the penal code gives judges discretion in murder cases for "extenuating circumstances," and socially conservative judges often use this to hand down only light punishment to perpetrators of honor killings.

# Turkmenistan

**Population:** 5,700,000  **Political Rights:** 7
**GNI/capita:** $950  **Civil Liberties:** 7
**Life Expectancy:** 67  **Status:** Not Free
**Religious Groups:** Muslim (89 percent), Eastern
Orthodox (9 percent), other (2 percent)
**Ethnic Groups:** Turkmen (77 percent), Uzbek (9 percent),
Russian (7 percent), Kazakh (2 percent), other (5 percent)
**Capital:** Ashgabat

**Ten-Year Ratings Timeline (Political Rights, Civil Liberties, Status)**

| 1994 | 1995 | 1996 | 1997 | 1998 | 1999 | 2000 | 2001 | 2002 | 2003 |
|------|------|------|------|------|------|------|------|------|------|
| 7,7NF | 7,7NF | 7,7NF | 7,7NF | 7,7NF | 7,7NF | 7,7NF | 7,7NF | 7,7NF | 7,7NF |

**Overview:** The effects of the November 25, 2002 alleged assassination attempt against President Saparmurat Niyazov, which triggered a crackdown against suspected critics of the regime, continued to be felt in 2003. Among those arrested and convicted for their supposed involvement in the plot was Boris Shikhmuradov, an exiled prominent leader of the political opposition. The incident precipitated a series of wide-reaching repressive measures, including the reintroduction of the exit visa system, a new restrictive law on nongovernmental organizations (NGOs), a broader definition of acts of treason, and increased surveillance of the movements of foreign nationals and Turkmen citizens. Meanwhile, Ashgabat's relations with Russia were strained over its unilateral abrogation of a dual citizenship agreement with Moscow, although the two countries also signed a lucrative energy deal.

The southernmost republic of the former Soviet Union, Turkmenistan was conquered by the Mongols in the thirteenth century and seized by Russia in the late 1800s. Having been incorporated into the U.S.S.R. in 1924, Turkmenistan gained formal independence in 1991 after the dissolution of the Soviet Union.

Niyazov, the former head of the Turkmenistan Communist Party, was the sole candidate in elections to the newly created post of president in October 1990. After the adoption of a new constitution in 1992, he ran unopposed again and was re-elected for a five-year term with a reported 99.5 percent of the vote. The main opposition group, Agzybirlik, which was formed in 1989 by leading intellectuals, was banned. In a 1994 referendum, Niyazov's tenure as president was extended for an additional five years, until 2002, which exempted him from having to run again in 1997 as originally scheduled. In the December 1994 parliamentary elections, only Niyazov's Democratic Party of Turkmenistan (DPT), the former Communist Party, was permitted to field candidates.

In the December 1999 elections to the National Assembly (Mejlis), every candidate was selected by the government and virtually all were members of the DPT. According to government claims, voter turnout was 98.9 percent. The Organization for Security and Cooperation in Europe (OSCE), citing the lack of provision for nongovernmental parties to participate and the executive branch's control of the nomination of candidates, refused to send even a limited assessment mission. In a further consolidation of Niyazov's extensive powers, parliament unanimously voted in late December to make him president for life. With this decision, Turkmenistan became the first country in the Commonwealth of Independent States to formally abandon presidential elections.

Although Niyazov continued to exercise widespread power throughout the country in 2002, cracks in his regime became more visible during the year. Several high-level government defections, along with a purge by Niyazov of Turkmenistan's intelligence service, highlighted growing political tensions and challenges to the government. On November 25, Niyazov survived an alleged assassination attempt in Ashgabat when gunmen fired at the president's motorcade. The incident sparked a widespread crackdown against the opposition and perceived critics of the regime, drawing condemnation from foreign governments and international organizations, including the OSCE and the United Nations.

While some observers speculated that Niyazov himself had planned the shooting as an excuse to increase repression of his political enemies, others maintained that it was a failed attempt by certain members of the opposition to oust the president from power. According to the government, former foreign minister and opposition leader Boris Shikhmuradov, along with three other former high-ranking officials living in exile, had organized the attack. He was alleged to have returned to Turkmenistan from exile in Russia with the help of the Uzbek authorities, an accusation that soured already strained relations with Uzbekistan. Shikhmuradov was arrested on December 25 and made a televised confession four days later that critics maintain had been coerced. On December 30, he was sentenced to life in prison following what human rights groups condemned as a Soviet-style show trial. Two of the alleged co-conspirators received life sentences in absentia, while many other suspects were given lengthy prison sentences.

Parliamentary and local elections, which serve essentially to reinforce the president's control over the country's legislative process, were held on April 6, 2003. Voters were provided with virtually no information about the candidates, who were selected by the authorities based on their loyalty to Niyazov and proof of their Turkmen ancestry several generations back. Official turnout was reported at over 99 percent.

Relations with Russia were strained following Ashgabat's unilateral withdrawal in late April from a 1993 dual citizenship agreement with Moscow. Less than two weeks earlier, the two countries had signed a protocol ending dual citizenship, at the same time that they adopted a long-term lucrative energy agreement. However, Russia maintained that the protocol was not retroactive and would not enter into force until ratified by Russia's parliament at some future date. After Turkmen authorities set a deadline of June 22 for the selection of either Russian or Turkmen citizenship, many Russians holding dual citizenship reportedly frantically applied to leave Turkmenistan or risk automatically becoming Turkmen citizens. Meanwhile, the protocol provoked strong opposition from members of Russia's parliament and the media, who accused Moscow of having sold out its people in exchange for the purchase of Turkmen natural gas.

**Political Rights and Civil Liberties:** Citizens of Turkmenistan cannot change their government democratically. President Saparmurat Niyazov enjoys virtually absolute power over all branches and levels of government. In recent years, the government has undergone a rapid turnover of personnel as Niyazov has dismissed many officials whom he suspects may challenge his authority.

The country has two parliamentary bodies: the unicameral Mejlis (Assembly), composed of 50 members elected by popular vote for five-year terms, and the Halk Maslahaty (People's Council), officially described as the country's highest representative body, composed of both elected and appointed members. Neither body enjoys genuine independence from the executive. In August 2003, the Halk Maslahaty approved changes to the constitution stipulating that its approximately 2,000 members would remain in permanent session, rather than meeting only about once a year to address major issues, as was previously the practice. Following the November 2002 assassination attempt on Niyazov, the president announced early parliamentary elections for April 2003. The 1994, 1999, and 2003 parliamentary elections were neither free nor fair.

Niyazov has established an extensive cult of personality, including erecting monuments to his leadership throughout the country. In 1994, he renamed himself Turkmenbashi, or leader of the Turkmen. He has enacted bizarre decrees, including ordering the renaming of the days of the week and months of the year after himself and his mother.

Only one political party, the Niyazov-led Democratic Party of Turkmenistan, has been officially registered. Opposition parties have been banned, and their leading members face harassment and detention or have fled abroad. In September 2003, four prominent opposition groups in exile met in Prague, Czech Republic, where they pledged to unite as the Union of Democratic Forces. Their goal is the replacement of Niyazov's government with one based on democratic principles. Some analysts have cited the wave of post-assassination attempt reprisals as the impetus for the long-divided opposition to put aside enough of their differences to join forces.

Freedom of speech and the press is severely restricted by the government, which controls all radio and television broadcasts and print media. Reports of dissenting political views are banned, as are even mild forms of criticism of the president. In September 2003, Saparmurat Ovezberdiev, a correspondent for Radio Free Europe/Radio Liberty and the producer of a controversial local radio program in Ashgabat, was arrested and detained for three days and threatened with a 30-year prison sentence. In November, he was beaten by two men believed to be agents of the state security service. Subscriptions to foreign newspapers are severely restricted. Some Russian television programs are available, although their broadcast is delayed to allow time for Turkmen censors to review content. Foreign journalists have few opportunities to visit Turkmenistan and are often limited to certain locations. The state-owned Turkmentelekom is the only authorized Internet provider in the country.

The government restricts freedom of religion through strict registration requirements and other measures. Only Sunni Muslims and Russian Orthodox Christians have been able to meet the registration criterion of having at least 500 members. Members of religious groups that are not legally registered by the government, including Baptists, Pentecostals, Jews, and Jehovah's Witnesses, have been fined, beaten, and imprisoned by security forces. In November 2003, a new law on religion was adopted that criminalizes religious activities by bodies that are not registered with the Ministry of Justice.

The government places significant restrictions on academic freedom. The works of various writers reportedly have been placed on a blacklist because of their interpretation of Turkmen history. The *Rukhnama*, a quasi-spiritual guide allegedly authored by Niyazov, is required reading throughout the school system and has largely replaced many other traditional school subjects. In February 2003, Niyazov signed a decree on foreign exchange restrictions for most students studying abroad. The decision, which will severely limit the ability of students to complete their studies, appeared to reflect the authorities' fears that those studying abroad are potential dissenters.

The state security services regularly monitor the activities of citizens and foreign nationals, limiting open and free private discussion. Security officers use such surveillance techniques as wiretapping, the interception of mail, and the recruitment of informers. As part of the post-November 25 crackdown, Niyazov reportedly directed law enforcement bodies to monitor carefully people's conversations in public places and called on people to assist the police by informing on their fellow citizens.

While the constitution guarantees peaceful assembly and association, these rights are restricted in practice. Public demonstrations against state policies are extremely rare. In Ashgabat, all public gatherings—and even private events such as weddings—must be registered in advance with city authorities.

Unregistered nongovernmental organizations (NGOs) face harassment and criminal prosecution for their activities. After the November 25 alleged assassination attempt, the authorities increased their monitoring and harassment of civil society activists across the country. In March, the director of the Dashoguz Ecological Club, Farid Tukhbatullin, was sentenced to three years in prison for allegedly having heard about the upcoming plot against Niyazov while attending a human rights conference in Moscow and failing to alert the authorities. After the case received widespread international condemnation, Niyazov pardoned Tukhbatullin in April, but only after he "repented" his alleged crime. In November 2003, a new law on NGOs entered into force that stipulates that unregistered groups are subject to confiscation of their property; violators of the law may face up to one year in prison.

The government-controlled Colleagues Union is the only central trade union permitted. There are no legal guarantees for workers to form or join unions or to strike, although the constitution does not specifically prohibit these rights. Strikes in Turkmenistan are extremely rare.

The judicial system is subservient to the president, who appoints and removes judges for five-year terms without legislative review. The authorities frequently deny rights of due process, including public trials and access to defense attorneys. In early 2003, the government broadened the definition of treason to cover a wide range of activities, including attempting to undermine the public's faith in the president's policies and failing to inform the authorities of a wide range of crimes. Those arrested and sentenced for their complicity in the alleged assassination attempt against Niyazov suffered ill-treatment or torture and were convicted in closed trials; many of their relatives were targeted for harassment and intimidation. Human Rights Watch condemned as a violation of due process the fact that parliament, rather than the courts, sentenced three alleged organizers of the attack to life in prison. Although officials stated that approximately 70 people were arrested in the course of the investigation, human rights groups insisted that at least 200 had been detained.

Police abuse of suspects and prisoners, often to obtain confessions, is reportedly widespread, and prisons are overcrowded and unsanitary. In October 2003, Niyazov signed his annual prisoner pardon, granting amnesty to some 7,000 convicts. However, those convicted in the November 25 alleged assassination plot were excluded from the possibility of amnesty as part of their sentences.

Employment and educational opportunities for ethnic minorities are limited by the government's policy of promoting Turkmen national identity and its discrimination against non-ethnic Turkmen. The revocation of the Russian-Turkmen dual citizenship agreement in 2003 increased Russian emigration from Turkmenistan. In early 2003, Niyazov reportedly ordered the forced relocation of part of the Uzbek population living along the border with Uzbekistan and their replacement with ethnic Turkmen. The decree appeared to be connected to a plan to relocate so called "unworthy" people from regions along the Uzbek border after Uzbeks came under suspicion following the alleged assassination attempt against Niyazov.

Freedom of movement is severely restricted, with citizens required to carry internal passports that note the bearer's place of residence and movements into and out of the country. Since the November 25 alleged assassination attempt, travel within the country is more closely monitored, with travelers having to pass through various identity check posts. In February 2003, the exit visa system, which officially had been abolished in January 2002, was reintroduced for Turkmen citizens. Obtaining exit visas is difficult for most nonofficial travelers and allegedly often requires payment of bribes to government officials. Those banned from travel abroad include young men of conscription age. In March, the State Service for the Registration of Foreign Citizens was established to monitor the activities of foreign visitors. Foreigners would be required to stay only in pre-approved hotels and check in within 24 hours of arrival in the country. Anyone breaking these and other related rules would be subject to a heavy fine and risk deportation.

A continuing Soviet-style command economy and widespread corruption diminish equality of opportunity. Profits from the country's extensive energy exports rarely reach the general population, most of whom live in poverty.

Traditional social and religious norms mostly limit professional opportunities for women to the roles of homemaker and mother, and anecdotal reports suggest that domestic violence is common. Women under the age of 35 reportedly are not eligible for exit visas unless they have at least two children.

# Tuvalu

**Population:** 10,000    **Political Rights:** 1
**GNI/capita:** $1,930    **Civil Liberties:** 1
**Life Expectancy:** 66    **Status:** Free
**Religious Groups:** Church of Tuvalu [Congregationalist] (97 percent), other (3 percent)
**Ethnic Groups:** Polynesian (96 percent), Micronesian (4 percent)
**Capital:** Funafuti

**Ten-Year Ratings Timeline (Political Rights, Civil Liberties, Status)**

| 1994 | 1995 | 1996 | 1997 | 1998 | 1999 | 2000 | 2001 | 2002 | 2003 |
|------|------|------|------|------|------|------|------|------|------|
| 1,1F | 1,1F | 1,1F | 1,1F | 1,1F | 1,1F | 1,1F | 1,1F | 1,1F | 1,1F |

**Overview:**

Intense political competition brought Tuvalu's parliament largely to a standstill in 2003. After a no-confidence vote in parliament and two by-elections, Prime Minister Sautafu Sopoanga regained majority control of the legislature toward the end of the year after agreeing to appoint opposition members to his cabinet.

Tuvalu became part of the Gilbert and Ellice Islands in the British protectorate in 1916. During World War II, the United States used Tuvalu's northernmost atoll as a base to fight the Japanese. In 1974, the Ellice Islanders voted to separate from the Micronesian Gilbertese, and attained independence on October 1, 1978, under the precolonial name of Tuvalu.

Sopoanga narrowly defeated Amasone Kilei in a parliamentary leadership vote following the July 2002 general elections. The incumbent, Kolou Telake, failed to win a seat. Telake was in office for barely half a year, having become prime minister in December 2001 after his predecessor, Faimalaga Luka, was ousted in a no-confidence vote. Luka, in turn, had become prime minister only in February of that year after the sudden death in office of Ionatana Ionatana.

Prime Minister Sopoanga lost power after a by-election in May 2003, but he refused to concede. Results of the May election paved the way for the fifth change of leadership in the past three years. Such frequent changes as a result of no-confidence votes in parliament have sustained a debate in the last decade over whether citizens should be allowed to choose their leader directly rather than through parliament, which is driven by factional politics. On July 3, the opposition took Sopoanga to court for refusing to convene parliament after the election of the new speaker in mid-June following an intervention by the governor-general, who also ordered that parliament be convened. Parliament eventually reconvened following by-elections in October, which gave Sopoanga a majority in parliament when opposition members agreed to join his cabinet.

The country continues to be concerned about the threat of climate change and rising sea levels to the future of the low-slung islands. Several years ago, the government asked Australia to agree to take its entire population in the event the islands are flooded, but Canberra refused.

**Political Rights and Civil Liberties:** Citizens of Tuvalu can change their government through elections. Queen Elizabeth II is the head of state and is represented by the governor-general who must be a citizen of Tuvalu. Parliament appointed Faimalaga Luka the new governor-general in September 2003. The prime minister, who is chosen by parliament, leads the government. Prime Minister Saufatu Sopoanga was first elected to power in the July 2002 general election. The unicameral, 15-member parliament is elected to four-year terms. A six-person council administers each of the country's nine atolls. Council members are chosen by universal suffrage to four-year terms. There are no formal political parties, but there are no prohibitions against their formation.

The constitution provides for freedom of speech and the press, and the government generally respects these rights in practice. In 2001, the country's sole radio station, Radio Tuvalu, was privatized. The government voiced objections to some comments made on the station in 2001 but did not interfere with broadcasts. The sole television station, owned and operated by the government, went off the air in 2001 for financial reasons. Broadcasts limited to a few hours each day were resumed in 2002. Many residents use satellite dishes to access foreign programs. There is one fortnightly newspaper, *Tuvalu Echoes*. The first Internet connection was made in 1999. There are no government restrictions on access, but penetration is largely limited to the capital due to cost and connectivity issues.

Religious freedom is generally respected in practice. The vast majority of the population, some 97 percent, are Congregational Protestants. Religion is a big part of life and Sunday service is commonly considered the most important weekly event. Academic freedom is also generally respected.

Nongovernmental groups across all levels of society provide a variety of health, education, and other services for youths, women, and the population at large. Workers are free to organize unions and choose their own labor representatives. Since most of the population is engaged in subsistence farming or fisheries, the only registered trade union is the Tuvalu Seamen's Union, with approximately 600 members who work on foreign merchant vessels. Workers have the right to strike, but no strikes have ever taken place. Both private and public sectors generally use nonconfrontational deliberations to resolve labor disputes rather than legal procedures.

The constitution provides for an independent judiciary, and the government generally respects this provision in practice. Tuvalu has a two-tier judicial system. The higher courts include the privy council, the court of appeal, and the High Court. The lower courts consist of senior and resident magistrates, the island courts, and the land courts. The chief justice, who is also the chief justice of Tonga, sits on the High Court approximately once a year. A civilian-controlled, 70-member police constabulary is the country's only security force.

Two-thirds of the population engages in subsistence farming. Increasing salination of the soil is a serious concern. The country also generates income through other means, including sale of coins and stamps, money sent back by islanders working overseas, sale of tuna fishing licenses to foreign ships, and lease of its country Internet ".tv" domain name. It also derives about 10 percent of its annual budget from the Tuvalu Trust Fund, a well-run overseas investment fund set up by the United Kingdom, Australia, and South Korea in 1987 to provide development assistance.

Although there is general respect for human rights, traditional customs and social norms encourage discrimination against women and limit their roles in society.

# Uganda

**Population:** 25,300,000
**GNI/capita:** $260
**Life Expectancy:** 44
**Political Rights:** 5*
**Civil Liberties:** 4
**Status:** Partly Free
**Religious Groups:** Roman Catholic (33 percent), Protestant (33 percent), Muslim (16 percent), indigenous beliefs (18 percent)
**Ethnic Groups:** Baganda (17 percent), Ankole (8 percent), Basogo (8 percent), Iteso (8 percent), Bakiga (7 percent), Langi (6 percent), Rwanda (6 percent), other (40 percent)
**Capital:** Kampala
**Ratings Change:** Uganda's political rights rating improved from 6 to 5 due to a Constitutional Court ruling removing key restrictions on political party activity

**Ten-Year Ratings Timeline (Political Rights, Civil Liberties, Status)**

| 1994 | 1995 | 1996 | 1997 | 1998 | 1999 | 2000 | 2001 | 2002 | 2003 |
|------|------|------|------|------|------|------|------|------|------|
| 5,5PF | 5,4PF | 4,4PF | 4,4PF | 4,4PF | 5,5PF | 6,5PF | 6,5PF | 6,4PF | 5,4PF |

**Overview:**

In March 2003, Uganda's Constitutional Court overturned a controversial prohibition on political party activities, which had long formed the basis for suppression of political pluralism. Opposition parties continued to protest, however, about perceived restrictive party registration requirements and the predominant status of the ruling National Resistance Movement (NRM). Public statements by President Yoweri Museveni also raised the possibility that he would seek to lift the existing two-term presidential limit in time for elections in 2006.

Uganda has experienced considerable political instability since independence from Britain in 1962. An increasingly authoritarian president, Milton Obote, was overthrown by Idi Amin in 1971. Amin's brutality made world headlines as hundreds of thousands of people were killed. Amin's 1978 invasion of Tanzania finally led to his demise. Tanzanian forces and Ugandan exiles routed Amin's army and prepared for Obote's return to power in the fraudulent 1980 elections. Obote and his backers from northern Uganda savagely repressed his critics, who were primarily from southern Ugandan ethnic groups. Approximately 250,000 people were killed as political opponents were tortured and murdered and soldiers terrorized the countryside. Obote was ousted for a second time in a 1985 army coup. Conditions continued to worsen until the Museveni-led National Resistance Army entered the capital of Kampala in January 1986.

The NRM—for years, the only de-facto party functioning party—has ruled since a 1986 ban by President Museveni on most formal political party activities, including the sponsoring of candidates for elections and the staging of political rallies. In June 2000, a referendum was held on whether to lift the ban. Almost 90 percent of those voting supported continuation of the current de facto single-party system. Opposition parties had called for a boycott, however, and overall voter turnout was just over 50 percent.

Museveni and the NRM comfortably won presidential and legislative elections in 2001. However, the elections were held under conditions that called their legitimacy into serious question. Reports by human rights groups and donor countries concerning the March presidential election noted that state media and other official resources were mobilized in support of Museveni's successful candidacy, and that the ban on most formal party activities further hindered the opposition. Most observers believe, however, that Museveni would have won in a multiparty contest and described the actual balloting and vote tabulation processes as largely transparent. The opposition, which claimed that the elections were rigged, boycotted the subsequent parliamentary elections in June that confirmed the NRM's hold on the legislature; The NRM's comfortable majority was buttressed by dozens of special-interest representatives nominated by the president.

The 2002 Suppression of Terrorism Bill, which defines any act of violence or threat of violence for political, religious, economic, or cultural ends as a terrorist act, imposes harsh penalties on suspected terrorists and has raised fears that it could be used against political opponents. The unlawful possession of arms is also defined as terrorism. Publishing news that is "likely to promote terrorism" can result in up to 10 years' imprisonment.

In May 2002, parliament passed the Political Organizations Law barring the formation and registration of new parties until 2005, while old political parties are required to register afresh within six months or face dissolution. In 2003, the Constitutional Court ruled that the law was unconstitutional, as it effectively prevented political parties from carrying out their activities. Under the law, parties were not allowed to hold rallies, take part in elections, or have offices outside the capital, Kampala. Concerns exist that a continuing requirement that parties must register in order to be legalized will be used to prohibit or impede their functioning. The government has emphasized that all parties can only exist and operate after registering and paying the necessary registration fees. As part of these changes, leaders of the NRM were preparing in late 2003 to register it as a political party.

Despite the Constitutional Court's ruling, the NRM continues to dominate the nation's political life through direct and indirect means. The parliament has become increasingly assertive, however, occasionally rejecting appointments or policy initiatives proposed by the executive branch.

Regional tensions diminished somewhat during the year, as Ugandan military forces withdrew from the eastern part of the Democratic Republic of Congo (DRC). These units had been sent to suppress rebels who had been perpetrating attacks across the border into Uganda. International human rights groups, however, have criticized Uganda for continuing to support armed militias in eastern DRC. A cult-based guerrilla movement, the Lord's Resistance Army, continued a gruesome insurgency in northern Uganda, with human rights violations committed on both sides. Uganda has 1.5 million people living with HIV or AIDS. The latest records show that the rate of prevalence has gradually fallen from a national average of 30 percent in 1992 to about 6 percent today, the lowest in the sub-Saharan region.

**Political Rights and Civil Liberties:** Ugandans do not have the right to elect their government democratically. The only open multiparty elections were held in 1961 in preparation for the country's independence from Britain. In 1986, President Yoweri Museveni banned most political party activities. Uganda's 1995 constitution extended the ban for five years until the results of a 2000 referendum on the establishment of a multiparty system; voters overwhelmingly rejected the proposal. Arguing that majoritarian democracy exacerbates religious and ethnic tensions in Africa, President Yoweri Museveni substituted a "no-party" system with only one, supposedly nonparty political organization—the National Resistance Movement (NRM)—allowed to operate unfettered. Some space is allowed for parliament to function; it has, for example, occasionally censured government ministers accused of corruption and has forced budgetary amendments.

A Constitutional Review Commission (CRC) was established by Museveni in 2001 to examine possible adaptations to the constitution. Issues being discussed include the future of political parties, presidential term limitations, federalism, the size of parliament, and voter and candidate eligibility. Critics suggest that the commission does not reflect the broad spectrum of Ugandan public opinion. In 2003, the stature of the CRC was weakened by repeated pronouncements by the cabinet that it would reject any recommendations by the commission inconsistent with its own positions. Key issues include the two-term presidential limitation and the possible future federal form of government. Museveni himself made public statements that raised the possibility that he would seek to lift the two-term presidential limit in time for the 2006 elections.

There is some freedom of expression. Independent and print media outlets, including more than two dozen daily and weekly newspapers, are often highly critical of the government and offer a range of opposition views. Buttressed by legislation limiting press freedoms, however, the government at times selectively arrests or harasses journalists. A sedition law remains in force and is applied selectively to journalists and other persons who hold views that are at variance with those of the NRM. The Suppression of Terrorism Bill levies a possible death sentence on anyone publishing news "likely to promote terrorism." Several private radio stations and private television stations report on local political developments. The largest newspapers and broadcasting facilities that reach rural areas remain state owned. Governmental corruption is reported. Opposition positions are also presented, but the coverage is often not balanced. Journalists have asked parliament to enact a freedom-of-information act.

There is no state religion, and freedom of worship is constitutionally protected and respected. Various Christian sects and the country's Muslim minority practice their creeds freely.

Nongovernmental organizations (NGOs) currently make a significant contribution to Uganda's social, cultural, and political life. They encourage the expression of different views and, significantly, have been willing to address politically sensitive issues. The existence and activities of NGOs are, however, subject to stringent legal restrictions. All NGOs in Uganda must be approved and registered by a government-appointed board composed mostly of government officials, including security officials, before they are allowed to operate. Security forces have halted numerous political rallies, some through force, and leading opposition activists have been harassed and, sometimes, subjected to arbitrary arrest.

The National Organization of Trade Unions, the country's largest labor federation, is independent of the government and political parties. An array of essential workers are barred from forming unions. Strikes are permitted only after a lengthy reconciliation process.

The judiciary is still influenced by the executive despite increasing autonomy. It is also constrained by inadequate resources and the army's occasional refusal to respect civilian courts. With parliamentary approval, the president names a judicial commission that oversees judicial appointments. At times, the government liberally applies the charge of treason against nonviolent political dissidents. Local courts are subject to bribery and corruption. Prison conditions are difficult, especially in local jails. More than 500 prisoners die annually as a result of poor diet, sanitation, and medical care.

Serious human rights violations by rebel groups and the Uganda People's Defense Forces have been reported. The Ugandan Human Rights Commission (UHRC), for example, issued a report in 2003 noting an increase in torture by the state and stating that "about 1,277 people (soldiers, rebels and civilians) lost their lives between January and September 2002 due to Operation Iron Fist." The UHRC also criticized the army's "shoot to kill" operations, which it called illegal. In 2003, the cabinet proposed to merge the UHRC with the office of the Inspector General of Government (IGG). Groups such as the Uganda Law Society have opposed this, noting that the commission provides an important measure of transparency on the extent to which human rights are being respected.

Manipulation and exploitation of ethnic divisions pose a serious, continuing threat to peace in Uganda. Baganda people in the country's south continue to demand more recognition of their traditional kingdom. Northern ethnic groups complain of governmental neglect; that region especially is subject to continuing guerrilla activities.

Uganda has legislated quotas for women officials in all elected bodies from village councils to the national parliament. Almost 20 percent of Uganda's parliament is female. One-third of local council seats must, by law, go to women. Currently, however, there are no laws protecting women from domestic violence. A battered woman can only file a case based on assault, and often the police ignore the context and seriousness of the crime. Draft laws such as the Domestic Relations Bill, the Equal Opportunities Act, and the Sexual Offenses Act have been introduced in parliament, but they have not yet been voted upon. A recent study conducted by Johns Hopkins University shows that about one woman in three living in rural areas experiences verbal or physical threats from her partner.

# Ukraine

**Population:** 47,800,000 **Political Rights:** 4
**GNI/capita:** $720 **Civil Liberties:** 4
**Life Expectancy:** 68 **Status:** Partly Free
**Religious Groups:** Ukrainian Orthodox [Moscow and Kyiv Patriarchates], Ukrainian Catholic, Protestant, Jewish
**Ethnic Groups:** Ukrainian (78 percent), Russian (17 percent), other (5 percent)
**Capital:** Kyiv

**Ten-Year Ratings Timeline (Political Rights, Civil Liberties, Status)**

| 1994 | 1995 | 1996 | 1997 | 1998 | 1999 | 2000 | 2001 | 2002 | 2003 |
|------|------|------|------|------|------|------|------|------|------|
| 3,4PF | 3,4PF | 3,4PF | 3,4PF | 3,4PF | 3,4PF | 4,4PF | 4,4PF | 4,4PF | 4,4PF |

**Overview:**

The erosion of the rule of law in Ukraine was characterized by further attacks on press freedom in 2003. In addition, the major reform party was violently attacked by a mob that opposition forces claimed had been organized by the ruling elite. Promising leads in the country's most significant case of political murder—that of journalist Heorhiy Gongadze—were not fully pursued despite credible allegations about the operation of a political death squad. In the face of widespread public support for an opposition candidate for the October 2004 presidential election, parties linked to the ruling elite and supportive of incumbent lame duck president Leonid Kuchma lunched efforts at constitutional reform that would strip most powers from the presidency.

In December 1991, Ukraine ended more than 300 years of Russian ascendancy when voters ratified a declaration of independence and elected Leonid Kravchuk president. In 1994, Communists came in first in parliamentary elections, and Leonid Kuchma, a former Soviet director of military production, defeated Kravchuk in the presidential poll. In the first years of his presidency, Kuchma struggled against a Communist-influenced parliament to effect reforms. However, over time, his government became the target of domestic and international criticism for extensive and high-level corruption and for the erosion of basic political and free speech rights.

In the 1999 presidential election, Kuchma defeated Communist Party leader Petro Symonenko in the second round of voting with 56.21 percent of the vote. Symonenko received only 37.5 percent. Observers declared the election unfair because of harassment of independent media, biased coverage by state media, intimidation of candidates and their supporters, and illegal campaigning by state officials. The murder in 2000 of independent journalist Heorhiy Gongadze, in which credible evidence appeared to implicate Kuchma in the crime, sparked mass public demonstrations and calls for the president's dismissal.

Despite polls that showed reform-minded prime minister Viktor Yushchenko with an approval rating of 63 percent, a coalition of the Communist Party and parties controlled by economic oligarchs ousted Yushchenko on April 26, 2001, who was replaced by Anatoly Kinakh. The subsequent strong showing of Yushchenko's Our Ukraine bloc in the parliamentary elections of 2002, where it emerged as the single largest political force in a party-list vote, marked the first electoral success for the democratic opposition since independence. Although Yushchenko eventually failed to muster enough support to form a new government, his bloc's strong support in the party-list vote signaled the growing strength of democratic forces in the country and galvanized thousands who took to the streets during the year to demonstrate against President Kuchma's growing authoritarianism.

The opposition's strong showing notwithstanding, government pressures on the large bloc of "independent" deputies enabled Kuchma to shape a working parliamentary majority. Since the 2002 election, Ukraine has continued to be plagued by pervasive corruption and ongoing violations of basic rights. Kuchma has also come under increased scrutiny from Western and other democratic leaders because of evidence—believed to be credible by the U.S. government—that he had authorized the sale of a powerful radar system to Saddam Hussein's Iraq in violation of a UN embargo.

According to the Organization for Security and Cooperation in Europe (OSCE), the parliamentary elections of March 2002 "brought Ukraine closer to meeting international commitments and standards for democratic elections." However, following the election, Yushchenko accused government authorities of falsifying the vote— particularly in single-mandate districts, where opposition candidates did poorly and where pro-government candidates captured some three-quarters of their seats— and declared that "democracy is the loser." Ultimately, pro-Kuchma forces led by For a United Ukraine received enough post election support from the Social Democratic Party of Ukraine–United (SDPUu), the Communists, independent candidates, and even members of Our Ukraine to dominate parliament. Prime Minister Kinakh remained in power until November 2002, when Kuchma dismissed the government allegedly for failing to implement economic reforms. Kinakh was replaced as prime minister late in 2002 by Viktor Yanukovych, a former convicted felon and representative of the Russian-speaking Donbas region, where economic oligarchs tightly control the local media and political life.

Since the 2002 parliamentary election, and the ascendancy of President Kuchma's chief of staff Viktor Medvedchuk, authoritarian policies have been reinforced and there is unassailable evidence of pervasive government interference in the media. In 2002, Mykola Tomenko, the chair of the parliamentary Committee for the Freedom of Expression, released documents containing directives from the presidential administration to national television channels on acceptable news items and coverage. The instructions, known as *temnyky* (theme directives), were said to be issued weekly, and failure to comply can result in various forms of harassment such as tax audits, canceled licenses, and libel suits.

Public opinion data throughout 2003 showed strong support for Yushchenko, who ran ahead of all other potential candidates by at least a margin of nearly two to one. With the unpopular Kuchma barred from seeking a third term in office, parties linked with the ruling elite proposed constitutional amendments that would strip the presidency of most of its power and create a parliamentary republic. At the end of the year, these efforts had not borne fruit, but the pro-Kuchma majority hoped to revise the constitution in 2004.

In November, opposition leaders released what they said were instructions from the presidential administration to local government officials demanding efforts to undermine opposition meetings and rallies and to deny the opposition coverage in local mass media. Late in the year, a conference organized by backers of opposition front-runner Yushchenko was disrupted by a violent mob in the eastern city of Donetsk.

Ukraine's relations with Russia appeared to be strengthened with the signing on September 19 of an agreement to create a Common Economic Space that could eventually link the two countries with Belarus and Kazakhstan in a common market and customs union. However, in October, relations suffered after Russia unilaterally constructed a dam encroaching on Ukraine's territory in the Kerch straits near the Sea of Azov. The action precipitated a major diplomatic crisis, as Ukraine reinforced its security presence in the disputed area, Tuzla Island.

**Political Rights and Civil Liberties:** Ukrainian voters have been able to change their government democratically, although growing evidence suggests there is no longer a level playing field in terms of legal protections, media access, and unfettered campaigning. A May 2003 mayoral election saw the de-registration of the front-runner and opposition candidate, opening the way for the victory of the candidate backed by the presidentially appointed regional governor. State pressures on other major mayoral elections were also registered in the summer of 2003, and election-monitoring groups warned that these were a harbinger of potential massive interference in future elections.

Citizens elect the president and delegates to the Verkhovna Rada, the 450-seat unicameral parliament. Under an election law adopted in 2001, half of parliament is elected in proportional voting and half in single-mandate constituencies. The president appoints the prime minister and other cabinet members. The next presidential election will take place in October 2004, and President Leonid Kuchma is constitutionally ineligible to seek a third term.

The 1996 constitution guarantees freedom of speech and expression, but the government has frequently violated these rights through direct and well documented interference in media content. Opposition figures who command a large public following are given little media coverage and are frequently subjected to unbalanced reporting on nationwide television, which is either state owned or controlled by economic oligarchs closely associated with the president and the government. State media reflect a pro-Kuchma bias, while private media typically reflect the views of their owners. Under a law that took effect in 2001, libel no longer carries criminal charges. Journalists who report on corruption or criticize the government are particularly subject to harassment and violence, and press freedom groups noted numerous cases in 2003. In April, Ukraine's Human Rights Ombudsman, Nina Karpachova, reported that over the previous 10 years, 36 media workers had been killed, and that there had been numerous beatings and acts of intimidation against journalists. She also reported on frequent cases of the freezing of bank accounts of media outlets and confiscation of print runs of newspapers. As in the case of other political killings and the assassinations of journalists, the murder of investigative journalist Heorhiy Gongadze remained unresolved, and new leads have not been resolutely pursued.

The constitution and the Law on Freedom of Conscience and Religion define religious rights in Ukraine, and these are generally well respected. There are limited restrictions on the activities of foreign religious organizations, and all religious groups with more than 10 members must register with the state. In 2002, President Kuchma established a commission to explore mechanisms for restoring religious property seized under communism. Acts of anti-Semitism are consistently investigated and condemned by state authorities.

Academic freedom is generally respected, although students who engage in opposition political activity are subject to threats of expulsion or suspension. New private universities are playing an important role in augmenting state supported higher education.

Ukraine has several thousand nongovernmental organizations and an increasingly vibrant civil society. The constitution guarantees the right to peaceful assembly but requires advance notification to government authorities. In recent years, organizations critical of the government have been subjected to surveillance and harassment, especially at the hands of tax authorities. Some demonstrations and civic meetings have been dispersed or violently suppressed. A conference of democratic forces, organized by the leading opposition party bloc, Our Ukraine, was disrupted by a violent mob in the eastern city of Donetsk in October.

Trade unions function, but strikes and protests are infrequent. The leader of the country's largest national labor federation was forced to withdraw from an opposition parliamentary faction as the result of an orchestrated threat to his union leadership organized by allies of the presidential administration. A smaller independent labor federation that includes miners and railway workers is closely linked with democratic opposition parties.

The judiciary consists of the Supreme Court, regional courts, and district courts. There is also a Constitutional Court. The constitution guarantees equality before the law, but the president, members of parliament, and judges are immune from criminal prosecution unless parliament consents. The judiciary is inefficient and subject to corruption. Although the Constitutional Court as a rule has functioned independently, the retirement in 2003 of its well-regarded chief justice has raised questions about its ongoing independence. Other courts lack independence. Judges are often penalized for independent decision making, and there is significant evidence of routine interference in judicial decisions by the executive branch.

In 2002, the Council of Europe's Committee for the Prevention of Torture issued a report that criticized the Ukrainian police for using methods of interrogation that could be considered torture. These include electric shocks, cigarette burns, asphyxiation, and suspension by the arms or legs. The report, based on visits to Ukraine between 1998 and 2000, also noted overcrowding, inadequate facilities for washing and cleaning, lack of adequate food supplies in prisons, and extended detention of suspects. In August 2003, the issue of political killings resurfaced with the death of former militia officer Ihor Honcharov in police custody. Honcharov's attorney alleged that his 43-year-old client, who was arrested on suspicion of criminal activity, died as a result of beatings administered in prison. Posthumously released affidavits from Honcharov charged that a death squad directed by officers from the militia and operating with the knowledge of Ukraine's highest ranking officials, including President Kuchma, was responsible for the murder of journalist Heorhiy Gongadze. Several individuals whose names had surfaced in conjunction with the death squad allegations were held at various times of the year in criminal detention. In November, a city council member whose name had surfaced in conjunction with death squad activities escaped assassination as his automobile exploded in a busy Kyiv street.

In response to ongoing allegations of criminal attacks on opposition figures, the prosecutor general in charge of investigating these cases was dismissed from office and replaced with an official analysts regarded to be more resolutely loyal to the president.

The government generally respects personal autonomy and privacy, and the constitution guarantees individuals the right to own property, to work, and to engage in entrepreneurial activity. However, crime, corruption, and the slow pace of economic reform have effectively limited these rights. In 2001, the Constitutional Court struck down the country's Soviet-era *propiska* system, which had required individuals to register with the Interior Ministry in their place of residence. Opponents of the provision had long argued that the regulation violated freedom of movement. Under a 2001 law, the purchase and sale of land, thus far severely limited, will be broadly allowed beginning in 2005.

Gender discrimination is prohibited under the constitution, but women's rights are not a priority for government officials. In some settings, women face discrimination in employment, but there is little effective redress through existing anti-discrimination mechanisms. The sexual trafficking of women abroad remains a major problem and a threat to women's rights and security.

# United Arab Emirates

**Population:** 3,900,000
**GNI/capita:** $19,750
**Life Expectancy:** 74
**Religious Groups:** Muslim [Shi'a (16 percent)] (96 percent), other (4 percent)
**Ethnic Groups:** Arab and Iranian (42 percent), other [including South Asian, European, and East Asian] (58 percent)
**Capital:** Abu Dhabi

**Political Rights:** 6
**Civil Liberties:** 6*
**Status:** Not Free

**Ratings Change:** The United Arab Emirates' civil liberties rating declined from 5 to 6 due to a technical reevaluation of the state of personal autonomy and equality of opportunity.

**Ten-Year Ratings Timeline (Political Rights, Civil Liberties, Status)**

| 1994 | 1995 | 1996 | 1997 | 1998 | 1999 | 2000 | 2001 | 2002 | 2003 |
|------|------|------|------|------|------|------|------|------|------|
| 6,5NF | 6,5NF | 6,5NF | 6,5NF | 6,5NF | 6,5NF | 6,5NF | 6,5NF | 6,5NF | 6,6NF |

**Overview:**

The United Arab Emirates (UAE) took no major steps in improving its poor political rights and civil liberties record in 2003. Political discourse was focused on regional issues, particularly the war in Iraq, with a few protests breaking out in opposition to the war.

For most of its history, the territory of the UAE—a federation of seven separate emirates formerly known as the Trucial States—was controlled by various competing tribal forces. Attacks on shipping in waters off the coast of the UAE led British forces to conduct raids against the tribes in the nineteenth century. In 1853, the tribal leaders signed a treaty with the United Kingdom agreeing to a truce, which led to a decline in the raids on shipping. Though never formal British colonies, the territories of the UAE were provided protection by the British, and tribal leaders of the emirates often referred their disputes to the United Kingdom for mediation.

In 1971, the United Kingdom announced that it was ending its treaty relationships with the seven emirates of the Trucial States, as well as Bahrain and Qatar. Six of the seven states entered into a federation called the United Arab Emirates, and Ras al-Khaimah, the seventh state, joined in 1972. The 1971 provisional constitution kept significant power in the hands of each individual emirate.

In contrast to many of its neighbors, the UAE has achieved some success in diversifying its economy beyond dependency on the petroleum sector, building a leading free trade zone in Dubai and a major manufacturing center in Sharjah, as well as investing resources to develop its profile as a leading center for tourism in the region. In 2001, the government cracked down on corruption with arrests of senior officials. In the wake of the September 11, 2001 attacks on the World Trade Center and Pentagon, the government introduced reforms in its financial services and banking sectors to cut down on terrorist financing.

Economic reform has not been matched by political reform in the UAE, which has a closed political system in which the views of citizens are not taken into account. Recent reforms undertaken in the governance sector are generally more closely related to issues of trade, commerce, and the economy than to the enhancement of political rights and civil liberties. Political power remains in the hands of traditional tribal leaders. Shaikh Zayed bin Sultan Al-Nahyan, the current president, has ruled since the UAE was founded.

The year 2003 did not see any important events and major changes in the UAE's record on political rights and civil liberties. In March, the government did not interfere with protests against the Iraq war that took place in several locations around the country.

**Political Rights and Civil Liberties:** Citizens cannot change their government democratically. The UAE has never held an election. All decisions about political leadership rest in the hands of the dynastic rulers of the seven separate emirates of the UAE. These seven leaders select a president and vice president, and the president appoints a prime minister and cabinet. The UAE has a 40-member Federal National Council with delegates appointed by the seven leaders every two years. However, the council serves only as an advisory body, reviewing proposed laws and questioning federal government ministers.

The UAE does not have political parties. Rather, the allocation of positions in the government is largely determined by tribal loyalties and economic power. Abu Dhabi, the major oil producer in the UAE, has controlled the presidency of the UAE since its inception. Citizens have limited opportunities to express their interests through traditional consultative sessions.

Although the UAE's constitution provides for freedom of expression, in practice the government severely restricts this right. Laws prohibit criticism of the government, ruling families, and friendly governments, and they also include vague provisions against statements that threaten society. As a consequence, journalists commonly practice self-censorship, and the leading media outlets in the UAE frequently publish government statements without criticism or comment. However, Dubai has a "Media Free Zone" where few restrictions on print and broadcast media produced for audiences outside of the UAE have been reported.

The UAE's constitution provides for freedom of religion. Islam is the official religion, and the majority of citizens are Sunnis. The government controls content in nearly all Sunni mosques. Shia minorities are free to worship without interference. Academic freedom is limited, with the Ministry of Education censoring textbooks and curriculums in both public and private schools. In addition, the government banned six university professors in 2002 from lecturing at the university because of their political views.

The government places limits on freedom of assembly and association. Small discussions on politics in private homes are generally tolerated, but there are limits on citizens' ability to organize broader gatherings. Public meetings require government permits. In March, the government did not interfere in protests in Al Ain, Dubai, and Ras Al-Khaimah against the Iraq war.

All nongovernmental organizations (NGOs) must register with the UAE's Ministry of Labor and Social Affairs, and registered NGOs reportedly receive subsidies from the government. In August, the government closed the Zayed Center for Coordination and Follow-up, a think tank, for publishing anti-Jewish literature and allowing anti-Semitic language on its Web site. The government explained that the closure was necessary, saying that the think tank's activities contradicted the principles of interfaith tolerance.

The UAE has no labor unions, although the government has mediated labor disputes. Foreign nations, who make up the vast majority of the UAE's workforce, are generally not offered labor protections. In July, the government issued a ban on a long-standing practice of employers forcing foreign employees to surrender their passports as a condition of employment.

The judiciary is not independent, with court rulings subject to review by the UAE's political leadership. An estimated 40 to 45 percent of judges in the court system are noncitizen foreign nationals. The constitution bans torture. However, Sharia (Islamic law) courts sometimes impose flogging sentences for individuals found guilty of drug use, prostitution, and adultery. In 2002, the Dubai police established a Human Rights Department to rehabilitate prisoners, monitor prison conditions, and conduct programs for crime victims.

The constitution provides for equality before the law. In practice, women's social, economic, and legal rights are not always protected because of incomplete implementation of the law and traditional biases against women. Women are underrepresented in government, although there are small signs of limited openings for women, with women receiving appointments at various levels of government in 2003.

# United Kingdom

**Population:** 59,200,000  **Political Rights:** 1
**GNI/capita:** $25,120  **Civil Liberties:** 1
**Life Expectancy:** 78  **Status:** Free
**Religious Groups:** Anglican, Roman Catholic,
Muslim, Protestant, Sikh, Hindu, Jewish
**Ethnic Groups:** English (82 percent), Scottish (10 percent),
Irish (2 percent), Welsh (2 percent), other [including Indian
and Pakistani] (4 percent)
**Capital:** London

**Ten-Year Ratings Timeline (Political Rights, Civil Liberties, Status)**

| 1994 | 1995 | 1996 | 1997 | 1998 | 1999 | 2000 | 2001 | 2002 | 2003 |
|------|------|------|------|------|------|------|------|------|------|
| 1,2F | 1,2F | 1,2F | 1,2F | 1,2F | 1,2F | 1,2F | 1,2F | 1,1F | 1,1F |

**Overview:**  British political discussion in 2003 was dominated by the war in Iraq. Despite the opposition of a majority of Britons before the war, British forces played a major role both in military operations and in the postwar occupation of the country. A scandal over whether the government had exaggerated the threat from Iraq dogged the prime minister, Tony Blair, and members of his cabinet throughout the summer. Blair was also under pressure to deliver the improvements in public services that he had promised before his Labour government's landslide reelection in 2001. However, the main opposition Conservative Party largely failed to capitalize on the prime minister's weakness.

The English state emerged before the turn of the first millennium and was conquered by Norman French invaders in 1066. Celtic-speaking Wales and Ireland were incorporated into the kingdom over the course of the centuries; Scotland joined on more favorable terms with the creation of Great Britain in 1707. The Glorious Revolution of 1688-1689 began a gradual—but eventually total—assertion of the powers of parliament, as Britain became one of the world's first democracies, with a significant extension of voting rights in 1832.

Separatism has persisted in the Celtic lands; most of Ireland won independence after World War I, with Protestant-majority Northern Ireland remaining part of the United Kingdom. Most of Britain's global empire, the most important portion of which was India, became independent in the decades after World War II, although many of Britain's former colonies maintain links with the country through the Commonwealth.

Significant powers were devolved to a Scottish parliament (and fewer to a Welsh assembly) established by the current Labour Party government, which was first elected in 1997, and reelected in 2001. Peace negotiations restored home rule to Northern Ireland in 1998, but it has since been suspended because of breakdowns in the peace process.

Despite a promise to focus on public services, particularly the ailing health and transport systems, Tony Blair's second term as prime minister has been dominated by his support of the U.S.-led war in Iraq. Blair strongly supported George Bush, the U.S. president, in the UN Security Council and on the world stage, despite anger within his own Labour party and demonstrations on the streets of London, including one on February 15, 2003, that was believed to be the largest in British history. Support for the war increased, however, with the coalition's initial swift and thorough military success.

After the end of the initial hostilities, however, the government suffered renewed criticism surrounding the case it had made for the war in the run-up to the conflict. On May 29, a BBC radio reporter alleged that a confidential source had told him that the government had "sexed up" claims that Saddam Hussein could deploy weapons of mass destruction in 45 minutes. A subsequent parliamentary inquiry cleared the government of the charge of misleading the British people. However, the focus turned to the government's attack on the BBC. The source for the BBC's report, a Ministry of Defense scientist, committed suicide, apparently because of pressure from the scrutiny that he had endured after the report aired. The government was accused of "outing" the scientist to discredit him and of trying to intimidate the BBC. The broadcasting corporation itself also came under fire, as elements of the initial broadcast were shown to be incorrect and the BBC's head stood by the story without thoroughly investigating its veracity. The prime minister's press secretary and confidant, Alastair Campbell, resigned, although he claimed that his resignation had nothing to do with the investigation.

In the wake of the war, Blair made mild public criticisms of some aspects of U.S. policy, in an attempt to show that he did not blindly follow the U.S. president's lead. In addition, the prime minister hoped to patch things up with his European Union (EU) allies. Notably, in late 2003, the British government apparently softened its opposition to an EU-only military planning cell, which Britain fears could compete with and undermine NATO.

The government has yet to deliver the major improvements in public services, especially health and transport, that it had promised, and its reelection will depend largely on such improvements materializing in the coming years. Another major issue of political economy, whether or not to adopt the euro, was prominent in 2003. However, the Treasury announced that its five tests for joining the euro-zone had not been met, making membership highly unlikely in the current parliament, which is set to end by 2006.

Despite the prime minister's struggles, the opposition Conservative Party floundered in 2003, and deposed its leader, Iain Duncan-Smith, in October. He was replaced by Michael Howard, formerly home secretary and the Conservative's shadow chancellor of the exchequer.

**Political Rights and Civil Liberties:** The British can change their government democratically. Each of the 659 members of the House of Commons is elected in a single-member district. This procedure multiplies the power of the two largest parties, Labour and the Conservatives, at the expense of third parties. The Liberal Democrats are the most disadvantaged; although they won 16.8 percent of the vote in the 2001 election, they received only 7.9 percent of the seats in the House of Commons. (Labour won a crushing majority of seats, 62.5 percent, with just 40.8 percent of the vote.) The separation of powers is weak, with the prime minister and all members of his cabinet also being members of the legislature. The executive has in recent years become more powerful at the expense of the House of Commons. The monarch, currently Queen Elizabeth II, is the head of state but plays only a ceremonial role. The opposition party plays a crucial role in the Commons; although it is unable to block legislation, it holds ministers accountable in parliamentary debates that are widely covered in the press.

After a period of centralization under Conservative governments from 1979 to 1997, the Labour Party made constitutional reform a key part of its 1997 election platform. In government, it has delivered a far-reaching (though asymmetrical) devolution of power to Northern Ireland, Scotland, and Wales. The first elections to the Scottish Parliament and the Welsh Assembly were held in 1999. The Scottish body has more power (including some tax-raising powers) than its Welsh counterpart, largely because of stronger separatist sentiment in Scotland. Welsh nationalism is largely cultural; with official protection and encouragement, the number of Welsh-language speakers actually grew 17 percent from 1991 to 2001. The Northern Ireland Assembly was suspended in October 2002 after complications in the peace process.

The government is largely free of pervasive corruption. Transparency International, a corruption watchdog, ranked Britain eleventh in its Corruption Perceptions Index for 2003, putting it in a tie for fifth place within the EU.

The media market in Britain is free, lively, and competitive. Many daily newspapers across a broad spectrum of political opinions compete for readers. Although broadcasting is dominated by the state-owned BBC, the corporation is editorially independent of the government. In fact, Britain's biggest 2003 scandal was the battle over the "sexed up" dossier in which the BBC claimed that the government exaggerated evidence of Iraqi weapons of mass destruction, and the government's (probably overdone) efforts to exculpate itself. While the episode tarnished the reputations of both the government and the BBC, more generally, it was a sign of the healthy political debate that is possible in Britain. Internet access is not restricted by the government.

Although the Church of England and the Church of Scotland are established churches, the government both prescribes freedom of religion in law and protects it in practice. Scientology is not recognized as an official religion for charity purposes. Muslims and other religious minorities complain of discrimination. The government respects academic freedom.

Civic organizations and NGOs are allowed to operate freely, and the freedom to assemble is respected, as demonstrated by protests against the government's participation in the Iraq war in February 2003. The right to organize in unions is protected. Trade unions have traditionally played a strong role in the Labour Party, though this is weakening as the party moves to the center and seeks a bigger role for the private sector in traditional public sector areas, such as health care.

A historical oddity in the justice system was removed in 2003 when the post of Lord Chancellor was abolished. The position, the second-oldest office in Britain after the monarchy, combined a legislative seat in the House of Lords, a senior executive position in the cabinet, and a powerful judicial position as, effectively, the top judge in the country. As such, it was a serious breach of the separation of powers (already weak in Britain), and the Labour government abolished it in 2003, creating the cabinet position of secretary for constitutional affairs. However, the top judges in the land remain the Law Lords, a combination of legislative and judicial authority that weakens judicial independence. The police maintain high professional standards, and prisons generally meet international standards.

Britain has large numbers of immigrants and second-generation children of immigrants, who receive equal treatment under the law. In practice, their living standards are lower than the national average. Women also receive equal treatment under the law, but are under-represented in politics and the top levels of business.

# United States of America

**Population:** 291,500,000
**GNI/capita:** $34,280
**Life Expectancy:** 77
**Political Rights:** 1
**Civil Liberties:** 1
**Status:** Free
**Religious Groups:** Protestant (56 percent), Roman Catholic (28 percent), Jewish (2 percent), other (14 percent)
**Ethnic Groups:** White (77 percent), black (13 percent), Asian (4 percent), Amerindian (1.5 percent), Pacific Islander (0.3 percent), other (0.2 percent)
**Capital:** Washington, D.C.

**Ten-Year Ratings Timeline (Political Rights, Civil Liberties, Status)**

| 1994 | 1995 | 1996 | 1997 | 1998 | 1999 | 2000 | 2001 | 2002 | 2003 |
|------|------|------|------|------|------|------|------|------|------|
| 1,1F | 1,1F | 1,1F | 1,1F | 1,1F | 1,1F | 1,1F | 1,1F | 1,1F | 1,1F |

**Overview:**

Political developments in the United States of America in 2003 were dominated by the war in Iraq and the challenge of rebuilding that country in the face of a campaign of guerrilla attacks and terror carried out by loyalists of the former regime of Saddam Hussein.

By year's end, a growing domestic debate had broken out concerning the mounting number of casualties among U.S. military personnel, aid workers, and Iraqis who were cooperating with the coalition forces that had occupied the country. It seemed likely that Iraq would be a central issue of the 2004 presidential contest unless the United States proved able to restore to Iraq a measure of stability and security.

Founded in 1776 during a revolution against British colonial rule, the United States began the modern movement for freedom and self-government in the world. The current system of government began functioning in 1789, following the ratification of the constitution. Because the founders of the United States distrusted concentrations of centralized government power, they established a system in which the federal government has three competing centers of power (executive, legislative, and judicial branches) and left many powers with the state governments and the citizenry.

The United States launched a war in Iraq on March 19, 2003. In just three weeks, the United States and its coalition allies routed Hussein's forces and captured Baghdad with minimal casualties. Although much of the country was quickly pacified, key regions, including Baghdad, remained in a condition of chaos. Saddam Hussein himself apparently remained in hiding, and irregular forces loyal to him used a variety of tried-and-true tactics—car bombs, mines, hit-and-run assaults, assassinations, suicide bombings, and the destruction of physical infrastructure—in a campaign to undermine the effectiveness of the occupying authorities.

The war in Iraq has had no appreciable impact on domestic civil liberties. Hundreds of journalists from around the world covered the early stages of the Iraq war through a process known as "embedding," under which arrangements were made for journalists to travel with military units onto the field of conflict. The embedding process allowed a great deal of live coverage of the war, and journalists were subjected to practically no censorship by military authorities. The U.S. media have provided extensive coverage of the postwar events in Iraq and have regularly reported on the string of guerrilla assaults and bombings directed at U.S. troops and Iraqis, as well as charges that the administration of President George W. Bush mishandled important aspects of Iraq policy and misled the American people about the justification for the war. A robust and increasingly partisan debate over Iraq policy has emerged, spearheaded by several leading candidates for the Democratic presidential nomination. There have also been a number of marches and demonstrations against the war in major U.S. cities.

At the same time, aspects of the administration's domestic campaign against terrorism continued to draw sharp criticism from civil libertarians, human rights organizations, and organizations representing Muslims and Arab Americans. The Department of Homeland Security and its affiliated agencies began effective operations in the last year. Much attention was directed at the USA Patriot Act, a comprehensive law expanding the federal government's role in the war on domestic terrorism that was adopted shortly after the attacks of September 11, 2001. Critics have claimed that administration policy is overly secretive, discriminates against immigrants from countries with majority Muslim populations, tips the balance of governing power from the legislative and judicial to the executive branch, erodes due process protections for criminal suspects, and unnecessarily expands the government's surveillance and investigative powers.

Some of the most controversial measures are directed at immigrants and visitors from predominantly Muslim countries. These include special interrogations of immigrants and students from selected Muslim countries and new screening procedures for young men from specified countries, mostly in the Middle East and South Asia, who are seeking visas to enter the United States. Organizations representing Arab Americans and Muslims have accused the Justice Department of practicing a form of racial profiling. The Justice Department has defended these policies on the ground that those responsible for recent acts of terror against the United States, including the suicide attacks of September 11, come primarily from predominantly Islamic countries and that al-Qaeda and other terrorist organizations continue to plan terror operations against the United States. Ironically, the furor over the treatment of Muslims has contributed to an enhancement of the influence of Arab American organizations, which have become more assertive in protesting alleged abuses and more involved as a lobbying force in political affairs and election campaigns.

A number of critics, including both Democrats and Republicans in Congress, have accused the Justice Department of being overly secretive in the implementation of antiterrorism policies and of violating the country's tradition of open government. The Justice Department has curbed the number of government documents made available to the public through the Freedom of Information Act. Critics contend that the new policy affects areas of government that have nothing to do with national security.

The administration's reliance on special military tribunals to prosecute prisoners captured during combat in Afghanistan and held at the U.S. military facility at Guantanamo, Cuba, has also been the target of criticism. The administration claims that under international law, those captured in Afghanistan do not meet the standards for prisoner-of-war (POW) status, but rather fall into the category of illegal combatants, and thus do not qualify for the rights extended by the Geneva Convention to POWs. Critics assert that the military tribunals would deprive defendants of due process and are concerned because the verdicts of the tribunals cannot be appealed to a higher civilian court. In another controversial move, the Justice Department has sought to label two U.S. citizens as illegal combatants. The cases are before the court system; if the labeling is approved, it is likely the two defendants would be brought to trial before military tribunals as well.

The Patriot Act's expansion of the government's surveillance powers has also raised concern. The law allows the Federal Bureau of Investigation access to the personal records of U.S. citizens, including medical history, library activities, educational background, Internet usage, and finances. An especially bitter controversy erupted over the government's assertion of the right to investigate the books that people borrow and the material they gain access to on publicly available computers in public libraries. The American Library Association condemned the Justice Department's policy, and some librarians vowed to refuse cooperation with federal agents. In response to the public outcry, the Justice Department issued a report indicating it had not made use of the power to investigate the reading habits of Americans.

The Supreme Court issued two decisions in 2003 that may have an important impact on minority rights. In one case, the court decided that state-funded universities have the right to adopt admissions policies that give preference to African

Americans and other minorities, but only when race is considered as one of many factors in determining admission. The court also struck down a Texas state law that criminalized homosexual acts between consenting adults. In the wake of this ruling, gay rights organizations stepped up their campaign to achieve the legalization of same-sex marriage, while conservative groups criticized the decision as the federal courts usurping the authority of state legislatures.

Although the next presidential election does not take place until November 2004, campaigning for the presidency was the dominant political event throughout 2003. The nine announced Democrats took part in a series of debates on foreign and domestic policy. Meanwhile, President Bush faces no opposition within his Republican Party and is expected to amass a reelection campaign war chest in excess of $200 million. The president and several Democratic candidates have announced that they will forgo public matching funds, a key strategy in recent plans to reform campaign finance, in order to avoid being subject to spending caps on their campaigns.

The most notable political development of the year was the successful campaign to recall Governor Gray Davis of California. The power of recall is seldom resorted to in American politics. However, in the wake of allegations of broken campaign promises and mismanagement of the state's finances, California's voters chose, in effect, to remove Davis from office. To succeed him, the state's voters chose Arnold Schwarzenegger, an Austrian immigrant, former bodybuilding champion, and movie star.

**Political Rights and Civil Liberties:** The United States has a highly competitive political system dominated by the two major parties, Republican and Democratic. Although the Republican Party currently controls the presidency and both houses of Congress—the Senate and the House of Representatives—the margin of domination is slight. In the House, the breakdown is 229 Republicans, 205 Democrats, and 1 Independent; in the Senate there are 51 Republicans, 48 Democrats, and 1 Independent.

In electing a president, the United States uses a unique system that combines a popular vote and the ballots cast by an electoral college. The electoral college apportions votes to each state based on population; the electors then cast all the ballots of a particular state for the candidate who won the popular vote in that state, no matter what the margin. The electoral college vote determines the winner of the election. Under this system, it is possible for a candidate to win the presidency even though an opposing candidate may have won a greater number of popular votes nationwide. In 2000, this system led to the anomalous situation in which the winning candidate, George W. Bush, actually received fewer popular votes than his nearest rival, Al Gore, the Democratic nominee. Some also contended that Bush's victory was tainted by a controversy over ballot-counting procedures in the state of Florida. After nearly a month of dispute, the election was decided by the Supreme Court, the nation's highest tribunal, which in effect handed the election to Bush. Subsequently, Congress adopted legislation to forestall similar problems from materializing in future elections.

The two principal parties choose candidates for the presidency and Congress through a primary system, in which citizens enrolled in the party vote directly for their preferred candidate. The system gives more influence to rank-and-file party members and detracts from the influence of the party leadership.

Although the two-party system that prevails in the United States discourages the rise of new, independent parties, both major parties have shown themselves open to the participation and influence of constituency groupings. The Democratic Party in particular espouses a set of policies that are strongly influenced by constituency groups that participate in its internal affairs: African Americans, trade unions, feminist organizations, gay rights groups, and environmentalists. On occasion, candidates representing third parties or particular causes have exerted a significant impact on presidential politics. The most recent example of this phenomenon was Ross Perot, who gained nearly 20 percent of the presidential vote in the 1992 election as the candidate of the Reform Party.

In the U.S. federal political system, a great deal of government responsibility devolves to the individual states. Most law enforcement matters are dealt with at the state level, as is education, and states have been given wide powers to raise revenues through various forms of taxation. Some states give citizens wide powers to influence legislation through institutions of direct democracy like the referendum. The state of California is notable for the number and kind of measures that are placed before the voters; recent referendums involved the rights of undocumented immigrants, the level of property taxes, and affirmative action plans for minority groups.

The federal government in the United States has a high degree of transparency. A substantial number of auditing and investigatory agencies function independently of party influence or the influence of incumbent officials. The efforts of these entities are reinforced by an impressive number of private watchdog organizations that focus on such disparate issues as political campaign spending, open government, the impact of business lobbying on the legislative process, and the defense budget. Federal agencies regularly place information relevant to their mandate on Web sites to broaden public access.

The United States has a free, diverse, and constitutionally protected press. In recent years, a debate has arisen over the impact of media consolidation, accomplished through the purchase of large press entities—television networks, newspapers, and weekly magazines—by giant corporations with little or no previous interest in journalism. The Federal Communications Commission has rules in place to prevent a single entity from purchasing more than a certain percentage of the media in a given market, but those rules were loosened during 2003. The commission's ruling, however, has been challenged, and its fate is currently before the federal court system. Critics assert that the continuation of the consolidation trend will lead to a press with a homogenized message and an unwillingness to challenge corporate power. Others, however, point to the trend among many Americans to look to the Internet as a prime source of news as evidence that media diversity remains strong.

The United States has a long tradition of religious freedom. Adherents of practically every major religious denomination, as well as many smaller groupings, can be found throughout the country, and religious belief and religious service attendance is high. There is an ongoing debate over the role of religion in public life, often centered on the question of whether government subsidies to schools sponsored by religious denominations meet constitutional standards. Issues such as "gay marriage" and "partial birth abortion" and even the place of the words "under God" in the Pledge of Allegiance are heavily loaded with religious overtones and serve to mobilize certain constituencies to engage in the political process. The chief justice of the supreme court of the state of Alabama was removed from office in November for disobeying a court order to remove a monument to the Ten Commandments from the State Courthouse. That decision reflects a long-standing trend by the courts of leaning in the direction of a separation between religion and the state.

Although a contentious debate has emerged over the university's role in society, academic life is notable for a healthy level of intellectual freedom. In 2003, academics and students participated in vigorous debates over public policy issues, especially the war in Iraq, the global economy, and U.S. policy toward Israel. Controversies have broken out at a number of the country's prestigious universities over what is characterized as "political correctness," by which is meant a climate of intolerance toward opinions, usually voiced by political conservatives, that diverge from the campus mainstream. Conservatives have been particularly critical of speech codes adopted by many universities to regulate the tone of discourse over race, ethnicity, and gender. The judiciary has struck down a number of these speech codes as infringements on freedom of speech.

Private discussion and public debate are vigorous. There were a number of demonstrations against the war in Iraq as well as public declarations issued by committees of war critics. An impressive number of organizations devoted to political causes or public policy issues have emerged over the years, including groups that represent racial minorities, the disabled, homosexuals, the poor, those who want to expand the role of religion in public life, gun owners, and industry interests. The United States is unique in the openness of its system to advocacy efforts by groups that want to influence the course of U.S. foreign policy.

Trade unions by law are guaranteed the right to organize workers and engage in collective bargaining with employers. The right to strike is also guaranteed. Over the years, however, the strength of organized labor has declined to the point where less than 9 percent of the private workforce is represented by unions, one of the lowest figures among stable, economically advanced democracies. An important factor in labor's decline is the country's labor code, which is regarded as an impediment to organizing efforts. Union organizing efforts are also impeded by strong resistance from employers and the federal government's failure to enforce the law against labor code violators strictly. Several attempts to modify core labor laws have been defeated in Congress over the years. At the same time, trade unions remain an important force in political life. In recent years, unions have become more directly involved in Democratic Party affairs, and unions are expected to serve as a crucial source of campaign funds and volunteer workers for the Democrats in the 2004 presidential election.

The judiciary plays a more central role in the governing system than in most other established democracies. Judicial independence is respected, though the influence of the court system has become a source of sometimes bitter contention over the years, with critics claiming that judicial authority has expanded into areas of governance that are best left to the legislative branch.

There is a strong rule of law tradition in the United States. At the same time, a number of controversies have emerged over the treatment of poor and especially minority defendants in criminal law cases. African Americans and Hispanics constitute a large portion of defendants in criminal cases involving murder, rape, assault, and robbery. The police in a number of large cities have been accused of using unnecessary force in dealings with black and Hispanic criminal suspects, although the number and intensity of complaints have declined in the past few years and most urban police departments mandate some form of human rights training for new officers. Some police departments have also come under criticism for "racial profiling," a practice whereby members of a particular racial or ethnic group are targeted for investigations or searches. President Bush has spoken out against racial profiling, and in 2003, he issued an executive order banning the practice by federal authorities except in cases involving national security. Nevertheless, civil libertarians and Arab American organizations have claimed that the Justice Department, as part of its offensive against domestic terrorism, has engaged in the profiling of men who have come to the United States from countries in the Middle East or South Asia. In response, Justice Department officials contend that a measure of profiling is essential in the war against terrorism given the Middle Eastern or South Asian origins of the majority of those involved in terrorist plots against the United States.

Civil liberty and other groups have advanced a broad critique of the criminal justice system, contending that there are too many Americans (especially minority Americans) in prison, that prison sentences are often excessive, and that too many people are prosecuted for minor drug offenses. During 2003, there was a movement in a number of states toward shorter prison sentences and earlier releases for convicted felons. Concern has also been raised about prison conditions, especially the disturbing levels of violence and rape and the reportedly inadequate medical attention for prisoners with mental illness. As evidence of a growing controversy over the death penalty, several states have announced a moratorium on capital punishment while studies are undertaken on the death penalty's fairness.

Citizens of the United States enjoy a high level of personal autonomy. The right to own property is protected by law, and business entrepreneurship is encouraged as a matter of government policy.

The United States is one of the world's most racially and ethnically diverse societies. In recent years, the country's population dynamics have shifted in important ways, as Americans of Latin American ancestry have replaced African Americans as the leading minority group, and the percentage of whites in the population has declined somewhat. A complex variety of policies and programs are designed to protect the rights of minorities, including laws to prevent discrimination on the job, affirmative action plans for university admissions, quotas to guarantee representation in the internal affairs of some political parties, and policies to ensure that minorities are not treated unfairly in the apportionment of government-assistance efforts. African Americans, however, continue to lag in economic standing, education, and other social areas. Black Americans are more likely to live in poverty, less likely to own businesses, less likely to have gained a university degree, and more likely to have served time in prison than members of other groups, including many recent immigrant groups.

The United States has a long history of liberal immigration policies. In recent years, there has been some debate over the degree to which new immigrants are assimilating into American society. Most observers, however, believe that the country has struck a balance that both encourages assimilation and permits new immigrants to maintain certain religious or cultural customs. The United States has in recent years not faced the kind of controversy that has erupted in other countries over the wearing of the *hijab* (headscarf) by Muslim girls in public schools.

The United States has been less successful in devising a policy for dealing with undocumented immigrants, several million of whom live and work in the country at any one time. Many immigrants' rights advocates assert that the country would not be able to meet labor needs if illegal immigration were curbed. At the beginning of his administration, President Bush indicated he was prepared to reach an agreement with Mexico to establish policies to regulate the flow of migrant workers who cross the border into the United States. After the events of September 11, negotiations with Mexico were dropped, and the administration adopted a tougher stance toward undocumented workers and visitors whose visas have expired. The Bush administration has drawn particular criticism for policies that, civil libertarians contend, discriminate against immigrants and visa applicants from countries in the Middle East and South Asia. These measures subject those from predominantly Muslim countries to special registration requirements, interviews by law enforcement officials, and lengthy visa application procedures. Concern has also been expressed about the federal government's policy of holding asylum seekers in detention facilities while their applications are being assessed. At the same time, the United States has not reduced the number of legal immigrants allowed into the country, which is high by global standards.

Women have made important strides toward equality over the past several decades. Women are heavily represented in the law, medicine, and journalism, and predominate in the university programs that train students for these professions. Although the average compensation of female workers is less than 80 percent of that for male workers, women with recent university degrees have effectively attained parity with men.

# Uruguay

**Population:** 3,400,000   **Political Rights:** 1
**GNI/capita:** $5,710   **Civil Liberties:** 1
**Life Expectancy:** 75   **Status:** Free
**Religious Groups:** Roman Catholic (66 percent),
Protestant (2 percent), Jewish (1 percent),
other (31 percent)
**Ethnic Groups:** White (88 percent), mestizo (8 percent),
black (4 percent)
**Capital:** Montevideo

**Ten-Year Ratings Timeline (Political Rights, Civil Liberties, Status)**

| 1994 | 1995 | 1996 | 1997 | 1998 | 1999 | 2000 | 2001 | 2002 | 2003 |
|------|------|------|------|------|------|------|------|------|------|
| 2,2F | 2,2F | 1,2F | 1,2F | 1,2F | 1,2F | 1,1F | 1,1F | 1,1F | 1,1F |

**Overview:**
Disputes with neighboring Brazil over regional free trade, and with Argentina over specific human rights issues festering since the 1970s, dominated Uruguay's political debate in 2003. The center-right government of President Jorge Batlle, steering an independent course, remained the region's only vociferous opponent of the last

unelected dictator in the hemisphere—Cuba's Fidel Castro. In mid-2003, a bond restructuring avoided a potentially catastrophic economic default.

After gaining independence from Spain, the Oriental Republic of Uruguay was established in 1830. The Colorado Party dominated a relatively democratic political system throughout the 1960s.

In 1998, the centrist National Party, racked by mutual accusations of corruption, joined the opposition Colorado Party in supporting the latter's presidential nominee, Batlle, a 72-year-old senator and five-time presidential candidate whose father and great-uncle had been respected Colorado Party presidents. Faced with dismal economic prospects and a choice between presidential candidates representing the moderate right or an eclectic left, in 1999, Uruguayans gave Batlle 52 percent of the vote. On taking office, the new president incorporated several National Party members into his cabinet.

Batlle immediately sought an honest accounting of the human rights situation under a former military regime whose widely acknowledged viciousness had turned Uruguay's reputation as the "Switzerland of Latin America" on its head. Batlle also showed equally firm determination to reduce spending and taxes and to privatize previously sacrosanct state monopolies. In 2001, crises in the rural sector and an increase in violent crime, in what was still one of Latin America's safest countries, dominated much of the public's attention, as did growing labor unrest. Montevideo, with 1.4 million inhabitants, is Uruguay's only large city and contains most of its highest crime areas.

A devaluation and default in Argentina at the end of 2001 shrank Uruguay's international reserves 80 percent in six months, with the country losing its coveted investment grade status on Wall Street—one of only four in Latin America to have such a status—in February 2002. In July, the government was forced to impose a week-long bank holiday, Uruguay's first in 70 years, to stanch a run on the country's banks. The spillover effect from Argentina's melting economy was blamed for a day of violence in August, when looters ransacked businesses and labor unions staged antigovernment protests that brought much of Montevideo to a standstill. In the meantime, Batlle caused a huge diplomatic flap by calling his neighbors in Argentina "a bunch of thieves" and predicting that his Argentine counterpart, Eduardo Duhalde, might be forced to leave the presidency at any moment. In October, the Blanco Party withdrew its members from Batlle's government.

Toward the end of 2003, the leftist Broad Front, headed by Tabare Vasquez, a moderate and former mayor of Montevideo, appeared favored to win the October 2004 presidential elections, despite a small economic rally following the worst economic crisis in the country's history. Vasquez remained enigmatic about his own economic plans should he win the presidency. The emergence of an invigorated left appeared to be linked in part to the government's promotion of an unpopular law that allowed the national oil refinery to establish joint ventures with transnational petroleum companies.

The political situation with Argentina remained tense, particularly after the new Argentine president, Nestor Kirchner, joined his Brazilian counterpart, Luiz Inacio "Lula" da Silva, at a Broad Front political rally. Meanwhile, the luster of Batlle's human rights record appeared to dim after he chose as a naval attaché in Buenos Aires a navy captain accused of being responsible for the deaths of two Argentines when both countries were ruled by military dictatorships. Uruguay also firmly rejected efforts by the Argentine government to create an alliance between the Cuban regime and the regional free trade partnership known as Mercosur.

**Political Rights and Civil Liberties:** Citizens of Uruguay can change their government democratically. The 1967 constitution established a bicameral congress consisting of the 99-member Chamber of Deputies and the 31-member Senate, with every member serving a five-year term. The president is also directly elected for a five-year term. In 1999, for the first time, Uruguayan parties selected a single presidential candidate in open primary elections. Previously, the parties had fielded a number of candidates, and the candidates with the most votes then accumulated the votes cast for the others.

Uruguay, long a haven for anonymous foreign bank deposits as a result of its strict banking secrecy laws, has also taken measures to regulate financial activities in order to reduce the potential for money laundering. October 1998 saw the passage of antidrug legislation that made narcotics-related money laundering a crime. The Financial Investigations Unit (FIU) was established in order to present more complete evidence in narcotics-related prosecutions. On the request of the Central Bank, financial institutions must provide certain information, and banks (including offshore banks), currency exchange houses, and stockbrokers are required to report transactions of more than $10,000. The FIU also requires all entities under its jurisdiction to report suspicious financial transactions to a financial information analysis unit.

The Transparency Law (Ley Cristal) entered into force in January 1999. It criminalizes a broad range of potential abuses of power by governmental officeholders, including the laundering of funds related to public corruption cases. It also requires financial disclosure statements to be filed by high-ranking officials. Public officials who know of a drug-related crime or incident and do nothing about it may be charged with a "crime of omission" under the Citizen Security Law. Uruguay ranks near the top of public transparency ratings for Latin America issued annually by Transparency International.

Constitutional guarantees regarding free expression are generally respected. The press is privately owned, and broadcasting is both commercial and public. Numerous daily newspapers publish, many associated with political parties; there are also a number of weeklies. In 1996, a number of publications ceased production because of a government suspension of tax exemptions on the import of newsprint. In addition, a June 1996 decree requires government authorization to import newsprint. Internet access is unrestricted.

Freedom of religion is a cherished political tenet of democratic Uruguay and is broadly respected. The government does not restrict academic freedom.

Civic organizations have proliferated since the return of civilian rule. Numerous women's rights groups focus on violence against women, societal discrimination, and other problems. Workers exercise their right to join unions, bargain collectively, and hold strikes. Unions are well organized and politically powerful. Strikes are sometimes marked by violent clashes and sabotage.

The judiciary is relatively independent, but has become increasingly inefficient in the face of escalating crime, particularly street violence and organized crime. The court system is severely backlogged, and suspects under arrest often spend more time in jail than they would were they to be convicted and serve the maximum sentence for their crime. Allegations of police mistreatment, particularly of youthful offenders, have increased; however, prosecutions of such acts are also occurring more frequently. Prison conditions do not meet international standards.

President Jorge Batlle's pro-human rights stance appeared to waiver in 2003. In November Batlle announced that the case of the daughter-in-law of Argentine poet Juan Gelman, detained in Buenos Aires in 1976 and later allegedly made to disappear in Uruguay, was included in a 1986 law that effectively granted amnesty to Uruguay's military and police accused of committing right violations during the military's 12-year regime. Efforts by that regime in the mid-1970s to kill U.S. Congressman Ed Koch of Manhattan, a fierce critic of the Uruguayan military, were also confirmed by independent investigators in 2003 after having been first reported in 1993.

The small black minority continues to face discrimination. Uruguay's continuing economic crisis has forced thousands of formerly middle-class citizens to join rural migrants in the shantytowns ringing Montevideo.

Violence against women continues to be a problem. However, the government generally protects children's rights and welfare, and has placed the education and health of children as a top priority.

# Uzbekistan

**Population:** 25,700,000　**Political Rights:** 7
**GNI/capita:** $450　**Civil Liberties:** 6
**Life Expectancy:** 70　**Status:** Not Free
**Religious Groups:** Muslim [mostly Sunni] (88 percent),
Eastern Orthodox (9 percent), other (3 percent)
**Ethnic Groups:** Uzbek (80 percent), Russian (6 percent),
Tajik (5 percent), Kazakh (3 percent), other (6 percent)
**Capital:** Tashkent

**Ten-Year Ratings Timeline (Political Rights, Civil Liberties, Status)**

| 1994 | 1995 | 1996 | 1997 | 1998 | 1999 | 2000 | 2001 | 2002 | 2003 |
|------|------|------|------|------|------|------|------|------|------|
| 7,7NF | 7,7NF | 7,6NF | 7,6NF | 7,6NF | 7,6NF | 7,6NF | 7,6NF | 7,6NF | 7,6NF |

**Overview:**　Throughout 2003, Uzbekistan continued its repressive policies against human rights defenders, independent journalists, opposition political activists, and suspected members of banned Islamic groups in an attempt to silence dissent. Despite limited gestures toward greater political openness—including allowing two unregistered opposition political groups to hold meetings—the government's policy toward critics of the regime remained essentially unchanged. During the weeks surrounding a key meeting in Tashkent of representatives from the European Bank for Reconstruction and Development (EBRD), the authorities harassed or detained political dissidents and relatives of religious prisoners. While lifting restrictions on the convertibility of the national currency, the government resisted most international pressure to adopt reforms to the country's largely centrally planned economy.

Located along the ancient trade route of the famous Silk Road, Uzbekistan was incorporated into Russia by the late 1800s. The Uzbekistan Soviet Socialist Republic was established in 1924, and its eastern region was detached and made a separate Tajik Soviet republic five years later.

On December 29, 1991, more than 98 percent of the country's electorate approved a popular referendum on the Uzbekistan's independence. In a parallel vote, Islam Karimov, former Communist Party leader and chairman of the People's Democratic Party (PDP), the successor to the Communist Party, was elected president with a reported 88 percent of the vote The only independent candidate to challenge him, Erk (Freedom) Party leader Mohammed Solih, charged election fraud. Solih fled the country two years later, and the party was forced underground. The opposition group Birlik (Unity) was barred from contesting the election and later refused legal registration as a political party, and the Islamic Renaissance Party (IRP) and other religious-based groups were banned entirely. Only pro-government parties were allowed to compete in elections to the first post-Soviet legislature in December 1994 and January 1995. A February 1995 national referendum to extend Karimov's first five-year term in office until the year 2000 was allegedly approved by 99 percent of the country's voters.

The government's repression of members of the political opposition and of Muslims not affiliated with state-sanctioned religious institutions intensified following a series of deadly bombings in Tashkent in February 1999. The authorities blamed the attacks, which they described as an assassination attempt against Karimov, on the Islamic Movement of Uzbekistan (IMU), an armed group seeking the overthrow of Uzbekistan's secular government and its replacement with an Islamic state. The state justified its increasing crackdowns against moderate secular and religious groups under the pretext of fighting violent Islamist organizations, including the IMU.

Of the five parties that competed in the December 1999 parliamentary election, which was strongly criticized by international election observers, all supported the president and differed little in their political platforms. In the January 2000 presidential poll, Karimov defeated his only opponent, Marxist history professor Abdulhasiz Dzhalalov, with 92 percent of the vote. Uzbekistan's government refused to register genuinely independent opposition parties or permit their members to stand as candidates. Meanwhile, in August 2000, the IMU engaged in armed clashes with government troops in Uzbekistan; the following month, the U.S. government placed the IMU on its list of international terrorist organizations for its ties to Osama bin Laden's terrorist network, al-Qaeda, and the Taliban. As part of its declared effort to prevent renewed invasions by the IMU, Uzbekistan subsequently placed land mines along portions of its borders with Kyrgyzstan and Tajikistan, leading to protests by both governments and reports of accidental deaths of civilians in the region.

After the September 11, 2001 attacks on the Pentagon and the World Trade Center, Uzbekistan became a key strategic ally of the United States in its military operations in Afghanistan. Tashkent's decision to permit the deployment of U.S. troops on its territory for search-and-rescue and humanitarian operations was widely seen as an effort to obtain various concessions from the West, including economic assistance, security guarantees, and reduced criticism of its poor human rights record. In March 2002, the United States and Uzbekistan signed a Declaration on Strategic Partnership and Cooperation Framework, in which both countries agreed to cooperate on economic, legal, humanitarian, and nuclear proliferation matters. Uzbekistan's continued collaboration with the U.S.-led antiterrorism campaign in 2002 led to American commitments of increased financial assistance in exchange for promises from Karimov of political reforms. However, there was little evidence at year's end of substantive changes to the Uzbek government's repressive policies.

In early May 2003, the EBRD held its annual meeting in Tashkent, the first large-scale EBRD function in Central Asia. The choice of the meeting venue, which traditionally serves as a showcase for the host nation, stirred considerable controversy. In March, the EBRD set a one-year deadline for compliance with three broad benchmarks for reform in Uzbekistan: greater political openness and freedom of the media, free functioning of civil society groups, and implementation of the recommendations of the UN Special Rapporteur on Torture. While welcoming these benchmarks, international human rights and political observers criticized the EBRD for failing to use its leverage to press Karimov for more concrete economic and political change. The observers noted that in the weeks surrounding the meeting, police intensified harassment of human rights defenders and relatives of religious prisoners in an attempt to prevent them from staging public protests about government abuses. In late November, Human Rights Watch concluded that Uzbekistan had made no real progress toward meeting the EBRD benchmarks.

Despite continued pledges by Karimov to implement economic reforms, the government took only limited steps to loosen its tight control over the country's economy. In October, Uzbekistan finally announced plans to ease restrictions on the convertibility of the national currency, the som, after years of pressure from international financial institutions. However, some analysts predict that pressure on the country's foreign exchange reserves will soon lead to a growing spread between the official exchange rate and the black market rate.

**Political Rights and Civil Liberties:** Citizens of Uzbekistan cannot change their government democratically. President Islam Karimov and the executive branch dominate the legislature and judiciary, and the government severely represses all political opposition. The national legislature largely confirms decisions made by the executive branch. The 1994–1995 and 1999 parliamentary elections and the 2000 presidential poll, in which only pro-government candidates could participate, were neither free nor fair. In a January 2002 nationwide referendum, 91 percent of voters allegedly approved amending the country's constitution to extend the presidential term from five to seven years. Karimov's current term in office will therefore end in 2007, rather than in 2005. In a parallel vote, 93 percent of voters officially supported replacing the country's 250-member single-chamber legislature with a bicameral parliament. Independent observers raised serious doubts about the validity of the referendum, citing the presence of police in polling stations and the fact that some people had been able to vote on behalf of several individuals. In April 2003, parliament adopted legislation providing former presidents immunity from prosecution and lifelong state-funded security for them and their immediate family.

No genuine political opposition groups function legally or participate in the government. A 1997 law prohibits parties based on ethnic or religious affiliations and those advocating subversion of the constitutional order. Members of unregistered secular opposition groups, including Birlik and Erk, are subject to discrimination, and many are in exile abroad. In a small gesture toward opening political life in the country, the authorities allowed both Erk and Birlik to hold open meetings in Tashkent in 2003. However, in an indication that this development did not represent a fundamental change in the authorities' policy toward the opposition, neither group was allowed to register officially as a political party. In addition, police briefly detained two Erk members a week before its meeting, searching their homes and seizing books, computers, and various documents. Corruption is reportedly widespread throughout various levels of government, with bribery to obtain lucrative positions a common practice.

The state imposes strict limits on freedom of speech and the press, particularly with regard to reports on the government and President Karimov. The government controls major media outlets and newspaper printing and distribution facilities. The country's private broadcast and print media outlets generally avoid political issues, are largely regional in scope, and suffer from administrative and financial constraints. Although official censorship was abolished in May 2002, the responsibility for censoring material was transferred to newspaper editors, who were warned by the State Press Committee that they would be held personally accountable for what they publish. Self-censorship is widespread, while the few journalists who dare to produce probing or critical reports of the authorities face harassment, physical violence, and closure of their media outlets. The government has blocked a number of non-Uzbek news Web sites, and access to controversial information on the Internet remains extremely difficult.

The year saw a renewed crackdown on the media in Uzbekistan. In a case that attracted international attention, independent journalist and human rights activist Ruslan Sharipov, who had written widely on government corruption, was sentenced on August 13, 2003 to five and a half years in prison on charges of homosexuality—which is a criminal offense in Uzbekistan—and sexual relations with a minor. Sharipov reportedly confessed to the charges under duress, citing concerns for the safety of his mother and legal defenders, and was tortured while in custody. In September, an appeals court reduced his prison sentence to four years. On August 28, Sharipov's attorney, Surat Ikramov, was abducted and assaulted by a group of masked men; Ikramov had been helping to organize a peaceful protest outside of parliament scheduled for the following day. Authorities reportedly used politically motivated charges to detain or arrest other journalists, including Tokhtomurad Toshev, editor of the newspaper *Adolat*; Oleg Sarapulov, an assistant to an independent journalist; Ergash Babajanov, a journalist and member of Birlik; and Khusnutddin Kutbiddinov and Yusuf Rasulov, correspondents with Radio Free Europe/Radio Liberty and Voice of America, respectively.

The government exercises strict control over Islamic worship, including the content of imams' sermons, and is suspicious and intolerant of followers of Muslim organizations not sanctioned by the state. Many members of such groups have been arrested or imprisoned on charges of anti-constitutional activities, often under the pretext of the government's fight against militant Islamists. Muslim prisoners are frequently tortured for their religious convictions or to compel them to renounce their beliefs. Authorities have targeted members of the banned Hizb-ut-Tahrir (Islamic Party of Liberation), an international movement calling for the creation of an Islamic caliphate throughout the Muslim world. Suspected members have been forced to give confessions under torture, and their family members have been subjected to interrogation, arrest, and extortion.

The government permits the existence of certain mainstream religions, including approved Muslim and Jewish communities, as well as the Russian Orthodox Church and some other Christian denominations. As of June 2003, the authorities had registered some 2,100 religious congregations and organizations. However, the activities of other congregations are restricted through legislation that requires all religious groups to comply with burdensome state registration criteria. Involvement in religious activities carried out by unregistered groups is punishable by fines or imprisonment, and meetings held by such groups have been raided and participants interrogated and arrested. The 1998 Law on Freedom of Conscience and Religious Organizations prohibits activities including proselytizing and private religious instruction, and requires groups to obtain a license to publish or distribute materials.

The government grants academic institutions a degree of autonomy, though freedom of expression remains limited, according to the 2003 U.S. State Department country report on human rights practices. While professors generally are required to have their lectures pre-approved, implementation of this restriction vary, the report stated; university professors reportedly practice self-censorship.

Open and free private discussion is limited by the *mahalla* committees, a traditional neighborhood organization that the government has turned into an official system for public surveillance and control. According to a 2003 Human Rights Watch report, the mahalla committees maintain files on those considered to be overly pious in their religious expression and alert the police of so-called suspicious religious and other activities.

Although nonpolitical associations and social organizations are usually allowed to register, complicated regulations and governmental bureaucracy make the process difficult. Unregistered nongovernmental organizations (NGOs), including the Human Rights Society of Uzbekistan (HRSU), do not exist as legal entities and can face difficulties operating. In a positive development, Yuldash Rasulov, an HRSU member, was released from prison in January 2003 under a December 2002 presidential amnesty. Rasulov, who had helped people persecuted for their religious beliefs, was sentenced to seven years in prison in September 2002 on charges of attempting to overthrow the constitutional order and distributing extremist literature. Other human rights activists endured arrest, beatings, and intimidation throughout the year. On August 20, Mutabar Tajibaeva, the leader of a human rights group called Yuraklar, was beaten by a group of women while attending a demonstration against local law enforcement officials in the Ferghana Valley; Tajibaeva believes that the authorities organized the attack.

Despite constitutional provisions for freedom of assembly, the authorities severely restrict this right in practice. Law enforcement officials have used force to prevent demonstrations against human rights abuses in the country, and participants have been harassed, detained, and arrested. In recent years, there have been some small protests by family members of people jailed for allegedly being members of violent Islamic groups. Larger protests by merchants were staged across the county in response to new costly regulations that the government had imposed on them; some clashes between police and demonstrators were reported.

The Council of the Federation of Trade Unions is dependent on the state, and no genuinely independent union structures exist. Organized strikes are extremely rare. However, according to an August 2003 article by the Institute for War and Peace Reporting, workers at two large factories in the city of Ferghana held several strikes that month to protest unpaid wages; most of the promised concessions from management reportedly failed to materialize, and workers were pressured or threatened.

The judiciary is subservient to the president, who appoints all judges and can remove them from office at any time. Police routinely physically abuse and torture suspects to extract confessions, which are accepted by judges as evidence and often serve as the sole basis for convictions. Law enforcement authorities reportedly often plant narcotics, weapons, and banned religious literature on suspected members of Islamic groups or political opponents to justify their arrest. Executions are regarded as state secrets, and relatives are sometimes not informed until months after the execution has occurred.

Prisons suffer from severe overcrowding and shortages of food and medicine. The Jaslyk prison camp is notorious for its extremely harsh conditions and ill-treatment of religious prisoners. Inmates, particularly those sentenced for their religious beliefs, are often subjected to ill-treatment or torture, and Human Rights Watch has documented a number of torture-related deaths in custody during the last few years. An estimated 6,000 to 7,000 political prisoners are being held in Uzbekistan's penal institutions.

Although racial and ethnic discrimination is prohibited by law, the belief that senior positions in government and business are reserved for ethnic Uzbeks is widespread. Some members of minority groups have declared themselves to be ethnic Uzbeks in an effort to improve their employment and other opportunities.

The government severely limits freedom of movement and residence within the country and across borders. There are widespread restrictions on foreign travel, including the use of a system of exit visas, which are often issued selectively. Permission is required from local authorities to move to a new city, and the authorities rarely grant permission to those wishing to move to Tashkent. Bribes are often paid to obtain the necessary registration documents.

Widespread corruption, bureaucratic regulations, and the government's tight control over the economy limit most citizens' equality of opportunity. There has been little reform in the country's large and predominantly centrally planned agricultural sector, in which the state sets high production quotas and low purchase prices for farmers. In October 2003, the authorities adopted tough measures to prevent impoverished farmers from smuggling cotton—one of Uzbekistan's top exports—to neighboring countries for higher prices. A government decree issued the same month requiring that non-food items be sold in stores rather than less costly market stalls and that merchants use expensive cash registers sparked angry protests by merchants in a number of towns.

Women's educational and professional prospects are restricted by traditional cultural and religious norms and by ongoing economic difficulties throughout the country. Victims of domestic violence are discouraged from pressing charges against their perpetrators, who rarely face criminal prosecution. According to a 2003 Human Rights Watch report, mahalla committees enforce government policy to prevent divorce by frequently denying battered wives access to the police or courts and holding them responsible for the abuse they experience. The trafficking of women abroad for prostitution remains a serious problem.

# Vanuatu

**Population:** 200,000
**GNI/capita:** $1,080
**Life Expectancy:** 67
**Political Rights:** 2*
**Civil Liberties:** 2
**Status:** Free
**Religious Groups:** Presbyterian (36.7 percent), Anglican (15 percent), Roman Catholic (15 percent), indigenous beliefs (7.6 percent), Seventh-Day Adventist (6.2 percent), Church of Christ (3.8 percent), other (15.7 percent)
**Ethnic Groups:** Melanesian (98 percent), other [including French, Vietnamese, and Chinese] (2 percent)
**Capital:** Port Vila
**Ratings Change:** Vanuatu's political rights rating declined from 1 to 2 due to a technical reevaluation of the country's political life and electoral process.

**Ten-Year Ratings Timeline (Political Rights, Civil Liberties, Status)**

| 1994 | 1995 | 1996 | 1997 | 1998 | 1999 | 2000 | 2001 | 2002 | 2003 |
|------|------|------|------|------|------|------|------|------|------|
| 1,3F | 1,3F | 1,3F | 1,3F | 1,3F | 1,3F | 1,3F | 1,3F | 1,2F | 2,2F |

**Overview:**

In 2003, the government passed new laws to deter money laundering. Also during the year, the National Council of Chiefs instituted measures to restrict the free movement of people between provinces.

Vanuatu, an archipelago of 83 islands lying 1,300 miles northeast of Sydney, Australia, was occupied by the British and French under an Anglo-French "condominium" in 1906 until its independence in 1980. This legacy continues to split society along linguistic lines, from politics to religion to economics.

The left leaning Vanua'aku Party led the country from 1980 until 1991. That year, a split within the party allowed Maxime Corlot, leader of the francophone Union of Moderate Parties (UMP) to become Vanuatu's first French-speaking prime minister. After the 1995 elections, Carlot was succeeded by Serge Vohor, who headed a dissident faction of the UMP. Barak Sope took over from Vohor in 1999; Sope was ousted by a no-confidence vote and convicted of a felony two years later. Current prime minister Edward Natapei of the Vanua'aku Party has been in power since 2001, in a coalition government with the UMP. The UMP won the most seats of any party in the May 2002 legislative elections, capturing 15 seats compared to the Vanua'aku Party's 14.

The government has tightened laws to tackle money laundering and tax evasion to protect its offshore banking business. In May 2003, the Organization for Economic Cooperation and Development (OECD) removed Vanuatu from the list of uncooperative tax havens for the country's efforts to improve transparency of its tax and regulatory systems and its plan to establish effective exchange of information for tax matters by the end of 2005. The OECD list was created in 2000, and it includes Nauru, the Marshall Islands, and other countries and territories that have insufficient safeguards to prevent tax evasion and money laundering.

In another economic matter, the government passed a new law in January to stop all mixed-race and naturalized citizens from farming kava, a native herb that has gained popularity among health supplement consumers in the West.

In September, the National Council of Chiefs passed a motion to require people to carry permits for movement between provinces because of concerns about crime in the capital.

## Political Rights and Civil Liberties:

Citizens of Vanuatu can change their government democratically. The constitution provides for parliamentary elections based on universal suffrage once every four years. The 52 members of parliament choose from among themselves a prime minister to lead the government. The prime minister appoints his own cabinet, the Council of Ministers. Members of parliament and the presidents of six provincial governments also form an electoral college to select the president for a five-year term. The president serves as the head of state, a largely ceremonial post. The National Council of Chiefs works in parallel with parliament, exercising authority mainly over language and cultural matters.

In recent years, leadership has changed many times through no-confidence votes, and parliamentary coalitions were formed and dissolved with increasing frequency throughout the 1990s. Fraud and bribery have also been common problems in elections.

The government generally respects freedom of speech and of the press. The weekly *Port Vila Press* and daily *Vanuatu Daily Post* provide readers with international, national, and local news, and there is limited government-owned broadcast media available. Most media deliver information in Bismala, English, and French. The number of mobile phone and Internet users is rising, but is still very small because of high costs and difficulties in access outside the capital of Port Vila.

The government generally respects freedom of religion in this predominantly Christian country. There were no reports of restrictions on academic freedom. Port Vila is host to the Emalus Campus of the University of the South Pacific, which offers undergraduate and postgraduate training.

There have been no reports of government restrictions on civil society groups, and nongovernmental organizations are active in a variety of spheres. Many receive support from foreign private foundations and bilateral aid donors. Workers can organize unions and bargain collectively. There are five independent trade unions organized under the umbrella Vanuatu Council of Trade Unions, representing nearly 40 percent of the country's 25,000 workforce.

Although the judiciary is generally independent, it is weak and inefficient. Lack of resources has kept the government from hiring and retaining qualified judges and prosecutors. As a result, criminal defendants are often held for long periods in pretrial detention. Prison conditions are poor for the country's approximately 30 inmates. Vanuatu has no armed forces. The Vanuatu Mobile Force is a paramilitary wing of the small police force. Both are under the command of a civilian police commissioner. There have been some reports of abuse by the police, but such incidents appear to be infrequent and not widespread or severe.

The vast majority of the population is engaged in either subsistence farming or fishing. Tourism, the civil service, and offshore banking provide employment in the service sector.

Violence against women is common and is particularly severe in rural areas. Spousal rape is not a crime, and no specific law addresses wife beating or sexual harassment. The police and courts display general hesitation to intervene or impose stronger punishment for offenders. Most cases go unreported because women are not aware of their rights, fear reprisal, or are discouraged by family pressure. In the economic sphere, women are largely limited to traditional roles as wives and mothers. Policies drafted as part of a reform program to protect and further the rights of women have not been implemented. Many women's rights leaders consider village chiefs to be major obstacles to improving conditions for women. The practice of "bride price payment," used in the majority of marriages, is also seen to encourage the view of women as property.

# ⬇ Venezuela

**Population:** 25,700,000
**GNI/capita:** $4,760
**Life Expectancy:** 73
**Religious Groups:** Roman Catholic (96 percent), Protestant (2 percent), other (2 percent)
**Ethnic Groups:** Spanish, Italian, Portuguese, Arab, German, African, indigenous people
**Capital:** Caracas

**Political Rights:** 3
**Civil Liberties:** 4
**Status:** Partly Free

**Trend Arrow:** Venezuela received a downward trend arrow due to growing political violence, an unabated wave of common crime, and credible reports of the increasing participation of Cuban nationals in the country's security and intelligence services.

**Ten-Year Ratings Timeline (Political Rights, Civil Liberties, Status)**

| 1994 | 1995 | 1996 | 1997 | 1998 | 1999 | 2000 | 2001 | 2002 | 2003 |
|------|------|------|------|------|------|------|------|------|------|
| 3,3PF | 3,3PF | 2,3F | 2,3F | 2,3F | 4,4PF | 3,5PF | 3,5PF | 3,4PF | 3,4PF |

**Overview:**

During 2003, President Hugo Chavez appeared on a collision course with a political opposition that seemed determined to force his resignation before the end of his elected term. However, the opposition also faced questions about its own democratic commitment given a 2002 failed coup attempt and its promotion of an unsuccessful general strike in February 2003, as well as more practical concerns about its own cohesion and effectiveness.

The Republic of Venezuela was established in 1830, nine years after independence from Spain. Long periods of instability and military rule ended with the establishment in 1961 of civilian rule and the approval of a constitution. Until 1993, the social democratic Democratic Action Party (AD) and the Social Christian Party (COPEI) dominated politics. Former president Carlos Andres Perez (1989–1993) of the AD was nearly overthrown by Chavez and other nationalist military officers in two 1992 coup attempts in which dozens were killed. In 1993, Perez was charged with corruption and removed from office by congress. Rafael Caldera, a former president (1969–1974) of the COPEI and a populist, was elected president in late 1993 as head of the 16-party National Convergence, which included Communists, other leftists, and right-wing groups. With crime soaring, public corruption unabated, oil wealth drying up, and the country in its worst economic crisis in 50 years, popular disillusionment with politics deepened.

In 1998, Chavez, a twice unsuccessful military coup leader, made his antiestablishment, anticorruption populist message a referendum on the long-ruling political elite—famous for its interlocking system of privilege and graft, but also for its consensual approach to politics—in that year's presidential contest. As the country's long-ruling political parties teetered at the edge of collapse, last-minute efforts to find a consensus candidate to oppose Chavez were unsuccessful, and he won with 57 percent of the vote, taking the reins of the world's fifth-largest oil-producing country in February 1999.

A constituent assembly dominated by Chavez followers drafted a new constitution that strengthened the presidency and allowed Chavez to retain power until 2013. After Venezuelans approved the new constitution in a national referendum on December 15, 2000, congress and the Supreme Court were dismissed. Although he was reelected as president, new national elections held in July 2000 marked a resurgence of a political opposition that had been hamstrung in its efforts to contest Chavez's stripping of congress and the judiciary of their independence and power. Opposition parties won most of the country's governorships, about half the mayoralties, and a significant share of power in the new congress. That November, Chavez's congressional allies granted him special fast-track powers that allowed him to decree a wide range of laws without parliamentary debate.

Chavez was deposed by dissident military officers working with major opposition groups in April 2002, after 19 people died in a massive protest against his government. However, he was reinstated two days later when loyalist troops and supporters gained the upper hand in the streets and in barracks around the country. Opponents cited Article 350 of the 1999 constitution, which permits citizens not to recognize a government that infringes on human and democratic rights—an article that was included by Chavez to justify his own 1992 coup attempt. However, throughout the year, the country was wracked by protests by a broad spectrum of civil society and saw unprecedented discontent among military officers. In August, charges against four alleged military coup leaders were dismissed on the grounds of insufficient evidence. In October, an estimated one million Venezuelans marched in Caracas demanding that Chavez call either early elections or a referendum on his rule—and threatening a general strike if he did not accede.

In early February 2003, a devastating 62-day national strike against Chavez was ended after it failed to force him from office. Organized by the opposition umbrella group, Coordinadora Democratica, as well as the major business association and the country's largest federal trade union, the protest crippled Venezuela's oil industry and created serious hardships around the country. The post-strike situation was painted starkly by *The New York Times*: "More than 5,000 industrial companies failed last year, nearly 20 percent of the population is unemployed, inflation is soaring and 56 percent of Venezuelans work in the informal economy, many of them selling trinkets and fruit on the streets."

Following Chavez's successful quashing of the politically motivated strike, opponents quickly mobilized behind a recall referendum, which is allowed under the 1999 constitution promoted by the president and his supporters. Because he is at the end of the third year of his six-year term, Chavez will be obligated to hold the vote if 20 percent of the electorate calls for such a move. A first attempt to collect the necessary signatures succeeded in gathering 2.8 million at a time when polls show 65 percent of Venezuelans would vote to oust Chavez, but was declared invalid by the National Elections Council (CNE). Opponents quickly mobilized to collect new signatures, but hope for a vote in 2003 appeared to fade, as the CNE has 30 days to validate a petition and then set a date for voting within 60 days.

A leading human rights group, Cofavic, warned that Venezuela's lax justice system was creating a climate of growing political violence. Noting that in the 12-month period ending April 2003, fifty-seven people were killed and more than 300 wounded by gunfire "in a context of political violence," it described an atmosphere of "total impunity" where aggressors are rarely brought to justice. In September, a judge upheld rebellion charges, punishable by a maximum 24-year prison sentence, against 13 civilians accused of participating in the 2002 military coup. The last half of 2003 was marked by a series of government social services initiatives, including urban health care and literacy programs supported by the Cuban government, that appeared to give Chavez a lift in popularity in the face of the potential presidential-recall referendum. The increase in political violence in the country came as a ferocious wave of common crimes continued unabated.

**Political Rights and Civil Liberties:** Citizens can change their government democratically, although supporters of President Hugo Chavez appear at times on the verge of mob rule, particularly as constitutional checks and balances have been removed. The July 2000 elections were considered by international observers to be free and fair. Under the constitution approved in 1961, the president and a bicameral congress are elected for five years. The Senate has at least two members from each of the 21 states and the federal district of Caracas. The Chamber of Deputies has 189 seats. A constitution adopted in 1999 strengthened the presidency and allowed Chavez to retain power until 2013.

On the national level, there are no independent government institutions. The military high command is loyal to a single person—the president—rather than to the constitution and the law. Chavez's party controls the National Assembly (though narrowly), as well as the Supreme Justice Tribunal (TSJ), whose members are elected by the National Assembly to a single 12-year term. It also controls the Citizen Power branch of government created to fight corruption by the 1999 constitution. This branch is made up of the offices of the ombudsman (responsible for compelling the government to adhere to the constitution and laws), the comptroller general (who controls the revenues and expenses incurred by the government and serves as the watchdog for the national patrimony), and the public prosecutor (who provides opinions to the courts on the prosecution of criminal cases and brings to the attention of the proper authorities cases of public employee misconduct and violations of the constitutional rights of prisoners or accused persons).

The Chavez government has done little to free the government from excessive bureaucratic regulations, registration requirements, and/or other forms of control that increase opportunities for corruption, relying instead on attacking persons and social sectors it considers to be corrupt and selectively enforcing good government laws and regulations against its opponents. In the past two years, the opposition has sued Chavez on charges that include misusing government stabilization funds to refusing to declare campaign funds from foreign sources. At the same time, Chavez's Plan Bolivar 2000 social programs were authorized to carry out their business in hard-to-audit cash transactions.

A 2003 study by the World Bank found that Venezuela has one of the most regulated economies in the world. New regulations and controls over the economy have ensured that public officials have retained the ample opportunities for personal enrichment enjoyed under the previous governments.

On a positive note, on April 7, 2003, the Law Against Corruption was put into effect. It establishes a citizen's right to know and sets out the state's obligations to give Venezuelans a thrice-yearly rendition of public goods and expenses, except those security and national defense expenditures as exempted by law. The law also requires most public employees to present a sworn declaration of personal assets within 30 days of assuming a post, as well as 30 days after leaving it; allows for the extradition of corrupt officials and their prohibition from holding office in the future; and includes a prohibition on officials having secret foreign bank accounts.

Venezuela's constitution provides for freedom of the press, and there are few blatant legal restrictions on media freedom. Both the print and broadcast media operated without restriction in 2003, and there are no journalists in prison as a result of their professional work. However, a climate of permanent intimidation and hostility against the press has been established in the past few years, in large part as a result of strong anti-media rhetoric by the government and a significant anti-Chavez slant on the part of media owners. The state allocates broadcast licenses in a biased fashion and engages in favoritism in the distribution of government advertising revenues.

In 2003, Chavez's government proposed several measures to tighten its control over opposition newspapers and television and radio stations, which would allow for a "selective censorship" of opposition media as the country moves toward a referendum on Chavez's presidency. These include a ban on the transmission of "violent" images and sounds from 7 A.M. to 7 P.M., a restriction that media owners say would force them to delay broadcasting news of street riots or terrorist attacks. The government does not restrict Internet access.

Freedom of religion, which the constitution guarantees on the condition that its practice not violate public morality, decency, or the public order, is generally respected by the government. Academic freedom traditionally is generally respected. However, government funding was withheld from the country's universities, and the rectors of those institutions charged that the government did so to punish them; all of the major public university rectors were elected on anti-government platforms.

Although professional and academic associations generally operate without official interference, the Supreme Court ruled in 2000 that NGOs that receive funding from foreign governments or whose leaders are not Venezuelan are not part of "civil society." As a result, they may not represent citizens in court or bring their own legal actions. However, the government has not moved to implement the court's decision. The president and his supporters have sought to break what they term a "stranglehold" of corrupt labor leaders on the job market, a move that labor activists say tramples on the rights of private organizations. Opposition and traditional labor leaders say that challenges by insurgent workers' organizations mask Chavez's intent to create government-controlled unions; the president's supporters maintain that the old labor regime amounted to little more than employer-controlled workers' organizations. Security forces frequently break up strikes and arrest trade unionists, allegedly under the guidance of Cuban security officials.

Until Chavez took power, the judicial system was headed by a nominally independent Supreme Court that was nevertheless highly politicized, undermined by the chronic corruption (including the growing influence of narcotics traffickers) that permeates the entire political system, and unresponsive to charges of rights abuses. An unwieldy new judicial code, which has helped to reduce the number of people jailed while awaiting arraignment, has hampered some law enforcement efforts, resulting in low rates of conviction and shorter jail terms even for convicted murderers. Police salaries are woefully inadequate.

Widespread arbitrary detention and torture of suspects, as well as dozens of extrajudicial killings by the often-corrupt military security forces and the police, have increased as crime continues to soar. Since the 1992 coup attempts, weakened civilian governments have had less authority over the military and the police, and overall rights abuses are committed with impunity.

Since Chavez's election, Venezuela's military, which is largely unaccountable to civilian rule, has become an active participant in the country's social development and delivery of public services. The 1999 constitution assigns the armed forces a significant role in the state but does not provide for civilian control over the military's budget, procurement practices, or related institutional checks. A separate system of armed forces courts retains jurisdiction over members of the military accused of rights violations and common criminal crimes, and decisions cannot be appealed in civilian court.

Venezuela's indigenous peoples number approximately 316,000 people belonging to 27 ethnic groups. The formal rights of Venezuela's Native Americans have improved under Chavez, although those rights, specifically the groups' ability to make decisions affecting their lands, cultures, traditions, and allocation of natural resources, are seldom enforced, as local political authorities rarely take their interests into account. Indigenous communities typically face deforestation and water pollution. Few Indians hold title to their land; many say that they do not want to, as they reject market concepts of individual property, preferring instead that the government recognize those lands traditionally held by them as native territories. At the same time, indigenous communities trying to defend their legal land rights are subject to abuses, including murder, by gold miners and corrupt rural police. The constitution creates three seats in the National Assembly for indigenous people and also provides for "the protection of indigenous communities and their progressive incorporation into the life of the nation." In the July 2000 national elections, in addition to the three indigenous candidates elected to the National Assembly, eight were elected to regional legislative congresses and four Indians won mayoralties. The lack of effective legal rights, however, has created an unprecedented migration by Indians to poverty-stricken urban areas.

Women are more active in politics than in many other Latin American countries and comprise the backbone of Venezuela's sophisticated grassroots network of nongovernmental organizations.

# Vietnam

**Population:** 80,800,000 **Political Rights:** 7
**GNI/capita:** $410 **Civil Liberties:** 6
**Life Expectancy:** 72 **Status:** Not Free
**Religious Groups:** Buddhist, Hoa Hao, Cao Dai, Christian, indigenous beliefs, Muslim
**Ethnic Groups:** Vietnamese (85-90 percent), other [including Chinese, Muong, Thai, Meo, Khmer, Man, and Cham] (10-15 percent)
**Capital:** Hanoi

## Ten-Year Ratings Timeline (Political Rights, Civil Liberties, Status)

| 1994 | 1995 | 1996 | 1997 | 1998 | 1999 | 2000 | 2001 | 2002 | 2003 |
|------|------|------|------|------|------|------|------|------|------|
| 7,7NF | 7,7NF | 7,7NF | 7,7NF | 7,7NF | 7,7NF | 7,6NF | 7,6NF | 7,6NF | 7,6NF |

**Overview:**
Vietnam's authoritarian rulers continued in 2003 a crackdown, begun two years earlier, that has seen dozens of religious and political dissidents detained or jailed. Many are ethnic minorities from the Central Highlands region who protested for greater religious freedom or tried to flee to Cambodia. Authorities have also targeted urban intellectuals who used the Internet to call for political reforms or share information with overseas Vietnamese.

Vietnam won independence from France in 1954 after a century of colonial rule followed by occupation by the Japanese during World War II. At independence, the country was divided into the Western-backed Republic of South Vietnam and the Communist-ruled Democratic Republic of Vietnam in the north. Following a decade-long war that killed tens of thousands of soldiers and civilians, North Vietnam defeated the U.S.-backed South in 1975 and reunited the country in 1976.

Victorious on the battlefield, the Communist government proved unable to feed its people. The centralized economy grew at anemic rates, and fertile Vietnam had to import rice. The government responded with reforms in 1986 that dismantled collectivized farms and encouraged small-scale private enterprise. Spurred by the reforms, Vietnam's economy grew by 7.6 percent a year on average, and output doubled between 1991 and 2000, according to World Bank figures. The Southeast Asian nation is now the world's second-biggest rice exporter.

The Communist Party of Vietnam (CPV) in 2001 signaled its intent to continue market reforms, but at a gradual pace, when it tapped as its new party leader Nong Duc Manh, now 62, who is known for stressing pragmatism over ideology. In choosing

Manh, a northerner, and then in 2002 reelecting Prime Minister Phan Van Khai and state President Tran Duc Luong, the party also preserved the leadership troika's traditional balance between northern, central, and southern Vietnam.

While economic liberalization has muddled along, political reforms have been ruled out entirely, as evidenced by Vietnam's May 2002 parliamentary elections. The CPV vetted all candidates for the 498-seat body, and the number of nonparty lawmakers shrank to 51 from 68.

The government's latest crackdown on dissent began in 2001 after several thousand mainly Christian hill tribesmen held protests in the Central Highlands demanding greater religious freedom, increased land rights, and political autonomy for the region. More than 70 hill tribesmen, known as Montagnards, are serving lengthy prison terms for participating in protests or trying to flee to Cambodia, according to the New York–based Human Rights Watch. The organization released what it said were letters by church leaders in Dak Lak province detailing recent rights violations by officials, including beatings of church leaders, destruction of churches, and widespread confiscation of villagers' farmland. Hill tribesmen routinely complain that their lands increasingly are being converted by lowland Vietnamese into plantations for coffee and other cash crops.

Meanwhile, urban intellectuals seeking political reforms continued to be arrested, sentenced to long jail terms, placed under house arrest, or otherwise harassed by Vietnamese authorities.

Vietnam's leadership continues to be divided over the pace and depth of privatization and other market reforms. Moderates see deep-rooted reforms as the ticket to modernizing the impoverished country and creating enough jobs to stave off social unrest. Hard-liners, though, fear that further loosening the state's control over the economy will undermine the tight grip on power held by the ruling CPV. They realize that farmers, who now work for themselves, and other private sector workers cannot be monitored as easily as those who depend on the state for their livelihood. Moreover, while the government has sold off thousands of small firms, privatization of large companies would very likely throw millions out of work, possibly leading to a social backlash.

**Political Rights and Civil Liberties:** Ruled by the Communist Party of Vietnam (CPV) as a single-party state, Vietnam is one of the most tightly controlled countries in the world. The CPV's powerful Central Committee is the peak decision-making body in Vietnam, and the National Assembly generally follows the party's dictates when it comes to passing laws. Assembly delegates, however, influence legislation, question state ministers, air grassroots grievances, and, within limits set by the party, debate legal, social, and economic matters. They also regularly criticize officials' performance and governmental corruption and inefficiency. The party-controlled Fatherland Front, however, vets all assembly candidates and allows only CPV cadres and some independents to run.

Eager to portray itself as representing the masses, the regime not only allows the National Assembly to be used as an outlet for grassroots complaints, but also has tried to address bread-and-butter concerns with a 1998 decree that directs local officials to consult more with ordinary Vietnamese. In many provinces, however, complaints by villagers reportedly get bogged down in the bureaucracy.

The leadership increasingly also allows farmers and others to hold small protests over local grievances, which often concern land seizures. Thousands of Vietnamese also try to gain redress each year by writing letters to or personally addressing officials. In addition to land matters, citizens complain about official corruption, economic policies, government inefficiency, and opaque bureaucratic procedures. In an October speech to the National Assembly, Deputy Prime Minister Nguyen Tan Dung acknowledged "public discontent" with officials, "especially due to corruption, wastefulness, embezzlement of state property, harassment of people, dishonesty, fraud, and weak discipline."

The government made a show of addressing these concerns in 2003 in Vietnam's largest-ever corruption case, which involved an organized-crime empire in the south. The three-month trial of 155 officials and organized-crime figures ended in June with 16 officials receiving prison terms for taking bribes and other offenses and a southern gang leader and five of his cronies sentenced to death for murder and other gangland-related crimes. The Berlin-based Transparency International's 2003 Corruption Perceptions Index ranked Vietnam in a six-way tie for 100th place out of 133 countries rated.

All media in Vietnam are tightly controlled by the party and government. Officials have punished journalists who overstepped the bounds of permissible reporting by jailing or placing them under house arrest, taking away their press cards, or closing down their newspapers. The media also are kept in check by a 1999 law that requires journalists to pay damages to groups or individuals that are found to be harmed by press articles, even if the reports are accurate. At least one suit has been filed under this law, although it was withdrawn. While journalists cannot report on sensitive political or economic matters or openly question the CPV's single-party rule, they sometimes are allowed to report on high-level governmental corruption and mismanagement.

The regime tightened its control over Internet use in May by formally banning Vietnamese from receiving or distributing antigovernment e-mail messages and by setting up a special body to monitor Internet communications and prosecute violators. The government also requires owners of domestic Web sites to submit their Web site content to the government for approval. Authorities also block nearly 2,000 Internet Web sites, according to the Paris-based Reporters Sans Frontieres.

The regime sharply restricts religious freedom by regulating religious organizations and clergy and cracking down on independent religious groups and their leaders. All religious groups and most individual clergy must join a party-controlled supervisory body, one of which exists for each religion that the state recognizes— Buddhism; Roman Catholicism; Protestantism; Islam; Cao Daiism, a synthesis of several religions; and the Hoa Hao faith, a reformist Buddhist church. Besides registering, religious groups must get permission to build or refurbish places of worship; run religious schools or do charitable work; hold conventions, training seminars, and special celebrations; and train, ordain, promote, or transfer clergy.

As a result of these regulations, religious groups generally have trouble expanding schools, obtaining teaching materials, publishing religious texts, and increasing the number of students training for the clergy. Cao Daiists have largely been barred since 1975 from ordaining new priests, although some new priests recently have been ordained, while Protestants are generally prohibited from training new clergy.

In a positive development in this area, officials in January agreed to allow Protestants in southern Vietnam to reopen a long-closed seminary, according to Compass Direct, a U.S.-based news service that reports on persecution of Christians. Meanwhile, the government effectively maintains veto power over Vatican appointments of Roman Catholic bishops in Vietnam.

The regulations particularly affect groups that are unable or unwilling to obtain official recognition, including some Buddhist and Hoa Hao religious bodies from the former South Vietnam and underground Protestant house churches. Unregistered groups are considered illegal and often face harassment. For years, the government has tried to undermine the independent Unified Buddhist Church of Vietnam (UBCV). Officials have released several prominent UBCV monks in recent years, but continue to harass church members. Buddhists make up three-quarters of Vietnam's population, although it is not known how many belong to the UBCV.

Amnesty International said in 2002 that several members of the Hoa Hao faith recently had been jailed on charges that the London-based rights group believes are linked solely to their religious practices. Ethnic minority, underground Protestant worshippers in the Central Highlands and northwestern provinces also face severe abuses. Local officials in some provinces reportedly at times jail worshippers, forbid Protestant gatherings, withhold government food rations from believers, and bar children of Protestant families from attending school beyond the third grade.

Vietnamese officials reportedly launched a new campaign in February to convince ethnic minority Protestants in at least some northwestern provinces to renounce their faith, providing incentives such as money or goods to those who abandon their religion. Hmong and other ethnic minority Protestants, particularly in the northern provinces of Lao Cai and Lai Chau and in the Central Highlands, have complained for years that they are at times jailed, harassed, or otherwise pressured by local officials to abandon their religious faith. At the same time, unregistered religious groups in some parts of Vietnam are allowed to worship with little or no interference.

Academic freedom is limited, as university professors must stick to party views when teaching or writing on political topics.

Despite the many restrictions on their rights, ordinary Vietnamese, particularly those living in Hanoi and Ho Chi Minh City, increasingly are free of government intrusion into their daily lives. The regime continues to rely on informers, block wardens, and a household registration system to keep tabs on individuals, but this surveillance is now directed mainly at known dissidents rather than the entire population.

Human rights organizations and other private groups with rights-oriented agendas are banned. Trade unions remain state controlled, although hundreds of independent "labor associations" are permitted to represent many workers at individual firms and in some service industries. In any case, the vast majority of Vietnamese workers are small-scale farmers in rural areas who are not unionized in any way. Enforcement of child labor, workplace safety, and other labor laws is poor. Workers frequently have taken matters into their own hands, staging dozens of strikes in recent years, generally against foreign and private companies.

Vietnam's judiciary is subservient to the CPV with the party closely controlling the courts at all levels and exerting strong influence over political and other high-profile cases. According to Amnesty International, even in ordinary criminal cases, defendants often lack sufficient time to meet with their lawyers and to prepare and present an adequate defense. Defense lawyers cannot call or question witnesses and sometimes are permitted only to appeal for leniency for their clients. While defendants have a constitutional right to counsel, Vietnam's scarcity of lawyers often makes this right impossible to enforce. Moreover, many lawyers reportedly are reluctant to take human rights and other sensitive cases because they fear that later they will be hit with sudden tax audits or otherwise harassed.

Police at times beat suspects and detainees. Vietnamese jails tend to be overcrowded and provide inmates with insufficient food and poor sanitation. Inmates generally are required to work, but receive little or no wages. Amnesty International said in 2002 that it had documented dozens of cases of Vietnamese prisoners who were denied adequate medical care, shackled as a form of punishment, or held in solitary confinement for long periods.

The death penalty is applied mainly for violent crimes, but sometimes also against Vietnamese convicted of nonviolent crimes, including economic and drug-related offenses. Of the 931 people sentenced to death between 1997 and 2002, for example, 310 were convicted of offenses involving illegal narcotics, according to official statistics. It is not clear how many of these sentences actually have been carried out.

While the government has long cracked down on dissent, the actual number of political prisoners is unknown. The latest crackdown has targeted, among others, Vietnamese who use the Internet to criticize the government or share information with overseas Vietnamese groups. Since 2001, at least 10 Vietnamese Internet dissidents have been arrested, with 6 of them sentenced to long jail terms after unfair trials, Amnesty International said in November. They include Pham Hong Son, who was sentenced in June to 13 years in prison on espionage charges. He was arrested after sending an article on democracy to friends and senior party cadres. Authorities in early 2003 also arrested and beat some of the more than 100 Montagnards who recently were forcibly returned to Vietnam after crossing into Cambodia, Human Rights Watch said in March. The government denies holding any prisoners on political grounds.

In addition to facing restrictions on religious freedom, Vietnam's ethnic minorities face unofficial discrimination in mainstream society, and local officials reportedly sometimes restrict minority access to schooling and jobs. Minorities also generally have little input into development projects that affect their livelihoods and communities.

Vietnamese women increasingly work in universities, the civil service, and the private sector, though in the latter they continue to face unofficial discrimination in wages and promotion. Many women reportedly are victims of domestic violence. Despite some governmental initiatives to protect women, trafficking of women and girls, both within Vietnam and to China, Cambodia, and other countries, continues unabated.

# Yemen

**Population:** 19,400,000  **Political Rights:** 5*
**GNI/capita:** $450  **Civil Liberties:** 5
**Life Expectancy:** 60  **Status:** Partly Free
**Religious Groups:** Muslim [including Sunni and Shi'a],
other
**Ethnic Groups:** Arab [majority], Afro-Arab, South Asian
**Capital:** Sanaa
**Ratings Change:** Yemen's political rights rating improved from 6 to 5, and its status from Not Free to Partly Free, due to the holding of parliamentary elections that were legitimate but flawed.

**Ten-Year Ratings Timeline (Political Rights, Civil Liberties, Status)**

| 1994 | 1995 | 1996 | 1997 | 1998 | 1999 | 2000 | 2001 | 2002 | 2003 |
|------|------|------|------|------|------|------|------|------|------|
| 5,6NF | 5,6NF | 5,6NF | 5,6NF | 5,6NF | 5,6NF | 5,6NF | 6,6NF | 6,5NF | 5,5PF |

**Overview:**

Yemen took a small step forward in improving the mechanisms and structures for continuing its transition to democracy in 2003 by holding parliamentary elections. However, the ruling party's lack of confidence in its own ability to compete in a fully democratic system impeded more substantial progress. The status of detainees held incommunicado remained an issue of concern during the year.

As part of the ancient Minaean, Sabaean, and Himyarite kingdoms, Yemen has a long history stretching back nearly three thousand years. For centuries, a series of imams controlled most of northern Yemen and parts of southern Yemen. The Ottoman Empire ruled many of the cities from the sixteenth to the nineteenth century, and the British Empire controlled areas in the southern part of the country in the first part of the twentieth century, including the port of Aden. Yemen was divided into two countries, the Yemen Arab Republic of the north and the People's Republic of South Yemen, which ultimately unified in 1990 after decades of conflict and tensions.

In the face of widespread poverty and illiteracy, tribal influences that limit the central government's authority in certain parts of the country, a heavily armed citizenry, and the threat of radical Islamist terrorism, Yemen has managed to take some limited steps to improve its record on political rights and civil liberties in the 13 years since its unification.

In 1999, President Ali Abdullah Saleh won a five-year term in the country's first nationwide direct presidential election, gaining 96.3 percent of the vote. Saleh's only opponent came from within the ruling General People's Congress (GPC), and his term in office was extended from five to seven years in a 2001 referendum.

Yemen's April 2003 parliamentary election, its third in the last decade, took place despite concerns that popular unrest resulting from the war in Iraq might lead to a postponement. International election observers noted that Yemen had made substantial improvements in electoral management and administration. On the surface, the elections were competitive with the opposition Islah Party taking seats in constituencies that were former strongholds of the ruling party. However, there were numerous problems with the election. Voter registration was characterized by widespread fraud and cheating, and underage voting was a widespread problem. Rather than opening the door for increased political pluralism, Yemen's parliamentary election was a missed opportunity, marred by cheating on the part of all major political parties and by reports of intimidation, use of state resources, and control of certain media outlets by the ruling party.

In addition to the parliamentary elections, another leading story in Yemen in 2003 was the continued incommunicado detention of individuals suspected of having ties to Islamic extremist groups such as al-Qaeda. Authorities in the government estimated the number of detainees at 200 to 300 individuals. The minister of the interior told parliament that a number of these individuals had been released because they had changed their views, while others remained in detention because they still held on to their militant views. Some of the releases were part of an Islamically oriented approach to rehabilitation, begun when President Saleh asked Judge Hamood Al-Hitar to form a "Dialogue Committee" to persuade fundamentalists to renounce violence and their fanatical views.

**Political Rights and Civil Liberties:** Citizens of Yemen cannot change their government democratically. Yemen is a republic headed by a popularly elected president, with a bicameral parliament composed of a 301-seat popularly elected House of Representatives and an 111-member Majlis Al-Shura or Consultative Council appointed by the president. The House of Representatives has legislative authority, and the Majlis Al-Shura serves in an advisory capacity.

Yemen is one of the few countries in the Arab world to organize regular elections on national and local levels, with limited competition among the ruling GPC party; two main opposition parties, Islah and the Yemeni Socialist Party (YSP); and a handful of other parties. On the surface level, Yemen appears to have a relatively open democratic system. In reality, Yemen's politics are monopolized by the ruling party, the GPC, which has increased the number of parliament seats it holds from 145 in 1993 to 237 in the current parliament.

Yemen's government suffers from the absence of any real system of checks and balances of power and any significant limits on the executive's authority. Although local council members are popularly elected—the most recent local election was held in 2001—President Ali Abdullah Saleh appoints all local council chairpersons, who wield most of the decision-making authority.

Corruption is an endemic problem at all levels of government and society. Despite recent efforts by the government to step up efforts to fight corruption and institute a civil service reform program, Yemen lacks most legal safeguards to protect against conflicts of interest. Chief auditing and investigative bodies charged with fighting corruption are not sufficiently independent of the executive authorities.

Article 103 of the Press and Publications Law outlaws direct personal criticism of the head of state and publication of material that "might spread a spirit of dissent and division among the people" or "leads to the spread of ideas contrary to the principles of the Yemeni Revolution, [is] prejudicial to national unity or [distorts] the image of the Yemeni, Arab, or Islamic heritage." Although newspapers have some degree of freedom, the print media do not seem to have a strong impact across much of society, which has a high rate of illiteracy, estimated at 54 percent. The state maintains a monopoly over the media that matter the most—television and radio. Access to the Internet is not widespread, and the government reportedly blocks Web sites it deems offensive.

Article 2 of the constitution states that Islam is the religion of state, and Article 3 declares Sharia (Islamic law) to be the source of all legislation. Yemen has few religious minority groups, and their rights are generally respected in practice. Strong politicization of campus life, including tensions between the ruling GPC and opposition Islah parties, places limits on academic freedom.

Yemenis have the right to form associations, according to Article 58 of the constitution. Yemen has several thousand nongovernmental organizations, although some observers question the viability and independence these organizations. The government respects the right to form and join trade unions, but some critics claim that the government and ruling party elements have stepped up efforts to control the affairs of these organizations.

The judiciary is nominally independent, but in practice it is weak and susceptible to interference from the executive branch. Government authorities have a spotty record of enforcing judicial rulings, particularly those issued against prominent tribal or political leaders. The lack of a truly independent judiciary impedes progress in all aspects of democracy and good governance; without an independent arbiter for disputes, people often resort to tribal forms of justice or direct appeals to the executive branch of government.

Arbitrary detention occurs, sometimes because of a lack of proper training of law enforcement officials, and at other times because of a lack of political will at the most senior levels of government. One prominent example of the latter from 2003 was the arrest inside the presidential building and detention without charge of members of the Jahm tribe. The Jahm tribal leaders reportedly had a dispute with officials while in the presidential office, and they were subsequently detained, initially in a military prison. They were ultimately released after mediation from another tribal leader, not because of any procedure related to the courts or the rule of law.

Yemen is relatively homogenous ethnically and racially. The Akhdam, a small minority group, lives in poverty and faces social discrimination.

Women are afforded most legal protections against discrimination and provided with guarantees of equality. In practice, women continue to face pervasive discrimination in several aspects of life. Women are vastly under-represented in elected office. Despite the best efforts of women's rights groups to increase the number of women in parliament, only one woman won a seat in the 2003 parliamentary elections, out of 301 total seats. At the local government level, women won only 38 seats out of 6,676 in the 2001 local elections. The number of women registered to vote increased nearly sevenfold in the past decade, from half a million in the 1993 parliamentary elections to more than three million in the 2003 parliamentary elections.

A woman who seeks to travel abroad must obtain permission from her husband or fathers to receive a passport and travel. A woman does not have the right to confer citizenship on her foreign-born spouses, and the process of obtaining Yemeni citizenship for a child of a Yemeni mother and a foreign-born father is in practice more difficult than that for a child born of a Yemeni father and a foreign-born mother.

# ↑ Zambia

**Population:** 10,900,000　**Political Rights:** 4
**GNI/capita:** $320　**Civil Liberties:** 4
**Life Expectancy:** 41　**Status:** Partly Free
**Religious Groups:** Christian (50-75 percent),
Muslim and Hindu (24-49 percent), indigenous
beliefs (1 percent)
**Ethnic Groups:** African (99 percent), other
[including European] (1 percent)
**Capital:** Lusaka
**Trend Arrow:** Zambia received an upward trend arrow due to the formal inclusion of
civil society groups in the country's constitutional review process and the president's
aggressive efforts to root out government corruption.

**Ten-Year Ratings Timeline (Political Rights, Civil Liberties, Status)**

| 1994 | 1995 | 1996 | 1997 | 1998 | 1999 | 2000 | 2001 | 2002 | 2003 |
|------|------|------|------|------|------|------|------|------|------|
| 3,4PF | 3,4PF | 5,4PF | 5,4PF | 5,4PF | 5,4PF | 5,4PF | 5,4PF | 4,4PF | 4,4PF |

**Overview:**　The legitimacy of Zambian President Levy Mwanawasa's
2001 electoral victory remained under scrutiny in 2003, with
some 80 witnesses testifying about voting irregularities in
a petition to the country's High Court by three of the losing candidates to recount
the votes. The results of September parliamentary by-elections, which increased the
number of seats held by the ruling Movement for Multiparty Democracy (MMD),
were rejected by the main opposition party, which also boycotted a national conference on constitutional reform.

President Kenneth Kaunda and the United National Independence Party (UNIP)
ruled Zambia from independence from Britain in 1964 until the transition to a
multiparty system in 1991. Kaunda's regime grew increasingly repressive and
corrupt as it faced security and economic difficulties during the long guerrilla wars against
white rule in neighboring Rhodesia (now Zimbabwe) and Portuguese-controlled
Mozambique. UNIP's socialist policies, combined with a crash in the price of copper,
Zambia's main export, precipitated an economic decline unchecked for two decades.

In the face of domestic unrest and international pressure, Kaunda permitted free
elections in 1991. Former labor leader Frederick Chiluba and his MMD won convincingly. By contrast, the November 1996 presidential and parliamentary polls lacked
legitimacy, largely because of a series of repressive measures instituted by the government. State resources and media were mobilized extensively to support Chiluba
and the ruling MMD, and serious irregularities plagued election preparations. Voter
lists were incomplete or otherwise suspect; independent monitors estimated that
more than two million people were effectively disenfranchised. Candidate eligibility
requirements were changed, which resulted in the exclusion of Kaunda, the most
credible opposition candidate. Most opposition parties boycotted the polls, in which
the MMD renewed its parliamentary dominance. International observer groups that
did monitor the polls, along with independent domestic monitors and opposition
parties, declared the process and the results to be fraudulent.

Prior to the December 2001 presidential elections, President Chiluba supported a move within his party to change the constitution so that he could run for a third term. Dissension within his party, the opposition, and civil society forced him to back off from that plan. Instead, the MMD nominated Mwanawasa, who narrowly won the vote by only 29 percent against a divided opposition. Both domestic and international election monitors cited serious irregularities with the campaign and election. President Mwanawasa must now defend his victory before the country's High Court, but it is unlikely that a ruling will come in time to affect his current term in office. During concurrent parliamentary elections, the MMD captured 69 seats out of 150 elected members.

A motion by opposition legislators to impeach Mwanawasa on charges of graft and nepotism was defeated in August 2003. Although widely perceived as former president Chiluba's handpicked candidate, Mwanawasa has backed wide-ranging legal inquiries into alleged corruption by Chiluba and his senior associates while they were in power. Meanwhile, hotly contested by-elections in September increased the number of seats held by the MMD to 75. The main opposition party rejected the results.

Under pressure to introduce electoral reforms and to allow a constituent assembly to draft a new constitution, Mwanawasa organized a national conference in October that drew more than 600 delegates. However, the country's main opposition parties boycotted the forum, and the press was barred from covering the deliberations. The government had originally sought to steer the reform process through a handpicked Constitutional Review Commission, but agreed to a more representative and transparent process after intense criticism from civil society groups.

Zambia's privatization program slowed in 2003, after the government sold off 257 state-owned companies out of 280 enterprises earmarked for privatization since the mid-1990s. Some of these deals, especially in the mining sector, have allegedly involved significant corruption. Relations deteriorated with the IMF and foreign donors in 2003 because of a $125 million budget deficit, although the country has continued to receive limited debt relief from the World Bank. New business formation is slowed by the country's weak financial structures.

The country is among those suffering most from the AIDS pandemic; government figures indicate that Zambia already has more than 700,000 AIDS orphans. UNAIDS estimated infection rates in 2002 at 21.5 percent.

**Political Rights and Civil Liberties:** The ability of Zambians to change their government democratically is not yet consolidated. While Zambians' constitutional right to change their government freely was honored in the 1991 elections, both the 1996 and 2001 elections won by the ruling MMD were subjects of intense controversy. President Levy Mwanawasa, who was reprimanded by Acting Chief Justice Ernest Sakala in 2002 for intimidating witnesses during the 2001 presidential election, has said he intends to drag the case out until the next election. Zambia's president and parliament are elected to serve concurrent five-year terms. The National Assembly includes 150 elected members, as well as 8 members appointed by the president and the speaker of the house.

High levels of corruption have burdened development, although President Mwanawasa has taken the initiative in rooting out state graft. He earned praise for banning cabinet ministers and senior officials from bidding on government contracts and for sacking his own vice president, Enoch Kavindele, for involvement in an irregular oil contract. Zambia ranked 92 out of 133 countries on Transparency International's 2003 Corruption Perceptions Index.

The government dominates broadcasting, although an independent radio station, Radio Phoenix, presents nongovernmental views. The Public Order Act, among other statutes, has at times been used to harass and intimidate journalists. In November, police raided the offices of the privately owned Omega television station in the capital and ordered it to cease broadcasting, following a dispute over the station's license. Other tools of harassment have included criminal libel suits and defamation suits brought by MMD leaders in response to stories on corruption. Reporters Sans Frontieres ranked Zambia 86 out of 166 countries in a 2003 study of press freedom.

The independent media supported the 2002 introduction into parliament of the Freedom of Information, Broadcasting, and Independent Broadcasting Authority draft legislation. The law aims to facilitate easier access to information held by government and quasi-governmental organs, transform the state-owned and government-controlled Zambia National Broadcasting Corporation (ZNBC) from a government propaganda organ to a public broadcaster, and establish an independent regulator to regulate broadcasting. However, in November 2002, Vice President Kavindele abruptly withdrew the bill, citing global security concerns after the September 11, 2001, terrorist attacks in the United States. The government does not restrict access to the Internet.

Constitutionally protected religious freedom has been respected in practice. The government does not restrict academic freedom.

Nongovernmental organizations (NGOs) engaged in human rights promotion, such as the Zambian Independent Monitoring Team, the Zambian Civic Education Association, and the Law Association of Zambia, operate openly. In 1999, however, the government drafted a policy that would closely regulate NGOs.

Zambia's trade unions remain among Africa's strongest, and union rights are constitutionally guaranteed. The Zambia Congress of Trade Unions, an umbrella for Zambia's 19 largest unions, operates democratically without governmental interference. The 1993 Industrial and Labor Relations Act protects collective bargaining rights, and unions negotiate directly with employers. About two-thirds of the country's 300,000 formal (business) sector employees are union members.

The judicial system, which has at times been subject to political influence, is under considerable pressure, with several high-level cases pending. In February, Chiluba was formally charged with theft of state funds during his tenure as president, having lost his immunity from prosecution the year before. His trial, on 168 counts of theft related to an overseas bank account, is set to begin in early December. Four other officials face similar charges.

The court system is severely overburdened. Pretrial detainees are sometimes held for years under harsh conditions before their cases reach trial. The Magistrates and Judges Association identified congestion in prisons and delayed trials as extremely serious problems; malnourishment and poor health care in prisons cause many deaths. More than 200 people were on death row in Zambia awaiting execution in 2001, according to Amnesty International. In 1997, eight people were executed, and between 1998 and 2000, at least 97 people were sentenced to death. Customary courts of variable quality and consistency, whose decisions often conflict with both national law and constitutional protections, decide many civil matters. The government human rights commission investigated frequent complaints about police brutality and denounced the torture of coup suspects, but has no power to bring charges against alleged perpetrators.

Societal discrimination remains a serious obstacle to women's rights. A 1998 regional human development report noted that Zambia was one of the lowest-performing countries in southern Africa in terms of women's empowerment. Women are denied full economic participation and are discriminated against in rural land allocation. A married woman must have her husband's permission to obtain contraceptives. Discrimination against women is especially prevalent in traditional tribunals that are courts of first instance in most rural areas. Spousal abuse and other violence against women are reportedly common. Following a report by Human Rights Watch on the sexual abuse of women and girls and its role in the spread of HIV/AIDS, President Mwanawasa promised in 2003 to create a government program to combat gender-based violence.

# ⬇ Zimbabwe

**Population:** 12,600,000
**GNI/capita:** $480
**Life Expectancy:** 41
**Religious Groups:** Christian (25 percent), indigenous beliefs (24 percent), other [including Muslim] 51 percent
**Ethnic Groups:** Shona (82 percent), Ndebele (14 percent), other (4 percent)
**Capital:** Harare

**Political Rights:** 6
**Civil Liberties:** 6
**Status:** Not Free

**Trend Arrow:** Zimbabwe received a downward trend arrow due to government repression of political opponents, civil society activists, and independent media representatives.

**Ten-Year Ratings Timeline (Political Rights, Civil Liberties, Status)**

| 1994 | 1995 | 1996 | 1997 | 1998 | 1999 | 2000 | 2001 | 2002 | 2003 |
|------|------|------|------|------|------|------|------|------|------|
| 5,5PF | 5,5PF | 5,5PF | 5,5PF | 5,5PF | 6,5PF | 6,5PF | 6,6NF | 6,6NF | 6,6NF |

**Overview:**

Zimbabwe in 2003 descended into further crisis as the authoritarian government of President Robert Mugabe continued to quash dissent. Economic collapse deepened and food shortages increased along with increasingly rampant corruption, as the government proceeded with its ruinous policy of moving white farmers off commercial lands. A series of strikes called by opponents and trade unions generated harsh government retaliation. Mass arrests, sustained attacks, and severe restrictions were harnessed against opposition members, independent media, and civic organizations.

Zimbabwe gained independence in 1980 after a guerrilla war against a white-minority regime that had declared unilateral independence from Britain in 1965 in what was then Southern Rhodesia; Mugabe has ruled the country since then. For a few years, Zimbabwe was relatively stable, although from 1983 to 1987, the government suppressed resistance from the country's largest minority group, the Ndebele, to dominance by Mugabe's majority ethnic Shona group. Severe human rights abuses accompanied the struggle, which ended with an accord that brought Ndebele leaders into the government.

The 2000 parliamentary elections, in which 57 members of the opposition Movement for Democratic Change (MDC) were elected out of a total of 150 seats, were deemed by observers to be fundamentally flawed prior to balloting. MDC candidates and supporters faced violence and intimidation, and a constitutional provision empowering Mugabe and allied traditional leaders to appoint one-fifth of parliament's members helped to ensure the ruling Zimbabwe African National Union-Patriotic Front's (ZANU-PF) continued majority in parliament. Voter registration and identification procedures and tabulation of results were judged by independent observers in some constituencies to have been highly irregular. The heavily state-controlled media offered limited coverage of opposition viewpoints, and ZANU-PF used state resources heavily in campaigning.

Mugabe issued a pardon for thousands of people, most from ZANU-PF, for crimes committed during the election campaign, including assault, arson, kidnapping, torture, and attempted murder. According to the Zimbabwe Human Rights Forum, the rights of more than 18,000 people were violated, and more than 90 percent of the alleged perpetrators were ZANU-PF supporters or government officials.

Mugabe claimed victory in a deeply flawed 2002 presidential election that failed to meet minimum international standards for legitimacy, although a number of African leaders refused to condemn the elections. The election pitted Mugabe against the MDC's Morgan Tsvangirai, a popular trade union leader who was arrested and charged with treason in 2003 after organizing national strikes.

Parliamentary by-elections held in 2003 in two districts near the capital, Highfield and Kuwadzanaw, were marred by intimidation of the MDC, which nonetheless won the polls. Party members were prevented from undertaking normal campaign activities and were detained, beaten, and harassed.

In recent years, Mugabe has turned against student groups, labor unions, and white landowners to create the country's worst crisis since independence. War veterans and youth militias continued in 2003 to occupy and disrupt opposition strongholds and white-owned land, with the overt or complicit backing of the government. The government harshly retaliated against a series of national stay-aways and strikes organized by the MDC and trade unions during the year.

An estimated 400 white-owned farms remain out of the 4,500 that existed when land invasions began in 2000. The land reform has destroyed commercial farming, on which exports, foreign exchange, and 400,000 jobs had depended. Unemployment exceeds 70 percent, and inflation, which was at an annual rate of 32 percent in 1998, raged at nearly 600 percent in 2003. Aid agencies have warned that nearly half of Zimbabwe's 12 million people need emergency food aid, largely because of faults in the redistribution policy. Party officials handling distribution have manipulated food aid that arrives, withholding relief from suspected opposition supporters.

Zimbabwe is in arrears to internal and external creditors, which has led to suspension of disbursements and credit lines. This situation has created shortages of key imports, such as fuel. Concern about the land-reform program was one reason that the IMF suspended its financial support to Zimbabwe.

**Political Rights and Civil Liberties:** Zimbabweans cannot change their government democratically. President Robert Mugabe and the ZANU-PF, which have dominated the country's political landscape since independence, enjoy wide incumbency advantages that enhance their ability to manipulate political structures to ensure continued control. Although the grip of the ZANU-PF on parliament has weakened in recent years, the party remains the predominant power through its control over the security forces, the media, and much of the economy. Since 1987, there have been at least 15 amendments to the constitution by the ZANU-PF—including scrapping the post of prime minister in favor of an executive president and abolishing the upper chamber of parliament, the Senate—that have given the government, and particularly members of the executive, more power. In turn, popular opposition to Mugabe has deepened, with trade unions often at the forefront, while the opposition MDC has experienced rapid growth.

The year 2003 saw increased activity by ZANU-PF youth militias, which have disrupted meetings and campaigning by opposition members. Political violence prevalent in the countryside has increasingly spread to urban areas as security forces target church leaders and civic organizations, according to the New York based Human Rights Watch. Mugabe has on several occasions invoked the Presidential Powers Act, which enables him to bypass normal governmental review and oversight procedures.

Corruption is rampant. Much of the seized land has gone to ZANU-PF officials, who often have no farming background, instead of the landless black Zimbabweans who were supposed to benefit.

Freedom of the press is severely restricted. There are no privately owned radio or television stations in Zimbabwe, and the state-controlled newspapers and radio and television stations are seen as mouthpieces of the government and provide negative coverage of opposition activities. The Parliamentary Privileges and Immunities Act has been used to force journalists to reveal their sources regarding reports on corruption before the courts and parliament. Internet access is limited but growing.

The 2002 Access to Information and Protection of Privacy Act (AIPPA), which gives the information minister sweeping powers to decide who can work as a journalist in Zimbabwe, has been used to silence media critics of the government. AIPPA created a governmental commission that hands out "licenses" allowing journalists to work, and those operating without a license face fines or prison. Authorities in September closed down the one independent daily newspaper, *The Daily News*, which had been harshly critical of Mugabe, for failing to register for an AIPPA license. A subsequent application for a license was rejected, and five of the newspaper's directors were arrested. Several other Zimbabwean journalists were assaulted or detained in 2003. Foreign reporters face difficulty gaining approval to work in the country and are allowed to stay for only a short time when approval is granted. An American journalist who had worked in the country for 23 years was expelled in May, even though his deportation order was awaiting a Supreme Court hearing.

Freedom of religion is generally respected, but academic freedom is limited.

There is a small, though active, nongovernmental (NGO) sector. Several groups focus on human rights, including the Catholic Commission for Justice and Peace, the Zimbabwe Human Rights Organization, and the Legal Relief Fund. However, NGOs report increased difficulty in operating. Public demonstrations and protests are essentially illegal under the 2002 Public Order and Security Act, which forbids criticism of the president, limits public assembly, and allows police to impose arbitrary curfews. Meetings are often declared illegal or disrupted by party militias or security forces. Intelligence agencies are among law enforcers empowered to disperse "illegal" assemblies or arrest participants.

The right to collective action is limited by provisions of the Labor Relations Act, which allow the government to veto collective bargaining agreements that it argues would harm the economy. Strikes are allowed except for industries declared "essential" under the act. Mugabe has used his presidential powers to declare strikes illegal, and labor organizers are common targets of government harassment. Most notably, security forces arrested more than 400 people in response to a two-day general strike in March; many were beaten or tortured while in police custody.

Despite coming under increasing pressure by the regime, the judiciary at times acts independently. In the past, courts struck down or disputed government actions, most notably regarding illegal occupation of farms. The government, however, has repeatedly refused to enforce court orders and has replaced senior judges or pressured them to resign. In December 2002, the Supreme Court ruled that the government's land-reform program was legal, but subsequent rulings in the separate High Court have determined that many eviction orders were illegal. Some farmers who had been evicted from their properties were granted a temporary reprieve allowing them to return until the Administrative Court confirmed the confiscation of their farms.

Security forces, particularly the Central Intelligence Organization, often ignore basic rights regarding detention, search, and seizure. With a decline in law and order, war veterans have taken over traditional policing roles in land redistribution. The military, too, is assuming more policing in food distribution and elections. According to Human Rights Watch, the government has taken no clear action to halt the rising incidence of torture and mistreatment of suspects held by police or intelligence services. Prison conditions are harsh and degrading.

The prices of many major commodities and food staples are controlled by the government, and state-linked companies dominate many sectors. The current political turmoil and investment flight does not bode well for the private business environment.

Women enjoy extensive legal protections, but de facto societal discrimination and domestic violence persist. Rape is used as a political weapon by youth militias. The Supreme Court issued a ruling relegating African women to the status of "junior males" within the family, declaring that those who marry under customary law must leave their original families behind and are therefore barred from inheriting their property. Married women cannot hold property jointly with their husbands. Access to education for women is especially difficult in rural areas, and women have borne the brunt of the hardships of the agrarian reforms.

# Armenia/Azerbaijan
## Nagorno-Karabakh

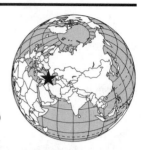

**Population:** 150,000    **Political Rights:** 5
**Religious Groups:** Armenian   **Civil Liberties:** 5
Apostolic [majority], other    **Status:** Partly Free
**Ethnic Groups:** Armenian (95 percent), other (5 percent)

### Ten-Year Ratings Timeline (Political Rights, Civil Liberties, Status)

| 1994 | 1995 | 1996 | 1997 | 1998 | 1999 | 2000 | 2001 | 2002 | 2003 |
|------|------|------|------|------|------|------|------|------|------|
| 7,7NF | 6,6NF | 6,6NF | 5,6NF | 5,6NF | 5,6NF | 5,6NF | 5,6NF | 5,5PF | 5,5PF |

**Overview:** Internationally mediated efforts to find a political settlement to the protracted Nagorno-Karabakh conflict made little progress in 2003. With presidential elections scheduled for both Armenia and Azerbaijan during the year, neither country's leadership appeared willing to risk a public backlash by agreeing to compromises over the disputed territory's status. Meanwhile, a mounting number of cease-fire violations led to concerns over a possible threat of renewed larger-scale confrontations.

The Nagorno-Karabakh Autonomous Region, a territory largely populated by ethnic Armenians inside the former Soviet republic of Azerbaijan, was established in 1923. In February 1988, Nagorno-Karabakh's regional legislature adopted a resolution calling for union with Armenia. The announcement triggered the first mass violence related to the conflict with attacks against Armenians in the Azerbaijani city of Sumgait several days later.

Successive battles and counteroffensives were fought over the next several years between various Armenian, Azerbaijani, and Nagorno-Karabakh forces. At its inaugural session in January 1992, Nagorno-Karabakh's new legislature adopted a declaration of independence, which was not recognized by the international community. By the time a Russian-brokered cease-fire was signed in May 1994, Karabakh Armenians, assisted by Armenia, had captured essentially the entire territory, as well as six Azerbaijani districts surrounding the enclave. Nearly all ethnic Azeris had fled or been forced out of the enclave and its surrounding areas, and the fighting had resulted in thousands of casualties and an estimated one million refugees.

In December 1994, the head of Nagorno-Karabakh's state defense committee, Robert Kocharian, was selected by the territory's parliament for the newly established post of president. Parliamentary elections were held in April and May 1995, and Kocharian defeated two other candidates in a popular vote for president in November of the following year. In September 1997, Foreign Minister Arkady Ghukasian was elected to replace Kocharian, who had been named prime minister of Armenia in March of that year.

In the territory's June 2000 parliamentary vote, 123 candidates representing five parties competed for the assembly's 33 seats. The ruling Democratic Union Artsakh (ZhAM), which supported Ghukasian, enjoyed a slim victory, winning 13 seats. The

Armenian Revolutionary Federation–Dashnaktsutiun won 9 seats, the Armenakan Party captured 1 seat, and formally independent candidates, most of whom supported Ghukasian, won 10. International observers described the electoral campaign and voting process as calm and largely transparent, although problems were noted with the accuracy of some voter lists.

In February 2001, former Defense Minister Samvel Babayan was found guilty of organizing a March 2000 assassination attempt against Ghukasian and sentenced to 14 years in prison. His supporters insisted that the arrest was politically motivated, as Babayan had been involved in a power struggle with Ghukasian. Others, however, welcomed the arrest and conviction of Babayan, who had been accused of corruption and reportedly wielded considerable political and economic power in the territory.

Ghukasian was reelected to a second term as president on August 11, 2002, with 89 percent of the vote. His closest challenger, former parliament speaker Artur Tovmasian, received just 8 percent. Voter turnout was close to 75 percent. Observers from countries including the United States, the United Kingdom, and France reported no serious violations. While a number of domestic and international nongovernmental organizations concluded that the elections marked a further step in Nagorno-Karabakh's democratization, they did voice some criticisms, including the limited access for the opposition to state-controlled media. Azerbaijan's Foreign Ministry described the election as a violation of international norms, insisting that a legitimate vote could be held only after a peaceful resolution to the conflict.

With both Armenia's president, Robert Kocharian, and Azerbaijan's president, Heydar Aliev, poised to seek reelection in 2003—and the domestic political risk associated with either leader's making significant public concessions over the territory during a campaign year—few observers expected any breakthroughs in the conflict during 2003. An upsurge in shooting incidents along the ceasefire line in the summer, which both Armenian and Azerbaijani officials accused the other side of instigating, fueled concerns of a further and more widespread escalation of violence. Meanwhile, speculation grew over the impact of Aliev's failing health and the October election of his son, Ilham, to succeed him as president on prospects for a negotiated settlement to the conflict.

Despite continued high-level discussions in the framework of the Organization for Security and Cooperation in Europe's Minsk Group—which was established a decade earlier to facilitate dialogue on a political settlement on Nagorno-Karabakh's status—a resolution of the long-standing dispute remained elusive at year's end. While Yerevan insists that Nagorno-Karabakh should be left outside Azeri jurisdiction, Baku maintains that the territory may be granted broad autonomy while remaining a constituent part of Azerbaijan. Azerbaijan also has refused to negotiate with Ghukasian, who has demanded direct representation in the peace process.

**Political Rights and Civil Liberties:** A self-declared republic, Nagorno-Karabakh has enjoyed de facto independence from Azerbaijan since 1994 while retaining close political, economic, and military ties with Armenia. Parliamentary elections in 1995 and 2000 were regarded as generally free and fair, as were the 1996 and 1997 presidential votes. However, the elections were considered invalid by most of the international community that does not recognize

Nagorno-Karabakh's independence. Nagorno-Karabakh's electoral law calls for a single-mandate system to be used in parliamentary elections; lawmakers have rejected the opposition's demands for the inclusion of party-based lists.

The territory officially remains under martial law, which imposes restrictions on civil liberties, including media censorship and the banning of public demonstrations. However, the authorities maintain that these provisions have not been enforced since 1995, a year after the cease-fire was signed.

The government controls many of the territory's broadcast media outlets, and most journalists practice self-censorship, particularly on subjects dealing with policies related to Azerbaijan and the peace process. Some observers maintain that the government used the attempted murder of President Arkady Ghukasian in 2000 as a pretext to intensify attacks against its critics.

The registration of religious groups is required under Nagorno-Karabakh's 1997 law on religion. The Armenian Apostolic Church, which is the territory's predominant religion, is the only faith registered with the state. According to Forum 18, a religious-freedom watchdog group based in Norway, members of various minority faiths, including Pentecostals, Adventists, Baptists, and Jehovah's Witnesses, have faced restrictions on their activities. In 2003, a local Baptist was beaten, was threatened with mind-altering drugs, and had threats made against his wife by law enforcement officials for distributing religious literature on the street, Forum 18 reported; authorities denied that any threats were made against him.

Freedom of assembly and association is limited, although political parties and unions are allowed to organize.

The judiciary, which is not independent in practice, is influenced by the executive branch and powerful political and clan forces. Former defense minister Samvel Babayan alleged that he had been physically assaulted during his interrogation and detention as a suspect in the failed assassination attempt against President Ghukasian in March 2000. The presiding judge in the case announced that the subsequent guilty verdict against Babayan was based on pretrial testimony in which Babayan confessed to the charges, although he later retracted his admission of guilt, claiming that it had been obtained under duress. The republic's government announced that it had replaced the death penalty with life imprisonment as of August 1, 2003.

The majority of those who fled the fighting continue to live in squalid conditions in refugee camps in Azerbaijan, while international aid organizations are reducing direct assistance to the refugees. Landmine explosions continue to result in casualties each year, with children and teenagers among the most vulnerable groups. According to the International Committee of the Red Cross, at least 50,000 anti-personnel mines were laid during the war, although in many cases, records of minefield locations were never created or were lost. The HALO Trust, a British nongovernmental organization, is the major de-mining group operating in the territory.

Nagorno-Karabakh's fragile peace has failed to bring significant improvement to the economy, particularly in the countryside, and pensioners are particularly hard hit. Widespread corruption, a lack of substantive economic reforms, and the control of major economic activity by powerful elites limit equality of opportunity for most residents.

# China
## Hong Kong

**Population:** 7,400,000
**Religious Groups:** Mixture of local religions (90 percent), Christian (10 percent)
**Ethnic Groups:** Chinese (95 percent), other (5 percent)

**Political Rights:** 5
**Civil Liberties:** 3
**Status:** Partly Free

### Ten-Year Ratings Timeline (Political Rights, Civil Liberties, Status)

| 1994 | 1995 | 1996 | 1997 | 1998 | 1999 | 2000 | 2001 | 2002 | 2003 |
|------|------|------|------|------|------|------|------|------|------|
| -- | -- | -- | 6,3PF | 5,3PF | 5,3PF | 5,3PF | 5,3PF | 5,3PF | 5,3PF |

**Overview:**
Using street protests and the ballot box, Hong Kong residents in 2003 put democratic reform squarely on the territory's political agenda. Some 500,000 residents took to the streets in a July protest that forced unpopular Chief Executive Tung Chee-hwa to shelve controversial internal security legislation. In addition, voters strongly backed pro-democracy candidates in local elections in November. The record turnout and strong support for pro-democracy politicians suggested that many ordinary Hong Kong residents want the government to introduce direct elections for the chief executive and entire legislature once these changes become legally possible beginning in 2007.

Located at the mouth of the Pearl River on the southern Chinese coast, Hong Kong consists of Hong Kong Island and Kowloon Peninsula, both ceded in perpetuity to Britain by China in the mid-1800s, and the mainland New Territories, which Britain "leased" for 99 years in 1898. Hong Kong's transition to Chinese rule began in 1984, when Britain agreed to return the territory to China in 1997 in return for Beijing's pledge to maintain the capitalist enclave's legal, political, and economic autonomy for 50 years.

London and Beijing later drafted a mini-constitution for Hong Kong, called the Basic Law, that laid the blueprint for introducing direct elections for 18 seats in the territory's 60-member legislature, known as the Legislative Council (Legco), in 1991 and gradually expanding the number to 30 over 12 years. Hong Kong's last colonial governor, Christopher Patten, infuriated Beijing with his attempt to deepen democracy by giving ordinary residents greater say in choosing Legco's indirectly elected seats. After China took control of Hong Kong as planned in 1997, Beijing retaliated by disbanding the partially elected Legco and installing a provisional legislature for ten months, which repealed or tightened several of the territory's civil liberties laws.

As chief executive since the handover, Tung has seen his popularity wane as Hong Kong struggles to regain its economic vigor in the wake of the regional financial crisis that began in 1997. He was chosen for the top job by a Beijing-organized committee in 1996 after Chinese leaders indicated that he was their preferred choice.

Capitalizing on Tung's unpopularity, pro-democracy parties picked up several seats in the most recent Legco elections, held in 2000. They won 16 of Legco's 24 directly elected seats and 21 of 60 overall. Final results gave the main opposition

Democratic Party 12 seats and the conservative, pro-Beijing Democratic Alliance 11, with smaller parties and independents taking the remaining seats.

The political crisis that engulfed Tung's administration in 2003 began the previous year, when the government first publicized details of proposed internal security laws. Human rights activists, religious figures, and others argued that Hong Kong lacks sufficient democratic checks and balances to ensure that the laws are not abused. Many warned that the laws could be used to undermine press and academic freedoms, criminalize public advocacy of independence for Tibet or Taiwan, or target groups that Beijing opposes, such as the Falun Gong spiritual movement.

Even some members of the business community, which generally supports Tung's conservative administration, warned that the laws could stifle the free flow of information and undermine Hong Kong's competitive advantage as an outpost of the rule of law in China. The government responded by saying that the laws carried sufficient safeguards and that it was simply carrying out its responsibilities under the Basic Law. The Basic Law requires the government to introduce laws that criminalize subversion, secession, treason, sedition, theft of state secrets, and the maintenance of links with foreign political groups that could harm national security.

Thrown on the defensive by the July 1, 2003, protest—the largest on Chinese soil since the 1989 Tiananmen demonstrations—Tung shelved the security legislation indefinitely on September 5 after it became clear that key supporters in Legco would not vote for the unpopular bills. Against this backdrop, the Democratic Party portrayed the November 23 local elections as a referendum on democratic reform. Led by lawyer Yeung Sum, the party won nearly 80 percent of the seats it contested, while the Democratic Alliance won only 38 percent of the seats it stood for.

Exit polls showed that 80 percent or more of voters interviewed favor direct elections for the chief executive and for all of Legco's seats. While the Basic Law allows direct elections for Tung's post in 2007 and for the entire Legco in 2008, any changes would have to be approved by China's rubber-stamp National People's Congress (NPC), Hong Kong's chief executive, and Legco. Tung, who was reelected to a second 5-year term in 2002 by an 800-member committee of lawmakers, religious figures, and interest-group representatives, has promised public consultations in 2004 or 2005 on changes to the electoral system.

The more immediate political test will be the September 2004 Legco elections, where half of the body's 60 seats will be directly elected. Tung relies on the Democratic Alliance and pro-business Liberal Party to pass legislation, but pro-democracy parties are looking to gain control of Legco for the first time.

Demands for political reform have been fueled in part by Hong Kong's economic gloom. The economy staggered through its third technical recession in six years in the first half of 2003 as retail and tourism were battered by the deadly severe acute respiratory syndrome (SARS) virus, which killed 299 people in Hong Kong before abating in mid-year. Unemployment hit a record high of 8.7 percent in the May-July reporting period before falling to 8.3 percent later in the year.

While the government was expecting the economy to grow by around 2 percent for the full year, the outlook continued to be clouded by persistent deflation, high budget deficits, and the wealth-erasing effects of a 60 percent fall in residential and commercial property prices since 1997. Hong Kong also faces the longer-term challenge of preserving its status as an international trade, shipping, and finance center, and its niche as a gateway for trade and investment with China, in the face of competition from Shanghai and other mainland cities.

**Political Rights and Civil Liberties:** Hong Kong residents enjoy most basic rights, but the legal footing for many of these rights is less secure than before the handover and voters cannot change their government through elections.

Criticism of Chief Executive Tung Chee-hwa's performance and concern over his proposed security laws has focused attention on the limited democratic checks and balances in Hong Kong. Most notably, the chief executive wields strong executive powers and is appointed rather than elected. The 800-member committee that reelected Tung in 2002 consisted of the 60 members of Hong Kong's Legislative Council (Legco); Hong Kong's 36 delegates to China's NPC; 40 representatives of religious groups; 41 members of an official Chinese consultative body; and 623 interest group representatives chosen in July 2000 by a narrow electorate of just 180,000 voters. Those 180,000 voters, representing labor, business, and the professions, also chose 30 of the 60 seats in the 2000 Legco elections. Six other seats were chosen by the same 800 people who reelected Tung, leaving only 24 directly elected seats.

Moreover, the Basic Law restricts Legco's law-making powers. It prohibits legislators from introducing bills affecting Hong Kong's public spending, government operations, or political structure. Legco members can introduce bills concerning government policy, but only with the chief executive's prior approval. The government in certain cases has used a very broad definition of "government policy" in order to exercise its right to block Legco bills. In addition, for an individual member's bill to pass, it must have separate majorities among Legco members who are directly elected and those who represent interest groups.

Beyond these formal limits on elections and legislative power, many ordinary Hong Kong residents have criticized what they see as collusion between the administration and a handful of powerful businessmen. They point, for example, to the government's decision in 2000 to bypass the routine bidding process in awarding a contract to develop the Cyberport industrial park to Richard Li, a son of Li Ka-shing, Hong Kong's wealthiest businessman.

Despite these concerns, even the government's staunchest critics generally acknowledge that Hong Kong residents enjoy the same basic rights that they had enjoyed before the handover. Many of these rights, however, are now on less solid legal footing. While the International Covenant on Civil and Political Rights continues to be formally incorporated into Hong Kong's 1991 Bill of Rights, the provisional legislature that served for 10 months after the handover watered down certain provisions of the Bill of Rights and rolled back certain laws protecting worker's rights. It also amended laws to give officials the power to cite national security concerns in denying registration to nongovernmental organizations (NGOs), de-registering existing groups, and barring public protests.

In practice, the press continues to be outspoken on many issues. Hong Kong's hundreds of newspapers and magazines routinely carry articles critical of the Hong Kong and Beijing governments, statements by Chinese dissidents and supporters of Taiwanese independence, and reports of official corruption on the mainland. Many media outlets, however, practice some self-censorship when reporting on Chinese politics, powerful local business interests, and the issues of Tibetan and Taiwanese independence. The press faces no direct pressure, but some editors and publishers believe that advertising revenues or their business interests in China could suffer if they appear to be hostile to China or to local tycoons.

Religious freedom is respected in Hong Kong, with Buddhism and Taoism having the most adherents. Practitioners of the Falun Gong and other spiritual groups can practice without interference. Meanwhile, university professors can write and lecture freely, and political debate on campuses is lively and robust.

Hong Kong NGOs continue to be vigorous, and none have been denied registration under the post-1997 national security provisions. Similarly, thousands of protests have been staged since the handover, and the government has never invoked its power to bar protests on national security grounds. Some protest organizers, however, say that the "designated areas" to which some protests are confined are often locations where the rallies receive little public attention. Some organizers also complain about the need to obtain prior approval for assemblies and demonstrations. Three political activists were sentenced to three months' probation in 2002 for organizing an unauthorized rally. The case marked the first time since the handover that protesters were sanctioned for holding a demonstration without obtaining police permission in advance.

Hong Kong's trade unions are independent, but the law restricts some basic labor rights and does not protect others. Most importantly, the provisional legislature in 1997 removed both the legal basis for collective bargaining and legal protections against summary dismissal for union activity. More than 22 percent of Hong Kong workers who receive regular wages or salaries are unionized. While strikes are legal in the territory, many workers have to sign employment contracts stating that job walkouts are a basis for summary dismissal.

Hong Kong's common law judiciary is independent. Many human rights activists and others argue, however, that the Tung administration has undermined the territory's rule of law. They cite what they see as the government's preferential treatment of Richard Li and other well-connected business leaders as well as its intervention in a 1999 immigration case. In that case, the government asked China's NPC to interpret the Basic Law's provisions on immigration to Hong Kong from the mainland. The NPC's ensuing interpretation effectively overturned an earlier ruling by Hong Kong's Court of Final Appeal. Critics alleged that the NPC's involvement raised doubts over whether any Court of Final Appeal decision is truly final. The Basic Law requires Hong Kong courts—though not the government—to seek from the NPC an interpretation of the Basic Law on issues that touch on Beijing's responsibilities to the territory or concern the relationship between Beijing and Hong Kong.

Hong Kong's police force continues to be dogged by complaints from residents of being assaulted by officers. While few of these complaints are substantiated, the UN Human Rights Committee and local rights groups have called for a more independent police oversight body to replace the current, executive-appointed body.

Ethnic minorities are well represented in the civil service and many professions. Hong Kong residents of Indian descent and other minorities regularly allege, however, that they face discrimination in renting apartments, landing private sector jobs, getting treated in public hospitals, and competing for public school and university slots. The press regularly carries accounts of apparent discrimination against minorities and also against newly arrived mainland Chinese.

Women in Hong Kong have equal access to schooling and are entering medicine and other professions in increasingly greater numbers. In the private sector, however, they continue to face discrimination in landing jobs and getting fair salaries and promotions. Women also make up an outsized share of low-level workers, and relatively few women are judges, lawmakers, or senior civil servants.

The government funds programs to curb domestic violence and prosecutes violators, but violence against women in the home persists, and punishments generally are lenient. Meanwhile, credible reports suggest that some Hong Kong residents illegally force their foreign household help to accept less than the minimum wage and provide them with poor living conditions. Traffickers bring women into Hong Kong for prostitution and to work as household help and use the territory to transit trafficking victims.

# China
## Macao

**Population:** 470,000
**Religious Groups:** Buddhist
(50 percent) Roman Catholic
(15 percent), other (35 percent)
**Ethnic Groups:** Chinese (95 percent), other
[including Macanese and Portuguese] (5 percent)

**Political Rights:** 6
**Civil Liberties:** 4
**Status:** Partly Free

### Ten-Year Ratings Timeline (Political Rights, Civil Liberties, Status)

| 1994 | 1995 | 1996 | 1997 | 1998 | 1999 | 2000 | 2001 | 2002 | 2003 |
|------|------|------|------|------|------|------|------|------|------|
| 6,4PF | 6,4PF | 6,4PF | 6,4PF | 6,4PF | 6,4PF | 6,4PF | 6,4PF | 6,4PF | 6,4PF |

**Overview:**

China took steps in 2003 to help boost Macao's economy, easing trade and travel restrictions in the territory.

Ruled by Portugal for 443 years beginning in 1557, Macao was the first European outpost in the Far East, the leading gateway for European trade with China until the 1770s, and a hideaway for buccaneers and Chinese criminal gangs until becoming, more recently, a bawdy city of casinos and prostitution. The territory's road to reunification with the mainland began in 1987, when China and Portugal agreed that Beijing would regain control over Macao in 1999 and that the enclave would maintain its legal system and capitalist economy for 50 years.

Macao lacks the vibrant banking, trading, and real estate industries found in Hong Kong, just 40 miles to the east along the south China coast. Its economic fortunes recently have been tied largely to tourism and the casino industry, as well as to textile and garment exports. When Macao's economy slid into recession in 1995, it was partly because a surge in gang-related violence, including killings and attacks on several local civil servants and Portuguese officials, hurt tourism, which makes up around 40 percent of gross domestic product (GDP). The regional financial crisis that began in 1997 prolonged the recession, which ended in 2000.

Gangland violence tailed off significantly in the lead-up to the handover to Chinese rule, which took place in December 1999. China reportedly helped Macao crack down on crime groups, and the outgoing Portuguese jailed a major crime boss.

Despite concerns before the handover that China would renege on its pledges to respect Macao's autonomy, there has been little sign that Beijing is trying to pressure the administration of Edmund Ho, the territory's appointed top official. Still, these concerns remain for some Macao residents, in part because the territory's press and civic groups are less vigorous than those in Hong Kong. Moreover, under the 1987 Sino-Portuguese deal, Macao's chief executive, like Hong Kong's, is appointed by an elite committee rather than popularly elected. Ho, a Canadian-educated banker, was the committee's consensus choice to be the first chief executive. The committee's 199 members were themselves appointed by a Beijing-selected committee.

Concerns about Beijing's influence in the territory may have been allayed somewhat by the fact that Macao's sole pro-democracy party was the largest single vote-getter in the September 2001 legislative elections, the first since the handover. Led by Ng Kuok-cheong, the Association for a New Democratic Macao party took 2 of the 10 directly elected seats in the 27-member body. Business-backed candidates won 4 seats, and the pro-China camp won another 4. Ten other seats, chosen by special interest groups, were uncontested. Ho appointed the remaining seven seats. Macao's legislature, in any case, has little influence under a political setup that puts most power in the hands of Chief Executive Ho.

In a long-expected move, the government in 2002 broke casino magnate Stanley Ho's 40-year monopoly on Macao's $1.99 billion gaming industry by awarding him only one of three new licenses to operate casinos in the territory. Analysts say that increased competition should boost an industry that already accounts for an estimated one-third of Macao's $6.2 billion GDP and about half of the government's annual revenues.

Beijing said in August that it would ease restrictions on travel to Macao, as well as to Hong Kong, for some mainland residents. In October, China and Macao signed a trade pact that will grant Macao firms access to China's legal, banking, and telecom sectors and eliminate Chinese tariffs on 273 types of goods made in the territory.

**Political Rights and Civil Liberties:** Residents of Macao cannot change their government through elections, although they do enjoy many basic rights and freedoms.

Macao's mini-constitution, known as the Basic Law, calls for the government to be led by a powerful chief executive who is subject to few democratic checks and balances. Aside from its provisions on governmental structure, the Basic Law is "riddled with ambiguities," fails to guarantee several basic rights, and grants Beijing emergency powers that are vaguely worded, the human rights group Amnesty International said in 1999. Like the Portuguese governors who served in the waning years of colonial rule, Macao's chief executive is appointed and holds broad executive powers. Meanwhile, legislators are barred from introducing bills relating to Macao's public spending, its political structure, or the operation of its government.

In addition, bills relating to government policies must receive the chief executive's written approval before they can be submitted.

The legislature elected in 2005 will have two additional seats, both of them directly elected. After 2009, the Basic Law allows lawmakers, by a two-thirds vote and subject to the chief executive's approval, to draw up a new mix of directly and indirectly elected seats.

Outside of a handful of opposition politicians like Ng Kuok-cheong, of the Association for a New Democratic Macao party, Macao has few outspoken voices for greater political freedom or for more transparency in business and government.

Most of the enclave's ten daily newspapers, including the top-selling *Macao Daily*, are pro-Beijing. None take an independent political line. The press also offers little coverage of people, groups, or activities that challenge Macao's conservative political and business establishment or that call for greater political rights.

Macao residents of all faiths generally can worship freely. Practitioners of the Falun Gong spiritual movement, whose followers on the mainland have been suppressed ruthlessly, routinely perform their exercises in Macao's parks. Police, however, often photograph practitioners and at times take them to stationhouses for checks of their identity documents that can last for several hours, according to the U.S. State Department's human rights report for 2002, released in March 2003. University professors and other educators can write and lecture without interference.

Human rights groups, such as the Macao Association for the Rights of Laborers, operate freely, though they generally have little impact on the territory's political life. Critics say that Macao's dominant labor confederation, the Federation of Trade Unions, is more of a political front for mainland Chinese interests than an advocate for better wages, benefits, and working conditions. Several small private sector unions and two of Macao's four public sector unions are independent. Laws protecting striking workers from dismissal are inadequate, and government enforcement of labor laws is lax.

Some observers question whether Macao's judiciary is robust enough to protect fundamental liberties should they be threatened in the future. The judiciary is still finding its footing following delays in translating laws and judgments into Chinese from Portuguese. The courts are also grappling with a severe shortage of local bilingual lawyers and magistrates. Only about 10 of the 94 lawyers in private practice can read and write Chinese. In addition, the chief executive appoints judges without legislative oversight. Judicial candidates are recommended to the chief executive by a commission that he himself names. Prisons meet international standards, and there have been few recent reports of police abuse.

Foreign workers often work for less than half the wages paid to Macao residents, live in controlled dormitories, and owe huge sums to the firms that brought them to the enclave, according to the U.S. State Department report. Macao workers, meanwhile, complain that their bargaining power is eroded by the territory's many foreign laborers, who make up around 12 percent of the workforce.

Women in Macao are gaining a greater foothold in business and increasingly holding senior government posts. They are, however, still under-represented in politics and the civil service. Traffickers continue to bring women from abroad into Macao for prostitution, although there are no accurate figures on the scale of the problem.

# China
## Tibet

**Population:** 5,300,000*     **Political Rights:** 7
**Religious Groups:** Tibetan     **Civil Liberties:** 7
Buddhist [majority], other     **Status:** Not Free
(including Muslim and Christian)
**Ethnic Groups:** Tibetan, Chinese
* This figure from China's 2000 census includes 2.4 million
Tibetans living in the Tibet Autonomous Region (TAR) and
2.9 million Tibetans living in areas of Eastern Tibet that,
beginning in 1950, were incorporated into four Chinese provinces.

### Ten-Year Ratings Timeline (Political Rights, Civil Liberties, Status)

| 1994 | 1995 | 1996 | 1997 | 1998 | 1999 | 2000 | 2001 | 2002 | 2003 |
|------|------|------|------|------|------|------|------|------|------|
| 7,7NF | 7,7NF | 7,7NF | 7,7NF | 7,7NF | 7,7NF | 7,7NF | 7,7NF | 7,7NF | 7,7NF |

**Overview:**     China continued its tight control over Tibet in 2003, jailing dissidents, managing the daily affairs in major Buddhist monasteries and nunneries, and carrying out the first known case of a possibly politically motivated execution in many years.

China's occupation of Tibet has marginalized a Tibetan national identity that dates back more than 2,000 years. Beijing's modern-day claim to the region is based on Mongolian and Manchurian imperial influence over Tibet in the thirteenth and eighteenth centuries, respectively. Largely under this pretext, China invaded Tibet in late 1949 and, in 1951, formally annexed the Central Asian land. In an apparent effort to undermine Tibetan claims to statehood, Beijing split up the vast region that Tibetans call their traditional homeland. It incorporated roughly half of this region into four different southwestern Chinese provinces beginning in 1950. The rest of this traditional homeland was named the Tibet Autonomous Region (TAR) in 1965.

The defining event of Beijing's rule so far took place in 1959, when Chinese troops suppressed a local uprising by killing an estimated 87,000 Tibetans in the Lhasa area alone. The massacre forced the Tibetan spiritual and political leader, the fourteenth Dalai Lama, Tenzin Gyatso, to flee to Dharamsala, India, with 80,000 supporters. More recently, Mao's Cultural Revolution devastated Tibet. China jailed thousands of monks and nuns, and nearly all of Tibet's 6,200 monasteries were destroyed.

As resistance to Beijing's rule continued, Chinese soldiers forcibly broke up mainly peaceful protests throughout Tibet between 1987 and 1990. Beijing imposed martial law on Lhasa and surrounding areas in March 1989 following three days of antigovernment protests and riots during which police killed at least 50 Tibetans. Officials lifted martial law in May 1990.

In a flagrant case of interference with Tibet's Buddhist hierarchy, China in 1995 detained six-year-old Gedhun Choekyi Nyima and rejected his selection by the Dalai Lama as the eleventh reincarnation of the Panchen Lama. The Panchen Lama is Tibetan Buddhism's second-highest religious figure. Officials then stage-managed the selection of another six-year-old boy as the Panchen Lama. Since the Panchen

Lama identifies the reincarnated Dalai Lama, Beijing potentially could control the identification of the fifteenth Dalai Lama. The government has also tried to control the identification and education of other religious figures.

Since the 1989 demonstrations led to a blanket repression of dissent, Tibetans have mounted few large-scale protests against Chinese rule. In addition to jailing dissidents, Chinese officials have stepped up their efforts to control religious affairs and undermine the exiled Dalai Lama's religious and political authority. Foreign observers have reported a slight easing of repression since late 2000, when Beijing tapped the relatively moderate Guo Jin-long, a veteran party official, to be the TAR's Communist Party boss. Guo replaced Chen Kui-yan, the architect of recent crackdowns. Guo, who reportedly is in poor health, was replaced in 2003 by one of his deputies, Yang Chuan-tang.

Chen's departure in 2000 may have been linked to Beijing's anger over the escape to India in late 1999 of the teenager recognized by the Dalai Lama, and accepted by China, as the seventeenth Karmapa. The Karmapa is the highest-ranking figure in the Karma Kargyu school of Tibetan Buddhism. Beijing had interfered in the Karmapa's selection and education as part of an apparent effort to create a generation of more pliant Tibetan religious leaders.

China in recent years has made a series of goodwill gestures that may be aimed at influencing international opinion on Tibet. Beijing has freed several Tibetan political prisoners before the end of their sentences. It also hosted visits by envoys of the Dalai Lama in 2002 and again in 2003, the first formal contacts between Beijing and the Dalai Lama since 1993. Neither side gave details of the meetings, although the two sides' positions on the purpose and desirability of holding more structured talks in the future are known to be far apart. Since 1988, the Tibetan government-in-exile's official policy has been to seek negotiations on genuine autonomy for Tibet, having dropped earlier demands for independence. China's official statements, however, suggest that it is willing to have contacts with the Dalai Lama, but not to hold negotiations with him on Tibet's political future.

**Political Rights and Civil Liberties:** Under Chinese rule, Tibetans enjoy few basic rights and lack the right to determine their political future. The Chinese Communist Party rules the TAR and traditional Tibetan areas in nearby Qinghai, Sichuan, Gansu, and Yunnan provinces through appointed officials whose ranks include some Tibetans. No Tibetan, however, has ever held the peak post of TAR party secretary. In a leadership shuffle in the spring of 2003, Jampa Phuntsog, formerly vice chairman of the TAR People's Congress, became chairman of the TAR regional government, while his predecessor in that post, Legchog, was named chairman of the TAR People's Congress. The most powerful Tibetan Communist official, Ragdi, was made vice chairman of China's National People's Congress.

China controls the flow of information in Tibet, tightly restricting all media and regulating Internet use.

Chinese officials permit Tibetans to take part in many religious practices, but since 1996, they have also strengthened their control over monasteries under a propaganda campaign that is aimed largely at undermining the Dalai Lama's influence as a spiritual and political leader. Under this "patriotic education campaign," government-run "work teams" visit monasteries to conduct mandatory sessions on Beijing's version of Tibetan history and other political topics. Officials also require monks to sign a declaration agreeing to reject independence for Tibet, denounce the Dalai Lama, not listen to Voice of America radio broadcasts, and reject the boy whom the Dalai Lama identified as the eleventh Panchen Lama.

The intensity of the patriotic education campaign recently has died down somewhat. Chinese officials say that the campaign ended in 2000 while acknowledging that patriotic education continues at some monasteries and nunneries. In any case, hundreds of monks and nuns have been expelled from monasteries or have left voluntarily since the campaign began.

In addition to trying to coerce monks and nuns to renounce their beliefs, the government oversees day-to-day affairs in major monasteries and nunneries through state-organized "democratic management committees" that run each establishment. Authorities limit the numbers of monks and nuns permitted in major monasteries, although these restrictions are not always enforced. Officials have also restricted the building of new monasteries and nunneries, closed many religious institutions, and demolished several others. Tibetans who are state workers or Communist Party cadres face restrictions on religious practice that are stricter in some years than others. State workers also face constant pressure not to show any form of loyalty to the Dalai Lama.

In universities, professors cannot lecture on politically sensitive topics, and many reportedly are required to attend political education sessions. Moreover, independent trade unions, civic groups, and human rights groups are illegal.

Tibetan political dissidents face particularly severe human rights abuses. Security forces routinely arrest, jail, and torture dissidents to punish nonviolent protest against Chinese rule, according to the U.S. State Department, the London-based Tibet Information Network (TIN) watchdog group, and other sources. The party-controlled judiciary has jailed many Tibetans for distributing leaflets, putting up posters, holding peaceful protests, putting together lists of prisoners, possessing photographs of the Dalai Lama, and displaying Tibetan flags or other symbols of cultural identity.

Chinese jails held some 150 Tibetan political prisoners as of February 2003, many of them in China's Sichuan and Qinghai provinces, according to TIN. The group said that it also had unconfirmed reports of 10 to 20 additional political prisoners. The overall number of Tibetan political prisoners has declined recently, and the pattern of arrests has changed. Political arrests inside the TAR have declined sharply since 1996, TIN says, while arrests of Tibetans on political grounds outside the TAR have increased, particularly in Kardze in the traditional Tibetan area of Kham, now part of China's Sichuan province. Forty Tibetan political prisoners have died since 1987 as a result of prison abuse, according to TIN.

In the first known case in many years of a Tibetan being executed on possibly politically motivated grounds, former monk Lobsang Dhondup, 28, was executed in January 2003. He had been convicted in a closed trial in connection with a series of bombings in Sichuan province that killed one person. Official Chinese accounts said that leaflets calling for Tibetan independence were found at the scene of at least one explosion. A senior lama, Tenzin Deleg Rinpoche, 53, received a suspended death sentence in the same case.

In jails and detention centers throughout Tibet, security forces routinely beat, torture, or otherwise abuse inmates and detainees. "Poor conditions of detention coupled with widespread torture and abuse make life extremely harsh for all those jailed in Tibet," the human rights group Amnesty International said in 2002. In one of the most notorious cases of prison abuse in recent years, officials responded to protests at Lhasa's Drapchi Prison in 1998 by torturing and beating to death nine inmates, including five nuns and three monks. Forced labor reportedly is used in some prisons, detention centers, "re-education through labor" camps, and prisoner work sites, according to the U.S. State Department's human rights report for 2002, released in March 2003. Prisoners often receive some payment and can earn sentence reductions for their work.

Because they belong to one of China's 55 recognized ethnic minority groups, Tibetans receive some preferential treatment in university admissions and government employment. Tibetans, however, generally need to learn Mandarin Chinese in order to take advantage of these preferences and for many private sector jobs. Many Tibetans are torn between a desire to learn Chinese in order to compete for university slots and jobs and the realization that increased use of Chinese threatens the survival of the Tibetan language. Chinese has long been the main language of instruction in high schools and many middle schools and reportedly is now being used to teach several subjects in a number of Lhasa primary schools.

Tibetans reportedly are facing increased difficulties in obtaining passports. Up to 3,000 Tibetans, many without valid travel documents, cross the border into Nepal each year. Many seek to study or settle in India.

In the private sector, employers favor Han Chinese for many jobs and give them greater pay for the same work. Tibetans also find it more difficult than Han Chinese to get permits and loans to open businesses.

Thanks in part to subsidies from Beijing and favorable tax and other economic policies, living standards have improved somewhat in recent years for many Tibetans. Much of Tibet's recent growth, however, has been concentrated in urban areas and the state sector, thereby largely bypassing most Tibetans, who are mainly rural. Han Chinese have been the main beneficiaries of the growing private sector and many other fruits of development. This is seen most starkly in Lhasa and other Tibetan cities where Han Chinese and members of China's Muslim Hui minority run most small businesses. Moreover, the flow of ethnic Han and Hui into Tibet in recent decades has altered the region's demographic makeup and helped to marginalize Tibetan cultural identity.

Tibetan women are subject to China's restrictive family planning policies, which are somewhat more lenient toward Tibetans and other ethnic minorities. Officials generally limit urban Tibetans to having two children. They also frequently pressure party cadres and state workers to have only one child. While farmers and herders often have three or more children, reports in recent years suggested that local officials in certain counties were limiting these rural Tibetans to two children.

# Georgia
## Abkhazia

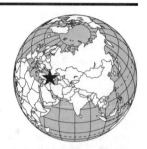

**Population:** 250,000
**Religious Groups:** Muslim, Christian
**Ethnic Groups:** Abkhaz [majority], Georgian

**Political Rights:** 6
**Civil Liberties:** 5
**Status:** Not Free

### Ten-Year Ratings Timeline (Political Rights, Civil Liberties, Status)

| 1994 | 1995 | 1996 | 1997 | 1998 | 1999 | 2000 | 2001 | 2002 | 2003 |
|------|------|------|------|------|------|------|------|------|------|
| -- | -- | -- | 6,5NF | 6,5NF | 6,5NF | 6,5NF | 6,5NF | 6,5NF | 6,5NF |

**Overview:**

A decade after separatist forces defeated Georgian government troops for control of the breakaway republic of Abkhazia, no significant advance was reached in 2003 on finding a lasting political solution to the conflict. In what appeared to be a small step forward, Russia and Georgia agreed in principle to the repatriation of Georgian refugees to Abkhazia and the restoration of rail communication between the two countries via Abkhazia. In April, the territory's government stepped down after just four months in office, following demands by a group representing the republic's war veterans that it resign.

Annexed by Russia in 1864, Abkhazia became an autonomous republic of Soviet Georgia in 1930. The year after the 1991 collapse of the Soviet Union, Abkhazia declared its independence from Tbilisi, igniting a war between Abkhaz secessionists and Georgian troops that lasted nearly 14 months. In September 1993, Abkhaz forces, with covert assistance from Russia, seized control of the city of Sukhumi, ultimately defeating the Georgian army and winning de facto independence for the territory. As a result of the conflict, more than 200,000 residents, mostly ethnic Georgians, fled Abkhazia, while casualty figures were estimated in the thousands. An internationally brokered cease-fire was signed in Moscow in 1994, although a final decision on the territory's status remains unresolved.

In the October 1999 elections for president of Abkhazia, Vladislav Ardzinba, the incumbent and the only candidate running for office, was reelected. The Organization for Security and Cooperation in Europe (OSCE), the United Nations, and other international organizations refused to recognize the vote as legitimate. In a concurrent referendum on independence, the results of which were not accepted by any state, a reported 98 percent of voters supported independence for Abkhazia. Georgia denounced the polls as illegal and as an attempt to sabotage peace talks.

Tensions in the Kodori Gorge, an area controlled partly by Georgia and partly by Abkhazia, underscored the precariousness of the region's fragile peace. In October 2001, a group reportedly consisting of Chechen rebels and Georgian partisans clashed with Abkhaz troops following a deadly raid on a village in the gorge. The downing of a UN helicopter and the bombing of several Abkhaz villages by aircraft that Georgian authorities alleged had come from Russia intensified the conflict. Tbilisi responded by sending troops to the upper part of the gorge in what it said was an operation to protect ethnic Georgians living there from separatist attacks. Despite a UN-brokered protocol calling for the withdrawal of Georgian forces that was signed by Russia and Georgia in 2002, Abkhaz officials insisted that Georgia had not pulled out all its troops from the Kodori Gorge. Georgian authorities countered that the protocol did not require the withdrawal of other military detachments, including border guards.

Deputies loyal to Ardzinba won a landslide victory in the March 2002 parliamentary elections when the opposition Revival and People's Party withdrew most of its candidates in protest over the conduct of the campaign. Officially backed candidates, who won all 35 seats in the legislature, ran unopposed for 13 of them. Among the problems cited during the elections were that ethnic Georgians displaced by the war were not able to vote, official radio and television promoted pro-government candidates, and the head of the Central Election Commission had disqualified a number of candidates supported by the opposition. As in previous elections in Abkhazia, the international community declared the elections to be illegitimate.

After just four months in office, the government of Prime Minister Gennady Gagulia, who had developed a reputation for political weakness and inefficiency, resigned on April 8, 2003. Gagulia stepped down following pressure from Amtsakhara, an increasingly powerful opposition political movement representing primarily veterans of the 1992–1993 war, which had threatened to organize a mass rally if he remained in office. On April 22, Defense Minister Raul Khadjimba was named to succeed Gagulia. Subsequently, Amtsakhara also called on Ardzinba to resign as president because of his poor health; Ardzinba, who was undergoing medical treatment in Moscow for an undisclosed illness and who was no longer actively involved in the daily running of the government, insisted that he had no intention of stepping down before the next presidential election, in October 2004.

Ongoing efforts to advance the peace process apparently took a small step forward in 2003, even as negotiations between Tbilisi and Sukhumi continued to be stalled over the primary issue of the region's final political status: while Tbilisi holds that Abkhazia must remain a constituent part of Georgia, Sukhumi insists on the territory's independence from Georgia, a status that has not been recognized by the international community. In a March meeting in the southern Russian city of Sochi, Russian president Vladimir Putin and then-Georgian president Eduard Shevardnadze agreed provisionally to allow Georgian internally displaced persons (IDPs) who fled the war in Abkhazia to begin returning to their homes, first to the southernmost Gali region. The focus on IDP returns had emerged from discussions held the previous month in Geneva by the Friends of the Secretary-General—a subgroup of the UN Security Council composed of delegates from the United States, the United Kingdom, France, Germany, and Russia and tasked with helping to mediate a solution to the conflict. In exchange for beginning the repatriation of refugees, Georgia would sanction the resumption of rail links from Sochi to Tbilisi via Abkhazia.

Other agreements reached in March included an extension of the Russian peacekeeping force—deployed under the aegis of the Commonwealth of Independent States (CIS) following the 1994 cease-fire—until either Georgia or Abkhazia demands its withdrawal, and the repair of the Inguri hydroelectric power station to supply power to the region. Just two months earlier, Georgia had insisted that the renewal of the peacekeeping force would be contingent on Russia's suspension of passenger rail service between Sukhumi and Sochi—which had resumed in December 2002 without Georgia's consent, as stipulated by a 1996 CIS resolution—and of a cessation of Moscow's issuing of Russian passports to residents of Abkhazia.

However, as of November 30, questions remained about the effective implementation of these agreements. Despite such plans as deploying a UN civilian police force in Gali to help provide security for the IDPs, most refugees remained skeptical about their prospects of returning in the near future. Meanwhile, domestic political tensions in Georgia that eventually led to Shevardnadze's resignation in November contributed to the lack of progress on reaching a settlement on the territory's status.

**Political Rights and Civil Liberties:** Residents of Abkhazia can elect government officials, but the more than 200,000 displaced Georgians who fled the region during the war in the early to mid-1990s could not vote in the October 1999 presidential, March 2001 local, or March 2002 parliamentary elections. International organizations, including the OSCE, as well as the Georgian government, criticized the polls as illegitimate. Although the November 1994 constitution established a presidential-parliamentary system of government, the president exercises extensive control of the region. The ethnic Georgian Abkhazian Supreme Council has been a government in exile in Tbilisi since being expelled from Abkhazia in 1993. Opposition political parties include Aitara (Revival). Amtsakhara, a political group representing primarily veterans of the 1992–1993 war, is becoming a growing force in the territory's political life.

Several independent newspapers are published in the territory. Electronic media are controlled by the state and generally reflect government positions.

Reliable information on freedom of religion is difficult to obtain. Although a presidential decree bans Jehovah's Witnesses and members have been detained by the authorities in recent years, none were in detention at year's end, according to a representative of the group. Abkhazia's Ministry of Education prohibits instruction in the Georgian language in the territory's schools, the 2003 U.S. State Department's human rights report for Georgia stated. Local residents in the Gali district, whose population is largely ethnic Georgian, were denied access to education in their mother tongue.

Most nongovernmental organizations operating in Abkhazia rely on funding from outside the territory.

Systemic problems in the territory's criminal justice system include a failure to conduct impartial investigations and to bring alleged perpetrators to justice, according to the 2003 U.S. State Department report. Other areas of concern include defendants' limited access to qualified legal counsel, violations of due process, and the lengthiness of pretrial detentions. An independent legal aid office in the southern Gali district has provided free legal advice to the local population since 2002. According to a February 2003 statement adopted by Abkhazia's parliament, which called on the territory's government to address a perceived rise in crime, criminal gangs in the territory are increasingly joining forces with counterparts in Georgia and southern Russia.

Personal security in the conflict zone continued to be a concern in 2003. Since the cease-fire, a small, unarmed UN Observer Mission in Georgia (UNOMIG) has monitored the cease-fire and attempted to resolve violations, while a CIS peacekeeping force of some 1,800 troops, dominated by Russian troops, has patrolled the region. The 1994 cease-fire has at times been tenuous, with incidents of violence and kidnappings, including of members of the UNOMIG and the CIS peacekeeping force, taking place during the year.

Travel and choice of residence are limited by the ongoing conflict. Approximately 200,000 ethnic Georgians who fled Abkhazia during the early 1990s are living in western Georgia, most in the Zugdidi district bordering Abkhazia. Most of these IDPs are unable or unwilling to return because of fears for their safety.

Equality of opportunity and normal business activities are limited by widespread corruption, the control by criminal organizations of large segments of the economy, and the continuing effects of the war. Abkhazia's economy is heavily reliant on Russia; the territory uses the Russian ruble as its currency, and many residents earn income by trading citrus fruits across the border in Russia.

# India
## Kashmir

**Population:** 11,000,000  
**Religious Groups:**Muslim  
(64.2 percent), Hindu  
(32.2 percent), Sikh (2.4 percent),  
Buddhist (1.2 percent)  
**Political Rights:** 5  
**Civil Liberties:** 5  
**Status:** Partly Free  

**Ethnic Groups:** Kashmiri [majority], Dogra, Ladakhi, Gujjar, Bakerwal, Dard, Balti, other

**Ten-Year Ratings Timeline (Political Rights, Civil Liberties, Status)**

| 1994 | 1995 | 1996 | 1997 | 1998 | 1999 | 2000 | 2001 | 2002 | 2003 |
|------|------|------|------|------|------|------|------|------|------|
| 7,7NF | 7,7NF | 7,7NF | 7,7NF | 6,6NF | 6,6NF | 6,6NF | 6,6NF | 5,5PF | 5,5PF |

**Overview:** Following the election of a new state government in late 2002, hopes were high that a corner had been turned in the conflict over the territory of Kashmir, where a continuing insurgency has killed at least 40,000 civilians, soldiers, and militants since 1989. Although the Congress–People's Democratic Party (PDP) coalition promised to provide a "healing touch" by encouraging economic growth and reducing corruption, it has had a limited ability to effectively address the issue of human rights violations or to negotiate a solution to the conflict. In April 2003, the Indian government launched a new peace initiative aimed at the Kashmiris, and in October it announced a series of confidence-building measures designed to improve relations with Pakistan. However, overall progress on finding a political solution to the conflict remained slow and unsteady during the year.

After centuries of rule in Kashmir by Afghan, Sikh, and local strongmen, the British seized control of the Himalayan land in 1846 and sold it to the Hindu maharajah of the neighboring principality of Jammu. The maharajah later incorporated

Ladakh and other surrounding areas into what became the new princely state of Jammu and Kashmir. At the partition of British India into the new nations of India and Pakistan in 1947, Maharajah Hari Singh attempted to preserve Jammu and Kashmir's independence. However, after Pakistani tribesmen invaded, the maharajah agreed to Jammu and Kashmir's accession to India in return for promises of autonomy and eventual self-determination.

Within months of gaining their independence, India and Pakistan went to war in Kashmir. A UN-brokered cease-fire in January 1949 established the present-day boundaries, which gave Pakistan control of roughly one-third of Jammu and Kashmir, including the far northern and western areas. India retained most of the Kashmir Valley along with predominantly Hindu Jammu and Buddhist-majority Ladakh.

Under Article 370 of India's constitution and a 1952 accord, the territory received substantial autonomy. However, New Delhi began annulling the autonomy guarantees in 1953, and in 1957, India formally annexed the part of Jammu and Kashmir under its control. Seeking strategic roads and passes, China seized a portion of Kashmir in 1959. India and Pakistan fought a second, inconclusive, war over the territory in 1965. Under the 1972 Simla accord, New Delhi and Islamabad agreed to respect the Line of Control (LOC), which demarcates the Indian- and Pakistani-held parts of Kashmir, and to resolve Kashmir's status through negotiation.

The armed insurgency against Indian rule gathered momentum after 1987, when the pro-India National Conference Party won state elections that were marred by widespread fraud and violence, and authorities began arresting members of a new, Muslim-based, opposition coalition. Militant groups with links to political parties assassinated several National Conference politicians and attacked government targets in the Kashmir Valley. The militants included the Jammu and Kashmir Liberation Front (JKLF) and other pro-independence groups consisting largely of indigenous Kashmiris, as well as Pakistani-backed Islamist groups that want to bring Kashmir under Islamabad's control.

As the violence escalated, New Delhi placed Jammu and Kashmir under federal rule in 1990 and attempted to quell the mass uprising by force. By the mid-1990s, the Indian army had greatly weakened the JKLF, which abandoned its armed struggle in 1994. The armed insurgency has since been dominated by Pakistani-backed extremist groups, which include in their ranks many non-Kashmiri fighters from elsewhere in the Islamic world. Although opposition parties joined together to form the All Parties Hurriyat Conference (APHC) in 1993, they boycotted the 1996 state elections, and the National Conference was able to form a government under party leader Farooq Abdullah.

In August 2000, Hizbul Mujahideen, the largest armed group in Kashmir, initiated a dialogue with the Indian government, but talks broke down when India refused to include Pakistan in the discussions. The two neighbors had engaged in a limited war in 1999 after Pakistan had seized strategic heights on the Indian side of the LOC. A summit held in 2001 failed to resolve the two countries' long-standing differences over Kashmir. Militants stepped up their attacks in the aftermath of the summit, with an increasing focus on targeting Hindu civilians in the southern districts of the state. In addition, a leading moderate separatist politician, Abdul Ghani Lone, was assassinated in May 2002, probably by a hard-line militant group.

Seeking legitimacy for the electoral process, New Delhi encouraged all political parties to participate in the fall 2002 state elections, but was unsuccessful in persuading the APHC to contest the polls. However, in a surprise result, the ruling National Conference lost 29 of its 57 assembly seats, while the Congress Party and the PDP made significant gains, winning 16 and 20 seats respectively. In November, the two parties formed a coalition government headed by the PDP's Mufti Mohammad Sayeed. The new government promised to address issues of human rights violations, corruption, and economic development, and urged the central government to hold peace talks with separatist political groups. Sayeed also created a committee within the state assembly to study all autonomy-related issues.

After initial signs of improvement during the new government's honeymoon period, the incidence of both violence and human rights violations rose to previous levels: an estimated 3,000 people were killed during 2003. Progress in finding a solution to the conflict moved at a slow pace, largely because the main groups could not agree on an overall framework within which negotiations should be conducted. Additional complications have arisen as a result of factional infighting within militant groups, such as the Hizbul Mujahideen, and between moderates and hard-liners within the APHC. Nevertheless, during the year, the Indian government showed a greater willingness than before to initiate a dialogue with various Kashmiri groups, including the APHC. At the same time, authorities in New Delhi attempted to improve relations with Pakistan via a series of "confidence-building measures" announced in October, including a resumption of transport links between the two countries. In November, Pakistan declared a cease-fire across the LOC, to which India reciprocated, and the two governments plan to hold talks over Kashmir in 2004.

**Political Rights and Civil Liberties:** India has never held a referendum on Kashmiri self-determination as called for in a 1948 UN resolution. The state's residents can nominally change the local administration through elections, but historically, elections have been marred by violence, coercion by security forces, and balloting irregularities. Militants commonly enforce boycotts called for by separatist political parties, threaten election officials and candidates, and kill political activists as well as civilians during the balloting. During the campaign period leading up to the 2002 elections for the 87-seat state assembly, over 800 people, including more than 75 political activists and candidates, were killed. However, the balloting process itself was carefully monitored by India's Election Commission, and turnout averaged just over 40 percent. Most independent observers judged the elections to be fair but not entirely free, largely because of the threat of violence.

Although Jammu and Kashmir was returned to local rule in 1996, many viewed the National Conference government as corrupt, incompetent, and unaccountable to the wishes and needs of Kashmiris. A report issued by the International Crisis Group noted that official corruption is "widespread" and corruption cases are seldom prosecuted. Much corrupt behavior and illegal economic activity can be traced directly to political leaders and parties and to militant groups. Although the new state government made a commitment to address issues of corruption and governance, progress in improving both has been slow.

The insurgency has forced Kashmiri media outlets to "tread carefully in their reporting," according to the Committee to Protect Journalists. In recent years, militant groups have kidnapped, tortured, killed, and threatened numerous journalists, causing some self-censorship. Unidentified gunmen murdered local editor Parvaz Mohammed Sultan in January, and in April, a bomb attack on state-owned media outlets left five people dead. In addition, authorities occasionally beat, detain, or otherwise harass journalists. Kashmiri journalist Iftikhar Ali Gilani, who was detained under the Official Secrets Act in 2002, was released in January after the military admitted that the case against him was baseless. Though it is generally not used, under India's 1971 Newspapers Incitements to Offenses Act (in effect only in Jammu and Kashmir), district magistrates can censor publications in certain circumstances. Other forms of pressure have also been employed against the media; in January, Reporters Sans Frontieres criticized a decision by the state government to stop placing official advertisements in the independent *Kashmir Observer* newspaper, thus depriving it of an important source of revenue. Despite these restrictions, however, newspapers do report on controversial issues such as alleged human rights abuses by security forces. Civilians' right to communicate was enhanced when the use of mobile phones was legalized in August.

Freedom to worship and academic freedom are generally respected by Indian and local authorities. For the first time in over a decade, the state government granted permission to separatist groups who wished to organize a procession in order to mark the anniversary of Prophet Muhammad's birthday. However, Islamist militant groups do target Hindu and Sikh temples or villages for attack; a number of such instances, in which dozens of civilians were killed, occurred during the year.

Although local and national civil rights groups are permitted to operate, the Indian government has banned some international groups from visiting the state. Several human rights activists have been killed since 1989, and only a few individuals and groups continue to do human rights work. The APHC, an umbrella group of 23 secessionist political parties, is allowed to operate, although its leaders are frequently subjected to preventive arrest and its requests for permits for public gatherings are routinely denied. The Indian government has also denied permission for APHC leaders to travel to Pakistan. Politically motivated strikes, protest marches, and antigovernment demonstrations take place on a regular basis, although some are forcibly broken up by the authorities.

Under heavy pressure from both the government and militants, the judiciary barely functions, according to the U.S. State Department's 2003 human rights report. The government frequently disregards judicial orders quashing detentions, and security forces refuse to obey court orders, while militants routinely threaten judges, witnesses, and the families of defendants. Many judicial abuses are facilitated by the 1978 Public Safety Act and other broadly drawn laws, which allow authorities to detain persons for up to two years without charge or trial. Although detentions under the security laws are nonrenewable, authorities frequently re-arrest suspects on new charges and impose new detentions; Amnesty International's 2003 report noted that hundreds of people remain held in preventive detention under such legislation. The new state government promised in November 2002 to review cases of detainees being held without trial and to release those against whom there were no charges. Although a screening committee met several times early in 2003 and several political prisoners were released, progress in implementing this commitment remains slow. The Prevention of Terrorism Act (POTA), which became law in March

2002, gives authorities wide powers of interrogation and detention while expanding the definitions of punishable crimes and prescribing severe punishments for a broad range of criminal acts. While it was not used to arrest Kashmiris in 2003 (as promised by the new state government), many of those arrested under POTA in 2002 remained in detention.

Two other broadly written laws, the Armed Forces Special Powers Act and the Disturbed Areas Act, allow Indian forces to search homes and arrest suspects without a warrant, shoot suspects on sight, and destroy homes or buildings believed to house militants or arms. Moreover, the Special Powers Act requires New Delhi to approve any prosecution of Indian forces. While the state human rights commission examines some human rights complaints, it cannot directly investigate abuses by the army or other federal security forces or take action against those found guilty of violations. Efforts to bring soldiers to justice have been rare. However, in 2003, the new state government did undertake several initiatives to improve accountability. In June, it announced that 118 security force personnel had been punished for having committed rights violations.

In a continuing cycle of violence, several thousand militants, security force personnel, and civilians are killed each year. Approximately 500,000 Indian security forces based in Kashmir, including soldiers, federal paramilitary troops, and the police, carry out arbitrary arrests and detentions, torture, "disappearances," and custodial killings of suspected militants and alleged civilian sympathizers. From 3,000 to 8,000 people are estimated to have "disappeared" during the course of the insurgency. As part of the counterinsurgency effort, the government has organized and armed pro-government militias composed of former militants. Members of these groups act with impunity and have reportedly carried out a wide range of human rights abuses against pro-Pakistani militants as well as civilians. Local activists report that human rights violations continue to occur at levels similar to those of previous years.

Armed with increasingly sophisticated and powerful weapons, and relying to a greater degree on the deployment of suicide squads, militant groups backed by Pakistan continued to kill pro-India politicians, public employees, suspected informers, members of rival factions, soldiers, and civilians. Militants also engage in kidnapping, rape, extortion, and other forms of terror. Repeated violence against Kashmiri Hindus throughout the year, such as the killing of 24 Hindus in Nadimarg in March, is part of a pattern since 1990 that has forced several hundred thousand Hindus to flee the region. Until the cease-fire declared in November, shelling by Indian and Pakistani troops along the LOC killed numerous civilians during the year, displaced thousands more, and disrupted schools and the local economy.

Female civilians continue to be subjected to harassment and intimidation, including rape and murder, at the hands of both the security forces and militant groups. Women have also been targeted by the Lashkar-e-Jabbar militant group, which issued an ultimatum in 2001 that all Muslim women wear *burqas*, or head-to-toe coverings; members of the group threw acid at and sprayed paint on several women who refused to comply with the directive. In late 2002, another militant group active in Rajouri district declared that no girls over the age of 12 should attend school.

# Indonesia
## West Papua

**Population:** 1,800,000
**Religious Groups:** Christian, Muslim, animist
**Ethnic Groups:** Melanesian [240 different peoples] (50 percent), Indonesian (50 percent)

**Political Rights:** 5
**Civil Liberties:** 4
**Status:** Partly Free

**Ten-Year Ratings Timeline (Political Rights, Civil Liberties, Status)**

| 1994 | 1995 | 1996 | 1997 | 1998 | 1999 | 2000 | 2001 | 2002 | 2003 |
|------|------|------|------|------|------|------|------|------|------|
| 7,7NF | 7,7NF | 7,7NF | 7,7NF | 7,6NF | 6,5PF | 5,5PF | 5,5PF | 5,4PF | 5,4PF |

**Overview:**

Five years after the downfall of former Indonesian strongman Suharto ushered in greater political and social freedoms in troubled Papua, serious human rights abuses continued in 2003 in Indonesia's easternmost province, as security forces mounted a crackdown following a raid by armed attackers on a military outpost. Meanwhile, a military court in April handed down light sentences to four soldiers convicted in the killing of a pro-independence leader in 2001.

Located on the western side of rugged New Guinea island, Papua has been dominated by outside powers for nearly two centuries. The Dutch set up the first European outpost in New Guinea in 1828 and formally took control of the South Pacific island's western side under an 1848 agreement with Britain. That deal paved the way for Britain and Germany to colonize the eastern side, which today is the independent state of Papua New Guinea. The Japanese occupied the Dutch-controlled side of New Guinea during World War II. The Netherlands ceded its territory to Indonesia in 1963 under a UN agreement calling for Jakarta to hold a referendum on self-determination by 1969.

Seeking an independent homeland, a group of tribesmen calling themselves the Free Papua Movement (OPM) began waging a low-grade insurgency against Indonesian rule in the mid-1960s. As the violence continued, Jakarta gained UN approval to formally annex Papua after holding a tightly controlled "Act of Free Choice" referendum in the summer of 1969. The 1,025 traditional leaders who took part in this sham referendum voted unanimously against independence.

As the OPM stepped up its hit-and-run attacks against the far more powerful Indonesian forces, the army launched a counteroffensive in 1984 that drove hundreds of villagers into neighboring Papua New Guinea. That year, Indonesian troops also killed the prominent Papuan anthropologist Arnold Ap. The army carried out more major anti-OPM offensives in 1989.

While the OPM and other tiny, armed groups continue to mount sporadic antigovernment attacks, civilian groups have become the main voices for Papuan independence ever since Indonesia's democratic transition began in 1998. The Papua Presidium Council, a forum for Papuan leaders seeking peaceful independence, held a congress in the spring of 2000 that called on Jakarta to recognize a 1961 Papuan declaration of independence under Dutch rule that was never recognized internationally.

Jakarta tolerated the congress, but violence in the town of Wamena later in 2000 raised tensions and pushed the two sides even farther apart. That October, security forces in Wamena killed two people while breaking up a pro-independence ceremony. Amid mounting tensions in the town, security forces shot dead 11 more people, and local Papuans killed 19 immigrants from other parts of Indonesia.

The Papuan independence movement suffered a major blow when the leader of the Presidium Council, Theys Eluay, was killed in 2001. A military court in April 2003 convicted two officers and two soldiers for their involvement in Eluay's killing, but handed down light jail sentences of up to three and a half years. Throughout 2001, a series of alleged rebel attacks and security force crackdowns caused thousands of villagers to flee their homes.

Tensions rose again in 2003 as police and soldiers carried out sweeps in the Wamena area after unknown attackers broke into a local military command in April, killing two soldiers and stealing arms. Indonesian forces arrested at least 30 people in connection with the attack, one of whom died in custody allegedly as a result of torture. Police in July shot dead one man and wounded two others while breaking up a pre-dawn ceremony in Wamena that raised the pro-independence Morning Star flag.

Meanwhile, the U.S. Federal Bureau of Investigation is investigating whether the military was involved in an ambush in 2002 that killed two Americans and an Indonesian near the giant Grasberg mine in Tembagapura. The military has denied involvement. Owned by the local subsidiary of the U.S.-based Freeport McMoRan, the gold and copper mine came under scrutiny in the 1990s over environmental concerns and allegations that Indonesian forces guarding the site committed rights abuses against local Papuans.

**Political Rights and Civil Liberties:** Papuans enjoy many basic rights previously denied to them under former President Suharto. Security forces, however, continue to commit serious human rights abuses, and several Papuans recently have been jailed for peaceful, pro-independence activities.

Moreover, while Papuans can vote in Indonesian elections, they continue to lack the right to determine Papua's political future. They had no input into the so-called New York Agreement of 1962 between the Netherlands and United Nations that transferred Papua from Dutch to Indonesian control in 1963. Moreover, the 1969 referendum that ratified Indonesian rule was neither free nor fair. The New York Agreement did not specify procedures for the referendum, but the agreement did call for it to be held "in accordance with international practice," a standard that Jakarta arguably ignored. The Indonesian military reportedly coerced the traditional leaders who took part into approving Jakarta's rule. The UN special observer reported that, "the administration exercised at all times a tight political control over the population."

Papua's many independent newspapers and magazines generally are permitted to report on the territory's pro-independence movement and other local political news. However, journalists who try to expose abuses by security forces often come under pressure to halt their investigations. Radio and television stations generally are less outspoken than their print counterparts.

Most Papuans follow either Christianity or indigenous beliefs, and all generally can worship freely. University professors and other educators generally can write and lecture without interference.

Meanwhile, human rights, social welfare, and environmental nongovernmental groups generally operate freely. Prominent local human rights groups, however, such as the Institute for Human Rights Study and Advocacy, have had their activities monitored and members harassed by police. Trade unions have limited influence given the relatively low number of Papuans who have wage-earning jobs.

Papua's court system is fairly rudimentary, and corruption among judges reportedly is common. Moreover, courts continue to jail peaceful independence activists. Around 20 of the more than 50 Papuans who have been tried since late 1998 in connection with separatist activities are believed to be peaceful pro-independence activists, the human rights group Amnesty International reported in July. Amnesty said in early October that two prisoners of conscience currently were in jail in Papua, both in connection with a December 2002 flag-raising ceremony.

Indonesian forces in Papua have assaulted, tortured, and killed villagers while searching for suspected rebels and have also killed Papuans while searching for ordinary criminal suspects, according to the U.S. State Department's human rights report for 2002, released in March 2003. Some detained suspects are tortured or brutally beaten, the New York based Human Rights Watch said in 2002. Meanwhile, the OPM and other small, armed, separatist groups in recent years have killed several soldiers and police and have also briefly kidnapped several foreigners in order to bring attention to their cause.

Critics say that the presence of large numbers of non-Papuans in the territory threatens to marginalize the Papuans' distinct Melanesian culture and makes it harder for them to find work. Local governmental agencies and private mining outfits reportedly tend to fill job openings with immigrants rather than Papuans. Moreover, immigrants dominate small business and reportedly discriminate against indigenous Papuans. The October 2000 killings in Wamena of at least 19 immigrants from other parts of Indonesia were the worst of several incidents in recent years where Papuans violently attacked or otherwise harassed non-Papuans. Some 170,000 non-Papuans came to Papua from Indonesia's overcrowded main islands under a largely defunct "transmigration" program that began in the 1970s. Thousands more immigrated on their own.

Indonesian rule has helped modernize Papua and develop its economy. Most of the benefits, however, have been reaped by the military, foreign investors, and immigrants from other parts of the archipelago. Papuans also have little control over the territory's abundant natural resources. Indigenous Papuans say that officials continue to expropriate their ancestral lands and grant mining, logging, and energy contracts without adequate consultation or compensation, while investing little in local development projects. Papua recently received an increase in funds from Jakarta under a 2001 Indonesian law giving the province 80 percent of local forestry, fishery, and energy revenues. Many Papuans say, however, that they have seen few tangible benefits from the money.

Traditional norms relegate women to secondary roles in family and public life, contributing to unofficial discrimination against women in education and employment.

# Iraq
## Kurdistan

**Population:** 4,000,000　**Political Rights:** 5
**Religious Groups:** Sunni　**Civil Liberties:** 4
Muslim [majority]　**Status:** Partly Free
**Ethnic Groups:** Kurds, Assyrian, Armenian, Iraqi Turkmen

### Ten-Year Ratings Timeline (Political Rights, Civil Liberties, Status)

| 1994 | 1995 | 1996 | 1997 | 1998 | 1999 | 2000 | 2001 | 2002 | 2003 |
|------|------|------|------|------|------|------|------|------|------|
| 4,4PF | 4,4PF | 6,6NF | 6,6NF | 6,6NF | 6,6NF | 6,6NF | 5,5PF | 5,4PF | 5,4PF |

**Overview:**　As U.S.-led coalition forces swept away the brutal dictatorship of Iraqi president Saddam Hussein and began forging a new Iraqi polity in 2003, the autonomous Kurdish enclave in northern Iraq remained largely under the control of the Kurdistan Democratic Party (KDP) and the Patriotic Union of Kurdistan (PUK), though some governing responsibilities were relinquished to the Coalition Provisional Authority (CPA). Kurdish jubilation over the fall of Iraq's Baathist regime was tempered by the deterioration of living conditions, difficulties in the repatriation of Kurdish refugees to areas outside of the enclave, and uncertainty over the future political status of the autonomous zone.

Since the withdrawal of Iraqi military forces and administrative personnel from northern Iraq and the establishment of a U.S.-enforced no-fly zone north of the 36th parallel in 1991, most of the three northern provinces of Erbil, Duhok, and Suleimaniyah have been under the control of Massoud Barzani's KDP and Jalal Talabani's PUK. Elections in the Kurdish self-rule area were held in 1992, and the KDP and PUK shared power in the nascent Kurdish Regional Government (KRG) for two years. Disputes over power and revenue sparked a three-year civil war, from 1994 to 1997. The two rival Kurdish groups set up separate administrations, with the KDP controlling the western region from its headquarters in Erbil, and the PUK controlling the southeast from its headquarters in Suleimaniyah. In 1998, the two groups agreed to unify their separate administrations and hold new elections, but implementation of the agreement remained stalled by disputes over revenue and the composition of a joint regional government. In 2001, however, the two rival factions eased restrictions on travel between their respective sectors and resumed dialogue. The KDP-PUK rapprochement deepened in 2002 as the United States prepared for a possible invasion of Iraq to oust Saddam Hussein.

In spite of this rivalry, northern Iraq experienced rapid development during the 1990s. With their 13 percent share of Iraqi revenue from the UN oil-for-food program, and customs duties from Iraqi-Turkish trade, the Kurdish authorities built schools, roads, hospitals, and sewage systems, and engaged in other development projects. Anxious to win international support for long-term Kurdish self-governance, both the KDP and the PUK allowed a flourishing of political and civil liberties not seen elsewhere in the Arab world.

KDP and PUK fighters (*peshmerga*) fought alongside coalition forces during the March-April 2003 invasion of Iraq. However, their relations with the CPA were strained after Kurdish forces moved into the northern cities of Kirkuk and Mosul and expelled Arabs who had taken ownership of Kurdish homes and property seized by the former regime. The CPA also put pressure on the KDP and PUK to begin dissolving their militias, but they refused, insisting that the 50,000 to 60,000 fighters under their control be transformed into a regional self-defense force similar to the U.S. Army National Guard, which maintains locally recruited units in each state.

Although residents of the autonomous Kurdish enclave escaped the acute insecurity that plagued much of Iraq during the year, their living standards declined as a result of the sharp drop in the overland trade of diesel fuel to Turkey and the discontinuation of the UN oil-for-food program. Moreover, the cash-strapped Kurdish authorities came under pressure from the CPA to stop collecting taxes. The CPA began paying the salaries of civil servants in the Kurdish enclave, but these wages fell as much as 75 percent below their prewar salaries, sparking widespread discontent.

Conscious of the former Iraqi regime's legacy of anti-Kurdish repression, the overwhelming majority of Iraqi Kurds are reluctant to relinquish the independence they have enjoyed for more than a decade. In negotiations with the CPA and non-Kurdish groups over the country's political future, Kurdish leaders demanded the creation of a decentralized federal state with a strong Kurdish regional government in control of northern oil resources.

**Political Rights and Civil Liberties:** Iraqi Kurds cannot change their government democratically, as factional strife has precluded parliamentary elections since 1992 and national elections have not yet been held. The KDP and the PUK have separate administrations and cabinets for the territories under their control. While municipal elections held by the PUK in February 2000 were generally free and fair, the May 2001 municipal elections in the KDP enclave were marred by Assyrian Christian allegations of vote rigging and intimidation of boycott supporters by Kurdish police.

Freedom of expression is generally protected. The KDP and PUK have allowed approximately 200 print publications, 2 satellite television channels, around 20 local television stations, and scores of radio stations to operate in areas under their control. Most, however, are affiliated with political parties. While few media outlets are, in fact, independent, there is an open climate for discussion of political issues. Internet access and satellite dishes are available without restriction.

Religious freedom is protected, though there have been several reported incidents of Muslim-on-Christian mob violence in recent years. Academic freedom in areas under KDP and PUK control is protected, although Turkmen student groups have complained of harassment.

Freedom of association is also protected. Around 30 licensed political parties have been established, representing a broad ideological and sectarian spectrum. However, the activities of the Iraqi Turkmen Front (ITF) and the Iraqi Workers Communist Party (IWCP) have been curtailed in recent years. Scores of human rights groups and other nongovernmental organizations operate freely. Both Kurdish factions have enacted laws protecting workers' rights.

While the Kurdish authorities have been much more tolerant of ethnic and religious minorities than the former government of Saddam Hussein, Assyrian Christian and Turkmen groups have complained about human rights abuses. Both Kurdish factions have forced Assyrian and Turkmen schools to fly the Kurdish flag and teach the Kurdish language. In February, KDP forces in Erbil reportedly arrested and detained the ITF's security chief.

The KDP and the PUK maintain separate judicial systems in areas under their control, but reliable information about judicial integrity is difficult to obtain. Reportedly, hearings are conducted, adjudicated, and enforced by local officials of the two parties. The two groups also run separate prisons and detention facilities, where human rights violations, including denial of due process and torture, have occurred. However, both sides regularly grant access to their prisons to delegations from the International Committee of the Red Cross.

Women face social and legal discrimination in Iraqi Kurdistan. Local women's organizations report widespread "honor killings" of women who deviate from traditional social norms, especially in areas under the control of the KDP, which relies strongly on tribal support. The PUK has abolished legal provisions legitimizing honor killings; in 2002, the Independent Women's Organization reported that the number of honor killings in PUK territory declined from 75 in 1991 to 15 in 2001. Women are under-represented in both administrations, but less so in that of the PUK, which has a 500-strong battalion of female *peshmerga* and several senior female officials in its regional government. In July 2003, the PUK appointed a woman, Mudira Abu Bakr, town prefect for the northern Dukan region. A few months later, PUK leader Nasreen Mustafa Sideek Barwari became the lone female minister in the cabinet of Iraq's provisional government.

# Israel
## Israeli-Administered Territories

**Population:** 3,390,000 (1,226,000: **Political Rights:** 6
Gaza; 2,164,000: West Bank). In   **Civil Liberties:** 6
addition, there are some 220,000   **Status:** Not Free
Israeli settlers in the West Bank,
20,000 in the Golan Heights, and 7,500 in the Gaza Strip.
Approximately 172,000 Jews and 170,000 Arabs live in
East Jerusalem.
**Religious Groups:** Muslim, Jewish, Christian
**Ethnic Groups:** Palestinian, Jewish, Bedouin
*Note:* The areas and total number of persons under Israeli jurisdiction changed periodically during the year as a result the fluid nature of Israel's military presence in the West Bank and Gaza Strip.

**Ten-Year Ratings Timeline (Political Rights, Civil Liberties, Status)**

| 1994 | 1995 | 1996 | 1997 | 1998 | 1999 | 2000 | 2001 | 2002 | 2003 |
|------|------|------|------|------|------|------|------|------|------|
| -- | -- | 6,5NF | 6,5NF | 6,5NF | 6,5NF | 6,6NF | 6,6NF | 6,6NF | 6,6NF |

**Overview:**    Despite international efforts to urge Israel and the Palestinian Authority (PA) to pursue peace based on a "road map" toward eventual Palestinian statehood, and a seven-week Palestinian cease-fire, the two parties remained locked in violent conflict throughout 2003. While Israel did not fulfill its obligations under the road map to freeze settlement activity in the West Bank, the PA failed to abide by the demands to crack down on terrorism. Israel maintained its siege of Yasser Arafat's compound in Ramallah, isolating the Palestinian leader and deciding in principle to "remove" him. Citing the PA's unwillingness to confront terrorism, Israel targeted and killed several operatives and political leaders of radical Palestinian groups, generally after devastating suicide bombings in Israel; several unarmed Palestinian civilians died in the attacks. Israel also staged several raids into Palestinian-ruled territory in the West Bank and Gaza Strip in an attempt to combat terrorism. Israel continued construction of a controversial security fence in the West Bank designed to prevent terrorists from infiltrating the country. Two joint Israeli-Palestinian nongovernmental peace initiatives garnered limited domestic support on both sides. Approximately 2,500 Palestinians and 900 Israelis have been killed since the outbreak of the Palestinian uprising in September 2000.

After Palestinian rejection of a UN partition plan in 1947, Israel declared its independence on the portion of land allotted for Jewish settlement. The fledgling state was jointly attacked by neighboring Arab states in Israel's 1948 War of Independence. While Israel maintained its sovereignty, Jordan seized East Jerusalem and the West Bank, and Egypt took control of the Gaza Strip. In the 1967 Six-Day War, Israel came to occupy the West Bank, Gaza, the Sinai Peninsula, East Jerusalem, and the Golan Heights.

After 1967, Israel began establishing Jewish settlements in the West Bank and

Gaza Strip, an action regarded as illegal by most of the international community. Israel maintains that these settlements are legal since under international law the West Bank and Gaza are in dispute, with their final legal status to be determined through direct bilateral negotiations based on UN Security Council Resolutions 242 and 338. The settlements have become a major sticking point in negotiations between Israel and the Palestinians and in relations between Israel and the international community. The PA- and U.S.-backed road map demands a freeze on settlements, something that Israel did not sufficiently honor in 2003.

In what became known as the *intifada* (uprising), Palestinians living in the West Bank and Gaza began attacking mainly settlers and Israel Defense Forces troops (IDF) in 1987 to protest Israeli rule. A series of secret negotiations between Israel and Arafat's Palestine Liberation Organization (PLO) conducted mainly in Oslo, Norway, produced an agreement in September 1993. The Declaration of Principles provided for a PLO renunciation of terrorism, PLO recognition of Israel, Israeli troop withdrawals, and gradual Palestinian autonomy in the West Bank and Gaza.

Most of Gaza and the West Bank town of Jericho were turned over to the PA in May 1994. Following the assassination of Israeli prime minister Yitzhak Rabin in November 1995 by a right-wing Jewish extremist opposed to the peace process, Israel, under the stewardship of Prime Minister Shimon Peres, began redeploying its forces from six major Palestinian cities in the West Bank and Gaza.

The January 1996 elections for the PA's first Legislative Council and for the head of the council's executive authority were considered to be generally free and fair. Independents won 35 of the 88 council seats, while Arafat's Fatah movement won the remainder. Arafat became chairman of the executive authority with 88 percent of the vote.

After a wave of Palestinian suicide bombings in early 1996, Peres lost a general election to Likud party leader Benjamin Netanyahu, who stayed in office until 1999. Labor Party leader Ehud Barak was elected prime minister in May of that year; he immediately pursued negotiations with Syria over the Golan Heights. Intensive peace negotiations between Israel and Syria broke down in January 2000 over disagreements on final borders around the Golan Heights. The key sticking point centered on which country should control a strip of shoreline along the eastern edge of the Sea of Galilee, located below the western slopes of the Golan. The sea serves as Israel's primary fresh water source. Prior to losing the Golan in 1967, Syria had used the territory to shell northern Israeli towns.

Under the provisions of Oslo implemented so far, the Palestinians have had full or partial control of up to 40 percent of the territory of the West Bank and 98 percent of the Palestinian population. However, Palestinian jurisdiction has eroded considerably since the eruption of the second intifada in September 2000, when the IDF temporarily re-entered some PA-controlled territory.

At Camp David in July 2000 and at Taba, Egypt, in the fall and in early 2001, Israeli and Palestinian leaders engaged in negotiations under U.S. sponsorship. For the first time, Israel discussed compromise solutions on Jerusalem, agreeing to some form of Palestinian sovereignty over East Jerusalem and Islamic holy sites in Jerusalem's Old City. Israel also offered all of the Gaza Strip and more than 95 percent of the West Bank to the Palestinians. The Palestinian leadership rejected the Israeli proposals. Some analysts suggested that Arafat was not confident that Israeli offers guaranteed contiguity of Palestinian territory in the West Bank or that Israel would recognize a "right of return," allowing Palestinian refugees to live in Israel.

Following a controversial visit by Likud party leader Ariel Sharon to the Temple Mount in Jerusalem in September 2000, the Palestinians launched an armed uprising. The site, considered the third holiest in Islam, is home to al-Aqsa mosque and was once the site of the Jewish temple. Snap Israeli elections in February 2001 took place against the backdrop of continuing Palestinian violence. Sharon, promising Israelis both peace and security from terrorism, trounced Barak at the polls. Sharon was reelected in national elections in January 2003.

Violence continued to rage throughout the Israeli-administered territories in 2003. Insisting that the PA was not preventing terrorism, Israel responded to successive waves of Palestinian suicide bombings by staging several incursions into Palestinian-ruled territory, destroying many weapons factories and killing many members of radical Islamist groups such as Hamas and Islamic Jihad, as well as members of the secular Tanzim and al-Aqsa Martyrs Brigades, both offshoots of Arafat's mainstream Fatah movement. Israel ceased to distinguish between militants and so-called political leaders of the groups, insisting that both were directly responsible for terrorism. In September, Israel attempted to assassinate Hamas leader Sheikh Ahmed Yassin.

The IDF also staged several raids into the Gaza Strip, especially in response to rocket fire from there into Israel. Israeli troops also tried to destroy arms-smuggling tunnels from Egypt into Gaza, killing civilians and razing many Palestinian homes and farming groves in the process.

While Israeli responses were generally carefully executed, many innocent bystanders were wounded or killed in the raids, which were often carried out by helicopter gunships or undercover units. Israel denied the deliberate targeting of civilians, asserting that Palestinian gunmen and other militants were intentionally positioning themselves among civilian populations, thus placing them in danger.

Israel faced intense international criticism for its handling of the Palestinian uprising. The United Nations condemned Israel for using disproportionate lethal force against Palestinian demonstrators. Although the IDF has disciplined some soldiers for apparent excessive use of force, Israeli human rights organizations have criticized the army for not being more vigilant.

The conflict in the territories resembled guerrilla warfare as Palestinians adopted more sophisticated tactics. Successful attacks were carried out against Israeli tanks in the Gaza Strip, a tactic used widely by Hezbollah against Israeli forces in southern Lebanon throughout the 1990s. Several analysts concluded that Iranian- and Syrian-backed Hezbollah cells in the West Bank and Gaza train Palestinians.

Israel and the PA took some steps toward implementing a road map to peace put forward in April 2003 by the United States, Russia, the UN, and the European Union (EU). The multi-stage, performance-based plan demanded concrete Palestinian moves against terrorist groups, to be followed by Israeli troop pullbacks and relaxation of curfews and travel restrictions. The plan also called for a freeze on Israeli settlement activity. Progress toward these goals was conditioned on the PA's first implementing sweeping political and economic reforms and establishing an "empowered prime minister" who would replace Arafat as lead Palestinian negotiator and as head of Palestinian security services.

In April, in accordance with the road map, Yasser Arafat appointed Mahmoud Abbas as the new Palestinian prime minister. Abbas negotiated a three-month cease-fire (*Hudna*) among Palestinian radical groups at the end of June. While attacks against Israel markedly decreased, isolated attacks, including a suicide bombing, did take place. The PA continued to refuse to dismantle the groups. Hamas and Islamic Jihad called off the cease-fire in August after Israel assassinated Ismail Abu Shanab, a Hamas official in Gaza. The assassination came 48 hours after 18 people were killed by a Hamas suicide bombing aboard a bus in Jerusalem. The bombing violated the Palestinians' own cease-fire, to which Israel was not a party. Shortly after, Israel resumed operations in the West Bank and Gaza, reimposing roadblocks and sending troops back into Palestinian areas from which it had withdrawn during the lull in the violence.

Prime Minister Abbas resigned in September in protest over Yasser Arafat's refusal to allow him control of the various Palestinian security services, a key demand in the road map. He was replaced by Ahmed Qureia, who soon after his appointment similarly clashed with the Palestinian president. However, in the end, Qureia acquiesced to Arafat's dominance, as reflected in the creation of a Palestinian national security council, responsible for all security affairs and answerable solely to Arafat.

Israel continued construction of a controversial security fence along the West Bank side of the 1967 armistice line. Composed of high-wire fencing, ditches, security sensors, watchtowers, and in some parts concrete slabs, the fence is designed to prevent terrorists from infiltrating Israel. However, it is seen by Palestinians as a means to expropriate West Bank land and collectively punish ordinary Palestinians for atrocities committed by terrorists.

During the year, in partial accordance with the road map, Israel dismantled some illegal West Bank settlement outposts built without permits. Outposts normally consist of a handful of trailer homes placed mainly by religious Jews on uninhabited land. In October, the government announced plans to extend municipal services and security protection to some settlement outposts in the West Bank and Gaza and also issued new housing tenders for several hundred new apartment units in existing settlements, despite the road map's call for a freeze on Israeli settlement activity in the territories. In November, Prime Minister Sharon told a gathering of his Likud party that Israel would have to give up some settlements as part of a peace arrangement with the Palestinians.

Earlier in the fall, after devastating suicide bomb attacks in Israel, the Israeli cabinet decided in principle to "remove" Yasser Arafat from power at a time of its choosing, stating that he was the chief impediment to peace and that no progress could take place as long as he maintained political control over Palestinian affairs. However, in October, Sharon publicly ruled out killing Arafat as a policy option.

In November, the IDF's chief of staff, Lieutenant General Moshe Yaalon, publicly criticized Sharon's policies, saying they were strengthening terrorist organizations and undermining moderate Palestinian politicians. General Yaalon's remarks followed warnings by four former heads of the Shin Bet, Israel's domestic security service, that the government's policies were leading the country to "catastrophe."

A group of former Israeli and Palestinian politicians put forward in the fall of 2003 a private peace initiative negotiated in secret in Geneva, Switzerland. Premised on terms discussed by Israeli and Palestinian negotiators at Taba, Egypt, from December 2000 to January 2001, the nongovernmental "Geneva accord" called for an independent Palestinian state in the West Bank and Gaza Strip, the removal of Jewish settlements in those areas, the division of Jerusalem, and sole Palestinian control of the Temple Mount in Jerusalem's Old City with international monitoring. In return, Palestinians would pledge peace. There was also a vague reference to the Palestinians' dropping their demand for a "right of return" of refugees to Israel. The accord drew some limited support in the Israeli and Palestinian communities, but their respective leaders paid it little attention. An additional plan, proposed by former Shin Bet chief Ami Ayalon and Palestinian academic and peace activist Sari Nusseibeh also achieved limited support.

Peace talks with Syria did not take place during the year.

**Political Rights and Civil Liberties:** After Israel's annexation of East Jerusalem in 1967, Arab residents there were issued Israeli identity cards and given the option of obtaining Israeli citizenship. However, by law, Israel strips Arabs of their Jerusalem residency if they remain outside the city for more than three months. Arab residents have the same rights as Israeli citizens except the right to vote in national elections (they can vote in municipal elections). Many choose not to seek citizenship out of solidarity with Palestinians in the West Bank and Gaza Strip, believing East Jerusalem should be the capital of an independent Palestinian state. East Jerusalem's Arab population does not receive a share of municipal services proportionate to its numbers. Arabs in East Jerusalem have the right to vote in Palestinian elections.

Druze and Arabs in the Golan Heights, who were formerly under Syrian rule, possess similar status to Arab residents of East Jerusalem. They cannot vote in Israeli national elections, but they are represented at municipal levels.

International press freedom groups criticized Israel for preventing journalists from accessing conflict zones in the West Bank and for harassing Palestinian journalists. In January, the IDF closed two TV stations and one radio station in Hebron during antiterrorism operations. In April, Israeli troops shot and killed Nazih Darwazeh, an Associated Press Television News cameraman filming clashes in the West Bank city of Nablus. Israel denied deliberately targeting Darwazeh. In May, James Miller, a British cameraman, was killed after being shot in apparent crossfire between IDF troops and Palestinian gunmen in Gaza. He was filming a documentary about arms smuggling in the Rafah refugee camp. The same month, British photojournalist Tom Hurndall was shot in the head by IDF troops as they battled gunmen in the West Bank. The Committee to Protect Journalists has reported that several journalists have suffered gunshot wounds since 2000.

Israel generally recognizes the right to freedom of worship and religion. On several occasions during the intifada, Israel has restricted Muslim men under 40 from praying on the Temple Mount compound in Jerusalem's Old City, for fear of violent confrontations. Palestinians have deliberately damaged Jewish shrines and other holy places in the West Bank.

In January, after suicide bombings in Tel Aviv killed 22 people, Israel's Security Cabinet temporarily closed some Palestinian universities and prevented members of a PA delegation from traveling to London for meetings with British officials.

Freedom of assembly is generally respected. However, Israel has imposed strict curfews in the West Bank at various times since September 2000. There are many Palestinian nongovernmental organizations and civic groups. Labor affairs in the West Bank and Gaza are governed by a combination of Jordanian law and PA decisions. Workers may establish and join unions without government authorization. Palestinian workers seeking to strike must submit to arbitration by the PA Labor Ministry. No laws in the PA-ruled areas protect the rights of striking workers. Palestinian workers in Jerusalem are subject to Israeli labor law.

Palestinians accused by Israel of security offenses in Israeli-controlled areas are tried in Israeli military courts. Security offenses are broadly defined. Some due process protections exist in these courts, though there are limits on the rights to counsel, bail, and appeal. Administrative detention is widely used. Most convictions in Israeli military courts are based on confessions, sometimes obtained through physical pressure. Israel outlawed the use of torture as a means of extracting vital security information in 2000, but milder forms of physical coercion are permissible in cases where the prisoner is believed to have immediate information about impending terrorist attacks. Human rights groups still criticize Israel for engaging in what they consider torture. Confessions are usually spoken in Arabic and translated into Hebrew for official records.

While Palestinians have recourse to Israel's highest civilian courts to protest home demolitions and Israel's tactics in carrying out targeted assassinations, decisions made in their favor are rare.

In July, Israel released several hundred Palestinian prisoners. While the releases were not required under the road map, they were a key Palestinian demand to build confidence in the peace process. Some of those released went on to carry out attacks against Israelis, including suicide bombings.

During the year, Israel continued its controversial policy of destroying the homes of families of suicide bombers, claiming that the policy serves as a deterrent. Throughout the Palestinian uprising, Israel has also destroyed many homes in the West Bank and Gaza Strip on the grounds that they provide cover for gunmen and bombers. Additionally, Israel has destroyed some Palestinian structures built without permits, especially in East Jerusalem. Building permits are difficult for West Bank Palestinians to obtain.

In October, the IDF killed several Palestinians and destroyed many homes and much farmland during fighting with gunmen in the Rafah refugee camp in the Gaza Strip. Israel was attempting to destroy tunnels originating in Egypt used to smuggle arms to Gaza; many of the tunnels led to private homes in Rafah. In one raid, the IDF destroyed 230 homes, displacing 1,200 people, according to the International Committee of the Red Cross. Israel claimed it had uncovered 70 tunnels since 2000 and that destroying homes was a necessary part of preventing arms smuggling.

In March, Rachel Corrie, an American peace activist attached to the International Solidarity Movement (ISM) was killed while protesting in a closed military zone in the Gaza Strip. She died after an Israeli army bulldozer crushed her as she protested in front of it. After an extensive inquiry, the incident was ruled an accident by the IDF. Israel, in an attempt to control the movement of international protestors into active combat zones, expelled some ISM members and restricted the movements of other activists into and around the territories.

Violence between Palestinians and settlers is not uncommon. Several Jewish settlers in the West Bank and Gaza Strip were ambushed and killed by Palestinian gunmen or attacked with mortar fire. Some were targeted while traveling in cars or buses, and others were attacked while in their homes and schools. Attacks by settlers against Palestinians have also taken place. In September, three settlers were convicted of planning a bomb attack at a Palestinian school in the West Bank.

Construction of Israel's security barrier in the West Bank disconnected hundreds of Palestinians from their farming fields and denied them and others easier access to other parts of the West Bank. The fence cut off one town, Qalqilya, from open access to the farms that normally supply its markets. Some Palestinian buildings, irrigation networks, and fields were destroyed to accommodate construction of the fence. Israel said that it replanted Palestinian trees and crops in areas not affected by the fence. Israel also incorporated access gates for use by Palestinians, but many complained of substantial inconveniences and hardship. Israel insisted that the fence was not a permanent border, that it was a temporary solution to an ongoing terrorist threat. A report issued by UN secretary-general Kofi Annan in November said that the barrier would cause serious human suffering once completed, separating nearly 700,000 Palestinians from their farms, jobs, and schools.

All West Bank and Gaza residents must have identification cards in order to obtain entry permits into Israel, including East Jerusalem. Israel often denies permits to applicants with no explanation. Even senior Palestinian officials are subject to long delays and searches at Israeli checkpoints in the West Bank.

The Israeli army maintained roadblocks and checkpoints throughout the West Bank in 2003 to prevent terrorists from entering Israel. The measure denied Palestinians easy passage from one town to another, making access to jobs, hospitals, and schools extremely difficult. The restrictions of movement between and among Palestinian towns and cities have been denounced as collective punishment. Travel for Palestinians between the West Bank and Gaza is extremely difficult. Israel exercises overall military control at border crossings between the West Bank and Jordan and between the Gaza Strip and Egypt.

The Palestinian economy has been seriously affected by the intifida and the Israeli closures of the West Bank and Gaza. According to the World Bank, unemployment in Palestinian areas reached 50 percent in 2003. Thousands of Palestinians rely on access to jobs in Israel. At various times during the year, Israel permitted several thousand Palestinian workers to enter the country.

# Israel
## Palestinain Authority-
## Administered Territories

**Population:** 3,390,000
(1,226,000: Gaza; 2,164,000:
West Bank). In addition,
there are some 220,000 Israeli settlers in the West Bank,
20,000 in the Golan Heights, and 7,500 in the Gaza Strip.
Approximately 172,000 Jews and 170,000 Arabs live in East Jerusalem.

**Political Rights:** 5
**Civil Liberties:** 6
**Status:** Not Free

**Religious Groups:** Muslim, Christain
**Ethnic Groups:** Palestinian, Bedouin
*Note:* The areas and total number of persons under Palestinian jurisdiction changed periodically during the year as a result of the fluid nature of Israel's military presence and activities in the West Bank and Gaza Strip.

**Ten-Year Ratings Timeline (Political Rights, Civil Liberties, Status)**

| 1994 | 1995 | 1996 | 1997 | 1998 | 1999 | 2000 | 2001 | 2002 | 2003 |
|------|------|------|------|------|------|------|------|------|------|
| -- | -- | 5,6NF | 5,6NF | 5,6NF | 5,6NF | 5,6NF | 5,6NF | 5,6NF | 5,6NF |

**Overview:**

Palestinians continued their *intifada* (uprising) in 2003, which led to Israeli incursions into areas previously ceded to Palestinian control. Israel intermittently reoccupied some West Bank towns and cities, carried out armed raids, and imposed strict curfews and roadblocks in and around Palestinian areas. The Israeli measures, sometimes resulting in Palestinian civilian deaths, generally occurred after terrorist attacks against Israelis by Palestinian Islamist groups and by more secular groups such as Tanzim and the al-Aqsa Martyrs Brigades, which are affiliated with Palestinian chairman Yasser Arafat's Fatah movement. Crises gripped Palestinian politics throughout the year, with two separate appointments to the post of prime minister in accordance with the U.S.-backed "road map" to peace put forward in April. The plan called for consolidating Palestinian security services under the prime minister; Arafat's refusal to do so prompted the first prime minister to resign. The Israeli government decided in principle to "remove" him from power, although it ruled out killing him. A seven-week cease-fire (*hudna*) declared by the Palestinian Authority (PA) and radical Palestinian groups ended in renewed violence against Israel. The PA did not carry out all its obligations under the road map, including foremost the need to confront and dismantle terrorist groups. The rule of law eroded in some Palestinian cities, where violent armed gangs generally operated unchallenged.

In the 1967 Six-Day War, Israel came to occupy Sinai, the West Bank, Gaza, East Jerusalem, and the Golan Heights. Israel annexed Jerusalem's Old City and East Jerusalem in 1967 and the Golan Heights in 1981.

Palestinians living in the West Bank and Gaza began an intifada in 1987, primarily attacking targets of the Israel Defense Forces (IDF) to protest Israeli rule. Israel and Arafat's Palestine Liberation Organization (PLO) conducted a series of secret negotiations in Oslo, Norway, producing an agreement in September 1993. Premised on the land-for-peace formula articulated in UN Security Council Resolution 242 of November 1967, the Declaration of Principles provided for Israeli troop withdrawals and gradual Palestinian autonomy in the West Bank and Gaza in exchange for an end to Palestinian terrorism and recognition of Israel.

Elections for the first PA Legislative Council and for head of the council's executive authority, held in January 1996, were considered to be generally free and fair. Arafat's Fatah movement won 53 of the 88 council seats, and independents won 35. Arafat gained the chairmanship of the executive authority with 88 percent of the vote.

In May 1994, Israel turned over most of Gaza and the West Bank town of Jericho to the PA. Over the next two years, Israel redeployed its forces in the West Bank and Gaza. Israel concluded its redeployment from six major Palestinian cities in December 1995 and agreed to withdraw troops from 80 percent of Hebron in January 1997. As a result of the provisions of the Oslo agreement implemented, the PA has had full or partial control of up to 40 percent of the territory of the West Bank, and 98 percent of the Palestinian population. However, the IDF has reentered some PA-controlled territory several times since the eruption of the second intifada in September 2000.

In the United States at Camp David in July 2000 and at Taba, Egypt, in the fall of 2000 and early 2001, Prime Minister Ehud Barak and U.S. president Bill Clinton engaged the Palestinian leadership in far-reaching negotiations. Israel discussed for the first time compromise solutions on Jerusalem, agreeing to some form of Palestinian sovereignty over East Jerusalem and Islamic holy sites in Jerusalem's Old City. Israel also offered all of the Gaza Strip and more than 95 percent of the West Bank to the Palestinians. However, the Palestinian leadership rejected the Israeli offers. Some analysts suggested that Arafat was not satisfied that Palestinian territory in the West Bank would be contiguous and that Israel would recognize a "right of return" that would allow Palestinian refugees to live in Israel. Following a controversial visit by Likud party leader Ariel Sharon to the Temple Mount in Jerusalem in September 2000, the Palestinians initiated an armed uprising. The site, considered the third holiest in Islam, is home to al-Aqsa mosque and was once the site of the Jewish temple. Snap Israeli elections in February 2001 took place against the backdrop of continuing Palestinian violence. Sharon, promising Israelis both peace and security from terrorism, trounced Barak at the polls. Sharon was reelected in national elections in January 2003.

Violence raged throughout Palestinian areas in 2003. In response to successive waves of suicide bombings inside Israel and attacks on Jewish settlers and IDF personnel in the West Bank and Gaza, Israeli forces carried out several incursions into Palestinian-ruled territory, killing and arresting many suspected militants throughout the year.

Israel killed several top Hamas and Islamic Jihad figures and other radical Islamists suspected of committing or preparing attacks against Israel. Palestinians condemned Israel for the killings—often carried out by helicopter gunships or undercover units—and labeled them "assassinations." Israel also faced international criticism for the killings, which it termed "targeted killings." Israel justified the policy on the grounds that its repeated requests that the PA detain Palestinians suspected of planning or carrying out attacks had gone unheeded. Hamas and Islamic Jihad reject Israel's right to exist and are committed by their respective charters to its destruction. The U.S. government classifies the organizations as terrorist groups, making no distinction between their so-called military and political wings. In September, the European Union (EU) officially labeled Hamas a terrorist organization. Both groups routinely recruit Palestinians—including young men and women—to carry out suicide attacks. Fatah's al-Aqsa Martyrs Brigades also became increasingly involved in suicide attacks in 2003.

Israeli reprisal raids and killings of Palestinian militants sometimes resulted in the deaths of numerous Palestinian civilians. Israel denied the intentional targeting of civilians, saying that Palestinian gunmen and other militants were deliberately positioning themselves among civilians, thus putting them in harm's way.

In October, the Popular Resistance Committee, composed of breakaway members of Hamas, Fatah, and the Palestinian police, killed three Americans with roadside explosives as a U.S. diplomatic convoy traveled in the Gaza Strip. The involvement of former members of the Palestinian police suggested that elements within the PA may have collaborated in the attack. The incident marked the first deliberate attack against American targets by Palestinians in the Gaza Strip or West Bank. While the PA made some arrests, the U.S. government was not satisfied that the PA was engaged in a determined effort to apprehend the culprits. In November, the United States offered a reward of $5 million for information leading to the arrests of the attackers.

Israel and the PA took some steps toward implementing a road map to peace put forward by the United States, Russia, the United Nations, and the EU. The multistage, performance-based plan is premised on demonstrative Palestinian commitments to ending violence, to be followed by Israeli troop pullbacks and easing of curfews and travel restrictions on Palestinians. The road map also calls for a freeze on Israeli settlement activity once Palestinian terrorism ends. Progress toward these goals was conditioned on the PA's first implementing sweeping political and economic reforms and establishing an "empowered prime minister" committed to combating and dismantling violent Palestinian organizations, and who would replace Arafat as lead Palestinian negotiator and as head of Palestinian security services.

Jewish settlements in the West Bank and Gaza have become a major sticking point in negotiations between Israel and the Palestinians and in relations between Israel and the international community. The road map demands a freeze on settlement activity. While Israel dismantled some illegal outposts in the West Bank—composed mostly of small, makeshift trailers—it did not remove all outposts, nor did it cease construction activity in existing settlements.

In March, the Palestinian parliament approved the creation of the post of prime minister. In April, Yasser Arafat appointed Mahmoud Abbas as the new prime minister but refused to relinquish control over Palestinian security services or over negotiations with Israel. Arafat also rejected Abbas's proposed cabinet, endangering the possibility of reform and setting the stage for an inevitable political crisis.

The two men immediately clashed over the reorganization of Palestinian security services, with Abbas trying to abide by road map demands that he consolidate and take control over more than one dozen separate security agencies. Arafat blocked the appointment of Muhhamad Dahlan to head the Interior Ministry, which has control over security affairs. Israeli and American officials generally favored Dahlan for his pragmatism. With Arafat in charge, radical Palestinian groups and militias acted with relative impunity, helping to further undermine the rule of law in the West Bank and Gaza.

Prime Minister Abbas was able to negotiate a three-month cease-fire (*hudna*) between the PA and radical Palestinian groups at the end of June. However, he refused to confront and dismantle the groups, as required by the road map. While attacks against Israel did markedly decrease during the hudna, isolated attacks took place, including a suicide bombing. Israel argued that the radical groups used the downtime afforded by their cease-fire to rebuild their arsenals, regroup, and plan future attacks. Israel accused Arafat of providing funds to armed groups opposed to the cease-fire, including the al-Aqsa Martyrs Brigades.

Hamas and Islamic Jihad called off the cease-fire in August after Israel assassinated Ismail Abu Shanab, a Hamas official, in Gaza. The assassination came 48 hours after a Hamas suicide bombing aboard a bus in Jerusalem killed 18 people, in violation of the Palestinians' own cease-fire, to which Israel was not a party. With the ending of the cease-fire, Israel resumed antiterrorist operations in the West Bank and Gaza, reimposing roadblocks and sending troops back into Palestinian areas from which it had withdrawn during the lull in violence.

In September, relations between Arafat loyalists and Prime Minister Abbas worsened. An armed standoff between Arafat supporters and Palestinian police at a civil service building in Gaza underscored Abbas's ultimate inability to affect meaningful political reform, including replacing the heads of key political posts. The standoff arose after Mohammad Abu Sharia, an Arafat loyalist, refused orders from Abbas to give up his post as civil service commissioner. Also in September, Palestinian police ended a violent two-day clash with Hamas that followed the arrest of seven Hamas members suspected of kidnapping a policeman.

Abbas resigned in early September in protest against Arafat's refusal to hand over control of the various Palestinian security services and because of threats made against him by radical groups, including the al-Aqsa Martyrs Brigades. Abbas also blamed his resignation on Israel, particularly its failure to freeze settlement activity.

Ahmed Qureia, a longtime lead Palestinian negotiator in talks with Israel, replaced Abbas in September. However, like his predecessor, Qureia ruled out a crackdown on armed radical groups. Soon after his appointment, he clashed with Arafat over control of security forces. Arafat responded by consolidating all security authority in a new national security council answerable solely to himself. Though Qureia initially threatened to resign unless Arafat relented to his demand for control over security services and cabinet appointments, the prime minister ultimately acquiesced to Arafat's continued exclusive authority. Despite U.S. and Israeli efforts to sideline him—including Israel's besiegement of Arafat's Ramallah compound—Arafat remained at the center of Palestinian political life all year. Moreover, despite U.S. and Egyptian assistance, Qureia was unable to reach long-lasting cease-fire arrangements with radical Palestinian groups.

Later in September, after devastating suicide bomb attacks in Israel, the Israeli cabinet decided in principle to "remove" Arafat from power at a time of its choosing, stating that he was the chief impediment to peace. In October, Israeli Prime Minister Ariel Sharon publicly ruled out killing Arafat as an option.

In the fall, a group of former Israeli and Palestinian politicians revealed a private peace initiative negotiated in secret in Geneva, Switzerland. Based largely on the terms of reference discussed by Israeli and Palestinian negotiators at the Taba, Egypt, talks in December 2000-January 2001, the nongovernmental "Geneva accord" envisioned an independent Palestinian state in the West Bank and Gaza Strip, the dismantling of Jewish settlements in those areas, the division of Jerusalem, and sole Palestinian control of the Temple Mount in Jerusalem's Old City with international monitoring. In return, Palestinians would pledge peace and possibly drop their demand for a "right of return" of refugees to Israel. While the accord drew some limited support from the Israeli and Palestinian publics, their respective leaders largely ignored it. Another peace plan, headed by former Shin Bet chief Ami Ayalon and Palestinian academic and peace activist Sari Nusseibeh, also garnered limited support.

**Political Rights and Civil Liberties:** Palestinian residents of the West Bank, Gaza, and East Jerusalem chose their first popularly elected government in 1996. Independents won 35 of the 88 Palestinian Legislative Council seats, while members of Yasser Arafat's Fatah party won the remainder. Arafat became chairman of the council's executive authority with 88 percent of the vote. Despite some irregularities, particularly in East Jerusalem, international observers regarded the vote as reasonably reflective of the will of the voters. The Legislative Council has complained of being marginalized by the executive authority. Although it has debated hundreds of draft laws, few have been signed into law. The Palestinian government indefinitely postponed local elections in May 1998, citing the threat of Israeli interference. As per agreements with Israel, the council has no real authority over borders or defense policy.

The creation of the post of prime minister in March—and the subsequent appointments to the post—came about largely as a result of international pressure; there were no elections held.

Palestinian residents of the West Bank, Gaza, and East Jerusalem do not have the right to vote in national elections in Israel. Arabs in East Jerusalem, while holding Israeli identity cards and given the right to vote in Jerusalem municipal elections, can also vote in Palestinian elections.

The PA continued to face accusations of autocratic leadership, mismanagement, and political corruption. Arafat's autocratic tendencies have put him at odds with the Legislative Council. Despite a temporary surge in popularity when Israel threatened to expel him, Arafat faced enormous internal and international pressure to institute widespread political and economic reforms.

Arafat frequently scuttles the legislative process or refuses to sign council rules into law. In February, the Palestinian Committee for Drafting the Constitution submitted a revised basic law to Arafat. According to Palestinian officials, he signed the law in May. The Palestinian Legislative Council had passed the constitution-like law in 1997, although for years, Arafat refused to endorse it. Once enacted, the law would presumably curtail Arafat's own authority. In April, the PA revealed a draft constitution. The constitution would strengthen the judiciary, one of the weakest Palestinian institutions.

Throughout 2003, the new Palestinian finance minister, Salam Fayad, tried to make the PA's finances more transparent. In February, *Forbes* magazine estimated Yasser Arafat's personal worth to be at least $300 million. Arafat reportedly has diverted international funds donated to the PA toward weapons purchases and support for terrorism, allegations supported by Israeli and U.S. intelligence. An IMF audit in September revealed that Arafat had diverted $900 million in public money to a special account under his control.

Rampant corruption within the PA and the rapid deterioration of both civil order and the ability of the PA to deliver basic services have benefited Hamas, a radical, violent Islamic group that operates an extensive private charitable social services network. Vocal opposition to Israel and to the Oslo accords has turned Hamas into a growing political alternative to Arafat's Fatah party.

Under a 1995 Palestinian press law, journalists may be fined and jailed and newspapers closed for publishing "secret information" on Palestinian security forces or news that might harm national unity or incite violence. However, another press law, also signed in 1995, stipulates that Palestinian intelligence services do not reserve the right to interrogate, detain, or arrest journalists on the basis of their work. Nonetheless, several small media outlets are pressured by authorities to provide favorable coverage of Arafat and the PA. Arbitrary arrests, threats, and the physical abuse of journalists critical of the PA are routine. Official Palestinian radio and television are government mouthpieces. Palestinians generally have unfettered access to the Internet.

Journalists covering the Israeli-Palestinian conflict and Palestinian political affairs face harassment by the PA. PA officials reportedly threaten journalists who file stories deemed unfavorable. PA-affiliated militias have also warned Israeli journalists to stay out of Palestinian areas. International press freedom groups have called on the PA to cease harassment of journalists.

In January, Palestinian intelligence agents raided Al-Jazeera TV's Gaza bureau without a warrant, detaining a correspondent. In September, five armed men claiming they were members of al-Aqsa Martyrs Brigades, raided the Arabiya satellite TV bureau in Ramallah, smashing equipment and threatening to kill workers. The station had received threats over what was perceived to be biased reporting in favor of Israel.

Arafat has yet to ratify a 1996 law passed by the Palestinian Legislative Council that guarantees freedom of expression. In July, hundreds of Palestinians ransacked the Ramallah offices of Khalil Shikaki, a Palestinian pollster. The protestors, who also physically attacked Shikaki, were angry over a poll released by Shikaki's institute that showed most Palestinian refugees would not choose to return to Israel proper if Israel granted them the "right of return"; the PA insists on the "right of return" in negotiations with Israel.

The PA generally respects freedom of religion, although no law exists protecting religious expression. The basic law declares Islam the official religion of Palestine and also states that "respect and sanctity of all other heavenly religions—Judaism and Christianity—shall be maintained." The PA requires all Palestinians to be affiliated with a religion, which must be indicated on identification cards. Personal status law, which governs marriage and divorce, is based on religious law; for Muslims, it is derived from Sharia, and for Christians, from ecclesiastical courts. Some Palestinian Christians have experienced intimidation and harassment by radical Islamic groups and PA officials. In August, Muslim squatters seized Christian-owned land in Bethlehem. Several other similar illegal land seizures have reportedly taken place. In October, Palestinians torched and nearly completely destroyed Joseph's tomb, a Jewish shrine in Nablus.

Palestinian schools teach hatred of Israel and textbooks and curriculums promote its destruction. Student life at Palestinian universities is often heavily politicized. Pressure from student groups affiliated with Palestinian political and religious organizations sometimes has a chilling effect on the work of students.

The PA requires permits for rallies and demonstrations and prohibits violence and racist sloganeering. Nonetheless, anti-Israel and anti-Semitic preaching and incitement to violence are regular features of daily mosque prayer services and official radio and television broadcasts. The PA also operates children's military training summer camps, which are usually named after suicide bombers and where violence against Jews is praised and glorified.

Labor affairs in the West Bank and Gaza are governed by a combination of Jordanian laws and PA decisions. Workers may establish and join unions without government authorization. Palestinian workers seeking to strike must submit to arbitration by the PA Labor Ministry. There are no laws in the PA-ruled areas to protect the rights of striking workers. Palestinian workers in Jerusalem are subject to Israeli labor law.

Palestinian judges lack proper training and experience. Israeli demands for a Palestinian crackdown on terrorism have given rise to state security courts, which lack almost all due process rights. There are reportedly hundreds of administrative detainees currently in Palestinian jails and detention centers. The same courts are also used to try those suspected of collaborating with Israel or of drug trafficking. Defendants are not granted the right to appeal sentences and are often summarily tried and sentenced to death. Executions often take place immediately after sentencing and are carried out by firing squad. According to the Palestinian Human Rights Monitoring Group, alleged collaborators are routinely tortured in Palestinian jails and are denied the right to defend themselves in court. These practices are not prohibited under Palestinian law.

The limits of Palestinian justice and the further breakdown of the rule of law were underscored several times during the year. Offshoots of Arafat's Fatah party controlled the largely anarchic West Bank cities of Jenin and Nablus with impunity. In July, members of the al-Aqsa Martyrs Brigades detained and beat Haider Irsheid, Jenin's governor, accusing him of collaborating with Israel. Arafat ordered his release five hours after his detention, leading to speculation that Arafat had himself ordered Irsheid's abduction and beating after the governor had publicly called for the disarmament of the Martyrs Brigades. In Nablus, hundreds of people protested the uncontrolled presence of gunmen after a young mother was shot and killed in the street during an attempted abduction of someone else. In November, gunmen attempted to assassinate the city's mayor, Ghassan Shaka.

Armed militias sometimes summarily execute Palestinians accused of collaborating with Israel. These murders, which sometimes take place publicly, generally go unpunished. In July, masked gunmen entered a Ramallah courtroom and shot and killed a suspected collaborator. The next month, masked gunmen believed affiliated with the al-Aqsa Martyrs Brigades killed another man in Ramallah also suspected of collaborating with Israel. The Brigades also murdered another alleged collaborator in Ramallah. In October, Brigades members, together with Islamic Jihad gunmen, shot and killed two suspected collaborators in the West Bank town of Tulkarm; they later displayed the bodies in the central square of the town's refugee camp, underscoring the impunity Palestinian militia enjoy.

In October, al-Aqsa Martyrs Brigades publicly threatened to execute Palestinians who sell land to Jews. In 1997, the PA issued a death penalty edict for Arabs who sell land to Jews.

Violence between Palestinians and settlers is not uncommon. In 2003, several Jewish settlers in the West Bank and Gaza Strip were ambushed and killed by Palestinian gunmen. Some were targeted while traveling in cars or buses. Others were attacked while in their homes and schools. These attacks generally went unpunished by the PA. Settlers sometimes attack Palestinians. In September, three settlers were convicted by an Israeli court of planning a bomb attack at a Palestinian school in the West Bank. Israeli police prevented the attack from taking place.

The intifada, and Israeli closures of the Palestinian territories, have exacted a serious toll on the Palestinian economy. According to a World Bank study issued in March, two million Palestinians—60 percent of the total population—live below the poverty line of two dollars of income per day. The study cited unemployment at 50 percent. Economic output plunged as tens of thousands of Palestinians who normally work in Israel were denied entry into the country at various times during the year in response to terrorist attacks.

While Palestinian women are under-represented in most professions and encounter discrimination in employment, they do have full access to universities and to many professions. Personal status law, derived in part from Sharia (Islamic law), puts women at a disadvantage in matters of marriage, divorce, and inheritance. Rape, domestic abuse, and "honor killings," in which unmarried women who are raped or who engage in premarital sex are murdered by a relative, are not uncommon. Since societal pressures prevent reporting of such incidents, the exact frequency of attacks is unknown. According to media reports, an average of one honor killing per week takes place in the West Bank and Gaza. These murders often go unpunished, or perpetrators serve extremely short prison sentences.

# Moldova
## Transnistria

**Population:** 620,000
**Religious Groups:** Christian
Orthodox (94 percent),
other [including Roman Catholic,
Protestant and Muslim] (6 percent)
**Ethnic Groups:** Moldovan (40 percent), Ukrainian
(28 percent), Russian (23 percent), other (9 percent)

**Political Rights:** 6
**Civil Liberties:** 6
**Status:** Not Free

### Ten-Year Ratings Timeline (Political Rights, Civil Liberties, Status)

| 1994 | 1995 | 1996 | 1997 | 1998 | 1999 | 2000 | 2001 | 2002 | 2003 |
|------|------|------|------|------|------|------|------|------|------|
| -- | -- | 6,6NF | 6,6NF | 6,6NF | 6,6NF | 6,6NF | 6,6NF | 6,6NF | 6,6NF |

**Overview:**

Some slight progress toward resolving the status of the breakaway Moldovan region of Transnistria was made during 2003, as the Russian military continued to remove weapons stockpiles from Transnistria in keeping with international agreements, and a number of international actors announced their support for a plan to reintegrate Transnistria with Moldova.

The Dnestr Moldovan Republic (DMR), bounded by the Dniester River to the west and the Ukrainian border on the east, is a breakaway region in the eastern part of Moldova with a large population of ethnic Russians and ethnic Ukrainians. In Moldova, the region is called Transnistria. The DMR broke away from Romanian-speaking Moldova in 1991, when the Moldovan Soviet Socialist Republic declared independence from the Soviet Union. At the time, pro-Russian separatists in Transnistria feared that Moldova would join neighboring Romania. They reacted by declaring independence, establishing the DMR, and setting up an authoritarian presidential system. With weapons and other assistance from Russia's Fourteenth Army, the DMR leadership fought a military conflict with Moldova that ended in a 1992 cease-fire. Since that time, the separatist regime has existed as a para-state, strong enough to resist absorption by Moldova yet too weak to gain outright international recognition as a sovereign nation.

Over the past several years, the Organization for Security and Cooperation in Europe (OSCE), Russia, and Ukraine have attempted to mediate a final settlement between Moldova and the DMR. They also participate in the Joint Control Commission that monitors compliance with the 1992 cease-fire. Nevertheless, despite Russia's acceptance of the 1999 Adapted Convention Forces in Europe Treaty, under which Russia was supposed to have removed its forces and weapons stockpiles from the DMR, the question of the DMR's political status remains unsettled.

Parliamentary elections in December 2000 resulted in a victory for separatist leader Igor Smirnov's supporters. In December 2001, "presidential" elections were held, but were severely flawed. One potential contender was barred from participating in the race, and another, the mayor of Benderi, was dismissed from his position. Workers were reported to have been threatened with the loss of their jobs and students with expulsion if they did not vote for the government's candidate. Smirnov was declared the victor, in some areas winning by a considerable margin. In the northern region of Kamenka, for example, he received 103.6 percent of the vote, indicating significant ballot-stuffing.

After Moldovan elections in 2001, in which Communist Party leader Vladimir Voronin was elected president, there were some hopes that a quicker resolution to the Transnistrian conflict would be achieved. Negotiations have, however, made little progress over the past several years. The lingering presence in Transnistria of 1,300 Russian soldiers and of a supply of Russian weapons—the second largest weapons stockpile in Europe, with some 22,000 tons in all—has further complicated a resolution of the dispute. In 1999, Russia agreed to an OSCE initiative for the removal of all Russian weapons and troops by December 2002. As the withdrawal deadline approached, Russia announced that it would not meet its obligation and attempted to refashion the force as "guarantors" of any eventual diplomatic settlement. In response to this development, the OSCE extended the deadline by 12 months. During the course of 2003, some movement was seen on the issue; by April, 10 trainloads of Russian military equipment had left Tiraspol for Moscow.

During the year, a Joint Constitutional Committee composed of members of the Moldovan government and DMR representatives worked on a plan to create a federal structure for Moldova that would allow for Transnistria's reintegration, but little progress was achieved. The most important substantive problem remains the different visions between the Moldovan preference for a federal state with a recognizable center and the DMR authorities' preference for a "common state" but one that would be more of a confederation of two very distinct entities. Since Russia has accepted the federalization plan for Moldova, however, many observers believe it is only a matter of time before the DMR's authorities have to accept this outcome as well.

**Political Rights and Civil Liberties:** Residents of Transnistria cannot elect their leaders democratically, and they are also unable to participate freely in Moldovan elections. While the DMR maintains its own legislative, executive, and judicial branches of government, no country recognizes its sovereignty. The DMR's legislative body, the Council of People's Deputies, was transformed into a unicameral body with 43 members in 2000.

A local faction of the Communist Party of Moldova is the only group in opposition to the government; however, its influence is limited. No other democratic alternatives to the current regime exist, as all other parties and political formations have ceased to operate in Transnistria.

The DMR government controls most print and electronic media in Transnistria and restricts freedom of speech. Independent newspapers and television stations do exist, but they frequently experience harassment for criticizing the government. Authorities have also confiscated copies of independent newspapers. In 2001, DMR president Igor Smirnov issued a decree on the creation of a state editorial committee to oversee the activity of all print and electronic media. The committee's members include the ministers of security, justice, foreign affairs, and information. In May, a court in the city of Bender ordered the closure of one of Transnistria's few independent newspapers, *Novaya Gazeta*, and the paper's editors were fined approximately $5,000 after they were found guilty of libel. Outside observers believed that the trial was politically motivated. There is no information on government policy relating to the Internet.

Authorities have denied registration to some religious groups (such as Baptists and Methodists) and prevented them from distributing literature or leading public meetings. The government also limits the ability of religious groups to rent space for prayer meetings. DMR authorities discriminate against ethnic Moldovans, who constitute 40 percent of the region's population. Several Jehovah's Witnesses were arrested during the course of the year on charges of proselytizing. There is no information on government policy with regards to academic freedom.

The DMR authorities severely restrict freedom of assembly, and on the few occasions when permits have been granted for groups to protest, the organizers have been harassed. The authorities have also organized "spontaneous" counter-rallies on such occasions. Freedom of association is similarly circumscribed. In June, the Supreme Court upheld a 2001 ruling forbidding the formation of a nascent political party. Nongovernmental organizations (NGOs) have reportedly been harassed by police officials, who invite NGO leaders for "informational discussions" or pressure landlords of properties being used by NGOs not to renew leases. Trade unions are holdovers from the Soviet era, and the United Council of Labor Collectives works closely with the government.

The judiciary is not independent. Politically motivated killings and police harassment have been reported, and political prisoners are frequently denied access to lawyers. Police can detain suspects for up to 30 days. Prison conditions are considered harsh, and prisons are severely overcrowded. The police continue to use torture and arbitrary arrest and detention, especially against political opponents of the current government.

Domestic violence against women is a problem, and women are under-represented in most positions of authority. In the absence of a strong central authority in Transnistria, many observers claim that the region has become a "criminal black hole" in Europe for various forms of smuggling and trafficking in human beings for purposes of prostitution.

# Morocco
## Western Sahara

**Population:** 260,000
**Religious Groups:** Muslim
**Ethnic Groups:** Arab, Berber

**Political Rights:** 7
**Civil Liberties:** 6
**Status:** Not Free

### Ten-Year Ratings Timeline (Political Rights, Civil Liberties, Status)

| 1994 | 1995 | 1996 | 1997 | 1998 | 1999 | 2000 | 2001 | 2002 | 2003 |
|------|------|------|------|------|------|------|------|------|------|
| 7,6NF | 7,6NF | 7,6NF | 7,6NF | 7,6NF | 7,6NF | 7,6NF | 7,6NF | 7,6NF | 7,6NF |

**Overview:**

Prospects for a settlement of the dispute in Western Sahara remained low in 2003 despite a renewed call for negotiation by UN Secretary-General Kofi Annan. Significant differences continue to divide the principal parties to the conflict, Morocco and the Polisario. Amnesty International noted an increase in reports of torture or ill-treatment used against Sahrawi activists. While human rights groups welcomed the Polisario's release of 243 Moroccan prisoners of war, they reiterated calls for the repatriation of the 914 remaining prisoners.

Western Sahara was a Spanish colony from 1884 until 1975, when Spanish forces withdrew from the territory following a bloody two-year conflict with the Polisario Front. Moroccan claims to the territory date to Moroccan independence in 1956. Mauritania also laid claim to the southern portion of the territory. In 1976, Morocco and Mauritania partitioned the territory under a tripartite agreement with Spain, but the Polisario declared the establishment of an independent Sahrawi Arab Democratic Republic (SADR) and fought to expel foreign forces. Mauritania renounced its claims to the land and signed a peace agreement with the Polisario in 1979, prompting Morocco to seize Mauritania's section of territory.

In 1991, the United Nations brokered an agreement between Morocco and the Polisario that called for a cease-fire and the holding of a referendum on independence to be supervised by the newly created Mission for a Referendum in Western Sahara (MINURSO). However, the referendum, initially scheduled for January 1992, was repeatedly postponed after Morocco insisted that the list of eligible voters include an additional 48,000 people who, according to the Polisario and most international observers, were Moroccan nationals.

In the ensuing years, Morocco has attempted to cement its hold on Western Sahara by offering incentives such as free housing and salaries to Sahrawis who relocated from the territory to Morocco. At the same time, the Moroccans have repeatedly rebuffed UN attempts to broker a lasting solution to the conflict. On ascending the Moroccan throne in 1999, King Muhammad made some important gestures toward reconciliation including releasing prisoners and allowing limited activity for Sahrawi human rights groups.

In his October 16, 2003 report to the Security Council, Annan advised Morocco to accept by January 1, 2004 a peace plan proposed by Special Representative James Baker. The proposed plan would make the territory a semiautonomous part of Morocco during a four- to five-year transition period. A referendum would then let residents choose independence, continued semiautonomy, or integration with Morocco. The addition of a third option, continued semiautonomy, weighs in Morocco's favor by allowing residents who cannot fathom integration with Morocco an option short of independence. While initially opposed, the Polisario, under intense pressure from Algiers, has accepted the plan. The Moroccan government continues to voice its opposition to the plan, saying it cannot accept any referendum in which independence is an option. Instead, the Moroccans have called on Algeria to negotiate an end to the conflict. The Algerian government has ruled out bilateral talks, calling on Rabat to accept the peace plan.

Earlier this year, both Morocco and the Polisario agreed to a package of confidence-building measures promoted by MINURSO and the UN High Commissioner for Refugees (UNHCR). The measures include limited telephone and personal mail services. The exchange of family visits constitutes a third element of the confidence-building measures. However, implementation of the confidence-building measures has been problematic, with both parties unable to agree to the terms of limited phone and mail service. Family visits have yet to be included as an agenda item in discussion between the parties.

**Political Rights and Civil Liberties:**   Sahrawis have never been able to elect their own government. The Moroccan government organizes and controls local elections in the Moroccan-held areas of the territory. Only Sahrawis whose views are consonant with the Moroccan government hold seats in the Moroccan parliament. In general, political rights for residents of Western Sahara remain severely circumscribed.

Freedom of expression remains very restricted. Moroccan security forces reportedly closely monitor the political views of Sahrawis. Police and paramilitary forces resort to repressive measures against those suspected of supporting the Polisario and independence. Private media and Internet access are virtually nonexistent.

The overwhelming majority of Sahrawis are Sunni Muslim, and the Moroccan authorities generally respect freedom of worship. Restrictions on religious freedom in Western Sahara are similar to those found in Morocco. Academic freedoms are severely restricted.

Freedom to assemble or to form political organizations is quite restricted. For example, Sahrawis are largely unable to form political associations or politically oriented nongovernmental organizations. On June 18, 2003, the Sahara branch of the Forum for Truth and Justice, a human rights organization, was dissolved on the charge that the group had undertaken illegal activities that could disturb public order and undermine the territorial integrity of Morocco. Nonviolent demonstrations are often dispersed with excessive force by security forces, particularly in the form of beatings.

Little organized labor activity occurs. The same labor laws that apply in Morocco are applied in Moroccan-controlled areas of the territory. Moroccan unions are present in these areas, but not active.

The civilian population living in Moroccan-controlled areas of Western Sahara is subject to Moroccan law. International human rights groups have reported that activists in the territories have been tried and imprisoned on politically motivated charges. Several reported being tortured during detention. Indeed, arbitrary killing, arrest, and incommunicado detention by Moroccan security forces continue. The Polisario released 243 Moroccan prisoners of war in September, but continues to hold 914 Moroccan prisoners. The UN secretary-general reiterated demands that the Polisario release the remaining prisoners, who are currently held in six detention centers in Tindouf, Algeria, as well as in Polisario-controlled areas of Western Sahara.

Freedom of movement within Western Sahara is limited in militarily sensitive areas, within both the area controlled by Morocco and the area controlled by the Polisario. UN monitors maintain that Sahrawis living in the territory under Moroccan control had difficulty obtaining Moroccan passports. As in Morocco itself, women are subjected to various forms of legal and cultural discrimination. Female illiteracy is very high, especially in rural areas.

# Pakistan
## Kashmir

**Population:** 4,200,000
**Religious Groups:** Muslim
[Shi
a majority, Sunni minority]
(99 percent), other (1 percent)
**Ethnic Groups:** Kashmiri, Punjabi, Balti, Gujjar, Ladakhi,

**Political Rights:** 7
**Civil Liberties:** 5
**Status:** Not Free

**Ten-Year Ratings Timeline (Political Rights, Civil Liberties, Status)**

| 1994 | 1995 | 1996 | 1997 | 1998 | 1999 | 2000 | 2001 | 2002 | 2003 |
|------|------|------|------|------|------|------|------|------|------|
| -- | -- | -- | -- | -- | -- | -- | -- | 7,5NF | 7,5NF |

**Overview:**

Relations between archrivals India and Pakistan showed signs of a thaw as Pakistani leader General Pervez Musharraf faced sustained international pressure in 2003 to intensify his crackdown on the Islamist militant groups that operate in Indian-administered Kashmir. India has made Pakistan's cooperation a key condition for resuming talks over the disputed territory, and although Musharraf promised to rein in militant activities, incursions continue to be reported. Meanwhile, nationalist and pro-independence groups in Pakistani-administered Kashmir continued to agitate for increased political representation. In August, Shabir Choudhury, the leader of the Jammu and Kashmir Liberation Front (JKLF), accused the Pakistani government of denying human rights to the Kashmiri people. Violent protests erupted in the same month among Shias in Gilgit over the government's decision to introduce a new educational curriculum in the Northern Areas.

For centuries, Kashmir was ruled by Afghan, Sikh, and local strongmen. In 1846, the British seized control of the territory and sold it to the Hindu maharajah of the neighboring principality of Jammu. The maharajah later incorporated Ladakh and other surrounding areas into the new princely state of Jammu and Kashmir. When British India was partitioned into India and Pakistan in 1947, Maharajah Hari Singh tried to maintain Jammu and Kashmir's independence. However, after Pakistani tribesmen invaded, he agreed to cede Jammu and Kashmir to India. In return India promised autonomy and eventual self-determination for the territory.

India and Pakistan went to war over Kashmir within months of gaining their independence. As part of a UN-brokered cease-fire in January 1949 that established the present-day boundaries, Pakistan gained control of roughly one-third of Jammu and Kashmir, including the far northern and western areas, as well as a narrow sliver of land adjoining Indian-held Kashmir. India retained most of the Kashmir Valley along with Jammu and Ladakh.

Unlike India, Pakistan never formally annexed the portion of Kashmir under its control. The Karachi Agreement of April 1949 divided Pakistani-administered Kashmir into two distinct entities, Azad (free) Kashmir and the Northern Areas. The Northern Areas consist of the five districts of Gilgit, Ghizer, Ghanche, Diamer, and Baltistan. Pakistan retained direct administrative control over the Northern Areas, while Azad Kashmir was given a larger degree of nominal self-government.

For several decades, an informal council administered Azad Kashmir. A legislative assembly was set up in 1970, and the 1974 interim constitution established a parliamentary system headed by a president and a prime minister. However, the political process in Azad Kashmir has been suspended on several occasions by the military rulers of Pakistan. In 1977, General Zia ul-Haq dissolved the legislative assembly and banned all political activity for eight years, while in 1991, the prime minister of Azad Kashmir was dismissed, arrested, and imprisoned in Pakistan.

Chronic infighting among the state's various political factions has also allowed Islamabad to interfere with ease in the electoral process. In the 1996 state elections, Sultan Mahmud Chaudhary's Azad Kashmir People's Party (AKPP) emerged with a majority of seats. The outgoing Muslim Conference (MC) had boycotted the elections, accusing the AKPP of vote rigging and fraud. In elections held in July 2001 with a 48 percent turnout, the MC swept back into power, winning 30 out of 48 seats. However, General Musharraf installed a serving general as the president of Azad Kashmir later that month, amid speculation that Islamabad intended to reassert its control over the territory.

The lack of political representation in the Northern Areas has fueled demands for both formal inclusion within Pakistan and self-determination. In 1988, Gilgit was wracked by unrest after the majority Shias demanded an independent state. The Pakistani army suppressed the revolt with the help of armed Sunni tribesmen from a neighboring province. In May 1999, the Pakistani Supreme Court directed the government to act within six months to give the Northern Areas an elected government with an independent judiciary. After the verdict, the Pakistani government announced a package that provided for an appellate court and an expanded and renamed Northern Areas Legislative Council (NALC). Elections to the NALC were held under the military government in 2000, but the NALC continues to have few real financial and legislative powers. In August, the NALC submitted a proposal to the Pakistani government that called for a more autonomous form of provincial government along the lines of what currently exists in Azad Kashmir.

In January 2001, twelve small Kashmiri separatist groups in Azad Kashmir and the Northern Areas announced the formation of the All Parties National Alliance, which committed itself to fighting for an independent Kashmir and demanded that both India and Pakistan release jailed members of the group. While the Pakistani authorities have readily provided support to armed militants fighting in India, they have been less tolerant of groups that espouse Kashmiri self-determination. In June, policemen in Gilgit fired on Nawaz Khan Naji, the acting chairman of the Balawaristan National Front (BNF).

Since early 2002, Musharraf has been under pressure to curb the activities of Pakistan-based militant groups. In May 2003, citing law-and-order concerns, Pakistani authorities banned the leader of a militant group from entering Azad Kashmir. However, when Musharraf banned the movement of militants from the Pakistani portion of Kashmir into the Indian-held section of Kashmir in June, hard-line Islamist groups in Azad Kashmir organized protest rallies denouncing his decision and vowed to continue their armed insurgency.

**Political Rights and Civil Liberties:** The political rights of the residents of Pakistani-administered Kashmir remain severely limited. Neither the Northern Areas nor Azad Kashmir has representation in Pakistan's national parliament. The Northern Areas are directly administered by the Pakistani government and have no constitution guaranteeing them fundamental rights, democratic representation, or the separation of powers, according to Amnesty International. Executive authority is vested in the minister for Kashmir affairs, a civil servant appointed by Islamabad. An elected Northern Areas Legislative Council (NALC) serves in an advisory capacity and has no authorization to change laws or spend revenue. In November 1999, the new military government permitted previously scheduled elections to the NALC to take place; candidates who won seats included independents as well as representatives of several political parties. Elections for local governmental posts were held in July 2000.

Azad Kashmir has an interim constitution, an elected unicameral assembly headed by a prime minister, and a president. However, Pakistan exercises considerable control over both the structures of governance and electoral politics. Islamabad's approval is required to pass legislation, and the minister for Kashmir affairs handles the daily administration of the state. Twelve of the 48 seats in the Azad Kashmir assembly are reserved for Kashmiri "refugees" in Pakistan, and the elections to these seats are the subject of some manipulation.

In addition, candidates in elections are required to support the accession of Kashmir to Pakistan. According to Human Rights Watch, authorities barred at least 25 candidates from the pro-independence JKLF from contesting the July 2001 elections after they refused to sign a declaration supporting the accession of all of Kashmir to Pakistan. Several hundred JKLF supporters, including its chief, Amanullah Khan, were arrested while protesting against the decision. Fifteen other nationalists who agreed to the "accession" clause competed in the elections, but none won a seat.

Azad Kashmir receives a large amount of financial aid from the Pakistani government, but successive administrations have been tainted by corruption and incompetence. A lack of official accountability has been identified as a key factor in the poor socio-economic development of both Azad Kashmir and the Northern Areas.

The Pakistani government uses the constitution and other laws to curb freedom of speech on a variety of subjects, including the status of Kashmir. In recent years, authorities have banned several local newspapers from publishing. In October 2000, the district magistrate revoked the publication license of the independent weekly *K-2* for "promoting anti-Pakistan feelings"; the ban remained in effect until July 2001. In addition to pressure from the authorities, journalists face some harassment from other, non-state actors. In June 2002, political party activists attacked the office of the weekly *Naqqara*, a Gilgit-based newspaper, and assaulted the staff. While the Northern Areas have no local broadcast media, a local radio station was inaugurated in Azad Kashmir in 2002 and the government also announced plans to launch a satellite television station.

Pakistan is an Islamic republic, and there are numerous restrictions on religious freedom. In addition, religious minorities face unofficial economic and societal discrimination and are occasionally subject to violent attack. Shia Muslims, who form the majority of the population in the Northern Areas, include a large number of Ismailis, a group that follows the Aga Khan. Sectarian strife between the majority Shia population and the increasing number of Sunni Muslims (many of whom are migrants from elsewhere in Pakistan) continues to be a problem.

In June 2001, Sunni organizations protested against the local administration's decision to supply different school textbooks for Shia students. In 2003, violent protests erupted among Shias in Gilgit over the government's decision to introduce a new educational curriculum in the Northern Areas. The Aga Khan Rural Support Program, run by the Aga Khan Foundation, an international development organization that focuses on Ismaili Shia communities worldwide, has in recent years been subjected to harassment and violence from extremist Sunni religious leaders.

Freedom of association and assembly is restricted. The constitution of Azad Kashmir forbids individuals and political parties from taking part in activities prejudicial to the ideology of the state's accession to Pakistan. Political parties that advocate Kashmiri independence are allowed to operate, but not to participate in elections. According to Amnesty International, some people who do not support the accession of Azad Kashmir to Pakistan have been dismissed from their jobs and denied access to educational institutions. A number of nationalist political parties have been formed in the Northern Areas that advocate either self-rule or greater political representation within Pakistan. However, their leaders are subject to harassment, arbitrary arrest, and long jail terms. The BNF estimates that more than 70 individuals are facing sedition or treason cases as a result of their political activities.

In recent years, police have suppressed antigovernment demonstrations, sometimes violently, in both Azad Kashmir and the Northern Areas. These have included rallies by nationalist political organizations, as well as student protests. The Asian Human Rights Commission reported that in September 2002, police attacked protestors demonstrating peacefully against the Mangla Dam extension in Mirpur, arresting 13 people and injuring others. However, in June, more than 500 protestors in Azad Kashmir were able to hand a petition to the United Nations asking that India refrain from shelling civilian targets along the Line of Control.

Nongovernmental organizations (NGOs) are generally able to operate freely. In July, the independent Human Rights Commission of Pakistan established an office in Gilgit to monitor the human rights situation in the region. However, employees of NGOs that focus on women's issues are sometimes subjected to threats and other forms of harassment from religious leaders and Islamist militant groups.

The judiciary of the Northern Areas consists of district courts and a chief court, whose decisions are final. The Northern Areas Council Legal Framework Order of 1994 provides for a court of appeals, but this court has not yet been established. The territory continues to be governed by the colonial-era Frontier Crimes Regulations (FCR), under which residents are required to report to local police stations once a month. Law enforcement agencies have reportedly used torture on political activists who have been detained or imprisoned. Azad Kashmir has its own system of local magistrates and high courts, whose heads are appointed by the president of Azad Kashmir. Appeals are adjudicated by the Supreme Court of Pakistan.

A number of Islamist militant groups, including members of al-Qaeda, have bases in, and operate from, Pakistani-administered Kashmir with the tacit permission of Pakistani intelligence. Several militant groups that advocate the accession of Kashmir to Pakistan receive weapons and financial aid from the Pakistani government in support of their infiltrations into Indian-administered Kashmir. Under pressure from the United States, General Musharraf undertook several steps to curb infiltrations across the LOC, such as banning the main militant groups and persuading them to close some of their training camps in Azad Kashmir. However, by 2003, militant activity had increased to previous levels. Tension between the Islamist, pro-Pakistan groups and the pro-independence Kashmiri groups has reportedly intensified. In April, police in Azad Kashmir arrested more than a dozen Kashmiri militants over fears of a possible clash between two rival groups.

Until a bilateral ceasefire was declared in November, shelling between Indian and Pakistani forces around the Line of Control in Kashmir continued to kill or displace numerous civilians throughout the year. The Azad Kashmir government manages relief camps for refugees from Indian-administered Kashmir, which are funded by the Pakistani government. The appropriation of land in the Northern Areas by non-Kashmiri migrants from elsewhere in Pakistan, which has been tacitly encouraged by the federal government and army, has led to dwindling economic opportunities for the local population as well as an increase in religious and ethnic tensions.

The status of women in Pakistani-administered Kashmir is similar to that of women in Pakistan. Domestic violence, rape, honor killings, and other forms of abuse continue to be issues of concern. Women are not granted equal rights under the law and their educational opportunities and choice of marriage partner remain circumscribed.

# Russia
## Chechnya

**Population:** 1,200,000
**Religious Groups:** Muslim
[majority], Russian Orthodox
**Ethnic Groups:** Chechen (83 percent), other [including
Russian and Ingush] (17 percent)

**Political Rights:** 7
**Civil Liberties:** 7
**Status:** Not Free

**Ten-Year Ratings Timeline (Political Rights, Civil Liberties, Status)**

| 1994 | 1995 | 1996 | 1997 | 1998 | 1999 | 2000 | 2001 | 2002 | 2003 |
|------|------|------|------|------|------|------|------|------|------|
| -- | -- | -- | -- | 6,6NF | 7,7NF | 7,7NF | 7,7NF | 7,7NF | 7,7NF |

**Overview:**
In 2003, the inhabitants of Chechnya continued to be victimized by a debilitating, long-term civil war that has included acts of terrorism, disappearances, and war crimes perpetrated by various parties to the conflict. Human rights groups estimate that over 150,000 fatalities have occurred since war in Chechnya began in 1994, and hundreds of thousands have been wounded and displaced.

A small Northern Caucasus republic covered by flat plains in the north-central portion and by high mountains in the south, Chechnya has been at war with Russia for most of its history since the late 1700s. In February 1944, the Chechens were deported en masse to Kazakhstan under the pretext of their having collaborated with Germany during World War II. Officially rehabilitated in 1957 and allowed to return to their homeland, they remained politically suspect and were excluded from the region's administration.

Following election as Chechnya's president in October 1991, former Soviet Air Force Commander Dzhokhar Dudayev proclaimed Chechnya's independence. Moscow responded with an economic blockade. In 1994, Russia began assisting Chechens opposed to Dudayev, whose rule was marked by growing corruption and the rise of powerful clans and criminal gangs. Russian president Boris Yeltsin sent 40,000 troops into Chechnya by mid-December and attacked the capital, Grozny, precipitating a lengthy conflict that claimed tens of thousands of lives. As casualties mounted, Russian public opposition to the war increased, fueled by criticism from much of the country's then-independent media. In April 1996, Dudayev was killed by a Russian missile.

A peace deal was signed in August 1996, resulting in the withdrawal of most Russian forces from Chechnya. However, a final settlement on the republic's status was put off until 2001. In May 1997, Russia and Chechnya reached an accord recognizing the elected President Aslan Maskhadov as Chechnya's legitimate leader.

Following incursions into neighboring Dagestan by renegade Chechen rebels and deadly apartment bombings in Russia which the Kremlin blamed on Chechen militants, then-Russian prime minister Vladimir Putin launched a second military offensive on Chechnya in September 1999. Russian troops conquered the flat terrain in the north of the republic, but progress slowed considerably as they neared heavily defended Grozny. Amid hostilities, Moscow withdrew recognition of Maskhadov.

Russia's indiscriminate bombing of civilian targets caused some 200,000 people to flee Chechnya, most to the tiny neighboring Russian republic of Ingushetia. After federal troops finally captured Grozny in February 2000, the Russian military focused on rebel strongholds in the southern mountainous region. Russian security sweeps led to atrocities in which civilians were regularly beaten, raped, or killed. Russian forces were subject to almost daily guerrilla bomb and sniper attacks by rebels. The renewed campaign enjoyed broad popular support in Russia fueled by the media's now one-sided reporting favoring the official government position.

Following the September 11, 2001 terrorist attacks on New York and Washington, D.C., Moscow defended its actions in Chechnya as part of the broader war on global terrorism, asserting a connection between Chechen separatists and terrorists linked to Osama bin Laden. No connections have been proven.

Prominent Russian and Chechen leaders met in Liechtenstein in August 2002 to discuss a peace plan. However, progress toward peace remained elusive, as Chechen rebels have continued to engage in guerrilla warfare against Russian troops. In an ordeal covered live by Russian television, a group of Chechen rebels stormed a Moscow theater on October 23, 2002, taking 750 people hostage. Over 120 hostages died, most from the effects of a sedative gas that Russian troops used to incapacitate the rebels. Russian authorities reported that all 41 of the rebels had been killed.

Reliable estimates suggest that at least 5,000 Chechens, mostly civilians, died as a result of the conflict in 2003. Independent military analysts believe approximately 1,200 Russian troops were killed during the year. In addition, rights groups estimate that an average of 50 people disappear each month, usually as a result of abductions believed to originate with Russian forces.

While some 85,000 Russian troops are estimated to remain in Chechnya, in 2003, Russian officials attempted to demonstrate to the international community that authority is being ceded to Chechens. In an effort to deflect international criticism and domestic unease about the protracted conflict, Russia's government seeks to transfer significant responsibility for policing and governing to Chechen leaders who favor remaining part of the Russian Federation. In 2003, this strategy came in two stages: a highly-touted and highly tainted referendum and an election to determine Chechnya's executive and legislative leadership.

The March 23, 2003 referendum on a new Chechen constitution took place in the absence of open and free media, with opponents of the referendum and opponents of its questions effectively silenced. Russian government social and humanitarian agencies were mobilized to pressure Chechens to participate. On the day of the vote, Russian soldiers and Chechen police forced villagers to take part in the vote. Ballot security was put in the hands of the Russian military, which transported ballots to and from polling stations. Such direct involvement by the Russian military placed the accuracy of the ballot tabulation under question. According to current law, Russian military and police personnel serving on the territory of any Russian political entity are entitled to take part in a local vote.

Chechnya's Moscow-appointed administration said results indicated a voter turnout of 85 percent, with 96 percent of voters in favor of ratifying the Kremlin-backed constitution. Yet an independent survey of voter sentiments conducted by the Russian rights group Memorial found that 80 percent of the indigenous population opposed the referendum. Local rights groups reported largely empty polling places, contrary to official local state-radio reports, which claimed long lines of voters.

After the referendum, Russian authorities moved quickly toward presidential and legislative elections, which were held on October 5, 2003. A poll conducted by the independent Public Opinion polling group in the summer of 2003 showed only 14.4 percent of the population favoring the Kremlin-backed candidate, Akhmad Kadyrov. When the official results were tabulated, Kadyrov was said to have won with 81 percent of the vote and a voter turnout that was said to be nearly 88 percent. The absence of leading alternative candidates, the disqualification of a leading competitor by the courts, the resignation of rival candidates after Kremlin pressure, and reported physical threats paved the way for Kadyrov's tainted victory. The Organization for Security and Cooperation in Europe criticized the elections for not offering voters significant choice and the U.S. government judged them as "seriously flawed." Journalists who monitored the election reported sparse participation and many virtually empty polling places.

Kadyrov is a former mufti who served as the civilian administrator of the region before the elections. There are numerous credible reports that he and his associates are involved in corruption and the diversion of Russian aid for private gain. Chechen, Russian, and international monitoring groups worry that the transfer of some authority to Kadyrov will empower brutal and corrupt leaders and will result in a further deterioration of human rights.

**Political Rights and Civil Liberties:** The resumption of war in Chechnya in 1999 led to the total evisceration of the political rights of Chechens. Residents of the republic currently do not have the means to change their government democratically. Claims by the Russian government that they were returning the region to democratic rule by means of a March 2003 referendum lack credibility. The referendum was orchestrated by the Kremlin, with no opportunity for debate, widespread vote rigging, and official results that indicated a voter turnout of 85 percent and nearly unanimous support for a new constitution. According to domestic and international analysts, the results were heavily doctored. The subsequent presidential and parliamentary elections of October 5, 2003, did not resemble a competitive democratic political process. Candidates representing a genuine alternative were not on the ballot, and other pro-Russian candidates were forced off the ballot as a result of political pressure and intimidation. Political debate was stifled in an atmosphere of repression and censorship. Moreover, the official election results are believed to reflect widespread falsification. Under the authoritarian rule of President Akhmad Kadyrov, there is no party pluralism and politicians who advocate Chechen state independence are unable to work openly and freely.

The previous presidential elections in 1997—conducted by separatist authorities—were characterized by international observers as reasonably free and fair. President Aslan Maskhadov fled the capital city in December 1999, and the parliament elected in 1997 ceased to function. In June 2000, President Putin enacted a decree establishing direct presidential rule over Chechnya, appointing Kadyrov, a Muslim cleric and Chechnya's spiritual leader, to head the republic's administration. The new "elected" president is linked to a network of criminal Chechen groups and is denounced by Maskhadov and separatist Chechens as a traitor. Some pro-Moscow Chechens distrust him for his support for the republic's independence during the first Chechen war.

The disruptive effects of the war severely hinder news production and the free flow of information. Russian state-run television and radio broadcast in Chechnya, although much of the population remains without electricity. The local administration of President Kadyrov effectively controls all other broadcast and most print media, which predominantly reflect official viewpoints. There are three licensed television broadcasters, whose content is pro-regime. The Chechen rebel government operates a Web site with reports about the conflict and other news from its perspective. The editors of an independent weekly, *Groznensky Rabochy,* left Chechnya in 1999. The paper is now edited in Moscow and has limited distribution in Chechnya amid increased government restrictions on media coverage of the conflict. The paper's editor reports that there is widespread self-censorship by reporters who fear violent reprisals from rebels and pro-government forces.

The Russian military imposes severe restrictions on journalists' access to the Chechen war zone, issuing accreditation primarily to those of proven loyalty to the Russian government. Few foreign reporters are allowed into the breakaway republic, and when they are allowed entry, access is restricted by military and police authorities as journalists covering the war must be accompanied at all times by military officials.

Most Chechens are Muslims who practice Sufiism, a mystical form of Islam characterized by the veneration of local saints and by groups practicing their own rituals. The Wahhabi sect, with roots in Saudi Arabia and characterized by a strict observance of Islam, has been banned. Since the start of the last war in 1994, many of the republic's schools have been damaged or destroyed, and education in Chechnya has been sporadic. Most schools have not been renovated and continue to lack such basic amenities as textbooks, electricity, and running water.

Some charitable nongovernmental organizations (NGOs) working in humanitarian, cultural and social issues are allowed to operate. An important but small Western-supported NGO, the LAM Center for Complex Research and Popularization of Chechen Culture, conducts activities in Russia to promote inter-group understanding and makes small grants to a small network of embattled NGOs. However, associational and trade union life is dominated by pro-regime organizations and any groups and NGO activists that are viewed as sympathetic to the cause of Chechen independence are subject to persecution. In the face of the ongoing conflict, some Chechen NGO activists have left the region and are now working among refugees in the neighboring republic of Ingushetia.

Amid widespread conflict, the rule of law is virtually nonexistent. Civilians are subject to harassment and violence, including torture, rape, and extra-judicial executions, at the hands of Russian soldiers. Senior military authorities have shown disregard for these widespread abuses. There are worries that the new police and security structures under the control of President Kadyrov are likely to contribute to additional widespread rights abuses. According to a report in Britain's *Guardian* in October 2003, Kadyrov has assembled a well-paid private army of 4,000 former rebels, policemen, and hired guns. Chechen rebel fighters have targeted Chechen civilians who have cooperated with Russian government officials or who work for the pro-Moscow administration.

Extra-judicial killings, disappearances, and other war crimes are rarely investigated and even more rarely punished. In an unprecedented development, on July 25, 2003, a military court in Rostov-on-Don, Russia found Russian Colonel Yuri Budanov guilty of kidnapping and murdering a Chechen woman and sentenced him to 10 years in a maximum security prison. The court concluded that Budanov was sane at the time he killed the 18-year-old woman three years ago. In December 2003, a Russian military court initiated the trial of four soldiers for murders alleged to have been committed in the Shattoi region of Chechnya in January 2002.

Russian troops engage in so-called "mopping-up" operations in which they seal off entire towns and conduct house-to-house searches for suspected rebels. During these security sweeps, soldiers have been accused of beating and torturing civilians, looting, and extorting money. Thousands of Chechens have gone missing or been found dead after such operations. In 2002, Chechnya issued new rules for troops conducting sweeps, including identifying themselves and providing a full list of those detained, but rights activists have accused federal troops of widely ignoring these rules. Human rights groups report the ongoing operation of illegal filtration camps by Russian authorities and Kadyrov's security forces. The camps detain and "filter" out Chechens suspected of ties to rebel groups, with filtration often used as a euphemism for murder.

While precise estimates by independent monitoring agencies are unavailable, close approximations suggest that at the end of 2003, there were nearly 100,000 refugees in camps outside of Chechnya. Many were living in appalling conditions in tent camps, abandoned buildings, or in cramped quarters with friends or relatives. They are under intense pressure to return to their war-ravaged conflict zone despite ongoing concerns for personal security, as well as a lack of employment and housing opportunities. There were tens of thousands of additional internally displaced persons inside the region and well over 100,000 additional long-term homeless.

Travel to and from the republic and inside its borders is severely restricted. After the resumption of war, the Russian military failed to provide safe exit routes from the conflict zones for noncombatants. Bribes are usually required to pass the numerous military checkpoints.

Widespread corruption and the economic devastation caused by the war severely limit equality of opportunity. Ransoms obtained from kidnapping and the lucrative illegal oil trade provide money for Chechens and members of the Russian military. Much of the republic's infrastructure and housing remains damaged or destroyed after years of war, with reconstruction funds widely believed to have been substantially misappropriated by corrupt local authorities. In the capital city of Grozny, the long-term conflict has devastated civilian life, with over 60 percent of all buildings completely destroyed. Much of the population ekes out a living selling produce or other goods at local markets. Residents who have found work are employed mostly by the local police, the Chechen administration, the oil and construction sectors, or at small enterprises, including cafes. There are signs of an emerging struggle between what is referred to as the "Kadyrov clan" and other corrupt economic interest and criminal groups.

While women continue to face discrimination in a traditional, male-dominated culture, the war has resulted in many women becoming the primary breadwinners for their families. Russian soldiers reportedly rape Chechen women in areas controlled by federal forces.

# Serbia
## Kosovo

**Population:** 2,100,000    **Political Rights:** 5
**Religious Groups:** Muslim    **Civil Liberties:** 5
(majority), Serbian    **Status:** Partly Free
Orthodox, other
**Ethnic Groups:** Albanian (90 percent), Serb, Muslim, Montenegrin, Turk, Croat, Roma (10 percent)

**Ten-Year Ratings Timeline (Political Rights, Civil Liberties, Status)**

| 1994 | 1995 | 1996 | 1997 | 1998 | 1999 | 2000 | 2001 | 2002 | 2003 |
|------|------|------|------|------|------|------|------|------|------|
| 7,7 NF | 7,7 NF | 7,7 NF | 7,7 NF | 7,7 NF | 7,7 NF | 6,6NF | 6,6NF | 5,5PF | 5,5PF |

**Overview:** Tensions rose in the NATO-occupied Serbian province of Kosovo during the course of 2003, as the United Nations labeled an ethnic Albanian extremist group a "terrorist organization" and attacks on non-Albanian ethnic minorities intensified over the summer. Local ethnic Albanian politicians, meanwhile, were warning the international community that without a quick resolution of Kosovo's "final status," demands for independence could explode into serious violence against both the local non-Albanian population in the province and the international presence in Kosovo.

Control over Kosovo was a source of conflict between ethnic Albanians and Serbs throughout the twentieth century. The current round of troubles began in the early 1980s after the death of Yugoslav dictator Josip Broz Tito, when Albanians in the province began a series of demonstrations in favor of independence and/or republic status within the former Yugoslavia. The tensions accelerated after former Serbian strongman Slobodan Milosevic came to power and began to revoke much of Kosovo's autonomy. For most of the 1990s, an uneasy but generally nonviolent status quo was maintained between the Yugoslav government and the Kosovo Albanians, who developed an entire parallel society in Kosovo, replete with quasi-governmental institutions, hospitals, and school systems.

In late 1997, a guerrilla movement called the Kosovo Liberation Army (KLA) began a series of attacks on Serb targets in the province, provoking harsh reprisals from Yugoslav government forces. The fighting intensified in 1998, and at one point during the summer, up to 300,000 ethnic Albanians were forced from their homes. In March 1999, NATO launched a 78-day air campaign against the Federal Republic of Yugoslavia (FRY) to force it to relinquish control over the province. During the war, Yugoslav military forces and paramilitary gangs forced hundreds of thousands of ethnic Albanians out of the province.

Under the terms of United Nations Security Council Resolution (UNSCR) 1244 of June 1999, a NATO-led peacekeeping force (KFOR) assumed responsibility for security in Kosovo. UNSCR 1244 turned Kosovo into a protectorate of the international community, while officially maintaining Yugoslav sovereignty over the province.

Since international forces moved into Kosovo in mid-1999, a campaign of reverse ethnic cleansing has been taking place. Some 200,000 non-Albanian ethnic minority group members have been forced to flee the province. Most of the non-Albanian population remaining in Kosovo live in small clusters of villages or in urban ghettoes under round-the-clock KFOR protection. The largest Serb population is concentrated in a triangle-shaped piece of territory north of the Ibar River.

Kosovo's last elections for a provincial assembly, held on November 17, 2001, were contested by 26 political parties. Ibrahim Rugova's Democratic League of Kosovo (LDK), considered relatively moderate by international officials, won a plurality in the elections, gaining some 45.7 percent of the votes cast; former KLA leader Hashim Thaci's Democratic Party of Kosovo came in second with 25.7 percent; and the mainly Serb Return Coalition won 11.3 percent. The elections brought out more than 64 percent of eligible voters.

Municipal elections were held in Kosovo on October 25, 2002, after a campaign that international observers claimed was "generally free and fair." The election results confirmed the continuing dominance of the LDK over the PDK, while Ramush Haradinaj's Alliance for the Future of Kosovo (AAK) made a strong showing in western Kosovo.

In 2003, violence against non-Albanian ethnic minorities in the province increased, and the security situation deteriorated in general. In the spring, members of the so-called Albanian National Army (AkSH), which included members of the Kosovo Protection Corps, attempted to blow up a bridge in northern Kosovo. The United Nations (UN) afterward declared the AkSH a terrorist organization. In June, three members of a Serb family in Obilic were brutally murdered in their home in the middle of their village. In August, a group of Serb children swimming in a river were mowed down by machine-gun fire; two were killed and several injured. Amnesty International reported in 2003 that "minorities in Kosovo continue to be denied access to their basic human rights, and to any effective redress for violations and abuses of these rights."

Non-Albanian ethnic minorities have not been the only victims of persecution by extremists in the province. Over the past four years, criminal elements associated with the former KLA and Thaci's PDK and Haradinaj's AAK have repeatedly been accused of murdering political opponents. One prominent assassination occurred in January, when a leading member of Rugova's LDK, Tahir Zemaj, was murdered in western Kosovo, along with two members of his family. Problems with witness protection have also been significant in Kosovo over the past year. In one recent case, Ilir Selimaj, a former KLA fighter, was assassinated in April after testifying in a war crimes case against former colleagues.

The first face-to-face meetings between officials from the highest levels of the Kosovo and Serbia-Montenegro (the new official name for the FRY as of February 2003) governments was held in Vienna, Austria, on October 14, but international officials characterized the session as a "dialogue of the deaf," with both sides engaging mainly in grandstanding for their respective publics. Nevertheless, the meeting was seen as a necessary first step in bringing the two sides together so that talks over final status can eventually begin.

In December, the United Nations Interim Mission in Kosovo (UNMIK) unveiled its effort to move Kosovo towards "final status" negotiations. Its "standards before status" approach called for Kosovo institutions, politicians, and society to reach certain performance benchmarks on issues such as the creation of democratic institutions, the establishment of the rule of law, freedom of movement for minorities, refugee return, the resolution of property rights issues. Also in December, UNMIK began the process of turning over several aspects of self-government to local Kosovo institutions, including specific powers over agriculture, the media, culture, and the environment. Still, at the end of the year, it was clear that the slow pace in the evolution of Kosovo's post-1999 status was not enough to satisfy most Kosovo Albanians. In October, the first large-scale demonstrations against the international presence in Kosovo were held, and the Kosovo Albanian prime minister, Bajram Rexhepi, openly warned the international community that these protests were "only the beginning."

## Political Rights and Civil Liberties:

According to UNSCR 1244, ultimate authority within Kosovo resides with the UN Special Representative in the province, who is appointed by the UN secretary-general. The Special Representative, who also serves as chief of UNMIK, is responsible for implementing civilian aspects of the agreement ending the war. Elections in Kosovo in the post-1999 period, organized by the international community, have been considered "generally free and fair." In the October 2002 municipal elections, contested by more than 60 political entities, voter turnout was approximately 54 percent. There was a disproportionately low Serb turnout because of continuing complaints about the lack of freedom of movement to and from polling places.

Freedom of expression is limited because of the overall lack of security in the province. Although a wide variety of print and electronic media operate in Kosovo, journalists report frequent harassment and intimidation. A survey conducted by the Organization for Security and Cooperation in Europe (OSCE) Mission in Kosovo in December 2001 found that 78 percent of the journalists questioned did not feel free to do investigative journalism without fear of reprisal. There were no reports of government attempts to restrict access to the Internet.

The Albanian population in Kosovo, which is predominantly Muslim, on the whole enjoys freedom of belief and religious association, but there have been consistent, systematic attacks on Orthodox churches and other holy sites associated with the Serb population. Since NATO took control of Kosovo, more than 100 churches and other properties belonging to the Serbian Orthodox Church have been destroyed or damaged. There were also reports in 2003 from Kosovo's small Protestant community that "Islamic extremists" were attending services so that they could identify worshipers and later harass them. There were several reported incidents of attacks on Protestant places of worship. Academic freedom, however, has not been restricted.

Freedom of assembly, especially in flashpoints for ethnic conflict such as the divided city of Mitrovica, is occasionally restricted by UNMIK and/or KFOR because of security concerns. Both domestic and foreign nongovernmental organizations (NGOs) generally function freely, although lack of donor funding in the past two years has forced a large number of NGOs to stop operating. Current UNMIK regulations governing workers rights allow for workers to join unions, although there is no explicit right to association. Similarly, the law does not recognize the right to strike, although no attempt is made to prevent workers from striking. The largest union in Kosovo, BSPK, claims to represent some 100,000 workers.

Kosovo lacks a functioning criminal justice system. Ethnic Albanian judges are generally unwilling to prosecute cases involving Albanian attacks on non-Albanians, and the physical safety of non-Albanian judges brought into Kosovo to try cases is difficult to guarantee. Criminal suspects who have been arrested under the UN Special Representative's power to order executive detentions are frequently released on the orders of local judges.

The lack of a functioning judicial system in Kosovo is considered one of the main stumbling blocks to the resolution of Kosovo's final status. Despite the hundreds of murders that have occurred in Kosovo since 1999, almost no one has been arrested for such crimes. These difficulties are compounded by a local "code of silence" in dealing with authorities. During the course of 2003, several of the witnesses involved in the case of the "Dukagjini group" accused of murdering Albanian political opponents in western Kosovo were assassinated.

Several leading members of the former KLA are under investigation for war crimes by the International Criminal Tribunal for the Former Yugoslavia (ICTY) for actions committed before, during, and after the NATO intervention. The KLA's successor organization, the Kosovo Protection Force, has been widely implicated in numerous violent acts since its formation in 1999. In December 2003, the UN Special Representative in Kosovo, Harri Holkeri, suspended 2 generals and 10 other officers from the unit, after the individuals in question were implicated in a number of these incidents.

Freedom of movement continues to be a significant problem in Kosovo for ethnic minorities. During the course of 2003, Amnesty International issued a report noting that non-Albanians in Kosovo "find themselves subjected to both direct and indirect discrimination when seeking access to basic civil, political, social, economic and cultural rights."

Gender inequality continues to be a serious problem in Kosovo Albanian society. Patriarchal societal attitudes often limit a woman's ability to gain an education or to choose her own marriage partner. In many rural areas of Kosovo, women are effectively disenfranchised by "family voting," in which the male head of a household casts ballots for the entire family.

Trafficking is a major problem in Kosovo, which serves as a place of transit for women trafficked from Eastern to Western Europe, a point of destination, and a source for trafficked women and children. The presence of a large international military force and of numerous civilian agencies provides a relatively affluent clientele for the trafficking trade in the province. NGOs estimate that 80 percent of the clients at brothels in Kosovo are locals and 20 percent are foreigners. Efforts to protect trafficked human beings in the province often backfire because of the pervasive influence of organized crime syndicates; in January, the offices of the Center for Protection of Women and Children in Pristina were broken into and computer hard drives with the personal testimonies of approximately 650 women who had reported human rights abuses were stolen. Officials of the center noted that UNMIK had failed to investigate four previous break-ins at the center.

# Turkey
## Cyprus

**Population:** 230,000    **Political Rights:** 2
**Religious Groups:** Muslim    **Civil Liberties:** 2
(99 percent), other    **Status:** Free
[including Greek Orthodox] (1 percent)
**Ethnic Groups:** Turkish (99 percent), other [including Greek]
(1 percent)

**Ten-Year Ratings Timeline (Political Rights, Civil Liberties, Status)**

| 1994 | 1995 | 1996 | 1997 | 1998 | 1999 | 2000 | 2001 | 2002 | 2003 |
|------|------|------|------|------|------|------|------|------|------|
| 4,2PF | 4,2PF | 4,2PF | 4,2PF | 4,2PF | 4,2PF | 2,2F | 2,2F | 2,2F | 2,2F |

*Note: See Cyprus (Greek) under Country Reports.*

**Overview:** The thwarted reunification process between the Greek and Turkish halves of Cyprus dominated Turkish Cypriot politics in 2003. Though there was some progress made, no agreement was reached by the deadline of March 2003 set by the UN and secretary-general Kofi Annan, who has worked hard to bring about a resolution. Though the failure of talks was widely blamed on the intransigence of Rauf Denktash, the long-time Turkish Cypriot leader, an election in Greek Cyprus shortly before the deadline may have contributed as well. As a result of the talks' failure, Greek Cyprus will join the European Union (EU) while Turkish Cyprus will remain out for the time being.

Annexed by Britain in 1914, Cyprus gained independence in 1960 after a ten-year guerrilla campaign by partisans demanding union with Greece. In July 1974, Greek Cypriot National Guard members, backed by the military junta in power in

Greece, staged an unsuccessful coup aimed at unification. Five days later, Turkey invaded northern Cyprus, seized control of 37 percent of the island, and expelled 200,000 Greeks from the north. Currently, the entire Turkish Cypriot community resides in the north, and property claims arising from the division and population exchange remain key sticking points in the reunification negotiations.

A buffer zone, called the "Green Line," has divided Cyprus since 1974. The capital, Nicosia, is similarly divided. The division of Cyprus has been a major point of contention in the long-standing rivalry between Greece and Turkey in the Aegean. Tensions and intermittent violence between the two populations have plagued the island since independence. UN resolutions stipulate that Cyprus is a single country in which the northern third is illegally occupied. In 1982, Turkish-controlled Cyprus declared its independence as the Turkish Republic of Northern Cyprus (TRNC), an entity recognized only by Turkey.

The UN-sponsored negotiations over reunification of the island broke down in 2003 over a range of issues. For the Greek side, former Greek Cypriot president Glafcos Clerides was seen as having conceded too much to his Turkish counterpart, Denktash, especially on the right of Greek Cypriots to return to land lost after the Turkish invasion; they also note that Turkish Cypriots control 37 percent of the island's land, but are only 17 percent of its population. This helped lead to the election in February of Tassos Papadopoulos, usually considered more intransigent than his predecessor. Denktash, for his side, insisted that the plan did not offer Turkish Cypriots sufficiently strong guarantees of equal rights in a united Cyprus. The Greek Cypriots would like a full federation, while Denktash has insisted on a looser confederation, with only a few powers, including foreign representation, given to the central government.

In April, shortly after the Greek-Cypriot government signed the EU accession treaty, the Turkish-Cypriot authorities loosened border crossings with the south. This move, greeted with joy on both sides, came after some pressure not only from Turkish Cypriots, who strongly back negotiations with their Greek-Cypriot neighbors, but from Turkey itself. The new government of Turkey, elected in November 2002, is less willing than past governments to indulge the Turkish-Cypriot leadership's stubbornness on negotiations, because Turkey's own chances of getting into the EU hinge on (among other considerations) a resolution of the island's division. Turkey's prime minister, Recep Tayyip Erdogan, initially strongly supported the UN peace plan. However, under some pressure from the Turkish military, which still sees Cyprus as a crucial strategic asset, he has backed away somewhat from this position.

Denktash's popularity suffered in 2003, thanks to a perception that he has been too stubborn in the reunification negotiations. Turkish Cypriots, who are considerably poorer than their Greek neighbors, will see the wealth gap widen when the southern half of the island becomes part of the EU and receives development funding. (Turkish Cypriots overwhelmingly support EU membership; one poll showed 88 percent in favor of joining.) There is also increasing resentment of the 30,000 Turkish troops stationed in Cyprus. Pressure from an ever more irritated public could cost Denktash in the legislative elections to be held in December 2003. If the opposition gains control of the government, it could pressure Denktash, who will turn 80 in January 2004, to resign and appoint a negotiator more amenable to agreement on reunification.

**Political Rights and Civil Liberties:** Turkish Cypriots can change the government of the TRNC democratically. The president and legislature are elected to a term of not longer than five years. Legislative elections will be held in December 2003, and Rauf Denktash's current term as president is set to expire by April 2005. The powers of the president are largely ceremonial; Denktash wields influence by his status as the traditional leader of the Turkish Cypriot community and by his control over the center-right governing coalition of the National Unity Party and the Democratic Party. Turkey continues to play a strong role in TRNC politics, through both its military presence and its large financial contributions. However, for the 2003 legislative elections, the Turkish government has openly backed away from becoming involved. The 1,000-odd Greek and Marionite Christian residents of the north are disenfranchised, but many vote in elections in the Republic of Cyprus.

The criminal code allows the government to jail journalists for what they write, and the government has been hostile to the independent press. For example, it harassed and eventually forced the closure of *Avrupa*, an opposition paper, for criticizing President Denktash. Two editors from *Avrupa*'s successor, *Afrika*, have also been imprisoned for insulting the president. They were each originally sentenced to six months' jail time, but their sentences were cut to six weeks on appeal and they were freed immediately.

An agreement with Greek-Cypriot authorities dating from 1975 provides for freedom of worship for both communities in both parts of the island.

Civic groups and nongovernmental organizations generally operate without restrictions, and there is a free and competitive party political scene. There is freedom of assembly. In February, 70,000 Turkish Cypriots marched through the Turkish half of Nicosia angrily shouting slogans at Denktash. Workers may form independent unions, bargain collectively, and strike.

The judiciary is independent, and trials generally meet international standards of fairness. Turkish-Cypriot police, under the control of the Turkish military, sometimes abuse due process rights and civilians are sometimes tried in military courts. Prison conditions generally meet international standards.

Personal autonomy improved with the loosening of border controls with the Greek half of Cyprus in early 2003. However, Turkish Cypriots have difficulty traveling because most governments do not recognize their travel documents. In August, the TNRC signed an agreement with Turkey to ease trade between the countries. The agreement, intended to help the TNRC export its goods via Turkey, was condemned by the EU.

Women are under-represented in government. There are legal provisions for equal pay for equal work, but these are often disregarded.

# United Kingdom
## Northern Ireland

**Population:** 1,700,000
**Religious Groups:** Protestant (58 percent), Roman Catholic (42 percent)
**Ethnic Groups:** Irish [majority]

**Political Rights:** 2
**Civil Liberties:** 2
**Status:** Free

**Ten-Year Ratings Timeline (Political Rights, Civil Liberties, Status)**

| 1994 | 1995 | 1996 | 1997 | 1998 | 1999 | 2000 | 2001 | 2002 | 2003 |
|------|------|------|------|------|------|------|------|------|------|
| 4,3PF | 4,3PF | 4,3PF | 3,3PF | 3,3PF | 3,3PF | 2,2F | 2,2F | 2,2F | 2,2F |

**Overview:**

The Northern Ireland assembly based at Stormont, whose work stopped in October 2002 after a dispute between Catholic and Protestant parties over the decommissioning of arms by former terrorists, remained suspended throughout 2003. An election in November for a new assembly gave the largest share of seats to the more extreme parties on both sides of the divide, including one that flatly rejects the Good Friday agreement of 1998 that set up the power-sharing agreement. The assembly will not continue working until some form of cooperation reemerges.

After the Anglo-Irish Treaty of 1921, the Irish Free State (now the Republic of Ireland) was created out of most of the island of Ireland, with six Protestant-majority counties in the Irish province of Ulster remaining in the United Kingdom as the British province of Northern Ireland. Catholics now constitute a majority in four of the six counties, causing concern among Protestants, who are largely descended from English and Scottish settlers.

A nonviolent Catholic civil rights movement emerged in the 1960s. When Britain sent troops—which are still there today—trouble in the province increased, and sectarian violence grew during the 1970s. The Northern Irish parliament, established by the British in 1920, was suspended in 1972. Terrorist acts were committed by extremists on both sides of the Catholic (Republican) and Protestant (Unionist) divide. Negotiations over peace began in 1996. In 1997, a cease-fire by the Irish Republican Army (IRA) and an agreement by Sinn Fein, the IRA's political wing, to participate in peace talks was secured.

With the help of a former U.S. senator, George Mitchell, the Good Friday agreement was reached in 1998. It established the principle of consent, under which it was agreed that Northern Ireland's status would not change without the consent of a majority of its population, and established several cross-border institutions with the rRpublic of Ireland. The constitution of the republic was amended to remove its claim to the North. All of the major political parties, save one hard-line Protestant party, the Democratic Unionists, signed the agreement. The governments of Britain and the Irish republic strongly supported it as well, and it passed referendums both in the North and in the republic. The agreement created a 108-member Northern Ireland assembly at Stormont in Belfast.

Parties in favor of the agreement dominated the assembly's first elections in 1998, and a power-sharing government was installed with David Trimble, of the moderate Ulster Unionist Party, as first minister. Sinn Fein also took part in the government. The agreement required decommissioning of weapons by the IRA, however, and over the life of the assembly, frustration mounted with the IRA's slow, secretive, and therefore difficult-to-verify moves to put its weapons "beyond use." In October 2002, the assembly was suspended after police raided Sinn Fein headquarters and found documents that may be useful to terrorists; Trimble demanded that Sinn Fein be ejected from the government.

Efforts to restart the peace process sputtered over the course of 2003. In November, fresh elections were held and, as feared, gave increased power to the rejectionist Democratic Unionists and to Sinn Fein, now the largest unionist and republican parties, respectively. The moderate Catholic and republican Social Democratic and Labour Party had the worst results. Talks will begin to restore cooperation. To the surprise of many, the Reverend Ian Paisley, the Democratic Unionists' fiery leader, has said that his party hopes to be "constructive."

**Political Rights and Civil Liberties:** The people of Northern Ireland may vote for members of the British Parliament sitting in London and for the Northern Ireland Assembly, which ran many local affairs before it was suspended. A free and fair election was held in November 2003 for the assembly, and the political system is open to the rise and fall of competing parties including the Ulster Unionists (moderate unionist), Democratic Unionists (hard-line unionist), the Social Democratic and Labour Party (moderate republican), Sinn Fein (republican, linked to the IRA), and the Alliance Party (interdenominational unionist). The government is largely free of pervasive corruption.

A free and competitive media market esists in Northern Ireland. Newspapers across a broad spectrum of political opinions compete for readers. Although broadcasting is dominated by the state-owned BBC, the corporation is editorially independent of the government. Internet access is unrestricted by the government.

Freedom of religion is protected by law and respected in practice. There is no established church in Northern Ireland, and most religions are officially classified as charities, with the corresponding tax benefits. The Anti-Terrorism, Crime and Security Act, enacted in 2001, increases the penalties handed out for assault, harassment, or criminal damage when the crime is "religiously aggravated."

Antiterrorism legislation may restrict the rights of assembly, association, or expression, but it is not generally used to do so, and Northern Ireland enjoys a vibrant civil society. Workers may bargain collectively and strike.

The judiciary is independent. The British cabinet post of Lord Chancellor, which combined executive, legislative, and judicial powers in one office, was abolished in 2003 in favor of a secretary of constitutional affairs. The Law Lords, sitting in the House of Lords of the British Parliament, constitute the highest court in Britain. Northern Irish citizens also have recourse to the European Convention on Human Rights, which was incorporated into Northern Irish law by the Northern Ireland Act of 1998.

In 1999, the Patten Report made recommendations for policing reform in the province. As a result, in 2001 the police force, the Royal Ulster Constabulary, long seen by Catholics as a tool of Protestant control, became the Police Service of Northern

Ireland. An ombudsman was created to provide an independent police-complaints system. The police force now accepts equal numbers of Catholics and Protestants as new recruits, regardless of how many applications from each group are received; it is currently 13 percent Catholic. Prison conditions are generally adequate, but an investigation into prison safety led to a government recommendation to separate unionist and republican paramilitary prisoners in one prison, Maghaberry.

Terrorist violence has subsided since 1998 and the signing of the Good Friday Agreement. However, high tensions and occasional low-level violence between the Catholic and Protestant communities remain. On August 7, 2003, Michael McKevitt, the man believed to be the head of the "Real" IRA, a dissident faction that rejects the peace process, was convicted of the offense of "directing terrorism" for his role in the 1998 bombing at Omagh, which killed 29. Bomb scares and hoaxes continue to be used as tools of intimidation and fear-mongering. In June 2003, a massive bomb was intercepted by police in transit in Londonderry.

Gender equality is guaranteed under law. Abortion law is more restrictive in Northern Ireland than in the rest of the United Kingdom, although some abortions are performed legally (usually to protect the mental or physical health of the mother). It has been estimated that 2,000 women travel from Northern Ireland to Great Britain each year to obtain abortions.

# United States
## Puerto Rico

**Population:** 3,900,000
**Religious Groups:** Roman Catholic (85 percent), other [including Protestant] (15 percent)
**Ethnic Groups:** White [mostly Spanish origin] (80.5 percent), other (11.5 percent), black (8 percent)

**Political Rights:** 1
**Civil Liberties:** 2
**Status:** Free

**Ten-Year Ratings Timeline (Political Rights, Civil Liberties, Status)**

| 1994 | 1995 | 1996 | 1997 | 1998 | 1999 | 2000 | 2001 | 2002 | 2003 |
|------|------|------|------|------|------|------|------|------|------|
| 1,2F | 1,2F | 1,2F | 1,2F | 1,2F | 1,2F | 1,2F | 1,2F | 1,2F | 1,2F |

**Overview:**

After several years of intense controversy, demonstrations, and acts of civil disobedience, the U.S. Navy abandoned the use of the small island of Vieques as a bombing range in 2003.

Puerto Rico acquired the status of a commonwealth of the United States following approval by plebiscite in 1952. Under its terms, Puerto Rico exercises approximately the same control over its internal affairs as do the 50 U.S. states. Although they are U.S. citizens, residents cannot vote in presidential elections and are represented in the U.S. Congress by a delegate to the House of Representatives who can vote in committee, but not on the floor.

Sila Maria Calderon, a member of the pro-commonwealth Popular Democratic Party (PDP), was elected governor in 2000. She captured 48.5 percent of the vote against 45.7 percent for her main rival, Carlos Pesquera of the pro-statehood New Progressive Party (NPP).

The controversy over Vieques was triggered in 1999, when a Puerto Rican civilian was killed accidentally during a bombing exercise. The incident ignited protests by Puerto Ricans and stimulated a debate over U.S. policy toward Puerto Rico. Governor Calderon sided with the protestors and urged a speedy shutdown of the bombing range and a handover of the territory involved to Puerto Rico. Calderon sponsored a referendum in 2001 in which voters opted strongly for the return of Vieques to Puerto Rican control. Subsequently, U.S. officials agreed to eliminate the bombing range and to shut down the Roosevelt Roads naval base, both of which were accomplished in 2003.

The island's relationship with the United States remains a fundamental issue. There have been several nonbinding referendums in which Puerto Ricans were asked to choose from among three options—a continuation of the commonwealth status, statehood, or independence. In the most recent referendum, in 1998, Puerto Rican voters opted to retain commonwealth status by a narrow margin over the statehood alternative. Any vote to change the island's status would have to be approved by the U.S. Congress. During her term, Governor Calderon has deemphasized the question of the island's status, focusing instead on economic development and crime prevention. Puerto Rico's status could emerge as an issue again after the next election for governor, scheduled for November 2004.

Governor Calderon has emphasized the fight against official corruption during her tenure. In an important case, Edison Misla Aldarondo, the former speaker of the Puerto Rican House of Representatives, was convicted of extortion and money laundering and sentenced to nearly six years in prison.

**Political Rights and Civil Liberties:** The commonwealth constitution, modeled after that of the United States, provides for a governor and a bicameral legislature, consisting of a 28-member Senate and a 54-member House of Representatives, elected for four years. As U.S. citizens, Puerto Ricans are guaranteed all civil liberties granted in the United States.

The press and broadcast media are well developed, varied, and critical.

Freedom of religion is guaranteed in this predominantly Roman Catholic territory, and a substantial number of evangelical churches have been established on the island in recent years. Academic freedom is guaranteed.

There is a robust civil society, with numerous nongovernmental organizations representing the interests of different constituencies. Freedom of assembly is guaranteed by law, and Puerto Ricans frequently mount protest rallies against government policies or policies of the United States. Trade union rights are respected by the government and unions are generally free to organize and strike.

The legal system is based on U.S. law, and a Supreme Court heads an independent judiciary. Crime is the most serious problem facing the island. More than 750 murders were committed in 2003, and the murder rate was three times the average for the United States. Puerto Rico is one of the Caribbean's main drug transshipment points, and a substantial percentage of murders are drug-related. Governor Sila Maria Calderon has made crime prevention a major priority of her administration. The effort, however, has been hampered by low police morale and an inadequate legal system.

A controversy has emerged over the issue of capital punishment. Although Puerto Rico prohibits the death penalty, Puerto Ricans are subject to the death penalty for crimes that violate U.S. federal law. Differences between Puerto Rican and U.S. departments of justice emerged in the case of two men accused of kidnapping (a federal crime) and murder in San Juan. The U.S. Justice Department is seeking the death penalty in the case.

In 2003, there was a surge in attempts by illegal migrants from various Caribbean countries, many traveling in flimsy boats, to reach Puerto Rico. Many were brought to the island by smugglers, who encouraged their migration efforts by warning that new U.S. policies would make illegal immigration more difficult in the future.

Laws granting equal rights for women in education, at the workplace, and in other aspects of society have been adopted. Women's rights organizations, however, claim that women are still subject to widespread discrimination.

# Survey Methodology—2004

## INTRODUCTION

The *Freedom in the World* survey provides an annual evaluation of the state of global freedom as experienced by individuals. Freedom is the opportunity to act spontaneously in a variety of fields outside the control of the government and other centers of potential domination. Freedom House measures freedom according to two broad categories: political rights and civil liberties. Political rights enable people to participate freely in the political process, including through the right to vote, compete for public office, and elect representatives who have a decisive impact on public policies and are accountable to the electorate. Civil liberties allow for the freedoms of expression and belief, associational and organizational rights, rule of law, and personal autonomy without interference from the state.

Freedom House does not maintain a culture-bound view of freedom. The methodology of the survey established basic standards that are derived in large measure from the Universal Declaration of Human Rights. These standards apply to all countries and territories, irrespective of geographical location, ethnic or religious composition, or level of economic development.

The survey includes both analytical reports and numerical ratings for 192 countries and 18 select territories. Each country and territory is assigned a numerical rating, which is calculated based on the methodology described below, on a scale of 1 to 7. A rating of 1 indicates the highest degree of freedom and 7 the least amount of freedom.

The survey findings are reached after a multi-layered process of analysis and evaluation by a team of regional experts and scholars. Although there is an element of subjectivity inherent in the survey findings, the ratings process emphasizes intellectual rigor and balanced and unbiased judgments.

The survey does not rate governments or government performance per se, but rather the real-world rights and freedoms enjoyed by individuals. Freedoms can be affected by state actions, as well as by non-state actors, including terrorists and other armed groups. Thus, the survey ratings generally reflect the interplay of a variety of actors, both governmental and nongovernmental.

In addition to country reports, *Freedom in the World* includes reports on a select group of territories based on their political significance and size. Freedom House divides territories into two categories: related territories and disputed territories. Related territories consist mostly of colonies, protectorates, and island dependencies of sovereign states that are in some relation of dependency to that state and whose relationship is not currently in serious legal or political dispute. Disputed territories are areas within internationally recognized sovereign states whose status is in serious political or violent dispute and that often are dominated by a minority ethnic group. This group also includes territories whose incorporation into nation-states is not universally recognized. In some cases, the issue of dispute is the desire of the majority of the population of that territory to secede from the sovereign state and either form an independent country or become part of a neighboring state.

## HISTORY OF THE SURVEY

Freedom House's first year-end reviews of freedom began in the 1950s as the *Balance Sheet of Freedom*. This modest report provided assessments of political trends and their implications for individual freedom. In 1972, Freedom House launched a new, more comprehensive annual study of freedom called *Freedom in the World*. Raymond Gastil, a Harvard-trained specialist in regional studies from the University of Washington at Seattle, developed the survey's methodology, which assigned countries political rights and civil liberties ratings and categorized them as Free, Partly Free, or Not Free. The findings appeared each year in Freedom House's *Freedom at Issue* bimonthly journal (later titled *Freedom Review*). The survey first appeared in book form in 1978 and continued to be produced by Gastil, with essays by leading scholars on related issues, until 1989, when a larger team of in-house survey analysts was established. Subsequent editions of the survey, including the 2004 edition, have followed essentially the same format.

## OVERVIEW OF RESEARCH AND RATINGS REVIEW PROCESS

This year's survey covers developments from January 1, 2003, through November 30, 2003, in 192 countries and 18 territories. The research and ratings process involved nearly two dozen analyst/writers and 12 senior-level academic advisors. The eight members of the core research team headquartered in New York, along with fifteen outside consultant writers, prepared the country and territory reports. The writers used a broad range of sources of information, including foreign and domestic news reports, academic analyses, nongovernmental organizations, think tanks, individual professional contacts, and visits to the region in preparing their reports.

The country and territory ratings were proposed by the writers of each related report. The ratings were reviewed on a comparative basis in a series of six regional meetings—Sub-Saharan Africa, Asia-Pacific, Central and Eastern Europe and the Former Soviet Union, Middle East and North Africa, Latin America and the Caribbean, and Western Europe—involving the writers and academic advisors with expertise in each region. The ratings were compared to the previous year's findings, and any major proposed numerical shifts or category changes were subjected to more intensive scrutiny. These reviews were followed by cross-regional assessments in which efforts were made to ensure comparability and consistency in the findings. Some of the key country reports were also reviewed by the academic advisors.

The survey's methodology is reviewed periodically by an advisory committee on methodological issues. Over the years, the committee has made a number of modest methodological changes to adapt to evolving ideas about political rights and civil liberties. At the same time, the time-series data are not revised retroactively, and any changes to the methodology are introduced incrementally in order to ensure the comparability of the ratings from year to year.

## RATINGS PROCESS

*(NOTE: see the full checklists and keys to political rights and civil liberties ratings and status at the end of the methodology essay.)*

**Raw Points** – The ratings process is based on a checklist of 10 political rights questions (grouped into three subcategories) and 15 civil liberties questions (grouped into four subcategories). Raw points are awarded to each of these questions on a scale of 0 to 4, where 0 points represents the smallest degree and 4 points the greatest degree of rights or liberties present. The only exception to the addition of 0 to 4 points per checklist item is Additional Discretionary Question B in the Political Rights Checklist, for which 1 to 4 points are subtracted depending on the severity of the situation. The highest number of points that can be awarded to the political rights checklist is 40 (or a total of up to 4 points for each of the 10 questions). The highest number of points that can be awarded to the civil liberties checklist is 60 (or a total of up to 4 points for each of the 15 questions).

To answer the political rights questions, Freedom House considers to what extent the system offers voters the opportunity to choose freely from among candidates and to what extent the candidates are chosen independently of the state. However, formal electoral procedures are not the only factors that determine the real distribution of power. In many countries, the military retains a significant political role, while in others, the king maintains considerable power over the elected politicians. In addition, elected governments must exhibit levels of accountability, openness, and transparency between elections.

In answering the civil liberties questions, Freedom House does not equate constitutional guarantees of human rights with the on-the-ground fulfillment of these rights. Both laws and actual practices are factored into the ratings decisions. For states and territories with small populations, particularly tiny island nations, the absence of trade unions and other forms of association is not necessarily viewed as a negative situation unless the government or other centers of domination are deliberately blocking their establishment or operation.

**Political Rights and Civil Liberties Ratings** – The total number of points awarded to the political rights and civil liberties checklists determines the political rights and civil liberties ratings. Each point total corresponds to a rating of 1 through 7, with 1 representing the highest and 7 the lowest level of freedom. (see Tables 1 and 2).

**Status of Free, Partly Free, Not Free** – Each pair of political rights and civil liberties ratings is averaged to determine an overall status of "Free," "Partly Free," or "Not Free." Those whose ratings average 1.0-2.5 are considered Free, 3.0-5.0 Partly Free, and 5.5-7.0 Not Free (see Table 3). [In previous years, countries or territories with a combined average score of 5.5 could be either Partly Free or Not Free, depending on the total number of raw points that they received.]

The designations of Free, Partly Free, and Not Free each cover a broad third of the available raw points. Therefore, countries and territories within any one category, especially those at either end of the category, can have quite different human rights situations. In order to see the distinctions within each category, a country or territory's political rights and civil liberties ratings should be examined. For example, countries at the lowest end of the Free category (2 in political rights and 3 in civil liberties, or 3 in political rights and 2 in civil liberties) differ from those at the upper end of the Free group (1 for both political rights and civil liberties). Also, a designation of Free does not mean that a country enjoys perfect freedom or lacks serious problems, only that it enjoys comparably more freedom than Partly Free or Not Free (or some other Free) countries.

**Indications of Ratings and/or Status Changes** – Each country or territory's political rights rating, civil liberties rating, and status is included in the statistics section that precedes each country or territory report. A change in a political rights or civil liberties rating since the previous survey edition is indicated with an asterisk next to the rating that has changed. A brief ratings change explanation is included in the statistics section.

**Trend Arrows** – Upward or downward trend arrows may be assigned to countries and territories. Trend arrows indicate general positive or negative trends since the previous survey that are not necessarily reflected in the raw points and do *not* warrant a ratings change. A country cannot receive both a numerical ratings change and a trend arrow in the same year. A trend arrow is indicated with an arrow next to the name of the country or territory that appears before the statistics section at the top of each country or territory report.

## GENERAL CHARACTERISTICS OF EACH POLITICAL RIGHTS AND CIVIL LIBERTIES RATING

### POLITICAL RIGHTS

**Rating of 1** – Countries and territories that receive a rating of 1 for political rights come closest to the ideals suggested by the checklist questions, beginning with free and fair elections. Those who are elected rule, there are competitive parties or other political groupings, and the opposition plays an important role and has actual power. Minority groups have reasonable self-government or can participate in the government through informal consensus.

**Rating of 2** – Countries and territories rated 2 in political rights are less free than those rated 1. Such factors as political corruption, violence, political discrimination against minorities, and foreign or military influence on politics may be present and weaken the quality of freedom.

**Ratings of 3, 4, 5** – The same conditions that undermine freedom in countries and territories with a rating of 2 may also weaken political rights in those with a rating of 3, 4, or 5. Other damaging elements can include civil war, heavy military involvement in politics, lingering royal power, unfair elections, and one-party dominance. However, states and territories in these categories may still enjoy some elements of political rights, including the freedom to organize quasi-political groups, reasonably free referenda, or other significant means of popular influence on government.

**Rating of 6** – Countries and territories with political rights rated 6 have systems ruled by military juntas, one-party dictatorships, religious hierarchies, or autocrats.

These regimes may allow only a minimal manifestation of political rights, such as some degree of representation or autonomy for minorities. A few states are traditional monarchies that mitigate their relative lack of political rights through the use of consultation with their subjects, tolerance of political discussion, and acceptance of public petitions.

**Rating of 7** – For countries and territories with a rating of 7, political rights are absent or virtually nonexistent as a result of the extremely oppressive nature of the regime or severe oppression in combination with civil war. States and territories in this group may also be marked by extreme violence or warlord rule that dominates political power in the absence of an authoritative, functioning central government.

## CIVIL LIBERTIES

**Rating of 1** – Countries and territories that receive a rating of 1 come closest to the ideals expressed in the civil liberties checklist, including freedom of expression, assembly, association, education, and religion. They are distinguished by an established and generally equitable system of rule of law. Countries and territories with this rating enjoy free economic activity and tend to strive for equality of opportunity.

**Rating of 2** – States and territories with a rating of 2 have deficiencies in a few aspects of civil liberties, but are still relatively free.

**Ratings of 3, 4, 5** – Countries and territories that have received a rating of 3, 4, or 5 range from those that are in at least partial compliance with virtually all checklist standards to those with a combination of high or medium scores for some questions and low or very low scores on other questions. The level of oppression increases at each successive rating level, including in the areas of censorship, political terror, and the prevention of free association. There are also many cases in which groups opposed to the state engage in political terror that undermines other freedoms. Therefore, a poor rating for a country is not necessarily a comment on the intentions of the government, but may reflect real restrictions on liberty caused by nongovernmental actors.

**Rating of 6** – People in countries and territories with a rating of 6 experience severely restricted rights of expression and association, and there are almost always political prisoners and other manifestations of political terror. These countries may be characterized by a few partial rights, such as some religious and social freedoms, some highly restricted private business activity, and relatively free private discussion.

**Rating of 7** – States and territories with a rating of 7 have virtually no freedom. An overwhelming and justified fear of repression characterizes these societies.

Countries and territories generally have ratings in political rights and civil liberties that are within two ratings numbers of each other. Without a well-developed civil society, it is difficult, if not impossible, to have an atmosphere supportive of political rights. Consequently, there is no country in the survey with a rating of 6 or 7 for civil liberties and, at the same time, a rating of 1 or 2 for political rights.

## ELECTORAL DEMOCRACY DESIGNATION

In addition to providing numerical ratings, the survey assigns the designation "electoral democracy" to countries that have met certain minimum standards. In determining whether a country is an electoral democracy, Freedom House examines several key factors concerning how its national leadership is chosen.

To qualify as an electoral democracy, a state must have satisfied the following criteria:

1) A competitive, multiparty political system.

2) Universal adult suffrage for all citizens (with exceptions for restrictions that states may legitimately place on citizens as sanctions for criminal offenses).

3) Regularly contested elections conducted in conditions of ballot secrecy, reasonable ballot security, and in the absence of massive voter fraud that yields results that are unrepresentative of the public will.

4) Significant public access of major political parties to the electorate through the media and through generally open political campaigning.

The electoral democracy designation reflects a judgment about the last major national election or elections. In the case of presidential/parliamentary systems, both elections must have been free and fair on the basis of the above criteria; in parliamentary systems, the last nationwide elections for the national legislature must have been free and fair. The presence of certain irregularities during the electoral process does not automatically disqualify a country from being designated an electoral democracy. A country cannot be listed as an electoral democracy if it reflects the ongoing and overwhelming dominance of a single party or movement over the course of numerous national elections; such states are considered to be dominant party states. Nor can a country be an electoral democracy if significant authority for national decisions resides in the hands of an unelected power, whether a monarch or a foreign international authority. A country is removed from the ranks of electoral democracies if its last national election failed to meet the criteria listed above, or if changes in law significantly eroded the public's possibility for electoral choice.

Freedom House's term "electoral democracy" differs from "liberal democracy" in that the latter also implies the presence of a substantial array of civil liberties. In the survey, all Free countries qualify as both electoral and liberal democracies. By contrast, some Partly Free countries qualify as electoral, but not liberal, democracies.

## POLITICAL RIGHTS AND CIVIL LIBERTIES CHECKLIST

### POLITICAL RIGHTS
### A. Electoral Process

1. Is the head of state and/or head of government or other chief authority elected through free and fair elections?

2. Are the legislative representatives elected through free and fair elections?

3. Are there fair electoral laws, equal campaigning opportunities, fair polling, and honest tabulation of ballots?

## B. Political Pluralism and Participation

1. Do the people have the right to organize in different political parties or other competitive political groupings of their choice, and is the system open to the rise and fall of these competing parties or groupings?

2. Is there a significant opposition vote, de facto opposition power, and a realistic possibility for the opposition to increase its support or gain power through elections?

3. Are the people's political choices free from domination by the military, foreign powers, totalitarian parties, religious hierarchies, economic oligarchies, or any other powerful group?

4. Do cultural, ethnic, religious, and other minority groups have reasonable self-determination, self-government, autonomy, or participation through informal consensus in the decision-making process?

## C. Functioning of Government

1. Do freely elected representatives determine the policies of the government?

2. Is the government free from pervasive corruption?

3. Is the government accountable to the electorate between elections, and does it operate with openness and transparency?

## Additional discretionary Political Rights questions:

A. For traditional monarchies that have no parties or electoral process, does the system provide for consultation with the people, encourage discussion of policy, and allow the right to petition the ruler?

B. Is the government or occupying power deliberately changing the ethnic composition of a country or territory so as to destroy a culture or tip the political balance in favor of another group?

*NOTE*: For each political rights and civil liberties checklist question, 0 to 4 points are added, depending on the comparative rights and liberties present (0 represents the least, 4 represents the most). However, for additional discretionary question B only, 1 to 4 points are subtracted, when necessary.

## CIVIL LIBERTIES

### D. Freedom of Expression and Belief

1. Are there free and independent media and other forms of cultural expression?

(Note: in cases where the media are state-controlled but offer pluralistic points of view, the survey gives the system credit.)

2. Are there free religious institutions, and is there free private and public religious expression?

3. Is there academic freedom, and is the educational system free of extensive political indoctrination?

4. Is there open and free private discussion?

## E. Associational and Organizational Rights

1. Is there freedom of assembly, demonstration, and open public discussion?

2. Is there freedom of political or quasi-political organization? (Note: this includes political parties, civic organizations, ad hoc issue groups, etc.)

3. Are there free trade unions and peasant organizations or equivalents, and is there effective collective bargaining? Are there free professional and other private organizations?

## F. Rule of Law

1. Is there an independent judiciary?

2. Does the rule of law prevail in civil and criminal matters? Are police under direct civilian control?

3. Is there protection from police terror, unjustified imprisonment, exile, or torture, whether by groups that support or oppose the system? Is there freedom from war and insurgencies?

4. Is the population treated equally under the law?

## G. Personal Autonomy and Individual Rights

1. Is there personal autonomy? Does the state control travel, choice of residence, or choice of employment? Is there freedom from indoctrination and excessive dependency on the state?

2. Do citizens have the right to own property and establish private businesses? Is private business activity unduly influenced by government officials, the security forces, or organized crime?

3. Are there personal social freedoms, including gender equality, choice of marriage partners, and size of family?

4. Is there equality of opportunity and the absence of economic exploitation?

## KEY TO RAW POINTS, POLITICAL RIGHTS AND
## CIVIL LIBERTIES RATINGS, AND STATUS

| Table 1 | | Table 2 | |
|---|---|---|---|
| **Political Rights (PR)** | | **Civil Liberties (CL)** | |
| **Total Raw Points** | **PR Rating** | **Total Raw Points** | **CL Rating** |
| 36-40 | 1 | 53-60 | 1 |
| 30-35 | 2 | 44-52 | 2 |
| 24-29 | 3 | 35-43 | 3 |
| 18-23 | 4 | 26-34 | 4 |
| 12-17 | 5 | 17-25 | 5 |
| 6-11 | 6 | 8-16 | 6 |
| 0-5 | 7 | 0-7 | 7 |

### Table 3

| **Combined Average of the PR and CL Ratings** | **Country Status** |
|---|---|
| 1.0 to 2.5 | Free |
| 3.0 to 5.5 | Partly Free |
| 5.5 to 7.0 | Not Free |

# Tables and Ratings

## Table of Independent Countries

| Country | PR | CL | Freedom Rating | Country | PR | CL | Freedom Rating |
|---------|----|----|----------------|---------|----|----|----------------|
| Afghanistan | 6 | 6 | Not Free | Dominica | 1 | 1 | Free |
| Albania | 3 | 3 | Partly Free | Dominican Republic | 3▼ | 2 | Free |
| Algeria | 6 | 5 | Not Free | East Timor | 3 | 3 | Partly Free |
| Andorra | 1 | 1 | Free | ↑ Ecuador | 3 | 3 | Partly Free |
| Angola | 6 | 5 | Not Free | Egypt | 6 | 6 | Not Free |
| Antigua and Barbuda | 4 | 2 | Partly Free | ↓ El Salvador | 2 | 3 | Free |
| Argentina | 2▲ | 2▲ | Free | Equatorial Guinea | 7 | 6 | Not Free |
| ↓ Armenia | 4 | 4 | Partly Free | Eritrea | 7 | 6 | Not Free |
| Australia | 1 | 1 | Free | Estonia | 1 | 2 | Free |
| Austria | 1 | 1 | Free | Ethiopia | 5 | 5 | Partly Free |
| Azerbaijan | 6 | 5 | Not Free | ↓ Fiji | 4 | 3 | Partly Free |
| Bahamas | 1 | 1 | Free | Finland | 1 | 1 | Free |
| Bahrain | 5 | 5 | Partly Free | France | 1 | 1 | Free |
| Bangladesh | 4 | 4 | Partly Free | ↓ Gabon | 5 | 4 | Partly Free |
| Barbados | 1 | 1 | Free | The Gambia | 4 | 4 | Partly Free |
| ↓ Belarus | 6 | 6 | Not Free | Georgia | 4 | 4 | Partly Free |
| Belgium | 1 | 1 | Free | Germany | 1 | 1 | Free |
| Belize | 1 | 2 | Free | Ghana | 2 | 2▲ | Free |
| Benin | 2▲ | 2 | Free | Greece | 1 | 2 | Free |
| Bhutan | 6 | 5 | Not Free | Grenada | 1 | 2 | Free |
| Bolivia | 3▼ | 3 | Partly Free | ↓ Guatemala | 4 | 4 | Partly Free |
| ↑ Bosnia-Herzegovina | 4 | 4 | Partly Free | Guinea | 6 | 5 | Not Free |
| Botswana | 2 | 2 | Free | Guinea-Bissau | 6▼ | 4▲ | Partly Free |
| Brazil | 2 | 3 | Free | Guyana | 2 | 2 | Free |
| Brunei | 6 | 5 | Not Free | ↓ Haiti | 6 | 6 | Not Free |
| Bulgaria | 1 | 2 | Free | ↓ Honduras | 3 | 3 | Partly Free |
| Burkina Faso | 4 | 4 | Partly Free | Hungary | 1 | 2 | Free |
| Burma | 7 | 7 | Not Free | Iceland | 1 | 1 | Free |
| Burundi | 5▲ | 5 | Partly Free | India | 2 | 3 | Free |
| Cambodia | 6 | 5 | Not Free | Indonesia | 3 | 4 | Partly Free |
| ↓ Cameroon | 6 | 6 | Not Free | Iran | 6 | 6 | Not Free |
| Canada | 1 | 1 | Free | Iraq | 7 | 5▲ | Not Free |
| Cape Verde | 1 | 1▲ | Free | Ireland | 1 | 1 | Free |
| Central African Republic | 7▼ | 5 | Not Free | Israel | 1 | 3 | Free |
| | | | | Italy | 1 | 1 | Free |
| Chad | 6 | 5 | Not Free | ↓ Jamaica | 2 | 3 | Free |
| Chile | 1▲ | 1 | Free | Japan | 1 | 2 | Free |
| China | 7 | 6 | Not Free | Jordan | 5▲ | 5 | Partly Free |
| Colombia | 4 | 4 | Partly Free | Kazakhstan | 6 | 5 | Not Free |
| Comoros | 5 | 4 | Partly Free | Kenya | 3▲ | 3▲ | Partly Free |
| Congo (Brazzaville) | 5▲ | 4 | Partly Free | Kiribati | 1 | 1 | Free |
| ↑ Congo (Kinshasa) | 6 | 6 | Not Free | Kuwait | 4 | 5 | Partly Free |
| Costa Rica | 1 | 2 | Free | Kyrgyzstan | 6 | 5 | Not Free |
| Côte d'Ivoire | 6 | 5▲ | Not Free | Laos | 7 | 6 | Not Free |
| Croatia | 2 | 2 | Free | Latvia | 1 | 2 | Free |
| Cuba | 7 | 7 | Not Free | Lebanon | 6 | 5 | Not Free |
| Cyprus | 1 | 1 | Free | Lesotho | 2 | 3 | Free |
| Czech Republic | 1 | 2 | Free | ↑ Liberia | 6 | 6 | Not Free |
| Denmark | 1 | 1 | Free | Libya | 7 | 7 | Not Free |
| Djibouti | 5▼ | 5 | Partly Free | Liechtenstein | 1 | 1 | Free |

| Country | PR | CL | Freedom Rating |
|---------|-----|-----|----------------|
| Lithuania | 1 | 2 | Free |
| Luxembourg | 1 | 1 | Free |
| ⬆ Macedonia | 3 | 3 | Partly Free |
| Madagascar | 3 | 3▲ | Partly Free |
| Malawi | 3▲ | 4 | Partly Free |
| Malaysia | 5 | 4▲ | Partly Free |
| Maldives | 6 | 5 | Not Free |
| Mali | 2 | 2▲ | Free |
| Malta | 1 | 1 | Free |
| Marshall Islands | 1 | 1 | Free |
| Mauritania | 6▼ | 5 | Not Free |
| Mauritius | 1 | 2 | Free |
| Mexico | 2 | 2 | Free |
| Micronesia | 1 | 1▲ | Free |
| Moldova | 3 | 4 | Partly Free |
| Monaco | 2 | 1 | Free |
| Mongolia | 2 | 2 | Free |
| Morocco | 5 | 5 | Partly Free |
| Mozambique | 3 | 4 | Partly Free |
| Namibia | 2 | 3 | Free |
| Nauru | 1 | 1▲ | Free |
| Nepal | 5▼ | 4 | Partly Free |
| Netherlands | 1 | 1 | Free |
| New Zealand | 1 | 1 | Free |
| ⬇ Nicaragua | 3 | 3 | Partly Free |
| Niger | 4 | 4 | Partly Free |
| Nigeria | 4 | 4▲ | Partly Free |
| North Korea | 7 | 7 | Not Free |
| Norway | 1 | 1 | Free |
| Oman | 6 | 5 | Not Free |
| Pakistan | 6 | 5 | Not Free |
| Palau | 1 | 1▲ | Free |
| Panama | 1 | 2 | Free |
| Papua New Guinea | 3▼ | 3 | Partly Free |
| Paraguay | 3▲ | 3 | Partly Free |
| Peru | 2 | 3 | Free |
| Philippines | 2 | 3 | Free |
| Poland | 1 | 2 | Free |
| Portugal | 1 | 1 | Free |
| ⬆ Qatar | 6 | 6 | Not Free |
| Romania | 2 | 2 | Free |
| ⬇ Russia | 5 | 5 | Partly Free |
| Rwanda | 6▲ | 5 | Not Free |
| St. Kitts and Nevis | 1 | 2 | Free |
| St. Lucia | 1 | 2 | Free |
| St. Vincent and the Grenadines | 2 | 1 | Free |
| Samoa | 2 | 2 | Free |
| San Marino | 1 | 1 | Free |
| Sao Tome and Príncipe | 2▼ | 2 | Free |
| Saudi Arabia | 7 | 7 | Not Free |
| Senegal | 2 | 3 | Free |
| ⬇ Serbia and Montenegro | 3 | 2 | Free |

| Country | PR | CL | Freedom Rating |
|---------|-----|-----|----------------|
| Seychelles | 3 | 3 | Free |
| Sierra Leone | 4 | 3▲ | Partly Free |
| Singapore | 5 | 4 | Partly Free |
| Slovakia | 1 | 2 | Free |
| Slovenia | 1 | 1 | Free |
| Solomon Islands | 3 | 3 | Partly Free |
| Somalia | 6 | 7 | Not Free |
| South Africa | 1 | 2 | Free |
| South Korea | 2 | 2 | Free |
| Spain | 1 | 1 | Free |
| Sri Lanka | 3 | 3▲ | Partly Free |
| Sudan | 7 | 7 | Not Free |
| Suriname | 1 | 2 | Free |
| Swaziland | 7▼ | 5 | Not Free |
| Sweden | 1 | 1 | Free |
| Switzerland | 1 | 1 | Free |
| Syria | 7 | 7 | Not Free |
| Taiwan (Rep. of China) | 2 | 2 | Free |
| Tajikistan | 6 | 5 | Not Free |
| Tanzania | 4 | 3 | Partly Free |
| Thailand | 2 | 3 | Free |
| Togo | 6 | 5 | Not Free |
| ⬇ Tonga | 5 | 3 | Partly Free |
| Trinidad and Tobago | 3 | 3 | Partly Free |
| Tunisia | 6 | 5 | Not Free |
| Turkey | 3 | 4 | Partly Free |
| Turkmenistan | 7 | 7 | Not Free |
| Tuvalu | 1 | 1 | Free |
| Uganda | 5▲ | 4 | Partly Free |
| Ukraine | 4 | 4 | Partly Free |
| United Arab Emirates | 6 | 6▼ | Not Free |
| United Kingdom* | 1 | 1 | Free |
| United States | 1 | 1 | Free |
| Uruguay | 1 | 1 | Free |
| Uzbekistan | 7 | 6 | Not Free |
| Vanuatu | 2▼ | 2 | Free |
| ⬇ Venezuela | 3 | 4 | Partly Free |
| Vietnam | 7 | 6 | Not Free |
| Yemen | 5▲ | 5 | Partly Free |
| ⬆ Zambia | 4 | 4 | Partly Free |
| ⬇ Zimbabwe | 6 | 6 | Not Free |

PR and CL stand for Political Rights and Civil Liberties. 1 represents the most free and 7 the least free category.

⬆⬇ up or down indicates a general trend in freedom.

▲▼ up or down indicates a change in Political Rights or Civil Liberties since the last survey.

The freedom ratings reflect an overall judgment based on survey results. See the essay on survey methodology for more details.

\* Excluding Northern Ireland.

Note: The ratings in this table reflect global events from January 1, 2003, through November 31, 2003.

## Table of Related Territories

| Country | PR | CL | Freedom Rating |
|---|---|---|---|
| China | | | |
|   Hong Kong | 5 | 3 | Partly Free |
|   Macao | 6 | 4 | Partly Free |
| United Kingdom | | | |
|   Northern Ireland | 2 | 2 | Free |
| United States | | | |
|   Puerto Rico | 1 | 2 | Free |

## Table of Disputed Territories

| Country | PR | CL | Freedom Rating |
|---|---|---|---|
| Armenia/Azerbaijan | | | |
|   Nagorno-Karabakh | 5 | 5 | Partly Free |
| China | | | |
|   Tibet | 7 | 7 | Not Free |
| Georgia | | | |
|   Abkhazia | 6 | 5 | Not Free |
| India | | | |
|   Kashmir | 5 | 5 | Partly Free |
| Indonesia | | | |
|   West Papua | 5 | 4 | Partly Free |
| Iraq | | | |
|   Kurdistan | 5 | 4 | Partly Free |
| Israel | | | |
|   Israeli-Administered territories | 6 | 6 | Not Free |
|   Palestinian Authority-Administered territories | 5 | 6 | Not Free |
| Moldova | | | |
|   Transnistria | 6 | 6 | Not Free |
| Morocco | | | |
|   Western Sahara | 7 | 6 | Not Free |
| Pakistan | | | |
|   Kashmir | 7 | 5 | Not Free |
| Russia | | | |
|   Chechnya | 7 | 7 | Not Free |
| Serbia & Montenegro | | | |
|   ⬇ Kosovo | 5 | 5 | Partly Free |
| Turkey | | | |
|   Cyprus | 2 | 2 | Free |

# Combined Average Ratings: Independent Countries

| | | | |
|---|---|---|---|
| **FREE** | Poland | Paraguay | Azerbaijan |
| **1.0** | St. Kitts and Nevis | Seychelles | Bhutan |
| Andorra | St. Lucia | Solomon Islands | Brunei |
| Australia | St. Vincent and | Sri Lanka | Cambodia |
| Austria | the Grenadines | Trinidad and Tobago | Chad |
| Bahamas | Slovakia | | Cote d'Ivoire |
| Barbados | South Africa | **3.5** | Guinea |
| Belgium | Suriname | Fiji | Kazakhstan |
| Canada | | Indonesia | Kyrgyzstan |
| Cape Verde | **2.0** | Malawi | Lebanon |
| Chile | Argentina | Moldova | Maldives |
| Cyprus | Benin | Mozambique | Mauritania |
| Denmark | Botswana | Sierra Leone | Oman |
| Dominica | Croatia | Tanzania | Pakistan |
| Finland | Ghana | Turkey | Rwanda |
| France | Guyana | Venezuela | Tajikistan |
| Germany | Israel | | Togo |
| Iceland | Mali | **4.0** | Tunisia |
| Ireland | Mexico | Armenia | |
| Italy | Mongolia | Bangladesh | **6.0** |
| Kiribati | Romania | Bosnia-Herzegovina | Afghanistan |
| Liechtenstein | Samoa | Burkina Faso | Belarus |
| Luxembourg | Sao Tome and | Colombia | Cameroon |
| Malta | Principe | The Gambia | Central African |
| Marshall Islands | South Korea | Georgia | Republic |
| Micronesia | Taiwan | Guatemala | Congo (Kinshasa) |
| Nauru | Vanuatu | Niger | Egypt |
| Netherlands | | Nigeria | Haiti |
| New Zealand | **2.5** | Tonga | Iran |
| Norway | Brazil | Ukraine | Iraq |
| Palau | Dominican Republic | Zambia | Liberia |
| Portugal | El Salvador | | Qatar |
| San Marino | India | **4.5** | Swaziland |
| Slovenia | Jamaica | Comoros | United Arab Emirates |
| Spain | Lesotho | Congo (Brazzaville) | Zimbabwe |
| Sweden | Namibia | Gabon | |
| Switzerland | Peru | Kuwait | **6.5** |
| Tuvalu | Philippines | Malaysia | China |
| United Kingdom | Senegal | Nepal | Equatorial Guinea |
| United States | Serbia and | Singapore | Eritrea |
| Uruguay | Montenegro | Uganda | Laos |
| | Thailand | | Somalia |
| **1.5** | | **5.0** | Uzbekistan |
| Belize | | Bahrain | Vietnam |
| Bulgaria | **PARTLY FREE** | Burundi | |
| Costa Rica | **3.0** | Djibouti | **7.0** |
| Czech Republic | Albania | Ethiopia | Burma |
| Estonia | Antigua and Barbuda | Guinea-Bissau | Cuba |
| Greece | Bolivia | Jordan | Libya |
| Grenada | East Timor | Morocco | North Korea |
| Hungary | Ecuador | Russia | Saudi Arabia |
| Japan | Honduras | Yemen | Sudan |
| Latvia | Kenya | | Syria |
| Lithuania | Macedonia | **NOT FREE** | Turkmenistan |
| Mauritius | Madagascar | **5.5** | |
| Monaco | Nicaragua | Algeria | |
| Panama | Papua New Guinea | Angola | |

# Combined Average Ratings: Related Territories

**FREE**

**1.5**
Puerto Rico (US)

**2.0**
Northern Ireland (UK)

**PARTLY FREE**
**4.0**
Hong Kong (China)

**5.0**
Macao (China)

# Combined Average Ratings: Disputed Territories

| | | |
|---|---|---|
| **FREE** | Nagorno-Karabakh | Kashmir (Pakistan) |
| **2.0** | (Armenia/Azerbaijan) | Transnistria (Moldova) |
| Cyprus (Turkey) | | |
| | **NOT FREE** | **6.5** |
| **PARTLY FREE** | **5.5** | Western Sahara |
| **4.5** | Abkhazia (Georgia) | (Morocco) |
| West Papua (Indonesia) | Palestinian Authority- | |
| Kurdistan (Iraq) | Administered Territories | **7.0** |
| | (Israel) | Chechnya (Russia) |
| **5.0** | | Tibet (China) |
| Kashmir (India) | **6.0** | |
| Kosovo | Israeli-Administered | |
| (Serbia & Montenegro) | Territories (Israel) | |

# Electoral Democracies (117)

| | |
|---|---|
| Albania | Jamaica |
| Andorra | Japan |
| Argentina | Kenya |
| Australia | Kiribati |
| Austria | Latvia |
| Bahamas | Lesotho |
| Bangladesh | Liechtenstein |
| Barbados | Lithuania |
| Belgium | Luxembourg |
| Belize | Macedonia |
| Benin | Madagascar |
| Bolivia | Malawi |
| Botswana | Mali |
| Brazil | Malta |
| Bulgaria | Marshall Islands |
| Canada | Mauritius |
| Cape Verde | Mexico |
| Chile | Micronesia |
| Colombia | Moldova |
| Costa Rica | Monaco |
| Croatia | Mongolia |
| Cyprus | Mozambique |
| Czech Republic | Namibia |
| Denmark | Nauru |
| Dominica | Netherlands |
| Dominican Republic | New Zealand |
| East Timor | Nicaragua |
| Ecuador | Niger |
| El Salvador | Nigeria |
| Estonia | Norway |
| Finland | Palau |
| France | Panama |
| Germany | Papua New Guinea |
| Ghana | Paraguay |
| Greece | Peru |
| Grenada | Philippines |
| Guatemala | Poland |
| Guyana | Portugal |
| Honduras | Romania |
| Hungary | Russia |
| Iceland | St. Kitts and Nevis |
| India | St. Lucia |
| Indonesia | St. Vincent and the Grenadines |
| Ireland | Samoa |
| Israel | San Marino |
| Italy | Sao Tome and Principe |

Senegal
Serbia and Montenegro
Seychelles
Sierra Leone
Slovakia
Slovenia
Solomon Islands
South Africa
South Korea
Spain
Sri Lanka
Suriname
Sweden

Switzerland
Taiwan
Thailand
Trinidad and Tobago
Turkey
Tuvalu
Ukraine
United Kingdom
United States
Uruguay
Vanuatu
Venezuela

# The Survey Team

## CONTRIBUTING AUTHORS

**Martin Edwin "Mick" Andersen** is an investigative reporter and a historian. He has worked as a special correspondent for *Newsweek* and *The Washington Post* in Argentina, a staff member of the Senate Foreign Relations Committee, and senior adviser for policy planning with the criminal division of the U.S. Justice Department. He serves as the Latin America analyst for *Freedom in the World*.

**Gordon N. Bardos** is Assistant Director of the Harriman Institute at Columbia University. His research interests focus on problems of nationalism and ethnic conflict, and he is a frequent commentator on the Balkans in the U.S. and European press. He serves as the Balkans analyst for *Freedom in the World*.

**Gary C. Gambill** is the Editor of the *Middle East Intelligence Bulletin* and a Research Associate at the Middle East Forum. He has written extensively on Lebanese and Syrian politics, authoritarianism in the Arab World, and American foreign policy in the region. He serves as a Middle East analyst for *Freedom in the World*.

**Michael Gold-Biss** is Assistant Vice President for International Programs at Texas A&M International University in Laredo. He is the author of *The Discourse on Terrorism: Political Violence and the Subcommittee on Security and Terrorism, 1981-1986* and co-editor with Richard Millett of *Beyond Praetorianism: The Latin American Military in Transition*. He holds a doctorate in international relations from American University. He serves as the Central America and Caribbean analyst for *Freedom in the World*.

**Thomas W. Gold** frequently teaches as an adjunct professor of political science at the City University of New York. He has researched and written extensively on Italian and European politics and is the author of *The Lega Nord and Contemporary Politics in Italy* (Palgrave, 2003). He earned his doctorate from the New School for Social Research and received a Fulbright Fellowship to conduct research in Italy from 1996 to 1997. He serves as a Western Europe analyst for *Freedom in the World*.

**Michael Goldfarb** is Senior Press Officer at Freedom House. He has worked as a reporter in Israel for United Press International and as a writer for Time.com, the Web site of *Time* magazine. He serves as a Middle East analyst for *Freedom in the World*.

**Charles Graybow** is a former managing editor of both *Nations in Transit*, a Freedom House survey of democratization in East-Central Europe and Eurasia, and of *Freedom in the World*. He has participated in human rights missions to several Asian and West African countries. He serves as the East and Southeast Asia analyst for *Freedom in the World*.

**Robert Lane Greene** writes for Economist.com and *The Economist*, as well as a foreign affairs column for the Web site of the *New Republic* magazine. Previously, he was the editor of country analysis at Economist.com. He holds a master's degree from Oxford University in European politics, where he was a Marshall Scholar. He serves as a Western Europe analyst for *Freedom in the World*.

**Adrian Karatnycky** is Senior Scholar and Counselor at Freedom House, advising the organization on programs, policy, and research. From 1996 until 2003, he served as president of Freedom House. He is co-author of three books on East European politics and editor or co-editor of 16 volumes of studies on global political rights, civil liberties, and political transitions. He serves as the Russia, Ukraine, and Belarus analyst for *Freedom in the World*.

**Karin Deutsch Karlekar** is a Senior Researcher at Freedom House and the editor of Freedom House's annual *Freedom of the Press* survey. She was the author of the Afghanistan and Sri Lanka reports for Freedom House's *Countries at the Crossroads 2004* survey of democratic governance. Ms. Karlekar holds a PhD in Indian history from Cambridge University and previously worked as a consultant for Human Rights Watch and as an editor at the Economist Intelligence Unit. She serves as the South Asia analyst for *Freedom in the World*.

**Brian M. Katulis** works as a research and strategy consultant to several organizations, including ARD Incorporated, Freedom House, the National Democratic Institute, and Pal-Tech Incorporated. He previously worked on international political research and strategy projects in a dozen countries as a senior associate with Greenberg Quinlan Rosner Research. His experience includes work on the Policy Planning Staff at the Department of State and the Near East and South Asian Directorate of the National Security Council during the Clinton administration. He serves as a Middle East analyst for *Freedom in the World*.

**Judith Matloff** is an Adjunct Professor at the Columbia Graduate School of Journalism. She worked as a foreign correspondent for 20 years and wrote a book about Angola, *Fragments of a Forgotten War*. Her last two assignments abroad were as Africa Bureau Chief and Moscow Bureau Chief for *The Christian Science Monitor*. She serves as an Africa analyst for *Freedom in the World*.

**Edward R. McMahon** holds a joint appointment as Research Associate Professor in the Departments of Political Science and Community Development and Applied Economics at the University of Vermont. Previously, he was dean's professor of applied politics and the director of the Center on Democratic Performance at Binghamton University (SUNY). He has also served as regional director for West, East, and Central Africa at the National Democratic Institute for International Affairs and as a diplomat with the U.S. Department of State. He serves as an Africa analyst for *Freedom in the World*.

**Aili Piano** is a Senior Researcher at Freedom House and an editor of *Freedom in the World*. She was the author of the Georgia report for Freedom House's *Countries at* *the Crossroads 2004* survey of democratic governance. Previously, she wrote reports for several editions of *Nations in Transit*, a Freedom House survey of democratization in East-Central Europe and Eurasia. Before joining Freedom House, Ms. Piano worked as a diplomatic attache at the Estonian Mission to the United Nations. She serves as the Central Asia and Caucasus analyst for *Freedom in the World*.

**Arch Puddington** is Director of Research at Freedom House and an editor of *Freedom in the World*. He has written widely on American foreign policy, race relations, organized labor, and the history of the Cold War. He is the author of *Broadcasting Freedom: The Cold War Triumph of Radio Free Europe and Radio Liberty* and has just completed a biography of the late trade union leader, Lane Kirkland. He serves as the United States and Canada analyst for *Freedom in the World*.

**Sarah Repucci** is a Researcher at Freedom House and an editor of Freedom House's *Countries at the Crossroads 2004* survey of democratic governance. She has written articles on the European Union and transatlantic cooperation. She serves as a Western Europe analyst for *Freedom in the World*.

**Mark Yaron Rosenberg** is a Research Assistant at Freedom House. He is a recent Phi Beta Kappa graduate of the University of California, Berkeley, where he earned a BA with highest honors in political economy, and was previously employed at the Export-Import Bank of the United States. He serves as the Baltic states analyst for *Freedom in the World*.

**Cindy Shiner** is a freelance journalist who has spent much of her time in Africa. She has written for *The Washington Post*, done broadcasts for National Public Radio, and worked as a consultant on Africa issues for Human Rights Watch. She serves as an Africa analyst for *Freedom in the World*.

**Yves Sorokobi** is a freelance journalist and human rights professional. An analyst and commentator on Africa, he has worked as Africa program coordinator for the Committee to Protect Journalists and as a senior communications consultant with the International AIDS Vaccine Initiative. He serves as an Africa analyst for *Freedom in the World*.

**Christopher Walker** is Director of Studies at Freedom House and an editor of Freedom House's *Countries at the Crossroads 2004* survey of democratic governance, for which he was the author of the Azerbaijan report. He has written extensive analyses of European and Eurasian political and security affairs. He serves as the Central Europe analyst for *Freedom in the World*.

**Anny Wong** is a political scientist with the RAND Corporation. Her research covers science and technology policy, international development, homeland security, and U.S. relations with Asia-Pacific countries. She serves as the Pacific Islands analyst for *Freedom in the World*.

**Mona Yacoubian** is an independent consultant specializing in the Middle East and North Africa. She has provided analysis and guidance on political reform, women's empowerment, and civil society promotion in the Arab world to clients including the World Bank and the U.S. Department of State. She serves as the North Africa analyst for *Freedom in the World.*

## ACADEMIC ADVISERS

**Adotei Akwei** is Senior Africa Advocacy Director for Amnesty International USA.

**David Becker** is Associate Professor in the Department of Government, Dartmouth College.

**Charles Gati** is Senior Adjunct Professor in European Studies in the Paul H. Nitze School for Advanced International Studies, Johns Hopkins University.

**Thomas Lansner** is Adjunct Assistant Professor of International Affairs in the School of International and Public Affairs, Columbia University.

**Peter M. Lewis** is Associate Professor in the School of International Service, American University.

**Thomas O. Melia** is Director of Research in the Institute for the Study of Diplomacy at the Edmund A. Walsh School of Foreign Service, Georgetown University, where he is also an adjunct professor.

**Alexander J. Motyl** is Professor in the Department of Political Science and Deputy Director of the Center for Global Change and Governance, Rutgers University-Newark.

**Andrew Moravcsik** is Professor of Government and Director of the European Union Program, Harvard University.

**Phillip Oldenburg** is an independent scholar. He currently serves as Senior Lecturer in the Department of Government, University of Texas at Austin, and as Adjunct Research Associate at the Southern Asian Institute, Columbia University.

**Daniel Pipes** is Director of the Middle East Forum and a columnist for the *New York Post* and *The Jerusalem Post.*

**Arturo Valenzuela** is Professor of Government and Director of the Center for Latin American Studies in the Edmund A. Walsh School of Foreign Service, Georgetown University

**Bridget Welsh** is Assistant Professor of Southeast Asian Studies in the Paul H. Nitze School for Advanced International Studies, Johns Hopkins University.

**Linda Stern**, copy editor
**Ida Walker**, proofreader
**Mark Wolkenfeld**, production coordinator
**Elizabeth Howell**, intern
**Jeff Moorhead**, intern
**Renee Manuel**, intern

# Sources

## PUBLICATIONS/BROADCASTS

ABC Color [Paraguay], www.abc.com.py
Africa Confidential, www.africa-confidential.com
Africa Daily, www.africadaily.com
Africa Energy Intelligence, www.africaintelligence.com
AFRICAHOME dotcom, www.africahome.com
AfricaOnline.com, www.africaonline.com
Aftenposten Norway, www.aftenposten.no
Agence France Presse (AFP), www.afp.com
allAfrica.com, www.allafrica.com
Al-Ray Al-'am [Kuwait], www.alraialaam.com
Al-Raya [Qatar], www.raya.com
Al-Thawra [Yemen], www.althawra.gov.ye
Al-Watan [Qatar], www.al-watan.com
American Broadcasting Corporation News (ABC), www.abcnews.go.com
Andorra Times, www.andorratimes.com
Arab News [Saudi Arabia], www.arabnews.com
Asia Times, www.atimes.com
Associated Press (AP), www.ap.org
Australia Broadcasting Corporation News Online, www.abc.net.au/news
Bahrain Post, www.bahrainpost.com
Bahrain Tribune, www.bahraintribune.com
Baltic News Service, www.bns.lt
Bangkok Post, www.bangkokpost.co.th
British Broadcasting Corporation (BBC), www.bbc.co.uk
Cabinda.net, www.cabinda.net
Cable News Network (CNN), www.cnn.com
Cameroon Tribune, www.cameroon-tribune.cm
The Central Asia-Caucasus Analyst (Johns Hopkins University), www.cacianalyst.org
The Christian Science Monitor, www.csmonitor.com
CIA World Factbook, www.cia.gov/cia/publications/factbook
Civil Georgia, www.civil.ge
Daily Excelsior [India-Kashmir], www.dailyexcelsior.com
Daily Star [Bangladesh], www.dailystar.net
Danas [Serbia and Montenegro], www.danas.co.yu
Dani [Bosnia-Herzegovina], www.bhdani.com
Dawn [Pakistan], www.dawn.com
Der Standard [Austria], www.derstandard.at
Deutsche Presse-Agentur [Germany], www.dpa.de
Deutsche Welle [Germany], www.dwelle.de

Die Zeit [Germany], www.zeit.de
The East Africa Standard [Kenya], www.eastandard.net
East European Constitutional Review (New York University), www.law.nyu.edu/eedr
The Economist, www.economist.com
The Economist Intelligence Unit reports
EFE News Service [Spain], www.efenews.com
El Mercurio [Chile], www.elmercurio.cl
El Nuevo Herald [United States], www.miami.com/mld/elnuevo
El Pais [Uruguay], www.elpais.com.uy
El Tiempo [Colombia], www.eltiempo.com
El Universal [Venezuela], www.eluniversal.com.ve
Election Watch, www.electionwatch.org
Expreso [Peru], www.expreso.co.pe
Far Eastern Economic Review, www.feer.com
Federal Bureau of Investigation Hate Crime Statistics, www.fbi.gov/ucr/2003/03semimaps.pdf
The Financial Times, www.ft.com
Finnish News Agency, http://virtual.finland.fi/stt
Folha de Sao Paulo, www.folha.com.br
Foreign Affairs, www.foreignaffairs.org
Foreign Policy, www.foreignpolicy.com
Frankfurter Allgemeine Zeitung [Germany], www.faz.net
The Friday Times [Pakistan], www.thefridaytimes.com
The Frontier Post [Pakistan], www.frontierpost.com
Global News Wire, www.lexis-nexis.com
Globus [Croatia], www.globus.com.hr
The Good Friday Agreement [Northern Ireland], www.nio.gov.uk/issues/agreement.htm
The Guardian [Nigeria], www.ngrguardiannews.com
Gulf Daily News [Bahrain], www.gulf-daily-news.com
Gulf News Online [United Arab Emirates], www.gulf-news.com
Gulf Times [Qatar], www.gulf-times.com
Haveeru Daily [Maldives], www.haveeru.com.mv
The Hindustan Times [India], www.hindustantimes.com
Iceland Review, www.icelandreview.com
The Independent [United Kingdom], www.independent.co.uk
Index on Censorship, www.indexonline.org

*India Today*, www.india-today.com
*The Indian Express*, www.indian-express.com
*Insight Magazine*, www.insightmag.com
Integrated Regional Information Networks
  (IRIN), www.irinnews.org
Inter Press Service, www.ips.org
Interfax News Agency, www.interfax-news.com
*International Herald Tribune*, www.iht.com
*Irish Independent*, www.unison.ie/irish_independent
*Irish Times*, www.ireland.com
*The Jordan Times*, www.jordantimes.com
*Journal of Democracy*,
  www.journalofdemocracy.org
*Kashmir Times* [India-Kashmir],
www.kashmirtimes.com
*Kathmandu Post*, www.nepalnews.com.np/ktmpost.htm
*Khaleej Times* [United Arab Emirates],
  www.khaleejtimes.com
*Kuensel* [Bhutan], www.kuenselonline.com
*Kurier* [Austria], www.kurier.at
*Kuwait Post*, www.kuwaitpost.com
*La Jornada* [Mexico], www.jornada.uam.nx
*La Nacion* [Argentina], www.lanacion.com.ar
*La Repubblica* [Italy], www.repubblica.it
*La Tercera* [Chile], www.tercera.cl
*Lanka Monthly Digest* [Sri Lanka],
  www.lanka.net/LMD
Latin American Regional Reports,
  *www.latinnews.com*
Latin American Weekly Reports,
  *www.latinnews.com*
*Le Figaro* [France], www.lefigaro.fr
*Le Monde* [France], www.lemonde.fr
*Le Temps* [Switzerland], www.letemps.ch
Lexis-Nexis, www.lexis-nexis.com
*The Los Angeles Times*, www.latimes.com
*The Messenger* [Georgia],
  www.messenger.com.ge
*The Miami Herald*, www.miami.com/mld/miamiherald
*Mirianas Variety* [Micronesia], www.mvariety.com
*Mopheme News* [Lesotho], www.lesoff.co.za/news
*The Moscow Times*, www.themoscowtimes.com
*Nacional* [Croatia], www.nacional.hr
*The Nation*, www.thenation.org
*The Nation* [Thailand],
  www.nationmultimedia.com
*The Nation Online* [Malawi],
  www.nationmalawi.com
National Public Radio (NPR), www.npr.org
*National Review*, www.nationalreview.com
*Neue Zurcher Zeitung* [Switzerland],
  www.nzz.ch
*The New York Times*, www.nytimes.com

*The New Yorker*, www.newyorker.com
*NIN* [Serbia and Montenegro], www.nin.co.yu
*Noticias* [Argentina],
  www.noticias.uolsinectis.com.ar
*Notimex* [Mexico], www.notimex.com
*Novi Reporter* [Serbia and Montenegro]
*O Estado de Sao Paulo*, www.estado.com.br
O Globo [Brazil], www.oglobo.globo.com
OFFnews [Argentina], www.offnews.info
*Oman Arabic Daily*, www.omandaily.com
*Oman Daily Observer*,
  www.omanobserver.com
*Oslobodjenje* [Bosnia-Herzegovina],
  www.oslobodjenje.com.ba
*Outlook* [India], www.outlookindia.com
*Pagina/12* [Argentina], www.pagina12.com.ar
PANAPRESS, www.panapress.com
*The Pioneer* [India], www.dailypioneer.com
Political Handbook of the World, http://phw.binghamton.edu
*Politika* [Serbia-Montenegro],
  www.politika.co.yu
*The Post* [Zambia], www.zamnet.zm/zamnet/post/post.html
Radio Australia, www.abc.net.au/ra
Radio France Internationale, www.rfi.fr
Radio Free Europe-Radio Liberty reports,
  www.rferl.org
Radio Lesotho, www.lesotho.gov.ls/radio/radiolesotho
Radio New Zealand, www.rnzi.com
*Reporter* [Serbia and Montenegro]
Reuters, www.reuters.com
*Ritzau* [Denmark], www.ritzau.dk
*Semana* [Colombia], www.semana.com
*Slobodna Bosna* [Bosnia-Herzegovina],
  www.slobodna-bosna.ba
Solomon Islands Broadcasting Corporation,
  www.sibconline.com.sb
*The Somaliland Times*,
  www.somalilandtimes.net
*South Asia Tribune* [Pakistan],
  www.satribune.com
*South China Morning Post* [Hong Kong],
  www.scmp.com
*The Statesman* [India],
  www.thestatesman.net
*Straits Times* [Singapore],
  www.straitstimes.asia1.com.sg
*Suddeutsche Zeitung* [Germany],
  www.sueddeutsche.de
*Tageblatt* [Luxembourg], www.tageblatt.lu
Tamilnet.com, www.tamilnet.com
Tax-News.com, www.tax-news.com
*This Day* [Nigeria], www.thisdayonline.com
*The Tico Times* [Costa Rica],
  www.ticotimes.net
*Time*, www.time.com

The *Times of Central Asia*, www.times.kg
The *Times of India*, www.timesofindia.net
*Transcaucasus: A Chronology*,
www.anca.org/anca/transcaucasus.asp
Turkistan Newsletter
*U.S. News and World Report*,www.usnews.com
U.S. State Department Country Reports on
Human Rights Practices, www.state.gov/g/drl/
rls/hrrpt
U.S. State Department Country Reports on
Human Trafficking Reports, www.state.gov/
g/tip
U.S. State Department International Religious
Freedom Reports, www.state.gov/g/drl/irf
Venpres [Venezuela], www.venpres.gov.ve
Voice of America, www.voa.gov
The *Wall Street Journal*, www.wsj.com
The *Washington Post*,
www.washingtonpost.com
The *Washington Times*,
www.washingtontimes.com
The *Weekly Standard*,
www.weeklystandard.com
World of Information Country Reports,
www.worldinformation.com
Xinhua, www.xinhuanet.com
Yemen Observer, www.yobserver.com
*Yemen Times*, www.yementimes.com

## ORGANIZATIONS

Afghan Independent Human Rights
Commission, www.aihrc.org.af
Afghanistan Research and Evaluation Unit,
www.areu.org.pk
American Civil Liberties Union, www.aclu.org
Amnesty International, www.amnesty.org
Annan Plan for Cyprus, www.cyprus-un-
plan.org
Asian Center for Human Rights [India],
www.achrweb.org
Asian Human Rights Commission [Hong
Kong], www.ahrchk.net
Balkan Human Rights Web,
www.greekhelsinki.gr
Bangladesh Center for Development,
Journalism, and Communication,
www.bcjdc.org
British Helsinki Human Rights Group,
www.oscewatch.org/default.asp
Cabindese Government in Exile,
www.cabinda.org
Cambridge International Reference on
Current Affairs, www.circaworld.com
The Carter Center, www.cartercenter.org
Centre for Monitoring Electoral Violence [Sri
Lanka], www.cpalanka.org/cmev.html
Centre for Policy Alternatives [Sri Lanka],
www.cpalanka.org

Committee for the Prevention of Torture,
www.cpt.coe.int
Committee to Protect Journalists, www.cpj.org
Council of Europe, www.coe.int
Ditshwanelo – The Botswana Centre for
Human Rights, www.ditshwanelo.org.bw
Election Commission of India, www.eci.gov.in
Eurasia Group, www.eurasiagroup.net
European Bank for Reconstruction and
Development, www.ebrd.org
European Commission Against Racism and
Intolerance, www.ecri.coe.int
European Institute for the Media,
www.eim.org
Forum 18, www.forum18.org
Forum for Human Dignity [Sri Lanka],
www.fhd.8m.net
Forum of Federations/Forum des Federations,
www.forumfed.org
Global Rights, www.globalrights.org
The Government of Botswana Website,
www.gov.bw
Habitat International Coalition, http://
home.mweb.co.za/hi/hic/
Heritage Foundation, www.heritage.org
Hong Kong Human Rights Monitor,
www.hkhrm.org.hk
Human Rights Center of Azerbaijan, http://
mitglied.lycos.de/hrca
Human Rights Commission of Pakistan,
www.hrcp-web.org
Human Rights First,
www.humanrightsfirst.org
Human Rights Watch, www.hrw.org
INFORM (Sri Lanka Information Monitor)
Institute for Democracy in Eastern Europe,
www.idee.org
Institute for Security Studies, www.iss.co.za
Institute for War and Peace Reporting,
www.iwpr.net
Inter American Press Association,
www.sipiapa.com
International Bar Association, www.ibanet.org
International Campaign for Tibet,
www.savetibet.org
International Centre for Ethnic Studies,
www.icescolombo.org
International Commission of Jurists,
www.icj.org
International Confederation of Free Trade
Unions, www.icftu.org
International Crisis Group, www.crisisweb.org
International Federation of Journalists,
www.ifj.org
International Foundation for Electoral
Systems, www.ifes.org
International Freedom of Expression
Exchange, www.ifex.org

International Helsinki Federation for Human Rights, www.ihf-hr.org
International Institute for Democracy and Electoral Assistance, www.idea.int
International Labour Organization, www.ilo.org
International Legal Assistance Consortium, www.ilacinternational.org
International Monetary Fund, www.imf.org
International Press Institute, www.freemedia.at
International Republican Institute, www.iri.org
International Society for Fair Elections And Democracy [Georgia], www.isfed.ge
Jamestown Foundation, www.jamestown.org
Kashmir Study Group, www.kashmirstudygroup.net
Kyrgyz Committee for Human Rights, www.kchr.elcat.kg
Macedonian Information Agency, www.mia.mk
The Malawi Human Rights Commission
Malta Data, www.maltadata.com
Media Institute of Southern Africa, www.misa.org
National Democratic Institute for International Affairs, www.ndi.org
The National Endowment for Democracy, www.ned.org
National Human Rights Commission [India], www.nhrc.nic.in
National Peace Council of Sri Lanka, www.peace-srilanka.org
National Society for Human Rights [Namibia], www.nshr.org.na
Nicaragua Network, www.nicanet.org
Observatory for the Protection of Human Rights Defenders, www.omct.org
Odhikar [Bangladesh], www.odhikar.org
Office of the High Representative in Bosnia and Herzegovina, www.ohr.int
Open Society Institute, www.soros.org
Organization for Security and Cooperation in Europe, www.osce.org
Pacific Media Watch, www.pmw.c20.org
People's Forum for Human Rights [Bhutan]
Population Reference Bureau, www.prb.org
Refugees International, www.refugeesinternational.org
Reporters Sans Frontieres, www.rsf.org
Republic of Angola, www.angola.org
Royal Institute of International Affairs, www.riia.org
Save the Children, www.savethechildren.org
Shan Women's Action Network, www.shanwomen.org
South African Human Rights Commission, www.sahrc.org.za
South African Press Association, www.sapa.org.za

South Asia Analysis Group [India], www.saag.org
South Asia Terrorism Portal [India], www.satp.org
Tibet Information Network, www.tibetinfo.net
Transitions Online, www.tol.cz
Transparency International, www.transparency.org
Turkish Ministry of Foreign Affairs, www.mfa.gov.tr
United Nations Development Program, www.undp.org
United Nations High Commissioner on Human Rights, www.unhchr.ch
United Nations Interim Mission in Kosovo, www.unmikonline.org
United Nations Population Division, www.un.org/esa/population
U.S. Department of State, www.state.gov
University Teachers for Human Rights-Jaffna, www.uthr.org
Washington Office on Latin America, www.wola.org
The World Bank, www.worldbank.org
World Markets Research Centre, www.wmrc.com
World Press Freedom Committee, www.wpfc.org

## ABOUT FREEDOM HOUSE

Founded in 1941 by Eleanor Roosevelt and others, Freedom House is the oldest non-profit, nongovernmental organization in the United States dedicated to promoting and defending democracy and freedom worldwide. Freedom House supports the global expansion of freedom through its advocacy activities, monitoring and in-depth research on the state of freedom, and direct support of democratic reformers throughout the world.

**Advocating Democracy and Human Rights:** For over six decades, Freedom House has played an important role in identifying the key challenges to the global expansion of democracy, human rights, and freedom. Freedom House is committed to advocating a vigorous U.S. engagement in international affairs that promotes human rights and freedom around the world.

**Monitoring Freedom:** Despite significant recent gains for freedom, hundreds of millions of people around the world continue to endure dictatorship, repression, and the denial of basic rights. To shed light on the obstacles to liberty, Freedom House issues studies, surveys, and reports on the condition of global freedom. Our research is meant to illuminate the nature of democracy, identify its adversaries, and point the way for policies that strengthen and expand democratic freedoms. Freedom House projects are designed to support the framework of rights and freedoms guaranteed in the Universal Declaration of Human Rights.

**Supporting Democratic Change:** The attainment of freedom ultimately depends on the actions of courageous men and women who are committed to the transformation of their societies. But history has demonstrated repeatedly that outside support can play a critical role in the struggle for democratic rights. Freedom House is actively engaged in these struggles, both in countries where dictatorship holds sway and in those societies that are in transition from autocracy to democracy. Freedom House functions as a catalyst for freedom by working to strengthen civil society, promote open government, defend human rights, enhance justice, and facilitate the free flow of information and ideas.